SCIENCE EVIDENCE REVIEW

ADMISSIBILITY AND USE OF EXPERT
EVIDENCE IN THE COURTROOM

MONOGRAPH NO. 9

Cynthia H. Cwik, Jules Epstein, and Carol Henderson, Editors

Cover by Jill Tedhams/ABA Publishing.

The materials contained herein represent the opinions of the authors and editors, and should not be construed to be the views or opinions of the law firms or companies with whom such persons are in partnership with, associated with, or employed by, nor of the American Bar Association or the Section of Science and Technology Law unless adopted pursuant to the bylaws of the Association.

Nothing contained in this book is to be considered as the rendering of legal advice for specific cases, and readers are responsible for obtaining such advice from their own legal counsel. This book is intended for educational and informational purposes only.

© 2013 American Bar Association. All rights reserved.

No part of this publication may be reproduced, stored in a retrieval system, or transmitted in any form or by any means, electronic, mechanical, photocopying, recording, or otherwise, without the prior written permission of the publisher. For permission, contact the ABA Copyrights and Contracts Department by e-mail at copyright@americanbar.org or fax at 312-988-6030, or complete the online request form at http://www.americanbar.org/utility/reprint.

Printed in the United States of America.

17 16 15 14 13   5 4 3 2 1

Cataloging-in-Publication Data is on file with the Library of Congress

Scientific Evidence Review: Admissibility and Use of Expert Evidence in the Courtroom—Monograph No. 9
Edited by: Cynthia H. Cwik, et al.
ISBN: 978-1-61438-997-2

Discounts are available for books ordered in bulk. Special consideration is given to state bars, CLE programs, and other bar-related organizations. Inquire at Book Publishing, ABA Publishing, American Bar Association, 321 North Clark Street, Chicago, Illinois 60654-7598.

www.ShopABA.org

TABLE OF CONTENTS

EDITORS' NOTE xiii

BIOGRAPHIES OF EDITORS AND AUTHORS xv

INTRODUCTION xxvii
    A. *Frye*'s "General Acceptance" Test xxvii
    B. *Daubert v. Merrill Dow* xxviii
        1. *Daubert's* multi-factor reliability test xxviii
    C. The Judge's Gatekeeping Role under *Daubert* xxviii
    D. *General Electric v. Joiner*: Appellate Courts Must Defer to the Trial
       Court's Decision Whether to Admit Expert Testimony xxix
    E. *Kumho Tire v. Carmichael*: The Judge's Gatekeeping Function Applies
       to All Expert Testimony xxix
    F. Revised Rule 702 xxx
    G. Post-*Daubert* Trilogy Developments in the Supreme Court xxx
    H. Expert Admissibility Issues on the Horizon xxxii

CHAPTER I
EXPERT EVIDENCE IN THE FIRST CIRCUIT 1
    A. Key Decisions Applying *Daubert* and *Joiner* 1
        1. U.S. Court of Appeals for the First Circuit 1
            a. Key Decisions 1
            b. Procedural Considerations 7
            c. Standard of Review 8
            d. Technical or Specialized Evidence 8
            e. Preservation of Admissibility Issues for Appeal 9
            f. U.S. District Court for the District of Maine 9
            g. U.S. District Court for the District of Massachusetts 11
            h. U.S. District Court for the District of New Hampshire 14
            i. U.S. District Court for the District of Puerto Rico 15
            j. U.S. District Court for the District of Rhode Island 17
    B. Expert-Related Rules and Procedural Issues in Federal Court 18
        1. Districts of Maine, New Hampshire, Puerto Rico, and Rhode Island 18
        2. District of Massachusetts 18
        3. Discovery and Trial Practice 19
    C. State Law Expert Issues 19
        1. Expert Evidence in Massachusetts State Courts 19
            a. *Daubert*, in Part, Determines Admissibility 19
        2. Expert Evidence in Maine State Courts 22
            a. State Law Determines Admissibility of Scientific Evidence 22
        3. Expert Evidence in New Hampshire State Courts 22
            a. *Daubert* Applies to Determinations of Admissibility
               of Scientific Evidence 22
        4. Expert Evidence in Rhode Island State Courts 23
            a. *Daubert* Guides Issues of Admissibility of Scientific Evidence ... 23
    D. Local Practice Tips and Suggestions 23

CHAPTER II
EXPERT EVIDENCE IN FEDERAL AND STATE COURTS
WITHIN THE SECOND CIRCUIT 25
- A. **Expert Evidence in Federal Courts within the Second Circuit** 25
  1. Key Decisions in the Second Circuit on Expert Evidence.................25
  2. Expert-Related Rules and Procedural Issues 34
     a. Local Rules 34
     b. The Expert Report 35
     c. Failure to Comply with Expert Disclosure Requirements...........35
     d. Costs..38
     e. Admissibility Hearings 41
     f. Post-2010 Discovery of Expert Materials under Rule 26 42
     g. Use of Rule 706..45
  3. Practice Tips and Suggestions for Second Circuit Courts 45
- B. **Expert Evidence in New York State Courts** 46
  1. New York Courts Continue to Apply *Frye*............................46
  2. Rules and Procedures Governing Expert Disclosure in New York State Courts ...52
  3. Local Practice Tips for New York State Courts 57
  4. The Future of *Frye* and *Daubert* in New York State Courts 58
- C. **Expert Evidence in Connecticut State Courts** 59
  1. Key Decisions Applying *Daubert* and *Kumho*........................59
  2. Expert-Related Rules and Procedural Issues in Connecticut State Courts 62
- D. **Expert Evidence in Vermont State Courts** 63
  1. Key Decisions Applying *Daubert* and *Kumho*........................63
  2. Expert-Related Rules and Procedural Issues in Vermont State Courts 65
  3. Local Practice Tips and Suggestions for Vermont State Courts.........66

CHAPTER III
EXPERT EVIDENCE IN THE THIRD CIRCUIT 69
- A. **Key Decisions Applying the Principles of *Daubert*, *Joiner*, and *Kumho Tire* in Federal Courts in the Third Circuit** 69
  1. Introduction 69
- B. **Expert Qualifications** 70
- C. **Reliability**..72
  1. General Standards Governing Reliability 72
  2. Application of the Reliability Requirement...........................74
- D. **The "Fit" Requirement**...79
- E. **Expert-Related Rules and Procedural Issues in Federal Courts in the Third Circuit**...82
  1. Rule 104(a) Inquiry 82
  2. Hearing Requirement...83
  3. Depositions 83
  4. Expert Reports 84
  5. Pretrial Orders 84
  6. Relationship to State Law 85
  7. Appellate Review of Exclusion of Expert Testimony 85
- F. **State-Law Expert Issues** 85
  1. Introduction 85
  2. Expert Evidence in Delaware State Courts 85
     a. Delaware Courts Apply *Daubert* and *Kumho Tire*................85

   b. Delaware's Five-Part Test for Admissibility of Expert Evidence 86
   c. Procedural Issues 91
  3. State-Law Expert Issues in New Jersey State Courts. 92
   a. Beyond the Ken of the Average Juror 93
   b. Reliability. 94
   c. Expert Qualifications 98
   d. Procedural Issues 99
  4. Expert Evidence in Pennsylvania State Courts 100
   a. Pennsylvania Applies the *Frye* Standard 100
   b. When Does *Frye* Apply? 101
   c. What Must Be Generally Accepted? 102
   d. Application of the *Frye* Test. 102
   e. Qualification of Experts. 103
   f. Procedural Issues 105

CHAPTER IV
EXPERT EVIDENCE IN THE FOURTH CIRCUIT 107
 A. Key Decisions Applying *Daubert* in the Fourth Circuit 107
  1. Introduction 107
   a. Development of the *Daubert* Standard 107
   b. Whether the Evidence Is Helpful. 109
   c. Appellate Review. 110
   d. Procedural Issues 112
  2. Evidence Based on the Natural or Hard Sciences 113
   a. Product Design / Engineering 113
   b. Environmental Engineering / Hydrogeology / Appraisal. 115
   c. Medical Causation 116
  3. Hybrid Fact-Opinion Testimony 118
   a. Chemistry. 118
  4. Evidence Rooted in the Social Sciences 119
   a. Psychology. 119
   b. Economics 120
   c. "Identification" Experts 121
   d. Miscellaneous Criminal "Experts" 123
 B. State-Law Expert Issues. 124
  1. Expert Evidence in Maryland State Courts 125
  2. Expert Evidence in North Carolina State Courts 125
   a. General Standards 125
   b. Expert-Related Rules and Procedural Issues 126
  3. Expert Evidence in South Carolina State Courts 127
  4. Expert Evidence in Virginia State Courts 127
  5. Expert Evidence in West Virginia State Courts 129

CHAPTER V
EXPERT EVIDENCE IN THE FIFTH CIRCUIT 133
 A. Key Fifth Circuit Decisions Applying *Daubert*, *Kumho*, and *Joiner* 133
  1. Qualifications. 133
  2. Methodology 134
   a. Methodology—Toxicology. 134
   b. Methodology—Damages. 135

- c. Methodology—Statistics.. 135
- d. Methodology—Valuation. 136
- B. **Decisions in the Federal District Courts** **136**
  - 1. Texas Cases 136
    - a. Expert Qualifications 136
    - b. Procedural Issues 137
    - c. Helpfulness 138
    - d. Methodology Cases 138
    - e. Disqualification 139
  - 2. Louisiana Federal Court Cases 139
    - a. Expert Qualifications 139
    - b. Helpfulness 140
    - c. Methodology 140
    - d. Criminal 141
  - 3. Mississippi Cases. 141
    - a. Procedure 141
    - b. Qualifications. 142
    - c. Products Liability. 142
    - d. Toxicology 143
- C. **Expert-Related Rules and Procedures in Federal Court.** **143**
  - 1. Texas Federal Courts 143
  - 2. Louisiana Federal Courts 144
  - 3. Mississippi Federal Courts. 144
- D. **State-Law Expert Issues** **144**
  - 1. Expert Evidence in Texas State Courts 144
    - a. Texas Rules and Procedures. 144
    - b. Texas Case Law 146
  - 2. Expert Evidence in Louisiana State Courts 150
    - a. Procedural Rules 150
    - b. Evidentiary Framework 152
    - c. Recent Cases 152
  - 3. Expert Evidence in Mississippi State Courts. 153
    - a. Procedural Rules 153
    - b. Evidentiary Framework 153
    - c. Recent Cases 154

CHAPTER VI
EXPERT EVIDENCE IN THE SIXTH CIRCUIT. 159
- A. **Introduction.** **159**
- B. **Expert Qualification Cases.** **159**
  - 1. Sixth Circuit 159
  - 2. District Courts. 161
- C. **Methodology Cases** **164**
  - 1. Product Design 164
    - a. Sixth Circuit. 164
    - b. District Courts. 167
  - 2. Human Factors and Accident Reconstruction 169
    - a. Sixth Circuit. 169
    - b. District Courts 170

      3. Fire Origin 170
          a. Sixth Circuit 170
          b. District Courts 171
      4. Toxic Torts 172
          a. Sixth Circuit 172
          b. District Courts 172
      5. Antitrust 173
          a. Sixth Circuit 173
          b. District Courts 174
      6. Biomedical and Biomechanical Engineering 176
          a. Sixth Circuit 176
      7. Medical Causation 178
          a. Sixth Circuit 178
          b. District Courts 179
      8. Differential Diagnosis 181
          a. Sixth Circuit 181
          b. District Courts 184
      9. Damages 185
          a. Sixth Circuit 185
          b. District Courts 185
     10. Police Practices / Excessive Force 187
          a. Sixth Circuit 187
     11. Civil Rights 189
          a. Sixth Circuit 189
          b. District Courts 189
     12. Other 190
          a. Sixth Circuit 190
          b. District Courts 191
D. Procedural Issues **192**
      1. Sixth Circuit 192
      2. District Courts 194
E. *Daubert* in Criminal Cases **195**
      1. Eyewitness Identification 195
          a. Sixth Circuit 195
      2. DNA Evidence 196
          a. Sixth Circuit 196
      3. Handwriting Analysis and Polygraphs 197
          a. Sixth Circuit 197
      4. Other 197
          a. Sixth Circuit 197
          b. District Courts 198
      5. Criminal Procedural Issues 199
          a. Sixth Circuit 199
F. State-Law Expert Issues **200**
      1. Expert Evidence in Tennessee State Courts 200
          a. Evidentiary Standards 200
          b. Expert-Related Rules and Procedural Issues 201
      2. Expert Evidence in Kentucky State Courts 201
          a. Evidentiary Standards 201
          b. Expert-Related Rules and Procedural Issues 202

3. Expert Evidence in Ohio State Courts 202
   a. Evidentiary Standards 202
   b. Expert-Related Rules and Procedural Issues 203
4. Expert Evidence in Michigan State Courts 203
   a. Evidentiary Standards 203
   b. Expert-Related Rules and Procedural Issues 203
G. **General Practice Tips** **204**
   1. Selection and Retention of Experts 204
   2. Expert Interrogatory Responses and Expert Reports 205
   3. Expert Affidavits and Declarations 205
   4. Depositions 205
   5. Trial 205
   6. Post-Trial Motions 206

CHAPTER VII
EXPERT EVIDENCE IN THE SEVENTH CIRCUIT 207
A. **Key Decisions Applying *Daubert* in Federal Courts** **207**
   1. Introduction 207
   2. Cases Discussing Specific Types of Scientific Evidence 210
      a. Product Design/Engineering 210
      b. Environmental Engineering/Hydrology 213
      c. Psychology 214
      d. Medical Causation 216
      e. Business Practices and Economic Damages 220
B. **State Law Expert Issues** **221**
   1. Expert Evidence in Illinois State Courts 221
      a. Evidentiary Standard 221
      b. Expert Related Rules and Procedural Issues 224
      c. Qualification 224
      d. Discovery 225
      e. Fees 225
   2. Expert Evidence in Indiana State Courts 226
      a. Evidentiary Standard 226
      b. Other Expert Related Rules and Procedural Issues 227
   3. Expert Evidence in Wisconsin State Courts 227
      a. Evidentiary Standard 227
      b. Other Expert Related Rule and Procedural Issues 228

CHAPTER VIII
EXPERT EVIDENCE IN THE EIGHTH CIRCUIT 229
A. **Key Eighth Circuit Decisions Applying *Daubert*—Civil Cases** **229**
   1. Medicine and Toxicology 230
   2. Product Design, Human Factors, and Warnings 237
   3. Environmental Science 244
   4. Fire Cause and Origin 244
   5. Psychiatry and Emotional Harm 246
   6. Economic, Accounting, and Statistical Testimony 247
   7. Accident Reconstruction 251
   8. Professional Malpractice 252

		9. Daubert Procedural Issues—Civil Cases........................253
		a. Preserving *Daubert* Challenge on Appeal....................253
		b. Exclusion as a Sanction for Noncompliance with Scheduling Order.......253
		c. Recovery of Costs Following Successful *Daubert* Motion..............254
		d. *Daubert* and Class Certification..........................254
B.	**Key Eighth Circuit Decisions Applying *Daubert*—Criminal Cases**............**254**
	1.	Gas Chromatography/Mass Spectrometry ("GC/MS") Testing...............254
	2.	DNA Evidence..255
	3.	Acid-Phosphate Tests...................................256
	4.	Inductively Coupled Plasma-Atomic Emission Spectrography (ICP) and Voice Spectrography Evidence........................256
	5.	Polygraph Evidence....................................257
	6.	Psychological and Psychiatric Testimony........................258
	7.	Drug Trafficking......................................258
	8.	Fingerprint Evidence...................................260
	9.	Other Categories of Criminal Forensic Evidence....................260
	10.	Daubert Procedural Issues—Criminal Cases......................262
		a. Preserving *Daubert* Challenges for Appeal...................262
		b. Necessity of *Daubert* Hearings..........................262
		c. Adequacy of Disclosure of Anticipated Trial Testimony..............263
		d. Intrusion on Jury's Role..............................263
C.	**Key Decisions Applying *Daubert* in the District Courts of the Eighth Circuit**..................................**263**
	1.	Arkansas..263
	2.	Iowa...267
	3.	Minnesota...274
	4.	Missouri..282
	5.	Nebraska..289
	6.	North Dakota.......................................293
	7.	South Dakota.......................................297
D.	**Expert Evidence in the State Courts of the Eighth Circuit**..................**299**
	1.	Arkansas..299
		a. *Daubert* Test Guides Admissibility.......................299
		b. Expert-Related Rules and Procedural Issues in Arkansas..............302
	2.	Iowa...302
		a. A Liberal Variation of *Daubert*.........................302
		b. Expert-Related Rules and Procedural Issues in Iowa................304
	3.	Minnesota...304
		a. A *Frye*-Based Standard of "General Acceptance" and "Foundational Reliability"........................304
		b. Expert-Related Rules and Procedural Issues in Minnesota.............308
	4.	Missouri..309
		a. Different Standards in Civil and Criminal Cases..................309
		b. Expert-Related Rules and Procedural Issues in Missouri..............312
	5.	Nebraska..313
		a. The *Daubert* Standard Governs Admissibility..................313
		b. Expert-Related Rules and Procedural Issues in Nebraska.............316
	6.	North Dakota.......................................317
		a. Admissibility Governed by North Dakota Rule of Evidence 702.........317
		b. Expert-Related Rules and Procedural Issues in North Dakota...........318

7. South Dakota 318
   a. Admissibility Governed by *Daubert* Test 318
   b. Expert-Related Rules and Procedural Issues in South Dakota 320

CHAPTER IX
EXPERT EVIDENCE IN THE NINTH CIRCUIT 323
A. Key Ninth Circuit Decisions Applying *Daubert* and *Joiner*...................323
   1. Expert Evidence of Medical Causation 324
   2. Other Types of Scientific Expert Evidence 330
   3. Nonscientific Expert Evidence.......................................333
B. Expert-Related Rules and Procedural Issues in Federal Courts 336
   1. Class Certification Issues...336
   2. Daubert Hearings..336
   3. Court-Appointed Experts...337
   4. Failure to Comply with Expert Disclosure Requirements..................339
   5. Appellate Review..340
C. State Law Expert Issues 341
   1. Expert Evidence in Alaska State Courts 341
      a. *Daubert* Applies to Determinations of Admissibility
         of Scientific Evidence 341
      b. Expert-Related Rules and Procedural Issues in Alaska State Courts........344
   2. Expert Evidence in Arizona State Courts..............................345
      a. *Daubert* Now Sets the Standard for Admissibility of Scientific Evidence ...345
      b. Expert-Related Rules and Procedural Issues in Arizona State Courts.......347
   3. Expert Evidence in California State Courts............................347
      a. Evidentiary Standards 347
      b. Constitutional Issues 354
      c. Expert-Related Rules and Procedural Issues in California State Courts.....355
   4. Expert Evidence in Hawaii State Courts 358
      a. A Modified *Daubert* Test Governs Admissibility 358
      b. Expert-Related Rules and Procedural Issues in Hawaii State Courts 359
   5. Expert Evidence in Idaho State Courts 359
      a. *Daubert* Guides Issues of Admissibility 359
      b. Expert-Related Rules and Procedural Issues in Idaho State Courts 361
   6. Expert Evidence in Montana State Courts 361
      a. *Daubert* Applies to "Novel" Scientific Evidence.....................361
      b. Expert-Related Rules and Procedural Issues in Montana State Courts......363
   7. Expert Evidence in Nevada State Courts 363
      a. State Law Determines Admissibility 363
      b. Expert-Related Rules and Procedural Issues in Nevada State Courts 365
   8. Expert Evidence in Oregon State Courts 365
      a. State Law Governs Admissibility 365
      b. Expert-Related Rules and Procedural Issues in Oregon State Courts 369
   9. Expert Evidence in Washington State Courts 370
      a. *Frye* and State Law Determine Admissibility 370
      b. Expert-Related Rules and Procedural Issues in Washington State Courts....372

CHAPTER X
EXPERT EVIDENCE IN THE TENTH CIRCUIT 375
- A. **Key Decisions Applying *Daubert*, *Joiner*, and *Kumho Tire*** 375
  1. U.S. Court of Appeals for the Tenth Circuit 375
     a. Reversals for Failure to Make Specific Findings or Too Greatly Limiting the *Daubert* Record 375
     b. Deference to Trial Court Under Abuse of Discretion Standard 377
     c. *Daubert* in Other Civil Cases..379
     d. *Daubert* in Criminal Cases..379
- B. **Expert Related Rules and Procedural Issues** 380
  1. Expert Designation and Expert Reports................................380
  2. Expert Qualifications..381
  3. Sanctions for Expert Disclosure Infractions 382
- C. **Expert Witness Issues under State Law** 383
  1. Colorado...383
  2. Kansas...385
  3. New Mexico...386
  4. Oklahoma...388
  5. Utah...389
  6. Wyoming..390

CHAPTER XI
EXPERT EVIDENCE IN THE ELEVENTH CIRCUIT 393
- A. **Key Decisions Applying *Daubert*** 393
  1. Decisions of the Eleventh Circuit 393
  2. District Court Cases...399
     a. Alabama District Court Cases 400
     b. Florida District Court Cases......................................404
     c. Georgia District Court Cases 408
- B. **Expert-Related Rules and Procedural Issues** 414
  1. Alabama—Northern District 414
  2. Alabama—Middle District..414
  3. Alabama—Southern District 415
  4. Florida—Northern District 415
  5. Florida—Middle District 416
  6. Florida—Southern District..416
  7. Georgia—Northern District 418
  8. Georgia—Middle District 420
  9. Georgia—Southern District 421
- C. **State Law Expert Issues** 421
  1. Expert Evidence in Alabama State Courts..............................421
     a. Alabama Previously Applied Three Standards for Admitting Expert Evidence..421
     b. Alabama Expert Evidence Admissibility In Most Civil Cases Filed On or After January 1, 2012 423
     c. Expert Related Rules and Procedures in Alabama State Court 426
  2. Expert Evidence in Florida State Courts 427
     a. Florida remains among the minority of state courts using the test set forth in *Frye v. United States*, 293 F. 1013, 1014 (D.C. Cir. 1923), to determine the admissibility of expert evidence 427

        b. Beyond the Exceptions—Recent Florida Cases Applying the Frye test for admissibility of Expert Evidence 434
        c. Expert Related Rules and Procedural Issues 435
   3. Expert Evidence in Georgia State Courts 438
        a. Civil Cases 439
        b. Criminal Cases 443
        c. Expert Related Rules and Procedures in Georgia State Court 443

Chapter XII
EXPERT EVIDENCE IN THE DISTRICT OF COLUMBIA 445
A. Expert Evidence in the District of Columbia Circuit 445
   1. Key Decisions Applying Daubert v. Merrell Dow Pharm., Inc., 509 U.S. 579 (1993). 445
        a. *Ambrosini v. Labarraque*, 101 F.3d 129 (D.C. Cir. 1996) 445
        b. Other Cases 448
   2. Expert-Related Rules and Procedural Issues 451
B. Expert Evidence in Local District of Columbia Courts. 451
   1. Key Decisions 451
        a. *Dyas v. United States*, 376 A.2d 827 (1977) 452
        b. Other Cases 454
   2. Expert-Related Rules and Procedural Issues 456

Chapter XIII
THE NAS AND THE COURTS: A THREE-YEAR PERSPECTIVE 459
A. Latent Print Evidence. 460
B. Ballistics Evidence. 462
C. Questioned Documents (Handwriting) Analysis 463
D. Towards a "Systems" Approach. 463
E. Conclusion 465

Chapter XIV
EXPERT WITNESS QUALIFICATIONS AND TESTIMONY 467
A. Introduction. 467
B. Selecting an Expert 467
   1. Qualifications. 468
   2. Experience as an Expert Witness 468
   3. Education and Training 468
   4. Membership in Professional Associations 469
C. Increased Scrutiny of Experts 469
D. Weight of the Evidence 470
E. Conclusion 471

INDEX. 473

EDITORS' NOTE

It is our pleasure to present the Ninth Monograph of *Scientific Evidence Review*, a publication of the Section of Science and Technology Law of the American Bar Association. In this Monograph, we provide a complete update of Monograph No. 8, which focused on state and federal court expert evidence issues, including the *Daubert-Joiner-Kumho Tire* trilogy. We are pleased to present an introductory overview on United States Supreme Court decisions regarding expert admissibility issues. We then provide the circuit by circuit chapters written by experienced attorneys with knowledge of the application of the rules regarding expert evidence in their specific jurisdictions. Finally, we include an article examining the impact on court decisions of the National Research Council's 2009 report about the scientific foundation underlying forensic testimony and an article about factors to take into account when selecting an expert. In short, the Monograph should provide the reader with quick access to the governing expert evidence rules in federal and state courts across the country.

The editors very much appreciate the hard work of those who have contributed to this Monograph, including Krishana Whittington of Jones Day who generously provided us with her extensive technical expertise and spent many hours on this project. We also acknowledge the contributions of Sarah Orwig of the American Bar Association.

We generally have made only minor stylistic changes to the papers. While the papers are intended to be an objective statement of the law, the reader should note that the editors and the Section may not necessarily agree with all of the statements in these papers. These views are not necessarily the views of the editors or the editors' clients. Furthermore, the editors have generally relied on the authors to verify the accuracy of their statements and citations. The reader should make an independent verification of these statements and citations before advocating any position in reliance on them.

The editors invite the readers to contact them with any thoughts or comments regarding this or future monographs.

Cynthia H. Cwik
Jules Epstein
Carol Henderson

BIOGRAPHIES OF EDITORS AND AUTHORS

EDITORS

Cynthia H. Cwik

Cynthia Cwik is a partner with the San Diego office of Jones Day. She has extensive experience in complex litigation and class actions, including mass tort and product liability cases, consumer class actions, and environmental and securities cases. She has represented clients in multidistrict litigation proceedings, arbitrations, mediations, and trials. She has been selected seven times as a California "Top Female Litigator" by *The Los Angeles/San Francisco Daily Journal*.

Ms. Cwik has considerable experience with scientific issues and expert witnesses, and she has had significant victories in high-profile matters involving scientific issues. She was featured in a front page article in *The San Diego Daily Transcript*, which described how her attention to scientific detail led to courtroom success. In one case, Ms. Cwik won motions to exclude the testimony of five of the plaintiffs' experts and had the claims of all of the trial plaintiffs dismissed. A journalist described Ms. Cwik as "formidable" and "the mastermind behind the team's savvy attack." The journalist added that Ms. Cwik's "step-by-step dismantling of [plaintiffs'] case was a study in discipline and focus." In another case, after a three-week evidentiary hearing on the science issues, she won motions to exclude the testimony of all seven of plaintiffs' medical causation experts and won summary judgment with regard to the claims of the 14 trial plaintiffs.

Ms. Cwik has been very active in the ABA Section of Science and Technology Law for many years. She has served as co-editor of Scientific Evidence Review for more than a decade. She is the current co-chair of the Life and Physical Sciences Division, and she has served as co-chair of the Scientific Evidence Committee and the Interdisciplinary Committee.

She has been active in other bar and community organizations. She is the current Chair of the Executive Committee of the Yale Law School Association. She previously served as President of the San Diego Chapter of the Federal Bar Association and as a Lawyer Representative to the Ninth Circuit Judicial Conference. She also has been the Co-Chair of the Children at Risk Committee of the San Diego County Bar Organization. Ms. Cwik is a frequent lecturer and has made presentations to many organizations, including the Association of General Counsel, the National Judicial College, and the ABA.

She graduated from Yale College in 1983 (summa cum laude) and from Yale Law School in 1987. She was a Law Clerk to the Honorable Thomas J. Meskill, U.S. Court of Appeals, Second Circuit (1987–1988).

Jules Epstein

Jules Epstein is Associate Professor of Law at Widener University School of Law, where he teaches Evidence, Criminal Procedure and Criminal Law. He is faculty for the National Judicial College, teaching Evidence and Capital Case courses. Professor Epstein has taught courses on eyewitness evidence nationally to judges, lawyers, and law enforcement; published extensively on the subject, and testified as an expert witness in *State v. Henderson* in New Jersey.

In the area of forensics, Professor Epstein has worked on two DNA workgroups and in capital case and forensics trainings for the national Institute of Justice, and more recently on a working group on latent print issues for the National Institute for Standards and Technology. Professor Epstein has lectured on forensics to judges and attorneys nationally, and is co-editor of THE FUTURE OF EVIDENCE (ABA 2011). Professor Epstein graduated from the University of Pennsylvania in 1975 and from the University of Pennsylvania School of Law in 1978.

Carol Henderson

Carol Henderson is the founding director of the National Clearinghouse for Science, Technology and the Law (NCSTL) and a Professor of Law at Stetson University College of Law. Professor Henderson planned and managed NCSTL's development since 2002. NCSTL provides the only comprehensive, searchable database of science, technology and law in the world (www.ncstl.org) with hits from 170 countries and more than 138,000 data entries. NCSTL received the 2010 August Vollmer Excellence in Forensic Science Award for Innovation in Forensic Technology from the International Association of Chiefs of Police.

Recognized as an international authority on science and law, Professor Henderson has presented more than 275 lectures and workshops to thousands of forensic scientists, attorneys, judges, law enforcement and military personnel worldwide on the topics of scientific evidence, courtroom testimony, and professional responsibility. She has lectured in Argentina, Australia, Bahrain, Canada, Finland, Germany, Hong Kong, Italy, Japan, Portugal, Scotland, Spain and Taiwan.

Professor Henderson has more than sixty publications on scientific evidence, law and ethics. She edited the *Encyclopedia of Forensic and Legal Medicine* (2005), which received the Minty Prize from the British Medical Association. Her most recent book, which she co-edited, is *The Future of Evidence: How Science & Technology Will Change the Practice of Law*. It was published by the American Bar Association (ABA) in 2011. The 5th edition of *Scientific Evidence in Civil and Criminal Cases*, which she co-authored, was published in 2008 and the supplement was published in 2009. She is presently a co-editor and author for the ABA's forthcoming *Scientific Review: Admissibility and Use of Expert Evidence in the Courtroom, Monograph No. 9*.

Professor Henderson is a Past President of the American Academy of Forensic Sciences, and Chair of the Scientific Evidence Committee of the American Bar Association's Science and Technology Law Section. She also served on the Forensic Committee of the International Association of Chiefs of Police. She is a member of the editorial boards of the *Journal of Clinical Forensic Medicine*, and the *Forensic Science, Medicine and Pathology Journal*. She served on the *Journal of Forensic Sciences* editorial board from 2003 to 2012. She has also served on working groups for the National Institute of Justice.

Professor Henderson has appeared in both the popular and professional media, including National Public Radio, Fox News, CBS "48 Hours," The John Walsh Show, Montel, TruTV, Court TV, the American Bar Association Journal and Lawyers Weekly USA. She testified before Congress regarding the National Academy of Sciences report on Forensic Science.

Professor Henderson received her BA from the University of Florida and her JD from George Washington University in 1980. Prior to receiving her JD she worked for the Federal Bureau of Prisons and the Department of Justice Criminal Division. She began her legal career as an Assistant United States Attorney in Washington, D.C.

ASSISTANT EDITORS

Sarah A. Bennington

Sarah A. Bennington is an associate at Jones Day. She joined the New Lawyers Group (NLG) in 2012, which provides new lawyers the opportunity to gain exposure to different practice areas before making a commitment to a specific practice. Ms. Bennington is a summa cum laude graduate of the University of California, Irvine School of Law. During law school, she worked in the Community and Economic Development Clinic where she handled transactional and litigation matters pertaining to California mobile home residency law. Ms. Bennington is also a member of the Lawyers Club of San Diego and the San Diego County Bar Association.

Kelly V. O'Donnell

Kelly O'Donnell is an associate at the San Diego office of Jones Day who represents clients in federal and state courts in San Diego and throughout California. He has experience with commercial disputes, unfair competition, antitrust, credit reporting under federal and state laws, product liability, health care, trade secret misappropriation and patent litigation, often in complex multiparty or multijurisdictional actions.

In addition to his work at the trial court level, Mr. O'Donnell has won appellate victories for clients. Mr. O'Donnell also represents clients in criminal and civil investigations involving possible violations of federal laws such as the Anti-Kickback Statute, the Foreign Corrupt Practices Act, the False Claims Act, and the Food, Drug, and Cosmetic Act. Kelly has helped clients defend qui tam actions, respond to subpoenas, and prepare grand jury and trial witnesses. In his pro bono practice, Mr. O'Donnell has obtained successful results at both the trial and appellate levels. In 2011, he was named in *The Daily Transcript* as one of the top young attorneys in San Diego.

Mr. O'Donnell graduated from the University of California, Los Angeles in 2004 (cum laude) and from the University of California, Hastings College of Law in 2007 (magna cum laude). Kelly was a Law Clerk to the Honorable Marilyn L. Huff, U.S. District Court, Southern District of California (2007–2008).

Evan M. Roberts

Evan M. Roberts is an associate at Jones Day and is currently a member of the firm's New Lawyers Group. Mr. Roberts is a graduate of the University of Washington and University of California, Berkeley School of Law. During law school, he served as the Senior Submissions Editor for the Berkeley Business Law Journal and received Jurisprudence Awards in Holistic Leadership and Psychology of Diversity and Discrimination. He has written on topics including corporate governance, boardroom diversity and management strategy.

Evan Rosen

Evan Rosen is a third year student at Stetson University College of Law in Gulfport, FL. He holds a BA in Communication Studies from The College of Charleston, Charleston, SC. While at Stetson Law, Mr. Rosen has worked as a Research Assistant for the National Clearinghouse of Science, Technology and the Law.

Mr. Rosen is currently an intern at the Florida Attorney General's Office, Children's Legal Services division. He has previously held the position of intern for the Hon. Lynn Leibovitz of the Superior Court of the District of Columbia; the Miami-Dade County Health Department; the United States Marshals Service; and Living Cities, a philanthropic collaborative of 22 of the world's largest foundations and financial institutions that helps revitalize urban neighborhoods by supporting community development.

Community involvement is important to Mr. Rosen. He is a founding member of the Juvenile Justice Initiative at the Law School, a program that educates juveniles and the community about the consequences of criminal punishment. He has served on the Student Bar Association for two years and is past chairman of the Pro Bono Committee. He is a student volunteer with the Community Law Program that connects attorneys engaged in pro bono service to individuals who otherwise would be unable to afford assistance. Mr. Rosen is a recipient of the Cecil C. and Augusta M. Bailey Scholarship, at Stetson University College of Law, granted on the basis of character, academic achievement and meritorious leadership in the field of law.

AUTHORS

Expert Evidence in the Supreme Court

Donald B. Ayer

Don Ayer, a partner at Jones Day's Washington office, is considered as one of the firm's most experienced Supreme Court lawyers, with 19 arguments before the Court, and the immediate past-President of the American Academy of Appellate Lawyers. He has argued more than 60 other appeals. His experience covers subject areas ranging from criminal appeals to business torts to a wide range of constitutional and technical statutory and regulatory issues. He also has been lead counsel in 20 federal court jury trials.

Before entering private practice in 1990, Mr. Ayer served for ten years in the United States Department of Justice as an Assistant U.S. Attorney in San Francisco, as United States Attorney in Sacramento, as Principal Deputy Solicitor General under Solicitor General Charles Fried, and as Deputy Attorney General. He has also served as president of the Edward Coke Appellate Inn of Court, and currently teaches a course in Supreme Court Advocacy at Georgetown University Law Center and Duke University Law School.

Mr. Ayer is listed in The Best Lawyers in America (appellate practice), Who's Who in America, Who's Who in the World, Chambers USA (National Appellate), Washingtonian Magazine's Best Lawyers in Washington (Supreme Court), and D.C. Magazine's Top 100 Lawyers in Washington, D.C. He is a member of the ALI and a Fellow of the American Bar Foundation.

Mr. Ayer graduated from Stanford University in 1973 (BA, History, with great distinction), and from Harvard University in 1975 (JD). He was a Law Clerk to the Honorable Malcolm R. Wilkey, U.S. Court of Appeals, D.C. Circuit (1975 Term), and to the Honorable Justice William H. Rehnquist, U.S. Supreme Court (1976 Term).

Nathaniel Garrett

Nat Garrett, an associate at Jones Day, focuses his practice primarily on appellate litigation and motions practice in state and federal courts. He has handled appeals involving legal issues in numerous areas of the law, including bankruptcy, business torts, consumer class actions, constitutional, criminal, environmental, labor and products liability.

Mr. Garrett has briefed appeals in the United States Supreme Court and in numerous federal and state appellate courts and has argued before the Ninth Circuit Court of Appeals and California Court of Appeal.

Mr. Garrett serves as an Appellate Lawyer Representative to the Ninth Circuit Judicial Conference and is a member of the Ninth Circuit's Criminal Justice Act Appeals Panel. He also is a member of the Edward J. McFetridge American Inn of Court.

Mr. Garrett graduated from Yale University (BA, cum laude, 2000) and Stanford University (JD 2006). He was a Law Clerk to the Honorable Raymond C. Fisher, U.S. Court of Appeals for the Ninth Circuit (2006–2007), and to the Honorable Charles R. Breyer, U.S. District Court for the Northern District of California (2007–2008).

First Circuit

Rory FitzPatrick

Rory FitzPatrick is a partner at Cetrulo LLP and is responsible for complex litigation in diverse substantive areas including securities law, contract disputes, environmental regulation, products liability and constitutional law. He has been actively involved in the trial and management of cases in federal and state courts in Massachusetts, New York and other jurisdictions around the country for more than 30 years. He has tried complex commercial disputes, both jury trials and bench trials.

Mr. FitzPatrick also has argued frequently in state and federal appellate courts. He has been involved in a variety of multiparty, multi-jurisdiction litigation and class actions involving claims of personal injury and property damage arising from exposure to such substances as asbestos, lead pigment, silica, various chemicals and pharmaceutical products. He has handled the defense of class actions in a number of state and federal jurisdictions as well as a number of commercial arbitrations.

Mr. FitzPatrick graduated from Manhattan College (BA 1967), Harvard University (MA 1969), and Harvard Law School (JD 1974).

Second Circuit

Konrad L. Cailteux

Konrad Cailteux is a partner in Weil Gotshal & Manges LLP's New York office, where he specializes in defending US and foreign corporations in product liability actions, mass tort matters, class actions and other complex litigation, in both trial courts and appellate courts. Mr. Cailteux has served as lead trial counsel and national coordinating counsel in cases that encompass a wide range of allegations, including wrongful death, defective products, False Claims Act violations, sovereign immunity, and Alien Tort Statute violations. These cases have concerned diverse subjects, including high-tech fibers, pharmaceuticals, silicone gel breast implants, clinical trials, electrical and construction equipment, HVAC systems, PCBs, nuclear power plant construction, and alleged human rights violations. He has also handled numerous matters before the Judicial Panel on Multidistrict Litigation, as well as civil and criminal investigations by federal agencies and state attorneys general. Among Mr. Cailteux's more notable recent cases is *Zeppetella v. Second Chance Body Armor & Toyobo Co., Ltd.*, a highly publicized wrongful death case involving a police officer who was killed in the line of duty when his bullet-resistant vest was allegedly penetrated by an assailant's bullet. Defending Toyobo Co., Ltd., the manufacturer of the fiber used to manufacture the ballistic fabric in the bullet-resistant vest, against defective product claims and other allegations, Mr. Cailteux and the Weil trial team convinced the jury to return an extremely favorable verdict for Toyobo, including no finding of a product defect.

Mr. Cailteux is co-editor of Weil Gotshal's Product Liability Monitor, a blog discussing key trends and developments in the product liability/mass tort field (http://product-liability.weil.com). He is also an active member of several committees of the American Bar Association. He has lectured and written on a number of issues involved in the defense of product liability and mass tort suits, including class actions, the admissibility of expert evidence, medical monitoring, the False Claims Act, the Alien Tort Statute, and managing complex litigation. Mr. Cailteux has also prepared amicus briefs for the United States Supreme Court in numerous high profile cases involving issues of critical importance in the product liability and mass tort area, including the landmark Supreme Court cases, *State Farm Mutual Auto Ins. v. Campbell* (vacating excessive punitive damages award) and *Kumho Tire Co. v. Carmichael* (excluding expert testimony under Daubert). He received his law degree from Hofstra University School of Law, where he was managing editor of the law review, and is a graduate of the United States Military Academy. Prior to attending law school Mr. Cailteux served in the United States Army for five years, reaching the rank of Captain.

Isabella C. Lacayo

Isabella C. Lacayo is an associate in Weil Gotshal & Manges LLP's Litigation department. Ms. Lacayo works primarily on the defense of product liability and mass tort matters as well as other complex litigation. She has represented major domestic and foreign corporations in complex commercial litigations and appeals in federal and state courts. Ms. Lacayo's practice focuses on contract claims, defective product allegations, personal injury claims, False Claims Act violations and sovereign immunity. Her diverse experience includes defending companies in litigations relating to the 9/11 terrorist attacks and the Holocaust. In addition, she has advised companies on the product liability issues of entities targeted for purchase or acquisition. Ms. Lacayo has also assisted in the drafting of amicus curiae briefs on issues impacting product liability and mass tort law.

Ms. Lacayo is a regular contributor to Weil's Product Liability Monitor, a blog discussing key trends and developments in the product liability/mass tort field (http://product-liability.weil.com). She has written for other publications on various subjects, including jurisdiction, motion practice and discovery. Ms. Lacayo received her JD in 2006 from the Benjamin N. Cardozo School of Law where she was an editor of the Cardozo Law Review. She received her BA in Government and French in 2002 from Georgetown University.

Arvin Maskin

Arvin Maskin is a partner at Weil Gotshal & Manges LLP and is Co-Chair of the Product Liability and Mass Tort Practice Group. He has served as lead counsel in some of the largest mass tort and product liability litigations in the country. Formerly with the US Department of Justice in Washington DC, he was the government's lead counsel in such seminal matters as the "Agent Orange" litigation. He has been consistently successful in handling a broad range of domestic and international matters, including the defense, coordination and resolution of product liability, mass tort and consumer fraud litigations, in some cases seeking billions of dollars, involving asbestos, breast implants, food products, industrial chemicals and their by-products, genetic research, lead paint, aircraft, automotive products, electrical and navigation equipment, and pharmaceuticals and medical devices, as well as counseling relating to industrial, consumer and OTC products, FDA, EPA, NHTSA and Consumer Product Safety Act compliance, product recalls (domestic and international), the False Claims Act, the Alien Tort Statute, Congressional investigations, deceptive trade practice claims brought by state attorneys general, product distribution, marketing and labeling, risk avoidance, internal investigations, food tampering, crisis management and strategic media communications. Mr. Maskin is often sought in the defense of high-stakes, high-profile mass tort matters. He has been a lead counsel and negotiator in connection with World War II forced and slave labor class actions involving eight different nations, and has served as lead counsel in the defense and resolution of 33 separate state consumer fraud class actions and an MDL concerning some 170 million automobile and light truck tires. He has handled mass tort class actions and related consumer fraud and personal injury litigations throughout the country involving the sale of hundreds of thousands of bullet-proof vests, including related suits brought by the U.S. Department of Justice under the False Claims Act seeking hundreds of millions of dollars.

Currently, Mr. Maskin is Co-Chairman of the ABA Subcommittee on Complex Torts Committee of the Committee on Corporate Counsel, Litigation Section. He was immediate past co-chairman of the ABA Mass Tort and Product Liability Subcommittee of the Committee on Corporate Counsel. He was also past Chairman of the Toxic and Hazardous Substances and Environmental Law Committee of the Torts and Insurance Practice Section of the ABA. He has been appointed to the Task Force on Mass Torts of the US Chamber of Commerce, and serves as a member of the Boards of Advisors of BNA's Civil Trial Manual, Toxics Law Reporter and Product Safety & Liability Reporter, Leader Publications Products Liability Law & Strategy, among others. Mr. Maskin also serves as a member of the Legal Policy Advisory Board of the Washington Legal Foundation. Mr. Maskin has been recognized by Benchmark Litigation as a "National Litigation Star" in Product Liability (2009–2012) and a "New York Star" in Product Liability (2011 and 2012). He is a graduate of Georgetown University and received his JD from the Georgetown University Law Center.

Theodore E. Tsekerides

Theodore Tsekerides, a partner based in Weil Gotshal & Manges LLP's New York office, concentrates his practice in product liability and complex commercial litigation matters. Mr. Tsekerides' experience includes coordinating national litigation and evaluating a variety of product liability/mass tort matters, including medical devices, over-the-counter pharmaceutical products, breast implants, consumer products, construction equipment and matters alleging groundwater contamination. Mr. Tsekerides is one of the principal attorneys defending Seacor Holdings and its subsidiaries in the multi-district litigation relating to the Deepwater Horizon oil spill pending in federal court in New Orleans. He is also on the trial team representing ExxonMobil in litigation pending in the State of New Hampshire alleging MTBE contamination. Mr. Tsekerides was also one of the lead attorneys representing Lend Lease in all aspects of the World Trade Center debris removal litigation, which involved over 10,000 claims brought by plaintiffs alleging respiratory and other injuries as a result of the clean-up of the Ground Zero site. He was also extensively involved in efforts that resulted in passage of legislation in the United States Congress addressing the claims of these plaintiffs and other injured parties, as well as providing legal protections for contractors such as Lend Lease who assisted in the clean-up. In addition, Mr. Tsekerides' experience includes representing Fortune 500 companies in a variety of complex contractual disputes. He is one of the lead attorneys representing ESPN in connection with litigation and trials involving licensing agreements and Most Favored Nations provisions and represents SiriusXM in litigation regarding music licensing issues.

He is co-editor of Weil's Product Liability Monitor, a blog discussing key trends and developments in the product liability/mass tort field (http://product-liability.weil.com). Mr. Tsekerides is a graduate of Columbia University and received his JD from Brooklyn Law School.

Third Circuit

Robert M. Palumbos

Robert M. Palumbos is an associate at Duane Morris LLP who practices in the area of commercial litigation. Prior to entering private practice, Mr. Palumbos served as judicial clerk to the Honorable Marjorie O. Rendell of the U.S. Court of Appeals for the Third Circuit. Mr. Palumbos is a magna cum laude graduate of the University of Pennsylvania Law School and a graduate of Johns Hopkins University.

John J. Soroko

John J. Soroko is the Chairman and Chief Executive Officer of Duane Morris LLP. Mr. Soroko practices in the area of litigation, with particular emphasis on general business, corporate and securities matters, including the defense of securities and other class actions. Mr. Soroko is listed in Chambers USA: America's Leading Lawyers for Business as a "Leader in Pennsylvania" and one of the leading lawyers in Pennsylvania in the areas of both general commercial litigation and securities litigation. He also is listed as a SuperLawyer in the area of commercial litigation by Law & Politics and Philadelphia magazines. Mr. Soroko is a graduate of New York University School of Law and a graduate of Haverford College.

James H. Steigerwald

James H. Steigerwald is a partner at Duane Morris LLP and practices in the firm's Commercial, Securities and Antitrust Litigation Group. Mr. Steigerwald has significant experience with securities litigation, partnership and shareholder disputes, and franchise and distribution law. He graduated with honors from Cornell Law School and Harvard College.

Shannon Hampton Sutherland

Shannon Hampton Sutherland is a partner at Duane Morris LLP. Ms. Sutherland represents clients nationally in complex commercial litigation, and has significant experience in restrictive covenant, trade secret, and unfair competition claims. Ms. Sutherland is a cum laude graduate of the American University, Washington College of Law, and a summa cum laude graduate of Temple University. Prior to entering the practice of law, Ms. Sutherland had experience in global logistics.

Fourth Circuit

J. Michael Showalter

J. Michael Showalter is an associate with Schiff Hardin LLP in Chicago. He practices litigation, with an emphasis on environmental and complex commercial disputes involving technical and scientific issues. Mr. Showalter received an undergraduate degree from Columbia College of Columbia University, and a JD from Vanderbilt University. Before joining Schiff Hardin, Mr. Showalter practiced law in Virginia and West Virginia and served as a law clerk for United States Magistrate Judge (now District Judge) Michael F. Urbanski of the Western District of Virginia and Chief United States District Judge David A. Faber of the Southern District of West Virginia. Mr. Showalter is admitted to practice in West Virginia, Virginia, New York, and Illinois and various federal courts.

Fifth Circuit

Clifton T. Hutchinson

Cliff Hutchinson is a litigation partner in the Dallas, Texas office of K & L Gates LLP, where he focuses on disputes involving complex technical and scientific issues and evidence.

Mr. Hutchinson received an undergraduate degree in Industrial Engineering from Georgia Tech in 1969 and his JD from Southern Methodist University School of Law in 1980 (cum laude), where he was Texas Survey Editor of the Southwestern Law Journal. Mr. Hutchinson is admitted to practice in Texas and California and before the United States Patent and Trademark Office.

Sixth Circuit

C.E. Hunter Brush

C.E. Hunter Brush is an associate in the Nashville office of Butler, Snow, O'Mara, Stevens & Cannada, PLLC, where he is part of the Commercial Litigation Group and the Government, Environmental, and Energy Group. Mr. Brush is a graduate of The University of the South (Sewanee) and The University of Tennessee College of Law, where he was an Editor for *Transactions: The Tennessee Journal of Business Law*.

Brian Jackson

Brian Jackson is a member in the Nashville office of Butler, Snow, O'Mara, Stevens & Cannada, PLLC, where he is part of the Pharmaceutical, Medical Device and Healthcare Industry Team and the Appellate and Written Advocacy Group. Although he has first chair jury trial experience in various substantive areas of litigation, today Mr. Jackson primarily represents pharmaceutical companies in the defense of product liability claims, including federal MDL proceedings, coordinated state proceedings and related global litigation. He has acted as *Daubert* counsel in jurisdictions around the United States and he regularly makes presentations on law and practice relating to expert witnesses.

Mr. Jackson has been listed in *Best Lawyers in America* and Mid-South *Super Lawyers* since 2010 and is a member of the International Association of Defense Counsel. He is a graduate of The University of the South (Sewanee) and Vanderbilt University Law School, where he was Associate Editor of the *Vanderbilt Law Review*.

Seventh Circuit

Helen E. Witt

Helen E. Witt is a partner and trial lawyer in the Chicago office of Kirkland & Ellis LLP. Her practice is concentrated in the areas of class actions and mass torts. In addition to her practice, Ms.

Witt has been a member of the Board of Directors of the Legal Assistance Foundation of Metropolitan Chicago, the Chicago Chapter of the Federal Bar Association and the Visiting Committee for the University of Chicago Law School. She has also taught Trial Practice and Complex Civil Litigation at the University of Chicago Law School, and various classes and workshops at Northwestern University Law School, the University of Michigan Law School and Loyola University Law School.

Ms. Witt earned a BA in Economics from Yale College and a JD from the University of Chicago Law School.

Eighth Circuit

Ryan T. Dunn

Ryan Dunn, an associate at Faegre Baker Daniels, focuses his practice on environmental and products liability litigation. Ryan has worked on a number of expert-related motions on topics including groundwater contamination and corrosion of metals and has assisted with presentations on topics including low- and no-injury claims by plaintiffs in tort cases. Mr. Dunn is admitted in courts in Minnesota and California and served as a law clerk to two trial court judges in Los Angeles Superior Court after graduating from the UCLA School of Law.

Christin Eaton Garcia

Christin Garcia, a partner at Faegre Baker Daniels, defends product liability or consumer fraud cases for drug and supplement manufacturers and has represented petroleum or chemical companies in environmental and toxic tort cases. She often addresses the science, presenting both company and independent expert witnesses and challenging plaintiff experts, and has served as national science counsel in several lawsuits. She has designed and implemented strong challenges to expert witness testimony in explosion, chemical exposure and drug cases. Ms. Garcia graduated from Duke University (AB magna cum laude 1988) and from the University of Michigan Law School (JD cum laude 1992).

Demoya R. Gordon

Demoya Gordon is a litigation associate at Faegre Baker Daniels LLP. Her experience includes medical device and pharmaceutical litigation, food litigation, general products liability litigation, and estates and trusts litigation. Ms. Gordon received a BA from Macalester College and a JD from the University of California, Berkeley. During law school, she was a member of the California Law Review and served as symposium editor for The Berkeley Journal of African American Law and Policy and submissions and projects editor for the Berkeley Journal of Gender, Law, and Justice.

Shelby L. Myers

Shelby Myers, a litigation associate in Faegre Baker's Denver office, focuses her practice on products liability defense. She has been involved in multidistrict and complex product liability litigation involving medical device manufacturers and pharmaceutical companies. Ms. Myers received a BA from the University of Colorado in Boulder and a JD from the University of California, Berkeley. During law school, Ms. Myers was a member of the California Law Review and clerked with the Neighborhood Justice Clinic of the East Bay Community Law Center in Berkeley, California.

Joseph M. Price

Joe Price has practiced with Faegre Baker Daniels since 1972 and is the senior partner in the product liability and environmental group. His practice focuses on complex litigation, mass tort and class action product liability defense, especially litigation involving medical devices and pharmaceuticals. Mr. Price's experience includes litigation involving mammary implants, orthopaedic prostheses, urologic implants, cardiovascular devices, a wide variety of prescription and over-the-counter drugs, and various chemicals. Other major medical products litigation in which Mr. Price has taken an active role as defense counsel includes the Dalkon Shield and other IUDs, cardiac defibrillators, oral contraceptives, PPA, Diet Drugs, SSRI Psychotropics, herbal supplements and vaccines. He also served as national counsel for a major Fortune 500 Company in several toxic tort cases. Mr. Price is also a recognized expert in the area of obesity/fast food litigation and has vast experience in trial/jury consulting and psychology. Mr. Price graduated from the University of Minnesota (BA 1969) and from the University of Minnesota Law School (JD magna cum laude 1972).

Ninth Circuit

Cynthia Cwik

Nathaniel Garrett

Kelly O'Donnell

Tenth Circuit

Linnea ("Nea") Brown
Nea Brown is a partner at Temkin Wielga & Hardt LLP. She is an accomplished trial lawyer whose professional passion is trying cases. Her practice primarily focuses on environmental, energy, and natural resources litigation. She provides strategic and vibrant representation in complex and contentious matters. Her ability to prepare cases adeptly for settlement or, if necessary, for trial is respected by adversaries and has resulted in clients' trust.

Ms. Brown graduated from Stanford University with Departmental Honors (Human Biology). She received her JD from New York University. She is admitted to practice in all state courts in Colorado and California. She is also admitted to practice in the Federal District Courts in Colorado, California (Northern and Central Districts), Kentucky, and Michigan (Eastern District) and in the 5th, 9th, and 10th Circuit Courts of Appeal. She has also appeared in courts in Texas, Oregon, New Mexico, and Wyoming. She is listed in The Best Lawyers in America (Mass Tort Litigation), in Chambers and Partners, and in Colorado SuperLawyers. In addition, she was honored as one of Colorado's top women lawyers in Law Week Colorado (2009). She was a partner with a major Denver-based law firm, before joining Temkin Wielga & Hardt.

Eleventh Circuit

Daniel A. Cohen
Daniel A. Cohen, Special Counsel with Kasowitz Benson Torres and Friedman LLP, focuses his practice on complex commercial litigation, Title IX, labor and employment, and higher education law. Mr. Cohen serves as a Special Assistant Attorney General to represent certain public institutions in Title IX gender equity matters. Mr. Cohen earned a JD from Vanderbilt University School of Law and a BA, *magna cum laude*, with distinction, from Duke University.

D. Anne Jarrell
Anne Jarrell is an associate at Kasowitz Benson Torres and Friedman LLP with a practice focusing on complex business litigation with an emphasis on breach of contract and fraud actions. She is experienced at handling cases to trial in state and federal courts throughout the U.S. In addition, Ms. Jarrell has presented numerous CLE presentations on ethics to corporate clients and attorneys. Licensed to practice in Georgia and New York, she graduated from Emory University

School of Law, where she was awarded Order of Advocates and additional advocacy honors and scholarships.

John North

John North, a partner in Kasowitz Benson Torres and Friedman LLP's intellectual property group, focuses his practice on patent litigation, trade secret and trademark disputes. A significant number of Mr. North's patent cases have involved unfair competition claims, including PRE and Walker Process claims as well as patent misuse and Lanham Act claims. Many international corporations have relied on Mr. North to take the lead counsel role in major patent litigations, including an electronics focused major entertainment company, some of the world's largest pharmaceutical corporations and a cutting-edge minerals technologies company. Prior to joining Kasowitz in May 2011, Mr. North was a partner at Sutherland Asbill & Brennan LLP, where he chaired the firm's intellectual property group.

Mr. North spends considerable time in court handling trials and hearings, and takes a "hands on" approach to his cases. He has handled cases involving a wide range of technologies including interactive program guides, consumer products, electronic coupons, computerized healthcare information systems and other electronics issues, pharmaceuticals, various chemical products, medical products, paint, textile dye processes and a variety of minerals technologies.

Mr. North graduated from Duke University (BA magna cum laude 1984) and from Emory Law School (JD cum laude 1987).

Misty Peterson

Misty Peterson is a litigation associate at Kasowitz Benson Torres and Friedman LLP where she focuses on business litigation and toxic tort actions. Prior to joining Kasowitz, she served as in-house compliance counsel to an automobile insurance group. Ms. Peterson earned a JD at the University of Georgia School of Law, where she served as Senior Articles Editor of the Journal of Intellectual Property Law. She received a BA in English and a Certificate in Women's Studies from the University of Georgia.

D. Alan White

Alan White is an associate with Kasowitz Benson Torres and Friedman LLP where he practices with the firm's intellectual property group. Mr. White earned a JD, *with honors*, from Emory University School of Law, where he was a Robert W. Woodruff Fellow. He served as the Executive Notes and Comments Editor for the *Emory Law Journal*, and received the ABA/BNA Award for Excellence in the Study of Intellectual Property Law. Prior to attending law school, Alan earned a PhD in Medical Sciences-Genetics from the University of Florida, where he researched the mechanisms of inherited retinal disorders and associated gene therapies, and subsequently conducted related postdoctoral research. He earned a BS in Genetics from the University of Georgia.

Paul G. Williams

Paul Williams is an associate with Kasowitz Benson Torres and Friedman LLP where he practices primarily in the area of complex civil litigation, particularly business and commercial litigation, unfair competition litigation and international litigation. He has handled effectively numerous complex commercial cases involving contractual disputes and business torts at the trial and appellate levels in both state and federal courts. Mr. Williams successfully represented U.S. and foreign telecommunications companies before federal district and circuit courts and the U.S. Supreme Court in matters involving governmental assertion of the state secrets privilege. Mr. Williams also has experience in bankruptcy litigation cases regarding fraudulent transfers and intellectual property cases involving trademark infringement.

Mr. Williams earned a JD, *cum laude*, and an LLM in International and Comparative Law from Duke University School of Law, where he was Notes Editor for the Duke Journal of Comparative & International Law. He also received a BS, with Merit, in English from the United States Naval Academy, an MA in Medieval Studies from the University of London, and an MFS, with Distinction, in Forensic Sciences from National University.

District of Columbia Circuit

Scott Jones

Scott Jones is a senior associate in the Washington, D.C. office of Latham & Watkins. Mr. Jones has extensive experience in the white collar criminal defense practice, representing corporate clients before the DOJ on matters ranging from national security and trade sanctions to health care fraud. Mr. Jones also has significant experience advising clients facing SEC enforcement actions. In these two spheres, Mr. Jones has represented clients in all phases of the litigation process—developing preliminary response strategies, conducting internal investigations, navigating through negotiations, and preparing and implementing long-term compliance solutions.

Christine Rolph

Christine Gregorski Rolph serves as the Global Co-chair of Latham & Watkins' Product Liability, Mass Torts & Consumer Class Actions Practice and is a partner in the firm's Washington, D.C. office. She has been recognized as a Products Liability Litigation Star by Euromoney's Benchmark Institutions and also was named a leading attorney in both the Consumer Products and Mass Tort Defense areas by The Legal 500 US 2012. As a result of praise from clients and peers, Ms. Rolph was named in Benchmark Litigation's 2012 list of "local Litigation Stars" in Washington, D.C. for her products liability work. Benchmark also recognized Ms. Rolph as one of the "Top 250 Women in Litigation" in its inaugural list this year. Ms. Rolph has extensive expertise in litigating consumer class actions, toxic torts, product liability/consumer fraud suits and multi-plaintiff matters. She has represented clients in various high-stakes environmental, chemical and complex commercial matters in federal and state courts.

Ms. Rolph graduated from Duke University (BA 1994) and from the University of Virginia School of Law (JD 1997).

NAS REPORT

Jules Epstein (see above)

Expert Witness Qualifications and Testimony

Carol Henderson (see above)

Kurt W. Lenz

Kurt W. Lenz earned his BA *magna cum laude* from Duquesne University. Mr. Lenz earned his JD from Duquesne University School of Law, where he was Executive Editor of the school's *Business Law Journal* and a member of the Moot Court Honor Board. He then practiced law for ten years as a commercial litigator at firms in Pennsylvania and New York. Most recently, Mr. Lenz has had teaching appointments at Stetson University College of Law and the University of Miami School of Law. Mr. Lenz has published in the areas of scientific evidence and expert testimony in criminal and civil trials.

INTRODUCTION

by

Donald B. Ayer
Nathaniel P. Garrett
Jones Day
51 Louisiana Ave., N.W.
Washington, D.C. 20001
dbayer,jonesday.com
Jones Day
555 California St., 26th Floor
San Francisco, CA 94104
ngarrett,jonesday.com

The United States Supreme Court set forth the standards governing admissibility of expert witnesses' testimony under the Federal Rules of Evidence in a series of cases colloquially referred to as the *Daubert* trilogy: *Daubert v. Merrill Dow Pharmaceuticals, Inc.*, 509 U.S. 579 (1993), *General Electric Co. v. Joiner*, 522 U.S. 136 (1997), and *Kumho Tire Co. v. Carmichael*, 526 U.S. 137 (1999). At the broadest level, the *Daubert* trilogy replaced the so-called *Frye* standard, which required that expert opinion based on a scientific technique be generally accepted as reliable in the relevant scientific community, with a multi-factor analysis that requires the trial judge to ascertain whether the proffered expert testimony rests "on a reliable foundation."

A. *FRYE*'S "GENERAL ACCEPTANCE" TEST

Until the Supreme Court rendered its 1993 opinion in *Daubert*, federal courts generally utilized the "general acceptance" standard articulated in *Frye v. United States*, 293 F. 1013 (D.C. Cir. 1923), as the governing standard for determining the admissibility of novel scientific evidence at trial. The *Frye* test has its origin in a short 1923 decision concerning the admissibility of evidence derived from a precursor to the polygraph machine. In rejecting the expert's testimony as inadmissible, the court declared that "while courts will go a long way in admitting expert testimony deduced from a well-recognized scientific principle or discovery, the thing from which the deduction is made must be sufficiently established to have gained general acceptance in the particular field in which it belongs." *Id.* at 1014.

Although application of the *Frye* test was common until *Daubert*, its merits were heavily debated after 1975, when the Federal Rules of Evidence became federal law. On one hand, certain courts and commentators concluded that *Frye* had been entirely superseded by the Rules of Evidence, which, they maintained, established a lower threshold for determining the admissibility of expert evidence. *See, e.g., United States v. Jakobetz*, 955 F.2d 786, 794 (2d Cir. 1992). On the other hand, certain courts and commentators took the position that *Frye* and the Federal Rules were compatible, and that while the Federal Rules determined whether the expert was qualified to express, *Frye* set the standard for determining whether the expert's conclusion rested on a well-founded methodology. *See, e.g., Christophersen v. Allied-Signal Corp.*, 939 F.2d 1106, 1110 (5th Cir. 1991) (en banc).

In 1993, the Supreme Court conclusively settled the issue by siding with the former camp in *Daubert*, holding that "the *Frye* test was superseded by the adoption of the Federal Rules of Evidence." 509 U.S. at 587.

B. *DAUBERT V. MERRILL DOW*

In *Daubert*, the Supreme Court abandoned the *Frye* test in favor of a multi-factor reliability standard predicated on the plain text of the Federal Rules of Evidence. In *Daubert*, children born with birth defects alleged that their injuries were caused by their mothers' ingestion of Bendectin, a prescription antinausea drug marketed by the defendant. 509 U.S. at 582. In opposing summary judgment, the plaintiffs proffered the testimony of eight experts who concluded, on the basis of test tube and live animal studies, that Bendectin can cause birth defects. *Id.* at 583. Relying on *Frye*, the Ninth Circuit affirmed the district court's decision not to admit the plaintiffs' evidence, holding that the experts' reliance on animal studies could not be shown to be "generally accepted" as a reliable technique. *Id.* Vacating and remanding the Ninth Circuit's decision, the *Daubert* opinion established both a new standard and a new process for evaluating the reliability of expert testimony.

1. *Daubert's multi-factor reliability test*

The Supreme Court rejected *Frye*'s standard on the ground that the Federal Rules governing admissibility of expert testimony do not establish "general acceptance" as an absolute prerequisite to admissibility. Rather, Rule 702, which governs expert testimony, provided: "If scientific, technical, or other specialized knowledge will assist the trier of fact to understand the evidence or to determine a fact in issue, a witness qualified as an expert by knowledge, skill, experience, training, or education, may testify thereto in the form of an opinion or otherwise." Based on the plain text of Rule 702, the Court held that expert testimony is admissible if the expert proposes to testify to: (1) scientific knowledge that; (2) will assist the trier of fact to understand or determine a fact in issue. *Daubert*, 509 U.S. at 592.

According to *Daubert*, a conclusion qualifies as "scientific knowledge" if the proponent can demonstrate that it is the product of sound "scientific methodology" derived from the scientific method. *Daubert*, 509 U.S. at 589. In ascertaining whether proffered testimony meets this standard, the Court encouraged federal courts to consider several factors, including: (1) whether the theory or technique can be and has been tested; (2) whether the theory or technique has been subjected to peer review and publication; (3) the known or potential rate of error and the extent and maintenance of standards controlling the technique's operation; and (4) the theory or technique's degree of acceptance within the scientific community. *Id.* at 593–94. In this way, the "general acceptance" standard established by *Frye* is one consideration, though not a determinative one, in ascertaining whether to admit expert testimony. Ultimately, the *Daubert* opinion establishes a more "flexible," and arguably liberal, standard of admissibility than the previously prevailing *Frye* test. *Id.* at 594.

C. THE JUDGE'S GATEKEEPING ROLE UNDER *DAUBERT*

In an effort to assuage the defendant's concern that abandonment of *Frye* would result "in a 'free-for-all' in which befuddled juries are confounded by absurd and irrational pseudoscientific assertions," the *Daubert* Court emphasized that the Federal Rules of Evidence require trial judges to play "a gatekeeping role." *Daubert*, 509 U.S. at 596–97. Procedurally, therefore, *Daubert*'s greatest development was its encouragement to trial judges to ensure, before the evidence ever reaches a jury, "that an expert's testimony both rests on a reliable foundation and is relevant to the task at hand." *Id.* at 597.

D. *GENERAL ELECTRIC V. JOINER*: APPELLATE COURTS MUST DEFER TO THE TRIAL COURT'S DECISION WHETHER TO ADMIT EXPERT TESTIMONY

Four years after *Daubert*, the Supreme Court again addressed the admissibility of scientific expert testimony in *General Electric v. Joiner*, 522 U.S. at 136. In *Joiner*, the Supreme Court clarified that appellate courts must review a district court's decision whether to admit expert testimony under the deferential "abuse of discretion" standard.

The plaintiff in *Joiner* was an electrician who worked with coolant fluid contaminated with polychlorinated biphenyls ("PCBs"). 522 U.S. at 139. The plaintiff, a smoker, sued the manufacturer of the coolant after he developed lung cancer, alleging that his exposure to PCBs "promoted" his cancer. *Id.* at 139–40.

To oppose summary judgment, the plaintiff proffered the opinions of experts that PCBs can promote cancer and that plaintiff's exposure was likely responsible for his cancer. *Joiner*, 522 U.S. at 140. The trial court deemed the experts' testimony inadmissible, finding that it did not rise above "subjective belief or unsupported speculation." *Id.* After the court of appeals reversed, the defendants sought certiorari on the ground that the court should have applied abuse of discretion review. *Id.* at 141.

The Supreme Court reversed, holding that the trial court's admissibility ruling should have been reviewed for abuse of discretion. *Joiner*, 522 U.S. at 142. Applying that standard, the Supreme Court held that the trial judge did not abuse its discretion because the plaintiff's experts relied on animal studies involving massive amounts of PCB exposure that were so dissimilar to the facts that they did not support the conclusion that plaintiff's more limited exposure caused his cancer. *Id.* at 145. The Supreme Court also found that the experts' conclusions could not be justified by reference to four epidemiological studies, because none of those studies drew a firm link between exposure to PCBs and lung cancer. *Id.* at 145–46. While accepting that trained experts can extrapolate from existing data, the Court held that "nothing in either *Daubert* or the Federal Rules of Evidence requires a district court to admit opinion evidence that is connected to existing data only by the *ipse dixit* of the expert." *Id.* at 146.

E. *KUMHO TIRE V. CARMICHAEL*: THE JUDGE'S GATEKEEPING FUNCTION APPLIES TO ALL EXPERT TESTIMONY

Finally, in *Kumho Tire v. Carmichael*, the Supreme Court held that the judge's gatekeeping function identified in *Daubert* applies to all expert testimony, including that which is non-scientific. Moreover, a trial judge determining the admissibility of an expert's testimony may consider one or more of the factors identified in *Daubert*, but also may consider other measures of reliability if appropriate under the facts.

In *Kumho Tire*, the plaintiff was involved in an automobile accident after the right rear tire of his minivan blew out. 526 U.S. at 142. The plaintiff sued the tire's maker and distributor, claiming that the tire was defective. *Id.* The plaintiff relied heavily upon an engineering expert in tire failure analysis who testified that a defect must have caused the blowout. *Id.* at 142–45. The trial court examined the expert's methodology under the reliability factors set forth in *Daubert* and excluded the expert's testimony. *Id.* at 145. Upon reconsideration, the trial court acknowledged that *Daubert* should be applied flexibly, and that other factors court argue in favor of admissibility, but nonetheless reaffirmed its exclusion ruling. *Id.* at 146. The court of appeals reversed, holding that the *Daubert* factors apply only where an expert relies on the application of scientific principles rather than on skill- or experience-based observation. *Id.*

The Supreme Court reversed, holding that the evidentiary rationale underlying *Daubert* is not limited to "scientific" knowledge. *Kumho Tire*, 526 U.S. at 148. The Court also concluded that it would prove difficult, if not impossible, for judges to distinguish between "scientific" knowledge and "technical" or "other specialized" knowledge. *Id.*

The Court also agreed with the trial court's conclusion that it could consider factors other than those identified in *Daubert* when determining the admissibility of expert evidence. The Court confirmed that the *Daubert* factors were "meant to be helpful, not definitive." *Kumho Tire*, 526 U.S. at 151. In certain cases, the *Daubert* factors might not apply at all. *Id.* In other cases, the court may consider other factors, depending on the facts of that case. *Id.* at 150. Either way, "[t]he trial court must have the same kind of latitude in deciding *how* to test an expert's reliability, and to decide whether or when special briefing or other proceedings are needed to investigate reliability, as it enjoys when it decides *whether or not* that expert's relevant testimony is reliable." *Id.* at 152. "Thus, whether Daubert's specific factors are, or are not, reasonable measures of reliability in a particular case is a matter that the law grants the trial judge broad latitude to determine." *Id.* at 153.

F. REVISED RULE 702

Since *Kumho Tire*, Rule 702 has been amended to reconcile the rule's text with the *Daubert* trilogy and to address other longstanding concerns. In particular, Rule 702 now provides that "[a] witness who is qualified as an expert by knowledge, skill, experience, training, or education may testify in the form of an opinion or otherwise if: (a) the expert's scientific, technical, or other specialized knowledge will help the trier of fact to understand the evidence or to determine a fact in issue; (b) the testimony is based on sufficient facts or data; (c) the testimony is the product of reliable principles and methods; and (d) the expert has reliably applied the principles and methods to the facts of the case."

Under the revised rule and governing Supreme Court jurisprudence, it is clear that courts' analyses of the admissibility of expert testimony must be fact intensive, and the outcome will vary depending on the circumstances. The rule, and the governing Supreme Court opinions, provide ample leeway to trial judges in performing their "gatekeeping" role, a flexible approach that inevitably results in a wide variety of rulings in the lower courts, as described in the following sections.

G. POST-DAUBERT TRILOGY DEVELOPMENTS IN THE SUPREME COURT

Since the Supreme Court decided the last of the *Daubert* trilogy cases in 1999, the Court has remained relatively quiet about expert admissibility issues, allowing the lower federal courts to develop admissibility doctrines on their own. In that time, the Supreme Court has considered expert admissibility issues in two important, if tangential, respects.

First, following the Supreme Court's reconceptualization of the Confrontation Clause in *Crawford v. Washington*, 541 U.S. 36 (2004), that Court has dealt several times with the Clause's application to use in criminal cases of expert reports and certificates of forensic analysis and tests. *See Melendez-Diaz v. Massachusetts*, 557 U.S. 305 (2009); *Bullcoming v. New Mexico*, 131 S.Ct. 2705 (2011); *Williams v. Illinois*, 132 S.Ct. 2221 (2012). In *Crawford*, the Court reversed its holding in *Ohio v. Roberts*, 448 U.S. 56, 66 (1980), which had looked to reliability of the disputed evidence, and held there is no right of confrontation for evidence falling "within a firmly rooted hearsay exception," or in other cases where "particularized guarantees of trustworthiness" can be shown. *Crawford* rejected the reliability test and, looking to original materials, held that Confrontation Clause demanded a right of confrontation for all evidence that was "testimonial" in character. 541 U.S. at 51.

In *Melendez-Diaz*, the State of Massachusetts charged the defendant with distributing cocaine, and placed into evidence certificates of analysis showing the results of a forensic analysis performed on plastic bags found to contain cocaine. The Supreme Court's five member majority ruled that these certificates were affidavits which fell within the core class of testimonial statements covered by the Sixth Amendment's Confrontation Clause. *Melendez-Diaz*, 557 U.S. at 311. The Court explained that the opportunity for cross-examination was critical because, like expert witnesses generally, an analyst's lack of proper training or deficiency in judgment could be exposed through questioning. *Id.* at 320. Four Justices dissented, noting that the decision "sweeps away an accepted rule governing the admission of scientific evidence," and pointing out the practical problems likely to ensue if experts must always appear in court in criminal cases to secure the admission of forensic evidence. 557 U.S. at 330.

In *Bullcoming*, the Supreme Court, again by a vote of 5-4, extended its opinion in *Melendez-Diaz*, and held that the accused's right of confrontation is not satisfied by offering the surrogate testimony of someone other than the analyst who made the certification. 131 S.Ct. at 2710. In doing so, the Court held that the right to confrontation prevails even if the expert's analysis is obviously reliable; "the analysts who write reports that the prosecution introduces must be made available for confrontation even if they possess 'the scientific acumen of Mme. Curie and the veracity of Mother Teresa.'" *Id.* at 2715 (citation omitted). The dissenters—the same four as in *Melendez-Diaz*—noted that the "Crawford approach was not preordained," suggested that it "is time to return to solid ground," and rejected the majority's extension of *Melendez-Diaz* "to bar the reliable, commonsense evidentiary framework the State sought to follow in this case." 131 S.Ct. at 2728.

The present precariousness of the Supreme Court's doctrine in this area was highlighted by the Court's decision in *Williams*, where the Court upheld testimony by a forensic expert who had tested a DNA sample from the defendant, and compared it with a report of a similar DNA profile of a sample taken from the rape victim that was prepared by a different laboratory, Cellmark. Although the prosecution did not offer any witness from Cellmark or attempt to introduce that report into evidence, it did ask the testifying expert who had examined the defendant's DNA sample whether there was a "computer match" between the DNA source taken from the victim and the defendant's DNA, to which the expert replied in the affirmative. *Williams*, 132 S.Ct. at 2236.

The plurality opinion, on behalf of the four *Melendez-Diaz* and *Bullcoming* dissenters, upheld testimony and the bench trial conviction for rape. Its analysis was offered as completely consistent with the prior cases, *Williams*, 132 S.Ct. at 2240, but was not supported by any of the other five members of the Court. The plurality noted that under Federal Rule of Evidence 703, an expert may base an opinion on facts that are made known to the expert, although such reliance does not constitute admissible evidence of the underlying information, and the material relied upon is not itself put into evidence. *Williams*, 132 S.Ct. at 2235. While federal law generally bars an expert from disclosing such inadmissible evidence to a jury, the Federal Rules place no restriction on the revelation of such information to a judge serving as factfinder. *Id.* With respect to the Confrontation Clause, the majority rejected the notion that the expert improperly vouched that the matching DNA sample was found on the victim; instead, the Court found, the expert simply assumed that fact, and from Cellmark's report concluded that the two DNA samples matched. *Id.* at 2236. Because the witness' testimony did not attempt to establish the truth of the matter asserted—*i.e.*, that the sample tested by Cellmark was, in fact, taken from the victim's body—the Court found no violation of the Sixth Amendment. *Id.*

This plurality view governed the outcome of the case only because Justice Thomas concurred in the judgment, based on this entirely separate belief that testimonial statements for purposes of the

Confrontation Clause must be of a very formal character, akin to affidavits and sworn testimony, that is lacking here. *Williams*, 132 S.Ct. at 2255. Justice Thomas nonetheless wrote an opinion that was highly critical of the plurality view, and substantially echoed the concerns expressed by the *Williams* dissenters about the prejudice to defendants inherent in the majority's approach, and its departure from the prior precedents. *Id.* at 2262.

The second post-*Daubert* trilogy area of jurisprudence relevant to scientific testimony concerns the entry of judgment as a matter of law. In *Weisgram v. Marley Co.*, 528 U.S. 440 (2000), The plaintiff prevailed at trial on his claims for wrongful death after the district court, over objection, allowed three experts to testify that an alleged defect in the decedent's heater caused the fatal fire. On appeal, the court of appeals found that the testimony should have been excluded, that the remaining evidence was insufficient to support the verdict, and entered judgment for the defendant. The question presented was whether, under that set of facts, an appellate court may enter judgment for the losing party, or must instead remand the case to the district court for a new trial determination. *Id.* at 443. Affirming, the Supreme Court held that federal rule of civil procedure 50 permits an appellate court to direct the entry of judgment as a matter of law when it determines that expert evidence was erroneously admitted at trial under *Daubert* and that the remaining, properly admitted evidence is insufficient to constitute a submissible case. *Id.* at 446.

H. EXPERT ADMISSIBILITY ISSUES ON THE HORIZON

Numerous issues concerning the admissibility of expert testimony remain unresolved by the Supreme Court. The Court plans to address at least one of those issues in its 2012 Term, by deciding whether a district court may certify a class action without resolving whether the plaintiff class has introduced admissible evidence, including expert testimony, to show that the case is susceptible to awarding damages on a class-wide basis. *See Comcast Corp. v. Behrend*, —- S.Ct. —— (June 25, 2012) (granting petition for writ of certiorari).

In *Behrend*, the Supreme Court is expected to resolve whether expert testimony, which frequently is required to establish class-wide damages in order to obtain class certification under Federal Rule of Civil Procedure 23, must comport with the admissibility standards set forth in Federal Rule of Evidence 702 and the *Daubert* trilogy. The district court certified a class action in *Behrend*, and the Third Circuit affirmed, holding that whether the expert's methodology was sufficiently reliable under *Daubert* was a merits issue that has "no place in the class certification inquiry." *Behrend v. Comcast Corp.*, 655 F.3d 182, 207 (3d Cir. 2011). Certain justices already have expressed skepticism of the view that *Daubert* does not apply to expert testimony at the certification stage of class-action proceedings. *See Wal-Mart Stores, Inc. v. Dukes*, 131 S.Ct. 2541, 2553-54 (2011) ("The District Court concluded that *Daubert* did not apply to expert testimony at the certification stage of class-action proceedings. We doubt that is so. . . ."). Whatever the Supreme Court ultimately decides, it is sure to affect how and to what extent expert testimony is used at the class certification stage.

CHAPTER I
EXPERT EVIDENCE IN THE FIRST CIRCUIT

by

Rory FitzPatrick
Robert J. L. Moore[1]
Cetrulo & Capone LLP
2 Seaport Lane
Boston, MA 02111
(617) 217-5500

A. KEY DECISIONS APPLYING *DAUBERT* AND *JOINER*[2]

1. *U.S. Court of Appeals for the First Circuit*

a. Key Decisions

(1) Ruiz-Troche

The First Circuit's most comprehensive discussion of the *Daubert* expert evidence rule came in a personal injury case. *Ruiz-Troche v. Pepsi Cola of Puerto Rico Bottling Co.*, 161 F.3d 77 (1st Cir. 1998), *rev'g* 177 F.R.D. 82 (D.P.R. 1997). The *Ruiz-Troche* decision is important for two reasons. First, it establishes that the proponent of the scientific evidence need only show that the expert's conclusion has been arrived at in a scientifically sound and methodologically reliable fashion, not that the expert's opinion or methodology is beyond reproach. Second, the court established the framework by which trial courts in the First Circuit should analyze expert admissibility issues: they must review the proffered testimony according to the purpose or purposes for which the expert proposes to testify.

In *Ruiz-Troche*, the court considered whether the trial court abused its discretion in granting a motion *in limine* that excluded a defense expert who proposed to testify as to toxicology and causation issues. *Id.* at 79–80. The case involved a car accident in which six people were killed when Julio Elvin Ruiz Cintron (Ruiz) changed lanes to pass a slower vehicle and collided head-on with

---

[1] The authors would like to thank and acknowledge the work of Alex M. Spisak, a student at Suffolk University School of Law, for his assistance in preparing this update. The authors also acknowledge the work of Sarah C. Kellogg, Amy B. Abbot, J. Patrick Kennedy, Kristina E. Barclay, and Mark W. Freel in drafting the prior versions of this chapter, which appeared in *Scientific Evidence Review Monograph No. 8*.

[2] Due to the volume of cases applying *Daubert* and *Joiner*, this chapter is not an exhaustive discussion of every decision discussing these cases.

an oncoming truck. The ensuing negligence action was brought in diversity by a surviving child and relatives of certain of the deceased.

The toxicology section of Ruiz's autopsy report reflected the presence of cocaine and cocaine metabolites. The defendants sought to introduce this report and expert testimony regarding the significance of these findings to bolster their defense that Ruiz was contributorily negligent. Defendants' expert, a doctor in pharmacology, proposed to testify that, in his opinion, based on the toxicology results finding cocaine and cocaine metabolites in Ruiz's body, Ruiz had snorted at least 200 milligrams of cocaine within one hour before the accident. *Id.* at 82. The expert also proposed to testify that "cocaine impairs senses and capabilities affecting driving, diminishes perception, and increases the willingness to take risks." *Id.* The plaintiffs moved to exclude defendants' proffered expert testimony.

The trial court held a pretrial conference to address the expert testimony admissibility issue. Plaintiffs sought exclusion of the expert's dosage and impairment opinion on the ground that levels of cocaine contamination from the toxicology report cannot be correlated to dosage or impairment levels with the degree of certainty required for expert testimony. *Id.* at 82–83. The defendants responded that the pharmacologist's methodology was sufficiently reliable to withstand *Daubert* scrutiny. At the court's request, defendants agreed to submit copies of the eighteen articles cited in their expert's report. The district court, however, issued an order excluding the proffered testimony after having received only fourteen of the articles. *Id.* at 82. The district court ruled that there was no "scientific basis" for the expert's dosage opinion and that his impairment opinion likewise failed to pass the *Daubert* reliability test. *Id.*

On appeal, the First Circuit (Selya, J.) reviewed the evidentiary ruling according to the purposes for which the expert proposed to testify. First, as to the proffered dosage opinion, the appeals court carefully reviewed the articles cited in the expert report, and found that "[t]he publication of these pieces and their exposure to peer review serve as an independent indicia of reliability of the . . . technique" employed by the expert in developing his opinions. *Id.* at 84. The court recognized that certain of the articles pointed out flaws that might tend to reduce the accuracy of the methodology employed. However, the court found that the trial court had "set the bar too high" by rejecting the testimony because certain statements in the articles "cast doubt on [the expert's] position." Rather, the court held that:

> *Daubert* neither requires nor empowers trial courts to determine which of several competing scientific theories has the best provenance. It demands only that the proponent of the evidence show that the expert's conclusion has been arrived at in a scientifically sound and methodologically reliable fashion.

Id. at 85 (citations omitted). The First Circuit concluded that the proffered dosage opinion, on balance, satisfied Rule 702's expert admissibility standard and should have been admitted.

The appeals court next addressed the proffered impairment testimony. The court noted that in order for their expert's dosage opinion to be meaningful, the defendants "had to show a correlation between cocaine use in the dosage suggested by [their expert's] opinion and an impairment affecting the cocaine user's fitness to drive." *Id.* To supply this correlation, their expert proposed to testify that cocaine intoxication resulting from such a dosage "results in impairments of perception, reflexes, reaction time, and judgment, and that such a degree of intoxication increases one's 'sense of mastery' and thus promotes risk taking," all of which "adversely affect the ability to drive safely." *Id.* Although the trial court concluded that it is generally accepted that "cocaine causes impairment," it rejected admission of the expert's opinion for this purpose on the ground that the degree of impairment cannot be "scientifically deduced" because people "metabolize cocaine differently." *Id.* at 86.

The First Circuit also reversed this holding, finding that the trial court impermissibly "conflated the dosage and impairment issues." *Id.* Critically, the court found that the trial court had applied "a standard of scientific certainty to the impairment testimony beyond that which *Daubert* envisions." *Id.* The trial court erred by imposing as a threshold requirement "that science be able to declare that a precise quantity of cocaine in the bloodstream produces an equally precise degree of impairment." *Id.* The appeals court found that this standard would change the role of the trial court under *Daubert* "from that of gatekeeper to . . . armed guard." *Id.* In short, the appeals court held that *Daubert* does not require the trial court to "solicit a level of assurance that science realistically cannot achieve" in order to permit admission of scientific evidence. *Id.*

(2) Milward

The First Circuit, in the 2011 opinion *Milward*, expounded on *Ruiz-Troche*. *Milward v. Acuity Specialty Prods. Grp., Inc.*, 639 F.3d 11 (1st Cir. 2011). In reversing a District Court ruling that expert testimony was inadmissible, the *Milward* court provided further explanation of (A) the nature of the gatekeeper function played by trial courts determining the admissibility of expert evidence, (B) what constitutes reliable methodology underlying an expert opinion, and (C) how the First Circuit views the "abuse of discretion" standard. *Id.* at 14.

Brian Milward and his wife brought suit against multiple chemical companies after he was diagnosed with a rare form of leukemia (APL) in 2004. The plaintiffs alleged that his disease was caused by exposure to defendants' benzene-containing products during the time he worked as a refrigeration technician, from 1973 until 2007. *Id.* at 13.

At the request of the defendants, the trial was bifurcated. *Id.* The issue of general causation—whether exposure to benzene could cause APL, the specific form of leukemia that afflicted Mr. Milward—would be determined at the onset. *Id.* Courts had not previously found a scientific link between exposure to benzene and APL. *Id.*

To establish general causation, the plaintiffs proffered toxicologist Dr. Martyn Smith as an expert. *Id.* His opinion that exposure to benzene can cause APL relied to a material extent on peer-reviewed studies that were contradicted by other peer-reviewed literature on the subject. *Id.* at 21. Dr. Smith explained that he applied his years of experience and acumen in the field in evaluating the relative merits of the contradictory studies, and that the weight of the evidence supported his opinion on general causation. *Id.* at 19.

After a four-day evidentiary hearing, the District Court ruled the testimony of Dr. Martyn Smith inadmissible under Federal Rule of Evidence 702. *Id.* at 13. The District Court determined that "Dr. Smith's proffered testimony that exposure to benzene can cause APL lacks sufficient demonstrated scientific reliability to warrant its admission under Rule 702," *Milward v. Acuity Specialty Prods. Grp., Inc.*, 664 F. Supp. 2d 137, 140 (D. Mass. 2009), as he did not derive his operative opinion with reliable methodology. *Id.*

Once the District Court ruled, the parties agreed to allow judgment to enter in defendants' favor, for purposes of facilitating an appeal to the First Circuit. 639 F.3d 11, 13 (1st Cir. 2011).

On appeal, the First Circuit reversed and remanded the District Court's ruling on the admissibility of Dr. Smith's testimony. The District Court's reasoning for preventing Dr. Smith's testimony, the First Circuit held, "placed undue weight on the lack of general acceptance of Dr. Smith's conclusions and crossed the boundary between gatekeeper and trier of fact." *Id.* at 22. Specifically, the First Circuit determined, the District Court erred in three respects.

First, the First Circuit held that the District Court incorrectly determined that Dr. Smith's opinion lacked general acceptance. *Id.* The mere fact that causes of APL other than benzene exist did not give rise to a lack of certainty in Dr. Smith's opinion sufficient to render it unreliable. *Id.* Insufficient support of an expert's opinion is an issue for the trier of fact, the First Circuit noted, whereas a trial court performs its gatekeeper function with respect to the reliability of support of an expert's opinion. *Id.*

Second, the First Circuit held that the District Court erred in ruling that the studies on which Dr. Smith relied did not support his opinion. *Id.* at 24. The District Court "read too much into the paucity of statistically significant epidemiological studies." *Id.* The lack of epidemiological studies linking benzene exposure to APL cannot be used to discount the possibility in the way the presence of numerous studies contradicting Dr. Smith's opinion would discount his findings. *Id.* The rareness of APL renders it difficult or impossible to gather a statistically significant number of afflicted subjects to perform an epidemiological study. *Id.* Further, the absence of such a study cannot preclude Dr. Smith from using sound scientific reasoning to link the cancer to benzene exposure. *Id.* at 25. Much like the issue of general acceptance, the First Circuit held, because Dr. Smith used valid scientific reasoning and methodology to determine his opinion, it was up to the jury to decide if Dr. Smith's testimony was believable, not the District Court. *Id.* at 24.

Third, the First Circuit held that the District Court's ruling confused biological plausibility with probability, in a manner that affected the outcome of the ruling. *Id.* at 25. The District Court mistakenly interpreted Dr. Smith's opinion to mean that benzene could possibly cause APL, rather than "the sum of his testimony was that a weighing of [factors commonly used by epidemiologists to assess causality] including biological plausibility, supported the inference that the association between benzene exposure and APL is genuine and causal." *Id.* at 26.

In *Milward*, the First Circuit explained in detail the applicable "abuse of discretion" standard, holding that the District Court exceeded its role as gatekeeper when it "repeatedly challenged the factual underpinnings of Dr. Smith's opinion, and took sides on questions that are currently the focus of extensive scientific research and debate—and on which reasonable scientists can clearly disagree." *Id.* at 22. In this way, the First Circuit stressed that the trial court's role as gatekeeper was restricted to determining whether an expert's opinion is reliable and properly supported. The finder of fact, the First Circuit continued, must determine whether an expert is believable.

(3) Other important decisions

The First Circuit has issued other significant decisions interpreting *Daubert* in the civil litigation context. In *Baker v. Dalkon Shield Claimants Trust*, 156 F.3d 248 (1st Cir. 1998), the First Circuit addressed whether the trial court erred by excluding certain gynecological test results and expert testimony proffered by the defendant relating to evidence of a sexually transmitted disease for the purpose of providing an alternative causation theory regarding plaintiff's infertility. *Id.* at 250–51. Following a *voir dire* hearing, the trial court granted plaintiff's motion *in limine* on the ground that the proffered testimony was "nothing more than a guess" and its likely prejudicial effect outweighed its probative value. *Id.* at 251. On appeal, the First Circuit (Boudin, J.) reviewed the evidence in detail and held that the trial court had committed reversible error because the proffered testimony rested on a scientific method and was "self-evidently relevant" because it "offer[ed] a scientific explanation directly pertinent to the central issue in the case, namely, whether the [defendant's product] caused" plaintiff's infertility. *Id.* at 253. As to the risk of prejudice to plaintiff from introduction of evidence regarding her sexually transmitted disease, the appeals court held that her counsel could adequately protect against undue prejudice by effective cross-examination. *Id.* at 254. The First Circuit vacated the judgment and remanded the case for a new trial. *Id.* at 255; *see also Mitchell v. United States*, 141 F.3d 8, 14–17 (1st Cir. 1998) (trial court properly analyzed expert testimony admissibility factors under *Daubert* in its decision to allow plaintiff's medical experts to testify as to the relative benefits and risk from use of particular medication following a surgical procedure).

In *Feliciano-Hill v. Principi*, 439 F.3d 18 (1st Cir. 2006), the First Circuit addressed whether a proposed expert's testimony and report met the standards of *Daubert* and Rule 702 where (1) the expert's opinion differed from that of the treating physician and (2) the proposed expert failed to support his diagnosis with citations to published authorities. The court (Lipez, J.) found that "[t]he mere fact that two experts disagree is not grounds for excluding one's testimony." *Id.* at 25. The court noted that even if one were to assume that the plaintiff's expert was more qualified than the defendant's expert, the district court could not have excluded the defendant's expert testimony on that ground alone. *Id.* The court also rejected the plaintiff's argument that the defendant's expert's testimony did not meet the *Daubert* standard because he failed to support his diagnosis with citations to published authorities. The court noted that the doctor/expert was called on to make a routine diagnosis pertaining to a common condition well within his expertise. The court found the expert's "training and experience placed his report and testimony well above the Rule 702/*Daubert* bar." *Id.* The court elaborated further by stating, "[i]ndeed, even in more complicated cases when an examining physician calls upon training and experience to offer differential diagnosis . . . most courts have found no *Daubert* problem." *Id.*

Similarly, in *Gaydar v. Sociedad Instituto Gineco-Qururgico Y Planificacion Familiar*, 345 F.3d 15 (1st Cir. 2003), the court (Lipez, J.) found that a "proffered expert physician need not be a specialist in a particular medical discipline to render expert testimony relating to that discipline." *Id.* at 24; *see also Therrien v. Town of Jay*, 489 F. Supp. 2d 116 (D. Me. 2007) (holding that under *Daubert*, internist could testify as an expert about traumatic injury and timing); *Bado-Santana v. Ford Motor Co.*, 482 F. Supp. 2d 192 (D.P.R. 2007) (allowing expert to testify under *Daubert* about mild traumatic brain injury even though she was not a neurologist or physician and had not interviewed the patient's treating psychiatrist and psychologist); *Akerson v. Falcon Transport Co.*, CV-06-36-B-W, 2006 U.S. Dist. LEXIS 84870 (D. Me. Nov. 21, 2006) (holding that an emergency room physician and a physician's assistant had a proper foundation upon which to base their expert opinions and that their opinions met *Daubert* requirements). In the district court, the plaintiffs prevailed on medical malpractice claims against the defendants, an abortion clinic and doctors. Defendants appealed, contending, in part, that the plaintiffs' expert, a general practitioner, was not qualified to testify as an expert regarding ectopic pregnancies because he was not a doctor of obstetrics or gynecology. The First Circuit found that the district court properly admitted the expert's testimony, finding "[t]he mere fact that [the expert] was not a gynecologist does not mean that he was not qualified to give expert testimony regarding [plaintiff's] pregnancy. . . . In fact, it would have been an abuse of discretion for the court to exclude [the doctor's] . . . testimony on the sole basis that his medical specialty was something other than gynecology or obstetrics." 343 F.3d at 24–25.

In 2012, the First Circuit affirmed a District Court of Maine ruling excluding an expert's testimony. *Samaan v. St. Joseph Hosp.*, 670 F.3d 21, 31 (1st Cir. 2012). In *Samaan*, the district court determined that, while a proffered expert was qualified and utilized reliable methodology, "the results produced through that methodology left an analytical gap." *Id.* at 32. The First Circuit noted that *Daubert* analysis goes beyond an expert's qualifications and methods and additionally requires the trial judge "to ensure an adequate fit between the expert's methods and his conclusions." *Id.* Plaintiff's expert Dr. Ravi Tikoo opined, through his use of odds ratios and efficacy rates, that the defendants' failure to administer an intravenous shot of tissue plasminogen activator (t-PA) resulted in the plaintiff's inability to recover from his stroke-related injury. *Id.* at 33. Using several peer-reviewed articles and studies, Dr. Tikoo attempted to argue that over 50 percent of individuals given a timely injection of t-PA improve, and that, had the plaintiff been given an injection, he likely would not have suffered from the stroke-related injury. *Id.* The First Circuit emphasized that "correlation is not causation." *Id.* Dr. Tikoo misconstrued the figures in his numerical analysis and did not take into account the number of stroke patients who recovered without the use of t-PA and those who did not recover despite the injection of t-PA. *Id.* at 34. The First Circuit held that "the methods that Dr. Tikoo employed and the data that he presented were simply too distant from the conclusion that he drew, thus negating an adequate fit." *Id.* at 35.

Many of the First Circuit's other significant decisions interpreting *Daubert* have arisen in the criminal context. In *United States v. Sepulveda*, 15 F.3d 1161 (1st Cir. 1993), *cert. denied*, 512 U.S. 1223 (1994), the criminal defendants faced drug trafficking conspiracy charges. *Id.* at 1172–75. The government proposed to offer the testimony of an experienced law enforcement "expert" who would explain the drug distribution "business" to the jury. *Id.* at 1182. The defendants moved *in limine* to exclude the expert's testimony. After receiving the government's proffer, the trial court denied the defendants' motion *in limine*. The First Circuit (Selya, J.) upheld the trial court's decision, explaining that the trial judge properly performed the "gatekeeping function" by determining that it was "reasonably likely that the expert possess[ed] specialized knowledge [that would] assist the trier better to understand a fact in issue." *Id.* at 1183. Although the expert's testimony at trial later turned out to lack an adequate foundation, and thus was stricken by the court, the trial court properly performed its role under *Daubert* by first examining the proposed testimony at the pretrial stage.

In *United States v. Shay*, 57 F.3d 126 (1st Cir. 1995), the court addressed whether Rule 702's admissibility requirement could be satisfied by the testimony of a psychology expert who proposed to testify that a criminal defendant suffered from a mental disorder that may have caused him to make false but incriminating statements to the police and a cell mate that the government planned to use during his prosecution. *Id.* at 130–34. The trial court prevented the defense from offering this expert testimony without conducting a pretrial hearing, on the ground that the jury was capable of assessing the reliability of the defendant's incriminating statements without the testimony. *Id.* at 130. The First Circuit (Barbadoro, J.) reversed, holding that the expert was qualified and prepared to offer specialized expert-opinion testimony that may have been helpful to the jury in assessing the reasons for the defendant's incriminating statements. *Id.* at 133. The court remanded the case to the trial court and instructed it to hold an evidentiary hearing to address the expert admissibility issue in the first instance. *Id.* at 134; *see also United States v. Kayne*, 90 F.3d 7, 11–12 (1st Cir. 1996) (holding that expert testimony as to the value of rare coins was properly admitted by the trial court; issues as to consistency of standards and market assessment factors are properly subject of cross-examination, not the admissibility determination); *United States v. Brien*, 59 F.3d 274, 276–78 (1st Cir. 1995) (failing to adopt blanket rule regarding admissibility of expert testimony on eyewitness identification); *United States v. Alzanki*, 54 F.3d 994, 1005–06 (1st Cir. 1995) (trial court properly performed gatekeeping function by holding *voir dire* before admitting expert testimony of a "victimologist").

In *United States v. Ayala-Pizarro*, 407 F.3d 25 (1st Cir. 2005), the court considered the line between expert testimony under Rule 702 of the Federal Rules of Evidence and lay witness testimony under Rule 701. In this case, the defendant challenged his criminal conviction, arguing that the district court erred in permitting the arresting police officer to testify about his experience with drug points and heroin packaging. The defendant argued that the police officer crossed the line from being a fact witness to being an expert witness and that because no prior notice had been given, a Rule 702 violation had occurred. The First Circuit (Lynch, J.) agreed with the government that neither testimony about drug distribution points nor testimony regarding heroin packaging constitutes expert testimony. The court noted that the line between expert testimony and lay opinion testimony is not easy to draw. *Id.* at 28. "Indeed, the same witness—for example, a law enforcement officer—may be qualified to 'provide both lay and expert testimony in a single case." The court found that the police officer's testimony about drug points and heroin packaging was not expert testimony because it was based on the requisite personal knowledge under Rule 702 and also met the requirements of Rule 701 because it was based on particularized knowledge that he had by virtue of his position as a police officer. *Id.* The testimony required no special expertise and was based on the officer's personal observations and experience with drug arrests. *Id.* at 29; *see also United States v. Santana,*

342 F.3d 60, 68 (1st Cir. 2003) (holding that agent's testimony as to his personal observations is not expert testimony). Moreover, the defendant was free to test the reliability of the officer's perceptions through cross-examination. Accordingly, the court found that the officer's testimony was properly admitted as lay witness testimony under Rule 701.

b. Procedural Considerations

As for procedural considerations, the First Circuit has held that *Daubert* can be applied by trial courts to exclude evidence when ruling on summary judgment motions that involve expert evidence admissibility issues, but should do so with extreme caution. *See Cortes-Irizarry v. Corporacion Insular de Seguros*, 111 F.3d 184 (1st Cir. 1997). In addition, the court has held that trial courts have an obligation to apply the *Daubert* standards to proffered expert evidence even absent any objection by a party. *See Hoult v. Hoult*, 57 F.3d 1, 4 (1st Cir. 1995).

In *Cortes-Irizarry v. Corporacion Insular de Seguros*, 111 F.3d 184 (1st Cir. 1995), the court addressed the appropriateness of applying *Daubert* to exclude expert evidence at the summary judgment stage of a proceeding. Appealing a trial court's denial of its summary judgment motion, the defendants contended that the trial court erred in failing to exclude the opinions advanced by the plaintiff's experts, despite the fact that they failed to object. *Id.* at 188–89. The plaintiff responded that the trial court's *Daubert* "gatekeeping" role is strictly a "time-of-trial phenomenon" that cannot be used to exclude testimony when ruling on a summary judgment motion. *Id.* at 188. Rejecting plaintiff's contention, the First Circuit (Selya, J.) stated that "[t]he *Daubert* regime can play a role during the summary judgment phase of civil litigation. If proffered expert testimony fails to cross *Daubert's* threshold for admissibility, a district court may exclude that evidence from consideration when passing upon a motion for summary judgment." *Id.* (citations omitted).

Nevertheless, the court warned that the *Daubert* "gatekeeping" function must be handled with extreme caution in connection with summary judgment rulings. Noting that "[a] trial setting normally will provide the best operating environment for the triage which *Daubert* demands," the court stated that "[v]oir dire is an extremely helpful device in evaluating proffered expert testimony," and that "this device is not readily available in the course of summary judgment proceedings." *Id.* The court further noted that *Daubert* normally involves a "complex factual inquiry" such that courts will be "hard-pressed in all but the most clear-cut cases to gauge the reliability of expert proof on a truncated record." *Id.* The court held:

> Because the summary judgment process does not conform well to the discipline that *Daubert* imposes, the *Daubert* regime should be employed only with great care and circumspection at the summary judgment stage.
>
> We conclude, therefore, that at the junction where *Daubert* intersects with summary judgment practice, *Daubert* is accessible, but courts must be cautious—except when defects are obvious on the face of a proffer—not to exclude debatable scientific evidence without affording the proponent of the evidence adequate opportunity to defend its admissibility.[3]

Moreover, consistent with *Daubert's* teaching that the job of "gatekeeping" ultimately rests with trial courts (and not necessarily the parties), in *Hoult v. Hoult*, 57 F.3d 1, 4 (1st Cir. 1995), the court held that *"Daubert* . . . instruct[s] district courts to conduct a preliminary assessment of

---

[3] *Id.* (footnote omitted). The court failed to explain what types of procedural mechanisms would be acceptable to permit a complete development of the expert evidence record at the summary judgment stage. However, the court cast some doubt on the effectiveness of using *in limine* hearings and the submission of serial affidavits by expert witnesses. *Id.* at 188 n.3.

the reliability of expert testimony, even in the absence of an objection." *Id.* In *Hoult,* the defendant contended in a postjudgment motion under Fed. R. Civ. P. 60(b)(1) that the trial court committed error by permitting the plaintiff's expert to testify at trial, despite having failed to lodge any objection to the expert at or before trial. The trial court denied defendant's motion for a new trial on the ground that *Daubert* does not require trial courts to act as a "gatekeeper" of expert testimony absent an objection by one of the parties. *Id.*

On appeal, the First Circuit (Torruella, C.J.) affirmed the trial court's holding that it had not committed an error that would require vacating the judgment and granting a new trial. However, the court disagreed with the trial court's interpretation of *Daubert.* The First Circuit held that *Daubert* "instruct[s] district courts to conduct a preliminary assessment of the reliability of expert testimony, even in the absence of an objection." *Id.* Nevertheless, trial courts in the First Circuit are not required to make, *sua sponte,* explicit rulings on the record regarding the admissibility of expert testimony absent a formal objection or a motion *in limine.* The court reasoned:

> We think *Daubert* and Rule 104(a) place some burden on the district court judge to make preliminary evaluations with respect to the reliability of evidence, but we decline to "shackle the district court with a mandatory and explicit" reliability analysis. Rather, we assume that the district court performs such an analysis *sub silentio* throughout the trial with respect to all expert testimony.

Id. at 5.

c. Standard of Review

Prior to the issuance of the Supreme Court's decision in *Joiner,* the First Circuit had not addressed whether *Daubert* required a more stringent standard of review than "abuse of discretion" when reviewing a trial court's expert-evidence "gatekeeping" rulings made at the summary judgment stage. *See Ed Peters Jewelry Co. v. C & J Jewelry Co.,* 124 F.3d 252, 259 n.4 (1st Cir. 1997); *Cortes-Irizarry,* 111 F.3d at 189 n.4. However, it is now clear that the First Circuit follows the Supreme Court's holding on this point. Appellate courts review threshold evidentiary determinations made in connection with summary judgment motions for abuse of discretion. *See Schubert v. Nissan Motor Corp.,* 148 F.3d 25, 29 (1st Cir. 1998) (holding determination as to admissibility of evidence for purposes of a summary judgment proceeding is reviewed for abuse of discretion prior to turning to de novo summary judgment examination); *EEOC v. Green,* 76 F.3d 19, 24 (1st Cir. 1996) (discussing district court's broad authority to prescribe the evidentiary materials it will consider in deciding a motion for summary judgment and the application of the abuse of discretion standard upon appellate review).

d. Technical or Specialized Evidence

The First Circuit has addressed evidentiary issues in several cases in which parties have contended that *Daubert* and its principles should apply to expert testimony that is not purely scientific in nature. In this regard, the First Circuit is one of several circuits that, shortly following the issuance of *Daubert,* indicated that trial courts should screen all proffered expert testimony—whether it relates to strictly scientific principles or not—to ensure that it "both rests on a reliable foundation and is relevant to the task at hand," as required by Fed. R. Evid. 702 and 403. *Vadala v. Teledyne Indus., Inc.,* 44 F.3d 36, 39 (1st Cir. 1995).

In *Vadala v. Teledyne Indus., Inc.,* the First Circuit affirmed the trial court's decision to exclude proffered expert engineering testimony regarding the cause of an airplane engine failure on the ground that the factual basis and reasoning relied on by the expert were faulty. *Id.* at 38–39. Even following its decision in *Vadala* (but before the Supreme Court issued its decision in *Kumho Tire Co., Ltd. v. Carmichael*, 526 U.S. 137 (1999)), however, the First Circuit had in several instances noted that the question of whether the principles of *Daubert* must be applied to determine the admissibility of "technical" or "other specialized" evidence was an "open one." *Acosta-Mestre v. Hilton Int'l of Puerto Rico, Inc.*, 156 F.3d 49, 53 (1st Cir. 1998) (holding that it need not decide whether the trial court erred in refusing to permit plaintiff's mechanical engineer to testify as to design defects because any such error was harmless); *see also Bogosian v. Mercedes-Benz of North Am., Inc.*, 104 F.3d 472, 479 (1st Cir. 1997) (holding that the trial court's ruling preventing plaintiff's automotive repair expert from testifying was not an abuse of discretion because the proffered testimony did not rest on "a reliable factual and methodological foundation"). In light of the Supreme Court's decision in *Kumho Tire,* it is now clear that courts in the First Circuit must apply the principles of *Daubert* to nonscientific expert evidence.

e. Preservation of Admissibility Issues for Appeal

In *United States v. Diaz,* 300 F.3d 66 (1st Cir. 2002), the First Circuit addressed the sufficiency of objections to expert testimony on *Daubert* grounds in order to preserve the issue for appeal. The defendant, charged with malicious destruction of property by fire, filed a "Pretrial Memorandum" that stated that "[t]he only anticipated legal issue potential[ly] would be the qualification of the experts, so-called, under the standards of the *Daubert* trilogy." *Id.* at 70. At trial, the government offered expert testimony regarding the cause of the fire. As the government concluded its examination of the expert with questions concerning the expert's opinion as to the cause of the fire, defense counsel objected by stating, "Objection: *Daubert.*" *Id.* at 75. At the close of the defendant's case, defense counsel renewed his motion for acquittal "for the same reasons [he had] previously stated . . . [and] under Rule 702 that the opinions of the two experts be excluded under the *Daubert* analysis as I have previously mentioned." *Id.* at 72. Diaz was convicted and appealed on the ground that admission of the expert testimony was improper because the expert's methods were not valid or reliable. *Id.* at 72–73. The government countered that Diaz failed to properly preserve his objection and thus lost his right to raise the issue on appeal. *Id.* at 74.

Judge Lipez, writing for the unanimous panel, stated that "litigants must raise a timely objection to the validity or reliability of expert testimony under *Daubert* in order to preserve a challenge on appeal to the admissibility of that evidence" under an abuse of discretion standard. *Id.* (citing *United States v. Gilbert,* 181 F.3d 152, 162–63 (1st Cir. 1999)). In the absence of a timely objection, the court will review a substantive challenge to the reliability of expert witness testimony under a plain error analysis. *Id.* at 76. The court held that the district court reasonably interpreted defense counsel's objections as pertaining to the qualifications of the expert witness, and not to the reliability of the expert's methods or the application of those methods. *Id.* at 75–76. The court accordingly held that Diaz's objections were "woefully deficient for the purpose of advising the district court that [he] was raising a challenge to the reliability of the experts' methods and the application of those methods under Rule 702." *Id.* at 75. Thereafter, the court, examining the record for the expert's methodology, found that there was no plain error in admitting the experts' testimony. *Id.* at 77.

f. U.S. District Court for the District of Maine

Four notable rulings have arisen in the District of Maine following the issuance of *Daubert.* In *Coffin v. Orkin Exterminating Co., Inc.*, 20 F. Supp. 2d 107 (D. Me. 1998), plaintiff sued a pest extermination company under negligence and strict liability theories for causing her to contract a disease known as multiple chemical sensitivity (MCS). The defendant moved *in limine* to exclude plaintiff's proposed expert, a medical doctor who examined and treated her, from testifying about MCS generally and opining that plaintiff acquired MCS as a result of her exposure to pesticides applied by the defendant. *Id.* at 109. The defendant moved to exclude the expert testimony "on the ground that the diagnosis of MCS and the theories underlying it are unreliable and lack a scientifically valid basis." *Id.*

The trial court (Brody, J.) assessed the reliability of the proffered medical evidence using the four-part test set forth in *Daubert. Id.* at 110. The court noted that several federal courts had previously addressed the issue of admissibility of expert medical testimony on MCS under *Daubert* and that in each instance the court had concluded that it was too speculative to meet the requirement of "scientific knowledge." Rather than engaging in a comprehensive discussion of the reasons that the proposed testimony was too speculative to survive the defendant's motion, the court adopted the reasoning and conclusions set forth in two of those cases. *Id.* (citing *Frank v. New York*, 972 F. Supp. 130 (N.D.N.Y. 1997) and *Summers v. Mo. Pac. R.R. Sys.*, 897 F. Supp. 533 (E.D. Okla. 1995), *aff'd*, 132 F.3d 599 (10th Cir. 1997)). In order to address the plaintiff's argument that the studies relied on in previous cases were outdated, the court reviewed more recent articles submitted by plaintiff in support of her expert's testimony and concluded that "individually and as a whole, they do not support [her] argument that MCS's etiology has progressed from the plausible to scientific knowledge capable of assisting a fact-finder." *Id.* at 111 (footnote omitted). Accordingly, the court found that expert testimony concerning MCS was not sufficiently reliable and, therefore, such testimony was inadmissible.

In *Reali v. Mazda Motor of Am., Inc.*, 106 F. Supp. 2d 75, 78 (D. Me. 2000), the court held that under *Daubert*, the court must consider only the methodology underlying an expert's opinion, not the end result. The plaintiff claimed that the defendant's allegedly defective seat design resulted in the plaintiff's mild traumatic brain injury. *Id.* at 76. The defendant moved *in limine* under *Daubert* to exclude the testimony of plaintiff's expert on the ground that the expert used unreliable scientific principles. *Id.* at 76–77. The expert had utilized a computer model to determine whether the automobile seat could have been designed so that the passenger in the accident at issue would not have suffered the same injuries. *Id.* at 77. The defendant objected to the expert's assumption and estimate of an extremely important variable, "Delta V," which represented the change in velocity of the car as it struck another object. *Id.*

The expert used a 12 m.p.h. Delta V based on his review of photographs of the vehicle after the collision in combination with the vehicle's empirical bumper rating. *Id.* The defendant's own experts developed a range in which the Delta V could have been as high as 11 m.p.h., which fell only 1 m.p.h. below that of the plaintiff's expert. *Id.* The court (Hornby, C. J.) excluded the evidence finding that, while the plaintiff's expert possessed over twenty-five years of biomechanical engineering experience, the method of "eyeballing accident photographs" had not been shown to be an acceptable, accurate, or reliable manner of generating a Delta V value. *Id.* at 78–79. The fact that the expert's unscientifically derived estimate was nearly the same as the defendant's figure was irrelevant. *Id.* at 78.

In *Fullerton v. Gen. Motors Corp.*, 408 F. Supp. 2d 51 (D. Me. 2006), the plaintiffs claimed that the injured party was hurt when she was struck by a defectively designed motor vehicle manufactured by the defendant. The defendants argued that the plaintiffs' expert's testimony characterizing a feature of the car ("illusory park") as a defect was not permitted under *Daubert* because the expert conceded at deposition that the condition of "illusory park" is a characteristic that is common to the vast majority of vehicles." *Id.* at 57 (internal quotations omitted). The district court (Cohen, J.) denied defendants' motion to exclude the testimony of plaintiff's expert on this basis, finding that neither *Daubert* nor *Kumho* "require that, in order to be identified as a 'defect' by an expert witness, a design feature or condition of the injury-causing item be unique to that item or common to less than some specified percentage of all such items available in the stream of commerce. First Circuit case law allows expert testimony under these conditions." *Id.*

Daubert analysis has also been applied to criminal cases in the District of Maine. In *United States v. Raymond*, the court (Hornby, J.) precluded the prosecution's expert witness from testifying because his methodology could not be deemed reliable. 700 F. Supp. 2d 142 (D. Me. 2010). The prosecution attempted to use the expert testimony of Kenneth V. Lanning, a former federal agent with over thirty years of experience in the Federal Bureau of Investigation dealing with behavioral science. *Id.* Defendant James Raymond was indicted on two counts of transporting a minor across state lines with the intent of engaging in illegal sexual activity. *Id.* at 143. The prosecution intended to call Lanning as an expert witness to testify about the behavioral patterns of child molesters and certain characteristics of "compliant child victims." *Id.* Defendant Raymond moved to exclude Lanning's testimony pursuant to Federal Rule of Evidence 702. *Id.* Lanning's testimony was to be based on a book and article he authored that "did not give the facts or data Lanning used" and had not been subject to the rigorous peer review required under *Daubert*. *Id.* at 147. The court noted that it did not "know whether Lanning's opinions are generally accepted in the community of psychologists and behavioral scientists for predicting illicit intent or victim truthfulness," and did "not know whether Lanning's professional field reaches reliable results beyond suggesting useful leads for law enforcement investigation." *Id.* at 152. In allowing the defendant's motion, the court concluded that "Lanning's categorization of behavioral characteristics of child molesters and child victims is the 'subjective, conclusory approach' that cannot be 'reasonably assessed for reliability' under Rule 702," *id.* at 149, and "that the proposed testimony fails almost all the admissibility tests for allowing such testimony in a courtroom," *id.* at 153.

g. U.S. District Court for the District of Massachusetts

The U.S. District Court for the District of Massachusetts has issued several important decisions applying the principles of *Daubert*. At issue in *Sutera v. Perrier Grp. of Am., Inc.*, 986 F. Supp. 655 (D. Mass. 1997), was whether plaintiff's medical expert, an oncologist, had sufficient grounds to testify that plaintiff's exposure to low doses of benzene from drinking bottled water caused his leukemia. *Id.* at 656–60. Applying the test from *Daubert*, the court (Saris, J.) found plaintiff's proffered expert testimony to be lacking in several respects. First, the court reviewed epidemiological studies that were relied on by the expert in issuing his causation opinion and concluded that none of the studies associated plaintiff's specific type of leukemia to benzene exposure at levels that plaintiff experienced. *Id.* at 662–63.

The court next reviewed "mechanistic peer-reviewed studies" cited by plaintiff's expert to support his causation opinion but found them lacking because (1) the levels of exposure were significantly higher than that experienced by the plaintiff, (2) one of the studies involved exposing human cells that were already cancerous and thus provided no evidence of initial causation, and (3) the studies failed to establish the validity of absorption mechanics that were important to the expert's proposed causation opinion. *Id.* at 663–64. Furthermore, the court found the expert's "risk assessment" approach equally unavailing in light of contrary scientific evidence cited by defendant's experts. *Id.* at 664–67. Finally, the court reviewed the expert's qualifications and found him to be unqualified to provide an opinion as to whether there was a causal link between plaintiff's leukemia and his benzene exposure. *Id.* at 667. While plaintiffs' expert was an oncologist and hematologist and therefore was qualified to testify as to medical issues in his field, he had "no expertise in epidemiology, toxicology, biostatistics or risk-assessment," all of which are critical to the causation opinion that he proposed to provide. *Id.* Accordingly, the court found that the plaintiffs failed to offer reliable scientific evidence tending to show a causal link between plaintiff's leukemia and his benzene exposure. As a result, the court granted the defendant's motion for summary judgment. *Id.* at 668.

In *Shahzade v. Gregory*, 923 F. Supp. 286 (D. Mass. 1996), the plaintiff, a victim of alleged sexual abuse by the defendant, sought to introduce evidence relating to alleged repressed memories recovered during psychotherapy. The defendant filed a motion *in limine* to exclude the repressed memory evidence. *Id.* at 287. The court (Harrington, J.) denied the defendant's motion, concluding that, under Rule 702 of the Federal Rules of Evidence and *Daubert*, the proffered testimony was based on a reliable scientific theory. *Id.*

The court described the test for admission of expert testimony as involving two steps: (1) the expert must qualify as an expert, and (2) the expert must offer testimony relating to reliable scientific knowledge. *Id.* After simply concluding, without analysis, that the expert was qualified, the court examined the reliability of the scientific testimony under Rule 702 and *Daubert*. *Id.* According to the court, "[t]he reliability standard is grounded in Rule 702's requirement that an expert's testimony relate to 'scientific knowledge,'" and "[t]o qualify as 'scientific,' the theory must be grounded in the methods and procedures of science." *Id.* (quoting *Daubert*, 509 U.S. at 590). In addition, "in order to qualify as 'scientific knowledge,' an inference or assertion must be derived by the scientific method." *Id.* The court specifically stated that, where *scientific* evidence is at issue, "reliability is based upon scientific validity." *Id.* (citing *Daubert*, 509 U.S. at 590–91 n.9). The court concluded that the plaintiff had "satisfied the four *[Daubert]* foundational factors which are to be considered, although not independently determinative, in order to introduce evidence relating to repressed memories." *Id.* at 290. The court further stated that, with respect to repressed memory evidence, "[f]or the law to reject a diagnostic category generally accepted by those who practice the art and science of psychiatry would be folly." *Id.*

In *United States v. Lowe*, 954 F. Supp. 401 (D. Mass. 1996), the defendant moved pursuant to Rules 702, 901, and 403 to exclude evidence that his DNA profile matched the DNA sample taken using a rape kit from an alleged rape victim, her clothing, and her car. *Id.* at 402. The defendant argued that the court should find the new method of analyzing DNA evidence unreliable under *Daubert*. The government argued that a "full-blown *Daubert* analysis" of the new technique was not necessary. The district court (Saris, J.) presided over four days of extensive evidentiary hearings before denying the defendant's motion under Rule 702 and *Daubert*.

Acknowledging its "gatekeeping" role as set forth in *Daubert*, the court stated that it was required by *Daubert* to make "'a preliminary assessment of whether the reasoning or methodology underlying the testimony is scientifically valid and of whether that reasoning or methodology properly can be applied to the facts in issue.'" *Id.* at 410 (quoting *Daubert*, 509 U.S. at 592–93). While recognizing that the Supreme Court "deliberately avoided prescribing a definitive test" for reliability of scientific evidence in *Daubert*, the court considered the "nonexclusive factors" outlined in *Daubert* in making its assessment of the admissibility of the prosecution's expert scientific evidence. *Id.* at 410. Moreover, the court admonished that Rule 403 considerations must still be taken into account in determining the admissibility of scientific evidence. *Id.* at 411. The court analyzed the new technique using the *Daubert* factors and determined that "the Government . . . established the scientific validity, and thus the evidentiary reliability," of the new technique employed in the DNA analysis, "as required by *Daubert*." *Id.* at 421.

In *Kearney v. Philip Morris, Inc.*, 916 F. Supp. 61 (D. Mass. 1996), the plaintiff brought a product liability action against a cigarette manufacturer arising out of a fatal house fire caused by a cigarette. The defendant-manufacturer moved for summary judgment. The district court (Keeton, J.) granted the defendant's motion, finding that the plaintiff failed to prove the cause-in-fact requirement of his case. *Id.* at 65.

The plaintiff had proffered expert testimony regarding the cause-in-fact element. *Id.* Without making a determination as to the admissibility of the expert evidence, the court ruled that the testimony of the plaintiff's experts did not "fit" the facts of the case and therefore summary judgment was warranted. *Id.* The court stated that it must "determine whether the proposed testimony is relevant and fits the facts of the case." *Id.* (quoting *Shay*, 57 F.3d at 133; citing *Daubert*, 509 U.S. at 591–92). Because "a finder of facts reasoning from all of the evidence proffered by plaintiff in this case could not come to a reasoned finding that plaintiff's experts' observations . . . fit the facts of this case," the court granted summary judgment. *Id.* at 69.

In *Whiting v. Boston Edison Co.*, 891 F. Supp. 12 (D. Mass. 1995), the defendant nuclear power station moved *in limine* to exclude the testimony of experts offered by plaintiff employee's estate on the basis of the experts' qualifications and the reliability of the scientific methods and theories on which their opinions were based. *Id.* at 13–14. The district court (Stearns, J.) granted the defendant's motion.

Acknowledging its role as "gatekeeper" under *Daubert*, the court identified two "gateposts" that "frame the exercise of a judge's discretion" in determining the admissibility of expert testimony. *Id.* at 24. First, a witness must be qualified under Fed. R. Evid. 702 in the specific subject for which the witness's testimony is offered. *Id.* Second, the scientific testimony or evidence must be reliable. *Id.* (citing *Daubert*, 509 U.S. at 589–90). The court concluded that neither of the plaintiff's experts was qualified to testify in the fields for which their testimony was proposed. *Id.* at 25. The court further found that the theory as to which the experts proposed to testify "fails all of the *Daubert* reliability factors." *Id.*; *see also United States v. Patrick*, 6 F. Supp. 2d 51, 55–56 (D. Mass. 1998) (authentication of audiotape recording is proper subject of expert testimony; criminal defendant's proposed expert, a sound recording engineer, was not qualified to render expert testimony as to authenticity of the voice on the audiotape); *Jensionowski v. Beck*, 955 F. Supp. 149, 150–51 (D. Mass. 1997) (experienced polygraph examiner was not competent to testify as to the scientific validity of polygraph technique and the truthfulness of polygraph testimony; an expert psychophysiologist might provide foundation for admission of such evidence).

In *United States v. Frabizio*, 445 F. Supp. 2d 152 (D. Mass. 2006), the government charged the defendant with possession of child pornography and sought to introduce testimony of a forensic examiner of photographic evidence. The defendant moved to exclude the proffered testimony as unreliable under *Daubert*. The district court (Gertner, J.) held that it was too difficult for the jury or even a seasoned expert to discern, using only visual means, whether the images portrayed real children or were computer generated to the level of certainty required in a criminal prosecution. Moreover, even if visual observation was sufficient, the expert's methodology did not meet the reliability requirements set forth in *Daubert*. Therefore, the court found that the forensic examiner's testimony would not be helpful and must be excluded. *Id.* at 155.

The court framed the threshold question before the court as "whether visual observation is at all appropriate to the task at hand: distinguishing real images from virtual ones." *Id.* The court stated:

> If it is possible to distinguish the real from the virtual with the naked eye, then the specialized observational skills of a Daubert-qualified photograph expert could help the jurors make their own observations of the evidence. As such, the photograph expert's testimony might be admissible, assuming *Daubert*'s other requirements were satisfied.
>
> On the other hand, if visual observation, even by a seasoned observer, cannot distinguish real and computer-generated images in this case, then observation alone fails to address the threshold question and is therefore irrelevant. The testimony of a photograph expert would be inadmissible; an individual with expertise in computer-generated images would be required.

Id. (citation omitted). After three days of hearings and multiple briefings on the *Daubert* issues, the court found that "it is extremely difficult, if not impossible, for a photographic expert, let alone a lay observer, to determine whether the images involved" are real or were created or manipulated through digital technology. "If photographic experts as a general matter are inadequate to the task of identifying computer-generated images, then no level of experience in that field will suffice to qualify one as an expert." The court further held that had the images been identifiable as genuine or computer manipulated, the expert's methodology, which consisted of eyeballing the images and recording his results did not meet the reliability standards under *Daubert*. *Id.* at 162.

In *Lobsters, Inc. v. Evans*, 346 F. Supp. 2d 340 (D. Mass. 2004), the plaintiffs appealed a decision of the defendant, National Marine Fishery Service, which assessed a $250,000 fine against the plaintiffs and revoked their fishing permits for fishing in closed waters and making a false statement to the Coast Guard regarding the size of their catch. The administrative law judge decided against the plaintiffs based largely on evidence secured by the use of a vessel-tracking system, which established that the fishermen had entered the closed area. *Id.* at 344. On appeal to the district court, the plaintiffs argued that such evidence should not have been admitted because the defendant did not demonstrate that the evidence met the *Daubert* standard for reliability. *Id.* The court (Gorton, J.) found that while the rule of *Daubert* does not apply to administrative proceedings because the Federal Rules of Evidence do not govern such proceedings, "the spirit of *Daubert* does apply to administrative proceedings because 'junk science' has no more place in administrative proceedings than in judicial ones." *Id.* (quoting *Niam v. Ashcroft*, 354 F.3d 652, 660 (7th Cir. 2004)). Ultimately, the court found that evidence based on the tracking system was reliable and properly admitted at the hearing. *Id.* at 345.

In *Smith v. Gen. Elec. Co.*, No. 91-12912-RGS, 2004 U.S. Dist. LEXIS 7011 (D. Mass. Apr. 23, 2004), the plaintiff, an executrix for a deceased employee of the defendant, brought a wrongful-death action against the employer. The plaintiff sought to introduce expert testimony that "chronic low-level exposure to inhaled or ingested plutonium and americium alpha emitters can cause the onset of CML (chronic myelogenous leukemia) in human beings." *Id.* The court framed the issue as whether "the 'gatekeeping' rule of *Daubert* precludes a jury from considering a novel and controversial scientific theory of causation that, while plausible, is nonetheless on the outer rim of supportable science." *Id.* at *1 (citation omitted). "The question to which the court sought an answer" was whether the "plaintiff presented a sufficiently plausible theory of general causation to withstand defendant's motion to exclude her expert witness on the subject." *Id.* at *17. The court (Stearns, J.) concluded that testimony concerning plaintiff's general causation hypothesis should be permitted and that while such hypotheses might not survive a trial on the merits, they "are not so divorced from a scientific method of investigation that they can be dismissed as quackery or armchair conjecture. Hence, as I understand *Daubert*, my role is over, and the role of the jury begins." *Id.* at *16. Accordingly, the court denied defendant's motion to exclude plaintiff's expert witness.

Finally, in *McGovern ex rel. McGovern v. Brigham & Women's Hosp.*, 584 F. Supp. 2d 418 (D. Mass. 2008), the district court (Young, J.), in precluding the plaintiff's expert from testifying, acknowledged that if there exists a gap between concrete evidence and the conclusions drawn by an expert, the expert's testimony is inadmissible. There, the plaintiff brought a medical malpractice claim against a hospital and doctor after the use of a vacuum extraction during the delivery of plaintiff child. *Id.* at 420. The child suffered a stroke during the delivery that resulted in severe complications later in life. *Id.* at 422. In moving to preclude plaintiff's expert Dr. Marc Engelbert, the defendants pointed out that Dr. Engelbert's testimony regarding the standard of care in the process of vacuum-assisted delivery was "not supported by even one peer reviewed publication available" at the time of the delivery. *Id.* at 425. In her reply to defendants' motion, plaintiff supplemented her answer with some articles regarding the risks of vacuum extraction deliveries, but the court ruled that "these materials suggested that vacuum extraction may present risk . . . however as to Dr. Engelbert's proposed testimony about specific causation . . . there was simply too great an analytical gap between the data and the opinion proffered." *Id.* at 425–26.

h.   U.S. District Court for the District of New Hampshire

Three significant decisions interpreting *Daubert* have arisen in this district. In *Pacamor Bearings, Inc. v. Minebea Co., Ltd.*, 918 F. Supp. 491 (D.N.H. 1996), a manufacturer brought an action against its competitors alleging false advertising and unfair competition. The defendants filed a motion *in limine* to preclude the plaintiff's proposed damages expert from testifying. *Id.* at 506. The district court (Devine, S. J.) denied the defendants' motion.

The court stated that "Rule 702 consists of three distinct but related requirements ... which are intended to guide the trial judge in ensuring that an expert's testimony both rests on a reliable foundation and is relevant to the task at hand." *Id.* (quoting *Shay*, 57 F.3d at 132 and *Vadala*, 44 F.3d at 39 (internal quotations omitted)). According to the court, the "gatekeeping function" requires the trial judge to determine whether it is reasonably likely that the expert possesses specialized knowledge that will assist the trier of fact, or whether a lay person would be qualified to decide the issue without having specialized knowledge. *Id.* The court denied the defendants' motion because the "evidence in support of the motion *in limine* ... address[ed] the weight and/or credibility of plaintiffs' proposed expert testimony rather than the admissibility of the same *qua* expert opinion." *Id.* at 507.

In *Grimes v. Hoffmann-LaRoche, Inc.*, 907 F. Supp. 33 (D.N.H. 1995), the plaintiff filed a product liability action against a drug manufacturer and a medical malpractice action against a doctor for injuries that she claimed were caused by a prescription drug. The defendants moved to exclude the testimony of the plaintiff's expert and for summary judgment. The district court (Barbadoro, J.) granted the defendants' motions.

The court stated that, after *Daubert*, "expert testimony must satisfy three requirements in order to survive a Rule 702 objection: first, the expert must be qualified; second, the expert's testimony must be reliable; and third, it must 'fit' the facts of the case." *Id.* at 34 (citing *Shay*, 57 F.3d at 126). With respect to the reliability requirement, the court stated that the four *Daubert* factors, in addition to the "general acceptance" test of *Frye*, should be considered when making the reliability determination. *Id.* at 35. After examining the methodology underlying the opinion of the plaintiff's expert, the court determined that the expert's opinion failed *Daubert*'s reliability and fit requirements. *Id.* at 38.

Lastly, in *St. Laurent v. Metso Minerals Indus., Inc.*, No. 04-CV-14-SM, 2005 U.S. Dist. LEXIS 20436 (D.N.H. Sept. 13, 2005), plaintiffs asserted claims against a rock-crushing machine manufacturer and others, alleging design defects in the machine and failure to warn. The manufacturer moved to exclude the plaintiffs' expert's testimony that provided opinions on warnings and an alternative design for the rock-crushing machine, arguing that the proffered testimony failed to meet the criteria of admission under Rule 702. Looking to the standards employed in other circuits, the court (Muirhead, Mag.) held that the expert's testimony should be excluded because it failed to satisfy "either the *Daubert* factors, or any other set of reasonable reliability criteria." *Id.* at *24. The court found it significant that the expert "did not create any prototypes of his alternative design, or do any testing to support his alternative design theory, which is perhaps the most important *Daubert* factor." *Id.* at *22. Similarly, the expert did not rely on any engineering drawings, industry standards, or peer review. Nor did he draft any proposed warnings or demonstrate any other indicia of reliability of his alternative design. Although the reliability inquiry under Rule 702 is flexible, "nothing in either *Daubert* or the Federal Rules of Evidence requires a district court to admit opinion evidence which is connected to existing data only by the *ipse dixit* of the expert." *Id.* at *22–23 (quoting *Gen. Elec. Co. v. Joiner*, 522 U.S. 136, 146 (1997)).

i. U.S. District Court for the District of Puerto Rico

In *Gonzalez v. Exec. Airlines, Inc.*, 236 F.R.D. 73 (D.P.R. 2006), an airline passenger sued an airline company, alleging that she suffered the effects of post-traumatic stress disorder after the airplane on which she was a passenger made a hard landing. The plaintiff intended to rely on the testimony of her treating psychiatrist and did not intend to present an expert witness. The defendants moved to compel the psychiatrist to produce an expert report. The court (Pieras, S. J.) held that the determinative issue is the scope of the proposed testimony. As long as the testimony of the psychiatrist was limited to the topics of the nature and treatment of the plaintiff's psychological condition, and the opinions that he presented were limited to those he formed as part of his treatment of the plaintiff, the treating psychiatrist would not be bound by the expert witness requirements of Rule 26.[4] The court stated that its ruling denying defendant's motion to compel did not leave the defendant unprotected because the defendant had the right to gather information concerning the nature of the psychiatrist's testimony, care, and treatment through discovery.

In its discussion of the Federal Rules of Evidence and *Daubert*, the court noted that it is "particularly wary of when plaintiffs claim to be suffering from PTSD as a result of defendant's actions," and it "pays heed to the fact that psychologists are not psychiatrists." *Id.* at 80–81. Consistent with its obligation to screen evidence of scientific, technical, or other specialized knowledge to ensure that it is relevant and reliable, "the court will not admit the testimony of a treating psychologist as an expert until verifying that the patient was referred . . . by a psychiatrist, and further verifying that the psychologist" is qualified. *Id.* at 81.

In *McNeil-PCC, Inc. v. Merisant Co.*, No. 04-1090 (JAG), 2004 U.S. Dist. LEXIS 27733 (D.P.R. July 29, 2004), the manufacturer of Splenda no-calorie sweetener sued Merisant for trade dress infringement for marketing a no-calorie sweetener in the same color packaging as Splenda, as well as false advertising. The plaintiff also sought a preliminary injunction to enjoin defendant from continued sales of the allegedly infringing product. At the preliminary injunction hearing, the plaintiff offered into evidence a consumer survey indicating that consumers had attached secondary meaning to plaintiff's trade dress. *Id.* at *27. The defendant argued that the survey was unreliable and should be excluded from consideration.

The Supreme Court's holdings in *Daubert*, "which require that certain standards be met before expert scientific testimony can be accepted and relied upon by a tribunal, apply to survey research." *Id.* at *35. In general, however, "courts are loathe to exclude consumer surveys from evidence." *Id.* "'The majority rule is that while technical difficulties can reduce a survey's weights, they will not prevent the survey from being admitted into evidence.' So long as the survey is conducted according to accepted principles, 'survey evidence should ordinarily be found sufficiently reliable under *Daubert*.'" *Id.* at *35–36 (citations omitted). The court (Garcia-Gregory, J.) found the plaintiff's survey to satisfy these standards, and therefore defendant's motion to exclude was denied. *Id.* at *36–37.

In *Rodriguez Cirilo v. Garcia*, 908 F. Supp. 85 (D.P.R. 1995), defendant police officers moved for summary judgment as to the plaintiffs' Section 1983 claim. The district court (Laffitte, J.) granted the defendants' motion, in part because the expert testimony offered by the plaintiffs as to causation was not based on a reliable foundation. *Id.* at 92. To support their allegation that the defendants' failure to arrest their attacker was the cause of the plaintiffs' injuries, and therefore establish causation for their Section 1983 claim, the plaintiffs offered the testimony of a clinical psychologist. *Id.* at 91. The court stated that "a trial judge has a 'gatekeeping' function to ensure that an expert's reasoning and methodology are valid and that the expert's testimony can properly be applied to the facts at issue." *Id.* at 91–92. Because the plaintiffs' expert did not examine the attacker prior to preparing his opinion, the court found that the "opinion does not rest on a reliable foundation," and thus the expert opinion was held inadmissible. *Id.* at 92.

In *Fedelich v. Am. Airlines*, 724 F. Supp. 2d 274 (D.P.R. 2010), the District Court of Puerto Rico (Casellas, J.) granted the defendant's motion to exclude plaintiff's expert because the

---

[4] *Id.* at 80. In making this finding, the court stated: "Though *Daubert* and its progeny facially deal with the admissibility of the testimony of experts in their proffer of opinion testimony, which is exempt from the 'usual requirement of first-hand knowledge,' by implication and by the application of common sense, the judge's duty to screen scientific or specialized evidence extends beyond that of expert witnesses, but also to the proverbial 'percipient witness who happens to be an expert.'" *Id.* at 81. (internal citations omitted).

expert's opinion was "subjective, conclusory, and cannot reasonably be assessed for reliability." *Id.* at 281. The defendant, American Airlines, moved to exclude the plaintiff's expert, S. Melville McCarthy, who opined that the placement of an emergency stop box at a baggage carousel was negligent and caused plaintiffs' injury. *Id.* at 274. The court noted, "McCarthy's testimony seems to be based more on subjective elements than objective analysis." *Id.* at 282. Specifically, the court found, the expert's opinion was based on a photographic inspection, rather than an in-person inspection, and made numerous baseless assumptions. *Id.* at 280. Consequently, the court ruled, the record was "insufficient to demonstrate that McCarthy used a reliable methodology to reach his conclusions." *Id.*

Despite the admonition from the First Circuit that trial courts should exercise extreme caution when excluding expert testimony prior to trial, the U.S. District Court for the District of Puerto Rico has applied *Daubert* quite liberally when ruling on summary judgment motions that involve expert evidence on admissibility issues. *See id.*; *see also Silca v. Am. Airlines, Inc.*, 960 F. Supp. 528 (D. P.R. 1997) (the district court (Fuste, J.) granted summary judgment for defendant on plaintiffs' product liability action, in part because the testimony of plaintiffs' two proposed experts was inadmissible under *Daubert*); *Bericochea-Cartagena v. Suzuki Motor Co.*, 7 F. Supp. 2d 109, 112 (D.P.R. 1998) (in denying defendants' motion for summary judgment, partly because the opinion of plaintiffs' expert was admissible, the district court (Dominguez, J.) held that the *Daubert* analysis was inapplicable to proffered expert testimony that was not based on "unique, untested or controversial methodologies or techniques").

j. U.S. District Court for the District of Rhode Island

In *Hartford Ins. Co. v. Gen. Elec. Co.*, 526 F. Supp. 2d 250 (D.R.I. 2007), the defendants, a manufacturer and a distributor, moved to exclude the plaintiffs' experts from opining that (A) a fire that destroyed the plaintiffs' house originated at the defendants' water dispenser, and (B) that said water dispenser caused the fire. The court (Smith, J.) first addressed plaintiffs' origin expert. Defendants argued that plaintiffs' expert on this point was unqualified and proffered unsupported speculation as an opinion, due to the expert's failure to document the scene properly or collect any evidence from the scene. *Id.* at 257. The court ruled that the arguments defendants were making "are more appropriately aimed at the weight to be accorded [the expert's] opinion and not its admissibility." *Id.* When an expert is qualified to opine on a topic and the methods used pass the *Daubert* test, "vigorous cross-examination, presentation of contrary evidence, and careful instruction on the burden of proof are the traditional and appropriate means of attacking shaky but admissible evidence," not exclusion. *Id.* at 257–58 (quoting *Daubert*, 509 U.S. at 596).

The court next considered the plaintiffs' causation experts. On cross-examination during deposition, plaintiffs' experts were questioned at length about the bases for their opinions that the defendants' negligent design of their product caused the defect that resulted in the fire destroying plaintiffs' home. *Id.* at 259. The court reviewed this testimony and found that the opinions proffered by plaintiffs' experts were "nothing more than rank speculation." *Id.* at 253. *Daubert* requires that scientific knowledge "connotes more than subjective belief or unsupported speculation." *Id.* (quoting *Daubert*, 509 U.S. at 590). With no supporting scientific material, the court ruled, the experts' testimony was "no more than unsupported speculation, and [was] thus inadmissible." *Id.* at 260.

In *Polidore v. McBride*, 2010 WL 3666971 (D.R.I. 2010), the court (Lisi, C. J.) precluded plaintiff's accident reconstruction expert after conducting *Daubert* analysis to "determine whether the reasoning or methodology underlying [the proffered expert] testimony is scientifically valid and . . . whether that reasoning or methodology properly can be applied to the facts in issue." *Id.* at *5. The defendants moved for summary judgment and to exclude the plaintiff's accident reconstruction expert. *Id.* at *1. The plaintiff's expert testimony intended to demonstrate that the accident resulting in the plaintiff's decedent's death was caused entirely by the actions of the defendants. *Id.* at *4. In ruling the expert's testimony inadmissible, the court focused on the fact that the expert "merely reviewed the materials provided to him by plaintiffs' counsel and based his conclusions entirely on his interpretation of the facts and statements contained in those materials." *Id.* at *6. The expert did not conduct any additional research and measurements relating to the accident, nor interview any witnesses or law enforcement officers who were present at the scene of the accident. *Id.* The court determined that "such conclusions and opinions lack the reliability required by *Daubert* and would provide no assistance to a reasonable jury in assessing the present evidence." *Id.* at *7.

B. EXPERT-RELATED RULES AND PROCEDURAL ISSUES IN FEDERAL COURT

1. *Districts of Maine, New Hampshire, Puerto Rico, and Rhode Island*

The federal courts in the states within the First Circuit, with the exception of Massachusetts, have not, as a general matter, promulgated local rules that modify the Federal Rules of Civil Procedure in any material respect with regard to practice and procedure involving experts and expert reports. For example, the local rules of the U.S. District Courts for the Districts of Maine, New Hampshire, Puerto Rico, and Rhode Island do not contain specific rules governing expert discovery or trial practice. Thus, the Federal Rules of Civil Procedure apply without modification in those districts. Since the Federal Rules of Civil Procedure do not specifically address such matters as the conduct of expert depositions and whether a pretrial hearing must be held to address objections to the admissibility of expert testimony, those issues are left to the parties to work out by agreement, or may be addressed at the pretrial conference or in the court's pretrial orders.[5]

2. *District of Massachusetts*

The U.S. District Court for the District of Massachusetts, by contrast, has adopted a local rule that establishes so-called special procedures for handling experts. Rule 26.4(A) of the Local Rules of the U.S. District Court for the District of Massachusetts provides that, unless otherwise directed by court order, expert disclosures pursuant to Fed. R. Civ. P. 26(a)(2) "shall be made at least 90 days before the final pretrial conference." Following receipt of expert disclosures, a party that intends to object to an expert's qualifications or to any exhibit related to the proposed testimony must "give written notice of the ground of objection, together with supporting authority, to all other parties no later than the time for such objections provided in [Local Rule] 16.5(c)." Local Rule 26.4(A) of the U.S. District Court for the District of Massachusetts. The parties are obligated first to meet and confer in an attempt to resolve any such objections. In the event the parties are unable to resolve their dispute, objections are submitted to the court for resolution as part of the joint pretrial memorandum. Local Rule 16.5 (C) & (D) of the U.S. District Court for the District of Massachusetts.

At the final pretrial conference, judges of the U.S. District Court for the District of Massachusetts are required to consider (1) precluding the appearance of any expert witness who was not

---

[5] For example, New Hampshire Local Rule 16.3 states that at the final pretrial conference "the court may consider and take appropriate action" on evidentiary problems, including expert witnesses.

timely identified, (2) precluding the use of any expert testimony at trial that would be "at variance with any written statement or any deposition testimony," (3) limiting the use of expert depositions (including videotaped depositions) at trial, and (4) "making any other ruling on the admissibility of expert testimony at trial." Local Rule 26.4(B) of the U.S. District Court for the District of Massachusetts. The obvious purpose of this rule is to reduce the chance that "ambush" techniques will be employed at trial.

3. *Discovery and Trial Practice*

Discovery and trial practice with respect to experts are strictly scrutinized and may provide a basis for challenging a judgment on appeal when the rules are not followed. A prime example is procuring expert testimony that goes beyond the scope of disclosure in the expert report or during discovery. In *Licciardi v. TIG Ins. Grp.*, 140 F.3d 357 (1st Cir. 1998), the First Circuit (Selya, Boudin, Lynch, J. J.) addressed whether the trial court committed reversible error by permitting defendant's medical expert to testify, over plaintiff's objection, as to causation issues that were not disclosed in his Fed. R. Civ. P. 35 expert report or in supplemental interrogatory responses served after the jury had been impaneled (which, indeed, confirmed that the subject of the expert's testimony would be the same as was disclosed in his prior expert report). *Id.* at 360–62. Noting that the trial court's decision to permit defendant's medical expert to testify as to an important undisclosed causation issue was extremely prejudicial to plaintiff, the First Circuit vacated the defense judgment and remanded the case for a new trial. *Id.* at 363–67.

C. STATE LAW EXPERT ISSUES

1. *Expert Evidence in Massachusetts State Courts*

a.   *Daubert*, in Part, Determines Admissibility

Massachusetts courts utilize the *Daubert* standard in concert with the standard set out by the Massachusetts Supreme Judicial Court in *Commonwealth v. Lanigan*, 419 Mass. 15 (1994), to determine the admissibility of a scientific expert's opinion. In *Lanigan,* the court accepted the basic reasoning of *Daubert* but went on to state, "[w]e suspect that general acceptance in the relevant scientific community will continue to be the significant, and often the only, issue. We accept the idea, however, that a proponent of scientific opinion evidence may demonstrate the reliability or validity of the underlying scientific theory or process by some other means, that is, without establishing general acceptance." *Id.* at 26. Massachusetts state courts consistently apply the *"Daubert-Lanigan"* standard. *See, e.g., Peter Palandjian v. Foster*, 446 Mass. 100, 106–07 (2006); *Commonwealth v. Patterson*, 445 Mass. 626, 627–28 (2005); *Commonwealth v. Zimmerman*, No. 06-P-1240, 2007 Mass. App. LEXIS 1050, at *4 (Oct. 3, 2007); *Federico v. Ford Motor Co.*, 67 Mass. App. Ct. 454, 457 (2006).

Until the Massachusetts Supreme Judicial Court rendered its decision in *Commonwealth v. Lanigan*, 419 Mass. 15 (1994), Massachusetts courts used the *Frye* "general acceptance" test to determine the reliability of a scientific theory underlying scientific opinion evidence. *Id.* at 24. In *Lanigan,* the defendant challenged his conviction for rape and indecent assault and battery on the ground that the trial court erred in admitting incriminating DNA evidence. *Id.* at 16. The court concluded that the commonwealth had established the reliability of the process underlying its expert testimony as to the DNA evidence and affirmed the defendant's conviction. *Id.* at 27.

While acknowledging that it traditionally had applied the *Frye* test when determining the admissibility of expert testimony based on scientific knowledge, the court recognized the "risk that reliable evidence might be kept from the factfinder by strict adherence to the *Frye* test" and insisted that it had always instructed Massachusetts courts to apply the *Frye* test flexibly. *Id.* at 24. According to the court, the "ultimate test . . . is the reliability of the theory or process underlying the expert's testimony." *Id.* at 25. The commonwealth urged the court to adopt the reasoning of *Daubert* and to abandon the *Frye* general acceptance test. *Id.* The court stated that the Supreme Court recognized "general acceptance" as a relevant factor in determining admissibility of expert testimony based on a scientific theory but admonished that it was not the sole test. *Id.* The court described the other factors set forth in *Daubert* and opined that "[t]he general proposition set forth in the *Daubert* opinion seems sound, although that opinion gives little guidance for the application of that proposition to the facts of a given case." *Id.* (citing *Daubert*, 509 U.S. at 598–99 (Rehnquist, C. J., concurring in part, dissenting in part)). The court adopted the *Daubert* test as follows:

> We accept the basic reasoning of the *Daubert* opinion because it is consistent with our test of demonstrated reliability. We suspect that general acceptance in the relevant scientific community will continue to be the significant, and often the only, issue. We accept the idea, however, that a proponent of scientific opinion evidence may demonstrate the reliability or validity of the underlying scientific theory or process by some other means, that is, without establishing general acceptance.

Id. at 26.

Many of Massachusetts's significant decisions have arisen in the criminal context. In *Commonwealth v. Senior*, 433 Mass. 453 (2001), the court reaffirmed that it had adopted *Daubert* "in part" by its holding in *Lanigan*. *Id.* at 458. The court continues to apply "the *Daubert-Lanigan* standard" where "the ultimate test . . . is the reliability of the theory or process underlying the expert's testimony," which can be established without a showing of general acceptance. *Id.* (quoting *Lanigan*, 419 Mass. at 24).

Commonwealth v. Pytou Heang, 458 Mass. 827 (2011), is significant both as a challenge to the specificity of an expert's conclusion and as a directive for discovery and trial presentation practices in forensic evidence cases. Reviewing a challenge to firearms identification evidence [matching projectiles and spent cartridge casings from a crime scene to a weapon found in an apartment], the Massachusetts Supreme Judicial Court first gave approval to the trial judge's ruling that "the trooper could testify 'to a degree of scientific certainty' that the recovered projectiles were fired by the nine millimeter firearm seized at 17 Morris Street provided he also admitted that he could not exclude the possibility that the projectiles were fired by another nine millimeter firearm." *Id.* at 844. The court then set guidelines for future cases involving firearms identification evidence: first, that examiners extensively document their findings and provide that documentation in discovery, *id.* at 847; second, that any opinion evidence be preceded by an explanation of the "the theories and methodologies underlying the field of forensic ballistics," *id.*; and finally, that any opinion of a match be expressed to a reasonable degree of "ballistics certainty" rather than "scientific certainty," *id.* at 848.

In *Commonwealth v. Patterson*, 445 Mass. 626 (2005), a criminal defendant moved to exclude all fingerprint evidence from his retrial on the grounds that the commonwealth's latent fingerprint identification techniques were unreliable and inadmissible under *Daubert* and *Lanigan*. *Id.* at 627–28. On appeal, the court held that the "the underlying theory and process of latent fingerprint identification, and the ACE-V method in particular, are sufficiently reliable to admit expert opinion testimony regarding the matching of a latent impression with a full fingerprint." *Id.* at 628. The commonwealth, however, failed to establish the general reliability of latent fingerprint identification. *Id.* "It needed to establish that the theory, process, and method of latent fingerprint identification could be applied reliably to simultaneous impressions not capable of being individually matched to any of the fingers that supposedly made them." *Id.* "The procedure we adopted in *Lanigan* includes ensuring not only the reliability of the abstract theory and process underlying an expert's opinion, but the particular application of that process." *Id.* at 648. After applying an independent *Daubert-Lanigan* inquiry, the court found that the commonwealth did not establish that "the application of the ACE-V method to simultaneous impressions is generally accepted by the fingerprint examiner community or that a review of the other *Daubert* factors favors admission of evidence based on such an application." *Id.* at 655. As a result, the court vacated the trial court's denial of defendant's motion to exclude the fingerprint evidence and remanded the case for further proceedings. *Id.*

In *Commonwealth v. Bradway*, 62 Mass. App. Ct. 280 (2004), the defendant appealed a judgment of the superior court that found him to be a sexually dangerous person and committed him to a treatment center. *Id.* at 280–81. The defendant argued that the trial judge erred in admitting expert testimony from state-qualified examiners[6] without assessing such testimony for reliability under *Daubert*. *Id.* at 281. The court stated that "[w]hether the testimony of qualified examiners is admissible absent a determination that the anticipated testimony meets the standards set by *Daubert* . . . is an issue of first impression for the appellate courts of Massachusetts." *Id.* at 283. The court denied defendant's motion and held that qualified examiners did not need to undergo such analyses because the legislature had "made a considered decision to draw on qualified and experienced professionals in the field to bring to bear their knowledge and informed judgment on the necessary, but difficult, task of evaluating whether sex offenders are likely to reoffend." *Id.* at 287. Thus, the appeals court found that the trial court properly admitted the qualified examiners' testimony as to the sexual dangerousness of an offender.

In *Commonwealth v. Glyman*, Nos. 02-499, 02-500, 2003 Mass. Super. LEXIS 431 (Dec. 15, 2003), the defendants, who were charged with offenses arising from falsifying a will, challenged the admissibility of expert testimony concerning handwriting analysis. The defendants sought to exclude the expert testimony on the ground that it did not meet the standard of reliability required by *Lanigan*. However, "Massachusetts, like other jurisdictions, has long admitted handwriting comparison by a qualified expert." *Id.* at *2. "Massachusetts courts have considered the reliability of such testimony to be so firmly established as to obviate the need for preliminary screening." *Id.* at *3. Finding that an evidentiary hearing is neither required nor warranted, and that the expert's qualifications were sufficient, the court denied defendants' motion to exclude. *Id.* at *13–14.

Lastly, in *Commonwealth v. Pasteur*, 66 Mass. App. Ct. 812, the court held that "[t]o preserve an objection to expert testimony pursuant to *Lanigan*, a defendant must file a pretrial motion and request a hearing on the subject." *Id.* at 826. In *Pasteur*, the defendant argued that the trial court improperly admitted the opinion testimony of a pathologist called by the commonwealth. The defendant maintained that there was an inadequate showing that the expert's methodology was sufficiently reliable. The court found, however, that the defendant waived any objection to the admissibility of the expert testimony by failing to make a proper pretrial objection. Moreover, at a voir dire of the pathologist, the defense failed to make an inquiry relevant to the expert's methodology. As a result, the Court of Appeals denied the defendant's appeal.

---

[6] A qualified examiner must be "a physician who is licensed . . . [and] who is either certified in psychiatry by the American Board of Psychiatry and Neurology or eligible to be so certified, or a psychologist who is licensed." *Id.* at 284. "The examiner must also have 'two years of experience with diagnosis and treatment of sexually aggressive offenders' and be designated by the Commissioner of Correction." *Id.* (quoting Mass. Gen. Laws ch. 123A, § 1).

2. Expert Evidence in Maine State Courts

a. State Law Determines Admissibility of Scientific Evidence

The Supreme Judicial Court in Maine has declined to adopt the *Daubert* standard outright. *Searles v. Fleetwood Homes of Pa.*, 878 A.2d 509, 516 n.2 (Me. 2005) ("[W]e decline [defendant's] invitation to adopt the *Daubert* standard in the present case"); *see also Hall v. Kurz Enters.*, No. CV-04-44, 2006 Me. Super. LEXIS 94, at *8 (May 3, 2006) (holding that "controlling law in Maine" governs the issue); *Mills-Stevens v. Travelers Ins. Co.*, No. CV-03-362004, 2004 Me. Super. LEXIS 194 (Aug. 13, 2004) ("*Daubert* was decided on grounds that are not binding on Maine courts"). Despite the court's unwillingness to adopt *Daubert,* the Maine standard is very similar to that set out in *Daubert*. In fact, the Superior Court of Maine noted in *Hall v. Kurz Enter.*, 2006 Me. Super. LEXIS 94 at *9 (2006), that there is very little difference between the analyses under Maine law and *Daubert*—"the principle and purpose" of the two inquiries are the same.

Under controlling law in Maine, the ultimate test for the admissibility of expert testimony is whether (1) the testimony is relevant pursuant to Rule 401 of the Maine Rules of Evidence and (2) it will assist the trier of fact in understanding the evidence or determining a fact in issue. 878 A.2d 509, 515–16 n.2 (Me. 2005) (quoting *State v. Williams*, 388 A.2d 500, 504 (Me. 1978)). "To meet the two-part standard for the admission of expert testimony, the testimony must also meet a threshold level of reliability." *Id.* at 516. In determining whether the threshold level of reliability has been met, a trial court may consider whether "the scientific matters involved in the proffered testimony have been generally accepted or conform to the generally accepted explanatory theory." *Id.* at 516 (quoting *Williams*, 388 A.2d at 504). General acceptance is not a prerequisite for admission; rather, the court has latitude to determine whether the proffered evidence is sufficiently reliable to be held relevant. *Id.*

Lastly, the Supreme Judicial Court has cited *Daubert* with approval. *See, e.g., Flippo v. L.L. Bean, Inc.*, No. CV 00-446, 2004 Me. Super LEXIS 171, at *5 (Jan. 7, 2004) (applying *Daubert* exclusively). For example, in *State v. MacDonald*, 718 A.2d 195 (Me. 1998), the Supreme Judicial Court addressed whether a trial court properly excluded defendant's proffered expert testimony that the accused suffered from adult children of alcoholics syndrome (a condition not recognized by the definitive treatise on psychological studies). In an effort to cast doubt on the veracity of the accused's incriminating statement made to the police shortly after discovery of the crime, the expert would have opined that the accused is more likely than a person not suffering from this condition to have lied to protect others. Citing the test from *Daubert,* the court affirmed the trial court's exclusion of the testimony primarily on the ground that the condition is not generally accepted in the field of psychiatry and has not been supported by published studies. *Id.* at 198–99; *see also Green v. Cessna Aircraft Co.*, 673 A.2d 216, 218–19 (Me. 1996) (citing *Daubert* with approval in affirming trial court's decision rejecting plaintiff's proffered expert opinion as to mechanical causes of airplane crash because it was based on assumptions not supported by evidence of record).

3. Expert Evidence in New Hampshire State Courts

a. *Daubert* Applies to Determinations of Admissibility of Scientific Evidence

The New Hampshire Supreme Court adopted the *Daubert* standard in *Baker Valley Lumber, Inc. v. Ingersoll-Rand*, 148 N.H. 609 (2002) (holding that the trial court erred in its application of the formerly used *Cressley* test and adopting *Daubert*). The court stated that "[a]lthough *Daubert* is binding only in federal court, the text of New Hampshire Rule of Evidence 702 is identical to the federal rule at the time of the *Daubert* decision. . . . Today, we apply the *Daubert* standard to New Hampshire Rule of Evidence 702." *Id.* at 614 (citations omitted). The court "emphasize[d] that our adoption of *Daubert* does not require a trial court to conduct a pretrial hearing in every case involving disputed expert testimony. The decision to hold such an evidentiary hearing rests within the trial court's sound discretion. . . . Pre-trial hearings, thus, should be limited to the 'less usual or more complex cases where cause for questioning the expert's reliability arises.'" *Id.* at 617 (quoting *Kumho Tire Co. v. Carmichael*, 526 U.S. 137, 152 (1999)).

4. Expert Evidence in Rhode Island State Courts

a. *Daubert* Guides Issues of Admissibility of Scientific Evidence

The highest court in Rhode Island has cited *Daubert* with approval but has declined to expressly adopt the standards outlined therein. Rather, the Supreme Court of Rhode Island drew guidance from the principles set forth in *Daubert* when it formulated the standard Rhode Island trial courts should use when determining the admissibility of expert scientific testimony. *See DiPetrillo v. Dow Chem. Co.*, 729 A.2d 677, 685–86 (R.I. 1999). In practice, however, the courts refer to the state court standard interchangeably with the term *"Daubert* analysis." *See Roe v. Gelineau*, 794 A.2d 476, 483 (R.I. 2002); *see also Mills v. State Sales, Inc.*, 824 A.2d 461, 470 (R.I. 2003); *Youngsaye v. Susset*, No. 03-2892, 2007 R.I. Super. LEXIS 127 (Sept. 10, 2007); *Dodson v. Ford Motor Co.*, No. PC 96-1331, 2006 R.I. Super. LEXIS 113 (Aug. 17, 2006).

In *DiPetrillo v. Dow Chemical Co.*, 729 A.2d 677 (R.I. 1999), the Supreme Court of Rhode Island discussed the standard that should govern a trial court's decision concerning the admissibility of novel, complex scientific evidence. *Id.* at 685. Specifically, the court offered "guidance on the standard for admissibility that should govern preliminary hearings and hearings out of the presence of the jury." *Id.* at 686. In its discussion, the court walked through the four prongs of the *Daubert* analysis and noted that although the court has declined to expressly adopt the *Daubert* standard, the court has "endorsed its principles." *Id.* The court instructed trial justices, in their discretion, to "control the gateway for expert scientific testimony by conducting pursuant to Rule 104 an early, preliminary assessment of the evidence." *Id.* "Faced with a proffer of expert scientific testimony . . . the trial judge must determine at the outset . . . whether the expert is proposing to testify to (1) scientific knowledge that (2) will assist the trier of fact to understand or determine the fact in issue." *Id.* at 687 (quoting *Daubert I*, 509 U.S. at 592–93).

In *State v. Quattrocchi*, 681 A.2d 879 (R.I. 1996), the court held that the trial court erred in failing to hold an evidentiary hearing on defendant's objection to the admissibility of expert testimony regarding suppressed memories of childhood sexual assault. *Id.* at 884. The court "le[ft] for another day the emphasis to be placed on general acceptance as set forth in both *Frye* and *Daubert* as opposed to the three other factors set forth in *Daubert*." *Id.* at n.2; *see also State v. Morel*, 676 A.2d 1347, 1355 (R.I. 1996) (citing *Daubert* with approval in interpreting its identical counterpart to Fed. R. Evid. 702 to uphold trial court's admission of DNA evidence on sound scientific bases).

D. LOCAL PRACTICE TIPS AND SUGGESTIONS

As in other courts, expert-related discovery and trial practice in courts located in the geographic area of the First Circuit are critical to the outcome of many cases. This is particularly true in complex civil cases involving intellectual property and other technology matters, where expert testimony is invaluable in educating the finder of fact (whether judge or jury) about the merits of your position. Although the courts located in the First Circuit historically have not been populated with large numbers of cases involving intellectual property and technology, greater numbers of these types of cases are being brought and, thus, the judges are increasingly becoming familiar with the types of issues they present.

A critical factor to successfully litigating such cases is finding the right expert. Although there is no "magic formula" to selecting the most qualified expert for a particular issue, consideration should be given to the expert's qualifications (educational degrees, specialized training, licenses to practice, length of practice in the field, relevant work or research experience, publications, teaching experience, membership in professional organizations, and prior experience as an expert witness), experience in the legal arena (including deposition and trial experience), and possible conflicts of interest (with respect to parties and issues). Consideration should also be given to whether the expert will be supported by a research assistant or assistants who can assist with discovery and other matters (usually in a more cost-effective manner) or will handle everything him- or herself.

Finding appropriate candidates to serve as experts can be difficult but must be undertaken as early in the case as possible to ensure that your litigation team is in place once discovery commences. Moreover, it is always prudent to contact and retain the best experts in the field before they are retained by your opponents. Other attorneys who have experience litigating similar cases and faculty members at local universities are valuable resources who often provide helpful recommendations for possible expert witnesses during the search and identification process.

Expert reports should be complete enough, at a minimum, to provide the information required by Fed. R. Civ. P. 26(a)(2)(B). Depositions of experts who are expected to testify at trial are conducted only after submission of the expert report and, as a practical matter, should be scheduled only after counsel has had an adequate opportunity to review and understand the contents of the expert report. A prudent course is to share your opponent's expert report with your own expert on that issue in order to obtain assistance in conducting written and deposition testimony as to that expert. If the pretrial schedule permits sufficient time to conduct written discovery of experts prior to conducting depositions, that opportunity should be utilized. Motions to exclude an expert witness from appearing at trial and motions *in limine* should be filed at the earliest available opportunity (usually shortly following the date on which expert discovery closes), but no later than the last date on which such motions can be filed, so that they will be ripe for consideration at the final pretrial conference. In the Boston metropolitan area this procedure is generally followed, in contrast with other courts within the First Circuit. Both Fed. R. Civ. P. 26(a)(1) and 26(a)(2)(B) allow parties to proceed either by stipulation or court order as alternatives to the procedure described above. In fact, such a course of conduct is the prevailing practice in courts of the First Circuit of Boston.

Successful cross-examination of expert witnesses is particularly difficult because counsel is rarely as proficient in the subject matter at issue as the expert. One strategy that has been used effectively by experienced cross-examiners of expert witnesses is to avoid challenging the expert's specialized knowledge, but rather to attack the predicate facts and underlying premises on which the expert's conclusions are based. In addition, expert witnesses are sometimes prone to think only within the "box" of their particular subject matter; points oftentimes can be scored by cross-examining an expert with respect to an issue that is not directly addressed in his or her expert report, but that is necessarily implicated by the conclusions drawn by the expert (for instance, damages).

CHAPTER II
EXPERT EVIDENCE IN FEDERAL AND STATE COURTS WITHIN THE SECOND CIRCUIT

by

**Arvin Maskin
Konrad L. Cailteux
Theodore E. Tsekerides
Isabella C. Lacayo[1]
Weil, Gotshal & Manges LLP
767 Fifth Avenue
New York, New York 10153
(212) 310-8000**

A. EXPERT EVIDENCE IN FEDERAL COURTS WITHIN THE SECOND CIRCUIT

1. Key Decisions in the Second Circuit on Expert Evidence

The role of the district court as "gatekeeper" with broad discretion to determine the admissibility of expert testimony is well settled in the Second Circuit.[2] In performing this "gatekeeping role," district courts are charged with a two-fold responsibility: to determine whether proffered testimony is relevant and sufficiently reliable. *Lynch v. Trek Bicycle Corp.*, 374 Fed. App'x 204, 206 (2d Cir. 2010) (citing *Amorgianos v. Nat'l R.R. Passenger Corp.*, 303 F.3d 256, 265 (2d Cir. 2002)); *Moltner v. Starbucks Coffee Co.*, 399 Fed. App'x 630, 631–32 (2d Cir. 2010). In order to be relevant, the testimony must be helpful to the jury, that is, it must "assist the trier of fact to understand the evidence or to determine a fact in issue." Fed. R. Evid. 702; *see also United States v. Farhane*, 634 F.3d 127 (2d Cir. 2011); *Major League Baseball Props., Inc. v. Salvino, Inc.*, 542 F.3d 290, 310 (2d Cir. 2002) ("[A] trial judge must determine at the outset . . . whether the expert is proposing to testify to (1) scientific knowledge that (2) will assist the trier of fact to understand or determine a fact in issue.") (quoting *Daubert v. Merrell Dow Pharmaceuticals*, 509 U.S. 579, 592 (1993)). Performing this analysis requires courts to "be guided by the indicia of reliability identified in Rule 702," *Moltner*, 399 Fed. App'x at 632, as well as the considerations laid out in *Daubert* and *Kumho Tire*. *See Nimely v. City of New York*, 414 F.3d 381, 396 (2d Cir. 2005). These factors do not constitute a "definitive checklist" for admissibility, but rather act as guideposts to inform the court in performing its gatekeeping function. *See also George v. Ford Motor Co.*, No. 03 Civ. 7643, 2007 WL 2398806,

---

[1] The authors wish to thank associate Jesse Morris and summer associates Jennifer Ramos, Molly Weston, Rachel Liebert, and Daniel Cohl for their invaluable assistance in preparing this review of expert evidence in the courts of the Second Circuit.

[2] It is equally well settled that the principles first discussed in *Daubert* apply to all forms of expert testimony, as established in *Kumho* and reflected in Rule 702.

at *3 (S.D.N.Y. Aug. 17, 2007); *Adesina v. Aladan Corp.*, 438 F. Supp. 2d 329, 342 (S.D.N.Y. 2006). Where the usefulness of testimony is questionable, courts tend to favor admitting the evidence, if the testimony could at all be useful.[3]

The district court applies a flexible, case-specific inquiry in determining the admissibility of expert evidence. *Amorgianos*, 303 F.3d at 265–66; *see also Wick v. Wabash Holding Corp.*, 801 F. Supp. 2d 93, 109 (W.D.N.Y. 2011).[4] The latitude given to the district court applies not only to the ultimate decision whether to admit or exclude expert testimony, but also as to the factors to consider in making the determination. *Olin Corp. v. Certain Underwriters at Lloyd's London*, 468 F.3d 120, 133 (2d Cir. 2006); *see also United States v. Carmona*, 361 Fed. App'x 166, 170 (2d Cir. 2010) (district courts have "broad latitude" with respect to admissibility of expert testimony) (citing *Kumho*, 526 U.S. at 153). Additionally, even where the district court determines that there are certain deficiencies in an expert's testimony, it may nonetheless admit the testimony where such deficiencies go to the weight of the proffered testimony rather than its admissibility.[5]

Recognizing that expert testimony is often indispensable to support a party's claim or defense, courts within the Second Circuit are hesitant to exclude proffered testimony without giving the proponent of the testimony a full opportunity to be heard on issues of admissibility. *See George v. Ford Motor Co.*, 2007 WL 2398806, at *4 (noting that although plaintiff's expert failed to meet the *Daubert* standards, a hearing on the admissibility of the expert's testimony was warranted, as the *Daubert* standards are suggestive factors, not rigid prerequisites to admissibility). In *George v. Ford Motor Co.*, the court stated that, based on the expert report, the expert testimony proffered by plaintiffs did not meet three of the four criteria laid out in *Daubert* for evaluating admissibility. 2007 WL 2398806, at *3.[6] Nevertheless, characterizing the *Daubert* factors as "guideposts" rather than strict prerequisites, the court ordered a hearing to determine admissibility. *Id.* at *4.[7] This result

---

[3] *See United States v. Jackobetz*, 955 F.2d 786, 797 (2d Cir. 1992) (noting that "doubts about whether an expert's testimony will be useful should generally be resolved in favor of admissibility unless there are strong factors such as time or surprise favoring exclusions") (quoting 3 WEINSTEIN & BERGER, WEINSTEIN'S EVIDENCE, § 702[03], at 702–36 (1989)); *see also Borawick v. Shay*, 68 F.3d 597, 610 (2d Cir. 1995); *UMG Recordings, Inc. v. Lindor*, 531 F. Supp. 2d 453, 456 (E.D.N.Y. 2007); *Schwab v. Philip Morris USA, Inc.*, 449 F. Supp. 2d 992, 1137 (E.D.N.Y. 2006).

[4] This breadth of the court's discretion is based on the notion that "the rejection of expert testimony is the exception rather than the rule." Fed. R. Evid. 702, advisory committee's note; *see also E.E.O.C. v. Morgan Stanley & Co.*, 324 F. Supp. 2d 451, 456 (S.D.N.Y. 2004).

[5] *See Olin*, 468 F.3d at 133–34 (district court did not abuse its discretion in allowing expert to testify even though it found that some of the expert's conclusions were not well supported). In *Olin*, the district court admitted the expert testimony on the basis that weaknesses in the expert's conclusions could be pointed out to the jury during cross-examination. The court held that this was a better technique of attacking weak expert testimony than wholesale exclusion. *Id.* at 134; *see also Amorgianos*, 303 F.3d at 267; *Deutsch v. Novartis Pharms. Corp.*, 768 F. Supp. 2d 420, 482 (E.D.N.Y. 2011) ("Plaintiffs' arguments regarding the personal experiences of the experts or the articles they reviewed go to the weight and not the admissibility of the opinions").

[6] The court held that the fourth *Daubert* factor—known error rate—did not apply to the case, but noted that the expert acknowledged that he had no way of estimating how frequently his theory would predict that electromagnetic interference would cause sudden acceleration in a cruise control system. 2007 WL 2398806, at *3.

[7] After the *Daubert* hearing, the court admitted the proffered expert testimony. *George v. Ford Motor Co.*, No. 03 Civ. 7643, 2007 WL 4355048, at *1 (S.D.N.Y. Dec. 11, 2007).

is consistent with jurisprudence in the Second Circuit, recognizing that while the *Daubert* factors provide guidance, the determination of admissibility must remain flexible.[8]

Although recognizing the liberalized view toward admissibility of expert evidence, in fulfilling their gatekeeper function, courts within the Second Circuit continue to scrutinize expert testimony to ensure that it is reliable and relevant. In that regard, an expert's testimony must be based on the expert's knowledge, not speculation or conjecture. *See, e.g., Fernandez v. Cent. Mine Equip. Co.*, 670 F. Supp. 2d 178, 185 (E.D.N.Y. 2009); *DiBella v. Hopkins*, 403 F.3d 102, 121 (2d Cir. 2005); *In re Rezulin Prods. Liab. Litig.*, 309 F. Supp. 2d 531, 541 (S.D.N.Y. 2004). Courts compare the witness's area of knowledge, education, experience, or skill with the subject of the proffered testimony to determine whether the testimony is proper.[9] In order to verify that an expert's testimony is more than mere subjective speculation, and to permit a sufficient evaluation of reliability, Second Circuit courts demand that experts specifically explain the methodology by which their ultimate conclusions were reached.[10] However, "[a] minor flaw in an expert's reasoning or a slight modification of an otherwise reliable method will not render an expert's opinion *per se* unreasonable." *Amorgianos*, 303 F.3d at 267.[11] In making this evaluation, courts must look to the totality of a witness's background and qualifications.[12]

The reliability analysis, while meticulous, is by no means rigid. The focal point of the inquiry centers upon the Supreme Court's instruction in *Kumho* that the trial court ascertain whether the expert "employ[ed] in the courtroom the same level of intellectual rigor that characterizes the

---

[8] *See, e.g., Borawick v. Shay*, 68 F.3d 597, 610 (2d Cir. 1995) (emphasizing *Daubert*'s holding that the determination of admissibility must be flexible); *Celebrity Cruises Inc. v. Essef Corp.*, 434 F. Supp. 2d 169, 176 (S.D.N.Y. 2006) (noting that *Daubert* requires flexibility in determining admissibility).

[9] *See United States v. Chin*, 371 F.3d 31, 40 (2d Cir. 2004); *see also United States v. Diallo*, 40 F.3d 32, 35 (2d Cir. 1994) (determining witness was competent to testify as an expert because of his extensive knowledge and work as a commodities analyst); *Delehanty v. KLI, Inc.*, 663 F. Supp. 2d 127, 133 (E.D.N.Y. 2009) (finding expert unqualified because of his lack of specialization in the field for which testimony was proffered); *United States v. Ojeikere*, No. 03 CR 581JGK, 2005 WL 425492, at *4 (S.D.N.Y. Feb. 18, 2005) (noting that "[i]n certain fields, experience is the predominant, if not sole, basis for a great deal of reliable expert testimony").

[10] *See, e.g., Reigel v. Medtronic, Inc.*, No. 99-CV-0649, 2003 WL 25556778, at *5 (N.D.N.Y. Dec. 2, 2003); *Lippe v. Bairnco Corp.*, 288 B.R. 678 (S.D.N.Y. 2003); *Donnelly v. Ford Motor Co.*, 80 F. Supp. 2d 45 (E.D.N.Y. 1999); *Trouble v. Wet Seal Inc.*, 179 F. Supp. 2d 291 (S.D.N.Y. 2001).

[11] *See also Gross v. Bare Escentuals Beauty, Inc.*, 641 F. Supp. 2d 175, 191 (S.D.N.Y. 2008); *Alfa Corp. v. OAO Alfa Bank*, 475 F. Supp. 2d 357, 360 (S.D.N.Y. 2007); *Adel v. Greensprings of Vermont, Inc.*, 363 F. Supp. 2d 683, 686 (D. Vt. 2005); *Pugliano v. United States*, 315 F. Supp. 2d 197, 199 (D. Conn. 2004); *Demar v. DL Peterson Trust*, No. 1:05-CV-0103, 2006 WL 2987314, at *2 (N.D.N.Y. Oct. 13, 2006).

[12] *See Rosco, Inc. v. Mirror Lite Co.*, 506 F. Supp. 2d 137, 144–45 (E.D.N.Y. 2007); *see also, e.g., Hollman v. Suffolk Cnty.*, 06-CV-3589 JFB ARL, 2011 WL 2446428, at *14 n.13 (E.D.N.Y. June 15, 2011); *Chooseco LLC v. Lean Forward Media LLC*, No. 1:07-CV-159, 2009 U.S. Dist. LEXIS 2522 (D. Vt. Jan. 13, 2009); *Humphrey v. Diamant Boart, Inc.*, 556 F. Supp. 2d 167, 174–75 (E.D.N.Y. 2008); *Emig v. Electrolux Home Prods. Inc.*, 06-CV-4791, 2008 WL 4200988, at *4 (S.D.N.Y. Sept. 11, 2008); *Tiffany (NJ) Inc. v. eBay, Inc.*, 576 F. Supp. 2d 457, 458 (S.D.N.Y. 2007); *Keenan v. Mine Safety Appliances Co.*, CV-03-0710 TCP ARL, 2006 WL 2546551, at *2 (E.D.N.Y. Aug. 31, 2006); *Smith v. Herman Miller, Inc.*, CV-03-5358, 2005 WL 2076570 (E.D.N.Y. Aug. 26, 2005).

practice of an expert in the relevant field" in formulating his expert opinion. *See Kumho*, 526 U.S. at 152. Whether the proposed expert testimony reaches this threshold varies based upon the nature of the testimony and the methods used by the expert. While the factors listed in Rule 702, as well as those enunciated in *Daubert*, are often an appropriate starting point, Second Circuit courts will generally consider any factor that could be relevant to its admissibility analysis. *See, e.g.*, *In re Omeprazole Patent Litig.*, 490 F. Supp. 2d 381, 401 (S.D.N.Y. 2007). Other factors courts consider include: the foundation for the opinion,[13] failure to test theories,[14] personal knowledge or experience,[15] and whether the opinion is "speculative or conjectural."[16] Additionally, in performing its reliability analysis, the district court "must focus on the principles and methodology employed by the expert, without regard to the conclusions the expert has reached or the district court's belief as to the correctness of those conclusions." *Amorgianos*, 303 F.3d at 267 (citing *Daubert*, 509 U.S. at 595). The expert's conclusions are relevant, though, as a court may conclude that there is too large an analytical gap between the data and the expert's opinion, connected by nothing more than the *ipse dixit* of the expert. In these situations, *Joiner* instructs a district court to exclude such testimony.[17]

A district court's determination regarding the admissibility of expert testimony is afforded great weight. In reviewing these decisions, the Second Circuit uses an abuse of discretion standard. *See Chin v. Port Authority of N.Y. & N. J.*, 685 F.3d 135, 161 (2d Cir. 2012) ("A district court's exclusion of expert testimony is reviewed for abuse of discretion and 'a decision to admit or exclude expert scientific testimony is not an abuse of discretion unless it is 'manifestly erroneous'" (*citing Amorgianos*, 303 F.3d at 265)); *Nimely*, 414 F.3d at 292.

Under this standard, the Second Circuit will only reverse district court decisions to admit or exclude expert evidence that are "manifestly erroneous." *See Zerega Ave. Realty Corp. v. Hornbeck Offshore Transp., LLC*, 571 F.3d 206, 213 (2d Cir. 2009); *Zaremba v. Gen. Motors Corp.*, 360 F.3d 355, 357 (2d Cir. 2004).[18]

---

[13] *See Nimely v. City of New York*, 414 F.3d 381, 396–97 (2d Cir. 2005) (noting that *Daubert* and Rule 702 mandate exclusion of opinions based on data, methodology, or studies that are inadequate to support the conclusions reached).

[14] *See Zaremba v. Gen. Motors Corp.*, 360 F.3d 355 (2d Cir. 2004).

[15] *See, e.g.*, *In re Zyprexa Prods. Liability Litig.*, 489 F. Supp. 2d 230, 286 (E.D.N.Y. 2007); *Rivera v. Mill Hollow Corp.*, No. 96 CIV. 8150, 2000 WL 1175001, at *1 (S.D.N.Y. 2000).

[16] *Highland Capital Mgmt., L.P. v. Schneider*, 379 F. Supp. 2d 461, 473 n.2 (S.D.N.Y. 2005) (quoting *Boucher v. U.S. Suzuki Motor Corp.*, 73 F.3d 18, 21 (2d Cir. 1996)); *see also, e.g.*, *Major League Baseball Props., Inc. v. Salvino, Inc.*, 542 F.3d 290, 311 (2d Cir. 2008) ("[a]dmission of expert testimony based on speculative assumptions is an abuse of discretion") (quoting *U.S. Suzuki Motor Corp.*, 73 F.3d at 22); *Dora Homes, Inc. v. Epperson*, 344 F. Supp. 2d 875, 889 (E.D.N.Y. 2004) (rejecting expert's "subjective" and speculative opinion as "patently devoid of reliability"); *U.S. Info. Sys., Inc. v. Int'l Bd. of Elec. Workers Local Union Number 3, AFL-CIO*, 313 F. Supp. 2d 213, 227 (S.D.N.Y. 2004) (one factor for courts to consider in determining reliability is "whether the expert's technique can be challenged in some objective sense, or whether it is instead simply a subjective, conclusory approach that cannot reasonably be assessed for reliability").

[17] *See, e.g.*, *Ruggiero v. Warner-Lambert Co.*, 424 F.3d 249, 253 (2d Cir. 2005); *Amorgianos*, 303 F.3d at 266; *Lewis v. FMC Corp.*, 786 F. Supp. 2d 690, 705 (W.D.N.Y. 2011); *Berk v. St. Vincent's Hosp. & Med. Ctr.*, 380 F. Supp. 2d 334, 350 (S.D.N.Y. 2005).

[18] *See also Chin*, 371 F.3d at 40 (noting that it is not an abuse of discretion "merely because [the Second Circuit] would have disagreed" with the district court's decision); *United States v. Taubman*, 297 F.3d 161, 164 (2d Cir. 2002) (same); *United States v. Schatzle*, 901 F.2d 252, 257 (2d Cir. 1990).

Notwithstanding the broad discretion given to the district courts, the Second Circuit will remedy situations where a district court's admission or exclusion of expert testimony is improper. In *Nimely*, an expert for the defendant—a police officer accused of shooting the plaintiff in the back—testified that it was his opinion that the police officer perceived that the plaintiff was facing him and holding a weapon, even though the medical evidence showed that the plaintiff was shot in the back. 414 F.3d at 389. This testimony was based on the short period of time over which the events at issue took place and the consistency between the testimony of the officer and his partner at their pretrial depositions. The expert also testified—over continued objections by plaintiff's counsel—that, given the investigation and surrounding circumstances that were sure to follow a shooting by an officer, there would be no reasons for the officer to lie, and therefore, he based his conclusions on the presumption that the officers' testimony was credible. *Id.* at 394. The only explanation given by the expert for rejecting the notion that the officers were lying was that such a lie would be "easily disproved." *Id.* at 395.

The Second Circuit held that admission of this testimony was erroneous on several grounds and required a new trial. *Id.* at 398. By testifying that he rejected the possibility that the officers were lying in reaching his conclusions, the expert was essentially instructing the jury as to an issue that was exclusively within its province—the credibility of the officers as witnesses. *Id.* This testimony essentially informed the jury as to the result to reach and sought to substitute the expert's judgment for the jury's. *Id.* The Second Circuit, and other circuits, have consistently held that expert opinions constituting evaluations of witness credibility are inadmissible under Rule 702, "even where such evaluations are rooted in scientific or technical expertise." *Id.*[19]

In analyzing the admissibility of expert testimony, courts within the Second Circuit are mindful that certain factors go to the weight of the proposed expert testimony rather than its admissibility. Such factors include: whether the expert has employed the best method available,[20] whether gaps or inconsistencies exist with respect to the expert's testimony,[21] and whether the expert's opinion, model, or test lacks a real-world equivalent. *See, e.g.*, *Jarvis v. Ford Motor Co.*, No. 92 Civ. 2900, 1999 WL 461813 (S.D.N.Y. July 6, 1999); *Guild v. Gen. Motors Corp.*, 53 F. Supp. 2d 363 (W.D.N.Y. 1999). Where such factors form the primary basis of a party's objection to the admission of its opponent's expert, courts in the Second Circuit will generally deny the motion to exclude the testimony and allow a jury to determine its value.

When experts testify that there are safer alternative designs in products liability cases, Second Circuit courts require more than a mere hypothetical design before the expert testimony will be admitted. *See, e.g.*, *Kass v. W. Bend Co.*, No. 02-CV-3719, 2004 WL 2475606, at *13 (E.D.N.Y. Nov. 4, 2004) (characterizing the failure to operate or test a proposed alternative design as a "fatal oversight [that] flies in the face of established engineering and scientific methodology"), *aff'd* 158 Fed. App'x 352 (2d Cir. 2005). In *Zaremba v. General Motors Corp.*, the plaintiffs were involved in an automobile accident in which the Pontiac Trans Am they were in rolled over. 360 F.3d 355. The

---

[19] *See also United States v. Lumpkin*, 192 F.3d 280, 289 (2d Cir. 1999); *United States v. Duncan*, 42 F.3d 97, 101 (2d Cir. 1994); *Hill v. City of New York*, No. 03-CV-1283, 2007 WL 1989261, at *5 (E.D.N.Y. July 5, 2007); *United States v. Paracha*, No. 03 CR 1197, 2006 WL 12768, at *23 (S.D.N.Y. Jan. 3, 2006).

[20] *See, e.g.*, *Adel*, 363 F. Supp. 2d at 689 (admitting plaintiff's expert testimony over defendants' objection that more advanced testing methods than the one used by plaintiff's expert existed went to the weight of the expert evidence, not its admissibility, and noting that Rule 702 and *Daubert* do not require an expert to use the best method available, only that the evidence be relevant and reliable); *Reyes v. Delta Dallas Alpha Corp.*, No. 92 Civ. 4418, 2000 WL 526851 (S.D.N.Y. May 4, 2000).

[21] *See, e.g.*, *SR Int'l Bus. Ins. Co., Ltd. v. World Trade Ctr. Props., LLC*, 467 F.3d 107, 134 (2d Cir. 2006) (citing *Campbell v. Metro. Prop. & Cas. Ins. Co.*, 239 F.3d 179, 186 (2d Cir. 2001)); *In re Ephedra Prod. Liab. Litig.*, 393 F. Supp. 2d 181, 189 (S.D.N.Y. 2005).

driver was killed, and the two passengers were injured—one of them suffering brain damage. The Trans Am was a "T-top" model with removable glass panels separated by a longitudinal bar running down the center of the car's roof. The plaintiffs alleged that the vehicle was defectively designed and that rather than having a single support bar running down the middle of the roof, there should have been two longitudinal "roof rails" running along each side of the car. In support of their theories, the plaintiffs sought to introduce expert testimony regarding this safer alternative design based on a reconstruction of the accident. 360 F.3d at 356–57.

General Motors challenged the proffered expert testimony on the basis that it was not grounded in a reliable methodology. The district court agreed, concluding that "[e]ssentially the [expert's] design ha[d] no concrete basis in reality." *Id.* at 357. Among the reasons for this conclusion were that the expert: (1) made no prototype of his proposed alternative design, (2) conducted no tests of his design, (3) offered no calculations in support of the safety of his design, (4) had not subjected his alternative design to peer review and evaluation, and (5) had presented no evidence that others in the automobile design community accepted his untested propositions. *Id.*[22] Accordingly, the court held that although the proffered experts were qualified in their field, their testimony was "based on unfounded speculation and [was] unreliable under *Daubert* principles." *Id.* With the expert testimony excluded, the court granted summary judgment to the defendants.

The Second Circuit held that the district court did not commit manifest error in excluding the plaintiffs' experts. It noted that the experts did not satisfy any of the four *Daubert* factors, and cited the decisions of numerous courts in excluding expert testimony regarding a safer alternative design "where the expert failed to create drawings or models or administer tests." *Id.* at 358–59. The court rejected the plaintiffs' argument that their expert's testimony was reliable based on tests performed by GM on a design similar to the expert's proposed alternative design in which GM concluded that the modified design would have "improved 'bending performance' and 'tortional performance.'" *Id.* at 359. Even accepting this as true, the plaintiffs' expert could not show that his hypothetical design "would have resulted in greater safety in the rollover accident at issue." *Id.* In the absence of a prototype of his design, and without performing calculations and tests regarding the hypothetical alternative design, the Second Circuit held that the district court's decision to exclude the expert was not manifestly erroneous. Based on the affirmance of the district court's exclusion of the plaintiffs' expert, the Second Circuit also affirmed the grant of summary judgment to GM. *Id.* at 360.

There is no obligation for the opponent of expert testimony to offer testimony from a rebuttal expert in order for a proffered expert to be excluded. In *Brooks v. Outboard Marine Corp.*, 234 F.3d 89, 91 (2d Cir. 2000), the Second Circuit held that the initiation of a court's gatekeeping function is not contingent upon the presentation of opposing expert testimony. In *Brooks*, the hand of plaintiff's fourteen-year-old son was amputated in a boating accident when the boy's arm became entangled with a boat's propeller. Plaintiff claimed that the boat's motor was "unreasonably dangerous" due to the lack of a propeller guard and a defective gearshift mechanism that engaged with only minimal pressure. *Brooks*, 234 F.3d at 90.

In an initial one-page report, plaintiff's expert concluded that either a propeller guard or an emergency shutdown device (otherwise known as a kill switch), would have prevented the accident in its entirety or, in the alternative, reduced its severity. Thereafter, the only additional evidence produced by plaintiff's expert was a videotape generally demonstrating the operation of a kill switch. Defendant moved to exclude plaintiff's expert on the ground that the expert lacked the proper qualifications to testify and that his theory regarding the impact of a kill switch was untested and unsup-

---

[22] Plaintiffs also sought to introduce testimony of a medical expert to testify as to the reduced injuries plaintiffs would have sustained if the alternative design proposed by plaintiff's engineering expert had been implemented. This testimony was rejected based on the fact that, *inter alia*, the medical expert relied on the testimony of the rejected engineering expert to support his conclusions. 360 F.3d at 357.

ported by an actual examination of the boat at issue or an interview with any witness. The magistrate judge excluded the expert's opinion as unreliable and speculative. Without the expert testimony, the magistrate recommended that defendant receive summary judgment because plaintiff could not make out her prima facie case of causation. Over plaintiff's objection, the district court adopted the magistrate's recommendation. *Id.* at 91.

On appeal, plaintiff argued that the order dismissing his expert was untimely because the defendant had not presented contradictory expert testimony. The Second Circuit held that the trial court's gatekeeping role is not dependent upon a challenge from an opposing expert. Indeed, the court noted that neither *Daubert* nor *Kumho* required a rebuttal expert before proffered expert testimony could be "sufficiently called into question." *Id.*

Further, in finding that the district court did not abuse its discretion by excluding plaintiff's expert, the Second Circuit held that "[t]he failure to test a theory of causation can justify a trial court's exclusion of the expert's testimony." *Brooks*, 234 F.3d at 92.[23] In *Brooks*, plaintiff's expert not only failed to reconstruct the accident or test his "kill switch" theory, but the expert never inspected the allegedly defective boat or motor, never spoke to any of the individuals involved in the incident, and was unaware of several key facts.

Second Circuit courts have shown a willingness to adapt to technology in expert-related issues as well. In *Alfa Corp. v. OAO Alfa Bank*, the defendants challenged plaintiff's proffered expert on several grounds, one of them being his reliance on the Internet Web site *Wikipedia* as a source supporting his opinion. 475 F. Supp. 2d at 361–63. The court noted that judicial opinions frequently cited to Internet Web sites—including *Wikipedia*—which suggests that courts do not consider such sources to be inherently unreliable. *Id.* at 361–62. While recognizing that there may be issues of reliability with *Wikipedia* (enhanced by the ability of anonymous users to modify entries), the court held that the expert could testify and the defendants could challenge his testimony by "apply[ing] the tools of the adversary system to his report." *Id.* at 362.[24]

---

[23] Second Circuit courts on several other occasions have excluded expert testimony due at least in part to the expert's failure to test a proffered theory. *See, e.g., Lynch v. Trek Bicycle Corp.*, 374 Fed. App'x 204, 207 (2d Cir. 2010) ("district court was not required to accept [expert's] testimony regarding . . . speculative and untested theories regarding the cause of [plaintiff's] accident"); *Zaremba*, 360 F.3d 355; *Kass*, 2004 WL 2475606, at *6 ("[c]ourts have repeatedly rejected expert testimony where a proposed theory or alternative design was not properly tested for safety or utility"); *Rypkema v. Time Mfg. Co.*, 263 F. Supp. 2d 687, 693 (S.D.N.Y. 2003) (court excluded expert testimony regarding a design defect on the latch attached to an aerial lift bucket where expert proposed the use of a different style latch, but did not test alternative design with the suggested latch, and expert was opposed by an equally qualified expert for defendant who had performed tests on the product at issue); *Colon v. BIC USA, Inc.*, No. 00 Civ. 3666, 2001 WL 1631402 (S.D.N.Y. Dec. 19, 2001) (excluding expert's testimony regarding design defect of safety lock on cigarette lighter because expert failed to test his proposed alternate design or point to a comparable design in the marketplace). *But see Martin v. Shell Oil Co.*, 180 F. Supp. 2d 313 (D. Conn. 2002) (refusing to exclude plaintiff's expert and holding that an expert's opinion need only be testable, not that it necessarily be tested).

[24] The court noted that citing a Web site in a judicial opinion is not necessarily the same as using it as a source for an expert opinion, but it does indicate that courts do not view the Internet as inherently unreliable, and therefore, it may be an appropriate source upon which an expert may partially base his opinion. *Alfa Corp.*, 475 F. Supp. 2d at 361–62 (citing *Phillips v. Pembroke Real Estate, Inc.*, 459 F.3d 128, 133 n.3 (1st Cir. 2006). *See, e.g., Reuland v. Hynes*, 460 F.3d 409, 422 n.1 (2d Cir. 2006) (Winter, J. dissenting); *Sacirbey v. Guccione*, No. 05 Civ. 2949, 2006 WL 2585561, at *1 n.2 (S.D.N.Y. Sept. 7, 2006); *Applied Interact, LLC v. Vermont Teddy Bear Co.*, No. 04 Civ. 8713, 2005 WL 2133416, at *11 (S.D.N.Y Sept. 6, 2005).

Where proffered expert testimony meets the standards of reliability indigenous to the expert's field, courts in the Second Circuit appear inclined to admit the testimony. *See In re Fosamax Prods. Liab. Litig.*, 645 F. Supp. 2d 164, 183 (S.D.N.Y. 2009) (permitting testimony on causation from experts that had published peer-reviewed articles on the subject matter, noting that this is a significant indication that the research is accepted by other scientists). For example, in *Katt v. City of New York*, 151 F. Supp. 2d 313 (S.D.N.Y. 2001), the plaintiff, a former civilian employee of the New York City Police Department ("NYPD"), claimed that she was subjected to a hostile working environment and sexual harassment in violation of federal, state, and city antidiscrimination laws. Defendants asserted that plaintiff's failure to seek redress through the administrative grievance mechanism provided by the police department was an affirmative defense barring recovery. In response, plaintiff argued that her fear of retaliation as well as the NYPD's "code of silence" would have rendered any attempt to use the police department's internal adjudication system entirely ineffective. To support her assertion, plaintiff offered the testimony of a criminologist and former New York City police officer who testified that police culture strongly disfavoring complaints or truthful testimony about officer misconduct is effectively conveyed to civilian employees and would have reasonably discouraged plaintiff from filing the otherwise required complaints. *Id.* at 324–26.

In its posttrial motion for judgment as a matter of law, defendants argued that by failing to cite empirical evidence regarding the existence of a code of silence and basing his conclusions entirely upon anecdotal data such as interviews and conversations with NYPD officers, plaintiff's expert utilized a flawed methodology and should have been precluded from testifying. The court offered two separate grounds for rejecting defendants' challenges. First, based in part upon the judge's personal familiarity with the "standards and practices of academic criminology," the court held that plaintiff's expert had employed a level of intellectual rigor consistent with his particular field of social science. In an effort to understand the actual practices of law enforcement officials, plaintiff's expert acted reasonably in relying upon interviews with officers, criminals, and victims as well as his personal observations as a police officer and trained sociologist. While the court acknowledged that statistical methods are sometimes used to analyze the results of this type of data, it determined that no statistical study would have adequately assessed police culture with respect to reporting misconduct. *Id.* at 355–57; *see also Benjamin v. Kerik*, No. 75 CIV 3073, 2000 WL 278085 (S.D.N.Y Mar. 14, 2000) (admitting expert testimony based upon anecdotal evidence concerning the importance of attorney-client meetings in providing a criminal defense and the effect of the burdensome practices and procedures of the New York City Department of Corrections for conducting such meetings).

Further, the court found that the defendants' challenges, aimed at discrediting the skill and knowledge of plaintiff's expert, were more relevant to weight than admissibility. The court noted that defendants had a full and fair opportunity to expose any shortcomings of the expert's testimony to the jury. Indeed, the jury was made aware that plaintiff's expert did not base his opinion on statistical information and depended upon hearsay information to obtain his data. *Katt*, 151 F. Supp. 2d at 357–58.

Defendants additionally attempted to exclude the expert's testimony as irrelevant because the jurors, as citizens of New York City and in light of mass media coverage of the NYPD, did not need expert testimony to understand the so-called code of silence. However, citing well-settled precedent, the court held that the particular facts of a case may make the jury's general knowledge of a subject incomplete or inaccurate and that in such cases expert testimony sufficiently assists the jury so as to be relevant and admissible.[25] Accordingly, the court found that the testimony of plaintiff's expert

---

[25] *See also United States v. Amuso*, 21 F.3d 1251, 1264 (2d Cir. 1994) (permitting expert testimony on crime-family terminology and practices despite the prevalence of such information in the

was properly admitted because it was helpful to the jury's understanding of why the plaintiff reasonably chose to forsake established complaint procedures. *Id.* at 358–59.

The decision in *Freitas v. Michelin Tire Corp.*, No. Civ. 3:94CV1812, 2000 WL 424187 (D. Conn. Mar. 2, 2000), further illustrates that courts in the Second Circuit carefully examine all aspects of an expert's testimony to parse through and separate the reliable from the unreliable. The plaintiff in *Freitas*, the administrator of the decedent's estate, charged that a defect in both design and warning caused the victim's death when he attempted to inflate one of defendant's tires on a mismatched wheel. Defendant alleged that the expert testimony presented by each of plaintiff's experts was unreliable and irrelevant. *Id.* at *1.

With respect to the design defect claim, plaintiff offered the testimony of an engineering expert who opined that defendant's 16-inch tires were defective because they fit on a 16.5-inch wheel and exploded at low inflation pressures. The expert based his conclusions on his experience as a tire engineer, his own mathematical calculations, burst tests he had previously conducted on other mismatched tires, other burst tests performed by reliable testers, sworn testimony, reports of other experts, and documents from the defendant and others in the tire industry. The court concluded that the design defect expert's testimony was appropriately grounded in his extensive experience, training, and education, and was firmly supported by "reliable data including information of a type reasonably relied upon by experts in the field." *Id.* at *2. The court also held that any further dispute about the quality of the sources used by the expert or the lack of textual authority would go to the weight rather than admissibility of the testimony. *Id.*

By contrast, the court held that while relevant, the testimony of plaintiff's other expert concerning an alleged warnings defect was insufficiently reliable for admission. That expert insisted that an adequate warning located on the sidewall of defendant's tires would, more likely than not, have been noticed and read, thereby preventing the decedent's injury. This opinion was based upon the expert's own research and studies, in which he determined that adequate warnings, if noticed, would favorably alter people's behavior. However, on cross-examination at a *Daubert* hearing, the plaintiff's expert admitted that he was unaware of any studies that considered the effect of warnings on the sidewalls of actual tires and that none of his own studies tested the noticeability of "on-sidewall" warnings. Rather, the expert asserted that other field tests concerning the matching and mounting of tire and wheel components by service-station workers creates a valid inference that warnings would be recognized and read. The court found this linkage insufficient, holding that the expert's conclusion was not supported by empirical data and was nothing more than unsupported speculation. *Id.* at *4.

Courts within the Second Circuit have also been guided by the Supreme Court's admonition in *Joiner* that "nothing in either *Daubert* or the Federal Rules of Evidence requires a district court to admit opinion evidence that is connected to existing data only by the *ipse dixit* of the expert" and that "a court may conclude that there is simply too great an analytical gap between the data and the opinion proffered." *Gen. Elec. Co. v. Joiner*, 522 U.S. 136, 146 (1997). For example, in *Zwillinger v. Garfield Slope Hous. Corp.*, No. CV94-4009, 1998 WL 623589, at *10–11, 23 (E.D.N.Y. Aug. 17, 1998), plaintiff sought to recover for injuries allegedly caused by emissions from newly installed

---

media because the operational methods of crime families is beyond the knowledge of the average citizen). *But see LinkCo, Inc. v. Fujitsu LTD*, No. 00 Civ. 7242, 2002 WL 1585551, at *3 (S.D.N.Y. July 16, 2002) (holding expert testimony that was based only on a review of deposition testimony and documents produced in discovery to be inadmissible because it "address[ed] evidence and issues that [were] within the understanding of the jury"); *Grdinich v. Bradlees*, 187 F.R.D. 77, 82 (S.D.N.Y 1999) (excluding as irrelevant expert testimony concerning whether ironing boards were safely displayed because such a concept was within the understanding of the jury).

carpeting. Defendants moved for summary judgment, contending that plaintiff's proffered expert was unqualified to testify, and that the testimony upon which plaintiff intended to base her claim—that emissions from the carpet caused her to develop an immunotoxicity syndrome known as multiple chemical sensitivity ("MCS")—was inadmissible because it failed to meet *Daubert*'s reliability and relevance requirements. The defendants maintained that because the plaintiff's only proffered causation testimony was inadmissible, they were entitled to judgment as a matter of law.

Although the district court found that plaintiff's proffered expert was qualified to testify, the court agreed that the expert's analysis and conclusions failed to meet the standard for admissibility set forth by *Daubert*. *Id.* at *13–15. Moreover, the district court found that in evaluating the conclusions the expert had drawn from his research and treatment of plaintiff, it was readily apparent that there was too great an analytical gap between his data and the opinions he offered. Consequently, the court excluded the expert's testimony. Among its reasons for discrediting the expert's research was that the research was likely "marred by a high rate of error," *id.* at 18, since the expert did not use a control group, and because the expert's theories of causation were neither empirically tested nor subject to peer review. *Id.* at 17. Because the excluded testimony had been plaintiff's only proffered evidence on causation, the court granted defendants' summary judgment motion. *Id.* at 23.

2. *Expert-Related Rules and Procedural Issues*

a. Local Rules

The 2000 Amendments to the Federal Rules of Civil Procedure eliminated the authority of district courts and individual judges to alter or "opt out" of national disclosure requirements by local or individual rule. The amendments invalidated both formal local rules as well as "standing" orders, issued by either individual judges or the court, that exempted parties from the national rule. However, judges are still able to fashion contrary rules on a case-specific basis where the national requirements are inappropriate for the specific circumstances of a particular case.

In addition, practitioners should be aware of local rules and individual judges' rules that may add requirements to those found in the Federal Rules of Civil Procedure. For example, Local Rule 26.3 of the Northern District of New York provides for disclosure of expert witnesses, including, unless otherwise stipulated by the parties, a curriculum vitae and a written report pursuant to Fed. R. Civ. P. 26(a)(2)(B) prior to the completion of discovery, in accordance with the deadlines set by the Uniform Pretrial Scheduling Order or other court order. Failure to meet the requirements of this rule may result in sanctions or preclusion of testimony. Several individual judges' rules require submission of specific information relating to expert witnesses. The Honorable Deborah Batts of the Southern District of New York, for example, requires parties to include a "brief summary of the testimony of each expert (one page at most)" in a joint pretrial statement.[26] And the Honorable Jesse Furman in the same court requires that "motions to exclude testimony of experts . . . be made by the deadline for dispositive motions" and specifies that they are not to be treated as motions *in limine*.[27]

---

[26] Individual Practices of Judge Deborah A. Batts, *available at* http://www.nysd.uscourts.gov/cases/show.php?db=judge_info&id=436.

[27] Individual Practices of Judge Jesse M. Furman, *available at* http://www.nysd.uscourts.gov/cases/show.php?db=judge_info&id=637.

b. The Expert Report

The determination of the sufficiency of an expert report is not subject to any hard and fast rule in the Second Circuit other than those established by Federal Rule of Civil Procedure 26(a)(2)(B)[28] and Federal Rule of Evidence 702. *Robinson v. Suffolk Cnty. Police Dep't*, No. CV 08-1874 (AKT), 2011 U.S. Dist. LEXIS 119356, at *6–8 (E.D.N.Y. Oct. 17, 2011). Generally, the report must be prepared and signed by the expert, contain a complete statement of the expert's opinions and the basis and reasons for those opinions, disclose the data or other information considered by the witness in forming the opinions, and list the cases in which the expert has provided expert testimony at either trial or deposition during the preceding four years. Further, the report should set forth the substance of the expert's opinion and reflect the substance of the testimony the expert is expected to present on direct examination. *See Bank Brussels Lambert v. Credit Lyonnais (Suisse), S.A.*, No. 93 Civ. 6876, 2000 WL 1762533, at *1 (S.D.N.Y. Nov. 30, 2000); Advisory Committee Notes for the 1993 amendments to Federal Rule 26(a)(2).

After submitting an expert report, an expert may have a duty to supplement the report if the original report contains information that is incomplete or incorrect and that is not otherwise known to the parties in the course of discovery. FED. R. CIV. P. 26(e)(1). A court will assume that once submitted, an expert report reflects the expert's "full knowledge and complete opinions on the issues for which his opinion has been sought." *Sandata Tech., Inc. v. Infocrossing, Inc.*, 69 Fed. R. Serv. 3d 776 (S.D.N.Y. 2007). The duty to supplement is not an invitation to submit an additional report as a rebuttal to opposing party's own expert report where the originally submitted report was deficient. *Sandata*, 69 Fed. R. Serv. 3d, at *5–6 (holding that supplemental reports by defendant's expert witness were not admissible since they did not fall under the duty to supplement since the later reports were responsive to issues raised by the plaintiff rather than rectifying incomplete or incorrect information); *see also Lidle v. Cirrus Design Corp.*, 08 CIV. 1253 BSJ/HBP, 2009 WL 4907201, at *6 (S.D.N.Y. Dec. 18, 2009) (not permitting submission of supplemental expert report where report did not correct incomplete or incorrect information and was based on the same information relied on for the initial report).

Any additions or changes to an expert's report must be disclosed by the time a party's Rule 26(a)(3) pretrial disclosures are due. FED. R. CIV. P. 26(e)(2); *see also Sandata*, 69 Fed. R. Serv. 3d, at *3. Late reports, whether original or supplemental, are subject to sanctions according to Rule 37(c)(1). *See Innis Arden Golf Club v. Pitney Bowes, Inc.*, 3:06 CV 1352, 2009 WL 5873112, at *3–4 (D. Conn. Feb. 23, 2009) (rejecting supplemental expert report where the report neither corrected nor supplemented incomplete information and whose late submission was neither justified nor harmless).

c. Failure to Comply with Expert Disclosure Requirements

Pursuant to Federal Rule 37(c)(1), failure to meet the disclosure requirements of Rule 26(a)(2) results in preclusion of such testimony at trial. The rule sets out two exceptions for the automatic preclusion: substantial justification for nondisclosure or harmless error from the nondisclosure. Fed. R. Civ. P. 37(c)(1). Given the "drastic" nature of exclusion of expert testimony as a remedy and the critical need for the use of expert testimony, however, courts within the Second Circuit have generally reserved the exclusion sanction for truly egregious cases, and granted such sanctions only "in those rare cases where a party's conduct represents flagrant bad faith and callous disregard" of the Federal Rules. *See, e.g., Sterling v. Interlake Indus., Inc.*, 154 F.R.D. 579, 587 (E.D.N.Y. 1994). Since the 2000

---

[28] *See, e.g., In re Kreta Shipping, S.A.*, 181 F.R.D. 273, 275 (S.D.N.Y. 1998) (citing Federal Rule 26(a)(2)(B) and advisory committee notes in analyzing the sufficiency of claimant's expert reports).

amendments to the Federal Rules of Civil Procedure no longer require a demonstration of bad faith, however, the Second Circuit has held that the previous bad faith standard should not be read into Rule 37(c)(1). *Design Strategy, Inc. v. Davis*, 469 F.3d 284, 296 (2d Cir. 2006); *see also Degelman Indus. Ltd. v. Pro-Tech Welding & Fabrication, Inc.*, No. 06–CV–6346, 2011 WL 6754059, at *2 (W.D.N.Y. June 8, 2011) (noting that the 2000 amendments do not require a finding of bad faith and instead applying the substantial justification or harmless error analysis to determine whether to exclude expert testimony).

Where a party's failure to disclose experts is inexcusable, courts will take the "drastic remedy" to exclude the experts. In *Bastys v. Rothschild*, No. 97 Civ. 5154, 2000 WL 1810107, at *26 (S.D.N.Y. Nov. 21, 2000), the district court excluded the affidavits of three of the plaintiff's experts for failure to disclose their identity and reports during discovery. At the close of discovery, plaintiff had not disclosed any expert witnesses he intended to call at trial. On September 22, 1999, the defendants moved for summary judgment, and on September 28, 1999, the district court ordered that no further expert discovery would be available to plaintiff. In opposition to the defendants' summary judgment motions, plaintiff sought to use affidavits of three expert witnesses. The defendants argued that the court should decline to consider the affidavits based on the plaintiff's failure to identify such experts as required by Rule 26(a)(2).

Although noting the drastic nature of excluding expert testimony, and the notion that exclusion should only be applied in rare cases, the district court nonetheless held that exclusion was mandated under Rule 37(c)(1). *Id.* at *27. The district court found that neither of the exceptions recognized in Rule 37 for excusing noncompliance with Rule 26 disclosure requirements were present. The plaintiff did not articulate any justification for his failure to comply with the disclosure requirements. And the district court held that the plaintiff's failure to disclose was not harmless because, based on the plaintiff's decision not to identify any expert witnesses, defendants did not retain their own experts. Thus, the district court held that preclusion of the plaintiff's experts was appropriate. *Id.*

Rather than creating a rule for automatic exclusion, though, the Second Circuit has developed a range of factors courts should consider before precluding expert testimony. These factors include: "(1) the party's explanation for the failure to comply with the discovery order; (2) the importance of the testimony of the precluded witness; (3) the prejudice suffered by the opposing party as a result of having to prepare to meet the new testimony; and (4) the possibility of a continuance." *See Softel, Inc. v. Dragon Med. & Scientific Commc'n, Inc.*, 118 F.3d 955, 961 (2d Cir. 1997), *cert. denied*, 523 U.S. 1020 (1998).[29]

For example, in *Patterson v. Balsamic*, 440 F.3d 104 (2d Cir. 2006), the defendant challenged the district court's grant of plaintiff's motion *in limine* seeking to preclude the testimony of defendant's expert witnesses for failure to disclose their identity in a timely fashion. The Second Circuit laid out the four factors to be considered when determining whether the district court abused its discretion in precluding the expert testimony. *Id.* at 117 (quoting *Softel*, 118 F.3d 955). After evaluat-

---

[29]   *See also Great White Bear, LLC v. Mervyns, LLC*, No. 06 Civ. 13358(RMB)(FM), 2008 U.S. Dist. LEXIS 41977, at *15 (S.D.N.Y. May 27, 2008) (noting that although the language of Rule 37(c)(1) is mandatory, the Second Circuit has adopted a discretionary test); *Kolerski v. United States*, No. 06CV422S, 2007 WL 2325856, at *3 (W.D.N.Y. Aug. 13, 2007) (denying defendant's motion to preclude plaintiff's expert even though plaintiff could not justify her failure to disclose, where testimony was crucial to plaintiff's case, defendant could not show prejudice by allowing late disclosure, and an extension of the scheduling order would cure any prejudice the delay may have caused); *Atkins v. Cnty. of Orange*, 372 F. Supp. 2d 377, 396 (S.D.N.Y. 2005) (finding that even though expert's report was deficient and did not fully comply with Rule 26, on balance, the factors used to evaluate the propriety of excluding expert testimony under Rule 37 favored admission).

ing the factors, the Second Circuit determined that the district court had not abused its discretion in precluding the defendant's experts from testifying at trial.

In analyzing the first factor, the Second Circuit noted that there was not substantial justification for the delay in disclosing the expert witnesses and the substance of their testimony. Although defendant's counsel had only recently been substituted as counsel, and thus, had only learned of the existence of the expert witnesses shortly before trial, the court held that this did not excuse the failure of defendant's prior counsel to disclose the experts. Further, defendant's counsel waited for three weeks after plaintiff's Rule 26(a) disclosures, during which time counsel was aware of the identity of the experts even by his own admission. The district court refused to excuse the late disclosure, and the Second Circuit agreed. *Id.*

With respect to the second factor—the importance of the excluded witness's testimony—defendant's counsel did not establish the importance of the proffered testimony to the district court. While counsel offered to explain what the testimony would be on the day of trial, he did not explain how that testimony was important to the defendant's case, even though the district court gave counsel the opportunity to present such an explanation. Although on appeal the defendant argued that the proffered testimony was critical to his case, the Second Circuit held that the district court did not abuse its discretion in finding against the defendant on this factor. *Id.* at 117–18.

The Second Circuit ruled that the third factor—prejudice to the opposing party—clearly weighed in favor of exclusion. The defendant sought to identify four additional expert witnesses just ten days before trial was set to begin. Plaintiff would have to prepare to meet this new evidence, none of which was submitted in connection with the defendant's prior summary judgment motion. Even when the defendant disclosed the identity of the proffered experts, he did not disclose the subject matter of their testimony. Finally, although the prejudice to the plaintiff may have been cured through a continuance, there was no indication in the record that the defendant ever sought a continuance. Given the history of the case, the Second Circuit refused to hold that the district court abused its discretion by excluding defendant's proffered experts rather than issue a continuance on its own initiative. Based on the Second Circuit's review of the factors to be considered before precluding expert testimony, it held that the district court properly ruled against the defendant. *Id.* at 118.

Although a continuance of the proceedings will often diminish the prejudice to the party opposing the submission of untimely expert disclosure, courts within the Second Circuit will not use this tool to excuse the failure of counsel to adhere to discovery rules. *See In re Teligent, Inc.*, 358 B.R. 45, 57 (Bankr. S.D.N.Y. 2006) (noting that "[w]hile a continuance is always possible . . . [d]eadlines should be observed," and that expert evidence will be precluded where the other factors favor preclusion) (citing *Millenium Expressions, Inc. v. Chaus Mktg., Ltd.*, No. 02 Civ. 7545, 2006 WL 288353, at *2 (Feb. 6, 2006)). Rather, courts will look to the other factors to determine whether preclusion is warranted, and whether a continuance would lessen, or eliminate, the prejudice to the party opposing the expert evidence. Where, however, other factors make preclusion unnecessary, courts will admit the expert testimony and take necessary steps—such as grant a continuance or other scheduling modification to allow the opposing party a full opportunity to counter the expert evidence—to ensure that a party does not benefit from its failure to disclose to the detriment of the opposing party. *See, e.g., Houlihan v. Invacare Corp.*, No. CV 2004-4286, 2006 WL 1455469, at *1 (E.D.N.Y. May 24, 2006) (permitting plaintiff's expert to submit supplemental report, but requiring plaintiff to bear all of the costs for defendant to re-depose plaintiff's expert on supplemental issues); *Cartier, Inc. v. Four Star Jewelry Creations, Inc.*, No. 01 Civ. 11295, 2003 WL 22471909, at *2 (S.D.N.Y. Oct. 31, 2003) (refusing to preclude plaintiff's proffered expert testimony where there was no showing of bad faith on the plaintiff's part and any prejudice could be cured by allowing defendant to depose plaintiff's expert even though discovery had closed).

In *Grdinich v. Bradlees*, 187 F.R.D. 77 (S.D.N.Y. 1999), the court refused to preclude plaintiff's expert even though plaintiff submitted its expert reports over a month after they were due. The court found that plaintiff's decision to suspend expert preparation in light of ongoing settlement negotiations and mediation efforts substantially justified his nondisclosure. Indeed, the court noted that plaintiff's month-and-a-half-long delay did not exhibit the "flagrant bad faith" or "callous disregard" otherwise required for preclusion. Further, the court rejected the defendant's claim that plaintiff's failure to comply with Rule 26 prejudiced its case because defendant did not retain its own expert upon concluding that plaintiff had no intention of offering expert testimony. Rather, the court held that any prejudice to the defendant could simply be remedied by allowing defendant additional time to name its own expert and to depose plaintiff's. *Id.* at 79.

In *Fritter v. Dafina, Inc.*, 181 F.R.D. 215 (N.D.N.Y. 1998), however, the court precluded the defendant's expert from testifying concerning opinions he had not disclosed in his initial report. There, the court set a deadline for the production of expert reports, and defendant's expert submitted a timely report. Subsequently, plaintiff deposed defendant's expert and learned that the expert had conducted additional testing and videotaping following the court-imposed deadline. Plaintiff's counsel refused to depose the expert with respect to the later testing, maintaining that the testing violated the court's order. The defendant argued that the subsequent testing merely affirmed the conclusions reflected in the expert's report and offered to permit further deposition of its expert. The court refused, finding: "Only one month is insufficient time for plaintiffs to complete such tests. Any delay in the trial date, which has been set for quite some time, would considerably inconvenience the parties and the court." Accordingly, the court excluded the defendant's expert's supplemental testimony and evidence. 181 F.R.D. at 217; *see also Ferriso v. Conway Org.*, No. 93 Civ. 7962, 1995 WL 580197, at *1 (S.D.N.Y. Oct. 3, 1995) (upholding magistrate's order precluding expert from testifying at trial concerning matters beyond the scope of expert's written report but recognizing without deciding that, assuming no prejudice to adversary, report could be amended); *Gold v. Dalkon Shield Claimants Trust*, No. 5:82-CV-383, 1998 WL 422900, at *1 (D. Conn. July 16, 1998), *aff'd*, 189 F.3d 460 (1999), *cert. denied*, 529 U.S. 1068 (2000) (awarding summary judgment to the defendant where the plaintiff failed to comply with the dictates of Federal Rule 26(a)(2)(B) in identifying an expert to meet plaintiff's burden of proof on causation).

These cases demonstrate that the sanctions for failing to comply with the expert disclosure requirements under the Federal Rules will turn primarily upon factors concerning prejudice to the opposing party and the court. So long as the defect may be cured without causing undue delay to the proceedings and irreconcilable damage to the opposing party, a court will most likely fashion a remedy that allows supplements to an expert's report but at the offending parties' expense. However, practitioners proceed at their peril if the expert report is untimely or fails to contain the information required under the Federal Rules, particularly if such noncompliance may delay the case. Because there is no guarantee that a court will allow a supplemental or untimely disclosure, the better practice is to ensure at the outset that the report contains all of the expert's opinions and supporting bases and to coordinate with the expert to ensure timely disclosure. If it appears that the deadline cannot be met, practitioners should seek a conference with the court early on in discovery to alert the court of the potential need for additional time and the reasons such extension is required.

d. Costs

In practice, parties to an action typically agree to be responsible for their own expert's fees regardless of whether or not the fees are generated as a result of opposing parties' discovery demands. Where the parties have comparable financial abilities and the number of expert depositions is substantially the same, such an arrangement is even more likely. However, no provision in either the Federal or Local Rules compels parties to consent to a stipulation on expert costs. The apportionment of expert costs is best resolved prior to the discovery scheduling order so that the matter may be included in the case management order.

In cases where the parties fail to stipulate to expert costs, Federal Rule 26(b)(4)(E) governs the assignment of payment responsibilities.

> (E) Payment. Unless manifest injustice would result, the court must require that the party seeking discovery:
>
> (i) pay the expert a reasonable fee for time spent in responding to discovery under Rule 26(b)(4)(A) or (D); and
> (ii) for discovery under (D), also pay the other party a fair portion of the fees and expenses it reasonably incurred in obtaining the expert's facts and opinions.[30]

The fact that the rule also applies to experts who are not required to submit an expert report indicates that the rule is focused on the deposition process rather than the reporting process. *See Lamere v. N.Y. State Office for the Aging*, 223 F.R.D. 85, 93 (N.D.N.Y. 2004) (noting that "it is not the reporting requirement that generates a reasonable fee be paid but, rather, the deposition process itself, which blankets all experts" based on the fact that rule applies to experts who do not have to create any expert report). Additionally, the rule uses the general language of "time spent in responding to discovery" in discussing covered costs, and Second Circuit courts have generally held that the rule permits recovery of fees for activities such as preparation for and travel to a deposition, in addition to the time spent at the deposition itself. *See Packer v. SN Servicing Corp.*, 243 F.R.D. 39, 43 (D. Conn. 2007).[31]

---

[30] The pre-December 1, 2007, version of the rule stated that the court "shall" require the party seeking discovery to pay the covered costs, whereas the amended version uses the term "must." The advisory committee notes state that the rule has been amended as part of the "general restyling of the Civil Rules to make them more easily understood and to make style and terminology consistent throughout the rules." It also notes that the changes "are intended to be stylistic only," and the changes have not had an impact on courts' decisions in cost-sharing disputes. The rule was also updated in 2010, but only to reflect renumbering. Further, while there do not appear to be any cases in the Second Circuit defining what "manifest injustice" may be, the advisory committee notes to the Federal Rules contemplate that such a situation may arise where the party seeking discovery is indigent. *See E.E.O.C. v. Johnson & Higgins, Inc.*, No. 93 CIV. 5481 LBS AJP, 1999 WL 32909, at *4 (S.D.N.Y. Jan. 21, 1999) (holding that the parties in the case could afford to pay the expert costs but noting that implicit in the reasonable fee requirement and manifest injustice caveat of Rule 26(b)(4)(E) is the concept that "a 'rich' party should not be allowed to agree to pay excessively high fees to its expert in order to prevent a 'poorer' opposing party from being able to afford to depose the expert."); *see also Robinson v. Sikorsky Aircraft Corp.*, 142 F. App'x 489, 492 (2d Cir. 2005) (While noting that a court "may deny costs on account of a losing party's indigency," the court refused to waive deposition costs because of plaintiff's inability to pay since the plaintiff did not present the argument on a timely basis and it was meritless since "indigency *per se* does not automatically preclude an award of costs." (citing *Whitfield v. Scully*, 241 F.3d 264, 270 (2d Cir. 2001)). Moreover, courts may compel the party whose expert is being deposed to pay the expert's fees as a sanction for failing to comply with expert discovery requirements.

[31] *See also Conte v. Newsday, Inc.*, No. CV 06–4859, 2012 WL 37545, at *3–4 (E.D.N.Y. Jan. 9, 2012) (requiring defendant to pay plaintiff's experts for ten hours of deposition preparation even though each of the experts spent over fifty hours preparing); *American Ref-Fuel Co. of Niagara, LP v. Caremeuse N.A.*, No. 02-CV-814C(F), 2007 WL 2283768, at *2 (W.D.N.Y. Aug. 6, 2007) (directing plaintiff, as the party seeking the discovery at issue, to compensate

Although Rule 26(b)(4)(E) establishes a party's right to reimbursement for its expert's fees in responding to discovery, parties often dispute what constitutes a "reasonable" fee. The party seeking reimbursement bears the burden of establishing the reasonableness of the fees sought. *See New York v. Solvent Chem. Co.*, 210 F.R.D. 462, 468 (W.D.N.Y. 2002). Where a party fails to meet its burden of establishing the reasonableness of expert fees, courts can exercise their discretion to lower fees that they find to be excessive. *See Mannarino v. United States*, 218 F.R.D. 372, 374 (E.D.N.Y. 2003); *see also Garnier v. Ill. Tool Works*, No. 04CV1825, 2006 WL 1085080, at *4 (ordering expert to be reimbursed at rate of $350/hour rather than the $450/hour sought based on a comparison with the rates of other, similarly qualified experts). *But see Jimico Enters. v. Lehigh Gas Corp.*, No. 1:07-CV-0578, 2011 U.S. Dist. LEXIS 112514, at *38 (N.D.N.Y Sept. 30, 2011) (granting expert fee requested by plaintiff where defendant had not contested the reasonableness of the amount). Generally, courts have determined that it is reasonable for experts to charge the same hourly rate for preparation time as they charge for the time in the deposition. *See McCulloch v. Hartford Life & Accident Ins. Co.*, No. Civ. 3:01CV1115, 2004 WL 2601134, at *2 (D. Conn. Nov. 10, 2004). *But see Garnier*, 2006 WL 1085080, at *4 (reimbursing expert for travel time at a rate of $125/hour but awarding $350/hour for time spent preparing for and attending deposition).

Courts usually limit how much preparation time can be reimbursed under the rule so as to avoid the "great risk of abuse in compensating a party for his expert's deposition preparation time, since that time usually includes much of what ultimately is trial preparation work for the party retaining the expert." *Constellation Power Source, Inc. v. Select Energy, Inc.*, No. 3:04CV983, 2007 WL 188135, at *7 (D. Conn. Jan. 23, 2007). However, given the broad discretion given to district courts to shape discovery matters, there is no bright-line rule for determining how much preparation time should be reimbursable, and decisions vary greatly. For example, in *New York State Office for the Aging*, 223 F.R.D. at 93, the court held that the defendant had to reimburse plaintiff's treating physician, who was testifying as an expert, at the physician's normal hourly rate of $185/hour for preparation time, but the court held that this reimbursement was limited to one and a half hours of preparation time for a three-and-a-half-hour deposition. On the other hand, in *Flaherty v. Connecticut*, No. 3:04 CV 2140, 2006 WL 4475013 (D. Conn. Aug. 23, 2006), the court ordered that the expert be reimbursed for twelve hours of preparation time for a four-hour deposition, a three-to-one ratio.

Courts within the Second Circuit have developed a nonexclusive list of factors to guide the determination as to whether an expert's fee is reasonable. Those factors include: (1) the witness's area of expertise; (2) the education and training required to provide the expert insight that is sought; (3) the prevailing rates of other comparably respected available experts; (4) the nature, quality, and complexity of the discovery responses provided; (5) the cost of living in the particular geographic area; (6) any other factor likely to be of assistance to the court in balancing the interests implicated by Rule 26; (7) the fee being charged by the expert to the party who retained him; and (8) fees traditionally charged by the expert on related matters. *Id.* at 645; *see also Garnier*, 2006 WL 1085080, at *2.[32] None of the factors has "talismanic qualities," but rather are designed to assure that parties maintain the ability to engage competent experts at competitive rates while at the same time preventing opposing parties that wish to depose such experts from having to pay excessive rates. *See*

---

defendant's expert seven hours of preparation time plus travel time at the rate of $125 per hour). *But see Lent v. Fashion Mall Partners*, 223 F.R.D. 317, 318 (S.D.N.Y. 2004) (requiring defendant to pay for plaintiff's expert's preparation time, but requiring plaintiff to pay for expert's travel time and expenses between Georgia and New York where plaintiff made no showing that an acceptable expert was not available in the New York area).

[32] Courts may also look to factors such as the fees being charged by the expert to the party proffering the testimony and the fees traditionally charged by the expert on related matters. *See Mathis v. NYNEX*, 165 F.R.D. 23, 25 (E.D.N.Y. 1996).

Magee v. Paul Revere Life Ins. Co., 172 F.R.D. 627 (E.D.N.Y. 1997); *see also Carovski v. Jordan*, No. 06CV716S, 2008 WL 4501907, at *4 (W.D.N.Y. Sept. 30, 2008). The weight to be given to any particular factor depends on the circumstances before the court. S*ee Goldwater v. Postmaster Gen.*, 136 F.R.D. 337, 340 (D. Conn. 1991); *see also Solvent Chem.*, 210 F.R.D. at 468.

The court in *Magee* was asked to determine the reasonableness of the fee requested by defendant's expert, a psychiatrist. The expert indicated that he would only appear for a deposition upon receipt of a $2,000 deposition fee. Plaintiff objected that the Federal Rules did not require payment in advance of the deposition and that the requested fee was unreasonable. 172 F.R.D. at 644. The expert subsequently reduced his demand to $1,300 but stated that he would only submit to a two-hour deposition ($250 per hour for one hour of preparation, $350 per hour for one hour of travel to the deposition, and $350 per hour for two hours of testimony). The plaintiff, however, maintained its objection and requested that the court set the expert's fee.

The court concluded that the requested fee of $350 per hour was unreasonable and reduced the amount to $250 per hour for all purposes. *Magee*, 172 F.R.D. at 645. The court was swayed by the fact that the expert only charged defendant $250 per hour to examine the plaintiff and that both plaintiff's treating and expert psychiatrists charged $120 and $250 per hour, respectively. Further, the court concluded that the fee was significantly higher than expert psychiatric fees found to be reasonable in other cases. *Id.* at 646.[33]

e. Admissibility Hearings

Second Circuit courts have been guided by *Daubert*'s direction that Rules 104(a) and 702 of the Federal Rules of Evidence require the district court, in its role as gatekeeper, to make a preliminary determination as to the admissibility of expert evidence. To that end, district courts have discretion to conduct pretrial *Daubert* hearings to assist in determining the admissibility of expert evidence. *See United States v. Yousef*, 327 F.3d 56, 148 (2d Cir. 2003).[34] For example, in *Graham v. Playtex Prods., Inc.*, 993 F. Supp. 127 (N.D.N.Y. 1998), the defendant filed a motion for summary judgment seeking the dismissal of plaintiff's warranty and product liability claims. Although the court granted the defendant's motion as to plaintiff's warranty claims, the court reserved judgment on the product liability claims until after it held a *Daubert* hearing to determine the admissibility of plaintiff's expert testimony. After considering the evidence presented at the *Daubert* hearing, the court found the experts' testimony admissible. Accordingly, it denied defendant's summary judgment motion as to plaintiff's product liability claims.[35]

Nothing in *Daubert*, its progeny, or the Federal Rules mandates that the trial court grant a hearing to a party objecting to the admission of expert evidence. *See Colon ex rel. Molina v. BIC USA, Inc.*, 199 F. Supp. 2d 53, 71 (S.D.N.Y. 2001). However, the Second Circuit has noted that, in gen-

---

[33] As discussed below, *Magee*'s holding on "core" work product materials has been superseded by the 2010 amendments to Rule 26. The remainder of *Magee*'s holding, however, remains good law.

[34] Further, where a *Daubert* hearing is conducted, district courts are offered broad discretion in determining the procedures governing the hearing. *Id.* (citing *Kumho*, 526 U.S. at 152).

[35] *See also Deutsch v. Novartis Pharms. Corp.*, 768 F. Supp. 2d 420, 464 (E.D.N.Y. 2011) (scheduling a *Daubert* hearing to determine admissibility of expert evidence); *Freitas v. Michelin Tire Corp.*, No. 3:94CV1812, 2000 WL 424187 (D. Conn. Mar. 2, 2000) (court held a *Daubert* hearing to determine admissibility of testimony by plaintiff's design-defect and warning-defect experts); *Jarvis v. Ford Motor Co.*, No. 92 Civ. 2900, 1999 WL 461813 (S.D.N.Y. July 6, 1999) (*Daubert* hearing held to determine whether testimony of plaintiff's design-defect expert was admissible).

eral, *Daubert* hearings are "highly desirable" because they allow parties to present expert evidence and conduct cross-examination of the proposed expert. *See Borawick v. Shay*, 68 F.3d 597, 608 (2d Cir. 1995) (affirming the exclusion of expert testimony even though the district court did not hold a pretrial hearing). As the Supreme Court suggested in *Kumho*, courts in the Second Circuit have held that a trial judge "must have the same kind of latitude in deciding *how* to test an expert's reliability, and to decide whether or when special briefing or other proceedings are needed to investigate reliability, as it enjoys when it decides *whether or not* that expert's relevant testimony is reliable." *Bank Brussels Lambert v. Credit Lyonnais (Suisse) S.A.*, Nos. 93 Civ. 6876, 94 Civ. 2713, 2000 WL 1694321 (S.D.N.Y Nov. 13, 2001), at *1 (quoting *Kumho*, 526 U.S. at 152) (emphasis in original). Accordingly, a district court may determine the admissibility of expert evidence without conducting a hearing. Factors affecting a court's decision whether to conduct a hearing include the nature of the case and the issues to be determined.[36]

f.   Post-2010 Discovery of Expert Materials under Rule 26

In late 2010, three significant changes to Federal Rule of Civil Procedure 26 governing disclosures surrounding expert witnesses went into effect. First, Rule 26(b)(4)(C) now grants work-product protection to communications between attorneys and experts required to provide a report under Rule 26(a)(2)(B), regardless of the form of the communication. There are, though, three exceptions to this new general rule: communications relating to the expert's compensation, communications that "identify facts or data that the party's attorney provided and that the expert considered in forming the opinions to be expressed," and communications that "identify assumptions that the party's attorney provided and that the expert relied on in forming the opinions to be expressed." Fed. R. Civ. P. 26(b)(2)(C)(i)–(iii).

This work-product protection explicitly extends to drafts, including electronic drafts, of expert reports under the new Rule 26(b)(3)(B) (*"Trial-Preparation Protection for Draft Reports or Disclosures.* Rules 26(b)(3)(A) and (B) protect drafts of any report or disclosure required under Rule 26(a)(2), regardless of the form in which the draft is recorded"). With regard to disclosure of draft expert reports, Rule 26(b)(3)(B) effectively superseded *W.R. Grace & Co.-Conn. v. Zotos International, Inc.*, No. 98–CV–838S(F), 2000 WL 1843258 (W.D.N.Y. Nov. 2, 2000), which required defendant to produce prior drafts of an expert's report to plaintiff.

Second, the new Rule 26(a)(2)(B)(ii) (formerly known as Rule 26(a)(2)(B)) replaced the requirement that "the data or other information considered by the witness in forming opinions" be disclosed with a requirement that "facts or data considered by the witness" be disclosed. This, along with the

---

[36] *See, e.g., Colon*, 199 F. Supp. 2d at 71 (noting that "[n]othing in *Daubert,* or any other Supreme Court or Second Circuit case, mandates that the district court hold a *Daubert* hearing before ruling on the admissibility of expert testimony," and that a *Daubert* hearing may be unnecessary where the evidentiary record is well developed); *LaBarge v. Joslyn Clark Controls, Inc.*, No. 03-CV-169S, 2006 WL 2795612, at *6 (W.D.N.Y. Sept. 26, 2006) (excluding plaintiff's proffered expert as unreliable without the need for a *Daubert* hearing); *see also Rexall Sundown, Inc. v. Perrigo Co.*, 651 F. Supp. 2d 9, 25 (E.D.N.Y. 2009) (finding that a *Daubert* hearing was not necessary where defendant's objections were solely based on written materials and no issues needed to be disputed at a hearing); *Berk v. St. Vincent's Hosp. & Med. Ctr.*, 380 F. Supp. 2d 334, 352 (S.D.N.Y. 2005) (court excluded plaintiff's expert testimony as unreliable by applying the *Daubert* factors based on the briefing submitted to the court without need for a formal *Daubert* hearing).

new Rule 26(b)(4)(C) reversed the pre-2010 Second Circuit trend, which generally required disclosure of all materials considered by an expert, including those otherwise privileged or protected.[37]

Third, Rule 26(a)(2)(C) added a new requirement that, for experts not required to submit a formal report under Rule 26(a)(2)(B), parties must include in their expert witness disclosures notice of the subject matter the expert is expected to present evidence on and "a summary of the facts and opinions to which the witness is expected to testify." This amendment was explicitly intended to respond to courts that had de facto expanded Rule 26(a)(2)(B) by ruling "that experts not described in Rule 26(a)(2)(B) must provide (a)(2)(B) reports." Advisory Committee on Federal Rules of Civil Procedure, Report of the Civil Rules Advisory Committee of May 8, 2009, at 2.

Because the revisions are relatively new, Second Circuit case law interpreting the new rules is sparse and, as of this writing, no Second Circuit decision has explicitly ruled on a relevant Rule 26 issue since the amendments took effect. However, New York and Connecticut district courts have had occasion to rule on such issues. The court in *Ziegenfus v. John Veriha Trucking*, No. 10 Civ. 5946, 2012 WL 1075841 (S.D.N.Y. Mar. 28, 2012), analyzed Rule 26(a)(2)(C) in considering a motion for summary judgment. In *Ziegenfus*, the plaintiff sued to recover damages for injuries sustained after her vehicle and defendant's tractor-trailer collided. *Id.*, slip op. at 2. The plaintiff was examined by two doctors that corroborated she sustained injuries as a result of the accident. *Id.* However, at no point did the plaintiff move to make the two examining physicians expert witnesses. *Id.* The defendant filed for summary judgment and, in her response to the motion, plaintiff submitted affidavits from the two doctors describing her injuries. *Id.*, slip op. at 3.

In analyzing whether plaintiff had made her prima facie case (where the discovery deadline for submitting expert reports had long passed), the court noted that "even when a party is not required to include a written report with its expert disclosure," the party must still disclose "(i) the subject matter on which the witness is expected to present evidence under Federal Rule of Evidence 702, 703, or 705; and (ii) a summary of the facts and opinions to which the witness is expected to testify." *Id.*, slip op. at 5 (quoting Fed. R. Civ. P. 26(a)(2)(C)). The court quoted the Advisory Committee report as stating that "physicians or other health care professionals and employees of a party who do not regularly provide expert testimony" were required to provide summaries under Rule 26(a)(2)(C). *Id.* The district court went on to find, regarding the plaintiff's treating physician, that even if the plaintiff was not required to submit a Rule 26(a)(2)(B) report, "Plaintiff was required to disclose him as an expert and, at a minimum, provide Defendants with a summary of his opinions about Plaintiff's medical condition." *Id.*, slip op. at 7 (citing Fed. R. Civ. P. 26(a)(2)(C)). Because the plaintiff had failed to make these (and other) disclosures, the proffered expert testimony was precluded. *Id.*, slip op. at 7, and, ultimately, the court granted defendant's motion for summary judgment. *Id.*, slip op. at 9.

Another district court relied on the Advisory Committee notes on this amendment as support for the proposition that Rule 26 contemplates multiple categories of experts, including those other than the specially retained experts who are required to provide a report under Rule 26(a)(2)(B). *Franz v. New England Disposal Techs.*, No. 10–CV–201A, slip op. at 2 (W.D.N.Y. Nov. 9, 2011) (distinguishing expert testimony as provided by ongoing medical providers versus experts hired to provide an opinion and allowing testimony of the plaintiff's medical providers even though they did not submit expert reports, reasoning that because the medical providers were not specifically hired

---

[37] For examples of pre-2010 amendment Second Circuit practice, see *Sparks v. Seltzer*, No. 05-CV-1061, 2007 WL 295603, at *2 (E.D.N.Y. Jan. 29, 2007); *Baum v. Vill. of Chittenango*, 218 F.R.D. 36, 40 (N.D.N.Y. 2003); *Lugosch v. Congel*, 219 F.R.D. 220, 250 (N.D.N.Y. 2003); *Aniero Concrete Co. v. N.Y.C. Sch. Constr. Auth.*, No. 94 CIV. 9111, 2002 WL 257685 (S.D.N.Y. Feb. 22, 2002); *Herman v. Marine Midland Bank*, 207 F.R.D. 26 (W.D.N.Y. 2002); and *Mfg. Admin. & Mgmt. Sys., Inc. v. ICT Group, Inc.*, 212 F.R.D. 110, 116–18 (E.D.N.Y. 2002).

to provide expert testimony and instead developed their knowledge via treatment of the plaintiff, no report was necessary).

One district court took a narrow view of the expanded work-product protection, finding that the preparatory notes of an expert were not protected from discovery, as they were neither attorney-expert communications nor draft reports. *Dongguk Univ. v. Yale Univ.*, No. 3:08-CV-00441, 2011 WL 1935865, at *1 (D. Conn. May 19, 2011). In *Dongguk*, the defendant sought the disclosure of certain documents created by plaintiff's expert witness. The documents sought were two handwritten notes memorializing the results of tests conducted by the expert and a memorandum from the plaintiff's attorneys to the expert. *Id.* In making its determination, the court explicitly relied on the Advisory Committee's Note to the amendments to support its decision. *Id.* (stating that "Rules 26(b)(4)(B) and (C) do not impede discovery about the opinions to be offered by the expert or the development, foundation, or basis of those opinions. For example, the expert's testing of material involved in litigation, and notes of any such testing, would not be exempted from discovery . . . ." (quoting Advisory Committee Note to the 2010 Amendment of Rule 26(b)(4)).

After an *in camera* review of the disputed documents, the court decided that the handwritten notes were subject to discovery. With respect to the memorandum, the court permitted a partial redaction, mandating discovery of statements that were "facts or assumptions, provided by Dongguk's attorney and relied on by [the expert] in forming her opinion" and were not protected from discovery because they fell under the Rule 26(b)(4)(C)(ii) ("facts or data") and 26(b)(4)(C)(iii) ("assumptions") exceptions. *Id.*, slip op. at 2. However, other statements in the same memorandum were protected under the expanded work-product protection because they did not fall under any of the exceptions. *Id.* ("[T]he discovery authorized by the exceptions does not extend beyond those specific topics." (quoting Advisory Committee Note on 2010 Amendment of Rule 26(b)(4)(C))). Another court, considering a similar issue also after *in camera* review, found a letter from a consultant to counsel to be protected from disclosure under Rule 26(b)(4)(C) and therefore never needed to reach the issue of attorney-client privilege. *GenOn Mid-Atlantic, LLC v. Stone & Webster, Inc.*, No. 11 Civ. 1299, 2011 WL 5439046, at *15 (S.D.N.Y. Nov. 10, 2011).

One court has interpreted this provision without *in camera* review of particular documents. In *Pope v. City of New York*, No. 10 Civ. 4118, 2012 WL 39349 (S.D.N.Y. Jan. 5, 2012), defendants sought "production of an unclear universe of documents from plaintiff's medical expert." *Id.*, slip op. at 2. In particular, defendants asked for communications between the expert and plaintiff's counsel, insofar as those communications fell under one of the three enumerated exceptions in Rule 26(b)(4)(C). *Id.* Plaintiff's counsel asserted that her communication with the expert had concerned only one of the excepted categories, compensation. *Id.* The court "assume[d], although counsel is not specific, that plaintiff has produced the compensation communication" and ordered that, if the plaintiff had not, he must "do so promptly." *Id.*

Pope further noted that defendants charged, as a "fall-back position," that "the court should review any other documents claimed by plaintiff not to come within the three cited categories." *Id.* Because it had "no reason to question the representations of plaintiff's counsel in this respect," the court denied this application. *Id.*

In *S.E.C. v. Nadel*, No. CV 11-215, 2012 WL 1268297, slip op. at 4 (E.D.N.Y. Apr. 16, 2012), the district court clarified the limits of the Rule 26(b)(4)(C)(i) exception. There, the district court ruled against requiring disclosure of the annual compensation of an Iowa State University professor who also served as an SEC "employee" under an intergovernmental agreement. *Id.*, slip op. at 2. The court reasoned that because the expert had not received additional compensation for providing this opinion beyond his ordinary annual salary, there was no reason to believe his compensation might have biased him (the general reasoning for requiring disclosure of expert compensation). *Id.*, slip op. at 2–3. While the court rejected defendants' argument that the professor must disclose his salary, it did order an *in camera* review of certain documents, including the expert's compensation as a professor and the intergovernmental agreement that permitted the university professor to work with the SEC, since the veracity of those documents was questioned. *Id.*, slip op. at 4.

g. Use of Rule 706

Courts in the Second Circuit, primarily in the Southern and Eastern Districts of New York, have utilized Rule 706 of the Federal Rules of Evidence to appoint experts to assist in complex litigation. Among the district court judges, perhaps the one best known for his innovative use of 706 experts is Judge Jack B. Weinstein of the Eastern District of New York. Judge Weinstein has utilized Rule 706 to appoint experts in several mass tort litigations to assist the court, and the parties, in addressing complex issues. *See, e.g., In re Breast Implant Cases*, 942 F. Supp. 958 (E. & S.D.N.Y. 1996) (appointing panel of experts to identify neutral experts to aid the court in breast implant litigation); *In re Joint E. & S. Dist. Asbestos Litig.*, 830 F. Supp. 686 (E.D.N.Y. & S.D.N.Y. 1993) (utilizing Rule 706 to establish a panel of experts to assist in reaching a determination as to the fairness of a proposed settlement for the payment of asbestos claims); *In re DES Cases*, No. CV 91-3784, 1991 WL 270477, at *1 (E.D.N.Y. Dec. 6, 1991) (appointing special master to report to the court on use of a panel of economists and medical experts to assist in settling DES cases).

Judge Weinstein, however, is not alone in his use of court-appointed experts to assist the court in addressing complex issues. Other district court judges in the Southern and Eastern Districts also have used 706 experts to provide assistance on matters such as the substantive law of foreign nations, *Carbotrade S.p.A. v. Bureau Veritas*, No. 92 Civ. 1459, 1998 WL 397847, at *1 (S.D.N.Y. July 16, 1998) (Koeltl, J.); computer technology, *Cerruti 1881 S.A. v. Cerruti, Inc.*, 169 F.R.D. 573 (S.D.N.Y. 1996) (Mukasey, J.);[38] copyright infringement, *Harbor Software, Inc. v. Applied Sys., Inc.*, 936 F. Supp. 167 (S.D.N.Y. 1996) (Baer, J.); and patent infringement, *Unique Concepts, Inc. v. Brown*, 659 F. Supp. 1008 (S.D.N.Y. 1987) (Pollack, J.). *But see Gold v. Dalkon Shield Claimants Trust*, No. B-82-383, 1998 WL 351466, at *2 (D. Conn. June 3, 1998), *aff'd,* 189 F.3d 460 (2d Cir. 1999), *cert. denied,* 529 U.S. 1068 (2000) (refusing to appoint an expert under Rule 706 because, among other things, the litigation did "not raise any complex scientific issues which the Court needs expert guidance to understand").

In addition, other courts have used the "threat" of appointing their own experts under Rule 706 in order to prompt the parties to agree upon an expert. For example, in *Mancuso v. Consolidated Edison Co.*, No. 93 Civ. 0001, 1993 WL 525241, at *1 (S.D.N.Y. Dec. 13, 1993), the court indicated that unless the parties appointed a neutral expert to conduct inquiries into PCB contamination, it would appoint its own expert under Rule 706. *See also Derico v. Int'l Bus. Mach. Corp.*, No. 93 Civ. 0823, 1993 WL 106799, at *1 (S.D.N.Y. Apr. 6, 1993) (indicating that unless the parties appointed a neutral expert to conduct inquiries into PCB contamination, the court would appoint its own expert under Rule 706).

3. Practice Tips and Suggestions for Second Circuit Courts

In addition to the other suggestions provided above, attorneys practicing in the Second Circuit should keep in mind that the district courts, especially in the Southern and Eastern Districts of New York, have been exposed to large and complex litigation where expert issues, both with respect to procedure and admissibility, often arise. This is particularly true with respect to litigation concerning scientific evidence. These courts are willing to work in conjunction with the parties to fashion appropriate and in some cases innovative mechanisms and procedures through which to address

---

[38] *See also Gutman v. Klein*, No. 03CV1570(BMC)(RML), 2008 WL 4682208 (E.D.N.Y. Oct. 15, 2008).

expert issues. If a party contests the use of an expert or the sufficiency of a report, it is best to raise such objections early in the process, before substantial judicial resources are expended. The courts are usually receptive to legitimate and timely objections or requests.

B. EXPERT EVIDENCE IN NEW YORK STATE COURTS

1. *New York Courts Continue to Apply* Frye

The New York Court of Appeals has resisted the *Daubert* approach to evaluating the admissibility of expert evidence and continues, with few exceptions, to apply the principles set forth in *Frye. See People v. Wesley*, 83 N.Y.2d 417, 423 n.2 (1994). For the most part, New York State courts determine whether an expert's relevant testimony regarding scientific principles will be admitted according to "whether the accepted techniques, when properly performed, generate results accepted as reliable within the scientific community generally." *Id.* at 422.[39] To determine whether a technique has gained general acceptance, the *Frye* test "emphasizes 'counting scientists votes, rather than on verifying the soundness of a scientific conclusion.'" *Parker v. Mobil Oil Corp.*, 7 N.Y.3d 434, 447 (2006) (citing *Wesley*, 83 N.Y.2d at 422); *see also Zito*, 28 A.D.3d at 44 ("[G]eneral acceptance does not necessarily mean that a majority of the scientists involved subscribe to the conclusion. Rather it means that those espousing the theory or opinion have followed generally accepted scientific principles and methodology in evaluating clinical data to reach their conclusions.").

However, the court of Appeals recently acknowledged that "the *Frye* inquiry is separate and distinct from the admissibility question applied to all evidence—whether there is a proper foundation—to determine whether the accepted methods were appropriately employed in a particular case." *Parker*, 7 N.Y.3d at 447. In a footnote that signaled a departure from more than a decade of general adherence to *Frye*, the *Parker* court observed that cases employing *Daubert* analysis "are instructive" to the determination of admissibility "to the extent that they address the reliability of an expert's methodology." *Id.* at 448 n.4.

The issue in *Wesley* was whether DNA profiling evidence was properly admitted at trial. Applying *Frye*, the court analyzed whether the expert testimony was based upon scientific principles or procedures that had gained general acceptance. Following a *Frye* hearing (akin to a *Daubert* hearing), the trial court determined that the relevant scientific community accepted DNA evidence as reliable. The intermediate appellate court and the New York Court of Appeals affirmed in a plurality opinion. However, with respect to the application of *Frye*, the Court was unanimous in finding:

> [W]here the scientific evidence sought to be presented is novel, the test is that articulated in *Frye v. United States*, in essence whether there is general acceptance in the relevant scientific community that a technique or procedure is capable of being performed reliably.

83 N.Y.2d at 435 (Kaye, J., concurring) (citations omitted).

---

[39] The Court of Appeals has reaffirmed its commitment to *Frye's* "general acceptance" standard, at least with respect to assessing the validity of expert testimony based on novel scientific principles or techniques. *See People v. Lee*, 96 N.Y.2d 157, 162 (2001) (articulating "general acceptance" in the relevant scientific community as the test for admissibility of novel scientific theories or techniques); *see also Zito v. Zabarsky*, 28 A.D.3d 42, 44 (2d Dep't 2006) (applying *Wesley* and *Frye* to permit plaintiff's expert to testify where "a synthesis of various studies or cases" indicated that the expert's methodology had gained general acceptance in the scientific community).

Further, *Wesley* described a three-step inquiry to be applied by courts when considering novel scientific evidence. The first step is the *Frye* inquiry, articulated above. After conducting the *Frye* inquiry, the second step requires courts to consider "'whether the accepted techniques were employed by the experts in this case.'" *Wesley*, 83 N.Y.2d at 429 (quoting *People v. Middleton*, 54 N.Y.2d 42, 50 (1981)). This second step focuses on the specific reliability of the procedures employed by the expert or laboratory, and creates the foundation for the admissibility of the evidence.[40] Lastly, if the evidence satisfies both steps, then it is admissible and the jury must consider the weight of the evidence. *Wesley*, 83 N.Y.2d at 429.

Following *Wesley*, New York courts have continued to apply *Frye*'s "general acceptance" standard to questions concerning the admission of novel scientific principles or techniques. *See, e.g., Giordano v. Market Am., Inc.*, 15 N.Y.3d 590, 601 (NY 2010) ("Our courts follow Frye . . . in making 'general acceptance' the test for admitting expert testimony about scientific principles or discoveries.").[41] For example, in *DeMeyer v. Advantage Auto*, 797 N.Y.S.2d 743 (Sup. Ct. Wayne Cty. 2005), the court ordered a *Frye* hearing to determine the admissibility of expert testimony based on historical case reports offered by the plaintiff to prove that plaintiff's decedent's mesothelioma and death had been caused by occupational exposure to asbestos. Defendants sought to preclude evidence of the historical reports on the grounds that the scientific and medical communities required epidemiological studies, rather than historical case reports, in order to determine the cause of a particular disease. The plaintiff argued that the court should admit the evidence and cited to multiple legal opinions, including three unreported decisions from New York state trial courts, allowing non-epidemiological evidence of disease causation. *Id.* at 313–15.

The court was not persuaded, finding that "most of these cases were decided in federal courts or other jurisdictions, which have adopted the Daubert standards for admissibility of expert testimony." *Id.* at 749. Quoting Chief Judge Kaye, the *DeMeyer* court noted that "the difference [between *Frye* and *Daubert*] is that *Frye* looks to consensus within the scientific community as an indicator of reliability, while *Daubert* requires judges to evaluate both the validity of the expert reasoning and its application to the case." *Id.* at 750.[42] Having drawn this distinction, the court declined to apply *Daubert*, noting that:

> Over the years, since *Wesley*, several trial courts, in New York, have decided to apply the *Daubert* standard rather than the general acceptance standard set forth in *Frye*. Nevertheless, whenever directly confronted with the issue, appellate courts have consistently rejected the idea that *Daubert* should be the controlling standard in New York rather than *Frye*.

---

[40] The foundational inquiry "is the same that is applied to all evidence, not just to scientific evidence." *Wesley*, 83 N.Y.2d at 425.

[41] *See also Kelly v. Metro-N. Commuter R.R.*, 74 A.D.3d 483, 484 n.1 (1st Dep't 2010) (noting New York courts' adherence to the *Frye* standard); *Lascano v. Lee Trucking*, N.Y.L.J., Oct. 3, 2007, p. 27, col. 2 (Sup. Ct. N.Y. Cty. Sept. 7, 2007) (Tingling, J.) (excluding plaintiff's expert following a *Frye* hearing where the expert relied on LS-DYNA simulations to show crashworthiness of an alternative design without performing any real-life crash test on his proposed design). The court in *Lascano* did not accept the plaintiff's reliance on various crash tests performed by third parties, finding that the conditions those tests were conducted under were too dissimilar from the facts of the case before it to meet the general acceptance requirement.

[42] *See also Castrichini v. Rivera*, 669 N.Y.S.2d 140 (Sup. Ct. Monroe Cty. 1997) ("[U]nder *Daubert*, the party proffering evidence need only show the reliability of the methodology, and in addressing that question the court and the parties are not limited to what is generally accepted. Under *Frye*, the party proffering scientific evidence had to show it was based on the method generally accepted in the scientific community."). *Id.* at 146 n.3.

Based upon a review of case law, both in the State of New York, as well as other jurisdictions, this court is unable to discern a consensus regarding the general acceptance of the methodology used by plaintiff's experts to arrive at an opinion making a causal connection between exposure to asbestos friction products and mesothelioma.

797 N.Y.S.3d at 751.[43]

Since *Wesley*, some lower courts in New York have applied *Daubert*'s standard of admissibility where the expert evidence does not involve a novel scientific principle or technique. For example, in *Wahl v. American Honda Motor Co.*, 693 N.Y.S.2d 875 (Sup. Ct. Suffolk Cty. 1999), the court held that the testimony of an engineer offered to establish the existence of design defects in a products liability action was admissible under *Daubert*. The defendant sought to preclude this testimony on the grounds that it had not gained general acceptance in the engineering community. While the court acknowledged *Frye*'s applicability to novel scientific evidence, it held that where "testimony is based upon . . . recognized technical or other specialized knowledge, . . . the stricter general acceptance standard of *Frye* is not applicable." *Id.* at 877.

Instead, the court applied the expert screening factors enunciated in *Daubert*. These factors include (1) whether the expert's concept has been tested; (2) whether it has been subjected to peer review; (3) what the known rate of error is; (4) whether the concept is generally accepted by the scientific community to which it belongs. *Id.* at 877–78. "*Daubert*['s] 'gatekeeping' inquiry is a flexible one, and . . . the trial court has broad discretion in the manner in which it determines reliability in light of the particular facts and circumstances of the particular case." *Id.* at 877 (citing *Kumho Tire*, 526 U.S. 137, 151 (1999)). After conducting a hearing, the court in *Wahl* held that the engineer's testimony was based upon recognized principles of mathematics and engineering, and was therefore sufficiently trustworthy and reliable to be presented to the jury. *See also Frankson v. Brown & Williamson Tobacco Corp.*, No. 29415/00, 2004 WL 1433068, at *2 n.3 (Sup. Ct. Kings Cty. June 22, 2004) (Kramer, J.) (applying *Daubert* to defendant's proposed introduction of a memorandum

---

[43] *See also People v. Whitaker*, 289 A.D.2d 84 (1st Dep't 2001) (appellate court affirmed lower court's decision to admit testimony of a blood splatter analysis expert without a *Frye* hearing because the procedures employed in this analysis did not involve novel scientific techniques); *People v. Wooten*, 283 A.D.2d 931 (4th Dep't 2001) (appellate court affirmed lower court's decision to deny *Frye* hearing where the use of luminol, a chemical used during an investigation to detect the existence of blood at a crime scene, is universally accepted and therefore not considered novel scientific evidence); *People v. Johnston*, 273 A.D.2d 514, 517 (3d Dep't 2000) (where defendant was charged with sexually abusing children, the court held that *Frye's* "stricter 'general acceptance' test" would apply to determine the admissibility of the expert testimony of a psychologist concerning "children's susceptibility to suggestive interrogation"); *People v. Fortin*, 706 N.Y.S.2d 611 (Sup. Ct. Nassau Cty. 2000), *aff'd*, 289 A.D.2d 590 (2d Dep't 2001) (*Frye* hearing held to determine the admissibility of expert testimony relating to a psychological syndrome called Parental Alienation Syndrome). Likewise, in *Selig v. Pfizer, Inc.*, 713 N.Y.S.2d 898 (Sup. Ct. N.Y. Cty. 2000), the plaintiff sought to introduce expert testimony to establish a link between the plaintiff's use of Viagra with his suffering of a heart attack. The defendant sought to preclude this testimony on the grounds that the expert's methodology and theory of causation were not generally accepted in the scientific community. Plaintiff responded by arguing that a *Frye* hearing was not appropriate because the scientific principles on which the expert relied were not novel. The court held that *Frye's* "general acceptance" test applied even though the expert's testimony was not based on "an outwardly novel scientific technique." Specifically, the court noted that because the expert's conclusions were "allegedly novel," there was an issue as to whether the expert's testimony was supported by accepted scientific methods. *Id.* at 902.

summarizing scientists' opinions that smoking was not a health hazard; court believed it was "within its discretion to apply [*Daubert*] where, as here, the document contains the rankest of hearsay and its admission was sought on the grounds that it provided a kind of 'negative' notice to defendants").

Similarly, in *Giangrasso v. Ass'n for the Help of Retarded Children*, N.Y.L.J., Mar. 19, 2001, p. 33, col. 2 (Sup. Ct. Suffolk Cty. Jan. 23, 2001) (Oshrin, J.), the trial court applied *Daubert* to determine the admissibility of expert testimony concerning a variety of issues surrounding special education. The plaintiff, a mentally retarded adult, alleged that she was sexually assaulted and molested by an employee of the bus service that took her to and from a workshop operated by the Association for the Help of Retarded Children ("AHRC"). The plaintiff sought to introduce expert testimony on the custom and usage in the special education field on several issues, such as the hiring, training, and supervision of bus drivers and the duty of schools to monitor the transportation contractors.

Both defendants—the bus company and AHRC—sought to preclude such testimony on the grounds that the plaintiff did not need expert testimony on issues of negligent hiring, retention, supervision, or control. AHRC further argued that the plaintiff's expert failed to articulate any industry custom or standard that the defendants allegedly violated. The plaintiff argued that the expert was qualified to testify as an expert in these areas, that the expert's testimony would assist the trier of fact, and that *Frye's* "general acceptance" test did not apply, but that the expert testimony satisfied the "reliability" test enunciated in *Daubert* and *Kumho Tire*.

The court rejected the defendants' argument that no expert testimony was necessary, stating that expert testimony is appropriate when "it would help to clarify an issue calling for professional or technical knowledge, possessed by the expert and beyond the ken of the typical juror." *Id.* According to the court, expert testimony is also appropriate where the jurors have a general awareness of an area but are in need of further clarification. While the court further acknowledged the applicability of *Frye's* "general acceptance" test where the proposed evidence is "scientific or technical in nature," it classified plaintiff's expert testimony as "professional" in nature, and concluded that the *Daubert* factors are more appropriately applied to plaintiff's expert than *Frye's* "general acceptance" test. *Id.*; *see also Hofmann v. Toys "R" Us-N.Y. Ltd. P'ship.*, 272 A.D.2d 296 (2d Dep't 2000).[44]

Other New York State courts have examined expert evidence under both *Frye* and *Daubert*. In *Clemente v. Blumenberg*, 705 N.Y.S.2d 792, 800 (Sup. Ct. Richmond Cty. 1999), the court deemed a portion of an engineer's expert testimony concerning various principles of mechanics inadmissible under both *Frye* and *Daubert*. While the court confirmed New York's adherence to *Frye's* "general acceptance" standard, it also expressed some doubt as to its continuing validity in the scientific arena.

> [T]he accelerated pace at which science travels is today far faster than the speed at which it traveled in 1923 when *Frye* was written. Breakthroughs in science which are valid may be relevant to a case before the courts. Waiting for the scientific community to "generally accept" a novel theory which is otherwise valid and reliable as evidence may deny a litigant justice before the court. A Trial Judge's role as a gatekeeper of evidence is not a role created by *Daubert* and rejected by the Court of Appeals; it is an inherent power of all trial court Judges to keep unreliable evidence ("junk science") away from the trier of

---

[44] In *Hofmann,* the Appellate Court affirmed the lower court's decision to grant defendant summary judgment where plaintiff's proposed expert report failed to create any triable issue of fact. There, the plaintiff submitted a report of an expert who sought to establish that the defendant created a dangerous condition by placing boxes of diapers on a top shelf in the store and failing to alert customers to the dangers associated with removing these items. The court, citing *Daubert* and *Kumho Tire*, held that the plaintiff failed to establish the expert's knowledge, training, experience, or education in areas such as consumer safety or package retrieval.

fact regardless of the qualifications of the expert. A well-credentialed expert does not make invalid science valid merely by espousing an opinion . . . .

There may be more than one valid scientific or technical opinion on a particular point which may be generally accepted by the relevant scientific community. The opinions presented need not be the majority opinion. There may be valid minority opinions which are scientifically valid which may rightfully be presented to the trier of fact.

Id. at 799, 800.

The court concluded that the portion of the engineer's testimony relating to the use of repair costs and photographs to calculate the change in velocity of the vehicles at impact failed under *Frye* because the source of the expert's data, as well as the methodology he employed, was not generally accepted in the relevant scientific community. *Id.* at 800. The court also noted that the expert's opinion could be excluded under *Daubert* and *Kumho Tire* because the data and the methodology are not scientifically valid. *Id.*

Likewise, in *Harris v. Long Island R.R. Co.*, 787 N.Y.S.2d 837 (Sup. Ct. Kings Cty. 2004), the court deemed an industrial hygienist's testimony concerning the cause of a railroad employee's carpal tunnel syndrome inadmissible under both *Frye* and *Daubert*. Noting that the expert's proposed testimony deviated from accepted procedures in the field of industrial hygiene, the court ruled the testimony inadmissible under *Frye*. However, as if to bolster its conclusion rhetorically, the court concluded in dictum that the testimony would not even pass muster under the less restrictive *Daubert* analysis. Citing a federal case that ruled expert testimony inadmissible under similar facts, the court observed that the expert's methodology deviated from accepted procedure; that he had even less familiarity with the defendant's facilities than the expert in the federal case; and that he based the entirety of his testimony on a short interview with the plaintiff. The court concluded that the "testimony thus would not be admissible even under the *Daubert* standard."[45]

As discussed above, the Court of Appeals has recently indicated that the role of the trial judge as a gatekeeper may extend beyond merely ascertaining whether a methodology has gained general acceptance in the relevant scientific community. In *Parker v. Mobil Oil Corp.*, plaintiff was diagnosed with acute myelogenous leukemia ("AML") after prolonged exposure to benzene over the course of his career as a gas station attendant. 7 N.Y.3d at 442. On the issue of medical causation, plaintiff's expert proposed to testify that plaintiff's AML was caused by benzene exposure but did

---

[45] *See also Duffy v. Bristol-Meyers Prods.*, No. 403726/03, 2006 WL 1358427, at *3 (Sup. Ct. New York Cty. May 16, 2006) (acknowledging the instructiveness of the *Daubert* standard of relevance and reliability in determining whether to grant a *Frye* hearing); *Tavares v. New York City Health & Hosps. Corp.*, No. 45757/00, 2003 WL 22231534, at *18 (Sup. Ct. Kings Cty. June 23, 2003) (held plaintiff's expert's opinion that infant plaintiff's cerebral palsy was caused by hypoxia or asphyxia during labor admissible under *Frye* and *Daubert*); *Stanley Tulchin Assocs. v. Grossman*, No. 1236/99, 2002 WL 31466800, at *4 (Sup. Ct. Nassau Cty. Oct. 10, 2002) (expert's testimony concerning methodology used to calculate plaintiff's lost profits admissible under *Frye* and *Daubert*); *People v. Hyatt*, No. 8852/00, 2001 WL 1750613, at *2–3 (Sup. Ct. Kings Cty. Oct. 10, 2001) (court reviewed admissibility of expert testimony concerning the validity of latent fingerprint evidence under both *Frye* and *Daubert*); *People v. Berberich*, N.Y.L.J., Jan. 11, 2000, p. 33, col. 4 (Sup. Ct. Westchester Cty.) (court affirmed New York's continuing adherence to *Frye* yet found the evidence to be inadmissible under both *Frye* and *Daubert*). *But see Clotter v. New York City Hous. Auth.*, No. 14220/96, 2001 WL 1666444 (Sup. Ct. Bronx Cty. Dec. 10, 2001) (court ordered hearing to determine the scientific validity of an isolated blood-lead-level reading and cited *Daubert* as the governing standard).

not cite to studies linking AML to exposure to benzene in gasoline and did not quantify plaintiff's exposure to benzene.

Because the correlation between benzene exposure and AML was well documented, the court observed that "there is no particular novel methodology at issue for which the court needs to determine whether there is general acceptance." *Id.* at 447; *see also Jackson v. Nutmeg Techs., Inc.*, 43 A.D.3d 599 (3d Dep't 2007) (eschewing *Frye* analysis and engaging in Parker's "foundational inquiry" where "plaintiffs' experts relied upon epidemiological studies, which are by no means a novel methodology for demonstrating a causal relationship between a chemical compound and a set of symptoms or a disease"). Thus, the court found it unnecessary to apply *Frye*, which only governs admissibility in cases involving the introduction of novel scientific evidence. Furthermore, the Court of Appeals rejected the Appellate Division's requirement that the amount of plaintiff's exposure needed to be exactly quantified in order for the expert's testimony to be in accord with generally accepted scientific norms. *Parker*, 7 N.Y.3d at 447. Instead, the court in *Parker* proceeded to the second inquiry delineated in *Wesley*, observing that the relevant question was "more akin to whether there is an appropriate foundation for the experts' opinions, rather than whether the opinions are admissible under *Frye*." *Id.* The court went on to describe what would constitute an appropriate foundation, noting that "it is well-established that an opinion on causation should set forth a plaintiff's exposure to a toxin, that the toxin is capable of causing the particular illness (general causation) and that plaintiff was exposed to sufficient levels of the toxin to cause the illness (specific causation)." *Id.* at 448; *see also Coratti v. Wella Corp.*, No. 106168/01, 2006 WL 3718247, at *7 (Sup. Ct. New York Cty. Dec. 15, 2006) (expert testimony inadmissible where plaintiffs failed to provide "information regarding the amount of the chemicals phenylenediamaine and resorcinol required to cause [plaintiff's] alleged illnesses and . . . failed to quantify [plaintiff's] exposure").

In determining whether the plaintiff's evidence fulfilled these requirements, the *Parker* court cited a number of federal cases, each of which analyzed the admissibility of evidence under *Daubert*. *Id.* at 448.[46] The court observed that cases applying *Daubert* were "instructive to the extent that they address the reliability of an expert's methodology." *Id.* at 448 n.4. Like numerous experts deemed unreliable under the federal *Daubert* standard, plaintiff's experts failed to demonstrate that exposure to benzene "as a component of gasoline" caused plaintiff's AML, lacked epidemiological evidence of causation, and failed to quantify plaintiff's exposure to benzene in an acceptable manner. *Id.* at 449–50; *see also Coratti*, No. 106168/01, 2006 WL 3718247. The court therefore held that the experts' conclusions were insufficiently reliable on the issue of causation and refused to admit plaintiff's evidence. *Id.* at 450; *see also Ratner v. McNeil-PPC, Inc.*, 91 A.D.3d 63, 73 (2d Dep't 2011) (stating that "where a plaintiff's qualified experts offer no novel test or technique, but intend to testify about a novel theory of causation, where such opinion is supported by generally accepted scientific methods, it is proper to proceed directly to the foundational inquiry of admissibility, which is whether the theory is properly founded on generally accepted scientific methods or principles").

In the wake of *Parker*, courts have struggled to determine the role of *Frye*'s general acceptance test in the area of novel theories of causation. In *In re Neurontin Product Liability Litigation*, the court noted that, after *Parker*, "if the methodology is not novel and the issue is whether the methodology leads to a reliable theory of causation, the theory should arguably be scrutinized not under *Frye* for general acceptance, but under foundational principles for reliability." 897 N.Y.S.2d 671, at *3 (Sup. Ct. New York Cty. May 15, 2009). Furthermore, the court applied *Parker*'s proposition that a "*Daubert*-type analysis of the plaintiff's expert's methodology is relevant where the scientific

---

[46] *See, e.g., McClain v. Metabolife Intl. Inc.*, 401 F.3d 1233 (11th Cir. 2005); *Wright v. Williamette Indus. Inc.*, 91 F.3d 1105 (8th Cir. 1996); *Westberry v. Gislaved Gummi AB*, 178 F.3d 257 (4th Cir. 1999); *Heller v. Shaw Indus., Inc.*, 167 F.3d 146 (3d Cir. 1999); *Hayman v. Norfolk & W. Ry. Co.*, 243 F.3d 255 (6th Cir. 2001).

issue is . . . whether the methodology employed by the plaintiff's expert leads to a reliable theory or opinion on causation." *Id.* at *2. In conducting the "*Daubert*-type analysis," the use of federal cases evaluating reliability under *Daubert* is permitted. *Id.*

However, the court also stated that post-*Parker* courts have "continued to hold, or left open the possibility that novel opinions on causation should be scrutinized at a *Frye* hearing rather than in a foundational inquiry undertaken at trial." *In re Neurontin Prod. Liab. Litig.*, No. 117852, 2009 WL 1979936, at *3 n.3 (Sup. Ct. New York Cty. May 15, 2009).[47]

2. Rules and Procedures Governing Expert Disclosure in New York State Courts

Section 3101(d) of New York's Civil Practice Law and Rules ("CPLR") governs expert disclosure in New York State courts. That section provides in pertinent part:

1. Experts. (i) Upon request, each party shall identify each person whom the party expects to call as an expert witness at trial and shall disclose in reasonable detail the subject matter on which each expert is expected to testify, the substance of the facts and opinions on which each expert is expected to testify, the qualifications of each expert witness and a summary of the grounds for each expert's opinions. However, where a party for good cause shown retains an expert an insufficient period of time before the commencement of trial to give appropriate notice thereof, the party shall not thereupon be precluded from introducing the expert's testimony at the trial solely on the grounds of noncompliance with this paragraph. In that instance, upon motion of any party, made before or at trial, or on its own initiative, the court may make whatever order may be just . . . .

(iii) Further disclosure concerning the expected testimony of any expert may be obtained only by court order upon a showing of special circumstances and subject to restrictions as to scope and provisions concerning fees and expenses as the court may deem appropriate.

Thus, expert disclosure in New York State court under CPLR § 3101(d) is triggered only by a demand from opposing counsel. *See Collins v. Greater N.Y. Sav. Bank*, 194 A.D.2d 514, 514 (2d Dep't 1993) (noting the burden lies on the party seeking information to affirmatively request expert disclosure). Such a request for expert disclosure under CPLR § 3101(d) is "of a continuing nature," and requires a party to supplement expert information upon retention of an expert. *See Dunn v.*

---

[47] *See, e.g., Leffler v. Feld*, 51 A.D.3d 410 (1st Dep't 2008) (stating that "the court correctly concluded that the theory of causation . . . was a novel one and thus warranted a *Frye* hearing."); *Fraser v. 301-52 Townhouse Corp.*, 57 A.D. 3d 416, 418 (1st Dep't 2008) (upholding lower court's decision to preclude expert testimony, noting that "whether plaintiff's theory of causation is scrutinized under the *Frye* inquiry applicable to novel scientific evidence or under the general foundational inquiry applicable to all evidence, the conclusion is the same . . . "); *People v. Abney*, No. 3314/05, 2011 WL 2026894, at *15 (Sup. Ct. New York Cty. May 5, 2011) (stating that "the same general acceptance as reliable in the scientific community test applies even in cases where causation and scientific techniques that are not novel are at issue" and granting in part and denying in part defendant's motion to introduce expert evidence of witness identification); *People v. Hampson*, No. 2006NA021294, 2009 WL 2569058, at *2 (Sup. Ct. Nassau Cty. Aug. 21, 2009) (In deciding to admit expert testimony, the court held that "it is still important to view the evidence under the *Frye* standard as it has evolved, even when applying it to a novel conclusion drawn from more established methodology").

Medina Mem'l Hosp., 502 N.Y.S.2d 633, 636 (Sup. Ct. Erie Cty. 1986) (citing *Salander v. Cent. Gen. Hosp.*, 496 N.Y.S.2d 638, 642 (Sup. Ct. Nassau Cty. 1985). Under the CPLR, there is no specific form that a request for expert disclosure must take.[48]

Upon receipt of a request for expert disclosure, a party must respond by identifying each expert the party expects to call at trial;[49] a reasonably detailed description of the subject matter on which the expert is expected to testify; the substance of the facts and opinions on which the expert is expected to testify; the expert's qualifications; and a summary of the grounds for each expert's opinion. CPLR § 3101(d)(1)(i).

With respect to the expert's qualifications, courts have interpreted this requirement to include a "reasonably detailed" statement as to the expert's skill, training, knowledge and experience. For example, in *Strach v. Doin*, 288 A.D.2d 640, 642 (3d Dep't 2001), the plaintiff sought to introduce testimony relating to the value of her personal property that was sold by defendant at an auction. However, the court found that plaintiff's description of her expert's qualifications as having "attended numerous auctions and sales" and "spoken with dozens of individuals" to be conclusory and therefore insufficient to satisfy the requirements of Section 3101(d)(1)(i). *See also Deitch v. May*, 713 N.Y.S.2d 278, 279–80 (Sup. Ct. Rockland Cty. 2000) (court discussed the balance it must strike in a medical malpractice action between a party's right to omit the name of the expert witness with the party's burden of disclosing the expert's qualifications).

Further, courts have repeatedly stated that a party must disclose only "the substance" of the expert's facts and opinions, as distinct from *all* of the facts and opinions on which the expert relies. *Krygier v. Airweld, Inc.*, 176 A.D.2d 700, 701 (2d Dep't 1991); *Renucci v. Mercy Hosp.*, 124 A.D.2d 796, 797 (2d Dep't 1986). Absent agreement between the parties, there is no requirement that the expert prepare a report of the type contemplated by the Federal Rules of Civil Procedure or that materials relied upon by the expert be produced. New York State's disclosure requirement is minimal. Finally, Section 3101(d)(1)(i) does not impose a specific time period in which a party must respond to a request for expert disclosure.[50]

Because the CPLR does not require that a party produce a report prepared by its expert, issues do not normally arise regarding the sufficiency of an expert report. The typical disclosure of an expert under Section 3101(d) contains no more than the limited information specified above. The issues that are most often disputed include whether the expert was disclosed in a timely fashion and with sufficient identification of the issues on which the expert is to testify.

---

[48] There has been some disagreement as to whether a request for expert data may be made in a demand for a bill of particulars. *See Bellen v. Baghei-Rad*, 148 A.D.2d 827 (3d Dep't 1989) (acknowledging validity of a 3101(d) request contained in a demand for a bill of particulars); *cf. Coleman v. Richards*, 138 A.D.2d 556 (2d Dep't 1988) (holding that, since a demand for a bill of particulars is not an evidentiary disclosure device, it is not an appropriate document in which to make a 3101(d) request).

[49] In an action for medical, dental, or podiatric malpractice, the CPLR excuses a party responding to a disclosure request from revealing the names of the experts but requires the disclosure of all other information specified in the statute. *See* CPLR § 3101(d)(1)(i).

[50] *Rowan v. Cross Cnty. Ski & Skate, Inc.*, 42 A.D.3d 563, 564 (2d Dep't 2007) (quoting *Hernandez-Vega v. Zwanger-Pesiri Radiology Group*, 39 A.D.3d 710, 710–11 (2d Dep't 2007)); *see also Shopsin v. Siben & Siben*, 289 A.D.2d 220, 220 (2d Dep't 2001) (quoting *Cutsogeorge v. Hertz Corp.*, 264 A.D.2d 752, 753–54 (2d Dep't 1999)). However, parties should consult the court's local rules to ensure compliance with any time limits imposed therein. *See, e.g., Gushlaw v. Roll*, 290 A.D.2d 667, 667 (3d Dep't 2002) (Third Judicial District established a local rule that requires a party respond to a demand for expert disclosure before the filing of the note of issue).

In the event that a party fails to comply with the statutory requirements of the CPLR or unduly delays in responding to a request for disclosure, courts are free to "make whatever order may be just." CPLR § 3101(d)(1)(i). When making a determination as to the appropriate penalty, courts focus on whether the delay was intentional or willful and whether the opposing party suffered prejudice as a result of the delay. For example, in *Silverberg v. Community General Hospital*, 290 A.D. 2d 788 (3d Dep't 2002), the appellate court affirmed the trial court's order denying certain defendants' motion to preclude where plaintiff responded to defendants' expert disclosure request almost four months prior to the scheduled trial date. The court found that the plaintiff did not exhibit any willful or intentional behavior, and the defendants failed to establish that they suffered any prejudice as a result of the plaintiff's delay.

Even where a delay is found to be intentional or willful, courts may nevertheless permit testimony if the delay is not prejudicial to the opposing party. In *Gayz v. Kirby*, for example, the Second Department held that even though there was "evidence . . . that the plaintiff's belated disclosure of her expert information in response to defendant's demand therefore was intentional," the expert's testimony was nevertheless admissible because "any potential prejudice to the defendants was ameliorated by the Supreme Court granting an adjournment of the trial." 41 A.D.3d 782, 782 (2d Dep't 2007). The court therefore reversed the trial court's preclusion of the expert's testimony. *Id.*; *see also Johnson v. Greenberg*, 35 A.D.3d 380 (2d Dep't 2006) (admitting plaintiff's expert testimony where prejudice was ameliorated by Supreme Court marking the action "off" the trial calendar and by plaintiff timely moving to restore the action in conjunction with providing the expert witness information that the defendants sought).

Recent decisions out of the Second Department have rendered the timeliness requirement of CPLR § 3101(d)(1)(i) ambiguous. Going against New York State courts' general trend of leniency, the Second Department held that a trial court did not abuse its discretion by rejecting the affidavits of a plaintiff's expert where the expert was not identified until after the note of issue and certificate of readiness were filed (indicating that all discovery was complete and the case ready for trial). *Constr. by Singletree Inc. v. Lowe*, 55 A.D.3d 861, 863 (2d Dep't 2008); *see also Yax v. Dev. Team Inc.*, 67 A.D.3d 1003, 1004 (2d Dep't 2009) (holding that the trial court should not have considered the expert affidavit, "since the defendant did not provide an excuse for failing to identify the expert in response to the plaintiff's discovery demands, and the plaintiff was unaware of the expert until he was served with the expert's affidavit in opposition to his summary judgment motion"); *Gerardi v. Verizon N.Y.*, 66A.D.3d 960, 961 (2d Dep't 2009) (finding that a plaintiff's expert report should have been precluded where there was no good cause for the expert not being disclosed prior to the filing of the note of issue and certificate of readiness to be filed). In spite of this decision, the Second Department has since stated that: "CPLR 3101(d)(1)(i) does not require a party to respond to a demand for expert witness information at any specific time nor does it mandate that a party be precluded from offering expert testimony merely because of noncompliance with the statute, unless there is evidence of intentional or willful failure to disclose and a showing of prejudice by the opposing party." *Browne v. Smith*, 65 A.D.3d 996, 997 (2d Dep't 2009); *see also Hayden v. Gordon*, 91 A.D.3d 819, 820 (2d Dep't 2012) (finding that the Supreme Court did not err in considering the submitted expert affidavit, "since there was no evidence that the failure to disclose the identity of their expert witness . . . was intentional or willful, and there was no showing of prejudice to the appellant"); *Acca v. Clemons Props., Inc.*, No. 102925/08, 2010 WL 5479906, at *2–3 (Sup. Ct. Richmond Cty. Dec. 27, 2010) (rejecting the holding in *Construction by Singletree, Inc.* in favor of the holding in *Browne*).

Trial courts in the Second Department have struggled to differentiate between the two diverging opinions, some falling in line with *Singletree*, others with *Browne*. *See Deitch v. May*, 713 N.Y.S.2d 278; *Renucci v. Mercy Hosp.*, 124 A.D.2d 796. Furthermore, one trial court recently noted that "[b]etween these rather opposing views, fall a growing number of post-*Singletree* opinions that either permit or require preclusion of expert testimony where there is post-note disclosure, and where the proffering party fails to show 'good cause' or 'valid excuse' for the late disclosure."[51]

The First Department has also rejected expert testimony when it was not disclosed in a timely fashion. In *Lissak v. Cerabona*, 10 A.D.3d 308 (1st Dep't 2004), the appellate division held that the trial court erred when it permitted testimony by experts for whom disclosure had been given on the eve of trial. The appellate court determined that defendant had not shown good cause for delayed service when the 3101(d) disclosures described testimony adverse to the interests of a co-defendant who had been represented by the same counsel and who had settled and been released during trial. *Id.* at 308. Additionally, the appellate court observed that the attorney's conflict of interest did not amount to "good cause," noting that the "conflict of interest and the resulting tactics were a course charted by the defense, and the last-minute change in strategy made possible by the hospital's settlement of the claim against it should not be permitted to inure to plaintiffs' detriment." *Id.* at 310; *see also Klatsky v. Lewis*, 268 A.D.2d 410 (2d Dep't 2000) (plaintiffs' reason for calling new expert on the eve of trial did not constitute "good cause").[52]

As an alternative to precluding expert testimony, courts can impose less drastic penalties against the offending party. For example, in *Herd v. Town of Pawling*, 244 A.D.2d 317 (2d Dep't 1997), the appellate court reversed the trial court's order that precluded the plaintiff's experts from testifying at trial because the plaintiff's disclosure failed to comply with the requirements of Section 3101(d). Although the appellate court agreed that the plaintiff's disclosure was deficient in various respects, the court determined that preclusion was unwarranted. Instead, the court allowed the plaintiff one final opportunity to comply but assessed plaintiff's counsel a monetary penalty for its conduct in causing delay and creating additional motion practice. *Id.* at 318; *see also Cela v. Goodyear Tire & Rubber Co.*, 286 A.D.2d 640 (1st Dep't 2001) (although the appellate court found that plaintiff's conduct raised an inference of intentional withholding of expert disclosure, it noted that the defendant failed to establish any prejudice as a result of the delay, and therefore conditionally granted the defendant's motion to preclude unless plaintiff's counsel paid $1,000 to defendant's counsel).

Similarly, in *Rook v. 60 Key Centre, Inc.*, 239 A.D.2d 926 (4th Dep't 1997), the court reversed an order that precluded an expert economist from testifying because the expert disclosure did not reveal the basis for the expert's conclusion. In reversing, the Fourth Department determined that "[a] less drastic remedy, such as further disclosure of the basis for the economist's opinions, would have sufficed and would have better served the policies underlying the expert disclosure statute." *Id.* at 927; *see also McDermott v. Alvey, Inc.*, 198 A.D.2d 95, 95 (1st Dep't 1993) (reversing the lower court and allowing the plaintiff's expert to testify even though the plaintiff waited until the eve of trial to respond to the demand under § 3101(d)(1)(i) but fining the plaintiff's counsel $1,500 for its "lack of diligence"); *Einheber v. Bodenheimer*, No. 114682, 2006 WL 1835019, at *6 (Sup. Ct. N.Y. Cty. May 5, 2006) (court merely required plaintiff to supplement his disclosures to specify

---

[51] *Herrera v. Lever*, No. 723/10, 2012 WL 874788, at *3 (Sup. Ct. Kings Cty. Mar. 15, 2012) (citing *Banister v. Marquis*, 87 A.D.3d 1046 (2d Dep't 2011); *Kopeloff v. Arctic Cat, Inc.*, 83 A.D.3d 890, 891 (2d Dep't 2011); *Stolarski v. Di Simone*, 83 A.D.3d 1042, 1044 (2d Dep't 2011)).

[52] *But see Chapman v. State*, 227 A.D.2d 867 (3d Dep't 1996) (court considered claimants' *pro se* status and apparent good-faith effort to provide an adequate response to the disclosure request and declined to preclude claimants' expert testimony despite the fact that claimants' notice was deficient because it did not contain the substance of the expert's opinions and a summary of the grounds for each opinion).

against which defendants each expert would testify when the sole deficiency in the disclosures was the failure to so specify).[53]

Unlike the Federal Rules, the CPLR makes no provision for the automatic deposition of an opposing party's testifying expert. *See* FED. R. CIV. P. 26(b)(4)(A).[54] Rather, a party seeking to depose an adversary's expert must request the court's permission to do so "upon a showing of special circumstances." CPLR § 3101(d)(1)(iii); *Feldman v. N.Y. State Bridge Auth.*, 40 A.D.3d 1303 (3d Dep't 2007) (finding no "special circumstances" meriting the deposition of defendant's expert and ordering plaintiff to disclose "further explanatory information" when defendant's expert had deciphered raw data and plaintiff's expert was unable to do so without "further explanatory information"). "Special circumstances" are most often found where physical evidence has been examined by one expert and subsequently lost or destroyed before the opposing expert has an opportunity to examine it.[55] While loss or destruction of evidence constitute acceptable "special circumstances" in the lion's share of cases, "special circumstances" may also be found where the court finds that a "unique factual situation" counsels toward permitting the deposition of a party's expert. *See Brooklyn Floor Maint. Co. v. Providence Wash. Ins. Co.*, 296 A.D.2d 520, 522 (2d Dep't 2002) (defendant demonstrated special circumstances justifying deposition of plaintiff's expert when plaintiff could not answer basic questions regarding its bookkeeping practices, or regarding specific entries in the corporation's financial records, and indicated that the expert was the only person who could answer those questions). In either case, a party seeking to take expert depositions must provide more than mere "conclusory allegations" as to the nature of the special circumstances. *See, e.g., Feldman v. N.Y. State Bridge Auth.*, 40 A.D.3d 1303 (3d Dep't 2007); *Melendez v. Roman Catholic Archdiocese of N.Y.*, 277 A.D.2d 64 (1st Dep't 2000) (court found that no special circumstances existed where the plaintiff's expert report sufficiently detailed the nature of the expert's testimony and specified the extent of plaintiff's psychological injuries and diagnosis). Finally, even if the court grants a party permission to depose an expert, the court may limit the content of the inquiries and impose fees and other expenses as it deems appropriate.[56]

---

[53] *But see Corning v. Carlin*, 178 A.D.2d 576, 577 (2d Dep't 1991) (affirming the trial court's decision to preclude the plaintiff from offering an expert witness at trial where the plaintiff "failed to show good cause why she did not retain an expert until the very eve of trial and then failed to disclose his existence until after opening statements had been made").

[54] CPLR Section 3101(d)(1)(ii) does provide certain circumstances under which the deposition of an expert may be taken in cases involving medical, dental, or podiatric malpractice.

[55] *Dixon v. City of Yonkers*, 16 A.D.3d 542 (2d Dep't 2005) (court permitted plaintiff to depose defendant's expert where the complaint alleged that decedent's death was caused by a falling tree, which was removed from the accident scene within forty-eight hours, and defendant's expert examined the tree before it was rendered unavailable to the plaintiff); *Kaufman v. Lund Fire Prods. Co.*, 8 A.D.3d 242 (2d Dep't 2004) (court permitted plaintiff to depose defendant's expert where pieces of equipment, which were examined by defendant's expert in their original state, had been altered prior to inspection by plaintiff); *Rosario v. Gen. Motors Corp.*, 148 A.D.2d 108, 113 (1st Dep't 1989) (court permitted further expert disclosure pertaining to the facts surrounding the expert's inspection of the evidence where such evidence was destroyed prior to the opposing party's inspection); *see also Mead v. Benjamin*, 201 A.D.2d 796, 797 (3d Dep't 1994) (appellate court affirmed lower court's decision permitting defendant to depose plaintiff's expert witness in an action against plaintiff's former attorneys for negligent legal representation, upon finding that the "unique factual situation" qualified as "special circumstances" under Section 3101(d)(1)(iii)).

[56] *See McDonald v. Finley's Inc.*, 20 A.D.3d 900 (4th Dep't 2005) (special circumstances justified plaintiff's deposition of defendant's expert as to factual issues and permitted

The CPLR contains no rule analogous to Rule 706 of the Federal Rules of Evidence. Nevertheless, New York State courts, primarily in New York County, have employed special masters akin to court-appointed experts to assist in complex scientific litigation.[57] For example, in the asbestos litigation, a special master was appointed to assist the court in administering thousands of individual lawsuits filed in New York State.[58] In addition, in the breast implant litigation, a state court justice combined resources with her counterparts in the federal courts in New York in order to address expert evidentiary issues. In the breast implant litigation, the New York State and federal courts agreed "to a unique cooperative endeavor whereby a *Daubert* hearing would be held in [a federal judge's] court and the parties would use the record of that hearing in future proceedings in state court for rulings on the admissibility of scientific evidence and expert testimony." *In re New York State Silicone Breast Implant Litig.*, 982, 656 N.Y.S.2d 97, 98 (Sup. Ct. N.Y. Cty. 1997) (citation omitted).

3. *Local Practice Tips for New York State Courts*

Expert disclosure in New York State courts under CPLR Section 3101(d) is triggered only by a demand from opposing counsel. Therefore, attorneys litigating in New York State court should serve their demand for expert disclosure early in the litigation (perhaps with the answer for the defendant and soon thereafter for the plaintiff) to avoid surprise and to put the burden on the adversary to comply. Although the CPLR does not prescribe a fixed time in which a party must respond to an expert disclosure request, the time periods for all disclosure, including expert disclosure, are usually agreed upon by the parties and embodied in a preliminary conference order. In the absence of such an order, the parties should respond within a reasonable time period—one that precludes an adversary from claiming that they suffered prejudice as a result of any delay. In the absence of an order, a party should also attempt to reach an agreement with opposing counsel on the dates for expert disclosures. Furthermore, practitioners should consult the rules of the court in which they are litigating to ensure their compliance with the applicable local rules governing the timing of expert disclosure. Although the CPLR does not require that the disclosure request take a specific form, a party should make sure they include at a minimum the items required under Section 3101(d).

Notwithstanding that the CPLR eschews expert depositions, the parties may agree to allow their experts to be deposed in certain circumstances and, as noted above, the court may also order such depositions. Parties in complex commercial litigation may find that making their experts available provides valuable insight into the opinions of their adversary's experts. If both parties agree, they

---

discovery of factual portions of expert's report; plaintiff was not permitted to inquire about expert's factual conclusions or discover those portions of the expert's report embodying conclusions or opinions); *Coello v. Progressive Ins. Co.*, 6 A.D.3d 282 (1st Dep't 2004) (court's finding of special circumstances permitted plaintiff to depose defendant's expert as to his factual observations of a car's condition, but plaintiff was not permitted to depose the expert as to his opinions); *Taft Partners Dev. Group v. Drizin*, 277 A.D.2d 163, 163 (1st Dep't 2000) (court limited scope of inquiries to the factual circumstances of the observations of the experts and prohibited any inquiry as to the experts' opinions). *Accord Tedesco v. Dry-Vac Sales, Inc.*, 203 A.D.2d 873, 874 (3d Dep't 1994).

[57] *See* Article 43 of the CPLR, which sets forth the procedures for appointing a referee.

[58] *See* New York City Asbestos Litig. Case Mgmt. Order (Sept. 20, 1996 *amended* May 26, 2011) *available at* http://www.nycal.net/PDFs/cmo/CMO_revised_052611.pdf; *see also N.Y. City Asbestos Litig. v. A.O. Smith Water Prods.*, No. 112742/04, slip op. at 1 (N.Y. Sup. Ct. Sept. 15, 2005) (granting plaintiff's motion for the joint trial of four cases and describing the process of utilizing a special master to efficiently deal with the high volume of cases involved in the asbestos litigation).

can devise a mechanism through which the experts are deposed and can request that the court set a schedule for the depositions.

If the parties cannot agree, they can seek a court order compelling the expert's deposition. However, as noted above, the parties must demonstrate exceptional circumstances. A party can also gain disclosure of the opposing party's experts' opinions without their agreement by filing a dispositive motion, that is, one for summary judgment. The opposing party is then forced to disclose its experts' opinions to oppose the motion. In this manner, even if unsuccessful, the moving party will gain some insight into its adversary's expert's position. Of course, this tactic will also reveal the views of the moving party's own expert.

Given the limited scope of expert disclosure under New York State court practice, if it is apparent that a case will be decided primarily upon the strength of expert testimony, practitioners should consider, as early in the discovery process as possible, whether to attempt to obtain additional expert disclosure from their adversaries, either voluntarily through agreement between the parties or through court intervention.

4. The Future of Frye and Daubert in New York State Courts

Unlike expert disclosure in federal practice, the CPLR significantly limits the amount of information a party is entitled to receive in response to a request for expert disclosure.[59] This procedural distinction between the Federal Rules and the CPLR likely explains why challenges to expert evidence in New York State courts are not as prevalent as in federal courts. Thus, at the start of a trial in state court, parties are not ordinarily armed with the information necessary to move the court to preclude expert testimony using the factors set forth in *Daubert* and *Kumho*.[60]

Although the New York Court of Appeals has consistently renewed its adherence to *Frye*'s "general acceptance" standard when determining the admissibility of expert testimony based on novel scientific principles, it is becoming increasingly clear that the lower courts are paying closer attention to the principles of reliability enunciated in *Daubert* and *Kumho Tire*. Counsel has the opportunity to argue that, even if specific proffered testimony is "generally accepted," it should nonetheless be excluded as unreliable given the facts of the case. And, courts retain the discretion and flexibility to admit only expert testimony that is reliable and will be helpful to the jury.

Finally, since the standard to be applied to evidence not properly classified as "novel science" still remains uncertain, practitioners should be prepared to defend their expert evidence, or, alternatively, oppose their adversary's expert evidence, under the standards of both *Frye* and *Daubert*.

---

[59] The limitations placed upon expert discovery under Section 3101(d) seem to conflict with Section 3101(a)'s "full disclosure" mandate. Section 3101(a) provides that "[t]here shall be full disclosure of all matter material and necessary in the prosecution or defense of an action. . . ." Expert testimony serves the critical function of aiding the fact-finder in his or her understanding of issues that are not within the fact-finder's common or ordinary knowledge. Given the importance of expert testimony during a trial, it would be hard to categorize expert testimony as anything other than "material and necessary."

[60] As a result, parties may not uncover the validity or invalidity of an expert's testimony until the trial is underway. However, this lack of pretrial information does not mean that a litigant cannot challenge the proffer of expert testimony at trial.

C. EXPERT EVIDENCE IN CONNECTICUT STATE COURTS

1. Key Decisions Applying Daubert and Kumho

The Connecticut Supreme Court has adopted *Daubert* for governing the admissibility of scientific evidence in Connecticut. *State v. Porter*, 698 A.2d 739, 743 (Conn. 1997). Connecticut Code of Evidence § 7-2 regarding expert testimony is also similar to Federal Rule of Evidence 702 and adopts the principles enunciated in *Daubert*:

> A witness qualified as an expert by knowledge, skill, experience, training, education or otherwise may testify in the form of an opinion or otherwise concerning scientific, technical or other specialized knowledge, if the testimony will assist the trier of fact in understanding the evidence or in determining a fact in issue.

Conn. Code of Evid. § 7-2; see *Poulin v. Yasner*, 64 Conn. App. 730, 740, 781 A.2d 422, 430 (2001). However, Connecticut has not adopted *Kumho* and extended the *Daubert* analysis to nonscientific evidence that is technical or requires specialized knowledge. *State v. Sorabella*, 891 A.2d 897, 934 (Conn. 2006) (noting that "*Porter* applies only to expert scientific evidence" and declining to consider adopting *Kumho* for expert testimony based on technical or other specialized knowledge because the defendant failed to raise the claim in the trial court). The commentary to § 7-2 notes that *Kumho* was decided subsequent to *Daubert* and *Porter* and clarifies that the Connecticut Code of Evidence takes no position on whether *Porter* applies to expert testimony based on technical or specialized knowledge, and states that § 7-2 "should not be read either as including or precluding the *Kumho Tire* rule." Conn. Code of Evid. § 7-2, Commentary. Thus, whether the Connecticut Supreme Court will extend *Porter* by adopting *Kumho* remains unresolved.

Under *Porter*, Connecticut trial courts perform a gatekeeper function, determining whether the proffered scientific evidence meets the two *Daubert* requirements of reliability and relevance for admissibility. *Porter*, 698 A.2d at 744, 747. When a party seeks to introduce scientific testimonial evidence, the trial court must assess the validity of the methodology underlying the opinion pursuant to a *Porter* two-step analysis. *Prentice v. Dalco Elec., Inc.*, 907 A.2d 1204, 1212 (Conn. 2006). The trial court should conduct a *Porter* hearing to conduct the analysis for the proposed testimony and decide whether to admit it. *Id.*

The first *Porter* requirement for admissibility is scientific reliability. A trial court should find scientific evidence to be sufficiently reliable if it is "scientifically valid, meaning that it is scientific knowledge rooted in the methods and procedures of science; and is more than subjective belief or unsupported speculation." *Porter*, 698 A.2d at 744 (citing and quoting *Daubert*, 509 U.S. 579, 590 (1993)). In order for the court to be able to perform its gatekeeper function and determine whether the proffered scientific evidence is reliable, the proponent must articulate the methodology underlying the scientific evidence. *Prentice*, 907 A.2d at 1210. When assessing scientific reliability, the trial court should focus solely on the validity of the principles and methodology underlying the expert opinion, not on the opinion itself. *Porter*, 698 A.2d at 753.

The second *Porter* requirement is relevance, and a trial court should find this requirement met if the scientific evidence is "demonstrably relevant to the facts of the particular case in which it is offered, and not simply . . . valid in the abstract." *Porter*, 698 A.2d at 745. Therefore, the proponent of scientific expert testimony must establish that the testimony is derived from and based upon a scientifically reliable methodology (a methodology meeting the first *Porter* requirement). *Maher v. Quest Diagnostics, Inc.*, 847 A.2d 978, 994 (Conn. 2004).

In Connecticut, certain scientific evidence will not be subject to a *Porter* threshold admissibility analysis if it is based on scientific principles that have become so well established as to be subject to judicial notice. *State v. West*, 877 A.2d 787, 805 (Conn. 2005) (citing *Porter*, 698 A.2d at 755 n.30); *Maher*, 847 A.2d at 989 (some "scientific principles are considered so reliable within the relevant medical community that there is little or no real debate as to their validity and it may be presumed as a matter of judicial notice"). Under these circumstances, the proposed scientific evidence would clearly withstand the *Porter* reliability analysis and would be admitted upon a showing of relevance. *West*, 877 A.2d at 805. Thus, "if a trial court determines that a scientific methodology has gained general acceptance [in the scientific community], then the *Daubert* inquiry will generally end and the conclusions derived from that methodology will generally be admissible." *Id.* at 807 (quoting *Porter*, 698 A.2d at 754). In *Porter*, the Connecticut Supreme Court noted that ordinary fingerprint identification is the type of evidence that is generally accepted and so well established so as not to require a *Porter* hearing. *Porter*, 698 A.2d at 755 n.30; *see also West*, 877 A.2d at 807–08 (finding that microscopic hair analysis does not require a *Porter* analysis because it is so well established and generally accepted); *State v. Kirsch*, 820 A.2d 236 (Conn. 2003) (finding that blood alcohol testing was universally accepted and recognized as reliable and, therefore, did not require a *Porter* reliability determination).

The Connecticut Supreme Court has also identified a narrow category of "exceptional situations" where courts may find no need for a *Porter* hearing because the proposed evidence, "although ostensibly rooted in scientific principles and presented by expert witnesses with scientific training, [is] not scientific for the purposes of our admissibility standard for scientific evidence." *Prentice*, 907 A.2d at 1214 (citing and quoting *Maher*, 847 A.2d at 989 n.22). Thus, certain evidence does not require the court to undertake a validity assessment under *Porter* because it is "neither scientifically obscure nor instilled with an aura of mystic infallibility" and merely places a jury in a position to assess the evidence without abandoning common sense and sacrificing independent judgment. *Id.* at 1215 (citation omitted). For example, the court held that a validity determination was unnecessary for the state's proposed testimony of a criminologist regarding visible characteristics of, and similarities between, strands of hair. *State v. Reid*, 757 A.2d 482, 487–88 (Conn. 2000). The court explained that since the witness would present enlarged photographs of the hair samples and explain how he had compared them, the jury was free to use its own powers of observation and comparison and decide for itself whether the hairs matched. *Id.* Thus, no *Porter* determination would be necessary. *Id.* Similarly, the court found no need for a *Porter* hearing when the state introduced a podiatrist's testimony as to the likelihood that a certain pair of sneakers would fit on the defendant's feet. *State v. Hasan*, 534 A.2d 877 (Conn. 1987). The court did not consider the testimony to be scientific evidence because the podiatrist merely compared the sneakers to the defendant's feet and, therefore, it was not subject to analysis under *Porter* but, rather, under traditional admissibility standards discussed below. *Id.*

The *Porter* court stressed that *Daubert* is a conceptual approach to the admissibility of scientific evidence and, therefore, its analysis was not meant to be a mechanical, clearly defined test for trial courts to apply when evaluating the admissibility of scientific evidence. *Porter*, 698 A.2d at 751–52. Accordingly, the court identified several nonexclusive factors for trial courts to consider for admissibility: general acceptance in the relevant scientific community; whether the methodology underlying the scientific evidence has been tested and subjected to peer review; the known or potential rate of error; the prestige and background of the expert witness supporting the evidence; the extent to which the technique at issue relies upon subjective judgments made by the expert rather than on objectively verifiable criteria; whether the expert can present and explain the data and methodology underlying the testimony in a manner that assists the jury in drawing conclusions therefrom; and whether the technique or methodology was developed solely for purposes of litigation. *Prentice*, 907 A.2d at 1210. Despite all these factors, *Porter* is only a threshold inquiry as to the admissibility of scientific evidence; other evidentiary rules must also be satisfied. For example, the trial court should exclude evidence that passes a *Porter* threshold inquiry when the prejudicial impact of the scientific testimony substantially outweighs its probative value. *Porter*, 698 A.2d at 757.

Trial courts should generally admit expert testimony if the following factors are met: "(1) the witness has a special skill or knowledge directly applicable to a matter in issue, (2) that skill or knowledge is not common to the average person, and (3) the testimony would be helpful to the court or jury in considering the issues." *State v. McClendon*, 730 A.2d 1107, 1114 (Conn. 1999). The trial court should exclude scientific evidence "only when the methodology underlying such evidence is sufficiently invalid to render the evidence incapable of helping the fact finder determine a fact in dispute." *Porter*, 698 A.2d at 756. The proposed evidence need not be conclusive to be admissible and can even be "susceptible to different interpretations," so long as the fact finder can reasonably construe it in a way that it would be relevant. *Id.* at 755–56. Thus, simply because a judge believes that a particular technique has flaws that may lead to inaccurate conclusions does not render such evidence incapable of assisting the fact finder and, therefore, such evidence often should be admitted. *Id.* at 756.

The trial court has broad discretion in ruling on the qualifications of experts and the admissibility of expert evidence, and a trial court's decision "will be overturned only upon a showing of a clear abuse of the court's discretion." *State v. St. John*, 919 A.2d 452, 459–60 (Conn. 2007) (citation omitted); *McClendon*, 730 A.2d at 1114. When reviewing a trial court's determination for abuse of discretion, "every reasonable presumption should be made in favor of the correctness of the trial court's ruling." *State v. Griffin*, 869 A.2d 640, 646 (Conn. 2005); *see also State v. Victor O.*, 20 A.3d 669, 678 (Conn. 2011). Thus, a trial court's ruling on the admissibility of evidence is given great deference. *Id.*

In *State v. Griffin*, the Connecticut Supreme Court reviewed a trial court's refusal to admit the testimony of a clinical psychologist regarding the Grisso test—a test used to measure a defendant's understanding of *Miranda* warnings and his choice to waive his rights. *Griffin*, 869 A.2d at 643–44. The trial court had concluded, based on a *Porter* analysis, that the psychologist's testimony regarding the Grisso test and her expert opinion based on the test results were inadmissible because the defendant had failed to prove that the methodology employed was scientifically valid. *Id.* at 643. On appeal, the defendant maintained that the trial court erred when it subjected the Grisso test to a *Porter* hearing. The Connecticut Supreme Court disagreed, finding that the Grisso test was a scientific instrument or tool subject to a *Porter* analysis. *Id.* at 649–50. The defendant also contended that the trial court improperly concluded that the proposed testimony failed to meet the *Porter* standard. *Id.* at 650. Again, the Connecticut Supreme Court disagreed, finding that the trial court properly considered the relevant *Porter* factors and reasonably found them to be lacking because the Grisso test had neither been subject to peer review nor was it generally accepted as scientifically valid. *Id.* at 652. Accordingly, the Connecticut Supreme Court affirmed the trial court's determinations. *Id.*

In *Maher v. Quest Diagnostics, Inc.*, the Connecticut Supreme Court reversed the judgment of the trial court and remanded the medical malpractice case for a new trial because the trial court improperly admitted the plaintiff's expert testimony. *Maher*, 847 A.2d at 981. The expert was an oncologist that testified as to what stage plaintiff's cancer would likely have been one year before plaintiff was diagnosed. *Id.* at 985. His expert opinion was based on what the oncologist determined was the relevant "doubling time" of plaintiff's cervical cancer and working backwards in time. *Id.* The Connecticut Supreme Court first concluded that the oncologist's testimony was the type of scientific evidence that required a *Porter* hearing because the principles underlying the testimony were not so well established as to be presumed reliable. *Id.* at 984, 988. The court then found that while the trial court had conducted a *Porter* hearing, it had improperly determined that the evidence was admissible because the plaintiff failed to adequately articulate the methodology that formed the basis for the oncologist's testimony as to doubling time in cervical cancer. *Id.* at 986, 994. In particular, the plaintiff failed to produce any evidence as to the reliability of the propositions underlying the testimony and also failed to show that the propositions had any support in the scientific community. *Id.* at 995. Thus, the court concluded that the trial court had assessed the reliability of the methodology by "mere reliance on an expert witness' belief that [the] methodology [was] reliable" and had, therefore, abused its discretion in admitting the testimony into evidence. *Id.*

2. *Expert-Related Rules and Procedural Issues in Connecticut State Courts*

Chapter 13 of the Connecticut Practice Book governs the procedure relating to the use and discovery of expert evidence in Connecticut, containing similar provisions as FED. R. CIV. P. 26(a)(2) and 26(b)(4) and mandating full and continuing disclosure. *See* Conn. Practice Book §§ 13-4; 13-15. Connecticut substantially rewrote the section of its Practice Book governing expert evidence in 2008, 2009, and 2010, including internally restructuring large portions of the chapter.

Each party must "disclose each person who may be called by that party to testify as an expert witness at trial, and all documents that may be offered in evidence in lieu of such expert testimony . . . ." Conn. Practice Book § 13-4(a). That party is further required to disclose, via filing with the court and service on opposing counsel, "the name, address and employer of each person who may be called by that party to testify as an expert witness at trial, whether through live testimony or by deposition." Conn. Practice Book § 13-4(b). This disclosure must additionally include "the field of expertise and the subject matter on which the witness is expected to offer expert testimony; the expert opinions to which the witness is expected to testify; and the substance of the grounds for each such expert opinion," except under certain circumstance when the expert is a health care provider who treated the patient as described in Connecticut Practice Book § 13-4(b)(2).[61] Conn. Practice Book §13-4(b)(1). This disclosure requirement may be satisfied by referencing in the disclosure document and producing to all parties "a written report of the expert witness containing such information." *Id.* Such information must be supplemented if the party expecting to call the expert discovers additional or new information or discovers that a prior disclosure was incorrect or has become incorrect since the party made the disclosure. Conn. Practice Book §§ 13-4(a), 13-15.

Subject to exceptions for treating health care providers and specific party agreements, parties disclosing expert witnesses are obligated to produce on request "all materials obtained, created and/or relied upon by the expert in connection with his or her opinions . . . within fourteen days prior to that expert's deposition" unless otherwise specified by the Schedule for Expert Discovery. Conn. Practice Book § 13-4(b)(3). For materials already produced to the other parties, the party calling the expert must create a list of such materials. *Id.* There is an exception under this rule for expert witnesses that are not being compensated, and in those instances, it becomes the duty of the party adverse to the expert to obtain these materials "by subpoena or other lawful means." *Id.*

Barring a judicial order otherwise (for "good cause shown") or an agreement by the parties, the deposing party is responsible for paying fees and expenses of the expert for the deposition, excluding preparation time. Conn. Practice Book § 13-4(c)(2). These fees and expenses, unless otherwise ordered, are limited to "a reasonable fee" for the witness's time at the deposition and traveling to and from the deposition and "reasonable expenses actually incurred for travel . . . and lodging." *Id.* Parties must file with the court lists of "documents or records" they expect to submit in evidence in

---

[61] The section reads: "If the witness to be disclosed hereunder is a health care provider who rendered care or treatment to the plaintiff, and the opinions to be offered hereunder are based upon that provider's care or treatment, then the disclosure obligations under this section may be satisfied by disclosure to the parties of the medical records and reports of such care or treatment. A witness disclosed under this subsection shall be permitted to offer expert opinion testimony at trial as to any opinion as to which fair notice is given in the disclosed medical records or reports. Expert testimony regarding any opinion as to which fair notice is not given in the disclosed medical records or reports must be disclosed in accordance with subdivisions (1) of subsection (b) of this section." Conn. Practice Book § 13-4(b)(2).

lieu of live expert testimony, but should not file copies of the actual "documents or records" with the court. Conn. Practice Book § 13-4(d). Similarly, any party wishing to call as a witness at trial any expert previously disclosed under Section 13-4 by another party must file a notice of disclosure "(1) stating that the party adopts all or a specified part of the expert disclosure already on file; and (2) disclosing any other expert opinions to which the witness is expected to testify and the substance of the grounds for any such expert opinion." Conn. Practice Book § 13-4(e). This disclosure must be "made within thirty days of the event giving rise to the need for that party to adopt the expert disclosure as its own," with the specific example given of "the withdrawal or dismissal of the party originally disclosing the expert." Conn. Practice Book § 13-4(g)(3).

For an expert retained but not intended to be called as a trial witness, a party other than the retaining party may get discovery from that expert only under the provisions of Connecticut Practice Book § 13-11 or "upon a showing of exceptional circumstances under which it is impracticable for the party seeking discovery to obtain facts or opinions on the same subject by other means." Conn. Practice Book § 13-4(f). Connecticut Practice Book Section 13-11, in turn, governs only court-ordered physical and mental examinations, particularly those of persons in custody or of plaintiffs in personal injury suits, similar to the provisions of Rule 35 of the Federal Rules of Civil Procedure. Conn. Practice Book § 13-11.

The revised Connecticut Practice Book Section 13-4(g) sets out a timeline for expert discovery that governs in the absence of an alternate judicial order or agreement among the parties. Conn. Practice Book § 13-4(g). Parties must submit a Schedule for Expert Discovery on a prescribed form within 120 days after the return date of a civil action; if the parties cannot agree on a schedule, they must notify the court, which will set a scheduling conference. Conn. Practice Book § 13-4(g)(1). The Practice Book provides no specific guidance for setting deadlines within the schedule, except noting that the proposed deadlines "shall be realistic and reasonable, taking into account the nature and relative complexity of the case, the need for predicate discovery and the estimated time until the case may be exposed for trial." *Id.* In the event that a new party is added after a Schedule for Expert Discovery is approved, an amended schedule must be filed with the court for approval "within sixty days after such new party appears, or at such other time as the court may order." Conn. Practice Book § 13-4(g)(2).

Once a Schedule for Expert Discovery is set, it may be modified by agreement of the parties so long as the modifications do not disrupt an assigned trial date. Conn. Practice Book § 13-4(g)(4). In addition, absent agreement, a party may file a motion to modify. *Id.* Such motions shall be granted unless the requested modification would cause "undue prejudice" to another party or "undue interference" with the trial schedule, or was the result of the requesting party's bad-faith disclosure delay. *Id.*

Parties may face sanctions for failure to comply with Section 13-4, after an appropriate hearing. Conn. Practice Book § 13-4(h). Preclusion of an expert's testimony, however, is disfavored. An expert witness's testimony may only be precluded if two findings are made. *Id.* First, there must be a finding that preclusion, "including any consequence thereof on the sanctioned party's ability to prosecute or defend the case," is a proportional sanction to the relevant noncompliance. Second, there must also be a finding that the relevant noncompliance "cannot adequately be addressed by a less severe sanction or combination of sanctions." *Id.*

D. EXPERT EVIDENCE IN VERMONT STATE COURTS

1. Key Decisions Applying **Daubert** *and* **Kumho**

The Vermont Supreme Court has adopted the principles of *Daubert* in considering the admissibility of scientific expert evidence in Vermont State courts. *See USGen New England, Inc. v. Town of Rockingham* ("*USGen*"), 177 Vt. 193, 201, 838 A.2d 269, 275 (2004) ("In Vermont, we adopted the *Daubert* analysis, concluding that because our rules of evidence are 'essentially identical to the federal ones on admissibility of scientific evidence' it makes sense to adopt admissibility principles similar to those used in the federal courts."); *985 Assocs., Ltd. v. Daewoo Elecs. Am., Inc.*, 183 Vt. 208, 212, 945 A.2d 381, 383 (2008); *State v. Streich*, 163 Vt. 331, 342, 658 A.2d 38, 46 (1995); *State v. Brooks*, 162 Vt. 26, 30, 643 A.2d 226, 229 (1993). In 2004, Vermont Rule of Evidence 702 was amended to explicitly adopt and include the *Kumho* holding such that Vermont courts apply the *Daubert* approach to nonscientific evidence that is technical or requires specialized knowledge. *See* 2004 Amendment to V.R.E. 702 (effective July 1, 2004); *USGen*, 177 Vt. at 201, 838 A.2d at 275; *State v. Kinney*, 171 Vt. 239, 250 n.2, 762 A.2d 833, 842 (2000) (following *Kumho* before V.R.E. 702 was amended).

Under *Daubert* and *Kumho,* trial courts act as "gatekeepers" by screening expert testimony to ensure that it is reliable and helpful to the issue before allowing the jury to hear it. *USGen*, 177 Vt. at 201, 838 A.2d at 276 (citing *Amorgianos v. Nat'l R.R. Passenger Corp.*, 303 F.3d 256, 265–66 (2d Cir. 2002)). If the court finds that the proffered evidence meets both *Daubert* prongs of relevance and reliability, the expert may be presented; otherwise, the evidence is excluded and never presented to the jury.[62] *USGen*, 177 Vt. at 201, 838 A.2d at 276. The Vermont Supreme Court has emphasized that *Daubert* is only an admissibility standard: "the admitted evidence does not alone have to meet the proponent's burden of proof on a particular issue, and, of course, the expert witness remains subject to cross-examination." *USGen*, 177 Vt. at 201, 838 A.2d at 276 (citation omitted).

With regard to the first *Daubert* prong, evidence will be deemed relevant if it "will assist the trier of fact to understand the evidence or to determine a fact in issue." *State v. Streich*, 163 Vt. at 343, 658 A.2d at 47 (citation omitted). And, with regard to the second *Daubert* prong, the four nonexclusive factors for a trial judge to evaluate in determining reliability, as originally set out in *Daubert*, are: (1) whether the theory or technique is capable of being tested; (2) whether the theory or technique has been subjected to peer review and publication; (3) the known or potential rate of error associated with the technique; and (4) whether the theory or technique has been generally accepted by the scientific community. *Id.* at 343, 658 A.2d at 47. To determine the reliability of expert testimony, the court examines the "factual basis, data, principles, methods, or their application" and whether the evidence is based upon sufficient facts or data. *USGen*, 177 Vt. at 204, 838 A.2d at 278 (quoting *Kumho*, 526 U.S. at 149); V.R.E. 702.

The trial judge should allow the trier of fact to evaluate "[a] contest over the 'science' or the specific result" of any expert testimony and not preclude a party from proving the reliability and accuracy of its expert's analysis. *Brooks*, 162 Vt. at 31, 643 A.2d at 229. In the case of a bench trial, "Daubert must still be followed, albeit in a somewhat more relaxed manner" because "in the absence of a jury, the screening function of the judge is diminished." *USGen*, 177 Vt. at 204, 838 A.2d at 278.

The trial court's discretion to admit expert evidence is highly discretionary because "the trial court is in the best position to assess the expert's credibility." *USGen*, 177 Vt. at 204, 209, 838 A.2d at 278, 281–82 ("We stress that the trial court has wide discretion to determine the qualifications of an expert witness"). As such, the trial court's decision with respect to the admissibility of expert evidence will

---

[62] The trial court must also consider other general requirements of admissibility, such as V.R.E. 104(a) (preliminary questions concerning an expert's qualifications are for the court), 402 (evidence which is not relevant is not admissible), 403 (relevant evidence is to be excluded if danger of unfair prejudice substantially outweighs its probative value), 703 (otherwise inadmissible hearsay is permitted if it is normally relied upon by experts in the field), and 706 (the court may procure the assistance of an expert of its choosing), in making its admissibility determination. *See Streich*, 163 Vt. at 344 n.3, 658 A.2d at 48; *Brooks*, 162 Vt. at 30, 643 A.2d at 229.

be reviewed under an abuse-of-discretion standard. *USGen*, 177 Vt. at 202–03, 838 A.2d at 276–77 ("Although we have not specifically articulated a standard of review for *Daubert* rulings, we have held that admissibility decisions under V.R.E. 702 are reviewed only for abuse of discretion. . . . [W]e conclude that a special standard of review for *Daubert* challenges is inappropriate."); *see also State v. Forty*, 187 Vt. 79, 94, 989 A.2d 509, 519 (2009) ("Although we have some concerns as to the trial court's V.R.E. 702 analysis, we find that the trial court did not abuse its discretion in excluding the expert). Accordingly, the reviewing court will reverse the trial court's decision only if it was "made for reasons clearly untenable or was unreasonable" and there is a "clear showing of judicial error." *USGen*, 177 Vt. at 203, 838 A.2d at 277 (citing *Quenneville v. Buttolph*, 175 Vt. 444, 833 A.2d 1263 (2003)).

In *USGen*, the owner of a hydroelectric power plant appealed as improper the court's admission of an expert's testimony regarding the valuation of the plant for property tax purposes. *USGen*, 177 Vt. at 194, 838 A.2d at 271. According to the appellant, the expert used an improper methodology in his economic analysis, rendering his testimony insufficiently reliable. *Id.* at 199, 838 A.2d at 274. The Vermont Supreme Court affirmed the trial court, finding that while the appellant's arguments potentially affected the weight that should be given to the expert's testimony, they did not negate admissibility under *Daubert*. *USGen*, 177 Vt. at 208, 838 A.2d at 280–81.

Similarly, in *Boehm v. Willis*, 180 Vt. 615, 618–19, 910 A.2d 908, 913 (2006), the Vermont Supreme Court affirmed the trial court's ruling that a doctor's testimony was admissible in a personal injury car-accident case. The plaintiff argued that the testimony had been improperly admitted because the doctor, having no specialty in neurology or orthopedics, was not qualified to form an opinion on plaintiff's injury. *Id.* The plaintiff also argued that the doctor had an insufficient basis for forming his opinion because he had limited access to plaintiff's medical records and only examined plaintiff for fifteen minutes. *Id.* The Vermont Supreme Court agreed with the trial court, finding that: "plaintiff's arguments for excluding [the doctor's] testimony all went against the weight of [the doctor's] testimony, not its admissibility." *Id.*

2. *Expert-Related Rules and Procedural Issues in Vermont State Courts*

Vermont Rule of Civil Procedure 26(b)(4) governs the presentation of expert evidence in Vermont and is similar to its counterpart in the Federal Rules of Civil Procedure. Under Vermont's Rule 26(b)(4)(A), a party has a right to discover the identity, and the substance of the testimony, of an opposing party's expert witness and to take the expert's deposition. *Hutchins v. Fletcher Allen Health Care, Inc.*, 172 Vt. 580, 581, 776 A.2d 376, 378 (2001).[63] If a party fails to disclose its intent to offer an expert witness's testimony within a discovery deadline, the trial court may prevent that party from offering the expert testimony. *Id.* A party may discover facts known or opinions held by

---

[63] Unlike the Federal Rules, the Vermont Rules do not require the disclosure of an expert report, but a party can ascertain information about another party's experts through interrogatories: "A party may through interrogatories require any other party to identify each person whom the other party expects to call as an expert witness at trial, to state the subject matter on which the expert is expected to testify, and to state the substance of the facts and opinions as to which the expert is expected to testify and a summary of the grounds for each opinion." VT. R. CIV. P. 26(b)(4)(A)(i). A party has the right to depose any person who has been identified in the responses to the interrogatories as a testifying expert. VT. R. CIV. P. 26(b)(4)(A)(ii). A party may also "obtain by request for production or subpoena any final report of the opinions to be expressed by an expert who has been identified in an answer to an interrogatory posed pursuant to subparagraph (A)(i) as an expert whose opinions may be presented at trial, as well as the basis and reasons for the opinions and any exhibits that will be used to summarize or support them." VT. R. CIV. P. 26(b)(4)(A)(iii).

nontestifying experts who have been retained in anticipation of litigation or preparation for trial only "upon a showing of exceptional circumstances under which it is impracticable for the party seeking discovery to obtain facts or opinions on the same subject by other means" or as provided in Rule 35(b). VT. R. CIV. P. 26(b)(4)(D).[64] When seeking discovery of a nontestifying expert, the party must pay "a fair portion of the fees and expenses incurred by the [other] party in obtaining facts and opinions from the expert," unless the result would be a manifest injustice. VT. R. CIV. P. 26(b)(4)(E)(ii).

Rules 26(b)(4)(B) and (C) were added to the Vermont Rules of Civil Procedure in 2012 in order to reflect amendments made to the Federal Rules of Civil Procedure. VT. R. CIV. P. 26 reporter's notes. Vermont Rule 26(b)(4)(B) extends the trial preparation protections from Rule 26(b)(3) to "drafts of any disclosure of an expert that is required under subparagraph (A)(i) and drafts of any report prepared by such an expert." VT. R. CIV. P. 26(4)(B). Subparagraph (C) protects communications between a party's attorney and an expert identified in response to an interrogatory, with exceptions for communications that relate to data or assumptions provided by the attorney and relied upon by the expert in forming opinions or that relate to the expert's compensation. VT. R. CIV. P. 26(4)(C).

3. *Local Practice Tips and Suggestions for Vermont State Courts*

In Vermont, trial courts tend to favor permitting witnesses, including expert witnesses, to testify rather than precluding testimony and, thus, allowing the jury to make a credibility determination about the weight that should be given to the testimony. For example, in *Koplewitz v. Hamilton*, No. 103-2-01, 2004 WL 5657981 (Vt. Super. Ct. July 28, 2004), defendants sought exclusion of plaintiff's expert witnesses' testimony, arguing that the expert doctors were not qualified to offer opinions on causation of plaintiff's injuries by carbon monoxide poisoning. The court acknowledged its role as gatekeeper under *Daubert* but noted that the trial court should not deprive the jury of expert testimony that may be helpful, even if there are some limitations or weaknesses in an expert's methodology or qualifications, because the opposing party may make those limitations or weaknesses clear to the jury. The court found that defendants' arguments, which may affect the weight given to the testimony, did not undermine the doctors' qualifications or the reliability of the doctors' underlying reasoning or methodology so as to make the testimony inadmissible. Thus, the court denied defendants' motion and admitted the expert doctors' testimony.

Similarly, in *Parah v. Lakeside Pharmacy, Inc.*, No. S0195-02, 2004 WL 5576898 (Vt. Super. Ct. Sept. 30, 2004), a wrongful-death case, defendant sought exclusion of a doctor's testimony, arguing that he was not qualified to testify and that his opinions and conclusions on causation of decedent's loss of consciousness were not reliable. The court found that the defendant's arguments regarding the doctor's professional qualifications went to the weight rather than relevance and reliability of the evidence. With respect to defendant's contention that the doctor relied on an improper methodology, the court found that the methodology was a generally accepted form of scientific reason and that defendant's arguments again went to weight, not admissibility. Accordingly, the court denied defendant's motion and permitted the testimony.

Trial courts in Vermont, though, will exercise their right to exclude expert evidence when there are clear admissibility issues. In *Trickett v. Ochs*, No. 267-11-00, 2005 WL 5895218 (Vt. Super. Ct. Mar. 10, 2005), defendants sought exclusion of plaintiffs' expert witness testimony on the health hazards of diesel fumes. The court acknowledged its function as a gatekeeper that should not allow expert testimony to be offered unless it is both reliable and relevant. Defendants argued, and the

---

[64] Vermont Rule of Civil Procedure 35 pertains to physical and mental examinations made under court order when the physical or mental condition of a party is in controversy. Rule 35(b) requires the party taking an examination to deliver a copy of the examiner's report to the requesting party. VT. R. CIV. P. 35(b).

court agreed, that the expert's testimony failed *Daubert*'s reliability analysis: the expert, an engineer, had based his testimony on informal self-study; his theory about the correlation between diesel-fume odors and actual particulate concentrations had not been tested, published, or subjected to peer review; and, there was no evidence regarding the general acceptance of his theories in the scientific community. Therefore, the court deemed the expert's testimony to be unreliable and inadmissible.

Practitioners are encouraged to refer to the Vermont Judiciary's online database of select trial-court opinions to learn more about how Vermont trial courts are applying *Daubert*.[65]

---

[65] *See Legal Community Civil Opinions*, VERMONT JUDICIARY, http://www.vermontjudiciary.org/search/tcdecisioncvl.aspx (last visited July 9, 2012).

CHAPTER III
EXPERT EVIDENCE IN THE THIRD CIRCUIT

by

John J. Soroko
James H. Steigerwald
Shannon Hampton Sutherland
Robert M. Palumbos[1]
Duane Morris LLP
30 South 17th Street
Philadelphia, PA 19103
(215) 979-1000

A. KEY DECISIONS APPLYING THE PRINCIPLES OF *DAUBERT*, *JOINER*, AND *KUMHO TIRE* IN FEDERAL COURTS IN THE THIRD CIRCUIT

1. Introduction

Long before the Supreme Court's decision in *Daubert v. Merrell Dow Pharmaceuticals, Inc.*, 509 U.S. 579 (1993), the Third Circuit had already rejected *Frye's* "general acceptance" standard for the admissibility of scientific expert testimony. *See United States v. Downing*, 753 F.2d 1224, 1237 (3d Cir. 1985) ("[W]e conclude that 'general acceptance in the particular field to which a [scientific technique] belongs' . . . should be rejected as an independent controlling standard of admissibility"). In fact, in *Daubert*, the Supreme Court discussed Chief Judge Becker's concept of "fit" and cited his decision in *United States v. Downing*, 753 F.2d 1224, in the course of largely adopting the Third Circuit's approach. *See Daubert*, 509 U.S. at 585, 591, 594 (citing *Downing*, 753 F.2d 1224); *see also In re Paoli R.R. Yard PCB Litig.*, 35 F.3d 717, 741 (3d Cir. 1994) (noting that *Daubert* had largely adopted the Third Circuit's test for scientific expert testimony), *aff'd in part, rev'd in part on other grounds*, 221 F.3d 449 (3d Cir. 2000) (hereinafter "*Paoli II*"). After *Daubert*, the Third Circuit has continued to apply its three-pronged test to the admissibility of expert testimony. Under that test, expert testimony must (1) be qualified, (2) be based on reliable and scientifically valid methodology, and (3) "fit" the facts of the case. *See Paoli II*, 35 F.3d at 741–43. As discussed below, the Third Circuit has repeatedly applied this approach post-*Daubert*. *See, e.g., Oddi v. Ford Motor Co.*, 234 F.3d 136 (3d Cir. 2000); *Heller v. Shaw Indus., Inc.*, 167 F.3d 146 (3d Cir. 1999), *cert. denied*, 532 U.S. 921 (2001); *Paoli II*, 35 F.3d 717.

---

[1] The authors thank Erica Fruiterman and Meghan Claiborne for their assistance in connection with this chapter. Ms. Fruiterman and Ms. Claiborne will graduate in 2013 from Temple University Law School and Emory University Law School, respectively, after which time they will join Duane Morris LLP.

Until the Supreme Court's decision in *Kumho Tire Co. v. Carmichael*, 526 U.S. 137 (1999), the Third Circuit wrestled with *Daubert*'s applicability outside scientific subject matter.[2] For example, the Third Circuit refused to apply *Daubert* to examine the reliability of an expert's testimony about the safety conditions of a railroad track. *See Lauria v. Nat'l R.R. Passenger Corp.*, 145 F.3d 593, 599 n.7 (3d Cir. 1998). In accordance with *Kumho Tire*, the Third Circuit now applies *Daubert*'s standards to determine the admissibility of all expert testimony.

In its role as the "gatekeeper," the court must exclude expert evidence that does not satisfy the requirements of *Daubert*. However, the Third Circuit has been clear that "the court is *only* a gatekeeper, and a gatekeeper alone does not protect the castle. *United States v. Mitchell*, 365 F.3d 215, 245 (3d Cir. 2004). So long as there are "good grounds" for the expert's opinion, *Daubert*, 509 U.S. at 590, the court must leave it to the adversarial process to test expert evidence and to the fact finder to evaluate and weigh it. *Mitchell*, 365 F.3d at 245.

B. EXPERT QUALIFICATIONS

The Third Circuit recognizes that "a broad range of knowledge, skills, and training qualify an expert as such." *Lauria*, 145 F.3d at 598 (quoting *Paoli II*, 35 F.3d at 741); *see also Hammond v. Int'l Harvester Co.*, 691 F.2d 646, 653 (3d Cir. 1982) (permitting engineer who taught high school automobile repair class and had experience selling agricultural equipment to testify in product liability action regarding defective design of tractor). Therefore, the Third Circuit has "eschewed imposing overly rigorous requirements of expertise and ha[s] been satisfied with more generalized qualifications." *Lauria*, 145 F.3d at 598 (quoting *Paoli II*, 35 F.3d at 741); *see also In re Paoli R.R. Yard PCB Litig.*, 916 F.2d 829, 855 (3d Cir. 1990) ("insistence on a certain kind of degree or background is inconsistent with our jurisprudence"). For example, in *Lauria v. National Railroad Passenger Corp.*, 145 F.3d 593 (3d Cir. 1998), the plaintiff sued the defendant for failing to provide a reasonably safe work environment after the plaintiff slipped and was injured while crossing a rail yard. The plaintiff offered the testimony of a foreman/maintenance engineer who was prepared to testify that the defendant should have discovered and removed a piece of wood that contributed to the plaintiff's accident. The district court excluded the expert's opinion, in part, because he was not sufficiently qualified. Noting the witness's twenty years of experience as a trackman, machine operator, assistant supervisor, supervisor, and self-employed safety consultant, the Third Circuit concluded that the witness was sufficiently qualified as an expert and reversed the district court's ruling. *See id.* at 599.

In the medical area, the Third Circuit places great weight on the testimony of treating physicians, even when they are not necessarily specialists in the applicable field.[3] For example, in *Holbrook v. Lykes Bros. Steamship Co.*, 80 F.3d 777 (3d Cir. 1996), the Third Circuit examined a district court ruling that precluded a treating physician from testifying about a pathology report or from providing his diagnosis to the jury because the physician was not an oncologist or a specialist in "definitive cancer diagnosis." The Third Circuit reversed the lower court and held:

---

[2] Third Circuit cases applying *Daubert* in the nonscientific setting pre-*Kumho Tire* have done so in a more "general manner." *See Robert Billet Promotions, Inc. v. IMI Cornelius Inc.*, No. 95-1376, 1998 U.S. Dist. LEXIS 16080, at *27–29 (E.D. Pa. Oct. 13, 1998) (applying *Daubert* to accountant's estimate of contractual damages).

[3] By contrast, the Third Circuit has expressed its reservations about allowing nonmedical experts to testify about the cause of a party's illness. *See Heller*, 167 F.3d at 159 ("We note preliminarily that we are doubtful that a non-medical expert . . . is qualified to testify as to the cause of someone's illness"); *cf. Corrigan v. Methodist Hosp.*, 874 F. Supp. 657, 660 (E.D. Pa. 1995) ("We find that . . . non-medical doctors can testify as to causation of illness if they have an expertise in that area").

It would be inconsistent and run counter to the Rules' liberal policy of admissibility to allow an outside expert, hired solely for litigation purposes, to rely on and testify about a pathology report, but exclude testimony by the treating physician who ordered the report and relied on it for life and death decisions about the patient's treatment. Opinions by physicians who have neither examined nor treated a patient have less probative force, as a general matter, then [sic] they would have if they had treated or examined him.[4]

The Third Circuit has also relied on a liberal approach to evaluate expert qualifications of nontreating physicians. In *Schneider v. Fried*, 320 F.3d 396, 399 (3d Cir. 2003), the Third Circuit held that a nontreating physician who possessed "eminent academic credentials" as a cardiologist should be admitted to testify as a medical expert regarding the standard of care for interventional cardiologists. The court rejected the argument that the physician should have been excluded from testifying as an expert because he was "an invasive cardiologist (diagnosing and treating heart conditions) and not an interventional cardiologist (performing angioplasties)," and therefore not qualified as an expert in the subspecialty at issue. *Id.* at 407. Because the proposed expert was "highly knowledgeable about cardiology" and "had regular contact with and advised interventional cardiologists," he had the proper qualifications to give an expert opinion, "especially considering that the requirement that a witness have specialized knowledge has been interpreted liberally." *Id.*

The Third Circuit's liberal approach does not, however, render meaningless *Daubert*'s requirement regarding qualifications. In *Surace v. Caterpillar, Inc.*, 111 F.3d 1039 (3d Cir. 1997), the Third Circuit affirmed the lower court's preclusion of an expert who was called to testify about the defective warning system of a "profiler" road machine. The plaintiff was a road-crew member working behind a profiler. The profiler had a blind spot that prevented its operator from seeing behind the machine. Although the profiler had a visual and audible warning system, the plaintiff argued that the signals were inadequate due, in part, to the phenomenon of habituation. Among other experts, the plaintiff called an electromechanical engineer to testify that the profiler's warning signals were not sufficient. While the proffered expert had experience as an engineer, "habituation was the crux of his theory of liability." *Id.* at 1056. The expert was precluded from testifying because the expert admitted that he relied on another expert for his conclusions regarding habituation and that he had not read any literature about habituation or participated in habituation testing or study. *Id.* at 1055–56.

Similarly, the "marginal nature" of the expert's qualifications in *Elcock v. Kmart Corp.*, 233 F.3d 734 (3d Cir. 2000), marked the "outer limit" of the Third Circuit's liberal approach to expert qualification. *Id.* at 744. In *Elcock*, the district court found a psychologist qualified to testify as an expert in vocational rehabilitation, even though the expert's qualifications were a "close call." *Id.* at 740. Although the expert had no formal training as a vocational expert, the Third Circuit affirmed the district court because the expert had experience helping drug addicts return to work, had read the relevant literature and attended conferences in the field of vocational rehabilitation, had consulted the *Dictionary of Occupational Titles*, and had testified previously as a vocational rehabilitation expert. *Id.* at 743–44. Although the Third Circuit found that the expert's experience related more to the "micro" level of vocational rehabilitation than to the "macro" level of vocational rehabilitation, and that the expert's qualifications were of a "marginal nature," the Third Circuit found that

---

[4] *Holbrook*, 80 F.3d at 782. The court also concluded that the district court erred by precluding a doctor who practiced in pulmonary and internal medicine from testifying about radiation as a cause for cancer. Although the district court had concluded that the doctor did not have the required specialization in cancer and radiation, the Third Circuit determined that the doctor's expertise in lung diseases qualified him to testify that radiation was not the cause of the plaintiff's mesothelioma. *See id.* at 780, 783.

the district court had not abused its discretion in resolving a "close call" in favor of qualifying the expert. *Id.* at 744.

"Because of [the Third Circuit's] liberal approach to admitting expert testimony, most arguments about an expert's qualifications relate more to the weight to be given the expert's testimony than to its admissibility." *Holbrook*, 80 F.3d at 782. Unless an expert's testimony strays from his field of expertise, as in *Surace*, challenges to the expert's qualifications will generally be more successful during cross-examination to undercut the expert's credibility. "[I]t is an abuse of discretion to exclude testimony simply because the trial court does not deem the proposed expert to be the best qualified or because the proposed expert does not have the specialization that the court considers most appropriate." *Pineda v. Ford Motor Co.*, 520 F.3d 237, 244 (3d Cir. 2008) (quoting *Holbrook*, 80 F.3d at 782). Such challenges, however, may still help to exclude expert opinion as unreliable when other circumstances are also present.[5]

C. RELIABILITY

1. General Standards Governing Reliability

Following *Daubert*, the Third Circuit requires scientific testimony to be based on a reliable and scientifically valid methodology. *See, e.g., Paoli II*, 35 F.3d at 742. This reliability prong requires an expert to have "good grounds" for his opinion and "assures that the expert's opinions are based on science rather than 'subjective belief or unsupported speculation.'" *Holbrook*, 80 F.3d at 784 (quoting *Daubert*, 509 U.S. at 590); *see also In re TMI Litig. Cases Consol. II.*, 193 F.3d 613, 669 (3d Cir. 1999), *amended by* 199 F.3d 158 (3d Cir. 2000). To determine whether a scientific technique or method is reliable, courts are to consider "all relevant factors that may bear on the reliability of the proffered evidence." *United States v. Velasquez*, 64 F.3d 844, 849 (3d Cir. 1995). The Third Circuit uses the following nonexclusive factors pulled from *Daubert* and *Downing*, 753 F.2d 1224 (3d Cir. 1985):

> (1) Whether a method consists of a testable hypothesis; (2) whether the method has been subject to peer review; (3) the known or potential rate of error; (4) the existence and maintenance of standards controlling the technique's operation; (5) whether the method is generally accepted; (6) the relationship of the technique to methods which have been established to be reliable; (7) the qualifications of the expert testifying based on the methodology; and (8) the non-judicial uses to which the method has been put.

Paoli II, 35 F.3d at 742 n.8; *Oddi*, 234 F.3d at 145. Even if the trial court admits testimony against objections to the expert's qualifications, the strength or weakness of the qualifications will still be considered when the court considers the reliability of the expert's opinion. *See United States v. Mitchell*, 365 F.3d 215, 242 (3d Cir. 2004) ("[T]he binary question whether an expert is or is not qualified to testify to a particular subject is analytically distinct, under Rule 702, from the more finely textured question whether a given expert's qualifications enhance the reliability of his testi-

---

[5] Thus, challenges to an expert's qualifications supplement challenges to the reliability of the expert's testimony. *See, e.g., Burton v. Danek Med. Inc.*, No. 95-5565, 1999 U.S. Dist. LEXIS 2619 (E.D. Pa. Mar. 1, 1999) (neurologist not qualified to testify in product liability/ negligence action related to spinal fusion surgery where he had no experience with spinal fusion surgeries or products, and expert's opinion was not reliable because opinion was based on materials provided by plaintiff's counsel, was prepared for litigation, and did not use differential diagnosis).

mony"); *Elcock*, 233 F.3d at 744 (noting that the "marginal nature of [the expert's] qualifications also enters into the *Daubert* calculus"). These factors are "simply useful signposts, not dispositive hurdles that a party must overcome in order to have expert testimony admitted." *Heller*, 167 F.3d at 152. Thus, "a party seeking to exclude [or to admit] expert testimony must do more than enumerate the factors . . . and tally the number that are or are not met by a particular expert's testimony." *Id.*

The *Daubert* standard for reliability applies to all expert testimony in federal courts. *See Kumho Tire*, 526 U.S. 137. In determining the reliability of nonscientific testimony, particularly in product liability cases, the Third Circuit will also look at several nonexclusive factors "as indicia of reliability." *Milanowicz v. Raymond Corp.*, 148 F. Supp. 2d 525, 532–33, 536 (D.N.J. 2001) (holding that an engineer's opinion that improperly designed forks on a forklift caused the plaintiff's severed finger in a product liability case failed to meet *Daubert* standards of reliability because the opinion was not based on relevant literature or testing). These factors include (1) federal design and performance standards; (2) standards established by independent organizations; (3) relevant literature; (4) evidence of industry practice; (5) product design and accident history; (6) illustrative charts and diagrams; (7) data from scientific testing; (8) the feasibility of suggested modification; and (9) the risk utility of suggested modification. *Id.* at 536. If an expert cannot rule out all obvious alternative causes for a product's failure, the testimony will not meet the *Daubert* reliability requirement. *Id.* at 536.

Although the Third Circuit has not held that a district court can *never* consider the credibility of an expert witness in assessing reliability, the Third Circuit requires a case-by-case assessment before engaging in such considerations. *See Elcock*, 233 F.3d at 745. The district court may need to evaluate the expert's general credibility, but the court's fact-finding role under Fed. R. Evid. 104(a) is circumscribed in the context of a reliability inquiry. *Id.*

The Third Circuit acknowledges that under *Daubert* "the focus . . . must be solely on principles and methodology, not on the conclusions that they generate." *Oddi*, 234 F.3d at 145 (quoting *Daubert*, 509 U.S. at 595); *see also Paoli II*, 35 F.3d at 744–45 ("A judge frequently should find an expert's methodology helpful even when the judge thinks that the expert's technique has flaws sufficient to render the conclusions inaccurate"). Nevertheless, under *Joiner*, "a district court must examine the expert's conclusions to determine whether they could reliably follow from the facts known to the expert and the methodology used." *Heller*, 167 F.3d at 153; *see also Montgomery Cnty. v. Microvote Corp.*, 320 F.3d 440, 448–49 (3d Cir. 2003) (affirming the exclusion of expert testimony where the expert could not describe how the data that formed the basis of his opinion had been gathered); Fed. R. Evid. 702.

> [B]ecause conclusions and methodology are not entirely distinct from one another. Trained experts commonly extrapolate from existing data. But nothing in either *Daubert* or the Federal Rules of Evidence requires a district court to admit opinion evidence that is connected to existing data only by the *ipse dixit* of the expert. A court may conclude that there is simply too great an analytical gap between the data and the opinion proffered.

Gen. Elec. Co. v. Joiner, 522 U.S. 136, 146 (1997). Thus, using "reliable methods . . . cannot sanitize an otherwise untrustworthy conclusion." *Oddi*, 234 F.3d at 146 (citing *Joiner*, 522 U.S. at 146); *see also Childs v. Gen. Motors Corp.*, 1998 U.S. Dist. LEXIS 10991 (E.D. Pa. July 22, 1998) (excluding expert's opinion, in part, because conclusion that a design defect existed was not consistent with the expert's tests).

Under the Third Circuit's interpretation of *Daubert*, where the expert fails to clearly explain his method "in rigorous detail" and makes it nearly impossible for the opponent's experts to duplicate the expert's subjective methods, there exists no testable hypothesis for which there are controlling standards. *See, e.g., Elcock*, 233 F.3d at 747 (citing *Paoli II*, 35 F.3d at 742); *Furlan v. Schindler*

Elevator Corp., No. 10-6870, 2012 U.S. Dist. LEXIS 44751 (E.D. Pa. Mar. 30, 2012) (expert's opinion was not reliable because it was not based on "methods and procedures of science" but on the expert's own intuition). When a witness's testimony is based on experience, the witness "must apply his experience reliably to the facts; his opinions must be well-reasoned, grounded in his experience, and not speculative." *Roberson v. City of Philadelphia*, No. 99-3574, 2001 U.S. Dist. LEXIS 2163, at *14, 23 n.15 (E.D. Pa. Mar. 2, 2001) (a purported expert on police practices may give conclusions based on his experience and training, but he must explain how his experiences (1) lead to his conclusions, (2) provide a sufficient basis for his opinion, and (3) reliably apply to the facts of the case) (citing Fed. R. Evid. 702 & Adv. Comm. Notes (2000)). Even where a purported expert has years of experience, without evidence on which the judge can base a reliability determination, such as relevant literature to submit the methodology to peer review and tests to verify the error rate of the underlying theory, the opinion will not pass muster under the *Daubert* standards.[6]

2. Application of the Reliability Requirement

In contrast to other federal courts of appeals, the Third Circuit does not require experts to base their testimony concerning the causation of illnesses on published studies. *See Heller*, 167 F.3d at 155–56; *Yarchak v. Trek Bicycle Corp.*, 208 F. Supp. 2d 470, 499 (D.N.J. 2002) (denying defendant's motion to exclude testimony of plaintiff's medical expert that prolonged bicycle riding caused plaintiff's erectile dysfunction on the grounds that the medical studies and articles he referenced did not establish a general causal link between bicycle riding and impotence because the Third Circuit does not require published studies for general causation). In *Heller*, the Third Circuit noted that an expert could base his causation theory on a differential diagnosis and strong temporal relationship between the alleged cause and the plaintiff's illness without relying on published studies if the methodology was otherwise reliable. *See id.* The Third Circuit supported its rejection of the require-

---

[6]   *See Calhoun v. Yamaha Motor Corp., U.S.A.*, 350 F.3d 316, 324 (3d Cir. 2003) (holding that proposed expert with degrees in naval architecture and marine engineering had no basis to opine reliably on the safety of a Jet Ski design where he had conducted no relevant testing with Jet Skis, had no professional experience with Jet Skis, and had not even operated a Jet Ski at the time he wrote his expert report); *Oddi*, 234 F.3d at 156, 158 (finding that the purported expert's opinion on a design defect did not satisfy the *Daubert* standard where the expert conducted no tests and failed to calculate any of the forces on the plaintiff or his vehicle during the accident, but instead relied primarily on his own intuition) *(Daubert* requires more than "haphazard intuitive inquiry"); *Booth v. Black & Decker, Inc.*, 166 F. Supp. 2d 215, 221 (E.D. Pa. 2001) (finding that the purported expert's opinion on a design defect did not satisfy *Daubert* when he did not test his hypothesis concerning the device in question, sketch the kind of device he recommended, produce an example of the recommended device, conduct practical research on how to incorporate the device into the product in question, or install the device on a model for testing); *Rapp v. Singh*, 152 F. Supp. 2d 694, 706 (E.D. Pa. 2001) (under *Oddi*, an expert cannot intuitively evaluate even a "blatant defect," but rather must perform tests and calculations to support his methodology); *Hamilton v. Emerson Elec. Co.*, 133 F. Supp. 2d 360, 371–72 (M.D. Pa. 2001) (finding that the purported expert's opinion on a brake's design defect was inadequate under *Daubert* where the witness merely assumed that the brake must have failed at the time of the accident because it failed after the accident, and failed to demonstrate that his hypothesis could be tested). *But see United States v. Davis*, 397 F.3d 173, 178–79 (3d Cir. 2005) (holding that police officer's twelve years of experience relating to narcotics were, without more, a sufficient basis to provide a reliable opinion regarding the methods of operation of drug dealers).

ment that experts rely on published studies by analogizing such a rule to the "*Frye*-like bright line standard." *Id.* at 155. In contrast to such rigid standards, the court asserted that expert testimony "must be evaluated practically and flexibly without bright-line exclusionary [or inclusionary] rules." *Id.* Moreover, the Third Circuit refused to exclude testimony that preceded published studies when physicians do not wait for such studies to make "life and death" decisions. *Id.* at 155–56.

In *Paoli II*, the Third Circuit examined proffered expert testimony that relied on differential diagnosis to determine the cause of a plaintiff's illness. The court noted that differential diagnosis "generally is a technique that has widespread acceptance in the medical community." *Paoli II*, 35 F.3d at 758; *see also Burton*, 1999 U.S. Dist. LEXIS 2619, at *15 ("Courts have insisted repeatedly that an expert may not give opinion testimony regarding specific causation if the expert failed to perform a differential diagnosis.") (citing *Rutigliano v. Valley Bus. Forms*, 929 F. Supp. 779, 786 (D.N.J. 1996), *aff'd*, 118 F.3d 1577 (3d Cir. 1997)). Because differential diagnosis involves assessing causation with respect to a particular individual, however, the steps taken by the doctor will vary from case to case. Thus, "no particular combination of techniques chosen by a doctor to assess an individual patient is likely to have been generally accepted." *Paoli II*, 35 F.3d at 758; *see also Johnson v. Vane Line Bunkering, Inc.*, No. 01-5819, 2003 U.S. Dist. LEXIS 23698, at *19 (E.D. Pa. Dec. 30, 2003) ("Physicians are not required to review every record or perform every conceivable test in order to reach a reliable conclusion as to causation"). Nevertheless, conducting a physical examination, taking a patient's medical history, and using laboratory testing are all methods that strengthen conclusions based on differential diagnosis and "their absence makes it much less likely that a differential diagnosis is reliable." *Id.* Accordingly, the Third Circuit admits expert testimony based on differential diagnosis and concerning the cause of a party's illness unless (1) the expert engaged in "very few standard diagnostic techniques by which doctors normally rule out alternative causes and the doctor offer[s] no good explanation as to why his or her conclusion remain[s] reliable," or (2) the opposing party points to some alternative likely cause of the party's illness and the expert offers no explanation as to why his or her opinion is still accurate. *Id.* at 760; *see also Heller*, 167 F.3d at 156 (expert using differential diagnosis need not rule out all possible alternative causes of a party's illness but must have some explanation for why his or her conclusion remains reliable); *United States v. Fleet Mgmt.*, 332 F. App'x 753 (3d Cir. 2009) (affirming the exclusion of an expert who failed to consider any alternative explanations for the discharge of an oily waste by a ship because "the very hallmark of [differential diagnosis] is the elimination of alternative causes"); *Johnson*, 2003 U.S. Dist. LEXIS 23698, at *12 (noting that the Third Circuit requires that the physician "'employed sufficient diagnostic techniques to have good grounds for his or her conclusion'" (quoting *Paoli II*, 35 F.3d at 764) and has not adopted the Eighth Circuit's standard requiring a physician to rule out every possible cause of a party's illness).

Applying its test for expert testimony based on differential diagnosis, the Third Circuit concluded that the exclusion of expert causation testimony was proper where experts had not personally examined the patients or performed other standard tests. *See Paoli II*, 35 F.3d at 764; *see also Miller v. United States*, 287 F. App'x 982 (3d Cir. 2008) (affirming the exclusion of an expert who based his opinion that a bus accident had caused plaintiff's injuries solely on the plaintiff's subjective complaints and the resolution of his symptoms after surgery, and the expert did not review the plaintiff's medical records). On the other hand, the Third Circuit reversed the lower court's exclusion of expert testimony where the expert had personally examined patients, reviewed their medical records, and taken their medical histories.[7]

---

[7] *See id.* at 767. In *Kannankeril v. Terminix Int'l Inc.*, 128 F.3d 802 (3d Cir. 1997), the court examined a lower court's exclusion of expert testimony regarding the causation of a plaintiff's illness where the expert had not met or examined the plaintiff. The court held that "[a] doctor needs only one reliable source of information showing that a plaintiff is ill; either a physical test or medical records will suffice for this." *Kannankeril*, 128 F.3d at 807.

In addition to approving of the exclusion of testimony applying differential diagnosis without sufficient grounds (the lack of personal examination or review of the appropriate records), *Paoli II* held that federal courts must also exclude expert conclusions that rest on unreliable data.[8] Thus, the Third Circuit affirmed the district court's exclusion of an exposure expert's testimony regarding the level of polychlorinated biphenyls (PCBs) in the plaintiffs' blood when the test results were unreliable. The expert had also recalculated test results for the level of PCBs in the plaintiffs' blood by multiplying the levels by a factor between two and a half and three. The expert's estimate relied on the apparently "sloppy" practices of the lab that had conducted the tests and also the comparison of three unrelated samples to another lab's results. After finding that such recalculation methodology was novel, not subject to critical scrutiny, and based on inaccurate assumptions, the district court also excluded the expert's recalculation testimony. Noting that the testing lab generally produced similar results to the lab with which the expert had compared the earlier results, the Third Circuit deferred to the district court's conclusion and upheld its exclusion of the recalculation evidence. *See Paoli II*, 35 F.3d at 773.

As with differential diagnosis, the Third Circuit also generally considers multiple regression analysis to be a reliable scientific method.[9] "Therefore, the results of such a study should be accepted [into evidence], assuming that it was done properly." *Petruzzi's IGA Supermarkets Inc. v. Darling-Del. Co.*, 998 F.2d 1224, 1238 (3d Cir. 1993) ("There is no dispute that when used properly multiple regression analysis is one of the mainstream tools in economic study and it is an accepted method of determining damages in antitrust litigation"). Thus, expert testimony based on multiple regression analysis was held to be appropriate in an antitrust case to examine differences in industry prices paid to new and existing accounts. *See id.* at 1238–41; *see also In re Indus. Silicon Antitrust Litig.*, No. 95-2104, 1998 U.S. Dist. LEXIS 20464 (W.D. Pa. Oct. 13, 1998) (denying motion to preclude expert's testimony based on multiple regression analysis where expert used market variables to control for the industry's price and concluded that prices increased by $1.92 for some products as a result of alleged conspiracy). Parties challenging multiple regression analyses as unreliable must do more than simply identify factors not considered by an expert. Instead, opposing parties must introduce evidence supporting their contention that the failure to include certain variables actually changed the analysis or made it unreliable. *See In re Indus. Silicon Antitrust Litig.*, 1998 U.S. Dist. LEXIS 20464, at *9–10.

In *Heller*, the Third Circuit reviewed a district court's exclusion of an environmental expert's testimony that volatile organic compounds (VOCs) emitted from the defendant's carpet caused the plaintiffs' illnesses. The expert's conclusion rested on three calculations. First, the expert tested the VOC levels in the plaintiffs' closet shortly before and after the defendant's carpet was removed.

---

[8] *Paoli II*, 35 F.3d at 747–48; *see also Daddio v. A.I. duPont Hosp. for Children*, 650 F. Supp. 2d 387 (E.D. Pa. 2009) (holding that "[i]t would not be proper to permit [an expert] to testify that unspecified, undocumented organ damage caused the decedent to be unable to combat pleural effusions" because "[s]uch guesswork is not based on methods and procedures of science"); *JMJ Enters., Inc. v. Via Veneto Italian Ice, Inc.*, NO. 97-CV-0652, 1998 U.S. Dist. LEXIS 5098 (E.D. Pa. Apr. 14, 1998) (holding damages expert's testimony unreliable where it relied on tax returns that did not accurately reflect plaintiff's operations and on unwarranted assumptions, and ignored existing data), *aff'd,* 178 F.3d 1279 (3d Cir. 1999).

[9] Even when the court determines as a matter of law that a method is reliable enough to form the basis of expert testimony, the court may still allow expert testimony criticizing the reliability of the method or technique. For example, in *Velasquez,* 64 F.3d at 850, the court found that "the field of handwriting analysis consists of 'scientific, technical or other specialized knowledge' properly the subject of expert testimony under Rule 702." Nevertheless, the court also found that another expert could testify about the lack of reliability and credibility of handwriting analysis. *See id.* at 851-52.

Because the VOC levels were higher before the carpet was removed and all other factors remained the same, the expert concluded that the carpet emitted VOCs. The expert's tests, however, found VOC levels far below those known to cause health problems for humans. As a result, the expert's second calculation divided the generally accepted occupational limits on exposure to the VOCs by a factor of 420. The expert justified his reduction of the acceptable background limits by noting that those limits are based on a forty-hour work week for an average healthy adult. Thus, the expert divided the limits by 4.2 (assuming an individual spent the entire 168-hour week in the home) and then further divided the limits by 100 to account for the presence of children, older adults, or unhealthy adults. Finally, the expert explained the low levels of VOCs found in the carpet by estimating that the carpet had emitted far more VOCs when initially installed. The expert used a back-extrapolation methodology to calculate his estimate for the VOCs at the time of the carpet's installation.

The Third Circuit affirmed the district court's order that granted summary judgment in favor of the defendant after excluding the plaintiffs' expert testimony. The Third Circuit determined that the environmental expert's testimony was unreliable for several reasons. First, dividing the occupational VOC limits by 420 was "suspect." While another study had also concluded that the occupational limits were too high for homes, the study divided the limit by only 10 instead of 420. Next, without ruling on the admissibility of back-extrapolation results generally, the Third Circuit determined that the expert's use of the methodology was flawed and unreliable. For example, the expert had relied on the assumption that emission rates declined exponentially by half-lives. Available evidence, however, indicated that "the actual rate of decline of emissions from carpet is nothing like half-life progression." Additionally, the expert merely relied on the declining emission rate without considering factors such as the size of rooms, air flow, and other factors that affect the air concentration of VOCs. Thus, because the expert's back-extrapolation method was unreliable and the expert's tests revealed VOC levels below acceptable rates, the Third Circuit concluded that the district court had not abused its discretion by excluding the environmental expert's testimony.

Similarly, in *Citizens Financial Group, Inc. v. Citizens National Bank of Evans City*, 383 F.3d 110 (3d Cir. 2004), the Third Circuit affirmed a decision by the district court to exclude expert testimony regarding likelihood of confusion in a trademark dispute because the proffered testimony was based on a consumer survey that was "too fundamentally flawed to be admissible." *Id.* at 120. The proposed expert had interviewed people at two malls to determine whether there was a likelihood of confusion between the trademarks at issue in the case. The Third Circuit affirmed the district court's holding that this survey encompassed the wrong "universe" of consumers and that the methodology used in the survey questions was vague and imprecise. Because these "fatal flaws" made the survey too unreliable to satisfy the standards of *Daubert*, the district court had acted appropriately as a "gatekeeper" in excluding this evidence. *Id.*

The district court in *United States v. Lightman* granted the plaintiff's motion to exclude the defendant's expert's modified allocation of responsibility for response costs at Superfund sites because the expert's methodology was "arbitrary and not based on any recognized methodology." No. 92-4710, 1999 U.S. Dist. LEXIS 21646, at *7–8 (D.N.J. 1999). In finding that the expert's methodology was "too speculative to pass muster under Rule 702," the district court reasoned that the expert failed to demonstrate any support for the assumption that increasing the distribution of site contaminants by a factor of two would also increase the site costs by a factor of two. *Id.* at *12–13.

In *Mendler v. Aztec Motel Corp.*, No. 09-2136, 2011 U.S. Dist. LEXIS 140928 (D.N.J. Dec. 7, 2011), the plaintiff in a slip-and-fall case offered an expert to prove defendants failed to satisfy industry standards by not installing a grab bar in a motel bathroom. However, the expert offered no evidence of the standard in the hotel industry and provided no evidence of even one hotel that abided by the cited requirements by installing grab bars in each bathroom. He relied instead on reports discussing industry guidelines that were between ten and thirty years old. The district court precluded the testimony as no more than "subjective belief." *Id.* at *12.

In a landmark decision, *United States v. Plaza*, Judge Pollak of the United States District Court for the Eastern District of Pennsylvania considered whether to admit expert opinion on the "match" between a latent and a rolled fingerprint. 179 F. Supp. 2d 492 (E.D. Pa. 2002) (hereinafter "*Plaza I*"), rev'd by 188 F. Supp. 2d 549 (E.D. Pa. 2002) (hereinafter "*Plaza II*"). Although Judge Pollak initially excluded the proffered fingerprint identification evidence, 179 F. Supp. 2d at 509, 513, on rehearing he reassessed the application of several *Daubert* factors and admitted the fingerprint-match testimony. 188 F. Supp. 2d at 564, 571.

On the heels of Judge Pollak's decisions in *Plaza*, the Third Circuit took up the issue of whether fingerprint analysis satisfies the standards of *Daubert*. In *United States v. Mitchell*, the government conducted two experiments in anticipation of a *Daubert* hearing in the district court in order to show the reliability of latent fingerprint identification through concrete and testable evidence. First, the government surveyed the law enforcement agencies of all fifty states, plus the District of Columbia, Canada's Royal Canadian Mounted Police, and Scotland Yard, to ask (1) whether the agency currently accepted fingerprints as a means to make identifications; (2) whether the agency had ever found two individuals to have the same fingerprints; (3) whether the agency could match the defendant's fingerprints on a ten-print card with any fingerprints in its database; and (4) whether the agency could match the latent prints at issue in the case with any prints in its database. *Id.* at 223–24. The survey revealed that all fifty-three agencies used fingerprints to identify individuals and that none had ever found two individuals who had the same fingerprints. *Id.* at 224.

The second experiment the government performed was a statistical analysis using a set of fifty thousand prints in the FBI's fingerprint database to test the proposition that each set of fingerprints is unique. "Based on statistical extrapolation . . . , the experimenters put the chances of a single full-rolled print matching another full-rolled print from anyone in the world other than the person who deposited the print at approximately one in ten to the eighty-sixth power (i.e., 1 chance in 1 followed by 86 zeroes), a very low probability indeed." *Id.* at 225. The experiment also "put the probability of a latent partial print matching the full print of anyone in the world other than the person who deposited the print at approximately one in ten to the sixteenth power (i.e., 1 in 10,000,000,000,000,000), also a very low probability." *Id.* at 226.

In a lengthy opinion authored by Judge Becker, the Third Circuit affirmed the district court's admission of latent fingerprint identification evidence against the defendant. *Id.* at 246. The court held that the "testability" factor under *Daubert* weighed in favor of admitting the evidence, as did the error rate, its general acceptance, and reliability of the techniques involved. *Id.* Although the court did not "announce a categorical rule that latent fingerprint identification evidence is admissible in [the Third] Circuit," the court stated that its decision should provide "strong guidance" in favor of the admission of fingerprint identification evidence. *Id.* In the future, "a district court would not abuse its discretion by limiting, in a proper case, the scope of a *Daubert* hearing to novel challenges to the admissibility of latent fingerprint identification evidence—or even dispensing with the hearing altogether if no novel challenge was raised." *Id.*

In *United States v. Gricco*, No. 01-90, 2002 U.S. Dist. LEXIS 7564 (E.D. Pa. Apr. 26, 2002), the Eastern District of Pennsylvania reevaluated the reliability of expert handwriting-match testimony under the *Daubert* standard. In *Gricco*, the district court accepted the reliability of "questioned document analysis," the same type of handwriting analysis methodology that the Third Circuit accepted in an "exercise of caution" before *Kumho Tire* in *United States v. Velasquez*. *See Velasquez*, 64 F.3d at 850.

Initially, the district court noted that the expert explained in detail the methodology she used, which consisted of determining whether a questioned document and sample contain a sufficient amount of writing and individual characteristics to analyze, looking at objective characteristics in both the questioned document and sample, making comparisons and weighing the evidence, and not writing a report until two examiners agreed on the result. *See Gricco*, 2002 U.S. Dist. LEXIS 7564, at *7–8 n.2. The district court further reasoned that the expert's methodology was reliable because it satisfied other *Daubert* factors. The handwriting analysis consisted of a testable hypothesis because other handwriting comparisons and existing databases of handwriting samples showed that no two persons have the same handwriting. *See id.* at *17–18. Moreover, clear standards, promulgated by the Scientific Working Group for Forensic Document Examination, controlled the method of handwriting analysis. *See id.* at *19. Next, the district court found that the expert's methodology was generally accepted in the field by law enforcement agencies in the United States and worldwide. *See id.* at *20. Additionally, the district court found that the expert's extensive experience with handwriting analysis and her certification by the American Board of Forensic Document Examiners qualified her as an expert in the field. *See id.* at *20 n.9, 21. Finally, the district court noted that the expert's method of handwriting analysis had been put to many nonjudicial uses, including for the Smithsonian and the United States Postal Service. *See id.* at *21.

In *United States v. Ford*, 481 F.3d 215 (3d Cir. 2007), the Third Circuit held that shoeprint analysis is a reliable method under *Daubert*. The defendant was convicted of participating in the robbery of two banks. He was linked to the scene of the crime, in part, by three partial shoeprints that were similar to the type of imprints that would be made by the shoes that the defendant was wearing when he was apprehended. The district court found that "there was a general acceptance of shoeprint analysis in both federal courts and the forensic community, the theory had been subject to peer review and publication, potential error rate is known, and there are standards and techniques commonly employed in the analysis." *Id.* at 218. It held that there was "sufficient underlying information"—the partial shoeprints and the shoes the defendant was wearing when apprehended—to reliably express an opinion concerning the similarities between the prints and the inability to rule out based upon any differences between them. The Third Circuit affirmed the district court's decision as a proper exercise of its gatekeeping function. *Id.* at 219.

In *United States v. Walker*, 657 F.3d 160 (3d Cir. 2011), the government introduced a police officer as an expert to render the opinion in a Hobbs Act prosecution that cocaine is manufactured outside of Pennsylvania and transported into the state. The defendant argued that the testimony was unreliable because the witness was not a chemist and was unable to distinguish ordinary cocaine from synthetic cocaine. *Id.* at 168. The Third Circuit affirmed the use of the testimony. The witness was a thirty-year veteran of cocaine-trafficking investigations who had experience in approximately 100 cocaine investigations a month, spoke with drug traffickers daily, and regularly participated in investigations involving the importation of cocaine in Harrisburg and the surrounding region. The court found that the expert's experience formed a sufficient foundation for his testimony because the expert had numerous opportunities to investigate the geographic origins of the cocaine sold in Harrisburg and did not have to be a professional chemist to gather reliable information on whether cocaine was being synthetically produced locally or transported into the state.

D. THE "FIT" REQUIREMENT

Even if an expert is sufficiently qualified and has "good grounds" for an opinion, there must also be a "connection between the scientific research or test result to be presented, and particular disputed factual issues in the case." *Downing*, 753 F.2d at 1237. Thus, an expert's analysis must "fit" the facts of the case[10] by providing the jury with the "relevant information, necessary to a reasoned

---

[10] *See Phillips v. Tilley Fire Equip. Co.*, No. 97-0033, 1998 U.S. Dist. LEXIS 18553, at *16–17 (E.D. Pa. Nov. 23, 1998) (holding that testimony designed to rebut the defense that jokes were not racial was not relevant where defense was that plaintiff initiated and encouraged racial joking and also noting that expert testimony not necessary to explain racial aspect of threat to have plaintiff "strung up"); *Belofsky v. Gen. Elec. Co.*, 1 F. Supp. 2d 504, 507 (D.V.I. 1998) (excluding expert's opinion that refrigerator was defectively designed and could have injured plaintiff by closing by itself where opinion did not match fact that, when examined, refrigerator had to be manually closed).

decision of the case." *Magistrini v. One Hour Martinizing Dry Cleaning*, 180 F. Supp. 2d 584, 595 (D.N.J. 2002) (citing *Paoli II*, 35 F.3d at 743). "In other words, the expert's testimony must be relevant for the purposes of the case and must assist the trier of fact." *Schneider*, 320 F.3d at 404. This requirement, however, does not impose a heavy burden on the proponent of such evidence. *See United States v. Mathis*, 264 F.3d 321, 335 (3d Cir. 2001), *cert. denied*, 152 L. Ed. 2d 148, 122 S. Ct. 1211 (2002) (citing *Oddi*, 234 F.3d at 145 (noting that the fit requirement is "not intended to be a high one")).

In *Heller*, the Third Circuit reviewed the proffered testimony of a doctor who specialized in internal medicine and allergy-immunology. The doctor utilized differential diagnosis to determine that the plaintiffs' illnesses were the result of VOCs emitted by the defendant's carpet. *Heller*, 167 F.3d at 153–54. The district court excluded the doctor's testimony because he could not identify any studies indicating what level of VOCs would cause the plaintiff's illnesses, failed to rule out all other possible causes of the illnesses, and relied on a weak temporal relationship. *Id.* at 154. The Third Circuit held that the district court erred by requiring the doctor to base his testimony on a published study and by requiring him to rule out all alternative causes instead of showing good grounds for his opinion. *Id.* at 155–57.

Despite its errors, Chief Judge Becker concluded that the district court had not abused its discretion by excluding the doctor's opinion because his testimony did not "fit" the data that preceded it. For example, the doctor heavily relied on the temporal relationship between the installation of the carpet and the onset of the plaintiffs' illnesses to support his conclusion. One of the plaintiffs, however, experienced health problems even before the carpet was installed, and another plaintiff did not suffer any symptoms until two weeks after the carpet had been installed. Moreover, two weeks after the carpet was removed, the plaintiffs moved back into their home and one plaintiff began to experience the symptoms again. *Id.* at 157–58.

In *Habecker v. Clark Equipment Co.*, 36 F.3d 278 (3d Cir. 1994), *cert. denied sub nom. Clark Equip. Co. v. Habecker*, 514 U.S. 1003 (1995), the plaintiff sued a manufacturer after her husband had been thrown from a forklift and killed while backing the machine down a ramp. The plaintiff alleged that the forklift was defective because it did not have an operator-restraint system. At trial, the plaintiff proffered the testimony of a safety director who had investigated the accident and conducted simulations. In upholding the district court's exclusion of the expert's testimony, the Third Circuit noted that in the simulation the ramp was pulled away from the trailer instead of moving on its own, there was no forklift operator, the height of the fork was disregarded, the forklift was not moving backward, and there was no attempt to duplicate the forklift's velocity. As a result, the Third Circuit noted that the evidence from the simulation did not appear to fit the facts of the case and would not assist the trier of fact to determine how the accident occurred. *Habecker*, 36 F.3d at 290; *see also Buzzerd v. Flagship Carwash of Port St. Lucie, Inc.*, 397 F. App'x 797 (3d Cir. 2010) (affirming preclusion of expert testimony that lacked a reliable method for an opinion on the "central issue that the jury would have been called to decide," and therefore did not satisfy the fit requirement).

Similarly, in *Saldana v. Kmart Corp*, a slip-and-fall case, the plaintiff sued the defendant for failing to clean up auto wax on the floor of the defendant's store. 84 F. Supp. 2d 629 (D.V.I. 1999), *aff'd in part, rev'd in part on other grounds*, 260 F.3d 228 (3d Cir. 2001). The defendant filed a motion *in limine* to exclude the pour tests of the plaintiff's safety engineer. The expert handheld two bottles of auto wax, one unshaken and one shaken, above the floor at a pouring angle and timed how long it took for the entire bottle to empty. *Saldana*, 84 F. Supp. 2d at 634. The expert then left the wax from one bottle on the floor for five minutes and measured the size of the puddle at twelve inches. *Id.* The expert conducted these tests on her own kitchen floor, which was older than the defendant's floor but had a similar vinyl surface. *Id.* at 635. The district court denied the defendant's motion *in limine* as to the unreliability and unreplicability of the pour tests. *Id.* at 635. However, the district court granted the defendant's motion *in limine* as to the expert's extrapolation of the test results so as to opine that the wax must have been on the defendant's floor for at least eight minutes to create a twenty-four-square-inch puddle. *Id.* Since there was no evidence in the record that the puddle was twenty-four inches across until after the plaintiff spread out the puddle during her own fall and recovery, the district court held that the extrapolation testimony did not fit the facts of the case. *Id.* at 635.

In *United States v. Mathis*, 264 F.3d 321 (3d Cir. 2001), although the government did not contest the expert's qualifications, methods, principles, or data, the government asserted that the testimony did not meet the "fit" requirement. *Id.* at 335. The government challenged three aspects of the expert's testimony. First, the government asserted that, contrary to the expert's "double identification" theory, the case did not involve any double identification because the eyewitness had seen the defendant's face only once. *Id.* at 336. The Third Circuit found that the government misconstrued the substance of the expert's testimony regarding the double identification theory, since, despite its name, the theory did not require the witness to see the defendant more than once. *Id.* Next, the government argued that the expert's opinions regarding the weak relationship between the accuracy of eyewitness testimony and testimonial confidence did not fit the facts of the case because it presented "nothing more than a general thesis on the correlation between confidence and accuracy." *Id.* at 337. The Third Circuit determined, however, that the government again had misconstrued the expert's evidence, because the expert actually testified about the relationship between these two variables under the specific facts of the case at hand. *Id.* Finally, the government argued that the expert's opinions about "weapons focus" were irrelevant, because they did not apply to a police officer accustomed to the use of firearms. *Id.* at 338. Once again, the Third Circuit rejected the government's challenge and found that its arguments were more appropriate for cross-examination, not for the purposes of exclusion under Rule 702. *Id.* Since the court later found that the evidence should also not have been excluded under Rule 403, the Third Circuit determined that the district court had abused its discretion in excluding the expert's testimony. *Id.* at 342. Nevertheless, taking the record as a whole, the Third Circuit viewed the district court's exclusion of the testimony as harmless error and therefore affirmed. *Id.* at 343–44.

In *United States v. Schiff*, 602 F.3d 152 (3d Cir. 2010), the Third Circuit reviewed a pretrial ruling by a district court to preliminarily exclude a government expert in a securities fraud case. The government proffered the expert to testify that drops in the stock price of Bristol-Myers Squibb were a result of corrective announcements by the company. Under the efficient market theory, a drop in stock price after an announcement of information shows that the information is material. However, if similar information is disclosed on multiple days, and there is no measurable movement in the stock price after the initial disclosure, then a drop in the stock price after the second disclosure must have been caused by a different factor. *Id.* at 174. The government only asked the expert to testify about the change in stock prices on the day after the announcement. The defendants argued that it was impossible to tell if the announcement on the second day was material without seeing the impact of the first day's disclosures on the price of the stock. *Id.* at 174–75. Without evidence concerning the stock price on the day of the announcement, the court found that the expert's testimony failed the *Daubert* "fit" requirement that the testimony be sufficiently tied to the facts of the case. However, the court did leave the government the option of producing a fact witness at trial to remedy the "fit" issue. The Third Circuit affirmed. *Id.* at 176–77.

Since the primary concern of the "fit" requirement is to ensure that the expert testimony will assist the trier of fact under Rule 702, expert testimony will also be excluded where it is of limited probative value and may confuse the jury instead of assisting it. For example, the Third Circuit has approved of the use of an expert to discuss whether a voice exemplar was suggestive. *See Virgin Islands v. Sanes*, 57 F.3d 338, 341 (3d Cir. 1995). In the same case, however, it was held not to be error to have precluded the expert from comparing the reliability of voice identification with the reliability of eyewitness identification because such testimony would be of little probative value and would have wasted the court's time. *Id.*

E. EXPERT-RELATED RULES AND PROCEDURAL ISSUES IN FEDERAL COURTS IN THE THIRD CIRCUIT

1. Rule 104(a) Inquiry

"Under Rule 104(a), the district court makes preliminary determinations [of] whether the proposed expert witness is qualified and whether the testimony to be given is admissible under Rule 702." *Holbrook*, 80 F.3d at 781. The district court must assess "whether the reasoning or methodology underlying the testimony is scientifically valid" and "whether that reasoning or methodology properly can be applied to the facts in issue." *Oddi*, 234 F.3d at 144. "This does not mean that plaintiffs have to prove their case twice—they do not have to demonstrate to the judge by a preponderance of the evidence that the assessments of their experts are correct, they only have to demonstrate by a preponderance of evidence that their opinions are reliable." *Paoli II*, 35 F.3d at 744. Thus, a district court should admit an expert opinion if the proponent of the testimony demonstrates by a preponderance of the evidence that the expert is qualified, and has good grounds to support his or her opinion, and the testimony will assist the jury, even if the district court believes that the expert is incorrect. *See id.* at 744–45 ("A judge frequently should find an expert's methodology helpful even when the judge thinks that the expert's technique has flaws sufficient to render the conclusions inaccurate"); *see also Oddi*, 234 F.3d at 144 (stating that the proponent must satisfy his burden under 104(a) "by a preponderance of the proof"); *Daubert*, 509 U.S. at 592.

The Third Circuit no longer defers to experts on the issue of the data on which they may reasonably rely.[11] When assessing the reliability of an expert's testimony under Rule 702, judges are also now to examine the reliability of the expert's data under Rule 703. *See Montgomery Cnty.*, 320 F.3d at 448 ("While FRE 702 is the 'primary locus' of a District Court's gatekeeping role, it also must look to other rules, including FRE 703"). This independent evaluation of the expert's data relies on the same policy considerations underlying inquiries under Rule 702 and essentially requires that there be good grounds to rely on the data to reach the expert's conclusion. *Paoli II*, 35 F.3d at 749.

The Rule 702 analysis "partly incorporates Rule 403 analysis but leaves some room for Rule 403 to operate independently." *Paoli II*, 35 F.3d at 746; *see also Carter*, 2000 U.S. Dist. LEXIS 13860, at *8 (noting that a court may exclude polygraph evidence under Rule 403 even if the court finds the evidence to be scientifically valid and relevant to the facts in issue under Rule 702). Nevertheless, "[i]f expert testimony survives the rigors of Rules 702 and 703, then Rule 403 becomes an unlikely basis for exclusion, especially in the pretrial setting." *Petruzzi's IGA Supermarkets*, 998 F.2d at 1239. For example, the Third Circuit has held that an "exceptionally well-qualified expert" cannot be excluded under Rule 403 on the grounds that the expert's sterling credentials may impress the jury so much as to cause unfair prejudice with respect to the issue about which the expert will testify. *United States v. Rutland*, 372 F.3d 543, 546 (3d Cir. 2004). Likewise, expert testimony should not be excluded merely because it is complicated and may overwhelm the jury. To illustrate the role of Rule 403, the Third Circuit stated that "a judge might use [it] to exclude an expert's critique of eyewitness testimony even though the critique met the requirements of Rule 702" if there was other evidence of the defendant's guilt that would make efforts to criticize the eyewitness testimony a waste of time. *Paoli II*, 35 F.3d at 746. If a district court applies Rule 403 to exclude an expert's opinion in the pretrial setting, then the court must have a "record complete enough on the point at issue to be considered a virtual surrogate for a trial record." *Petruzzi's IGA Supermarkets*, 998 F.2d at 1240 (holding that district court abused its discretion by excluding expert's opinion under Rule 403 without a sufficiently developed record) (quoting *In re Paoli R.R. Yard PCB Litig.*, 916 F.2d 829, 859–60 (3d Cir. 1990)).

---

[11] Before *Paoli II*, the Third Circuit held that the opinion of one expert that data is reliable had been enough to render the data reliable. *See Paoli II*, 35 F.3d at 748 (citing *Deluca v. Merrell Dow Pharms. Inc.*, 911 F.2d 941 (3d Cir. 1990), *cert. denied*, 510 U.S. 1044 (1994)).

2. Hearing Requirement

Although the Third Circuit does not require a *Daubert in limine* hearing, "whenever a *Daubert* objection is raised to a proffer of expert evidence, . . . when the ruling on admissibility turns on factual issues, . . . at least in the summary judgment context, failure to hold such a hearing may be an abuse of discretion." *Padillas v. Stork-Gamco, Inc.*, 186 F.3d 412, 418 (3d Cir. 1999) (hereinafter "*Padillas II*") (finding that the district court abused its discretion by failing to provide plaintiffs with a *Daubert* hearing in complex litigation) (citing *Cortes-Irizarry v. Corporacion Insular de Suguros*, 111 F.3d 184, 188 (1st Cir. 1997) ("Given the complex factual inquiry required by *Daubert*, courts will be hard-pressed in all but the most clearcut cases to gauge the reliability of expert proof on a truncated record")); *Crowley v. Chait*, 322 F. Supp. 2d 530, (D.N.J. 2004) ("Where the ruling on admissibility turns on factual issues in the summary judgment context, failure to hold a hearing may be an abuse of discretion"). The Third Circuit considers *in limine* hearings to be an "important" and the "most efficient" way of making a *Daubert* reliability determination in complex cases, especially considering the liberality of the *Daubert* assessment. *See Padillas II*, 186 F.3d at 417; *see also Carter v. City of Philadelphia*, No. 97-CV-4499, 2000 U.S. Dist. LEXIS 13860, at *9 (E.D. Pa. Sept. 11, 2000) (deferring a ruling on the validity and reliability of a polygraph examination in a civil rights action until after a *Daubert* hearing, "[g]iven the complexity" of the determination), *aff'd*, 35 F. App'x 36 (3d Cir. 2002). However, if the record provided by deposition testimony of the expert and the other evidence in the record provides the trial court with enough information to determine whether an expert should be precluded from testifying, a *Daubert* hearing on reliability is not required.[12] In *Elcock v. Kmart Corp.*, 233 F.3d 734 (3d Cir. 2000), the Third Circuit acknowledged that the court's gatekeeping function extends to cases involving both scientific and nonscientific testimony. Accordingly, the necessity of a *Daubert* hearing is determined under the same guidelines for all expert testimony. *Elcock*, 233 F.3d at 744–45 (remanding to the district court to conduct a *Daubert* hearing because, without a hearing, the court could not determine how the expert reached his opinion).

3. Depositions

Before the preliminary hearing regarding the admissibility of expert testimony, each party will presumably have the opportunity to depose the other party's experts. In the Third Circuit, depositions of experts should be permitted in most cases.[13] This requirement also extends to experts engaged solely to testify at the pretrial hearing, and not at trial, regarding the admissibility of another expert. *See Paoli II*, 35 F.3d at 739. Normally, "the party taking the expert's deposition will bear the costs

---

[12] *See United States v. Mornan*, 413 F.3d 372 (3d Cir. 2005) (holding that it was not plain error for a district court not to conduct an extensive *Daubert* analysis on the record); *Mitchell*, 365 F.3d at 346 (stating that "a district court would not abuse its discretion by limiting . . . the scope of a *Daubert* hearing to novel challenges to the admissibility of latent fingerprint identification evidence—or even dispensing with the hearing altogether if no novel challenge was raised"); *Oddi*, 234 F.3d at 152–53 (finding no abuse of discretion for failure to hold a *Daubert* hearing when the evidentiary record regarding the expert testimony was extensive, consisting of a preliminary report, an amended report prepared after review of the deposition testimony of a defense expert, an affidavit prepared in defense to the defendants' *Daubert* challenge, and two depositions); *Crowley*, 322 F. Supp. 2d at 537 ("[A]n *in limine* hearing is not required in all cases in which a *Daubert* objection is raised to a proffer of expert evidence").

[13] See Thomas L. Cooper, *Admissibility of Expert Testimony—Daubert Revisited: Expert Testimony—Its Admissibility in Pennsylvania State and Federal Courts*, 73 Pa. B. Ass'n. Q. 57, 70 (Apr. 2002) (citing *Paoli II*, 35 F.3d at 733).

charged by the expert for the testimony." *Reed v. Binder*, 165 F.R.D. 424, 427 (D.N.J. 1996). In limited circumstances, however, where it would be manifestly unjust to require the deposing party to bear the costs, the party proffering the expert must pay the costs associated with the deposition. *See id.* at 426–27 (finding that plaintiffs did not have to pay expert costs for depositions where plaintiffs were impoverished and defendant's experts submitted incomplete expert reports).

4. Expert Reports

In accordance with Fed. R. Civ. P. 26(a)(2)(B), parties must submit expert reports containing an expert's conclusions and the facts and grounds relied on by the expert for his or her opinion. "The test of a report is whether it was sufficiently complete, detailed and in compliance with the Rules so that surprise is eliminated, unnecessary depositions are avoided, and costs are reduced." *Reed*, 165 F.R.D. at 429; *F. P. Woll & Co. v. Fifth & Mitchell St. Corp.*, No. 96-5973, 1999 U.S. Dist. LEXIS 894 (E.D. Pa. Feb. 4, 1999) (finding report to be sufficient where it set forth expert's opinions, data relied on, and reasons for opinions, and where opposing party had three weeks to depose the expert but failed to do so). Incomplete reports may expose proffering parties to sanctions, such as exclusion of the expert's testimony,[14] limitation of the expert's testimony to matters within the scope of his or her report,[15] or imposing expert deposition costs. *See Reed*, 165 F.R.D. at 429–31 (imposing costs of expert depositions on party offering the experts where reports did not contain experts' compensation, publications, prior testimony, or sufficiently discuss the basis for the expert opinions). Similarly, expert reports that do not sufficiently set forth an expert's methodology and qualifications may be excluded in connection with the opposition of a motion for summary judgment if the expert's testimony is inconsistent with the report. *See Bowersfield v. Suzuki Motor Corp.*, 151 F. Supp. 2d 625, 632 (E.D. Pa. 2001) (holding that an expert could give substantially more detailed testimony on his methodology at the *in limine* than was set forth in his report, since the conclusions the expert reached at the hearing were consistent with the report and any prejudice to the defendant could be cured by granting leave to file supplemental expert reports).

5. Pretrial Orders

District courts are entitled to enforce their pretrial orders. Thus, when a party fails to list an expert witness as required in its discovery responses or a pretrial memorandum, a district court may then refuse to permit the witness to testify as an expert. *Habecker*, 36 F.3d at 289. Moreover, "such an order will not be disturbed absent a clear abuse of discretion." *Id.* (citation omitted). In *Paoli II*, the Third Circuit held that the district court had abused its discretion by precluding an expert from testifying about one aspect of his testimony because the substance of that portion of the testimony had not been revealed by the court's deadline. The expert, however, had been identified by the deadline and the substance of his testimony was covered in a deposition shortly after the discovery deadline. *Paoli II*, 35 F.3d at 792–93.

---

[14] *See In re TMI Litig. Cases Consol. II*, 911 F. Supp. 775, 828–29 (M.D. Pa. 1996) (excluding expert testimony where reports were submitted eight months after court-imposed deadline), *aff'd in part, rev'd in part on other grounds,* 193 F.3d 158 (3d Cir. 1999).

[15] *See Johnson v. Vanguard Mfg., Inc.*, No. 01-1589/01-1742, 2002 U.S. App. LEXIS 8849, at *4 (3d Cir. May 8, 2002) (finding that the district court did not abuse its discretion when it excluded the portion of the plaintiff's expert's testimony based on observations not recorded in the expert's report) ("Pursuant to Fed. R. Civ. P. 26(a)(2)(B), . . . [a] party that fails to disclose evidence required by Rule 26(a) will not be allowed to use that evidence unless the failure to disclose the evidence is harmless"); *Baird v. Goldstein*, No. 95-6920, 1998 U.S. Dist. LEXIS 6347 (E.D. Pa. May 1, 1998), *aff'd,* 178 F.3d 1278 (3d Cir. 1999).

6. Relationship to State Law

In cases applying state law, where requirements concerning the expert's degree of certainty may affect the burden of proof, experts must meet the state standard. For example, when Pennsylvania or New Jersey law applies, an expert testifying about the cause of an illness must do so with a reasonable degree of medical certainty, but an expert in Delaware court need only testify with a reasonable degree of medical probability.[16]

7. Appellate Review of Exclusion of Expert Testimony

Consistent with its liberal approach to the admission of expert testimony,[17] the Third Circuit has taken a "hard look" at district court opinions excluding such testimony because of the "enormous power of the district court to foreclose submission of a party's case to a jury on the basis of a threshold determination of nonreliability of opinion evidence." *See Paoli II*, 35 F.3d at 733. In light of *Joiner*, however, the Third Circuit now reviews *Daubert* decisions carefully but with deference. *See Schneider*, 320 F.3d at 404 ("We review the decision to admit or reject expert testimony under an abuse of discretion standard."); *Heller*, 167 F.3d at 149, 151 (consistent with *Joiner*, this deferential review is for abuse of discretion).

F. STATE-LAW EXPERT ISSUES

1. Introduction

This section discusses the approaches to handling expert testimony of the state courts of the three states within the Third Circuit: Delaware, New Jersey, and Pennsylvania. Delaware, like the Third Circuit, considers factors beyond the general acceptance of a subject to determine the admissibility of expert testimony. New Jersey, on the other hand, requires that expert testimony be generally accepted, unless it is offered in a toxic tort case where a more flexible approach is applied. Pennsylvania also has not yet departed from the *Frye* general-acceptance approach.

2. Expert Evidence in Delaware State Courts

a. Delaware Courts Apply *Daubert* and *Kumho Tire*

Recognizing that Rule 702 of the Delaware Rules of Evidence is identical to Federal Rule 702, in *M. G. Bancorporation, Inc. v. Le Beau*, 737 A.2d 513, 522 (Del. 1999), the Supreme Court of Delaware expressly adopted the holdings of *Daubert* and *Kumho Tire* as the proper interpretation

---

[16] *See Heller*, 167 F.3d at 153 n.4 (applying Pennsylvania law); *Kannankeril*, 128 F.3d at 802 (applying New Jersey law); *State v. Steen*, No. 99A-04-016-NAB, 1999 Del. Super. LEXIS 407, at *6–7 (Del. Super. Ct. July 29, 1999) (applying Delaware law). Additionally, even where a degree of certainty is not required, the opposing party may still inquire about the certainty with which the expert holds his or her opinion on cross-examination. *See Holbrook*, 80 F.3d at 785.

[17] *See Lauria*, 145 F.3d at 598 ("We have consistently maintained that Rule 702 is to be interpreted liberally").

of Del. R. Evid. 702.[18] After *Le Beau*, there is no question in Delaware that *"Daubert* applies to *all* expert testimony on 'scientific,' 'technical' or 'other specialized' matters" and that "the factors mentioned in *Daubert* do not constitute a 'definitive checklist or test' but, rather, must be 'tied to the facts' of a particular 'case.'" *Id.* at 521 (citing *Kumho Tire*, 526 U.S. 137) (cited in *New Haverford P'ship v. Stroot*, 772 A.2d 792, 799 (Del. 2001) (noting that the "trial court has flexibility in deciding whether the so-called *Daubert* factors are appropriate in a given case")). Moreover, there must be "'a valid . . . connection to the pertinent inquiry as a precondition to admissibility.' When the 'factual basis, data, principles, methods, or their application' in an expert's opinion are challenged, the trial judge must decide if the expert's testimony 'has a reliable basis in the knowledge and experience' of the relevant discipline." *Le Beau*, 737 A.2d at 523 (citing *Daubert*, 509 U.S. at 592); *see also Kumho Tire*, 526 U.S. at 149. For a court to admit expert testimony, both the expert's methodology and ultimate conclusion must be reliable. *See Le Beau*, 737 A.2d at 522 (cited in *Price*, 790 A.2d at 1210).

b. Delaware's Five-Part Test for Admissibility of Expert Evidence

In addition to *Daubert*, based on the Delaware Rules of Evidence and *LeBeau*, the Supreme Court of Delaware requires a five-step test before a court may admit expert testimony:

(1) the witness is "qualified as an expert by knowledge, skill, experience, training or education" (Del. R. Evid. 702);
(2) the evidence is relevant and reliable (Del. R. Evid. 401 & 402);
(3) the expert's opinion is based upon information "reasonably relied upon by expert in the particular field" (Del. R. Evid. 702);
(4) the expert testimony will "assist the trier of fact to understand the evidence or to determine a fact in issue" (Del. R. Evid. 703); and
(5) the expert testimony will not create unfair prejudice or confuse or mislead the jury (Del. R. Evid. 403).[19]

The party seeking to introduce the expert testimony has the burden of establishing these prerequisites to admissibility by a preponderance of the evidence. *See Bowen*, 906 A.2d at 795. In determining

---

[18] In *Le Beau*, the issue before the court was the admissibility of the capital market approach to valuation of banks and bank holding companies. The Delaware Supreme Court upheld the lower court's rejection of the approach because it was not "generally accepted in the financial community for valuing banks and/or bank holding companies" and it "contained an inherent minority discount that made its use legally impermissible in a statutory appraisal proceeding." *Le Beau*, 737 A.2d at 523.

[19] *See, e.g., Spencer v. Wal-Mart Stores E., LP*, 930 A.2d 881, 888 (Del. 2007) (citing *Goodyear v. Hyster Co.*, 845 A.2d 498, 503 (Del. 2004)); *Sturgis v. Bayside Health Assoc. Chartered*, 942 A.2d 579, 584 (Del. 2007); *Bowen v. E. I. DuPont de Nemours & Co., Inc.*, 906 A.2d 787, 795 (Del. 2006); *Tolson v. State*, 900 A.2d 639, 645 (Del. 2006) (cited in *Alderman v. Clean Earth*, C.A. No. 04C-06-181-FSS, 2007 Del. Super. LEXIS 125, at *6 (Del. Super. Apr. 30, 2007)); *Eskin v. Carden*, 842 A.2d 1222, 1227 (Del. 2004) (citing *Cunningham v. McDonald*, 689 A.2d 1190, 1193 (Del. 1997) (citing *Nelson v. State*, 628 A.2d 69, 74 (Del. 1993))), *aff'd, Mason v. Rizzi*, 843 A.2d 695 (Del. 2004); *see also Candlewood Timber Grp., LLC v. Pan Am. Energy, LLC*, C.A. No. 04C-12-139 RRC, 2006 Del. Super. LEXIS 209, at *36 (Del. Super. May 16, 2006); *Family Health of Del., Inc. v. Brar*, C.A. No. 02C-04-011 WLW, 2004 Del. Super. LEXIS 224, at *5 (Del. Super. May 28, 2004) (citations omitted). Some courts also add a separate sixth prong to the test: "The probative value of the evidence upon which the expert relies substantially outweighs the risk of prejudice." (Del. R. Evid. 703). *See, e.g., Brandt v. Rokeby Realty Co.*, C.A. No. 97C-10-132-RES, 2006 Del. Super. LEXIS 280, at *9 (Del. Super. July 7, 2006).

whether the proponent has met its burden, however, the court must focus on the reliability of the proffered expert's methodology, not the correctness of his conclusions. *See, e.g., In re Asbestos Litig.*, 911 A.2d 1176, 1200-01 (Del. Super. 2006) (citing *Daubert*, 509 U.S. at 595; *In re Paoli R.R. Yard PCB Litig.*, 35 F.3d 717, 744 (3d Cir. 1994), *cert denied sub nom. Gen. Elec. Co. v. Ingram*, 513 U.S. 1190 (1995)).

(1) Expert Qualifications

In *Spencer v. Wal-Mart Stores East, LP*, 930 A.2d 881 (Del. 2007), the plaintiff/appellant, who had allegedly suffered injuries as a result of a slip and fall in Wal-Mart's parking lot, sought to introduce the expert testimony as to the maintenance and snow removal in the parking lot. *See id.* at 887–88. After a pretrial hearing, the trial court excluded the proffered testimony because (1) the expert's qualifications as an architect did not qualify him to testify in the areas of maintenance and snow removal; (2) he formed his opinion by assembling statements from various snowplowing and safety publications; and (3) his testimony would not assist the jury because he primarily restated the legal standard of care. *See id.* at 884, 888 (citing *Spencer v. Wal-Mart Stores E., L.P.*, 2006 Del. Super. LEXIS 230, at *5–7 (Del. Super. June 5, 2006)).

The Supreme Court of Delaware rejected the appellant's contention that the proffered expert had sufficient education, experience, and training to opine on snow and ice control. *See Spencer*, 930 A.2d at 888–89. Although the proffered expert had taken a two-day course addressing snow and ice abatement procedures and had assisted with his father's snowplowing business, the remainder of his education and experience related to architecture, not to snow and ice removal. *See id.* at 888–89.

In *Rodriguez v. State*, 30 A.3d 764 (Del. 2010), the Supreme Court of Delaware considered whether a latent fingerprint examiner, who had attended an FBI course on tire track and shoeprint analysis and testified on that subject before Delaware courts, could offer reliable testimony on boot and tire tracks found at an arson scene. *Id.* at 765. The court held that the district court did not abuse its discretion by finding that the fingerprint examiner qualified as an expert in tire track and shoeprint analysis under Rule 702. *Id.* at 770.

In reaching this conclusion, the court relied in part on the expert's substantial expertise in fingerprint analysis. *Id.* at 769–70. Although the court acknowledged that tire track/shoeprint analysis was a distinct forensic discipline from fingerprint analysis, the court emphasized that they share a similar analytic process (both examine "impression evidence"). Thus, the expert's training in fingerprint analysis was relevant to whether the expert was qualified to offer his opinion on the boot print and tire tracks found at the scene of the arson. *Id.*

In *Bowen v. E. I. DuPont de Nemours & Co.*, 906 A.2d 787 (Del. 2006), the Supreme Court of Delaware considered whether the trial court properly excluded the plaintiff/appellant's proffered expert in dermal absorption based on the trial court's conclusion that the doctor was not qualified to offer a dermal absorption opinion and, even assuming, *arguendo*, that he was qualified, his testimony was not admissible because his underlying methodology was not reliable. *See id.* at 795.

The court recognized that, although "at times an expert may be qualified by criteria outside of his formal training or designated specialty, [the court] must scrutinize an expert's qualifications with due regard for the specialization of modern science." *Id.* at 796 (internal quotations and citations omitted). The proffered expert admitted that the model he employed was the least favored method of measuring dermal absorption but was not qualified, either formally or otherwise, to opine why it was appropriate to choose the least favored, as opposed to other methods.[20] Accordingly, the court affirmed the trial court's exclusion of the proffered testimony. *See id.* at 795–97.

---

[20] *See id.* The court went on to conclude that, in addition to the proffered expert's lack of qualification to provide expert testimony on dermal absorption, his methodology was also unreliable because he failed to inquire about any existing studies and failed to even consider other "more favorable" methods of measuring dermal absorption before reaching his conclusion. *See id.* at 796–97.

In *Norman v. State*, 968 A.2d 27 (2009), the Supreme Court of Delaware held that police officers must be qualified as experts before identifying controlled substances. *Id.* at 28. Prior to *Norman*, however, the court had allowed a drug dealer to offer lay witness testimony identifying a particular substance as cocaine, based on the principle that a "lay witness with familiarity and experience" with a drug may identify that drug. *Wright v. State*, 953 A.2d 188, 195 (Del. 2008).

The court distinguished *Norman* from *Wright*, reasoning that a drug dealer could offer lay opinion on the substance's identity because his knowledge came from the daily buying, selling, and packaging of cocaine, whereas a police officer could only offer expert testimony because her knowledge came from her training and experience apprehending criminals involved in drugs. *Id.* at 31. The court found that the police officer's knowledge was "specialized" and therefore within the scope of D.R.E. 702, while the drug dealer's knowledge fell within the scope of D.R.E. 701 because his knowledge came from his everyday activity. *Id.*

(2) Relevance and Reliability

As the Supreme Court of Delaware has explained, a proffered expert's qualification to opine within a recognized field does not automatically guarantee reliable and admissible testimony. *See Goodyear*, 845 A.2d at 503. Rather, the "trial judge's inquiry should include whether the proffered expert and the purported 'field of expertise' itself can produce an opinion that is sufficiently informed, testable and, in fact, verifiable on an issue to be determined at trial" such that the judge is "satisfied that any generalized conclusions are applicable to the particular facts of the case." *Id.* (citations omitted).

In *Crowhorn v. Boyle*,[21] the Delaware Superior Court excluded the testimony of the defendant's expert because the expert's reasoning was neither scientifically valid nor applicable to the facts of the case under the *Daubert* standard. *See Crowhorn*, 793 A.2d at 433 (citing *Daubert*, 509 U.S. at 593). In *Crowhorn*, the defendant attempted to offer the expert testimony of an orthopedic surgeon that, although the plaintiff's back pain continued for more than six weeks, the pain the plaintiff experienced beyond the six-week mark could not be causally related to the collision with the defendant. *Id.* at 424. Under the *Daubert* standard, the court found that the studies on which the expert had relied did not factually support his conclusion and that the expert had not explained why the plaintiff would fall into the small percentage group in which the expert placed him. The court reasoned:

> Even if peer-reviewed sources existed to support [the doctor's] proposition that seventy-five percent of chronic back pain sufferers "get better" in six weeks (and there is no evidence in the record suggesting that they do), that fact would have no application to [the plaintiff] because [the doctor] offers no basis for placing [the plaintiff] among the seventy-five percent of quick healers, as opposed to the twenty-five percent who suffer longer.

Id. at 433.

---

[21] 793 A.2d 422 (Del. Super. 2002) (cited in *Atwell v. Rhis, Inc.*, C.A. No. 02C-12-003 WLW, 2006 Del. Super. LEXIS 429, at *3–4 (Del. Super. Sept. 11, 2006) (reasoning that the court must make a preliminary assessment of whether the proffered expert's reasoning or methodology is "scientifically valid and of whether that reasoning and methodology can be properly applied to the facts in issue.")).

In *Cunningham v. McDonald*,[22] the Delaware Supreme Court focused on the reliability of an expert's blood alcohol extrapolation tests. The expert used blood-test results taken by the hospital and by the police to calculate the plaintiff's blood alcohol content at the time of a car accident. The two samples, however, produced significantly different results. As a result, the expert averaged the results to calculate his estimate. Despite the plaintiff's argument that such a methodology rendered the expert's conclusions to be mere speculation and guesswork, the Delaware Supreme Court found that the averaging was "a common, accepted method of reconciling data." *Cunningham*, 689 A.2d at 1194.

In *Pfizer, Inc. v. Advanced Monobloc Corp.*, No. 97C-04-037-WTQ, 1999 Del. Super. LEXIS 509 (Sept. 24, 1999), the Delaware Superior Court refused to admit an expert's testimony on the value of twenty years' worth of lost sales to the plaintiff because, by failing to evaluate underlying factors "that were clearly present in the mix," the expert testimony did not meet the *Daubert* standard for reliability. *Id.* at *2. Moreover, the expert made unacceptable "analytical leaps without explanation" by making comparisons between two products without explaining the differences between them and why those differences would not affect his conclusions. *Id.* at *14. Even though the court "never questioned [the witness's] qualifications to be an expert," the court refused to admit the testimony because testimony based on unsupported conclusions does not meet the *Daubert* gatekeeping requirements. *Id.* at *16, 18; *see also Bowen*, 906 A.2d at 796–97.

(3) Based on Information Relied on by Experts in Field

"It is clearly the law in Delaware that an expert witness must first identify the facts and data upon which he bases his opinion and the reasons for it before being permitted to testify as to that opinion." *Cebenka v. Upjohn Co.*, C.A. No. 80C-AP-67, 1988 Del. Super. LEXIS 179 (May 27, 1988) (citations omitted); *see also Fensterer v. State*, 509 A.2d 1106 (Del. 1986) (citing *Eaton v. State*, 394 A.2d 217, 219 (Del. 1978)) ("Generally speaking, an expert witness is expected to state the entire basis for his opinion") (citations omitted). As the Delaware Superior Court has explained, "even if an expert's opinions are ultimately wrong, as long as he is qualified as an expert and his opinions are based upon information reasonably relied upon by others in the field, the testimony is admissible." *Brar*, 2004 Del. Super. LEXIS 224, at *5 (citing *Conway v. Bayhealth Med. Ctr.*, C.A. No. 99C-06-039 WLW, 2001 Del. Super. LEXIS 115, at *7 (Mar. 26, 2001)). On the other hand, an "expert" opinion based solely on the proffered expert's own experience will not suffice.[23]

---

[22] 689 A.2d 1190 (Del. 1997) (cited in *Goodyear*, 845 A.2d at 503 (explaining that the expert's opinion must be informed, testable, and verifiable, and any generalized conclusions must be applicable to the particular facts of the case)).

[23] *See Costalas v. Safeway, Inc.*, C.A. No. 04C-12-122-JRJ, 2007 Del. Super. LEXIS 291, at *3 (Oct. 1, 2007) (excluding proffered expert testimony because the "'reliability' requirement ensures that the expert's opinion is based upon proper factual foundation and sound methodology. Julio fails to offer any factual basis for his opinion other than his 'experience.' This is not enough. The Court will not accept Julio's opinion that the 'industry practice' with regard to inspection frequency is every 30 minutes simply because he says so. Accordingly, because Julio's opinion is not based on sufficient facts or data and is not the product of reliable methods, it fails to meet the *Daubert* [standard]."); *Juliano v. Am. Honda Motor Co.*, C.A. No. 04C-01-263-PLA, 2006 Del. Super. LEXIS 459, at *8–9 (Nov. 8, 2006) (rejecting expert opinion where proffered expert relied merely on a review of records and his own subjective experience instead of objectively ruling out other possible diagnoses of the alleged problem).

(4) Assisting the Trier of Fact

For an expert's testimony to assist the trier of fact under Del. R. Evid. 702, it must involve specialized knowledge that is "not possessed by the average trier of fact who lacks the expert's skill, training, or education." *Wheat*, 527 A.2d at 272. Generally, such testimony will fail to assist the jury when it discusses matters within the province of the jury, such as the credibility of a witness. *See, e.g.*, *State v. Capano*, 781 A.2d 556, 595 (Del. 2001) (noting that, in general, a witness may not offer expert testimony on the credibility of another witness) (citing *Wheat*, 527 A.2d at 275). "If jurors, without the assistance of the expert, are as capable of answering a question as an expert, then the expert's opinion would not be helpful and is not admissible under D.R.E. 702." *Jolly v. State*, No. 445, 1994, 1995 Del. LEXIS 429, at *3 (Del. Nov. 22, 1995); *see also Harrigan v. Del. Transit Corp.*, C.A. No. 05C-10-258-JOH, 2007 Del. Super. LEXIS 358, at *6–7 (Nov. 30, 2007) (reasoning that expert evidence is not admissible where it "embraces matters in which the jury is just as competent as the expert to consider and weigh the evidence and draw the necessary conclusions").

The proposed testimony will also be rejected if the proffered expert's background and analysis fail to meaningfully align with the facts and necessities of the case. In *Goodridge v. Hyster Co.*, 845 A.2d 498 (Del. 2004), the Delaware Supreme Court examined whether the plaintiff/appellant's proposed expert testimony, that the forklift involved in the accident should have been equipped with backup warning indicators, would meaningfully assist the jury. *Id.* at 501, 504. The proffered expert was a Certified Hazard Control Manager, Master Level I; had received an M.A. degree from The Center for Safety at New York University; performed consulting work for labor organizations and industry, with a concentration on safety consulting; had been employed as a safety inspector for OSHA for ten years, during which he visited approximately 800 workplaces, evaluated more than 10,000 products, and investigated more than 500 fatal accidents; and published an article titled "Professional Safety" in *The Journal of the American Society of Safety Engineers*. *Id.* at 500. The proffered expert, however, was not a forklift designer or an engineer, had never operated a forklift, and was uncertain whether he had even ever seen the type of forklift involved in the accident. *Id.* at 501, 502, 504. His opinion, the trial court found, was based on culling together "snippets" from various safety publications. *Id.* at 501. As the trial court reasoned, without a qualified expert to put those safety publications into context, the jury would have to speculate to apply the literature to the facts of the case. *Id.* Accordingly, the trial court held, and the Supreme Court of Delaware affirmed, that the proffered testimony would not meaningfully assist the trier of fact. *Id.* at 501, 503, 504.

(5) No Unfair Prejudice, Confusion, or Misleading the Trier of Fact

As with each of the five steps to admissibility of expert evidence, whether evidence will confuse or mislead a jury is highly contextual. *See Mason v. Rizzi*, 843 A.2d 695 (Del. 2004). The critical inquiry is whether the opinion will "actually assist the trier of fact in fairly resolving the underlying factual dispute, or will it confuse the issue by shifting the fact finders' attention from the particular to the universal? That is, will the fact finder be confused about the expert opinion's application to the specific facts of the case at hand?" *Id.* at *13.

In *Mason v. Rizzi*, the trial court excluded the defendant/appellant's biomechanical expert testimony regarding the relatively low force of the subject rear-end collision. *Id.* at *7, 8, 13–16. As the trial court reasoned, although such testimony is relevant in some cases, it had too much potential to mislead jurors in the case at hand where (1) the motorist's preexisting condition rendered her unusually susceptible to an impact and (2) the expert only proffered an opinion based on the impact on normal spines. *Id.* Accordingly, the Supreme Court of Delaware affirmed the trial court's exclusion of the testimony. *Id.*

Generally speaking, however, doubts concerning the usefulness of expert testimony should be resolved in favor of admissibility. *See Bowen v. E. I. du Pont de Nemours & Co.*, C.A. No. 97C-06-194, 2005 Del. Super. LEXIS 239, at *31 (June 23, 2005), *aff'd*, *Bowen*, 906 A.2d 787; *see also* 4-702 Weinstein & Berger, Weinstein's Fed. Evid. § 702.03 [2][b] at 702-35-36 (2d ed. 2002). "Where the question of admissibility is a close one, exclusion of the expert evidence is not appropriate where cross-examination, the presentation of contrary evidence and careful instruction regarding the burden of proof will insure that the jury is not misled or confused." *Bowen*, 2005 Del. Super. LEXIS 239, at *31 (citing *Daubert*, 526 U.S. at 596). Where the fact finder is a judge, there is an even heightened presumption favoring admissibility because there is little, if any, risk that the finder of fact will be deceived or misled by any potentially unhelpful testimony. *See Brar*, 2004 Del. Super. LEXIS 224, at *6 ("Further, as this is a bench trial, there is no concern that a jury will be confused or misled by his testimony").

c. Procedural Issues

Before introducing expert testimony, the party offering the expert must list the expert witness during pretrial discovery.[24] Objections to the admissibility of testimony from experts not listed in pretrial discovery are waived, however, unless raised at trial.[25]

---

[24] In the civil context, see *Coleman v. Pricewaterhouse Coopers, LLC*, 902 A.2d 1102, 1008 (Del. 2006) (noting that the rules of civil procedure require a party to designate expert witnesses during pretrial discovery) (citing *Duphily v. Del. Elec. Coop.*, 662 A.2d 821, 836 (Del. 1995) (holding that "[t]he rendering of . . . expert testimony require[s] that [the expert witness] be designated as such in pre-trial discovery and appropriately qualified at trial")); *Russell v. K-Mart Corp.*, 761 A.2d 1, 3 (Del. 2000) ("In Delaware, 'the requirement of a party to comply with discovery directed to identification of expert witnesses and disclosure of the substance of their expected opinion is a pre-condition to the admissibility of expert testimony at trial.'") (quotations omitted); *Sammons v. Doctors for Emergency Servs., P.A.*, 913 A.2d 519, 529-31 (Del. 2006) (holding that the trial court did not abuse its discretion in restricting the areas of trial testimony to only those areas actually disclosed in pretrial filings and interrogatory responses before the scheduling order deadline, even though additional areas of testimony were later disclosed during the expert's deposition) (citing *Stafford v. Sears, Roebuck & Co.*, 413 A.2d 1238 (Del. 1980) (party who listed witness as expert but then failed to list expert in response to interrogatory could not offer witness's testimony by claiming he was fact witness without submitting supplemental discovery response)). In the criminal context, see *Wheat v. State*, 527 A.2d 269 (Del. 1987) (the state must provide notice in advance of trial before presenting expert testimony to assist the jury in evaluating the testimony of child sexual-abuse victims); *Hopkins v. State*, 893 A.2d 922, 930 n.22 (Del. 2006) (reasoning that, although the appellant correctly cited the general rule set forth in *Wheat*, the court must engage in a contextual inquiry about whether the state violated its discovery obligations in each case).

[25] *See Greene v. Beebe Med. Ctr.*, No. 343, 1994, 1995 Del. LEXIS 244, at *5–6 (July 9, 2005) (holding that party on appeal waived objection to qualification of opposing party's expert by failing to raise objection at trial) (citing *Yankanwich v. Wharton*, 460 A.2d 1326 (Del. 1983)); *State v. Stevens*, C.A. No. 00A-02-008, 2001 Del. Super. LEXIS 167, at *9 (May 15, 2001) (same), *aff'd*, 784 A.2d 1081 (Del. 2001); *see also* Off. Cmt. to Del. R. Evid. 703 (explaining that any party who wishes to exclude expert-basis information must raise an objection).

The court may limit the expert's testimony to areas specifically addressed in his report and other submissions. *See Russell*, 761 A.2d at 3–4 (holding that the superior court did not err in ruling that the "expert['s] testimony at trial would be limited to subjects discussed in his reports and letters"). Similarly, if the substance of the expert's proposed testimony is contained in his deposition, the opposing party is entitled to rely on that deposition testimony in anticipation of trial. *See id.*

Fact witnesses who have expertise in the subject at issue need not be listed as experts to testify, but their opinions will then be limited to those facts. For example, where a defendant electrical company called its senior engineer, not listed as an expert, to testify in a case involving the height of the defendant's electrical wires, the witness could testify about the practices of his company, but not about the appropriate height for wires under the law. *See Duphily*, 662 A.2d at 835–36.

Opposing parties may pursue discovery of expert witnesses expected to testify at trial through interrogatories or, by order of the court, through other means. *See* Del. Sup. Ct. R. 26(b)(4)(A)(i)–(ii). Upon a showing of "exceptional circumstances," parties may also discover facts or opinions of experts not expected to be called for trial. *See* Del. Sup. Ct. R. 26(b)(4)(B). With respect to interrogatories or expert reports for expert witnesses expected to testify at trial, opposing parties generally do not have to pay any costs. For further expert discovery, the court may, or, in the case of nontestifying experts, shall, require discovering parties to share the expert's fees and expenses. *See* Del. Sup. Ct. R. 26(b)(4)(C).

Where practical, motions regarding the admissibility of expert testimony should be considered through motions *in limine* prior to trial. *See Lagola v. Thomas*, 867 A.2d 891, 898 (Del. 2005) ("The trial judge's role as a gatekeeper should be performed outside the presence of the jury either through motions in limine prior to trial or during preliminary voir dire by counsel of a proposed expert.") (citing *Price v. Blood Bank of Del.*, 709 A.2d 1203, 1212 (Del. 2002)). Parties should conduct *voir dire* outside the presence of the jury. *See id.* Finally, direct and cross-examination by counsel "should occur prior to the court's questioning" to "ensure an orderly and impartial presentation of expert testimony." *See Price*, 709 A.2d at 1212.

The proponent of expert testimony should supply the court, in the normal course, with the expert's deposition testimony, as well as any supporting affidavits, to assist the court in assessing the necessity of a *Daubert* hearing. *See Candlewood Timber Group, LLC v. Pan Am. Energy, LLC*, C.A. No. 04C-12-139 RRC, 2006 Del. Super. LEXIS 209, at *41–42 (Del. Super. May 16, 2006). It is appropriate to submit an affidavit by the proposed expert to clarify questions of reliability, especially where the case presents particularly complex circumstances. *See id.*

An appellate court reviews a trial court's decision to exclude expert testimony for abuse of discretion. *See Sturgis v. Bayside Health Ass'n. Chartered*, No. 146, 2007, 2007 Del. LEXIS 557, at *8 (Del. Dec. 26, 2007).

3. *State-Law Expert Issues in New Jersey State Courts*

The "starting point" for determining the admissibility of proffered expert testimony in New Jersey State courts is Rule 702 of the New Jersey Rules of Evidence (N.J. R. Evid. 702). *State v. Torres*, 874 A.2d 1084, 1092–93 (N.J. 2005). The rule provides that, "[i]f scientific, technical or other specialized knowledge will assist the trier of fact to understand the evidence or to determine a fact in issue, a witness qualified as an expert by knowledge, skill, experience, training, or education may testify thereto in the form of an opinion or otherwise." N.J. R. Evid. 702 (quoted in *Agha v. Feiner*, 198 N.J. 50, 62, 965 A.2d 141, 148 (N.J. 2009); *Brenman v. Demello*, 191 N.J. 18, 31, 921 A.2d 1110 (N.J. 2007) (quoting *State v. Townsend*, 897 A.2d 316 (2006)); *Torres*, 874 A.2d at 1093). Notably, this rule lacks the three further requirements of the corresponding Federal Rule that such evidence may only be admitted "if (1) the testimony is based upon sufficient facts or data, (2) the testimony is the product of reliable principles and methods, and (3) the witness has applied the principles and methods reliably to the case." *Cf.* N.J. R. Evid. 702 and Fed. R. Evid. 702.

Using Rule 702 as the starting point, the Supreme Court of New Jersey has articulated the three basic requirements for the admission of expert testimony in New Jersey State courts as follows:

(1) the intended testimony must concern a subject matter that is beyond the ken of the average juror;
(2) the field testified to must be at a state of the art that an expert's testimony could be sufficiently reliable; and
(3) the witness must have sufficient expertise to offer the intended testimony.

Brenman, 191 N.J. at 31–32 (quoting *Torres*, 874 A.2d 1084 (citations omitted)).

a. Beyond the Ken of the Average Juror

Traditionally, New Jersey has required that expert testimony concern a subject matter that is "so distinctively related to some science, profession, business or occupation as to be beyond the ken of the average layman." *See State v. McLean*, 205 N.J. 438, 453–56, 16 A.3d 332, 341–43 (2011) (noting that it is impermissible to use expert testimony to "shore up" a police officer's testimony about straightforward facts); *Kelly*, 97 N.J. at 208. The New Jersey Supreme Court has also stated that "[e]xpert opinion is admissible if the general subject matter at issue, or its specific application, is one with which an average juror might not be sufficiently familiar," *State v. Berry*, 140 N.J. 280, 290–93, 658 A.2d 702 (1995), or "if the trial court determines that the expert testimony would 'assist the jury in comprehending the evidence and determining the issues of fact.'" *Id.* (quoting *State v. Odom*, 116 N.J. 65, 70, 560 A.2d 1198, 1201 (1989)). The trial judge determines whether the proffered testimony will help the jurors before an expert may testify. *See State v. Torres*, 183 N.J. 554, 567, 874 A.2d 1084 (2005); *State v. J.Q.*, 252 N.J. Super. 11, 26, 599 A.2d 172 (App. Div. 1991), *aff'd*, 130 N.J. 554, 617 A.2d 1196 (N.J. 1993).

In *Brenman v. Demello*, 921 A.2d at 1118, the plaintiff asserted that expert testimony was required to correlate the amount of vehicle damage in an automobile accident with the extent of injuries to the occupants. The Supreme Court of New Jersey disagreed that the issue was beyond the ken of the average juror. *See id.* at 1118–19. The court reasoned:

[I]n most cases, there is a relationship between the force of impact and the resultant injury, and the extent of that relationship remains in the province of the factfinder. . . . [The exceptions to those cases] inhabit, however, the margins of common knowledge. Juries are entitled to infer that which squarely resides at the center of everyday knowledge: the certainty of proportion, and the resulting recognition that slight force most often results in slight injury, and great force most often is accompanied by great injury.

Id.

In *State v. Henderson*, the Supreme Court of New Jersey reevaluated the legal standard for admitting eyewitness identification evidence and addressed the use of expert testimony to evaluate such evidence at trial. *See State v. Henderson*, 208 N.J. 208, 297–98, 27 A.3d 872, 925 (2011). The court stated that "there will be times when expert testimony will benefit the trier of fact," but that "experts may not opine on the credibility of a particular eyewitness." *Id.* at 297–98 (citing *State v. Frisby*, 174 N.J. 583, 595, 811 A.2d 414 (2002)). Although the court acknowledged the "usefulness" of expert testimony relating to eyewitness identification, the court anticipated that "with enhanced jury instructions there will be less need for expert testimony." *Id.* at 298. The court went on to highlight the advantages of jury charges over expert testimony.

New Jersey courts have held that experts may testify about matters such as illegal drug trafficking,[26] posttraumatic stress disorder,[27] the transmission of the HIV virus,[28] and the use and results of a horizontal gaze nystagmus (HGN) test. *See State v. Doriguzzi*, 760 A.2d 336, 341 (App. Div. 2000) (finding that HGN testing is "so esoteric that it is beyond the ken of the average person" and therefore "qualifies as an appropriate subject for expert testimony"). By contrast, the danger of displaying a wild animal and the danger of hanging invisible wire between two pillars[29] are not beyond the ken of the average juror and, therefore, are not appropriate subjects for expert testimony. Moreover, courts do not permit expert testimony regarding questions of law[30] or the credibility of other witnesses or parties. *See State v. Henderson*, 208 N.J. 208, 297, 27 A.3d 872 (2011); *State v. Vandeweagh*, 177 N.J. 229, 239, 827 A.2d 1028 (2003).

b. Reliability

The standard of reliability required for the subject of expert testimony in New Jersey appears to remain the *Frye* standard of general acceptance. In 1996, in *State v. Fertig*, 143 N.J. 115, 668 A.2d 1076 (N.J. 1996), the New Jersey Supreme Court stated in dicta that "we abandoned the *Frye* 'general acceptance' test for the admission of expert evidence. . . . Generally speaking, our current test is whether expert testimony derives from a sound methodology supported by some consensus of experts in the field." *Id.* (determining whether the hypnotically induced testimony of an independent witness was admissible). However, one year later, the state Supreme Court returned to the *Frye* standard holding that "the test in criminal cases remains whether the scientific community generally accepts the evidence." *State v. Harvey*, 151 N.J. 117, 170, 699 A.2d 596, 621 (1997), *cert. denied*, 528 U.S. 1085 (2000).

In *In re R.S.*,[31] the Supreme Court suggested that the more stringent *Frye* standard should be used in cases where there is a "significant liberty interest at stake," such as in civil commitment proceedings. *In re R.S.*, 801 A.2d at 220 (using the *Frye* standard to assess the admissibility of expert testimony based on actual risk assessments of recidivism under the New Jersey Sexually Violent Predator Act), *aff'g* 339 N.J. Super. 507, 773 A.2d 72 (App. Div. 2001) (stating that the test "in criminal and civil cases alike, is whether the specific scientific community generally accepts the evidence" and applying the same test to behavioral-science expert testimony as to physical-science expert testimony). Without distinguishing between civil and criminal cases, the Superior Court has indicated that, "in New Jersey, with the exception of toxic tort litigation, *Frye* remains the standard" of reliability. *Doriguzzi*, 760 A.2d at 341. Although in certain contexts there is a lower standard because of the "extraordinary and unique burdens facing plaintiffs who seek to prove causation," as a general

---

[26] *See Berry*, 658 A.2d 702; *Odom*, 560 A.2d 1198.
[27] *See State v. Hines*, 303 N.J. Super 311, 313, 696 A.2d 780 (App. Div. 1997).
[28] *See State v. Smith*, 262 N.J. Super. 487, 520–521, 621 A.2d 493 (App. Div. 1993), *cert. denied*, 134 N.J. 476, 634 A.2d 523 (N.J. 1993).
[29] *See McColley v. Edison Corp. Ctr.*, 303 N.J. Super. 420, 428–29, 697 A.2d 149 (App. Div. 1997).
[30] *See Bedford v. Riello*, 392 N.J. Super. 270, 278–79 (App. Div. 2007), *rev'd on other grounds* 195 N.J. 210 (2008); *Healy v. Fairleigh Dickinson Univ.*, 287 N.J. Super. 407, 413, 671 A.2d 182 (App. Div. 1996), *cert. denied*, 519 U.S. 1007 (1996); *State v. Grimes*, 235 N.J. Super. 75, 80, 561 A.2d 647 (App. Div. 1989).
[31] 173 N.J. 134, 801 A.2d 219 (N.J. 2002); *see also State v. Harvey*, 151 N.J. at 169–70, 699 A.2d at 621 (noting that the *Frye* standard applies in criminal cases).

rule, New Jersey courts still require expert testimony to be based on generally accepted techniques or methodology. *Rubanick v. Witco Chem. Corp.*, 125 N.J. 421, 433, 593 A.2d 733 (N.J. 1991).

When required, parties proffering expert testimony may prove its general acceptance in three ways:

- by expert testimony as to the general acceptance, among those in the profession, of the premises on which the proffered expert witness based his or her analysis;
- by authoritative scientific and legal writings indicating that the scientific community accepts the premises underlying the proffered testimony; and
- by judicial opinions that indicate the expert's premises have gained general acceptance.[32]

General acceptance by the scientific community "entails the strict application of the scientific method, which requires an extraordinarily high level of proof based on prolonged, controlled, consistent, and validated experience." *Rubanick v. Witco Chem. Corp.*, 125 N.J. 421, 436, 593 A.2d 733 (N.J. 1991). The standard does not, however, require unanimity or infallibility. *See, e.g., State v. Tate*, 102 N.J. 64, 83, 505 A.2d 941 (1986) (reliability "does not depend upon unanimous belief or universal agreement within the scientific community"); *In re R.S.*, 801 A.2d at 220 ("When seeking to satisfy [the *Frye*] standard . . . a party need not show unanimous acceptance by the relevant community"). When applying the standard, the most important factor is the assurance of reliability. *See In re R.S.*, 801 A.2d at 220. For example, actuarial risk assessments on which expert testimony on recidivism is based need not be "the best methods which could ever be devised to determine risk of recidivism. What is required is that they produce results that are reasonably reliable for their intended purpose." *Id.* at 221.

A novel scientific method "achieves general acceptance only when it passes from the experimental to the demonstrable stage." *State v. Harvey*, 151 N.J. 117, 699 A.2d 596, 622 (1997), *cert. denied*, 528 U.S. 1085 (2000). Proponents of newly devised scientific methods bear the burden to "clearly establish" their general acceptance. *Id.* at 621; *see also Suanez v. Egeland*, 353 N.J. Super. 191, 196, 801 A.2d 1186 (2002) (holding trial court erred by permitting introduction of biomechanical studies to support theory that a low-impact car crash cannot cause serious injury because expert, who was educated and trained in physics and mechanical engineering (not anatomy or physiology), was not competent to establish scientific reliability of studies). *But see Hisenaj v. Kuehner*, 194 N.J. 6, 20–22 (2008) (distinguishing *Suanez*, reversing appellate court decision, and holding that trial court did not abuse its discretion by allowing expert testimony of a biomechanical engineer concerning the probability that a low-impact car collision caused a chronic injury). In *State v. Harvey*, the New Jersey Supreme Court examined the admissibility of the polymarker DNA test. The court held that the technique is generally accepted even though there have not been many opinions admitting the evidence and not many articles supporting the methodology. The court recognized "the correlation between the number of published articles and the general acceptance of a subject" but held that there was no "magic number" of publications required. 151 N.J. at 174, 699 A.2d at 623. In addition to a few articles, the court cited to numerous lectures and presentations on the subject, and also a few judicial opinions that supported the state's expert and her opinion that such methods were reliable.

---

[32] *State v. Cavallo*, 88 N.J. 508, 521, 443 A.2d 1020 (N.J. 1982); *see also State v. Rosales*, 202 N.J. 549, 562, 998 A.2d 459 (N.J. 2010); *Hisenaj v. Kuehner*, 194 N.J. 6, 17, 942 A.2d 769 (N.J. 2008); *State v. Moore*, 188 N.J. 182, 206, 902 A.2d 1212 (2006); *Torres*, 874 A.2d at 1093; *Doriguzzi*, 760 A.2d at 341.

New Jersey courts have held that the following subjects of scientific testimony are generally accepted by the relevant scientific communities: battered woman syndrome,[33] child sexual-abuse accommodation syndrome,[34] shaken baby syndrome,[35] dot-intensity analysis to interpret DNA test results,[36] breath-testing devices to measure blood alcohol concentration,[37] the matching of bullets found in a defendant's possession with those found in the victim's body,[38] and bite-mark analysis.[39] By contrast, the courts have not yet recognized the general acceptance of voiceprint analysis,[40] sodium amytal (truth serum) tests,[41] horizontal gaze nystagmus (HGN) tests,[42] phenol-

---

[33] *See Kelly*, 97 N.J. at 210 (battered-woman-syndrome expert testimony admissible for self-defense argument); *Frost*, 242 N.J. Super. 601, 610, 577 A.2d 1283 (admitting battered-woman-syndrome expert evidence for prosecution).

[34] *See State v. J.Q.*, 130 N.J. 554, 566–574, 617 A.2d 1196 (1993) (noting child sexual-abuse accommodation syndrome testimony can be admissible to explain why certain behavior that might seem inconsistent with alleged abuse might not be inconsistent with such abuse, but holding that such testimony was not admissible to demonstrate that abuse in fact occurred); *State v. W.B.*, 205 N.J. 588, 609–11 (2011).

[35] *See State v. Compton*, 304 N.J. Super. 477, 484–87, 701 A.2d 468 (App. Div. 1997), *cert. denied*, 153 N.J. 51 (1998).

[36] *See Harvey*, 151 N.J. at 177, 699 A.2d at 625 (finding that the expert evidence presented demonstrated the reliability of the polymarker test and that challenges to dot-intensity analysis went to the weight of the testimony, not its admissibility).

[37] *See State v. Chun*, 194 N.J. 54, 65, 943 A.2d 114 (2008) (ordering modifications to Alcotest device but affirming its use).

[38] *See State v. Noel*, 723 A.2d 602 (N.J. 1999) (holding that statistical probability evidence is not a prerequisite to the admission of expert testimony on the composition of lead bullets and finding that challenges to the testimony go to the weight, not the admissibility, of the testimony).

[39] *See State v. Timmendequas*, 161 N.J. 515, 624, 737 A.2d 55, 115 (N.J. 1999) (upholding lower court's admission of testimony by a physician to a medical certainty that the bite mark on the defendant's hand was made by the victim against defendant's objection that bite-mark analysis is scientifically unreliable because at least thirty jurisdictions have found bite-mark analysis to be generally accepted and no state has rejected it).

[40] *See Windmere, Inc. v. Int'l Ins. Co.*, 105 N.J. 373, 383–87, 522 A.2d 405 (N.J. 1987).

[41] *See State v. Pitts*, 116 N.J. 580, 622, 562 A.2d 1320 (N.J. 1989).

[42] *See Doriguzzi*, 760 A.2d at 337 (finding that an HGN test is a scientific test that must meet the *Frye* standard and surveying the decisions of other jurisdictions and relevant scientific studies to hold that the court could not take judicial notice of the general acceptance of the reliability of HGN testing without a more fully developed factual record below and more agreement among the jurisdictions and authoritative texts).

phthalein tests,[43] false confessions,[44] or linkage analysis to establish that the same person committed two crimes.[45]

In *Khan v. Singh*, 200 N.J. 82, 99, 975 A.2d 389, 400 (2009), the New Jersey Supreme Court considered expert testimony introduced to provide the foundational proofs required for a *res ipsa loquitur* charge in a medical malpractice case. *Id.* at 100. The court held that the expert was not able to demonstrate that it was common knowledge in the medical community that the injury would not have happened in the absence of negligence. *Id.* at 102. It was not the expert's lack of firsthand knowledge that led to the court's conclusion, but rather the plaintiff's failure to point to an alternate source of support for the expert's assertion—for example, the medical literature—that his opinion was commonly accepted in the profession. *Id.*

In addition to proving a subject's general acceptance, the party proffering the evidence must "show that the technique, methodology, or procedure was correctly used to produce that evidence." *State v. Marcus*, 294 N.J. Super. 267, 275 (App. Div. 1996), *cert. denied*, 157 N.J. 543, 724 A.2d 803 (N.J. 1998). Accordingly, courts will exclude expert testimony that simply provides a "net opinion" without any description of the factual evidence, reasoning, or methodology supporting a conclusion. *See Pomerantz Paper Corp. v. New Cmty. Corp.*, 207 N.J. 344, 372–74, 25 A.3d 221, 237–38 (2011); *Jimenez v. GNOC Corp.*, 670 A.2d 24, 27–28 (App. Div. 1996), *cert. denied*, 145 N.J. 374, 678 A.2d 714 (1996). Thus, in *Jimenez v. GNOC Corp.*, the trial court properly struck an expert's opinion where the expert could not support his conclusion with any facts indicating why the defendant was negligent or how the defendant's actions contributed to an escalator malfunction. *See Jimenez*, 670 A.2d at 27–28.

New Jersey has a lower standard for the admissibility of scientific evidence in toxic tort cases. Instead of focusing on the general acceptance of a scientific subject, courts focus on the methodology and reasoning of testimony proffered in toxic tort cases. Thus, an expert's toxic tort causation testimony must be

> based on a sound, adequately-founded scientific methodology involving data and information of the type reasonably relied on by experts in the scientific field. The evidence must be proffered by an expert who is sufficiently qualified by education, knowledge, training, and experience in the specific field of science. The expert must possess a demonstrated professional capacity to assess the scientific significance of the underlying data and information, to apply the scientific methodology, and to explain the bases for the opinion reached.

Rubanick, 125 N.J. at 449; *see also Kemp v. State*, No. A-80, 2002 N.J. LEXIS 1260, at *46 (calling the *Rubanick-Landrigan* standard an "important part of [New Jersey] jurisprudence").

---

[43] *See State v. Pittman*, 419 N.J. Super. 584, 595, 18 A.3d 203 (App. Div. 2011).

[44] *See State v. Rosales*, 202 N.J. 549, 565, 998 A.2d at 469 (2010) (finding that trial court properly excluded psychiatrist's testimony about false confessions because testimony was not about a field that is at a "state of the art" to be considered sufficiently reliable). *But see State v. King*, 387 N.J. Super. 522, 542–46 (App. Div. 2006) (finding expert's testimony that defendant's personality disorders are consistent with his claim of false confession to be sufficiently reliable).

[45] *See State v. Fortin*, 162 N.J. 517, 525–27, 745 A.2d 509, 513–14 (2000) (finding linkage analysis to be insufficiently reliable to meet the standards set forth in *Harvey* when the method has an uneven success rate and, since only a few people were involved in this type of analysis, there are no peers to test the expert's theories and duplicate his results) (citing *State v. Cavallo*, 88 N.J. 508, 443 A.2d 1020 (1982) (excluding rapist-profile evidence)).

In *Landrigan v. Celotex Corp.*, 127 N.J. 404, 605 A.2d 1079 (N.J. 1992), the New Jersey Supreme Court examined the admissibility of expert testimony based on epidemiological studies regarding the causal relationship between colon cancer and asbestos exposure. The court explained that experts relying on epidemiological studies must "be able to identify the factual bases for their conclusions, explain their methodology, and demonstrate that both the factual bases and the methodology are scientifically reliable." *Landrigan*, 27 N.J. at 417. In addition, the court asserted that every step of an expert's analysis must be examined. *Landrigan* suggests that courts undertaking such analyses look at published works related to the methodology, a witness's qualifications, the data relied on, whether the data is of a type ordinarily relied on by such experts, and the expert's reasoning to determine whether the testimony is reliable. *Id.* at 417–21.

Landrigan ultimately reversed and remanded a lower court opinion that had excluded two experts who relied on epidemiological studies. One of the experts based his conclusion that asbestos exposure caused the plaintiff's cancer on studies indicating that such exposure increased an individual's risk of colon cancer and the absence of other risk factors (determined by reviewing the plaintiff's medical records and answers to interrogatories). The New Jersey Supreme Court reversed the Appellate Division's ruling that individual causation testimony could not be based on epidemiological studies but instructed the court on remand to examine the validity of the expert's methodology and assumptions. *Id.* at 418–21. Moreover, *Landrigan* held that nonphysicians could testify about the cause of an individual's cancer based on epidemiological studies. *Id.* at 422–23.

c. Expert Qualifications

An expert may be qualified by virtue of his knowledge, skill, experience (even when limited), training, or education. Experts must "be suitably qualified and possessed of sufficient specialized knowledge to be able to express [an expert opinion] and to explain the basis of that opinion." *State v. Moore*, 122 N.J. 420, 458–59, 585 A.2d 864 (1991); *see also Agha v. Feiner*, 198 N.J. 50, 62, 965 A.2d 141 (2009); *State v. Bealor*, 187 N.J. 574, 592, 902 A.2d 226, 237 (2006) (noting that New Jersey police officers, by virtue of their training, are eligible to qualify as experts on marijuana intoxication under N.J.R.E. 702. New Jersey courts are fairly liberal in admitting experts and generally leave it to the jury "to determine the credibility, weight and probative value" of an expert's testimony. *Rubanick v. Witco Chem. Corp.*, 242 N.J. Super. 36, 48, 576 A.2d 4 (App. Div. 1990), *mod. on other grounds*, 125 N.J. 421 (1991). Although witnesses may qualify as experts "by reason of study without practice or practice without study," *Moore*, 122 N.J. at 457–60, the court may require that the expert be licensed if the subject matter "falls distinctly within the province of a particular profession." *State v. Frost*, 242 N.J. Super. 601, 615, 577 A.2d 1282 (App. Div. 1990), *cert. denied*, 127 N.J. 321, 604 A.2d 596 (1990). Furthermore, when a theory or methodology is not generally accepted, the expert must be qualified within the specific field of science. For example, a pharmacologist may not testify as an expert about the causation of birth defects from ingesting certain drugs when the proffered witness's qualifications with respect to the drug are limited to the review of articles. *Thompson v. Merrell Dow Pharms., Inc.*, 229 N.J. Super. 230, 241, 551 A.2d 177 (App. Div. 1988).

In *State v. Torres*, 874 A.2d 1084, 1097 (N.J. 2005), the New Jersey Supreme Court considered whether an experienced police officer who specialized in street-gang investigations was qualified to provide expert testimony on gang hierarchy, organization, and discipline. Vasquez had worked in law enforcement for twenty years and as an organized-crime investigator for several of those years. *Id.* In these capacities, his duties included tracking and assessing gang trends, instructing and lecturing on gang alliances and suppression techniques, and handling investigations for groups and organizations, primarily Hispanic, combating street gangs. *Id.* He had also interviewed ten to fifteen members, including arrestees, informants, and cooperating witnesses, of the gang at issue;

attended ten classroom sessions of specialized training concerning street gangs, including forty to eighty hours of training concerning the gang at issue; and taught, as a certified instructor, approximately 100 law enforcement seminars. *Id.* Based on Vasquez's experience and training, the New Jersey Supreme Court affirmed the trial court's ruling that he was qualified to testify as an expert concerning gang activity. *Id.* The court also held that, if properly qualified, an expert may provide gang-related testimony. *Id.* at 1087.

d. Procedural Issues

The court has discretion to exclude areas of expert testimony that were not covered in the required written reports exchanged during discovery. *See Ferrante v. Sciaretta*, 839 A.2d 993, 997 (N.J. App. Div. 2003) (reasoning that, "when an expert report is furnished, the expert's testimony at trial may be confined to the matters of the opinion reflected in the report," but "testimony about the predicates and conclusions set forth in the report are not foreclosed") (internal quotations and citations omitted); *McCalla v. Harnischfeger Corp.*, 215 N.J. Super. 160, 521 A.2d 851 (App. Div. 1987) ("[W]hen an expert's report is furnished, 'the expert's testimony at trial may be confined to the matters of opinion reflected in that report,' . . . however, the logical predicates for and conclusions from statements made in the report are not foreclosed"), *cert. denied*, 108 N.J. 219, 528 A.2d 37 (1987). For example, a court may exclude expert testimony regarding statistics where the statistics were not in the expert's report or any discovery material. *See Mauro v. Owens-Corning Fiberglas Corp.*, 225 N.J. Super. 196, 206, 542 A.2d 16 (App. Div. 1988), *aff'd sub nom.*, 116 N.J. 126, 561 A.2d 257 (N.J. 1989). However, appellate courts have instructed the lower courts to avoid excluding such testimony when there is "(1) the absence of a design to mislead, (2) absence of the element of surprise if the evidence is admitted, and (3) absence of prejudice which would result from the admission of the evidence." *Ratner v. Gen. Motors Corp.*, 241 N.J. Super. 197, 202, 574 A.2d 541 (App. Div. 1990). In one case, the Appellate Division affirmed a trial court decision to admit expert testimony that exceeded the scope of the experts' reports where the opposing party "should [not] have been surprised, except as they had failed to depose the experts, and thus were unaware of the details of the experts' opinions." *Congiusti v. Ingersoll-Rand Co.*, 306 N.J. Super. 126, 703 A.2d 340 (App. Div. 1997).

Treating physicians may be permitted to testify about their opinions concerning the condition of their patient or cause of their patient's illness or injury even when not listed as expert witnesses in discovery. *Ginsberg v. St. Michael's Hosp.*, 292 N.J. Super. 21, 32–33, 678 A.2d 271 (App. Div. 1996). For example, in *Stigliano v. Connaught Labs.*, 658 A.2d 715, 716 (N.J. 1995), the plaintiffs sued a doctor and laboratory after a vaccination allegedly caused a child's seizure disorder. At trial, the lower court precluded the defendants from calling the child's subsequent treating physicians to testify because they were not qualified and because of the physician-patient privilege. The New Jersey Supreme Court, however, held that the plaintiff waived the physician-patient privilege by putting her illness at issue. Furthermore, the court ruled that the physicians' testimony should have been admissible since the doctors were not retained for the purposes of litigation but rather for treatment. Thus, the testimony of treating physicians may be admissible as fact witness testimony. *Stigliano*, 658 A.2d at 719.

In fact, although the use of experts is generally permissive and offered at the discretion of the parties,[46] expert testimony may be required to establish elements of certain claims, such as the

---

[46] *See Brenman*, 921 A.2d at 1120–21 (rejecting a *per se* rule requiring expert testimony as a foundation for the admissibility of a photograph of vehicle damage offered to show a correlation between the vehicle damage and the cause or extent of injuries claimed by an occupant).

existence of a duty and questions of causation. *See Phillips v. Gelpke*, 921 A.2d 1067, 1073 (N.J. 2007). N.J. R. Evid. 704, which provides that "[t]estimony in the form of any opinion or inference otherwise admissible is not objectionable because it embraces an ultimate issue to be decided by the trier of fact," is essentially identical to Federal Rule 704(a). The New Jersey Rule, however, lacks the counterpart to Federal Rule 704(b), which prohibits expert-opinion testimony regarding whether a criminal defendant possessed the requisite mental state or condition constituting an element of the crime or offense. *See* N.J. R. Evid. 704; Fed. R. Evid. 704(b).

Despite the absence of this language in N.J. R. Evid. 704, in *State v. Nesbitt*, 888 A.2d 472 (N.J. 2006), the New Jersey Supreme Court cautioned that, even though expert testimony may embrace the ultimate facts or issues to be determined by the jury, as the gatekeeper of evidence, a trial court must nevertheless take care to instruct the jury on the proper weight to be given to expert testimony and to emphasize that, ultimately, the decision about the defendant's guilt rests solely with the jury. *See id.* at 476–78 (citations omitted).

Appellate review of expert-evidence issues, at least in criminal cases, goes beyond the record developed in the trial court "to account for and consider the latest and most reliable scientific developments in the field under review . . . ." *State v. Calleia*, 997 A.2d 1051, 1059 (N.J. App. Div. 2010), *rev'd on other grounds*, 20 A.3d 402 (N.J. 2011).

4. Expert Evidence in Pennsylvania State Courts

Pennsylvania permits expert testimony that will "assist the trier of fact." Pa. R. Evid. 702. Expert testimony, however, must concern subject matter beyond the knowledge, information, skill, or experience of the average layperson, *see* Pa. R. Evid. 702; *Grady v. Frito-Lay, Inc.*, 789 A.2d 735, 740 (Pa. Super. 2001) (citation omitted), *rev'd in part*, 576 Pa. 546, 839 A.2d 1038 (2003), and may not go to the veracity of a party. *See, e.g., Commonwealth v. Balodis*, 747 A.2d 341, 344 (Pa. 2000) (reversing and remanding because the trial court improperly admitted expert testimony by a social worker on the disclosure patterns of abused children in violation of the rule that "expert testimony as to the veracity of a particular class of people, of which the victim is a member, is inadmissible") (citing *Commonwealth v. Dunkle*, 529 Pa. 168, 602 A.2d 830 (1992) (excluding expert testimony about the behaviors of abused children because an average layperson could understand the behavior without an expert's assistance)). The expert must express his or her opinion with reasonable certainty[47] and the expert "must testify as to the facts or data on which the opinion or inference is based." Pa. R. Evid. 705; *see also Newcomer v. Workmen's Comp. Appeal Bd.*, 692 A.2d 1062 (Pa. 1997) (expert may base opinion on facts of which he has no personal knowledge but the facts must be supported by evidence in the record).

a. Pennsylvania Applies the *Frye* Standard

In *Grady v. Frito-Lay, Inc.*, 576 Pa. 546, 839 A.2d 1038 (2003), the Supreme Court of Pennsylvania rejected the *Daubert* test and reaffirmed the use of the *Frye* standard to determine the admissibility of evidence involving novel science. The court stated, *"Frye's* 'general acceptance' test is a proven and workable rule, which when faithfully followed, fairly serves its purpose of assisting the courts in determining when scientific evidence is reliable and should be admitted." *Id.* at 557, 839 A.2d at 1044.

---

[47] *See McMahon v. Young*, 276 A.2d 534 (1971); *see also Eaddy v. Hamathy*, 694 A.2d 639 (Pa. Super. 1997) (plaintiff not permitted to proceed to trial for medical malpractice claim where plaintiff's expert report did not express the requisite degree of medical certainty).

The *Grady* court based its adherence to the *Frye* test on the principle that scientists are in a better position than judges to determine the reliability of scientific evidence. Further, the *Grady* court noted that "the *Frye* test, which is premised on a rule—that of 'general acceptance'—is more likely to yield uniform, objective, and predictable results among the courts, than is the application of the *Daubert* standard, which calls for a balancing of several factors." *Id.* at 557, 839 A.2d at 1045.

In a concurring opinion, Justice Newman criticized the approach of the *Grady* court. Rule 702 of the Pennsylvania Rules of Evidence is modeled after Federal Rule of Evidence 702. Justice Newman noted that the United States Supreme Court "expressly stated that *Frye* was an 'austere standard, absent from, and incompatible with, the Federal Rules of Evidence.'" *Id.* at 568, 839 A.2d at 1051 (quoting *Daubert*, 509 U.S. at 589). Therefore, Justice Newman asserted she could not join an opinion that interpreted the same language but reached the opposite conclusion of the United States Supreme Court in *Daubert*. *Id.*

b. When Does *Frye* Apply?

The Supreme Court of Pennsylvania "has made it clear that *Frye* is not implicated every time science comes into the courtroom; rather, it applies only to proffered expert testimony involving novel science." *Commonwealth v. Dengler*, 586 Pa. 54, 69, 890 A.2d 372, 382 (2005); *see also Commonwealth v. Chmiel*, 30 A.3d 1111, 1140 (Pa. 2011). For example, in *Commonwealth v. Blasioli*, 713 A.2d 1117 (Pa. 1998), the Pennsylvania Supreme Court applied the *Frye* standard to the admissibility of "novel scientific evidence," such as DNA statistical evidence. *Id.* at 1119; *Chmiel*, 30 A.3d at 1140. In *Grady*, the court held that *Frye* applied to bar the proffered testimony of a chemical engineer who calculated the force necessary to fracture Doritos chips and concluded they were too hard to be swallowed safely after being chewed. By contrast, the Supreme Court of Pennsylvania has also held that the testimony of an expert witness regarding whether an offender is a sexually violent predator is not subject to the *Frye* test. *Dengler*, 586 Pa. at 71, 890 A.2d at 382.

In *Betz v. Pneumo Abex, LLC*, No. 38 WAP 2010 (Pa. May 23, 2012), the Pennsylvania Supreme Court provided further guidance on the admissibility of novel scientific evidence. *Id.* at *42–45. The issue in the case was the admissibility of a medical expert's theory that "each and every exposure" to asbestos—no matter what the level or duration—contributed substantially to the development of asbestos-related disease. *Id.* at *2. The court explained that the expert's opinion was both internally irreconcilable and inconsistent with Pennsylvania case law because the expert simultaneously claimed that a single asbestos fiber, among millions, is substantially causative and that asbestos-related disease is dose responsive. *Id.* at *47–53. The court held that the trial judge did not abuse his discretion by excluding such testimony on the ground that the expert witness had not applied accepted scientific methodology in reaching his conclusions. *Id.* at *53.

On the question of the *Frye* hearing itself, the court found the trial court's decision to conduct a *Frye* hearing to be appropriate and consistent with the trial judge's duty to screen scientific evidence. *Id.* at *42–45. The court held that the term "novel" should apply not only to new science but also to the use of recognized scientific methods in novel ways to arrive at an opinion for use in litigation. *Id.* at *43–44. In addition, the court found that where an expert fails to clearly articulate his or her methodology, or where the conclusions drawn by the expert are outside or beyond the scope of the expert's scientific field, scrutiny by the court is appropriate under *Frye*.[48]

---

[48] *Id.* at *42–43. The court noted that the expert in question—a pathologist—would not ordinarily be called upon to attribute specific causation, but rather that his usual focus would be upon diagnosis based on empirical review. The pathologist in question could not cite to specific research he had performed or to any other methodological basis on which he offered his "every fiber" opinion. *Id.*

c. What Must Be Generally Accepted?

Under the *Frye* standard, the general acceptance test applies only to the expert's methodology, not to his conclusions. *See Cooper, supra* note 13, at 65 (citing *Daubert*, 509 U.S. at 594; *Paoli II*, 35 F.3d at 746). In *Grady*, the Supreme Court of Pennsylvania held that this approach is sensible because "it imposes appropriate restrictions on the admission of scientific evidence, without stifling creativity and innovative thought." *Chmiel*, 30 A.3d at 1140 (quoting *Grady*, 576 Pa. at 558, 839 A.2d at 1045).

d. Application of the *Frye* Test

When *Frye* applies, if a scientific expert is qualified, will testify about a matter beyond the knowledge of an average layperson, and holds his or her opinion with reasonable certainty, and the party proffering the expert's testimony has complied with the discovery requirements, then the court must examine whether the expert's methodology is generally accepted in the relevant community. Pennsylvania courts have strictly applied this general acceptance standard (the *"Frye* standard") because:

> The requirement of general acceptance in the scientific community assures that those most qualified to assess the general validity of a scientific method will have the determinative voice. Additionally, the *Frye* test protects prosecution and defense alike by assuring that a minimal reserve of experts exists who can critically examine the validity of a scientific determination in a particular case. Since scientific proof may in some instances assume a posture of mystic infallibility in the eyes of a jury of laymen, the ability to produce rebuttal experts, equally conversant with the mechanics and methods of a particular technique, may prove to be essential.

Topa, 369 A.2d 1277 (quoting *United States v. Addison*, 498 F.2d 741, 744 (D.C. Cir. 1974)).

In *Topa*, the Pennsylvania Supreme Court examined the proffered expert testimony of a police lieutenant based on voiceprint analysis of a telephone call. The court noted that the testimony of one expert could not meet the *Frye* standard for proving general acceptance. Moreover, citing published studies and opinions by experts in the field, as well as case law discussing expert testimony regarding the reliability of voiceprint identification, the court held that the technique had not been generally accepted in the scientific community. Thus, the Pennsylvania Supreme Court held that the trial court erred by admitting the expert's voiceprint testimony and remanded the case for a new trial. *Id.* at 1281–82.

In *Commonwealth v. Crews*, 640 A.2d 395 (Pa. 1994), the Pennsylvania Supreme Court examined the admissibility of DNA evidence. At trial, the prosecution's expert witness testified that the defendant's DNA patterns in three of four genetic loci matched the DNA patterns obtained from semen found in the victim. The expert did not testify about the statistical probability of the DNA matching a person other than the defendant. Instead, the expert testified that "he did not know of a single instance where different individuals that are unrelated have been shown to have matching DNA profiles for three of four probes" and that the semen more likely than not was the defendant's. *Id.* at 397, 402, 408.

On appeal, the Pennsylvania Supreme Court affirmed both the trial court's admission of evidence matching the defendant's DNA and its exclusion of evidence discussing the statistical probability of such DNA matching another person. Based on numerous scientific articles, many judicial opinions, and expert testimony in the pretrial setting, the court concluded that comparison of DNA samples was generally accepted in the scientific community. *Id.* at 400–01. The court held, however, that there was not enough evidence in the record to establish that the statistical relevance of a DNA match had been generally accepted. *Id.* at 402 n.4.[49] Confronted with the defendant's argument that DNA evidence is meaningless without establishing the likelihood of a match, the court explained that the evidence was relevant because it tended to make the defendant's guilt more likely than it would have been without such evidence. *Id.* at 402–03. A concurring opinion pointed out that the expert's statements still suggested a statistical likelihood of the match and should have been excluded. *Id.* at 408 (Cappy, J. concurring).

Using the *Frye* test, Pennsylvania courts have found that the results of a horizontal gaze nystagmus test (field sobriety test) are not admissible because the test is not generally accepted. *See Commonwealth v. Apollo*, 603 A.2d 1023 (Pa. Super. Ct. 1992). Similarly, hypnotically refreshed testimony,[50] the results of polygraph tests,[51] and the causal relationship between low-voltage electric shocks and cardiomyopathy[52] have been excluded because their reliability has not yet been generally accepted within the scientific community. On the other hand, Pennsylvania courts have accepted expert testimony regarding battered woman's syndrome to support a self-defense theory in a murder trial[53] and tool mark identification.[54]

In criminal cases, the Pennsylvania Supreme Court has imposed a ban on experts who testify about how a class of witnesses thinks or behaves, viewing such testimony as an improper comment on credibility. Thus, expert testimony on eyewitnesses,[55] rape victim behaviors,[56] and child sexual-assault victims[57] has been prohibited. This categoric rejection may be modified, as in 2012 when the court heard argument on whether expert evidence in eyewitness cases should be allowed, and included in the grant of allowance of appeal the question of whether "the court [should] permit expert scientific testimony, whether it be for the defense or prosecution, on how the mind works as long as such testimony has received general acceptance within the scientific community." *Commonwealth v. Walker*, 2011 Pa. LEXIS 939 (2011).

e. Qualification of Experts

Qualifying a witness as an expert is not difficult in Pennsylvania, as "[i]t is well established . . . that the standard for qualification of an expert witness is a liberal one." *Miller v. Brass Rail Tavern, Inc.*, 664 A.2d 525, 528 (Pa. 1995). Therefore, formal education is not required and a witness's

---

[49] Subsequent cases have held that such statistical evidence is generally accepted. *See Blasioli*, 685 A.2d 151 (1996); *Commonwealth v. Timbers*, 116 Dauphin Co. Reps. 368 (1996).

[50] *See Commonwealth v. Nazarovitch*, 436 A.2d 170 (Pa. 1981) (excluding hypnotically refreshed testimony since many researchers speculated about the reliability of this method of recall).

[51] See *Commonwealth v. Chester*, 526 Pa. 578 (1991).

[52] *See Thomas*, 760 A.2d at 1180.

[53] *See Commonwealth v. Stonehouse*, 555 A.2d 772 (Pa. 1989) (plurality).

[54] *See Commonwealth v. Foreman*, 797 A.2d 1005, 1018 (Pa. Super. Ct. 2002) (citing *Commonwealth v. Graves*, 456 A.2d 561 (Pa. Super. Ct. 1983)).

[55] *Commonwealth v. Simmons*, 662 A.2d 621, 631 (Pa. 1995).

[56] *Commonwealth v. Gallagher*, 547 A.2d 355 (Pa. 1988).

[57] *Commonwealth v. Davis*, 541 A.2d 315 (Pa. 1988).

training and experience may qualify him or her as an expert.[58] As the Pennsylvania Supreme Court has stated:

> The test to be applied when qualifying a witness to testify as an expert witness is whether the witness has any reasonable pretension to specialized knowledge on the subject under investigation. If he does, he may testify and the weight to be given to such testimony is for the trier of fact to determine.

Pa. R. Evid. 702 cmt. (quoting *Miller*, 664 A.2d at 528). Thus, in *Miller*, the trial court erred by excluding the testimony of a coroner regarding the time of a person's death simply because the coroner did not have a medical degree. *Miller*, 664 A.2d at 529.

Similarly, in *Commonwealth v. Arroyo*, 723 A.2d 162 (Pa. 1999), the appellant claimed that the lower court erred in admitting the expert testimony of a witness qualified only as a forensic pathologist where such evidence was admitted on issues involving the fields of biomechanics and occupant kinematics. 723 A.2d at 170. The Pennsylvania Supreme Court held there was ample evidence to support a finding that an expert witness had a "reasonable pretension" to knowledge of biomechanics and occupant kinematics where the witness had received extensive training in crime-scene reconstruction, which involves biomechanics, authored several articles regarding occupant kinematics, and lectured and testified extensively on issues involving those fields. *See id.* at 170–71 (applying a liberal standard for qualification of an expert witness).

Finally, in *West Phila. Therapy Ctr. v. Erie Ins. Grp.*, 751 A.2d 1166 (Pa. Super. 2000), the trial court excluded the expert testimony of a chiropractor, reasoning that he was not qualified as an expert because he was not certified by the National Board of Chiropractic Examiners, had only been practicing for six years, had improperly indicated that he was board certified on his curriculum vitae, and could not remember the name of the organization that had accredited his chiropractic college. *Id.* at 1168–69. The Superior Court held that the trial court erred in excluding the expert testimony because, even though the chiropractor was not board certified, he had attended a four-year chiropractic college, completed an internship at a chiropractic college, completed an externship at a chiropractic center, attended many postgraduate seminars, completed twenty-four hours of continuing education annually, and was board eligible in chiropractic rehabilitation and licensed for chiropractics in the commonwealth. *Id.* at 1168.

---

[58] *See id.; see also Grady*, 789 A.2d at 740 (holding that an expert need not have formal training in the area of testimony as long as the witness can demonstrate greater knowledge than the average layperson); *Commonwealth v. Puksar*, 740 A.2d 219, 226 (Pa. 1999) (doctor with experience in physics, gravity, and what blood does in certain cases, and with experience determining the origin, cause, and manner of blood spatter in hundreds of cases, could testify regarding bloodstain pattern interpretation), *cert. denied*, 531 U.S. 829 (2000); *Rutter v. Ne. Beaver Cnty. Sch. Dist.*, 437 A.2d 1198, 1202 (Pa. 1981) (former football coach may testify that another coach did not conduct his practices in conformity with the safety standards of other Pennsylvania schools) (plurality opinion); *McDaniel v. Merck, Sharp & Dohme*, 533 A.2d 436, 440 (Pa. Super. Ct. 1987) ("Although the witness must demonstrate some special knowledge or skill, there is no requirement that a witness acquire that knowledge as a result of formal schooling; expertise acquired by experience is expertise nonetheless.") (citations omitted). *But see Flanagan v. Labe*, 690 A.2d 183 (Pa. 1997) (nurse not qualified to testify regarding the identity and cause of a plaintiff's medical condition).

f. Procedural Issues

Although Pennsylvania courts generally do not permit opposing parties to depose experts,[59] the Pennsylvania Rules of Civil Procedure "favor the liberal discovery of expert witnesses." *Jones v. Constantino*, 631 A.2d 1289 (Pa. Super. Ct. 1993) (affirming lower-court order for new trial where expert report only contained conclusory statement that defendant was not negligent but testimony went into facts and reasoning beyond scope of report). Accordingly, if an opposing party has submitted discovery requests regarding an expert's opinion or the bases for such opinion, the expert may not testify beyond the scope of his or her report. *See id.*; *see also Christiansen v. Silfies*, 667 A.2d 396 (Pa. Super. Ct. 1995) ("fair scope" involves inquiry as to whether report provided sufficient notice to opposing party to prepare rebuttal witness). *But see Brady v. Ballay, Thornton, Maloney Med. Assocs., Inc.*, 704 A.2d 1076 (Pa. Super. Ct. 1997) (trial court did not err by admitting expert's testimony even though it exceeded the fair scope of the expert's pretrial report where there was no unfair surprise or prejudice to the opposing party). This requirement ensures "that the expert's report will be sufficiently comprehensive and detailed to inform an opposing party of the expert's testimony at trial." *Havasy v. Resnick*, 415 Pa. Super. 480, 492, 609 A.2d 1326, 1331 (Pa. Super. Ct. 1992), *app. dismissed*, 537 Pa. 114, 641 A.2d 580 (Pa. 1994); *see also* Pa. R. Civ. P. 4003.5 cmt. (6) (limiting expert testimony to the scope of the pretrial report prevents "incomplete or 'fudging' of reports which would fail to reveal fully the facts and opinions of the expert or his grounds therefor"). "However, [experts] shall not be prevented from testifying as to facts and opinions on matters on which [they have] not been interrogated in the discovery proceedings."[60] An expert's testimony may be precluded altogether when the party proffering the testimony has not complied with discovery requests. *See* Pa. R. Civ. P. 4019(a)(1)(iii); *see also Dion v. Graduate Hosp., Univ. of Penn.*, 360 Pa. Super. 416, 520 A.2d 876 (Pa. Super. Ct. 1987) (affirming preclusion of expert testimony where party did not comply with discovery or court order). It is important to note that Pa. R. Civ. P. 4003.5 applies only to expert opinions acquired or developed in anticipation of litigation. Thus, a county coroner who examined a body in the performance of his official duties did not fall under Rule 4003.5 because his opinion was not developed in anticipation of litigation. *Miller*, 664 A.2d at 485–88.

A motion to exclude expert testimony that relies on novel scientific evidence on the ground that it is inadmissible under Pa. R. Evid. 702 or 703 must contain the name and credentials of the potential expert, a summary of the expert's testimony with specific reference to the portion the movant seeks to exclude, the specific basis for exclusion, the evidence on which the movant relies, and copies of all relevant expert reports and curriculum vitae. *See* Pa. R. Civ. P. 207.1(a). The court has discretion to determine whether, "in the interest of justice," the motion to exclude should be

---

[59] Only upon good cause shown, and upon payment of fees and expenses, may the opposing party depose an expert. Pa. R. Civ. P. 4003.5 cmt.

[60] *See* Pa. R. Civ. P. 4003.5(c) and cmt. (6) ("[W]here the full scope of the expert's testimony is presented in the answer to interrogatories or the separate report as provided in subdivisions (a)(1) and (2), this will fix the permissible limits of his testimony at trial. But, if the inquirer limits his inquiry to one or more specific issues only, the expert is free to testify at trial as to any other relevant issues not including the discovery"). In the criminal context, prosecutors must disclose to the defendant's attorney "results or reports of scientific tests, expert opinions, and written or recorded reports of polygraph examinations or other physical or mental examinations of the defendant, which are in the possession" of the prosecutor. Pa. R. Crim. P. 305(B)(1)(e). This does not, however, require prosecutors to have experts create written reports. *See Commonwealth v. Blasioli*, 454 Pa. Super. 207, 225, 685 A.2d 151, 160 (1996), *aff'd*, 713 A.2d 1117 (Pa. 1998).

addressed before trial. *See* Pa. R. Civ. P. 207.1(3). In making this determination, the court should consider several factors:

> the dispositive nature or significance of the issue to the case, the complexity of the issue involved in the testimony of the expert witness, the degree of novelty of the proposed evidence, the complexity of the case, the anticipated length of trial, the potential for delay of trial, and the feasibility of the court evaluating the expert witness testimony when offered at trial.

Pa. R. Civ. P. 207.1, Official Note.

Although depositions of expert witnesses and evidentiary hearings are available to the court to determine a motion to exclude expert testimony that relies on novel scientific evidence, these depositions "should be utilized in limited circumstances." Pa. R. Civ. P. 207.1, Official Note (citing Pa. R. Civ. P. 4003.5). Moreover, although a "hearing is not necessarily required, the better practice in complex cases would appear to provide for such a hearing." *Grady*, 789 A.2d at 740 n.3.

CHAPTER IV
EXPERT EVIDENCE IN THE FOURTH CIRCUIT

by

J. Michael Showalter
Schiff Hardin LLP
233 S. Wacker Drive
Suite 6600
Chicago, IL 60606
mshowalter@schiffhardin.com

Daubert v. Merrell Dow Pharmaceuticals, Inc., 509 U.S. 579 (1993), has governed the admissibility of scientific testimony for nearly twenty years. The related cases *General Electric Co. v. Joiner*, 522 U.S. 136 (1997), and *Kumho Tire Co. v. Carmichael*, 526 U.S. 137 (1999), are almost fifteen years old. Accordingly, the Fourth Circuit's methodology for evaluating *Daubert* challenges has a settled predictability. Generally, questions related to the admissibility of expert evidence similarly follow predictable paths in the Fourth Circuit constituent state courts.

A. KEY DECISIONS APPLYING *DAUBERT* IN THE FOURTH CIRCUIT

1. Introduction

a. Development of the *Daubert* Standard

The *Daubert* standard in the Fourth Circuit developed with fits and starts. The first Fourth Circuit case to apply *Daubert* was *United States v. Bynum*, which involved the admission of evidence that had been offered at trial under the *Frye v. United States* standard of "general acceptance." 3 F.3d 769 (4th Cir. 1993), *cert. denied*, 510 U.S. 1132 (1994) (discussing *Frye v. United States*, 293 F. 1013 (1923)). The *Bynum* court explained that, under *Daubert*, expert testimony must rely on scientific knowledge and must assist the trier of fact. 3 F.3d at 773. "Scientific knowledge" is "generated through the scientific method—subjecting testable hypotheses to the crucible of experiment in an effort to disprove them." *Id.* "An opinion that defies testing, however defensible or deeply held, is not scientific." *Id.* The *Bynum* court noted that although evidence may be considered scientific, "the district courts need not admit all 'scientific' evidence without any regard to its reliability." District courts may consider whether the evidence has been subject to peer review, contains a known rate of error, and whether it enjoys "widespread acceptance" in the community. *Id.* The *Bynum* court found that the scientific evidence met the new *Daubert* standard since the government had adequately explained the hypotheses underlying the technique, listed numerous publications in which the technique had been subjected to peer review, and concluded that the technique enjoyed general acceptance in its field. *Id.*

The Fourth Circuit decision in *United States v. Dorsey*, 45 F.3d 809 (4th Cir. 1995), *cert. denied*, 515 U.S. 1168 (1995), clarified what was meant by "scientific knowledge." The court again applied

Daubert, using a two-prong test requiring both "scientific *knowledge*" and assistance to the trier of fact. *Id.* Three years later, the Fourth Circuit revisited the topic of scientific knowledge in *Cavallo v. Star Enterprise*, 100 F.3d 1150 (4th Cir. 1996), *cert. denied*, 522 U.S. 1044 (1998). The *Cavallo* court summarized that in lieu of the *Frye* test, *Daubert* allowed the district courts to implement a flexible inquiry into the validity of scientific methodology or reasoning. *Id.* at 1158. *Cavallo* introduced the five-factor test now commonly associated with *Daubert*. *Id.*[1] The *Daubert* factor referencing rate of error stated, "[I]n the case of a particular scientific technique, the court ordinarily should consider the known or potential rate of error and the existence and maintenance of standards controlling the technique's operation." *Daubert*, 520 U.S. at 594 (citations omitted).

The *Cavallo* court simply split the one sentence into two distinct factors. Since *Cavallo*, the fifth factor has been incorporated into and cited favorably by district courts in the Fourth Circuit. *See, e.g., Higgins v. Diversey Corp.*, 998 F.Supp. 598, 605 n.7 (D. Md. 1997); *Ballinger v. Atkins*, 947 F.Supp. 925, 927 (E.D. Va. 1996). The inquiry should focus on whether the science has been (1) tested, (2) published, (3) determined to have a particular rate of error, (4) standardized and controlled, and (5) generally accepted. *Id.* "Although *Daubert* eliminated the requirement of general acceptance, the five factors it established still require that the methodology and reasoning used by a witness have a significant place in the discourse of experts in the field." *Id.* at 1159.

Shortly after *Cavallo* rephrased the test for scientific knowledge, the Fourth Circuit took up a technical knowledge case. In *Freeman v. Case Corp.*, 118 F.3d 1011, 1016 n.6 (4th Cir. 1997), *cert. denied*, 522 U.S. 1069 (1998), the court drew a distinction between scientific knowledge and technical knowledge, acknowledging that the Supreme Court had left open the question of whether the *Daubert* analysis applied outside the scientific context. In *Freeman*, the court declined to perform a *Daubert* preliminary assessment analysis since the challenge to the testimony involved the expert's conclusions and not the reliability or relevance of the testimony itself. *Id.* The court reasoned that in cases where an expert relies on his or her experience and training and not a particular methodology to reach his conclusions, the application of *Daubert* is unwarranted. *Id.*; *see also Binakonsky v. Ford Motor Co.*, 133 F.3d 281, 290 (4th Cir. 1998) (*Daubert* is inapplicable to fact witnesses who are neither engaged as experts nor paid to testify); *Talkington v. Atria Reclamelucifers Fabrieken BV*, 152 F.3d 254, 265 (4th Cir. 1998) (*Daubert* does not apply when a witness merely bases conclusions on experience and training and there is no challenge to methodology or technique). Thus, the Fourth Circuit applied *Daubert* outside the scientific context when the reliability of the testimony, the relevance of the testimony, or a particular methodology comes into question but did not apply *Daubert* to mere facts or conclusions of a technical expert.

In 1999, the Fourth Circuit acknowledged that the United States Supreme Court held that *Daubert* applied to all experts, not just scientific experts. In *Ballance v. Wal-Mart Stores, Inc.*, 1999 U.S. App. LEXIS 7663, at *14 (4th Cir. 1999) (unpublished opinion), the Fourth Circuit noted that "*Daubert*'s 'gatekeeping' obligation requires a district court to make a preliminary assessment of all expert testimony, not just 'scientific' testimony." Despite the broadening of types of testimony reviewed, the *Ballance* court noted that a significant point made by *Kumho Tire* was that a district court retains wide discretion in permitting or excluding expert testimony. *Id.*

---

[1] Until *Cavallo*, Fourth Circuit cases cited four factors: testing, peer review, rate of error, and general acceptance. *Cavallo* listed an additional factor: standards and controls over the methodology's implementation. Although the case is cited as adding a fifth factor, that factor already appeared in the *Daubert* opinion.

b. Whether the Evidence Is Helpful

Once the science is determined to be valid from a scientific perspective, then it will be reviewed for applicability to the facts in issue. In evaluating the relevance of the evidence, the court adopts the concept of "fit." *See, e.g., United States v. Powers*, 59 F.3d 1460, 1472 (4th Cir. 1995) (proffered testimony on characteristics of a fixated pedophile did not "fit" the case and would not assist the trier of fact since it did not show that those who are not fixated pedophiles are less likely to commit incest abuse). The *Cavallo* court addressed this point by noting that *Daubert* itself instructed that the applicability determination will be made by reference to other rules of evidence, such as the relevance and prejudice provisions of Rules 401 and 403. *Cavallo*, 100 F.3d at 1158. Essentially, a scientifically based expert opinion shall not come before a jury unless it "fits" with the underlying background facts of the case.

The *Dorsey* court also discussed *Daubert*'s second prong of the admissibility test, that is, helpfulness to the trier of fact. The court warned that a judge must be mindful of other evidentiary rules, such as Rule 403, to keep powerful expert evidence from misleading the jury. *Dorsey*, 45 F.3d at 813; *see also Westberry v. Gislaved Gummi AB*, 178 F.3d 257 (4th Cir. 1999) (courts must recognize that due to the difficulty of evaluating their testimony, expert witnesses have the potential to be both powerful and quite misleading); *United States v. Davis*, 602 F. Supp. 2d 658, 684 (D. Md. 2009) ("The Court is mindful that 'expert testimony may be assigned talismanic significance in the eyes of lay jurors and, therefore, the district courts must take care to weigh the value of such evidence against its potential to mislead or confuse'"). The court further quoted *Daubert* in its passage discussing the balance that is struck by the Rules of Evidence and the possibility that valid science may be excluded as "designed not for the exhaustive search for cosmic understanding but for the particularized resolution of legal disputes." *Dorsey*, 45 F.3d at 814 (quoting *Daubert*, 509 U.S. at 595–97). The court also relied on an earlier interpretation of Rule 702 in its discussion of helpfulness to the trier of fact. "[I]n determining whether a particular expert's testimony is sufficiently helpful to the trier of fact to warrant admission into trial, the district court should consider whether the testimony presented is simply reiterating facts already 'within the common knowledge' of the jurors." *Id.* at 814 (citing *United States v. Harris*, 995 F.2d 532 (4th Cir. 1993)).

Helpfulness, however, is not limited to the issue of whether the testimony "fits" the case. Quite understandably, expert testimony is not helpful if it consists of speculation. "A reliable expert opinion must be based on scientific, technical, or other specialized knowledge and not on belief or speculation, and inferences must be derived using scientific or other valid methods." *Oglesby v. Gen. Motors Corp.*, 190 F.3d 244, 250 (4th Cir. 1999). As the Supreme Court explained in *Kumho Tire*, the objective of *Daubert*'s gatekeeping requirement is to "make certain that an expert . . . employs in the courtroom the same level of intellectual rigor that characterizes the practice of an expert in the relevant field." 526 U.S. at 152. The Fourth Circuit has made clear that experts are not permitted to speculate; where experts engage in unsupported speculation, their testimony must be excluded. *See, e.g., Oglesby*, 190 F.3d at 250 (excluding testimony where the expert "admitted, however, that he did not know the type or composition of the plastic [used in a defective ladder]. He did not ask the manufacturer; he did not analyze the part; he did not test it; he did not apply any calculations"); *Cooper v. Smith & Nephew, Inc.*, 259 F.3d 194, 202 (4th Cir. 2001) ("Thus, if an expert utterly fails to consider alternative causes or fails to offer an explanation for why the proffered alternative cause was not the sole cause, a district court is justified in excluding the expert's testimony"). However, a professional expert's qualifications are to be examined broadly; an expert need not have conducted research identical to the questions before a court.

Casey v. Geek Squad is instructive in this regard. *See Casey v. Geek Squad Subsidiary Best Buy Stores, L.P.*, 823 F. Supp 2d 334, 344–45 (D. Md. 2011). *Casey* involved a claim for damages for personal injuries that occurred proximate to when a computer was serviced by a Best Buy technician.

See id. at 338–39. Plaintiff's expert testified that an electric shock incurred by the plaintiff was a "but for" result of the actions of the technician. *Id.* at 343. After defendant lodged a *Daubert* challenge based on the expert's purported lack of reliable methodology applied to data, the court concluded that the sources the expert relied upon—namely an expert report offered by the defense—were insufficient to demonstrate the reliability of the expert's testimony. *Id.* at 343–44. The court also found the expert's methodology—conducting a visual examination of the computer without any testing—insufficient to justify the expert's conclusions. *Id.* at 344. "Without any reference in the record to a recognizably reliable methodology employed in his investigation, and in light of the evidence showing that [the expert] conducted a visual examination of the computer away from the site of the original shock, using no tools other than a magnifying glass and his hands, while the computer was turned off and not plugged in to an electrical source, this Court is unable to find that [the expert] conclusions meet the reliability requirement of Rule 702." *Id.* at 345 n.9 (additionally explaining that the expert's testimony did not qualify as "experiential" because the expert failed to demonstrate how his experience "leads to the conclusion he reached," citing cases including *United States v. Wilson*, 484 F.3d 267, 274 (4th Cir. 2007)). The court concluded with a note that it is appropriate to exclude expert testimony "that is connected to existing data only by the *ipse dixit* of the expert." *Id.* (citing *Joiner*, 522 U.S. at 146).

c. Appellate Review

(1) Generally

In evaluating district court decisions on *Daubert* issues, the Fourth Circuit applies an abuse-of-discretion standard. *See United States v. Grimmond*, 137 F.3d 823, 831 (4th Cir. 1998) ("A district court's evidentiary rulings are reviewed under the narrow abuse of discretion standard"). *United States v. Barnette*, 211 F.3d 803 (4th Cir. 2000), illustrates the limits of the abuse-of-discretion standard. Although a trial judge's decision on whether to admit expert testimony under *Daubert* receives great deference, the Fourth Circuit will reverse if there is "a clear error in judgment on the part of the district court." *Id.* at 816 (citing *Westberry v. Gislaved Gummi AB*, 178 F.3d 257, 261 (4th Cir. 1999)). *Barnette* rejected a challenge that the trial court impermissibly allowed at the sentencing phase expert psychiatric testimony that defendant was a psychopath.

District courts are given broad procedural, as well as substantive, leeway. In *United States v. Beasley*, 495 F.3d 142 (4th Cir. 2007), the court noted that the district court did not abuse its discretion by not holding a *Daubert* hearing because the challenged expert's training and experience were clear on the record then before the district court.[2] This said, the latitude granted to the district court is not unlimited. In *Westfield Insurance Co. v. Harris*, 134 F.3d 608, 611 (4th Cir. 1998), a fire marshal's expert testimony as to the causation of fire was stricken from the record. The district court

---

[2] *Id.* at 150 (stating that the expert's "credentials, which were substantial, included: training in numerous law enforcement courses on identification of narcotics . . . participation as a member of a local narcotics agency in the seizure of cocaine in its various stages on its way to becoming crack cocaine; and witnessing on video the full process of turning powder cocaine into crack cocaine. This training and experience qualified [the expert] to give testimony on the process of making crack cocaine from cocaine powder. Accordingly, the district court did not abuse its discretion in allowing him to testify as an expert, without conducting a Daubert hearing."); *see also United States v. Thomas*, No. 10-4725, 2012 WL 2951410, at *4–5 (4th Cir. July 20, 2012) (more recent discussion of the same principle, that is, that a district court's careful examination of a technical expert for whom the standard *Daubert* criteria are less relevant will be sufficient to overcome a challenge to admissibility).

concluded, among other things, that it was improper for the marshal to rely on other expert reports. *Id.* at 612. The Fourth Circuit, upon review, pointed out that Rule 703 expressly authorizes expert opinions based on opinions and observations of others if they are of the type reasonably relied on by experts in the field. *Id.* The Fourth Circuit found that the reports and data relied on by the marshal were ordinarily relied on by him in investigating fires. *Id.* at 613. Therefore, the district court had abused its discretion in striking the testimony. *Id.* Although the abuse-of-discretion standard grants the district courts freedom to exercise their judgment in admitting expert testimony, it is not without limits. The appellate court is "obligated to assess the full record and the reasons assigned," and will reverse "if the decision was 'guided by erroneous legal principles' or 'committed a clear error of judgment in the conclusion it recorded upon a weighing of relevant factors.'" *Sharpe v. Director, Office of Workers' Compensation Programs*, 495 F.3d 125, 130 (4th Cir. 2007) (citing *Westberry*, 178 F.3d at 261). Even if an abuse of discretion occurs, such a ruling "is reversible only if it affects a party's substantial rights." *Schultz v. Capital Int'l Sec., Inc.*, 466 F.3d 298, 310 (4th Cir. 2006) (applying Fed. R. Evid. 103(a)).

(2) Evidence Must Meet the Preponderance Standard

In *Maryland Casualty Co. v. Therm-O-Disc, Inc.*, 137 F.3d 780 (4th Cir.), *cert. denied*, 525 U.S. 827 (1998), the Fourth Circuit held that a party seeking to admit evidence under *Daubert* must establish that the evidence is appropriate by a preponderance of the evidence. In *Therm-O-Disc*, the appellate panel affirmed the district court's decision to allow expert scientific testimony from an experienced electrical engineer on the issue of causation by acknowledging the district court's discretion in applying the *Daubert* factors:

> Beyond establishing the two criteria of reliability and helpfulness, the Court has left the means by which these criteria are evaluated to the sound discretion of the district judge . . . In addition, this circuit has taken the position that the *Daubert* court "was not formulating a rigid test or checklist," and was "relying instead on the ability of federal judges to properly determine admissibility."

Id. at 785 (citing *Benedi*, 66 F.3d at 1384).

The *Therm-O-Disc* court rejected the argument that there were further considerations a district court needed to make in order to comply with *Daubert*. The court noted that *Daubert* makes no mention of a burden of proof regarding the decision to admit expert testimony, but does require a burden of production, that is, producing evidence for the trial court to evaluate whether the evidence is reliable and helpful. *Id.* at 782–83. As the *Therm-O-Disc* court stated:

> As in all questions of admissibility, the proffering party must come forward with evidence from which the court can determine that the proffered testimony is properly admissible. However, there is no requirement in *Daubert*, or any other controlling authority, that the proffering party must "prove" anything to the court before the testimony in question can be admitted.

Id. at 783.

Further explaining this reasoning, the *Therm-O-Disc* court noted that *Daubert* did reference another case for the proposition that matters should be established by a preponderance of proof. *Id.* at 783 n.9 (citing *Bourjaily v. United States*, 483 U.S. 171 (1987)). The Fourth Circuit does not interpret "preponderance of proof" to refer to a burden of proof, especially when case law distinguishes between the two concepts. *Id.* "[T]he preponderance standard ensures that before admitting evidence, the court will have found it more likely than not that the technical issues and policy concerns addressed by the Federal Rules of Evidence have been afforded due consideration." *Id.* Proponents of expert testimony do not need to prove their case twice, by proving first to a judge and then to a jury that expert opinions are correct. *Id.* at 783. The proponents only have to prove to a judge that the expert opinions are reliable before the opinions can be heard by a jury. *Id.*

In recent years, the Fourth Circuit has increasingly formalized its willingness to evaluate "experiential" testimony in a less formal manner than it does "scientific" testimony. *See United States v. Moreland*, 437 F.3d 424, 431 (4th Cir. 2006); *United States v. Wilson*, 484 F.3d 267, 274–75 (4th Cir. 2007). In *Wilson*, the court noted that "[a] district court's reliability determination does not exist in a vacuum, as there exist meaningful differences in how reliability must be examined with respect to expert testimony that is primarily experiential in nature as opposed to scientific." *Id.* Although "'experience alone—or experience in conjunction with other knowledge, skill, training or education—may . . . provide a sufficient foundation for expert testimony,'" "the district court must . . . require an experiential witness to 'explain how [his] experience leads to the conclusion reached, why [his] experience is a sufficient basis for the opinion, and how [his] experience is reliably applied to the facts.'" *Id.* (quoting Fed. R. Evid. 702 advisory committee's note) (alterations in original).

d. Procedural Issues

Federal Rule of Civil Procedure 26(a)(2) of the Federal Rules of Civil Procedure imposes specific requirements for the disclosure of expert testimony. Rule 26(a)(2)(A) provides that each "party shall disclose to other parties the identity of any person who may be used at trial to present evidence under Rules 702, 703, or 705 of the Federal Rules of Evidence." The required disclosures must be made as directed by the court's scheduling order or, if none, no later than ninety days prior to the trial, and must be supplemented when required under Rule 26(e)(1). Rule 26(a)(2)(C).

Rule 37(c)(1) provides the remedy for failing to disclose evidence under Rule 26. It provides that "[a] party that without substantial justification fails to disclose information required by Rule 26(a) . . . is not, unless such failure is harmless, permitted to use as evidence at trial, at a hearing, or on a motion any witness or information not so disclosed." Fed. R. Civ. P. 37(c)(1) (emphasis added). It is the burden of the party facing sanctions to show that the failure to comply was either substantially justified or harmless.

Where a *Daubert* challenge is likely, district courts require the parties to (1) disclose the identity of all expert witnesses expected to testify at trial; (2) provide, among other things, the experts' written, signed reports stating all opinions to be offered and support for such opinions; and (3) make the experts available for deposition after the reports are submitted. After a challenge is made, the failure to address any of these items will likely result in the court excluding (or limiting) the questioned expert.

The Fourth Circuit has demonstrated a willingness to exclude expert testimony based on failures to disclose. In *Carr v. Deeds*, 453 F.3d 593, 601–04 (4th Cir. 2006), when a plaintiff failed to provide any explanation for a failure to disclose an expert witness, the Fourth Circuit relied on this failure to uphold the district court's exclusion of the witness's testimony. Exhibiting a high degree of skepticism to the proffering party's explanation that the failures to disclose were "inadvertent," the Fourth Circuit followed precedent, stating:

> Rule 26 disclosures are often the centerpiece of discovery in litigation that uses expert witnesses. A party that fails to provide these disclosures unfairly inhibits its opponent's ability to properly prepare, unnecessarily prolongs litigation, and undermines the district

court's management of the case. For this reason, "[w]e give particularly wide latitude to the district court's discretion to issue sanctions under Rule 37(c)(1)."

Id. (citing *Saudi v. Northrop Grumman Corp.*, 427 F.3d 271, 278–79 (4th Cit. 2005) (internal citation omitted)).

The Fourth Circuit concluded that "[e]very litigant in federal court is plainly entitled under Rule 26(a)(2)(B) to be given the information spelled out therein, and none shoulder the burden to independently investigate and ferret out that information as best they can and at the expense of their client. . . . The available penalty for failure to comply with [the Rule] is equally plain, and if a litigant refuses to comply with the requirements of the rule, he does so at his peril." *Id.* (citing *Saudi*, 427 F.3d at 274).

The contours of expert disclosures are often set forth in local rules. The Southern District of West Virginia has addressed the adequacy of expert reports specifically in a reported decision. In the case of *Smith v. State Farm Fire & Casualty Co.*, 164 F.R.D. 49, 53–54 (S.D. W. Va. 1995), a motion to compel based on inadequacy of reports provided by plaintiffs' expert witnesses, the court held that the contents of the majority of the reports were insufficient under Fed. R. Civ. P. 26 and Local Rule 3.01. The court also clarified the meaning of "retained" or "specially employed." *See id.* at 54–56.

2. *Evidence Based on the Natural or Hard Sciences*

a. Product Design / Engineering

Since *Daubert*, courts in the Fourth Circuit have decided a number of *Daubert* challenges in the product design and engineering area. A party seeking to admit, or challenge, such evidence will likely follow a well-trodden path. Speaking generally, since *Kumho Tire* effectively opened the door to this type of testimony, the contours of expert admissibility in this area mirror *Daubert* applications in other areas.

In *Freeman v. Case Corp.*, 118 F.3d 1011 (4th Cir. 1997), the technical expert testimony of a mechanical engineer was admitted in a product liability case regarding the close proximity of the speed-control pedal to the brake pedal. The court declined to address the question of whether the *Daubert* analysis applied outside the scientific context, because the challenge to the testimony involved the expert's conclusions and not the reliability or relevance of the testimony itself. *Id.* at 1016 n.6 (citations omitted). However, the court reasoned that in cases where an expert relies on his experience and training and not a particular methodology to reach his conclusions, the application of *Daubert* was unwarranted. *Id.* Without the gatekeeping of *Daubert*, the technical testimony was allowed into evidence. *Freeman* has largely been rendered irrelevant by the *Kumho Tire* decision.

In *Oglesby v. General Motors Corp.*, 190 F.3d 244 (4th Cir. 1999), the Fourth Circuit reviewed a mechanical engineer's testimony as to an alleged defect in the manufacturing of a radiator hose part. *Kumho Tire* had come down before oral arguments were heard. *Id.* at 249. Although the district court did not have the benefit of *Kumho Tire*, its analysis reached the same result that a *Daubert* analysis would have produced. *Id.* at 251. The district court excluded the engineer's testimony because it was based on incorrect and untested assumptions, an error in logic, and a failure to follow general engineering principles. *Id.* at 250–51. The court recognized the evidence's flaws and concluded that the expert's opinion lacked any probative value because it lacked reliability, foundation, and relevance. *Id.* at 251. "A reliable expert opinion must be based on scientific, technical or other specialized *knowledge* and not on belief or speculation, and inferences must be derived using scientific or other valid methods." *Id.* at 250 (emphasis in original). The Fourth Circuit found no error in the district court's exercise of discretion in excluding the testimony. *Id.*

In *Simo v. Mitsubishi Motors North America, Inc.*, 2007 U.S. App. LEXIS 19421, at *11 (4th Cir. Aug. 15, 2007), the Fourth Circuit upheld the admissibility of testimony from a mechanical engineer, the bulk of whose experience in the relevant field came from twenty-plus years of experience in performing stability testing on vehicles in "litigation consulting-type work." As a result of "hundreds and hundreds of tests associated with vehicle stability [and] vehicle rollover resistance," the expert had specialized knowledge concerning the tests manufacturers employ and experience in evaluating different design modifications in protecting against rollovers. In admitting the expert's testimony, the Fourth Circuit also relied on internal automobile company documents, test data, deposition testimony of automobile-manufacturer engineers, and other materials related to the design and development of various vehicles, as well as documents authored by the NHTSA and professional societies of automobile engineers. *Id.* at *12. Because the engineer offered testimony that several vehicles on the market did not have the tendencies to roll over as did the Mitsubishi Montero at issue in *Simo*, the expert's failure to testify about design suitability was not fatal. *Id.*

In *Boss v. Nissan North America, Inc.*, 228 F. App'x 331, 336–37 (4th Cir. 2007) (unpublished), the Fourth Circuit upheld the exclusion of four design experts who testified that an automobile's power-steering mechanism was defectively designed, and a particle that was lodged in the power-steering system's spool valve caused a steering malfunction that resulted in a crash. As all four experts relied on the same theory—particle jamming—the court analyzed their exclusion together. *Id.* at 337–38. Applying *Daubert*, the Fourth Circuit held that the experts' testimony that "a significant number of particles" could jam the spool valve was unreliable because (1) the probability of a particle causing a spool jam has never been established, (2) the experts never determined how much force would be determined to crush or shear a lodged particle, (3) the risk of steering malfunction caused by particle jamming is not generally accepted in the engineering community, and (4) the experts never ruled out human error as an alternative cause of the crash. *Id.* at 338.

Buckman v. Bombardier Corp., 893 F. Supp. 547 (E.D.N.C. 1995), an Eastern District of North Carolina decision, illustrates another trial court's application of *Daubert* in the product design area. In *Buckman*, the plaintiff brought a product liability action against Bombardier Corporation, the manufacturer of a *Sea Doo* recreational watercraft. Bombardier moved to exclude evidence offered by the plaintiff's expert witness who testified as to four areas of defects in the *Sea Doo*: (1) the stop-switch malfunction, (2) the lack of rudder and keel, (3) the crashworthiness of the *Sea Doo*, and (4) the lack of a built-in signaling device. The court applied the five factors of *Daubert* to each area of mechanical defect.

With respect to the stop-switch malfunction, the expert conducted a comparative test with the vehicle in question and a similar vehicle fitted with a stop-switch capacitor to determine whether the *Sea Doo* would cut the engine in choppy water. The court found the test to be weak and based on an untested assumption, but nonetheless a scientifically valid exercise of the use of controls and procedures. However, portions of the test that were conducted under dissimilar conditions from those of the accident were ruled invalid. The court did not consider the peer-review factor, finding it inapplicable to the comparative test. The third *Daubert* factor, rate of error, could not be determined through statistical calculations. With respect to objective standards, the expert witness set the standards himself, thus the court found that they were not objective or fair. Finally, there being no relevant scientific community for the comparative test, the court did not consider the last *Daubert* factor.

The court granted the defendant's motion to exclude the rudder and keel redesign theory set forth by the plaintiff's expert. The expert had conducted no testing on the new design. The court found that this "untested guess" at a safer design was the type of hypothetical science *Daubert* sought to exclude.[3] The court similarly granted the defendant's motion to exclude the built-in signaling device redesign theory, because the expert failed to test the built-in signaling device.

In *Pugh v. Louisville Ladder, Inc.*, 361 Fed. Appx. 448, 452–54 (4th Cir. 2010), the Fourth Circuit reviewed a district court's admission of testimony from two engineers who evaluated the structural failure of a ladder. In evaluating these experts' testimony, the court noted that "the proponent of expert testimony does not have the burden to 'prove' anything, but must 'come forward with evidence from which the court can determine that the proffered testimony is properly admissible." *Id.* at 452–53 (citing *Therm-o-Disc*, 137 F.3d at 784). The court noted that defendant, in challenging proffered opinions of an expert, "focused almost entirely on the contention that [the experts'] conclusions were falsifiable." *Id.* at 453–54. Instead of basing its opinion in this area, the district court correctly focused its analysis on whether the opinions were the product of appropriate methodology. *Id.* at 455–56. Having found that the experts' opinions were methodologically valid, the court upheld the district court's admission of them. *Id.* at 455–57.

b. Environmental Engineering / Hydrogeology / Appraisal

The courts of the Fourth Circuit also apply *Daubert* in a straightforward fashion in the environmental engineering context. In *Carroll v. Litton Systems, Inc.*, 47 F.3d 1164 (4th Cir. 1995), *cert. denied*, 516 U.S. 816 (1995), the Fourth Circuit's analysis under Fed. R. Evid. 702 paralleled an analysis for reliability under *Daubert*. The plaintiffs who had obtained drinking water from private wells brought a claim against a manufacturer alleging groundwater contamination at a plant site and surrounding wells between 1967 and 1974. The district court concluded that the testimony of plaintiffs' expert that defendant's contamination entered the residential wells in 1970 was inadmissible under Fed. R. Evid. 702 because it was not based on any evidence that contamination had seeped into the wells in those years. By definition, without such evidence, the scientific testimony was not helpful to the trier of fact.

Further, the district court found the plaintiffs' expert testimony on the amount of contamination in plaintiffs' wells since 1970 inadmissible because his concept and approach regarding the environmental half-life for the contamination was rejected by his peers and subject to an extremely high rate of error. Accordingly, the court concluded that the testimony of both witnesses, as well as the testimony of three physicians who relied, in part, on one of the expert's calculations, was also not sufficiently reliable.

In *Adams v. NVR Homes, Inc.*, 141 F. Supp. 2d 554 (D. Md. 2001), the District of Maryland reviewed several experts under the standards of both *Daubert* and *Kumho Tire*. An engineer's testimony focused on remediation of a contaminated site and its effects on nearby residences. *Id.* at 560. His testimony as to the amount of methane gas during exposure time and after remediation was found relevant since it would be germane to establishing the reasonableness and duration of any sustained emotional injuries. *Id.* at 561. Although the engineer's expert testimony was related to emotional injuries, he was not allowed to render an opinion concerning the duration of plaintiffs'

---

[3] This is not to say that the presentation of hypothetical facts to experts is inappropriate, so long as those facts are established independently by other evidence. *See, e.g., Newman v. Hy-Way Heat Sys., Inc.*, 789 F.2d 269, 270 (4th Cir. 1986) ("It is fixed law that an expert can give his opinion on the basis of hypothetical facts, but those facts must be established by independent evidence properly introduced." (quotation omitted)); *Casey v. Geek Squad Subsidiary Best Buy Stores, L.P.*, 823 F. Supp. 3d 334, 344 (D. Md. Nov. 10, 2011) (same). Indeed, as demonstrated by these cases, the presentation of hypothetical facts to experts has been long accepted.

reasonable "window of anxiety" since he was not a psychologist or a psychiatrist and was not qualified to offer an expert opinion as to any aspect of plaintiffs' mental condition. *Id.*

The *Adams* court also reviewed the admissibility of a certified mapping scientist's testimony. Here, the court found that the scientist's testimony did not fit the plaintiffs' claims, that is, the scientist looked at ground disturbance when the claim centered on quarry activity. *Id.* at 566. In addition, the scientist's testimony was unreliable since it did not utilize the generally accepted scientific methodology, that is, stereographic photographs would have enabled him to see three-dimensional objects, but he only used aerial photographs. *Id.*

The *Adams* court also reviewed the proffered testimony of an experienced and certified real estate appraiser. The court allowed the opinion as to the ten-year effect the stigma associated with environmental contamination would have on the plaintiffs' property values, because it believed that the opinion was grounded on "a reliable basis in the knowledge and experience in the discipline." *Id.* at 567 (citing *Kumho Tire*, 526 U.S. at 149). Although the *Adams* court acknowledged that *Daubert* commands that in-court science must do the speaking and not merely the scientist, it found that the essentially nonscientific discipline of real estate appraisal was sufficiently reliable and contained a reasonable nexus to underlying data to be admissible as expert testimony in this case. *Id.* (citing *Cavallo*, 100 F.3d at 761). Any questioning of the expert's data would go to the weight, not the admissibility, of the testimony. *Id.*

East Tennessee Natural Gas v. 7.74 Acres in Wythe County, Virginia, 228 Fed. App'x 323, 327–28 (4th Cir. 2007), involves an evaluation of the testimony of appraisers, and particularly whether the appraisers used appropriate comparables. After cross-motions to exclude were filed, the court noted that it would need to hear the full expert testimony before deciding whether the experts had used incorrect methodology to determine the highest and best use of the involved property. *Id.* at 328. The judge also observed that, because he was not the trier of fact, he "would be on a very slippery slope to start saying what is a proper comparable and what is not a proper comparable." He concluded: "I am not prepared to say that because the comparables are open to very severe cross-examination, that they're not proper comparables. At this point in time, I think that is an issue for the jury to determine, not the Court." *Id.* The Fourth Circuit affirmed, indicating that neither party actually challenged the methodology used by the other; instead, they made challenges based on data. These challenges could be better evaluated through cross-examination. *Id.* (citing *TFWS, Inc. v. Schaefer*, 325 F.3d 234, 240 (4th Cir. 2003), for the proposition that a data-based, not methodology-based challenge "does not mount a true *Daubert* challenge").

c. Medical Causation

In *Westberry v. Gislaved Gummi AB*, 178 F.3d 257, 262 (4th Cir. 1999), the Fourth Circuit evaluated whether differential diagnosis, or differential etiology, can establish causation absent supporting epidemiological data. The questioned expert concluded that occupational exposure to high levels of talc caused the plaintiff's sinus problems. *Id.* at 264. Following prior Fourth Circuit case law, the court noted that

> Differential diagnosis . . . is a scientific technique of identifying the cause of a medical problem by eliminating the likely causes [of a disease or medical condition] until the most probable one is isolated. . . . A reliable differential diagnosis typically, though not invariably, is performed after "physical examinations, the taking of medical histories, and the review of clinical tests, including laboratory tests" and generally is accomplished by determining the possible causes for the patient's symptoms and then eliminating each of these potential causes until reaching one that cannot be ruled out or determining which of those that cannot be excluded is the most likely.

Id. at 262 (citing *Kannankeril v. Terminix Int'l, Inc.*, 128 F.3d 802, 807 (3d Cir. 1997)).

In *Westberry*, the court excused the expert's inability to quantify the plaintiff's precise exposure to talc, noting that plaintiff's testimony established that he had been exposed to a substantial amount of talc. *Id.* at 264–65. Further supporting the expert's conclusion derived through differential diagnosis was the strong temporal connection between the onset of the plaintiff's exposure to talc and the worsening of the plaintiff's health. *Id.* at 265. The expert indicated that the plaintiff's sinus problems began shortly after his exposure to talc occurred, and the plaintiff's symptoms abated when his contact with talc became less pronounced. *Id.* Additionally, the court noted that even though the expert's differential diagnosis did not completely foreclose all other possible causes of the plaintiff's sinus condition, the expert did make clear that he considered and excluded these conditions. *Id.* at 266. Finally, plaintiff's expert failed to conduct a physical examination of plaintiff and did not speak with any of plaintiff's treating physicians. *Id.* While an expert "may reach a reliable differential diagnosis without personally performing a physical examination," *Kumho Tire* emphasizes that the purpose of Rule 702's gatekeeping function is to "make certain that an expert . . . employs in the courtroom the same level of intellectual rigor that characterizes the practice of an expert in the relevant field." *Id.* (citing *Westberry*, 178 F.3d at 262, and Kumho Tire, 526 U.S. at 152).[4]

In *Cooper v. Smith & Nephew, Inc.*, 259 F.3d 194, 202–03 (4th Cir. 2001), the Fourth Circuit, applying *Westberry*, upheld the exclusion of an expert using a differential-diagnosis methodology for a host of reasons. The plaintiff's medical causation expert testified that a medical device that had been implanted in his back caused a nonunion between two of his vertebrae. *Id.* at 197. The plaintiff's medical causation expert, a practicing orthopedic surgeon, sought to testify that he was of the opinion that the medical device was defective when it was implanted into the plaintiff's back. *Id.* at 198. The expert sought to testify that the medical device was necessarily defective because a nonunion between plaintiff's vertebrae occurred, and that the device's failure necessarily caused the nonunion. *Id.* at 200–01.

The Fourth Circuit upheld the district court's exclusion of this testimony, noting that "*Daubert* requires more than an assertion that if there is a lack of surgical success, there is *ipso facto* a product defect, and hence causation is established. [The expert's] methodology simply failed to provide any medical evidence as to what caused [plaintiff's] injuries . . . rather [he] seems to have inferred causation from the existence of a non-union alone." *Id.* The court noted that defense experts had provided several alternative explanations for plaintiff's nonunion, and while the alternative causes suggested by a defendant normally affect the weight . . . and not the admissibility of an expert's testimony . . . a "differential diagnosis that fails to take serious account of other potential causes may be so lacking that it cannot provide a reliable basis for an opinion on causation." *Id.* (citing *Westberry*, 178 F.3d at 265).

On a related point, *Cavallo v. Star Enterprises*, 892 F. Supp. 756 (E.D. Va. 1995), establishes that case reports alone cannot provide the requisite epidemiological evidence necessary to admit expert evidence. In *Cavallo*, a toxicologist relied on case studies in which people exposed to organic compounds suffered respiratory illnesses. The court held that reliance on case studies alone to form a conclusion was inconsistent with the scientific method. *Id.* at 769. "[C]ase reports are not reliable scientific evidence of causation, because they simply describe reported phenomena without

---

[4] Decisions since *Westberry* evaluating differential diagnosis tend to follow its language closely. *See, e.g.*, *In re Digitek Prods. Liab. Litig.*, 821 F. Supp. 2d 822, 837–839 (S.D. W. Va. 2011) (in a medical products claim, emphasizing *Westberry* factors in conjunction with factors considered in conjunction with two factors discussed in *McClain v. Metabolife Int'l, Inc.*, 401 F.3d 1233, 1240 (11th Cir. 2005), namely (1) whether questionable scientific principles have been used and unsubstantiated analogies drawn; and (2) whether the opinions rely on overreaching or speculative methodologies).

comparison to the rate at which the phenomena occur in the general population or in a defined control group; do not isolate and exclude potentially alternative causes; and do not investigate or explain the mechanism of causation." *Id.* at 765 n.18 (citing *Casey v. Ohio Med. Prods.*, 877 F. Supp. 1380, 1385 (N.D. Cal. 1995)). The Fourth Circuit upheld the exclusion as within the district court's discretion. *See* 100 F.3d at 1159 (4th Cir. 1996).

3. Hybrid Fact-Opinion Testimony

Medical causation evidence routinely opens the door to so-called hybrid fact-opinion testimony. A hybrid fact-opinion witness, such as a treating physician, presents a challenging inquiry to the court in determining whether *Daubert* should apply or not. In *Binakonsky v. Ford Motor Co.*, the Fourth Circuit upheld the district court's decision to allow a medical examiner's testimony regarding physical observations of the body, as well as her opinion as to what caused the trauma. 133 F.3d 281 (4th Cir. 1998). The Fourth Circuit held that *Daubert* did not apply since it pertains to the scientific validity of an expert's methodology and not to a fact witness's findings. In the *Binakonsky* case, the medical examiner did not make her findings as a result of being hired as an expert or prepare her report in preparation for trial. *Id.* at 290. The Fourth Circuit found that the defense was essentially challenging the medical examiner's observations and not her methodology. *Id.* (citing *Freeman*, 118 F.3d at 1016 n.6 (for the proposition that *Daubert* is inapplicable to testimony based on experience and training)). Similar to *Freeman*, discussed above, the *Binakonsky* court draws a distinction between conclusions drawn from observations and opinions based on methodologies, clearly removing the *Daubert* analysis from the former type of testimony.

However, in an earlier case, the Fourth Circuit appeared to be more open to using *Daubert* in hybrid medical testimony cases. In *Benedi v. McNeil-P.P.C., Inc.*, 66 F.3d 1378 (4th Cir. 1995), the Fourth Circuit reviewed the introduction of liver-disease expert testimony under the *Daubert* standard. The defense contended that since the plaintiff's experts did not rely on epidemiological data in forming their opinions, their testimony was inadmissible under *Daubert*. *Id.* at 1384. The *Benedi* court found that *Daubert* did not restrict expert testimony to a particular methodology. *Id.* It held that, "[u]nder the *Daubert* standard, epidemiological studies are not necessarily required to prove causation, as long as the methodology employed by the expert in reaching his or her conclusion is sound." *Id.* The plaintiff's treating physicians based their conclusions on physical observations and medical history. The plaintiff's other experts relied on a similar methodology. The *Benedi* court decided that in light of the medical community's daily use of the same methodologies in diagnosing patients, it would not declare such methodologies invalid and unreliable. *Id.* The Fourth Circuit affirmed the finding by the lower court that the plaintiff's experts satisfied *Daubert*'s test of relevance and reliability. *Id.* at 1385.

The District of Maryland reviewed another chemical-exposure matter in the case of *Comber v. Prologue, Inc.*, 2000 U.S. Dist. LEXIS 16331 (D. Md. 2000). Again, the expert testimony on the long-term sensitivity to chemical vapors remained unsubstantiated. The plaintiff's own doctor testified that he performed no tests, that he could not identify peer-reviewed scientific literature, and that the medical community did not generally accept his diagnosis. *Id.* The *Comber* court correctly recognized that the plaintiff had failed to submit evidence meeting any of *Daubert*'s requirements. *Id.* The *Comber* court also noted that a "host of federal courts" refused to recognize the multiple-chemical-sensitivity syndrome as acceptable scientific evidence under the *Daubert* standard. *Id.*

a. Chemistry

United States v. Bynum, 2000 U.S. Dist. LEXIS 16331 (D. Md. 2000) (citing *Frye v. United States*, 293 F. 1013 (1923)), involved the admission of evidence that had been offered at trial under the *Frye* standard. The government presented two chemists who explained their chromatographic analyses of crack-cocaine samples seized from the defendant. *Bynum*, 3 F.3d at 772 (4th Cir. 1993). The *Bynum* court found that although the testimony had been offered under *Frye*, it met the new *Daubert* standard since the government had adequately explained the hypotheses underlying the technique, listed numerous publications in which the technique had been subjected to peer review, and concluded that gas chromatography enjoys general acceptance in the field of forensic chemistry. *Id.*

In *Cooper v. Laboratory Corp. of America Holdings, Inc.*, 150 F.3d 376, 380 (4th Cir. 1998), the Fourth Circuit examined another report in the field of chemistry and held that an employee's witness was not qualified as an expert in the field of urine alcohol testing since he was not a toxicologist and had no experience in forensic toxicology, beyond a general knowledge of chemistry. The court found that since he could not qualify as an expert in a particular scientific field, he could not testify as an expert under *Daubert*. *Id.*[5] His qualifications were reviewed nonetheless as a technical expert under Fed. R. Evid. 702 and were rejected since the witness did not have education, experience, or training in the field of urine alcohol testing apart from one course thirty years earlier and a general knowledge of chemistry. *Id.* at 380–81.

In *United States v. Daras*, 1998 U.S. App. LEXIS 26552 at *3, 4 (4th Cir. 1998) (unpublished opinion), the criminal defendant challenged the admissibility of a breath test on the alleged grounds that it was not a scientifically reliable device. The *Daras* court reasoned that *Daubert* merely requires that the proffered scientific evidence be relevant and reliable. *Id.* at *4 (citing *Benedi*, 66 F.3d at 1384). The criminal defendant did not challenge the relevance of the breath test in his driving under the influence trial, so the court narrowed its review to the reliability prong of the *Daubert* test. *Id.* The *Daras* court noted that the "reliability of the methodology, that is, the scientific technique by which breathalyzers measure breath alcohol content, is well established." *Id.* (citing *United States v. Reid*, 929 F.2d 990, 994 (4th Cir. 1991)). The government demonstrated the reliability of the equipment and the proper administration of the test. *Id.* at *6, 7. Accordingly, the district court properly admitted and relied on the results of the breathalyzer test.

4. *Evidence Rooted in the Social Sciences*

Where experts' methodologies are rooted in the social sciences, the application of *Daubert* becomes perhaps slightly less predictable. The courts of the Fourth Circuit have conducted lengthy examinations of social science experts in several areas, and the courts' decisions oftentimes appear to be driven by facts particular to individual cases. The rationale for this is likely that these experts often appear in criminal cases in support of the prosecution where the Fourth Circuit has been historically regarded as deferential to the government, or in Lanham Act cases where courts tend to perceive fact finders better positioned to evaluate challenges that are essentially nonmethodological factual disputes.

a. Psychology

Determinations on expert testimony in the field of psychology often turn on whether the proposed expert testimony may be proven unreliable. To this extent, the district court must weigh whether opposing evidence is sufficient to show unreliability. Since *Daubert*, several courts in the

---

[5] Similar cases, where medical or other experts masquerade as toxicologists, occur with certain frequency. *See In re Digitek Prods. Liab. Litig.*, 821 F. Supp. 2d 822, 840 (S.D. W. Va. 2011) (criticizing toxicological evidence offered by physician and a coroner who had a legal background on the grounds that neither expert had a background or experience with the toxicology of a particular substance).

Fourth Circuit have evaluated the admissibility of proposed testimony of experts in the field of psychology.

In *United States v. Powers*, 59 F.3d 1460 (4th Cir. 1995), *cert. denied*, 516 U.S. 1077 (1996), a clinical psychologist's testimony regarding results of an arousal test failed the "scientific validity" prong of *Daubert*. The court cited the four textual *Daubert* factors in concluding that the test results were inadmissible. The test was not generally accepted and produced a high percentage of false negatives. *Id.* at 1471.

In *United States v. Barnette*, 211 F.3d 803 (4th Cir. 2000), the use of a Psychopathy Checklist Revised was challenged as unreliable since it had not been standardized to meet the characteristics of the defendant. The only pieces of evidence put forth to challenge the reliability of the checklist were two articles by another doctor disputing the scientific validity of the checklist. The *Barnette* court held that "[a]bsent evidence indicating more than such a disagreement between professionals, we do not believe the district court needed to go further to evaluate reliability." *Id.* at 816.

In *United States v. Fitzgerald*, 80 F. App'x 857, 860 (4th Cir. 2003) (unpublished), the Fourth Circuit upheld the exclusion of a government forensic psychologist who sought to testify about the methodology and behavior of child molesters. The expert sought to testify that a child molester often begins by engaging in a seemingly innocuous behavior to gain a child's trust and then moves to a borderline behavior to test whether the child is receptive or suspicious. Applying *Daubert*, the Fourth Circuit upheld the exclusion of the expert, finding that the expert had not demonstrated that his theories regarding typical behavior of child molesters had been tested, or how testing supported his proffered theories. Additionally, the court found that the expert had not provided any indication that his work, or the work of authors having similar opinions, had ever been peer reviewed. *Id.* Additionally, the expert did not offer any other support for his opinions. As such, the expert's testimony was appropriately excluded. In a concurrence, Judge Traxler indicated that his decision was motivated by the "abuse of discretion" standard of review, and not by the substance of the proposed expert's testimony. *Id.* at 864–65.

In *Adams v. NVR Homes, Inc.*, 141 F. Supp. 2d 554 (D. Md. 2001), the District of Maryland reviewed the proffered testimony of a psychiatric expert. The court allowed the psychiatrist to testify about his epidemiologic study since its probative value outweighed the danger of unfair prejudice, confusion of the issues, or misleading the jury. *Id.* at 569. In addition, the court concluded that the epidemiologic study was relevant to his opinion that each plaintiff sustained emotional damage as a result of the environmental conditions. *Id.* at 570.

In *Black v. Rhone-Poulenc*, 19 F. Supp. 2d 592 (S.D. W. Va. 1998), the Southern District of West Virginia applied *Daubert* and its two-prong test along with its relevant factors. *Black v. Rhone-Poulenc* involved residents alleging injuries from exposure to chemicals during a fire at a plant. The Southern District of West Virginia held that the research, opinions, and testimony of a clinical psychologist who conducted a study of residents concerning the emotional effects of the chemical release were inadmissible due to flaws in methodology. The court specifically cited lack of record keeping (which precluded independent verification of the study), lack of appropriate peer review, a strong possibility of bias, failure to abide by established protocol, and several aspects of analysis as not satisfying the standard of "good science."

b. Economics

In Lanham Act cases, a plaintiff "asserting an implied falsehood must establish that the advertising tends to deceive or mislead a substantial portion of the intended audience." *PBM Products, LLC v. Mead Johnson & Co.*, 639 F.3d 111, 123 (4th Cir. 2011). This is generally done through the admission of consumer surveys. *Id.* "While there will be occasions when the proffered survey is so flawed as to be completely unhelpful to the trier of fact and therefore inadmissible, such situations will be rare." *Id.* (quoting *AHP Subsidiary Holding Co. v. Stuart Hale Co.*, 1 F.3d 611, 618 (7th Cir. 1993)). In these cases, methodological objections are usually addressed by the trier of fact. *Id.*

Two Fourth Circuit decisions in 2011 evaluated the admission of survey evidence. In *PBM Products*, defendant objected to surveys because, in defendant's view, plaintiff's expert surveyed the wrong universe of respondents. *Id.* The Fourth Circuit upheld the district court's rejection of this challenge on the grounds that plaintiff's challenge was close enough, finding that these critiques went to the weight of the evidence and not the admissibility. *Id.* at 123–34.

In *Belk v. Meyer*, also a Lanham Act case, the Fourth Circuit reviewed a challenge to a district court's decision to admit an expert in the field of the design and conduct of consumer survey research. *See* 679 F.3d 146, 161 (4th Cir. 2012). Plaintiff challenged the expert on the grounds that the expert only had "generalized marketing expertise," noting that "this was the first court case for which [the expert] had designed original research, consumer survey research in [his] career" and that he did not "have an understanding of basic concepts of trade dress." *Id.* at 161–62. The court rejected the challenge on the grounds that the expert's qualifications should be read more broadly through "consider[ing] the proposed experts full range of experience and training" and "not just his professional qualifications." *Id.* at 162 (citing cases including *Kumho Tire*, *United States v. Pansier*, 576 F.3d 726, 737 (7th Cir. 2009), and *Richmond Med. Ctr. for Women v. Herring*, 527 F.3d 128, 134 n. 1 (4th Cir. 2008), *rev'd en banc* 570 F.3d 165 (4th Cir. 2009). In this case, the testimony was reliable enough that any "methodological objections 'are properly addressed by the trier of fact.'" *Id.* at 163 (quoting *PBM Prods., LLC v. Mead Johnson & Co.*, 639 F.3d 111, 123 (4th Cir. 2011)).

c. "Identification" Experts

(1) Polygraph Evidence

In *United States v. Prince-Oyibo*, 320 F.3d 494 (4th Cir. 2003), the Fourth Circuit upheld the exclusion of a polygraph expert. The court noted that, prior to *Daubert*, the Fourth Circuit "consistently maintained a per se rule that the results of an accused's or witness' polygraph test are not admissible to bolster or undermine credibility." *Id.* at 497–98 (citing cases). The court noted that *Daubert* threw into question the continued viability of the Fourth Circuit precedent by "reserving the reliability assessment to the district courts." *Id.* at 498. This said, the *Prince-Oyibo* panel itself declined to find against the *per se* exclusion of polygraph evidence, counseling that only the Fourth Circuit sitting *en banc* could overturn the ban. *Id.* at 501.

Senior Judge Hamilton, in dissent, noted that "numerous courts have recognized that a *per se* rule banning the admission of polygraph evidence is inconsistent with *Daubert*." *Id.* at 505 (citing *United States v. Cordoba*, 104 F.3d 225, 228 (9th Cir. 1997); *United States v. Posado*, 57 F.3d 428, 434 (5th Cir. 1995); *United States v. Piccinonna*, 885 F.2d 1529, 1531–37 (11th Cir. 1989) (rejecting a *per se* ban on the admissibility of polygraph testimony)). In light of these cases, Judge Hamilton harmonized Fourth Circuit precedent on whether there was a *per se* ban on the admissibility of polygraph evidence to bolster or undermine the credibility of a witness, in the end concluding that the majority blatantly ignored changes that *Daubert* had effected on the law. *Id.* at 506. As such, Senior Judge Hamilton concluded that the district court should have given Prince-Oyibo the opportunity to demonstrate that his polygraph evidence was admissible post-*Daubert*. *Id.* at 507.

(2) Fingerprinting

Ostensibly applying *Daubert*, in *United States v. Crisp*, 324 F.3d 261, 265 (4th Cir. 2003), the Fourth Circuit upheld the admission of the government's fingerprinting expert over a defense objection. The defendant argued that the premises underlying fingerprinting evidence have not been adequately tested, that there is no known rate of error for latent fingerprint identifications, that fingerprint examiners operate without a uniform threshold of certainty required for a positive identification, and that fingerprint evidence has not achieved general acceptance in the relevant scientific community. *Id.* at 266. Instead of the usual reference directly to *Daubert*, the Fourth Circuit listed cases standing for the proposition that "[f]ingerprint identification has been admissible as reliable evidence in criminal trials in this country since at least 1911." *Id.*

When the court moved to the usual *Daubert* analysis, the court used the presumption established by the long history of fingerprint evidence being admissible to effectively shift the burden to the defendant to establish the inadmissibility of fingerprint evidence. *Id.* at 268. In applying the *Daubert* factors, the court noted that "while the principles underlying fingerprint identification have not attained the status of scientific law, they nonetheless bear the imprimatur of a strong general acceptance, not only in the expert community, but in the courts as well." *Id.* at 268-69 (citing *United States v. Havvard*, 260 F.3d 597, 601 (7th Cir. 2001) and *United States v. Llera Plaza*, 188 F. Supp. 2d 549, 572–73 (E.D. Pa. 2002)). The court cited approvingly language in *Havvard* indicating "that fingerprinting techniques have been tested in the adversarial system, that the individual results are routinely subject to peer review for verification, and the probability of error is exceptionally low." *Id.* (citing 260 F.3d at 601). Finally, the court emphasized the language in the *Daubert* opinion to the effect that "vigorous cross-examination, presentation of contrary evidence, and careful instruction on the burden of proof are the traditional and appropriate means of attacking shaky but admissible evidence. *Id.* at 270 (citing *Daubert*, 509 U.S. at 596).

Judge Michael's dissent in *Crisp* indicated that the majority's opinion failed to account for the significant changes occasioned by *Daubert* regarding the admissibility of fingerprint evidence. *See* 260 F.3d at 272. Particularly, the dissent noted that Federal Rule of Evidence 702 requires expert testimony to be "the product of reliable principles and methods." "Nothing in . . . *Daubert* suggests that evidence that was admissible under *Frye* is grandfathered in or is free of the more exacting analysis now required." *Id.* (citing *United States v. Saelee*, 162 F. Supp. 2d 1097, 1105 (D. Alaska 2001) (stating that "[t]he fact that [expert] evidence has been generally accepted in the past by courts does not mean that it should be generally accepted now, after *Daubert* and *Kumho*"). The dissent additionally noted that most criminal defendants do not have the resources to hire experts to effectively challenge fingerprint testimony once it is presented, and that the government failed to carry its burden to establish that the *Daubert* factors were fulfilled. *Id.* at 273–74.

Judge Michael's dissent has not persuaded the court to change its position in subsequent cases. The *Crisp* majority's language and methodology has been followed in subsequent opinions, including *United States v. Gary*, 85 F. App'x 908 (4th Cir. 2004). In *Gary*, the court noted that

> In light of *Crisp's* recent approval of the methodology used by the [fingerprint expert] in this case, and [defendant's] failure to provide any persuasive evidence of the expert's lack of qualifications, we find no abuse of discretion in admitting the expert's testimony concerning the latent fingerprint identification evidence.

Id. at 909 (citing *Crisp*, 324 F.3d at 268–69).

(3) Handwriting Analysis

United States v. Crisp also upheld the admission of the government's handwriting expert, who opined that certain handwriting matched a criminal defendant's. *United States v. Crisp*, 324 F.3d 261, 265–66 (4th Cir. 2003). The defendant's challenge to the handwriting expert was similar to his challenge regarding fingerprint evidence: that the basic premises behind handwriting analysis—that no two persons write alike, and that forensic document examiners can reliably determine authorship of a particular document by comparing it to known samples—cannot be tested, and no error rate regarding this technique has been established. *Id.* at 270. In addressing this challenge, the circuit approved the district court's admission of this evidence, noting that the other circuits that have considered the issue of handwriting experts post-*Daubert* have found such evidence admissible. *Id.* at 270 (citing cases from the Third, Sixth, Eighth, and Eleventh circuits). In upholding the admissibility of handwriting evidence, the court noted that the handwriting expert at issue had twenty-four years of experience in performing handwriting analysis and that the examiner had passed numerous proficiency tests establishing that he was a qualified handwriting examiner. *Id.* at 271. As with fingerprint analysis, the court's prime motivation for upholding the admissibility of handwriting analysis was the long history of such evidence being admissible. *Id.* (citing *Robinson v. Mandell*, 3 Cliff. 169, 20 F. Cas. 1027 (D. Mass. 1868)). Finally, the court noted that, to the extent a particular examiner's analysis is "flawed or flimsy, an able defense lawyer will bring that fact to the jury's attention, both through skillful cross-examination and by presenting expert testimony of his own." *Id.* at 271.

Judge Michael's dissent in *Crisp* was premised on the notion that handwriting analysis is not *per se* admissible in the wake of *Daubert*. While engaging in an exhaustive analysis of the *Daubert* factors discounting the post-*Daubert* admissibility of fingerprint evidence, the dissent also noted that some courts have taken the middle-ground position of permitting experts to testify to similarities between handwriting of unknown authorship and that of a known person. *Id.* at 278 (citing *United States v. Rutherford*, 104 F. Supp. 2d 1190, 1193 (D. Neb. 1999) and *United States v. Hines*, 55 F. Supp. 2d 62, 63–64 (D. Mass. 1999)).

(4) Eyewitness Identification

The Fourth Circuit has been skeptical regarding the use of expert witnesses in criminal cases raising a claim of mistaken identification. In *United States v. Davis*, the court upheld a trial judge's decision to exclude the expert testimony. 690 F.3d 226 (4th Cir. 2012). The appellate court cited to its earlier reasoning that "jurors using common sense and their faculties of observation can judge the credibility of an eyewitness identification, especially since deficiencies or inconsistencies in an eyewitness's testimony can be brought out with skillful cross-examination." 690 F.3d at 257 (quoting *United States v. Harris*, 995 F.2d 532, 534–535 (4th Cir. 1993)). The trial judge's decision was upheld both under this reasoning and because "even if it qualified as a proper subject of expert testimony, the probative value of the testimony, which was low, was outweighed by the danger of prejudice or confusing the jury." *Id.*

In *United States v. White*, a criminal defendant sought to admit the testimony of a psychologist who purported to be an expert in the field of eyewitness identification. *See United States v. White*, Case No. 3:07-CR-83, 2007 WL 1768718 (E.D. Va. June 15, 2007), at *4. The government in this case did not challenge the scientific basis for the expert's proposed testimony, but instead focused its challenge on whether the testimony would be helpful to a jury. *Id.* The Eastern District of Virginia judge concluded that he did not believe that the testimony would be helpful because the eyewitness in the case was a trained police officer; that most studies evaluating the reliability (or unreliability) of eyewitness identification were focused on college students; and that common sense and "skillful cross examination" could be used to explore the validity of the identification. *Id.* at *4–7. Accordingly, the court excluded the evidence. *Id.* at *7.

d. Miscellaneous Criminal "Experts"

The courts of the Fourth Circuit have also evaluated the admissibility of "expert" evidence regarding field sobriety tests, gang membership, comparison of individuals shown in photographs, and the expertise of an officer regarding controlled substances. In the case of *United States v. Horn*,

185 F. Supp. 2d 530 (D. Md. 2002), the District of Maryland considered whether the horizontal gaze nystagmus (HGN) test is sufficiently valid under the *Daubert* and *Kumho Tire* standards. In *Horn*, the defendant charged with driving while intoxicated challenged the validity of the HGN test to determine actual blood alcohol content. *Id.* at 533. The *Horn* court noted that the HGN test had been accepted as valid in many other cases but concluded that new developments or evidence may require a reevaluation of the conclusions previously reached by courts that did not have the benefit of more recent information. *Id.* at 536 n.15. "In short, neither science and technology may rest on past accomplishments—nor may the courts." *Id.*

The Fourth Circuit does not permit expert testimony regarding the comparison of persons shown in photographs. In *United States v. Dorsey*, 45 F.3d 809, 812 (4th Cir. 1995), the Fourth Circuit reviewed the application of the *Daubert* standard to the testimony of two forensic anthropologists who would testify that the defendant was not the person shown in bank surveillance photographs. In *Dorsey*, the district court rejected the expert scientific testimony due to its inability to help the trier of fact, noting that "the comparison of photographs is something that can be done by the jury without help from an expert." *Id.* (citing *United States v. Brewer*, 783 F.2d 841, 842 (9th Cir.), *cert. denied*, 479 U.S. 831 (1986)).

Regarding controlled-substance issues, in *United States v. Beasley*, the court noted that the district court did not abuse its discretion by not holding a *Daubert* hearing because the challenged expert's training and experience were clear on the record then before the district court. 495 F.3d 142, 150 (4th Cir. 2007) (stating that the expert's "credentials, which were substantial, included: training in numerous law enforcement courses on identification of narcotics . . . participation as a member of a local narcotics agency in the seizure of cocaine in its various stages on its way to becoming crack cocaine; and witnessing on video the full process of turning powder cocaine into crack cocaine. This training and experience qualified [the expert] to give testimony on the process of making crack cocaine from cocaine powder. Accordingly, the district court did not abuse its discretion in allowing him to testify as an expert, without conducting a Daubert hearing").

In *United States v. Thomas*, No. 10-4725, 2012 WL 2951410, at *4 (4th Cir. July 20, 2012), the Fourth Circuit affirmed a district court's decision to permit a police officer with broad experience working with gangs to testify regarding the history and organization of the Bloods gang, how different gang factions factored into the overall gang hierarchy, and on gang symbols. While noting that "the *Daubert* factors (peer review, publication, potential error rate, etc.) simply are not applicable to this kind of testimony . . . whose reliability depends heavily on the knowledge and experience of the expert, rather than the methodology or the theory behind it." *Id.* at *5. The court noted that the district court had conducted a broad review of the purported expert's training and experience, and its findings were "sufficiently diligent" to warrant upholding its decision to admit the relevant testimony. *Id.*

B. STATE-LAW EXPERT ISSUES

Expert practice in Maryland, Virginia, West Virginia, North Carolina, and South Carolina is largely analogous to practice in the federal courts. In every case where expert testimony is to be used, expert evidence should be thoroughly and adequately developed in discovery and the issue of admissibility should be resolved prior to trial, if at all possible. In order to give the issue of admissibility adequate and meaningful consideration, it should be raised at a hearing under state rules that are analogous to Fed. R. Evid. 104(a), by motion *in limine*, at the pretrial conference, or at a time agreed on by counsel and directed by the court. The admissibility of expert evidence must be challenged during trial. Failing to do so bars a later appeal. *See, e.g., C.B. Fleet Co. v. Smithkline Beecham Consumer Healthcare, L.P.*, 131 F.3d 430 (4th Cir. 1997) (in a false-advertising suit, plaintiff lost right to appeal defendant's use of expert evidence under *Daubert* regarding the reliability of tests that supported its advertising claims because plaintiff failed to challenge the admissibility of the evidence at trial).

Aside from these general concerns, state-specific considerations for the use of expert testimony are discussed in detail below. Speaking generally, Maryland courts apply a *Frye*-derived standard, while the remaining states apply either *Daubert* or what amounts to a close analogue to *Daubert*.

1. Expert Evidence in Maryland State Courts

Maryland applies the *Frye* standard to evaluate the admissibility of expert evidence. In *Reed v. State*, 283 Md. 374, 391 A.2d 364 (1978), the Maryland Court of Appeals adopted the *Frye* test for admissibility of novel scientific evidence. In *Reed* the court made clear that *Frye* sets forth only a legal standard that governs the trial judge's determination of a threshold issue. Testimony based on a technique that is found to have gained general acceptance in the scientific community may be admitted only if the trial judge determines that the proposed testimony will be helpful to the jury and that the expert is properly qualified. *Id.* at 389, 391 A.2d at 372. Applying what is known as the *Frye/Reed* standard, the court must determine that the scientific process or technique is generally accepted within the relevant scientific community. On July 1, 1994, Maryland adopted Rule 5-702 of its Rules of Evidence, modeled after Federal Rule 702. The adoption of this rule, however, did not modify the *Frye/Reed* standard.

Schultz v. State, 106 Md. App. 145, 664 A.2d 60 (Md. 1995), holds that Maryland Rule 5-702 is not intended to overrule *Reed* and other cases adopting the principles enunciated in *Frye*. The required scientific foundation for the admission of novel scientific techniques or principles is left to development through case law. Thus the *Frye/Reed* standard is still the standard utilized in Maryland to determine the admissibility of scientific evidence. 342 Md. 38, 673 A.2d 221 (Md. 1996); *State v. Blackwell*, 408 Md. App. 677, 971 A.2d 296 (Md. 2009) (continuing to apply *Schultz*).

Armstead v. State, 145 Md. App. 27, 801 A.2d 173, *cert. denied*, 369 Md. 661, 802 A.2d 439 (2002), addresses Maryland Code Section 10-915, providing that DNA evidence is admissible to prove identity, and finds that it eliminates the *Frye/Reed* hearing, as well as what the defendant termed the "inverse *Frye/Reed* hearing," to rebut the conclusion that this particular scientific technique has gained general acceptance in the relevant scientific community.

T-Up, Inc. v. Consumer Protection Division involved a judicial review of agency action in pursuing false-advertisement claims relating to products sold as cures or treatments for cancer or immunodeficiency diseases. *Id.* at 154, 664 A.2d at 64 n.3 (quoting Committee Note to Maryland Rule 5-702). Prior Maryland case law held that "a physician may testify as an expert witness, even if that physician is not a specialist in the area." *Id.* at 33, 801 A.2d at 189 (quoting *Radman v. Harold*, 279 Md. 167, 367 A.2d 472 (1977) and *Wolfinger v. Frey*, 223 Md. 184, 162 A.2d 745 (1960)). The *T-Up* court limited that ability to testify, stating "*Radman* does not give a holder of a medical degree carte blanche to opine on any subject having a medical context." *Id.* at 40, 801 A.2d at 191. In the end, the administrative law judge correctly exercised discretion in rejecting a physician as an expert when that physician had not conducted research in the immune disease area, had no formal education in the immune disease area, and had not conducted any systematic study or review of the effects of treatments on patients with immune or autoimmune diseases. *Id.* at 40–41, 801 A.2d at 191.

2. Expert Evidence in North Carolina State Courts

a. General Standards

North Carolina case law recognized factors outside *Frye*'s "general acceptance" rule long before *Daubert* established its test for scientific reliability and relevance. In *State v. Bullard*, 312 N.C. 129, 322 S.E.2d 370 (1984), the North Carolina Supreme Court discussed three factors in evaluating novel scientific evidence. First, the court looked at the witness's qualifications to be an expert. In this area, "the trial judge is afforded wide latitude of discretion when making a determination about the admissibility of expert testimony." *Id.* at 140, 322 S.E.2d at 376. The court cited earlier cases that held that determining the requisite skill of the witness to qualify as an expert falls within the exclusive province of the trial judge and will not be reversed on appeal unless there is "no evidence to support it." *Id.* (citations omitted). Secondly, the court reviewed the witness's scientific testimony for reliability. While not adhering exclusively to the *Frye* formula, the court stated the general rule for admitting new scientific methods is demonstrated accuracy and reliability that has become established and recognized. *Id.* at 146–147, 322 S.E.2d at 380 (citations omitted). Further, when no scientific precedent exists, scientifically accepted reliability based on judicial notice or other scientists' testimony, or both, justifies admission of the testimony of a qualified witness. *Id.* at 148, 322 S.E.2d at 381 (citations omitted). The court analyzed several cases, reviewed the expert's qualifications, and identified factors indicating reliability. The expert's use of established techniques, professional background in the field, use of visual aids before the jury so as not to ask the jury "to sacrifice its independence by accepting [a] scientific hypothesis on faith," and independent research all indicate scientific reliability. *Id.* at 151, 322 S.E.2d at 382. Finally, the court held that "relevant evidence is admissible if it 'has any logical tendency however slight to prove the fact at issue in the case.'" *Id.* at 154, 322 S.E.2d at 384 (citing *State v. Pratt*, 295 S.E.2d 462, 466 (1982)). Clearly, this case adopted factors outside of the *Frye* formula and established a three-part review—that is, qualifications, reliability and relevance—to admit scientific evidence.[6]

North Carolina adopted the *Daubert* test in *State v. Goode*, 341 N.C. 513, 461 S.E.2d 631 (N.C. 1995), a case involving expert testimony on bloodstain patterns. A preliminary assessment of whether the reasoning or methodology underlying the testimony is sufficiently valid and whether it can be properly applied to the facts is required prior to admitting expert testimony at trial. *Id.* at 527, 461 S.E.2d at 639. The court retained the three-factor analysis established in *Bullard*, describing the need for reliability, qualifications, and relevance in turn. "Reliability of a scientific procedure is usually established by expert testimony, and the acceptance of experts within the field is one index, though not the exclusive index, of reliability." *Id.* at 528, 461 S.E.2d at 640 (citing *Pennington*, 393 S.E.2d at 852–53). Reliability may be evidenced by the expert's use of established techniques, professional background in the field, use of visual aids before the jury so as not to sacrifice its independence by accepting the scientific hypothesis on faith, and independent research. *Id.* Once the court has determined the reliability, the next level of inquiry is the expert's qualifications. *Id.* at 529, 461 S.E.2d at 640. In this regard, the expert must, because of her expertise, be in a better position to have an opinion on the subject than the trier of fact. *Id.* (citations omitted). Finally, once qualified, the expert's testimony is still governed by relevancy. *Id.* at 529, 461 S.E.2d at 641. An expert's testimony will be relevant when such testimony can help the jury draw certain inferences from facts because the expert is better qualified than the jury to draw such inferences. *Id.* (citing *Bullard*, 322 S.E.2d at 376). Although *Goode* adopts the *Daubert* standard by reference, it continues to use the three-part test and factors established in earlier North Carolina case law.

b. Expert-Related Rules and Procedural Issues

Rule 26(b)(4) of the North Carolina Rules of Civil Procedure requires a written response to expert witness interrogatories but does not require the deposition of the opposing expert witness

---

[6] The case of *State v. Pennington*, 393 S.E.2d 847 (N.C. 1990), cites *Bullard* for its principles on admitting scientific evidence. *Pennington* also establishes DNA evidence as generally admissible subject to the regular attacks of relevancy, prejudice, impeachment, contamination, and chain of custody.

except by a court order. In practice, a court order is almost never required, and most expert witness depositions are conducted by agreement of counsel.

3. Expert Evidence in South Carolina State Courts

Even though Rule 702 of South Carolina's Rules of Evidence is identical to Fed. R. Evid. 702 and became effective September 3, 1995, South Carolina has not addressed the principles of *Daubert*, nor has it ever explicitly adopted the *Frye* standard. Instead, South Carolina "has employed a less restrictive standard in regard to the admissibility of scientific evidence." *State v. Ford*, 301 S.C. 485, 392 S.E.2d 781, 783 (S.C. 1990). In *State v. Jones*, 273 S.C. 723, 259 S.E.2d 120 (S.C. 1979), the admissibility of scientific evidence depended on whether the expert had relied on scientifically and professionally established techniques. The purpose of this *Jones* standard is to prevent the jury from being misled by the "aura of infallibility" that may surround unproven scientific methods. *State v. Morgan*, 485 S.E.2d 112, 117 (S.C. Ct. App. 1997). If this concern is implicated, the trial court must make a preliminary ruling on reliability before allowing the expert testimony to be admitted in evidence. *Id.* at 118. Reliability and general acceptance may be established by judicial notice, reliance on prior precedent, and evidentiary hearings. *Id.*

In *State v. Dinkins*, 319 S.C. 415, 462 S.E.2d 59 (1995) (decided under S.C. R. Crim. P. 24(a)), the court admitted DNA population-frequency statistics, finding that they would assist the jury in determining whether the defendant was, in fact, the plaintiff's attacker. The jury was then permitted to determine whether the DNA statistics were reliable. The court cited *Daubert* only for the proposition that "vigorous cross-examination, presentation of contrary evidence, and careful instruction on the burden of proof are the traditional and appropriate means of attacking shaky but admissible evidence." The court did not address the *Daubert* standard of reliability.

In *State v. Register*, 323 S.C. 471, 476 S.E.2d 153 (1996), *cert. denied*, 117 S. Ct. 988, 136 L. Ed. 2d 870 (1997), a *Jones* hearing on DNA evidence was not required. Similarly, in *State v. Morgan*, 326 S.C. 503, 485 S.E.2d 112, 117 (S.C. Ct. App. 1997), a *Jones* analysis was held inapplicable to the expert behavioral science testimony of a victim's postincident behavior.

In *State v. Council*, South Carolina again reviewed *Daubert* but declined to adopt it. In so doing, the court stated: "While this Court does not adopt *Daubert*, we find the proper analysis for determining admissibility of scientific evidence is now under the [South Carolina Rules of Evidence]." *State v. Council*, 335 S.C. 1, 28, 515 S.E.2d 508, 518 (S.C.), *cert. denied*, 528 U.S. 1050 (1999). The South Carolina Rule of Evidence at issue in this case was identical to the Fed. R. Evid. 702. *Id.* at 27, 515 S.E.2d at 517–18. In applying the rule, a "trial judge must find the evidence will assist the trier of fact, the expert witness is qualified, and the underlying science is reliable," and should apply the *Jones* factors to determine reliability. *Id.* at 28–29, 515 S.E.2d at 518. On the substantive issues, the trial court properly exercised its discretion in allowing the results of mitochondrial DNA analysis in evidence since, in part, the underlying science has been generally accepted by the scientific community, but disallowed the results of polygraph examinations since they were not generally reliable. *Id.* at 29–30, 34–36, 515 S.E.2d at 518–20.

4. Expert Evidence in Virginia State Courts

The Code of Virginia Section 8.01-401.3A is identical to Fed. R. Evid. 702. However, there is a significant amount of variation in how Virginia courts evaluate expert testimony. The Virginia Supreme Court has expressly declined to adopt the *Frye* test but has not embraced the principles of *Daubert* either. *See Spencer v. Commonwealth*, 393 S.E.2d 609, 621 (Va. 1990), *cert. denied*, 498 U.S. 908 (1990) (Spencer II); *see also O'Dell v. Commonwealth*, 364 S.E.2d 491, 504 (Va. 1988), *cert. denied*, 488 U.S. 871 (1988).

> When scientific evidence is offered, the court must make a threshold finding of fact with respect to the reliability of the scientific method offered, unless it is of a kind so familiar and accepted as to require no foundation to establish the fundamental reliability of the system, such as fingerprint analysis, . . . or unless it is so unreliable that the considerations requiring its exclusion have ripened into rules of law, such as "lie-detector" tests, . . . or unless its admission is regulated by statute, such as blood-alcohol test results, . . .
>
> In making the threshold finding of fact, the court must usually rely on expert testimony. If there is a conflict, and the trial court's finding is supported by credible evidence, it will not be disturbed on appeal. Even where the issue of scientific reliability is disputed, if the court determines that there is a sufficient foundation to warrant admission of the evidence, the court may, in its discretion, admit the evidence with appropriate instructions to the jury to consider the disputed reliability of the evidence in determining its credibility and weight.

Spencer, 393 S.E.2d at 621 (citations omitted).

Though the Virginia Supreme Court has not described in detail the inquiries to be made or factors to be considered when testing whether the reliability of the scientific method has been established, it has alluded to them. For example, in *Spencer v. Commonwealth (Spencer 1)*, 238 Va. 275, 289, 384 S.E.2d 775, 782–83 (1989), the court observed that the witnesses who were experts in their fields testified the technique at issue was reliable, that false positive results were eliminated by using a sufficient number of probes, that the testing was conducted in a reliable manner, that the technique is generally accepted, and that the technique is used in thousands of laboratories.

While the Virginia Supreme Court has not adopted all the features of *Daubert* as the controlling test in Virginia, the court has noted that "[p]rior to *Daubert*, . . . [it] discussed the trial court's role in making a threshold finding of scientific reliability when unfamiliar scientific evidence is offered." *John v. Im*, 263 Va. 315, 322 n.3, 559 S.E.2d 694, 698 n.3 (2002) (citations omitted). Thus, while not dispositive as a test in Virginia, the *Daubert* discussion concerning the factors that compose an analysis of scientific reliability certainly is instructive. *See Hasson v. Commonwealth*, 2006 Va. App. LEXIS 225, at *28 (Va. Ct. App. May 23, 2006). This accords with Virginia's tendency in this area to rely on federal cases to clarify their law. For instance, in *Avent*, the court relied on a federal case to support the finding that, "[f]ingerprint identification has long been recognized by the courts as [an] entirely appropriate [scientific method]." *Avent v. Commonwealth*, 209 Va. 474, 478, 164 S.E.2d 655, 658 (1968) (relying on *Stevenson v. United States*, 380 F.2d 590, 592 (D.C. Cir. 1967)).

"When scientific evidence is offered, the court must make a threshold finding of fact with respect to the reliability of the scientific method offered, unless it is a kind so familiar and accepted as to require no foundation to establish the fundamental reliability of the system, such as fingerprint analysis." *Spencer II*, 240 Va. at 97, 393 S.E.2d at 621. Moreover,

> Wide discretion must be vested in the trial court to determine, when unfamiliar scientific evidence is offered, whether the evidence is so inherently unreliable that a lay jury must be shielded from it, or whether it is of such character that the jury must be left to determine credibility for itself.

Id. at 98, 393 S.E.2d at 621.

Spencer II is suggestive of how Virginia courts would address situations where an expert has not followed accepted practice in conducting his or her inquiry. In the first instance, a party would have the opportunity to use the purported expert's failure to accord with industry standards in an effort to exclude the expert's testimony in its entirety. In some instances, not following an industry standard would likely lead to the testimony being inadmissible as having no adequate factual basis. *See*

Tittsworth v. Robinson, 252 Va. 151, 154, 475 S.E.2d 261, 263 (1996). The trial judge would have discretion to determine whether the purported expert's testimony was sound enough to bring before the jury. *See, e.g., Tarmac Mid-Atlantic, Inc. v. Smiley Block Co.*, 250 Va. 161, 166, 458 S.E.2d 462, 465 (1995) (stating that the admissibility of expert testimony is a matter within the sound discretion of the trial court, subject to an abuse-of-discretion review). If the expert *was* admitted, the party would then have the opportunity to argue before the jury that the expert's testimony was not worth much as he failed to follow accepted industry standards. *Accord Spencer II*, 240 Va. at 98, 393 S.E.2d at 621. As such, an expert's failure to follow accepted industry guidelines could go to *both* admissibility and weight.

Tarmac Mid-Atlantic, Inc. v. Smiley Block Co., 458 S.E.2d 462 (Va. 1995), illustrates these principles. In *Tarmac*, a buyer sought to introduce expert testimony, based on tests conducted on various samples of the seller's product, that the product supplied by the seller did not conform to industry standards. The Virginia Supreme Court stated that

> Expert testimony is admissible in civil cases to assist the trier of fact, if the evidence meets certain fundamental requirements, including the requirement that it be based on adequate foundation.... Expert testimony is inadmissible if it is speculative or founded on assumptions that have no basis in fact.... In addition, such testimony should not be admitted unless the trial court is satisfied that the expert has considered all the variables bearing on the inferences to be drawn from the facts observed.... Finally, the trial court should refuse to admit expert testimony unless there is proof of a similarity of conditions existing at the time of the expert's tests and at the time relevant to the facts at issue.

Id. at 465–66 (citations omitted).

In *Tarmac*, the product was the same at the time of its shipment as at the time of the expert's testing. There was no positive evidence to show any alteration of the product or the intermixture of foreign materials. Further, the expert had considered and excluded other variables that would affect his conclusions. The court held that there was a sufficient foundation for the admission of the expert's testimony.

As in federal court, testimony premised on speculation is inadmissible. In *Tittsworth v. Robinson*, 252 Va. 151, 475 S.E.2d 261 (Va. 1996), a driver suffered back injuries after a rear-end collision and brought a negligence claim against the driver of the vehicle that had been following him. An expert witness for the defense relied on experiments of similar types of rear-end collisions to conclude that the plaintiff driver could not have received the injuries from the accident as he alleged. The court addressed several requirements in determining the admissibility of this expert testimony:

> Testimony cannot be speculative or founded upon assumptions that have an insufficient factual basis.... [The testimony will be inadmissible] if the expert has failed to consider all the variables that bear upon the inferences to be deduced from the facts observed.... Further, where tests are involved, such testimony should be excluded unless there is proof that the conditions existing at the time of the test and at the time relevant to the facts at issue are substantially similar.

Id. at 263. Because the expert's testimony did not meet these fundamental requirements, the court ruled that it should have been excluded.

5. *Expert Evidence in West Virginia State Courts*

West Virginia courts apply *Daubert* to situations where the scientific or technical basis for expert testimony cannot be judicially noticed and a hearing must be held to determine the reliability of the testimony. In *Wilt v. Buracker*, 191 W. Va. 39, 443 S.E.2d 196 (1993), *cert. denied*, 511 U.S. 1129 (1994), a West Virginia state court ruled that *Daubert*'s analysis of Fed. R. Evid. 702, which is identical to Rule 702 of the West Virginia Rules of Evidence, should be followed in analyzing the admissibility of expert testimony.

The trial court's initial inquiry must consider whether the testimony is based on an assertion or inference derived from scientific methodology. Moreover, the testimony must be relevant to a fact in issue. Further assessment should then be made in regard to the expert's reliability by considering its underlying scientific methodology and reasoning. This includes an assessment of (a) whether the scientific theory and its conclusion can be and have been tested; (b) whether the scientific theory has been subject to peer review and publication; (c) whether the scientific theory's actual or potential rate of error is known; and (d) whether the scientific theory is generally accepted within the scientific community. *Id.* at 46, 443 S.E.2d at 203.

In *Wilt*, the willingness-to-pay studies offered by the plaintiffs' expert in support of hedonic damages had no relevance to a calculation of damages for the loss of enjoyment of life. Moreover, without a detailed explanation of the studies' methodologies, the expert testimony would not meet the reliability standard.

Importantly, whatever the evidentiary criteria may be in West Virginia's courts, crucial factors governing all evidentiary standards are that, in civil cases, West Virginia has no intermediate appellate courts, and, additionally, there is no mandatory right of appeal. Insofar as the trial court commits error in applying *Daubert*, a party may nevertheless have difficulty securing an appeal.

Under *Mayhorn v. Logan Medical Foundation*, 193 W. Va. 42, 454 S.E.2d 87 (W. Va. 1994), it was proper for the testifying expert to base his opinion on the report of another expert, even though the author of the report came to a different conclusion than the testifying expert, since the basic methodology employed by the testifying expert was scientifically valid and properly applied.

In *State v. Beard*, 194 W. Va. 740, 461 S.E.2d 486 (W. Va. 1995), the West Virginia Supreme Court cautioned that its switch from the *Frye* general acceptance standard to the *Daubert/Wilt* standard did not change its prior rulings on the inadmissibility of polygraph tests. "The reliability of such examinations is still suspect and *not* generally accepted within the relevant scientific community." *Id.* at 747, 461 S.E.2d at 493 (emphasis in original).

In *Gentry v. Mangum*, 195 W. Va. 512, 466 S.E.2d 171 (1995), a police officer was qualified to give expert testimony regarding whether a sheriff's failure to train deputies created unsafe working conditions. Such testimony did not present the kind of "junk science" problem that *Daubert/Wilt* was meant to address. Thus, it was not subject to *Daubert* analysis. The question of admissibility under *Daubert/Wilt* arises only if it is first established that the testimony deals with "scientific knowledge." In order to qualify as scientific knowledge, an inference or assertion must be derived by the scientific method. It is the circuit court's responsibility initially to determine whether the expert's proposed testimony amounts to "scientific knowledge."

In *Watson v. Theo Alloys Int'l, Inc.*, 209 W. Va. 234, 545 S.E.2d 294 (2001), the court reviewed a technical knowledge expert's testimony for admissibility. The court recognized that its prior holding in *Gentry* limited *Daubert* and *Wilt* to evaluations of scientific knowledge. *Id.* at 239, 545 S.E.2d at 299. The court also acknowledged that the United States Supreme Court, through *Kumho Tire*, had generally considered testimony in the field of engineering as technical rather than scientific. *Id.* at 240, 545 S.E.2d at 300. The West Virginia Supreme Court held that "unless an engineer's opinion is derived from the methods and procedures of science, his or her testimony is generally considered technical in nature, and not scientific. Therefore, a court considering the admissibility of such evidence should not apply the gatekeeper analysis set forth by [*Wilt* and *Gentry*]." *Id.* at 241, 545 S.E.2d at 301. From this case, it is evident that West Virginia has not adopted *Kumho Tire* and has continued to limit *Daubert* to scientific-evidence review.

In *State v. Leep*, 212 W. Va. 57, 569 S.E.2d 133 (2002), West Virginia reviewed the use of the *Frye* test over the *Daubert* factors with respect to scientific evidence. Here, the court concluded that *Frye*'s general acceptance standard was obsolete and was replaced by the judicial progression of *Daubert*, *Wilt*, *Gentry*, and Rule 702 of the Federal and West Virginia Rules of Evidence. *Id.* at 67, 569 S.E.2d at 143. However, the lower court's use of the *Frye* standard to determine the admissibility of scientific evidence fell within its discretion, since the *Frye* standard was much more onerous than the "reliable and relevant" standard presently applicable. *Id.*

In *State ex rel. Wiseman v. Henning*, 2002 W. Va. LEXIS 149 (2002), the West Virginia Supreme Court clarified the examination to be conducted by trial courts in making expert-witness decisions. The court reviewed West Virginia's case law on expert witnesses beginning with Rule 702 of the West Virginia Rules of Evidence, *Wilt*, and *Gentry*. With regard to the reliability of expert testimony, the court stated that "[w]hen a trial court examines the reliability of an expert's scientific testimony, the court should examine the soundness of the principles or theories, and the reliability of the process or method used to derive those principles or theories." *Id.* at *12. As *Gentry* held, "[t]he problem is not to decide whether the proffered evidence is right, but whether the science is valid enough to be reliable." *Id.* (quoting *Gentry*, 195 W. Va. at 523, 466 S.E.2d at 182). Although the expert's opinion that a cancer may be triggered by trauma may be novel and unorthodox, there was a sufficient degree of reliability underlying the formation of the opinion to make it reliable and admissible. *Id.* at *14.[7]

---

[7] This article is in part a revision of articles appearing in prior versions of this monograph. However, all errors and/or omissions are those of the current author.

CHAPTER V
EXPERT EVIDENCE IN THE FIFTH CIRCUIT

by

Clifton T. Hutchinson
K&L Gates
1717 Main Street, Suite 2800
Dallas, Texas 75201
(214) 939-5500

The Fifth Circuit pioneered the use of the Federal Rules of Evidence in careful gatekeeping of expert testimony[1] and continues to closely examine expert-opinion evidence following the guidelines of the Supreme Court and amended Rule 702. State courts within the circuit have adopted *Daubert* gatekeeping, following the federal guidelines or their own formulation of relevant factors.

A. KEY FIFTH CIRCUIT DECISIONS APPLYING *DAUBERT*, *KUMHO*, AND *JOINER*

Since the last monograph on this topic, the Fifth Circuit has frequently addressed issues with the admissibility of expert evidence, addressing a panoply of actual and claimed areas of specialized knowledge. The court consistently has applied the Supreme Court trilogy.

1. Qualifications

While questions regarding expert qualifications are less common after *Daubert*, a number of Fifth Circuit cases have addressed arguments regarding a witness's expertise. In *Huss v. Gayden*, 571 F.3d 442 (5th Cir. 2009), defendants proffered an expert board certified in internal medicine to opine that a drug did not cause plaintiff's heart condition. The trial court excluded the expert for lack of experience or training as to the cause of the disease; the expert was neither a cardiologist nor a toxicologist. The Fifth Circuit reversed, ruling that the expert need not have board certifications in radiology or toxicology to explain to the jury why certain medical studies did not establish a causal link, because the topic was of a general nature. *Id.* at 455. In a Katrina damage case, *Nunez v. Allstate Ins. Co.*, 604 F.3d 840 (5th Cir. 2010), the court excluded plaintiff's damages expert because his expertise consisted of a seven-day training course and one on-line self-study course, and he lacked training in the software used by Allstate to estimate damage. The court noted that four other judges in the Eastern District of Louisiana had excluded the expert, *inter alia*, for a lack of requisite qualifications. *Id.* at 848.

---

[1] *See, e.g.*, *Eymard v. Pan Am. World Airways (In re Air Crash Disaster at New Orleans, La.)* 795 F.2d 1230, 1234 (5th Cir. 1986) ("It is time to take hold of expert testimony in federal trials"); *Viterbo v. Dow Chem. Co.*, 826 F.2d 420 (5th Cir. 1987); *Brock v. Merrell Dow Pharmaceuticals, Inc.*, 874 F.2d 307 (5th Cir.), *modified*, 884 F.2d 166 (5th Cir. 1989).

2. *Methodology*

Daubert instructed federal courts to closely scrutinize the expert's methodology in arriving at his or her opinion. Thus the reliability of the methodology is frequently the focus of gatekeeping, as reflected in a number of recent Fifth Circuit opinions.

a. Methodology—Toxicology

Toxicology was often a topic for expert gatekeeping prior to *Daubert*,[2] and recent Fifth Circuit opinions reflect the type of careful analysis that has been the hallmark of the court with such testimony. In *Paz v. Brush Engineered Materials, Inc.*, 555 F.3d 383 (5th Cir. 2009), the plaintiff claimed to have contracted beryllium sensitization and chronic beryllium disease ("CBD") from exposure in his workplace. But plaintiffs' expert's diagnosis of CBD was based on an inaccurate assumption regarding pathology; in fact, the plaintiff did not have the markers required by scientific literature to diagnose the disease. Additionally, the expert in her own treatise on beryllium exposures, noted that beryllium sensitivity was merely a precursor to clinical illness, thus not a present injury according to the court. Hence the plaintiffs had no compensable injury, and their claims were properly dismissed.

In *Wells v. SmithKline Beecham Corp.*, 601 F.3d 375 (5th Cir. 2010), the plaintiff alleged that the drug he took for Parkinson's disease caused him to become a pathologic gambler. The plaintiff proffered three experts, but, in their depositions, the three witnesses agreed that the scientific literature did not establish a causal relationship. The experts relied on case studies, which, though not *per se* inadmissible, do not establish causation absent epidemiological support. Thus there was insufficient science to support the claim. *Id.* at 381 and n.33 (*quoting Rosen v. Ciba-Geigy Corp.*, 78 F.3d 316, 319 (7th Cir. 1996)("Law lags science, it does not lead it")).

To sustain a toxic tort claim, a plaintiff must provide evidence of the level of exposure to a substance that is harmful and evidence that the plaintiff was exposed to such quantities. *Seaman v. Seacor Marine L.L.C.*, 326 F. App'x 721, 723 (5th Cir. 2009) (*quoting Allen v. Pa. Eng. Corp.*, 102 F.3d 194, 199 (5th Cir. 1996)). In *Seaman*, the plaintiff claimed exposure to shipboard hydrocarbons, in particular a substance named Ferox, caused his bladder cancer. But the plaintiff's expert had no information about the duration, concentration, or other circumstances of the plaintiff's exposure to Ferox, and had no scientific literature showing a statistically significant link between Ferox and bladder cancer specifically. *Id.* at 726. The expert's testimony was "sadly lacking" and did not "come close to either general or specific causation." *Id.* at 728.

LeBlanc v. Chevron USA, Inc., 396 F. App'x 94 (5th Cir. 2010), is notable for the court's careful analysis of the scientific literature purportedly supporting general causation. The plaintiffs claimed their decedent contracted myelofibrosis with myeloid metaplasia ("MMM") from exposure to benzene. Their expert's scientific studies all had deficiencies, however, and could not show causation: some studies were not statistically significant; some were nonspecific and did not assess benzene alone; some expressly disclaimed a causal connection; and some were not scientific evidence at all but merely secondary literature. *Id.* at 99–100. The court also rejected the argument that the expert could establish causation based on his clinical experience without support from scientific literature. *Id.* at 100–01.

Wackman v. Rubsamen, 602 F.3d 391 (5th Cir. 2010), was an appeal from a wrongful death verdict against a defendant for morphine poisoning of an elderly cancer patient. The defendant argued that the plaintiff's expert's opinion that morphine caused death was unreliable, *inter alia*, because a liver toxicology test was affected by the presence of embalming fluid. But there was no evidence the embalming fluid would cause morphine levels to appear higher, and the decedent had a mor-

---

[2] *See, e.g.*, *Christophersen v. Allied Signal, Inc.*, 939 F.2d 1106 (5th Cir. 1991) (en banc).

phine level fourteen times higher than that reported in other morphine poisoning cases. The court determined that the alleged "analytical gaps" in the expert's testimony did not render the opinion inadmissible.

b. Methodology—Damages

Texas federal courts have conducted numerous intellectual property trials, and, not surprisingly, these cases have presented expert-evidence issues for the Fifth Circuit. In *MGE UPS Systems, Inc. v. GE Consumer and Indus., Inc.*, 622 F.3d 361 (5th Cir. 2010), the plaintiff sought damages for copyright infringement for software used in power-supply machines. The plaintiff's expert presented two theories for recovery, a calculation of MGE's lost profits and a calculation of a hypothetical reasonable royalty, but the district court struck both theories. In response to the ruling, MGE offered its general manager to testify as to reasonable royalty damages. Instead of hypothesizing a royalty to which the parties would have agreed, the witness only testified as to the royalty MGE would ask to *prevent* a competitor from entering the market, which the court found to be an inappropriate measure. *Id.* at 367 and n.2.

CQ, Inc. v. TXU Mining Co., 565 F.3d 268 (5th Cir. 2009), involved a breach of contract and trade-secret claim in connection with a coal-cleaning facility. The plaintiffs' expert calculated damages based on a reasonable royalty the plaintiffs might have negotiated for the use of their confidential information. The court ruled that the expert's reasoning was too speculative, requiring assumptions that the parties would have negotiated a long-term license absent breach of a confidentiality agreement. Such a hypothetical license "based on speculation and conjecture" could not reliably measure the plaintiffs' damages. *Id.* at 278–79.

Of course, a party should object to any improper damage-calculation methodology at trial, if not before. In *Garriott v. NCsoft Corp.*, 661 F.3d 243 (5th Cir. 2011), the plaintiff's expert measured damages for breach of a stock option agreement by valuing the stock after a dramatic post-breach price rise. The defendant argued on appeal that use of post-breach stock appreciation was an improper methodology, but had failed to object at trial, and the matter was not plain error so as to be considered for the first time on appeal. Additionally, even had there been a timely objection, the plaintiff adduced sufficient evidence to support the calculation, so it was not too speculative to be admissible.

c. Methodology—Statistics

Two Fifth Circuit opinions address the statistical methodology of regression analysis,[3] a technique commonly used by econometric experts to address damages and other issues. In *United States v. Valencia*, 600 F.3d 389 (5th Cir. 2010), the defendants were accused of filing false reports in order to manipulate natural-gas markets. The defendants questioned whether their alleged actions could have affected certain published indices, thus their allegedly false reports were not material. The government produced an expert who compared trade data with the published indices and found that removal of defendants' false trades *did* affect published figures. The defendants argued that the expert failed to employ a multiple-regression analysis to verify that a causal connection existed between the defendants' reports and published numbers. In this case, though, proof of the causal relationship was not essential; the government had only to prove defendants' actions were important to the publishers of the indices, not that they actually changed the numbers. *Id.* at 427–38. So, a regression analysis to eliminate all confounding or contributory factors was not necessary.

---

[3] *See* Daniel L. Rubinfeld, *Reference Guide on Multiple Regression* in REFERENCE MANUAL ON SCIENTIFIC EVIDENCE 303 (3d ed. Federal Judicial Center 2011).

In securities cases, a regression analysis called an event study is often used to correlate disclosure of information with a fluctuation in stock price. The expert in *Fener v. Operating Engineers Construction Ind. v. Misc. Pension Fund (Local 66)*, 579 F.3d 401 (5th Cir. 2009), used an event study to show causation between a disclosure of a newspaper's allegedly false circulation reports and stock declines. The disclosure press release had multiple parts, however, some unrelated to the alleged fraud. The plaintiffs were required to unbundle the various representations in their analysis and show that the specific disclosures at issue caused the decline. *Id.* at 409. The expert's event study treated the press release as one event, though, and did not separately examine the culpable disclosure. Thus the study could not be used to support loss causation, and the expert's opinion was insufficient.

d. Methodology—Valuation

Expert property appraisal was at issue in two recent circuit opinions related to tax claims. In *Whitehouse Hotel L.P. v Comm'r*, 615 F.3d 321 (5th Cir. 2010), the taxpayer claimed a charitable deduction for the donation of a historic-preservation easement burdening the Maison Blanche building in New Orleans. The IRS disallowed much of the deduction and imposed a penalty, relying on its expert's opinion that valued the easement at zero. The Fifth Circuit reversed and remanded to the Tax Court. The circuit court ruled that the government's expert, and the Tax Court, improperly failed to consider the effect of the easement on a contiguous building that was to be combined with the Maison Blanche. The taxpayer also argued that the government's appraiser should be excluded for failing to comply with the Uniform Standards of Professional Appraisal Practice (USPAP), but the court ruled that any such lack of compliance was relevant to the weight to be accorded the expert's report, not to its admissibility. *Id.* at 331–32.

Levy v. United States, 402 F. App'x 979 (5th Cir. 2010), concerned the valuation of raw land for estate tax purposes. The estate moved to exclude the government's expert for using purchase offers as part of the basis for valuation and for assuming the property would be rezoned. But offers of purchase are "admissible as evidence of fair market value when they are part of ongoing negotiations resulting in a contract with substantially the same terms." *Id.* at 982. Moreover, the rezoning was foreseeable, because, *inter alia*, it was anticipated in the city's comprehensive land-use plan. Accordingly, the trial court properly admitted the expert testimony.

B. DECISIONS IN THE FEDERAL DISTRICT COURTS

1. Texas Cases

a. Expert Qualifications

The focus of *Daubert* is on relevance and reliability, and Texas federal courts recognize that the admissibility threshold for expert qualifications is relatively low, as illustrated by *Raytheon Co. v. Indigo Sys. Corp.*, 598 F. Supp. 2d 817, 819 (E.D. Tex. 2009), which concerned the alleged theft of trade secrets for infrared imaging equipment. The defendant tendered an expert who had worked with the specific technology only on one project, forty years previously. The court found, however, that the expert had sufficient experience with similar technology that was relevant to the trade-secret claims.

In some instances, more specific knowledge is required to qualify the expert. In *Hopper v. M/V UBC Singapore*, 2010 WL 2787806 (S.D. Tex. July 14, 2010), the plaintiffs' engineering expert opined as to the speed of a vessel and the dynamics of an impact with a drowning victim. The expert's background in general mechanical engineering, though, did not qualify him to address the areas of hydrodynamics and maritime accident reconstruction that were relevant to the case. Also, his opinions were based on assumptions refuted by the undisputed evidence, so his testimony was not sufficiently reliable to assist the trier of fact.

The question of the need for specialized expertise arose in *Suzlon Wind Energy Corp. v. Shippers Stevedoring Co.*, 662 F. Supp. 2d 623 (S.D. Tex. 2009), which involved a fire during welding work on a wind turbine. The plaintiff's expert had no experience with welding or with wind turbines, but he was certified as a fire and explosion investigator and had conducted investigations that involved welding as the cause or origin. *Id.* at 665–66. The court ruled that his qualifications and experience as a fire investigator were sufficient.

In patent infringement cases, only an expert with "ordinary skill in the art" may offer expert testimony on technical matters. *See Byrne v. Wood, Herron & Evans, LLP*, 450 F. App'x 956, 962–63 (Fed. Cir. 2011). The defendant's expert in *Wright Asphalt Prods. Co. v. Pelican Refining Co.*, Civil Action No. H-09-1145 (S.D. Tex. May 29, 2012), held a Ph.D. and had forty years of experience in machinery and manufacturing. But the expert had no direct experience working as a binder formulator of asphalt mixtures, which was the product at issue. The court had ruled at a prior *Markman* hearing that approximately a decade of experience working in a binder lab would be necessary to qualify as a binder formulator. The expert could establish only about five weeks of work in asphalt formulation, so he was not qualified to provide technical testimony on the patents at issue.

The expert in *In re Texans CUSO Ins. Group, LLC*, 426 B.R. 194 (Bankr. N.D. Tex. 2010), presented opinions on the lost-profit damages of an insurance company. The expert held no insurance licenses and had no prior experience in the insurance industry, but he was a CPA and a certified fraud examiner with experience in the calculation of financial damages, so the court found him qualified. *See also Tesco Corp. v. Weatherford Int'l, Inc.*, 750 F. Supp. 2d 780, 795 (S.D. Tex. 2010) (expert with three degrees in engineering was qualified to testify on pipe-handling devices, although he had no education or experience specific to the type of equipment at issue). *But see MGM Well Services, Inc. v. Mega Lift Systems, LLC*, No. H-05-1634 (S.D. Tex. Jan. 16, 2007) (Ph.D. electrical engineer who had worked on oilfield equipment for Conoco was held unqualified because he did not have experience with the plunger-lift device at issue).

b. Procedural Issues

A motion to strike opposing experts on procedural grounds was considered in *Cooper v. Wal-Mart Transp., LLC*, 662 F. Supp. 2d 757 (S.D. Tex. 2009). The plaintiff identified two physician experts, who were employed by the Department of Veterans Affairs. But such employees may not provide expert opinions without the permission of the VA, and the VA denied Wal-Mart's requests for depositions. The trial court considered the factors set out in *Campbell v. Keystone Aerial Surveys, Inc.*,[4] analogizing the issue to late expert designations. The court noted that there was scant evidence as to the importance of the witnesses, and Wal-Mart would be prejudiced if they were allowed to testify without being deposed, so the court granted the motion to strike the experts. Similarly, the district court rejected late expert designations in *Rimkus Consulting Group, Inc. v. Cammarata*, Civil Action No. h-07-0405 (S.D. Tex. May 7, 2009). The plaintiff claimed new facts learned during discovery made clear the need for the experts, but the court found that the plaintiff did not explain such facts or establish that the proposed testimony was so important as to "*singularly* override the

---

[4] 138 F.3d 996, 1000 (5th Cir. 1998) ("(1) the importance of the witness's testimony; (2) the prejudice to the opposing party if the witness is allowed to testify; (3) the possibility that a continuance would cure potential prejudice; and (4) the explanation given for the failure to identify the witness").

enforcement of local rules and scheduling orders." *Id.* (*quoting Betzel v. State Farm Lloyd's*, 480 F.3d 704, 707–08 (5th Cir. 2007)).

c. Helpfulness

Expert testimony on general principles may be helpful in some instances if the opinion serves to educate the jury. But such testimony must be relevant to the issues in the case. In *Rolls-Royce Corp. v. Heros, Inc.*, 2010 WL 184313 (N.D. Tex. Jan. 14, 2010), Rolls-Royce claimed misappropriation of trade secrets, and Heros proffered an aviation expert to discuss FAA regulation and related industry safety. But the safety of the industry and an understanding of it would not assist the trier of fact in resolving any fact issue, and the court excluded that opinion. *Id.* at *6. The court did allow the expert's opinions regarding the FAA approval process.

d. Methodology Cases

Damages. A number of Texas federal court opinions addressed damages in intellectual property cases. In *IP Innovation LLC v. Red Hat, Inc.*, 705 F. Supp. 2d 687 (E.D. Tex. 2010), the plaintiff's expert invoked the "entire market value rule," premised on the theory that the patented apparatus substantially created the value of the component parts of the product. But most of the defendants' sales came from products that did not include the patented feature. The expert never tried to factor out such unrelated sales, and this methodological flaw rendered his opinion unreliable. *Id.* at 689–90. Moreover, the expert used an inflated royalty rate based on generic industry studies rather than specific prior royalty rates for the patents-in-suit. *Id.* at 691. The court precluded the expert's opinion. In *Mirror Worlds, LLC v. Apple, Inc.*, 784 F. Supp. 2d 703 (E.D. Tex. 2011), the plaintiff's expert based his damages calculation on a hypothetical royalty negotiation. But the expert evaluated damages as to the plaintiff's entire patent portfolio, not on a per-patent basis. *Id.* at 725. Moreover, although the plaintiff claimed it did not apply the entire market value rule, "it undisputedly used the entire market value of the accused commercial products in calculating its royalty base—and the accused products contain several features, both accused and non-accused." *Id.* at 726. The plaintiff could not apportion damages by simply giving a "haircut" to the hypothetical royalty rate. Accordingly, the expert did not provide a sufficient evidentiary record to support the damage award. *Id.* at 727. *See also Versata Software Inc. v. SAP America, Inc.*, Case No. 2:07-CV-153 CE (E.D. Tex. Sept. 9, 2011) (rejecting expert calculation that applied 93 percent royalty to defendant's total revenue).

Interplan Architects, Inc. v. C. L. Thomas, Inc., No. 4:08-CV-03181 (S.D. Tex. Oct. 9, 2010) concerned a claim for copyright infringement of architectural plans. The plaintiff offered an expert to opine on the defendants' gross revenues, which he calculated based on the total revenue of the defendants' convenience stores that allegedly used the infringing architectural designs. But the expert did not try to determine what portion of a store's gross revenue was attributable to the architectural design, therefore his methodology and the resulting calculation were unreliable.

Texas federal courts have expressed different views on the admissibility of expert opinion based on "litigation related" intellectual property licenses. In *Spreadsheet Automation Corp. v. Microsoft Corp.*, 587 F. Supp. 2d 794, 800-01 (E.D. Tex. 2008), the court held that an expert may not use evidence of royalty licenses obtained in settlements or under threat of litigation to calculate a hypothetical reasonable royalty. *See also Fenner Investments Ltd. v. Hewlett-Packard Co.*, No. 6:08-CV-273 (E.D. Tex. April 28, 2010) (royalties paid to avoid litigation are not a reliable indicator of the value of a patent). Judge Davis in *ReedHycalog UK, Ltd. v. Diamond Innovations Inc.*, 727 F. Supp. 2d 543 (E.D. Tex. 2010), rejected a bright-line rule in favor of a case-by-case analysis of the litigation licenses. The evidence in *ReedHycalog* consisted of five litigation licenses, which were consistent with nine nonlitigation licenses. The plaintiff agreed not to identify the licenses as resulting from litigation, so the judge ruled there would be no prejudice to their admission. *Id.* at 546–47.

The expert's damages calculation should match the theory of recovery. *Kozak v. Medtronic, Inc.*, 512 F. Supp. 2d 913 (S.D. Tex. 2007) involved a claim for misappropriation of trade secrets, but the plaintiff's expert offered a calculation based on a breach of contract claim using a contractual royalty rate. *Id.* at 916–17. The expert did not analyze such things as the actual loss due to the use of the trade secrets, the defendant's profits from such use, or a reasonable royalty for the use. The plaintiff's explanation that trade-secret damages "harmonized" with contract damages was merely a "post hoc rationalization" of the expert's opinion, which the court rejected.

In a personal injury case, calculation of lost-income damages begins with the gross earnings of the injured party at the time of the injury. *Culver v. Slater Boat Co.*, 722 F.2d 114, 117 (5th Cir. 1983) (en banc). In *Hopper v. M/V UBC Singapore*, 2010 WL 2787806 (S.D. Tex. July 14, 2010), the plaintiffs' economic expert used an earnings figure provided by the plaintiffs' counsel, even though the expert had actual payroll information showing less income. Moreover, he failed to deduct taxes and expenses as required by *Culver*. Thus his methodology was "woefully inadequate" and unreliable.

A review of expert testimony on punitive damages was one of a number of gatekeeping challenges addressed in *Burton v. Wyeth-Ayerst Labs.*, 513 F. Supp. 2d 708 (N.D. Tex. 2007). The plaintiffs' expert offered a schedule of financial calculations showing various punitive-damage awards as a percentage of certain of the defendant's financial measurements, such as net worth, total assets, and net income. *Id.* at 718. The court rejected the schedule to the extent it suggested a range of punitive damages to the jury. The expert chose the numbers because they "appeared" to him to be "significant," which the court stated was an improper basis for his testimony. The court also rejected as random speculation the expert's opinion that a punitive award of in excess of $1 billion would not jeopardize the defendant.

e. Disqualification

Lake Cherokee Hard Drive Technologies, LLC. v. Bass Computers, Inc., Case No. 2:10-CV-216-JRG (E.D. Tex. Mar. 5, 2012), presented an interesting issue of an expert witness with confidential information of the opposing party. In this patent infringement lawsuit, the plaintiff sought to retain as a consultant and potential testifying expert the inventor of the patents *sub judice* and a former senior director of a defendant. The Fifth Circuit applies a two-step analysis in such cases, questioning (1) whether the opposing party had a confidential relationship with the expert; and (2) whether the opposing party had disclosed relevant confidential or privileged information to the expert. *See Koch Ref. Co. v. Jennifer L. Boudreaux MV*, 85 F.3d 1178 (5th Cir. 1996). The parties did not dispute that the expert had signed a confidentiality agreement with the defendant, but the plaintiff argued that he did not receive confidential information related to the litigation. The court found, however, that the expert did receive relevant information as he worked on products similar to the accused products. Consequently, the court precluded the expert from assisting with infringement issues, but allowed his participation in other areas relating to claim construction and validity. The court reasoned that the public interest in allowing the plaintiff to consult with the actual inventor outweighed the defendant's confidentiality interest in those areas.

2. *Louisiana Federal Court Cases*

a. Expert Qualifications

Louisiana federal courts follow the Fifth Circuit's guidance that expert qualifications are not a top priority for gatekeeping. "As long as some reasonable indication of qualifications is adduced, the court may admit the evidence without abdicating its gatekeeping function." *Imperial Trading Co. v. Travelers Property Cas. Co.*, 2009 WL 2356292 (E.D. La. July 28, 2009) (*quoting Rushing v. Kansas City S. Ry. Co.*, 185 F.3d 496, 507 (5th Cir. 1999). Nevertheless, some topics do require a degree of specialization. In *Thomas v. City of Winnfield*, 2012 WL 1255265 (W.D. La. Apr. 13, 2012), plaintiff asserted a claim for wrongful death as a result of police use of a Taser shocking device. Plaintiff offered a forensic pathologist to opine as to the cause of death. But the witness was admittedly not an expert in cardiology, electricity, or the effects of electricity on the body. Moreover, the expert was unable to reference reliable scientific literature to support his opinion that the Taser caused the death. Plaintiff's engineering expert was similarly limited because, although he had a Ph.D. in mechanical engineering, he had no qualifications regarding the class of electrical device at issue.

b. Helpfulness

To be admissible, an expert's testimony must assist the fact finder to understand the evidence or determine a fact in issue. *Pipitone v. Biomatrix, Inc.*, 288 F.3d 239, 244–45 (5th Cir. 2002). If the matter at issue involves nothing more than lay common sense, expert testimony may not be necessary and therefore not helpful. *Alvarado v. Diamond Offshore Mgmt. Co.*, 2011 WL 4948031 (E.D. La. Oct. 18, 2011). Alvarado was injured at sea and brought a Jones Act claim. He retained a "certified safety professional" to offer expert opinions, but the expert's conclusions were only that defendant violated certain rules and regulations and that a certain task was unreasonably dangerous. No expertise was necessary to conclude that certain conduct violated rules or that the task, lifting large sacks, was unreasonably dangerous. "Therefore, [the expert's] report and anticipated testimony are unnecessary because they involve matters that are within the knowledge or experience of layman." *Id* at *3.

"Human factors" or "safety" experts are often tendered to cover a wide range of specialized topics in summary fashion. Such was the case in an MDL decision reported at *In re FEMA Trailer Formaldehyde Prods. Liab. Litig.*, No. 09-2892, 2009 WL 2169224 (E.D. La. July 15, 2009), involving a claim that formaldehyde contained in building materials in mobile homes rendered the homes unreasonably dangerous. Plaintiffs designated a human factors/warnings expert to opine that exposure to formaldehyde could cause serious health problems and that warnings were inadequate. But the expert was an industrial psychologist, not a medical doctor, toxicologist, industrial hygienist, engineer, or epidemiologist. "She seems to play the role of an 'über-juror' rather than as an expert, offering opinions that invade the province of the jury, which can reasonably be expected to consider and evaluate testimony from actual experts who have specialized, technical knowledge on the subject matter pertinent to this litigation, . . ." *Id.* at *3. The court ruled that the jury could handle these particular issues without expert help. "To be clear, the Court notes that no party will be permitted to introduce a human factors expert; no expert will be allowed to directly instruct the jury how it should dispose of a factual issue in this case." *Id.* at *4.

c. Methodology

Methodology—Damages. A damages expert must have some evidence to support his assumptions in formulating his opinions, but this foundation was lacking in *Sigur v. Emerson Process Management*, 492 F. Supp. 2d 565 (M. D. La. 2007), and the expert's testimony was excluded. The expert offered a damages analysis based on the assumption that plaintiff's lost sales were due to allegedly defamatory comments sent to plaintiff's customers. Plaintiff had no evidence, however, of any lost sales from the defamatory material, and the expert conceded that none of the customers had told him that their purchases would be adversely affected. Moreover, the expert did not consider whether any sales decline was due to the ordinary cyclical nature of plaintiff's business.

Methodology—Toxicology. In a toxic tort case, a plaintiff must show general causation and specific causation. General causation requires proof based upon medical studies with statistically significant results. *See Wagoner v. Exxon Mobile Corp.*, 813 F. Supp. 2d 771, 800 (E.D. La. 2011). In *Wagoner*, the plaintiff alleged that exposure to benzene caused decedent's multiple myeloma (MM). Defendants moved to exclude the plaintiff's experts on the grounds that their general causation opinions were not supported by scientific studies. The trial court gave a detailed review of these studies, however, and analyzed the two studies that had statistically significant findings. One of the studies dealt with exposure to crude oil, though, not benzene in particular. The other study, a meta-analysis, was not peer reviewed. Nevertheless, the trial court held that the expert's opinions were sufficiently reliable on the questions of general and specific causation.

d. Criminal

An interesting procedural issue arose in *U.S. v. Impastato*, 535 F. Supp. 2d 732 (E.D. La. 2008), involving the interplay of *Daubert* gatekeeping and Federal Rule of Criminal Procedure 16. Under Rule 16(a)(1)(G), a defendant may request summaries of expert testimony to be offered by the government. Under Rule 16(b)(1)(C), when a defendant makes such a request, he creates a reciprocal discovery obligation. In *Impastato*, the defendant made a Rule 16 request, but later withdrew it. As the government had not responded to the vital request for disclosure, the court ruled that the defendant could retract his request. But the question remained, how could the trial court comply with the Supreme Court's mandate to evaluate the reliability and accuracy of the expert testimony without the Rule 16 disclosures? The court resolved the dilemma by ordering an *in camera* submission.

3. *Mississippi Cases*

a. Procedure

Mississippi federal courts recognize that adherence to scheduling deadlines is critical. *See Metropolitan Prop. & Cas. Ins. Co. v. Clayco Constr. Group, LLC*, 2010 WL 1068159, at *1 (S.D. Miss. Mar. 18, 2010). Local Rules advise that "failure to make full expert disclosures by the expert designation deadline is grounds for prohibiting introduction of that evidence at trial," L.U. Civ. R. 26(a)(2), and late designation requires "a showing of good cause," L.U. Civ. R. 26(a)(2)(C), quoted at 2010 WL 1068159 at *1. Clayco offered expert testimony of the city fire inspector, though he had not been designated as an expert. Though both parties knew the witness had investigated the fire, Metropolitan would have been prejudiced by allowing him to offer opinion testimony without proper notice under Rule 26.

A somewhat different rule applies to expert treating physicians. Under Local Rule 26(a)(2)(D), when a plaintiff designates his treating physician as an expert, no written report is required, only a summary of the facts and opinions the expert will provide. In *Rosamond v. Great American Ins. Co.*, 2011 WL 4433582 (S.D. Miss. Aug. 4, 2011), the court denied a motion to strike a treating physician's affidavit, even though it offered an opinion on causation that went beyond matters covered in his medical records. *But see Previto v. Ryobi North America, Inc.*, 2010 WL 5185055 (S.D. Miss. Dec. 16, 2010) (excluding treating physician's supplemental opinion based on treatment by other providers); *Duke v. Lowe's Home Ctrs., Inc.*, 2007 WL 3094894, at *1 (N.D. Miss. Oct. 19, 2007) (without a report, treating physician limited to facts and opinions contained in records).

Reports are not required if the expert is not "retained," but the proponent must still disclose "a summary of the facts and opinions to which the witness is expected to testify." Local Rule 26(a)(2)(D). In *Doss v. NPC Int'l, Inc.*, 2010 WL 2900422 (N.D. Miss. July 20, 2010), plaintiffs designated two Department of Health officials with only an "extremely brief" explanation of their expected testimony. The filing failed to provide any facts related to the witnesses' investigations or even describe the opinions they would offer. Thus the court struck the experts for failure to comply with a proper disclosure.

O'Hara v. Travelers, Civil Action No. 2:11-CV-208-KS-MTP (S.D. Miss. 2012), considers the effect of the ghostwriting of the expert's report. The witness was offered as an expert on the cost of repair of a fire-damaged home and testified that he did not prepare or assist in the preparation of the expert reports disclosed by the plaintiff, but merely signed them at the plaintiff's request. Such a procedure violates the requirement of Rule 26 that the report be "signed and prepared" by the expert. Neither an attorney nor, as in this case, a party is permitted to "ghostwrite" a report. The court stated that by itself ghostwriting does not render testimony unreliable, but it is a factor to be considered. Here the expert also had not viewed the home until years after the loss, had never been inside, and had not considered the reports of the fire department and other experts. Thus he did not have sufficient facts or data under Rule 702(b) to be reliable.

b. Qualifications

Bossier v. State Farm Fire & Cas. Co., 2009 WL 4061501 (S.D. Miss. Nov. 20, 2009) presented an interesting question regarding an expert's qualifications under FRE 702 and his competency under FRE 601. Rule 601 mandates the application of state law competency rules when state law provides the rule of decision, as in this diversity case. Mississippi requires that engineers be certified in Mississippi in order to practice in their field, and the court ruled that providing testimony constitutes the practice of engineering so as to require state certification as a professional engineer. Defendant's witness had a Ph.D. in civil engineering and was clearly qualified under Rule 702, but he was not licensed in Mississippi. The court ruled that the standards of Rules 601 and 702 were cumulative; the expert was required to meet both, and, as he was not properly certified, he could not testify. *Id.* at *6.

Even a proper certification is not sufficient if the expert does not have knowledge or experience in the specific field at issue. The expert in *Lee v. Nat'l RR Passenger Corp. (Amtrak)*, 2012 WL 92363 (S.D. Miss. Jan. 11, 2012), was a licensed social worker, but her expertise in PTSD derived from one fifteen-hour continuing education course, which the court ruled was insufficient qualification for her to diagnose the disorder. Similarly, in *Ovella v. B&C Construc. & Equip., LLC*, 2011 WL 3665120 (S.D. Miss. Aug. 5, 2011), the court held that an architect was not qualified to testify as an expert in structural engineering, and in *Graves v. Toyota Motor Corp*, 2011 WL 4590772 (S.D. Miss. Sept. 30, 2011), the court precluded opinion testimony from two state troopers who investigated an auto accident on the ground that they were not trained in accident reconstruction.

The question of what degree of specialty is required for qualifications frequently arises in cases involving engineering. In *McSwain v. Sunrise Medical, Inc.*, 2010 WL 200004 (S.D. Miss. Jan. 24, 2010), the court limited the testimony of plaintiff's engineering expert because he lacked experience with wheelchairs, the product at issue. In *Gibson v. Invacare Corp.*, 2011 WL 2262933 (S.D. Miss. June 7, 2011), the court distinguished *McSwain*, and allowed the opinions of plaintiffs' mechanical engineering experts, though they did not have specific experience with walkers of the type involved in the accident at issue.

c. Products Liability

One signal for lack of reliability is that the expert formulated her opinions before having all the relevant information. This situation arose in *Elliot v. Amadas Ind., Inc.*, 796 F. Supp. 2d 796 (S.D. Miss. 2011), which involved an injury from an allegedly defective peanut combine. Plaintiffs' expert formulated his opinions before he had inspected the combine and before he knew the specific model of the combine. *Id.* at 807–08. He decided that a lockout mechanism was necessary before he knew if one could be incorporated into the design, and decided that additional warnings were necessary before he knew what warnings were already on the combine. *Id.* at 808. Moreover, the expert did not provide any technical basis for his alternative design, and had not tested it. *Id.* at 808–09. While no one issue was dispositive, in the aggregate they indicated that the proposed testimony was unreliable.

Of course, an expert may have difficulty evaluating an allegedly defective product if it was discarded before he was retained. In *Miller v. Genie Ind., Inc.*, 2012 WL 161408 (N.D. Miss. Jan. 19, 2012), plaintiffs claimed injury from an allegedly defective jib boom part on an aerial work platform. But, after the accident, plaintiffs discarded the jib boom. Nevertheless, plaintiffs' expert "confidently offer[ed] highly specific and nuanced conclusions regarding a piece of evidence which he has never laid eyes upon." *Id.* at *5. Further, the expert performed no testing of his theory of defect. The court questioned the reliability of a detailed opinion based on a product the expert had never examined and concluded that the expert's testimony should be stricken in its entirety.

Some courts have held that the failure to test an alternative design is less important if the expert can point to testing done by others or to the use of the alternative design within the industry. In *Hankins v. Ford Motor Co.*, 2011 WL 6046304 (S.D. Miss. Dec. 5, 2011), plaintiffs' expert claimed that the Ford's sunroof was defective and proposed six possible alternatives, one of which he had tested but under dramatically different conditions. The expert had not tested his proposals in connection with the vehicle at issue, but the court ruled "there is no requirement that the expert actually design, produce, and test their proposed design on the specific product at issue." *Id.* at *4 (*quoting Betts v. General Motors Corp.*, 2008 WL 2789524, at *8). *See also Willis v. Kia Motors Corp.*, 2009 WL 1974563 (N.D. Miss. 2009)(excluding evidence of patent designs but allowing evidence regarding alternative design that had actually been used in some limited number of vehicles).

d. Toxicology

Hill v. Koppers, Inc., 2009 WL 4908836 (N.D. Miss. Dec. 11, 2009), a toxic tort case, presents a dramatic example of experts changing their theories after filing their reports. The decedent Hill was diagnosed with pancreatic cancer in May 2004, passed away in July 2004, and his death certificate stated pancreatic cancer as his cause of death. Plaintiffs' experts filed initial reports in 2004 and 2005 assuming that Hill had pancreatic cancer. *Id.* at *4. In their depositions, however, the experts admitted that no scientific literature demonstrated that the chemicals involved caused pancreatic cancer. In 2009, five years after Hill's death, the experts submitted supplemental reports stating that Hill died of gastrointestinal cancer. *Id.* at *4. But the supplemental reports were untimely and did not explain how the diagnosis changed from pancreatic cancer to gastrointestinal cancer. Accordingly, the court ruled that plaintiff was precluded from asserting that Hill's death was not due to pancreatic cancer. As plaintiff's experts admitted they had no peer-reviewed scientific literature to establish general causation, the court excluded their opinions as unreliable.

C. EXPERT-RELATED RULES AND PROCEDURES IN FEDERAL COURT

1. Texas Federal Courts

Texas federal district courts have not generally altered federal rules practice dealing with experts, except for some specific deadlines that are established by the courts' initial scheduling orders. Specific details of each judge's procedures are available on the Internet. Some courts include a deadline for the filing of *Daubert* challenges.[5] The Eastern District has a specific local rule regarding expert disclosure, Local Rule CV-26 (b), "Disclosure of Expert Testimony":

> (1) When listing the cases in which the witness has testified as an expert, the disclosure shall include the styles of the cases, the courts in which the cases were pending, the cause numbers, and whether the testimony was in trial or deposition.
> (2) By order in the case, the judge may alter the type or form of disclosures to be made with respect to particular experts or categories of experts, such as treating physicians.

The Eastern District also has special rules for patent cases, attached as Appendix M to the Local Rules that address expert disclosures.

2. Louisiana Federal Courts

The three Louisiana federal districts have each adopted local rules, which don't provide additional gloss to expert procedure under Federal Rule 26. Nevertheless, individual divisions and courts may have specific requirements for dealing with experts, and counsel should consult with the district court to assure compliance with all relevant local guidelines. For example, the Western District's *Guide to Practice* has specific rules dealing with expert-witness fees.

3. Mississippi Federal Courts

Mississippi federal courts have adopted uniform local rules for the Northern and Southern Districts, which define required expert disclosures at Local Uniform Civil Rule 26. The local rule tracks Federal Rule 26, with some additions. If a party fails to designate an expert without the required full disclosure, the district court may strike the expert on motion or *sua sponte*. Parties must designate treating physicians and others who are not specially retained or employed, and disclose the subject matter and basis of their opinions. Local Uniform Civil Rule 7 governs motion practice, and Rule 7(b)(2)(C) provides that all motions challenging an opposing party's expert shall be filed no later than fifteen calendar days after the discovery deadline unless the schedule is modified in the Case Management Order.

D. STATE-LAW EXPERT ISSUES

1. Expert Evidence in Texas State Courts

a. Texas Rules and Procedures

Texas Rules of Evidence 701–03 are virtually identical to the federal rules. Expert discovery is available in similar fashion to the federal rules. A party may obtain initial disclosure of an expert's

---

[5] For example, Judge Sam Lindsay of the Northern District requires that *Daubert* challenges be filed at least ninety days before trial. *See* Court Procedural Rule IV.C, "Trial Procedures, Designation of Experts." *See* Requirements for District Judge Barbara M. G. Lynn, Case Management Procedures, Rule I.C. Status Report/Scheduling Order (parties can stipulate to extensions of deadlines, but the deadline for objecting to experts must be at least ninety days before trial).

identity, subject matter of testimony, and the general substance and basis of opinions under Tex. R. Civ. P. 194. The scope of discovery available for testifying and consulting experts is defined by Tex. R. Civ. P. 192, 194 of the Texas Rules of Civil Procedure ("TRCP"). The relevant sections of these rules are set out below:

192.3 Scope of Discovery

(e) *Testifying and Consulting Experts.* The identity, mental impressions, and opinions of a consulting expert whose mental impressions and opinions have not been reviewed by a testifying expert are not discoverable. A party may discover the following information regarding a testifying expert or regarding a consulting expert whose mental impressions or opinions have been reviewed by a testifying expert:

(1) the expert's name, address, and telephone number;
(2) the subject matter on which a testifying expert will testify;
(3) the facts known by the expert that relate to or form the basis of the expert's mental impressions and opinions formed or made in connection with the case in which the discovery is sought, regardless of when and how the factual information was acquired;
(4) the expert's mental impressions and opinions formed or made in connection with the case in which discovery is sought, and any methods used to derive them;
(5) any bias of the witness;
(6) all documents, tangible things, reports, models, or data compilations that have been provided to, reviewed by, or prepared by or for the expert in anticipation of a testifying expert's testimony;
(7) the expert's current resume and bibliography.

194.2 Content. A party may request disclosure of any or all of the following:

(f) for any testifying expert:
(1) the expert's name, address, and telephone number;
(2) the subject matter on which the expert will testify;
(3) the general substance of the expert's mental impressions and opinions and a brief summary of the basis for them, or if the expert is not retained by, employed by, or otherwise subject to the control of the responding party, documents reflecting such information;
(4) if the expert is retained by, employed by, or otherwise subject to the control of the responding party;
  (A) all documents, tangible things, reports, models or data compilations that have been provided to, reviewed by, or prepared by or for the expert in anticipation of the expert's testimony; and
  (B) the expert's current resume and bibliography.

195.1 Permissible Discovery Tools. A party may request another party to designate and disclose information concerning testifying expert witnesses only through a request for disclosure under Rule 194 and through depositions and reports as permitted by this rule.

195.2 Schedule for Designating Experts. Unless otherwise ordered by the court, a party must designate experts—that is, furnish information requested under Rule 194.2(f)—by the later of the following two dates: 30 days after the request is served, or—
(a) with regard to all experts testifying for a party seeking affirmative relief, 90 days before the end of the discovery period;
(b) with regard to all other experts, 60 days before the end of the discovery period.

Unlike the Federal Rules, the TRCP do not allow for the automatic disclosure or deposition of an opposing party's testifying expert. *See* TRCP 195.1. According to the TRCP, a party seeking disclosures from a testifying expert witness must request such disclosures in compliance with Rule 194.1. After such request has been made, parties are entitled to information regarding the expert's identity, the subject matter on which the expert will testify, and the general substance of the expert's mental impressions or opinions and a brief summary of the basis for them. *See* TRCP 194.2(f). If the expert is employed by or under the control of the responding party, the party requesting disclosure is also entitled to all documents, tangible things, reports, models, or data compilations that have been provided or used by the expert in anticipation of his or her testimony and a copy of his or her current resume and bibliography. *See* TRCP 194.2(f)(4).

Similar to the Federal Rules, discovery of nontestifying experts under the TRCP is more difficult. Under the TRCP, parties seeking discovery from a nontestifying expert can do so, but only if they comply with Rules 176 and 205 covering depositions from nonparties. *See* TRCP 195 cmt. 2. Information regarding purely consulting experts is not discoverable. *See* TRCP 195 cmt. 1. Unlike the Federal Rules, the TRCP also requires that "all reasonable fees charged by the expert for time spent in preparing for, giving, reviewing, and correcting the deposition must be paid by the party that retained the expert." TRCP 195.7.

b. Texas Case Law

Texas courts were among the first to adopt the guidelines of *Daubert*, through the Texas Supreme Court decisions in *Robinson* and *Havner*. Since the last Monograph, numerous Texas cases have continued to clarify the procedures for dealing with experts.

Qualifications. *Spin Doctor Golf, Inc. v. Paymentech, L.P.*, 296 S.W.3d 354 (Tex. App.—Dallas 2009, rev. denied), involved a defendant's credit card processing services for the plaintiff's golf club sales. The plaintiff designated its managing partner as its expert on lost-profit damages, based on his qualifications of thirty years of experience in evaluating business opportunities and his experience specifically with the golf club manufacturing business. But the court of appeals pointed out that lost profits testimony relates to accounting and finance, and the partner did not have the necessary experience in accounting principles. The expert's "experience in evaluating business opportunities, executing marketing plans for businesses, and monitoring business results for golf club manufacturers, no matter how extensive, does not amount to knowledge, skill, experience, training, or education so as to qualify him as an expert on the issue of lost profits." 296 S.W.3d at 360–61.

In medical malpractice cases, a frequent issue is whether a testifying expert must be a practitioner or have training in the same field as the defendant. In *Hayes v. Carroll*, 2010 WL 1930151 (Tex. App.—Austin, May 14, 2010), the issue concerned the placement of a bandage on plaintiff's leg during an emergency cardiac procedure. The bandage acted as a tourniquet, causing vascular damage. One of the plaintiff's experts was a board-certified vascular surgeon who claimed to be familiar with the appropriate standard of care for physicians and nurses in connection with what he termed a "basic medical skill." The defendants argued that the expert was not qualified to give an opinion on the standard of care in his specialties of emergency medicine, pulmonology, critical care, and intensive care nursing. The court of appeals stated that the focus for qualifications is not on the defendant's area of specialty but on the medical condition involved in the claim. 2010 WL 1930151 at *8; *see Moore v. Gatica*, 269 S.W.3d 134, 141 (Tex. App.—Fort Worth 2008, pet. denied) ("[A] physician 'who is not of the same school of medicine [as the defendant] is competent to testify if he has practical knowledge of what is usually and customarily done by a practitioner under circumstances similar to those confronting the defendant"). The court held there was no abuse of discretion in the trial court's accepting the qualifications of the expert to address the standard of care in treating the vascular condition at issue.

Barber v. Mercer, 303 S.W.3d 786 (Tex. App.—Fort Worth 2009), addressed a similar issue in a medical malpractice claim involving alleged negligence during a heart-bypass surgical procedure. Plaintiffs' expert, an anesthesiologist, opined as to the standard of care of the defendant general surgeon. The defendant surgeon objected that the anesthesiologist was not qualified to opine about the field of heart surgery, and the trial court granted his motion to dismiss. The expert filed a very detailed amended report (attached to the opinion), however, that claimed extensive experience and knowledge of the procedures in cardiac surgery and of the relevant standard of care. The court of appeals observed that plaintiffs' claim was for negligence in the positioning and padding of the patient during surgery and not to actual operating techniques. The anesthesiologist had knowledge of positioning and padding from his many years of work in operating rooms, so he was qualified, and the trial court abused its discretion in sustaining objections to the expert. 303 S.W.3d at 795–96; *see also Foster v. Richardson*, 303 S.W.3d 833 (Tex. App.—Fort Worth 2009) (internist who specialized in physical medicine and rehabilitation held qualified to opine as to standard of care of orthopedist in allegedly failing to follow proper diagnostic procedures).

In *Tenet Hospitals Ltd. v. Boada*, 304 S.W.3d 528 (Tex. App.—El Paso 2009), the plaintiffs sued the hospital, among others, for negligence in connection with emergency room treatment. The hospital appealed the trial court's denial of the hospital's motion to dismiss. The court of appeals ruled that Chapter 74 of the Civil Practice and Remedies Code applied to EMTALA claims. The court determined that the plaintiff's doctors' reports were inadequate as to negligence. But the report of the plaintiffs' nursing expert was timely and properly articulated the nursing standards of care and the claimed breaches. The problem is that a nurse is not qualified to render an expert opinion as to causation. This left plaintiffs with no admissible expert opinion on negligence causation, and those claims were dismissed. 304 S.W.3d at 543.[6]

Standard for reliability. In *E. I. DuPont de Nemours & Co. v. Robinson*, 923 S.W.2d 549, 556 (Tex. 1995), the Texas Supreme Court established guidelines for admissibility of expert evidence.[7] Following the United States Supreme Court decision in *Kumho Tire v. Carmichael*, 526 U.S. 137 (1999), Texas courts adopted a second method for testing the reliability of experience-based experts: whether an "analytical gap" exists between the expert's reasoning and his conclusion. *See Gammill v. Jack Williams Chevrolet*, 972 S.W.2d 713 (Tex. 1998). In *Mack Trucks, Inc. v. Tamez*, 206 S.W.3d 572 (Tex. 2006), the Texas Supreme Court emphasized that trial courts should still consider the *Robinson* factors when they would be helpful, whether the testimony was based on science or experience.

The issue of which of these reliability tests to apply was before the supreme court in a products liability case, *Whirlpool Corp. v. Camacho*, 298 S.W.3d 631 (Tex. 2009), and the court clarified its analysis, emphasizing the need for stringent gatekeeping. The Camachos sued Whirlpool after a fire destroyed their trailer home. Their expert blamed a defect in their Whirlpool clothes dryer, asserting

---

[6] One doctor's report was adequate to support the EMTALA claim, however, so plaintiffs' case continued on that theory.

[7] *Robinson* suggested the following factors for consideration: whether a theory has been tested; whether the expert opinion is subjective; whether the theory has been published and/or subjected to peer review; the potential rate of error; whether the theory is generally accepted; and whether the theory has been used nonjudicially. 923 S.W.2d at 557.

that the fire was caused by lint particles ignited by the dryer's heater element. A jury found that the dryer defect caused the fire, and the court of appeals affirmed judgment for the plaintiffs. *Whirlpool Corp. v. Camacho*, 251 S.W. 3d 88 (Tex. App.—Corpus Christi 2008). Noting that the plaintiffs' experts' testimony was based on experience, the court of appeals applied only the *Gammill* test, inquiring whether there was an "analytical gap" between the fire causation opinion and the basis on which it was founded, and rejected the use of specific *Robinson* factors. 251 S.W. 3d at 97.

The Texas Supreme Court recognized the hazard of a limitation on gatekeeping for "experience based" experts. If courts accept experience as a substitute for proof of reliability, then the expert may proffer "almost any type of data or subjective opinion" to fill the gaps in his testimony and insulate the opinion from meaningful review. 298 S.W.3d at 639. Accordingly, in most cases, the trial court should consider both the *Robinson* factors and the analytical gap test. *Id.* at 639–40. In any case, the analysis should be comprehensive. "When expert testimony is involved, courts are to rigorously examine the validity of facts and assumptions on which the testimony is based, as well as the principles, research, and methodology underlying the expert's conclusions and the manner in which the principles and methodologies are applied by the expert to reach the conclusions." 298 S.W.3d at 637. Moreover, "each material part of an expert's theory must be reliable." *Id.* So each step of the expert's analysis from data and assumptions to ultimate conclusion must be shown to be reliable under the appropriate indicia of the relevant field.

The court's focus in *Whirlpool* was on the first *Robinson* factor: whether the expert's theory had been or could be subject to testing. In this case, the plaintiffs' expert had not seen or read of a test showing that lint could back up into the dryer blower as he theorized. Nor had he personally tested this theory. Although dryer tests had been done by the CPSC and Whirlpool, the expert did not explain how these tests supported his ultimate conclusion on fire causation.

The court stressed that while testing is not always required, lack of relevant testing is a factor in determining that the expert's theory is unreliable. *Id.* at 642. The court also applied other *Robinson* factors, observing that the expert's theory was developed specifically for the litigation, had not been published or subjected to peer review, and had not been shown to be accepted as valid in the expert community. *Id.* at 643. Plaintiffs pointed to other objective evidence, but the court determined that the evidence as a whole did not support the expert's opinion. Without the expert's testimony, plaintiffs could not prove design defect, so the court reversed and rendered. *Id.*

Three months after *Whirlpool*, the Texas Supreme Court returned to the analytical gap test, addressing the opinions of an accident reconstructionist. "[W]e have found it appropriate in cases like this to analyze whether the expert's opinion actually fits the facts of the case. In other words, we determine whether there are any significant analytical gaps in the expert's opinion that undermine its reliability." 306 S.W.3d at 235. Several members of the Hughes family were killed when their GMC Yukon crossed the center line of a highway and struck a heavily loaded gravel truck. Although no fact witness supported this view, plaintiffs' expert opined that the truck veered into the other lane first, causing to Yukon to steer defensively into the truck. The expert based his opinion on various calculations, a review of documents, and a visit to the accident site.

The defendant objected that the expert made incorrect assumptions and selectively relied on some eyewitness testimony while rejecting the testimony that refuted his theory. The court disagreed, concluding that the expert's testimony was adequately tied to the physical evidence in the case so as to satisfy the "gap" test. *Id.* at 239–40. In a prior accident case, *Volkswagen of America, Inc. v. Ramirez*, 159 S.W.3d 897 (Tex. 2004), the court rejected the plaintiffs' reconstructionist on the ground that he had done no testing and had no publications to support his theory of the accident. Instead, the expert had applied the laws of physics to his review of the accident scene, testifying that "[a]ccident reconstruction is basically the application of laws of physics with respect to . . . describing the motion of [*sic*] vehicle before a collision, during a collision, and after a collision using basic scientific and some engineering principles, but all abiding by the laws of physics." 159 S.W.3d at 905.

In *TXI*, the court distinguished *Ramirez* on the ground that the expert testimony was "'not supported' by scientific analysis but rather rested upon the expert's 'subjective interpretation of the facts.'" 306 S.W.3d at 239–40. The apparent distinction is that the expert in *TXI* more carefully explained his reasoning, though there was no mention in the opinion that plaintiffs' expert did testing or had support from relevant literature.

Transcontinental Ins. Co. v. Crump, 330 S.W.3d 211 (Tex. 2010), a workers' compensation case, concerned the opinions of the plaintiff's treating physician. As the expert relied on differential diagnosis, a recognized medical technique, the plaintiff argued that the application of the *Robinson* factors should be less strict, and the court of appeals refused to apply *Robinson* at all. The Texas Supreme Court rejected this approach. "The mere fact that differential diagnosis was used does not exempt the foundation of a treating physician's expert opinion from scrutiny—it is to be evaluated for reliability as carefully as any other expert's testimony. Both the *Robinson* and *Gammill* analyses are appropriate in this context." *Id.* at 216. The supreme court then applied the *Robinson* factors and found the testimony reliable.

Procedure. As a general rule, a party must object at trial to preserve error regarding of expert testimony. The trial judge cannot act as a gatekeeper unless she or he is alerted to issues of reliability. But in some cases no objection is necessary, as the Texas Supreme Court pointed out in *City of San Antonio v. Pollock*, 284 S.W.3d 809 (Tex. 2009). In *Pollock*, the plaintiffs' infant daughter was diagnosed with acute lymphoblastic leukemia (ALL). The plaintiffs' backyard adjoined a city waste-disposal site, and analysis of gas samples from the landfill revealed traces of benzene, a known carcinogen at certain levels.

The plaintiffs sued the City, claiming their daughter's illness was caused by the mother's exposure to benzene while she was pregnant. One of the daughter's treating physicians testified as an expert in support of causation, citing studies showing an association between cancer and benzene among workers exposed at levels 200 times higher than those detected in the landfill gas analyses. The City did not object to the admission of plaintiffs' experts' opinions, although it argued in the trial court that the testimony was conclusory and insufficient to support a judgment. Ultimately the jury rendered a verdict for the Pollocks for close to $20 million, including $10 million in punitive damages.

In the court of appeals, the City argued, *inter alia*, that the Pollocks' experts' opinions were legally insufficient because they failed to meet the epidemiological standards established by *Havner*. *Merrell Dow Pharms., Inc. v. Havner*, 853 S.W.2d 706, 718 (Tex. 1997) (studies must show a doubling of the risk due to exposure to toxic substance). The lack of epidemiological support rendered their expert's evidence unreliable, thus it was no evidence at all, and no timely objection was necessary. But this was the same reasoning rejected by *Maritime Overseas Corp. v. Ellis*, 972 S.W.2d 402, 409–10 (Tex. 1998). "To preserve a complaint that scientific evidence is unreliable and thus, no evidence, a party must object to the evidence before trial or when the evidence is offered." 972 S.W.2d at 409. The court of appeals held that the City failed to preserve its *Havner* argument, reversed the award of punitive damages, but otherwise affirmed. 155 S.W.3d 322 (Tex. App.—San Antonio 2004).

On appeal, the Supreme Court cited two exceptions to the general rule of *Maritime Overseas*. If the expert's opinion is conclusory *or* the bases of the opinion provide no support, then no trial court objection is necessary to preserve error. 284 S.W.3d at 816–18. The difficulty with the test is determining what is "conclusory." Justice Medina in dissent writes that the distinction "apparently is the difference between something and nothing." *Id.* at 823. That is, if the expert simply relies on credentials and essentially says "take my word for it," stating a conclusion without any explanation; then the opinion is conclusory and no objection is necessary. *Id.* at 823–24, (quoting *Arkoma Basin Exploration Co. v. FMF Assocs. 1990-A, Ltd.*, 249 S.W.3d 380, 389–90 (Tex. 2008)). But the *Pollock* majority rejected such a bright-line approach in favor of more detailed appellate gatekeeping. While the Pollocks' medical expert did rely on "something," for example epidemiological studies linking benzene exposure to childhood leukemia, these studies were based on much higher levels of benzene exposure than those hypothesized by the Pollocks' expert, thus the studies provided no basis for the expert's conclusion. 284 S.W.3d at 819–20. Hence the expert's opinion was conclusory and could not support liability. *See also Wal-Mart Stores, Inc. v. Merrell*, 313 S.W.3d 837 (Tex. 2010) (fire origin expert did not eliminate other potential causes and "his specific causation theory amounted to little more than speculation" and was legally insufficient even if properly admitted).

To avoid waiver, must an objection to expert testimony be re-asserted at trial in response to each question seeking the objectionable opinion? The question arose in an oil-drilling dispute involving saltwater damage, *Discovery Operating, Inc. v. BP America Prod. Co.*, 2010 WL 1509796 (Tex. App.—Eastland, Apr. 15, 2010), in which BP's expert testified that the saltwater flow began when Discovery's drillers hit an underground cavern. Discovery objected on the ground that the testimony was merely speculation, unsupported by any facts developed in the case. The trial court overruled Discovery's first objection. Then BP asked another question on the issue, which was answered without objection. Discovery renewed its objection to a third question in the series, but was again overruled. Later the expert repeated his opinions without objection. The court of appeals held that Discovery was not required to repeat its objection but could assume that the trial court would make the same ruling for similar evidence. 2010 WL 1509796 at *22 (quoting *Atkinson Gas. Co. v. Albrecht*, 878 S.W.2d 236, 247 (Tex. App.—Corpus Christi 1994, *writ denied*)). Moreover, the fact that Discovery elicited the same testimony from the expert on cross-examination was not waiver, as it had previously been admitted over objection. *Id.*

Expert Reports and Designations. Texas Rule 194.2(f)(3) requires disclosure of "the general substance of the expert's mental impressions and opinions and a brief summary of the basis for them." Query: how detailed must these disclosures be? Can the disclosure be just subject matter or must it verge on a detailed outline of the expected testimony? A Beaumont case illustrates the pitfalls when a court finds a designation insufficient. *In re Commitment of Marks*, 230 S.W.3d 241 (Tex. App.—Beaumont, *no pet.*).

In this involuntary commitment case, the State's expert opined that Marks was feigning mental illness in an attempt to disprove the future likelihood of predatory acts of sexual violence. Marks had designated an expert, Dr. Dunham, to testify "whether Mr. Marks is an insane person who is in an insane condition of mind at a time when he is called to testify in this matter." In a pretrial deposition, Dr. Dunham testified that Marks suffered from a schizophrenic disorder, and Marks called him at trial to testify that he was not feigning the illness. The State objected because Dr. Dunham had not been designated specifically on feigned illness. The trial court sustained the objection and the court of appeals affirmed.

There seems little prejudice to the State in allowing expert testimony that simply covers the same ground disclosed in a deposition. The courts focused, though, on Marks's failure to make that express argument in a timely manner. At the time of the State's objection, Marks did not attempt either to show good cause for the lack of disclosure or to demonstrate lack of surprise and prejudice to the State. Marks did argue good cause and lack of prejudice in a motion for new trial, but the offer of proof was untimely because not made "as soon as practicable" pursuant to Texas Rule of Evidence 103(b). Marks was also untimely in his objection to the State's expert and his demand for a "gatekeeper hearing." The state had already elicited the expert's qualifications and much of his opinion at the time of the objection.

2. *Expert Evidence in Louisiana State Courts*

a. Procedural Rules

Article 1425 of the Louisiana Code of Civil Procedure ("LCCP") governs the discovery of expert testimony in Louisiana state courts. The applicable portion of this rule reads as follows:

A. A party may through interrogatories or by deposition require any other party to identify each person who may be used at trial to present evidence under Articles 702 through 705 of the Louisiana Code of Evidence.

B. Upon contradictory motion of any party or on the court's own motion, an order may be entered requiring that each party that has retained or specially employed a person to provide expert testimony in the case or whose duties as an employee of the party regularly involve giving expert testimony provide a written report prepared and signed by the witness. The report shall contain a complete statement of all opinions to be expressed and the basis and reasons therefore and the data or other information considered by the witness in forming the opinions. The parties, upon agreement, or if ordered by the court, shall include in the report any or all of the following: exhibits to be used as a summary of or support of the opinions; the qualifications of the witness, including a list of all publications authored by the witness within the preceding ten years; the compensation to be paid for the study and testimony; a listing of any other cases in which the witness has testified as an expert at trial or by deposition within the preceding four years. . . .

D. (1) Except as otherwise provided in Paragraph E of this Article, a party may, through interrogatories, deposition, and a request for documents and tangible things, discover facts known or opinions held by any person who has been identified as an expert whose opinions may be presented at trial. If a report from the expert is required under Paragraph B, the deposition shall not be conducted until after the report is provided.

(2) A party may, through interrogatories or by deposition, discover facts known by and opinions held by an expert who has been retained or specially employed by another party in anticipation of litigation or preparation for trial and who is not expected to be called as a witness at trial, only as provided in Article 1465 or upon a showing of exceptional circumstances under which it is impracticable for the party seeking discovery to obtain facts on the same subject by other means.

(3) Unless manifest injustice would result, the court shall require that the party seeking discovery pay the expert a reasonable fee for time spent in responding to discovery under this Paragraph; and with respect to discovery obtained under Subparagraph (2) of this Paragraph, the court shall also require, the party seeking discovery to pay the other party a fair portion of the fees and expenses reasonably incurred by the latter party in obtaining facts and opinions from the expert.

Similar to the Federal Rules, the LCCP provides for the use of interrogatories or depositions as methods for identifying an expert expected to be called at trial, revealing the subject matter of his testimony, and discovering the substance of the facts to which the expert is expected to testify. In addition, the LCCP tracks the language of the Federal Rules regarding experts who are retained in anticipation of litigation, but who are not expected to be called at trial. The facts known and the opinions held by these experts may be discovered only as provided in Article 1465 of the LCCP or "upon a showing of exceptional circumstances under which it is impracticable for the party seeking discovery to obtain facts on the same subject by other means." LCCP Art. 1425(2). According to both the LCCP and the Federal Rules, the party seeking discovery must pay the expert a reasonable fee for time spent responding to discovery.

In a significant departure from the Federal Rules, Louisiana protects from discovery drafts of the expert's report as well as "communications, including notes and electronically stored information or portions thereof that would reveal the mental impressions, opinions, or trial strategy of the attorney for the party who has retained the expert . . . " except on a showing of exceptional circumstances. Art. 1425.E.(1).

b. Evidentiary Framework

Louisiana Code of Evidence arts. 701–703 are virtually identical to the language of Federal Rules 701–703 prior to the 2000 amendments, and Louisiana has applied expert opinion gatekeeping in accord with federal court decisions. Louisiana has not adopted the 2000 Amendments to Federal Rule of Evidence 702, however, and one commentator has suggested that Louisiana courts "have not embraced the more restrictive *Daubert* interpretations rendered by some of their federal counterparts."[8]

Louisiana was one of the first states to expressly adopt the *Daubert* analysis, in *State v. Foret*, 628 So.2d 1116 (La. 1993). The Louisiana Supreme Court observed that since much of the Louisiana Code of Evidence is patterned after the Federal Rules, it is appropriate to utilize federal authority, especially where the language of the rules is virtually identical. Review of novel evidence under the *Foret* test requires an evidentiary hearing on reliability unless the specific method at issue has been proven "inherently reliable." *Id.* at 1123 n.8. *Foret* also expressly adopted *Daubert*'s four-factor guidelines for reliability. *Id.* at 1123. In *Independent Fire Ins. Co. v. Sunbeam Corp.*, 755 So.2d 226, 235–36 (La. 2000), the Supreme Court held that the *Daubert/Foret* standards should be considered by trial courts in deciding whether to admit expert opinion evidence in summary judgment proceedings.

c. Recent Cases

Procedural Issues. In *Cheairs v. State*, 861 So.2d 536, 542 (La. 2003), the Louisiana Supreme Court set out a three-step framework for analysis of expert testimony, derived in part from a federal Eleventh Circuit opinion,[9] which the court adopted: "(1) [whether] the expert is qualified to testify competently regarding the matters he intends to address; (2) [whether] the methodology by which the expert reaches his conclusions is sufficiently reliable as determined by the sort of inquiry mandated in *Daubert*; and (3) [whether] the testimony assists the trier of fact, through the application of scientific, technical, or specialized expertise, to understand the evidence or determine a fact issue." *Id.* The new analysis does not replace the *Daubert* analysis but instead is an addition in an effort to address all of the issues that arise when deciding whether to admit expert testimony. *Id.* at 542–43.

A formal hearing is essential to this procedure, as discussed in *Guardia v. Lakeview Regional Medical Center*, 13 So.3d 625 (La. App. 1 Cir. 2009). Prior to a summary judgment hearing, the defendant filed a motion *in limine* to exclude the plaintiff's expert. At the hearing, the trial court stated that the expert was not qualified and granted summary judgment. But the court did not hold a hearing on the expert and did not evaluate or analyze the relevant admissibility factors. Accordingly, the court of appeals held that the summary judgment was premature and therefore improper. *Id.* at 632.

Expert Qualifications. In a post-Katrina case, *Jouve v. State Farm Fire & Cas. Co.*, 74 So.3d 220 (La. Ct. App. 4th Cir. 2011), the court of appeals considered the qualifications of an expert offering an opinion on the cost of wind damage to property. The expert was not a licensed engineer or contractor, had not fully inspected the home at issue, and relied on a computer analysis prepared by his son. The expert's extensive experience was insufficient, given the additional problems with his failure to properly inspect the property or prepare the estimate at issue.

Methodology—Damages. An expert calculating economic damages must have a reliable basis reflecting the actual circumstances of the case. *Iles v. Ogden*, 37 So.3d 427 (La. Ct. App. 4th Cir. 2010), involved a wrongful death and expert testimony calculating, *inter alia*, future loss of support. Based on the expert's analysis, the trial court awarded $20 million for this future loss. But in making

---

[8] J. E. Cullens, Jr., *A Review of Recent* Daubert *Decisions of Louisiana State Courts*, 52 LA. B. J. 352, 356 (Feb./Mar. 2005).

[9] *See City of Tuscaloosa v. Harcros Chemicals, Inc.*, 158 F.3d 548, 562 (11th Cir. 1998).

his calculations, the expert used an estimated rate of return of 11 percent, representing the average rate of return for a stock portfolio. The decedent had been a conservative investor, however, with much of his portfolio invested in municipal bonds, and the court found that the investment strategy suggested by the expert "would as a matter of Louisiana law constitute mismanagement if made by a trustee to" someone in the plaintiff's circumstances. The appellate court ruled that the expert's use of the rate of return was error, and lowered the award to that proposed by the opposing expert.

3. *Expert Evidence in Mississippi State Courts*

a. Procedural Rules

Rule 26 of the Mississippi Rules of Civil Procedure ("MRCP") addresses the discovery of expert witnesses in Mississippi state courts. The relevant sections of this rule read as follows:

> **(4) Trial Preparations: Experts.** Discovery of facts known and opinions held by experts, otherwise discoverable under subsection (b)(1) of this rule and acquired or developed in anticipation of litigation or for trial may be obtained only as follows:
>
> (A)(i) A party may through interrogatories require any other party to identify each person whom the other party expects to call as an expert witness at trial, to state the subject matter on which the expert is expected to testify, and to state the substance of the facts and opinions to which the expert is expected to testify and a summary of the grounds for each opinion.
> (ii) Upon motion, the court may order further discovery by other means, subject to such restrictions as to scope and such provisions, pursuant to subsection (b)(4)(C) of this rule, concerning fees and expenses, as the court may deem appropriate.

In contrast to the Federal Rules, MRCP Rule 26 does not allow for the automatic deposition of an opposing party's testifying expert. As stated above, under MRCP Rule 26, a party seeking discovery of expert witnesses may through interrogatories require the disclosure of the identity of an expected expert witness, the subject matter of his testimony, the substance of the facts and opinions to which the expert will testify, and a summary of the grounds for these opinions. *See* MRCP 26(b)(4)(A)(i). This general rule is subject only to the exception that "the court may order further discovery by other means, subject to such restrictions as to scope and such provisions . . . concerning fees and expenses, as the court may deem appropriate." MRCP 26(b)(4)(A)(ii).

With the exception of the automatic deposition and initial mandatory disclosure obligations, the remainder of MRCP Rule 26 closely tracks the language found in the Federal Rules. Discovery of experts employed by parties in anticipation of litigation but not expected to be called at trial is available "only upon a showing of exceptional circumstances under which it is impracticable for the party seeking discovery to obtain facts or opinions in the same subject by other means." MRCP 26(b)(4)(B). In addition, the Federal Rules and the MRCP both require that barring manifest injustice, the party seeking discovery shall reasonably compensate the expert for responding to discovery requests or pay the opposing party reasonable fees in obtaining the requested information. *See* MRCP 26(b)(4)(C).

b. Evidentiary Framework

Mississippi Rules of Evidence (MRE) 701–703 are nearly identical to the language of Federal Rules of Evidence 701–703, following the 2003 amendments to the Mississippi Rules of Evidence. Mississippi has adopted the *Daubert* standard for the admission of expert testimony. *Miss. Transp.*

Comm'n v. McLemore, 863 So.2d 31 (Miss. 2003). Expert testimony must be relevant and based on fact, *Rebelwood Apartments RP, LP v. English*, 48 So.3d 483, 495 (Miss. 2010), and must concern matter that requires expertise so as to be helpful to the jury, *Utz v. Running & Rolling Trucking, Inc.*, 32 So.3d 450, 463–64 (Miss. 2010) (testimony re effect of dirt on taillights of truck did not require expert opinion). The standard of review for the admission or exclusion of expert opinion is an abuse of discretion. *Adcock v. Miss. Transp. Comm'n*, 981 So.2d 942, 946 (Miss. 2008).

c. Recent Cases

Procedure. A proponent of expert opinion must make an adequate proffer of the testimony to preserve error. MRE 103. In *Abernathy v. State*, 30 So.3d 320 (Miss. 2010), the defendant tendered a medical expert and described the proposed testimony in some detail to the trial court, seemingly in compliance with case law emphasizing the flexibility of Rule 103. See *Murray v. Payne*, 437 So.2d 47, 55 (Miss. 1993)(formal proffer of testimony not required). A divided Supreme Court held, however, that the defense failed to make an adequate record for review. *Id.* at 325. The court does not explicitly describe what *is* required, but counsel would be well advised to make a full formal proffer of the expert's testimony in response to a trial court's exclusion.

In *Hyundai Motor America v. Applewhite*, 53 So.3d 749 (Miss. 2011), the Supreme Court emphasized the necessity of timely objection to preserve error in expert testimony. In this wrongful death product liability case, plaintiffs' three experts were deposed long before trial, and defendant did not mount a pretrial *Daubert* challenge. Moreover, during trial, defendant did not object to one expert until after the witness had left the stand and did not object to another expert's testimony until it moved for directed verdict at the close of plaintiffs' case. For both experts, defendant waived its reliability objections. *Id.* at 755. Plaintiffs' third expert, however, failed to comply with discovery rules resulting in reversal. The expert, an accident reconstructionist, made a material substantive change to his calculations, which he tendered in an *errata* sheet to his deposition. But the *errata* sheet was not the proper form for a full and complete expert disclosure as required by Mississippi Rule of Civil Procedure 26(f). "The purpose of an *errata* sheet is to correct scrivener's errors or provide minor clarification; it is not a means of making material, substantive changes to a witness's testimony." *Id.* at 758. Expert discovery supplementation also was at issue in *Grant v. Ford Motor Co.*, 2012 WL 1592170 (Miss. Ct. App. May 8, 2012) (en banc), a products liability case. After the close of discovery, Ford filed a *Daubert* motion to exclude opinions of plaintiffs' biomechanics expert. In their responses, plaintiffs included three extremely lengthy affidavits of the expert containing new matter. The court quoted a federal district court opinion, *Avance v. Kerr-McGee Chem., LLC*, No. 5:04CV209, 2006 WL 3484246 (E.D. Tex. Nov. 30, 2006), in holding that the new material in the affidavits was untimely filed and allowing it would be unfair and prejudicial.

When a party raises a *Daubert* challenge, it is incumbent on the trial court to conduct a hearing on admissibility under MRE 702. In *Mitchell v. Barnes*, 2012 WL 1506004 (Miss. Ct. App. May 1, 2012), defendant filed a motion *in limine* to exclude plaintiff's expert testimony as unreliable. On the date of trial, defendant requested that the court hear the motion, but the court ruled that the issue should be raised on cross-examination. This approach failed to implement the gatekeeping function required by *McLemore* and constituted error.

Qualifications. MRE 702 "does not relax the traditional standards for determining that the witness is indeed qualified to speak an opinion on a matter within a purported field of knowledge." *McLemore*, 863 So.2d at 35. The question of expert qualifications thus continues to be an issue in numerous Mississippi cases.

As a general rule, an expert's precise title or certification is not as important as knowledge of the particular subject matter *sub judice*. In *Kilhullen v. Kansas City S. Ry.*, 8 So.3d 168 (Miss. 2009), a registered professional engineer was allowed to testify regarding a truck-train accident, though he had no specialized knowledge or training in accident reconstruction. The expert in *Investor Resource Svcs., Inc. v. Cato*, 15 So.3d 412 (Miss. 2009) had allowed her CPA license to lapse and had no experience in shareholder derivative suits. Nevertheless, she had more than twenty years of corporate and academic experience in business, which was sufficient to qualify her to offer an opinion on whether defendants properly fulfilled their duties as corporate officers and directors. *Id*. at 418–19.

But general expertise may be insufficient for specific issues. In *McKee v. Bowers Window & Door Co.*, 64 So.3d 926 (Miss. 2011), a general contractor with twenty-four years of experience was determined to be unqualified to opine in the specific field of window manufacture and design. The expert had no special education, training, or experience specific to windows and had never worked for a window manufacturer or seller. *Id*. at 934–35. A generalist mechanical engineer had no particular training or experience in the adequacy of warnings and his testimony on that topic was stricken in *Tucker v. Rees-Memphis, Inc.*, 17 So.3d 122 (Miss. Ct. App. 2009). In *Trapani v. Treutel*, 2012 WL 1399156 (Miss. Ct. App. Apr. 24, 2012), plaintiffs' insurance expert practiced as a claims adjuster, but his experience in procuring insurance for clients was very limited, and he was held unqualified to testify on insurance agency operations. *See also Grant v. Ford Motor Co.*, 2012 WL 1592170 (Miss. Ct. App. May 8, 2012) (expert who had taken only one brief course and had published no articles in the relevant field held not qualified to offer opinion regarding biomechanics).

Expert testimony is essential in medical malpractice cases, though testimony by a specialist may not be necessary. Qualifications depend on the expert's knowledge of the particular medical subjects involved. *See Troupe v. McAuley*, 955 So.2d 848, 858 (Miss. 2007) (neurosurgeon who had never performed middle-ear surgery held unqualified to opine re standard of care for such procedure). In *Worthy v. McNair*, 37 So.3d 609 (Miss. 2010), involving the death of an infant, the critical issue concerned pathology. Plaintiffs' expert was qualified in obstetrics but failed to establish his expertise in pathology and was properly excluded. Similarly, in *McDonald v. Mem. Hosp. at Gulfport*, 8 So.3d 175 (Miss. 2009), a board-certified pathologist and psychiatrist was not qualified to opine as to gastroenterology, while in *Hans v. Mem. Hosp. at Gulfport*, 40 So.3d 1270 (Miss. Ct. App. 2010), plaintiffs' expert was board certified in gastroenterology and internal medicine but was not qualified as to the emergency-room procedures at issue. *See also Paige v. Miss. Baptist Med. Ctr.*, 31 So.3d 637 (Miss. Ct. App. 2010) (internist practicing general medicine was not qualified to opine as to standard of care in surgical procedure; *Figueroa v. Orleans*, 42 So.3d 49 (Miss. Ct. App. 2010) (gastroenterologist not qualified to opine re standard of care in surgery case); *Parmenter v. J & B Enterprises, Inc.*, 2012 WL 539949 (Miss. Ct. App. Feb. 21, 2012) (precluding physician with no familiarity with standard of care of psychologist or psychiatrist from testifying as to plaintiff's alleged PTSD).

While a restricted medical license does not categorically preclude an expert from testifying, the expert in *Caldwell v. Warren*, 2 So.3d 751 (Miss. Ct. App. 2009), was specifically restricted from practicing in neurosurgery, the specialty at issue in the case. Accordingly, the witness was properly excluded.

Nurses are not qualified to testify as to medical causation, *Mid-South Retina, LLC v. Conner*, 72 So.3d 1048 (Miss. 2011), although they can offer opinions as to the standard of care in nursing. *Vaughn v. Miss. Baptist Med. Ctr.*, 20 So.3d 645, 654–55 (Miss. 2009).

The rules of evidence apply to death certificates, *Birkhead v. State*, 57 So.3d 1223 (Miss. 2011), and in *McKeown v. Pitcock*, 79 So.3d 520 (Miss. Ct. App. 2011), the court applied Rule 702 to exclude the death certificate of plaintiffs' decedent on the ground that the signatory to the certificate, a deputy coroner, was not qualified to give the listed opinion as to the cause of death.

Reliability and Methodology. Since *McLemore*, Mississippi courts have been careful in conducting their gatekeeping duties for expert testimony. While recognizing the wide berth given to expert opinion, courts require experts to satisfy the "scientific knowledge" element of Rule 702 by showing that their testimony is "supported and based on what is known" and "is more than subjective or unsupported speculation." *See Hill v. Mills*, 26 So.3d 322, 329 (Miss. 2010). Hill was a medical malpractice case in which the supreme court distinguished lack of reliability from the traditional "battle of the experts." Defendant's expert submitted substantial authoritative medical literature contradicting the opinion of plaintiffs' expert, who presented nothing in response. But "[a]n expert whose opinions are under scrutiny may not ignore allegations of unreliability and non-acceptance within the scientific community, but rather must respond with some evidence that the opinions are, in fact, accepted within the scientific community." *Id*. at 330. Accordingly, the trial court properly excluded the expert testimony as unreliable.[10]

The Mississippi Supreme Court considered lack of supporting evidence in another medical negligence case in *Patterson v. Tibbs*, 60 So.3d 742 (Miss. 2011). Plaintiffs' expert claimed that the deceased infant received a lethal dose of a painkiller prior to a surgery, but he had no support for his extrapolation of the amount of the drug administered in order to counter the peer-reviewed article proffered by opposing experts that rebutted his opinion. Finding the case analogous to *Hill*, the Supreme Court found that the expert's testimony was unreliable due to lack of support in any medical literature. *Id*. at 752.

Methodology—Toxicology. In *Sherwin-Williams Co. v. Gaines ex rel. Pollard*, 75 So.3d 41 (Miss. 2011), the Mississippi Supreme Court again addressed fundamental toxicological principles of dose response. "A dose-response ratio is critical to determining the causal connection between a poison and an injury." *Id*. at 45–46. Plaintiffs' experts claimed a single blood test showing a high lead level was sufficient to establish causation for a brain-injury claim. The experts extrapolated from that one data point to hypothesize both dose and duration, engaging in fallacious *post hoc ergo propter hoc* reasoning, which was mere speculation and inadmissible. Accordingly, the court reversed and rendered based on insufficient proof of causation. This recent decision seems to conflict with the court's opinion in *Franklin Corp. v. Tedford*, 18 So.3d 215 (Miss. 2009), which involved claims of neurological injury from exposure to propyl bromide ("1-BP"). The court recognized that the toxicology of 1-BP was "a relatively new field of study," and plaintiffs' experts did not know the lower level of toxicity for the chemical or the amount of exposure sustained by plaintiffs. Nevertheless, the court ruled that plaintiffs' experts were properly allowed to opine that plaintiffs had suffered injury from the chemical, based in part on the temporal relationship of symptoms and alleged exposure. The Supreme Court emphasized the need to carefully review allegedly supporting toxicological data in *Watts v. Radiator Specialty Co.*, 990 So.2d 143 (Miss. 2008). Plaintiffs' expert opined that benzene exposure in a solvent caused plaintiffs' non-Hodgkin's lymphoma, relying on eighteen case studies. But on close analysis, the court found that none of the studies concluded that there was such a causal link. *Id*. at 147. Thus there was a *Joiner* analytical gap between the data from the studies and the expert's proffered opinion, which was thus unreliable.

Methodology—Products Liability. The Mississippi Product Liability Act requires proof of a feasible design alternative in a defective design claim. In *Hyundai Motor America v. Applewhite*, 53 So.3d 749 (Miss. 2011), plaintiffs claimed a defectively designed automobile A-pillar, and their expert used a computer to simulate an alternative design. The Supreme Court held that such a simulation was sufficient, and plaintiffs were not required to build and test an actual model of the design. *Id*. at 755–57. In *Grant v. Ford Motor Co.*, 2012 WL 1592170 (Miss. Ct. App. May 8, 2012), plaintiffs' expert theorized that a seat belt unbuckled due to force on the buckle housing. The expert planned to perform demonstrations involving snatching and striking the buckles at trial. But the snatching demonstrations did not constitute proper testing of his theory, and his proposed alternative designs were not available when the car was built in 1996, so the opinions were wholly unreliable. *Id*. at *9–*11.

---

[10] See discussion of this rationale in the context of engineering opinion in *Smith v. Clement*, 983 So.2d 285 (Miss. 2008).

Methodology—Personal Injury Damages. In *Rebelwood Apartments RP, LP v. English*, 48 So.3d 483 (Miss. 2010), the Supreme Court addressed the methodology for the calculation of a personal injury plaintiff's lost earnings. Plaintiffs' economist expert used a national average for future income but ignored the decedent's actual earnings history. The Supreme Court rejected the earning-capacity methodology and added other specific rules for the estimation of a lost income stream. In addition to using actual earnings data when available, an expert must deduct for personal consumption, include fringe benefits only if they have been actually received, and use an objective standard for work-life expectancy. *Id.* at 494–97. In the analysis of future work life, a defendant is entitled to introduce evidence of factors that might influence life or employment expectancy. *Wackenhut Corp. v. Fortune*, 2012 WL 1174518, at *4 (Miss. Ct. App. Apr. 10, 2012). In *Wackenhut*, the court of appeals ruled that the defendant should have been allowed to introduce evidence of plaintiff's alcohol abuse for the limited purpose of showing diminished life expectancy or employability. In calculating medical expenses, an expert's opinion must be based on adequate evidence, not speculation. *City of Jackson v. Spann*, 4 So.3d 1029, 1038–39 (Miss. 2009) (rejecting expert's "guess" as to future surgical costs and estimate of future disability).

Methodology—Valuation. In an eminent domain case, the Supreme Court held that a valuation expert should use a recognized methodology. In *Dedeaux Utility Co. v. City of Gulfport*, 63 So.3d 514 (Miss. 2011), the court stated that the income-capitalization approach was appropriate to value intangible assets of a utility, rather than the condemnor expert's unrecognized methodology, which was inadmissible *ipse dixit*. Similarly, in *Gulf South Pipeline Co. v. Pitre*, 35 So.3d 494 (Miss. 2010), neither side's experts used a recognized methodology to evaluate the diminution in value of property due to the construction of a pipeline; thus their opinions were unreliable. Landowners may offer an opinion as to valuation based on their "unique view of the property," without being accepted as experts under Rule 702. *Miss. Transp. Comm'n v. Buchanan*, 2012 WL 1174578, at *5 (Miss. Ct. App. Apr. 10, 2012). Business valuation is a frequent issue in divorce cases. In Mississippi, an expert should not include goodwill in such a valuation. *See Yelverton v. Yelverton*, 961 So.2d 19, 29 (Miss. 2007) (husband's interest in car dealership); *Rhodes v. Rhodes*, 52 So.3d 430, 445–47 (Miss. Ct. App. 2011) (expert opinion excluded in part for failing to remove goodwill from calculation).

CHAPTER VI
EXPERT EVIDENCE IN THE SIXTH CIRCUIT

by

**Brian Jackson
C. E. Hunter Brush
Butlers, Snow, O'Mara, Stevens & Cannada, PLLC
150 Fourth Avenue North, Suite 1200
Nashville, TN 37219
(615) 503-9100**

A. INTRODUCTION

The Sixth Circuit applies a two-step *Daubert* inquiry. First, the district court should determine whether the expert testimony is reliable. Second, the district court must ensure that the testimony is relevant, that is, that it will assist the trier of fact in understanding the evidence or determining a fact in issue. *Smelser v. Norfolk Southern Railway*, 105 F.3d 299, 303 (6th Cir. 1996). In accordance with *General Electric Co. v. Joiner*, 522 U.S. 136 (1997), the Sixth Circuit employs an abuse-of-discretion standard to review the admission or exclusion of expert testimony. *Morales v. American Honda Motor Co.*, 151 F.3d 500, 515 (6th Cir. 1998).

Product liability cases have occupied a central role in the Sixth Circuit's *Daubert* jurisprudence. The court has examined a broad range of questions in the product liability context, including what witnesses are competent to testify regarding particular issues and what methodology can be used to establish that a product is defective or unreasonably dangerous. *See, e.g., Johnson v. Manitowoc Boom Trucks, Inc.*, 484 F.3d 426 (6th Cir. 2007). Another recurring issue has been the extent to which differential diagnosis may be used to establish both general and specific causation. After wrangling with that question for several years, the Sixth Circuit borrowed a test from the Third Circuit to clarify under what circumstances a differential-diagnosis causation opinion will be admissible. *Best v. Lowe's Home Centers, Inc.*, 563 F.3d 171 (6th Cir. 2009) (adopting *In re Paoli Railroad Yard PCB Litigation*, 35 F.3d 717 (3d Cir. 1994)).

B. EXPERT QUALIFICATION CASES

1. Sixth Circuit

Sigler v. American Honda Motor Co., 532 F.3d 469 (6th Cir. 2008).
Plaintiff was injured by an allegedly defective airbag. The district court granted summary judgment to defendant after excluding the testimony of plaintiff's experts, Mr. Griffin and Dr. Heisser. Griffin, a mechanic, proposed to testify about plaintiff's rate of speed at impact and the potential cause for the airbag malfunction. The district court determined that the mechanic, Griffin, was not qualified

to testify to physics, accident reconstruction, or airbag engineering. The district court excluded Heisser's testimony because he relied on assumptions tied to Griffin's testimony.

The Sixth Circuit agreed with the district court that Griffin lacked the expertise to testify about accident reconstruction. Moreover, the court noted that, while Griffin was qualified to analyze airbags, he had not examined the airbag in this case and therefore he could not reliably opine about why the airbag malfunctioned. However, the Sixth Circuit found that Heisser's assumptions were supported by evidence other than Griffin's opinions and that the district court abused its discretion in excluding Heisser's testimony.

Dickenson v. Cardiac and Thoracic Surgery of Eastern Tennessee, 388 F.3d 976 (6th Cir. 2004).
In this medical malpractice case, the plaintiff appealed the exclusion of the proffered testimony of expert witnesses. Plaintiff's expert Dr. Johnson testified about the alleged negligence of a pulmonologist in prematurely removing a ventilation tube after surgery. Johnson had practiced as a cardiac thoracic surgeon for more than thirty-five years, had performed thousands of heart-related operations, and had managed approximately two hundred patients within the last three years that required a ventilator in excess of three days. Despite this background, his testimony was excluded by the district court. The district court noted that Johnson was a cardiac thoracic surgeon, not a pulmonologist, that he was not trained in pulmonology, and that he had never previously qualified as an expert witnesses in a suit against a pulmonologist. The district court thought that Dr. Johnson's familiarity with ventilating medical equipment and the settings used on that equipment was lacking and noted that Johnson had never written an article on pulmonology and could not identify particular articles on the subject of pulmonology that he had read.

The Sixth Circuit observed that the law does not require an expert to demonstrate a familiarity with accepted medical literature or published standards in order for his testimony to be reliable in the sense contemplated by Federal Rules of Evidence 702. The court noted that the text of FRE 702 expressly contemplates that an expert may be qualified on the basis of experience and concluded that plaintiff had made a sufficient showing with respect to Johnson's experience. *Id.* at 980. The court noted that *Daubert*'s role of ensuring the courtroom door remains closed to junk science was not served by excluding testimony such as Johnson's that was supported by extensive relevant experience, such exclusion being rarely justified in cases involving medical experts as opposed to experts in the area of product liability. *Id.* at 982.

Surles ex rel. Johnson v. Greyhound Lines, Inc., 474 F.3d 288 (6th Cir. 2007).
A passenger attacked a bus driver with a box cutter and caused the bus to careen into a ditch. Plaintiff sued Greyhound for negligence in failing to equip the bus with a driver barrier. The jury awarded $8 million in damages. The Sixth Circuit found that the district court did not abuse its discretion in allowing plaintiff's expert witnesses, Martin and Watt, to testify. Martin had worked twenty-eight years with the Los Angeles Police Department, in his later years founding a threat-management unit. Among other things, the unit dealt with managing situations involving the violent mentally ill. In his subsequent role at a consulting firm, Martin worked with clients in the transportation industry on threat-assessment issues, oversaw the design of threat-assessment systems, and trained employees on interpersonal human aggression and managing violent employees. Although Martin did not have threat-assessment experience in the bus industry specifically, the Sixth Circuit found no clear error of judgment in allowing him to testify. Requiring experience in the very specialized area of commercial bus line threat assessment would be an unduly narrow approach to defining the requisite expert qualifications. Martin's unfamiliarity with those specific aspects of the subject at hand were deemed merely to affect the weight and credibility of the testimony, not its admissibility. *Id.* at 294.

Watt was employed as a forensic engineer and had received his educational training in a six-year mechanical engineering program, had worked in the transportation sector generally with a specific focus on buses for a period of several years, and in the early 1990s had designed an entry-resistant barrier to protect bus drivers from attacks by passengers. The district court acted within its discretion in qualifying Watt to testify. The district court did rule that neither Martin nor Watts would be permitted to offer opinions on the issue of foreseeability, noting that anyone could provide an opinion that such incidents were foreseeable in light of the number of prior incidents. In affirming the district court, the Sixth Circuit found that the experts had adequately explained how their experience led to the conclusions they reached, why that experience was a sufficient basis for their opinions, and how that experience was reliably applied to the facts.

2. District Courts

Sheet Metal Workers' National Pension Fund v. Palladium Equity Partners, LLC, 722 F. Supp. 2d 845 (E.D. Mich. 2010).
In this ERISA action involving withdrawal liability, plaintiffs alleged that defendants were alter egos of Haden Schweitzer Corporation and Haden Environmental Corporation (the "Haden Companies") as well as part of the same "controlled group" as the Haden Companies. Plaintiffs alleged that defendants were liable for the Haden Companies' withdrawal liability. Defendants hired Steven Adams, an attorney, to testify about the structure and function of defendants' private equity model as compared to similar entities in the industry, as well as to opine about the devastating effect that finding defendants liable would have on the private equity industry. Plaintiffs moved to strike this testimony on the basis that Adams was not qualified and that such testimony would not assist the fact finder.

The district court found that Adams was qualified to opine about the typical business model of private equity firms as he had twelve years of experience structuring private equity funds, served on numerous boards, and taught mergers and acquisition law. However, the district court found that Adams could not testify on the devastating effect that finding defendants liable would have on the private equity industry because "[s]uch policy-type arguments fall outside of the scope of expert testimony . . . and are irrelevant to [the] issues at hand."

Taylor v. Teco Barge Line, Inc., et al., 642 F. Supp. 2d 689 (W.D. Ky. 2009).
Plaintiff, a deckhand on a tugboat, suffered an injury while lifting heavy materials. Plaintiff hired Don J. Green, a marine liability expert, to opine about the Revised Lifting Equation issued by the National Institute for Occupational Safety and Health and to discuss the general duty standard adopted by the OSHA. The Lifting Equation assists with "the identification of ergonomic solutions for reducing the physical stresses associated with manual lifting." The general duty standard requires employers to maintain a workplace free from hazards likely to cause death or serious physical injury. Defendant moved to exclude Green's testimony.

The court found that, while Green had considerable experience in the maritime industry and experience as a safety consultant, he lacked experience in ergonomics and would therefore not be allowed to testify about the Lifting Equation. However, the district court found that, in light of his maritime and safety background, Green was qualified to testify as to whether the general duty standard was breached.

Saginaw Chippewa Indian Tribe v. Granholm, 690 F. Supp. 2d 622 (E.D. Mich. 2010).
The issue in this case was whether certain land in Michigan was "Indian Country" as defined by federal law. The resolution of that issue turned on the interpretation and context of several treaties signed between the federal government and a tribe and the history of the federal government's transition to the "reservation" program in the nineteenth century. The parties hired historical experts to address these issues, and each side challenged the qualifications of the other side's experts. Ultimately, the district court held that all of the experts were qualified to offer opinion testimony.

The court noted that the decisive issues were whether each expert possessed "specialized knowledge" that would assist the fact finder in determining a fact of consequence and whether the expert based his proposed testimony on sufficient research derived from reliable methods. The court noted that the core *Daubert* factors were not particularly helpful or applicable to historical experts, who deal in historical interpretation, not scientific testing. In evaluating the proposed testimony, the court considered the following:

> (1) whether the proposed expert's research and specialized knowledge was conducted for the purpose of the litigation or an independent purpose; (2) whether the proposed expert has improperly extrapolated an unfounded conclusion from a generally accepted premise; (3) whether the proposed expert has considered alternative explanations and conclusions; and (4) whether the proposed expert has conducted the litigation analysis with the same level of "intellectual rigor" used outside the courtroom.

Lee v. Metropolitan Govt. of Nashville and Davidson County, et al., 596 F. Supp. 2d 1101 (M.D. Tenn. 2009).

This Section 1983 action concerned a man on LSD who died after Nashville Metro police repeatedly used a Taser on him. Plaintiff employed two use-of-force experts, Ernest Burwell and Roger Clark, to address whether Metro properly trained its officers and whether excessive force was used. Defendants moved to exclude the proposed testimony of these experts on the basis that they were not qualified.

The district court examined *Berry v. City of Detroit*, 25 F.3d 1342 (6th Cir. 1994) and *Champion v. Outlook Nashville Inc.*, 380 F.3d 893, 902 (6th Cir. 2004) and observed that a police-practices expert may testify to the proper actions of an officer in a given situation, when that expert has sufficient credentials and his or her testimony will assist the fact finder in determining a fact in issue. Here, the district court held that both experts were qualified to opine on the relevant issues because both were former officers, served as police instructors, and were generally experienced with Tasers.

Bush v. Michelin Tire Corp., 963 F. Supp. 1436 (W.D. Ky. 1996).

In this product liability case, Plaintiffs sought to admit expert testimony that a tire was defectively designed. 963 F. Supp. at 1442. Defendant sought to disqualify the expert because he was not a formally trained engineer and had gained his knowledge from his work as a litigation consultant in other cases. *Id.* Without any discussion of *Daubert*, the court disagreed, stating that his experience was sufficient to establish expertise. *Id.* at 1442.

Defendant also objected to some of the studies and tests the expert offered in support of his opinion. *Id.* at 1443. The court cited *Daubert* and then analyzed each different study and test for its own admissibility, without specific reference to the factors cited in *Daubert*. *Id.* at 1443–45. The court noted that "[a]n expert may rely on evidence that is otherwise inadmissible in forming his opinion, if it is the type that is reasonably relied on by experts in the field," but that the "Sixth Circuit has placed limitations on the type of research on which an expert can rely for his opinion." *Id.* at 1445. The court concluded that three of the tests cited by the Plaintiff's expert were "inadequate to support an expert opinion," and that the expert could not refer to them or rely on them as a basis for his opinion, because the information had been gleaned from various other cases, and he did not have "any personal knowledge of the protocol, procedures, or raw data from the tests." *Id.* at 1445–46.

Rice v. Cincinnati, New Orleans and Pacific Ry. Co., 920 F. Supp. 732 (E.D. Ky. 1996).

An engineer-trainee sued his railroad employer for injuries he allegedly suffered in a collision with an automobile. 920 F. Supp. at 734. The plaintiff sought to admit expert testimony by several of the plaintiff's fellow trainmen that the engine cab was not properly designed and that the crossing was unsafe. *Id.* at 736. The court stated that this testimony might well have been admitted at one time, but that "a new era in the scrutiny of expert testimony was introduced by [*Daubert*]." *Id.* The court held that the trainmen were not qualified to offer expert opinion regarding the engine design, and that this issue would have to be addressed by an expert in ergonomics or train engine design. *Id.* at 737. The court likewise held that the trainmen did "not have the expertise to offer reliable testimony on crossing design." *Id.* at 737–38. Accordingly, the proffered testimony was excluded. *Id.* at 738.

Gibson Guitar Corp. v. Paul Reed Smith Guitars, LP, 325 F. Supp. 2d 841 (M.D. Tenn. 2004).
In this trademark-infringement action, plaintiff moved to exclude portions of the report of the defendant's expert, Ringo. The court noted the four criteria from *Daubert* and also added the five additional factors from the Sixth Circuit *Smelser* decision, 105 F.3d 299, 303 (6th Cir. 1997). Finally, the court noted that the Ninth Circuit had also considered the factor of whether the expert's opinion was the product of independent research or whether the opinion was formulated for litigation. The court ultimately excluded the opinion as failing the "fit" test of *Daubert* and being inappropriate to the legal issues remaining in the case.

Flanagan v. Altria Group, Inc., 423 F. Supp. 2d 697 (E.D. Mich. 2005).
Plaintiff in this tobacco litigation moved to exclude the testimony of the defense expert witness, Peterman. Peterman previously worked in the Bureau of Economics of the Federal Trade Commission (FTC) for eighteen years and after leaving the FTC worked with consulting firms specializing in economics, finance, and business. Defendant retained Peterman to offer expert testimony in tobacco litigation concerning the history of the FTC and its monitoring and regulation of cigarette advertising and marketing practices. In a prior Illinois state court case, Peterman's testimony was excluded as being unrelated to any potential areas of his expertise but instead being only a narrative summary of historical facts.

The court was concerned with Peterson's opinions about the meaning and significance of various actions of the FTC because he did not explain the economic principles or method on which his opinions were based. Ultimately, the court determined that it would analyze Peterson's opinion not as an economics expert applying economic analysis but instead as the opinion of one who acquired specialized knowledge through experience with the FTC's Bureau of Economics in connection with the FTC's regulation of cigarette advertising and promotion. Based on that experience, the court concluded that Peterson had acquired sufficient specialized knowledge to be permitted to testify.

De Jager Const., Inc. v. Schleininger, 938 F. Supp. 446 (W.D. Mich. 1996).
In a RICO action brought by a general contractor, plaintiff sought to use a CPA as an expert witness on damages. 938 F. Supp. at 447–48. The court cited its duty to determine the admissibility of such evidence under *Daubert* and observed that, while a CPA generally possesses the "specialized knowledge" to serve as an expert witness under the proper circumstances, the question of "[w]hether an 'expert' qualifies to answer specific questions in a particular case is a different issue." *Id.* at 448–49. The court then undertook an extremely detailed factual analysis of the substance of the proposed testimony, without reference to the *Daubert* framework. *Id.* at 449–55. The court concluded that the proposed testimony blurred "the distinction between substantive liability and a calculation of the damages," and that the expert selected portions of available material that supported his client's position, while ignoring other positions that did not support his client's claim. *Id.* at 449. Accordingly, the court held that this expert was not permitted to render any opinion regarding damages sustained by the plaintiff. *Id.* at 455.

Prater v. CSX Transportation, Inc., 2003 WL 21478892 (N.D. Ohio 2003).
In this FELA case, plaintiff, who worked for thirty years for Consolidated Rail Corporation as a car man, alleged that his working conditions caused carpal tunnel syndrome, shoulder pain and impairment, and herniated discs. Plaintiff moved to exclude defendant's expert on causation, Dr.

Howard Sandler. The court found little in Sandler's background to equip him to testify about musculoskeletal trauma and its effects. He had no formal or extensive medical training since medical school; he had not treated patients with musculoskeletal complaints; he had not been board certified in any of the professional specialties that come within the ambit of occupational medicine; he had not conducted research in any of those fields; and his professional writings were not the product of such research or the subject of peer review. Sandler's opinions in prior matters of occupational medicine across a broad range of bodily organs and functions had invariably been on behalf of the defense. While Sandler had been allowed to give opinion testimony in many other cases on occupational medicine issues, his background did not show that he had knowledge to support his proffered opinion that plaintiff's symptoms were not related to his railroad employment. The court thought it likely that Sandler was retained by defendants because they anticipated receipt of a favorable opinion. The court reached no specific conclusions about the adequacy of Sandler's methodology but noted the troubling absence of a record of measurements and observations. Sandler's testimony was excluded.

C. METHODOLOGY CASES

1. Product Design

a. Sixth Circuit

Lawrence v. Raymond Corp., No. 11-3935, 2012 WL 4748153 (6th Cir. 2012).
Plaintiff suffered an injury to her foot while operating a forklift. She alleged that the forklift was defectively designed and that its manufacturer had failed to warn her adequately about its dangers. Plaintiff hired Thomas Berry, a mechanical engineer, who opined that all forklifts without a latching door in the rear-entry are defectively designed and that such a door would have prevented plaintiff's injury. The district court excluded Berry's testimony on the grounds that it was unreliable and prepared solely for litigation.

On the reliability issue, the Sixth Circuit noted that forklift design cases require an expert to test the expert's proposed alternative design and be able to address the benefits and risks of the alternative design. Here, Berry only ran one test and that test was on a different type of forklift than the one that caused Lawrence's injury. The Sixth Circuit agreed that Berry's testimony was unreliable. The Sixth Circuit also noted that Berry himself admitted that almost all of his knowledge and experience about forklift design resulted from his work as a litigation expert and that he developed his latching-door theory while consulting on forklift accident litigation.

Newell Rubbermaid, Inc. v. Raymond Corp., 676 F.3d 521 (6th Cir. 2012).
In this product liability action arising from a forklift accident, the district court granted summary judgment to defendant after excluding the testimony of plaintiff's expert. The district court found that the expert's methods were unscientific in that they relied on anecdotal evidence, relied on improper extrapolation, failed to consider other potential causes, and lacked testing. The Sixth Circuit affirmed, citing a factually similar case, *Brown v. Raymond Corp.*, 432 F.3d 640 (6th Cir. 2005) (reasoning that a district court could exclude an expert's testimony when the expert did not test an alternative design), and observing that Plaintiff did not clarify the expert's methodology on appeal.

Johnson v. Manitowoc Boom Trucks, Inc., 484 F.3d 426 (6th Cir. 2007).
In this product liability case, plaintiff's guardian sued the manufacturer of a truck-mounted crane and appealed the district court's exclusion of proffered expert testimony by Friend, a registered professional engineer. Friend had a master's degree in engineering, taught engineering at a community

college for ten years, and since 1980 had been employed exclusively as an engineering consultant and testified in a wide range of design-defect cases, rendering opinions on the design of almost any type of machine. Friend's preparation for this case consisted primarily of document review including depositions, discovery responses, brochures, owner's and operator's manuals for a variety of truck cranes, standards for different kinds of mobile boom trucks, the OSHA accident report, and accompanying photographs. He also inspected and photographed the subject truck crane. Based on this research, Friend prepared a report in which he opined the truck crane was defectively designed because its outriggers were not electronically linked to crane operation via an interlocking system that would make the boom crane inoperable if any of the outriggers were not in contact with the ground. Friend noted particularly a brochure for a lift bucket-type truck that had such an interlocking system as early as 1978.

The Sixth Circuit observed that Friend had conducted no implementation or testing of the interlock concept. While testing is not an absolute prerequisite, when the subject easily lends itself to testing and substantiation, it is certainly preferable. The court stated that one way to overcome a testing requirement might be to show the expert has significant technical expertise in the specific area in which he is suggesting an alternative design. However, Friend had no such specialized expertise. Friend was also unsuccessful in arguing there was a general acceptance of interlocking outriggers at the time the truck crane was manufactured. Finally, the Sixth Circuit characterized Friend's testimony as being prepared for litigation, and not being testimony about matters growing naturally and directly out of research that Friend was conducting independent of the litigation. The Sixth Circuit approved consideration of the fact that the expert's opinions were conceived, executed, and invented solely in the context of this litigation as a factor weighing in favor of exclusion of the testimony. *Id.* at 435.

Davison v. Cole Sewell Corp., 231 F. App'x 444 (6th Cir. 2007).
Plaintiff's husband was injured when he was struck in the head and neck by a metal bracket that was a part of a display constructed and maintained by the defendants. The injuries ultimately led the husband to commit suicide. Plaintiff appealed from the exclusion of the testimony of her expert witness, Silverman, on the issues of negligence and proximate cause. Silverman opined that the accident was caused by some sort of failure of the display structure, listing sixteen possible causes for the alleged incident, such as insufficient screws, misaligned hinges, and insufficient inspection. It was impossible to establish the specific cause for the failure because the display was dismantled right after the accident occurred. Silverman reviewed deposition testimony, the report of the defendant's expert, and a report from the retail establishment where the accident occurred, but he based his opinion principally on photographs of a display in the store where the accident occurred, visits he made to another store, deposition testimony that a screw might have been missing, and Internet research about screws. There was no evidence that the other store had the same displays and, ultimately, Silverman could not identify the specific cause or causes of the accident. Because Silverman's causation testimony was essentially speculation and conjecture, and because there was not an adequate factual foundation for Silverman's hypothesis, the Sixth Circuit affirmed the exclusion of the testimony.

Pride v. BIC Corp., 218 F.3d 566 (6th Cir. 2000).
In her lawsuit against the defendant lighter manufacturer for the wrongful death of her husband, plaintiff sought to introduce the testimony of experts who opined that the defendant's lighters were defectively designed and unreasonably dangerous. 218 F.3d at 568–72. The trial court conducted a *Daubert* hearing, at which plaintiff's experts testified about their theories of the accident's cause. *Id.* at 571–72. In addition, defendant called two experts to assist the court in evaluating plaintiff's experts and their scientific methodologies. *Id.* at 573. After weighing all of the experts' testimony,

the magistrate judge recommended, and the district court agreed, to grant the defendant's motions to exclude plaintiff's expert witnesses. *Id.* at 574.

On appeal, the Sixth Circuit concluded that the district court had not abused its discretion in deciding that plaintiff's experts had used an unreliable methodology in forming their conclusions. *Id.* at 578. Thus, the Sixth Circuit affirmed the district court's order excluding the testimony of plaintiff's expert witnesses. *Id.* at 581.

American & Foreign Ins. Co. v. General Electric Co., 45 F.3d 135 (6th Cir. 1995).

Plaintiff insurance company brought a product liability case against General Electric for damages from a fire to a school insured by plaintiff. 45 F.3d at 136. Plaintiff raised various allegations of negligence with regard to a circuit breaker manufactured by GE. *Id.* The trial court excluded as unreliable the testimony of plaintiff's proffered expert, an electrical engineer, because the expert had not established any protocol for his testing, he had not taken any notes during the testing, and he had discarded the "raw data." *Id.* at 136–37. No one had witnessed the test, and the only evidence the expert had of the test was a summary graph of the results. *Id.* at 137. He also was unsure whether his equipment had been calibrated. *Id.* American argued on appeal that the trial court had erred by excluding the testimony. *Id.*

The Sixth Circuit recognized that *Daubert* establishes a standard of evidentiary reliability, where evidentiary reliability means, essentially, "trustworthiness." *Id.* at 138. "[B]y defining evidentiary reliability in terms of scientific validity . . . the *Daubert* Court has instructed the courts that they are not to be concerned with the reliability of the conclusions generated by valid methods, principles, and reasoning." 45 F.3d at 138 (quoting *United States v. Bonds*, 12 F.3d 540, 556 (6th Cir. 1993)). Instead, "they are only to determine whether the principles or methodology underlying the testimony itself are valid." *Id.* Under *Daubert*, the trial court must make a "preliminary assessment of whether the reasoning or methodology underlying the testimony is scientifically valid and whether that reasoning or methodology properly can be applied to the facts in issue." *Id.* The court then discussed the factors set forth in *Daubert*, which govern the analysis of "whether a theory or technique is scientific knowledge that will assist the trier of fact." *Id.*

Although the trial court's determination in this case was made before the *Daubert* decision, the Sixth Circuit held that the trial court properly analyzed the relevant considerations required by that case. *Id.* at 138–39. The inadequacies in the expert's testing and data collection prevented plaintiff from carrying its burden of showing that the testimony was reliable. *Id.* at 139. Accordingly, the Sixth Circuit held that the trial court did not abuse its discretion in excluding the testimony. *Id.*

Coffee v. Dowley Manufacturing Company, Inc., 89 F. App'x 927 (6th Cir. 2003).

In this product liability case, plaintiff appealed the trial court's decision to exclude the proffered testimony of his expert, Dr. Wilson, a professor of mechanical engineering, concluding that an automotive repair tool manufactured by defendant was defective. The Sixth Circuit affirmed, agreeing that Dr. Wilson's testimony failed to meet the standard set forth in Rule 702 and *Daubert*. Dr. Wilson utilized a purely analytical technique called finite element analysis that did not involve any physical testing as the basis of his testimony. Dr. Wilson never obtained a working exemplary tool. His first Rule 26 report was based on a critical error in his understanding of how the tool operated, and his initial results were wildly inaccurate. To the Sixth Circuit, this demonstrated Dr. Wilson's lack of experience about the subject matter of his testimony. Dr. Wilson further made several estimates with no factual foundation in important elements of his analysis.

Brock v. Caterpillar, Inc., 94 F.3d 220 (6th Cir. 1996).

Plaintiff brought a product liability suit for injuries suffered while operating a D9H Caterpillar bulldozer. 94 F.3d at 222. The trial judge permitted plaintiff's expert to testify about the feasibility of using an improved brake system in the D9H. *Id.* at 224. The Sixth Circuit held that this expert was qualified to testify "about matters pertinent to the condition and design of the braking system on the D9H machine at the pertinent time." *Id.* at 226. However, the court also held that the testimony of this expert as to the comparison between Caterpillar bulldozers that were substantially different or marketed and sold at a considerably later time was improper. *Id.* The court cited *Daubert*, explaining that "expert evidence can be both powerful and quite misleading. . . . Because of this risk, the judge in weighing possible prejudice against probative force under Rule 403 of the present rules exercises more control over experts than over lay witnesses." *Id.* (quoting *Daubert*, 509 U.S. at 595).

Brown v. Raymond Corp., 432 F.3d 640 (6th Cir. 2005).
Plaintiff alleged defendant's forklift was unreasonably dangerous due to defective design, defective brakes, and inadequate warnings. Plaintiff appealed from the district court's grant of summary judgment in favor of defendant on all claims, asserting that the district court improperly excluded the testimony of plaintiff's expert witnesses.

The district court excluded the testimony of experts Romansky and Driver. Romansky was a lawyer and an industrial engineer and would have testified that the forklift was unreasonably dangerous. Romansky admitted he had no special expertise in forklifts and that he had no alternative design to offer that would have eliminated the safety hazard. Driver was an experienced forklift operator and trainer who would have testified the Raymond's warnings were inadequate. Driver admitted he had not formulated or tested any alternative warnings. The Sixth Circuit found that Romansky's failure to present and test an alternative design justified the conclusion of the district court that his testimony would not assist the trier of fact. Similarly, "Driver's failure to propose alternative warnings subject to empirical testing rendered his testimony unreliable and irrelevant to the trier of fact." 432 F.3d at 648. The Sixth Circuit affirmed the exclusion of the expert witnesses as being within the discretion of the district court.

b. District Courts

Siegel v. Fisher & Paykel Appliances Holdings, Ltd., et al., 746 F. Supp. 2d 845 (W.D. Ky. 2010).
A range exploded while plaintiff was cooking, because a regulator inside the range leaked. The company that manufactured the regulator hired an engineering expert, Thomas Crane. That defendant, however, was summarily dismissed from the case. Nonetheless, plaintiff attempted to use Crane's testimony to further her own claim. The remaining defendant moved to exclude Crane's testimony.

Because the explosion completely destroyed the range, Crane could only test a used range of the same model and new range of a different model. From these tests, Crane expressed opinions about why the regulator malfunctioned. The court found that Crane's conclusions required too many speculative leaps, much like the expert in *Tamraz v. Lincoln Electric, Co.*, 620 F.3d 665 (6th Cir. 2010). Although the court excluded Crane's testimony, it also noted that "[c]onclusions based on accurate data, may rest on a modicum of reasonable, reliable, [sic] speculation, that is informed by the rigorous application of the scientific method, particularly where, as here, the product being evaluated has been destroyed by its failure."

Hoganson v. Mernard, Inc., 567 F. Supp. 2d 985 (W.D. Mich. 2008).
Plaintiff broke her femur when an electronic sliding door at defendant's store knocked her to the ground. Plaintiff employed an expert, Roger Davis, to estimate the rate and speed at which the door closed. While the district court noted that Davis, a mechanical engineer, was qualified under *Daubert*, the court also found that the method used by Davis to measure the rate and speed of the door was speculative because he did not take his measurements from the actual door in question. Unfortunately for plaintiff, the store removed that door shortly after the incident.

Meemic Ins. Co. v. Hewlett-Packard Co., 717 F. Supp. 2d 752 (E.D. Mich. 2010).
In this product liability action, a house fire was caused by an allegedly defective power adaptor. Defendants moved for summary judgment on grounds that plaintiff's electrical expert, McGuire, should be excluded as unreliable and therefore Plaintiff could not satisfy the causation element of its claim. Plaintiff argued that the court should allow McGuire to establish causation because he visually inspected the power adapter and because the origin of the fire was in the area of the printer. The district court disagreed, holding that plaintiff "failed to establish that McGuire's opinions represent[ed] reliable principles and methods" when (1) they were not based on scientifically valid principles, (2) were not duplicable, (3) had not been subjected to peer review or published, and (4) were not generally accepted as a method for determining that a defect in an electrical device caused a fire. Moreover, the court noted that McGuire's visual examinations and subsequent conclusions would not assist the jury, as the jury could make the same visual observations and draw their own conclusions from them.

Galloway v. Big G Express, Inc., 590 F. Supp. 2d 989 (E.D. Tenn. 2008).
In this product liability action, plaintiff was injured when the front windshield of the tractor trailer he was driving collapsed after water splashed onto the windshield. The parties each hired their own experts to determine whether the windshield was defective, and each party challenged the admissibility of the other party's experts.

The district court conducted a *Daubert* analysis for each expert and found that all experts and their opinions satisfied the *Daubert* standard. Of particular interest is the court's discussion of plaintiff's expert Dr. Booeshaghi, a mechanical engineer. Defendants principally attacked the admissibility of Booeshaghi's testimony on the basis that his underlying methodology used to prove general causation was "physically impossible in the real world." Ultimately, the district court found Dr. Booeshaghi's methodology to be sound. The court relied on *Jarvis v. Ford Motor Co.*, 283 F.3d 33 (2d Cir. 2002), where the Second Circuit concluded that such a "plausibility" argument goes to the weight of the proposed testimony, not its admissibility. Moreover, the district court agreed with *Jarvis* that, when an expert intends to testify about "'general causation and relies on modeling and a fault analysis to demonstrate known physical . . . principles,'" then the absence of a known rate of error is irrelevant.

Rose v. Truck Centers, Inc., 611 F. Supp. 2d 745 (N.D. Ohio 2009).
A truck driver and his wife suffered injuries after the truck's steering gear malfunctioned and the driver lost control of the vehicle. Plaintiffs filed a product liability action against the manufacturer and offered Philip Smith as an expert to testify as to the cause of the accident, specifically that defendant failed to properly torque the bolts that seal the steering gear.

Defendant moved for summary judgment, arguing that plaintiffs' expert was not qualified to testify about product defects and causation and, furthermore, that his opinions were unsupported by the facts of the case. The district court agreed, holding that, while Smith may be qualified as an expert on some issues, his testimony here exceeded the scope of his expertise because what he lacked in education and training—most notably, he was not an engineer—he did not make up for in experience. The court acknowledged that Smith had extensive experience as a mechanic, noting he was a mechanic by trade, was an ASE-certified master technician, held a diploma from Denver Auto & Diesel College, and received some training on TRW steering gears twenty years before; however, Smith did not demonstrate that he knew any more about mechanical engineering principles than an average juror.

Zuzula v. ABB Power T & D Co. 267 F. Supp. 2d 703 (E.D. Mich. 2003).
This product liability action was brought to recover for plaintiff's electrocution while installing an industrial fuse in high-voltage electrical switching gear designed and manufactured by ABB Power. Plaintiff's expert, Fagan, was a professor of electrical engineering whose private practice had principally involved the design of MRI and radar equipment, though he had designed one high-voltage piece of equipment. Fagan inspected and photographed the equipment at issue; read depositions;

reviewed accident reports, equipment manuals, and plan-operating procedures; and inspected high-voltage switching equipment manufactured by other vendors. He did not conduct testing of his theory of causation or create a model of a safer design, but Fagan produced an illustration of such a device utilizing computer graphics. The defendant's expert, Denbrock, was also an electrical engineer, but with over forty years of experience in planning, designing, engineering, constructing, and managing electric power systems. Denbrock had never designed equipment similar to that involved in the lawsuit but had been involved in purchasing such equipment. Denbrock offered the opinion that the equipment was properly designed and that plaintiff was not properly trained and must have attempted to bypass safety devices. The court found both experts to be qualified and Fagen's opinions to be grounded in principles of mechanics and electrical engineering that were generally accepted by the engineering community. Denbrock' s opinions were based on comparing equipment to prevailing standards and established codes, which the court indicated left something to be desired, but could still be relied on and provide some assistance to the jury.

Nagib v. Meridian Medical Technologies, Inc., 2005 WL 1077595 (S.D. Ohio 2005).
In this product liability action, plaintiff contended that defendants manufactured and sold a defective auto-injectable EpiPen containing a dose of epinephrine utilized to treat asthma attacks. During such an attack plaintiff and his fiancee were unable to remove the cap of the EpiPen and administer the epinephrine. The attack worsened and plaintiff suffered debilitating injuries and emotional distress. Defendant moved to exclude the testimony of Reese as a medical device expert. Reese's opinion was based on plaintiff's testimony that something with the EpiPen malfunctioned, but Reese did not know what in particular had malfunctioned because the EpiPen that plaintiff used had not been preserved. Reese did not review the EpiPen's design specifications or manufacturing procedures and could not identify a particular alleged defect in the product. The court found that Reese's proposed testimony and report would not help the trier of fact determine whether the EpiPen was negligently designed or manufactured, and excluded his testimony. Without Reese's testimony, plaintiff was unable to prove required elements of his claim, and summary judgment was granted to defendant.

Demaree v. Toyota Motor Corp., 37 F. Supp. 2d 959 (W.D. Ky. 1999).
Plaintiff sued the manufacturer of the automobile that she was driving at the time of an accident. Plaintiff asserted that the air bags in the car were defectively designed because their deployment threshold was set at a speed range that was too low. *Id.* at 963. Plaintiff introduced the testimony of an expert witness to prove that the deployment threshold was a defect in design of the air bags and that this defect proximately caused her injuries. *Id.* at 962–3. Defendants asked the court to exclude this testimony, arguing that it was unsupported by scientific evidence. *Id.* at 963. After noting several bases on which plaintiff's expert did *not* rely, the court concluded that the expert's testimony lacked "any of the usual indicia of reliability." *Id.* at 964. Furthermore, the court maintained that the expert's reliance on Toyota documents was insufficient and did not amount to scientific analysis. *Id.* at 965. Because the expert's opinion was "unpublished, unverified, and untested," the court held that the expert's testimony was inadmissible. *Id.* at 966–70.

2. *Human Factors and Accident Reconstruction*

a. Sixth Circuit

Clay v. Ford Motor Co., 215 F.3d 663 (6th Cir. 2000).
The Defendant car manufacturer appealed from a jury verdict finding that design defects in a Ford Bronco II caused the deaths in an accident, arguing, among other things, that the district court had abused its discretion in allowing the testimony of plaintiff's expert witness. 215 F.3d at 665. The Sixth Circuit agreed with the trial court that the expert testimony identifying defects in the

automobile and reconstructing the accident were relevant and reliable. *Id.* The court also concluded that the expert was qualified to testify. *Id.* at 667–68. The court, therefore, held that the trial court had not abused its discretion in admitting the testimony of plaintiff's expert.

The dissenting opinion, however, argued that the district court had "improperly abdicated its gatekeeping function under *Daubert*." *Id.* at 674. The dissenting judge believed that while the expert testimony was relevant, it was not reliable. *Id.* at 674–75. The opinion identified several deficiencies in the trial court's record concerning both the evidence of reliability and the use of the *Daubert* factors to evaluate the reliability of the testimony. *Id.* at 675–76. Furthermore, the opinion stated that even the general qualifications of the expert were questionable. *Id.* at 677. For these reasons, the dissenter argued that the expert testimony should have been excluded and that allowing the expert to testify was reversible error. *Id.* at 677.

b. District Courts

Pomella v. Regency Coach Lines, Ltd., 899 F. Supp. 335 (E.D. Mich. 1995).
Plaintiff sought to admit expert testimony regarding the cause of an automobile accident. 899 F. Supp. at 339. An accident reconstruction expert utilized an assumed value for a coefficient of friction for the highway to conclude that an oncoming car could have avoided the accident. *Id.* The court concluded that the proposed testimony was inadmissible because it was based on speculative estimates for the coefficient of friction of the highway and therefore did not assist the trier of fact. *Id.* at 341–43. In examining "scientific knowledge" under *Daubert*, "an expert's opinion must be supported by 'more than subjective belief and unsupported speculation' and should be supported by 'good grounds, based on what is known.'" *Id.* at 342 (quoting *Daubert*, 113 S. Ct. at 2795). A range of coefficients of friction for highways can vary from about 0.1 to about 0.75, and through the choice of a value of 0.25, the expert "eyeballed" in order to pick a value that was favorable to plaintiff's cause. *Id.* at 343. This "eyeballing" approach was "unscientific." *Id.* The "so-called proof that establishes a possible causal link does not satisfy the Plaintiff's burden." *Id.* at 341. Accordingly, the court granted summary judgment in favor of defendant. *Id.* at 343.

Darling v. J.B. Expedited Services, Inc., 2006 WL 2238913 (M.D. Tenn. 2006).
Plaintiff was struck and killed by a box truck. Plaintiff's survivor offered four experts, including Stopper, a private forensic consultant who had taught police academy motor-carrier safety and accident investigation training. Stopper claimed that plaintiff did not fall into the path of traffic, and that defendant's driver could not have traveled to the collision site within the allowable hours of service if he actually took the rest breaks he claimed in his driver logs. A safety consultant to the transportation industry, Dillard, opined that defendant's employer failed to properly train him, citing the absence of documented evidence of supervision, training, and guidance concerning hours of service and driver fatigue. Plaintiff also offered Dr. Mitler, an expert in sleep physiology who had previously conducted studies of driver fatigue, who opined that defendant's driver was fatigued and sleep deprived at the time of the crash, and Wylie, who had published studies on fatigue for the Federal Motor Carrier Safety Administration. The court found that all of the experts were qualified and that their testimony met the requirements of Fed. R. Evid. 702.

3. Fire Origin

a. Sixth Circuit

Hartley v. St. Paul Fire & Marine Insurance Co., 118 F. App'x 914 (6th Cir. 2004).
In this negligence action involving a space heater, the plaintiff's house burned. Plaintiff objected to the admission of expert testimony from Franklin, as Franklin was unable to eliminate other possible

causes of the fire or state with certainty the source of the accelerant. These alleged shortcomings were noted by the Sixth Circuit as bearing on the reliability of the expert's conclusions, not the admissibility of his opinion. *Id.* at 920.

b. District Courts

***Thompson v. State Farm Fire and Casualty Co.*, 548 F. Supp. 2d 588 (W.D. Tenn. 2008).**
Defendant insurance company denied plaintiff's claim on the grounds that a fire was incendiary. Defendant hired James Swain, an expert in fire cause and origin. Plaintiff moved to exclude Swain from testifying because he did not strictly adhere to the standards and protocols of the National Fire Protection Association 921 Guide for Fire and Explosion Investigations ("NFPA 921") when conducting his investigation. Defendants argued that Swain's underlying methodology was reliable because Swain relied in part on NFPA 921 and in part on his twenty-five years of experience as a professional investigator.

The district court found that, while strictly following NFPA 921 would tend to indicate that an investigator's methodology is reliable, a departure from these guidelines does not *per se* establish a lack of reliability. The district court reasoned that NFPA 921 does not prevent an investigator from considering a fire's temperature and growth rate, the presence of melted copper, or irregular burn patterns. Moreover, the court concluded that Swain was not disqualified for failure to obtain a "comparison sample" from an undamaged portion of the house as urged by NFPA 921, because Swain did obtain a sample that tested negative for ignitable fluids, and this sample could be used for comparison to his positive samples.

***Knotts v. Black & Decker, Inc.*, 204 F. Supp. 2d 1029 (N.D. Ohio 2002).**
Defendants in this product liability case moved to exclude the testimony of plaintiffs' experts. 204 F. Supp. 2d at 1034. The dispute in this case centered on whether defendant's battery recharger was the cause of a fire that killed two people.

Plaintiffs' first expert witness proposed to testify about the origin and cause of the fire. *Id.* at 1038. The court granted defendants' motion *in limine* to exclude this expert's testimony, because the expert relied to a large extent on witness statements and a fire investigation report. The court determined that this expert's testimony had no independent basis grounded in any reliable procedures or scientific methodology and, therefore, was inadmissible. *Id.* at 1040.

Plaintiffs' second expert witness proposed to testify about the capacity of the defendant's battery charger to malfunction and cause a fire due to its defective design. The court rejected the defendant's contention that the documents on which the expert relied were not properly authenticated, stating that the documents would be authenticated if the case proceeded to trial. Nevertheless, the court decided that the documents contained hearsay statements of witnesses who were not employees of the laboratory that generated the documents. *Id.* at 1041. The expert also relied on articles discussing battery chargers of various types, not just the defendant's chargers, in coming to his conclusions about the cause of the accident. *Id.* at 1045. The court was troubled not only by this reliance on articles that were only tangentially related to the battery charger at issue, but also by the expert's failure to complete any independent testing of defendants' battery charger. Believing that this expert opinion was "tenuous at best," the court concluded that this expert testimony was also inadmissible.

***Travelers Indemnity Co. v. Industrial Paper & Packaging Corp.*, 2006 WL 178 8967 (E.D. Tenn. 2006).**
This lawsuit involved a fire insurance company's subrogation claim to recover for a fire loss at an amusement complex. The defendant had serviced the HVAC system eight days before the fire and was alleged to have failed to warn about or remove the accumulation of diffusion fluid in the HVAC

system. The accumulation of the fluid allegedly led to the fire. Defendants moved to exclude the testimony of plaintiff's fire investigator, Rodney Fowler. Fowler did not conduct any testing regarding the combustibility or flammability of the diffusion fluid and had no personal knowledge or observations to bear out his assumption that diffusion fluid was present. Fowler was a qualified fire investigator, he interviewed witnesses to substantiate the presence of diffusion fluid, and he relied on the findings of a chemist as well as the material safety data sheet for diffusion fluid in forming his opinion. The court found that Fowler had generally followed the procedures of the National Fire Protection Association's Guide for Fire and Explosion Investigations, and held that Fowler would be permitted to testify as to the cause and origin of the fire.

4. Toxic Torts

a. Sixth Circuit

Downs v. Perstorp Components, Inc., 26 F. App'x 472 (6th Cir. 2002).
Plaintiff sued for injuries he suffered when exposed to a chemical product called Rubiflex SI 30690, which the defendant manufactured. To support his claim, the plaintiff offered the testimony of Dr. Kaye H. Kilburn, who diagnosed the plaintiff with chemical encephalopathy that he concluded was caused by exposure to Rubiflex. After conducting a *Daubert* hearing, the district court excluded Kilburn's testimony. The district court stated that the proposed testimony was not accepted by the medical community, was not properly tested, was not based on any research, and was extrapolated from unrelated information. On appeal, the Sixth Circuit agreed that Dr. Kilburn's proposed testimony was problematic, and it concluded that the trial court did not abuse its discretion in excluding the proffered testimony.

b. District Courts

Adams v. Cooper Industries, Inc., 2007 WL 1805586 (E.D. Ky. 2007).
In this action to recover for industrial contamination, the defendants attempted to exclude the testimony of a toxicologist and an air-modeling expert. The toxicologist determined the ordinary levels of dioxin-like compounds in the general population from published studies and compared those levels to plaintiffs' blood dioxin levels. Based on his review of the literature, the toxicologist opined that the source of elevated levels of dioxins in the plaintiffs' blood was from the combustion of the types of materials burned at defendant's facilities. The toxicologist defined as "abnormal" any dioxin blood level above the mean. By this definition, roughly one-half of the population would be deemed to have abnormal concentrations of dioxins. The court found that the use of this definition of "abnormality" caused the methodology to be unreliable and misleading. The court was also skeptical of the toxicologist's use of literature to conclude that the dioxin-like compounds in the plaintiffs' blood were attributable to combustion in the defendant's plant. The toxicologist's testimony was excluded.

The air-modeling expert utilized software called AERMOD to simulate the releases of PCBs from burners, oil, and coal-fired gaseous emissions from a low-level fired/burn box, as would be expected from defendant's facility. He then plotted the resulting data from AERMOD onto a map. The AERMOD software was determined to be reliable, the expert's opinions based on sufficient facts and data, and his methodology applied reliably to the facts of the case.

Mercer v. Rockwell Intern. Corp., 24 F. Supp. 2d 735 (W.D. Ky. 1998).
This case provides a brief description of the history of the *Joiner* case from the district court to the Eleventh Circuit and to the Supreme Court. Like *Joiner*, this case concerns PCBs, and the

expert doctor "sought to suggest a relationship between a limited exposure of PCB's on property, an unknown exposure to people who might purchase the property and an unknown and projected harm." *Id.* at 750. The court held that there was too great of an analytical gap between the data and the opinion offered, and that the doctor's opinion was even more speculative than the opinion offered in *Joiner. Id.* The court concluded that it was within its discretion to dismiss the case. *Id.* at 751.

Knous v. ConAgra Foods, Inc., 2006 WL 3087137 (W.D. Ky. 2006).
Plaintiff alleged that ConAgra negligently exposed him to carbon dioxide when he was driving a truck of frozen chicken from ConAgra's plant that was packed with dry ice. The defendant moved to exclude testimony from three causation experts and one industry standards expert. An expert that utilized scientific reasoning and methodology through a series of physiological reactions to reach his causation conclusions was allowed to testify. An expert whose causation opinion demonstrated backward reasoning was excluded. A third causation expert was allowed to testify based on his experience with cases involving carbon dioxide exposure. The industry standards expert was allowed to testify based on his experience with trucking safety and dealings with warning labels.

5. Antitrust

a. Sixth Circuit

In re Scrap Metal Antitrust Litigation, 527 F.3d 517 (6th Cir. 2008).
Plaintiffs produced scrap metal, ferrous (iron based) and nonferrous, as a byproduct of their manufacturing process, and they sold this scrap metal to defendants, who refined it and sold it to steel mills. Plaintiffs alleged that defendants violated the Sherman Act by unlawfully "allocating scrap metal generators among dealers, agreeing not to compete with one another, submitting rigged bids, setting prices for the purchase of unprocessed scrap metal, and imposing financial penalties on co-conspirators for disobeying allocation agreements." Pivotal to the plaintiffs' case was damages testimony from their expert economist, Dr. Jeffrey Leitzinger. Defendants moved to exclude Leitzinger from testifying, but the district court denied the motion, finding that defendants' attacks on Leitzinger went to the weight of the evidence, not to its admissibility. Plaintiffs received a $23 million judgment against one defendant for engaging in anticompetitive conduct relating to ferrous scrap metal sales.

On appeal, defendant argued that the district court erred in denying the motion to exclude Leitzinger's testimony. Leitzinger used the "during and after"/"before and after" method to determine what the plaintiff's profits would have been had the defendants not engaged in anticompetitive conduct. He used actual transaction data as well as index prices from the American Metal Market and Scrap Price Bulletin ("SPB") to generate his calculations. Specifically, "[b]y comparing the price spread during the conspiracy period with the price spread after the conspiracy period, [he] concluded that the results were consistent with anticompetitive conduct. . . ." Defendant asserted that the SPB data was not reliable because *Iron Age*, the publisher of the SPB, "issued a correction . . . stating that thirteen of the eighteen categories of processed ferrous scrap had been reported incorrectly for an unknown period of time." *Iron Age* issued corrections on December 7, 1998, and October 4, 1998—both within the relevant conspiracy period. However, Leitzinger accounted for ("backed out") these corrections "by subtracting them from the SPB index price" because he believed that the corrections only changed the price measuring point. Defendant submitted an affidavit of an *Iron Age* reporter who proclaimed that the corrections had nothing to do with price measuring points, and therefore, "by 'backing out' the corrections, Leitzinger made the SPB data . . . inaccurate."

The Sixth Circuit found that defendant's arguments went to the weight of the evidence, not to its admissibility, and further stated that "a determination that proffered expert testimony is reliable does not indicate, in any way, the correctness or truthfulness of such an opinion . . . [t]he task for the district court . . . is not to determine whether it is correct, but rather to determine whether it rests upon a reliable foundation, as opposed to, say, unsupported speculation." The court found that Leitzinger "performed his analysis according to a reliable method (the 'during and after' method) and reliably applied the method to the facts of this case."

Kentucky Speedway, LLC v. National Association of Stock Car Auto Racing, Inc., et al., 588 F.3d 908 (6th Cir. 2010).

In this antitrust action, the district court granted summary judgment to the defendants, in part because plaintiff's experts could not withstand scrutiny under *Daubert*. Plaintiff hired Dr. Zimbalist to define the Sanctioning Market and the Hosting Market, but he also opined about whether the defendants' behavior was anticompetitive. The district court struck Zimbalist's report because he did not consider other sports and forms of entertainment as possible substitutes in his interchangeability analysis and because his "Small but Significant Non-transitory Increase in Price" test failed under *Daubert* in that his version: "has not been tested; has not been subjected to peer review and publication; there [were] no standards controlling it; and there [was not a] showing that it enjoy[ed] general acceptance within the scientific community; [and] it was produced solely for this litigation." The district court struck Dr. Leffler's report because his report principally relied on Zimbalist's market analysis. The Sixth Circuit found no abuse of discretion in these findings.

Nilavar v. Mercy Health System—Western Ohio, No. 06-3819, 2007 WL 2264439 (6th Cir. Aug. 7, 2007).

Plaintiff sued Mercy Health System and its radiology group for violations of state and federal antitrust law and related state tort claims. The district court granted defendant's motion to exclude testimony of plaintiff's expert, Dr. Pisarkiewicz, and granted summary judgment to the defendants. Pisarkiewicz proposed to testify as to the defendant's market power in a geographic area utilizing the Elzinga-Hogarty test and the critical loss test. The Elzinga-Hogarty test provides scores that if sufficiently low demonstrate the existence of a cohesive geographic market and show defendant's market power. A 10 percent limit threshold is needed for a strong result. The expert's initial report found ratios of 4.8 percent and 25 percent. The expert refined his test through two additional iterations and finally obtained both ratios at 8.7 percent, within the 10 percent generally called for by the test.

The district court pointed out that Pisarkiewicz had excluded patients from the geographic market who required a procedure for which more than 90 percent of the patients left the market. But Pisarkiewicz admitted that some of the patients who left the area for services did so not because the services were not available, but because the services were perceived to be better elsewhere. The court found no proper justification for all of the exclusions and concluded that either the Elzinga-Hogarty test was improperly applied or that the expert had made an effort to manipulate the test. Pisarkiewicz also attempted to utilize the critical loss test, which assesses whether a market participant would be able to raise prices by 5 percent without a sufficient number of patients leaving the market. The district court noted that this test made no sense when a significant number of patients were leaving the geographic area in the absence of any price increase. The Sixth Circuit agreed with the district court's conclusion that the expert's opinion was flawed to the point of unreliability.

b. District Courts

J.B.D.L. Corp. v. Wyeth-Ayerst Laboratories, Inc., 2005 WL 1396940 (S.D. Ohio 2005).

In this antitrust action, the plaintiffs contended they were forced to pay an excessive price for Wyeth's drug Premarin due to Wyeth's anticompetitive and exclusionary conduct toward one of its competitors, Duramed. Premarin was Wyeth's brand of conjugated estrogen product, and Cenestin was the brand of Duramed's newer conjugated estrogen product. The plaintiffs relied on their economic experts, Leitzinger and Schondelmeyer, to establish the link between Wyeth's alleged anticompetitive conduct and supracompetitive price increases. Leitzinger concluded that as a result of Wyeth's limiting Cenestin's development as a competitor, Wyeth maintained its hold on customers and avoided the need for defensive pricing reactions. The court stated that Leitzinger assumed it was Wyeth's conduct alone that limited Cenestin's success, and not Duramed's decisions or marketing strategies or any clinical differences between the products. Leitzinger relied entirely on the opinion of Schondelmeyer for the proposition that Duramed undertook a substantial concerted marketing effort to promote Cenestin. In turn, Schondelmeyer relied on testimony from Duramed, who naturally blamed Wyeth almost exclusively for Cenestin's failure to achieve desired market share.

The court noted that while an expert may rely on another's expert opinion, neither Leitzinger nor Schondelmeyer offered any objective study on the effect of Wyeth's conduct. Furthermore, they ignored substantial evidence in the record contradicting their assumptions, including undisputed clinical and therapeutic differences in the drugs. Plaintiff's experts relied on basic economic theory to the effect that a dominant seller would lower its product price in response to market entry of competitors without substantive discussion, in spite of studies in the record indicating that brand-name drug prices actually rise in response to generic competition. The court stated that it need not accept an expert's assumption that is supported only by the *ipse dixit* of the expert. The court found that plaintiffs failed to establish a causative link between Wyeth's marketing conduct and Wyeth's price increases and granted Wyeth summary judgment.

State of Ohio ex rel. Montgomery v. Trauth Dairy, Inc., 925 F. Supp. 1247 (S.D. Ohio 1996).
The State of Ohio filed suit against thirteen dairies, alleging a conspiracy in violation of the Sherman Antitrust Act. Defendants sought to exclude the state's expert testimony regarding the dairies' business activities as demonstrated by statistical analysis. Defendants argued that the proposed experts were not qualified to testify, that the methodologies used by the experts were "fatally flawed," and that even if the methodologies were valid, the analysis could not distinguish between legal and illegal activity and therefore was of no use to the trier of fact. *Id.* at 1251.

The court mapped out the *Daubert* analysis, noting that the initial question was whether *Daubert* applied to the testimony offered by the state's experts. *Id.* at 1250–51. The proffered experts were two economists and a statistician, and the court stated that "[n]either economics nor statistics seems to completely qualify as 'scientific knowledge.'" *Id.* at 1252. However, the court concluded that the *Daubert* reasoning still applied, stating that the general framework applied to all expert testimony. *Id.* The court did recognize that the *Daubert* factors should be applied with the "clear understanding that they were devised specifically for scientific testimony." *Id.* The court concluded that "the *Daubert* analysis should be modified in the case of social science or other non-scientific expertise." *Id.* The court determined that, in this case, the proper inquiry was whether the proposed testimony would assist the trier of fact and whether "the proffered testimony [was] based upon valid economic, statistical or econometric methodologies and reasoning that [could] properly be applied to the facts of this case." *Id.*

The court noted that econometrics and regression analysis have been generally considered reliable disciplines, and the defendants' own expert conceded that one of the state's expert's regression analyses was testable, generally accepted, and reproducible. *Id.* at 1252. The defendants also argued that the plaintiffs' experts' control group was flawed and prejudiced the analysis, but the court stated that "[p]roblems in selection of a sample bear on the weight of the testimony, not its admissibility." *Id.* at 1253. Finally, the court concluded that the testimony satisfied the "fit" requirement of *Daubert* because the experts' analyses would assist the jury in assimilating complicated economic data. *Id.* at 1253–54.

6. Biomedical and Biomechanical Engineering

a. Sixth Circuit

Smelser v. Norfolk Southern Railway, 105 F.3d 299 (6th Cir. 1996).
Plaintiff brought suit against his employer for injuries suffered in an auto accident while driving to a job site in the company pickup truck. 105 F.3d at 301. Plaintiff's expert, a biomechanical engineer, gave his opinion that (1) the shoulder belt, but not the lap belt, in the company truck was defective; (2) these circumstances worked together to cause plaintiff's body to jackknife at the waist; and (3) the defective shoulder belt, not the rear-end collision, caused plaintiff's back injuries and aggravated neck injuries. *Id.* at 302. Defendant did not object to the expert's qualifications to testify as a biomechanical engineer but instead argued that methodology underlying his opinions on defect and causation was unreliable, and that his opinion on causation went beyond his expertise in biomechanics. *Id.*

The Sixth Circuit followed the guidance of *Daubert* in stating that "the party seeking to have the testimony admitted bears the burden of showing 'that the expert's findings are based on sound science, and this will require some objective, independent validation of the expert's methodology; the expert's bald assurance of validity is not enough.'" *Id.* at 303 (quoting *Daubert v. Merrell Dow Pharmaceuticals, Inc.*, (on remand), 43 F.3d 1311, 1316 (9th Cir. 1995)). The Sixth Circuit again noted the trial court's "gatekeeping function" under *Daubert*, which requires the trial court to examine the proffered testimony for reliability and relevance. 105 F.3d at 303. First, the trial court should determine "whether the experts' testimony reflects 'scientific knowledge,' whether their findings are 'derived by scientific method,' and whether their work product amounts to 'good science.'" *Id.* (quoting *Daubert*, 509 U.S. at 590, 593). If the expert's opinion is based on scientifically valid principles, it will satisfy Rule 702; if the basis of the opinion is only the expert's subjective belief or unsupported speculation, it will not satisfy Rule 702. 105 F.3d at 303. Second, the trial court "must ensure that the proposed expert testimony is relevant to the task at hand," and the testimony must "fit." *Id.* The court must examine whether the qualifications of a witness provide a foundation for a witness to answer a specific question, not merely examine the qualifications of the witness in the abstract. *Id.* (citing *Berry v. City of Detroit*, 25 F.3d 1342, 1351 (6th Cir. 1994)). The court must determine whether the expert's training and qualifications relate to the subject matter of his proposed testimony. 105 F.3d at 303.

In order to determine the reliability of an expert, a court must focus on the soundness of the expert's methodology and not the correctness of his conclusions; in so doing, a court should consider the factors enumerated in *Daubert*. *Id.* These factors may assist the court in determining "whether the analysis undergirding the experts' testimony falls within the range of accepted standards governing how scientists conduct their research and reach their conclusions." *Id.* (quoting *Daubert* (on remand), 43 F.3d at 1316). The court also recognized an additional factor proposed by the Ninth Circuit: "'whether the experts are proposing to testify about matters growing naturally and directly out of research they have conducted independent of the litigation, or whether they have developed their opinions expressly for purposes of testifying,' because the former 'provides important, objective proof that the research comports with the dictates of good science.'" 105 F.3d at 303 (quoting *Daubert* (on remand), 43 F.3d at 1317).

The Sixth Circuit observed that "*Daubert* teaches that expert opinion testimony qualifies as scientific knowledge under Rule 702 only if it is derived by the scientific method and is capable of validation." 105 F.3d at 304. The court concluded in *Smelser* that the plaintiff's proposed expert's opinion that the shoulder belt, but not the lap belt, failed in the auto accident could not have been based on "good science" because the expert

> (1) failed to perform any tests on the lap belt yet concluded it was in proper working condition; (2) conducted no testing to verify his conclusion the shoulder belt was damaged

in [a prior] accident; (3) failed to adequately document testing conditions and the rate of error so the test could be repeated and its results verified and critiqued; and (4) failed to discover, use or at least consider the degree the restraint system was actually mounted at in the subject vehicle and explain whether that information would affect his pendulum test for compliance with the federal safety standard.

Id. The court also held that the expert's opinion regarding causation of the plaintiff's injuries should have been excluded because it went beyond his expertise in biomechanics; the expert was not a medical doctor and was not qualified to testify as to the cause of the plaintiff's specific injuries. *Id.* at 305. Finally, the court concluded that the causation opinion also lacked reliability because the expert failed to review the plaintiff's medical history and failed to consider other important pieces of information. *Id.* For all of these reasons, the court concluded that the expert's opinion should not have been admitted. *Id.*

Mohney v. USA Hockey, Inc., 138 F. App'x 804 (6th Cir. 2005).

In this product liability action for spinal injuries due to alleged defects in a helmet, the district court excluded the testimony of plaintiff's experts doctors Collins and Johanson. Although Collins was recognized as a qualified expert in the field of biomedical engineering, the court found that his calculations and methods were suspect and unreliable. Collins's analysis was based on his personal review of the helmet and mask involved in the accident, and his research included watching a videotape of the incident, performing measurements of the helmet and mask, and incorporating these observations and measurements into mathematical calculations based on Newton's law of physics, a recognized and valid scientific method. However, Collins did not attempt to replicate the incident, perform any manner of accident reconstruction, or conduct any relevant technical or scientific testing of the helmet / face mask combination. In addition, Collins could not cite any published work to support his opinion, nor could he cite to general acceptance that spinal injury could occur from a face-first impact. Finally, Collins admitted that he did not utilize actual data but instead relied on a series of assumptions for the data input into the mathematical equations to support his theory.

The district court also excluded the testimony of Johanson, a qualified expert in the field of mechanical engineering, as he had not performed any tests but had simply based his opinions on visual inspection and measurements of the helmet and mask.

Nemir v. Mitsubishi Motors Corp., 381 F.3d 540 (6th Cir. 2004).

Plaintiff alleged that the latching failure of the seat belt in his car caused him to sustain serious injuries in an automobile accident. Plaintiff retained Dr. Horton, the former director of engineering for the manufacturer of the seat belt, and Horton planned to testify that the seat belt suffered from a design defect known as "partial latching," which caused the seat belt to unlatch during the accident. The district court ruled that Horton's testimony was inadmissible because of deficiencies in his methodology. *Id.* at 544. Horton was allowed to testify the seat-belt buckle was unreasonably dangerous because it allowed for partial engagement. However, he was unable to explain the basis for his conclusion because the district court prohibited Horton from testifying that he was able, on two out of twenty attempts, to create a partial latch of plaintiff's seat-belt buckle. The district court opined that Horton's method, in which he manipulated the buckle at varying speeds and angles, was scientifically unsound. The court also prohibited Horton from testifying about causation, because Horton did not demonstrate how he arrived at the conclusion the partial latch caused plaintiff's injuries as he did not eliminate other possibilities, such as the possibility that plaintiff was not wearing a seat belt at the time of the accident.

The court appointed two independent experts to help to determine whether the seat-belt buckle presented an inherently unreasonable risk of danger to the plaintiff. One of these experts, Manning, echoed Horton's conclusions, testifying that he had been able to partially engage the plaintiff's buckle during laboratory testing and that this was an unreasonably dangerous condition. The district court refused to allow plaintiff to call Manning to testify at trial.

On a previous appeal, the Sixth Circuit had ordered that Horton should be permitted to testify as to causation. The Sixth Circuit's earlier opinion is reported at 6 F. App'x 266, 275 (6th Cir. 2001): "The District Court, by requiring specific knowledge of the precise physiological cause of the accident held the expert up to entirely too strict a standard when considering the admissibility of the testimony." The Sixth Circuit added that having held the testimony on causation was admissible, Horton should not have been prohibited from testifying about his testing of the buckle, as it was not reasonable to admit Horton's causation testimony without permitting him to present the basis for his conclusions. 381 F.3d 554. Finally, the Sixth Circuit stated it was error to refuse to allow plaintiff to introduce the court-appointed expert Manning's testimony under FRE 706, noting Manning might be considered more credible than Horton, whom defendant described as a "hired gun." The case was reversed and remanded for assignment to another district judge.

7. Medical Causation

a. Sixth Circuit

Gass v. Marriott Hotel Services, Inc., 558 F.3d 419 (6th Cir. 2009).
Exterminators at a Maui hotel sprayed plaintiffs' room in response to a complaint about a dead cockroach. However, the exterminators sprayed the room while plaintiffs' belongings were in the room, prompting the plaintiffs to retrieve their belongings while the fumes were still present. Plaintiffs later became ill. Once home, they sought treatment from Dr. Robert DeJonge (husband of one of the plaintiffs), who referred tem to Dr. Gerald Natzke, a specialist in environmental medicine. Natzke examined the plaintiffs and diagnosed them with "acute pesticide exposure," but he could not identify the pesticide that caused their condition. However, he "did not rule out the possibility" that plaintiffs were exposed to SSI-550, which contains pyrethroids and other chemical compounds. SSI-550 was one of three pesticides used by the hotel. Natke did not run tests for other toxins.

In its *Daubert* analysis, the district court concluded that DeJonge and Natzke could testify to "'symptoms, tests, diagnosis, and treatment,'" but could not testify about causation because they did not demonstrate "'a scientifically reliable method to support their conclusions as to causation. . . .'" The Sixth Circuit held that the district court did not abuse its discretion by excluding the causation opinions. The circuit court concluded that the district court's exclusion comported with *Dickenson v. Cartdiac & Thoracic Surgery of Eastern Tenn., P.C.*, 388 F.3d 976 (6th Cir. 2004) that a medical doctor may testify to matters within his or her own professional experience, but if the physician lacks professional knowledge of a subject, then the testimony becomes less reliable under Fed. R. Evid. 702. Accordingly, the Sixth Circuit concluded that Dr. DeJonge and Dr. Natzke could rely on their professional education and/or experience to testify to diagnosis, but their medical experience did not "provide a basis to determine the exact chemical Plaintiffs were exposed to at the Marriott hotel."

Jahn v. Equine Services, PSC, 233 F.3d 382 (6th Cir. 2000).
After finding her champion pony dead in its stall, plaintiff filed suit, complaining that the defendants were negligent in their treatment of the pony. 233 F.3d at 386. Plaintiff sought to introduce the testimony of veterinarian Dr. George Mundy, who had considerable experience in the treatment of horses. *Id.* at 387. The plaintiff also intended to call Dr. Rhonda Robbins, a veterinarian specializing in horse medicine who had taught at the Auburn University veterinary school. *Id.* Both experts proposed to testify as to errors in the defendants' treatment of the pony, but neither could make a positive identification of the specific cause of the pony's death. *Id.* After conducting a *Daubert* hearing, the trial court excluded the testimony of both veterinarians. *Id.*

On appeal, however, the Sixth Circuit concluded that the district court erred in excluding the proffered testimony of the experts. *Id.* at 389. The court rejected the trial court's findings that the experts' conclusions were based on inadequate research or knowledge. *Id.* In addition, the court disagreed with the trial court's refusal to allow the testimony simply because the experts could not state with specificity the cause of the pony's death. *Id.* at 390. The court asserted that expert testimony "need not eliminate all other possible causes" to be admitted on the issue of causation. *Id.* Because the veterinarians based their opinions on factual analysis and scientific methodology, the court held that their expert testimony was improperly excluded. *Id.* at 391–93.

Glaser v. Thompson Medical Co., 32 F.3d 969 (6th Cir. 1994).
Plaintiff brought a product liability case against the defendant pharmaceutical company, alleging negligence and breach of warranty in the manufacture and distribution of the diet pill Dexatrim. 32 F.3d at 970. The plaintiff suffered severe head injuries from a fall; he alleged that the fall was caused by an intracranial bleed, which in turn he alleged was caused by the ingestion of Dexatrim. *Id.* at 970–71. The plaintiff's medical expert testified that Dexatrim can cause severe hypertension, which plaintiff contended caused the intracranial bleed. The trial court concluded that the plaintiff's expert's opinion was not based on a logical sequence of cause and effect and granted summary judgment in favor of the defendant. *Id.* at 971.

The Sixth Circuit reversed, holding that the testimony of plaintiff's expert was admissible under *Daubert*. *Id.* at 971–72. The medical expert's own testimony, literature (including peer-reviewed scientific evidence), and clinical and research experience provided a solid foundation for the conclusion that Dexatrim caused acute hypertension in the plaintiff. *Id.* at 972. The medical expert testified that his opinion was based on five studies he published on the topic, the published articles of other medical researchers, case reports, his experience treating patients who had ingested similar compounds, his clinical experience with these compounds in other studies, and his experience directing endocrine and obesity clinics. *Id.* at 972–75.

Rolen v. Hansen Beverage Co., 193 F. App'x 468 (6th Cir. 2006).
In this product liability action against a juice manufacturer, the plaintiff appealed from summary judgment granted to the defendant manufacturer after exclusion of plaintiff's expert witness on causation. The proposed expert, Dr. Houston, was an internist and was plaintiff's regular doctor before plaintiff consumed the defendant's product. Houston did not see plaintiff until more than three weeks after he drank the product and received treatment at the hospital. Houston's physical examination revealed that plaintiff's condition was basically normal with no abdominal tenderness or fever, and laboratory tests did not turn up any infection or any other biochemical abnormalities. Houston had no specialization in toxicology. Houston opined that Roland probably had staphylococcal food poisoning or some other type of bacterial infection from the ingestion of the product. However, the district court found that Houston's causation opinion was based on speculation solely from the absence of another obvious cause. The court did not find that. Houston had engaged in the kind of intellectual rigor that characterizes an acceptable differential diagnosis, but instead had merely based his opinion on the logical fallacy of *post hoc ergo propter hoc.* The Sixth Circuit affirmed.

b. District Courts

Schott, et al. v. I-Flow Corp., et al., 696 F. Supp. 2d 898 (S.D. Ohio 2010).
Defendant's infusion pump was designed to administer anesthetic to the shoulder following orthopedic surgery. Plaintiffs alleged that the pump caused chondrolysis, a severe and permanent damage to the shoulder joints. Defendants moved to exclude testimony of plaintiffs' general causation experts.

Defendant argued that the medical experts "have to take a leap of faith to offer their opinions regarding causation." According to defendant, while there may be an association or "strong suspicion" that the pump could cause chondrolysis, *Daubert* requires more. Defendant cited *Kilpatrick v. Breg, Inc.*, 2009 WL 2058384 (S.D. Fla. 2009), which excluded similar opinions for lack of reliable evidence. Plaintiffs argued that the purpose of *Daubert* was to "keep out bad science, not new science or controversial science, but bad science where the methods are improper and cannot be relied upon." *Id.* At 903. The court found that there "was more than adequate evidence that the expert opinions in this case have been published, subjected to peer review, and are generally accepted by the medical community," and that defendant's attack "boils down to semantics." *Id.* At 905. The testimony was therefore admitted.

In re Aredia and Zometa Products Liability Litigation, 754 F. Supp. 2d 934 (M.D. Tenn. 2010).
Plaintiffs alleged that prescription drugs caused them to develop osteonecrosis of the jaw. Defendants moved to exclude opinions expressed by plaintiffs' treating physicians that attributed the disease to the drugs. The court first noted that "a treating physician's expert opinion on causation is subject to the same standards of scientific reliability that govern the expert opinions of physicians hired solely for the purpose of litigation." *Id.* At 937. In the Sixth Circuit, "the ability to diagnose medical conditions is not the same as the ability to opine as an expert about the causes of those medical conditions." Id. (citing *Gass v. Marriott Hotel Services, Inc.*, 558 F.3d 419 (6th Cir. 2009)). Reviewing the qualifications and experience of the treating physicians in this case, the court concluded that, while they could testify as to their diagnoses of osteonecrosis, they would not be permitted to offer testimony about the cause of condition.

Hough v. State Farm Insurance Company, 2007 WL 1500181 (E.D. Mich. 2007).
Plaintiff sought no-fault insurance benefits from his insurer, and State Farm moved to exclude the testimony of plaintiff's treating physician and expert witness, Dr. Wheeler, regarding a discogram. A discogram is an invasive diagnostic procedure used to determine the cause of a patient's back pain by injecting a contrast dye into several discs of the spine and utilizing a CT scan to determine whether there is an abnormal disc morphology, coupled with recording the response of the patient to pain provocation in different portions of the spine. The insurance company's expert testified that many physicians were skeptical about the use of discograms. However, Dr. Wheeler was able to provide several studies evaluating the use and diagnostic accuracy of discography. The court determined that the procedure was sufficiently recognized to allow Dr. Wheeler to testify about the discogram. The court also permitted State Farm's witness to testify that in his opinion discography was not a valid or reliable procedure.

Smith v. Pfizer Inc., 714 F. Supp. 2d 845 (M.D. Tenn. 2010).
Plaintiff's husband Mr. Smith committed suicide after taking the prescription drug Neurontin, commonly prescribed for the off-label use of treating chronic pain. Plaintiff claimed defendants failed sufficiently to test the safety of Neurontin for off-label uses and failed to warn about the risk that the drug might give rise to suicidal ideations.

Defendants argued that there was no duty to warn because at the time plaintiff's husband committed suicide, there was no reliable evidence establishing a causal connection between Neurontin and suicide. Defendants offered Dr. Weiss Smith as an expert in epidemiology (the study of the risk of disease in population groups), pharmacoepidemiology (the study of the use and effects of medical products and drugs on humans), and pharmacovigilance (scientific and data-gathering activities related to the detection and assessment of adverse events). Smith contended that plaintiffs' analysis of adverse event data was flawed and that an FDA analysis on side effects was methodologically flawed and did not support the conclusion that Neurontin causes patients to commit suicide.

Plaintiffs moved to exclude this evidence on the basis that Smith had no expertise in making clinical assessments, writing FDA-compliant drug labels, suicidology, or pharmacovigilance practices. *Id.* at 850. Plaintiffs attacked Smith on a number of other grounds, including the methodology she used to search the adverse event database, the fact that she destroyed her underlying data, math mistakes, typographical errors, and arguably misleading citations. With respect to all of these issues, the court found that they did not affect the admissibility of the testimony, but could be highlighted during cross-examination.

Hansen v. United States, 2004 WL 2713078 (N.D. Ohio 2004).
Hansen was taken to the hospital after becoming ill with pneumonia. He went into cardiac arrest and died. Plaintiff brought negligence and medical malpractice claims against the hospital, doctors, and the doctors' employers. Plaintiff's expert Dr. Franklin expressed the opinion that the defendants failed to meet the standard of care by not triaging Hansen to the intensive care unit and by not monitoring his oxygen level. Defendants moved to exclude this testimony. Defendants also moved to exclude the testimony of Dr. Gluck, who proposed to testify that given Hansen's medical condition, he should have been placed in intensive care and given arterial blood gas. Both doctors would further testify that these failures in providing adequate medical care led to Hansen's death. The opinions of Gluck and Franklin were based on their experience rather than rigorous, peer-reviewed scientific studies. The court found that the opinions were reliable and flowed logically from the experts' opinions on the proper standard of care. The court found no need for plaintiff's experts to present masses of data on the survival rates of pneumonia patients but found that with their years of experience in critical care, the experts certainly had sufficient basis to testify as to what amounted to medical common sense.

Wynacht v. Beckman Instruments, Inc., 113 F. Supp. 2d 1205 (E.D. Tenn. 2000).
Defendant manufactured a chemical used in the lab where the plaintiff worked. 113 F. Supp. 2d at 1209–10. To prove that the chemicals that the defendant manufactured were the cause of her injuries, plaintiff sought to introduce the testimony of her physician, who had diagnosed plaintiff with approximately eighteen medical conditions. *Id.* at 1206–08. After applying the two-pronged test of *Daubert*, assessing the reliability and relevance of the proffered testimony of the plaintiff's expert, the court concluded that the expert could not offer a reliable opinion as to what had caused the plaintiffs' injuries. *Id.* at 1210–11. The court, therefore, granted the defendants' motion *in limine*. *Id.* at 1211.

Other Cases of Interest: *In re Heparin Products Liability Litigation*, 803 F. Supp. 712 (N.D. Ohio 2011) (addressing multiple challenges to causation testimony in pharmaceutical product liability cases); *Cooley v. Lincoln Electric Co.*, 693 F. Supp. 767 (N.D. Ohio 2010) (addressing claims that welding fume exposure led to neurological injuries).

8. *Differential Diagnosis*

a. Sixth Circuit

Best v. Lowe's Home Centers, Inc., 563 F.3d 171 (6th Cir. 2009).
In this case, the Sixth Circuit clarified when a differential diagnosis can be a valid and reliable basis for a medical-causation opinion under *Daubert v. Merrell Dow Pharmaceuticals, Inc.*, 509 U.S. 579 (1993).

A punctured container of Aqua EZ Super Clear Clarifier spilled on plaintiff's face as he retrieved it from a shelf at Lowe's. Plaintiff subsequently developed anosmia (loss of sense of smell). Dr. Francisco Moreno, a board-certified otolaryngologist with an undergraduate degree in chemical engineering, treated plaintiff following the incident. Moreno's diagnosis of anosmia was based on the University of Pennsylvania Smell Identification Test ("UPSIT"). After reviewing Best's medical history, a list of possible causes, and a Material Safety Data Sheet describing the active ingredients in Aqua EZ, Moreno opined that the inhalation of Aqua EZ could cause anosmia and had caused plaintiff's condition. In sum, Moreno performed a "differential diagnosis" to formulate his causation opinion.

The district court excluded Moreno's causation testimony, holding that conclusions amounted to "unscientific speculation" and therefore failed under the first prong of *Daubert* and Fed. R. Evid. 702. The district court relied on *Downs v. Perstorp Components, Inc.*, 126 F. Supp. 2d 1090 (E.D. Tenn. 1999), which set forth a list of "red flags" applicable to causation testimony—(1) improper extrapolation, (2) reliance on anecdotal evidence, (3) reliance on temporal proximity, (4) insufficient information about the case, (5) failure to consider other possible causes, (6) lack of testing, and (7) subjectivity.

The Sixth Circuit found that the district court failed to "recognize that differential diagnosis is a valid technique that often underlies reliable medical-causation testimony. . . ." The court reiterated its conclusion in *Hardyman v. Norfolk & W. Ry. Co.*, 243 F.3d 255, 260 (6th Cir. 2001) that differential diagnosis is "'a standard scientific technique of identifying the cause of a medical problem by eliminating the likely causes until the most probable one is isolated.'" The court recognized that not every differential diagnosis will meet *Daubert*'s reliability standard, and adopted the Third Circuit's differential-diagnosis test set forth in *In re Paoli Railroad Yard PCB Litigation*, 35 F.3d 717 (3d Cir. 1994), to help district courts evaluate causation opinions based on differential diagnosis:

> A medical-causation opinion in the form of a doctor's differential diagnosis is reliable and admissible where the doctor (1) objectively ascertains, to the extent possible, the nature of the patient's injury. . . . (2) 'rules in' one or more causes of the injury using a valid methodology, and (3) engages in 'standard diagnostic techniques by which doctors normally rule out alternative causes' to reach a conclusion as to which cause is most likely.
>
> In connection with the third 'rules out' prong, if the doctor 'engage[s] in very few standard diagnostic techniques by which doctors normally rule out alternative causes,' the doctor must offer a 'good explanation as to why his or her conclusion remain[s] reliable.' Similarly, the doctor must provide a reasonable explanation as to why 'he or she concluded that [any alternative cause suggested by the defense] was not the sole cause.'

563 F.3d at 179 (citations omitted) (quoting *Paoli*).

In applying this test to the case before it, the Sixth Circuit found that Moreno's causation opinion should have been admitted. The court noted that "*Daubert* attempts to strike a balance between a liberal admissibility standard for relevant evidence on the one hand and the need to exclude misleading 'junk science' on the other," and that Moreno's testimony "falls on the admissible side of the elusive line separating reliable opinions from 'junk science.'" *Id.* at 182.

Tamraz v. Lincoln Electric Co., 620 F.3d 665 (6th Cir. 2010).
Plaintiff, a welder for nearly twenty-five years, developed Parkinsonism, a neurological syndrome. Plaintiff sued several manufacturers of welding supplies, blaming manganese exposure for his condition. The crucial substantive issue in this case was the form of plaintiff's Parkinsonism—Parkinson's Disease or manganism. Parkinson's Disease has many causes, some unknown, while manganism is caused by overexposure to manganese. Plaintiff had at least four doctors examine him, all of whom reached a different conclusion about the type and cause of his Parkinsonism. At trial, Dr. Carlini, plaintiff's neurologist, opined that welding supplies had triggered "manganese-induced parkinsonism" in Tamraz. The jury awarded plaintiffs approximately $20 million in damages.

On appeal, the manufacturers challenged the admission of Carlini's opinion, arguing that it "was at most a working hypothesis, not admissible scientific 'knowledge.'" *Id.* at 670. The Sixth Circuit agreed, concluding that the testimony should have been excluded for several reasons. The court found that Carlini's line of reasoning depended on speculation and logical leaps. The court summarized Carlini's analysis as follows:

> [Plaintiff] was exposed to welding fumes presumably containing manganese; (2) he developed the symptoms of Parkinson's Disease (though not those of manganism); (3) scientists have identified genetic factors that cause some forms of otherwise 'idiopathic' Parkinson's Disease; (4) some literature has hypothesized that toxins combined with genetics may cause other cases of Parkinson's Disease; (5) manganese is known to cause manganism, so it would be a possible candidate for triggering Parkinson's Disease as well; (6) [Plaintiff] may have the genes for Parkinson's Disease; and (7) manganese may have triggered these genes and given [Plaintiff] parkinsonism.

Id at 670. "That is a plausible hypothesis. It may even be right. But it is no more than a hypothesis. . . . " *Id.*

Although the court recognized that experts may use a "differential etiology" or "differential diagnosis," Carlini's methodology failed under the "rule in" prong as well as the "rule out" prong of *Best v. Lowe's Home Centers, Inc.*, 563 F.3d 171 because "his efforts to 'rule in' manganese exposure as a possible cause or to 'rule out' other possible causes turned on speculation, not a valid methodology." *Id.* at 674. The court noted that

> most treating physicians have more training in and experience with diagnosis than etiology . . . [but] none of this means that physicians may not testify to etiology . . . only that courts must apply the *Daubert* principles carefully in considering it . . . [d]octors thus may testify to both, but the reliability of one does not guarantee the reliability of the other.

Id. at 673.

Pluck v. BP Oil Pipeline Co., 640 F.3d 671 (6th Cir. 2011).

Plaintiff developed Non-Hodgkin's lymphoma ("NHL"), which she alleged to have been caused by exposure to benzene. To prove general and specific causation, plaintiff offered Dr. James Dahlgren to testify that benzene is generally capable of causing NHL, and that plaintiff's NHL was caused by benzene. The district court excluded Dahlgren's testimony, finding that it was unreliable, suffered serious methodological flaws, and was based on speculation. Among other issues, Dahlgren formulated his opinions about dose without having any data about benzene level to which plaintiff was actually exposed.

The Sixth Circuit evaluated Dahlgren's differential diagnosis, using the "ruled in" and "ruled out" test from *Best v. Lowe's Home Centers, Inc.*, 563 F.3d 171 (6th Cir. 2009) and *Tamraz v. Lincoln Electric Co.*, 620 F.3d 665 (6th Cir. 2010). First, the court concluded that Dahlgren did not reliably "rule in" benzene as the cause of plaintiff's NHL because Dahlgren never ascertained her level of exposure. Rather, he concluded that continuous low-level exposure could have caused plaintiff's NHL because "'[t]here is no safe level for benzene in terms of causing cancer.'" Dahlgren's opinion that plaintiff's "'low-level exposure' to benzene caused her NHL [was] not grounded in 'sufficient facts or data,' nor [did] it reflect the 'reliable principles and methods' required by Rule 702." Dahlgren also failed to consider other sources of potential benzene exposure in his differential diagnosis, despite being aware of plaintiff's smoking habit. Therefore, he failed to "rule-out" possible alternative causes of plaintiff's NHL. The Sixth Circuit affirmed the exclusion of Dahlgren's testimony.

***Hardyman v. Norfolk and W. Ry. Co.*, 243 F.3d 255 (6th Cir. 2001).**
The plaintiff sued the defendant railroad under the Federal Employer's Liability Act (FELA). 243 F.3d at 257. The plaintiff claimed that he had developed carpal tunnel syndrome (CTS) as a result of his employment as a conductor and brakeman with the railroad. *Id.* The plaintiff sought to introduce the testimony of a specialist in occupational and environmental medicine, who proposed to testify about his "differential diagnosis" method for identifying the cause of the plaintiff's CTS. *Id.* at 261. Using this method, the specialist concluded that plaintiff's CTS was at least partly caused by his work for the defendant. *Id.*

While acknowledging that differential diagnosis is acceptable as a method for determining the cause of diseases, the district court refused to allow the specialist to testify for the plaintiff. *Id.* at 262. The district court required that the specialist offer a scientific study specifically addressing the relationship between CTS and work as a railroad brakeman before it would accept his testimony. *Id.* Furthermore, the district court refused to allow the introduction of the testimony of an ergonomist who had researched the plaintiff's work conditions and completed an extensive report about the specific tasks at work that contributed to the plaintiff's CTS. *Id.* at 263–64.

The Sixth Circuit, however, believed that the method of differential diagnosis should have been admitted under the *Daubert* standard. *Id.* at 265. After noting the wide latitude that district courts have in determining the admissibility of expert testimony, the Sixth Circuit held that the exclusion of the plaintiff's expert witnesses was not justified in this case. *Id.* at 267. Because the district court had abused its discretion in refusing to allow the plaintiff's experts to testify, the Sixth Circuit reversed the district court's decision and remanded the case. *Id.* at 269–70.

***Kolesar v. United Agri Products, Inc.*, No. 06-1416, 2007 WL 2492402 (6th Cir. 2007).**
In this lawsuit for negligent exposure to metam sodium, a toxic pesticide, the plaintiff appealed from the exclusion of the proffered testimony of his expert witness, Dr. Chen. Plaintiff consulted Chen approximately two weeks after the chemical spill and reported that he had been suffering from shortness of breath and wheezing since the exposure, and that he had no prior history of respiratory difficulty other than smoker's cough. Chen diagnosed the plaintiff as suffering from Reactive Airways Dysfunction Syndrome (RADS) caused by the chemical spill. Plaintiff argued that Chen's testimony was based on a valid differential diagnosis; however, Chen's conclusion was not the result of a careful study of plaintiff's prior medical records and did not initially take into account plaintiff's long history of asthma and smoking. In light of the methodological deficiencies in Chen's hypothesis, the Sixth Circuit concluded that the district court did not abuse its discretion in excluding her testimony.

b. District Courts

***Buck v. Ford Motor Co.*, 810 F. Supp. 2d 815 (N.D. Ohio 2011).**
This product liability action concerned an alleged electronic malfunction that caused a Ford Expedition to accelerate out of control. Plaintiff and defendant moved to exclude each other's experts. The court's discussion of electronics expert Samuel Sero is particularly noteworthy.

Sero intended to testify that the Expedition's speed control system was subject to electromagnetic interference that caused sudden acceleration. To reach this conclusion, he followed "a process of elimination," or in the view of the defendant, "differential diagnosis." Plaintiff contended that this methodology was in fact an accepted engineering failure analysis known as Failure Modes and Effects Analysis. But the court agreed that Sero was, in essence, using differential diagnosis to reach an opinion about the cause of the accident. The court subjected Sero's opinions to the differential-diagnosis test set forth in *Best v. Lowe's Home Centers, Inc.*, 563 F.3d 171 (6th Cir. 2009). Sero's theory failed to "rule in" EMI as a potential cause of sudden acceleration because it relied too heavily on general scientific and engineering principles without being tested or subjected to peer review.

Sero's underlying methodology was unreliable because Sero failed to supplement his conclusions derived from general engineering principles with reliable methodology that had not been verified through testing, accepted generally, or peer reviewed and/or published. Moreover, the district court found that Sero failed to "rule out" driver error.

Adams v. Cooper Industries, Inc., 2007 WL 2219 212 (E.D. Ky. 2007).
In this action for industrial contamination, the defendants moved to exclude the specific causation testimony of plaintiffs' experts. The experts employed differential etiology or differential diagnosis. The court stated that, in a toxic tort case, an opinion on causation requires (1) an analysis of whether the disease can be related to chemical exposure by a biologically plausible theory, (2) a determination of whether the plaintiff was exposed to the chemical in a manner that could lead to absorption in the body, and (3) that the expert have an opinion as to whether the dose to which the plaintiff was exposed was sufficient to cause the disease. Because the experts in this case made no effort to determine the dosage of industrial contaminants that the plaintiffs were exposed to, the court excluded the testimony.

9. Damages

a. Sixth Circuit

Tharo Systems, Inc. v. Cab Produkttechnik GmbH & Co Kg, 196 F. App'x 366 (6th Cir. 2006).
In this contract dispute, defendant argued that the district court erred by admitting testimony of plaintiff's damages expert, Mr. Bralas. Bralas estimated how much defendant overcharged plaintiff and he estimated the value to plaintiff of the technical information that defendant failed to provide. Bralas had been a CPA for approximately twenty years, was a partner in an accounting firm where he specialized in financial analysis in business disputes, and utilized the methodology called "benchmarking" to estimate the cost of developing the technology at issue. There was no evidence contradicting Bralas's testimony that benchmarking was recognized in his profession as a method to estimate cost and value, and he cited a text referencing this methodology. Bralas had testified in nearly 100 trials and worked as an auditor at an international accounting firm. Defendant, a German company, argued that Bralas's testimony should have been excluded because there was no evidence of his familiarity with German accounting principles, and he had no particular expertise in the technology involved in the contract. The Sixth Circuit found the trial court had fulfilled its gatekeeping duties in reviewing the evidence, and that defendant's criticisms of Bralas to the weight rather than the admissibility of his testimony.

b. District Courts

Younglove Construction, LLC v. PSD Development, LLC, et al., 782 F. Supp. 2d 457 (N.D. Ohio 2011).
Defendant alleged that the poor quality of materials and workmanship employed by plaintiff in building a feed mill diminished the value of that structure. Defendant retained Mr. Pelegrin, an industrial and commercial real estate appraiser. Because the unique facts of the case did not allow Pelegrin to employ his usual appraisal methods—measuring the useful life of assets and identifying comparable sales—Pelegrin applied an unusual method in reaching the conclusion that there was a 35 percent diminution in value. Pelegrin researched published articles and cases regarding the valuation of construction defects, drew comparisons from cases of environmental contamination, and interviewed fifteen real estate professionals to garner their reactions to the facts of the case. Pelegrin relied upon the report of his client's engineering expert, but he did not use the reports of plaintiff's

experts because he was not privy to them at the time. He also believed that plaintiff's engineers were not as reliable as the report of his client's engineers.

In moving to exclude the testimony, plaintiffs' main argument was that Pelegrin's interviews failed to comply with reliable survey methodology and therefore lacked scientific validity. *Id.* at 464. However, the court concluded that "although Mr. Pelegrin's interview method is far from unassailable, it is not so obviously unreliable" as to merit exclusion. *Id.* The court cited *Hawthorne Partners v. AT&T Technologies, Inc.* 1993 WL 311916 at *4 (N.D. Ill. 1993) ("Commercial real estate is not a branch of social science. Accordingly, in ruling on the admissibility of an appraisal expert's opinions, the court need not apply the same standards of methodological rigor required of social scientific inquiry."). Moreover, the court reasoned:

> as the unique qualities of a particular property increase and the number of possible 'comparables' decreases, the reliability of an appraisal will be subject to increasing question. But rational people rely on such appraisals in making commercial decisions. A court should not be too quick to reject an appraiser's opinion—where the appraiser is experienced and competent . . . simply because the circumstances are unique.

Id. at 466.

E.E.O.C. v. Freeman, 626 F. Supp. 2d 811 (M.D. Tenn. 2009).

In this Title VII action, plaintiffs sought to prove future damages through an economist, Dr. Mark Cohen. Among other things, Cohen projected the upper limit of the plaintiff's work life as being age 67. He based that opinion on the social security retirement age and his experience as a labor economist. Defendants moved to exclude Cohen's opinions.

The court noted that there was a dearth of contemporary data about the work life of women. "Accordingly, the Court finds that the *Daubert* factors are not helpful here. A theory about which little has been published cannot have been tested, subjected to peer review or publication, or analyzed with respect to error rate." *Id.* at 824. The court admitted the testimony.

TCE Systems, Inc. v. Thomas & Betts Corp., 2005 WL 3132207 (E.D. Mich. 2005).

TCE Systems sought damages from Thomas & Betts arising from breach of contract. Thomas & Betts attempted to exclude the report and proposed testimony of the plaintiff's witnesses. With respect to the proposed testimony of Mr. Henning, identified as a forgery specialist, his opinion about the obligations of Thomas & Betts to pay TCE for remaining invoices and extenuating damages resulting from nonconformance to contractual agreements between the parties was deemed to focus on legal conclusions. The court found that any value of Henning's report and proffered testimony would be substantially outweighed by the danger of prejudice, confusion of the issues, and misleading the jury, and granted the motion for exclusion. Defendant also offered the report and testimony of Dr. Misiolek on the issue of whether TCE developed and created products with design, function, and manufacturing processes that were valuable, original, and unique when provided to Thomas & Betts. The court found this to bear on whether trade secrets existed under the license agreements between the parties. The court also found that Misiolek's background as a professor in Lehigh University's materials science and engineering and mechanical engineering and mechanics departments provided sufficient qualifications for his opinions.

Finally, the defendant moved to exclude the testimony of CPA Jeffrey Mordaunt purporting to analyze and qualify the damages attributable to the conduct of Thomas & Betts. Mordaunt's report appeared to be more of a discussion of his view of the facts in the matter than an expert opinion. The court concluded that the risk of prejudice warranted excluding the Mordaunt report and related testimony.

Kurncz v. Honda North America, Inc., 166 F.R.D. 386 (W.D. Mich. 1996).
The plaintiff brought suit for injuries suffered while riding a three-wheeled recreational vehicle, and he sought to offer the testimony of an economist to aid the jury with statistical valuations of hedonic loss. 166 F.R.D. at 387–88. The court applied the *Daubert* two-part test: "(1) is the evidence reliable?; (2) is it relevant, i.e., does it 'fit' the case?" *Id.* at 388. The court then discussed the four factors listed in *Daubert* for determining whether the evidence is reliable.

The economic expert utilized a method for calculating the value of life according to a "willingness to pay model."[1] *Id.* at 388. The court noted that this model has been rejected by many courts as a "troubled science." *Id.* The model cannot be validated and has been criticized through peer review. *Id.* at 389. The model also is subject to tremendous variation in valuations and, therefore, may be subject to error. *Id.* at 389–90.

The court also held that this model does not "fit" within the meaning of Rule 702, and that the evidence was inadmissible under Rule 403. *Id.* at 390. Accordingly, the expert's testimony relating to the "willingness to pay" model was not allowed. *Id.*

Ellipsis, Inc. v. The Color Works, Inc., 428 F. Supp. 2d 752 (W.D. Tenn. 2006).
Plaintiff sued the defendant for failing to supply camouflage cell phone face plates in accordance with the parties' supply contract. The defendant challenged the admissibility of plaintiff's expert Patzer's lost-profits analysis. The court found that Patzer had relied exclusively on data provided by the plaintiff and had failed to verify the data or provide specific bases for assumptions and estimations made, thereby rendering his entire report unreliable. The court granted the defendant's motion to exclude the report and the testimony of the plaintiff's expert.

Hein v. Merck & Co., Inc., 868 F. Supp. 230 (M.D. Tenn. 1994).
The defendant in this tort action filed a motion *in limine* to exclude the testimony of an economic expert who proposed to testify as to the hedonic damages suffered by the plaintiff. 868 F. Supp. at 230. The court cited the four factors listed in *Daubert* and also proposed five additional factors. *Id.* at 231.

The proposed expert utilized "contingent valuation studies" to establish the trade-off people make between money and their risk of death to evaluate the lost enjoyment of life at a minimum of about $2,000,000 to a maximum of about $4,000,000 in the "willingness to pay" model. *Id.* at 232. The court stated that, unlike many other economic assumptions and predictions, there is no possible retrospective validation of this model of valuation. The court noted that this model is less than universally accepted. In considering the potential rate of error, the court observed that values for an anonymous life have varied in studies from $100,000 to $12,000,000. The court also concluded that there are "critical errors in the assumptions and methodology of the three models used to arrive at hedonic valuation." *Id.* at 233. Accordingly, the court concluded that the expert's testimony was "unreliable and invalid under the teaching of *Daubert*" and therefore inadmissible. *Id.* at 235.

10. Police Practices / Excessive Force

a. Sixth Circuit

Champion v. Outlook Nashville, Inc., 380 F.3d 893 (6th Cir. 2004).
In a civil rights action, the next of kin of the decedent, Champion, a 32-year-old mentally disabled man, brought suit against the caretaking service and Nashville police officers whose conduct gave

---

[1] Under this model, the value of human life is based on what an individual would pay for the reduced probability of dying. *Hein v. Merck & Co., Inc.*, 868 F. Supp. 230, 232 (M.D. Tenn. 1994).

rise to the series of events that culminated in Champion's death. Champion became self-destructive and his caretaker summoned the police. Plaintiffs alleged that the police officers used pepper spray and applied excessive pressure after Champion was handcuffed and hobbled. The police officers argued that the judge erred in allowing testimony from the plaintiffs' expert witness, Albert. Albert testified about the use of excessive force based on his particular knowledge of that subject. Albert had a PhD in sociology, was employed by the U.S. Department of Criminology, taught classes on police procedures and practices, participated in federal research funded by the Department of Justice evaluating the use of force by officers, trained officers in the use of force, worked with police departments to create use-of-force policies, had testified before Congress and state legislatures about police practices, and had authored over forty articles on the subject of police procedures, many of which appeared in journals. Albert opined that if the plaintiffs' witnesses' testimony were credited, the police officers' actions violated nationally recognized police standards governing excessive force.

The Sixth Circuit found that there was no error in admitting Albert's testimony because he had considerable experience in the field of criminology and because he was testifying concerning a discreet area of police practices about which he had specialized knowledge. The court distinguished the case from *Berry v. City of Detroit*, 25 F.3d 1342 (6th Cir. 1994), in which an expert was found unqualified to speak about the city government's policy of disciplining officers for alleged uses of excessive force.

Berry v. City of Detroit, 25 F.3d 1342 (6th Cir. 1994).

The estate of a victim fatally shot by a police officer brought a §1983 action against the city. 25 F.3d at 1344. The plaintiff used a former sheriff as an expert regarding police practices and procedures. *Id.* at 1349. The Sixth Circuit noted that *Daubert* was of limited help in this case because at the time application of the case was limited to scientific evidence. *Id.* at 1349. *But see Kumho Tire Co. v. Carmichael*, 526 U.S. 137 (1999). The *Berry* court provided an interesting distinction between scientific and nonscientific expert testimony by comparing the way an aeronautical engineer and a beekeeper might explain bumblebee flight characteristics to a jury. *Id.* at 1349–50. The engineer would understand the aerodynamics of flight, but if you wanted to prove that bumblebees always take off into the wind, a beekeeper with no scientific training at all would be an acceptable expert witness if a proper foundation were laid for his conclusions. This foundation would not relate to his formal training, but to his firsthand observations. *Id.* at 1349–50. The beekeeper may not know any more about flight principles than any juror, but in his experience has seen a lot more bumblebees than the jurors have. *Id.* at 1350. The court then concluded that if the ex-sheriff's testimony was admissible at all, it would have been from the viewpoint of the beekeeper, not the aeronautical engineer. *Id.* His testimony would not survive scrutiny under *Daubert* because his "theory" had neither been tested nor subjected to peer review and publication. *Id.*

The Sixth Circuit also discussed *Daubert*'s requirement that an expert's testimony rest on reliable foundation and be relevant to the task at hand. *Id.* at 1351. The court cited *United States v. Aozminski*, 821 F.2d 1186 (6th Cir. 1987), *aff'd in part and remanded in part*, 487 U.S. 931 (1988), which counseled against a trial court placing a general seal of approval on an expert after he has been qualified before any questions have been posed to the expert. 25 F.3d at 1351. The trial court in *Berry* accepted the qualification of the ex-sheriff as an expert in the field of proper police policies and practices, based on the testimony as to his background and experience in that field. *Id.* at 1352. The Sixth Circuit, however, observed that there is no such "field" as "police policies and practices," comparing the use of an ex-sheriff as an expert in policies and practices to the use of an attorney as an expert in "the law." *Id.* The court then noted that a divorce lawyer would be no more qualified to opine on patent-law questions than anyone else, and it is a mistake for a trial judge to declare anyone to be an expert generically as was done by the trial court in this case. *Id.* Accordingly, the Sixth Circuit reversed the jury verdict against the city of Detroit. *Id.* at 1356.

11. Civil Rights

a. Sixth Circuit

Thomas v. City of Chattanooga, 398 F.3d 426 (6th Cir. 2005).
Thomas appealed part of the summary judgment in favor of the city of Chattanooga in a civil rights action in light of the exclusion of the affidavit of the plaintiff's expert witness. The expert, Davidson, opined that based on his review of the complaints in forty-five lawsuits against the Chattanooga Police Department he could infer a policy, practice, or custom of the police department in condoning use of excessive force. While the Sixth Circuit acknowledged that in dealing with nonscientific testimony, an expert may rely on his experience in making conclusions, the Sixth Circuit noted that if the witness is relying solely or primarily on experience, then the witness must explain how that experience leads to the conclusion reached, and that the trial court's gatekeeping function required more than simply taking the expert's word for his opinion. *Id.* at 431. The court suggested Davidson would need to conduct more qualitative analysis to determine how many complaints would be excessive.

b. District Courts

King v. Enterprise Rent-A-Car Company, 231 F.R.D. 255 (E.D. Mich. 2004).
This action was brought by African American employees of the defendant, alleging race discrimination and seeking class certification. The plaintiffs attempted to use statistical evidence to establish a pattern and practice of discrimination, offering the expert testimony of Dr. Van Wingen. Defendants moved to exclude Dr. Van Wingen's reports and testimony. Dr. Van Wingen had no educational or professional background in the area of employment statistics, but plaintiffs contended that his general background in statistics was adequate for him to render an opinion. The plaintiffs did not present any evidence or authority to support that position. The court found Dr. Van Wingen's methodologies and rationale largely conclusory and gave little insight into how he reached his conclusions. Furthermore, Dr. Van Wingen combined various regions of the defendant's operations even though the uncontroverted evidence was that each region had a different means of assessing an employee's eligibility for promotion. Although Van Wingen asserted it was not necessary to analyze data by region, he did not provide any authority for this position, nor did he offer any authority to support his method of analyzing the data. The court granted the defendant's motion to exclude Dr. Van Wingen's reports and testimony because it was not clear that he had the requisite educational and professional background and because his reports did not establish his methodologies were based on sound scientific or statistical principles.

West Tennessee Chapter of Associated Builders and Contractors, Inc. v. City of Memphis, 300 F. Supp. 2d 600 (W.D. Tenn. 2004).
In this civil rights action challenging the enactment of a minority/women business enterprise program by the city of Memphis, the testimony of plaintiff's expert, Dr. Lallou, was offered to critique the disparity study conducted on behalf of the city of Memphis. Dr. Lallou was a political science professor with a long history of critiquing disparity studies through research, publications, and teaching. The court stated that social science and law do not subject studies to the same rigorous peer review as physics, chemistry, and the hard sciences. While agreeing that the city was correct when it argued that Lallou's methods were contested, the court noted that the city's own methods for determining contractor availability were also heavily contested.

Woodhull v. County of Kent, 2006 WL 2228986 (W.D. Mich. 2006).
The plaintiff in this action sought recovery for the death of her son, Michael Woodhull, who was alleged to have received inadequate medical care while in custody at the Kent County Jail. In order

to recover under 42 USC § 1893, the plaintiff needed to establish that the defendant had acted with "deliberate indifference." The court considered the question with respect to both sides' expert opinion evidence as one of relevance, not reliability. Whether a defendant acted with deliberate indifference is dependent on that defendant's subjective state of mind. The court held that no one, including an expert, can delve into a defendant's subjective state of mind. The court disregarded the opinions of both sides' experts, which expressed the legal conclusion that a defendant was or was not deliberately indifferent.

Mims v. Electronic Data Systems Corp., 975 F. Supp. 1010 (E.D. Mich. 1997).
In an age and race discrimination suit, the plaintiff sought to introduce statistical evidence in support of her claims. 975 F. Supp. at 1017–18. The plaintiff offered statistics regarding EDS's North American Operations group, which had some 14,000 members, but these statistics did not specifically show any discriminatory treatment in the plaintiff's division, which included only forty to fifty employees. *Id.* at 1018. The court stated that in order to utilize employment statistics, they must be "probative of an imbalance caused by a specific employment practice in the particular pool of workers to which the Plaintiff belongs." *Id.* Accordingly, the court granted summary judgment in favor of the defendant, concluding that the statistics offered by the plaintiff were not probative or relevant to her claims. *Id.* at 1018–19. The court stated that its "scrutiny of the proffered statistical evidence [was] in keeping with the Supreme Court's holding in *Daubert*," but the court did not discuss the application of *Daubert* to this case. *Id.* at 1018–19.

12. Other

a.   Sixth Circuit

Mike's Train House, Inc. v. Lionel, LLC, 472 F.3d 398 (6th Cir. 2007).
Defendant appealed a jury verdict holding it liable for misappropriation of trade secrets and unjust enrichment and awarding plaintiff more than $40 million. Plaintiff offered the testimony of Dr. Stein, a professor of mechanical engineering, to establish that defendant's design drawings had been copied from drawings developed for plaintiff by a Korean supplier. Stein developed a methodology for comparing similarities in the drawings. Based on twenty-one criteria, including factors such as the drawings' title and the part number assigned to the drawings, Stein concluded that approximately 55 percent of defendant's drawings had been copied from those of plaintiff's Korean supplier.

The Sixth Circuit concluded that the district court had abandoned its gatekeeping function by failing to make any findings regarding the reliability of Stein's testimony. Stein's methodology was new, had never been tested, had never been subjected to peer review, was not found to possess a known or potential rate of error, and did not enjoy general acceptance. Furthermore, Stein lacked an understanding of the Korean model-train design industry and thus was unable to identify aspects of the design drawings that might be indicative of copying. Stein also arbitrarily determined the weight applied to each of his twenty-one criteria. The Sixth Circuit noted a general suspicion of methodologies created for the purpose of litigation because expert witnesses are not necessarily always unbiased scientists. *Id.* at 408. Stein also testified concerning the similarities of his findings with the findings of Professor Lee, an expert who had testified in related Korean criminal proceedings, utilizing a regression analysis. Defendant did not challenge the general use of regression analysis but instead argued that this was not an appropriate method of allowing Stein's testimony regarding Lee's conclusions. The Sixth Circuit found that Stein's testimony was improperly admitted and likely had substantial effect on the verdict and therefore reversed and remanded the case.

Kilgore v. Carson Pirie Holdings, Inc., 205 F. App'x 367 (6th Cir. 2006).
In this premises liability action, the plaintiff fell while descending a stationary escalator and appealed the district court's grant of summary judgment after the exclusion of her expert witnesses. Plaintiff offered the testimony of Barnes, an architect prepared to testify about various dangers involving stationary escalators. To support his opinion, Barnes relied on several publications related to stationary stairs that were not applicable to escalators. The only publication critical of escalator risers mentioned the greater height of escalator risers relative to ordinary steps on a stairway, a defect not alleged to have caused the plaintiff's injury in question. The Sixth Circuit found that the testimony was arguably relevant, but it could not be said that the district court abused its discretion in excluding Barnes's testimony. Barnes's opinion that a stationary escalator should not be used because the appearance of the risers created an optical illusion was properly excluded, as he did not know what research or methodology underlay a supporting Web site article, and he had failed to conduct any independent research. Barnes's proposed testimony on appropriate steps was not supported by any evidence that the proposed steps were an industry standard or effective. Accordingly, the Sixth Circuit affirmed the exclusion of expert testimony, although the case was remanded due to another error in the grant of summary judgment.

b. District Courts

Whirlpool Properties, Inc. v. LG Electronics U.S.A., Inc., 2006 WL 62846 (W.D. Mich. 2006).
In this trademark-infringement case, plaintiff moved to exclude testimony of defendant's experts, Phillip Johnson and Robert Reitter, with respect to survey evidence. The court noted the general rule that methodological deficiencies in surveys relate to the weight to be given to their conclusions rather than to their admissibility, and that it would be a rare case when a proffered survey was so flawed as to be completely unhelpful to the trier of fact and therefore inadmissible. The plaintiff retained an expert, Cogan, not to conduct a survey, but to review and provide an opinion regarding surveys conducted by defendant's experts Johnson and Reitter. Cogan pointed out numerous potential defects in Johnson's survey, which was designed to ascertain whether consumers recognized the words "Whisper Quiet" as used by LG on panels of its home laundry equipment. Cogan criticized Johnson's selection of the universe of respondents, use of leading questions, and failure to adequately represent marketplace conditions. Reitter's survey was intended to assess customer confusion and trademark awareness. Plaintiff argued that Reitter's survey was flawed because it did not follow the survey template approved by the Seventh Circuit in *Union Carbide v. Ever-Ready, Inc.,* 531 F.2d 366, 387 (7th Cir. 1976). The court concluded that the absence of any competing survey evidence from Dr. Cogan showing divergent results significantly undermined plaintiff's arguments that defendant's evidence was so unreliable that it must be excluded. In the final analysis, the court concluded that plaintiff's objections went only to the weight, and not the admissibility, of the defendant's survey evidence.

Harvey v. Allstate Insurance Co., 2004 WL 3142227 (W.D. Tenn. 2004).
In this claim for insurance coverage for an automobile destroyed by fire, Allstate offered testimony of Pacheco, who performed key pathway analysis on the remains of the ignition lock assembly of the plaintiff's automobile. This analysis consisted of microscopically examining the striations within the lock to determine if any device other than a key of the proper type had been used in the automobile in question. Pacheco had extensive training in the forensic examination of vehicles, and the court allowed his testimony in this case, as he had also testified in many previous cases. Of particular interest, even though there was no literature on key-pathway analysis, Allstate submitted affidavits from a highly qualified engineer and from a criminal investor confirming that Pacheco had used all

the proper techniques of scientific examination. In its analysis, the court treated these affidavits as a form of peer review.

***Isely v. Capuchin Province*, 877 F. Supp. 1055 (E.D. Mich. 1995).**
In this civil action regarding alleged sexual abuse, the defendants filed a motion *in limine* to preclude expert testimony on posttraumatic stress disorder (PTSD) and repressed memory, arguing that the opinions lacked scientific reliability and validity. 877 F. Supp. at 1056. The court cited the language from *Daubert* and then discussed the application by courts from other jurisdictions of *Daubert*'s standards in the context of expert psychological testimony concerning sexual abuse, PTSD, repressed memory, and traumatic amnesia. *Id.* at 1057. Under *Daubert*, the plaintiff (that is, proponent of expert scientific testimony) first had to establish that the witness was qualified by virtue of her education and training to give such opinions. *Id.* at 1063. The plaintiff also had to establish that the expert had personal experience in treating people who have experienced PTSD and/or repressed memory. *Id.* at 1063–64. Once the proposed expert has established his or her personal background qualifications as an expert, the expert must then "provide further foundational testimony as to the validity and reliability of" the particular science the expert will testify about. *Id.* at 1064.

The court held that (1) the proposed expert established sufficient personal education, experience, and background qualifications necessary to testify as an expert on PTSD and repressed memories; (2) the proposed expert demonstrated sufficient scientific basis of support in the field of psychiatry for her theories to allow plaintiff to present them to the jury; and (3) the proposed expert would be permitted to testify regarding her theories and opinions on PTSD and repressed memory, including whether plaintiff's behavior was consistent with someone who suffered from such conditions and whether, in her opinion, the plaintiff suffered from repressed memory. *Id.* at 1064–67. However, she would not be permitted to testify that she believed the plaintiff or believed that the events he alleged actually occurred. *Id.* at 1067.

D. PROCEDURAL ISSUES

In the Sixth Circuit, there are only two local civil rules that specifically address expert testimony. Local Rule 43.2 of the Eastern District of Tennessee states that no more than three expert witnesses may be called to testify, except by leave of the court. Local Rule 12(c)(6) of the Middle District of Tennessee imposes the same restriction as the Eastern District, stating that no more than three expert witnesses may be called without prior approval of the trial judge. This local rule also stipulates that the case manager or judge may require that the direct testimony of an expert witness, other than a medical expert, be reduced to writing and provided to opposing counsel at least five days before trial. If so ordered, in lieu of ordinary direct examination, the witness will read the prepared statement.

In the Sixth Circuit, "a district court is not required to hold a formal hearing to determine whether a person is qualified to be a witness; rather, the court must merely make a determination as to the proposed expert's qualifications." *Morales v. American Honda Motor Co.*, 151 F.3d 500, 516 (6th Cir. 1998).

There is a dearth of case law from the individual Sixth Circuit district courts regarding the application of Federal Rule of Civil Procedure 26(a)(2), the evaluation of expert reports, and general expert procedural issues.

1. Sixth Circuit

***Hirsch v. CSX Transportation, Inc.*, 656 F.3d 359 (6th Cir. 2011).**
In this toxic tort case, the issue on appeal was whether the district court properly granted summary judgment on the basis that plaintiff's expert reports were insufficient to create a genuine

issue of material fact without first making a *Daubert* ruling. The Sixth Circuit quickly dispersed of this issue, noting that "[e]ven where an expert's evidence is ruled admissible under the *Daubert* standards, a district court remains free to decide that the evidence amounts to no more than a mere scintilla."

Nelson v. Tenn. Gas Pipeline Co., 243 F.3d 244 (6th Cir. 2001).

Plaintiffs brought suit claiming that they had suffered injuries from long-term exposure to a contaminant that the defendant had released into the environment. 243 F.3d at 248. The plaintiffs sought to establish the causation of their injuries with the expert testimony of Drs. Kilburn and Hirsch, who had studied the plaintiffs and others living in the community to determine the effects of the contaminants on their health. *Id.* The magistrate judge granted the defendants' motion to exclude the testimony of Drs. Kilburn and Hirsch, and because the plaintiffs could not establish causation of their injuries without the testimony, the magistrate judge granted the defendants' motion for summary judgment. *Id.* After the magistrate judge denied their motion to amend judgment, the plaintiffs appealed the decision to exclude the expert testimony and the entry of summary judgment. *Id.*

The Sixth Circuit rejected the plaintiffs' contention that the district court was required to hold a preliminary hearing regarding the proffered expert testimony. *Id.* at 248–49. The court concluded that the plaintiffs had not demonstrated that the district court had abused its discretion in excluding the expert testimony of the doctors. *Id.* at 249. The court also rejected the plaintiffs' argument that considerations of fair play and equity required that they be given an opportunity to cure their deficiency in causation by developing further expert testimony. *Id.* at 249–50. Finally, the court refused to accept the plaintiffs' contentions that the trial court adhered too strictly to the *Daubert* factors or that the trial court misunderstood the methodology that the doctors used in forming their opinions. *Id.* at 251–54. Accordingly, the Sixth Circuit affirmed the trial court's decision to exclude the expert testimony. *Id.* at 255.

Morales v. American Honda Motor Co., 151 F.3d 500 (6th Cir. 1998).

In this product liability case, the Sixth Circuit discussed the history of its requirements for the admissibility of expert testimony according to Fed. R. Evid. 702. The court noted that post-*Daubert*, pre-*Joiner* decisions reflected some inconsistency in the Sixth Circuit in choosing a standard of review to apply to expert testimony under Rule 702, *Cook v. American Steamship Co.*, 53 F.3d 135 (6th Cir. 1995), and set forth a three-part test for imposing a standard of review.[2] *United States v. Jones*, 107 F.3d 1147, 1150–56 (6th Cir. 1997), contained an in-depth, pre-*Joiner* discussion of the standard of review of expert testimony, and the court utilized an abuse-of-discretion standard, suggesting that the three-part test for imposing a standard of review was incorrect; the *Jones* court, however, did not explicitly overrule *Cook*. In *Morales*, the Sixth Circuit observed that any apparent conflict created by the *Cook* case was resolved by *General Electric Co. v. Joiner*, 522 U.S. 136 (1997), which requires that appellate courts utilize the abuse of discretion standard. 151 F.3d at 515.

---

[2] Preliminary fact finding under Fed. R. Evid. 104(a) (for example, a finding that the witness is qualified to testify as an expert on a certain subject) was reviewed for clear error. *Cook*, 53 F.3d at 738–39. A trial court's determination of whether proffered expert testimony was the subject of "scientific, technical or other specialized knowledge" was a question of law to be reviewed *de novo*. *Id.* at 738. Finally, the determination of whether the proffered expert opinion would assist the trier of fact to understand the evidence or to determine a fact in issue was reviewed for abuse of discretion. *Id.*

The Sixth Circuit held that the trial court did not abuse its discretion in allowing a product-safety specialist to testify as an expert without a Rule 702 hearing. *Id.* The trial court did hear testimony regarding the proposed expert's credentials (which were sufficient), and "a district court is not required to hold a formal hearing to determine whether a person is qualified to be a witness; rather, the court must merely make a determination as to the proposed expert's qualifications." *Id.* at 515–16.

The appellants also contended that the expert testified beyond the scope of his specialties. The court cited *Davis v. Combustion Eng'g, Inc.*, 742 F.2d 916, 919 (6th Cir. 1984), which stated that

> Rule 702 should be broadly interpreted on the basis of whether the use of expert testimony will assist the trier of fact. The fact that a proffered expert may be unfamiliar with pertinent statutory definitions or standards is not grounds for disqualification. Such lack of familiarity affects the witness' *credibility,* not his qualifications to testify.

151 F.3d at 516. The Sixth Circuit observed that the expert was cross-examined regarding his qualifications to testify in the areas in question, and the jury was free to give the expert's testimony as much credence as they felt it deserved. *Id.* Therefore, the appellants' argument on this issue also failed. *Id.*

United States v. Demjanjuk, 367 F.3d 623 (6th Cir. 2004).

In this denaturalization case, the government sought to revoke the citizenship of John Demjanjuk based on evidence he served as a guard in several Nazi training and concentration camps during World War II. Demjanjuk contended the district court erred in admitting and relying on Dr. Sydnor's testimony without a preliminary assessment of his archival search methodology. The Sixth Circuit noted the trial judge's broad discretion in the matter of admission or exclusion with expert evidence and that this discretion was particularly broad in a bench trial. *Id* at 633. Moreover, the expert's methodology was neither original nor controversial, and the Sixth Circuit found the trial judge acted within his discretion in admitting the testimony.

Deal v. Hamilton County Board of Education, 392 F.3d 840 (6th Cir. 2004).

In this nonjury case seeking to obtain an appropriate public education for plaintiffs' son, plaintiffs appealed the district court's failure to exclude certain expert testimony. The substance of the objections were directed at the witnesses' credibility. The Sixth Circuit noted that the "gatekeeper" doctrine was designed to protect juries and is largely irrelevant in the context of a bench trial. *Id.* at 852. The court held that even if the testimony were to be handled under the *Daubert* factors, it would readily meet the threshold for admissibility.

2. District Courts

Nisus Corporation v. Perma-Chink Systems, Inc., 327 F. Supp. 2d 844 (E.D. Tenn. 2003).

In this patent infringement lawsuit, the testimony of plaintiff Nisus Corporation's expert, Dr. McDaniel, did not survive a motion to exclude his testimony and opinions on the permeation of wood. The court concluded that Dr. McDaniel had failed to follow the generally accepted methodology, relied on inherently imprecise measurements, and failed to conduct a reproducible and reviewable procedure. Nisus then filed a motion for leave to file a supplemental expert report. The court held that the patentee was not entitled to file a supplemental expert report or to have additional testing done by a new expert using a different methodology, as it would have resulted in a complete reopening of expert discovery.

E. *DAUBERT* IN CRIMINAL CASES

1. *Eyewitness Identification*

a. Sixth Circuit

***United States v. Langan*, 263 F.3d 613 (6th Cir. 2001).**
Defendant, the founder of the Aryan Republican Army, was convicted of robbing two banks and of numerous firearms charges. 263 F.3d at 615. He was sentenced to life in prison without the possibility of parole, 35 years. *Id.* On appeal, the defendant sought to introduce the testimony of Dr. David F. Ross, a psychologist at the University of Tennessee. *Id.* at 618. Ross was prepared to testify concerning the phenomenon known as "unconscious transference," which would undermine the eyewitness testimony and a witness's identification of the defendant. *Id.* at 618–19. The district court conducted a *Daubert* hearing to determine whether Ross was qualified as an expert in eyewitness identification. *Id.* at 619. It concluded that Ross's testimony concerning the accuracy of eyewitness identification would not assist the jury and would improperly invade the province of the jury. *Id.* The court cited three reasons for refusing to allow Ross to testify at Langan's trial. *Id.* First, it believed that Ross's testimony concerning unconscious transference did not have a sufficient basis in science, failing to meet the standard set out in *Daubert*. *Id.* Second, the court recognized that Ross had published an article criticizing the theory of unconscious transference. *Id.* Finally, the court found Ross to be unqualified in the field of adult eyewitness identification because in the past Ross had focused his work on child eyewitness identification. *Id.*

The Sixth Circuit determined that the district court had not improperly excluded the expert testimony of Ross. *Id.* at 624. The court pointed out that trial courts have broad discretion in deciding whether to admit expert testimony. *Id.* at 622. While it refused to adopt the district court's reasoning regarding Ross's specialty in child eyewitness identification, the court found that the district court did not abuse its discretion in prohibiting Ross from testifying at trial. *Id.* at 623. Furthermore, the court concluded that the defendant had been given an adequate opportunity to cross-examine the eyewitness. *Id.* at 624. As a result, the Sixth Circuit affirmed the judgment of the district court. *Id.* at 627. As shown by *State v. Copeland*, 226 S.W.3d 287 (Tenn. 2007), a different result may prevail on experts on eyewitness testimony if a prior foundation is presented.

***United States v. Smithers*, 212 F.3d 306 (6th Cir. 2000).**
In this bank robbery case, the defendant sought to introduce the testimony of Dr. Solomon Fulero, an expert in eyewitness identification. 212 F.3d at 309–10. Fulero proposed to testify about factors affecting the accuracy of eyewitness identification, including such issues as the tendency of witnesses to focus on readily identifiable characteristics of people they observe, the effect that later events have on one's memory of a particular event, and the phenomenon of witnesses' memories being affected by talking to other witnesses. *Id.* at 310. In particular, Fulero proposed to testify that if the defendant had been the bank robber, the eyewitnesses would have seen a large scar on the defendant's neck. *Id.* After conducting a *Daubert* hearing, the trial court excluded the testimony of Fulero, deciding that the proposed testimony was not scientifically valid and that such testimony would invade the province of the jury. *Id.*

In his appeal to the Sixth Circuit, the defendant argued that under the holding of *United States v. Smith*, 736 F.2d 1103 (6th Cir. 1984), it was an abuse of discretion for the district court to exclude testimony about the reliability of eyewitness identification. *Id.* at 312. The court, however, disagreed with the defendant. *Id.* It stated that the proper test for determining the admissibility of expert testimony was articulated in *Daubert*. *Id.* at 313. After a discussion of the *Daubert* analysis, the court declared that the trial court had erred in excluding Fulero's testimony without conducting a complete *Daubert* hearing. *Id.* at 314.

The Sixth Circuit found it particularly troubling that the trial court seemed to exclude the expert testimony in order to "make the trial more interesting." *Id.* In addition, the court found fault with the trial court's failure to apply the *Daubert* factors in its evaluation of the proposed expert testimony. *Id.* at 315. It also rejected the dissent's argument that under Federal Rules of Evidence 403, the admission of the expert testimony would have caused undue delay, and the court maintained that the late introduction of Fulero's testimony was not a proper reason to exclude it. *Id.* at 316–17. After a complete discussion of the proper steps that the trial court should have taken under *Daubert*, the Sixth Circuit held that the trial court had abused its discretion in excluding Fulero's testimony. *Id.* at 317. Because this error was not harmless, the Sixth Circuit reversed the defendant's conviction and remanded the case back to the trial court. *Id.* at 318.

2. DNA Evidence

a. Sixth Circuit

United States v. Bonds, 12 F.3d 540 (6th Cir. 1993).
In this case, the FBI sought to admit DNA evidence in testimony that revealed a probability of 1 in 270,000 that an unrelated individual selected randomly from the community would have a DNA profile matching that of defendant, Bonds. 12 F.3d at 551. The trial court conducted a six-week-long *Frye* hearing, as this case reached the district court level before *Daubert* was decided. *Id.* The district court chose to admit the DNA evidence at trial. *Id.*

The Sixth Circuit described the effect of *Daubert* overruling *Frye*, noting that *Daubert* did not explicitly define scientific validity, but "it did begin to draw the parameters of this inquiry" by providing a nonexclusive list of factors. *Id.* at 555. The court then examined the list of factors discussed in *Daubert* and stated that

> the *Daubert* court has instructed the courts that they are not to be concerned with the reliability of the conclusions generated by valid methods, principles and reasoning. Rather, they are only to determine whether the principles and methodology underlying the testimony itself are valid. If the principles, methodology and reasoning are scientifically valid then it follows that the inferences, assertions and conclusions derived therefrom are scientifically valid as well. Such reliable evidence is admissible under Rule 702, so long as it is relevant.

Id. at 556. The court then proceeded with an extremely detailed *Daubert* analysis of the facts in this case to determine if the DNA evidence was properly admitted in the trial court. *Id.* at 557–68. The court determined that the evidence had been properly admitted at the trial level. *Id.* at 568.

United States v. Beverly, 369 F.3d 516 (6th Cir. 2004).
The defendant appealed his conviction for bank robbery, arguing that the introduction of mitochondrial DNA (mtDNA) evidence at trial was in error, as that evidence was not scientifically reliable. The Sixth Circuit first discussed mtDNA testing in general, noting that nuclear DNA testing is more precise but requires DNA extracted from a cell nucleus while mtDNA is found outside the nucleus in the mitochondrion. Thus, there is a significantly greater amount of mtDNA from which a sample can be extracted as compared to nuclear DNA, and the technique is very useful for minute samples. However, mtDNA typing is said to be a test of exclusion rather than one of identification. The Sixth Circuit observed that mtDNA testing had been admitted into evidence in North Carolina, Tennessee, South Carolina, New York, and Maryland in rulings that had been upheld on review. The trial court

found that the techniques utilized by the testing laboratory had been established and accepted by the scientific community, accepted by the courts, and subjected to review, and therefore admitted the expert testimony. The defense argued that the laboratory was not accredited and that the sample in this case was contaminated. The court found there was no error in admitting the testing results and that any issues concerning the conduct of the specific test in question were fully developed and subject to cross-examination. The testimony allowed was that, with a high degree of confidence, less than 1 percent of the population could be expected to have the same pattern as the mtDNA of the hair recovered from the bank robbery site, and that the defendant had the same pattern and thus could not be excluded as the source of the hair.

3. Handwriting Analysis and Polygraphs

a. Sixth Circuit

United States v. Jones, 107 F.3d 1147 (6th Cir. 1997).
Jones was a credit card fraud case in which the trial court allowed in evidence the testimony of the government's expert witness, a forensic document analyst, regarding analysis of the defendant's handwriting. The *Jones* court observed that in seventy years of applying the *Frye* test, courts did not treat handwriting analysis as a matter of scientific knowledge. 107 F.3d at 1157. The court then described scientific methodology according to the words of *Daubert*: "[Science] represents a process for proposing and refining theoretical explanations about the world that are subject to further testing and refinement." *Id.* (quoting *Daubert*, 509 U.S. at 590). The *Jones* court concluded that handwriting analysis is nonscientific, and therefore that the *Daubert* framework of analysis was not applicable. 107 F.3d at 1157–58.

The *Jones* court concluded, under an analysis not based on *Daubert*, that the handwriting expert's testimony was admissible. *Id.* at 1160. The court noted that the opposing party could still challenge the reliability of admitted evidence: "Vigorous cross-examination, presentation of contrary evidence, and careful instruction on the burden of proof are the traditional and appropriate means of attacking shaky but admissible evidence." 107 F.3d at 1161 (quoting *Daubert*, 509 U.S. at 596).

United States v. Sherwin, 67 F.3d 1208 (6th Cir. 1995).
In this case, the defendant sought to admit a polygraph test that allegedly proved he was truthful when he denied burning a building. 67 F.3d at 1216. The defendant argued that, under *Daubert*, the polygraph results were admissible pursuant to Rule 702. *Id.* The trial court disagreed, however, and excluded this polygraph evidence under Rule 403 because its probative value was outweighed by the prejudicial effect. *Id.* The Sixth Circuit held that the trial court did not abuse its discretion in excluding the results of the polygraph examination from evidence, noting that "unilaterally obtained polygraph evidence is almost never admissible under Rule 403." *Id.* (quoting *Conti v. Commissioner*, 39 F.3d 658, 663 (6th Cir. 1994)). The Sixth Circuit rejected the argument that *Daubert* was controlling in these circumstances, holding that "Rule 403 offers a basis for excluding polygraph results independent of *Daubert*." 67 F.3d at 1217.

4. Other

a. Sixth Circuit

United States v. Leblanc, 45 F. App'x 393 (6th Cir. 2002).
After he was convicted of sexually assaulting his six-year-old stepdaughter, the defendant appealed his conviction and challenged the exclusion of the expert testimony of a psychologist. The

psychologist intended to testify about the interview techniques that the police used to question the six-year-old victim, particularly the susceptibility of children to the suggestions of interviewers. After conducting a *Daubert* hearing, the district court refused to admit the psychologist's testimony. Specifically, the district court rejected the testimony because (1) the theories about which he would testify had not received general acceptance in the psychological community, (2) the psychologist's theories were "not repeatable" and subject to error, (3) the psychologist had not completed any research regarding his theories of interviewing techniques, (4) the psychologist appeared to be an advocate, and (5) the psychologist's proposed testimony would invade the jury's province.

After a discussion of the *Daubert* factors, the Sixth Circuit determined that the district court's reasoning was questionable. In particular, the court stated that the psychologist's testimony should not have been excluded based on either the lack of acceptance within the psychological community or because the theory was not repeatable. Furthermore, the court noted that other states had admitted such testimony in light of the significant body of research on the potential for coercive interview techniques in child sex-abuse cases.

Although it rejected at least two of the district court's reasons for excluding the expert's testimony, the Sixth Circuit determined that the testimony was properly excluded for one important reason. Like all evidence, expert testimony must be relevant to the case at hand and assist the trier of fact. In this case, the court found that the defendant did not demonstrate any link between the facts of this case and the testimony that the psychologist would provide. *Id.* Specifically, the defendant did not identify any incidents in which this victim was subjected to coercive interview techniques. For this reason, the Sixth Circuit concluded that the district court did not abuse its discretion in excluding the psychologist's testimony.

b.   District Courts

United States v. Martinez, 588 F.3d 301 (6th Cir. 2010).
In this criminal action involving the illegal distribution of controlled substances by an anesthesiologist, the Sixth Circuit affirmed the district court's decision to admit the expert testimony of Dr. Parren over defendant's objection that the testimony was speculative and failed under *Daubert*. The Sixth Circuit noted that any review of testimony under *Daubert* must focus on principles and methodologies—not conclusions. The Sixth Circuit found that Parren's testimony was based on his examination of the toxicology reports and patient files and was therefore sufficiently reliable.

United States v. Stone, 279 F.R.D. 434 (E.D. Mich. 2012).
Defendants were charged with several weapons violations and seditious conspiracy. To prove the motive and intent for the seditious conspiracy count, the government sought to use the testimony of Dr. Barkun, an expert on conspiracy beliefs and theories. The district court, however, found this testimony to be irrelevant and speculative under *Daubert* because the testimony failed to connect why conspiracy theorists might commit a criminal act. The district court noted that one does not have to be a conspiracy theorist to commit seditious conspiracy. Therefore, Barkun's testimony was excluded.

United States v. Poulsen, 543 F. Supp. 2d 809 (S.D. Ohio 2008).
In this health-care fraud case, the government challenged the admissibility of defendant's expert, Wayne Barnes, a former FBI agent with experience in health-care fraud cases. Defendant's intended to have Barnes sit through trial and then opine on the government's investigation based on his relevant work experience and observations throughout trial. The government argued that such testimony failed under *Daubert*'s reliability standard and also failed because Barnes did not articulate a

precise methodology. The district court allowed Barnes to testify, noting that Barnes did not need to articulate his methodology because his testimony was not based on science but on his own experience and further noting that experience testimony satisfies *Daubert*'s reliability standard.

United States v. Abdi, 2007 WL 2153234 (S.D. Ohio 2007).
Abdi was charged with conspiring to provide material support to terrorists and related crimes. The government moved to admit testimony by Dr. Gunarata as an expert with specialized knowledge in the field of international terrorism. Following the Sixth Circuit's holding in *United States v. Damrah*, 412 F.3d 618, 625 (6th Cir. 2005) and the need for flexibility in applying the *Daubert* factors to nonscientific expert testimony as explained in *First Tennessee Bank National Association v. Barreto*, 268 F.3d 319 (6th Cir. 2001), the court undertook to apply a flexible approach in applying *Daubert* to testimony concerning world terrorism, a nonscientific field. The court noted Dr. Gunarata's expertise in the field, found little merit in the defendant's claim that it would be impossible for an impressionable jury to sort fact from fiction, and granted the government's motion to allow the testimony.

5. Criminal Procedural Issues

a. Sixth Circuit

United States v. Cunningham, 679 F.3d 355 (6th Cir. 2012).
In this criminal action involving attorney fraud relating to fees collected in a class action lawsuit, the district court excluded the defendants' expert as being unqualified to testify about class action lawsuits, and in the alternative, excluded the expert because his opinions were generally inadmissible.

The Sixth Circuit noted that an expert may be qualified based on experience alone, but "[w]hether a proposed expert's experience is sufficient . . . depends on the nature and extent of that experience." While the Sixth Circuit observed that the defendants' expert was probably qualified, the court declined to rule on that issue and instead affirmed the district court's decision to exclude the expert's testimony on the basis that his report contained numerous misstatements of law and was therefore inadmissible. The court rejected the defendants' procedural argument that it was error for the district court to draft a memorandum opinion regarding the admissibility of defendant's expert prior to the *Daubert* hearing. The court noted that this was not error because *Daubert* hearings are not required and the issue was fully briefed by the parties prior to the hearing.

United States v. Stepp, 680 F.3d 651 (6th Cir. 2012).
In this case involving charges for possession of narcotics, the district court excluded the defendant's drug-dog expert on the basis that the Federal Rules of Evidence as well as *Daubert* did not apply to suppression hearings. The Sixth Circuit relied on *United States v. Ozuna*, 561 F.3d 728 (7th Cir. 2009) and *United States v. Diaz*, 25 F.3d 392 (6th Cir. 1994) to conclude that while a district court does not have to consider the Rules of Evidence and *Daubert* at a suppression hearing, "the district court must always consider any proffered expert's qualification and determine, in its discretion, what weight to afford that expert's testimony." The court determined that the district court in this case abused its discretion because it held itself to an erroneous standard when it believed that it could not consider the defendant's expert's testimony at all. However, the court further found that this error was harmless because the expert "lacked the necessary qualifications to offer even minimally credible or reliable testimony on the subject of dogs sniffing for narcotics" and because the government's expert offered credible evidence on the same subject.

***United States v. Roberts*, 830 F. Supp. 2d 372 (M.D. Tenn. 2011).**
In this case regarding defendant's building of a dam over a tributary of the Duck River in alleged violation of the Clean Water Act, both sides moved to exclude the other party's expert witnesses. The district court conducted a *Daubert* analysis for each expert's opinion, and the district court concluded that all of the opinions were admissible except for those of Hubbs, an expert biologist testifying on behalf of the government. The district court deemed his testimony inadmissible because his opinion relied upon making assumptions on issues that the government had not yet proved. Moreover, the district court noted that Hubbs's expert report was not reliable because it did not specifically analyze the effects that the particular dam in question would have on the Duck River, but instead analyzed the effects that a hypothetical dam would have on the Duck River.

F. STATE-LAW EXPERT ISSUES

1. Expert Evidence in Tennessee State Courts

a. Evidentiary Standards

In *McDaniel v. CSX Transportation, Inc.*, 955 S.W.2d 257, 265 (Tenn. 1997), the Supreme Court of Tennessee held that Tennessee Rules of Evidence 702 and 703 supersede the "general acceptance test" of *Frye v. United States*, 293 F. 1013 (D.C. Cir. 1923), in analyzing the admissibility of scientific evidence. Under Tennessee law, a trial court must determine whether the evidence will substantially assist the trier of fact to determine a fact in issue and whether the facts and data underlying the evidence indicate a lack of trustworthiness. The rules together necessarily require a determination as to the scientific validity or reliability of the evidence. *McDaniel*, 955 S.W.2d at 265.

The trial court is vested with substantial discretion in making this determination. *Hunter v. Ura*, 163 S.W.3d 686 (Tenn. 2005) (excluding medical expert's testimony on *possible* causes of death as not being helpful when the jury must determine *probable* cause). Although the Tennessee Supreme Court declined to expressly adopt *Daubert*, it did state that the list of factors enumerated in *Daubert* are useful in applying Tennessee Rules of Evidence 702 and 703:

> A Tennessee trial court may consider in determining reliability: (1) whether scientific evidence has been tested and the methodology with which it has been tested; (2) whether the evidence has been subjected to peer review and publication; (3) whether a potential rate of error is known; (4) whether, as formerly required by *Frye*, the evidence is generally accepted in the scientific community; and (5) whether the expert's research in the field has been conducted independent of litigation.

McDaniel, 955 S.W.2d at 265. The court also cited *Joiner v. General Electric*, stating that "the court need not weigh or choose between two legitimate but conflicting scientific views. The court instead must assure itself that the opinions are based on relevant scientific methods, processes, and data, and not upon an expert's mere speculation." *McDaniel*, 955 S.W.2d at 265.

The court has made it clear that the *Daubert* factors are neither exclusive nor subject to rigid application in any particular case. *Brown v. Crown Equipment Corp.*, 181 S.W.3d 268 (Tenn. 2005). Additional considerations may include the expert's qualifications for testifying on the issue and the relationship between the expert's knowledge and the basis of the expert's opinion. *State v. Stevens*, 78 S.W.3d 817 (Tenn. 2002). The Tennessee Supreme Court has also recently liberalized the admissibility of social and behavioral scientific evidence. In *State v. Copeland*, 226 S.W.3d 287 (Tenn. 2007), the court held that expert testimony on the issue of the reliability of eyewitness identification was admissible, overruling the prior holding of *State v. Coley*, 32 S.W.3d 831 (Tenn. 2000), which held this testimony had no scientific or technical underpinnings outside the common understanding of the jury, and therefore was not necessary to help juries understand the testimony of an eyewitness.

b. Expert-Related Rules and Procedural Issues

Tennessee Rules of Evidence 702 and 703 are similar to their federal counterparts with two noteworthy differences. Tennessee Rule of Evidence 702 requires that scientific evidence "*substantially* assist the trier of fact to understand the evidence or to determine a fact in issue," whereas the federal rule does not impose the "substantial" requirement. In light of this distinction, "Tennessee's courts require expert testimony to have greater probative force than may be required in federal courts." *State v. Scott*, 275 S.W.3d 395, 410 (Tenn. 2009); *Howell v. State*, 185 S.W.3d 319 (Tenn. 2006) (excluding opinion of expert on the issue of effectiveness of counsel in the appeal of a criminal conviction). Similarly, Tennessee Rule of Evidence 703 contains the statement that "[t]he courts shall disallow testimony in the form of an opinion or inference if the underlying facts or data indicate lack of trustworthiness," which is not found in its federal counterpart.

Procedurally, Tennessee Rule of Civil Procedure 26.02(4) follows former Federal Rule 26 regarding disclosure of expert testimony. The state rule does not make such disclosures mandatory, as does the current version of Fed. R. Civ. P. 26. Formal expert disclosures are not required for experts who are not retained, but whose opinions are based on the knowledge they have gained as participants or actors in the events giving rise to the case. *Alessio v. Crook*, 633 S.W.2d 770 (Tenn. Ct. App. 1982).

2. *Expert Evidence in Kentucky State Courts*

a. Evidentiary Standards

The Supreme Court of Kentucky expressly adopted the *Daubert* analysis in *Mitchell v. Commonwealth*, 908 S.W.2d 100, 101 (Ky. 1995). Kentucky, which had previously followed *Frye*, followed *Daubert*'s direction because Rule 702 of the Kentucky Rules of Evidence contains the same language as Federal Rule 702, which *Daubert* held to supersede the *Frye* standard. *Id.* at 101. Therefore, in Kentucky state court, a "trial court judge must conduct a preliminary hearing on the matter utilizing the standards set forth in *Daubert*." *Id.* at 102. In the case of *Goodyear Tire & Rubber Co. v. Thompson*, 11 S.W.3d 575 (Ky. 2000), the court adopted the reasoning of *Kumho Tire* and held that *Daubert* and *Mitchell* applied not only to testimony based on "scientific" knowledge, but also the testimony based on "technical" and "other specialized" knowledge.

The Kentucky Supreme Court announced the standard for admitting expert-opinion evidence in *Stringer v. Commonwealth*, 956 S.W.2d 883 (Ky. 1997), *cert. denied* 523 U.S. 1052, 118 S. Ct. 1374, 140 L.Ed.2d 522 (1998). Specifically, expert-opinion evidence is admissible so long as

> (1) the witness is qualified to render an opinion on the subject matter; (2) the subject matter satisfies the requirements of *Daubert; (3)* the subject matter satisfies the test of relevancy set forth in KRE 401, subject to the balancing of probativeness against prejudice required by KRE 403; and (4) the opinion will assist the trier of fact per KRE 702.

Mitchell was overruled in *Fugate v. Commonwealth*, 993 S.W.2d 931 (Ky. 1999), but only as to the case-specific holding in *Mitchell* that the admissibility of DNA evidence in a criminal case should be determined on a case-by-case basis. *Fugate* held that the PCR and RFLP methods of DNA analysis are so well accepted, that they are presumptively admissible under *Daubert*.

As for determining whether the subject matter of an expert's opinion satisfies the requirements of *Daubert*, the Kentucky Supreme Court adopted the view that the factors are a "nonexclusive" and "flexible" list. *Florence v. Commonwealth*, 120 S.W.3d 699, 702 (Ky. 2003). Moreover, Kentucky courts follow the rule that "once an appropriate appellate court holds that the *Daubert* test of reliability is satisfied, lower courts can take judicial notice of reliability and validity of the scientific method, technique or theory at issue." *Johnson v. Commonwealth*, 12 S.W.3d 258, 261 (Ky. 1999).

The Kentucky Supreme Court has reiterated its adoption of *Daubert* and *Kumho Tire* in *Toyota Motor Corp. v. Gregory*, 136 S.W.3d 35 (Ky. 2004). Under Kentucky Supreme Court precedent, review of the trial court's gatekeeper determination is only subject to a deferential abuse-of-discretion standard. *Miller v. Eldridge*, 146 S.W.3d 909 (Ky. 2004).

b. Expert-Related Rules and Procedural Issues

The applicable provisions of the Kentucky Rules of Evidence are substantially the same as the Federal Rules. In its rules of procedure, Kentucky also follows former Fed. R. Civ. P. 26.

3. Expert Evidence in Ohio State Courts

a. Evidentiary Standards

Ohio has repudiated the *Frye* standard, holding that "scientific opinions need not enjoy 'general acceptance' in the relevant scientific community in order to satisfy the reliability requirement of [Ohio] Evid. R. 702." *State v. Nemeth*, 694 N.E.2d 1332, 1338 (Ohio 1998).

In *Miller v. Bike Athletic Company*, 687 N.E.2d 735, 740 (Ohio 1998), the Supreme Court of Ohio followed the *Daubert* analysis, setting forth the factors to be considered in evaluating scientific evidence: "(1) whether the theory or technique has been tested, (2) whether it has been subjected to peer review, (3) whether there is a known or potential rate of error, and (4) whether the methodology has gained general acceptance." None of these factors, however, "is a determinative prerequisite to admissibility." *Nemeth*, 694 N.E.2d at 1339.

The Ohio Supreme Court has stated that the reliability requirement is "a threshold determination that should focus on a particular type of scientific evidence, not the truth or falsity of an alleged scientific fact or truth." *Id*. Rule 702(C) of the Ohio Rules of Evidence permits a witness to testify as an expert only if "[t]he witness' testimony is based on reliable scientific, technical, or other specialized information." This rule, however, does not define *reliable*; it leaves the definition of that standard to "further development through case-law." *State v. Nemeth*, 694 N.E.2d 1332, 1337 (Ohio 1998) (quoting Staff Note to Ohio Evid. R. 702).

In *Valentine v. Conrad*, 850 N.E.2d 683, 686 (Ohio 2006), the Ohio Supreme Court explained that under Rule 702, the qualification and reliability requirements for the admission of expert testimony are distinct. In that case, the majority excluded medical causation testimony based on differential diagnosis without supporting causation studies. *Id*. at 688. The dissent, however, would have admitted the testimony as reliable due to its statistical underpinnings. *Id*. at 689.

The Ohio Supreme Court later concluded that the relevance and reliability requirements for the admission of expert testimony are not always mutually exclusive because "'a determination regarding the scientific validity of a particular theory requires not only an examination of the trustworthiness of the tested principles . . . but also an analysis of the reliability of an expert's application of the tested principals. . . .'" *Terry v. Caputo*, 875 N.E.2d 72, 78 (Ohio 2007) (*quoting Cavallo v. Star Ent.*, 892 F. Supp. 756, 762–763 (E.D. Va. 1995)).

The court has also been rather liberal in allowing experts to reference facts from authoritative literature in support of their opinions. *Beard v. Meridia Huron Hospital*, 834 N.E.2d 323 (Ohio 2005).

b. Expert-Related Rules and Procedural Issues

The principal distinctions between the Ohio Rules of Evidence and the Federal Rules are contained in Rule 702. Ohio Rule 702 was effectively amended to its current form on July 1, 1994. Formerly, the Ohio rule mirrored Federal Rule of Evidence 702. The Ohio rule change was not intended to substantively change the law, however. The change was simply an attempt to clarify language in the Federal Rule that the Ohio Commission believed was too indefinite. Ohio Rule 702 currently states:

A witness may testify as an expert if all of the following apply:

The witness' testimony either relates to matters beyond the knowledge or experience possessed by lay persons or dispels a misconception common among lay persons;

The witness is qualified as an expert by specialized knowledge, skill, experience, training, or education regarding the subject matter of the testimony;

The witness testimony is based on reliable scientific, technical, or other specialized information. To the extent that the testimony reports the result of a procedure, test, or experiment, the testimony is reliable only if all of the following apply:

(1) The theory upon which the procedure, test, or experiment is based is objectively verifiable or is validly derived from widely accepted knowledge, facts, or principles;
(2) The design of the procedure, test, or experiment reliably implements the theory;
(3) The particular procedure, test, or experiment was conducted in a way that will yield an accurate result.

Like other states in the Sixth Circuit, Ohio Rule of Civil Procedure 26(b)(4) mirrors the former Fed. R. Civ. P. 26 in not mandating expert disclosure.

4. *Expert Evidence in Michigan State Courts*

a. Evidentiary Standards

In spite of several legislative attempts to adopt *Daubert*, Michigan courts followed *Frye*[3] until 2004. The *Daubert* principles were codified in MCL 600.2955(1) in 1996 as applicable to civil actions for injury to persons and property; however, not until MRE 702 was amended to conform to FRE 702, with staff notes explicitly endorsing *Daubert* and *Kumho Tire*, were these principles considered an evidentiary rule. The trial courts' obligation to ensure the reliability of expert evidence is considered even stronger under the Michigan rules than under FRE 702. *Gilbert v. Daimler Chrysler Corp.*, 407 Mich. 749, 780, 685 N.W.2d 391, 408 (Mich. 2004).

b. Expert-Related Rules and Procedural Issues

The principal distinction between the Michigan Rules of Evidence and the federal rules relating to expert testimony is the statement in MRE 703 that "underlying facts or data essential to an

---

[3] Michigan courts referred to the *"Davis/Frye"* rule, based on *Frye v. United States* and *People v. Davis*, 72 N.W.2d 269 (Mich. 1955).

opinion in inference *shall* be in evidence." The federal rule, however, requires that "[i]f of a type reasonably relied upon by experts in the particular field in forming opinions or inferences upon the subject, the facts or data need not be admissible in evidence." The Michigan Rule requires considerable planning and cooperation between counsel and expert witnesses to ensure the underlying facts essential to the expert's opinion are in evidence. Michigan has also codified requirements for expert testimony in medical malpractice cases, MCL 600.2169, incorporating the principles of *Daubert*, but imposing rigorous requirements of expert qualification. *Woodard v. Custer*, 476 Mich. 545, 719 N.W.2d 842 (Mich. 2006). Michigan also follows former Federal Rule of Civil Procedure 26 with respect to the disclosure of experts and their testimony (that is, no mandatory disclosure).

G. GENERAL PRACTICE TIPS

The proponent of the proffered expert testimony, not the party objecting to its admissibility, has the burden of establishing that the *Daubert* criteria are met; the party opposing the admissibility of the proffered expert testimony simply must make the appropriate objection, and the district court is required to conduct the *Daubert* analysis. If the party opposing the admissibility of the proffered expert testimony successfully "*Daubert*izes" the opponent's proffered expert testimony, the result can mean the difference between winning and losing. The inadmissibility of the proffered expert testimony may cause a failure of proof resulting in summary judgment, judgment as a matter of law, or a jury verdict against the party whose expert testimony was ruled inadmissible. And, because the district court's application of the *Daubert* criteria is reviewed on an abuse-of-discretion standard, the chances of a reversal on appeal are slight. For these reasons, it is imperative that litigants begin focusing on the *Daubert* guidelines from the outset of the litigation in instances where expert testimony is necessary.

1. *Selection and Retention of Experts*

From the moment that the determination is made that expert testimony in a particular field may be necessary or advisable, counsel must focus not only on what substantive opinions a prospective expert witness may provide, but also on whether the proposed expert testimony will meet the *Daubert* criteria. For example, can the expert show the procedure or scientific technique he used to arrive at his opinion within the relevant scientific community? Has the procedure or technique he used been tested and subjected to peer review and publication? What is the potential rate of error? All of these issues need to be addressed with the expert candidate at the front end, before he is designated as an expert witness in the litigation.

Has the expert candidate been retained to testify in connection with a federal court lawsuit in the past few years? If so, someone may have attempted to "*Daubert*ize" the expert in connection with other litigation. Check it out. Was there a ruling on the admissibility of the expert's opinions in that litigation? Even an unreported or trial transcript ruling that the expert's testimony is inadmissible would be highly persuasive to the district court judge in your case. One needs to do one's homework in this area; rest assured that the other side will.

Conversely, if the other side has retained and identified an expert witness who one believes is susceptible to being "*Daubert*ized," one should consider selecting and retaining on at least a consulting basis an expert witness regarding the methodology or procedures used by the opposing expert. The purpose of such a consulting (or possibly testifying) expert witness would not be to provide an opinion contradicting the opponent's substantive expert testimony, but rather to "*Daubert*ize" the other side's expert by establishing that the expert's methodology was flawed, unreliable, and therefore inadmissible.

2. Expert Interrogatory Responses and Expert Reports

When preparing responses to expert interrogatories and when preparing the expert report required by Rule 26(a)(2), one should pay particular attention to the *Daubert* criteria. It would be prudent for one to describe not only the substantive opinions to be offered by the expert, but also to provide the information necessary to establish that the admissibility criteria of *Daubert* are met. The interrogatory responses and expert report should describe what generally accepted procedure, analysis, or methodology was utilized in arriving at the conclusions at issue. Again, these are issues that must be dealt with early on and cannot wait until the eve of trial.

3. Expert Affidavits and Declarations

Expert affidavits and declarations, particularly when used in connection with a motion for summary judgment, should include more than just the expert's qualifications and his or her proffered substantive opinions. Again, a section of the affidavit or declaration should address the *Daubert* criteria and establish that the criteria for admissibility are met.

More and more frequently, the issue arises in connection with a party's opposition to a motion for summary judgment. For example, in a product liability case, the defendant moves for summary judgment on the grounds that there is no design defect. The plaintiff, as part of its opposition to the motion for summary judgment, submits the affidavit or declaration of an expert witness in order to raise a question of fact regarding the feasibility of alternative, safer designs. The summary judgment movant, either by way of a reply brief or by filing a separate motion to strike, will attempt to "*Daubert*ize" the plaintiff's expert's affidavit, challenging its admissibility under *Daubert*. If the district court grants the motion to strike, or otherwise deems the proffered expert testimony inadmissible, the result almost certainly will be summary judgment in favor of the product manufacturer. And given the abuse-of-discretion standard on appeal, the odds of reversal are slim. In such instances where the opponent may attempt to "*Daubert*ize" an expert's affidavit, rather than having to hurry to prepare a supplemental affidavit attempting to show that the *Daubert* criteria are in fact met, the better approach may be to address the *Daubert* criteria in the initial affidavit and affirmatively establish in the original affidavit that the *Daubert* criteria are met.

4. Depositions

It is imperative that one's expert be prepared for deposition questions not only on the substantive opinions he or she may offer at trial, but also on questions relating to the application of the *Daubert* criteria to his or her opinions and field of expertise. It is guaranteed that if the proposed expert witness cannot answer deposition questions on whether the expert's proffered opinions meet the *Daubert* criteria, a motion *in limine* seeking to exclude the expert's testimony from evidence at trial will follow shortly thereafter. At that point, it may be too late to try to rehabilitate an expert in whom one probably has by then invested significant time and money.

5. Trial

Hopefully, by the time of trial, the expert witness will be fully prepared to address the criteria set forth in *Daubert*. Remember, once the party opposing the admissibility of proffered expert testimony makes the appropriate objection, the district court must hold a hearing outside the presence of the jury and satisfy itself that the *Daubert* criteria are met. The trial notebook should include a section addressing the *Daubert* criteria as it relates to that particular expert witness, and counsel should be prepared to conduct a direct examination establishing that the *Daubert* criteria are satisfied. Conversely, the party opposing the admissibility of the proffered expert testimony should be prepared, primarily based on the deposition testimony of the proffered expert, to show that the *Daubert* criteria are not met, and that the proffered expert testimony should be ruled inadmissible. Pocket briefs on this issue are advisable for both the proponent of the expert testimony and the party objecting to its admissibility. This issue is crucial. In many instances, such as the design engineering expert discussed above in connection with a product liability case, a ruling that the proposed expert testimony is inadmissible may result in a directed verdict against one's client.

6. *Post-Trial Motions*

Post-trial motions for a new trial pursuant to Fed. R. Civ. P. 59 and for relief from judgment pursuant to Fed. R. Civ. P. 60 should include any challenges to the admissibility of expert testimony that erroneously were admitted into evidence at trial. Failure to raise the *Daubert* issues in connection with the motion for new trial may waive such issues as grounds for appeal.

Careful consideration of the *Daubert* criteria must take place at every step of the litigation process. Failure to do so frequently can make the difference between winning and losing.

CHAPTER VII
EXPERT EVIDENCE IN THE SEVENTH CIRCUIT

by

Helen E. Witt
Kirkland & Ellis LLP
300 North LaSalle St.
Chicago, IL 60654
(312) 862-2000
helen.witt@kirkland.com

A. KEY DECISIONS APPLYING *DAUBERT* IN FEDERAL COURTS

1. *Introduction*

The Seventh Circuit mandates a three-step *Daubert* inquiry to determine the admissibility of "scientific" evidence.[1] First, the district court must determine whether the witness is qualified. Next, it must determine whether the testimony has been subjected to the scientific method and is therefore reliable; it must rule out subjective belief or unsupported speculation. Finally, if reliable, the district court must determine whether the testimony will assist the trier of fact to understand the evidence or to determine a fact in issue. *See Myers v. Illinois Central R.R. Co.*, 629 F.3d 639, 644 (7th Cir. 2010); *Bielskis v. Louisville Ladder, Inc.*, 663 F.3d 887, 893–94 (7th Cir. 2011). The proponent of the expert's testimony bears the burden of proof with respect to the requirement for admissibility. *See Lewis v. CITGO Petroleum Corp.*, 561 F.3d 698, 704 (7th Cir. 2009). The proponent likewise bears the burden to "explain the methodologies and principles supporting the opinion." *Minix v. Canarecci*, 597 F.3d 824, 835 (7th Cir. 2010).

The legal standard applied by the district court in making its decision to admit or exclude expert testimony is reviewed *de novo*; its choice of factors to include within the legal framework and its ultimate conclusions are reviewed only for abuse of discretion. *See e.g. Lapsley v. Xtek, Inc.* 689 F.3d 802, 809 (7th Cir. 2012); *Winters v. Fru-Con Inc.*, 498 F.3d 734, 742 (7th Cir. 2007), *quoting Kempner Mobile Elecs., Inc. v. Southwest Bell Mobile Sys.*, 428 F.3d 706, 712 (7th Cir. 2005). In other words, once the district court has adequately applied the proper *Daubert* framework, the Seventh Circuit's "review of the determination to admit or exclude the evidence is deferential." *Lapsley v. XTEK, Inc.*, 689 F.3d 802 at 805. *See also Trustees of the Chicago Painters and Decorators Pension, Health and Welfare and Deferred Saving Plan Trust Funds v. Royal Int'l Drywall and*

---

[1] Although the Supreme Court has essentially abolished the often problematic distinction between scientific and nonscientific expert evidence by extending the basic gatekeeping obligation of *Daubert* to all expert testimony, *Kumho Tire Co. v. Carmichael*, 526 U.S. 137, 147–49 (1999), this chapter focuses primarily on cases involving "scientific" evidence, a category that has been liberally defined in practice by the Seventh Circuit.

Decorating, Inc., 493 F.3d 782, 787 (7th Cir. 2007), *citing Nutra Sweet Co. v. X-L Eng'g Co.*, 227 F.3d 776, 788 (7th Cir. 2000). But when the district court concludes that an expert's proferred testimony meets the *Daubert* standard and does not demonstrate that an adequate *Daubert* analysis has been performed, the admissibility determination is subject to *de novo* review. *Metavante Corp. v. Emigrant Savings Bank*, 619 F.3d 748, 760 (7th Cir. 2010). It must be clear that a sufficient assessment of the reliability of the expert's method was performed. *Naeem v. McKesson Drug Co.*, 444 F.3d 593, 608 (7th Cir. 2006).

In keeping with the Supreme Court's directives in *Daubert*, the Seventh Circuit affords district courts "wide latitude in performing its gatekeeping function and determining how to measure the reliability of expert testimony and whether the testimony itself is reliable." *Bielskis v. Louisville Ladder Co.*, 663 F.3d 887, 894 (7th Cir. 2011) (internal citation omitted.)

For purposes of the *Daubert* inquiry, Seventh Circuit judge and influential legal scholar Richard Posner has offered a helpful (and oft-invoked) interpretation of its underlying goal. The "object" of the gatekeeping function is to ensure "that when scientists testify in court they adhere to the same standards of intellectual rigor that are demanded in their professional work." *Rosen v. Ciba-Geigy Corp.*, 78 F.3d 316, 318-319 (7th Cir. 1996). "If they do, their evidence (provided of course that it is relevant to some issue in the case) is admissible even if the particular methods they have used in arriving at their opinion are not yet accepted as canonical in their branch of the scientific community. If they do not, their evidence is inadmissible no matter how imposing their credentials." *Id.* Lawyers practicing in the Seventh Circuit should thus pay close attention to the methodological consistency between an expert's outside professional work (if such exists) and his or her litigation opinion. *See Braun v. Lorillard Inc.*, 84 F.3d 230, 235 (7th Cir. 1996) (*Daubert* aimed at the abuse of "hiring of reputable scientists, impressively credentialed, to testify for a fee to propositions that they have not arrived at through the methods that they use when they are doing their regular professional work rather than being paid to give an opinion helpful to one side in a lawsuit.")

The *Daubert* gatekeeping function is not limited to experts designated to testify in jury trials in the Seventh Circuit, despite older case law suggesting that the primary purpose of the *Daubert* filter was "to protect juries from being bamboozled by technical dubious merit." *See e.g. Loeffel Steel Products, Inc. v. Delta Brands, Inc.*, 372 F.Supp. 2d 1104, 1123 (N.D. Ill. 2005). In particular, practitioners should be aware that the Seventh Circuit requires that a district court must rule "definitively" on a *Daubert* motion challenging an expert whose report or testimony is "critical," before ruling on a class certification motion. *See American Honda Motor Co. v. Allen*, 600 F.3d 813, 815-16 (7th Cir. 2010). *See also Messner v. Northshore University HealthSystem*, 669 F.3d 802, 813 (7th Cir. 2012) (cautioning district courts that the "time-honored and often acceptable approach" of giving an expert report "the weight it is due" rather than ruling on its admissibility is no longer sufficient when the expert testimony is critical to the class certification decision.)

Lawyers seeking to offer or bar scientific evidence in the Seventh Circuit should also keep in mind the power conferred upon district judges to appoint independent expert witnesses under Rule 706 of the Federal Rules of Evidence. Indeed, in an antitrust case, the court recommended that on remand the district court appoint its own expert to testify about the complex statistical evidence at issue, "rather than leave himself and the jury completely at the mercy of the parties' warring experts." *In re High Fructose Corn Syrup Antitrust Litigation*, 295 F.3d 651, 665 (7th Cir. 2002). The court also proposed a method for selecting the Rule 706 expert:

> The main objection to this procedure and the main reason for its infrequency are that the judge cannot be confident that the expert whom he has picked is a genuine neutral. The objection can be obviated by directing the party-designated experts to agree upon a neutral expert whom the judge will then appoint as the court's expert . . . . The neutral expert will

testify (as can, of course, the party-designated experts) and the judge and jury can repose a degree of confidence in his testimony that it could not repose in that of a party's witness.

Id.

The Seventh Circuit continues to urge district judges to consider this option. *See e.g., ATA Airlines, Inc. v. Federal Express Corp.*, 665 F.3d 882, 890 (7th Cir. 2011); *DeKoven v. Plaza Assoc.*, 599 F.3d 578, 583 (7th Cir. 2010) (suggesting that district judges consider appointing their own expert to conduct a survey in Fair Debt Collection Practices Act Cases).

Finally, lawyers seeking to offer expert scientific testimony in courts in the Seventh Circuit should recognize that the judges of that court have made clear that they expect a demonstrated high level of understanding of even the most technical and difficult scientific concepts from both district judges and lawyers presenting expert testimony. In *ATA Airlines, Inc., v. Federal Express Corp.*, 665 F.3d 882 (7th Cir. 2011), the court spent more than seven pages of its opinion, written by Judge Posner, dealing with an issue that had no effect on the outcome of the case before it, but that the court said raised important questions "bound to arise in future cases." *ATA Airlines,* 665 F.3d at 889. The issue involved a damage award based entirely on a regression analysis presented by a forensic accountant named Lawrence D. Morriss.

The court was not impressed with Mr. Morriss's testimony. It had been admitted over objection by the district court, which had identified multiple fatal errors. His regression, the court concluded, "had as many bloody wounds as Julius Caesar when he was stabbed twenty-three times by the Roman senators led by Brutus." *Id.* at 896. In the end, the court explained the messages it was conveying by its detailed analysis of a damages opinion irrelevant to its disposition of the case:

> We have gone on at such length about the deficiencies of the regression analysis in order to remind district judges that, painful as it might be, it is their responsibility to screen expert testimony, however technical; we have suggested aids to the discharge of that responsibility.[2]

Id.

The court also had advice for the lawyers, noting that "[t]he examination and cross-examination of Morriss were perfunctory and must have struck most, maybe all, of the jurors as gibberish." *Id.* at 896. And it suggested that at oral argument on appeal neither attorney seemed to understand the analysis. It ended its opinion with the following warning:

> If a party's lawyer cannot understand the testimony of the party's own expert, the testimony should be withheld from the jury. Evidence unintelligible to the trier or triers of fact has no place in a trial. *See* Fed. R. Evid. 403, 702.

Id.

---

[2] In addition to appointing independent experts, the court recommended that when faced with regression issues district judges consult the "Reference Guide on Multiple Regression," in *Reference Manual on Scientific Evidence* (3d Ed. 2011), or David Copes *Fundamentals of Statistical Analysis* (2005). *Id.* at 889–90.

2. Cases Discussing Specific Types of Scientific Evidence

a. Product Design/Engineering

Lapsley v. Xtek, Inc., 689 F.3d 802 (7th Cir. 2012), was a products liability case brought by a worker permanently disabled in an accident in a steel rolling mill. The plaintiff's expert, Dr. Gary Hutter, testified that an industrial grease jet manufactured by Xtek was defectively designed and had caused the accident. The defendant appealed denial of its *Daubert* motion after a jury verdict for the plaintiff, based in part on the brevity of the district court's analysis and the Seventh Circuit's opinion in *ATA Airlines, Inc. v. Federal Express Corp.*, 665 F.3d 882 (7th Cir. 2011). The Seventh Circuit affirmed. It found that the district judge had done more than state the general acceptability of Dr. Hutter's methods, and "provided specific examples that show he reviewed and understood the basis for Dr. Hutter's conclusions." 689 F.3d at 809. Because the opponent of the testimony had not identified, and the appellate court had not detected "any grave questions about the reliability of the calculations actually performed by Dr. Hutter," the court concluded that the district court's application of the *Daubert* framework, though brief, was sufficient to warrant deferential review. *Id.* at 809-10.

Based on that deferential review, the court concluded that Dr. Hutter's opinion was based on physics principles published centuries ago and used and tested by physicists and engineers for centuries. His approach, which started from known facts about the accident and the elimination of other possible causes, "until he was left with a hypothesis that was physically possible and that fit the evidence," was, in the court's view, "a good example of the scientific method." *Id.* at 810. The court also rejected the argument the expert's method and calculations were "inherently opaque" and concluded that the analysis was not "as difficult to understand as Xtek suggests." *Id.* at 810-811. The court reminded practitioners that as long as a court properly evaluates a proferred opinion for sufficient reliability, the opinion "is submitted to the 'capabilities of the jury and of the adversary system generally.'" *Id.* at 810, *quoting Daubert v. Merrel Dow Pharmaceuticals, Inc.*, 509 U.S. 579, 596 (1993).

Finally, the court took the opportunity in *Lapsley* to again caution lawyers and judges not trained in science that they may need to do more homework when dealing with scientific evidence:

> Law must apply itself to the life of a society driven more and more by technology and technological improvements. Judges and lawyers do not have the luxury of functional illiteracy in either of these two cultures. Sometimes, as in this case, effective presentation, cross-examination, and evaluation of expert testimony require lawyers and judges to fill in gaps in their scientific, engineering, or mathematics educations or refresh their memories about them.

Id. at 811.

Bielskis v. Louisville Ladder, Inc., 663 F.3d 887 (7th Cir. 2011), was a case filed by a worker injured when a mini-scaffold he was working on collapsed. The plaintiff's expert, Neil G. Mizen, opined that a castor stem on the scaffold has suffered a "brittle facture" as a result of being overtightened. The defendant's expert also concluded that the castor stem had sustained a "brittle facture," but determined that it failed because it was too loose, not too tight. *Bielskis*, 663 F.3d at 891-92. The district court judge excluded Mizen's testimony. It held that there was too great a leap, "without data or testing, from the accepted premise that a crack without plastic deformation is a brittle fracture to his ultimate conclusion that the castor stem broke because it was over-tightened." *Id.* at 892.

The Seventh Circuit affirmed the exclusion of Mizen's testimony as within the district court's discretion. It pointed to several specific insufficiencies that supported the district court's conclusion that his methodology "sounded more like the sort of '[t]alking off the cuff'—without data or analysis—that we have repeatedly characterized as insufficient." *Id.* at 894 (internal citation omitted). For example, Mizen described the scientific methodology he used as "basic engineering intelligence" and "solid engineering principles that any other engineer would use." *Id.* He made no attempt to test his hypothesis, and made incorrect assumptions about the size of the castor stem. *Id.* at 894-95. And he submitted nothing that supported his contention that his theory was consistent with a consensus view of the scientific community. Finally, the court noted that his personal evaluation of the failed castor with his naked eye could not be subjected to peer review. *Id.* at 895.

Winters v. Fru-Con Inc., 498 F.3d 734 (7th Cir. 2007), was a products liability case brought by a worker in a food processing plant whose hand was severed while he was attempting to dislodge a cake mix clot in a production tube. The plaintiff sought to offer the testimony of two experts. The first, Israelski, "was tendered as an expert in 'human factors.' Human factors is a discipline that incorporates a study of human behaviors, limitations, and capabilities into the design of products, systems and equipment." 498 F.3d at 741. The magistrate judge excluded the testimony after concluding "that Israelski's work was not performed in accordance to the standards of intellectual rigor required for admissibility. Thus, the proposed testimony was 'speculative and not the result of scientific procedure. Simply put, it is not reliable.'" *Id.*

The second expert, Kelsey, "was tendered as an expert in 'forensic engineering analysis in the area of mechanical systems.'" *Id.* The plaintiff offered Kelsey's testimony that the valve that severed his hand, and its associated control system, was defective and unreasonably dangerous. Kelsey proposed several alternatives, "but he did not test the alternatives." *Id.* The magistrate judge determined that the failure to test the alternatives "doomed his proposed opinion and excluded him from testifying." *Id.*

The Seventh Circuit affirmed both rulings based on the experts' failures to test their alternative designs or "to utilize any other method of research to compensate for their lack of alternative testing." *Id.* at 743. It reiterated that "[i]n alternative design cases, we have consistently recognized the importance of testing the alternative design' as a factor that the district court should consider in evaluating the reliability of the proposed expert testimony." 498 F.3d at 742, *quoting Dhillon v. Crown Controls Corp.* 269 F.3d 865, 870 (7th Cir. 2001.)

Fuesting v. Zimmer, Inc., 421 F.3d 528 (7th Cir. 2005), vacated in part on other grounds, 448 F.3d 936 (7th Cir. 2006), *cert. denied*, 127 S. Ct. 1151 (2007) was a strict liability and negligence case brought against the manufacturer of a prosthetic knee. The gist of the plaintiff's claim was that the method used to sterilize the knee at the time of manufacture constituted a design defect. 421 F.3d at 531. The plaintiff's proferred expert witness, James Pugh, was allowed to testify at trial, over objection, that the gamma irradiation method of sterilization used by the defendant caused polyethylene in the knee to oxidate and eventually fail. He further testified that better alternative methods of sterilization were available. The jury found in favor of the plaintiff.

On appeal, the Seventh Circuit held that Mr. Pugh's testimony should not have been admitted and that the district court's "*Daubert* factor analysis was not sufficient." 421 F.3d at 535. It found that "when subjected to a more thorough *Daubert* analysis, Pugh's testimony proves unreliable, as its juxtaposition against the *Daubert* guideposts plainly reveal." *Id.* at 536. In particular, the court noted that Pugh had not conducted any scientific tests or experiments to bolster this theory, did not produce or rely upon studies to verify his conclusions, extrapolated unjustifiably from basic polymer science to his complex conclusions, did not publish or otherwise subject his theory to peer review, and "developed his opinion expressly for this litigation." 421 F.3d at 536-537.

In short, the court concluded that Pugh's testimony stacked up "quite poorly against most all indicia of reliability, rendering the district court's decision to admit the opinion error." *Id.* at 537. Without the expert's opinions, the court ruled that the plaintiff could not establish a defect or negligence and remanded the case with instructions to direct a verdict in favor of defendant.

One final point of note in *Fuesting v. Zimmer* is the court's reference to the 2000 Advisory Committee's Notes to Federal Rule of Evidence 702. The court directed attention to those factors in addition to the "non-exhaustive" list of guideposts included in the *Daubert* opinion when evaluating the reliability of expert opinions:

> In addition to [the *Daubert*] factors, the 2000 Advisory Committee's Notes to Rule 702 suggest other benchmarks for gauging expert reliability, including (5) whether maintenance standards and controls exist; (6) whether the testimony relates to matters growing naturally and directly out of research they have conducted independent of the litigation, or developed expressly for purposes of testifying; (7) [w]hether the expert has unjustifiably extrapolated from an accepted premise to an unfounded conclusion; (8) [w]hether the expert has adequately accounted for obvious alternative explanations; (9) [w]hether the expert is being as careful as he would be in his regular professional work outside his paid litigation consulting; and (10) [w]hether the field of expertise claimed by the expert is known to reach reliable results for the type of opinion the expert would give. Fed. R. Evid. 702 advisory committee's note (2000 amends). 421 F.3d at 534-35.

Zenith Electronics Corp. v. WH-TV Broadcasting Corp., 395 F.3d 416 (7th Cir.) *cert. denied*, 545 U.S. 1140 (2005), was an action to recover payment for digital television converter boxes. Defendants counterclaimed for breach of contract and fraud premised on the claim that the boxes were defective. The district court excluded the testimony of the defendant/counterplaintiff's expert, Peter Shapiro, regarding the future growth and profitability of its business had the Zenith boxes been as promised, because Shapiro had too little support for his opinions.

Judge Easterbrook provided a pithy summary of the bases for the expert's proferred testimony and the appellate court's affirmance of its exclusion: "He was relying on intuition, which won't do." 395 F.3d at 418. The court went on to remind attorneys and would-be experts alike that Rule 702 requires more that the *ipse dixit* of the expert:

> A witness who invokes "my expertise" rather than analytic strategies widely used by specialists is not an expert as Rule 702 defines that term. Shapiro may be the world's leading student of MMDS services, but if he could not or would not explain how his conclusions met [Rule 702's] requirements, he was not entitled to give expert testimony. As we often reiterate: 'An expert who supplies nothing but a bottom line supplies nothing of value to the judicial process.' *Mid-State Fertilizer Co. v. Exchange Nat'l Bank*, 877 F. 2d 1333, 1339 (7th Cir. 1989).

395 F.3d at 419-20.

Czyszczon v. Universal Lighting Technologies, Inc., 2012 WL 2921510 (N.D. Ill. July 27, 2012), was a products liability case in which plaintiff alleged he was injured as a result of an electrical shock from a defective ballast designed and manufactured by Universal. The plaintiff offered the expert opinion of Robert Quinn in support of his theory, and Universal moved to exclude the testimony as without reliable factual or scientific foundation. 2012 WL 2921510 at *3. Universal pointed out that Quinn could not explain how a grounded fixture could shock the plaintiff or how the ballast actually caused the shock. And it demonstrated that Quinn had testified at deposition both that he could not say that it was more likely than not that a defect in the ballast caused the shock and that there was no way to know for sure what part of the fixture had caused the shock. Quinn nonetheless opined that although the cause of the shock was undetermined, it did occur in the ballast. *Id.* at *1.

Relying to a great extent on Quinn's deposition testimony, Judge Shadur[3] excluded his testimony; he found that it was precisely the type of "bottom-line" statement that is insufficiently reliable to be admissible: "At best, Quinn has badly and inexplicably contradicted himself, and such testimony cannot possibly assist the fact finder to understand evidence or determine a fact in issue[.]" *Id.* at *4.

b. Environmental Engineering/Hydrology

In *Dura Automotive Systems of Indiana, Inc. v. CTS Corp.*, 285 F.3d 609 (7th Cir. 2002), the plaintiff, Dura Automotive, sought to introduce the testimony of hydrogeologist Nicholas Valkenburg to show that the defendant, CTS Corp., was historically responsible for some of the contamination attributed to it by the E.P.A. After the expert report deadline, Dura Automotive sought to introduce affidavits from the groundwater modeling experts relied upon by Mr. Valkenburg, who himself had no such expertise. *Id.* at 612.

The Court of Appeals affirmed the district court's decision to treat the affidavits as untimely expert reports and to exclude Mr. Valkenburg's testimony as lacking adequate foundation. According to Judge Posner, who wrote the majority opinion (Judge Diane Wood dissented), "[a]n expert witness is permitted to use assistants in formulating his expert opinion, and normally they need not themselves testify"; however, "[a]nalysis becomes more complicated if the assistants aren't merely gofers or data gatherers but exercise professional judgment that is beyond the expert's ken." *Id.* at 612-13. This is especially true when "the soundness of the underlying expert judgment is in issue." *Id.* at 613.

In an oft quoted, though lengthy passage, the court made clear the pitfalls in a situation where experts attempt to rely on other experts:

> Now it is common in technical fields for an expert to base an opinion in part on what a different expert believes on the basis of expert knowledge not possessed by the first expert; and it is apparent from the wording of Rule 703 that there is no general requirement that the other expert testify as well. The Committee Notes to the 1972 Proposed Rule 703 give the example of a physician who, though not an expert in radiology, relies for a diagnosis on an X-ray. We too do not 'believe that the leader of a clinical medical team must be qualified as an expert in every individual discipline encompassed by the team in order to testify as to the team's conclusions.' But suppose the soundness of the underlying expert judgment is in issue. Suppose a thoracic surgeon gave expert evidence in a medical malpractice case that the plaintiff's decedent had died because the defendant, a radiologist, had negligently failed to diagnose the decedent's lung cancer until it was too advanced for surgery. The surgeon would be competent to testify that the cancer was too advanced for surgery, but in offering the additional and critical judgment that the radiologist should have discovered the cancer sooner he would be, at best, just parroting the opinion of an expert in radiology competent to testify that the defendant had x-rayed the decedent carelessly. The case would be governed by our decision in *In re James Wilson Associates*, 965 F.2d 160, 172-73 (7th Cir. 1992), where the issue was the state of repair of a building and 'the expert who

---

[3] Judge Shadur was a member and later chair of the Judicial Conference Advisory Committee on the Rules of Evidence, and headed the subcommittee specifically assigned to review and recommend to the entire committee revised versions of Rules 701, 702, 703 and the committee notes to those new versions. *See Scott v. City of Chicago*, 724 F. Supp. 2d 917, 921 (N.D. Ill 2010).

had evaluated the state—the consulting engineer—was the one who should have testified. The architect [the expert who did testify] could use what the engineer told him to offer an opinion within the architect's domain of expertise, but he could not testify for the purpose of vouching for the truth of what the engineer had told him—of becoming, in short, the engineer's spokesman.'

* * *

[T]he *Daubert* test must be applied with due regard for the specialization of modern science. A scientist, however well credentialed he may be, is not permitted to be the mouthpiece of a scientist in a different specialty. That would not be responsible science. A theoretical economist, however able, would not be allowed to testify to the findings of an econometric study conducted by another economist if he lacked expertise in econometrics and the study raised questions that only an econometrician could answer. If it were apparent that the study was not cut and dried, the author would have to testify; he could not hide behind the theoretician.

Id. at 614.

Applying this reasoning to Mr. Valkenburg's testimony and the affidavits, the court reached the same conclusion as the trial judge: the modelers' affidavits were actually expert reports that had not been disclosed in time. Specifically, Mr. Valkenburg lacked "the necessary expertise to determine whether the techniques were appropriately chosen and applied," and his colleagues "did not merely collect data for him to massage or apply concededly appropriate techniques in a concededly appropriate manner, or otherwise perform routine procedures." *Id.* at 615.

Other Relevant Cases

NutraSweet Co. v. X-L Eng'g Co., 227 F.3d 776, 787-90 (7th Cir. 2000) (district court properly ruled (1) analysis of aerial photos to determine the history of chemical dumping is well-accepted technique in hydrology and environmental engineering and thus bears sufficient indicia of reliability under *Kumho Tire*, and (2) plaintiff's expert did not need direct evidence or personal observation of illegal dumping to infer defendant was source of VOCs when he had soil gas results, groundwater migration test results, soil degradation analysis, and aerial photos).

Burns Philp Food, Inc., v. Cavalea Cont'l Freight, Inc., 135 F.3d 526, 530 (7th Cir. 1998) (trial court properly excluded testimony that diesel fuel on plaintiff's land came from adjacent landowner; expert's soil tests were unreliable because they were selective and result-oriented).

Ramsey v. Consol Rail Corp., 111 F. Supp. 2d 1030 (N.D. Ind. 2000) (hydrologist's proposed testimony, based on scientifically accepted groundwater flow modeling method, that contaminants from rail yard reached drinking well was inadmissible in well user's action against railroad, absent explanation of why all twelve tests during relevant eight-year period showed no contaminants).

c. Psychology

In *Tyus v. Urban Search Management*, 102 F.3d 256 (7th Cir. 1996), plaintiffs brought suit against the owners of an upscale apartment complex for allegedly violating the Fair Housing Act with racially discriminatory advertisement practices. The district court excluded the testimony of plaintiffs' two expert witnesses: Dr. Douglas Massey, a professor of sociology at The University of Chicago, who was to testify about the history and patterns of discrimination, "and Dr. John Tarini, a psychologist, statistician, and chair of the Department of Marketing Communication at Columbia College (Chicago), who would have testified about how advertising sends a message to its target market and how an all-White advertising campaign affects African-Americans." *Id.* at 262.

The Court of Appeals found the district court had erred in not applying *Daubert. Id.* at 263. Applying the *Daubert* framework, the Court of Appeals ruled the psychologist, Dr. Tarini, should have been permitted to testify. "[T]he materials on which Dr. Tarini relied, which were peer-reviewed articles accepted in his profession, and the particular methodology he used, were well within the range contemplated by Daubert for expert scientific testimony." *Id.* at 263-64. This methodology included "the well known 'focus group' method, to see how [certain ads] came across to African-American viewers." *Id.* at 264.

The Court of Appeals remanded the issue of the admissibility of Dr. Massey's testimony because of an inadequate record on the scope of his proposed testimony. *Id.*

In *United States v. Hall*, 93 F.3d 1337 (7th Cir. 1996), a criminal defendant sought to introduce the testimony of a social psychologist, Dr. Richard Ofshe, on the phenomenon of false or coerced confessions, and the testimony of psychiatrist, Dr. Traugott, on the defendant's "susceptibility to various interrogation techniques." *Id.* at 1341. The Court of Appeals, reversing the district court, held the testimony of both experts admissible under *Daubert*.

The Court of Appeals found that the fields of psychology and psychiatry presented a sufficiently reliable body of genuine specialized knowledge on the phenomenon of false confessions to pass muster under *Daubert. Id.* at 1342-43. Moreover, the testimony satisfied the "fit" prong of the Seventh Circuit's test: "It was precisely because juries are unlikely to know that social scientists and psychologists have identified a personality disorder that will cause individuals to make false confessions that the testimony would have assisted the jury in making its decision." *Id.* at 1345.

But see United States v. Mamah, 332 F.3d 475 (7th Cir. 2003) (proffered expert testimony by anthropologist and sociologist that defendant's confession was false was properly excluded. Expert's testimony was not based on sufficient facts or data to support the proposed conclusions: "As we have observed, experts' opinions are worthless without data and reasons." 332 F.3d at 477-78, *citing Kenosha v. Heublein*, 895 F.2d 418, 420 (7th Cir. 1990).)

Other Relevant Cases

Hoffman v. Caterpillar, Inc., 368 F.3d 709 (7th Cir. 2004) (expert in disability discrimination case was correctly precluded from testifying, based on reviewing a videotape, that plaintiff could operate a particular machine at mandated production levels; testimony would not assist the trier of fact as jury could view the videotape and assess plaintiff's performance independently.)

Bryant v. City of Chicago, 200 F.3d 1092, 1097-99 (7th Cir.) *cert. denied*, 531 U.S. 821 (2000) (expert's testimony that promotional examination for police lieutenant was valid and that final test scores could be used for rank-order promotions was admissible under *Daubert*, even though general scientific literature in area consisted of only one unpublished study; expert had extensive academic and practical experience in designing such evaluations, had based his opinions on job analysis that his firm had formulated, and had published numerous articles on employee selection and promotion testing generally).

Scott v. City of Chicago, 724 F. Supp. 2d 917 (N.D. Ill. 2010), was a Section 1983 action in which the plaintiff sought damages arising out of a determination in his criminal trial that his confession had been obtained in violation of his civil rights. Defendants offered the opinion testimony of Dr. Joel Silberberg, a psychiatrist, in support of their contention that Scott was not significantly depressed and had no damages. Silberberg relied on a report of a psychologist, Dr. Robert Hanlon, who had in turn based his conclusions on the results of psychologic diagnostic tests administered to Scott by his own expert psychologist, Dr. Paul Pasulka. Dr. Silberberg admitted that he was not personally qualified to interpret the diagnostic tests and relied on Dr. Hanlon's review of Dr. Pasulka's testing because of a code of practice that only a psychologist could comment on another psychologist's report. 724 F. Supp. at 921.

Relying heavily on the Seventh Circuit's opinion in *Dura Auto Sys. of Ind., Inc. v. CTS Corp.*, 285 F.3d 609 (7th Cir. 2002), the court excluded Dr. Silberberg's testimony, concluding that it "flunks the *Daubert-Kumho* gatekeeping test" because Dr. Silberberg was largely acting as a mouthpiece for another scientist whose expert judgment was really what was at issue.

Koutnik v. Brown, 396 F. Supp. 2d 978 (W. D. Wis. 2005), *aff'd*, 189 Fed. Appx. 546 (7th Cir. 2006) (defendant who was prison's "disruptive group coordinator" was qualified by years of training and experience to give opinion testimony regarding factors detrimental to prison's rehabilitative goals.)

Simon Prop. Group L.P. v. mySimon, Inc., 104 F. Supp. 2d 1033, 1040-52 (S.D. Ind. 2000) (proposed home page survey found inadmissible in trademark infringement suit to show likelihood of consumer confusion between Web sites of owner of shopping malls, whose site offered information about its brick-and-mortar malls and the retailers who operated stores in those malls, and operator of comparison shopping service, whose web site allowed a consumer to compare prices of online retailers, because the survey grossly distorted the marketplace conditions in which Internet users might actually encounter the two parties' marks together, failed to use the most basic control by not comparing potential confusion over other similarly named Web sites, and was designed to create "demand effects" that appeared to exaggerate unfairly any possible confusion about affiliation between the parties).

d. Medical Causation

Myers v. Illinois Central R.R. Co., 629 F.3d 639 (7th Cir. 2010), was a case brought by a railroad worker under the Federal Employer's Liability Act (FELA). Plaintiff sought to recover for "cumulative trauma injuries" he alleged had been caused by his almost thirty years of work in unsafe work environments caused by the railroad's negligence.

Plaintiff designated his three treating physicians and an ergonomist as experts in support of his causation theory. The district court excluded the testimony of all four experts, concluding that none of their opinions was based on reliable procedures or methods. With respect to the physicians, the court concluded that they did not have adequate understanding of the plaintiff's actual work for the railroad or his medical history to give a reliable opinion about what had caused his injuries. 629 F.3d at 642. As for the ergonomist, it found that because his analysis of railroad working conditions was not appropriately focused on the plaintiff's work in particular, he too could not give reliable testimony that the working conditions caused the injury. *Id.*

See also Meyers v. Nat'l R.R. Passengers Corp., 619 F.3d 729, 734-35 (7th Cir. 2010) (holding that a treating physician offered to provide causation testimony who did not make the causation determination in the course of treatment "should be deemed to be one 'retained or specially employed to provide expert testimony in the case,' and thus was required to submit an expert report in accordance with Rule 26(a)(2).")

A few months after *Myers* and *Meyers* were decided, the court decided *Banister v. Burton*, 636 F.3d 828 (7th Cir. 2011). The plaintiff in *Banister* sued the city of Chicago and two police officers under 42 U.S.C. § 1983 for injuries he sustained when he was shot by an undercover policeman from whom he thought he was buying drugs. A key issue was whether the plaintiff had pointed a gun, as the defendants contended, or was unarmed, as he claimed. The defendants maintained that Banister had thrown a gun that had been found forty feet from where he was shot.

The defendants called the trauma surgeon who had treated the plaintiff's gunshot wounds, Dr. Ross Fishman, as an expert to testify that the plaintiff was physically able to throw an object after being shot. The plaintiff moved *in limine* to bar the testimony on the grounds that Dr. Fishman was "not an expert in biomechanics or throwing." The district court allowed the testimony, concluding that a medical doctor could testify about whether a person he had examined was capable of throwing something. 636 F.3d at 830.

The Seventh Circuit affirmed. It held that while physicians may not give opinions which are beyond their requisite experience and unsupported by methodology simply because they are experienced physicians, testimony based on examination and application of training in anatomy was well within a trauma surgeon's requisite experience. The court also concluded that Dr. Fishman's testimony was not erroneously admitted even though defendants had failed to submit an expert report in compliance with Rule 26(a)(2)(B). Distinguishing its holding in *Meyers v. Nat'l R.R. Passenger Corp.*, 619 F.3d 729, 734-35 (7th Cir. 2010), it ruled that because Dr. Fishman's opinion related to the *effects* of an injury and not the *cause*, and was not formulated at the request of the city, but given at an earlier criminal trial, no expert report was required. 636 F.3d at 833.

Ervin v. Johnson & Johnson, Inc., 492 F.3d 901 (7th Cir. 2007), involved a plaintiff's claim that the prescription drug Remicade caused a blood clot that required a partial amputation of his leg. The district court excluded as unreliable the testimony of the plaintiff's internist and critical care specialist, Dr. Lee McKinley, that the use of Remicade (which Dr. McKinley had recommended) "was the major contributing factor to Ervin's thrombotic arterial occlusion and subsequent below knee amputation." 492 F.3d at 902-03. Dr. McKinley claimed to have based his opinion on the process of differential diagnosis which the court described as follows:

> Differential diagnosis generally provides a framework in which all reasonable hypotheses are ruled in as possible causes of a medical problem and some of these possible causes are then ruled out to the extent scientific evidence makes it appropriate to do so. The goal is to identify the last remaining, or most probable, ruled in cause of a medical problem.

492 F.3d at 903.

The Seventh Circuit affirmed the district court's exclusion of the testimony, agreeing that the expert had failed to use reliable methods. Specifically, the expert had failed to make scientifically valid decisions about which potential causes of the blood clot should be ruled in or out, could point to no epidemiologic data supporting his opinion and gave inappropriate weight to the temporal relationship between the taking of Remicade and the development of the blood clot.

In *Schultz v. Glidden Co.*, 2012 WL 968005 (E.D. Wis. March 21, 2012), the plaintiff brought suit against a paint manufacturer alleging that her husband died of acute myeloid leukemia (AML) contracted as a result of exposure to the known carcinogen benzene in paint he used in his job in an automobile manufacturing plant. The level of the decedent's exposure to benzene was calculated by plaintiff's industrial hygienist expert to be less than the minimum exposure necessary for benzene to cause AML as reflected in the medical and toxicological literature presented by the defendant's expert toxicologist.

The plaintiff's expert, Dr. Steven Gore, nonetheless opined that no safe threshold for exposure to benzene had been established, so that "any non-trivial exposure to that carcinogen during a time frame consistent with the range of latency periods with the disease should be considered as a probable substantial factor that contributed to the individual's cancer." 2012 WL 968005 at *3.

The district court excluded Dr. Gore's testimony on a number of grounds. It noted that "[t]he 'no-threshold' theory of causation in toxic tort cases has been roundly rejected by courts across the country." *Id.* Citing *Henrickson v. ConocoPhillips Co.*, 605 F. Supp. 2d 1142, 1166 (E.D. Wash. 2009), the court concluded that even though benzene has been shown capable of causing AML, it is "too difficult a leap" to say that any amount of exposure can cause AML and caused it in a particular patient. *Id.* In particular, the court noted that the no-threshold model cannot be falsified or validated, has no known rate of error and has been rejected by the overwhelming majority of the scientific community. The court also rejected the testimony because even the studies Dr. Gore relied on showed a shorter latency period than what the plaintiff's decedent would have experienced, and because he failed to rule out other potential causes, including heavy cigarette smoking, which he acknowledged may have contributed. Because he could not or did not explain how his opinion that benzene, not smoking, caused the AML, the court ruled that Dr. Gore's opinion was inherently unreliable. *Id.* at *4.

Moore v. P&G - Clairol, Inc., 781 F. Supp.2d 694 (N.D.Ill. 2011), was a products liability case brought by a seventeen-year-old student who alleged she had been injured as a result of a severe allergic reaction to a Clairol hair dye product. The plaintiff designated an organic chemist, Robert M. Moriarty, Ph.D., as her only expert witness. Moriarty opined that the dye was composed of dangerous chemicals that are skin irritants and allergenic, that the dye was unreasonably dangerous, and that the plaintiff's injuries were caused by her exposure to the dye.[4] *Id.* at 699.

The district court excluded all of Moriarty's opinions and granted summary judgment for Clairol, based on numerous infirmities in his methodology. In particular, the court noted that Moriarty had seemed to overlook the basic fact that "products that contain dangerous chemicals are not *per se*, unreasonably dangerous." *Id.* at 703. It determined that Moriarty's failures to investigate the amounts of the chemicals in the dye, the concentration or formulation of the chemicals in the dye, and the amount of each chemical required to cause a reaction in humans rendered his methodology unreliable. *Id.* The court also confirmed that, as a chemist, Moriarty was "not qualified to conclude that the dye caused plaintiff's injuries from a medical perspective." *Id.* at 705.

Finally, the court also excluded the causation testimony of the plaintiff's treating physicians because she had failed to disclose them as experts in accordance with Rule 26(a)(2) of the Federal Rules of Civil Procedure:

> The requirement that treating physicians are properly disclosed is particularly justified in a product liability suit like this one, where expert testimony is critically important because such testimony is almost always required on matters of causation and the jury is often asked to resolve a "battle of the experts."

In *Lemmermann v. Blue Cross Blue Shield of Wisconsin*, 713 F. Supp. 2d 791 (E.D. Wis. 2010), the plaintiff alleged that she had suffered serious respiratory injuries as the result of exposure to a pool chlorinating product that she claimed had exploded when she tried to dissolve it in a pitcher of water. She designated pulmonologist Dr. al-Saghir to provide the medical causation opinion that the plaintiff either suffered from Reactive Airways Dysfunction Syndrome ("RADS"), or an exacerbation of preexisting asthma as a result of her exposure to the fumes produced in the explosion. 713 F. Supp. 2d at 803.

The court excluded Dr. al-Saghir's testimony as a result of "striking flaws" in her methodology. *Id.* at 805. In particular, the court noted a "clear disconnect" between Dr. al-Saghir's concessions about the factors that lead to a proper diagnosis of RADS and the plaintiff's actual symptoms. *Id.* Dr. al-Saghir's failure to consider the plaintiff's full medical history and her blind reliance on information provided by the plaintiff even after it was shown to be false also left the court troubled. In addition, the court concluded that Dr. al-Saghir's opinion was insufficiently reliable because of a failure to account for obvious alternative explanations for the plaintiff's respiratory problems. This failure left her with no way to show the required bridge "between general principles and particular conclusions, and to vest thereby the opinion with requisite reliability." *Id.* at 806 (internal quotations excluded). The court also excluded the alternative opinion that the fumes caused an exacerbation of asthma as a result of the expert's total failure to provide evidence of the methodology on which that opinion was based.

Finally, the court likewise found unreliable Dr. al-Saghir's testimony that, whatever the proper diagnosis of plaintiff's condition, it had been caused by exposure to fumes from the explosion. It noted that courts in the Seventh Circuit have used the framework for evaluating an external cause of a particular medical ailment set out in the section titled "Reference Guide on Medical Testimony" in *Reference Manual on Scientific Evidence*. *Id.* at 807-08. That treatise lays out a basic four-step

---

[4] Moriarty also offered opinions about the adequacy of the warnings that were included with the product.

process for evaluating an external causation opinion including (1) characterization of the medical condition; (2) defining the nature and amount of exposure; (3) demonstration that scientific literature provides evidence that the exposure can cause the condition; and (4) application of the general knowledge to the specific case at issue. The court further noted that defining exposure requires identification of the agent, estimation of the level of exposure, determination of the temporal aspects of the exposure, and definition of the impact of exposure on the symptoms or the disease. *Id.* at 808. Because it did not appear that Dr. al-Saghir had evaluated most, if not all, of these factors, the court excluded her testimony in its entirety. *Id.* at 809.

In *Caraker v. Sandoz Pharmaceuticals Corp.*, 188 F. Supp. 2d 1026 (S.D. Ill. 2001), a mother brought a products liability action against a drug manufacturer after she allegedly suffered a stroke from taking Parlodel, a postpartum lactation-control drug. To show causation, plaintiff proffered the testimony of toxicologist Kenneth Kulig and neurologist Denis Petro. Both purportedly relied "on a differential diagnosis methodology, a methodology that involves 'ruling in' potential causes to develop a potential-cause checklist and then 'ruling out' potential causes one by one based on objective data and criteria. Causation is attributed to the last potential cause left on the list, or at least the most probable one if there are two left." *Id.* at 1030. The court excluded plaintiffs' experts, because they had not scientifically "ruled in" Parlodel as a potential cause of plaintiff's stroke.

According to the Court, when differential diagnosis "is used in the practice of science (as opposed to its use by treating physicians in the practice of medicine out of necessity) it must *reliably* 'rule in' a potential cause." *Id.* In support of their premise that Parlodel can cause a stroke, plaintiffs' experts pointed to several kinds of evidence, including epidemiological data, case reports, animal studies, and medical studies, none of which individually showed a causal connection. After examining this data, however, the Court found

> that their "ruling in" decision requires too many extrapolations from dissimilar data, too many analytical leaps and involves a loose application of purportedly objective scientific causation standards. For these and other reasons, the data these experts used to extrapolate their conclusions is suspect, and their opinions are more like personal opinions than products of any scientific methodology rigorously applied.

Id. at 1031. Without imposing an "absolute epidemiology requirement or any other requirement, except reliability and relevance," the court rejected "plaintiffs' experts' opinions inasmuch as they rely on selective use of statistically insignificant data from epidemiological studies." *Id.* at 1033-34. Moreover, plaintiffs' experts sought to shift the burden of proof by attacking the existing epidemiological evidence, which did not point to a causal link; as the court noted, however, the defendant "is not required to disprove a causal association." *Id.* at 1034.

The court also disapproved of plaintiffs' reliance on case reports. Although "an overwhelming amount of case reports of a temporal proximity between a very specific drug and a very specific adverse event might be enough to make a general causation conclusion sufficiently reliable," the court found plaintiffs' case reports made little attempt to isolate or exclude possible alternative causes and lacked adequate controls and analysis. *Id.* at 1034-35.

Likewise, none of plaintiffs' animal studies were designed to reveal the relevant causal link, and none so concluded. "Some studies involved almost poisonous doses; some involved animals that had a steel rod injected down their spinal cords so the animals had no intact nervous systems; some involved [the chemical's] reaction locally (*e.g.*, in a single isolated vein of an animal) as opposed to a systemic administration; and some were poorly document." *Id.* at 1037. Finally, the court also rejected plaintiffs' use of a "guilt by association" methodology, ruling that an inference from the health effects of one substance to those of another structurally different substance was unfounded in this case. *Id.* at 1039. In short, the court concluded, "the data points pulled from each 'type' of evidence are too limited, too disparate and too inconsistent. It amounts to a hollow whole of hollow parts." *Id.* at 1040.

Other Relevant Cases
Goodwin v. MTD Prods., Inc., 232 F.3d 600, 607-09 (7th Cir. 2000) (affirming that mechanical engineer without medical degree or medical training is not qualified to give expert testimony on medical questions, including the nature, scope, or cause of eye injury).

Michael v. Mr. Heater, Inc., 411 F. Supp. 2d 992 (W.D. Wis. 2006) (flaws in autopsy procedures go only to weight, not admissibility, of pathologist's opinion regarding cause of death.)

Lennon v. Norfolk and Western Ry. Co., 123 F. Supp. 2d 1143 (N.D. Ind. 2000) (treating neurologist's testimony that railroad worker's multiple sclerosis (MS) may have been precipitated by fall at work was unreliable, despite expert's differential diagnosis of MS and minority view within profession in support of his position, where expert had done no research or study on alleged association, and was not aware of most recent epidemiological studies showing lack of correlation between trauma and MS; consulting neurologist's testimony that worker's fall led to diffuse axonal injury and ultimately to demyelination was admissible, even if worker had not lost consciousness after fall, where relevant literature indicated statistically significant association between presences of diffuse axonal injury and falls, but did not rule out possibility that relatively minor trauma could lead to demyelination).

Walker v. Consol. Rail Corp., 111 F. Supp. 2d 1016, 1018-19 (N.D. Ind. 2000) (psychologist's inability to identify the cause of dormant schizophrenia did not require exclusion of his diagnosis that decedent's work-related accident was stressor that led to full, flagrant symptomatology).

e.   Business Practices and Economic Damages

In *Metavante Corp. v. Emigrant Savings Bank*, 619 F.3d 748 (7th Cir. 2010), the court affirmed the district court's allowance of the expert testimony of David Moffat, an expert on levels and measures of performance in the financial services industry. The defendant challenged the testimony on the grounds that the district court had not conducted a proper *Daubert* analysis and that the testimony was lacking a reliable foundation.

Agreeing that the district court's analysis of the reliability of the testimony had been improperly "conclusory," the court conducted a *de novo* review, but concluded that the testimony was in fact both relevant and reliable. 619 F.3d at 760-61. The court found that Moffat was properly qualified by experience to give the testimony, and had adequately explained how his opinions were based on what he had seen and experienced while working in the financial sector. It therefore concluded that the testimony "based on the usual business practice is reliable." *Id.* at 762.

In *United States v. Lupton*, 620 F.3d 790 (7th Cir. 2010), decided two days after *Metavante*, the court affirmed exclusion of the criminal defendant's proffered expert testimony about "the industry standards of practice governing commercial real estate brokers in Wisconsin[.]" 620 F.3d at 797. The court concluded that the district court was well within its discretion to exclude the testimony based on the view that it was in reality premised on interpretation of statutes and regulations, and not experiential knowledge of broker practices. The Seventh Circuit noted that the district court had "adhered to the *Daubert* framework," had received briefing and conducted a hearing on the issue, and laid out its various reasons for excluding the testimony. *Id.* at 799-800. It concluded that its exercise of discretion was therefore proper.

In *Naeem v. McKesson Drug Co.*, 444 F.3d 593 (7th Cir. 2006), an employment discrimination case, the court held that the district court's conclusory statements supporting its Rule 702 determination, without analysis of the expert's methodology "should not be given the deference normally afforded to a district court under the 'manifestly erroneous' standard." 444 F.3d at 608. It further held that the admission of the expert's testimony "regarding what is normal or usual business practice" was error because it was not founded in scientific, technical or specialized knowledge. *Id.* It affirmed the jury's verdict, however, based on the standard for reversal set forth in Rule 61 of the Federal Rules of Civil Procedure.

In *Target Market Publishing, Inc., v. ADVO, Inc.*, 136 F.3d 1139, 1142-45 (7th Cir. 1998), two parties formed a joint venture to produce a direct mail advertising publication. One of the parties brought suit against the other for breach of contract and breach of fiduciary duty. Plaintiff relied on the expert report of Bruce Burton, an accountant with Deloitte & Touche, to establish damages. *Id.* at 1142. The Burton report concluded that the plaintiff should have earned $1.4 million if defendant had not breached the joint venture agreement. *Id.*

The Court of Appeals affirmed the district court's decision to strike the testimony of the accountant. The Court of Appeals also rejecting plaintiff's argument that district courts are required to hold a hearing prior to excluding expert evidence. *Id.* at 1143.

The district court, which did not mention *Daubert*, granted summary judgment for defendant because the report relied upon assumptions "from which no reasonable inference of lost profits could be drawn." *Id.* at 1142. Invoking *Joiner*, the Court of Appeals agreed: "[t]he Burton report projecting $1.4 million in profits for the [joint] venture by the end of the twelvemonth contract period was based upon assumptions that do not legitimately support the conclusion." *Id.* at 1144.

In *Ayers v. Robinson*, 887 F. Supp. 1049 (N.D. Ill. 1995), the district court excluded testimony on "hedonic damages" incurred by the victim of a police shooting. The victim's estate offered the testimony of Professor Stanley Smith, the coauthor of a text on hedonic damages. In calculating hedonic damages incurred by the victim, Smith sought to establish a "benchmark" for measurement of an average human life, then make "adjustments" for the deceased. *Id.* at 1059. After a lengthy and detailed analysis, *id.* at 1059-64, the court found that this type of analysis did not rest upon any scientific method or procedure, as required under *Daubert*. Specifically, Smith's so-called willingness-to-pay methodology, which extrapolated a dollar value for life from what persons were willing to pay for safety devices such as automobile airbags, created widely divergent results. *Id.* at 1061. After looking at the academic literature, the court doubted "the basic assumption underlying the economic model—that the amount of individuals' willingness-to-pay for small reductions in the likelihood of death reflects how society values life." *Id.* at 1063.

Finally, the court also found a lack of "fit" between Smith's proposed testimony and the facts of the case "because the willingness-to-pay data upon which *Hedonic Damages* [Smith's text] relies goes to one thing (value of a statistical life) while the jury is called upon to determine a potentially very different figure (value of [victim's] life)." *Id.* at 1062.

Other Relevant Cases

Tuf Racing Prods., Inc. v. Am. Suzuki Motor Corp., 223 F.3d 585, 591 (7th Cir. 2000) (CPA was qualified to calculate the discounted present value of lost future earnings of terminated franchise because this "was a calculation well within the competence of a CPA").

Wsol v. Great No. Asset Mgmt., Inc., 114 F. Supp. 2d 720, 726 (N.D. Ill. 2000) (financial experts' reliance on Mills' methods of covariation and difference in preparing statistical analysis of financial performance of pension fund to show that trading cost was attributable to advisor's failure to execute commission recapture agreement with introducing broker was admissible in fund's action against advisor under ERISA for breach of fiduciary duty).

B. STATE LAW EXPERT ISSUES

1. Expert Evidence In Illinois State Courts

a. Evidentiary Standard

Illinois still follows the standard set in *Frye v. United States*, 293 F. 1013 (D.C. Cir. 1923), for evaluating scientific evidence. *In re Commitment of Simons*, 821 N.E.2d 1184, 1189 (Ill. 2004). The

Frye rule "dictates that scientific evidence is admissible at trial only if the methodology or scientific principle upon which the opinion is based is 'sufficiently established to have gained general acceptance in the particular field in which it belongs.'" *Id.* (quoting *Frye v. United States*). General acceptance does not require unanimity, consensus, or even majority acceptance; 'it is sufficient that the underlying method used to generate an expert's opinion is reasonably relied on by experts in the relevant field." *Id.*

There are two ways a court may determine whether a particular scientific principle or methodology is generally accepted: "(1) based on the results of a *Frye* hearing; or (2) by taking judicial notice of unequivocal and undisputed prior judicial decisions or technical writings on the subject." *People v. McKown*, 875 N.E.2d 1029, 1034 (Ill. 2007).

The Illinois Supreme Court has rejected the alternative "*Frye*-plus-accountability" standard that would allow trial courts to consider the *Daubert* factors in deciding whether to admit scientific evidence. *Donaldson v. Cent. Ill. Pub. Serv. Co.*, 767 N.E.2d 314, 325-26 (Ill. 2002), *abrogated in part by In re Commitment of Simons*, 821 N.E.2d 1184 (Ill. 2005). In rejecting this alternative standard, the Illinois Supreme Court emphasized that the role of the trial judge is to decide the general acceptance of a technique, while the role of the jury is to decide whether it will accept the expert's conclusion based on the technique. *Id. See also Northern Trust Co. v. Burandt and Armbrust, LLP*, 933 N.E.2d 432, 446 (Ill. App. Ct. 2010) (noting that *Frye* requires only that an expert's reliance on a particular methodology be "reasonable"; the validity and reliability of the opinion are not appropriate inquiries.)

For many years, the standard of review for a trial court's *Frye* ruling was abuse of discretion. However, since 2004, a trial court's decision about whether to admit scientific expert testimony is subject to a dual standard of review." *See In re Commitment of Simons*, 821 N.E.2d 1184, 1189 (Ill. 2004). A trial court's decisions as to whether a expert scientific witness is qualified and whether the expert's testimony is relevant remain committed to "the sound discretion of the trial court." *Id.* But a trial court's *Frye* analysis is subject to *de novo* review. *Id.* The *de novo* review standard is appropriate because general acceptance of a particular type of evidence "transcends any particular dispute" and because a decision on a particular type of evidence can "establish the law of the jurisdiction for future cases." *Id.* In reviewing a *Frye* ruling, an appeals court may consider evidence outside the trial record, including "legal and scientific articles, as well as court opinions from other jurisdictions." *Id. See also People v. McKown,* 875 N.E.2d 1029, 1037 (Ill. 2007) (appropriate to look at case law from other jurisdictions and technical writings to determine general acceptance of the reliability of the HGN test as indictor of alcohol impairment.)

A *Frye* analysis is required only for evidence that is both novel and scientific. *In re Marriage of Alexander*, 857 N.E.2d 766, 770 (Ill. App. Ct. 2006). "Scientific evidence is the product of scientific tests or studies." *People v. McKown*, 875 N.E.2d at 1035. While the "line that separates scientific evidence from nonscientific evidence is not always clear," where an expert's opinion is "derived solely from his or her observations and experiences, the opinion is generally not considered scientific evidence." *In re Marriage of Alexander,* 857 N.E.2d at 770. In *Alexander*, an expert measured the goodwill of a business using a technique he called "multiattribute utility theory." Noting that this methodology "does not rely on the application of scientific principles but incorporates basic math with the observations and experiences of the valuator," the court concluded that the method was not scientific evidence. *Id.* at 773. Thus, no *Frye* hearing was required.

In contrast, where an expert's opinion is "not derived solely from her observations and experience" but instead the expert "turned to and relied upon another source to provide a basis for her opinion," the opinion is scientific. *Id.* at 774-75. *See In re Marriage of Jawad*, 759 N.E.2d 1002 (Ill. App. Ct. 2001). In any case, the testimony of the expert that the method is scientific is irrelevant. *In re Alexander*, 857 N.E.2d at 771, 773. And even if a methodology is scientific, *Frye* does not apply if the methodology is not new or novel. *People v. Wilke*, 854 N.E.2d 275 (Ill. App. Ct. 2006). Whether scientific or experiential, however, mere speculation by an expert witness, or opinions based on guess or conjecture as to what may have happened is inadmissible. *Maggi v. RAS Development, Inc.*, 949 N.E.2d 731, 751 (Ill. App. Ct. 2011). But where there is "an evidentiary basis for the conflicting opinions of the experts offered by both sides," admission of the testimony is proper, and it is within the province of the jury to resolve the dispute. *Davis v. Kraff*, 937 N.E.2d 306, 320 (Ill. App. Ct. 2010) (citations omitted).

The failure to hold a *Frye* hearing before admitting evidence is harmless error if the methods the expert used are in fact generally accepted and the expert was subject to "vigorous cross-examination." *In re Darren M.*, 856 N.E.2d 624, 635-36 (Ill. App. Ct. 2006).

Specific Cases of Note

In re Commitment of Simons, 821 N.E.2d 1184, 1191-92 (Ill. 2004). Using the *de novo* review standard, the court approved the trial court's conclusion that actuarial risk assessment of sex offenders is proper scientific evidence. A psychologist conducting an actuarial risk assessment uses statistical personality trait data collected from past offenders. *Id.* at 1187. The psychologist compared a subject's personality traits to the data and determined the probability of reoffense. *Id.* at 1187. The fact that several other states allow this type of evidence was a persuasive factor in admitting actuarial risk assessment. *Id.* at 1191-92.

Donaldson v. Cent. Ill. Pub. Serv. Co., 767 N.E.2d 314 (Ill. 2002), *abrogated in part by In re Commitment of Simons*, 821 N.E.2d 1184 (Ill. 2005). In *Donaldson*, plaintiffs alleged that exposure to an environmental condition caused their children to develop an extremely rare form of cancer. The Supreme Court affirmed the trial judge's decision to allow plaintiffs' expert testimony. Significantly, the Court rejected the "*Frye*-plus-accountability" standard that had been followed by some Illinois appellate courts. *Id.* at 325-26. The court rejected the standard for two reasons. First, it is redundant: the "determination of the reliability of an expert's methodology is naturally subsumed by the inquiry into its general acceptance in the scientific community." *Id.* at 314. Second, it improperly assesses the underlying data: "[q]uestions concerning underlying data, and an expert's *application* of generally accepted techniques, go to the weight of the evidence, rather than its admissibility." *Id.* Thus, in strict adherence to the *Frye* standard, the court emphasized that the role of the trial judge is to decide the general acceptance of the technique, the role of the jury to decide whether it will accept the expert's conclusion based on the technique.

At issue in *Donaldson* was "extrapolation," the technique of extrapolating data and conclusions on causation from studies not directly related to the disease at issue. The court held that at least in the cause of rare diseases, extrapolation is appropriate because "medical science is simply unable to establish the cause and origin" of some diseases and "extrapolation offers those with rare diseases the opportunity to seek a remedy for the wrong they have suffered." *Id.* at 328. The court also found "that the method of extrapolation does not concern a technique new to science that may instill a sense of 'false confidence' or carry a misleading sense of scientific infallibility"; that "extrapolation by nature admits its fallibility"; and that therefore the "jury is left to judge the veracity of the expert's conclusion." *Id.* at 329.

Duran v. Cullinan, 677 N.E.2d 999 (Ill. App. Ct. 1997). In *Duran*, the parents of a child born with multiple birth defects sued the doctors who prescribed birth control pills to the mother of the child at a time when she was already pregnant, claiming that the contraceptives had caused the child's birth defects. There were no studies or other evidence linking the type of birth control pill prescribed to the particular birth defects suffered by the child. The plaintiffs' experts based their causation opinions, in large part, on extrapolation from studies showing other types of birth defects and animal studies showing that "oral contraceptives have significant teratogenic potential." *Id.* at 1001-02.

The trial court held that plaintiffs' experts' opinions were not admissible under *Frye*, because the experts' "extrapolation" methodology was not generally accepted in the scientific community.

Id. The Appellate Court reversed, rejected the trial court's reliance on the Ninth Circuit's opinion in *Daubert* and other federal cases:

> [W]e do not believe that the plaintiffs were required to present an epidemiological study showing the exact type of defect as long as the plaintiffs' experts' methodology in reaching their conclusions as to causation was sound.

Id at 1004.

Because the evidence in the trial court included "competing affidavits as to the method's general acceptance," the court held that the plaintiffs' experts' affidavits had to be taken as true and the weight to be afforded their opinions left to the jury. *Id.*

b. Expert Related Rules and Procedural Issues

In *Wilson v. Clark*, 417 N.E.2d 1322 (Ill. 1981), the Illinois Supreme Court adopted Rules 703 and 705 of the Federal Rules of Evidence. Thus, as in federal courts, an expert witness may base an opinion on information that has not been admitted into evidence so long as that information is reliable and is of a type reasonably relied upon by experts in that field. *See Modelski v. Navistar Int'l Transp. Corp.*, 707 N.E.2d 239, 244 (Ill. App. Ct. 1999).[5] An expert may give an opinion without disclosing the facts underlying it. The burden then shifts to the adverse party to elicit the underlying facts. *Aguilera v. Mount Sinai Hosp. Med. Ctr.*, 691 N.E.2d 1, 6 (Ill. App. Ct. 1997), *app. denied*, 699 N.E.2d 1030 (Ill. 1998). Note, however, that in affidavits in support of or in opposition to summary judgment, an expert must set forth "with particularity" the admissible facts which support the expert's conclusion. ILL. SUP. CT. R. 191; *Robidoux v. Oliphant*, 775 N.E.2d 987, 992 (Ill. 2002).

c. Qualification

Illinois has a specific rule outlining the requirements for qualifying an expert in any case filed after August 25, 2005 "in which the standard of care applicable to a medical professional is at issue." 735 ILCS 5/8-2501 provides that the court shall consider:

(a) Whether the witness is board certified or board eligible, or has completed a residency, in the same or substantially similar medical specialties as the defendant and is otherwise qualified by significant experience with the standard of care, methods, procedure, and treatments relevant to the allegations against the defendant;

(b) Whether the witness has devoted a majority of his or her work time to the practice of medicine, teaching, or university-based research in relation to the medical care and type of treatment at issue which gave rise to the medical problem of which the plaintiff complains;

(c) whether the witness is licensed in the same profession with the same class of license as the defendant if the defendant is an individual; and

---

[5] Federal Rule of Evidence 703 was amended in 2000 to provide a presumption against the disclosure to the jury of information relied on by an expert but not otherwise admissible. *See* Fed. R. Evid. 703, Advisory Committee Notes. No Illinois court has specifically adopted the amended version. *See Citibank v. McGladrey and Pullen LLP*, 953 N.E. 2d 38, 43 n.2 (Ill. App. Ct. 2011).

(d) whether, in the case against a nonspecialist, the witness can demonstrate a sufficient familiarity with the standard of care practiced in this State [Illinois].

The proposed expert is required to provide evidence of his active practice, teaching, or university-based research. 735 ILCS 5/8-2501. A party may not be qualified as an expert witness if he has been inactive for five years. *Id.* If the proposed expert is retired, he must additionally provide evidence of continuing education "for three years previous to giving testimony." *Id.*

Outside of this section, however, compliance with a professional licensing requirement is not a prerequisite to qualification of an expert witness in Illinois. *See Thompson v. Gordon*, 851 N.E.2d 1231, 1243 (Ill. 2006). The Illinois Supreme Court in *Thompson* found that the fact that the legislature had specifically provided for witness standards in medical malpractice cases weighed in favor of concluding that licensing was not a prerequisite in other witness contexts. *Id.* at 1242-43.

d. Discovery

Initial discovery of the identify and opinions of expert witnesses is accomplished by means of a written interrogatory pursuant to Illinois Supreme Court Rule 213(f)(2) and 213(f)(3). For experts who are not the party, the party's current employee, or the party's retained expert, in response to an interrogatory a party must "identify the subjects on which the witness will testify and the opinions the party experts to elicit." ILL. SUP. CT. R. 213(f)(2). If the expert is the party, the party's current employee, or the party's retained expert, the party must identify:

(i) the subject matter on which the witness will testify;
(ii) the conclusions and opinions of the witness and the bases therefor;
(iii) the qualifications of the witness; and
(iv) any reports prepared by the witness about the case.

ILL. SUP. CT. R. 213(f)(3). A party has a duty to "seasonably supplement or amend" an interrogatory answer when new or additional information subsequently becomes known. ILL. SUP. CT. R. 213(i). Unless a showing of good cause is made, upon objection, information not previously disclosed in a Rule 213(f) answer or a discovery deposition shall not be admitted. ILL. SUP. CT. R. 213(g); *Clayton v. County of Cook*, 805 N.E.2d 222 (Ill. App. Ct. 2004) (trial court erred in allowing expert testimony outside of the scope of 213(f) disclosure; listing factors to consider in determining the proper sanction).

Disclosure of expert opinions and testimony may also be required pursuant to Illinois Supreme Court Rule 218, providing for case management conferences and orders. ILL. SUP. CT. R. 218.

Depositions of expert witnesses may be taken pursuant to Supreme Court Rule 202. That rule continues the distinction in Illinois between "discovery" depositions and "evidence" depositions. Discovery and evidence depositions must be taken separately, unless the parties stipulate or the court orders otherwise. Discovery depositions may not exceed three hours, except by stipulation of the parties or by order. ILL. SUP. CT. R. 206(d).

e. Fees

Fees to an expert witness are governed by Illinois Supreme Court Rule 208 and 735 ILCS 5/2-1101. In general, those rules provide that the party taking a deposition or compelling the attendance of a witness at trial is responsible for the fees. In the case of a trial appearance of an expert witness pursuant to subpoena, including medical providers, when the fee cannot be agreed by the parties, the trial court shall conduct a hearing subsequent to the testimony to determine the reasonable fee to be paid. 735 ILCS 5/2-1101.

2. Expert Evidence In Indiana State Courts

a. Evidentiary Standard

Indiana Rule of Evidence 702(b) provides that "[e]xpert scientific testimony is admissible only if the court is satisfied that the scientific principles upon which the expert testimony rests are reliable." Ind. Evidence Rule 702(b). The Indiana Supreme Court has emphasized that "[t]his subsection differs from the Federal Rules of Evidence in its express requirement that expert testimony be based upon reliable scientific principles." *McGrew v. State*, 682 N.E.2d 1289, 1290 (Ind. 1997). *See also Person v. Shipley*, 962 N.E.2d 1192, 1194 n.1 (Ind. 2012) (noting differences in text of Indiana Rule 702 from Federal Rule of Evidence 702). Expert scientific evidence is admissible only if the trial court is satisfied that the opinion both assists the trier of fact and is based on reliable principles. *Person*, 962 N.E.2d at 1194.

The proponent of the testimony bears the burden of establishing the foundation and reliability of the scientific principles upon which the testimony is based. *Lytle v. Ford Motor Co.*, 814 N.E.2d 301, 308-09 (Ind. App. 2004). The trial court "must make a preliminary assessment of whether the reasoning or methodology underlying the testimony is scientifically valid and whether that reasoning or methodology properly can be applied to the facts in issue." *Id.* at 309 citing *Hottinger v. Trugreen Corp.*, 665 N.E.2d 593, 596 (Ind. App. 1996).

The reliability of scientific evidence under Indiana law can be determined using a variety of facts: "there is no specific 'test' or set of 'prongs' which must be considered in order to satisfy Indiana Evidence Rule 702(b)." *McGrew*, 682, N.E.2d at 1292. Those factors may include, but are not limited to:

> 1) whether the technique has been or can be empirically tested; 2) whether the technique has been subjected to peer review and publication; 3) the known or potential rate of error, as well as the existence and maintenance of standards controlling the technique's operation; and 4) general acceptance within the relevant scientific community.

Id. fn.5.

A decision with respect to the admissibility of scientific evidence is within the trial court's "broad discretion" and will be reversed only for abuse of discretion. *TRW Vehicle Safety Sys., Inc. v. Moore*, 936 N.E.2d 201, 216 (Ind. 2010). The trial court's decision is presumed to be correct and the losing party bears the burden of persuasion on appeal. *Id. See also Alsheik v. Guerrero*, 956 N.E.2d 115 (Ct. App. Ind. 2011).

Because of the differences in the text of the Indiana rule, federal case law interpreting the Federal Rules of Evidence is not controlling in Indiana, but may be helpful:

> [F]ederal case law interpreting the Federal Rules of Evidence is not binding upon the determination of state evidentiary law. Regarding *Daubert*, we noted only that "[t]he concerns driving *Daubert* coincide with the express requirement of Indiana Rule of Evidence 702(b) that the trial court be satisfied of the reliability of the scientific principles involved." *Steward*, 652 N.E.2d at 498. Contrary to the arguments made by the defendant, when analyzing Indiana Evidence Rule 702(b)—the adoption of which preceded *Daubert*—we find *Daubert* helpful, but not controlling.

McGrew, 682 N.E.2d at 1290. The *Frye* requirement of general acceptance, however, is clearly not the rule. *See Newhart v. State*, 669 N.E.2d 953, 955 (Ind. 1996). *See also Ford Motor Co. v. Ammerman*, 705 N.E.2d 539, 550 (Ind. App. 1999).

Finally, it is worth noting that unlike many other jurisdictions, Indiana does not require that medical causation opinions be given only by a physician. In *Person v. Shipley*, the Indiana Supreme Court noted

> that neither the criteria for qualifying under Rule 702 (knowledge, skill, experience, training or education) nor the purpose for which expert testimony is admitted (to assist the trier of fact) seems to support disallowing an otherwise qualified expert to offer an opinion regarding medical causation simply because he or she lacks a medical degree.

962 N.E.2d at 1196.

The court reasoned that an expert with a degree in Biomedical engineering who taught a course that covered the musculoskeletal system was qualified to give an opinion that an accident was not the likely cause of a lower back injury, and affirmed admission of the testimony. *Id.* at 1195. *See also Bennett v. Richmond*, 960 N.E.2d 782 (Ind. 2012) (allowing testimony of psychologist that car accident had caused traumatic brain injury).

b. Other Expert Related Rules and Procedural Issues

Discovery

Discovery of experts is governed by Rule 26(B)(4) of the Indiana rules of trial procedure. It provides for interrogatories requiring identification of each person the other party expects to call as an expert, a statement of "the subject matter on which the expert is expected to testify," a statement of the "substance of the facts and opinions to which the expert is expected to testify and a summary of the grounds for each opinion." Discovery by other means is only upon motion and order, and fees and costs may be provided. Rule 26(B)(4)(a)(ii).

3. *Expert Evidence In Wisconsin State Courts*

a. Evidentiary Standard

Testimony by experts in Wisconsin is governed by Sections 907.02 and 907.03 of the evidence chapter, which were adopted in 2011 to effectively adopt the federal *Daubert* standard. Those sections largely track Federal Rules of Evidence 702 and 703, and provide that the testimony of an expert witness must be "based upon sufficient facts or data," and be "the product of reliable principles and methods." The expert must also have "applied the principles and methods reliably to the facts of the case." Wis. Stat. § 907.02(1).

Wisconsin's enactment of these sections significantly changed the landscape for evaluation of scientific expert testimony. Prior to February 1, 2011, the threshold for admission of scientific evidence in the Wisconsin state courts was exceedingly low. The Wisconsin Supreme Court expressly rejected *Frye* in 1974, adopting instead a pure relevancy test. *Watson v. State*, 219 N.W. 2d 398, 403-04 (Wis. 1974). "Once the relevancy of the evidence is established and the witness is qualified as an expert, the reliability of the evidence is a weight and credibility issue for the fact finder and any reliability challenges must be made through cross-examination or by other means of impeachment." *State v. Peters*, 534 N.W.2d 867, 873 (Wis. App. 1995), citing *State v. Walstad*, 351 N.W.2d 469, 487 (Wis. 1984). Wisconsin judges did not previously evaluate the reliability of expert testimony or scientific evidence. *Ricco v. Riva*, 669 N.W.2d 193, 199-200 (Wis. App. 2003). Thus, cases predating 2011 may not be useful in considering a challenge to expert testimony in a case filed after January 31, 2011.[6]

b. Other Expert Related Rule and Procedural Issues

Discovery and Fees
Discovery of experts in Wisconsin is governed by Wis. Stat. § 804.01(2)(d), which provides for interrogatories, depositions, and, upon motion, other means. The party seeking discovery from an expert must pay the expert "a reasonable fee" for time spent in responding to discovery, "unless manifest injustice would result." Wis. Stat. § 804.01(2)(d)(3). A party seeking discovery from an expert may also be required to pay the other party "a fair portion of the fees and expenses reasonably incurred by the latter party in obtaining facts and opinions from the expert." *Id.*[7] A party is under a duty to supplement discovery responses regarding the identity of expert witnesses. § 804.01(5)(a)(2).

Court Appointed Experts
Wis. Stat. § 907.06(1) provides for court appointment of expert witnesses upon the judge's own motion or on the motion of any party. The compensation paid to a court appointed expert in a civil case shall be "reasonable compensation in whatever sum the judge may allow," and shall be paid by the parties in a proportion directed by the judge. Wis. Stat. § 907.06(2). Compensation paid to a court appointed expert is taxable as a cost, but without the limitation prescribed by Section 814.04(2). *Id.*

---

[6] Section 45(5) of the bill that adopted Sections 907.02 and 907.03 provided that, for civil actions, those sections "first apply to actions or special proceedings that are commenced on the [February 1, 2011] effective date of this subsection." 2011 Wis. Act 2, § 45(5). The Wisconsin Supreme Court confirmed that expert testimony in cases brought before February 1, 2011, are governed by the previous standards for admitting expert evidence. *See 260 North 12th St., LLC v. State of Wisconsin Dep't of Transp.*, 338 Wis.2 34, 808 N.W. 2d 372 (2011). The bill was silent with respect to criminal actions, leading commentators to believe that the new sections apply retrospectively in criminal cases.

[7] Wis. Stat. § 814.04(2) limits the recovery of expert fees as an item of cost to "an expert witness fee not exceeding $300 for each expert who testifies, exclusive of the standard witness fee and mileage which shall also be taxed for each expert[.]"

CHAPTER VIII
EXPERT EVIDENCE IN THE EIGHTH CIRCUIT

by

Christin Eaton Garcia
Ryan Dunn
Demoya Gordon
Shelby Myers
Joseph M. Price[1]

Faegre Baker Daniels LLP
2200 Wells Fargo Center
90 South Seventh Street
Minneapolis, MN 55402
(612) 766-7305

A. KEY EIGHTH CIRCUIT DECISIONS APPLYING *DAUBERT*—CIVIL CASES

Per Federal Rule of Evidence 702 and *Daubert* principles, the court should screen expert testimony to be sure: 1) it will be relevant to the finder of fact; 2) the expert is qualified to assist the trier of fact; and 3) the evidence is reliable and trustworthy. *Polski v. Quigley Corp.*, 538 F.3d 836, 839 (8th Cir. 2008). A party who offers expert testimony has the burden of establishing, by a preponderance of the evidence, that the testimony is admissible. *Id.* at 839, 841. In the *Polski* case, the Eighth Circuit affirmed the district court's exclusion of plaintiffs' expert who had not tested his theory that cold medicine sprayed from a bottle would travel in a straight line deep into the nose, so as to reach certain tissues and cause a loss of smell. Neither the expert nor anyone else had tested this theory, which had not been subjected to peer review or accepted in the scientific community, and which appeared to conflict with earlier writings by the expert. Exclusion accordingly was not an abuse of discretion, as the plaintiffs had not met their burden to establish a basis for admissibility.

Abuse of discretion is the basic standard by which the Eighth Circuit reviews a district court's decision to admit or exclude expert testimony. *Schmidt v. City of Bella Villa*, 557 F.3d 564, 570 (8th Cir. 2009), *citing Gen. Elec. Co. v. Joiner*, 522 U.S. 136, 143, 118 S. Ct. 512 (1997). The district court will not be reversed unless it has abused its discretion and the ruling had a substantial influence on the outcome of the case. *Schmidt*, 557 F.3d at 570 (affirming exclusion of testimony by a police officer outside his area of practical experience). The Eighth Circuit applies this standard differently,

---

[1] The authors thank Sarah Mulligan for her research support and also thank the authors of previous versions of this section, parts of which have been retained.

however, depending on the panel and the case. The words used to characterize it vary at times, often telegraphing the outcome.

1. Medicine and Toxicology

Kuhn v. Wyeth, Inc., — *F.3d* —, *2012 WL 3030730 (8th Cir. 2012)*
Thousands of menopausal hormone therapy (HT) cases have been consolidated through the multi-district litigation (MDL) process before a federal court in Arkansas. Most plaintiffs allege their breast cancer was caused by their use of the hormones estrogen and progestin. In this case, Wyeth succeeded in having the district court exclude testimony by plaintiff expert Dr. Donald Austin that the short-term use of HT for less than three years could cause breast cancer, as a general matter. Without this general causation testimony, plaintiffs' cases failed and were dismissed on summary judgment. The Eighth Circuit reversed.

At issue was the basis for the expert's opinion and his methods for reaching it. These were described in a written report and at a live hearing before the magistrate judge, who excluded the testimony in an order approved by the judge. In his report, Dr. Austin identified five observational studies that supported his current opinion on short-term use, which the defense said conflicted with his own earlier statement about results from the large Women's Health Initiative (WHI) randomized clinical trial. At the hearing, he admitted that two of the studies should not have been included in his report, which was prepared in about five hours with assistance from plaintiffs' counsel, to address an issue to which he had not given much thought before writing his report. Accordingly, three studies remained to support his opinion, and two of them were foreign. The parties debated the relevance of these studies to Wyeth's Prempro product, since the primary focus in these studies was on other HT types. Dr. Austin conceded that the last study he identified, which was conducted in U.S. women, did not reliably track duration of use. Wyeth argued that Dr. Austin "cherry picked" his three observational studies from a field including many that showed no risk for short-term Prempro use. "With no studies to reliably support his position, along with a failed effort to discredit WHI results," the magistrate judge excluded Dr. Austin's opinion as "not sufficiently reliable to be admissible under *Daubert*." See *Kuhn*, 2012 WL 3030730 at *13 (Judge Loken, dissenting).

It is telling that the majority stated the standard for review without embellishment: "We review . . . for an abuse of discretion." *Id.* at *4. The dissent added that, after this review, the court "must affirm unless [the district court's decision] is 'manifestly erroneous'." *Id.* at *13. Without expressly challenging this standard, the majority did reverse. In its long discussion about the framework for admissibility, the majority cited cases indicating that a party offering expert testimony need not demonstrate that the opinions are correct. It also cited the original *Daubert* decision for the concept that "shaky but admissible" testimony should be attacked through vigorous cross-examination, presentation of contrary evidence and careful instruction on the burden of proof.

The majority conducted an in-depth evidentiary review before concluding that Dr. Austin should have been allowed to testify, even though his theory was not supported by randomized trial data and may have conflicted with the WHI. Each of the three observational studies cited by Dr. Austin was addressed at length, with the court considering their limitations and concluding that they did offer relevant supporting evidence. The majority was not troubled by results from the WHI or statements by Dr. Austin about its meaning, since it said his burden was not to disprove the WHI's finding that short-term HT use did not cause breast cancer, but to establish a reliable basis for his own opinion that it did. Ultimately, the Eighth Circuit concluded that Dr. Austin presented "reliable epidemiological evidence to support his opinion that short-term use of Prempro increases the risk of breast cancer." Although "[t]here may be several studies supporting Wyeth's contrary position," the majority found that "it is not the province of the court to choose between the competing theories when both are supported by reliable scientific evidence." *Id.* at *12.

The dissenting judge concluded that the majority did not give adequate deference to the district court's review.

Junk v. Terminix Int'l Co., 628 F.3d 439 (8th Cir. 2010), cert. denied, 132 S. Ct. 94 (2011)
Plaintiff alleged her son's multiple medical conditions, including cerebral palsy and mental delay, were caused by exposure to numerous applications of the insecticide Dursban both *in utero* and after he was born. To establish that her son had been exposed to unsafe levels of the chemical, plaintiff offered testimony from Dr. Richard Fenske. He testified that he usually relied on a deterministic modeling method to estimate toxic exposure and dose, but that he could not use his model in this case because he lacked sufficient data. Instead, he compared the boy's exposure to published literature. The district court excluded Dr. Fenske's testimony, as he had not followed his own usual method and relied on a number of ungrounded assumptions in drawing a parallel between the boy's exposure and the situations described in the literature. This exclusion left insufficient basis for a neonatologist/pediatrician to testify that Dursban was a specific cause of the child's injuries, so the plaintiff was left without necessary expert support and the case was dismissed on summary judgment.

In affirming exclusion, the Eighth Circuit said it would reverse a trial court's decision only for a "clear and prejudicial abuse of discretion." 628 F.3d at 447. It was not an abuse of discretion to exclude Dr. Fenske's testimony for the reasons stated by the district court. Nor was it improper to exclude the physician who would have testified to specific causation, since the lack of an established exposure to unsafe levels of Dursban prevented her from "ruling in" the chemical as one plausible cause of the child's injuries, meaning she could not conduct an admissible differential diagnosis that would have "ruled out" other causes.

Barrett v. Rhodia, Inc., 606 F.3d 975 (8th Cir. 2010)
Plaintiff Barrett and his employer Clean Harbors alleged that his exposure to phosphorus pentasulfide (P_2S_5) at work caused an anoxic brain injury leading to dementia. The P_2S_5 came in drums and was used to stabilize hazardous waste for disposal. The drums were loaded onto a third floor platform and the chemical traveled down a chute to a platform twelve to fourteen feet below; at that level, the chute was opened and the P_2S_5 continued down to the ground level. On the day of the accident, a man opened a drum on the top floor and loaded it into the chute; Barrett was on the second level and "went down" and became unresponsive as soon as he opened the chute. The man on the top floor was later found dead.

When exposed to moisture, P_2S_5 dust can form hydrogen sulfide gas. High concentrations of this gas can cause unconsciousness and death. These dangers were well known and had led to OSHA recommendations that persons working with the chemical wear full protective clothing and a self contained breathing apparatus. Barrett and three nearby coworkers were not wearing protective masks or clothing. The man on the top platform was wearing a breathing device. The plaintiffs and defendant advanced competing theories for how the P_2S_5 came to be transferred to gaseous form.

During a post-accident investigation, an independent environmental company discovered hydrogen sulfide gas in the headspaces of other unopened P_2S_5 drums and in the at-issue drum. They estimated potential exposure levels for people at various distances, and indicated an exposure well below a toxic level for a person standing twelve feet away, which was about Barrett's distance.

Plaintiffs argued nonetheless that defects in the P_2S_5 drum had caused hydrogen sulfide gas to develop in the drum, which was released when it was opened and reached Barrett at a toxic concentration. Plaintiffs said that Rhodia failed to warn of this risk. Plaintiffs offered four experts in support. The medical experts said that Barrett sustained a brain injury resulting from exposure to a toxic concentration of hydrogen sulfide gas (Dr. Gerti Janss), that he suffered a brain injury resulting from exposure to hydrogen sulfide gas (treating physician Dr. Terry Himes) and that he suffered from a brain injury consistent with hydrogen sulfide gas poisoning and had been exposed to the gas at a toxic concentration (Dr. Anne Talbot). The safety engineer (Edward Ziegler) examined the worksite and observed the drums, but did not conduct any testing of the drums or chemicals. He said the drums were defective, hydrogen sulfide gas had formed in the at-issue drum, and this gas was released when it was opened, causing the injury. In response, defendant offered testimony from Dr. Michael Fox, Ph.D., who had conducted experiments and concluded that the P_2S_5 drum opened on the day of the accident could not have exposed Barrett to a sufficient concentration of hydrogen sulfide gas to cause serious injury. He attributed the injury instead to the inhalation of P_2S_5 dust, which was converted to gas in Barrett's lungs.

The district court granted in part Rhodia's exclusion motion, limiting the plaintiffs' experts to testimony about Barrett's symptoms and injuries and the conclusion that they were "consistent with" hydrogen sulfide gas exposure at certain levels. Finding the limited testimony insufficient to establish a *prima facie* case, the court granted summary judgment. In affirming these decisions, the Eighth Circuit said it would not reverse a district court's ruling on the admissibility of expert testimony "absent a clear and prejudicial abuse of discretion." 606 F.3d at 980. The district court acted within its allowed discretion when finding that neither Dr. Janss nor Dr. Talbot had any factual basis to support an opinion about the hydrogen sulfide gas levels to which Barrett was exposed. Likewise, it was proper to limit Dr. Himes, who had never before treated a patient suffering from P_2S_5 or hydrogen sulfide gas exposure and who did not consider any alternative causes for the injuries. Mr. Ziegler characterized his own role as focusing on "regulatory and safety" issues and admitted that he had relied on other experts for opinions about hydrogen sulfide gas concentration, source and dispersal. He had no prior experience with the gas or the chemical and did no research or testing. It therefore was proper to limit his testimony to general monitoring and safety practices at the plant. Notably, the court affirmed the decision to apply a *Daubert* analysis to the safety consultant's testimony, given the complexity of the issues.

Because all specific causation testimony had been excluded properly, and because plaintiffs had not established through admissible expert testimony that Barrett was exposed to hydrogen sulfide gas rather than P_2S_5 dust, the Eighth Circuit affirmed summary judgment. *Compare Bednar v. Bassett Furniture Mfg. Co., Inc.*, 147 F.3d 737 (8th Cir. 1998) (reversing summary judgment in a toxic tort case because plaintiffs had made a sufficient threshold showing of exposure to injurious levels of formaldehyde emanating from a dresser drawer) *and Wright v. Willamette Indus., Inc.*, 91 F.3d 1105 (8th Cir. 1996) (reversing the admission of expert testimony about airborne particulate exposure, given the expert's lack of knowledge about what amounts of wood fibers impregnated with formaldehyde involve an appreciable risk of harm to people who breathe them).

In re Baycol Prods. Litig., 596 F.3d 884 (8th Cir. 2010) (Flesner v. Bayer)
This decision addressed an individual plaintiff's appeal of a summary judgment order and certain expert witness exclusion orders underlying this result. Using an abuse of discretion standard, the Eighth Circuit affirmed the exclusion of a late-filed supplemental expert report on specific causation, on both procedural and substantive grounds. The district court acted within its discretion in refusing to allow the late report and also in determining that it contained an inadequate basis for admission. Without this and other expert testimony, plaintiff lacked sufficient evidence to get to a jury and the summary judgment was affirmed.

At issue was whether Baycol, a statin that had been removed from the market, had caused the plaintiff's muscle pains. The court found the proffered causation testimony "devoid of the factual basis necessary" to create a triable issue of fact. Plaintiff's expert Dr. Samuel Mayer conceded there were many tests that could have been done to diagnose myopathy, a particular kind of muscle pain that had been linked with Baycol, and that none of these tests had been conducted. He also agreed that plaintiff's slightly elevated creatine kinase (CK) levels could have alternative causes, and were so slight that the applicable medical standards would not raise a concern for myopathy arising from

Baycol use. Plaintiff's medical records indicated a long history of muscle pain, predating Baycol use and undercutting any reliance on temporal proximity to establish causation.

Scroggin v. Wyeth (In re Prempro Prods. Liab. Litig.), 586 F.3d 547 (8th Cir. 2009), cert. denied, 130 S. Ct. 3467 (2010)

Following a trial where plaintiff was awarded compensatory and punitive damages for failure to warn about breast cancer risk in connection with use of menopausal hormone therapy (HT) defendants appealed. One ruling challenged on appeal was the admission of testimony by plaintiff's specific causation expert, Dr. Elizabeth Naftalis. She characterized her analysis as a differential diagnosis. She said plaintiff's hormone receptor positive cancer needed hormones to grow, and said plaintiff's menopausal symptoms ruled out her own body's hormone production as a source. This left only the HT as a source. Defendants challenged this method on many grounds, including the failure to account for and rule out the plaintiff's other breast cancer risk factors. More fundamentally, a reliable "rule in" and "rule out" process to eliminate plausible alternative causes could not be undertaken for breast cancer, since the cause of breast cancer is most often not known.

The district court allowed the testimony and the Eighth Circuit affirmed, finding that Naftalis' explanations about other potential risk factors went to the weight of her opinions, not their admissibility. In addition, her testimony that external hormone pills were required to feed plaintiff's tumor, given plaintiff's insufficient internal hormone production, provided a sufficient basis to rule out other potential causes. Notably, Wyeth challenged the scientific basis and methods behind Naftalis' assertion that she could rule out a woman's own hormones as a cancer cause, based on symptoms. The court treated this as a "factual basis" for her testimony, appropriate for consideration by the jury. 586 F.3d at 566, n. 12.

Bland v. Verizon Wireless, (VAW) L.L.C., 538 F.3d 893 (8th Cir. 2008)

Reviewing for "clear and prejudicial" abuse of discretion, the Eighth Circuit here affirmed the exclusion of plaintiff's expert witness testimony and the resulting summary judgment. A Verizon employee had sprayed compressed air into plaintiff's water bottle as a joke, and plaintiff drank a few sips. On subsequent testing, difluoroethane (freon) was found in the water. Plaintiff brought suit, relying on her treating physician for testimony that her exposure to this chemical caused her to develop exercise-induced asthma.

In affirming the exclusion of this testimony, the court emphasized plaintiff's expert Dr. Nancy Sprince's concession that, in the majority of cases, the cause of exercise-induced asthma is unknown. This fact, combined with her failure to consider and rule out other potential causes of plaintiff's asthma, did not allow her to conduct an admissible differential diagnosis attributing the asthma to freon exposure. Nor could the expert adequately "rule in" the freon as a plausible cause to begin with, given her lack of knowledge about what level of exposure to freon may cause an appreciable risk of developing asthma or about the concentration or degree of plaintiff's individual exposure.

Allen v. Brown Clinic, P.L.L.P., 531 F.3d 568 (8th Cir. 2008)

Using an abuse of discretion standard and noting the "great latitude" district courts are given in fulfilling their gatekeeping function, the Eighth Circuit affirmed the admission of expert testimony presented by a medical malpractice defendant. The plaintiff alleged his perforated esophagus was caused negligently during the defendant's repair of his hiatal hernia. The defendant offered testimony by a general surgeon, who said it would be almost impossible to perforate the esophagus during this surgery and who identified several alternative causes that were more likely. He did not, however, testify to a reasonable degree of medical certainty that any one of the alternatives actually had caused the tear. In affirming the admission of this testimony, the court emphasized that it would be an impermissible shifting of the plaintiff's burden to prove causation if the defendant were required to "disprove" causation in order to offer expert testimony defending against plaintiff's allegations.

Olson v. Ford Motor Co., 481 F.3d 619 (8th Cir. 2007)
This product liability case arose from an automobile accident in which plaintiff's spouse lost control of his 1998 Ford Explorer as he was attempting to navigate a curve in the road. Plaintiff's spouse died at the scene. Plaintiff sued Ford Motor Company alleging that the accident occurred due to a defectively designed cruise control actuator cable. The case was tried to a jury, which found the decedent and defendant equally at fault, precluding any recovery by plaintiff under North Dakota law. Plaintiff appealed, contending the district court erred in admitting evidence of her husband's consumption of alcohol immediately prior to the accident.

The day after the accident, the county coroner drew a sample of decedent's vitreous humor, the clear fluid inside the eye, to test the alcohol level. The coroner had been unable to draw a blood sample. The state crime lab ran two tests on the vitreal sample, both showing .22 percent alcohol by weight. Several months later, at plaintiff's request, the crime lab retested the samples four more times, yielding different and lower results.

At trial, Ford offered the testimony of Dr. Alan Donelson, a pharmacologist. Based on the alcohol level in the decedent's vitreous humor, he said the blood alcohol level likely exceeded .10 at the time of the accident and impairment contributed to the crash. Plaintiff said this testimony should have been excluded because Donelson had no experience drawing or handling vitreal humor, or converting vitreal alcohol levels to blood alcohol levels. Because plaintiff failed to raise this issue in the district court, the Court of Appeals applied a plain error standard of review. The court found that Dr. Donelson was a pharmacologist qualified by education and experience to testify about how alcohol and drugs affect human beings, and while he had not previously calculated a blood-alcohol level from a vitreous-humor-alcohol level, the actual conversion was a matter of basic arithmetic that fell within his capabilities.

Plaintiff also said the testimony should have been excluded because the vitreal sample was unrepresentative and unreliable. Because plaintiff had raised this issue at trial, the admission was reviewed for abuse of discretion. The court rejected plaintiff's challenge, finding that it went only to the credibility of the factual basis for the opinion, which could be contested through direct examination of the state toxicologist and cross-examination of Donelson.

Plaintiff next argued that there was no proven, reliable method for converting a vitreous humor alcohol level to a blood alcohol level. The court found this tantamount to a *Frye* challenge, which was no longer by itself determinative of admissibility. Ford also had offered evidence that the technique was generally accepted, and the district court was entitled to credit this evidence.

Finally, plaintiff argued that Dr. Donelson had failed to take into account eyewitness testimony concerning whether the decedent was impaired on the night of the accident due to his alcohol consumption. The court found that a conflict between the testimony of an eyewitness and an expert does not mean the expert is unreliable. Cross-examination at trial could address any inconsistencies. Admission of the testimony therefore was affirmed.

Marmo v. Tyson Fresh Meats, Inc. 457 F.3d 748 (8th Cir. 2006)
Plaintiff claimed injuries from exposure to hydrogen sulfide emissions from wastewater treatment lagoons at defendant's beef processing plant. After trial on the merits of plaintiff's nuisance claim, plaintiff appealed the summary judgment dismissal of her physical injury claims, based on the trial court's limitation of her expert toxicologist's testimony on both procedural and substantive grounds. Both bases were affirmed.

The district court ruled that the toxicologist could testify that plaintiff's alleged injuries were "consistent with" hydrogen sulfide exposure, but could not testify regarding the ultimate issue of causation. The Eighth Circuit acknowledged previous decisions allowing a toxicologist to testify that exposure to a chemical caused a person's symptoms and injuries, citing *Bonner v. ISP Techs.,*

Inc., 259 F.3d 924, 928–31 (8th Cir. 2001) and *Loudermill v. Dow Chemical Co.*, 863 F.2d 566, 569–70 (8th Cir. 1988). But neither case set forth a blanket rule that toxicologists always may opine on causation. In this case, the toxicologist did not examine plaintiff or inquire about other toxic exposures. The toxicologist also failed to exclude confounding factors, leaving open the possibility of competing causes of disease and raising questions about the competency of the testimony. Plaintiff's expert also conceded that the causation standard she employed was a much lower standard than medical causation.

Larson v. Kempker, 414 F.3d 936 (8th Cir. 2005); 405 F.3d 645 (8th Cir. 2005)
Plaintiff, a convicted murderer, brought a claim under 42 U.S.C. § 1983 for prison officials' alleged failure to protect him from secondhand smoke. The plaintiff characterized his exposure to "unreasonably high levels" of tobacco smoke as cruel and unusual punishment in violation of the Eighth Amendment. The trial court granted a defense motion to exclude his expert, Dr. A. Jordan Wells, through whom plaintiff sought to introduce evidence on the adverse health effects of environmental tobacco smoke. The court's ruling centered on its finding that the expert had not done any of his own research on the subject, but was merely going to discuss the work of others. The Eighth Circuit found error in this holding, as Dr. Wells had participated in several government hearings and had authored numerous publications on secondhand smoke, including a 1992 EPA report, and was generally regarded as a leading expert on the issue. This error was deemed harmless, however, because even with the testimony, the plaintiff could not have met his burden to prove a level of exposure high enough to violate his Eighth Amendment rights.

Kudabeck v. Kroger Company, 338 F.3d 856 (8th Cir. 2003)
In *Kudabeck*, the trial court denied defendant's motion *in limine* seeking to exclude the testimony of the injured plaintiff's chiropractor. The Eighth Circuit reviewed the admission of the chiropractor's testimony for abuse of discretion. Defendant argued that the chiropractor's testimony was inadmissible because he failed to perform a differential diagnosis to exclude contributors to the plaintiff's degenerative disk disease other than work-related factors. Defendant also argued that the expert's testimony was unreliable because he failed to cite published studies to support his conclusion.

The court reviewed the testimony in detail and found that the expert's opinion was reliable because it was based on his education, training, and proper chiropractic methodology, including a thorough patient history, and was conducted in accord with his normal chiropractic practice. The court found defendant's challenges to be jury questions and concluded defendant had not demonstrated that the chiropractor had exceeded the boundaries of chiropractic medicine. The court went on to state that, even if it were to find that the evidence should have been excluded, the chiropractor's testimony likely did not affect the amount of the jury's award.

Bonner v. ISP Technologies, Inc., 259 F.3d 924 (8th Cir. 2001)
Plaintiff was twice exposed to FoamFlush, an organic solvent, while working on the assembly line of a urethane filter production plant. She claimed the exposure caused her to develop psychological problems, cognitive impairment, and Parkinsonian symptoms. Dr. Terry Martinez, a pharmacologist and toxicologist, and Dr. Raymond Singer, a neuropsychologist and neurotoxicologist, testified at trial on her behalf. The jury returned a $2.2 million verdict in her favor and ISP appealed, challenging the admission of the expert testimony.

The Eighth Circuit acknowledged plaintiff's requirement to prove that the at-issue exposure was capable of causing the alleged injuries and that it did, but also said that "[t]he first several victims of a new toxic tort should not be barred from having their day in court simply because the medical literature, which will eventually show the connection between the victims' condition and the toxic substance, has not yet been completed." The plaintiff need not produce "a mathematically precise table equating levels of exposure with levels of harm" to prove causation. ISP also challenged Dr. Martinez's reliance on case reports, animal studies, the temporal association between exposure and the plaintiff's symptoms, studies of chemicals with similar structures, and the plaintiff's medical records. While the Eighth Circuit recognized that case reports are not generally considered reliable evidence of causation, it nonetheless excused Martinez's reliance upon them because of "the immediacy of Bonner's acute symptoms to her exposure." The Eighth Circuit affirmed admission of the testimony.

Glastetter v. Novartis Pharms. Corp., 252 F.3d 986 (8th Cir. 2001)
In *Glastetter*, the plaintiff claimed that her use of Parlodel, a drug formerly prescribed for preventing postpartum lactation, caused her to suffer a stroke. Drs. Kenneth Kulig and Denis Petro both testified that Parlodel was the cause of Glastetter's stroke based on their differential diagnosis, for which they claimed support from published case reports, medical treatises, human dechallenge/rechallenge data, animal studies, internal Novartis documents, and the FDA's revocation of Parlodel's indication for lactation suppression. The trial court found that these various pieces of evidence did not support a conclusion that Parlodel could have caused Glastetter's stroke, and therefore excluded their testimony and granted summary judgment to Novartis. *Glastetter v. Novartis Pharms. Corp.*, 107 F.Supp.2d 1015 (E.D. Mo. 2000).

In a *per curiam* opinion, the Eighth Circuit affirmed. The court held that although the case reports "demonstrate a temporal association between Parlodel and stroke, or stroke-precursors, that association is not scientifically valid proof of causation." The treatises cited by plaintiffs "were largely grounded upon case reports and other anecdotal information," and one published treatise actually concluded that Parlodel does *not* cause vasoconstriction (the mechanism behind the plaintiff's stroke causation theory).

The court also rejected plaintiff's attempt to compare Parlodel's risk/benefit profile to other drugs in the same chemical family. "[T]his generic assumption that bromocriptine behaves like other ergot alkaloids carries little scientific value," the court held, because "[e]ven minor deviations in molecular structure can radically change a particular substance's properties and propensities." Similarly, the court was not persuaded by data from experiments where an observable reaction disappears following "dechallenge" (exposure is stopped), then reappears upon "rechallenge" with the drug. The court found this data more valuable than "run-of-the-mill case reports," but found no abuse of discretion in the trial court's decision to exclude it for lacking controls and using too small a patient sample. The plaintiff's animal studies also were excluded as insufficient to prove causation in humans. The court was careful to note, however, that epidemiological studies are not required to prove general causation in the Eighth Circuit.

Significantly, the court discounted the value of company documents and FDA pronouncements to support a causation opinion, finding that the company documents amounted to nothing more than the expression of a desire to perform more testing, and the FDA's decision to withdraw Parlodel's lactation suppression indication was based on a lower standard for evaluating causation than the proof-by-a-preponderance standard used in tort litigation. Of note, and in contrast to *Bonner v. ISP*, the Eighth Circuit in *Glastetter* expressed a conservative view towards causation theories that have yet to be validated by science.

Turner v. Iowa Fire Equip. Co., 229 F.3d 1202 (8th Cir. 2000)
Turner involved a claim by a supermarket employee that she developed reactive airway disorder syndrome (RADS) following exposure to fire extinguishing material consisting primarily of baking soda. In the month following the plaintiff's exposure, she developed blisters in her mouth and nose, black discharges, head pain, nose bleeds, and shortness of breath. Her pulmonologist, Dr. Hof,

opined that while Turner's profile was somewhat unusual due to the delayed development of symptoms following exposure, her RADS was nevertheless caused by the chemical exposure. Hof based his opinion on the plaintiff's lack of previous problems and the temporal association between the symptoms and the exposure. Hof acknowledged, though, that he had not ruled out alternative causes such as Turner's exposure to flour dust, ammonia cleaning products, or secondhand smoke. He also could not say what specific chemical in the extinguisher had caused Turner's reaction, and he misinterpreted the MSDS as containing a compound that it did not.

The court recognized that differential diagnosis—whereby an expert "rules in" the suspected cause and rules out alternative causes—is a scientifically valid methodology in the Eighth Circuit. In this case, however, it found that Dr. Hof's differential diagnosis was invalid, because it was intended only to treat Turner's condition, and not to determine medical causation. Thus, "Dr. Hof's diagnosis was, we believe, one which the medical community more properly identifies as 'differential' . . . rather than the type of *causal* diagnosis which the legal community calls 'differential.'" Because Dr. Hof arrived at his opinion "more as an afterthought" and "in an ad hoc manner," it lacked the reliability required of a *legal* differential diagnosis. The Eighth Circuit affirmed the district court's exclusion.

See also *Nat'l Bank of Commerce of El Dorado v. Associated Milk Producers, Inc.*, 191 F.3d 858 (8th Cir. 1999) (affirming exclusion of plaintiff's expert's opinion regarding aflatoxin M-1 as the cause of plaintiff's laryngeal cancer; addressing the different levels of proof needed to support a regulatory action level versus establishing tort liability; noting that the expert's differential diagnosis was "entitled to more weight than it was given by the district court," but the absence of proof of any correlation between aflatoxin M-1 and laryngeal cancer, plaintiff's inability to prove a threshold exposure level, and the litigation-driven nature of the expert's opinion were sufficient to "tip the scales" in favor of exclusion); *Hose v. Chicago & Northwestern Transp. Co.*, 70 F.3d 968 (8th Cir. 1996) (affirming admission of expert testimony regarding causation of manganese encephalopathy in plaintiff, a welder who alleged he was exposed to toxic fumes; despite limitations, PET scan and polysomnogram study results could be used to support the opinion); *Sorenson by and through Dunbar v. Shaklee Corp.*, 31 F.3d 638 (8th Cir. 1994) (affirming exclusion of expert testimony that plaintiffs' ingestion of alfalfa tablets caused their children's developmental disabilities; in addition to failing all of *Daubert*'s requirements, the proffered opinion testimony was not relevant because plaintiffs produced no evidence showing or providing a reliable inference that the alfalfa tablets they consumed actually contained ethylene oxide, the substance that allegedly caused the harm).

2. Product Design, Human Factors, and Warnings

In re Zurn Pex Plumbing Products Liability Litigation, 644 F.3d 604 (8th Cir. 2011)
In considering whether to certify a class of homeowners who had particular brass fittings connecting PEX tubes installed as part of their plumbing systems, the district court conducted a "focused *Daubert* inquiry" and admitted the testimony of two plaintiff experts, Roger Staehle and Wallace Blischke, about product defect. A class was certified on warranty and negligence claims, including homeowners whose pipes had not yet leaked, and defendants brought a Rule 23(f) interlocutory appeal of the class certification order. Zurn argued that the district court should have excluded the expert opinions and that it erred in declining to conduct a full *Daubert* inquiry before class certification. A majority of the Eighth Circuit panel affirmed, over a dissent.

The majority affirmed the district court's analysis, which it said considered the reliability of expert testimony in light of the evidence available at the class certification stage and which it characterized as consistent with precedent in *Blades v. Monsanto Co.*, 400 F.3d 562 (8th Cir. 2005). Using this approach, the Eighth Circuit did not find it an abuse of discretion to consider Dr. Staehle's tests, challenged by Zurn as applying an unrealistic amount of strain on the fittings. This "specific numbers" dispute went to the weight and accuracy, not to the method or admissibility, of the testimony. A trial court has "considerable" discretion regarding admissibility of expert testimony when factual bases for the testimony are disputed.

The majority also considered Dr. Blischke's testimony that 99 percent of homes would have a leak in at least one fitting within the twenty-five-year limited warranty period. In arriving at this conclusion, Blischke, a statistician, presumed a mean time to failure of forty years and an average household "count" of fifty fittings. Zurn disputed the basis for both presumptions, noting in particular that Blischke's assumed failure rate was based in part on a Zurn erosion test in which *no* fitting failed within forty years. The majority affirmed the district court's allowance of the testimony, finding it acceptable for the final admissibility decision to await full fact discovery.

The dissenting judge disagreed, finding it "counterintuitive" to allow district courts to use inadmissible expert testimony to resolve factual disputes at the class certification stage and finding the real concern to be not a premature expert analysis, but "that the case will proceed beyond class certification on the basis of *inadmissible*, unreliable expert testimony." 644 F.3d at 630 (emphasis in original). The dissenting judge would have remanded for a full *Daubert* inquiry, particularly given the significance of the presumed mean failure rate—and the resulting calculation that almost all homeowners would have at least one fitting fail under warranty—to the district court's conclusion that all homeowners had been injured in fact, even if their fittings had not yet leaked.

Notably, the majority supported its decision in part by saying the "main purpose" of exclusion under *Daubert* is to "protect juries from being swayed by dubious scientific testimony." "This interest," the court said, "is not implicated at the class certification stage where the judge is the decision maker." 644 F.3d at 613. In a subsequent Eighth Circuit decision, this aspect of *Zurn* was cited to support admission of a government compensation expert under the "relaxed *Daubert* standard" applicable in a bench trial. *David E. Watson, P.C. v. United States*, 668 F.3d 1008, 1015 (8th Cir. 2012).

Khoury v. Philips Medical Systems, 614 F.3d 888 (8th Cir. 2010)
Plaintiff doctor was injured while performing an angiogram, when a nurse without warning moved a monitor bank installed on a single ceiling track along with a radiation shield. Plaintiff grabbed the shield so it would not hit the patient, injuring his back. After some confusion, the claim was characterized as one for defect in the single track design.

The district court then excluded testimony from Dr. Andres, an ergonomics expert. Dr. Andres was qualified to address the force and biomechanical stress the plaintiff suffered when trying to block the device, but was not qualified in the design of medical devices or laboratories. Alternatively, his testimony was unreliable for lack of testing, insufficient examination and failure to consider the surrounding circumstances. The exclusion was affirmed.

DG&G, Inc. v. FlexSol Packaging Corp. of Pompano Beach, 576 F.3d 820 (8th Cir. 2009)
Plaintiff cotton gin operator sued for failure to warn and product defect when cotton bales became molded after being placed in polyethylene bags made by defendant FlexSol. The district court, which dismissed the claims on summary judgment, excluded expert testimony by Robert Bockserman, who had conducted inadequate tests on different bags. The Eighth Circuit affirmed.

Sappington v. Skyjack, Inc., 512 F.3d 440 (8th Cir. 2008)
The case arose out of a workplace accident involving a fatal fall from a scissors lift, which became unstable and fell over when its wheels dropped into a hole. The district court granted defendants' motion to exclude plaintiffs' expert testimony, leading to summary judgment on the products liability claim. Plaintiffs, decedent's mother and children, appealed.

The Eighth Circuit reversed. First, the court noted that Missouri law did not require plaintiffs to proffer expert testimony on this claim. Second, the Eighth Circuit rejected the district court's bases for excluding expert testimony. The Eighth Circuit concluded that the district court had fundamentally misunderstood the plaintiffs' theory of the case. Specifically, the Eighth Circuit found that the district court's analysis related to a claim plaintiffs did not make: that the scissors lift model the decedent was operating at the time of the accident should have been retrofitted with a "pothole protection" design feature found in the later model. Rather, the plaintiffs were contending that the accident would not have happened if the decedent had been operating the later model itself, and that this reasonable alternative design had been available and should have been used when the at-issue lift was made. Because the district court misconstrued plaintiffs' theory of the case, it erroneously found testing by Bryan Johnson to be irrelevant. Johnson tested the later lift model to determine whether it would have remained upright if the decedent had been operating it at the time he fell. The district court thought the appropriate test would have used the model decedent actually had been operating, retrofitted with pothole protection. In finding an abuse of discretion, the Eighth Circuit also discounted differences between the accident scene and the test conditions that had been cited by the district court.

The Eighth Circuit also found an abuse of discretion in the district court's exclusion of testimony by James Blundell, an associate professor of engineering, who relied on Johnson's testing as well as his own review of depositions, accident scene photographs, reports authored by plaintiffs' other experts, the OSHA investigation file, defendant manufacturer documents and testing, lift operation manuals and ANSI standards, among other materials. In addition to concluding that Johnson's tests were an admissible basis for the second expert's opinion, the appellate court found it appropriate for Blundell to rely on Skyjack's own product testing of the later lift model, as well as on evidence that another manufacturer began employing "pothole protection" in its lifts as early as 1987.

Notably, this decision cited favorably to the Eighth Circuit's earlier opinion in *Lauzon v. Senco Products, Inc.*, 270 F.3d 681 (8th Cir. 2001). There, the court characterized Rule 702 as an attempt to "liberalize the rules governing the admission of expert testimony" and called the rule "clearly one of admissibility rather than exclusion." *Sappington*, 512 F.3d at 448. Also cited was *Wood v. Minn. Mining & Mfg. Co.*, 112 F.3d 306 (8th Cir. 1997), for its holding that an expert's opinion should be excluded "only if it is so fundamentally unsupported that it can offer no assistance to the jury." Not all Eighth Circuit courts cite these cases. Not surprisingly, those that do typically find expert testimony to have been admissible.

Ahlberg v. Chrysler Corp., 481 F.3d 630 (8th Cir. 2007)
This case arose out of a fatal accident. An unattended child shifted a Dodge Ram truck out of park and into neutral or reverse with its engine running; the child's grandfather attempted to stop the truck, which had begun rolling down a driveway, and was fatally injured during his attempt.

At the Eighth Circuit, plaintiffs sought review of, among other things, the magistrate judge's ruling excluding the testimony of their expert witness Paul Sheridan, a former Chrysler employee who had chaired a minivan safety leadership team. During his employment at Chrysler, Sheridan had participated in retrofitting Chrysler vehicles with brake-shift interlock (BSI) devices. Chrysler had implemented BSI devices on some vehicle lines, but not the Dodge Ram truck at issue. The BSI device required the user of a vehicle to depress the brake pedal before shifting out of park in order to prevent unintended acceleration. Plaintiffs proffered Sheridan in support of their argument that the Dodge Ram truck's lack of a BSI device rendered it unreasonably dangerous. Plaintiffs contended that the only real qualification their expert needed was to understand generally how the BSI device worked and the risk posed by not incorporating it into the vehicle's design.

The Eighth Circuit held that the district court did not abuse its discretion by excluding Sheridan's testimony. Key to rulings in both courts was that Sheridan had employed no methodology in forming his opinion. Plaintiffs failed to describe Sheridan's techniques, and none were discernible from the record. Moreover, although Sheridan described himself as an engineer, he did not have an engineering degree. Rather, Sheridan attributed his engineering credentials to his experience in dealing with engineers and having been involved with technical issues at Chrysler. Indeed, plaintiffs argued that the relevant peer group for *Daubert*'s "peer review" consideration was Sheridan's coworkers at Chrysler. The court readily dismissed this contention, observing if that proposition were correct, then any employee could arguably be considered an expert on account of the fact that he or she worked with others. The court also held that plaintiffs' arguments concerning error rate and general acceptance failed because plaintiff did not address *any* methodology actually used by Sheridan.

Smith v. Cangieter, 462 F.3d 920 (8th Cir. 2006)

The survivors of passengers killed in a rental car accident and the injured driver of another car sued the rental car's manufacturer, among others. Plaintiffs offered an expert in mechanical engineering to testify that use of the car's part-time four-wheel drive on dry, asphalt roadways at highway speeds resulted in instability during steering and braking, which caused the accident. After a *Daubert* hearing, the district court excluded the testimony of plaintiffs' expert and granted the corporate defendants' motions for summary judgment.

The Eighth Circuit affirmed, noting that the expert's qualifications were not at issue, but only the reliability of his methodology. Plaintiffs' expert cited peer-reviewed articles indicating that part-time four-wheel drive systems can cause slippage and loss of traction. This testimony alone was insufficient to prove defect. Plaintiffs' expert did not offer the results of any testing to demonstrate that his theory was accurate, leaving no known rate of error. Plaintiffs' expert did not present accident data, produce testing performed by others or perform his own mathematical calculations to support his conclusions. His approach had not been considered by the scientific community and no supporting peer-reviewed articles existed. While plaintiffs argued that the expert had supported his opinion with several exhibits, including the vehicle's owner's manual, information regarding slippage in a competitor's vehicles and documents from an information website, the court concluded that none of these embodied any testing, accident data, or peer-reviewed analysis.

Pro Service Automotive, LLC v. Lenan Corp., 469 F.3d 1210 (8th Cir. 2006)

After losing a commercial automotive garage to a fire, plaintiff garage owners sued the manufacturer of a waste oil heater which they alleged caused the fire. The district court excluded the causation and design defect testimony of plaintiffs' experts and granted summary judgment for the defendant. On appeal, plaintiffs argued that the trial court erred in excluding the expert testimony of their causation witness, a chemical engineer and heating equipment expert, Alan Bullerdiek. Bullerdiek said a hole in an internal wall of the heater had allowed the development of localized hot spots that could start a fire either by overheating the airstream blowing through the heater or by conveying excess heat to the outer heater cabinet and consequently to nearby surfaces.

The Eighth Circuit affirmed the exclusion. Plaintiffs' expert performed no testing or other engineering analysis to support his opinion. Rather, he relied only on his expertise. He did not attempt to calculate where or how hot the theoretical "hot spots" were, or to identify a known or potential error rate for his analysis. He did not even provide a rough estimate as to how much heat would be transferred to these hot spots and whether it would be sufficient to ignite combustibles. His opinion was further compromised by his observation that the internal hole in the heater had been present during heater operation for weeks, or perhaps even months before the fire. He was unable to explain why the heater functioned without incident for that period. Without admissible causation testimony, the court affirmed the summary judgment ruling for defendant.

Wagner v. Hesston Corp., 450 F.3d 756 (8th Cir. 2006)

Plaintiff farmer sued a hay baler manufacturer and related entities after he lost his left hand and part of his arm in an accident. Defendants moved to exclude his expert testimony and for summary judgment. Both motions were granted. The Eighth Circuit affirmed, finding no abuse of discretion.

Plaintiff expert John Sevart had said defendants' hay baler was defective in design and manufacture because it was not adequately guarded, should have employed an alternate design and lacked an emergency stop system that would have prevented plaintiff's injuries. Sevart also said that feasible design alternatives were available and/or defendants should have retrofitted the hay baler with the expert's own proprietary guard and emergency stop design. Defendants did not contest Sevart's qualifications, but did challenge the reliability of his opinions.

The Eighth Circuit noted that testing is particularly important in analyzing the reliability of alternative design proposals. While Sevart had designed and tested a proposed baler guard, he offered only minimal evidence that he had used the modified baler in sufficiently varying conditions. His test methods were not well documented. Significantly, there was no evidence that the modified baler would in fact reduce the risk of serious injury or death; Sevart had not tested his conclusion that the modified baler would avoid injury by allowing the operator to extricate himself. Sevart had not evaluated the potential injuries involved if an operator did get entangled, or whether those injuries were more or less severe than those his design was intended to address.

In his several published papers related to agricultural machine guarding, Sevart never addressed a barrier guard for a hay baler. Cross-examination and review of Sevart's publications by the opposing party's experts did not substitute for peer review. The court rejected plaintiff's argument that Sevart's theory was generally accepted, noting no evidence in the record that any large round hay baler manufacturers had adopted Sevart's guard design. This factor weighed against admissibility, as did the fact that almost all of Sevart's tests of hay baler guards were conducted in the context of litigation.

His opinions about alternate "open throat" designs also were excluded, as the cited products were either inferior or lacking any evidence as to their effectiveness. Sevart did not meet his burden to show that defendants' own "open throat" model was available before the at-issue model was made, or that it produced bales of comparable quality.

As to the emergency stop device, Sevart did not even test the initial proposition that the lack of such a device worsened plaintiff's injuries or show that such a device would have prevented or lessened those injuries. He also failed to establish that the emergency stop device would not adversely affect the performance and maintenance of the hay baler.

Also excluded was testimony by Jonathan Chaplin, who opined that defendants' baler was defective in design and manufacture in many respects. Chaplin conducted no tests to support his opinions that the warning decal was confusing, that his alternate warning design was an improvement, or that the placement of the warning decal was ineffective; no other persons were consulted. Chaplin designed and conducted limited testing on an aluminum hay baler guard, but the court found this testing inadequate and there was no evidence it was subjected to peer review or was generally accepted in the agricultural engineering community. The court noted that his design was developed in connection with litigation and found his opinion speculative and inadmissible. Other aspects of his testimony were excluded as well.

Unrein v. Timesavers, Inc., 394 F.3d 1008 (8th Cir. 2005)
In this products liability case, the plaintiff was severely injured when her hand was caught in an industrial sander. The plaintiff's expert alleged that the sander was defectively designed because there was no "safeguarding" to block a user's hand from entering the infeed area of the device and no braking device that would quickly stop the conveyer belt feeding into the device. Although the machine was posted with the warning "Do not place hands between work piece and conveyor belt or near rolls," the expert argued that the warning was an inadequate substitute for a design solution. He proposed that the device should have been designed with a "continuous safety trip cord" around the infeed area and a brake easily accessible to the user. The trial court held that the expert did not show that these features were feasible or compatible with the sander's operation, and for that reason excluded the expert's testimony. The Eighth Circuit affirmed, upholding the principle that

"[a] expert proposing safety modifications must demonstrate by some means that they would work to protect the machine operators but would not interfere with the machine's utility." *See also Pestel v. Vermeer Mfg. Co.*, 64 F.3d 382 (8th Cir. 1995) (affirming exclusion of insufficiently tested opinion that a safety bar guard should have been used on a stump cutter; proposed bar guard was not ready for market or generally accepted in the industry).

Shaffer v. Amada America Inc., 2003 U.S. App. Lexis 19335 (8th Cir. 2003)

Plaintiff received a serious hand injury while repairing a press brake machine and brought an action alleging that the machine was defectively designed. The district court granted defendant seller's motion *in limine* to exclude the injured party's expert witness testimony and granted summary judgment. The Eighth Circuit affirmed.

The expert was a doctor of mechanical engineering. He was going to testify to various alleged defects in the press brake, including a treadle bar defect, the lack of an electric/pneumatic switch, and the lack of built-in safety sensors. But the court found that the expert had not designed or tested the devices he claimed would have prevented the accident, that there was no peer review of his theories, and that there was no evidence of the general acceptance of his abstract theory that certain devices could have prevented the accident. He had no experience with press brake designs. He had never designed a press brake or, for that matter, any of the safety equipment he proposed. He could not identify any code or standard applying to the design, manufacture, service, or operation of press brakes. The Eighth Circuit ruled that the expert's lack of design experience or expertise involving press brakes supported the district court's exclusion of his testimony.

Anderson v. Raymond Corporation, 340 F.3d 520 (8th Cir. 2003)

Plaintiff was injured while operating a standup power lift truck and sued the manufacturer for negligence and strict liability, alleging manufacturing and design defects and failure to warn. Plaintiff's expert witness opined that the lift truck was defectively designed because it had an open cockpit with no operator restraints; had no warnings regarding the potential hazards; and lacked a fail-safe design. The witness admitted he was not an expert in the design or engineering of standup lift trucks. He had never designed or consulted on the design of a standup lift truck, and had never designed a component part or a warning for a standup lift truck. He had not operated, or even seen a standup lift truck in operation before consulting on the case. Citing precedent from *Dancy v. Hyster Company*, 127 F.3d 649 (8th Cir. 1997), the Eighth Circuit found no abuse of discretion in the district court's decision that the expert was not qualified. The court further found that failure to hold a *Daubert* hearing before striking the expert was not an abuse of discretion.

Lauzon v. Senco Products, Inc., 270 F.3d 681 (8th Cir. 2001)

In *Lauzon*, a products liability case involving a pneumatic nailer, the trial court excluded the testimony of the plaintiff's expert on the ground that the expert could not reconcile his theory of defect with the record facts. The expert opined that the tool was defective because it could "double-fire"—deliver two nails when the user only intended one—and that this had occurred in Lauzon's case, driving the extra nail into the base of his thumb. Lauzon himself, however, testified that the nailer had *not* double-fired, and the only other witness to the accident submitted wavering statements, but with a similar message. The District of Minnesota excluded the expert's testimony for contradicting the record facts and for failing to meet *Daubert*'s requirements of relevance and reliability.

In reversing the trial court, the Eighth Circuit gave great weight to the expert's tests ruling out a manufacturing defect on the nailer gun plaintiff used. Having ruled out a manufacturing defect, the court held that the expert was justified in concluding the real and only remaining issue was defective design, because the gun could double-fire.

The Eighth Circuit said that experts should rule out alternative causes, but held that "this requirement cannot be carried to a quixotic extreme." The court was not persuaded that possible accident scenarios were important. Because use of an alternate nail gun design would have prevented injury under all scenarios, the expert testimony adequately addressed alternative cause.

Further, while acknowledging that research independent of litigation "provides important, objective proof that the research comports with the dictates of good science," the court found that the expert's history of testifying in forty previous nailer cases did not detract from reliability, but provided experience favoring admissibility.

When courts are in favor of admitting expert testimony, they often cite *Lauzon*.

Giles v. Miners, Inc., 242 F.3d 810 (8th Cir. 2001)
In *Giles*, a twelve-year-old girl suffered frostbite on her fingers when they stuck to the side of a reach-in "spot merchandising" freezer. The freezer was designed to operate with a layer of frost on the surface, which would have prevented the injury the girl suffered, but in this case the freezer had recently been defrosted and had not yet reaccumulated the protective frost layer. The plaintiff's expert, Gumz, opined that the freezer should have incorporated a "mesh guard" in order to prevent frostbite injuries from occurring in these circumstances. The district court excluded this testimony on the ground that Gumz had not analyzed how the proposed guard would interact with the freezer's proper functioning.

The Eighth Circuit affirmed, holding that "even if Gumz's testimony had been admitted, the plaintiffs did not have sufficient evidence to create a fact issue as to whether such an alternative design was feasible." The court also observed that the proposed guard "would violate government and industry design standards, which require a sanitary, easily cleanable surface, rather than one that allows the growth of mold and bacteria." Therefore, summary judgment on the products claim was affirmed, although the case was remanded to determine whether the store owner could have foreseen that injuries would occur if the freezer was placed in use before sufficient frost had accumulated.

See also Jaurequi v. Carter Mfg. Co., Inc., 173 F.3d 1076 (8th Cir. 1999) (affirming exclusion of opinion of mechanical engineering expert who "had not attempted to construct or even draw" the safety device he suggested should have been used on the combine that injured plaintiff; also affirming exclusion of a "human factors" expert who had not read the original warnings on the machine, designed warnings for any similar device, or tested the warnings that he claimed would have prevented plaintiff from getting injured); *Robertson v. Norton Co.*, 148 F.3d 905 (8th Cir. 1998) (reversing admission of a ceramics expert's testimony regarding the adequacy of warnings accompanying a grinding wheel; expressing concern that these opinions would invade the fact finding province of the jury, finding that the expert lacked qualification to address the warnings, and finding that the opinions were not "supported by the kind of scientific theory, practical knowledge and experience, or empirical research and testing" to qualify as valid under *Daubert*); *Dancy v. Hyster Co.*, 127 F.3d 649 (8th Cir. 1997) (affirming exclusion of expert testimony on safety guards for a lift truck because the expert had not tested his theory in any way, had not seen this type of device on any other lifts, and had not designed the device that he suggested would have prevented the injury); *Wood v. Minnesota Mining and Mfg. Co.*, 112 F.3d 306 (8th Cir. 1997) (affirming admission of a highway safety specialist's opinion that defendant did not properly construct a railroad crossing or provide reasonable warnings of the dangers the crossing presented); *Peitzmeier v. Henessey Industries, Inc.*, 97 F.3d 293 (8th Cir. 1996) (affirming exclusion of expert engineering testimony on alleged defects in a tire changer that exploded; witness had not designed or tested any of his proposed safety devices, conducted no experiments, and never subjected his proposed changes to peer review; court noted that testimony and cross-examination in other products liability cases could not take the place of scientific peer review).

3. Environmental Science

United States v. Dico, Inc., 266 F.3d 864 (8th Cir. 2001)
In this CERCLA action, the federal EPA sought to recover cleanup costs from Dico, Inc., due to its role in the contamination of the Des Moines public water supply with trichloroethylene (TCE) and other volatile organic compounds (VOCs). Dico had used TCE for many years as a degreaser and in other industrial applications. Dico disagreed with the EPA's assessment of liability and damages, however, and argued that a large portion of the contamination found on its site had migrated there from other sources. Following a bench trial, the district court awarded summary judgment to the EPA and awarded the specific amount of damages requested by the agency for groundwater remediation.

Dico argued on appeal that the trial court's decision to admit testimony from the government's expert hydrogeologist was error. Specifically, Dico maintained that the expert had failed to adequately account for alternative sources and pathways of contamination, relied on a computer model that did not accurately reflect the conditions at the site, took too few soil samples to enable a statistically reliable conclusion, and generally relied on insufficient data. The Eighth Circuit affirmed the admission, finding that the expert gave due consideration to alternative causes of the contamination. In addition, the court dismissed Dico's criticisms as affecting the weight and not the admissibility of the expert's testimony.

Wheeling Pittsburgh Steel Corp. v. Beelman River Terminals, Inc., 254 F.3d 706 (8th Cir. 2001)
Wheeling arose out of the 1993 flooding of the Mississippi River in St. Louis. Wheeling had stored approximately 3,000 tons of its steel in Beelman's riverside warehouse, which was ruined when the warehouse flooded. Wheeling claimed that Beelman should have warned Wheeling of the flood risk and should have moved the steel when it became apparent that the warehouse was going to be inundated. In its defense, Beelman relied in part on the testimony of an expert hydrologist, who testified that Beelman's actions were reasonable under the circumstances. The jury returned a verdict in favor of Beelman.

The Eighth Circuit reversed the district court's admission of testimony by Beelman's expert beyond his specific area of expertise: "[t]hough eminently qualified to testify as an expert hydrologist regarding matters of flood risk management, Dr. Curtis sorely lacked the education, employment, or other practical personal experiences to testify as an expert specifically regarding safe warehousing practices." Thus, it was error to allow "opinion testimony outside his area of expertise on ultimate issues of fact that the jury was required to answer—namely, whether Beelman's actions met the required standard of care for warehousemen."

4. Fire Cause and Origin

Presley v. Lakewood Engineering and Manufacturing, 553 F.3d 638 (8th Cir. 2009)
After sustaining property damage and personal injury in a house fire, plaintiffs sued Lakewood, alleging that a manufacturing defect in its space heater caused the fire. Plaintiffs' expert said he put this theory together "in pieces," through observations, testing, and established scientific principles. The district court excluded this testimony after a *Daubert* hearing, finding that the expert failed to apply reliably the governing fire investigation standard NFPA 921 to the facts of the case. The court found too great an inferential leap between the bases and the conclusions. Without the expert testimony, summary judgment was granted to defendant.

The Eight Circuit affirmed, finding no abuse of discretion. The court emphasized that its previous decision in *Fireman's Fund Ins. Co. v. Canon U.S.A., Inc.*, 394 F.3d 1054 (8th Cir. 2005) did not establish a bright-line rule requiring testing in all fire cases. Reliable opinions may be based on scientific observation and expertise. Experimental testing may be appropriate in certain circumstances, however, and an expert's failure to conduct experiments or use of inadequate experiments may be relevant to the *Daubert* assessment. In *Presley*, the *Daubert* assessment was affected both by the failure to conduct certain tests and by the lack of fit between tests that were conducted and the circumstances actually presented by the case. *Compare Shuck v. CNH American*, LLC, 498 F.3d 868 (8th Cir. 2007) (affirming the admission of expert testimony about the cause of a combine engine fire, based on the expert's observations and expertise, despite the lack of testing).

Hickerson v. District Pride Mobility Products Corp., 470 F.3d 1252 (8th Cir. 2006)

Plaintiff lost his wife and his home in a fire allegedly started by a defective motorized wheelchair. The district court granted defendant's motion to exclude plaintiff's expert witness because he was not an expert in the engineering or manufacturing of motorized wheelchairs or scooters, and subsequently granted defendant's motion for summary judgment. The Eighth Circuit reversed.

The Court of Appeals first noted that plaintiffs had not offered their expert to testify in the fields of electrical or mechanical design or engineering or to identify any specific alleged defect in the scooter. Rather, plaintiff offered him solely to opine on the cause and origin of the fire. Plaintiff relied entirely upon a *"res ipsa-type"* theory of implied product defect with respect to the scooter itself. The Eighth Circuit found that plaintiff's expert had extensive experience as a firefighter and fire investigator, and therefore was qualified to conduct a fire scene investigation and testify regarding the fire's origin. Defendant argued that the expert's conclusions were not supported by any reliable methodology, but the Court of Appeals was satisfied that the expert's examination of burn patterns as well as heat, fire, and smoke damage was sufficient to allow him to identify all possible causes and eliminate those other than the motorized scooter.

Weisgram v. Marley Co., 169 F.3d 514 (8th Cir. 1999); aff'd, 528 U.S. 440, 120 S. Ct. 1011 (2000)

This wrongful death case involved a claim against the manufacturer of a baseboard heating unit that allegedly caused a house fire. The plaintiff presented his case that the heater was defective through three expert witnesses: a fire chief, a "technical forensic expert," and a metallurgist. The Eight Circuit found an abuse of discretion in the district court's admission of this testimony.

While the fire chief "was qualified as a fire cause and origin expert," the court felt there was "no question that he was not qualified to offer an opinion that the Weisgram heater malfunctioned." The court concluded that his "qualification as a fire investigator did not give him free rein to speculate before the jury as to the cause of the fire by relying on inferences that have absolutely no record support." The "technical forensic expert" based his testimony almost entirely on the fire chief's observations; the court held that this testimony was also "rank speculation."

The metallurgist examined the thermostat and the "high limit control," a switch that shuts off the device at high temperatures. He opined that the thermostat was defective because it was susceptible to "welding shut" at high temperatures, creating a closed circuit and causing the device to overheat. He did no testing of this theory, however. Since he "admittedly had very limited experience with electrical contacts in small appliances and no experience with how contacts function in baseboard heaters," the court concluded that "[T]here is simply too great an analytical gap between the data and the opinion proffered." Because all three experts' testimony was speculative — and sometimes even mutually contradictory — the court excluded it and granted Marley's motion for summary judgment. Judge Bright dissented, arguing that the experts' qualifications, in addition to their examination of the fire artifacts, provided a sufficient factual basis for their testimony. He also contended that the appropriate relief for the erroneous admission of expert testimony was a new trial, not judgment as a matter of law for the defendant.

The Supreme Court granted *certiorari* to resolve the question of the appropriate relief following the Court of Appeals' finding that the district court's admission of expert testimony was an abuse of discretion. *Weisgram v. Marley Co.*, 528 U.S. 440, 120 S. Ct. 1011 (2000). The court, in an opinion by Justice Ginsburg, unanimously affirmed the Eighth Circuit's holding that F.R.C.P. 50(d) empowered it to grant judgment as a matter of law for the defense, and specifically held that the Eighth Circuit's refusal to remand for a new trial did not deprive the plaintiff of his Seventh Amendment right to a jury trial.

5. Psychiatry and Emotional Harm

Smith v. Rasmussen, 249 F.3d 755 (8th Cir. 2001)
In *Smith*, the Iowa Department of Human Services appealed the trial court's finding that the state owed Medicaid coverage to the plaintiff, a forty-one-year-old transsexual, for his sexual reassignment surgery. On appeal, the department challenged the district court's limitation of its expert's testimony to "general psychiatric principles and basic diagnostic criteria." The district court refused to allow the expert to testify regarding the effectiveness and necessity of sex reassignment surgery in general and for Smith in particular, holding that these specific areas were beyond his expertise. The Eighth Circuit upheld the trial court's limitation on the ground that the expert's testimony on the disputed subject "was based neither on his personal experience nor on his knowledge of the relevant discipline."

Nichols v. American Nat. Ins. Co., 154 F.3d 875 (8th Cir. 1998)
In *Nichols*, the district court admitted testimony in a sexual harassment case from defendant's psychiatric expert that the plaintiff had "poor psychiatric credibility," that she had difficulty in interpreting social settings, and that she had a tendency to blur fantasy with reality. The Eighth Circuit concluded that the testimony "sought to answer the very question at the heart of the jury's task—could [plaintiff] be believed?" The Court of Appeals found that the testimony was an impermissible comment on the plaintiff's credibility disguised by psychological labels, and accordingly held that the district court abused its discretion in admitting the testimony.

Jenson v. Eveleth Taconite Co., 130 F.3d 1287 (8th Cir. 1997)
In a case involving testimony from psychiatrists and psychologists on the issue of damages to plaintiffs in a sexual harassment suit for mental anguish, the Eighth Circuit found the proposed testimony to be both relevant and reliable. The plaintiffs in *Jenson* sought review of the district court's decision affirming the special master's report and recommendation for damages. The special master had found that there was "no scientifically developed psychiatric model or procedure for determining whether a particular stress caused a particular symptom or mental state." Because the evidence showed that most of the plaintiffs were subjected to outside stresses or trauma, the special master concluded that there was no reliable way of allocating proportionate causation.

The Eighth Circuit reversed, finding that the special master had abused his discretion in excluding expert testimony regarding the causation of plaintiffs' mental anguish. While the court did discuss the necessity that the proposed evidence be reliable, the decision that the evidence was admissible primarily turned upon a relevance inquiry: "The key question in these damages phases of the trial was the causal link between the actions of the defendants and the claimed emotional injuries of the plaintiffs. The evidence was therefore without doubt relevant to the issue before the court." The court further stated that the probative value of expert psychological proof regarding causation of the claimant's depression and emotional distress had been recognized by many courts.

Gier By and Through Gier v. Educational Service Unit No. 16, 66 F.3d 940 (8th Cir. 1995)
In *Gier*, plaintiffs proposed to introduce psychological testimony that their children were emotionally, physically, and sexually abused while attending an educational facility for handicapped individ-

uals. The district court excluded much of the testimony, concluding that psychologists' methodology lacked sufficient indicia of reliability under the first prong of *Daubert*. Specifically, the court found that the "Child Behavior Checklist" used by experts had not been validated for use with mentally retarded children and was insufficient on its own to establish abuse; the interview protocol did not provide specific guidance for conducting clinical interviews; the experts departed significantly from their normal practice when interviewing the children; and there was no known rate of error associated with the methodology. The court went on to find that even if the methodology were reliable for purposes of treatment, it would be reliable only to choose a course of psychotherapy and not to make factual conclusions in a legal proceeding.

6. *Economic, Accounting, and Statistical Testimony*

David E. Watson, P.C. v. United States, 668 F.3d 1008 (8th Cir. 2012)
Taxpayer sued the United States seeking a refund, based on his challenge to IRS assessments of employment taxes he owed on payments made to him by an S corporation. At the bench trial, government expert Igor Ostrovsky, a business valuation analyst, testified to the market value of plaintiff's accounting services. As the case evolved before trial, he made adjustments to his calculations to correct errors and account for new facts. Plaintiff disagreed with some facts and assumptions incorporated into his final opinion. The district court accepted his testimony and rendered a tax deficiency judgment against plaintiff.

The Eighth Circuit affirmed, giving substantial deference to the trial court and holding that disagreement about the assumptions underlying an expert's calculations does not lead to exclusion. Such issues should be addressed through cross-examination at trial and by presentation of opposing expert testimony. The appellate court discounted the importance of a *Daubert* analysis when the judge is the factfinder, concluding there was no abuse of discretion using a "relaxed *Daubert* standard in this bench trial." 668 F.3d 1008, 1015, *citing In re Zurn Pex Plumbing Prods. Liab. Litig.*, 664 F.3d 604, 613 (8th Cir. 2011).

Cole v. Homier Distributing Co., Inc., 599 F.3d 856 (8th Cir. 2010)
Plaintiff, a dealer in the sale, distribution and repair of tractors and other equipment, brought claims including breach of distributor agreements and violation of the Missouri Franchise Act. These claims were dismissed on summary judgment after the district court excluded testimony by plaintiff's disclosed expert, Dr. Bart Basi, and refused to consider supplemental evidence of damages. The Eighth Circuit affirmed the exclusion of Dr. Basi and affirmed in part the summary judgment dismissal for lack of other evidence proving damages.

The appellate court noted the wide discretion given to district courts on admissibility rulings and said an expert's opinion should be excluded if it is "so fundamentally unsupported that it can offer no assistance to the jury." Dr. Basi's report was factually flawed, because he assumed incorrectly that plaintiff lost the ability to sell Farm Pro equipment when defendant terminated the distributorship agreement. Defendant ended only the distributor status, however, and not the dealer status. The expert's lost-profits analysis accordingly was unsupported by the record and would offer no assistance to the jury. In addition, a twenty-five-year computation period based on plaintiff's retirement age failed to rise above the level of speculation and had nothing to do with an expected continuation of the contract, which could be terminated by either party for cause with ninety days' written notice.

Synergetics, Inc. v. Hurst, 477 F.3d 949 (8th Cir. 2007)
In this trade secrets case, former employees of a company that sold equipment used in eye surgeries appealed from an adverse jury verdict. Defendants asserted that the district court erred in denying

their motion *in limine* to exclude the expert testimony and report of Ronald Vollmar, a certified public accountant, financial analyst, and fraud examiner. Defendants argued that Vollmar's economic damages testimony should have been excluded because his opinions were based on an incorrect assumption regarding the number of suppliers in the relevant market. Because Vollmar was mistaken in this key assumption, defendants asserted that his testimony regarding the size of the market was unreliable and ignored significant competition.

Vollmar performed his damages assessment by using sales information provided by plaintiff's and defendants' companies. He identified common customers of both companies, then identified lost sales on products sold by defendants that were previously purchased from plaintiff and products sold by defendants that previously were only available from plaintiff.

The Eighth Circuit first observed the general rule that the factual basis of an expert's opinion goes to credibility, not admissibility, and that the appropriate way to deal with factual challenges is through cross-examination. The court found Vollmar's testimony was not so fundamentally unsupported that it could offer no assistance to the jury. Other methods for calculating damages may have been available, but so long as Vollmar's methods were generally sound, defendants' disagreement with his assumptions did not warrant exclusion of his testimony.

Margolies v. McCleary, Inc., 447 F.3d 1115 (8th Cir. 2006)

Plaintiff called an expert to testify to the damages resulting from a breach of contract. The expert was a certified public accountant with many years of experience in forecasting future business. The defendant, on appeal, claimed that the admission of the plaintiff's expert was improper because the opinion included unproven assumptions regarding market penetration, attainable market share, product classes covered by the agreement, and cost of market reentry. The Eighth Circuit found, however, that the expert had made assumptions only in areas where it was impossible to gather more concrete data due to the defendant's nonperformance. The assumptions represented the expert's best estimates, generated through consideration of past performance and potential for future performance, given current accepted market conditions. The court therefore affirmed the admission of his testimony. The court also noted that under Missouri law, the plaintiff is not required to prove the exact amount of his damages, and the expert's testimony was sufficiently reliable and relevant to meet the burden.

Wash Solutions, Inc. v. PDQ Mfg, Inc., 395 F.3d 888 (8th Cir. 2005)

In a dispute over lost profits, the defendant appealed an award of damages to the plaintiff. The defendant argued the plaintiff did not provide sufficient evidence to support a claim for future lost profits because the plaintiff's expert failed to address past sales performance and lacked knowledge of the car wash industry. After reviewing the admission for abuse of discretion, the Eighth Circuit affirmed. The court found it unnecessary for the expert to testify on historic sales performance, given the theory of recovery, and said no experience with the car wash industry was required. Plaintiff's expert was called upon only to calculate the net profit plaintiff would have made if it had received credit for certain purchases, a task the expert was qualified to perform based on his training and experience in accounting and financial reporting.

Nebraska Plastics, Inc. v. Holland Colors Americas, Inc., 408 F.3d 410 (8th Cir. 2005)

Nebraska Plastics, a manufacturer of polyvinyl chloride (PVC) products, partnered with defendant to develop pigmenting technology for the company's outdoor fencing products. Within a year of marketing the pigmented fencing, plaintiff began receiving complaints of rapid wear and discoloration. Defendant discovered that an ingredient in plaintiff's formula was unsuitable for colored outdoor products, due to its interaction with sunlight and moisture. The jury found that defendant wrongfully withheld this information so that it could continue supplying the ingredient to plaintiff.

Plaintiff was awarded damages for all warranty claims as of the date of trial, and an additional $1 million for future warranty claims. The district court excluded the plaintiff's expert testimony in support of the future damages claim, and granted defendant's motion for judgment as a matter of law on the future damages.

The Eighth Circuit affirmed the exclusion. The expert's calculation assumed that every pound of pigmented fencing product would eventually be the subject of a warranty claim. But the court found that the expert had failed to account for the fact that, depending on climate, sun exposure, and the color of the product, not all of the fencing would fade within the warranty period. As of the date of trial, warranty claims had been asserted for only 3.5 percent of the total amount sold. Since the expert "failed to take into account a plethora of specific facts tending to show limits on the amount of defective fencing that would be the subject of future warranty claims," the court found no abuse of discretion in the exclusion.

Marvin Lumber and Cedar Co. v. PPG Industries Inc., 401 F.3d 901 (8th Cir. 2005)

Marvin, a manufacturer of wood windows, alleged that PPG's wood preservative failed to perform as warranted, resulting in large numbers of claims against Marvin for premature deterioration of its products. Marvin prevailed at trial. On appeal, PPG challenged the trial court's admission, over a *Daubert* challenge, of a statistician's testimony that Marvin's wood-rot problems were attributable to the ineffectiveness of PPG's preservative. PPG argued that the statistician's study was litigation-based, that his underlying data was collected by an "unblinded" Marvin employee, that the sample size was too small and not collected from a representative geographical cross-section, and that the study failed to account for other causes of wood rot.

The Eighth Circuit affirmed the admission of the testimony. The court characterized PPG's arguments as directed to the factual basis for the expert's analysis, and "not to its evidentiary reliability." Thus, it was not an abuse of discretion to admit the testimony and let the jury decide its weight.

Craftsmen Limousine, Inc. v. Ford Motor Co., 363 F.3d 761 (8th Cir. 2004)

Plaintiff alleged that defendants, an automobile manufacturer and limousine manufacturer, had conspired in violation of the Sherman Act to prevent the plaintiff from advertising in trade publications and from attending trade shows. The plaintiff prevailed at trial.

The Eighth Circuit rejected the defendants' contention that the evidence was insufficient to establish a conspiracy, but it nevertheless vacated the judgment after concluding the district court erred in applying a "per se" analysis for the alleged Sherman Act violations. Because safety concerns were arguably a motivating factor behind the automobile manufacturer's actions, the court found that the jury should have analyzed the evidence under the "rule of reason." The court also concluded that the plaintiff's expert had sufficient education and experience to testify on damages, but that the testimony was inadmissible under Fed. R. Evid. 702 because his opinion failed to incorporate all material factors in the relevant market. The expert did not analyze whether general economic conditions or increased competition affected plaintiff's growth rate; his study simply assumed that defendants' actions were responsible for all of plaintiff's alleged losses. The Eighth Circuit held that this testimony was unreliable and did not aid the jury in determining whether there was an unreasonable restraint of trade in violation of the Sherman Act. The court vacated the damages award and sent the case back for a new trial on the Sherman Act claim, while leaving open the possibility that the expert could testify in the retrial if he reformulated his opinion according to the "rule of reason" analysis.

After remand, plaintiff retained an expert economist to conduct the analysis as described by the Eighth Circuit. His opinions were excluded and summary judgment was granted and appealed. Because the basis for exclusion was closely related to the substantive decision that the analysis did not fit the "rule of reason" test, the appellate court reviewed the record as a whole. The dismissal was affirmed. *Craftsmen Limousine, Inc. v. Ford Motor Co.*, 491 F.3d 380 (8th Cir. 2007).

Morgan v. United Parcel Service, 380 F.3d 459 (8th Cir. 2004)

A group of UPS employees appealed the dismissal of their individual and class claims of discrimination. In support of their claims, plaintiffs produced reports, statistical analyses, and models of UPS's employment data and practices prepared by two experts. UPS offered its expert's statistical analysis in response. UPS moved to bar the plaintiffs' expert testimony under *Daubert,* alleging faulty methodology and unreliable data. The district court granted summary judgment in favor of UPS on all class claims.

Plaintiffs' discrimination case hinged on a regression analysis by their experts. Contrary to the experts' conclusions, the district court found that any racial disparity in managers' pay was caused by factors other than race. Using an abuse of discretion standard, the Eighth Circuit deferred to the district court's ruling, finding that its analysis hinged on problems with plaintiffs' analysis that were arguably methodological. A key fact in the Eighth Circuit analysis was that the plaintiffs' experts excluded past pay. The experts admitted that if past pay were included, no statistically significant disparity would exist.

Meterlogic, Inc. v. KLT, Inc., 368 F.3d 1017 (8th Cir. 2004)

Meterlogic involved a claim for breach of a contract to distribute remote metering technology and services for copiers and other business machines. Plaintiff's expert was to testify regarding the discounted present value of plaintiff's defunct business. The trial court identified a number of flaws in the expert's analysis: He predicted financial results ten years into the future, even though the parties' contract extended only two years and either party could terminate at any time; he assumed plaintiff would be the sole vendor of the technology at issue, even though the contract was nonexclusive; he assumed the parties would have a level of market share that was not supported by any market research; he assumed an unrealistically high annual growth rate; he had no data or projections on how many devices would be sold; and he admitted his analysis was based on a speculative report that was intended only as an investment-planning tool. The district court concluded that the proposed testimony was so unreliable that it had no value to the finder of fact, and excluded it.

On appeal, plaintiff argued that the expert's testimony should have been admitted because the report on which it was based was an admission of a party opponent. But the Eighth Circuit observed that the expert's reliance on the report was only one of the many problems the district court had found with the expert's methodology. The Eighth Circuit found no abuse of discretion and affirmed the exclusion of the testimony.

Group Health Plan, Inc. v. Philip Morris USA, Inc., 344 F.3d 753 (8th Cir. 2003)

On behalf of their policyholders, health insurers brought consumer protection claims against cigarette manufacturers. The HMOs' expert, an economics professor at MIT and a treating physician at Massachusetts General Hospital, postulated a "counterfactual" world in which the tobacco companies' alleged misconduct never occurred. According to his theory, cigarettes in the "counterfactual world" would be safer because the defendants would not have blocked safety innovations; at the same time, people would smoke less because the defendants would not have hidden the dangers of smoking from the public. To arrive at a damages figure, he simply subtracted estimated smoking-related health care expenditures in the counterfactual world from the amount actually spent over the same period in the real world. The HMOs conceded that the expert's report involved some speculation, but said this was inevitable due to the impossibility of undoing the decades-long conspiracy.

The district court excluded the testimony, finding the analysis unduly speculative and criticizing the estimations as being nothing but an "inspired guess." This meant that the expert failed to establish a reliable causal nexus between the tobacco companies' alleged misconduct and the HMOs' claimed damages. While the Eighth Circuit found the proposed testimony more compelling than the trial judge did, the Eighth Circuit nevertheless affirmed, extending great deference to the district court and finding no clear error or abuse of discretion in the exclusion of the testimony.

Children's Broadcasting Corp. v. Walt Disney Co., 245 F.3d 1008 (8th Cir. 2001)
This case involved claims for breach of contract and misappropriation of trade secrets. After the jury awarded the plaintiff $20 million, the district court granted the defendant's motion for judgment as a matter of law and for a new trial. In granting the motions, the court held that the causation theory advanced by the plaintiff's expert lacked credible analysis and factual support, noting that his damages projections "went so far beyond realistic optimism as to be 'fairy-tale-like.'"

The Eighth Circuit reversed the judgment as a matter of law because the evidence "support[ed] the jury's finding that the breach of contract and the misappropriation of the advertiser list caused harm to Children's," and there was enough evidence to allow the jury to estimate Children's damages. The court affirmed the exclusion of the expert's testimony, however, because he failed to consider the effect of competition on Children's, his theory of causation was questionable, and his testimony was based on a report prepared before Children's claims were narrowed for trial. The court also found that the admission of Willis's testimony likely tainted the jury's damages calculation. Accordingly, the Eighth Circuit remanded the case for a new trial limited to damages.

Concord Boat Corp. v. Brunswick Corp., 207 F.3d 1039 (8th Cir. 2000)
In this antitrust action, a group of boat builders alleged that defendant had engaged in anticompetitive behavior in the market for recreational boat engines. To prove their damages, plaintiffs presented the testimony of an economist, Dr. Robert Hall. Dr. Hall calculated the estimated damages using a method known as the Cournot model, which predicts that as the number of firms competing in a market increases, the relative concentration of the market decreases and the equilibrium price falls toward the competitive level. Brunswick charged that its market share gains occurred for reasons wholly outside of the alleged misconduct, and that Hall's use of the Cournot model failed to distinguish between lawful and unlawful conduct. The trial court allowed Dr. Hall to testify, holding that Brunswick's argument was with the *application* of the Cournot model, rather than the model itself, which the court found reliable. The trial resulted in a plaintiff's verdict.

The Eighth Circuit reversed. The court found that "[n]ot all relevant circumstances were incorporated into the expert's method of analysis," and that Dr. Hall's use of the Cournot model "was not grounded in the economic reality of the [boat] engine market, for it ignored inconvenient evidence." Further, "[t]he model also failed to account for market events that both sides agreed were not related to any anticompetitive conduct." Consequently, Dr. Hall's testimony could not have supported the jury's verdict, which was identical to Dr. Hall's number. The court remanded for entry of judgment in Brunswick's favor.

See also *Blue Dane Simmental Corp. v. American Simmental Assoc.*, 178 F.3d 1035 (8th Cir. 1999) (affirming exclusion of an agricultural economist's opinion that changes in defendants' certification practices for cattle caused a decrease in their value; "[a]lthough Dr. Baquet utilized a method of analysis typical within his field, that method is not typically used to make statements regarding causation without considering all independent variables that could affect the conclusion," something the expert did not do).

7. *Accident Reconstruction*

Fireman's Fund Ins. Co. v. Canon U.S.A., Inc., 394 F.3d 1054 (8th Cir. 2005)
This case arose from a fire in a strip-mall video store. Insurers of property owners affected by the fire sought contribution from Canon, based the St. Paul Fire Department's finding that a Canon copier in the back of the store was the most likely origin of the fire. The insurers' experts attempted to recreate the accident in order to prove that the copier caught fire due to a design defect. The district court found, however, that the experts' reconstruction failed to comply with professional standards promulgated by the National Fire Protection Association, most notably NFPA 921, which requires

that hypotheses of fire origin be carefully examined against empirical data obtained from the scene. The district court found that the experts' experimental testing not only failed to generate a fire, but also bypassed a key fire safety feature built into the copier. The testing was designed to support the experts' hypothesis, but both the testing and the hypothesis failed to comport with evidence of the actual conditions at the scene, and the experts' testimony was therefore excluded.

The Eighth Circuit found no abuse of discretion. The court noted that experimental evidence "falls on a spectrum" in terms of the foundation required for its admissibility: "The more the experiment appears to simulate the accident, the more similar the conditions of the experiment must be to the actual accident conditions." The concern is that "accident reconstruction" testing that does not faithfully replicate the actual circumstances will confuse and mislead the jury. Since the testing in this case appeared to recreate the accident, the conditions needed to closely resemble those of the actual fire; because they did not, it was appropriate for the district court to exclude the testimony.

By contrast, when tests are done to demonstrate abstract or general scientific principles, the substantially similar requirement does not apply. This distinction was highlighted recently in *Dunn v. Nexgrill Industries, Inc.*, where the Eighth Circuit affirmed the exclusion of expert testimony that a propane gas grill started a fire. 636 F.3d 1049 (8th Cir. 2011). The district court did not abuse its discretion in finding that certain elements of the expert's tests suggested an effort to recreate the fire's cause and origin; yet in important ways, the test scenarios differed from the actual scene.

J.B. Hunt Transport, Inc. v. General Motors Corp., 243 F.3d 441 (8th Cir. 2001)

J.B. Hunt involved a collision between a Camaro and an eighteen-wheeler. The truck driver's employer settled with a severely injured passenger in the Camaro, then brought a contribution action against GM, alleging that the seats in the Camaro were not crashworthy. Plaintiff offered the testimony of an accident reconstructionist and a self-declared expert in "foamology." The trial court excluded both experts' testimony as unreliable and unsupported by the facts, and a defense verdict followed.

The Eighth Circuit held that the accident reconstructionist's testimony was properly excluded as lacking sufficient connection to the facts:

> Unlike defendants' accident reconstructionist, whose testimony utilized the testimony given by other witnesses, [plaintiff's expert's] theory was premised primarily upon his impressions of the photographs of the scratches in the paint of the vehicles involved in the accident. In fact, [plaintiff's expert] conceded he had insufficient evidence to completely reconstruct the accident as he theorized.

Since "[e]xpert testimony that is speculative is not competent proof and contributes nothing to a legally sufficient evidentiary basis," the district court properly excluded the reconstructionist's testimony. As for the "foamologist," his opinions relied heavily on the excluded reconstructionist's flawed account; further, the court found that he had "received no formal training or course work in foam (nor do we know of any that exists in this area)." Accordingly, the Eighth Circuit affirmed the trial court's exclusion of his testimony.

8. *Professional Malpractice*

In *First Union National Bank v. Benham*, 423 F.3d 855 (8th Cir. 2005), plaintiff, a bank and trustee of an Arkansas trust, brought a legal malpractice claim against the trust's counsel for failing to file a valuation action after the trust acquired stock through a merger. Plaintiff offered expert testimony from an Arkansas attorney regarding the standard of care. The district court excluded the expert's testimony based on his lack of relevant qualifications. The Eighth Circuit reversed.

The Eighth Circuit held that "[t]he district court's ruling cannot be reconciled with Rule 702, which expressly allows a witness to qualify as an expert based on his own knowledge, skill, experience, training, or education," which the court found adequate to address the issues in the case. The attorney had thirty-six years of experience with mergers and acquisitions and had been involved with several valuation actions over the course of his practice. It was therefore an abuse of discretion to exclude the testimony based on the expert's purported lack of qualifications.

While *Benham* allowed attorney expert testimony in the context of a professional malpractice claim, as a general rule legal opinion testimony is not permitted in the Eighth Circuit. In *In re Acceptance Insurance Companies Securities Litigation*, 423 F.3d 899 (8th Cir. 2005), the court made clear that "When expert opinions are little more than legal conclusions, a district court should not be held to have abused its discretion by excluding such statements."

9. *Daubert Procedural Issues—Civil Cases*

a. Preserving *Daubert* Challenge on Appeal

In *McKnight By and Through Ludwig v. Johnson Controls, Inc.* 36 F.3d 1396 (8th Cir. 1994), a case involving a car battery explosion, defendant appealed a $1.2 million jury verdict based in part on the trial court's admission of expert testimony. Defendant claimed that plaintiff's expert's testimony lacked sufficient foundation under *Daubert* and Rules 702 and 703. The Eighth Circuit held, however, that defendant failed to object to the expert's trial testimony at the time it was offered. The court held that "Without an objection and a proper request for relief, the matter is waived and will receive no consideration on appeal absent plain error." Eighth Circuit decisions since *McKnight* have reaffirmed that, to preserve a *Daubert* challenge for appeal, the opponent of the expert testimony must object before the testimony is given at trial. *See, e.g., Forklifts of St. Louis, Inc. v. Komatsu Forklift USA, Inc.*, 178 F.3d 1030, 1035 (8th Cir. 1999) (holding that, where Komatsu failed to object to specific points of damages expert's testimony at trial, "[f]or Komatsu to suggest that the district court abused its discretion by not excluding this testimony *sua sponte* borders on the absurd").

For an application of the plain error standard when no challenge was raised at trial, see *Olson v. Ford Motor Co.*, 481 F.3d 619 (8th Cir. 2007) (affirming admission of expert testimony on conversion of alcohol level measured in vitreous humor to expected blood alcohol level).

b. Exclusion as a Sanction for Noncompliance with Scheduling Order

The Eighth Circuit has affirmed trial courts' use of sanctions to punish noncompliance with discovery orders relating to experts. In *Sylla-Sawdon v. Uniroyal Goodrich Tire Co.*, 47 F.3d 277 (8th Cir. 1995), the court held that the district court was within its discretion in limiting the testimony of plaintiffs' expert, based on plaintiffs' "flagrant disregard" of the court's scheduling order. *Id.* at 283–84. Similarly, in *Hunt v. City of Minneapolis*, 203 F.3d 524 (8th Cir. 1999); *op. vacated, reh'g granted, op. refiled as modified* (Feb. 11, 2000), the Eighth Circuit affirmed dismissal based on plaintiffs' failure to, among other things, timely disclose expert witness pursuant to F.R.C.P. 26(a)(2)(B)).

In the *In re Baycol Products Litigation* decision, the Eighth Circuit affirmed exclusion of a plaintiff's supplemental expert witness report, amended to address specific causation issues after the defendant had deposed the expert and moved for summary judgment based on his initial report and deposition. 596 F.3d 884, 888 (8th Cir. 2010). The district court's "broad discretion" to establish and enforce discovery deadlines, as well as the lack of any good reason explaining the late change in approach by the expert, meant the district court had not abused its discretion. *Id.* Nor had a different trial court abused its discretion in denying plaintiff's attempt to withdraw her primary causation expert in the face of a motion *in limine* to exclude that expert, and to redesignate other experts to cover the issue. *Marmo v. Tyson Fresh Meats, Inc.*, 457 F.3d 748 (8th Cir. 2006). This would unfairly prejudice defendant, who had relied on plaintiff's designations to plan its strategy. *See also Miller v. Baker Implement Co.*, 439 F.3d 407 (8th Cir. 2006) (denying plaintiff's motion to designate a new witness after his experts were excluded, leading to summary judgment).

c. Recovery of Costs Following Successful *Daubert* Motion

Costs may be available to the winner of a *Daubert* motion. In *Glastetter*, Novartis recovered $15,525.26 in costs for expert witness fees and travel expenses, transcripts, deposition fees, and photocopying expenses. The Eighth Circuit affirmed the trial court's cost award. *Glastetter v. Novartis Pharms. Corp.*, 252 F.3d 986, 992–93 (8th Cir. 2001).

d. *Daubert* and Class Certification

In *Blades v. Monsanto Co.*, 400 F.3d 562 (8th Cir. 2005), a group of farmers brought a class action against several agribusiness firms for conspiring to inflate prices and limit production of corn and soybean seeds. Plaintiffs offered expert testimony to meet the requirement of commonality necessary to certify the class. The district court denied class certification because "[t]he dynamics of this localized industry make it highly unlikely that the existence and workings of the alleged conspiracy could be shown through common proof." On appeal, plaintiffs argued that the district court had improperly resolved disputes between the parties' experts that went to the merits. The Eighth Circuit held that the district court's findings "were properly limited to whether, if appellants' basic allegations were true, common evidence could suffice, given the factual setting of the case, to show classwide injury." In other words, the trial court appropriately considered the implications for class certification of the defendants' arguments, without actually deciding the reliability and admissibility of the plaintiffs' expert testimony under *Daubert*.

Citing *Blades*, a subsequent Eighth Circuit decision affirmed a district court's class certification order following a "focused" *Daubert* inquiry based on the information available at that time. *In re Zurn Pex Plumbing Prods. Liab. Litig.*, 644 F.3d 604, 613–14 (8th Cir. 2011). A dissenting opinion found error in the application, arguing that *Blades* addressed "the scope of the district court's fact finding with respect to conflicting expert testimony, not whether the testimony should have been admitted in the first place." 644 F.3d at 627. The dissent thought it important to conduct a full *Daubert* inquiry when the expert testimony is central to class certification and the reliability of the opinion has been challenged. In *Zurn*, a statistician's designation of a presumed failure rate for brass fittings was critical to the court's finding that all homeowners had been injured in fact, even if their fittings had not yet leaked, because this failure rate was incorporated into calculations predicting that almost all homeowners would have at least one fitting fail within the warranty period. The presumed rate was contrary to certain record evidence.

B. KEY EIGHTH CIRCUIT DECISIONS APPLYING *DAUBERT*— CRIMINAL CASES

1. *Gas Chromatography/Mass Spectrometry ("GC/MS") Testing*

In *United States v. $141,770.00 in United States Currency*, 157 F.3d 600 (8th Cir. 1998), Rafael Moreno-Pena appealed from a civil forfeiture action, in which the government seized $141,770.00

from Moreno-Pena as money used or intended to be used to facilitate illegal drug trafficking. It was determined that the money seized contained traces of drug residue after a drug-sniffing dog alerted to the money. To discredit the dog's positive alert, Moreno-Pena sought to introduce testimony from a forensic chemist that 99 percent of U.S. currency is contaminated with some amount of drug residue. In reaching his opinion, the chemist used bills brought to him by the narcotics division of certain police departments and tested for traces of drug residue using gas chromatography and mass spectrometry.

The Eighth Circuit held that the proposed testimony was properly excluded under *Daubert* as unreliable and irrelevant. The court noted that bills seized during narcotics investigations are not necessarily representative of the general population of currency in circulation. Therefore, the expert's sample was too small to support the conclusion that 99 percent of currency in circulation is contaminated with drug residue; at best, the test results showed that most bills that are seized in narcotics investigations contain traces of drug residue. The court then determined that the chemist's methodology did not bear any of the indicia of reliability set forth in *Daubert*, because (1) he had not submitted his results to peer review; (2) his rate of error was unknowable, but potentially quite high since he handled many bills without changing gloves; (3) his test results could not be replicated; and (4) he did not make use of controls.

Turning to the question of relevance or "fit," the court stated that even if the testimony were reliable, it was irrelevant. The authorities in this case determined the money was contaminated through the use of a drug-sniffing dog, not a gas chromatograph/mass spectrometer as used by the chemist. As a result, the chemist could not testify as to the level of contamination which must exist before a drug-sniffing dog will alert, or as to the percentage of currency which contains this level of contamination.

2. DNA Evidence

United States v. Gipson, 383 F.3d 689 (8th Cir. 2004)
Gipson involved an appeal from the District of Minnesota on a conviction of two counts of bank robbery. Defendant challenged the district court's denial of his motion to suppress expert testimony on a DNA test result. The Eighth Circuit found that there was no evidence to support the conclusion that the methodology used was so unreliable that it resulted in a material alteration. In applying the reliability requirement of *Daubert*, the Eighth Circuit drew a distinction between a challenge to a scientific methodology and a challenge to an application of the scientific methodology. When the application of a scientific methodology is challenged as unreliable under *Daubert* and the methodology itself is otherwise sufficiently reliable, outright exclusion of the evidence in question is warranted only if the methodology "was so altered [by a deficient application] as to skew the methodology itself." The Eighth Circuit further observed that the reliability of the proffered DNA test results may be challenged by showing that a scientifically sound methodology had been undercut by sloppy handling of the samples, failure to properly train those performing the testing, failure to follow the appropriate protocols and the like. In this case, the district court's ruling was affirmed.

United States v. Beasley, 102 F.3d 1440 (8th Cir. 1996)
In *United States v. Beasley*, hairs found inside a mask used during a robbery were tested using the polymerase chain reaction (PCR) method of DNA typing. The PCR method involves a natural replication process of the unknown DNA sample, which produces a sufficient quantity of pure sample to be tested against a known sample. The district court held an evidentiary hearing on the PCR method and found that the method met all of the *Daubert* reliability factors. Further, the court determined that the testing procedures were adequate and that any slight differences in the testing protocol would go to the weight of the DNA evidence, not its admissibility.

The Eighth Circuit affirmed and went on to note that "the reliability of the PCR method of DNA analysis is sufficiently well-established to permit the courts of this circuit to take judicial notice of it in future cases." The court reaffirmed the use of PCR testing in *United States v. Boswell*, 270 F.3d 1200 (8th Cir. 2001).

See also *United States v. Martinez*, 3 F.3d 1191 (8th Cir. 1993) (affirming admission of DNA restriction fragment length polymorphism (DNA/RFLP) test results; an alleged failure to properly apply a scientific principle would only justify exclusion "if a reliable methodology was so altered as to skew the methodology itself"). In *Martinez*, the Eighth Circuit held that the theories and techniques of DNA/RFLP were reliable and could be admitted on a "preliminary showing that the expert properly performed a reliable methodology," and that district courts in the future could take judicial notice of the reliability of such techniques but must hold a *Daubert* hearing if new DNA techniques were offered. For cases that have upheld the admission of DNA/RFLP profiling evidence following *Martinez*, see *United States v. Black Cloud*, 101 F.3d 1258 (8th Cir. 1996); *United States v. Richardson*, 537 F.3d 951, 960–61 (8th Cir. 2008) *United States v. Johnson*, 56 F.3d 947 (8th Cir. 1995). For additional cases regarding admission of DNA evidence despite deviations from testing protocol, see *United State v. Sinskey*, 119 F.3d 712, 717 (8th Cir. 1997) (holding that, although tests deviated from standard protocol for uses of an ammonia nitrate probe, the government produced testimony showing that deviations did not affect the reliability of test results; thus the evidence was admissible and the jury could decide what weight to give it); *United States v. Johnson*, 56 F.3d 947 (8th Cir. 1995) (holding that minor variations in certain steps of the standard protocol did not "substantially undermine the results"; any contrary testimony went to the weight of the evidence rather than its admissibility).

3. Acid-Phosphate Tests

United States v. Rodriguez, 581 F.3d 775 (8th Cir. 2009)
In *United States v. Rodriguez*, 581 F.3d 775 (8th Cir. 2009), the district court admitted the testimony of a government pathologist about the results of acid-phosphate tests conducted on the dead body of a rape victim which indicated the presence of semen in her vagina and cervix. Defendant objected to the pathologist's testimony under *Daubert*, arguing that it was based on the pathologist's own experience, rather than peer-reviewed research. The Eighth Circuit disagreed, pointing out that peer-reviewed publication is only one factor in the *Daubert* analysis. The Eighth Circuit also found significance in the fact that the government pathologist did not invent acid-phosphate testing. Moreover, the government pathologist was well-qualified as a licensed medical doctor with three decades of experience, and had extensive experience in criminal investigation, including sex crimes.

Defendant also argued that the testimony regarding acid-phosphate test results was unreliable because the pathologist's estimate that semen deposits were made within twenty-four to thirty-six hours of the victim's death was based on acid-phosphate measurements in living people. However, the Eighth Circuit reminded defendant that the factual basis of an expert opinion goes to the credibility of the testimony, not the admissibility, and held that the district court did not abuse its discretion by admitting the acid-phosphate test results.

4. Inductively Coupled Plasma-Atomic Emission Spectrography (ICP) and Voice Spectrography Evidence

United States v. Davis, 103 F.3d 660 (8th Cir. 1996)
In *United States v. Davis*, the district court allowed evidence of inductively coupled plasma-atomic emission spectrography (ICP) tests showing trace elements found in bullet fragments discharged during a bank robbery were identical in composition to bullets found in defendant's car. The court rejected defendant's argument that the comparison was irrelevant because it was impossible to know exactly how many bullets manufactured by the same company had the same elemental composition.

Noting that the weaknesses in the analysis went to weight, not admissibility, the Eighth Circuit affirmed: "[the defendant] was free to challenge the expert's conclusions and point out the weaknesses of the analysis to the jury during cross-examination."

United States v. Bahena, 223 F.3d 797 (8th Cir. 2000)

A prosecution for conspiracy to distribute methamphetamine, the Eighth Circuit considered the reliability of voice spectrography evidence. One of the defendants sought to introduce expert testimony that the voice recorded on several of the government's wiretaps was not his. After holding a *Daubert* hearing, the district court excluded the expert's testimony as unreliable, and the defendant was subsequently convicted.

The Eighth Circuit affirmed. The court held that exclusion of the expert's testimony under *Daubert* did not violate the defendant's Sixth Amendment right to compel witnesses in his defense, and that particular flaws in the expert's methodology—including his failure to adhere to recognized standards, and his use of copies instead of the original tapes—were sufficient to justify exclusion of his testimony. The Eighth Circuit pointed out, however, that spectrographic voice analysis is not inadmissible *per se*, and that numerous other decisions have admitted testimony based upon it.

5. *Polygraph Evidence*

The Eighth Circuit has been reluctant to admit polygraph results out of concern for relevance, prejudice, and reliability. In *United States v. Gianakos*, 415 F.3d 912 (8th Cir. 2005); 404 F.3d 1065 (8th Cir. 2005), the defendant faced charges for kidnapping with death resulting. At trial, the defendant sought to introduce failed polygraph results for two prosecution witnesses. The district court excluded the tests as relating to a collateral issue and as cumulative of other evidence. The Eighth Circuit observed that "[a] fundamental premise of our criminal trial system is that the jury is the lie detector." Because the witnesses testified at trial, the jury had ample opportunity to assess their truthfulness without reviewing the excluded polygraph results.

In *United States v. Rouse*, 410 F.3d 1005 (8th Cir. 2005), a jury convicted four men of aggravated sexual abuse. After the convictions the victims (nieces of the defendants) recanted their testimony. The district court did not find the recantations credible and denied defendants' motion for a new trial. On appeal, defendants challenged, among other things, the exclusion of polygraph test results from a male child witness that tended to support their testimony that the children had fabricated their trial testimony. The Eighth Circuit found no abuse of discretion in the trial court's refusal to consider the test results, because they did not meet the standards of any accepted polygraph procedure, and because the circumstances surrounding the test further undermined its reliability.

U.S. v. Greatwalker, 356 F.3d 908 (8th Cir. 2004), was an appeal from the District of North Dakota. Defendant appealed his first degree murder conviction in Indian country in violation of U.S. statute. Defendant contended that the district court should have allowed into evidence the results of lie detector tests taken by witnesses at the scene of the murder. The Eighth Circuit pointed out that before any expert evidence could be admitted, the party seeking its admission must lay a proper foundation for the district court to decide its reliability. Defendant never established or argued the results were reliable under *Daubert*, and, therefore, the polygraph results were inadmissible. The district court did not abuse its discretion in excluding the results of the polygraph examination.

See also United States v. Waters, 194 F.3d 926 (8th Cir. 1999) (polygraph evidence offered by defendant properly excluded under Fed. R. Evid. 403); *United States v. Jordan,* 150 F. 3d 895, 899 (8th Cir. 1998) (admission of tests would have been more prejudicial than probative); *United States v. Williams*, 95 F.3d 723 (8th Cir. 1996) (affirming exclusion of polygraph administered in connection with kidnapping investigation; agent who administered test could not say whether the procedure had been tested, subjected to peer review, was generally accepted in the scientific field, or what its rate of error was; court concluded that the results were more prejudicial than probative).

6. Psychological and Psychiatric Testimony

United States v. White Horse, 316 F.3d 769 (8th Cir. 2003), was appealed from the district of South Dakota. Defendant appealed his conviction for sexually molesting his six-year-old son. Defendant asserted on appeal that the district court abused its discretion by granting the government's motion to exclude a psychologist's testimony that defendant did not have a sexual interest in underage boys. In preparing for his testimony the psychologist interviewed defendant, administered a mental status examination and attempted to ascertain his sexual interest by means of what is called an "Abel Assessment." The district court gave detailed reasons for concluding that the Abel Assessment was neither scientifically valid nor a good fit for the specific facts of the case.

The Eighth Circuit agreed with the district court that there were significant concerns about how well each part of the Abel Assessment "fit" the facts of the case, and there was no evidence that the test had been validated with a statistically significant sample of Native Americans. Further, Dr. Abel stated in a prior paper that "incest only" cases were excluded from the testing of two of three predictive equations, because incest offenders often act for reasons other than sexual interest. The Eighth Circuit affirmed the district court's holding that the Abel Assessment was not admissible under Rule 702.

The Eighth Circuit has excluded psychiatric or psychological testimony where it creates a danger of confusing or misleading the jury or where it would lead the jury to adopt the expert's opinion on the "ultimate issues." *See United State v. Rouse*, 111 F.3d 561 (8th Cir. 1997) (limiting the testimony of psychologist as to issues that went to other witnesses' credibility); *United States v. Kime*, 99 F.3d 870, 884 (8th Cir. 1996) (affirming the exclusion of expert testimony on eyewitness identification in part because it cast doubt on the credibility of the eyewitness, an issue that is within the jury's domain). In a decision involving charges of sexual abuse of children, the Eighth Circuit excluded expert psychological testimony on interviewing techniques and the effects of interrogation on a young victim's testimony. *United States v. Reynolds*, 77 F.3d 253, (8th Cir. 1996). The court determined that because there was no evidence that the victim in this case had ever been interviewed, testimony on the effects of interrogations and interviewing was not relevant and thus properly excluded.

7. Drug Trafficking

United States v. Vesey, 338 F.3d 913 (8th Cir. 2003)
This appeal from the Northern District of Iowa arose from a conviction for delivery and possession with intent to deliver cocaine base and powder cocaine. The district court allowed the government's expert witness to testify that he had "never seen a drug user use a scale" and that those who used scales were "all people that are involved in distribution." Vesey argued that the admission of this evidence violated Fed. R. Evid. 704(b), which prohibits an expert from testifying as to whether a defendant had "the mental state or condition constituting an element of the crime charged." Vesey further maintained that the district court erred in finding the testimony of his own expert witness, a convicted drug trafficker and informant, unreliable and inadmissible under Fed. R. Evid. 702. Vesey sought to produce evidence of how illegal drug operations are normally conducted and to counter testimony of the government's expert witness through his expert.

The Court of Appeals held that the district court erroneously shifted the focus of its inquiry to the credibility of Vesey's expert, rather than the reliability of his methodology, and that the testimony should therefore have been admitted. The court found that Vesey's expert was qualified to testify as an expert based on the considerable number of drug deals that he had participated in. The Advisory Committee's note to Rule 702 states that experience-based expert testimony is reliable if the expert "explains how the experience leads to the conclusion reached, why that experience is sufficient basis for the opinion, and how that experience is reliably applied to the facts."

The court further held, however, that the error was harmless because several witnesses testified they had bought drugs from Vesey, and the jury heard a tape recording of an informant making a controlled buy from him. The police found $16,000 in cash in Vesey's home and nearly twenty-five grams of cocaine on his person. The court also observed that the jury might not have accorded much weight to Vesey's expert testimony, given his status as a convicted drug dealer and government informant.

United States v. Solorio-Tafolla, 324 F.3d 964 (8th Cir. 2003)

The defendant was convicted of a drug conspiracy offense but asserted that a law enforcement officer was improperly permitted to testify as an expert concerning drug trafficking without a *Daubert* hearing to determine his expert qualifications. Defendant contended that the officer's qualifications were not properly established prior to his testimony concerning drug prices and quantities, drug conspiracies, drug manufacturing, drug investigations, and drug packaging. The Eighth Circuit held that there was no requirement that the district court hold a *Daubert* hearing before qualifying an expert, and that it was well within the district court's discretion to allow law enforcement officials to testify as experts concerning the modus operandi of drug dealers. The officer in question was well-qualified to testify about drug-related issues, and the Eighth Circuit concluded that the district court did not err in admitting his expert testimony.

United States v. Robertson, 387 F.3d 702 (8th Cir. 2004)

Defendant appealed from the Eastern District of Missouri on a conviction for possession of a firearm during a drug trafficking crime. As in *Solorio-Tafolla*, defendant asserted that the district court abused its discretion by permitting two police detectives to testify as experts on drug trafficking. The Eighth Circuit affirmed the admission of the testimony. The detectives possessed the knowledge, skill, training, experience, and education to assist the trier of fact in understanding the business of drug trafficking. Moreover, the district court did not abuse its discretion in admitting the testimony without a preliminary *Daubert* hearing. *See also United States v. Spotted Elk*, 548 F.3d 641 (8th Cir. 2008) (Fed. R. Evid. 702 permits the district court to allow testimony from a police officer about how pieces of evidence found in the defendant's house and hotel room, such as little pieces of tinfoil or cash wrapped in Saran wrap, would have been used by drug dealers and users) and *United States v. Jeanetta*, 533 F.3d 651 (8th Cir. 2008) (affirming the district court discretion's to allow law enforcement officials to testify as experts concerning the modus operandi of drug dealers).

United States v. Sdoulam, 398 F.3d 981 (8th Cir. 2005)

Defendant was convicted on charges of conspiracy to distribute and actual distribution of pseudoephedrine with knowledge that it would be used to manufacture methamphetamine. At trial, the prosecution presented expert testimony that the amount of pseudoephedrine sold monthly through the defendant's store was 123 times the average amount based on a nationwide sample of convenience stores. The expert, a statistician, expressed this as "a ridiculous 730 standard deviations from the mean" and suggested that the chances such a large amount could be sold through normal business activity "would be infinitesimal." On appeal, Sdoulam challenged this testimony as an improper statement of the "statistical probability of guilt."

The admissibility of the testimony was affirmed. The Eighth Circuit agreed with the principle that a statistician's testimony cannot "serve to reduce the ultimate question of guilt or innocence to one of mathematical probabilities," but held that the expert in this case had adequate foundation for his statistical comparison and did not comment on the probability of the defendant's guilt or innocence.

8. Fingerprint Evidence

United States v. Janis, 387 F.3d 682 (8th Cir. 2004)
Defendant was convicted of possession of a firearm as a convicted felon. On appeal, defendant challenged the admission of expert fingerprint testimony from a police detective, as well as the district court's exclusion of testimony from defendant's treating physician concerning his wounds.

Defendant was admitted to the hospital after shooting himself in the leg. Subsequent investigation led authorities to discover that he had possession of unauthorized firearms as a convicted felon. The Eighth Circuit concluded that the exclusion of the doctor's testimony concerning defendant's wounds was not error since the number of gunshot wounds defendant suffered was irrelevant to the issue of whether he possessed and received the guns in question.

The district court was further found not to have abused its discretion by admitting expert fingerprint testimony linking the defendant to a 1987 felony conviction. The Eighth Circuit concluded that fingerprint evidence analysis is "generally accepted" and affirmed the district court's reliability determination.

United States v. Collins, 340 F.3d 672 (8th Cir. 2003)
Defendant was convicted of conspiracy and of possession with intent to distribute more than 500 grams of methamphetamine. He challenged the conviction on a variety of grounds, one of which was that the district court erred in failing to conduct a *Daubert* analysis on fingerprint evidence used to enhance his sentence. The district court admitted the fingerprint evidence to identify defendant as the same person convicted of prior offenses, and defendant challenged whether the fingerprints from his previous custody dates bore enough indicia of identity with his current fingerprints to support a conclusion that he had committed the prior crimes. He further argued that, despite his failure to challenge the admission of this evidence at the district court level, he was entitled to a review because it constituted plain error. The Eighth Circuit found that the admission of the prints was not plain error and that the fingerprint evidence received was generally accepted as to both admissibility and reliability. The conviction was affirmed.

9. Other Categories of Criminal Forensic Evidence

United States v. Montgomery, 635 F.3d 1074 (8th Cir. 2011)
The Eighth Circuit held that expert testimony on positron emission tomography (PET) showing abnormalities in the limbic and somatomotor regions of defendant's brain was improperly excluded by the district court in this death penalty case. Dr. Ruben Gur was prepared to testify that MRI and PET scans showed abnormalities in defendant's brain consistent with a diagnosis of pseudocyesis, a somatoform disorder in which the patient develops the delusion that she is pregnant. Defendant, who admitted to killing a pregnant woman, delivering the woman's baby, and taking it as her own, attempted to establish an insanity defense based on her expert's diagnosis of pseudocyesis. After a two-day *Daubert* hearing, the district court concluded that the MRI results were not admissible but the PET evidence would be allowed. However, before opening statements, the district court ruled that the PET evidence would be excluded because the government's experts were unable to replicate Dr. Gur's calculations. Because PET scans are reliable, the Eighth Circuit found this to be error.

The district court's error was harmless, nevertheless, because as the Eighth Circuit noted, PET scans can reliably measure brain activity, but are not used as a diagnostic aid for pseudocyesis and abnormalities. Moreover, the PET scan cannot predict behavior. The proffered testimony by Dr. Gur that the defendant killed the victim and kidnapped her child while in a delusional state was not admissible and any error in excluding the PET evidence was thus harmless.

United States v. Cawthorn, 429 F.3d 793 (8th Cir. 2005) vacated on other grounds, 552 U.S. 1136 (2008)
Defendant was convicted of a variety of drug and weapons offenses. The prosecution presented expert testimony that a positive hand-swab test for cocaine would not have resulted from casual contact. The expert supported his opinion with two studies: in the first, he swabbed the hands of bank tellers and a money counting machine, since a large percentage of U.S. currency carries cocaine residue; and in the second, he swabbed the steering wheels of vehicles impounded for drug activity. Neither of the two studies produced positive swab results and, on that basis, the expert concluded that the defendant's positive result must have resulted from more than incidental contact with cocaine. On appeal, defendant argued that the expert's studies were not sufficient to establish that a positive hand-swab test could not be the result of unintentional cocaine exposure. The Eighth Circuit held that the first study was specifically designed to examine the possibility of a positive result through contact with cocaine residue on currency, and found no error in the admission of the expert's testimony based on that study. The second study, however, was flawed because the expert did not establish that the impounded vehicles were involved in cocaine-related offenses. The trial court's erroneous admission of the second study was nevertheless harmless because other evidence supported the jury's verdict.

United States v. Nichols, 416 F.3d 811 (8th Cir. 2005)
Defendants, masterminds of a scheme to sell nonexistent vehicles from a nonexistent estate, were convicted on fraud and money-laundering charges. One of the defendants sought to introduce expert testimony from a religious studies professor concerning the beliefs held by defendants' church. The trial court excluded the testimony as irrelevant. On appeal, the defendant argued that his purpose in offering the testimony "was not simply [to profess] religious beliefs in an attempt to win sympathy or confuse the jury." Nevertheless, the Eighth Circuit held that "[t]he nature and sincerity of Nichols's religious beliefs was not before the court or necessary to Nichols's defense," and found no abuse of discretion in the exclusion of the professor's testimony.

United States v. Rushing, 388 F.3d 1153 (8th Cir. 2004)
Following an earlier remand, the Eighth Circuit reviewed the district court's exclusion of expert testimony in an immigration fraud case. The prosecution theory was that defendants had conspired to traffic two Chinese women into the United States so that one of the defendants could have sexual relations with them. The defense expert, a Pharm.D., opined that there was no sexual relationship between that defendant and the woman who testified for the government because the woman had hepatitis B and the defendant did not. The expert did not consider, however, that the woman may have had a low level of infectiousness at the time, that hepatitis B progresses differently in women than it does in men, and that it is generally less common for women to transmit hepatitis B infections to men than vice versa. The trial court excluded the proposed testimony, and the Eighth Circuit affirmed.

United States v. Larry Reed & Sons, 280 F.3d 1212 (8th Cir. 2002)
The government used computer analysis of satellite images to prove a farmer had submitted bogus crop insurance claims. The expert offering the testimony explained that his technique had been reviewed in "hundreds and hundreds" of academic articles, and that several universities employed the same method to promote agricultural productivity, assess hail damage, and for other purposes. The Eighth Circuit found no abuse of discretion in the trial court's decision to admit the testimony.

United States v. Ross, 263 F.3d 844 (8th Cir. 2001)
United States v. Ross involved a prosecution for a series of bank robberies. After holding an *in limine* hearing, the trial court admitted expert testimony from an FBI forensic examiner that boot and tire prints from the scene of one of the robberies matched evidence taken from the defendant. The Eighth

Circuit summarily affirmed, noting that it had previously upheld the use of footprint evidence (albeit in a pre-*Daubert* case, *United States v. Rose*, 731 F.2d 1337, 1345–46 (8th Cir. 1984)).

United States v. Iron Cloud, 171 F.3d 587 (8th Cir. 1999)

In *Iron Cloud*, the Eighth Circuit considered the admissibility of portable breath test (PBT) results as substantive evidence in an involuntary manslaughter trial. George Iron Cloud was charged with involuntary manslaughter for running over a pedestrian while giving a friend a ride home. The victim had a history of mental illness and a penchant for jumping in front of moving cars. Earlier on the day of the accident that killed him, he jumped in front of a police car and narrowly missed being hit. After the accident, defendant was administered a PBT, which recorded his blood-alcohol level at 0.14 percent.

Over defense objection, the trial court admitted the PBT results as substantive evidence. The Eighth Circuit concluded that this constituted error based on the numerous published decisions holding that PBT is only valid as a "screening test" and should only be admitted to show probable cause. The court further concluded that this error was not harmless, since the government sought to prove Iron Cloud's gross negligence through evidence of his intoxication. Judge Cynthia Hall of the Ninth Circuit, sitting by designation, concurred with the holding on the PBT's limited reliability, but dissented on the ground that other evidence provided sufficient proof of Iron Cloud's gross negligence.

See also *United States v. Triplett*, 195 F.3d 990 (8th Cir. 1999) (affirming exclusion of expert witness regarding lighting; testimony regarding methods that witness claimed were "based upon what he was visibly able to see by his own experience" was entirely subjective and concerned matters better left to the jury's common sense).

10. Daubert Procedural Issues—Criminal Cases

a. Preserving *Daubert* Challenges for Appeal

As seen in the Eighth Circuit's civil decisions, a litigant waives a *Daubert* challenge by failing to object to the expert's testimony before it is presented to the jury. In *United States v. Waters*, 194 F.3d 926 (8th Cir. 1999), a criminal defendant argued that the district court had erred in admitting the testimony of a social worker who specialized in child sexual abuse. Since he had not presented his *Daubert* argument to the district court, however, the Eighth Circuit refused to consider it.

b. Necessity of *Daubert* Hearings

A number of the Eighth Circuit's criminal decisions hold that for many categories of evidence, the trial court need not hold a *Daubert* hearing before admitting or excluding the expert testimony. In *Waters*, for example, defendant requested a *Daubert* hearing in order to show that his polygraph test results were reliable. Since defendant conceded he had no evidence establishing the reliability of the test, the Eighth Circuit found no abuse of discretion in the trial court's decision not to hold a hearing. The court also found that the trial court was within its discretion in excluding the polygraph evidence under Rule 403 on the ground that it was collateral and that the jury might give it undue weight. Similarly, in *United States v. Calderin-Rodriguez*, 244 F.3d 977 (8th Cir. 2001), the court found that no *Daubert* hearing was required to establish the reliability of digitally enhanced audio tapes, and in *United States v. Evans*, 272 F.3d 1069 (8th Cir. 2002), the court likewise held that a vice-squad officer could testify on prostitution rings without first undergoing a *Daubert* hearing.

Although a *Daubert* hearing is not required to admit expert testimony in the Eighth Circuit, the party offering the expert testimony must still prove by a preponderance of the evidence that the expert testimony is reliable and satisfies the admissibility tests under FRE 702. To establish that the proffered expert testimony is reliable and admissible, the proponent must show that the expert witness will use the witness's knowledge, skill, training, experience, or education to assist a trier of fact in understanding an area involving a specialized subject matter. *See Solorio-Tafolla*, 324 F.3d at 966. The proponent must also prove that the probative value of the expert testimony is not substantially outweighed by the danger of unfair prejudice, confusion of the issues, or misleading the jury. *See Id.* Thus, a detective with twenty years experience in the narcotics unit who received specialized training from the Drug Enforcement Administration and the National District Attorneys Association and had been involved in thousands of investigations was able to provide reliable testimony as to the modus operandi of drug dealers. *Id.*

c. Adequacy of Disclosure of Anticipated Trial Testimony

In *United States v. Conroy*, 424 F.3d 833 (8th Cir. 2005), defendant was convicted on federal charges of aggravated sexual abuse and abusive sexual conduct. On appeal, defendant argued that he did not receive sufficient notice of the bases for the prosecution expert's testimony concerning the absence of bodily fluids on a rug outside a victim's home. The Eighth Circuit held that "[w]hile the government's notice did not explain in detail the bases for [the expert's] opinions, and its use of a nonexclusive list is questionable," the district court did not abuse its discretion in finding the disclosure to be adequate. In addition, the expert was permitted to engage in some speculation regarding the lack of physical evidence, as long as she did not usurp the jury's role of determining whether the event actually occurred. The admission of the expert's testimony was therefore affirmed.

d. Intrusion on Jury's Role

The Eighth Circuit has been reluctant to impose hearings to determine the reliability of eyewitness identification testimony because it does not want to intrude on the jury's role in determining credibility and weighing the strength of evidence. The defendant in *United States v. Martin*, 391 F.3d 949 (8th Cir. 2004), sought to introduce expert testimony on the reliability of eyewitness identification. The district court held a hearing to determine whether to admit the testimony, in which the expert presented his qualifications, the validity of his field, and the ways his testimony might assist the jury in evaluating the accuracy of eyewitness identifications. Following the hearing, the district court excluded the testimony. The Eighth Circuit affirmed on the ground that the general reliability of eyewitness identification is a matter of common understanding and that evaluating the credibility of eyewitness identification testimony was a task best left to the jury. The proposed expert testimony was unnecessary and superfluous.

The United States Supreme Court has also refused to intrude on the jury's role in weighing eye witness testimony. In *Perry v. New Hampshire*, 132 S.Ct. 716 (2012), the Supreme Court rejected the defendant's argument that the due process clause requires a preliminary judicial inquiry into the reliability of eyewitness testimony. The court said that only after a showing of improper state conduct would due process require a trial court to screen the evidence for reliability before offering it to the jury. The court recognized that the jury, not the judge, traditionally determines the reliability of this type of evidence. In response to the defendant's argument that eyewitness evidence is "uniquely unreliable," the court stated that there were other safeguards built into the adversary system that caution juries against placing undue weight on eyewitness testimony of questionable reliability.

C. KEY DECISIONS APPLYING *DAUBERT* IN THE DISTRICT COURTS OF THE EIGHTH CIRCUIT

1. *Arkansas*

In re Prempro Prods. Liab. Litig., 738 F. Supp. 2d 887 (E.D. Ark. 2010)
Plaintiffs alleged that they developed breast cancer from hormone replacement therapy (HRT). At issue were defendants' motions to exclude plaintiffs' experts' testimony regarding general causation,

meaning whether estrogen-only HRT (EHRT) can cause breast cancer in the general population. Plaintiffs designated two experts: Dr. Jasenka Demirovic, an epidemiologist, and Dr. Marcelo Aldaz, a cell biologist. Dr. Demirovic evaluated the statistical relationship between use of EHRT and risk of breast cancer and Dr. Aldaz assessed the biological plausibility of a general causal relationship. The court excluded both experts' testimony.

With respect to Dr. Demirovic, the court found her testimony unreliable in large part because she relied on observational studies to contradict the findings of a generally accepted, decade-long clinical study called the Women's Health Initiative (WHI) study, which concluded that there was no increased risk of breast cancer with EHRT. The court noted that, unlike clinical studies, which are blinded and controlled, observational studies select patients from existing populations, based on whether or not they have or will be receiving treatment. Because this procedure lacks controls, observational studies are more susceptible to bias and other confounding factors, and so are less reliable than clinical studies, which are often referred to as the "gold standard." The court also found that Dr. Demivoric selected study data that best supported her opinion, while downplaying contrary findings or conclusions; relied on studies that found associations between EHRT that were either weak or not statistically significant; and did not understand the differences between different forms of EHRT. For these reasons, the court excluded her opinions.

With respect to Dr. Aldaz, the court found that he relied on a significant number of animal and tissue studies without explaining how these studies could be reliably extrapolated to predict the effects of EHRT in living humans. The court further noted that Dr. Aldaz failed to specify what level of exposure to EHRT would cause breast cancer in living humans. Thus, his opinion was also excluded.

Nelson v. Wal-Mart Stores, Inc., 2009 WL 330299 (E.D. Ark. 2009)

In this case, the plaintiffs alleged that the defendants' hiring practices had a discriminatory effect on African American applicants. Plaintiffs proffered two experts: Marc Bendick and Martin Shapiro. Bendick computed the expected representation of African American long-haul truck drivers at forty-seven transportation offices (TOs) of Wal-Mart stores from September 22, 2001 onward. Bendick estimated that the nationwide aggregate of African Americans among African American White over-the-road (OTR) drivers was 15.3 percent. Based on Bendick's findings, Shapiro analyzed the racial composition of truck driver hiring in Wal-Mart TOs.

Defendants moved to exclude both experts' opinions. Defendants argued that Bendick's testimony was not admissible because it was not based on sufficient facts or data and was not the product of reliable principles and methods because Bendick (1) improperly disregarded Wal-Mart's applicant flow data; (2) based his analysis on overly broad labor markets; (3) relied on overly broad census and EEO-1 population figures that did not reflect individuals interested in and qualified for Wal-Mart OTR driver positions; and (4) included in his analysis individuals who were not available for employment as Wal-Mart OTR drivers. Defendants also argued that Bendick's opinions were not relevant to the central issue of Wal-Mart's hiring of qualified OTR truck drivers from September 22, 2001 onward. Lastly, defendants asserted that, to the extent Shapiro's opinions and testimony were derivative of Bendick's flawed analysis, Shapiro's opinions and testimony were likewise unreliable and irrelevant.

The court admitted both experts' opinions. It found that Bendick's opinion was relevant and admissible even though Bendick disregarded Wal-Mart's applicant flow data. The court noted that the United States Supreme Court had held that applicant flow data may be relevant in determining if an employment practice had a discriminatory impact, but that there was no requirement that applicant flow data must be used. The court further noted that, while applicant flow data would generally be superior, it may not accurately depict the relevant labor market, especially when an employer uses discriminatory recruiting or hiring practices. In the instant case, plaintiffs alleged that

Wal-Mart's heavy reliance on word-of-mouth and informal recruitment practices deterred African American applicants. Thus, considering the specific facts of the case, the court found that plaintiffs' experts' exclusion of Wal-Mart's applicant flow data met *Daubert*'s standard.

Schipp v. Gen. Motors Corp., 443 F. Supp. 2d 1023 (E.D. Ark. 2006)

This case arose out of an automobile accident involving a General Motors Silverado. General Motors moved to exclude the testimony of two experts, both professors of mechanical engineering, regarding causation. At issue was the Silverado's torsion bar adjuster, which allegedly had broken prior to the accident and had caused the accident. The first expert opined, after visually inspecting the torsion bar adjuster, that the part broke some weeks or months prior to the accident as evidenced by the presence of rust at the fracture sites on the part. Yet, because expert failed to conduct any chemical analysis to confirm or refute his theory regarding the presence of rust at the fracture sites, the court found his opinion unreliable. In support of its finding, the court cited the ASM Handbook, General Practice in Failure Analysis, which identified the principal stages of a failure investigation and analysis, including: nondestructive testing, mechanical testing, microscopic examination and analysis, chemical analysis, analysis of fracture mechanics and testing under simulated service conditions, among other things. Because the expert failed to even conduct a chemical analysis to determine whether the deposits on the broken part comprised rust or dirt, his opinion was held to be unreliable. Moreover, the court noted that the expert did not use metallographic sectioning to analyze the material in the torsion bar adjuster to determine the presence or absence of inherent material flaws, although it was feasible to do so.

The first expert also opined that the torsion bar adjuster could have broken some weeks or months before the accident. At issue was whether the evidence showed that a fractured torsion bar adjuster could support the weight of the vehicle for any period of time. The court identified two ways that this issue could be analyzed: first, by mathematical calculations and second, by installing a fractured torsion bar adjuster on a Silverado and observing the effects. General Motors had performed both analyses, whereas the first expert at issue performed neither. While the first expert argued that General Motors' mathematical calculations failed to show that it was impossible for a fractured torsion bar to support the weight of a Silverado, the court noted that for purposes of defendant's *Daubert* motion the important point was that the expert had failed to demonstrate through any mathematical calculations that it was *possible* for a fractured torsion bar adjuster to sustain the weight of the Silverado for any period of time without breaking. Moreover, because the expert performed no physical testing of his theory, his opinion was no more than an untested hypothesis. His testimony was excluded.

The second challenged expert, on the other hand, did perform chemical analysis of the deposits on the fracture sites of the part at issue. And while he opined that the deposits were not composed of rust, he also opined that the deposits, whatever their makeup, would have taken weeks or months to form at the fracture site. He based his opinion on his past experience in examining fracture sites. As for whether a fractured torsion bar adjuster could support the weight of the vehicle, the second expert conducted no tests to demonstrate the reliability of his opinion that a compromised part could support the weight of a vehicle for some time. The court, thus, excluded his testimony as to both issues for the same reasons it excluded the testimony of the first expert.

McPike v. Corghi S.P.A., 87 F. Supp. 2d 890 (E.D. Ark. 1999)

Defendants moved to exclude plaintiff's expert witness who theorized that a design defect in a table top tire-changer caused a tire to fly into the air, injuring the plaintiff. The expert, Dr. Alan Milner, claimed that the machine acted as a "launch pad" when the tire and rim separated.

In *Peitzmeier v. Hennessy Indus., Inc.*, the Eighth Circuit had affirmed the district court's decision to exclude the same expert's testimony in another table top tire-changer case alleging design defect. In *Peitzmeier*, the record did not adequately demonstrate the design, testing, efficacy, feasibility, peer review, or general acceptance of the proposed safety devices the expert claimed were missing. The record in *McPike*, however, revealed that, at the time the machine in question was sold, "tire-changing machines incorporating Milner's proposed changes, had been manufactured and put on the market. The fact that machines including Milner's proposed changes have been manufactured and are in service negates the criticism based on the lack of testing, lack of a prototype, design development and the like." The district court denied defendants' motion to exclude plaintiff's expert witness.

Savage v. Union Pacific Railroad Co., 67 F. Supp. 2d 1021 (E.D. Ark. 1999)

In this toxic tort suit, plaintiff alleged that while working as a rail car repairman at defendant's facility, he was exposed to large quantities of toxic substances including benzene, diesel/furnace oil, car journal oil, carbon black, methylene chloride, creosote, and diesel fuels. Plaintiff developed various forms of cancer, including a basal carcinoma on his face (the only cancer at issue in the case because of the statute of limitations), which he attributed to the alleged exposure. To establish causation, plaintiff offered the expert testimony of Dr. Alan Boyd, who testified that exposure to petroleum products caused or contributed to plaintiff's skin cancer. The court found Dr. Boyd to be a highly qualified and credentialed expert in dermatology and dermatopathology who was knowledgeable in the diagnosis and treatment of skin cancers, "but he is not an oncologist or a toxicologist." Plaintiff's claim was brought under the Federal Employer's Liability Act (FELA). The Eighth Circuit has held that "under FELA, the plaintiff carries only a slight burden on causation." *See Paul v. Missouri Pacific R.R. Co.*, 963 F.2d 1058 (8th Cir. 1992). Under FELA, a plaintiff need only "provide a reasonable basis for a jury to conclude that the employer's negligence played any part, even the slightest, in producing the injury for which damages are sought." The court noted that tension exists between this standard and the *Daubert* standard for admission of expert testimony. Despite the lower burden of proof in FELA cases, the court held that *Daubert*'s standard of admissibility nevertheless still applies to each step in an expert's analysis. "Thus, if the expert's conclusion—or any inferential link that under girds it—fails under *Daubert* to provide any evidence of causation, it must be excluded . . . ."

The court found Dr. Boyd's testimony lacking in several respects. Citing *Wright v. Willamette Indus., Inc.*, the court noted that a plaintiff must demonstrate both plaintiff's actual exposure level and the levels of exposure that are hazardous to humans generally. Although Dr. Boyd testified that creosote was present at plaintiff's work site, he did not demonstrate sufficient knowledge regarding the specific exposure types or levels, since he did not know the extent of plaintiff's exposure and produced no scientific data showing the level necessary to initiate a basal cell carcinoma. *Id.* at 1033. As such, the court granted defendant's motion to exclude Dr. Boyd from testifying that the creosote at plaintiff's workplace caused or contributed to his cancer.

Nat'l Bank of Commerce of El Dorado v. Dow Chem., 965 F. Supp. 1490 (E.D. Ark. 1996), aff'd, 133 F.3d 1132 (8th Cir. 1998)

Plaintiffs, the guardians of the estate of Ashley Smits, claimed that Ashley's birth defects were caused by her *in utero* exposure to Dursban. The plaintiffs offered testimony by six experts, with one of the experts, Dr. Janette Sherman, serving as the lead expert for plaintiffs' causation theory. The district court held two full days of *Daubert* hearings and ruled that plaintiffs' experts should be excluded.

The court concluded that plaintiffs' experts failed to present any scientific evidence that fit the following "traditional" categories of scientific proof commonly recognized in the relevant field:

(1) Structure-activity relationship (determining the substance's similarity in chemical structure to an agent known to cause birth defects)

(2) In vitro studies (exposing tissue cultures to the substance to determine toxic effect)
(3) Animal studies (determining whether the substance causes birth defects in mammals)
(4) Epidemiological studies
(5) Secular trend data (comparing the societal incidence of birth defects to the overall population exposure to the agent in question)

965 F. Supp. at 1507–08.

Defendants also argued that plaintiff's experts had failed to employ proper scientific methodology in the relevant field of teratology (the study of birth defects and agents that cause them). Defendants' experts laid out a four-pronged approach to determining whether exposure to a substance causes birth defects:

(1) Epidemiological studies must consistently or repeatedly demonstrate a statistical association between exposure of the agent and an increase in the suspect congenital malformations, either a unique syndrome or a group of malformations. Secular trend data should also be consistent with the allegation, providing the alleged agent is in common use,
(2) A bona fide mammalian animal model of the teratogenesis must exist or can be developed, utilizing exposures comparable with those in the human,
(3) The animal model should demonstrate a dose-response curve within the exposure range of concern, and
(4) A plausible mechanism of teratogenesis can be, and is, established, so the teratogenic result makes biological sense.

The court took judicial notice of these commonly recognized standards in the field of teratology, and found that plaintiffs' evidence met none of them.

> The court concluded that Dr. Sherman was more of an advocate than a scientist: Dr. Sherman, in her testimony and in her written articles, comes across as an advocate. Of course, good and careful scientists may also end up as strong advocates of their scientific opinions. But candor should be a hallmark of a good scientist[s]. The court cannot avoid the conclusion on this entire record that Dr. Sherman's advocacy is based on suspicion and conjecture and litigation animus rather than science.

In the end, the court concluded that "Dr. Sherman's submissions and opinions are not derived from scientific methods and are nothing more than an invitation to the jury to speculate." *Id.* at 1520.

See also Pulice v. Smith and Nephew Richards, Inc., 1999 U.S. Dist. LEXIS 4476 (W.D. Ark 1999) (excluding opinions of plaintiff's expert, an osteopath, regarding defendant's spinal stabilization system; most of the expert's opinions were not "subjected to any scientific method" and "hardly more than a thinly veiled attempt to supply the finder of fact with no information other than what the expert believes the verdict should be" (internal quotations omitted).

2. Iowa

Junk v. Terminix Intern. Co. Ltd. P'ship, 2008 WL 5191865 (S.D. Iowa 2008); aff'd in relevant part, 628 F.3d 439 (8th Cir. 2010)

Plaintiff brought suit against a pest control company, alleging that the company's applications of insecticide in plaintiff's home caused her son's cerebral palsy, neurodevelopmental delay, and neurological deficits, and that the insecticide was unreasonably dangerous and had inadequate warnings. Defendant prevailed on the defective design claim by showing that the pesticide was not unreasonably dangerous, relying on statistical data that showed a very low percentage of applications of the pesticide resulted in a call to a poison control center and showing that plaintiff had not submitted a reasonable alternative design. On the inadequate warning claim, plaintiff provided expert testimony on the exposure of plaintiff's family to the insecticide and the application of the insecticide, but offered no testimony regarding the adequacy of the warnings or instructions. Thus, there was no disputed issue of fact on defendant's motion for summary judgment on the inadequate warning claim, and defendant prevailed.

Zach v. Centocor and Johnson & Johnson, 491 F. Supp. 2d 867 (S.D. Iowa 2007)
A mother and her child sued prescription drug manufacturers, alleging that the child suffered substantial and debilitating injuries as a result of using the drug Remicade. Defendants challenged the admissibility of plaintiff's causation expert, and moved for summary judgment. Following a *Daubert* hearing, the court granted defendants' motion to exclude his testimony. The court, on motion, granted summary judgment for defendants, finding that plaintiffs could not prevail as a matter of law because they had not identified any experts who would testify that the child's injuries were caused by Remicade other than the excluded expert. Because the court's opinion and order discussed personal information, including the child's medical history, it was filed under seal, making much of the court's reasoning not publicly available.

Housley v. Orteck International, Inc., 488 F. Supp. 2d 819 (S.D. Iowa 2007)
Housley involved a claim by a mechanic against a tire manufacturer for negligent failure to inspect, negligent manufacturing, and negligent assembly of a tire that exploded when plaintiff attempted to install it on a tractor. Plaintiff's expert was an insurance adjuster and not a forensic tire expert, and thus, according to the court, lacked qualifications, experience or credentials to testify as an expert. This was the first time the claims adjuster had ever adjusted a loss involving a tire explosion. The court held that the expert was not qualified to be considered an expert under Fed. R. Evid. 702. Accordingly, plaintiff did not demonstrate a genuine issue of material fact on his product liability claim and the court granted summary judgment for defendant.

Raymond v. USA Healthcare Center-Fort Dodge, LLC, 2007 U.S. Dist. LEXIS 36300 (N.D. Iowa 2007)
In *Raymond*, defendant sought to bar plaintiff from testifying that she had passed a polygraph test regarding events underlying the dispute. Defendant contended that polygraph evidence was generally inadmissible, at least in the absence of a stipulation of the parties, and that the polygraph evidence in question was inherently unreliable and otherwise objectionable. The district court noted that the Iowa Supreme Court has ruled polygraph examinations generally inadmissible because of their uncertain reliability, although testimony about a polygraph test might be admissible by stipulation or where a proper foundation has been laid. Defendant argued that in this case, plaintiff never attempted to provide a foundation for the polygraph results. The court agreed. Because there was no showing of reliability or an adequate foundation, the defendant's motion *in limine* to exclude plaintiff's polygraph evidence was granted.

McCabe et al. v. Macauley et al., 2007 U.S. Dist. LEXIS 14210 (N.D. Iowa 2007)
This case involved a claim by two teachers who attended a rally for President George W. Bush in order to protest the policies of the Bush administration and the war in Iraq. Plaintiffs were charged with criminal trespass, jailed, and strip searched, but eventually all charges against them were dropped. Plaintiffs brought suit for injuries they suffered in connection with their arrests. In support of their claims, plaintiffs designated two expert witnesses; one, a noted Iowa lawyer and former Iowa Supreme Court justice, offered opinions "regarding whether probable cause existed for the

arrests," and the other, a physician, opined that plaintiffs' injuries were not consistent with the appropriate and reasonable placement of handcuffs.

The state highway patrol and several officers challenged the admissibility of the opinions under *Daubert*. With respect to the first expert, defendants argued that probable cause was a question of law, and that judges, lawyers, professors, and other "legal" experts should be prohibited from interpreting the law for the court, or from advising the court about how the law should apply to the particular facts of the case. They argued that the proposed testimony would be irrelevant, unduly prejudicial, and would not assist the trier of fact in understanding the evidence. The court was unable to find any authorities that would permit the admission of the testimony, and could see no logical basis to do so. The doctor's testimony was not excluded, but defendants were given leave to reargue it at a later time.

At a subsequent phase of the case, these defendants sought to exclude plaintiffs' proffered security expert, a retired member of the Secret Service. *McCabe v. Macaulay*, 2008 WL 2980009 (N.D. Iowa 2008). The court granted the motion because the expert had given opinions on legal conclusions, which were the court's domain, and because the proffered expert lacked qualifications. The expert had not worked for the Secret Service for seventeen years and was unfamiliar with post-9/11 protocols. The court further held the expert's report and deposition were devoid of any valuable analysis.

Plaintiffs settled their claims against the state highway patrol officers and the case went to trial, without the expert's testimony, against other defendants involved in the arrest. The jailer who conducted the strip search admitted it was a violation of Fourth Amendment rights, and the jury awarded damages to plaintiffs of $500,000 and $250,000 against the jailer. After remittitur orders that were rejected by plaintiffs and a new trial, the plaintiffs appealed and the Eighth Circuit reversed the trial court's remittitur. The case was remanded for the trial court to take into account inflation when using a 1978 case to set the remittitur. *McCabe v. Parker*, 608 F.3d 1068 (8th Cir. 2010).

Chapman v. LaBone, 460 F.Supp.2d 989 (S.D. Iowa 2006)

Plaintiff was selected by his employer for a random drug screen and was fired after his results came back as "substituted, not consistent with normal human urine." Plaintiff brought a variety of claims against the laboratory that performed the urinalysis, alleging that the test results were false.

Defendant filed a motion to strike plaintiff's expert witness and for summary judgment. The laboratory argued that the expert was not competent under Fed. R. Evid. 702 and that affidavits opposing summary judgment contained opinions that had not been disclosed in the expert's reports. The trial court noted that the expert was certified to inspect laboratories that performed federally mandated occupational drug testing, and was therefore qualified to testify on the drug testing procedures at issue in the case. The portions of the expert's affidavits that were not previously disclosed were stricken, however. But because the plaintiff's expert eventually conceded that the laboratory's testing was more likely than not correct, although the court denied the laboratory's motion to exclude the expert's testimony, it nevertheless ordered summary judgment on all claims.

United States v. Meyer, 485 F. Supp. 2d 1001 (N.D. Iowa 2006)

As a condition of his probation, defendant had sixteen sweat patches applied and tested for drug use. The first patches tested negative, but the last eight were positive for cocaine. Defendant attempted to show that the sweat patch results were not reliable. The court reviewed the protocol for application and removal of the sweat patches and the qualifications of the probation officer who monitored the tests. There was no dispute that the proper protocol was followed in applying, removing, and preserving the patches, and that the laboratory followed accepted procedures in testing defendant's specimens. Defendant focused instead on an accidental contamination theory: he testified that he worked for a company that hauled repossessed cars, and that he touched steering wheels, gear shifts, and door handles of these cars. He offered no evidence that drugs were present in the cars, but speculated that drugs from these cars somehow contaminated his patches.

The court noted that the Eighth Circuit had not had the opportunity to address the reliability of sweat patches for monitoring illegal drug use, but cited the Tenth Circuit's opinion upholding the use of sweat patches in *United States v. Gatewood*, 370 F.3d 1055 (10th Cir. 2004); *vacated on other grounds*, *Gatewood v. United States*, 543 U.S. 1109, 125 S. Ct. 1013, 160 L.Ed.2d 1036 (2005). The court then found that defendant presented no reliable evidence that his sweat patches were contaminated, and that the sweat patch program established by a preponderance of the evidence that the defendant had used cocaine at least eight times in the past calendar year. Based on this finding, the court held that defendant had failed to abide by the conditions of his probation, and that revocation was the appropriate remedy.

Gregg v. Indian Motorcycle Corporation, 2006 U.S. Dist. LEXIS 65360 (N.D. Iowa 2006)

In *Gregg*, plaintiff alleged that a defect in his 2000 Indian Chief motorcycle caused him to lose control of the bike, leading to an accident. Plaintiff claimed that a bolt connecting the left shock absorber to the swing arm bolt gave way. Defendant claimed that the bolt was already broken at the time of the accident.

Plaintiff offered testimony from a mechanical engineer who had investigated several hundred mechanical failure accidents and fire events throughout his career, although never previously a motorcycle accident. The expert opined there was a misalignment of the left shock absorber, causing it to be cocked and pulled out at an angle, thereby exceeding the maximum misalignment specified by the shock manufacturer. In his opinion, the manufacturer should have advised dealers and owners about the risk of "weave" or "wobble" in some Indian Chief motorcycles and that owners should have been advised to replace the shock mount bolts.

The court ruled that the expert was qualified, that his opinions were relevant, and that his testimony would, if properly supported, be helpful to the jury. The court upheld the admissibility of his opinions that a broken shock absorber caused the motorcycle to go into a "weave" or "wobble," and that the too-flexible swing arm caused the rider to lose control of the bike. The court did strike certain of the expert's opinions, however, as not supported by anything other than his *ipse dixit*.

Plaintiff's second expert was a metallurgical engineer, who was also a seasoned expert witness with no experience in motorcycle accidents. He performed a failure analysis of the left rear shock mount bolt, and concluded that it had a fatigue crack that had propagated over time until stress loads caused it to fail. Defendant objected to his opinion on the ground that the expert was not qualified in the stress dynamics underlying motorcycle accidents. The court agreed, and precluded him from testifying at trial.

Williams et al. v. Security National Bank of Sioux City, Iowa, 358 F. Supp. 2d 782 (N.D. Iowa 2005)

Plaintiffs, remainder beneficiaries of a trust, brought various claims premised on alleged mismanagement by the trustee. The trustee challenged plaintiffs' accountant's testimony on the ground that he conceded the lack of sufficient information to reach any reliable, "final" opinions.

The court found that the proper resolution of the dispute was controlled by Rule 403, and not Rule 702. The court outlined the distinction between persons testifying as "experts" and persons with "expert" qualifications who testify as fact witnesses. In this case, it was clear that the accountant had "expert" qualifications, but the testimony that plaintiffs intended to elicit from him was purely "factual" and was based on his personal knowledge. To exclude it would effectively preclude the plaintiffs from presenting admissible evidence about what the trustee knew or had been advised at certain times during the trustee's management of the estate. The court concluded that under Rule 403, the probative value of what the accountant told the trustee outweighed the potential for prejudice, confusion, or the danger that the jury would give undue weight to his testimony as "expert."

The plaintiffs also designated as an expert a partner in a San Francisco law firm practicing in the area of probate and trust litigation. The trustee contended that the expert's conclusions were improper "legal opinions" and were also unreliable because he had no knowledge of Iowa trust law. The court found that the testimony did "sail perilously close to the line, if not over the line, between what is testimony on an ultimate issue and what is testimony on a conclusion of law." The court concluded, however, that it would decide the permissible scope of the expert's testimony at trial, since he would only be called as a rebuttal witness and his testimony would therefore depend on the defense experts' testimony.

Finally, defendant objected to the expert's testimony on damages because it was based on unverified information provided by third parties, which he then "plugged in" to an "off-the-shelf" software program. The trustee further contended that the expert disclaimed any damages opinions at his deposition, and that he was not qualified to opine on damages in any event because of his unfamiliarity with personal trust funds. The court concluded that the testimony was admissible and that the jury could weigh it accordingly.

Engineered Products Co. v. Donaldson Company, Inc., 313 F. Supp. 2d 951 (N.D. Iowa 2004)
Plaintiff filed a patent infringement action alleging that defendant's air filter indicator devices violated plaintiffs' patent. Plaintiff challenged defendant's liability and damages experts. Plaintiff's attack on the first expert raised issues of timeliness, but also whether the witness, a patent attorney, was qualified to testify as an expert in the relevant art. Plaintiff also argued that any expert legal testimony should be limited to Patent and Trademark Office procedures.

The court acknowledged that the first expert's report was untimely, but found "substantial justification" in defendant's failure to name the expert sooner. On the question of "legal opinion" testimony, the court noted that it alone bore the ultimate responsibility for instructing jurors on the law; however, the court was unable to find a rule barring patent attorneys from testifying on "ultimate issues" in patent infringement actions. In allowing the patent attorney to testify on the "ultimate issue" of infringement, the court distinguished the use of attorneys to testify on ultimate legal issues in patent cases from the general rule that prevents attorneys from instructing the jury on the law. This was consistent with opinion of the Federal Circuit in *Symbol Techs, Inc. v. Opticon, Inc.*, 935 F.2d 1569 (Fed. Cir. 1991) and other courts. Plaintiff's argument that the lawyer was not a "person skilled in the art" went to the weight of his testimony, not its admissibility.

Defendant next tried to exclude plaintiff's expert's testimony on lost profits. Defendant argued that the expert did not account for changes in demand, and further that he was not qualified to conduct an econometric analysis because he was an accountant and not an economist. The court ruled that the reasoning and methodology underlying the expert's testimony were valid and reliably applied to the facts at issue. The court observed that "vigorous examination, presentation of contrary evidence, and careful instruction on the burden of proof are not only traditional, but appropriate means of attacking" what defendant contended was shaky evidence.

See also Jeanes v. Allied Life Ins. Co., 168 F. Supp. 2d 958 (S.D. Iowa 2001) (determining lost future profits by projecting income based on historical growth rates is a common method and generally accepted in the relevant community; expert witness CPA was qualified and his opinions would assist the trier of fact; disagreements over the applicable growth rate go to weight of evidence, not admissibility.); *Transamerica Life Ins. Co. v. Lincoln Nat. Life Ins. Co.*, 2008 WL 4787173 (N.D. Iowa 2008) (citing *Engineered Products* and finding that patent attorney may not be expert on annuities, the subject at issue in the patent infringement case, but was properly qualified to given opinions; also cautioning that attorney expert's testimony must go beyond explaining the applicable law or giving legal conclusions).

Thomson v. Gummiwerk Kraiburg Elastik Beteiligungs GmbH & Co. et al., 2003 U.S. Dist. LEXIS 20414 (N.D. Iowa 2003)
Plaintiff worked at a rubber processing plant and was severely injured when he caught his hand in a mechanical press. He brought a product liability claim against the German manufacturer of the machine,

and designated an expert to testify that the press was defectively designed and that an alternative, safer design was available. Defendant argued that the expert's preliminary report was inadmissible under *Daubert* and that his supplemental report was untimely because it introduced new theories of liability.

The court found that the expert's testimony was not so fundamentally unsupported as to warrant exclusion. His opinion was based on his personal inspection of the evidence and his training and experience. To the extent that the defendants disagreed with the basis for his conclusions, defendants were free to cross examine the expert and highlight the facts that he did not prepare any drawings of his alternative design, and that he did not consider any hazards implicated by that design.

Pioneer Hi-Bred International, Inc. v. Ottawa Plant Food, Inc., 219 F.R.D. 135 (N.D. Iowa 2003)

Plaintiff sued to enforce its patents for hybrid and inbred seed corn. The parties challenged each others' proposed experts, and the court found that each of the experts was plainly qualified to offer expert opinions on various issues in patent cases. It was also likely that their testimony would assist the trier of fact to understand the evidence or determine a fact at issue.

The court made several decisions about admissibility of various aspects of the expert opinions on relevance grounds, finding that some of the opinions would not assist the jury or conflicted with the court's previous rulings. Defendant sought to exclude plaintiff's rebuttal expert, claiming that the testimony invaded the province of the jury. The court agreed that any testimony regarding the sufficiency of the evidence of infringement, or of willful infringement, was either irrelevant or invaded the province of the jury. The court believed that expert testimony on "willful infringement" would not assist the trier of fact to determine that issue, and that willful infringement was a matter for jury alone to decide. The court reserved for trial the question of the expert's competence to testify on matters such as the existence of a "two supplier" market, since it was unclear at that time whether the expert was qualified to offer such an opinion.

Finally, defendant moved to exclude expert testimony setting a reasonable royalty of $30 per bag, which was the same profit that plaintiff allegedly received for its conditional sales of the seed corn for purposes of growing corn for grain or forage. Defendant contended that plaintiff's expert did not perform any analysis to determine what a reasonable royalty for the right to resell would be. The court found that the motion boiled down to a disagreement with the expert's conclusions, which was not a basis to exclude the testimony.

Zeigler v. Fisher-Price, Inc., 2003 U.S. Dist. LEXIS 11184 (N.D. Iowa 2003)

Plaintiff sued a toy manufacturer alleging that a toy vehicle started a fire that damaged plaintiff's home, garage, and personal property. Plaintiff proposed to call two experts to testify about the fire's origin and cause. The manufacturer sought to preclude the experts' testimony under *Daubert*.

Plaintiff's first expert, a fire investigator, concluded after a rigorous investigation that the fire originated in the location of the toy vehicle and that the toy vehicle caused the fire. He based his conclusion on his interpretation of the location of the vehicle and the damage in that area. The court found that this expert followed a generally accepted methodology. Some of his conclusions were based on circumstantial evidence, but his reasoning and experience suggested that his opinions were reliable and would assist the jury.

The second expert had participated as a testifying witness for plaintiffs in several other cases involving the same toy vehicle. He came to his conclusions regarding how the toy vehicle caused the fire on the basis of documentary and photographic evidence. The court held that, because his conclusions represented common sense deductions, not scientific investigation, he was not qualified to give an expert opinion concerning the manufacturer's warranty, recordkeeping system, or the origin and cause of the fire. He was, however, qualified to testify concerning certain general issues which would assist the jury in determining whether the toy vehicle was a defective product.

Baker v. John Morrell & Co., 249 F. Supp. 2d 1138 (N.D. Iowa 2003)
An employee sued her employer under Title VII of the Civil Rights Act of 1964 for constructive discharge, disparate treatment, hostile work environment, and retaliation. A jury returned a verdict in the employee's favor. As part of the employer's motion for a new trial, it challenged the admission of testimony from plaintiff's treating physician that plaintiff's emotional distress was caused by her experience working for defendant.

The court ruled that the doctor's testimony was not so lacking in foundation or reliability that it should have been excluded. The physician had previously treated plaintiff for depression and referred her to a psychiatrist, who confirmed the treating physician's diagnosis. The sufficiency of the factual basis for the treating physician's testimony could be tested on cross examination, but it was not so deficient as to merit exclusion.

McGuire et al. v. Davidson Manufacturing Corporation, et al., 238 F. Supp. 2d 1096 (N.D. Iowa 2003)
Plaintiff fell from a six-foot wooden ladder and filed a products liability action against the manufacturer, proposing to call wood experts and engineering experts to testify that the ladder failed because it was defective. The manufacturer sought to exclude certain of the experts' testimony, claiming their opinions were not reliable under *Daubert*. The court held that the wood expert's opinion that the wood used in the ladder was brash or brittle due to high temperature drying was reached through a methodology that was proper under the circumstances. That testimony was not excluded. However, there was insufficient evidence to support the experts' opinion that brittleness in the wood actually caused the accident, so testimony related to this opinion was excluded. The court found no meaningful objection to the testimony of the engineering experts since they were merely applying well-established engineering techniques to the particular materials at issue in the case. Therefore, the motions to exclude the engineering experts' testimony were denied.

Shalom Hospitality, Inc. v. Alliant Energy Company, et al., 293 B.R. 211 (Bankr. N.D. Iowa 2003)
Debtor filed for bankruptcy under Chapter 7 of the bankruptcy code. Plaintiff trustee sought to recover pre-bankruptcy payments in a preference recovery action pursuant to 11 U.S.C. § 547. The trustee moved to exclude the testimony of the creditors' expert. That testimony related to calculation of the delinquencies in debtor's utility payments as part of the creditors' ordinary course of business defense. The court rejected the trustee's arguments that the expert's method of calculating the delinquency was not generally accepted and that this was not an appropriate area for expert testimony. The court found no reason not to apply an industry-standard methodology to debtor's payment history in order to determine whether payments during the preference period were made in the ordinary course. The court concluded that the testimony might be helpful, particularly with regard to the experts' analysis of ordinary business terms in the utility industry and the use of a "weighted day" calculation.

Krueger v. Johnson & Johnson, 160 F. Supp. 2d 1026 (S.D. Iowa 2001) (aff'd, 66 Fed. Appx. 661)
Following cervical fusion surgery that failed, plaintiff underwent a second surgery using an orthopedic device. For the second surgery, doctors implanted the Codman Anterior Cervical Plate System. The plate is designed to bear weight, allowing fusion to occur and the bony structure to heal. The plate is usually extracted from the body once fusion has occurred. While fusion was partially successful following the surgery, some of the screws that held the device in place had broken.

The patient and his wife sued the manufacturers of the plate system under negligence and strict liability theories. They retained an expert witness with degrees in metallurgy and engineering. After examining the screws and plate system that had been removed from plaintiff, the expert opined that the breaks were due to fatigue failure caused by a design defect.

The court granted defendants' motion to exclude the expert's testimony because neither his qualifications nor his proposed testimony satisfied the Rule 702 standard. Although the expert had evaluated a number of products over the course of his career, he had "no experience in the design of medical implants or any other medical devices." Citing cases from other jurisdictions, the court noted that "there appear to be only a narrow category of experts who are being found qualified to testify in cases of this nature across the country."

The court also found that the expert's opinions were based on insufficient facts: "He does not know how much pressure it takes to bend a screw in vivo and has never been involved in the testing of a medical device to be used inside the body." Finally, the court held that the expert base[d] his opinions on non-applicable principles and methods that are unreliable in this context and he applied them in an unreliable fashion."

See also *Stibbs v. Mapco, Inc., et al.*, 945 F. Supp. 1220 (S.D. Iowa 1996) (excluding plaintiffs' expert's testimony that a particle "of unknown size and composition" caused a propane water heater to explode; experts' opinion that the explosion dislodged the particle and caused the valve to return to function normally was untested and "essentially irrefutable").

3. Minnesota

In re Wholesale Grocery Prods. Antitrust Litig., 2012 WL 3031085 (D. Minn. 2012)

This matter consisted of two consolidated putative antitrust class actions. Defendants moved to strike the report and testimony of plaintiffs' economic expert, Dr. Jeffrey Leitzinger. Like defendants' economic experts, Dr. Leitzinger was proffered to opine about the extent to which common evidence could be used to determine the essential issues in the case.

The court denied defendants' *Daubert* motion, noting that the *Daubert* analysis had to be adapted to fit the procedural posture of the case: "At the class certification stage, the court, not a jury, is the decision maker, and therefore a less stringent analysis is required." The court noted that, at this stage, its only job was to scrutinize the reliability of expert testimony in light of the criteria for class certification and the current state of evidence. The court further noted that expert disputes at the class certification stage are resolved only to the extent necessary to determine the nature of the evidence that would be sufficient to make out a prima facie case of class liability and that "[t]he *Daubert* inquiry at [this] stage is to guard against certification of a class based on an expert opinion so flawed that it is inadmissible as a matter of law."

In light of these principles, the court denied defendants' *Daubert* motion. It found that, even accepting the reliability of Dr. Lietzinger's methodology, plaintiffs had not shown that common impact could be proven through common evidence. Therefore, the purpose of a *Daubert* inquiry at class certification, i.e., preventing a class from being certified based on dubious expert evidence, was not implicated. The court noted that the Eighth Circuit had recently held that expert disputes should be resolved only to the extent necessary to make a determination regarding the nature of the evidence sufficient for class certification. Because Dr. Leitzinger's methods, even if unchallenged, would be insufficient to demonstrate common impact, it was not necessary to resolve disputes regarding the reliability of his methods. Therefore, the court declined to conduct a full *Daubert* analysis at the class certification stage.

This decision seemingly contradicts the majority opinion in a recent U.S. Supreme Court case, *Wal-Mart Stores, Inc. v. Dukes*, 564 U.S. __, 131 S.Ct. 2541, 180 L.Ed.2d (2011). In *Wal-Mart*, the Supreme Court suggested that full *Daubert* scrutiny should apply to expert opinions proffered at the class certification stage. The majority opinion noted that it "doubted" the accuracy of the district court's conclusion that *Daubert* did not apply to expert testimony at the certification stage of class action proceedings. Thus, while *Wal-Mart* did not provide definitive guidance on the issue, it indicated that the Supreme Court would require district courts to conduct a full *Daubert* analysis of expert opinions proffered at the class certification stage.

Werth v. Hill-Rom, Inc., 2012 WL 1379660 (D. Minn. 2012)
In this case, plaintiffs were the parents of a newborn who sustained severe injuries while in the care of a hospital when a fire erupted in his bassinet. The hospital also joined in the action as a plaintiff. Plaintiffs brought a product liability suit against the manufacturer of the baby warmer that was covering the infant at the time. Plaintiffs hired a team of experts. The team's original report concluded that "ignition due to a hot [quartz] particle originating from the . . . warmer heater assembly and falling into the bassinet is the *most likely* ignition source for the . . . incident." However, a supplemental report stated that "to a reasonable degree of scientific and engineering certainty," the fire actually *"was caused by* . . . a hot particle originating from the warmer heater element assembly falling into the bassinet and igniting the oxygen-enriched solid combustibles." The supplemental report nowhere explained why it contained a more authoritative opinion on the fire's cause than the initial report and contained no discussion of additional testing or analyses performed following the initial report's preparation.

Defendant moved to exclude plaintiffs' expert team's opinions and testimony, arguing that the report provided no reasonable explanation for how a chip large enough to ignite the bassinet could have fallen though the tiny gap in the heater assembly. Plaintiffs responded that their experts complied with the protocol in the National Fire Protection Association (NFPA) publication *NFPA 921: Guide for Fire and Explosion Investigations*. The court was unconvinced and held that the report did not satisfy *Daubert*. The court noted that NFPA 21 was never mentioned in the nearly 300-page report and none of the experts mentioned it in their depositions. This alone justified exclusion. Also, even if the experts had properly disclosed their reliance on NFPA 921, this would not be sufficient, despite the standard's general acceptance among the fire investigation community. The experts failed to demonstrate they had applied the methodology reliably to the facts because neither the original nor the supplemental report indicated that the team had adequately tested its hypothesis, as required by NFPA 921. Plaintiffs' claim that, instead of physical testing, the experts had carried out "cognitive testing" or "thought experiments" did not pass muster under NFPA 921 or *Daubert*, particularly under the facts presented.

The court also noted that, during deposition testimony proffered after defendant's motion was filed, plaintiffs' experts tried to interject new explanations for how the fire occurred. These new explanations demonstrated that physical testing was feasible and that the experts recognized their opinion was flawed. Further, the court noted that the Eighth Circuit has repeatedly rejected expert testimony under similar circumstances. Finally, the court held that, even if the opinion was reliable, it would still likely be excluded under Rule of Evidence 403, which permits exclusion of evidence the probative value of which is outweighed by the danger of unfair prejudice, confusion of the issues, or misleading the jury.

Eldredge v. City of St. Paul, 809 F. Supp. 2d 1011 (D. Minn. 2011)
Plaintiff, a firefighter who suffered from a visual impairment called Stargardt's Macular Dystrophy, brought an action against the city of St. Paul and the fire department after he was terminated, alleging violations of the Americans with Disabilities Act (ADA), ADA Amendments Act and the Minnesota Human Rights Act (MHRA) after he was terminated. Plaintiff claimed that with reasonable accommodations he could perform his duties. Defendants argued that plaintiff could not perform the essential functions of a firefighter and that his requested accommodation created an undue hardship. Defendants filed a motion for summary judgment. Plaintiff filed motions for partial summary judgment and to exclude defendants' expert testimony.

Defendants proffered an ophthalmologist and two occupational health physicians who opined that plaintiff's visual condition prevented him from performing the duties required of a firefighter. Plaintiff argued that the experts' opinions were unreliable and irrelevant, largely because they lacked expertise in firefighting skills and one of them had not examined the plaintiff. The court rejected these arguments, holding that all three experts were qualified and had rendered sufficiently reliable opinions. The court noted that all three were physicians and "[t]heir findings are based on a number of years of experience in their respective specialty fields, a review of the records, and in some instances, an examination of Plaintiff." One expert also claimed experience working with firefighters and undergoing some of their training. The court also found that the opinions were relevant because defendants' experts, like plaintiff's, would proffer testimony regarding the central issue in the case: plaintiffs' medical condition and ability to work as a firefighter.

In re Viagra Prods. Liab. Litig., 658 F. Supp. 2d 936 (D. Minn. 2009); 659 F. Supp. 2d 950 (D. Minn. 2009)

Plaintiffs in this litigation filed product liability actions alleging that Viagra caused a vision loss disorder called non-arteritic anterior ischemic optic neuropathy (NAION) due to diminished blood flow to the frontal portion of the optic nerve. Defendant Pfizer moved to exclude plaintiffs' expert's testimony on general causation.

Plaintiffs' expert, Dr. Gerald McGwin, was the principal author of a study based on questions asked of thirty-eight patients who had been diagnosed with NAION and thirty-eight patients who had not. The information from the interviews was consolidated into an electronic data set, which Dr. McGwin used in his study without comparing the data set to the original survey forms. The study found that men with a history of myocardial infarction and Viagra/Cialis use had a statistically significant increased risk of suffering from NAION, and that men with hypertension and Viagra/Cialis use had a non-statistically significant increased risk of suffering from NAION. The court had previously denied Pfizer's *Daubert* challenge of Dr. McGwin, largely because it had found that his study was peer-reviewed, published, contained known rates of error, and resulted from generally accepted epidemiological research. The court had also noted that the study was conducted pre-litigation.

However, Pfizer later raised concerns about the accuracy of the data underlying the study. Most significantly, Pfizer uncovered evidence suggesting that, while the electronic data set coded a number of patients as having first taken Viagra or Cialis *before* being diagnosed with NAION, the original survey forms indicated that these patients had stated that they started taking Cialis or Viagra *after* their NAION diagnosis. Dr. McGwin later conducted a reanalysis of the data and sent a letter to the journal that originally published his article stating that "several aspects of [the] manuscript require[d] modification." He ultimately concluded the letter with a statement that "the results presented [in the letter] are consistent with those in our original manuscript with the exception that any increased risk appears to be limited to Viagra." Plaintiffs then moved to supplement Dr. McGwin's report. Pfizer renewed its *Daubert* challenge of Dr. McGwin and the court excluded his opinions as unreliable.

First, the court found that there were serious questions regarding the reliability of the study as originally published, most significantly because of discrepancies between the survey forms and the electronic data set that Dr. McGwin used to conduct his study. Second, the court found that McGwin's reanalysis also lacked reliability because it had not been published or peer-reviewed and it had been produced in reaction to concerns raised during litigation. The court also denied plaintiffs' motion to supplement Dr. McGwin's original report with a report that included his reanalysis, finding that the submission was untimely and was neither substantially justified nor harmless.

In another memorandum and order issued on the same day, the court also addressed several challenges to the plaintiffs' specific causation experts, despite acknowledging that its exclusion of Dr. McGwin's general causation opinions conclusively ended the plaintiffs' case. The court excluded the majority of plaintiffs' specific causation experts' opinions as unreliable. However, it held that the opinion of plaintiffs' FDA regulatory expert, Dr. Cheryl Blume, could not be excluded solely because it differed from the FDA's nonbinding "Guidance for Industry" publication. Neither could Dr. Blume's definition of a safety signal be excluded on the basis that it differed from the definition in the Guidance for Industry. The court found that Dr. Blume's definition had not been directly contradicted by any statute or regulation and appeared to be based on her interpretation of FDA regulations and her experience in applying those regulations.

In re Baycol Prods. Litig., 532 F. Supp.2d 1029 (D. Minn. 2007)

In this case, patients brought products liability claims against the manufacturer of Baycol, which was withdrawn from the market in 2001. The court ruled on numerous *Daubert* motions brought by defendants seeking to exclude portions of the testimony of several of plaintiffs' proposed experts. The most significant of these rulings are discussed.

The court first addressed the motion to exclude the testimony of Dr. John Farquhar, who opined that Baycol caused significantly greater muscle disease than other drugs in the same class, known as statins. Defendants argued that Dr. Farquhar improperly relied upon on Adverse Event Reports (AERs) in which prescription drug manufacturers receive information about adverse events reported by patients taking a particular drug. Defendants asserted that the medical and scientific consensus is that AERs cannot be used to determine a relative risk between medications, as one of plaintiffs' experts admitted. Defendants also pointed out that Dr. Farquhar combined data from the FDA U.S. AERs and the FDA Worldwide AERs without discerning whether there was any overlap in the data, or whether the definitions of AER terms varied from one country to another. Dr. Farquhar also did not take into account the fact that AERs are reported more frequently on initial marketing, with fewer reports over time. Finally, defendants asserted that in arriving at a "denominator" of total statin prescriptions, Dr. Farquhar failed to account for free samples given to patients in office visits.

The court held that Dr. Farquhar's meta-analyses of AER data comparing the toxicity of Baycol to other statins had not been tested or subjected to peer review and publication. Further, in light of the limitations inherent in AER data, there was insufficient evidence as to the known or potential rate of error and there was no evidence proffered to demonstrate that such an analysis was generally accepted. As to the articles cited by Dr. Farquhar, the court systematically distinguished the relevance or reliability of each. The court excluded Dr. Farquhar's opinion that Baycol was more dangerous than other statins under Rule 702 (but also noted that this holding did not preclude the admission of AER evidence for other purposes at trial).

Next, the court considered defendants' motion to exclude Dr. Farquhar's recalculation of a PacifiCare study. The court held that Dr. Farquhar was qualified to opine on the accuracy of the study, but excluded his recalculation of the study as scientifically unreliable. The court also granted defendants' motion to exclude the testimony of plaintiffs' biostatistician, Dr. Harland Austin because, like Dr. Farquhar, Dr. Austin had based his opinions about the risks of Baycol on his analysis of AERs and his recalculation of the PacifiCare study. In particular, the assumptions Dr. Austin made in order to recalculate the results of the PacifiCare study were based on analyses of AER data, which the court had determined were unreliable.

Plaintiffs also proffered several additional experts to testify as to the comparative toxicity of statins. The court excluded the opinions of two of these experts, largely because they relied on the findings of the experts whose opinions had already been excluded.

The court also addressed expert testimony regarding Bayer's conduct—specifically its state of mind and ethics—in dealing with FDA. The court determined that while expert testimony may be allowed as to the standard of care for pharmaceutical companies, an expert may not infuse his or her personal views as to whether a defendant acted ethically, responsibly, or recklessly inasmuch as those views are not "expert opinions" so much as personal opinions. Moreover, where plaintiffs' expert had not reviewed defendants' FDA submissions and did not definitively know what preclinical and clinical studies were conducted, he was not in a position to pass judgment on Bayer's clinical and preclinical work or its communications with the FDA. Accordingly, the court excluded the ethics testimony because it was speculative, lacked foundation, and would not assist the trier of fact.

Defendants also sought to exclude expert testimony that rhabdomyolysis may be diagnosed retrospectively on the basis of clinical information, including exposure to statins among other things. Defendants argued that these theories were not supported by studies, but were created solely for the litigation by extrapolation from the medical literature. After reviewing the relevant medical literature, the court agreed that rhabdomyolysis and/or myopathy could not be retrospectively diagnosed. The court precluded expert testimony to the effect that statin-induced rhabdomyolysis and/or myopathy could be diagnosed without objective findings.

Defendants also sought to exclude the opinion testimony of one of plaintiffs' experts that Baycol was more susceptible to drug-drug interactions because of its dual metabolic profile. Although the expert had conceded in deposition that his opinions were untested and that he was not aware of any publications supporting his theory, the court nevertheless denied defendants' motion. Similarly, the court permitted expert testimony on the mechanics of statin-induced myopathy, despite the fact that the mechanism of injury was not fully known at the time. The court noted that just because a theory is new or in the process of becoming generally accepted does not make it inadmissible. Plaintiffs' expert's opinion regarding the mechanics of injury was well-reasoned and based on relevant scientific literature as well as the expert's years of experience.

The court also permitted plaintiffs' expert testimony regarding the completeness or accuracy of the Baycol label based on the expert's knowledge of the risks of the drug and his own clinical experience. The court prohibited, however, any testimony as to whether the labeling complied with FDA regulations or should have included AER data, holding that plaintiffs' expert was not qualified in that regard.

In Re: St. Jude Medical, Inc. Silzone Heart Valves Prods. Liab. Litig., 493 F. Supp. 2d 1082 (D. Minn. 2007)

Plaintiffs brought product liability claims against the manufacturer of Silzone, a heart valve with a silver-lined sewing cuff intended to prevent endocarditis. Plaintiffs alleged that the silver coating damaged the tissue around the valve, causing it to fail. Defendants moved to preclude testimony of three of plaintiffs' experts.

Defendants challenged the first expert, Gregory J. Wilson, an anatomic pathologist, arguing that he was not qualified to opine on Silzone valves. The court found that Wilson's significant experience in biomaterials qualified him to opine on the issue despite his lack of experience specific to silver coatings.

Defendants also challenged the qualifications of plaintiff's expert Kevin E. Healy, who had not worked on mechanical heart valves or any silver-coated devices. The court again rejected defendants' argument, finding that Healy had sufficient expertise in biomaterials and the design of medical devices to qualify him to testify on the effects of silver leaching from the devices. Specifically, the court permitted Healy to testify that the Silzone coating caused local tissue damage because Healy had knowledge and experience in interactions between metals and human tissues.

Defendants also moved to exclude the testimony of Eric Butchart, a cardiothoracic surgeon with expertise in heart valve surgery. Butchart opined that Silzone had a direct toxic effect on tissues and blood components. Defendants argued that this opinion would require Butchart to have expertise in toxicology, pathology, hematology, biomaterials science, and metallurgy, of which he had none. But the court acknowledged that Butchart was an expert in the risk of thromboembolism after heart valve replacement, and that he had knowledge of the additional areas raised by defendants through reading the literature, talking to other experts, and attending medical conferences.

CardioVention, Inc. v. Medtronic, Inc., 483 F. Supp. 2d 830 (D. Minn. 2007)

CardioVention alleged that Medtronic had misappropriated its trade secrets, among other things. Medtronic challenged three of CardioVention's damages experts.

With respect to the first damages expert, Donald A. Gorowsky, Medtronic argued that two of his opinions must be excluded as "contrary to law." Medtronic asserted that Gorowsky had applied an incorrect measure of damages because he calculated unjust enrichment damages based on sales of Medtronic's existing perfusion line of products, as opposed to profits generated by Medtronic's sale of products incorporating the misappropriated trade secret. The court concluded, however, that Gorowsky's opinion was legally sufficient under the damages provisions of the Minnesota Uniform Trade Secrets Act.

Medtronic also sought to exclude Gorowsky's opinion that measured plaintiff's unjust enrichment damages according to the estimated loss of CardioVention's business value. Finding that courts have recognized that a plaintiff's actual damages can be measured by the value of the loss of the trade secret to the plaintiff under these circumstances, the court held this opinion admissible as well. Medtronic further objected that Gorowsky's opinions were premised on flawed and speculative facts. The court found that these attacks went to weight, not admissibility.

Medtronic also moved to exclude the expert testimony of John L. Heath, who used various valuation methods to estimate the fair market value of CardioVention. Medtronic asserted that, because Heath had an undisclosed financial interest in the outcome of the litigation, his testimony should be excluded. Without further elaboration, the court ruled that the possibility of a "success fee" for Heath went to the weight of his opinion, not the admissibility.

Maras v. Avis Rent A Car System, Inc., 393 F. Supp. 2d 801 (D. Minn. 2005)

Plaintiffs, a husband and wife, sued Avis rental car company and one of its employees over a minor accident involving the wife and the Avis employee. Plaintiffs alleged that the accident caused the wife's fibromyalgia. Defendants moved to exclude the testimony of plaintiffs' causation experts, family practice physician Dr. Jim Anagnostis and psychiatrist Dr. Andrew Klymiuk.

In support of their argument that plaintiffs' causation theory was unreliable, Defendants cited two Fifth Circuit cases excluding expert testimony that trauma causes fibromyalgia. Defendants argued that the scientific community's understanding of the causes of fibromyalgia had not advanced since the most recent Fifth Circuit ruling on the issue. In response, plaintiffs proffered two studies that they contended supported the medical community's acceptance of the experts' theory of causation. Plaintiffs also argued that because their experts reached their opinions after conducting a differential diagnosis, their testimony was necessarily reliable.

After briefly summarizing the Fifth Circuit cases, the court considered the two studies that plaintiffs cited as proof that their causation theory was generally accepted in the relevant community. With respect to the first, the court noted the authors' statements to the effect that their study only *suggested* that physical trauma was associated with the onset of fibromyalgia, that the cause of fibromyalgia remained unclear, and that further prospective studies were needed to confirm the association.

The court found that the second study was not a study at all, but a Web page suggesting generally that illness or injury can trigger fibromyalgia. The Website did not disclose the basis or methodology for its conclusion. Meanwhile, defendants presented studies characterizing the hypothesis that trauma causes fibromyalgia as an "open question" that merited further research. Based on legal precedent and the evidence presented, the court ruled that plaintiffs had failed to meet their burden under *Daubert* to show that their witnesses' testimony was reliable. The court found that plaintiffs' causation theory had not been verified by testimony or peer reviewed, and noted the experts' concessions in deposition testimony that the cause of fibromyalgia was unknown. The court also noted that the doctors' theory had no known potential rate of error and had failed to gain general acceptance.

Separately, plaintiffs asserted that their experts' opinions were necessarily reliable because they were formed after conducting differential diagnoses. The court, however, found that because neither doctor had a proper basis for "ruling in" the February 1999 accident as a potential cause of plaintiff's fibromyalgia, the differential diagnoses should be excluded. Accordingly, the court granted defendants' motion.

North Star Mutual Ins. Co. v. Zurich Ins. Co., 269 F. Supp. 2d 1140 (D. Minn. 2003)

In this case, which arose out of a loss due to fire, plaintiff insurer, North Star, sought a declaration that the insured's loss was in fact covered by another insurer, Zurich. North Star also alleged that the insured's broker negligently failed to secure replacement coverage with Zurich for the insured's loss and therefore was liable to North Star for reimbursement for the claim. Before the court were several motions including plaintiff's motion to extend the court's expert disclosure deadline.

Plaintiff sought leave to file an otherwise untimely expert report. Plaintiff's expert was the owner and CEO of several retail insurance agencies and president and CEO of a management consulting and appraisal company. Based on his review of discovery conducted in the case, the expert opined that the insured's agent in his communications with the defendant insurance broker had complied with the custom and practice of an agent in the circumstances, and that the broker did in fact bind Zurich to coverage for the insured's loss.

The court rejected both plaintiff's justifications for its untimeliness and plaintiff's arguments as to the reliability of his expert. The court held that the proffered expert testimony amounted to how one person (albeit a very experienced person) viewed a series of communications between an insurance agent and an insurance broker. The court noted that plaintiff's expert did not cite any treatise or anything beyond his own opinion to demonstrate the legitimacy of his opinion. Absent a connection to an independent authority, the court reasoned that the jury would have no means by which to ascertain the reliability of plaintiff's expert's view. Thus, the court denied plaintiff's motion for an extension of time to disclose expert reports.

Medalen v. Tiger Drylac U.S.A., Inc., 269 F. Supp. 2d 1118 (D. Minn. 2003)

In this product liability case, plaintiff sued manufacturers of powder-coat paint, Tiger Drylac and DuPont, asserting that exposure to defendants' products during the course of her employment caused her to develop skin cancer. Defendants moved for summary judgment based on the statutes of limitations, as well as for exclusion of the testimony and reports of plaintiff's experts as to causation. With respect to the expert testimony, defendants argued that plaintiff had failed to establish causation and likewise failed to establish the carcinogenicity of their products.

The court began its *Daubert* analysis by observing that, in order to prove causation in a toxic tort case, plaintiff must show that the agent was capable of causing injuries like those suffered by plaintiff and that it was in fact the cause of plaintiff's injuries. Citing Eighth Circuit authority, the court conceded that the first several victims of a new toxic tort should not be barred from recovery because the medical literature in support of their claims has not yet been developed. Rather, plaintiff needed only to proffer evidence from which a reasonable person could conclude that her exposure more likely than not caused her injury.

Defendant Tiger Drylac argued that its paint product contained only TGIC, which plaintiff's general causation expert Dr. Terry Martinez conceded was not a proven carcinogen. Thus, the court granted summary judgment as to that defendant. Dupont's products, on the other hand, contained nickel and chromium, which Dr. Martinez had stated were carcinogenic. DuPont challenged Dr. Martinez's assertion that the mere presence of nickel, chromium, and TGIC in its product was sufficient to make its product carcinogenic. The court agreed and proceeded to identify numerous flaws in Dr. Martinez's methodology. First, the court observed that Dr. Martinez had never examined or even talked to plaintiff. He also had not inspected or viewed plaintiff's workplace or assessed her employer's industrial hygiene practices. Dr. Martinez had no past experience with powder coatings; in forming his opinion, he relied solely on the case file materials he received from plaintiff's counsel and the results of a literature search on nickel, chromium, and TGIC.

Given his cursory literature review, the court found Dr. Martinez ill-equipped to opine as to the possible carcinogenicity of chromium or nickel without reference to dosage. Indeed, Dr. Martinez had made no effort to determine the dosage to which plaintiff was exposed. Thus, the court concluded that Dr. Martinez had failed to make the required threshold showing of exposure that would support a scientifically reliable causation opinion. A temporality argument was not well supported, particularly when Dr. Martinez failed to address any latency period. Moreover, Dr. Martinez conceded he could not even say for sure that these chemicals would be absorbed by the body. Thus, the court found his opinion to be without relevance or reliability, and granted defendants' motion for summary judgment on the issue of causation.

Because plaintiff argued that the testimony of Dr. Heath, her other expert, would also serve to "rule in" defendants' products as the cause of her cancer, the court proceeded to consider Dr. Heath's testimony. DuPont argued that Dr. Heath's testimony should be excluded because he failed to perform a valid differential diagnosis as to the cause of plaintiff's skin cancer. Specifically, DuPont asserted that the differential diagnosis Dr. Heath performed was for the purpose of diagnosing and treating plaintiff's condition, not determining its cause. Dr. Heath conceded he was not an expert in the causes of cancer. He also acknowledged he did not know the level of plaintiff's exposure to powder coatings. Dr. Heath conducted no independent research into any of the issues surrounding the case and had no expertise in toxicology. Thus, the court concluded Dr. Heath had no competent foundation to "rule in" powder coatings as the cause of plaintiff's cancer. Similarly, the court concluded Dr. Heath had no competent basis "rule out" other potential causes of plaintiff's skin cancer.

Carlen v. Minn. Comprehensive Epilepsy Program, P.A., 2001 WL 1078633 (D. Minn. 2001)

Plaintiff's decedent in this medical malpractice case was diagnosed with a low-grade brain tumor in 1980. After years of conservative management and little growth, the tumor became aggressively malignant in the spring of 1998. One day, she went to the emergency room after experiencing two seizures; she subsequently underwent brain surgery to "debulk" the tumor but she never recovered. Plaintiff, trustee in wrongful death of decedent's estate, sued the doctors on the ground that the tumor should have been operated on earlier. Plaintiff's expert opined that the decedent would have lived seven to eight months longer had she received earlier treatment. The court found, however, that this opinion lacked the relevance and reliability mandated by *Daubert*. First, the expert's argument that surgery, chemotherapy, and radiation could have slowed the growth of the tumor was "too vague to be sufficiently relevant under *Daubert*." The expert's seven-to-eight-month projection was also not validated by any showing of general acceptance or an acceptable error rate. On that basis, the court granted summary judgment to defendants.

Stevens v. City of Virginia, 2001 WL 391568 (D. Minn. 2001)

In *Stevens*, a civil claim against a police department, defendant sought to exclude expert testimony that plaintiff's seizures and headaches were consistent with a blow to the head that she allegedly received during her arrest. Defendant maintained that since the expert saw plaintiff in the context of treatment, he did not attempt to determine the cause of her symptoms, and therefore his testimony did not establish medical causation. The court found, however, that the expert did in fact consider causation when he examined plaintiff, and that he also conducted some testing to rule out alternative causes. On this basis, the court held that the expert satisfied *Daubert* and would be allowed to testify.

***Grinnell Mut. Reins. Co. v. Heritage Ins. Agency*, 2001 WL 902777 (D. Minn. 2001)**
This case involved a claim by an insurance underwriter against an agent for the agent's failure to notify the carrier of changes in the policyholder's status that materially increased the risk of loss. Both parties proffered expert testimony to explain the nature and scope of an insurance agent's duties. The defendant moved to exclude the plaintiff's expert's testimony as "factually unfounded extrapolations made exclusively from his subjective personal experience without reference to any reliable and tested industry standards, protocols, or guidelines." The court denied the motion, holding that the expert's forty years of experience in the insurance industry gave him sufficient foundation from which to offer opinions regarding "how a reasonable agent operating within the scope of the defined duty may balance his duties to the insurer and the insured," and "what may constitute good faith under the relevant or comparable circumstances." The court did restrict the expert from defining the scope of an agent's duty to an insurance company, however, because it that was a legal issue for the court to determine and instruct the jury accordingly.

***Am. Fam. Ins. Group v. JVC Americas Corp.*, 2001 WL 1618454 (D. Minn. 2001)**
Plaintiff's expert in this case opined that a defect in JVC's compact disc player started a fire that damaged the policyholders' home. He inspected the electrical artifacts salvaged from the fire, but performed almost no testing on any of the remains or the exemplar CD player that JVC provided. He based his opinion primarily on the burn patterns that he observed in the room where the fire started and on the remains of the appliance. The court found that the expert was not certified as a fire investigator and had no formal training in fire cause and origin analysis. Therefore, he was not qualified to render a causation opinion based on the burn patterns. In excluding testimony that mechanical stress inside the CD player had caused the fire, the court emphasized that "[the expert] made no attempt to determine through independent research and testing whether such mechanical stress could occur, whether it could produce fire and if so, how much stress was required to generate sufficient heat energy to produce fire." As a result, the court labeled his testimony "pure speculation" and granted summary judgment to JVC.

See also *Willert v. Ortho Pharm. Corp.*, 995 F. Supp. 979 (D. Minn. 1998) (excluding expert testimony regarding causal link between Floxin® and plaintiff's autoimmune hemolytic anemia and Guillain-Barre Syndrome; opinion lacked adequate scientific support because it did not "rule in" Floxin® or "rule out" other possible causes; case reports were "not reliable scientific evidence of causation, because they simply describe reported phenomena without comparison to the rate at which the phenomena occur in the general population or in a defined control group"); *Coffey v. County of Hennepin*, 23 F. Supp. 2d 1081 (D. Minn. 1998) (prohibiting a "clinical ecologist" from opining that plaintiff suffered from multiple chemical sensitivities (MCS); clinical ecologists not recognized within the medical community, "federal courts do not consider environmental illness or MCS a scientifically valid diagnosis," and plaintiff could not produce evidence showing that the methodology of diagnosing MCS had "progressed to a point that it is scientific knowledge capable of assisting a fact-finder").

4. Missouri

***Compare Lemmon v. Wyeth, LLC*, 2012 WL 3043014 (E.D. Mo., July 11, 2012) with *Parmentier v. Novartis Pharmaceuticals Corporation*, 2012 WL 2154347 (E.D. Mo., June 19, 2012)**
Two divisions of the United States District Court for the Eastern District of Missouri came to different conclusions regarding the admissibility of expert testimony based on "differential diagnosis" in two pharmaceutical cases. In *Lemmon*, the Eastern Division allowed testimony proffered by plaintiff that defendant's hormone replacement therapy caused plaintiff's breast cancer. The defense argued the testimony should be excluded because the expert did not properly apply the differential diagno-

sis technique; she failed to consider plaintiff's family history of breast cancer and failed to rule out plaintiff's endogenous hormones as a cause of cancer. The court rejected this argument, stating that because this same argument failed to persuade the Eighth Circuit in *Scroggin v. Wyeth*, 586 F.3d 547 (8th Cir. 2009), "this court likewise finds Defendants' contentions unpersuasive in this case."

On the other hand, in *Parmentier* the Southeastern Division excluded proffered expert testimony based on a differential diagnosis technique purporting to attribute plaintiff's osteonecrosis of the jaw (ONJ) with the use of defendant's cancer drug. In this case, the court looked closely at each of the plausible causes of ONJ that were "ruled in" and "ruled out" by the plaintiff's experts. The court noted that while the expert ruled out a number of possible causes of ONJ, he failed to rule out several other known causes including alcoholism and smoking. The court also took issue with the expert's ruling out of osteomyelitis where the plaintiff's own physician and oral surgeon had actually diagnosed the plaintiff with osteomyelitis. Due to the expert's "inadequate methodology and foundation," the expert testimony was excluded.

Maze v. Regions Bank, Inc., 265 F.R.D. 465 (W.D. Mo. 2009)

In a wrongful death case alleging that plaintiff's father's hip fracture from a fall at defendant's place of business caused his subsequent death, the district court analyzed the expert testimony of the orthopedic surgeon who performed the decedent's hip surgery. Although the decedent had not been seen by the orthopedic surgeon for months before his death, and the surgeon had not reviewed the decedent's medical records, the court allowed the surgeon's testimony on causation to defeat defendant's motion for summary judgment. The surgeon provided testimony that the decedent's broken hip, sustained as a result of his fall at defendant's business, "was a substantial factor which contributed to his subsequent death." The surgeon based his testimony on peer-reviewed orthopedic literature that states that within the first year of injury, the mortality rate for persons with hip fractures was 14 to 47 percent, irrespective of other health conditions. The surgeon's opinion was that "because the decedent here died within one year of his injury, such circumstance placed him within that 14- to 47-percent rate of mortality" and that this was "significant even at the low range." Defendant argued that the surgeon's opinion was irrelevant under *Daubert* because the surgeon failed to review the decedent's medical records prior to providing his testimony. The court concluded that these arguments went to the credibility of the expert, not the admissibility of the testimony. The court ruled that the plaintiff had met her burden of demonstrating the surgeon's expert testimony to be admissible.

In re Genetically Modified Rice Litigation, 666 F.Supp.2d 1004 (E.D. Mo. 2009)

Long-grain rice farmers and others involved in the rice business brought suit against a corporation that developed and marketed genetically modified rice, claiming damage from contamination of the U.S. rice supply. This multidistrict litigation, involving Missouri farmer plaintiffs, was the first of a series of bellwether trials. Both plaintiffs and defendants filed motions to exclude expert testimony on a number of issues, including damages. The district court denied most of the motions on expert testimony, concluding that the majority of objections went to the weight of the expert testimony, rather than the admissibility.

The district judge specifically discussed the *Daubert* motions on market damage. Plaintiffs' expert used a partial equilibrium model to estimate the decrease in demand for U.S. rice after the contamination was reported. On the other hand, defendants' expert applied an event study method to calculate the impact that the contamination had on prices for U.S. rice. Despite the differences in methodologies and conclusions, the district court found that both plaintiffs' and defendants' expert witnesses' testimony would assist the trier of fact, and was reliable, relevant and had a factual basis. The district court stated that "the court must be careful to examine methodology, and not the conclusions drawn from it" during a *Daubert* analysis. Thus, the court looked at whether each expert completed the required procedures, used data "typically" replied on, and accounted for relevant variables. Because both experts' methodologies met these requirements, both of the experts' testimony was admissible.

Metropolitan Life Insurance Company v. Bancorp Services, 421 F.Supp.2d 1196 (E.D. Mo. 2006), vacated on other grounds, 527 F.3d 1330 (D.C. Cir. 2008)

This case involved plaintiff insurance company's suit against defendant patent holder requesting a declaratory judgment of non-infringement and invalidity of a patent describing a system for administering and tracking the value of separate-account life insurance claims. The defendant included a declaration of David Klausner, an experienced engineer and software developer who also had experience with forensic investigation, including reverse engineering of computer programs. Klausner evaluated code to conclude whether the program was an infringement. Plaintiff argued that the expert's conclusions were inadmissible because his methodology was inadequate under the *Daubert* standard. Plaintiff did not suggest that the kind of code analysis the expert undertook was incorrect, merely that the expert analysis was incomplete. The court held that plaintiff's objection ultimately went to the credibility of the expert's conclusions rather than to the admissibility. Thus, the court found the expert's report admissible for the purposes of opposing plaintiff's summary judgment motion. Furthermore, the report created a genuine issue of material fact concerning various calculations of market and book value.

McIntosh v. Monsanto Company, 462 F. Supp.2d 1025 (E.D. Mo. 2006)

Plaintiff farmers sued soybean seed companies alleging, among others things, that defendants conspired to raise, fix, and stabilize the price of certain seeds in violation of Section 1 of the Sherman Act. The seeds at issue included a patented technology owned by one of the seed companies and licensed to numerous other companies. The complaint alleged that the owner seed company conspired to eliminate competition by entering into certain arrangements with other seed companies. Defendants moved for summary judgment. As part of defendants' motion for summary judgment, defendants sought to exclude plaintiffs' expert witness from testifying at trial on the grounds that his opinions were unreliable and his methodology deficient. The court denied defendants' motion, concluding that the expert's testimony was reliable and relevant.

The court pointed out that a review of the case law after *Daubert* showed that exclusion of expert testimony is the exception rather than the rule. The court held that it should resolve doubts regarding the usefulness of an expert's testimony in favor of its admissibility but it should not admit opinion evidence that is connected to existing data only by the "ipse dixit" of the expert.

In attacking plaintiff's expert's methodology, defendant argued that the expert's opinions regarding existence of a conspiracy were unreliable because they were imprecise and not supported with sufficient facts or data. Defendant claimed that plaintiff's expert improperly relied on defendant's own documents as evidence of a conspiracy and ignored other data relating to the pricing of the products in question. The court found that the expert based his opinion on a review of the documents in the case, application of economic theory and the expert's past experience in the antitrust field. There was no evidence that this type of methodology and the data were unreliable and not typically used in this field. The court pointed out that, under defendants' position, defendant's own experts would be subject to exclusion for employing similar methodology. Defendant's experts also reviewed defendants' documents to opine on the existence of a conspiracy. They just reached a different conclusion about them, according to the court. This type of disagreement did not render the expert's opinion unreliable.

Neither was the testimony rendered inadmissible under Rule 702 for the reason that the expert did not perform an extensive quantitative analysis in the case. Defendant's arguments about plaintiff's expert's conclusions went to the weight of the evidence, not its admissibility.

Menz v. New Holland North America, Inc., et al., 460 F. Supp. 2d 1058 (E.D. Mo. 2006)
Menz involved a husband and wife filing a personal injury claim against defendants, a tractor designer and manufacturer and other entities, alleging that the tractor was dangerous and defective. The designer and manufacturer of the tractor moved for summary judgment and to exclude testimony from plaintiff's expert.

Plaintiffs proposed to offer testimony from the expert about the need for rollover protection on the tractor, but the court held that the proposed testimony did not meet *Daubert's* requirement of reliability. The court found that summary judgment was warranted on the failure to warn claim because plaintiffs' expert testified that there were no warnings that could have been given that would have altered the husband's conduct at the time of the accident.

The court noted that plaintiffs' expert admitted that he was unable to verify a number of critical components of the accident including height of the loader, weight of the dirt in the loader, the speed at which the tractor was traveling, angle of the turn and slope of the ground as well as the depth of the ditch, soil conditions and whether the wheels contained ballast at the time of the accident. In light of those gaps, the court found that the expert's conclusion that the accident was caused by a defect in the tractor rather than the circumstances of the accident constituted inadmissible speculation.

The court further found that the expert's testimony regarding the absence of rollover protection failed to meet reliability requirements of *Daubert*. The expert had never tested his theory that plaintiff would not have suffered a serious injury had the tractor been equipped with the rollover protection. The expert had never even examined the rollover protection that was available for the tractor in question. Because he had not tested his theory, plaintiffs' expert was unable to establish with any degree of certainty the amount of force the rollover protection would have withstood, nor could he determine how the tractor would have landed had the tractor been equipped with rollover protection. The court concluded that the expert's testimony regarding the absence of rollover protection lacked a reliable basis in engineering science and was too speculative to be admissible.

Yapp v. Union Pacific Railroad Company, 301 F. Supp. 2d 1030 (E.D. Mo. 2004)
Plaintiffs alleged systemic racial discrimination in defendant's employee selection, training and compensation policies, practices, and procedures. Plaintiffs sought class certification, supporting their motion with expert reports of a statistician. Defendants opposed class certification and offered a report prepared by their own statistician. Plaintiffs moved to strike defendants' experts.

Plaintiffs' expert's statistical analyses were based on computer data provided by defendant and purported to demonstrate systemic, statistically significant, adverse impacts against African Americans in various aspects of defendant's job selection processes. Defendant's experts' report was based on statistical analysis that differed markedly from that of plaintiffs' expert because defendants' experts surveyed employees to assess the difference between the various departments in the railroad and the hiring practices used therein. Based on their survey, defendant's experts determined that the proper methods for analyzing the computer data was on a department-by-department basis with extra variables beyond minimum job qualifications. Plaintiffs argued the survey was scientifically invalid and that any statistical analysis based on the survey was unreliable. The court concluded that the survey methodology used by defendant's experts was not admissible scientific evidence.

Defendant argued that its experts never attempted to do a "scientific survey" because they saw no reason to do so. The court concluded that a valid scientific survey was necessary to support the experts' conclusions regarding additional hiring qualifications. The court disagreed with defendant's analysis, holding that the only scientific way to determine that the otherwise uniform aspects of the railroad hiring and selection process are controlled by specific departmental practices would be a scientific survey of the behavior of those departments.

While the court declined to adopt a rigid bar against participation of counsel in a study of employment procedures, under the facts of this case, the heavy involvement of defense counsel in the design and conduct of the survey indicated a lack of independence and thus a lack of scientific validity.

However, in a related case, the court in *Fast v. Applebee's International, Inc.*, 2009 WL 2391775 (W.D. Mo. 2009), allowed certain opinions by plaintiffs' expert regarding employment and tips based on a questionnaire prepared for the purposes of litigation. The court allowed plaintiffs' expert, a former employee of the Department of Labor, to express certain opinions about the validity of the questionnaire given to employees and whether certain questions correctly identified certain types of work because of the expert's substantial experience interpreting the FLSA. However, the court excluded the expert's testimony on what percentage of the plaintiffs' shift was spent performing preparation or maintenance work rather than tip-producing work and the expert's opinion that the results of the questionnaire could be extrapolated to the entire class of plaintiffs because the opinion "runs the risk of invading the province of the jury."

Sample v. Monsanto Company, 218 F.R.D. 644 (E.D. Mo. 2003)

Plaintiffs, a proposed class of corn and soybean farmers, claimed that defendants conspired to fix, raise, maintain, or stabilize prices on genetically modified soybean seeds and corn seeds in violation of the Sherman Act. The plaintiff farmers moved for class certification but the court denied their motion under Fed. R. Civ. P. 23(b)(3), concluding that individualized issues predominated over common questions. Specifically, the farmers could not show that both conspiracy and impact could be proven on a systemic class-wide basis. Plaintiffs had offered an expert witness to establish antitrust impact by constructing a hypothetical market free of the defendant's restraints alleged to be anti-competitive.

The court denied defendants' motion *in limine* to exclude the expert's opinion on the grounds that it was appropriate to consider all evidence at the class certification stage of the proceedings. The court considered all expert testimony offered by both sides in support of or in opposition to class certification. However, the court noted that plaintiffs' expert did not show that impact could be demonstrated on a class-wide basis. The court criticized plaintiffs' expert for presuming class-wide impact without any consideration of whether the markets or alleged conspiracy at issue actually operated in such a manner as to justify the presumption. The expert assumed the answer to the critical issue and plaintiffs asked the court to rely on the expert's conclusion as support for class certification. After considering all of the evidence submitted during the certification hearing, the court ruled that the impact of defendants' alleged antitrust violations could not be shown on a class-wide basis.

Prince v. Michelin North America Inc., 248 F. Supp. 2d 900 (W.D. Mo. 2003)

This product liability case against a defendant car maker and tire maker arose from an automotive fatality. The tire maker moved to exclude plaintiffs' expert, arguing that the witness was not an expert regarding tire manufacture or tire design. Plaintiffs argued that the expert was an expert regarding material sciences and failure analysis and therefore was qualified to testify on tire design and manufacture. The court ruled that the plaintiffs' expert's qualification in material sciences and failure analysis did not give him the necessary experience, either from his work as an educator and engineer or from any tests performed in connection with the case, to be qualified as an expert who could testify that the tire at issue failed due to defective design or manufacture.

The court stated that different areas of expertise need not be mutually exclusive. However, it was equally true that expertise in the fields of material sciences or failure analysis did not *per se* encompass expertise in areas of tire manufacture or tire design. Defendant did not contest the witness's expertise in the fields of material science or failure analysis, but rather argued that the expert had not proposed any reliable and relevant opinions regarding tire manufacture and tire design. The expert's qualifications were sufficient to allow him to offer opinions as to the behavior and state of the materials which composed the tire at issue and to offer his opinion as to how the behavior and state of the materials affected the failure of the tire at issue. Because the expert (1) made certain analytical leaps in his methodology, (2) did not state how his material science findings related to the tire at issue, (3) did not give any rate of error or general acceptance of the methodology and analysis he employed, (4) was limited in his experience regarding tire manufacture and design to what he had acquired in the instant litigation, (5) offered no alternative explanations for the alleged failure of the tire at issue, and (6) did not have the necessary experience from his work as an educator and engineer, he was disqualified as an expert who could testify that the tire at issue failed due to defective designed. The court held that he plaintiff's expert could offer opinions, however, about the behavior and state of the problems of materials in the tire and as to how the behavior and state of the problems of the materials affected the failure of the tire. The expert could not, however, speculate that the failure of the tire was caused by a manufacture or design.

Shaffer v. Amada America Inc., 335 F. Supp. 2d 992 (E.D. Mo. 2003), aff'd, 2003 U.S. App. Lexis 19335 (8th Cir. 2003)

This case involved plaintiffs' employee who was injured while servicing a press brake machine. The employee sued the machine's manufacturer claiming it was defectively designed. The court ruled that the employee's expert failed the Rule 702 and *Daubert* requirements for several reasons: (1) the expert's testimony was unreliable because it was not based on sufficient facts and data, (2) the expert had virtually no experience with press brakes, (3) the expert had never designed or tested the devices he claimed would have prevented the employee's accident, (4) the expert had no knowledge as to whether any of his proposals would have worked or would have interfered with normal operations in the press brake, (5) the expert offered no quantifiable evidence to support his theory as to the cause of the accident, (6) there was no peer review of the expert's theory of alternative design, and (7) there was no evidence of the general acceptance of the expert's abstract theory that his devices would have prevented the accident. The court granted defendant's motion to exclude the expert's testimony and ruled that there was no other evidence that the press brake was defective. Accordingly, summary judgment was granted.

The *Shaffer* holding was followed in a similar products liability case, *Arnold v. Amada North America, Inc.*, 2008 WL 3411789 (E.D. Mo. 2008). There, plaintiff's proffered expert did not have the qualifications of experience with press brake design and press brake manufacturing to provide an expert opinion on whether the press brake without hand-restraints was unreasonably dangerous. The district court also found that the proffered expert's methodology was unreliable because he did not know the basic facts that surrounded the accident at issue, he had not performed research regarding the design of the press brakes, and he never ran his own tests of the machine. Because plaintiff could not establish his claims without expert testimony, the court granted summary judgment for defendant.

Metropolitan St. Louis Equal Housing Opportunity Council v. Gundaker Real Estate Co., 130 F.Supp.2d 1074, 132 F.Supp.2d 1210 (E.D. Mo. 2001)

This litigation centered on claims of "racial steering," directing home seekers to certain neighborhoods based on their race, in St. Louis-area real estate sales. In order to prove their allegations of discriminatory practices, the Equal Housing Opportunity Council (EHOC) retained white and African American "testers" to approach the defendant's agents about potential home purchases. The African American and white "testers" were matched as closely as possible in familial status, age, and income, and were given a script to read to the agents. Based on the results of tests it conducted in 1996 and 1997, the EHOC concluded that the defendant was engaging in "racial steering."

The court held a *Daubert* hearing to determine whether the testers' reports were sufficiently reliable to allow plaintiff's experts to conclude that the defendant was in fact discriminating. The court found the tester data flawed both in terms of the methodology itself and the testers' execution of the methodology. Since all of plaintiffs' experts relied on the tester data, all of their testimony was excluded. In a subsequent order, however, the court held that the tester data could be presented to the jury as *factual* evidence of plaintiff's allegations, even though it was insufficient to support an expert conclusion on the ultimate issue of whether the defendant had engaged in racial steering. See *Metropolitan St. Louis Equal Housing Opportunity Council v. Gundaker Real Estate Co.*, 132 F.Supp.2d 1210 (E.D. Mo. 2001).

Thurman v. Missouri Gas Energy, 107 F.Supp.2d 1046 (W.D. Mo. 2000)
This case involved a natural gas pipeline explosion. The pipeline section that exploded was not excavated, so the cause of the failure could not be determined with certainty. Plaintiffs sought to exclude defense expert testimony that the pipeline failed due to an unforeseeable mechanical failure, rather than corrosion. The court granted plaintiffs' motion in part, holding that defendants' expert had failed to "explain how or why he arrived at his ultimate opinion." The court held, however, that the expert could testify regarding "the historical operations of the pipeline, the typical causes of failure in a pipeline as it ages, the historical frequency of these typical causes, why he believes some of the typical causes did not occur here, the facts which he believes preclude corrosion as a cause and the importance of excavation in determining pipeline failure." In short, the expert could testify about anything other than his opinion with respect to the cause of the pipeline explosion, the ultimate issue in the case.

The court followed the same pattern for the remainder of the experts on both sides: they could testify regarding the *basis* for their opinions, but would not be permitted to express opinions on the ultimate issues. The court explained that "[s]ince the pipeline was not excavated after the accident, no expert can offer a reliable opinion on the issue of ultimate causation so as to assist the jury in fixing the ultimate cause of the accident." Therefore, since the experts' testimony ultimately boiled down to unsolvable differences in their factual assumptions, "[t]he outcome should be determined by the jury on the basis of credibility versus reliability."

Nelson v. American Home Products Corp., 92 F.Supp.2d 954 (W.D. Mo. 2000)
After suffering a heart attack, plaintiff was prescribed defendant's antiarhythmic drug Cordarone. Approximately four months into his treatment, the plaintiff began to lose his eyesight. After his eyesight declined significantly, he sued, claiming that the drug had caused him to develop anterior ischemic optic neuropathy (AION). Defendant had previously sent out a notice to prescribers that it had received reports of AION associated with Cordarone use.

Addressing plaintiff's experts' opinions, the court held that their testimony was based entirely on litigation-driven research; that the experts relied heavily on defendant's FDA-mandated "Dear Doctor" letter, which did not provide a reliable basis for a causal conclusion; that they also relied on anecdotal case reports, which prove merely a temporal association between exposure and symptoms; and that they disagreed among themselves regarding the distinguishing marks and symptoms of the Cordarone-related condition they were attempting to prove. While the court recognized that, in principle, differential diagnosis constitutes a valid methodology, it held that the method was not properly applied in this case. "[A] differential diagnosis based solely on the assumption of causation due to a temporal relationship is inadmissible."

Davidson v. Besser Co., 1997 WL 321489 (E.D. Mo.)
In this products liability case, the Eastern District of Missouri considered the admissibility of expert testimony concerning a machine that fabricated concrete blocks. The plaintiff was injured when the machine started while he was trying to repair it. The expert opined that the machine design was

defective because it lacked an "interlock perimeter guard" to prevent it from starting during repair, an audible warning horn that would sound before the machine started, and proper warning labels.

The court held that the opinion as to the proposed "interlock device" was "unacceptably speculative" and did not fit the facts of the case. The expert apparently ignored that a tall screen barrier extended down one side of the machine, and he could not demonstrate that his proposed alternative design was feasible and would have prevented the plaintiff's injury.

The court allowed testimony that the machine should have incorporated an aural warning device, however, over the defense argument that the experts lacked a foundation for rendering such an opinion. The expert admitted that he lacked specific familiarity with the machine and had not tested an aural warning device on the machine. In addition, he had never designed a block-making machine, had done no research on whether the machine would be defective without an aural warning device, contacted no one in the industry to learn whether other manufacturers of block-making machines use such a device, and had not subjected his opinion to any sort of peer review. Nevertheless, the court held his testimony admissible due to his general experience designing and testing automatic start-up machines with aural warning devices.

Even though defendant sold an aural warning device separately, and the plaintiff's employer actually purchased the device but simply failed to install it, the court allowed the case to go to the jury on the theory that the block-maker was defective for not incorporating the warning device from the beginning.

See also Mascarenas v. Miles, 986 F. Supp. 582 (W.D. Mo. 1997) (excluding expert testimony that plaintiff's rare form of cancer was caused by his exposure to the pesticide Guthion 2L; plaintiff lacked proof that he was significantly exposed to Guthion 2L, lacked sufficient science to establish general cause, and plaintiff's experts did not "rule[] out, let alone attempted to rule out, any other possible causes" such as exposure to other pesticides); *Thomas v. FAG Bearings Corp., et al.*, 846 F. Supp. 1382 (W.D. Mo. 1994) (in a CERCLA case, expert testimony regarding the alleged responsibility of a third party defendant for environmental contamination lacked sufficient foundation and failed to meet the burden of proof of the proponent of the testimony; expert lacked factual data about the nature or depth of the alleged contamination, and could not testify "with any reasonable degree of scientific certainty that any cause [wa]s more than just a possibility").

5. *Nebraska*

Montes v. Union Pacific R.R. Co., 2011 WL 1343200 (D. Neb. 2011)

In this personal injury case, plaintiff proffered several expert witnesses, including his treating physician, Dr. Scott McMullen. According to plaintiff's expert disclosures, Dr. McMullen's opinions would be based on his review of plaintiff's medical records, his treatment of plaintiff, and his general training and experience. The disclosure also stated that Dr. McMullen was not specifically retained as an expert witness in the case. Plaintiff did not provide an expert report for Dr. McMullen.

Defendant moved to exclude Dr. McMullen's opinions, arguing that plaintiff had not provided expert reports in accordance with federal and local rules and also that Dr. McMullen's opinions lacked the required validity, reliability, and helpfulness under Rule 702 and *Daubert*. The court denied the motion because Dr. McMullen formed his causation opinions at the time of treatment and was therefore not deemed to be specifically retained to provide expert testimony in the case. Thus, he was not required to provide the more detailed expert disclosure required under Federal Rule of Civil Procedure 26(a)(2)(B).

Moreover, the court held that Dr. McMullen was an orthopedic surgeon who was competent to testify as to his treatment of the plaintiff and the opinions formed in connection of that treatment. Defendant's objections went to the weight of the evidence, not its admissibility.

WWW, Inc. v. Wounded Warriors, Inc., 2009 U.S. Dist. LEXIS 92521 (D. Neb. 2009), aff'd, 628 F.3d 1032 (8th Cir. 2011)

In this deceptive trade practices case, the defendant moved to exclude plaintiff's damages expert, Robert L. Kirchner, whom plaintiff retained to review relevant documents and determine the amount of "misdirected donations" that defendant had received, meaning the amount of donated funds that had been mistakenly given to the defendant by donors who intended to benefit plaintiff. Defendant argued that Kirchner's testimony was inadmissible because it would not be helpful to the jury, failed to rule out alternative explanations, and did not sufficiently connect with the facts of the case.

The court denied defendant's motion, finding its argument that Kirchner had applied uncomplicated mathematical principles to the donation data unpersuasive. The court found that Kirchner had relied on his experience in analyzing a substantial amount of financial data in forming his opinions, and that his testimony would be helpful to the jury's understanding of the evidence. In addition, Kirchner utilized and applied sufficiently reliable methodology in reaching his opinions. Defendant's challenges pertaining to Kirchner's failure to account for certain factors went to the weight of his testimony, not its admissibility.

Grant v. Pharmavite, 452 F. Supp. 2d 903 (D. Neb. 2006)

Defendants, manufacturers of the herbal supplement black cohosh, filed a motion to exclude the expert testimony of two experts in a product liability action brought by a husband and wife for alleged injury to the wife as a result of her ingestion of black cohosh. The wife allegedly contracted liver disease resulting in a liver transplant. One of plaintiff's two experts was a toxicologist who claimed that plaintiff's liver disease was more likely than not the direct result of use of black cohosh. The other expert was the wife's treating physician, a gastroenterologist, who intended to testify on the causation of plaintiff's liver disease. The court excluded both witnesses under *Daubert*.

The court first looked at the question of general causation. Plaintiffs sought to introduce the testimony of the toxicologist to establish general causation. The toxicologist started with an opinion, which he termed a "working hypothesis," that black cohosh was liver toxic. He did not test this working hypothesis and acknowledged that the hypothesis could be tested by controlled animal and human testing, which he did not do. Testing done by other scientists failed to determine that black cohosh was liver toxic and, in fact, the scientific research had consistently held that black cohosh was not liver toxic. The court held that, while it was not necessary that an opinion be backed by scientific research, an expert's testimony that contradicted all the existing research must, at a minimum, address or distinguish contradictory research. In this case, the expert had merely declared the research "wrong." The expert acknowledged that he lacked the information necessary to make an appropriate conclusion and also acknowledged that all the randomized, case-controlled, placebo control studies that had been done on the issue of black cohosh and liver toxicity had demonstrated no such toxicity.

Indeed, there was a body of epidemiology finding no association between black cohosh and liver toxicity. The district court ruled that, where there was a large body of contrary epidemiologic evidence, it was necessary to at least address it with evidence based on medically reliable and scientifically valid methodology. The court further pointed out that the toxicologist's theory was developed solely in connection with the litigation and that the expert failed to demonstrate that his opinion had been accepted let alone widely accepted. There was no evidence that the expert had shared his working hypothesis with any other scientist.

The court also ruled that the testimony of the treating gastroenterologist was insufficient to establish general causation. Although he was a physician, he was not a pharmacologist or a toxicologist. Prior to treating plaintiff he knew nothing about black cohosh. Only after the plaintiffs retained him did the doctor submit a case report on plaintiff's case for publication in which he linked her liver disease to black cohosh. But his case report contained several serious factual errors concerning plaintiff's medical history. He had omitted information that dealt with other possible causes of plaintiff's liver disease. The doctor also was not aware of case-controlled randomized double blind studies on black cohosh that consistently failed to demonstrate liver toxic effects. The doctor further acknowledged that 10 to 15 percent of liver disease was idiopathic, *i.e.*, that there is no known cause. He acknowledged that there was no evidence-based medicine establishing that black cohosh caused liver failure and that causation cannot be proven with a single case report.

With respect to the issue of specific causation, the toxicologist was excluded because he never examined plaintiff or her medical records, but instead relied only on a draft copy of the gastroenterologist case report, which failed to consider or even mention other known or suspected liver toxic exposures. The toxicologist acknowledged that, when attempting to analyze what may or may not have caused the patient's liver damage, it was important to have a full and complete history regarding the patient's potential exposures. Yet, plaintiff's toxicologist had never examined the plaintiff or her medical records.

The court also excluded the gastroenterologist's testimony because he had reached a scientifically invalid differential diagnosis by failing to include alternative causes. Furthermore, using a differential diagnosis to establish a specific cause was impermissible because general causation had not been proven.

In re Acceptance Ins. Cos., Inc. Sec. Litig., 352 F. Supp. 2d 940 (D. Neb. 2004), aff'd, 423 F.3d 899 (8th Cir. 2005)

Investors sued an insurance company and related entities, as well as three corporate officers, alleging securities fraud pursuant to various sections of the Security Exchange Act of 1934. The gravamen of the complaint was that defendants failed to disclose material information regarding the increasing number of California contractors' claims covered by the company and the attendant risk that the company faced in being under-reserved for losses.

Defendants sought summary judgment on multiple grounds. At issue was whether the corporations, through their officers, possessed material information that was required by law to be disclosed to the investing public and which was not disclosed. Defendants also moved to strike certain affidavits from plaintiffs' expert witnesses.

The court analyzed the expert reports in light of the *Daubert* and *Kumho* criteria. One expert was retained by the plaintiffs "to provide net loss and loss expense reserve estimates for the general liability primary line of business of Acceptance Insurance Companies." The court found that the expert's affidavit failed the first part of the *Daubert* analysis because the opinion was not supported by any discernible methodology. It was not clear which of the documents the expert identified were used by him in formulating his opinions. Moreover, the affidavit lacked an explanation of his methodology. The court ruled that the expert's affidavit provided little more than a bottom line opinion. After expert witness disclosures had been made and depositions taken, the expert's opinion may have been supported by an explanation, but the failure to include that foundation within the affidavit itself rendered it no use to the court.

Defendants also sought to strike the affidavit of a second CPA who was retained to give his expert opinion on whether Acceptance Insurance Companies' financial statements were prepared in accordance with Financial Accounting Standard No. 5. In his affidavit, the expert set forth some foundation for his opinions including an explanation of accounting theory and his interpretation of various accounting rules including Financial Accounting Standard No. 5. But the expert did not, however, explain how he reached his ultimate opinion, nor did he describe the analytical processes he employed to reach his opinion. Therefore, the court concluded that the affidavit did not satisfy the second part of *Daubert* and the affidavit was stricken.

Marmo v. IBP Inc. 360 F. Supp. 2d 1019 (D. Neb. 2005), aff'd Marmo v. Tyson Fresh Meats, Inc., 457 F.3d 748 (8th Cir. 2006)
Marmo involved a suit to recover damages for injuries allegedly sustained by plaintiffs as a result of exposure to hydrogen sulfide gas. Defendant filed a motion *in limine* to preclude testimony from plaintiffs' expert, a board-certified pathologist with substantial expertise in the nature and effects of poisons, including hydrogen sulfide gas. The expert interviewed all seventeen plaintiffs regarding their symptoms, and concluded, to a reasonable degree of scientific certainty, that plaintiffs' injuries were caused by exposure to hydrogen sulfide gas emissions.

The court granted the motion in part and denied it in part. The court held that the expert testify regarding the nature and effects of hydrogen sulfide gas and whether plaintiffs' injuries were "consistent with" exposure to the gas, but could not testify that plaintiffs' injuries were caused by exposure to hydrogen sulfide gas because the methodology underlying her opinion did not satisfy *Daubert*. The expert was not a medical doctor and did not examine plaintiffs or conduct a full differential diagnosis that would consider alternate causes; she did not perform statistical analysis of the population subject to the toxin; and the report was prepared solely for the purposes of litigation. In addition, the standard she used to reach her conclusion was lower than the standard used in the scientific community to reach a conclusion of causation. The expert testified that she understood the term "reasonable degree of scientific certainty" to mean more probable than not, and that it was a much lower standard than "scientific causation." While stating that the science of epidemiology uses a statistical measure of "95th confidence interval," the expert testified that the legal term "reasonable degree of scientific certainty" was not subject to measurement in terms of a percentage of error rate even though she used it to attribute causation.

U.S. v. Ramirez, 383 F. Supp. 2d 1179 (D. Neb. 2005)
Defendant, who was found in a car with a large quantity of marijuana, sought to offer testimony from a well-credentialed sociologist that it is not unusual for Hispanic immigrants to make cross-country travel arrangements with persons they have just met. The court held that the testimony was inadmissible because (1) it lacked probative value; (2) it amounted to little more than a recitation of ethnic or cultural stereotypes and thus had the potential to prejudice, mislead or confuse the jury; and (3) it invited the government to pursue similar but far more unflattering stereotypes when cross-examining the witness. The court stated that, "in short, and assuming (without deciding) that the testimony is admissible under *Daubert* principles and otherwise, the probative value of this very general testimony is nil."

Fitzpatrick v. Louisville Ladder Corp., 2001 WL 1568389 (D. Neb. 2001)
Plaintiff in this products liability case fell from a ladder on which he was standing to repair a conveyer belt. No one saw him fall, and he testified that he could not remember how he fell. His expert, Dr. John Morse, opined that the ladder was prone to excessive "racking"—where the ladder tips because one of its four legs is not level with the other three. Dr. Morse conceded, however, that the ladder at issue met industry standards for racking, that any ladder could rack, and that one could fall from a ladder without the ladder racking. At the close of plaintiff's case, defendant moved for judgment as a matter of law claiming that there was no evidence that the ladder had racked or that the alleged racking had caused the fall.

The court granted defendant's motion, finding "a complete failure of proof of the element of proximate cause." There was "no evidence from which the jury could find that this ladder did, indeed, rack," and similarly, there was "no evidence that racking, instead of mere loss of balance or other such occurrence, caused the fall." Citing *Lauzon v. Senco Products*, 270 F.3d 681 (8th Cir. 2011), the court held that Dr. Morse's opinion was technically admissible under *Daubert*, even though Morse was "unable to connect his theory in a meaningful way to the facts of this case." Although recognizing that "an expert's causation conclusion should not be excluded because he has failed to rule out every possible alternative cause," the court found the evidentiary support for

Morse's opinion "exceedingly thin." The court therefore rejected plaintiff's "circular argument" that "we can infer the ladder racked because the plaintiff fell," noting that this reasoning is tantamount to "adopting a *res ipsa loquitur* theory in a conventional negligence case." *But see Lauzon*, 270 F.3d at 694 (dismissing possibility of accidental injury as "specious" and holding that "the ruling out of the manufacturing defect simultaneously rules in a design defect").

U.S. v. Rutherford, 104 F. Supp. 2d 1190 (D. Neb. 2000)
In this prosecution for bank fraud and retaliating against a witness, defendant sought to exclude a government handwriting expert's testimony that defendant had authored certain incriminating documents. Defendant conceded that the government's witness was qualified to render opinions on similarities between his handwriting and the writing on the documents, but argued that the expert's methodology was not sufficiently sound to allow him to testify regarding the ultimate issue of authorship. The court granted the defendant's motion on the basis of "several scientific deficiencies," including the expert's failure to "blind" himself with respect to the purported author of the samples; the limited number of samples he reviewed; and his failure to analyze samples from others who could have authored the documents.

Uribe v. Sofamor, S.N.C., 1999 WL 1129703 (D. Neb. 1999)
Plaintiffs' experts Drs. Harold Alexander and Robert Pennell were excluded from testifying in this Nebraska bone screw case. In excluding them, the court first discussed the MDL court's order on the same subject, (*See In re Orthopedic Bone Screw Products Liability Litigation*, 1997 WL 39583 (E.D. Pa.)), which found that Dr. Alexander had little or no experience with bone screw devices before being retained by plaintiffs and that, while he was qualified to testify from an engineering standpoint, he was not qualified to render any medical causation opinions. In particular, the court relied on the MDL court's holding that:

> Plaintiffs cannot "piggyback" Dr. Alexander's exposure to other non-bioengineering subject areas onto his qualifications as an expert on orthopedic bioengineering and create a "one-size-fits-all" mass of qualifications warranting his elevation to expert rank in those other areas."

Dr. Alexander's testimony with respect to the engineering issues was also excluded, however, because he failed to identify a defect in the device, and because his testimony was "too generalized and irrelevant to specific plaintiffs to create a genuine issue of material fact regarding design defect."

Dr. Pennell's testimony was excluded on similar grounds. The court found that he reviewed records selected by plaintiff's attorneys rather than the whole set of medical records, that he had never performed the procedure he was critiquing, that he was not familiar with any of the relevant studies, that he had never treated any patients who had undergone the procedure, and that his specific causation opinion lacked foundation because he never examined plaintiff. In a holding reminiscent of the holding in *Fitzpatrick*, the court ultimately rejected Pennell's "*res ipsa*" theory:

> A trier of fact must not be permitted to assume that because a patient continues to experience back pain after an instrumented spinal fusion procedure, the hardware should be blamed.

6. *North Dakota*

Anderson v. Hess Corp., 592 F. Supp.2d 1174 (D.N.D. 2009)
Plaintiff alleged that she suffered from a respiratory injury known as reactive airways dysfunction syndrome due to "acute exposure" to gases emitted from defendant's tank battery. Plaintiff exhibited

symptoms and sought medical treatment within twenty-four hours of the alleged exposure, which occurred during the course of one night while she was sleeping. Plaintiff proffered five experts: Dr. Pedro A. Mendoza and Dr. Nicholas H. Neumann, both treating physicians retained to testify in accordance with plaintiff's medical records; Gail Joyce and Corrine Coughlin, both physician's assistants; and Tonya Anderson, a mental health professional who had treated the plaintiff. Defendant sought to exclude causation testimony by plaintiff's medical experts, arguing that none of them had performed any medical tests or investigated any alternative causes of plaintiff's injuries in order to make a differential diagnosis.

The court looked for evidence that each proffered expert had conducted a full differential diagnosis to consider possible alternate causes of plaintiff's injury and rule out all but the exposure to battery gas. Under this analysis, Dr. Neumann was allowed to testify, while Joyce, Coughlin, and Anderson were excluded. Noting that defendant had not deposed Dr. Mendoza, but instead based its argument on a review of plaintiff's medical records, the court deferred ruling on defendant's motion to exclude Dr. Mendoza's opinion until trial. The court stated that there was insufficient evidence of the methodology that Dr. Mendoza used to determine the cause of plaintiff's symptoms. Therefore, the court was unable to determine whether Dr. Mendoza's methodology was sufficiently reliable under Rule 702 and *Daubert*.

Symington v. Daisy Manufacturing Co., Inc., 360 F. Supp. 2d 1027 (D.N.D. 2005)

This case arose out of an accident involving an air gun in which plaintiff lost his eye when his friend shot a pellet at him. While the shooter had intentionally aimed the gun at plaintiff and pulled the trigger, he had not loaded any ammunition into the gun. In support of his case, plaintiff retained an expert to analyze the condition of the gun. Plaintiff's expert concluded that the gun was defective for a number of reasons, including a design flaw that allowed BBs to become lodged in the magazine of the gun, which gave the appearance that the gun was empty. In his deposition, plaintiff's expert was shown for the first time an X-ray of plaintiff's head which showed a pellet, instead of a BB, lodged in the back of plaintiff's right eye socket. After his deposition, plaintiff's expert supplemented his initial report and opined that the gun was defective because it allowed a pellet to enter and exit the BB feed hole.

In ruling on defendant's motion for summary judgment, the court first ruled on whether to accept plaintiff's expert's untimely supplementation. Finding that defendant had the substance of the supplemental report prior to the filing deadline, the court ruled that defendant was not prejudiced and that the court would therefore consider the late-filed expert affidavit. Next, the court addressed defendant's argument that plaintiff's supplementation was an "eleventh hour" attempt to contradict the expert's deposition testimony. The court disagreed, finding that plaintiff's initial opinion had been based entirely on the theory that a BB had injured plaintiff. As such, plaintiff's expert had not conducted any analysis prior to his deposition as to whether there was any defect in the gun as it related to pellets. Indeed, plaintiff's expert did not testify in deposition that the gun was not defective with regard to firing pellets. Thus, the supplemental report did not contradict the expert's deposition testimony and was potentially admissible.

The court then considered defendant's arguments regarding the qualifications of plaintiff's expert. The court acknowledged the expert's employment with the Michigan State Police for twenty-five years and his twenty-year experience in the state's Police Crime Laboratory as a firearms and toolmark examiner. The court also noted that he had examined thousands of firearms to determine how they function and that he had testified in court hundreds of times about the operation of a firearm as it related to whether a death was a homicide or an accident. The court referenced, among other things, the expert's extensive educational background and training related to firearms and that he had given expert opinions in more than thirty cases in state and federal courts regarding the design and operation of air guns. Moreover, the court observed that whether a design defect existed in an air gun was not an issue that would be readily obvious to a jury. Finally, the court found that the expert's opinion was based on his observation of the mechanics of the air gun and that the expert's report well described how the pellets entered the gun and could become lodged in the BB feed hole. The court held that plaintiff's expert satisfied the requirements of Rule 702.

Young v. All Erection & Crane Rental, Corp., 399 F. Supp. 2d 1028 (D.N.D. 2005)
Plaintiff, who was injured when operating a crane, brought suit against the crane rental companies alleging that the accident was caused by the improper adjustment of the crane crawler tracks. Defendants moved to exclude the testimony of plaintiff's three experts, arguing (1) the experts' opinions were not consistent, and (2) none of the experts could state to a reasonable degree of certainty that there was an improper adjustment to the crane track. Specifically, defendants asserted that, while each expert opined in his written report that the track was improperly adjusted, in deposition each expert conceded that he could not state his opinion to a reasonable degree of certainty.

The court began its analysis by noting that all of plaintiff's experts were mechanical engineers and that each had extensive experience dealing with cranes and crane safety. Moreover, the court noted that defendants had not challenged the experts' qualifications and, indeed, had conceded that the proposed testimony was based on technical or special knowledge that would be useful to the finder of fact. Thus, defendants attacked only the reliability of the testimony. With scant discussion, the court held that the alleged conflicts or contradictions in the written reports and the deposition testimony did not render the experts' opinions unreliable. The court did not address defendants' contention that the experts' opinions were not consistent among the experts themselves. In sum, the court ruled that the appropriate means of attacking each expert's opinion was through cross-examination and presentation of contrary evidence at trial.

Melberg v. Plains Marketing, L.P., 332 F. Supp. 2d 1253 (D.N.D. 2004)
This personal injury case arose out of an automobile accident in which plaintiff's van collided with a tractor/trailer driven by defendant's employee. Before the court were several motions *in limine* concerning two of defendant's experts and one of plaintiff's.

As to the first expert, defendant's accident reconstructionist, plaintiff contended that serious flaws compromised the expert's opinions with respect to the speed of plaintiff's van prior to braking and plaintiff's ability to respond to the danger given the speed of his van. In his report, defendant's expert had conceded that there was some uncertainty in his calculations. The court observed that the expert had made some mathematical adjustments to his calculations without sufficient explanation. Without further substantive analysis, the court concluded that defendant's expert's opinions were based on sufficient facts and data, were the product of reliable principles and methods and that the expert had applied the principles and methods to the facts of the case. Further, the court noted that vigorous cross-examination, presentation of contrary evidence and careful jury instruction were the proper means of attacking the expert's testimony.

The second expert, defendant's biomechanical engineer, proposed to opine that, if plaintiff had been wearing a safety belt at the time of the accident, he would not have sustained significant head trauma. Plaintiff asserted that defendant's expert's opinion was speculative because he did not follow an established methodology. The court summarily rejected plaintiff's assertion finding that defendant's expert had applied the principles and methods reliably to the facts as required under *Daubert* and *Kumho* and that it was within the province of the jury to decide issues of credibility and the weight to be accorded the expert's opinions.

As to the third expert, plaintiff's mechanical engineer, defendant moved to exclude his testimony as it pertained to crush measurements, total body simulation programs, and NHTSA frontal crash test video footage. The court briefly noted that expert testimony as to the speed of the vehicles and the nature and extent of plaintiff's injuries would be of assistance to the jury and that defendant had stipulated that plaintiff's expert was qualified to opine on those issues. With respect to whether the proposed evidence was reliable or trustworthy, the court assessed each basis for defendant's objections.

Because the NHTSA frontal crash test videos did not depict conditions sufficiently similar to the conditions involved in the underlying case, the court ruled the videos were not to be shown to the jury. However, both defendant's and plaintiff's experts were permitted to testify concerning the crash tests. Although the articulated total body (ATB) computer simulation program appeared "somewhat suspect," it was widely accepted as a tool for predicting the severity of automobile collision on human occupants. Accordingly, plaintiff's expert could testify about the two simulation runs of the ATB program. Plaintiff's expert was allowed to testify about a new crush analysis he made after correcting an error from his original report about the van weight, although the court permitted a supplemental deposition at plaintiff's cost prior to trial.

Schaaf v. Caterpillar, Inc., 286 F. Supp. 2d 1070 (D.N.D. 2003)

The parents of Jacob Schaaf, who was killed in a tractor accident, brought suit against the tractor manufacturer alleging that the tractor was defectively designed and unreasonably dangerous. Defendant moved to exclude the testimony of plaintiff's expert regarding the adequacy of the manufacturer's warnings on the basis that his opinions were outside his area of expertise. Plaintiffs argued that their expert was not proffered to opine regarding the adequacy of the warnings, but rather that Caterpillar failed to provide any warning which would be visible to individuals who might attempt to mount the machine when it was in motion, as Jacob Schaaf had done.

The court found that plaintiffs' expert was qualified to opine on the principles of the design process and applicability of relevant standards regarding safe product manufacturing. However, the court found plaintiffs' expert unqualified to testify as an expert concerning the adequacy of warnings (type of warnings, size, shape, content, color, etc.). Thus, the court ruled, in part, in defendant's favor finding that plaintiffs' expert would not be permitted to testify about the adequacy of the warnings on the tractor. However, he would be permitted to opine on general industry standards, accepted design processes for manufacture of agricultural equipment and machines and the application of relevant manufacturing standards.

Dickie v. Shockman, 2000 WL 33339623 (D.N.D. 2000)

This was the first reported decision in the District of North Dakota applying *Daubert*. *Dickie* involved a plaintiff who was severely burned when a fire broke out on her employer's farm. The fire was attributed to a leak in an underground pipe connecting propane tanks to a grain dryer. Plaintiff's expert, a metallurgist, testified regarding the development of a pinhole found in the pipe after the accident. Based on the size of the pinhole and a normal rate of corrosion, the expert calculated a range of time it would take for such a hole to form in the specific type of pipe. Defendants did not question the expert's qualifications, but argued that the expert's opinion was unduly speculative because he was only able to give a range of months for the pinhole formation rather than a specific date.

The court found that rates of corrosion and general metallurgical principles such as the properties of steel are outside the normal juror's knowledge, and thus the proffered testimony would be helpful in determining when the leak occurred. The court also found that the testimony would be reliable, as it was to be "based on extensive scientific/technical knowledge in metallurgical engineering." This specialized knowledge could be used to extrapolate the length of time it would take for a pinhole to form, an approach "generally accepted in the metallurgical engineering community." The court held that the expert's inability to pinpoint the exact date the leak began went to the weight of his testimony, not its admissibility.

The defendants also challenged the proposed testimony of plaintiff's mechanical engineer on the characteristics of propane and industry standards regarding its delivery. The court, citing Eighth

Circuit cases, held that expert testimony is properly admissible to establish industry standards where, as here, it would help the jury "to determine whether the defendants met their standard of care under the law." The court also allowed testimony regarding what constitutes "corrosion protection" of piping on the ground that it would assist the jury in understanding the meaning of the term as it is used in the industry. The court noted its concern regarding testimony by the engineer regarding warnings, as he was "not an expert in writing warnings and has never designed one" but allowed the testimony to the extent it focused on the *need* for a warning, rather than the *adequacy* or content of a warning.

7. South Dakota

Houwman v. Gaiser, 2011 WL 4345236 (D.S.D. 2011)
In this alienation of affections action, plaintiff sought to exclude defendant's expert's testimony. Plaintiff sued defendant based on an affair between defendant and plaintiff's wife, Brittney. The affair ultimately led plaintiff and Brittney to divorce. The expert, Dr. Susan K. Eleeson, was a marriage counselor and psychologist who had offered both joint and individual marriage counseling sessions to plaintiff and Brittney prior to the divorce.

Plaintiff argued that Dr. Eleeson's opinions should be excluded as unreliable under Rule 702 because Brittney had not been fully forthcoming with Dr. Eleeson. The court denied plaintiff's motion, finding that Dr. Eleeson's proffered testimony was relevant, that she was qualified to offer those opinions, and that the opinions were sufficiently reliable. The court found that Dr. Eleeson had "specialized knowledge of human interaction and expertise in marriage counseling" as well as an extensive counseling relationship with both plaintiff and Brittney. Thus, Dr. Eleeson could help the jury understand the marriage "through an analysis of their marital problems with a psychological or scientific lens" and could provide helpful information as to whether defendant had alienated Brittney's affections.

Although plaintiff argued that Dr. Eleeson's opinions were unreliable because Brittney had not immediately told Dr. Eleeson the whole truth about the affair, the court found that Dr. Eleeson knew the majority of the pertinent facts. Thus, the court held that Dr. Eleeson's testimony would not be excluded because "Rule 702 is one of inclusion, and her opinion is relevant, reliable, and would help the jury understand the issues in this case." The court noted that the plaintiff would have ample opportunity to expose the weaknesses in Dr. Eleeson's testimony on cross-examination.

Schumacher v. Tyson Fresh Meats, Inc., 69 Fed. R. Evid. Serv. 147 (D.S.D. 2006)
Plaintiff cattle producers filed suit against defendant meat packers, alleging that defendants knowingly used inaccurate pricing information to negotiate slaughter cattle prices in violation of the Packers and Stockyards Act. Each side moved to disqualify the other's experts. Plaintiffs alleged that four major meat packers knowingly used the inaccurate prices erroneously reported by the USDA to negotiate the purchases of slaughter cattle from plaintiffs.

The two issues for trial were defendants' knowledge and whether the incorrectly reported prices caused lower market prices to be received by plaintiffs. Plaintiffs proffered the expert report of an agricultural economist who, through a regression analysis, opined that defendants must have known of the reporting error and that defendants received more than a $22 million windfall as a result. Defendants sought to introduce the testimony of two economic experts. The first concluded that plaintiffs' expert's regression analysis was invalid. The expert also proffered his own "corrected" regression model which concluded that the reporting error had no effect on the relevant cattle prices. Defendants' second expert premised his opinions on the regression analysis performed by defendants' first expert and said there was no statistical basis for concluding the USDA reporting errors affected relevant cattle prices and there was no reason to believe defendants should have known the reported prices were erroneous.

Neither party disputed the general admissibility of regression analysis, which the court noted was an accepted form of scientific evidence. Rather, defendants challenged whether plaintiffs' expert's regression analysis was reliably applied to the facts of the case. The court found plaintiffs' expert report admissible, noting that the particular variables included in a regression analysis normally affects the probativeness of the analysis, not its admissibility. Defendants also argued that the court should exclude plaintiffs' expert's rebuttal report because it was prepared to correct the expert's initial report, not to rebut defendants' experts. The court ruled the rebuttal report admissible, finding that it was disclosed two weeks prior to the expert's deposition, in order to correct an error, and that it complied with the parties' duty to supplement expert disclosures under Rule 26.

For their part, plaintiffs argued that defendants' second expert did not perform his own regression analysis, but rather relied upon the analysis performed by defendants' first expert. Plaintiffs argued that such reliance was improper because the second expert did not test the first expert's data. The court summarily observed that experts may extrapolate from data supplied by other experts. Defendants' second expert's report, which purported to show there was no correlation between the USDA error and relevant cattle prices, was deemed a proper subject for expert testimony and, thus, admissible.

U.S. v. Rouse, 329 F. Supp. 2d 1077 (D.S.D. 2004)

Defendants, convicted in 1994 on charges of aggravated sexual abuse of five minors, moved for a new trial on the grounds that the victims and a child witness had recanted their testimony and taken polygraph tests. The court considered, among other things, the admissibility of polygraph evidence in the Eighth Circuit. After citing numerous Eighth Circuit cases discussing admissibility of polygraph evidence, the court found that, in the Eighth Circuit, polygraph evidence is no longer *per se* inadmissible and that it could be admitted in the absence of a stipulation and even over objection if the evidence independently meets *Daubert* standards.

After considering the expert dispute as to the application of *Daubert* factors and observing that they were not dispositive of the issue of reliability, the court then evaluated the specific polygraph evidence at issue. Among other factors, the test had been administered six years after the underlying facts allegedly occurred. Additionally, the witness, a minor, had by then been returned to his family, adult members of which did not believe the child's trial testimony regarding sexual assault. The court was not convinced that the polygraph testimony at issue was sufficiently reliable to determine the truthfulness of the witness's testimony.

U.S. v. White Horse, 177 F. Supp. 2d 973 (D. S.D. 2001)

A criminal defendant charged with sexually abusing his son proffered the testimony of Dr. Janz, who conducted a psychosexual evaluation of defendant. The court held an evidentiary hearing, primarily to determine the validity and reliability of the Abel Assessment, a two-part test for sexual interest in minors.

Applying the four *Daubert* factors to Part I of the Abel Assessment, the court found that (1) while it had been tested generally, it had not been sufficiently tested with regard to Native American subjects; (2) peer review of the Abel Assessment was sufficient; (3) a 24 percent rate of false negative results does not assist the trier of fact in understanding the evidence or determining a fact in issue; and (4) it had not achieved widespread acceptance within the scientific community. In balancing these four factors, the court held that Part I did not satisfy the *Daubert* admissibility requirements.

Testimony regarding the results of Part II was also excluded, as the results were inconclusive, according to Dr. Janz, and thus did not tend to make more or less probable the existence of any consequential fact. Moreover, the test may be inapplicable to incest cases, had not been subjected to peer review, and there was no evidence of acceptance in the relevant community.

Mattis v. Carlon Elec. Prods., 114 F. Supp. 2d 888 (D.S.D. 2000)
Plaintiff in this products liability case alleged that Carlon Cement, a product produced by defendants and used to bind sections of PVC pipe, caused his reactive airways dysfunction syndrome (RADS). A pulmonologist retained by plaintiff attributed plaintiff's breathing difficulties to RADS.

RADS was first described and named in a published article, which the court found had been properly subjected to peer review and generally accepted. The agents listed in the article as causes of RADS, however, did not include the four organic solvents found in Carlon Cement. Plaintiff's industrial hygiene expert attempted to bridge the gap by claiming that, like the etiological agents identified in the article, the four solvents in Carlon Cement were respiratory irritants. The article suggested that the development of RADS was related to the toxic effect of irritant exposure on the airways, but specifically stated that this conclusion was speculative and not substantiated.

The court noted the "analytical gap" between the clinical studies and the solvents at issue, but held that this was not fatal to the opinions of plaintiff's experts, as differential diagnosis "is a standard scientific technique of identifying the cause of a medical problem by eliminating the likely causes until the most probable one is isolated." Also, this perceived gap was partially "bridged by Defendant's own expert, who stated that he agrees both with the methodology in the article and with the conclusion that Carlon Cement solvents can cause RADS if they are present in high enough concentrations." The defendants' motion to exclude was therefore denied.

U.S. v. Black Wolf, 1999 U.S. Dist. LEXIS 20736 (D.S.D. 1999)
Defendant, accused of setting fire to a residence, moved to exclude the testimony of the state fire marshal who had investigated the scene and concluded that the fire was started by the use of an accelerant. Defendant urged the court to exclude the testimony, arguing that the investigator reached his conclusion without taking or analyzing samples of the building material, that his causation theory had not been subject to peer review, and that he used no scientific method or procedure in reaching his conclusions, which were "nothing more than subjective speculation." The court found, however, that under these circumstances rate of error and general acceptance "are not particularly appropriate and useful considerations." As such, the court held that the testimony was reliable, since the investigator's protocol was largely consistent with the procedures recommended by the National Fire Protection Association.

D. EXPERT EVIDENCE IN THE STATE COURTS OF THE EIGHTH CIRCUIT

1. Arkansas

a. *Daubert* Test Guides Admissibility

Arkansas courts apply a *Daubert* based test. Since the Arkansas Supreme Court's decision in *Farm Bureau Mut. Ins. Co. of Arkansas, Inc. v. Foote*, 14 S.W.3d 512 (Ark. 2000), Arkansas courts have used this admissibility analysis for all types of scientific evidence, not just "novel" methodologies. In *Farm Bureau*, the trial court rejected expert testimony concerning a dog's ability to detect the presence of accelerants after a fire because the proponent of the testimony failed to make any showing regarding the scientific validity of the evidence. The expert, a state police investigator, failed to produce a master's thesis which allegedly showed that "it has been proven in numerous cases that a dog's nose is more sensitive than the equipment used by forensic chemists." Without the study, the court could not verify the techniques used or the potential rate of error, or determine whether the theory had been tested, subjected to peer review, or otherwise embraced by the relevant scientific community. Therefore, the court held that the appellant had failed to carry its burden of proof on the issue of reliability under either *Daubert* or the pre-*Daubert* standard articulated in *Prater v. State*, 820 S.W.2d 429 (Ark. 1991).

In *Prater*, the Arkansas Supreme Court had adopted a "relevancy standard" for determining the admissibility of scientific evidence. The test required the trial court to inquire into:

(1) The reliability of the novel process used to generate the evidence;
(2) the possibility that admitting the evidence would overwhelm, confuse, or mislead the jury; and
(3) the connection between the novel process evidence to be offered and the disputed factual issues in the particular case.

Id. at 429. In *Moore v. State*, 915 S.W.2d 284 (Ark. 1996), the court clarified that, "in *Prater*, we rejected the majority approach for determining the admissibility of novel scientific evidence as set forth in *Frye v. United States* . . . [w]e instead adopted the more liberal standard of admissibility, based upon the relevancy approach of the Uniform Rules of Evidence, in particular Rules 401, 402 and 702." *Id.* at 294. The court in *Farm Bureau* noted that this "reliability approach" was comparable to the *Daubert* standard for admissibility of scientific evidence.

Before the Arkansas Supreme Court's decision in *Farm Bureau*, Arkansas trial courts would not apply the "reliability approach" if the expert evidence in question did not involve a novel methodology. *See, e.g., Whitson v. State*, 863 S.W.2d 794 (Ark. 1993) (holding Horizontal Gaze Nystagmus test to determine presence of alcohol not novel scientific method); *Moore v. State, supra* (trial court may take judicial notice of DNA analysis, no preliminary inquiry required); *cf. Houston v. State*, 906 S.W.2d 286 (Ark. 1995) (preliminary hearing required to determine admissibility of luminol testing for presence of blood because it was held to be a novel method).

After *Farm Bureau*, the Arkansas Court of Appeals applied *Daubert* in *Wood v. State*, 53 S.W.3d 56 (Ark. Ct. App. 2001). There, defendant, convicted of raping his two stepsons, appealed the exclusion of his expert's testimony that the antidepressant Paxil could cause a person to engage in deviant sexual behavior. The court of appeals held that the trial court properly excluded the evidence because the expert did not follow any accepted scientific method in arriving at her conclusion.

An expert's "professional accolades" are not dispositive on whether the expert can be qualified to give opinion testimony. In *Coca-Cola Bottling Co. of Memphis, Tenn. v. Gill*, 100 S.W.3d 715 (Ark. 2003), Plaintiff suffered a shock while setting up a concessions trailer at a school event. He and his wife sued the owner of the trailer, Coca-Cola Bottling, and the trailer's manufacturer, Waymatic, under theories of negligence and strict liability. At trial on the Coca-Cola claims, plaintiffs sought to qualify an expert witness on electricity. The proffered expert had received no formal education in electrical engineering, was never a formal apprentice to an electrician, did not then have an electrician's license or electrical engineering license, had not worked actively in "electrical matters" since 1970, and stated that he did not consider himself to be an electrical engineer. On the other hand, the expert had learned electrical engineering on the job and had served informally as "head electrician" at ALCOA for eighteen years, during which he was certified as an electrician. The trial court qualified him as an expert. The expert then testified that (1) a short in the wire from the trailer likely caused the incident, (2) the incident still would have been possible if the school's shed receptacle, where the trailer was plugged in, had been grounded and (3) had the trailer itself been grounded, the incident likely would not have occurred. The jury awarded plaintiffs $1.5 million.

On appeal, Coca-Cola argued that (1) the trial court abused its discretion in qualifying the expert witness on electricity, and (2) the trial court abused its discretion in refusing to strike the expert's testimony as incompetent. The Arkansas Supreme Court disagreed. First, it held that, under

Daubert and *Farm Bureau*, Ark. Rule Evid. 702 did not condition the admissibility of expert testimony "solely on an expert's professional accolades or lack thereof." Therefore the expert did not need to have a particular degree or license to testify as an expert on electricity. Further, the fact that the expert had not actively worked in the field for more than thirty years went to the weight of his expert testimony, not to his qualification. For these reasons, the trial court did not abuse its discretion in qualifying the expert. Second, the court held that prior testimony and the expert's own observations on the accident scene constituted a "sufficient basis of data" for his expert opinion. The dissent argued that the expert was not qualified as an electricity expert and that he had drawn inferences only the jury should have made.

Arkansas decisions demonstrate the degree of discretion trial courts have in evaluating expert testimony that is based on experience and knowledge rather than a "scientific" methodology. *Jackson v. State*, 197 S.W.3d 468 (Ark. 2004). In *Jackson*, at appellant's trial on charges of first-degree murder of a rival gang member, the prosecution sought to introduce expert testimony from an officer in a gang intelligence unit in the Little Rock Police Department. The officer testified that the appellant was the leader of a local gang and that, because he was the leader, he possessed authority over a younger gang member also involved in the crime. The jury convicted the appellant of first-degree murder and sentenced him to life imprisonment.

On appeal, appellant argued that the officer's expert testimony failed to meet the reliability standards of *Daubert*. According to the appellant, the officer did not possess the training or education necessary to ensure that his testimony would be unbiased and his conclusions based on "valid data-gathering techniques." The Arkansas Supreme Court held that the trial court did not abuse its discretion in qualifying the expert. The court noted that Arkansas courts had adopted both *Daubert* and *Kumho Tire*. Under these decisions, a trial court could apply the *Daubert* factors at its discretion. Given the nature of the expertise in this case, that discretion had not been abused. In particular, the officer's testimony was based on "experiences and the knowledge [he] garnered" working in the gang intelligence unit over a number of years. *Daubert* reliability factors were "simply inapplicable" to this kind of expert testimony, which "differs from expert testimony which rests purely on a scientific foundation."

In *Miller Brewing Co. v. Ed Roleson, Jr., Inc.*, 223 S.W.3d 806 (Ark. 2006), Plaintiff distributed beer for defendant brewery. After defendant sought to have a competing distributor purchase plaintiff's business, plaintiff sued for breach of contract, tortious interference with a business expectancy, civil conspiracy and violation of state franchise law. The jury found for plaintiff on the contract, conspiracy and state law claims, and the court awarded him $1.6 million.

On appeal, defendant argued that the trial court should have excluded plaintiff's expert witnesses on damages because their opinions, which had allegedly changed during the course of the litigation, were unreliable. The Arkansas Supreme Court held that the trial court had not abused its discretion. The court first recognized that, under Arkansas law, the trial court's discretion to admit expert testimony was broad. It then found that the defendant's arguments went to the weight of the testimony, not its admissibility. Moreover, the defendant had cross-examined the experts and could have introduced its own damages experts had it decided to do so.

Whether an expert's methodology has been tested can be an important factor in the admissibility analysis. *Green v. Alpharma, Inc.*, 284 S.W.3d 29 (Ark. 2008). In *Green*, Plaintiffs alleged that their child had developed leukemia as the result of his exposure to arsenic-laced chicken litter spread by farmers. The trial court prohibited certain testimony from plaintiffs' medical expert, specifically a table in the expert's report that collected the expert's opinions on ambient arsenic levels to which the plaintiff was allegedly exposed, finding that the methodology supporting the report did not meet the *Daubert* standards. The expert admitted that he was unsure if the formula he used to arrive at the results listed in the table, which had been used to calculate ambient levels of lead, had ever been used to calculate ambient levels of arsenic.

The Arkansas Supreme Court held that the trial court had not abused its discretion in limiting the expert's testimony. The court noted that the expert was no doubt qualified to give his opinions on the topic, but held that "[a] primary factor for a trial court to consider in determining the admissibility of scientific evidence is whether the scientific theory can be or has been tested." *Id.* at 46. Because the expert's theory had not been tested, and because the court found the trial court had not abused its "considerable" discretion in finding that the report did not satisfy any of the five *Daubert* factors, the Supreme Court affirmed the trial court's ruling limiting the testimony.

b. Expert-Related Rules and Procedural Issues in Arkansas

Rule 26 of the Arkansas Rules of Civil Procedure outlines the discovery of expert witnesses in a manner very similar to F.R.C.P. 26. Arkansas' Rule 26 provides that a party can be forced to identify each expert, "state the subject matter on which he is expected to testify, and ... state the substance of the facts and opinions to which the expert is expected to testify and a summary of the grounds for each opinion." *See* ARK. R. CIV. P. 26. In 2008, the Arkansas Rule 26 was amended to conform the rule to the current practice of allowing parties to depose witnesses without getting a court order allowing the deposition. *See id.* at 26(b)(4)(A).

Non-testifying experts who have been retained in anticipation of trial are discoverable under the same standard set by the Federal Rules. *See Id.* at 26(b)(4)(B). Similarly, Arkansas uses the language of Federal Rule 26 when discussing the payment of fees for the time a party's experts spend answering interrogatories. *See Id.* at 26(b)(4)(C).

2. Iowa

a. A Liberal Variation of *Daubert*

Iowa state courts have followed a "liberal rule on the admission of opinion testimony," as codified by Iowa Rule of Evidence 702. *Hutchinson v. American Family Mut. Ins.*, 514 N.W.2d 882, 885 (Iowa 1994). In the immediate aftermath of *Daubert*, the Iowa Supreme Court held that the *Daubert* decision merely reaffirmed Iowa's preexisting "liberal rule." In the years following, Iowa state courts applied *Daubert* in some cases, but not in others; generally, *Daubert* was applied only where the proposed expert testimony involved a novel area of scientific inquiry.

Finally, in *Leaf v. Goodyear*, 590 N.W.2d 525, 532 (Iowa 1999), the Iowa Supreme Court decided that it was "time for us to decide what role we should give to *Daubert* in expert-testimony cases. Should we apply it only in cases of a scientific—but not technical nature? Should the *Daubert* analysis be applied to all cases involving expert testimony? Or should we adopt a variation of *Daubert* that will encourage, but not require, use of portions of *Daubert*'s analysis? We elect the latter." In holding that Iowa courts are not required to apply *Daubert*, the court also clarified that neither are they precluded from doing so, as they "may find it helpful, particularly in complex cases, to use one or more of the relevant *Daubert* considerations in assessing the reliability of expert testimony."

In the *Goodyear* decision, the Iowa Supreme Court declined to apply *Daubert* to the testimony of a tire-design expert, finding it unnecessary since the witness' testimony "was quite simple to understand." Similarly, the Iowa Supreme Court found *Daubert* inapplicable to fire safety engineering experts in *Mercer v. Pittway Corp.*, 616 N.W.2d 602, 628 (Iowa 2000). The court also refused to apply *Daubert* to expert lighting safety testimony in a case where lights in a grain elevator allegedly ignited grain dust and caused an explosion. *Mensink v. American Grain, et al.*, 564 N.W.2d 376 (Iowa 1997). The court held in *Mensink* that *Daubert* applied only to expert evidence of a complex nature, which will ordinarily be scientific rather than "technical or other specialized knowledge."

Thus, in *Johnson v. Knoxville Community School District*, 570 N.W.2d 633 (Iowa 1997), the court held that *Daubert* did not apply to the testimony of a neuropsychiatrist who opined that the plaintiff's obsessive-compulsive disorder was not caused by his playground fall because the testimony "was not based on 'scientific knowledge' but rather constituted 'technical or specialized knowledge.'" The court subjected the expert's testimony to its "conventional Rule 702 analysis" and found it sufficiently reliable.

This decision departed somewhat from *Hutchison v. American Family Mut. Ins.*, 514 N.W.2d 882 (Iowa 1994), in which the court applied *Daubert* to a neuropsychologist's testimony concerning plaintiff's alleged closed head injury. In both cases, however, the court affirmed the admission of the experts' testimony. More recently, the Iowa Supreme Court has reaffirmed its position that *Daubert* is not appropriate in cases involving "technical or other specialized knowledge," and held that the foundational showing needed for such nonscientific evidence is correspondingly lower. *Ranes v. Adams Laboratories, Inc.*, 778 N.W.2d 677, 686 (Iowa 2010).

Iowa courts have applied *Daubert* in several other civil cases, usually finding the expert's testimony admissible. *See, e.g., Guidichessi v. ADM Milling Co.*, 554 N.W.2d 563, 566–67 (Iowa Ct. App. 1996) (citing *Daubert* in admitting testimony of railroad grade-crossing expert); *Carolan v. Hill*, 553 N.W.2d 882, 888–89 (Iowa 1996) (citing *Daubert* in reversing trial court's exclusion of nurse-anesthetist's testimony*); Williams v. Hedican,* 561 N.W.2d 817, 831 (Iowa 1997) (reversing trial court's exclusion of obstetrician's testimony, citing *Daubert* in holding that his testimony passed "good science" test). These decisions are consistent with Iowa courts' "liberal rule" regarding the admissibility of expert testimony.

Iowa appellate courts have also upheld trial court decisions excluding expert witnesses, however. In *Quad City Bank*, the Iowa Supreme Court upheld the trial court's exclusion of an expert accounting witness when the witness failed to show he was qualified to testify as an expert. *Quad City Bank & Trust v. Jim Kercher & Associates, P.C.*, 804 N.W.2d 83, 93–94 (Iowa 2011). The Iowa Supreme Court noted that the district court had made this ruling on an incorrect basis, that the expert was not a certified public accountant, but held that the expert's lack of qualifications to opine on whether an audit at issue in the case was negligent made the result of exclusion correct. *Id.* at 93. In *Ranes*, the Iowa Supreme Court affirmed a trial court's exclusion of the testimony of plaintiff's expert opining on whether a drug manufactured by the defendant was the cause of the plaintiff's myriad physical maladies. The court held that the expert did not practice a reliable methodology in reaching his opinion on causation. *Ranes*, 778 N.W.2d at 690–96.

State v. Stohr involved an appeal of a defendant who was prosecuted for operating while under the influence as a third or subsequent offender. 730 N.W.2d 674 (Iowa 2007). The trial court found that the state had not met the scientific reliability standard of a prior Iowa Supreme Court case with respect to the operation of the breath test device used to test defendant. The district court based its conclusion that the test results were unreliable on what it perceived to be uncertain internal standards and calibration methods, as well as the variable nature of the breath sample blown into the machine by defendant.

The Iowa Supreme Court held that the district court erred in suppressing defendant's breath test results. The Supreme Court held that all three of the requirements under Iowa Code § 321J.15, which sets forth the admissibility requirements for chemical analysis evidence in drunk driving cases, were satisfied. Under section 321J.15, a party seeking to introduce results of a chemical analysis must show that the analysis (1) was performed by a certified operator, (2) using a device intended to determine alcohol concentration, and (3) using methods approved by the commissioner of public safety. Defendant argued that the general rule for admission of scientific evidence must be superimposed on the statutory criteria; however, the Iowa Supreme Court suggested that its general rules for assessing admissibility of scientific evidence should control when a specific statutory process governed the admission of evidence.

b. Expert-Related Rules and Procedural Issues in Iowa

In Iowa state courts, Rule 1.508 of the Rules of Civil Procedure governs the discovery of experts and expert testimony. Rule 1.508 allows for expert discovery through interrogatories, and also provides a right to depose expert witnesses who will be testifying at trial. *See* I.C.A. Rule 1.508(1)(b)(1). Moreover, it specifically grants parties the discovery of "documents and tangible things including all tangible reports, physical models, compilations of data, and other material prepared by an expert or for an expert in anticipation of the expert's trial and deposition testimony." *Id.* at 1.508(1)(b)(2). The Iowa Rule confers on courts the power to require that a party put in writing "discoverable factual observations, tests, supporting data, calculations, photographs, or opinions of an expert who will be called as a witness" that are not in "tangible form." *See* I.C.A. Rule 1.508(1)(b)(3). Iowa courts have interpreted Rule 1.508(1) (formerly Rule 125(a)) to restrict expert discovery to opinions formed in anticipation of litigation; a party need not necessarily disclose opinions developed by the expert before being retained. *See id.* at 125(a)(1); *Day v. McIlrath*, 469 N.W.2d 676, 677 (Iowa 1991) ("[W]e do not believe that a treating physician's factual knowledge, mental impressions and opinions stand on precisely the same footing, especially in the early stages of litigation, as those of the retained expert contemplated by rule 125. Therefore we believe it would be inappropriate to employ all the disclosure procedures of rule 125."); *see also Duncan v. City of Cedar Rapids*, 560 N.W.2d 320 (Iowa 1997) ("Rule 125 applies to the discovery of facts known and mental impressions held by an expert and 'acquired or developed in anticipation of litigation.').

Under Rule 1.508, non-testifying experts who contribute work product relied upon by testifying experts are subject to the same discovery process as testifying experts. *See* I.C.A. Rule 1.508(2). As for non-testifying experts whose opinions are *not* used as a basis for a testifying witness, their opinions are discoverable in a manner identical to the Federal Rules. *Compare id., and* FED. R. CIV. P. 26(b)(4)(B).

Rule 1.508 provides for the payment of fees for time spent by experts in complying with discovery. *Compare* I.C.A. Rule 1.508(6), *with* FED. R. CIV. P. 26(b)(4)(C). In addition, there is language in Rule 1.508 which specifically excludes time spent in preparation for depositions from compensation and requires that the fee not be in excess of the expert's regular hourly or daily rate. *See* I.C.A. Rule 1.508(6).

3. Minnesota

a. A *Frye*-Based Standard of "General Acceptance" and "Foundational Reliability"

The Minnesota Supreme Court rejected *Daubert* in *Goeb v. Tharaldson*, 615 N.W.2d 800 (Minn. 2000), opting instead to stay with a *Frye*-based standard. That standard, otherwise known as "*Frye-Mack*," combines "general acceptance" with an examination of the "foundational reliability" underlying the expert's proposed testimony. The result is something of a hybrid approach, where the "general acceptance" question is critical, but where challenges to methodology and application are sometimes also considered under the rubric of "foundational reliability."

In *Goeb*, plaintiffs sued the manufacturer of a pesticide and the pest control company that applied it to their home in order to rid it of carpenter ants. Plaintiffs claimed that exposure to Dursban caused them generalized neurological damage, chemical sensitivity, and "chemical encephalopathy." In order to prove their claims, they offered the testimony of a toxicologist and a neurologist. The trial court found that "chemical encephalopathy" is not "clearly recognized to exist in the medical community," and it dismissed the case report that plaintiffs relied upon as "anecdotal rather than scientific." The trial court pointed out that the experts failed to account for the "NOEL" or "No Observable Effect Level" in forming the conclusion that Dursban had caused the Goebs' ailments.

The court then cited a long line of precedent holding that the "mere existence of an exposure to a chemical substance" does not prove a cause-and-effect relationship with an alleged condition.

The trial court also held that both of the plaintiffs' experts relied "to an inappropriate degree on a temporal relationship between an unquantified exposure and a claimed but unverified symptomatology." Neither expert performed an adequate differential diagnosis of the plaintiffs' claimed injuries, and as a result, "other potential[ly] operative medical, psychological or psychiatric causes" could not be ruled out. After reviewing the experts' supporting data, the court was "thoroughly convinced . . . that the literature sought by plaintiffs' experts to buttress their opinions is simply not supportive thereof . . . " The Minnesota Court of Appeals affirmed, holding that the trial court's decision was correct under either a *Frye* or *Daubert* analysis. *See Goeb v. Tharaldson*, 1999 WL 561956 (Minn. Ct. App. 1999).

The Minnesota Supreme Court affirmed the trial court's decision but, in so doing, reaffirmed the "*Frye-Mack*" standard and refused to adopt *Daubert*. Under the *Frye-Mack* standard, a trial court first determines whether the scientific technique has been generally accepted, and second—as established in *State v. Mack*, 292 N.W.2d 764 (Minn. 1980)—whether the particular evidence derived from the technique has a scientifically reliable foundation. The court noted that it had rejected previous challenges to *Frye-Mack*. *See, e.g., State v. Schwartz*, 447 N.W. 2d 422, 424 (Minn. 1989); *see also State v. Klawitter*, 518 N.W. 2d 577, 578 n.1 (Minn. 1994) (recognizing that the U.S. Supreme Court overruled *Frye*, but declining to express an "opinion on the continued vitality of the *Frye* rule in Minnesota"). Citing judges' lack of qualifications to decide scientific issues, and expressing concern over the "potential for non-uniformity in the law under *Daubert*," the court pronounced that *Frye-Mack* would continue to be the law in Minnesota. The court then applied the test to the plaintiffs' experts' testimony in *Goeb*, and held that the trial court did not abuse its discretion in excluding the testimony under the foundational reliability prong of *Frye-Mack*.

On the same day that it issued its decision in *Goeb*, the court also published *Sentinel Management Co. v. Aetna Cas. & Surety Co.*, 615 N.W.2d 819 (Minn. 2000), which involved a claim by property owners for asbestos-related damages under their insurance policies. The defendant argued that plaintiff's expert's testimony should have been excluded under *Frye-Mack*, on the ground that his four air samples could not be reliably extrapolated to the rest of the 450-unit building. Although the expert's evidence in this case appears to have been no more substantial than the evidence relied upon by the experts in *Goeb*, the Minnesota Supreme Court affirmed the trial court's decision to admit the evidence, finding that the defendant's criticisms went to the weight and not the admissibility of the testimony. The two decisions are consistent, however, in their substantial deference to the trial court's *Frye-Mack* analysis.

Many of the pre-*Goeb* Minnesota decisions on scientific evidence come from the criminal setting. *See, e.g., Ledin v. State*, 1997 WL 757156 (Minn. Ct. App. 1997) (recognizing "the development in the law regarding the admissibility of polygraph evidence in the wake of Daubert," but refusing on unrelated procedural grounds to grant petitioner a post-trial evidentiary hearing); *State v. Alt*, 504 N.W. 2d 38, 46 (Minn. 1993) (applying *Frye* to FBI crime lab DNA testing procedures; noting that "The [Minnesota] supreme court has allowed *Frye* to flourish"); *State v. Hodgson*, 512 N.W. 2d 95, 97 (Minn. 1994) (finding that bite-mark analysis passes *Frye*; "We need not address the issue of what impact Daubert should or will have in Minnesota . . . Suffice it to say, we are satisfied that basic bite-mark analysis by a recognized expert is not a novel or emerging type of scientific evidence"); *State v. Klawitter*, 518 N.W.2d 577 (Minn. 1994) (finding "Drug Recognition Expert" testimony concerning irregular eye movement admissible under *Frye*); *Barna v. Commissioner of Public Safety*, 508 N.W.2d 220 (Minn. Ct. App. 1993) (upholding alcohol dehydrogenase reaction method of determining blood alcohol content); *State v. Bauer*, 598 N.W.2d 352 (Minn. 1999) (demonstrative exhibit created with Photoshop software not subject to *Frye* analysis, since exhibit not offered as substantive evidence); *State v. Ritt*, 599 N.W.2d 802 (Minn. 1999) (trial court's exclusion of expert testimony regarding police interrogation techniques properly excluded as not adding "precision or depth" to jury's understanding of circumstances surrounding confession).

Since *Goeb*, the lion's share of Minnesota *Frye-Mack* decisions continues to arise in the criminal context. Among those, many have addressed the use of PCR-STR DNA test methods, the proper methodology for conducting those tests, and the propriety of testimony regarding the statistical inferences to be drawn from the results. The Minnesota Supreme Court has clarified over several decisions that the PCR-STR method has been "generally accepted" by DNA experts; that the reliability of PSR-STR test results is contingent upon the lab's compliance with the guidelines of the DNA Advisory Board (and not those of the Technical Working Group on DNA Analysis Methods, which have been superseded); and that the proper means of expressing the statistical likelihood of a random DNA match is through the "product rule." *See State v. Jones*, 678 N.W.2d 1 (Minn. 2004) (PCR-STR is generally accepted); *State v. Roman Nose*, 667 N.W.2d 386 (Minn. 2003) (DNA expert may testify to likelihood of a random match based on "product rule"); *State v. Kromah*, 657 N.W.2d 564 (Minn. 2003) (DAB guidelines supersede TWGDAM guidelines); *State v. Traylor*, 656 N.W. 2d 885 (Minn. 2003) (same); *Schneider v. State*, 725 N.W.2d 516 (Minn. 2007) (holding that it was not ineffective assistance of counsel to forego *Frye-Mack* challenge prior to admission of DNA evidence; tactical decision was within attorney's discretion and there was no showing that outcome would have been different).

In *State v. Bailey*, 732 N.W.2d 612 (Minn. 2007), the Minnesota Bureau of Criminal Apprehension revived a "cold case" by conducting DNA tests on a tissue sample that had been preserved on a slide. In order to access the sample, the BCA had to remove the cover slip from the slide, which they accomplished by heating it with a Bunsen burner. The test results showed matches on six of the test's ten loci, but the signals for the remaining four were too weak to interpret definitively. On his first appeal, *State v. Bailey*, 677 N.W. 2d 380 (Minn. 2004), defendant challenged the foundational reliability of the BCA's Bunsen burner technique. The Minnesota Supreme Court agreed and remanded for a *Frye-Mack* hearing on that question. On remand, the *Frye-Mack* hearing persuaded the trial court that the BCA's use of the Bunsen burner did not impact the foundational reliability of the test results. In his next appeal, defendant argued that the BCA should have done a study to confirm that the Bunsen burner would not affect the integrity of the sample. The court found no abuse of discretion in the admission of the evidence and testimony; there was no need for a validation study, as demonstrated by the subsequent BCA studies establishing the validity of the technique.

In *Loving*, the defendant contested the district court's admission of testimony on evidence of gunshot residue (GSR) found on the defendant's coat. *State v. Loving*, 775 N.W.2d 872 (Minn. 2009). Defendant did not take issue with the methodology of the scientific evidence—GSR testing through the use of a scanning electron microscope with an energy dispersive X-ray system (SEM/EDX)—because SEM/EDX testing for GSR has general acceptance in the scientific community. Instead, defendant argued that SEM/EDX analysis and the GSR evidence were unreliable. His argument was that, because GSR can be transferred in a number of ways, does not disintegrate, and can remain on clothing even after washing, the test is unable to determine how or when GSR lands on clothing. The Minnesota Supreme Court disagreed, stating that defendant's arguments about the inadequacy of the test's meaning went to the weight of the evidence, not its reliability. Foundational reliability for the evidence was met because both experts for the State and the defendant agreed that the SEM/EDX method was reliable for testing for GSR, the test had accurately identified GSR on the defendant's coat, and the expert performing the test followed approved procedures.

The Minnesota Supreme Court considered the evidentiary reliability of a positive dog-sniff "alert" for illegal drugs in *Jacobson v. $55,900 in U.S. Currency*, 728 N.W. 2d 510 (Minn. 2007). Plaintiff rented an apartment to a drug dealer who was later tried and convicted. The apartment contained a safe, which the plaintiff used for his business and to which he insisted his tenant had no access. When the police raided the apartment, they found $55,900 cash in the safe and seized it under a drug-related forfeiture statute. Plaintiff challenged the forfeiture on the ground that the government lacked adequate proof of a connection between the cash and illegal drugs. The government responded by introducing testimony from an expert dog handler that a dog specifically trained to detect drug odors, had "alerted" to the safe before the officers opened it. The Supreme Court upheld the admission of the dog handler's testimony, finding that the dog was well-trained and that the handler had enough training and experience to testify regarding the significance of the positive alert. Plaintiff's remaining criticisms of the handler's testimony went to weight rather than admissibility. As for the admissibility of the positive alert by itself, the court held that *Frye* did not apply because "the technique of using trained dogs to detect drug odors is neither emerging nor scientific." But the court expressed concerns over the "foundational reliability" of the alert, since the prosecution did not address how the storage conditions of the cash might have affected the dissipation of the drug odor. Thus, the court held that the positive alert could be admitted only if a complete foundation was laid for that evidence.

The Minnesota Supreme Court upheld the use of breath testing of drivers stopped for suspected drunk driving in 2012. *In re Source Code Evidentiary Hearings in Implied Consent Matters*, 816 N.W.2d 525 (Minn. 2012). The Supreme Court assigned to a district court a series of challenges to the use of the Intoxilyzer, a testing instrument that had been regularly used in Minnesota for many years. The challengers asserted that defects in the source code of the Intoxilyzer affected the reliability of test results from the machine. After an evidentiary hearing that lasted several days, the district court found the state's expert witnesses to be more credible and determined that the results of tests of the Intoxilyzer were reliable. The Minnesota Supreme Court affirmed on a 4-3 vote, finding no error in the district court's application of the preponderance of the evidence standard for reliability, no due process violation in the district court's pretrial determination that the challengers could not challenge the numerical test results at their individual hearings, and no abuse of discretion in the district court's practice of disregarding evidence of test results that showed a deficient sample.

A Minnesota Court of Appeals panel reaffirmed that the *Frye-Mack* standard is a more rigorous standard for admission of expert testimony in a case involving allegations that hormone replacement therapy (HRT) caused a plaintiff's breast cancer. *Zandi v. Wyeth*, 2009 WL 2151141 (Minn. App. 2009). The Court of Appeals, in affirming the trial court's decision to exclude plaintiff's medical experts and grant summary judgment for defendant for lack of causation evidence, agreed with the trial court that determining the cause of cancer in an individual "is not a generally accepted practice in the scientific or medical communities." Plaintiff's experts' epidemiological studies could not be the sole basis for the experts' opinions that HRT caused breast cancer, so plaintiff's experts relied on differential diagnosis. The court found that differential diagnosis had not been accepted as a method of diagnosing the cause of a person's breast cancer, that the experts' differential diagnoses were deficient for failure to rule out other causes, and that a test the experts offered to show specific causation was not a generally accepted means of showing causation. Thus, concluding that there was no method of diagnosing the specific cause of a woman's breast cancer that was generally accepted in the relevant scientific community—and thus no way for such a test to satisfy the *Frye-Mack* standard—the court affirmed summary judgment for the defendant.

The Minnesota Supreme Court has investigated the use of *Frye-Mack* to assess psychological theories in a series of decisions. In *State v. MacLennan*, 702 N.W. 2d 219 (Minn. 2005), the Minnesota Supreme Court confronted for the first time the theory of "battered child syndrome." The trial court conducted a *Frye-Mack* review and held that the syndrome was generally accepted from the standpoint of physical abuse, but not as a purely psychological syndrome. On appeal, the Minnesota Supreme Court questioned whether *Frye-Mack* was the appropriate standard to apply in the first place. The court expressed concern that *Frye* may be ill-suited to evaluate psychological and social science-based testimony (as distinguished from "hard science" fields like chemistry and toxicology). After reviewing decisions on the matter from other *Frye* jurisdictions, the court concluded that the proper standard to apply to "battered child syndrome" was Minnesota Rule of Evidence 702, not *Frye-Mack*.

The Minnesota Supreme Court revisited and refined an earlier holding that limited the ability of parties to offer evidence on typical rape victim behaviors. *State v. Obeta*, 796 N.W.2d 282 (Minn. 2011). In the opinion, the court made distinctions between its holding in *State v. Saldana*, 324 N.W.2d 227 (Minn. 1982), where it held that evidence on rape trauma syndrome was inadmissible, from the case at bar, where prosecutors were attempting to introduce evidence on delayed reporting of rape, lack of physical injuries in rape victims, and submissive conduct of rape victims during the assault. *Obeta*, 796 N.W.2d at 290–91. The Minnesota Supreme Court noted that only Minnesota and Pennsylvania categorically prohibited expert opinion on typical counterintuitive behaviors exhibited by adult victims of sexual assault. *Id.* at 292–93. The court remanded for a determination of whether the expert testimony was admissible pursuant to Minn. R. Evid. 702, but took no position on whether expert testimony that educates jurors about typical rape victim behaviors was based a novel scientific theory and therefore subject to *Frye-Mack*. *Id.* at 294, 294 n.9.

On the other hand, in 2012, the Minnesota Supreme Court limited the ability of a plaintiff bringing a claim against a Roman Catholic archdiocese to offer evidence on a theory of repressed and recovered memory. *John Doe 76C v. Archdiocese of Saint Paul and Minneapolis*, 817 N.W.2d 150 (Minn. 2012). Plaintiff alleged that he repressed his memories of four occasions when a priest molested him when plaintiff was a teenager, and despite heavy news coverage of other cases of abuse involving the priest in the mid-1980s, plaintiff alleged that he did not recount the incidents of abuse he suffered until 2002, which would have tolled the statute of limitations. The trial court held a three-day *Frye-Mack* hearing on the admissibility of the evidence, which the Minnesota Supreme Court recounted at length in its opinion, and found that plaintiff had failed to show that the repressed-memory theory was generally accepted in the relevant scientific community and failed to show that the theory was reliable. The appeals court reversed summary judgment for the defendant and remanded, finding that the trial court should not have applied the *Frye-Mack* test, citing MacLennan and likening the repressed memory syndrome to the "battered child syndrome" in that case. The Minnesota Supreme Court reversed the intermediate appeals court, reiterating that amendments to Rule 702 made foundational reliability, the same analysis as the second prong of the *Frye-Mack* test, the fourth part of the amended Rule 702. Citing *Jacobson*, the court found that the "foundational reliability" test went beyond simply whether the evidence was helpful, and instead, a court must analyze the proffered testimony in light of the purpose for which it was being offered, that the court must consider the underlying reliability, consistency, and accuracy of the expert's subject, and the proponent of the evidence must show that it is reliable in the particular case. Because the trial court had considered the purpose of the expert testimony, the reliability of the expert's underlying theory, and the reliability of the evidence in the case, the Minnesota Supreme Court reviewed only the district's court evidentiary ruling for an abuse of discretion. The Supreme Court found the trial court's decision to be amply supported by the record, and thus it was not improper for the district court to limit the evidence on the repressed memory theory.

b. Expert-Related Rules and Procedural Issues in Minnesota

Rule 26.02 of the Minnesota Rules of Civil Procedure contains the procedures for discovery of expert witnesses. Rule 26.02(e)(1)(A) says that a party can be required by another party to "identify each person whom the other party expects to call as an expert witness at trial, to state the subject matter on which the expert is expected to testify, and to state the substance of the facts and opinions to which the expert is expected to testify and a summary of the grounds for each opinion." MINN R. CIV. P. 26.02. The rule provides for discovery via interrogatories as a matter of right, *see Id.*, and does not grant an absolute entitlement to depose another party's experts as Fed. R. Civ. P. 26 does.

See FED. R. CIV. P. 26(b)(4)(A). Discovery in excess of the expert interrogatories is not granted in ordinary circumstances and is available only upon a good cause showing. *See* MINN. R. CIV. P. 26.02 advisory committee's note.

Minnesota Rule 26.02 does not contain the extensive expert testimony disclosure requirements of Fed. R. Civ. P. 26(a)(2)(B), although the special rules of practice for the Second Judicial District of Minnesota do provide for a small amount of special disclosure for expert witnesses. Rule 5 of the Special Rules provides that the joint disposition conference report *must* include "[a] list of each party's prospective witnesses, including each witness' name and address, employer and occupation, including expert witnesses and the particular area of expertise each expert will be addressing." MINN. SPEC. R. PRAC. (2nd Jud. Dist.) 6.

Minnesota has enacted a separate law for expert witness procedures in malpractice actions. Section 145.682 of the Minnesota statutes requires that a plaintiff in a malpractice case send the defendant an affidavit that identifies plaintiff's expert witnesses, "the substance of the facts and opinions" of anticipated expert testimony and a synopsis of the foundation for their conclusions. MINN. STAT. § 145.682, subd. 4 (1998).This affidavit must be signed by all the experts discussed within it and must be served on the defendant within 180 days of the initiation of the action. *Id.* In order to comply with section 145.682, "it is not enough simply to repeat the facts in the hospital or clinic record. The affidavit should set out how the expert will use those facts to arrive at opinions of malpractice and causation." *Sorenson v. St. Paul Ramsey Med. Ctr.*, 457 N.W.2d 188, 192–93 (Minn. 1990); *See also Stroud v. Hennepin County Med. Ctr.*, 556 N.W.2d 552 (Minn. 1996). The Supreme Court of Minnesota has indicated that the specificity demanded of the disclosure requirements in section 145.682 is the same or similar as that which is required in Rule 26. *See Sorenson*, 457 N.W. at 191. When a defendant moves to dismiss for noncompliance for section 145.682, however, the plaintiff can always use a forty-five-day safe harbor period to correct the deficiency. *Wesely v. Flor*, 806 N.W.2d 36, 41 (Minn. 2011).

Disputes frequently arise in criminal cases over the necessity of holding a *Frye* hearing prior to the admission of expert testimony or technical evidence. In *State v. Trevor Anthony Brown*, 2007 Minn. LEXIS 620, the Minnesota Supreme Court found no error in the trial court's admission of a digital copy of an analog videotape without first holding a *Frye* hearing. The court held that the conversion of the analog recording to a digital medium did not raise any issues of novel scientific evidence.

Similarly, some Minnesota Court of Appeals decisions since *Goeb* suggest that Minnesota courts need not apply scrutiny to as broad a range of expert testimony as federal courts must after *Kumho. See, e.g., Northern States Power Co. v. Burlington Northern & Santa Fe Rwy. Co.*, 2000 WL 1809143 (Minn. Ct. App. 2000) (trial court did not abuse discretion in admitting appraiser's testimony; arguably, *Frye* does not apply to expert evidence that is not "scientific;" also, expert's testimony had sufficient and reliable foundation).

4. *Missouri*

a. Different Standards in Civil and Criminal Cases

The Missouri Supreme Court adopted the *Frye* rule for criminal cases in 1972, *State v. Stout*, 478 S.W. 2d 368 (Mo. 1972), and first applied *Frye* in a civil case in 1985, *Alsbach v. Bader*, 700 S.W.2d 823 (Mo. 1985). In *Lasky v. Union Electric Co.*, 936 S.W.2d 797 (Mo. 1997), however, the Missouri Supreme Court held that Missouri Statute § 490.065—Missouri's equivalent to F.R.E. 702—governed the admissibility of expert testimony. Under that section, an expert's testimony (1) is admissible when the expert's testimony will assist the trier of fact, (2) is not objectionable because it embraces an ultimate issue to be decided by the trier of fact, (3) can be based upon facts or data made known to the expert at the hearing, must be of a type reasonably relied upon by experts in the field, and must be otherwise reasonably reliable, and (4) does not require the use of hypothetical questions so long as a reasonable foundation is laid, unless the court believes the use of a hypothetical question will make the expert's opinion more understandable or will be of greater assistance to the jury. Following *Lasky,* confusion persisted among Missouri appellate courts regarding whether *Frye* and/or *Daubert* still had a role in applying § 490.065 and deciding whether an expert's testimony met that standard. *Compare Long v. Missouri Delta Med. Ctr.,* 33 S.W.3d 629 (Mo. Ct. App. 2000) (affirming admission of economist's testimony regarding future care damages under *Frye* and Mo. Rev. Stat. § 490.065) *with Hobbs v. Harken,* 969 S.W.2d 318, 321 (Mo. Ct. App. 1998) (reversing trial court's admission of economist's future damages testimony without discussing whether *Frye* or *Daubert* applied).

Then, in *State Bd. of Registration for the Healing Arts v. McDonagh,* 123 S.W. 3d 146 (Mo. 2003), the Missouri Supreme Court held that § 490.065 is the *sole* standard for judging the admissibility of expert testimony. The court held that, "[t]o the extent that civil cases decided since *Lasky* apply *Frye* or some other standard, they are incorrect and should no longer be followed." In *McDonagh,* the Missouri State Board of Registration for the Healing Arts, which regulates the practice of medicine in Missouri, filed a complaint against Dr. Edward McDonagh. The agency sought to discipline Dr. McDonagh for administering ethylene diamine tetra-acetic acid (EDTA) to patients suffering from vascular disorders. Both before and during the hearing, the board moved to exclude expert testimony in support of EDTA therapy on the grounds that such testimony failed to meet *Frye* standards, but the motion was denied, along with the board's complaint.

On appeal, the board renewed its argument that expert testimony in support of EDTA therapy did not meet *Frye* standards and therefore should not have been admitted. In response, Dr. McDonagh argued that *Frye* conflicted with Missouri Statutes § 490.065, which governs the admissibility of expert testimony in civil cases. Unlike *Frye,* § 490.065 does not require general acceptance in a scientific community, but instead that the testimony be based on facts or data "reasonably relied upon by the experts in the relevant field." The Missouri Court of Appeals held that the testimony had been properly admitted. The Missouri Supreme Court reversed and remanded, however, holding that McDonagh's experts were not from the "relevant field" (in this case, vascular disease) and that McDonagh therefore had failed to present expert testimony regarding the applicable standard of care.

Since *McDonagh,* Missouri courts have reviewed expert testimony in a variety of settings. In *McGuire v. Seltsam,* 138 S.W.3d 718 (Mo. 2004), the Supreme Court reversed the trial court's admission of a defense psychiatrist's testimony that the plaintiff suffered from "somatization disorder." The court found that the psychiatrist simply "assumed" certain facts necessary to make the diagnosis; in other words, the expert "was making that assumption based upon her diagnosis and making her diagnosis, in part, based upon that assumption." The court held that "[t]his type of circular logic cannot form a reliable basis for an expert opinion." In *Doe v. McFarlane,* 207 S.W.3d 52 (Mo. Ct. App. 2006), the Court of Appeals affirmed expert testimony concerning the plaintiff's royalty and lost opportunity damages in a right-of-publicity case involving a former hockey player.

In *Brooks v. SSM Health Care,* 73 S.W.3d 686 (Mo. Ct. App. 2002), plaintiff Sally Brooks sued defendants SSM Health Care and Dr. Fernando DeCastro, alleging that the administration of a tissue plasminogen activator (tPA) by Dr. DeCastro caused Brooks to suffer bleeding, which in turn caused neurological problems. At trial Brooks sought to introduce expert testimony by Dr. Young, an emergency physician specializing in thrombolytic therapy and emergency cardiology. Dr. Young testified that Dr. DeCastro failed to use the degree of skill and learning ordinarily used by physicians in similar circumstances, and Dr. DeCastro's inappropriate administration of tPA caused bleeding, which led to plaintiff's neurological problems. After the jury found for Brooks, defendants moved for a new trial, arguing that Dr. Young had been unqualified to testify and his expert testimony had been improperly admitted. The trial court granted the motion.

On appeal, the Missouri Court of Appeals reversed the trial court's order and reinstated the jury verdict. The court found that defendants had not properly preserved a claim of error regarding the foundation of Dr. Young's testimony. Moreover, Dr. Young was qualified to testify about the cause of Brooks's bleeding, since the court found that physicians are generally competent to testify in fields where they are not specialists. For this reason, plaintiff's theory could be submitted to the jury and no new trial should have been granted.

In *M.C. v. Yeargin*, the Missouri Court of Appeals considered the admissibility of a physician's testimony that plaintiff, a rape victim, suffered post-traumatic stress disorder (PTSD) and brain damage as a result of the incident. *M.C. v. Yeargin*, 11 S.W.3d 604, 619 (Mo. Ct. App. 2000). Both sides' experts agreed that plaintiff had suffered PTSD, but differed over whether any organic brain damage had occurred. Over defendant's objection, the trial court admitted plaintiff's expert's opinion regarding plaintiff's alleged "diminished hippocampal volume," holding that there was a "sufficient and adequate basis" for the testimony. The Missouri Court of Appeals reversed, however, because the trial court did not specifically find that the expert's theory had been "generally accepted" under *Frye*.

The Missouri Supreme Court clarified the standard for admissibility of expert medical evidence in *Kivland*. The plaintiff in *Kivland* was the widow of a man who had been paralyzed from the waist down after spinal surgery and later committed suicide after filing his complaint alleging medical negligence. *Kivland v. Columbia Orthopaedic Group, LLP*, 331 S.W.3d 299 (Mo. 2011). The trial court prevented the plaintiff from offering expert testimony on proximate causation, but the Missouri Supreme Court reversed, "clarifying" section 490.065 and holding that a trial court is not required to consider the degree to which any of the section 490.065 factors were met, only whether the party offering the evidence satisfied the factors. *Id.* at 311. Thus, the trial court had erred in finding that the medical expert had to have relied on facts and data reasonably relied upon by experts in the field and that his testimony was inadmissible because he had no psychiatric diagnosis to explain the decedent's behavior. *Id.* at 312. Instead, the only requirement for being qualified to testify was whether the expert was qualified "by knowledge, skill, experience, training or education," and it was up to the jury to decide whether to accept the testimony. *Id.* at 311, 313. The medical expert's testimony assisted the plaintiff in making her case for proximate causation and the expert was qualified to testify, and thus the court reversed the judgment for defendant on the wrongful death claim. *Id.* at 313–14.

In *Goddard v. State*, 144 S.W.3d 848 (Mo. Ct. App. 2004), a jury heard the state's petition to have the defendant adjudged a sexually violent predator (SVP) and civilly committed. At the hearing, the state introduced the expert testimony of a doctor on the issue of whether defendant met the statutory definition of SVP. The doctor testified that the defendant did, citing his history of sexual offenses, his demeanor, his refusal to address the problem, his use of alcohol, and other related behaviors. The doctor also testified that he believed the defendant to be likely to reoffend based on his results under Static 99 and MnSOST-R, which were "actuarial instruments" derived from a nationwide study of sex offenders. The jury found the defendant to be a SVP, and the trial court ordered him committed to custody.

On appeal, the defendant argued that the trial court abused its discretion in admitting the portions of the doctor's testimony based on the actuarial instruments. The defendant claimed that the instruments failed to meet the requirements of Missouri Statutes § 490.065.3, under which the state had to establish that the tests were "reasonably relied upon by experts in the field in forming opinions." The Missouri Court of Appeals affirmed the verdict. It held, first, that although Section 490.065 governed the admission of expert testimony in Missouri, the defendant wrongly relied on subsection 490.065..3, whereas subsection 490.065.1 properly applied. Subsection 490.065.3 applies to the admission of "facts and data" on which an expert opinion is based, whereas subsection 490.065.1 applies to an expert's "general experience and knowledge." Further, the record showed that the tests were widely used in the scientific community, supported by field textbooks, the subject of peer review, and supported by "other evidence tending to show [their] scientific validity."

In criminal cases, Missouri continues to apply *Frye*, even after the Missouri Supreme Court's decision in *McDonagh. See, e.g., State v. Keightley*, 147 S.W. 3d 179, 187 n.7 (Mo. Ct. App. 2004). Missouri appears to be unique among states in the Eighth Circuit in its use of different standards for evaluating expert testimony in civil and criminal cases.

Missouri courts have upheld the RFLP and PCR/STR methods of DNA typing, as well as the "product rule" for determining the likelihood that a DNA match occurred by chance. *See, e.g., State v. Kinder*, 942 S.W.2d 313, 326–27 (Mo. 1996), *State v. Faulkner*, 103 S.W.3d 346 (Mo. Ct. App. 2003). Missouri decisions on DNA evidence are generally permissive; the manner in which DNA tests are conducted is considered more an issue of witness credibility and weight of the evidence, which are matters better left to the trial court and ultimately the jury. *See, e.g., State v. Davis*, 814 S.W. 2d 593 (Mo. 1991), *State v. Huchting*, 927 S.W.2d 411, 418 (Mo. Ct. App. 1996). In a first-degree murder case, the Court of Appeals held that the defendant was not prejudiced by the lack of a *Frye* hearing on DNA methods that, while not yet approved by Missouri courts, had been validated by other jurisdictions. *State v. Salmon*, 89 S.W. 3d 540 (Mo. Ct. App. 2002). In an earlier decision, however, the Court of Appeals excluded an expert's alternative methodology for interpreting DNA evidence. *State v. Love*, 963 S.W.2d 236 (Mo. Ct. App. 1997).

In other criminal cases involving expert challenges, the Missouri Court of Appeals has affirmed the admission of testimony regarding the amount of amphetamines that could be produced from seized precursor materials (*State v. Swain*, 977 S.W.2d 85, 86 (Mo. App. 1998), and excluded testimony from an "interrogation psychologist" as invading the jury's province (*State v. Davis*, 32 S.W.3d 603 (Mo. Ct. App. 2000)). One appeals court decision held that failure to request a *Frye* hearing to challenge testimony on "hair comparison analysis" amounted to ineffective assistance of counsel. *Butler v. State*, 108 S.W.3d 18 (Mo. Ct. App. 2003). In *State v. Daniels*, 179 S.W.3d 273 (Mo. Ct. App. 2005), the Court of Appeals held that it was an abuse of discretion for the trial court to allow the introduction of positive luminol test results, suggesting the presence of blood in defendant's home and vehicles, without first conducting a *Frye* hearing. Subsequent laboratory testing of samples from the home did not confirm the luminol results.

In Missouri, a *Frye* challenge is waived if the expert's testimony is not first objected to at trial. *Callahan v. Cardinal Glennon Hosp.*, 863 S.W.2d 852 (Mo. 1993) (expert challenge waived because appellant did not object to expert's testimony at trial); *Sanders v. Ahmed*, 364 S.W.3d 195, 209 (Mo. 2012) (defense attorneys waived *Frye* challenge on appeal where they failed to request that trial court strike expert's testimony).

b. Expert-Related Rules and Procedural Issues in Missouri

Rule 56.01 of the Missouri Rule of Civil Procedure is the main rule concerning the discovery of experts in Missouri state courts. Mo. R. Civ. P. 56.01. The rule states that a party can be required to disclose a testifying expert's "name, address, occupation, place of employment and qualifications to give an opinion," as well as the "general nature of the subject matter on which the expert is expected to testify, and the expert's hourly deposition fee." *Id.* at 56.01(b)(4)(a). It provides for discovery by interrogatory *and* deposition of the other party's experts who will be called at trial. *See Id.* at 56.01(b)(4)(a) & (b). Courts are to require the payment of a reasonable hourly fee to the expert by the party conducting the discovery by deposition, unless doing so would result in "manifest injustice." *Id.* at 56.01(b)(4)(b).

Missouri is unique among states within the Eighth Circuit in its treatment of "non-retained" experts. Rule 56.01(b)(5) provides that "[a] party, through interrogatories, may require any other party to identify each non-retained expert witness, including a party whom the other party expects to call at trial who may provide expert witness testimony by providing the expert's name, address, and field of expertise." *Id.* at 56.01(b)(5). However, the facts and opinions held by a non-retained expert are discoverable only in the same manner as lay witnesses generally. *See Id.* There is no language analogous to Federal Rule 26(b)(4)(B) which allows discovery of non-testifying experts "upon a showing of exceptional circumstances under which it is impracticable for the party seeking discovery to obtain facts or opinions on the same subject by other means."

5. Nebraska

a. The *Daubert* Standard Governs Admissibility

The Nebraska Supreme Court has adopted *Daubert* as the standard for evaluating expert testimony. In *Schafersman v. Agland Coop*, 631 N.W.2d 862 (Neb. 2001), the trial court admitted testimony from an expert veterinarian that contamination of defendant's feed caused plaintiffs' cows to suffer from "multiple mineral toxicity." Applying *Frye*, the Nebraska Supreme Court found that the expert had failed to rule out alternative causes of the cows' illness, did not examine or treat the cows, and was aware of no studies supporting his theory of "multiple mineral toxicity." Because the plaintiffs had not shown "general acceptance," or any other basis for validating their expert's testimony, the court held that the testimony should have been excluded.

It was not necessary to its decision in *Schafersman*, but the Nebraska Supreme Court nevertheless proceeded to adopt *Daubert*. The court reversed and remanded for a new trial, holding that just because the expert failed to pass *Frye* "does not necessarily preclude the Schafersmans from offering such testimony at a second trial" if the expert could be shown to meet the newly-adopted *Daubert* standard.

In *McNeel*, the Nebraska Supreme Court commented on the "fit" needed between expert opinions and the issues of the case, a FELA claim by a railroad engineer against his employer. *McNeel v. Union Pac. R.R.*, 753 N.W.2d 321 (Neb. 2008). In the case, the plaintiff was exposed to unidentified fumes which he alleged caused him a variety of maladies. *Id.* at 326. The trial court granted the defendant employer's motion to exclude the opinions of the plaintiff's medical experts, finding they lacked any evidence to a causative factor and were therefore irrelevant and inadmissible. *Id.* at 326–27. The Supreme Court affirmed this decision, holding that under *Daubert/Schafersman*, expert testimony lacks "fit" when "a large analytical gap must be made between the facts and the opinion." *Id.* at 332. Because the plaintiff's experts could not identify any toxic agent, there was too great an analytical leap to make between the defendant's actions and the plaintiff's injuries. But in *Golden v. Union Pac. R.R. Co.*, 804 N.W.2d 31 (Neb. 2011), another FELA case arising out of the same incident as *McNeel*, the Nebraska Supreme Court reversed summary judgment for the defendant. In *Golden*, the plaintiff provided expert testimony that presented genuine issue of material fact on whether plaintiff was exposed to the toxic substances emitted from within the locomotive, allowing him to move forward with his claims.

A number of Nebraska Supreme Court decisions attempt to delineate when scrutiny of expert testimony is warranted and when it is not. In a pre-*Schafersman* case, *Sheridan v. Catering Management, Inc.*, 558 N.W.2d 319 (Neb. Ct. App. 1997), plaintiff filed a workers' compensation claim alleging that her employer's application of pesticides in her workplace caused her to suffer brain damage. The court found that because the claim was made in Workmen's Compensation Court, the plaintiff's evidence did not have to meet the standards of either the *Frye* or the *Daubert* tests. Likewise, in litigation over a condemnation award, the Supreme Court held that *Daubert/Schafersman* did not apply to a valuation expert's testimony, and that criticism over the expert's use of certain comparables was really only a challenge to the foundation for the expert's testimony under Neb. R. Evid. 702. *City of Lincoln v. Realty Trust Group*, 705 N.W.2d 432 (Neb. 2005). The court has also held that a challenge to the admissibility of cellular phone records does not implicate *Daubert*. *State v. Gutierrez*, 726 N.W.2d 542 (Neb. 2007), *State v. Robinson*, 724 N.W. 2d 35 (Neb. 2006) (both abrogated on other grounds, *State v. Thorpe*, 783 N.W.2d 749, 757 (Neb. 2010). The Nebraska Supreme Court has also held that an expert civil engineer's testimony on causation in a case involving damage to a sewer system did not require *Daubert/Schafersman* analysis. *Village of Hallam v. L.G. Barcus & Sons, Inc.*, 798 N.W.2d 109, 120 (Neb. 2011).

In 2008, the court held that the testimony of a sexual assault nurse examiner about her examination of the victim was not opinion testimony and thus not subject to *Daubert/Schafersman*. *State v. Schreiner*, 754 N.W.2d 742, 754 (Neb. 2008). Similarly, when an opposing party attacked the factual basis of the opinion of a certified public accountant who analyzed financial documents to determine plaintiff's lost profits, the court held that a *Daubert/Schafersman* analysis was not required. *Aon Consulting, Inc. v. Midlands Financial Benefits, Inc.*, 748 N.W.2d 626, 640–41 (Neb. 2008). In cases involving non-novel expert testimony, a less probing *Daubert* analysis may suffice. *See, e.g., State v. Mason*, 709 N.W.2d 638 (Neb. 2006) (ballistics evidence not novel and therefore does not require extensive *Daubert* review). Similarly, in a bench trial, a trial court has greater flexibility in performing its "gatekeeping" function but may not abdicate it completely. *Fickle v. State*, 735 N.W.2d 754 (Neb. 2007).

The Nebraska Supreme Court clarified the *Daubert/Schafersman* test in a case challenging the use of the results of a horizontal gaze nystagmus (HGN) test as evidence in a criminal trial where defendant was accused of driving under the influence. *State v. Casillas*, 782 N.W.2d 882 (Neb. 2010). The trial court denied defendant's motion *in limine* to exclude the results of the HGN test and defendant's request to hold an evidentiary hearing on the validity of the HGN test, finding that the use of HGN did not warrant a *Schafersman* analysis. *Id.* at 891–92. The failure of the trial court to "carry out its gatekeeping duties under *Daubert/Schafersman*" was a harmless error, but the court still discussed how to apply *Daubert/Schafersman* in other settings. *Id.* at 895.

The *Casillas* court held that "[a]ll specialized knowledge falls generally under the rules of *Daubert/Schafersman*." Because HGN involved scientific knowledge, it was error to not apply the *Daubert/Schafersman* test. But depending on the type of specialized evidence and the circumstances of the case, Nebraska courts will have different duties. Thus, a pretrial *Daubert/Schafersman* hearing is not always required, and the "extensiveness" of the hearing is left to a trial court. Further, the party challenging the evidence bears no burden to make a showing that the proffered evidence is unreliable. Rather, it is "always the burden of the proponent of the evidence to establish the necessary foundation for its admission, including its scientific reliability under *Daubert/Schafersman*." All a challenging party needs to do to call into question specialized knowledge is "object with enough specificity so that the court understands what is being challenged and can accordingly determine the necessity and extent of any pretrial proceeding." *Id.* at 897. *See also State v. Huff*, 802 N.W.2d 77, 116–17 (Neb. 2011) (affirming denial of defendant's objection based upon *Daubert/Schafersman* when defendant failed to object with sufficient specificity). HGN had not been affirmed in Nebraska since the state adopted the *Daubert* test, so the trial court could not have taken judicial notice of precedent to satisfy its gatekeeping findings, but the court noted that the State could have made its prima facie case for admissibility of the HGN test results in reliance on case law under *Frye*. *Casillas*, 782 N.W.2d at 898.

In *Perry Lumber Co. v. Durable Services*, 710 N.W.2d 854 (Neb. 2006), the trial court held that plaintiffs' expert was qualified to testify concerning the origin but not the cause of a fire that damaged plaintiff's property. Because the expert had not only investigated the fire, but actually participated in fighting it, the expert was allowed to provide lay opinion testimony on causation based on his direct observation of the scene. The jury was instructed, however, that the expert was "not necessarily" an expert in this area, and that the jury should adjust the weight to be given the testimony accordingly. The Nebraska Supreme Court reversed, finding that the expert was sufficiently qualified to provide expert causation testimony, and that the court's comments unfairly and prejudicially diminished the credibility of his testimony. The court also held that no *Daubert* review of the expert's analysis was needed due to his compliance with applicable NFPA guidelines. Finally, the court upheld the admission of the defense expert's testimony that the plaintiff's expert did not have enough information to support his opinions; "[t]estimony critiquing the procedures and opinions of another expert is an acceptable form of expert testimony."

Clarifying the test for admissibility of causation testimony in epidemiological cases, the Nebraska Supreme Court held that under the *Daubert/Schafersman* test, a trial court need not require general acceptance of the causal link between an agent and a disease or condition if the expert's opinion is otherwise based on a reliable methodology. *King v. Burlington Northern Santa Fe Ry. Co.*, 762 N.W.2d 24, 44 (Neb. 2009). The facts that an expert's opinion that diesel exhaust could cause multiple myeloma was unpublished and that the expert had not personally conducted research on the subject were relevant to the *Daubert/Schafersman* test, but were not fatal to the expert's testimony because the expert had relied upon peer-reviewed studies to reach his opinion as to causation. The only questions for the trial court were whether the results of the epidemiological studies the expert relied upon were sufficient to support his opinion regarding causation and whether he reviewed the scientific literature or data in a reliable manner.

The *King* court also set forth four factors for Nebraska courts to use when determining the admissibility of expert testimony based on epidemiological evidence:

(1) strength of association or causal relationship, with the court setting a minimum limit for the relative risk factor at 1.0, allowing the significance of studies with weak positive associations to be "a question of weight, not admissibility";
(2) ruling out potential sources of error through testing for statistical significance, recognizing that tests for significance might not be needed where experts can show that others in the field would nonetheless rely on studies to support causation opinions;
(3) the number of studies supporting the causation opinion, or, in the normal situation, that there is more than one study showing a positive association, but allowing for trial courts to consider whether the expert has cherry-picked studies; and
(4) a method for reliably analyzing a body of evidence, or, in other words, a meta-analysis of existing studies to show the methodology is generally accepted in the field.

After setting forth these factors, the *King* court held that the trial court had improperly applied a "conclusive study" standard for admissibility of causation evidence. The court remanded for the trial court to decide whether "no reasonable expert would rely on the studies to find a causal relationship," not whether the parties disputed the studies' validity. *Id.* at 49.

The court then considered whether the expert performed a reliable differential etiology to rule out other possible causes. To determine whether an expert had performed a reliable etiology, a court must consider whether the expert considered a suspected agent that did not cause the disease and whether the expert completely failed to consider a cause that could explain the symptoms. In determining whether the expert erred in ruling out potential causes, the *King* court applied a test of whether the expert "had a reasonable basis" for concluding that one of the agents was the most likely cause and whether the expert had "good grounds" for eliminating other hypotheses. Such grounds depend upon the circumstances of the case but require more than unsupported speculation. *Id.*

When considering expert testimony from "nonscientists," the Nebraska Supreme Court focuses on the tightness of the connection between the expert's opinion and the record facts. In *Nebraska Nutrients v. Shepherd*, 626 N.W.2d 472 (Neb. 2001), the court held that plaintiff's damages experts had a sufficient factual basis to calculate prospective lost profits for an ethanol plant that never became operational. *See also Gary's Implement, Inc. v. Bridgeport Tractor Parts, Inc.*, 799 N.W.2d 249,

259–62 (Neb. 2011) (affirming admission of expert testimony from accountant who calculated lost profits based on comparisons between plaintiff's business and comparable businesses). Two decisions involving vocational rehabilitation experts had opposite results, based on the strength of the foundation for the expert's disability opinion. *Compare Phillips v. Industrial Machine*, 597 N.W.2d 377 (Neb. 1999) (vocational rehabilitation expert excluded because disability opinion not supported by any testimony from a medical doctor) *with Snyder v. Case*, 611 N.W.2d 409 (Neb. 2000) (testimony of vocational rehab expert properly admitted because opinion based on sufficient medical evidence).

Due to the powerful influence DNA testing can have in criminal trials, the Nebraska Supreme Court expanded the *Frye* test as applied to DNA evidence in *State v. Houser*, 490 N.W.2d 168 (1992). The need for additional safeguards resulted in the *"Frye-Houser"* test, which requires Nebraska courts to determine:

(1)   Whether the witnesses on the DNA issue are experts in the relevant scientific fields;
(2)   Whether the DNA testing used in the case under consideration is generally accepted as reliable if performed properly;
(3)   Whether the method of testing used in the case under consideration is generally accepted as reliable if performed properly;
(4)   Whether the tests conducted properly followed the method;
(5)   Whether the DNA evidence is more probative than prejudicial under Neb. Evid. R. 403; and
(6)   Whether statistical probability testimony interpreting the DNA evidence is more probative than prejudicial.

State v. Houser, 490 N.W.2d 168 (Neb. 1992). *See also State v. Carter*, 586 N.W. 2d 818 (Neb. 1998) (applying *Frye-Houser* test in approving PCR method of DNA analysis and population genetics evidence). But the Nebraska Supreme Court applied the *Daubert/Schafersman* test to a challenge to the use of PCR-STR testing in *Bauldwin* and found that the trial court had not abused its discretion in admitting the testimony discussing DNA evidence, suggesting that Nebraska courts will now apply *Daubert/Schafersman* to all challenges of this type. *State v. Bauldwin*, 811 N.W.2d 267, 287–89 (Neb. 2012). *See also State v. Edwards*, 767 N.W.2d 784, 803 (Neb. 2009) (holding that "methods and technique of DNA testing" used by experts were "accepted and practiced by others in the field" and thus did not require peer review of the tests at issue in the case).

Under Nebraska law, a litigant who calls an expert at trial waives the opportunity to challenge the admissibility of that expert's testimony on appeal. In *Kirchner v. Wilson*, 634 N.W.2d 760 (Neb. 2001), plaintiff called a defense expert as a witness, even though the defendant had withdrawn the expert from his witness list, for the purpose of attacking the expert's credibility. After suffering an adverse verdict, plaintiff then argued on appeal that the defense expert's testimony should not have been admitted because it did not meet *Frye*'s requirements for general acceptance. The Nebraska Supreme Court held that "[i]t is a well-established principle that a party cannot complain of an error which that party has invited the court to commit." Nebraska trial courts also have the discretion to allow other experts to testify at *Daubert/Schafersman* hearings as part of their gatekeeper function. *State v. Daly*, 775 N.W.2d 47, 65 (Neb. 2009). Thus, expert testimony at the evidentiary hearing on whether an expert was qualified to testify as to whether a criminal defendant was under the influence of drugs at the time he was stopped while operating a motor vehicle was proper, and the court affirmed the conviction.

b.   Expert-Related Rules and Procedural Issues in Nebraska

The procedures of discovery in Nebraska state courts are substantially similar to those in the Federal Rules. Rule 26 of the Nebraska Rules of Court states that a party may use interrogatories to discover the identity of the testifying expert witness, the "subject matter on which the expert is expected to testify, . . . the substance of the facts and opinions to which the expert is expected to testify and a summary of the grounds for each opinion." *See* NEB. CT. R. DISC.§ 6-326(b)(4)(A)(i). A special motion is required to gain discovery by other means. *Id.* at § 6-326(b)(4)(A)(ii). Nebraska has adopted essentially the same standards as the Federal Rules in regards to both discovery of non-testifying experts and the disbursement of fees for the time experts spend responding to interrogatories. *Id.* at § 6-326(b)(4)(B) & (C).

6. *North Dakota*

a. Admissibility Governed by North Dakota Rule of Evidence 702

Historically, the North Dakota Supreme Court had not made clear exactly which test North Dakota courts should use for admissibility of expert testimony. In *State v. Burke*, 606 N.W.2d 108 (N.D. 2000), for example, the court upheld the admissibility of PCR DNA testing evidence, noting that courts have found such evidence admissible under both the *Frye* and *Daubert* tests, but it did not indicate a preference for either test. Earlier cases, however, appeared to indicate a likelihood that North Dakota courts would follow the *Frye* standard. *See, e.g., City of Fargo v. McLaughlin*, 512 N.W.2d 700 (N.D. 1994) (holding that *Frye* need not be applied to Horizontal Gaze Nystagmus sobriety test due to objective nature of the test); *State v. Swanson*, 225 N.W.2d 283, 285 (N.D. 1974) (noting that since *Frye*, "the courts have been reluctant to allow the results of [polygraph] testing to be introduced in judicial proceedings," but refusing to address question of admissibility of polygraph evidence due to inadequate record).

In 2005, the North Dakota Supreme Court pointed to N.D.R. Evid. 702 without specifically enunciating a test or making a clear statement about the applicability of *Daubert*. *State v. Hernandez*, 707 N.W.2d 449 (N.D. 2005). Defendant, convicted in trial court of gross sexual imposition, appealed the judgment and an order denying his motions for a new trial. Defendant argued that the trial court had erred in allowing the State's handwriting expert to identify the defendant as the author of a letter handwritten in Spanish without properly exercising the gatekeeping function required by *Daubert* and *Kumho*. The court rejected defendant's argument stating, as a preliminary matter, that the North Dakota Supreme Court had never explicitly adopted *Daubert* and *Kumho*. Rather, under North Dakota law, the admission of expert testimony is governed by N.D.R. Evid. 702, which provides:

> If scientific, technical, or other specialized knowledge will assist the trier of fact to understand the evidence or to determine a fact in issue, a witness qualified as an expert by knowledge, skill, experience, training, or education, may testify thereto in the form of an opinion or otherwise.

The court observed that the rule envisioned generous allowance of the use of expert testimony if the witness is known to have some degree of expertise in the field in which the witness is proffered to testify. Indeed, the expert need not be a specialist in a highly particularized field or possess a special certification. Moreover, the court noted that past North Dakota Supreme Court decisions had implicitly recognized the admissibility of expert testimony regarding handwriting. The court then acknowledged the state's expert's lengthy employment as an agent for the North Dakota Bureau of Criminal Investigation, training in handwriting analysis and experience assisting in analyzing handwriting in one- to two-hundred cases. Thus, the court held that the lower court did not abuse its discretion in determining the private investigator was qualified to testify as an expert and that his testimony would assist the jury.

In *Westby v. Schmidt*, 779 N.W.2d 681 (N.D. 2010), a dissatisfied homeowner brought a suit against the contractor who built the plaintiff's home, alleging breach of contract. At trial, plaintiff offered an expert witness on construction standards and practices. Defendant argued, that the expert's testimony was not based on industry standards but instead rested on the expert's own personal preferences. In upholding the trial court's decision to allow two pieces of testimony into the case, the North Dakota Supreme Court cited *Hernandez* and the "broad discretion" to admit experts afforded by N.D. R. Evid. 702.

b. Expert-Related Rules and Procedural Issues in North Dakota

North Dakota's Rule 26, which covers the discovery of experts, is nearly identical to Federal Rule 26. Discovery entails the identity of every testifying expert witness, as well as the "subject matter on which the expert is expected to testify, ... the facts and opinions to which the expert is expected to testify and a summary of the grounds for each opinion." N.D.R. Civ. P. 26(b)(4)(A)(i) (2002). The rule provides for expert interrogatories to and also grants parties a right to depose all testifying experts, although it may be abrogated by the court in some circumstances: "[a] party may depose each person whom the other party expects to call as an expert witness at trial unless, upon motion, the court finds that the deposition is unnecessary, overly burdensome, or unfairly oppressive." *Id.* at 26(b)(4)(A)(i)&(ii). Thus, while several state courts within the Eighth Circuit require a motion to depose the other side's experts, North Dakota is distinctive in requiring a motion to *limit* the right to depose all expert witnesses testifying at trial.

The provisions within the rule that concern the discovery of retained, non-testifying experts and fee provisions for time in deposition and responding to discovery are identical to Federal Rule 26. *Id.* at 26(b)(4)(B)&(C); Fed. R. Civ. P. 26(b)(4)(B)&(C).

7. South Dakota

a. Admissibility Governed by *Daubert* Test

South Dakota was among the first states in the Eighth Circuit to adopt *Daubert*. *See State v. Hofer*, 512 N.W.2d 482, 484 (S.D. 1994) (applying *Daubert* in upholding scientific reliability of Intoxilyzer blood alcohol test). In *State v. Machmuller*, 630 N.W.2d 495 (S.D. 2001), the South Dakota Supreme Court found that the trial court abused its discretion in excluding expert testimony regarding calculation of blood alcohol levels based on weight, quantity consumed, and extrapolation charts. The court held that defendant's expert was a doctor with "considerable training and expertise in chemistry, pharmacology and medicine," and prosecutors stipulated to the fact that "chemistry and science" have established theories regarding alcohol consumption and how it affects blood alcohol. In *State v. Edelman*, 593 N.W.2d 419 (S.D. 1999), the court applied *Daubert* in validating the reliability of expert testimony regarding child sexual abuse accommodation syndrome as a method of explaining secrecy or delayed reporting of abuse, but not as a means of proving a victim's veracity. In another case involving child abuse, *In The Interest of T.A., Child*, 663 N.W.2d 225 (S.D. 2003), the court upheld testimony from a physician's assistant that she observed signs of abuse over objection that she was not a medical doctor.

In *State v. Guthrie*, 627 N.W.2d 401 (S.D. 2001), a murder case in which the defense claimed the decedent died by suicide, the North Dakota Supreme Court considered the admissibility of a psychological autopsy. The state offered the testimony of a psychologist and suicidologist whose testimony included an account of the common factors for persons at risk for suicide, a comparison of those factors to the case at issue, and an opinion that the decedent did not commit suicide. Defendant challenged the reliability of the foundation of the expert's opinion, arguing that psychological autopsies have not been subject to validity studies. The court noted that there were reliability studies, however, which assess "whether a group will reach the same conclusion given the same criteria." The court found no error in admitting testimony regarding risk factors for suicide generally and their application to the deceased, as trial courts are given broad latitude in deciding how to determine reliability. On the other hand, in *State v. Corey*, 624 N.W.2d 841, 845 (S.D. 2001), the court upheld limitations on a psychologist's testimony regarding the defendant's state of mind during a police interview because he "set out no scientific basis for the proposed testimony."

South Dakota courts have validated the PCR method of DNA analysis, *State v. Moeller*, (548 N.W.2d 465 (S.D. 1996)); *State v. Edelman*, (593 N.W.2d 419 (S.D. 1999)), and the "product rule" as a means of expressing DNA evidence statistically. *State v. Loftus*, 573 N.W.2d 167 (S.D. 1997). For postconviction DNA analysis to be admitted, however, the proponent must not only satisfy *Daubert*, but must also show that the testing does not impose an unreasonable burden on the state, and that a favorable result would likely result in acquittal. *See Jenner v. Dooley*, 590 N.W.2d 463 (S.D. 1999); *Davi v. Class*, 609 N.W.2d 107 (S.D. 2000). The trial court has substantial discretion in determining whether a *Daubert* hearing is necessary prior to the introduction of disputed evidence; similarly, there is no ineffective assistance of counsel where a defense attorney is unprepared for a *Daubert* hearing but later challenges the prosecution expert on cross-examination at trial. *Moeller v. Weber*, 689 N.W.2d 1 (S.D. 2004).

In a case where the trial court revoked a defendant's probation when his alcohol monitoring bracelet registered three "drinking events," the South Dakota Supreme Court held that the admission of expert evidence related to the bracelet satisfied the *Daubert* test. *State v. Lemler*, 774 N.W.2d 272 (S.D. 2009). At the trial, the prosecutors called as an expert the chief technology officer of the company that had manufactured the bracelets and compiled the data derived from the bracelets. The South Dakota Supreme Court noted that the fact that the expert had a financial stake in the product could be used as a factor to consider in whether he could be qualified as an expert, but held that the expert's qualifications in the field were sufficient for him to testify in the case. *Id.* at 279–80. Because the defendant's arguments amounted to a claim that the prosecution's expert could be incorrect, and because both parties agreed that the underlying scientific process was sound (even though variables could affect the conclusions), the court upheld the admission of the evidence. *Id.* at 282–86.

The South Dakota Supreme Court has applied *Daubert* in a variety of civil settings. Although the majority of the opinions concern challenges to the admissibility of expert trial testimony, the court has also acknowledged that *Daubert* may play an earlier role in class actions, where the decision whether to certify a class often depends on expert affidavits and scientific or technical evidence. *See In re South Dakota Microsoft Antitrust Litigation*, 657 N.W. 2d 668 (S.D. 2003).

The Supreme Court upheld admission of testimony by a fire cause and origin expert regarding alternative cause in *First Premier Bank v. Kolcraft Enterprises*, 686 N.W. 2d 430 (S.D. 2004). In *Kuper v. Lincoln-Union Elec. Co.*, 557 N.W.2d 748 (S.D. 1996), the court considered *Daubert*'s application in a civil case brought by a dairy farmer who alleged his herd was harmed by stray voltage. In *Supreme Pork*, the court considered the use of undisclosed expert testimony and other issues in a case involving an allegedly defective pressure washer installed at a pig farrowing facility. *Supreme Pork, Inc. v. Master Blaster, Inc.*, 764 N.W.2d 474 (S.D. 2009). The court upheld the trial court's ruling to admit exemplar evidence over the objection that it had not been previously disclosed and held that the challenged expert was entitled to rely upon hearsay and conversations with other experts in making his opinions. *Id.* at 481–83.

The court also applied *Daubert* in reversing the trial court's admission of the testimony of an economist regarding a plaintiff's disability rating, finding the opinion to be outside the economist's expertise. *Garland v. Rossknecht*, 624 N.W.2d 700 (S.D. 2001). But in *Reinfeld*, the court held that an expert vocational rehabilitation consultant's testimony on a plaintiff's lost earning capacity based upon the average salary in the plaintiff's field was properly admitted, but also noted that testimony of this type is not necessarily always admissible. *Reinfeld v. Hutcheson*, 783 N.W.2d 284, 292 (S.D. 2010). In another workers' compensation case, the court excluded a defense expert's testimony that the worker's electrical shock could have been avoided if the worker had used a portable ground fault circuit interrupter (GFCI); the court found that the testimony was purely anecdotal and that there was no indication that a GFCI could have prevented the shock in this instance. *Wells v. Howe Heating & Plumbing*, 677 N.W.2d 586 (S.D. 2004).

In *First Western Bank Wall v. Olsen*, 621 N.W.2d 611 (S.D. 2001), the court upheld a trial court's admission of an expert appraiser's testimony regarding valuation of a bank. The bank challenged the expert's credentials, noting that he had never valued a bank, but the court refused to "examine an expert's qualifications under such a restricted focus," and found the expert qualified, as he had prepared or supervised a considerable number of business valuation reports. *Id.*

In *Estate of Dokken*, 604 N.W.2d 487 (S.D. 2000), the South Dakota Supreme Court upheld the admissibility of a forensic psychologist's testimony regarding the testamentary capacity of the decedent. The will contestant argued that the psychologist's opinion did not rest on a reliable foundation because it was inconsistent with the testimony of another witness, but the court held that such "objections go to the weight of the evidence rather than the admissibility." *See also State v. Moeller*, 616 N.W.2d 424 (S.D. 2000) (finding no abuse of discretion in not holding a *Daubert* hearing on a soil expert's testimony, as there was no evidence that expert's methodology was unreliable, and *Kumho Tire* grants trial courts wide latitude in deciding how they test an expert's reliability).

The plaintiff in *Burley v. Kytec Innovative Sports Equipment*, 737 N.W.2d 397 (S.D. 2007), was injured by a track and field training device, the "Overspeed Trainer." She offered the testimony of a human factors expert from the University of South Dakota to support her claim that the warnings and instructions for the product were inadequate. The trial court found that, although the expert had "impressive credentials," he had no familiarity with ANSI standards, had never designed product warnings, and had not previously testified as a warnings expert. On that basis the trial court found that the expert was not qualified to render opinions on warnings and excluded his testimony.

The South Dakota Supreme Court reversed. The court observed that the expert's lack of testimonial experience was largely irrelevant, since "[m]ere experience as a practiced litigation witness is a poor touchstone for measuring genuine expert qualifications." The expert's ignorance of ANSI standards was also irrelevant, since the court found that defendants had not shown that any ANSI standards actually applied to this device. The court held that the expert was qualified to testify on the alleged deficiencies in the defendant's warnings and that the trial court had "set the bar too high." Having resolved the qualifications issue, the court remanded to the trial court for a determination on whether the expert's testimony was reliable.

On the other hand, in *Klutman*, plaintiff alleged that the artificial turf of a professional indoor football team was negligently installed and contributed to his knee injury. *Klutman v. Sioux Falls Storm*, 769 N.W.2d 440 (S.D. 2009). The defendant's proffered expert on medical causation was a chemical engineer with impressive credentials when it came to synthetic turf, but he had no expertise in medical causation. Thus, the South Dakota Supreme Court held that the trial court did not abuse its discretion in excluding the medical opinion from defendant's expert. *Id.* at 449–50.

b. Expert-Related Rules and Procedural Issues in South Dakota

Section 15-6-26 of the South Dakota Code lays out procedures dealing with the discovery of expert testimony. S.D. CODIFIED LAWS § 15-6-26(b)(4) (2001). Unlike the Federal Rules, section 15-6-26 grants discovery of experts that are going to testify at trial only through interrogatories. *See id.* at §15-6-26(b)(4)(A)(i). Access to expert witnesses through deposition may be granted by the court on motion. *See Id.* at §15-6-26(b)(4)(A)(ii). The rule states that parties can require the other party to "identify each person whom the other party expects to call as an expert witness at trial, to state the subject matter on which the expert is expected to testify, and to state the substance of the facts and opinions to which the expert is expected to testify and a summary of the grounds for each opinion." *Id.* at §15-6-26(b)(4)(A)(i). The provisions within the rule concerning the discovery of non-testifying experts and the payment of fees for complying with discovery requests are virtually identical to Federal Rule 26. *See Id.* at §15-6-26(b)(4)(D) & (E).

CHAPTER IX
EXPERT EVIDENCE IN THE NINTH CIRCUIT*

by

Cynthia H. Cwik
Nathaniel P. Garrett
Kelly V. O'Donnell
Matthew A. Samberg[1]
Jones Day
12265 El Camino Real, Suite 200
San Diego, California 92130
chcwik@jonesday.com
ngarrett@jonesday.com
kodonnell@jonesday.com
msamberg@jonesday.com

A. KEY NINTH CIRCUIT DECISIONS APPLYING *DAUBERT* AND *JOINER*

The circuit from which *Daubert* originated consistently requires district courts to fulfill their "gatekeeper" roles by excluding expert evidence that does not meet *Daubert*'s standard of "scientific reliability and relevance." *Ellis v. Costco Wholesale Corp.*, 657 F.3d 970, 982 (9th Cir. 2011); *see Barabin v. AstenJohnson, Inc.*, Case No. 10-36142, slip opn. at 7 (9th Cir. Nov. 16, 2012). In its "*Daubert II*" decision after the Supreme Court's remand, the Ninth Circuit provided a detailed structure for applying *Daubert* and stated that district courts cannot merely accept an expert's "bald assurance of validity," but must determine for themselves whether there exists "an objective, independent validation of the expert's methodology." *Daubert v. Merrell Dow Pharmaceuticals, Inc.*, 43 F.3d 1311, 1319 (9th Cir. 1995) (*Daubert II*) ("We've been presented with only the experts' qualifications, their conclusions, and their assurances of reliability. Under *Daubert*, that's not enough."). Echoing *Daubert II*, the Ninth Circuit continues to emphasize that a proponent of expert testimony explain and demonstrate the scientific reliability of the *methods* used in reaching the expert's conclusions. *See Avila v. Willits Environmental Remediation Trust*, 633 F.3d 828, 836–40 (9th Cir. 2011). "The test under *Daubert* is not the correctness of the expert's conclusions but the soundness of his methodology . . . ." *Primiano v. Cook*, 598 F.3d 558, 564 (9th Cir. 2010), *as amended*. District courts in the Ninth Circuit possess "broad latitude" not only in determining whether an expert's opinion is reliable, but also in deciding *how* to evaluate the reliability of the expert's testimony. *Avila*, 633 F.3d

---

[1] The authors wish to thank associates Sarah Bennington and Evan Roberts and summer associates Koree Blyleven and Greg Martin for their invaluable assistance with this update.

at 836–40 (upholding use of *prima facie* expert reports on exposure and causation, and affirming the ultimate exclusion of the expert opinions); *see Ellis*, 657 F.3d at 982.

1. Expert Evidence of Medical Causation

Expert testimony on medical causation continues to provide fertile ground for application of the *Daubert* standard in the Ninth Circuit. The Ninth Circuit recently affirmed a district court's decision to exclude medical testimony that "was not supported by the typical *Daubert* factors— testing, peer review, and general acceptance." *Wagner v. County of Maricopa*, 673 F.3d 977, 982 (9th Cir. 2012). In *Wagner*, the defendant county jail's "dress-out procedure" allegedly aggravated an inmate's mental instability, which in turn purportedly caused him to die of a cardiac arrhythmia. *Id.* at 979. The plaintiff's expert opined that the unexpected death was caused by an increase in symptoms of schizophrenia, which was "likely" due to the deceased's recollection of his treatment at the jail. *Id.* at 982. The Ninth Circuit concluded that the "district court's decision to exclude [the expert's] opinion that the dress-out procedure was 'probably' the cause of [the deceased's] death was a reasonable application of *Daubert*." *Id.* The Ninth Circuit emphasized that the expert failed to show how general facts regarding schizophrenia and cardiac arrhythmia allowed him to "determine the specific event" in this case. *Id.*

After the Supreme Court's decision in *Daubert*, several Ninth Circuit cases involving expert opinions on medical causation focused on whether the expert at issue developed his or her opinion independently of the litigation. *See Claar v. Burlington Northern Railroad Co.*, 29 F.3d 499, 502–03 (9th Cir. 1994) ("[S]cientists whose conviction about the ultimate conclusion of their research is so firm that they are willing to aver under oath that it is correct prior to performing the necessary validating tests could properly be viewed . . . as lacking the objectivity that is the hallmark of the scientific method."). In *Daubert II*, the Ninth Circuit reconsidered the plaintiffs' expert epidemiological and toxicological evidence regarding the drug Bendectin and limb-reduction birth defects. *Daubert II*, 43 F.3d at 1317. The court explained, "[t]hat an expert testifies based on research he has conducted independent of the litigation provides important, objective proof that the research comports with the dictates of good science." *Id.* If the proffered expert testimony is not based on independent research, the proponent of the testimony must offer some other "objective, verifiable evidence" of scientific validity. *See id.* One way to show this is by proof that the research and analysis supporting the expert's conclusions have been subjected to normal scientific scrutiny through peer review and publication. "That the research is accepted for publication in a reputable scientific journal after being subjected to the usual rigors of peer review is a significant indication that it is taken seriously by other scientists, i.e., that it meets at least the minimal criteria of good science." *Id.* at 1318.

Even absent such indicia of reliability, however, expert testimony may still be admitted if the expert explains precisely how the expert's conclusions were reached and points to some objective source—a learned treatise, the policy statement of a professional association, a published article in a reputable scientific journal or the like—to show that the expert has followed the scientific method, as it is practiced by (at least) a recognized minority of scientists in the expert's field. *Daubert II*, 43 F.3d at 1319. If the proponent of expert testimony makes the initial showing that the testimony was derived by the scientific method, the opposing party may challenge that showing by presenting evidence that the proposing party's expert "employed unsound methodology or failed to assiduously follow an otherwise sound protocol." *Id.* at 1318 n.10.

Applying these guidelines to the expert testimony at issue in the case, the *Daubert II* court once again affirmed the exclusion of the plaintiffs' expert testimony. In assessing scientific validity, the court found that (1) none of the plaintiffs' experts claimed to have studied the effect of Bendectin on limb reduction before being hired to testify, (2) none of the plaintiffs' experts had published their work on Bendectin in a scientific journal or solicited formal review by their colleagues, and, (3) although the plaintiffs' experts "relied on animal studies, chemical structure analyses, and epidemiological data, [the plaintiffs] neither explain[ed] the methodology the experts followed to reach their conclusions nor point[ed] to any external source to validate that methodology." *Id.* at 1317–19.

The *Daubert II* court also concluded that the plaintiffs' expert evidence was not "relevant to the task at hand," an inquiry that turns on "the governing substantive standard." *Id.* at 1315. The court determined that California tort law required plaintiffs to show "not merely that Bendectin increased the likelihood of injury, but that it more likely than not caused their injuries." *Id.* Thus, the court held that the plaintiffs' experts must be prepared to testify that the ingestion of Bendectin during pregnancy more than doubled the risk of birth defects, which, in epidemiological terms, requires evidence of a relative risk greater than 2.0. The court concluded that the plaintiffs' experts had failed to meet that standard, stating: "While plaintiffs' epidemiologists make vague assertions that there is a statistically significant relationship between Bendectin and birth defects, none states that the relative risk is greater than two." *Id.* at 1321. Accordingly, the Ninth Circuit again affirmed the exclusion of plaintiffs' expert evidence, as well as the summary judgment in favor of defendants.

The Ninth Circuit again affirmed exclusion of expert testimony on causation in *Lust v. Merrell Dow Pharmaceuticals,* 89 F.3d 594 (9th Cir. 1996). The plaintiff in *Lust* alleged that his birth defect, diagnosed as hemifacial microsomia, was caused by his mother's ingestion of Clomid, a fertility drug manufactured by Merrell Dow Pharmaceuticals. In support of his claim, the plaintiff offered the opinion of Dr. Alan Done, who opined that, because human epidemiological studies and animal studies reported a positive association between Clomid and a wide variety of birth defects, Clomid also should be able to cause hemifacial microsomia. *Id.* at 596. Dr. Done admitted, however, that he was not a teratologist, geneticist, or embryologist. He also admitted that no peer-reviewed article concluded that Clomid is a human teratogen, and that no human epidemiological or animal studies had found a positive association between the ingestion of Clomid and hemifacial microsomia. *See id.* After conducting an *in limine* hearing pursuant to Federal Rule of Evidence 104(a), the district court excluded Dr. Done's opinion and granted summary judgment in favor of Merrell Dow. *See id.*

In affirming the district court, the Ninth Circuit confirmed the analytical framework supplied by *Daubert II,* including considering whether the expert had developed his opinion outside the context of litigation and had subjected it to peer review. *See id.* at 597. The court noted that Dr. Done had not subjected his work to peer review. Furthermore, although Dr. Done had first rendered his opinion regarding Clomid in an article published in 1984, "he was at that time already a professional plaintiff's witness" and, therefore, it was "not unreasonable to presume that Dr. Done's opinion on Clomid was influenced by litigation-driven financial incentive." *Id.* The *Lust* court also agreed with the district court that Dr. Done had not explained how he reached his conclusions and had not pointed to any objective source showing that his method and premises were generally accepted by at least a recognized minority of teratologists. *See id.*

Finally, in a statement predictive of the "analytical gap" that the Supreme Court would identify in its subsequent opinion *General Electric Co. v. Joiner,* 522 U.S. 136, 188 S. Ct. 512 (1997), the *Lust* court rejected the plaintiff's argument that the district court had impermissibly examined Dr. Done's conclusions, rather than merely his methodologies. The court stated:

> When a scientist claims to rely on a method practiced by most scientists, yet presents conclusions that are shared by no other scientist, the district court should be wary that the method has not been faithfully applied. It is the proponent of the expert who has the burden of proving admissibility. To enforce this burden, the district court can exclude the opinion if the expert fails to identify and defend the reasons that his conclusions are anomalous.

Id. at 598. This aspect of the *Lust* decision has been cited by several courts, including the district court in *Carnegie Mellon University v. Hoffmann-LaRoche, Inc.,* 55 F. Supp. 2d 1024 (N.D. Cal.

1999). Citing both *Lust* and *Daubert II*, the *Carnegie Mellon* court excluded the opinions of one of the plaintiffs' expert witnesses as unreliable, largely because his conclusions were "at odds with the scientific findings in two learned treatises and sixteen published studies and were not supported by plaintiffs' other experts." *Id.* at 1033.

Several other Ninth Circuit courts have excluded medical causation testimony. *See, e.g., Avila v. Willits Environmental Remediation Trust*, 633 F.3d 828, 836–40 (9th Cir. 2011) (see below for a discussion of the process of *prima facie* expert reports used by the district court and upheld by the Ninth Circuit); *Schudel v. Gen. Elec. Co.*, 120 F.3d 991 (9th Cir. 1997) (holding that expert testimony that solvent exposure caused plaintiffs' physical ailments failed *Daubert* analysis); *Jones v. United States*, 933 F. Supp. 894 (N.D. Cal. 1996) (noting that scientific evidence regarding interaction between oral contraceptives and antibiotics did not satisfy the *Daubert* standard); *Valentine v. Pioneer Chlor Alkali Co.*, 921 F. Supp. 666 (D. Nev. 1996) (holding that scientific evidence that chlorine vapor caused plaintiffs' neurological disorders failed the *Daubert* standard); *Hall v. Baxter Healthcare Corp.*, 947 F. Supp. 1387 (D. Or. 1996) (finding that the plaintiffs' expert evidence attempting to link silicone breast implants to atypical connective tissue diseases did not meet the *Daubert* standard). *But see Kennedy v. Collagen Corp.*, 161 F.3d 1226 (9th Cir. 1998) (reversing the district court's exclusion of expert evidence because the expert had appropriately relied on scientific and clinical studies and had used traditional scientific methodology).

The Ninth Circuit has applied *Daubert* in the context of expert opinions based on animal studies. In *Domingo v. T.K.*, 289 F.3d 600 (9th Cir. 2002), *as amended*, the plaintiff brought a medical malpractice action following hip replacement surgery that left him with severe brain damage due to fat embolism syndrome (FES), a rare condition that was a known risk of the surgery. Plaintiff's expert sought to testify that, based on his professional experience and observations, as well as several studies of the topic, he had concluded to a reasonable medical probability that the plaintiff's FES was caused by the length of time the doctor spent trying to mallet into place the plaintiff's prosthesis. *Id.* at 604. The district court excluded plaintiff's expert and granted summary judgment in favor of defendants. *Id.* at 605.

In affirming the district court, the Ninth Circuit noted that the expert's theory "linking extended malleting to FES" was not widely accepted and, indeed, had never been published. *Id.* at 606. There existed no "objective source, peer review, clinical tests, establishment of an error rate, or other evidence" demonstrating that the expert "followed a valid, scientific method in developing his theory." *Id.* In addition, the expert failed to establish that the animal studies he used to support his theory were applicable to human operations. *Id.* "It is true that animal studies can be used to support theories on human health, but the district court retains its gatekeeper function in requiring analytical support for the extrapolation from animals to humans." *Id.* Plaintiff's expert in *Domingo* provided no such support. *Id.*

The Ninth Circuit's decision in *Metabolife Int'l v. Wornick*, 264 F.3d 832 (9th Cir. 2001), which the court cited in *Domingo*, involved a libel suit by the manufacturer of a diet pill against a news reporter and television station. The lawsuit arose from an investigative report that challenged the safety of Metabolife's diet pills and claimed that "you can die" from taking Metabolife's products. Metabolife sought to introduce several studies showing that its products were not harmful to humans, including an animal study involving mice and rats that was conducted in Asia. The defendants opposed the introduction of these Asian animal studies, arguing that they were inadmissible because of the "species gap" between humans and mice and rats and because the studies were high-dose, short-term studies that required experts to extrapolate the results to apply to the low-dose, long-term usage that would result from continued use. The district court had held that, "as a matter of law, animal studies are inadmissible due to the uncertainties in extrapolating from effects on mice and rats to humans." *Id.* at 842 (quotation marks and citation omitted). The Ninth Circuit rejected the lower court's decision, citing *Daubert II*, which "itself recognized that animal studies are not per se inadmissible and should be subjected to substantive analysis, just like other scientific evidence." *Id.* (citing *Daubert II,* 43 F.3d at 1319). Likewise, the Ninth Circuit noted that interdosage extrapolation was not *per se* inadmissible. *See id.* The court cautioned, however, that, while animal studies may provide useful data about human health in some cases, "[d]ifficulties with extrapolation" might render such studies unreliable under *Daubert* and "such a determination must be made on problems inherent to the studies themselves, not a general apprehension at inter-species and inter-dosage extrapolation." *Id.* at 843. Despite rejecting the reasons for exclusion proffered by the district court, the Ninth Circuit left open the possibility that the interspecies extrapolation and interdosage extrapolation of plaintiffs' animal studies would ultimately render the studies too unreliable and left this determination to the district court on remand. *See id.* at 842.

In addition to the Asian animal studies, Metabolife tried to introduce a "risk assessment" showing that its pills were not harmful. Metabolife's experts conducted a standard risk assessment that involved four stages: (1) hazard identification, (2) dose-response assessment, (3) exposure assessment, and (4) risk characterization. *Id.* at 844. In conducting the analysis, the experts consulted "a wealth of peer-reviewed articles, Food and Drug Administration adverse incident reports, studies, laboratory reports, and other scientific materials to formulate their opinions." *Id.* The district court excluded the experts' risk assessments because they did not explain precisely how they used the literature to form their conclusions. Instead, the experts simply listed the articles they consulted and concluded that, based on their review of these articles, Metabolife was not harmful. *See id.* The Ninth Circuit agreed with the district court that the methodology of the studies was open to the court's scrutiny. However, it overruled the district court's summary decision that the risk assessments were not adequately explained, finding that the court's role as gatekeeper required it to do more to examine the cited materials and determine how they relate to the expert's conclusions before determining if the studies met *Daubert's* requirements. *See id.*[2]

Following *Metabolife,* the district court in *Cloud v. Pfizer, Inc.,* 198 F. Supp. 2d 1118 (D. Ariz. 2001), excluded the testimony of expert witness Dr. Edwin E. Johnstone, who was offered to support the plaintiffs' argument that the antidepressant Zoloft causes suicide. After examining the materials cited by Dr. Johnstone, the *Cloud* court excluded Dr. Johnstone's opinions because, among other failings, Dr. Johnstone had failed to "plumb the depths of the relationship between the cited materials and conclusions drawn." *Id.* at 1133 (quoting *Metabolife,* 264 F.3d at 845). The district court found Dr. Johnstone's testimony unreliable because he was unable to cite competent materials to support his conclusion. First, Dr. Johnstone admitted he was not aware of any medical or scientific studies that showed that Zoloft increased the risk of suicide. *Id.* Second, the court concluded that the studies Dr. Johnstone used to support his conclusions were flawed; in fact, the authors of one of the cited studies themselves admitted that their study did not prove causation. *Id.* Lastly, the court rejected much of the literature because it consisted of case reports of particular patients who had committed suicide after taking Zoloft, concluding that mere "compilations of occurrences" did not constitute the reliable scientific evidence supporting expert opinion that *Daubert* required. *Id.* at 1134.

In the context of toxic torts, the Ninth Circuit has explained the level and type of scientific evidence required to establish medical causation relating to exposure to radiation and other alleged toxins. First, a pair of companion cases addressed causation issues relating to toxic exposure from a federal nuclear reservation. *See In re Berg Litig.,* 293 F.3d 1127 (9th Cir. 2002); *In re Hanford Nuclear Reservation,* 292 F.3d 1124 (9th Cir. 2002). In these cases, the Ninth Circuit clarified that

---

[2] The *Metabolife* court also held that experimentation outside the United States is not presumptively unreliable. Although "regulation of experimentation in the United States may bolster the reliability of results," there was no reason to assume that experimentation abroad was unreliable or would not meet admissibility standards. *See id.* at 843.

epidemiological evidence is necessary when there is no other scientific evidence of the agent's capacity to cause the claimed injuries. *See In re Hanford,* 292 F.3d at 1136–37. Conversely, when it is "recognized by scientific and legal authority" that the agent causes plaintiffs' claimed illnesses "at the lowest doses," epidemiological evidence is not necessary to establish general causation. *Id.* at 1137. Reaching this conclusion, the Ninth Circuit rejected the district court's ruling, which had required the plaintiffs to come forward with epidemiological evidence that plaintiffs' exposure "doubled the risk of suffering the alleged injuries." *Id.* at 1135–36; *In re Berg Litig.,* 293 F.3d at 1129; *cf. Daubert II, supra.*

Shortly after deciding these first two cases, the Ninth Circuit issued its decision in *Clausen v. M/V New Carissa,* 339 F.3d 1049 (9th Cir. 2003). The court concluded that evidence of a "differential diagnosis" (a technique used to determine which of several diseases with similar symptoms a patient is suffering from by systematically comparing and contrasting findings and eliminating hypotheses) is admissible so long as the expert offers an explanation for why certain causes were ruled out. *Id.* at 1057. Lack of a consensus in the medical community or peer-reviewed studies specifically proving causation does not necessarily bar admissibility of the opinion so long as the expert relies on objective, verifiable evidence. *Id.* at 1060–61. The Ninth Circuit, however, has recently reaffirmed the limits of the use of differential diagnosis in *Newkirk v. Conagra Foods,* 438 Fed. App'x 607, 609 (9th Cir. 2011), in which it concluded that the plaintiff's expert could not rely on a differential diagnosis to establish that the plaintiff's ailments were caused by exposure to microwave popcorn because he could not establish that the vapors in microwave popcorn were generally capable of causing the plaintiff's disease.

A recent decision in a complex toxic torts case underscores the district court's broad power to determine the method by which the testimony of an expert will be admitted or excluded. In *Avila v. Willits Environmental Remediation Trust,* 633 F.3d 828 (9th Cir. 2011), the plaintiffs claimed to suffer from medical ailments allegedly caused by chemical exposure. *Id.* at 831–32. As part of its case management procedure, the district court ordered any plaintiff who had never lived in the zone of operation, or who had moved there after operations had ceased, to "make a *prima facie* showing of exposure and causation." *Id.* at 833. The order required the plaintiffs to "set[] forth 'all facts' supporting . . . [the] plaintiffs' claimed exposure, together with a written statement from an expert describing the condition for which recovery was sought, identifying the chemical to which the plaintiff was exposed, explaining the route of exposure, opining on causation, and setting forth the scientific and medical basis upon which the opinion was based." *Id.* Ultimately, the district court struck the *prima facie* plaintiffs' expert report on exposure and causation, "finding that the report was wanting under Federal Rule of Evidence 702" and *Daubert. Id.*

On appeal, the plaintiffs subject to the *prima facie* order asked the Ninth Circuit to "disapprove of the process" because it bypassed traditional procedures. *Id.* The Ninth Circuit acknowledged that it had not directly addressed this type of order[3] before, but it upheld the order under the broad power of the district court to manage litigation found in Federal Rule of Civil Procedure 16. *Id.* Specifically addressing the *Daubert* question, the Ninth Circuit held that the *prima facie* process did not "skirt accepted procedure." *Id.* at 834. *Daubert* requires the district court to "determine at the outset . . . whether the expert's testimony will assist the trier of fact by assessing whether the method underlying the testimony is valid and reliable." *Id.* Further, the trial court has "broad latitude . . . in deciding how to determine the testimony's reliability." *Id.* (quoting *Mukhtar v. California State University,* 299 F.3d 1053, 1063 (9th Cir. 2002)). *See also Sullivan v. U.S. Dep't of the Navy,* 365 F.3d 827, 833–34 (9th Cir. 2004) (holding that *Kumho Tire* requires the district courts to apply the *Daubert*

---

[3] This type of order is often called a "Lone Pine Order" after *Lore v. Lone Pine Corp.,* 1986 WL 637507, (N.J. Super. Ct. Law Div. Nov. 18, 1986).

factors when they are reasonable measures of reliability, but that in determining the admissibility of specialized knowledge the factors are not intended to be exhaustive or restrictive).

The discretion of district courts is not unlimited, however. In *Barabin v. AstenJohnson, Inc.*, Case No. 10-36142 (9th Cir. Nov. 16, 2012), a case involving mesothelioma caused by exposure to asbestos, the Ninth Circuit reversed a district court's order of exclusion because the district court abused its discretion by failing to make a determination under *Daubert*. Slip Op. at 5.

In *United States v. Sandoval-Mendoza*, 472 F.3d 645 (9th Cir. 2006), a defendant accused of conspiring to sell drugs attempted to prove that he was entrapped by the government. The district court excluded the defense expert's testimony that Sandoval-Mendoza had a brain tumor that caused a predisposition to entrapment and susceptibility to suggestion. The court "based its ruling on the expert testimony's 'lack of scientific validity' and 'absence of ability to make a causal connection' between the tumor and inducement or predisposition." *Id.* at 654. The district court also reasoned that because the prosecution had an expert witness for rebuttal, expert testimony would be confusing to the jury. *Id.* On appeal, the Ninth Circuit determined that the district court abused its discretion in excluding the defendant expert's testimony. The court explained that expert evidence should not be excluded as unreliable merely because it does not conclusively prove the issue in question; "medical knowledge is often uncertain." *Id.* at 655. The court held that "[w]hen credible, qualified experts disagree, a criminal defendant is entitled to have the jury, not the judge, decide whether the government has proved its case." *Id.* at 654.

The Ninth Circuit considered whether the testimony of a doctor who could not establish why a medical device failed could still provide useful testimony to the jury in *Primiano v. Cook*, 598 F.3d 558 (9th Cir. 2010). In laying the foundation for its analysis, the court highlighted that the *Daubert* standard is "more open to opinion evidence" than the gatekeeping test under *Frye*. *Id.* at 564. In *Primiano*, the district court had excluded the opinion of the plaintiff's expert in a product liability case because he could not establish "why" the plaintiff's elbow replacement had failed. Importantly, the case was governed by Nevada tort law, which only requires the plaintiff to show that a dangerous malfunction occurred. *Id.* at 567. Emphasizing that expert testimony need only "assist" the trier of fact, the Ninth Circuit concluded that the expert's testimony that the device "failed to perform in the matter reasonably to be expected in light of [its] nature and intended function" was "enough to assist the trier of fact." *Id.*

The Ninth Circuit has also issued opinions focusing on the difference between relevance and reliability under *Daubert*. In *Stilwell v. Smith & Nephew, Inc.*, 482 F.3d 1187 (9th Cir. 2007), the plaintiff presented expert testimony of a metallurgist to argue that metal reconstruction nails installed to stabilize compound fractures in the plaintiff's leg were defectively designed. The district court excluded this testimony on the basis that the metallurgist lacked the medical expertise to determine whether the nails functioned as they were designed to medically. Thus, according to the district court, the expert's opinions lacked relevance to the ultimate issue. *Id.* at 1190–91. In reversing the district court's exclusion of the testimony, the Ninth Circuit first noted that the district court's analysis had "focused on the helpfulness, rather than reliability, of [the expert's] testimony." *Id.* at 1192. Further, in finding the expert's testimony lacking in relevance, the district court had set too stringent a standard. Explaining that relevance is not always a demanding inquiry, the Ninth Circuit held that "a district court may not exclude expert testimony [on relevance grounds] simply because the court can, at the time of summary judgment, determine that the testimony does not result in a triable issue of fact. Rather the court must determine [merely] whether there is `a link between the expert's testimony and the matter to be proved.'" *Id.* at 1192 (citation omitted).

In *Morin v. United States,* 244 F. App'x 142 (9th Cir. 2007), the Ninth Circuit affirmed the exclusion of an expert's testimony that a plaintiff's "plasmacytoma was caused by exposure to jet fuel and/or jet engine exhaust." *Id.* at 143. The court noted that the expert "did not conduct any independent research to support his conclusion," that "the studies he cited" did not "provide sufficient support" for his opinion, and that the expert "did not show whether or how he applied differential diagnosis in determining the cause of [the plaintiff's] plasmacytoma." *Id.* Thus, the expert's "method of reaching an opinion regarding specific causation was not sufficiently reliable to be admissible under Federal Rule of Evidence 702 and *Daubert."* *Id.* at 144; *see also In re Hanford Nuclear Reservation Litigation,* 497 F.3d 1005 (9th Cir. 2007) (affirming the exclusion of evidence where the defendant's data was unreliable); *Akkerman v. Mecta Corp.,* 247 F. App'x 895, 897 (9th Cir. 2007) (affirming the exclusion of a neurologist's testimony on the physiological effects of electroconvulsive therapy because the expert's opinions could not "be fairly characterized as having been subjected to peer review," since the "opinions were not derived from independent research," and plaintiff also failed to "demonstrate in some objectively verifiable way that the expert ha[d] both chosen a reliable scientific method and followed it faithfully") (quotation marks and citation omitted). *But see In re Hanford Nuclear Reservation Litig.*, 534 F.3d 986,1011 (9th Cir. 2008) (finding that the district court abused its discretion in barring the plaintiff from asking whether the expert had published peer reviewed articles on the toxin's ability to kill or damage thyroid cells because the fact that the expert had not written an article on the effects of the specific levels of radioiodine "I-103" at issue did not justify depriving the jury of the expert's general knowledge of causation). Thus, the Ninth Circuit has continued to endorse the role of the district court as a "gatekeeper" in evaluating medical causation evidence.

2. *Other Types of Scientific Expert Evidence*

Outside the medical causation context, Ninth Circuit courts have applied *Daubert* to various forms of scientific expert evidence. These have included polygraph results, testimony on the credibility of eyewitness identification, testimony on the credibility of witnesses generally, testimony on whether a criminal defendant's mental state was such that he could have been found to intend to commit fraud, methods of fingerprint identification, and certain forensic analyses of crime-scene evidence.

In *United States v. Cordoba,* 104 F.3d 225 (9th Cir. 1997), the court considered the admissibility of polygraph evidence in situations where the parties had not stipulated that the polygraph was admissible. The Ninth Circuit had previously established a *per se* rule excluding all such "unstipulated polygraph evidence," concluding that such evidence "interferes with, rather than enhances, the deliberative process." *Brown v. Darcy,* 783 F.2d 1389, 1397 (9th Cir. 1986). In *Cordoba,* however, the court held that the *per se* rule had been effectively overruled by *Daubert* and its "flexible inquiry." 104 F.3d at 227. The court emphasized that, by lifting the *per se* rule, it was "not expressing new enthusiasm for admission of unstipulated polygraph evidence." *Id.* at 228. Rather, the admissibility of such evidence is "for determination by the district judge, who must not only evaluate the evidence under Rule 702, but consider admission under Rule 403." *Id.* Because the district court had applied the invalidated *per se* rule, the *Cordoba* court remanded for reconsideration.

On remand, the district court again excluded the polygraph evidence, finding it inadmissible under both Rule 702 and Rule 403. *United States v. Cordoba,* 991 F. Supp. 1199 (C.D. Cal. 1998), *aff'd,* 194 F.3d 1053 (9th Cir. 1999). With respect to reliability under Rule 702, the district court explained:

> The court has carefully evaluated the proposed polygraph evidence under *Daubert.* The polygraph has been extensively tested, and has been the subject of extensive peer review and publication. While probably accepted in the scientific community as a useful diagnostic or investigative technique, it does not have "general acceptance" for use as courtroom evidence. The known or potential error rate of real-life polygraph tests is unknown, and fundamentally depends on the protocol followed during a particular examination. The

court finds there are no controlling standards to ensure proper protocol or provide a court with a yardstick by which a particular defendant's examination can be measured.

Id. at 1208. With respect to Rule 403, the court concluded that "[t]he polygraph testimony would be tantamount to testimony regarding the defendant's guilt or innocence," and that the evidence's "potential prejudice substantially outweighs its probative value." *Id.*; *see also United States v. Orians*, 9 F. Supp. 2d 1168 (D. Ariz. 1998) (excluding unstipulated polygraph evidence under both Rule 702 and Rule 403, relying on essentially the same reasoning as the district court in *Cordoba*).

The Ninth Circuit addressed unstipulated polygraph evidence again in *United States v. Benavidez-Benevidez*, 217 F.3d 720 (9th Cir. 2000), *cert. denied*, 531 U.S. 903 (2000). The Ninth Circuit affirmed the district court's exclusion of polygraph evidence and held that while a district court may conduct a Rule 702, 403, or 704(b) examination, it is not required to undertake each of the three examinations before denying admission of the evidence and need only cite one of the exclusionary rules to support its decision. "District courts are free to reject the admission of polygraph evidence on the basis of any applicable rule of evidence without analyzing all the other potential bases of exclusion." *Id.* at 724. Accordingly, the Ninth Circuit based its ruling solely on the lower court's analysis of the evidence under Rule 403. The Ninth Circuit later confirmed that a *Daubert* hearing is not required before excluding polygraph evidence because polygraph results may be excluded based on Rule 403 alone. *See United States v. Ramirez-Robles*, 386 F.3d 1234, 1246 (9th Cir. 2004), *cert denied*, 544 U.S. 1035 (2005). To date, therefore, it appears that unstipulated polygraph evidence has yet to have any more success under *Daubert* than under the *per se* exclusionary rule.

On the heels of *Daubert*, the Ninth Circuit also lifted its previous *per se* rule excluding expert testimony on the credibility of eyewitness identification. *See United States v. Amador-Galvan*, 9 F.3d 1414, 1417–18 (9th Cir. 1993). Applying *Daubert*, however, the Ninth Circuit has still affirmed the exclusion of such evidence, finding, among other things, that the proffered evidence would not assist the trier of fact because the district court conveyed essentially the same information by providing a comprehensive jury instruction on credibility determinations. *See United States v. Rincon*, 28 F.3d 921 (9th Cir. 1994). The *Rincon* court emphasized, however, that its result was "based upon an individualized inquiry, rather than strict application of the [*per se* rule]." *Id.* at 926. The court stated that its "conclusion does not preclude the admission of such testimony when the proffering party satisfies the standard established in *Daubert* by showing that the expert opinion is based upon 'scientific knowledge' which is both reliable and helpful to the jury in any given case." *Id.*

With regard to expert testimony regarding eyewitness credibility, the Ninth Circuit noted that the trial judge retains broad discretion in determining whether to admit such testimony. *Gurry v. McDaniel*, 149 Fed. App'x 593, 594 (9th Cir. 2005). The Ninth Circuit has stated that it has "repeatedly affirmed district court decisions to exclude the testimony of eyewitness-identification experts from federal criminal trials." *Howard v. Clark*, 608 F.3d 563, 573–74 (9th Cir. 2010). Representing the contrary position, one district court denied the government's motion to exclude expert testimony regarding eyewitness identification. *United States v. Feliciano*, No. CR-08-0932-01, 2009 BL 241206, at *1 (D. Ariz. Nov. 05, 2009). In reaching its decision, the court cited recent academic literature, consensus in the scientific community, the expert's credentials, and the potential helpfulness to the jury. *Id.* at *3–4.

The Ninth Circuit has also addressed the admissibility of expert testimony regarding a criminal defendant's "atypical belief system" as evidence of the defendant's mental state. In *United States v. Finley*, 301 F.3d 1000 (9th Cir. 2002), the defendant was accused of fraud after attempting to pass certain financial instruments he obtained at a "seminar" given by Leroy Schweitzer, leader of "a group of people calling themselves the 'Montana Freemen.'" *Id.* at 1002 n.l. The defendant sought to present expert testimony that, although he had not been diagnosed with a "mental condition which is reported in the DSM-IV," he "had an atypical belief system" that suggested he did not possess the requisite intent to commit fraud. *Id.* at 1004–05. The district court excluded the expert testimony, holding that it "would not be helpful to the jury" insofar as it amounted to little more than evidence of the defendant's credibility—an assessment normally left to the trier of fact. *Id.* at 1006–07.

The Ninth Circuit reversed, holding that the defendant's expert's testimony was reliable and relevant. *Id.* at 1007–16. Over the prosecution's objection that the expert had merely made a "subjective assessment of [the defendant's] truthfulness," the court found that the expert had "based his diagnosis on proper psychological methodology and reasoning." *Id.* at 1009. On the issue of relevance, the court explained that the expert's testimony went beyond "the common knowledge of the average layperson." *Id.* at 1013. Specifically, the expert's "testimony would have offered an explanation as to how an otherwise normal man could believe that these financial instruments were valid." *Id.* Thus, despite the absence of a formal diagnosis of mental illness, the district court had abused its discretion in excluding the defendant's expert's testimony. *See also United States v. Cohen*, 510 F.3d 1114, 1122–27 (9th Cir. 2007) (citing *Finley* and reversing the district court's exclusion of a psychiatrist's testimony that the defendant suffered from a "narcissistic personality disorder" that caused him to believe he was not violating the law in assisting others to file false tax returns); *cf. United States v. Anderson*, 94 F. App'x 487, 492 (9th Cir. 2004) (affirming exclusion of the testimony of an expert witness to demonstrate that the defendant "suffered from 'exceptionally and excessively rigid thinking,' because even if true, such thinking was irrelevant because it would not constitute a defense to willful violation of the tax laws"). *But see cf. United States v. Pelling*, 461 Fed. App'x 599, 600 (9th Cir. 2011) (citing *Finley* and affirming the district court's exclusion of expert testimony regarding an "impulse control disorder" as irrelevant and inadmissible where the defendant was found with erotica and nude photos in a motel room he shared with his twelve-year-old daughter).

The Ninth Circuit has also addressed the admissibility of certain types of forensic evidence. First, the court considered the admissibility of a method for testing blood stains for the presence of a certain preservative. In *Cooper v. Brown*, 510 F.3d 870 (9th Cir. 2007), a criminal defendant requested that a blood stain on a T-shirt be subjected to a mass-spectrometry test for the presence of the preservative ETDA, under the theory that if the stain contained the preservative, it may have been placed on the shirt at some point after the crime had occurred.[4] Although the testing was performed, the district court ultimately held that the results were inadmissible under *Daubert*. In affirming, the Ninth Circuit emphasized that "EDTA testing has not gained general acceptance in the scientific community." *Id.* at 880.

Second, the court has considered the reliability of fingerprint evidence. In *United States v. Calderon-Segura*, 512 F.3d 1104 (9th Cir. 2008), a defendant was convicted of unlawfully reentering the United States after having been deported. The defendant challenged "the testimony of a fingerprint expert that a fingerprint exemplar taken from [the defendant] matched the exemplar on his [prior] warrant of removal, which positively identified him as the same person who was previously deported." *Id.* at 1106. The district court held that the fingerprint evidence was admissible, and the Ninth Circuit affirmed. In doing so, the court contrasted the "inked" fingerprints taken in the present case from "latent" fingerprints, the identification of which can present difficulties. *Id.* at 1108. Having made this distinction, the court explained that, "[a]s other courts have recognized, fingerprint identification methods have been tested in the adversarial system for roughly a hundred years." *Id.* at 1109. Further, the court noted that although the defendant "offer[ed] evidence that inked prints can be less clear than latent prints in some cases, [the defendant] failed to show that the exemplars at issue in this case lacked clarity, were fragmented, or contained any other defects or artifactual

---

[4] ETDA, or ethylenediaminetetraacetic acid, gained notoriety during the O.J. Simpson trial. There, ETDA was found in blood samples taken from Simpson's home—leading the defense to suggest that they had been planted.

interference that might call into question the accuracy or reliability of their identification." *Id.; see also United States v. Aguilar*, 292 Fed. App'x 622, 624 (9th Cir 2008) (citing *Calderon-Segura* and affirming the district court's certification of an expert in fingerprint analysis). Thus, as with evidence of medical causation, the Ninth Circuit continues to recognize the discretion of district courts to evaluate other forms of scientific evidence.

3. Nonscientific Expert Evidence

The Supreme Court's decision in *Kumho Tire Co. v. Carmichael*, 526 U.S. 137, 119 S. Ct. 1167 (1999), confirmed that the district court's *Daubert* gatekeeper obligation applies to all expert evidence, regardless of whether that evidence can be deemed "scientific" in nature. *See also Claar v. Burlington Northern Railroad Co.*, 29 F.3d 499, 501 n.2 (9th Cir. 1994) (noting that the requirements of *Daubert* "apply to all proffered expert testimony—not just testimony based on novel scientific methods or evidence"). The Ninth Circuit applied *Kumho Tire* in *United States v. Hankey*, 203 F.3d 1160 (9th Cir. 2000), *cert. denied*, 530 U.S. 1268 (2000). In *Hankey*, the defendant claimed that the district court improperly assessed the reliability of expert testimony regarding the codefendants' gang affiliations and the gang's "code of silence." The defendant argued that the district court was required to evaluate the testimony in the same way the *Kumho Tire* court evaluated the methodology used by a tire-defect expert. The Ninth Circuit disagreed, finding that the extensive *voir dire* of the expert that the district court conducted was the most diligent review it could have undertaken given the type of the expert testimony proffered. *Id.* at 1169; *see also United States v. Murillo*, 255 F.3d 1169, 1178 (9th Cir. 2001), *cert. denied*, 122 S. Ct. 1342 (2002) (noting district court's *voir dire* as a basis for establishing the qualifications of a DEA agent as an expert witness).

The *Hankey* decision emphasized that Rule 702 is generally construed liberally and that judges have wide discretion in applying the rule. "Far from requiring trial judges to mechanically apply the *Daubert* factors—or something like them—to both scientific and nonscientific testimony, *Kumho Tire* heavily emphasizes that judges are entitled to broad discretion when discharging their gatekeeping function." *Id.; see also United States v. Mendoza-Paz*, 286 F.3d 1104, 1112–13 (9th Cir. 2002) (explaining that the reliability of expert testimony regarding the street value of narcotics is based on the expert's knowledge and experience, and thus its reliability should not be measured by a mechanical application of the *Daubert* factors).

In *United States v. Smith*, 520 F.3d 1097 (9th Cir. 2008), the Ninth Circuit considered an appeal brought by a prisoner after the prisoner was convicted of assault with a deadly weapon. The prosecution had offered the opinion of a physician's assistant employed by the prison, who testified that the knife that the defendant used was capable of causing "very fatal injuries." *Id.* at 1100. The district court allowed the testimony over the defendant's objections that the "expert" was only a physician's assistant and not a doctor, concluding that he was qualified based on an overseas medical degree and extensive experience in the prison. *Id.* The Ninth Circuit concluded that the expert's opinion was relevant to help determine the dangerousness of the weapon and that his opinion was reliable based on his education and experience. *Id.* at 1105. Further, the Ninth Circuit emphasized that Rule 702 does not require specific credentials in order to testify. *Id.* (citing *United States v. Garcia*, 7 F.3d 885, 889–90 (9th Cir. 1993). *But see United States v. Redlightning*, 624 F.3d 1090, 1115–16 (9th Cir. 2010), *cert denied*, 131 S. Ct. 2944 (2011) (affirming the exclusion of the testimony of a neuropsychologist who was proffered to testify regarding, *inter alia*, the "physical, medical symptoms of hypoglycemia" and the connection between the defendant's purportedly false confession and his post-traumatic stress disorder).

There are limits, however, to the district court's latitude in determining the reliability of nonscientific expert testimony. In *United States v. Hermanek*, 289 F.3d 1076 (9th Cir. 2002), the government had offered the testimony of an expert witness to interpret the wiretapped conversations of the defendants, who were accused of various drug-related offenses. In its offer of proof to the district court, the government presented affidavits and testimony regarding the witnesses' qualifications and conclusions; the district court qualified the witness as an expert and allowed him to testify. The Ninth Circuit reversed, finding that the reliability of the expert's methodology had not been adequately established:

> The district court relied solely on [the expert]'s general qualifications without requiring the government to explain the method [the expert] used to arrive at his interpretations. . . . As we said in *Daubert*, "[w]e've been presented with only the expert['s] qualifications, [his] conclusions and [his] assurances of reliability. Under *Daubert*, that's not enough." 43 F.3d at 1319.

Hermanek, 289 F.3d at 1094.

Hermanek did not foreclose the use of expert testimony to interpret drug jargon and, in 2006, the Ninth Circuit addressed a challenge to the use of expert testimony regarding drug jargon. *United States v. Decoud*, 456 F.3d 996 (9th Cir. 2006). The Ninth Circuit affirmed the admission of the testimony, concluding that the concerns with methodology and experience in *Hermanek* were not present in the case at bar. *Id.* at 1013–14. In a more thorough discussion, the Ninth Circuit subsequently approved of its use in *United States v. Freeman*, 498 F.3d 893 (9th Cir. 2007). In *Freeman*, the district court allowed the government to introduce the testimony of a detective regarding the meaning of coded language such as "iggidy" and "all gravy" that was intercepted during a drug investigation. *Id.* at 898. Citing *Kumho Tire*, the Ninth Circuit affirmed the certification of the detective as an expert in drug jargon. *Id.* at 901 (quoting *United States v. Griffith*, 118 F.3d 318, 321 (5th Cir. 1997) ("[Drug jargon] is a specialized body of knowledge, familiar only to those wise in the ways of the drug trade, and therefore a fit subject for expert testimony.")). The Ninth Circuit distinguished between expert and lay testimony, finding that the expert should not have been allowed to testify on ambiguous conversations that "did not consist of coded terms at all." *Id.* at 902 (finding the error harmless). A couple of years later, the Ninth Circuit affirmed both the admissibility of drug jargon experts and the distinction between lay and expert testimony in *United States v. Reed*, 575 F.3d 900 (9th Cir. 2009). The court cited both *Freeman* and the Advisory Committee Notes to Rule 702 which "expressly authorize the use of testimony by law enforcement officers concerning the meaning of words used by drug traffickers." *Id.* at 922.

Similarly, in *United States v. Sepulveda-Barraza*, 645 F.3d 1066 (9th Cir. 2011) the Ninth Circuit considered the admission of expert testimony regarding the structure and operation of drug trafficking organizations, which was offered to refute the defense theory that the defendant was an unknowing drug courier. The court found that there is no "per se rule of inadmissibility" and that this kind of testimony should be considered as any other—on a case-by-case basis to determine whether it is relevant, probative, and not unfairly prejudicial. *Id.* at 1071–72. *But see cf. United States v. Pineda-Torres*, 287 F.3d 860, 864–65 (9th Cir. 2002) (finding that expert testimony regarding drug trafficking organizations was improperly admitted because it attributed knowledge to the defendant "by attempting to connect him to an international drug conspiracy").

Returning to the issue of discretion discussed in *Hermanek*, in *Mukhtar v. California State University*, 299 F.3d 1053 (9th Cir. 2002), *as amended by* 319 F.3d 1073 (9th Cir. 2003), the Ninth Circuit confirmed the district court's discretion in making a determination of reliability in the case of expert evidence in an employment discrimination case yet ultimately reiterated the limits of the district court's discretion. Plaintiff Elsayed Mukhtar, a tenure-track professor, sued the California State University at Hayward and various individuals at the university over repeated denials of his tenure application, claiming employment discrimination. Mukhtar offered at trial, over the objection of defendants, the testimony of an expert witness who opined that racism was a factor in the denial of tenure. The Ninth Circuit described the district court's discretion in determining the reliability of this expert witness: "A trial court not only has broad latitude in determining whether an expert's testimony is reliable, but also in deciding *how* to determine the testimony's reliability." *Id.* at 1064 (citing *Hankey,* 203 F.3d at 1167; *Kumho Tire,* 526 U.S. at 152) (italics in original). However, the *Mukhtar* court cautioned that the district court's "broad latitude" in how it determines the reliability of expert evidence cannot be stretched too far: "Surely, however, the trial court's broad latitude to make the reliability determination does *not* include the discretion to abdicate completely its responsibility to do so." *Id.* After reviewing the trial transcript, the Ninth Circuit found that the district court had "said nothing about the *reliability* of the [expert's] testimony," and as a result, vacated the jury verdict and granted defendants a new trial. *Id.* at 1065; *cf. Jinro America, Inc. v. Secure Investments Inc.,* 266 F.3d 993, 1006 (9th Cir. 2001) (excluding proffered expert testimony as "so tinged with ethnic bias and stereotyping" as to be more prejudicial than probative). Later cases have construed *Mukhtar* to require an explicit determination of reliability on the record as part of the gatekeeping obligation of the trial courts. *See, e.g., United States v. Jawara,* 474 F.3d 565, 583 (9th Cir. 2007); *United States v. Barerra-Medina,* 139 F. App'x 786, 793 (9th Cir. 2005).

The Ninth Circuit analyzed the use of statistics-based expert testimony in *Obrey v. Johnson,* 400 F.3d 691 (9th Cir. 2005), where it emphasized the difference between reliability and credibility, and ultimately admitted statistical data to prove racial discrimination. In *Obrey,* the plaintiff sued the Secretary of the Navy, alleging that he was denied a promotion because of his race and that the Secretary of the Navy had a pattern of discriminating against qualified candidates of Asian-Pacific descent. *Id.* at 693. The plaintiff hired a statistician to analyze hiring statistics and provide a report. The report concluded that "there is no statistical evidence . . . that the selection process . . . was unbiased with respect to race." *Id.* at 694. The report was challenged as irrelevant and unreliable because qualifications of the applicants were not controlled for in the statistical analysis. The court concluded, however, that the statistical evidence was not irrelevant simply because it failed to control for the qualifications of the applicant pool. The fact that the report was not complete and was not able to prove the plaintiff's case did not go to the admissibility of the statistical data, but only the weight it should have been given. The court explained that so long as statistical evidence does not suffer from "serious methodological flaws," the usefulness or strength of the evidence does not affect its admissibility. *Id.* at 695–96. Although it could not prove the plaintiff's allegation of racial discrimination, the statistical evidence did analyze what it purported to analyze: the race of applicants hired for positions compared to the race of the entire applicant pool. Thus, the Ninth Circuit concluded that reliable and relevant statistics are admissible—and that concerns about the ability of the evidence to prove the issue in question may at times go only to weight and credibility.

The Ninth Circuit has also addressed the use of survey evidence and the expert testimony that stems from the survey results as a way to prove "actual confusion," a factor in evaluating a trademark infringement action. As an initial matter, "[i]n trademark cases, surveys are to be admitted as long as they are conducted according to accepted principles and are relevant." *Wendt v. Host Int'l, Inc.,* 125 F.3d 806, 824 (9th Cir. 1997). Any "[c]hallenges to survey methodology go to the weight given the survey, not its admissibility." *Id.* The Ninth Circuit revisited the question in *Fortune Dynamic Inc. v. Victoria's Secret Stores Brand Mgmt. Inc.,* 618 F.3d 1025 (9th Cir. 2010). Fortune Dynamic's survey evidence of consumer confusion was rejected by the district court based on flaws in the survey. *Id.* at 1037. The Ninth Circuit reversed, citing *Kumho Tire* and *Daubert* and concluding that "the results of the survey are relevant to the ultimate question whether Victoria's Secret's use of [the trademark] was likely to confuse consumers." *Id.* The court reiterated that any criticisms of the survey go to its weight. *Id.* at 1038 (citing *Daubert,* 509 U.S. at 596).

B. EXPERT-RELATED RULES AND PROCEDURAL ISSUES IN FEDERAL COURTS

1. Class Certification Issues

The Ninth Circuit recently considered the interplay between the *Daubert* standards and class certification in *Ellis v. Costco Wholesale Corp.*, 657 F.3d 970 (9th Cir. 2011). In *Ellis*, the parties relied on dueling experts to establish whether the plaintiffs satisfied the element of commonality required for class certification. The court held that under the Supreme Court's opinion in *Wal-Mart Stores, Inc. v. Dukes*, 131 S.Ct. 2541 (2011), a district court must consider the merits of the class members' substantive claims if they overlap with the commonality requirement. *Ellis*, 657 F.3d at 981. When a party uses expert opinions to establish commonality, the district court must ascertain not only whether the opinion is sufficiently reliable under *Daubert*, but also whether the opinion is sufficiently persuasive to establish commonality under Federal Rule of Civil Procedure 23(a)(2). *Id.* at 982. The court emphasized, however, that in conducting this analysis, the governing question is not whether the plaintiffs could actually prevail on the merits of their claims, but only whether common questions exist. *Id.* at 983 n.8.

2. Daubert Hearings

In *United States v. Alatorre*, 222 F.3d 1098 (9th Cir. 2000), deciding an issue of first impression, the Ninth Circuit held that district courts have discretion to decide whether to hold an evidentiary hearing on *Daubert* motions, and whether those hearings may be heard in the presence of the jury:

> Nowhere in *Daubert, Joiner,* or *Kumho Tire* does the Supreme Court mandate the form that the inquiry into relevance and reliability must take, nor have we previously spoken to this issue. Although the [Supreme] Court stated that the inquiry is a "preliminary" one, to be made "at the outset," this does not mean that it must be made in a separate, pretrial hearing, outside the presence of the jury.

Id. at 1102.

Repeatedly affirming *Alatorre* in its later decisions, the Ninth Circuit has continued to protect the district court's discretion regarding *Daubert* hearings. In *In re Hanford Nuclear Reservation Litigation*, 292 F.3d 1124 (9th Cir. 2002), the Ninth Circuit rejected the plaintiffs' argument that the district court had abused its discretion in granting defendants' *Daubert* motions without a hearing. After reversing the district court's ruling on defendants' *Daubert* motions on other grounds, the Ninth Circuit stated: "District courts are not required to hold a *Daubert* hearing before ruling on the admissibility of scientific evidence." *Id.* at 1138–39 (citing *Alatorre*, 222 F.3d at 1100); *see also Millenkamp v. Davisco Foods, Int'l*, 562 F.3d 971, 979 (9th Cir. 2009) (quoting the same); *United States v. Lopez-Martinez*, 543 F.3d 509, 514–15 (9th Cir. 2008) (noting that the district court is not required to conduct a formal *Daubert* hearing or insist the expert explain each logical step in his opinion under Supreme Court or Ninth Circuit precedent); *Morin v. United States*, 244 F. App'x 142, 144 (9th Cir. 2007) ("[T]he district court did not abuse its discretion in failing to hold an evidentiary hearing regarding the admissibility of [the plaintiff's expert's] proffered testimony, as [the plaintiff] did not request one and the district court had an adequate record."); *Hangarter v. Provident Life and Accident Ins. Co.*, 373 F.3d 998, 1018 (9th Cir. 2004) ("Even though the district court did not hold a formal *Daubert* hearing, the court's probing of [the expert's) knowledge and experience was sufficient to satisfy its gatekeeping role under *Daubert*."). Although finding that the district court did not abuse its discretion in refusing to hold an evidentiary hearing on defendants' *Daubert* motions, the *Hanford* court nonetheless "encourage[d] the [district] court to hold a hearing on remand." *In re Hanford*, 292 F.3d at 1139.

In addition, the Ninth Circuit has applied its decision in *Alatorre* to reject the argument that *Daubert* hearings need to be held outside the presence of the jury to comply with the district court's gatekeeping responsibility. *See Mendoza-Paz*, 286 F.3d at 1112 ("[Defendant]'s argument that the district court erred in failing to conduct the *Daubert* hearing outside the presence of the jury is foreclosed by our decision in *[Alatorre].*"); *cf. Hermanek*, 289 F.3d at 1095 n.7 (noting that, although district courts are not required to make Rule 702 determinations outside the presence of the jury, the district court should have ruled on "the potentially prejudicial qualifying testimony presented in this case" outside the presence of the jury).

3. *Court-Appointed Experts*

Under Federal Rule of Evidence 706, a United States district court may appoint one or more experts to assist the court in evaluating scientific evidence. Specifically:

> The court may on its own motion or on the motion of any party enter an order to show cause why expert witnesses should not be appointed, and may request the parties to submit nominations. The court may appoint any expert witnesses agreed upon by the parties, and may appoint expert witnesses of its own selection.

FRE 706(a). Indeed, in *Daubert II*, Judge Kozinski briefly cited to Rule 706 in his discussion of *Daubert* hearings, suggesting that district courts contemplate the occasional use of court-appointed experts to assist at such hearings. *See Daubert v. Merrell Dow Pharmaceuticals, Inc.*, 43 F.3d 1311, 1319 n.10 (9th Cir. 1995).

Courts in the Ninth Circuit have taken advantage of the power to appoint expert witnesses in a number of contexts. For example, in *Walker v. American Home Shield Long Term Disability Plan*, 180 F.3d 1065 (9th Cir. 1999), a participant of an ERISA plan who was diagnosed with fibromyalgia sued the plan administrator for wrongful termination of benefits. The plan administrator argued on appeal that the district court had improperly appointed an independent expert and accepted that expert's medical findings. The Ninth Circuit first clarified that the decision to appoint an expert under Rule 706 is reviewed for abuse of discretion. *Id.* at 1071. The court then held that the district court did not abuse its discretion in appointing an "independent expert to assist the court in evaluating contradictory evidence about an elusive disease of unknown cause." *Id.* at 1071; *see also Grant v. Bristol-Myers Squibb*, 97 F. Supp. 2d 986, 989–93 (D. Ariz. 2000) (excluding plaintiffs' expert testimony and granting partial summary judgment to defendant, relying, in part, on a court-appointed National Science Panel's finding that there was no association between breast implants and connective tissue disease); *cf. Lopez v. Scribner*, 2007 WL 1215420 (E.D. Cal. April 23, 2007) (declining plaintiff's request for a court-appointed expert to opine on whether defendants had been deliberately indifferent in failing to provide him with medically prescribed shoes, the court explained that "the issues [were] not so complex as to require the testimony of an expert to assist the trier of fact").

An expert appointed under Rule 706 "may be called to testify by the court or any party," and indeed *"shall* advise the parties of [his or her] findings." FRE 706(a) (emphasis added). Such an expert is thus subject to discovery: "the witness' deposition may be taken by any party . . . [and the] witness shall be subject to cross-examination by each party, including a party calling the witness." *Id.*

The Ninth Circuit has explained, however, that while expert witnesses appointed under Rule 706 are subject to discovery, "technical advisors" appointed under a district court's inherent power to manage litigation are not. In *Association of Mexican-American Educators (AMAE) v. California*, 231 F.3d 572 (9th Cir. 2000) (en banc), the plaintiffs argued that the district court "violated [FRE

706 by relying on the advice of an expert who was not subject to cross examination and did not prepare a report." *Id.* at 579. The Ninth Circuit found, however, that the expert in question "was appointed by the district court as a technical advisor," and "was not called as an expert witness." *Id.* at 590. The court explained that "district courts retain inherent authority to appoint technical advisors in appropriate cases," and that "Rule 706 applies to court-appointed *expert witnesses,* but not to technical advisors." *Id.* at 591 (emphasis in original). Thus, the discovery requirements of Rule 706 did not apply to the "technical advisor" in *AMAE,* and the district court did not err in refusing to permit such discovery.[5]

In *Federal Trade Commission v. Enforma Natural Products, Inc.,* 362 F.3d 1204 (9th Cir. 2004), the Ninth Circuit further clarified what distinguishes between "expert witnesses" and "technical advisors." *Id.* at 1212–15. The appellant in *Enforma* argued that the district court "erroneously deprived [it] of the ability to depose or cross-examine the court-appointed expert . . . or to view a report prepared by [the expert]." *Id.* at 1212. The appellee, however, argued that the expert in question was merely a "technical advisor" not subject to discovery. *Id.* The Ninth Circuit first reaffirmed that "[w]hen outside technical expertise can be helpful to a district court, the court may appoint a technical advisor." *Id.* at 1213 (citing *AMAE,* 231 F.3d at 590). The court then explained the differences between "technical advisors" and "expert witnesses":

> The role of a technical advisor is to organize, advise on, and help the court understand relevant scientific evidence. A technical advisor is a tutor who aids the court in understanding the 'jargon and theory' relevant to the technical aspects of the evidence. A technical advisor may not assume the role of an expert witness by supplying new evidence; nor may an advisor usurp the role of the judge by making findings of fact or conclusions of law. Technical advisors, acting as such, are not subject to the provisions of Rule 706, which govern court-appointed expert *witnesses.* A court-appointed expert is a witness subject to Rule 706 if the expert is called to testify or if the court relies on the expert as an independent source of evidence.

Id. (internal citations omitted) (emphasis in original).

The *Enforma* court found that it was unclear whether the district court had appointed an "expert witness" or merely a "technical advisor." As the court explained: "[The expert] was not a testifying expert witness in a formal sense. He was never placed under oath or called to testify at trial. He did not submit an expert report or any other independent evidence on the record." *Id.* at 1213. However, there was evidence that the expert had "offered his own opinion on the scientific evidence in the record" during a conference with the district court and the parties—but because the factual record was unclear, it was "impossible to determine whether [the expert] became the source of independent evidence or whether he merely advised the court with regard to the scientific issues in the case." *Id.* The Ninth Circuit thus remanded with instructions that the district court "clarify the status and role" of the expert. *Id.* at 1208.

Moreover, in *Enforma* the Ninth Circuit recommended that on remand the district court utilize certain "procedural safeguards" to protect against further misunderstanding. Endorsing an approach suggested by the dissent in *AMAE,* the court suggested that the district court:

---

[5] *See also Hall v. Baxter Healthcare Corp.,* 947 F. Supp. 1387, 1392 & n.8 (D. Or. 1996) (appointing experts in breast implant litigation under the court's "inherent authority as a federal district court judge to appoint independent advisors to the court"; and explaining that this would "keep the advisors independent of any ongoing proceedings" by avoiding Rule 706 requirements that "court-appointed experts, in effect, . . . act as additional witnesses subject to depositions and testifying at trial").

(1) utilize a fair and open procedure for appointing a neutral technical advisor; (2) address any allegations of bias, partiality, or lack of qualification; (3) clearly define and limit the technical advisor's duties; (4) make clear to the technical advisor that any advice he or she gives to the court cannot be based on any extra-record information; and (5) make explicit, either through an expert's report or a record of ex parte communications, the nature and content of the technical advisor's advice.

Id. at 1215 (citing *AMAE*, 231 F.3d at 611–14 (Tashima, J., dissenting)).

Finally, it should be noted that whether a district court wishes to appoint an "expert witness" under Rule 706 or a "technical advisor" under its inherent powers, there are resources available to assist the court in finding an appropriate expert. Specifically, the American Association for the Advancement of Science created a project entitled Court Appointed Scientific Experts (CASE) to do just that. *See* AMERICAN ASSOCIATION FOR THE ADVANCEMENT OF SCIENCE, COURT APPOINTED SCIENTIFIC EXPERTS, *at* www.aaas.org/spp/case/case.htm; *see also* Deborah C. Runkle, *Court Appointed Scientific Experts: Providing Objective Scientific Evidence to the Judiciary,* in ABA SCIENTIFIC EVIDENCE REVIEW, MONOGRAPH No. 7: CURRENT ISSUES AT THE CROSSROADS OF SCIENCE, TECHNOLOGY AND THE LAW, ABA Section of Science & Technology Law, Cynthia H. Cwik and Helen E. Witt, eds., pp. 19–38 (2005); Hon. Martin L.C. Feldman, *Court-Appointed Experts: A Judge's Perspective,* in ABA SCIENTIFIC EVIDENCE REVIEW, MONOGRAPH No. 5, ABA Section of Science & Technology Law, Cynthia H. Cwik and John L. North, eds., pp. 119–27 (2001).

4. *Failure to Comply with Expert Disclosure Requirements*

The Ninth Circuit has instructed district courts to look to five factors to determine whether the sanction of preclusion should be applied for failure to comply with expert disclosure requirements: (1) the public's interest in expeditious resolution of litigation, (2) the court's need to manage its docket, (3) the risk of prejudice to the other side, (4) the public policy favoring disposition of cases on their merits, and (5) the availability of less drastic sanctions. *See Wendt v. Host Int'l, Inc.,* 125 F.3d 806, 814 (9th Cir. 1997) (citing *Wanderer v. Johnston,* 910 F.2d 652, 656 (9th Cir. 1990)).

In *Wendt,* the district court issued an order precluding the defendant's expert from testifying for failure to comply with disclosure requirements. However, the procedural status of the case subsequently changed due to a successful appeal and change of counsel. *Id.* The Ninth Circuit held that the preclusion order should be vacated because, due to the new procedural posture of the case, a less drastic sanction was now available. The court explained: "At [the time the preclusion order was entered], counsel's failure to comply with discovery rules potentially prejudiced Host's and Paramount's ability to prepare adequately for trial. Today, that is not so. Both parties now have ample opportunity to begin the expert disclosure procedure anew." *Id.* The *Wendt* court noted, however, that, even though preclusion was no longer warranted, the district court had discretion to impose reasonable monetary sanctions on the plaintiff's former counsel for the disclosure failures. *Id.* Thus, *Wendt* suggested that prejudice to the other side and the availability of lesser sanctions are important factors. *See also Wanderer,* 910 F.2d at 656 (stating "the key factors are prejudice and availability of lesser sanctions" and finding prejudice to be an essential element in order to exclude expert testimony, as sanctions that interfere with a claim or defense would violate due process when imposed to punish violations that do not cause prejudice).

A decision that came a few years after *Wendt,* however, provided a standard under which district courts could more easily impose preclusion sanctions. In *Yeti by Molly Ltd. v. Deckers Outdoor Corp.,* 259 F.3d 1101 (9th Cir. 2001), the Ninth Circuit emphasized the language of Rule 37, which "forbid[s] the use at trial of any information required to be disclosed by Rule 26(a) that is not properly disclosed." *Id.* at 1106; Fed. R. Civ. P. 37(c)(1). The Ninth Circuit rejected the argument that district courts should be required to identify "willfulness, fault, or bad faith" before imposing preclusion sanctions, holding instead that the party facing the sanction bore the burden to show that the failure to disclose was substantially justified or harmless. *Id.* This approach of *Yeti* gained traction in the decade following the decision. *See Hoffman v. Constr. Protective Servs.*, 541 F.3d 1175, 1180 (9th Cir. 2008) (affirming exclusion where the expert failed to disclose damages; noting that exclusion under Rule 37(c)(1) was "appropriate 'even when a litigant's entire cause of action . . . [will be] precluded.'"); *Wong v. Regents of the University of California*, 379 F.3d 1097 (9th Cir. 2004) (upholding exclusion and affirming that the failure to disclose was neither substantially justified nor harmless even though the trial was several months away).

In 2012, the Ninth Circuit sought to synthesize these somewhat different approaches—and rein in the harsh results made possible by the *Yeti* line of cases. *R & R Sails, Inc. v. Insurance Co. of Pennsylvania*, 673 F.3d 1240, 1245–48 (9th Cir. 2012). In *R & R Sails*, the plaintiff sued his insurance company following the insurance company's failure to pay portions of a claim. The plaintiff repeatedly failed to disclose certain invoices that related to its claim for attorney's fees, and the district court ultimately excluded these documents. *Id.* at 1245–46. The Ninth Circuit found that the district court did not make "findings sufficient to support its preclusion of the invoices under Rule 37(c)(1)." *Id.* at 1247.

The Ninth Circuit acknowledged that, under the *Yeti* line of cases, a violation of Rule 26 might warrant preclusion of evidence, but noted that "evidence preclusion is, or at least can be, a 'harsh' sanction." *R & R Sails*, 673 F.3d at 1247. On the facts of *R & R Sails*, the court concluded that the exclusion of evidence constituted a "fatal blow" and "amounted to a dismissal of the claim." *Id.* Following this diagnosis, the Ninth Circuit cited back to *Yeti* and *Wendt* and "reaffirm[ed]" that when a sanction amounts to a dismissal of a claim, the district court must "consider whether the claimed noncompliance involved willfulness, fault, or bad faith . . . and also to consider the availability of lesser sanctions." *Id.* The Ninth Circuit concluded that this analysis falls under the "harmlessness inquiry required under Rule 37(c)(1)." *Id.* In a footnote, the court distinguished *Yeti* and *Hoffman*, saying that in those cases "the preclusion sanction did not amount to the dismissal of a cause of action." *Id.* at 1247 n.1.

Addressing a different matter of first impression relating to expert disclosure, the Ninth Circuit recently considered whether treating physicians are subject to the disclosure requirements of Rule 26(a)(2) in *Goodman v. Staples*, 644 F.3d 817, 824 (9th Cir. 2011). In general, treating physicians are exempt from the disclosure requirements. *Id.* at 819. In *Goodman*, the plaintiff suffered an injury after falling in the Staples store. The district court held that when the treating physician was asked to opine as to the cause of the plaintiff's injury, the physician had "been transformed into the same type of expert envisioned by the report requirement." *Id.* at 821–22. The Ninth Circuit affirmed, holding that when a treating physician "morphs into a witness hired to render expert opinions that go beyond the usual scope of a treating doctor's testimony, the proponent of the testimony must comply with Rule 26(a)(2)." *Id.* at 819–820. A physician is "only exempt from Rule 26(a)(2)(B)'s written report requirement to the extent that his opinions were formed during the course of treatment." *Id.* at 826. Because the treating physicians in this case were retained to form opinions as to issues outside of their course of treatment and reviewed documents to aid that determination, they were not exempt from the disclosure requirements. *Id.*

5. Appellate Review

In 2009, the Ninth Circuit considered the "familiar 'abuse of discretion' standard and how it limits [the] power [of] an appellate court to substitute [its] views of the facts, and the application of those facts to law, for that of the district court." *United States v. Hinkson*, 585 F.3d 1247, 1250 (9th Cir. 2009) (en banc). In reviewing a motion for a new trial where the defendant was charged with solicitation of murder of a federal official, the Ninth Circuit highlighted that the current abuse of discretion standard left the appellate courts with "no effective limit" on its power to substitute its judgment for that of the district court. *Id.* at 1251. Therefore, the Ninth Circuit established a new test for abuse of discretion. First, the appellate court must "consider whether the district court identified the correct legal standard for decision of the issue before it." Second, the appellate court must "determine whether the district court's findings of fact, and its application of those findings of fact to the correct legal standard, were illogical, implausible, or without support in inferences that may be drawn from facts in the record." *Id.* at 1251.

In *United States v. Redlightning*, 624 F.3d 1090, 1110 (9th Cir. 2010), *cert denied*, 131 S. Ct. 2944 (2011), the Ninth Circuit applied the abuse of discretion standard established in *Hinkson* to the review of evidentiary decisions regarding expert evidence. In *Redlightning*, the defendant confessed to a sexual assault and murder while taking a polygraph test. *Id.* at 1099. The defendant sought to offer expert testimony regarding false confessions, but the district court did not allow the testimony. *Id.* The Ninth Circuit first cited *United States v. Grace*, 504 F.3d 745, 759 (9th Cir. 2007), for the proposition that a district court's decision to exclude expert testimony is reviewed for abuse of discretion. *Redlightning*, 624 F.3d at 1110. Next, the Ninth Circuit considered the two-step *Hinkson* inquiry, concluding that the test is "useful also for purposes of assessing the district court's challenged decisions . . . to limit or exclude expert testimony." *Id.* The Ninth Circuit then affirmed the exclusion of the expert testimony in part because the testimony did not have a proper foundation. *Id.* at 1112–13.

C. STATE LAW EXPERT ISSUES

1. Expert Evidence in Alaska State Courts

a. *Daubert* Applies to Determinations of Admissibility of Scientific Evidence

In March 1999, the Alaska Supreme Court formally adopted the *Daubert* standard for determining the admissibility of scientific evidence. *See State v. Coon*, 974 P.2d 386 (Alaska 1999). Since then, as will be discussed *infra*, the court has narrowed its application of *Daubert* by limiting it to only scientific evidence, rather than experience-based evidence. *See, e.g., Thompson v. Cooper*, Nos. S-14142, S-14162 (Alaska Sept. 28, 2012) (pending publication in the Pacific Reporter); *Marsingill v. O'Malley*, 128 P.3d 151 (Alaska 2006); *Marron v. Stromstad*, 123 P.3d 992 (Alaska 2005). For experience-based expert evidence, the proponent must merely show that the witness has substantial experience in the field and that the testimony might help the jury. *See Thompson*, Nos. S-14142, S-14162 (Alaska Sept. 28, 2012).

Prior to the adoption of the *Daubert* standard in *Coon*, Alaska courts had adhered to the *Frye* test, despite several attempts by state prosecutors to argue that *Frye* had been superseded by the enactment of the Federal Rules of Evidence. *See Contreras v. State*, 718 P.2d 129 (Alaska 1986) (holding that testimony obtained through hypnosis is inadmissible); *Harmon v. State*, 908 P.2d 434, 439 (Alaska Ct. App. 1995) (holding that DNA testing is generally accepted within the scientific community and thus admissible).

In *Coon*, the defendant was convicted of making "terroristic" telephone calls. During trial, expert testimony regarding voice spectographic analysis was introduced and found admissible under *Frye*, as the technique was "generally accepted by courts" and was reliable. The trial court also found that the technique would be admissible under *Daubert*. *See Coon*, 974 P.2d at 388. On appeal, the

Alaska Supreme Court requested briefing on the issue of whether to retain *Frye* or adopt *Daubert*, even though the issue was not technically before it. *See id.* at 389.

In a thorough discussion, the court adopted *Daubert's* multiprong approach, relying on a common criticism of *Frye*—that it is "potentially capricious because it excludes scientifically reliable evidence which is not yet generally accepted, and admits scientifically unreliable evidence which although generally accepted, cannot meet rigorous scientific scrutiny." *Id.* at 393–94. Since *Frye* is thus both "unduly restrictive and unduly permissive," the court found the test to be inconsistent with the Alaska Rules of Evidence, which substantially resemble the Federal Rules, and which preclude the admissibility inquiry from focusing on any one factor, such as "general acceptance." *Id.* Applying *Daubert*, the court then found voice spectrograph analysis evidence to be admissible.

The *Coon* court downplayed concerns that adopting the *Daubert* standard would place undue burdens on state judges, by shifting their inquiry from a determination of whether scientists generally accept a given technique to an overall evaluation of reliability. Although the burden might be substantial, "[d]etermining reliability for judicial purposes is unavoidably the responsibility of trial courts, and should not be delegated to an expert's peers." *Id.* at 396. The court suggested that in complicated cases, courts may reduce their burden and increase the accuracy of their reliability evaluations by selecting independent expert witnesses and by appointing expert "advisors." *Id.*

Alaska courts have since applied the *Coon* standard in a number of circumstances. In a case analyzing the admissibility of behavioral profiles of abused children, the Alaska Supreme Court held that such expert testimony can be admitted and does not interfere with the jury's role of assessing witness credibility. *See L. C.H. v. T.S.*, 28 P.3d 915 (Alaska 2001). In *L. C.H.*, the defendant was convicted of sexually abusing his step-granddaughter and, on appeal, argued that profile testimony should have been limited. The court held that profile evidence is admissible in rebuttal to claims that certain conduct by the victim is inconsistent with sexual abuse. *Id.* at 924; *see also Russell v. State*, 934 P.2d 1335, 1343 (Alaska Ct. App. 1997). Such profile evidence is relevant to the jury's ability to determine guilt or innocence, so long as the jury's province to determine credibility is not invaded. *See L. C.H.*, 28 P.3d at 927. The court explained that this form of expert testimony is admissible if it is not mere "vouching evidence," which occurs when experts are called upon to state that an individual fits a victim profile. *Id.* at 925.

In *John's Heating Svc. v. Lamb*, 46 P.3d 1024 (Alaska 2002), the Alaska Supreme Court applied its *Coon* test and upheld the admission of expert medical causation testimony in a chronic carbon monoxide poisoning case. Although noting that other jurisdictions had cautioned against causation opinions based on "unwarranted extrapolations," the Alaska Supreme Court found that the expert testimony was "generally reasonable." *Id.* at 1035. The court based its decision, in part, on a recognition that the ethical limitations of testing on humans "excuses the lack of [empirical] testing to some extent. In this case, the lack of empirical testing does not render the theory so unreliable as to require exclusion." *Id.* The *John's Heating* court also expressly declined to hold that medical causation opinions based on differential-diagnosis methodologies (i.e., the consideration of alternative diagnoses to explain a patient's condition) are inadmissible. *Id.* at 1036. The court's decision was influenced by "the medical community's daily use of the same [differential-diagnosis] methodologies in diagnosing patients." *Id.*

In *Samaniego v. City of Kodiak*, 80 P.3d 216, 220 (Alaska 2003), the Alaska Supreme Court declined to apply the *Coon* test to psychiatric testimony because the testimony was "simply a diagnosis" that resulted from a typical psychiatric examination. The court found that psychological and psychiatric exams had been repeatedly recognized as legitimate by the courts, and thus that merely attacking the expert's testimony was not enough to subject the diagnosis to an evaluation under the *Coon* factors. Instead, courts can take judicial notice of admissibility when evidence is of the type that has been "repeatedly admitted in previous cases," such as a routine exam and diagnosis. *Id.*

The Alaska Court of Appeals has addressed the reliability of expert opinions based on portable breath test devices designed to test blood alcohol content. *See Guerre-Chaley v. State*, 88 P.3d 539,

542 (Alaska Ct. App. 2004). In *Guerra-Chaley,* although the court made no determination regarding the reliability of the specific breath test itself, it clarified the relationship between expert testimony and the underlying data or scientific tests that give rise to such data. *Id.* at 543. Even though an expert witness is permitted to base an opinion on information that is not independently admissible pursuant to Evidence Rule 703, the proponent of the expert's testimony must still show that the test or method used to collect the data meets the *Daubert/Coon* test for admissibility of scientific evidence. *Id.* Similarly, in the DNA analysis context, the Alaska Court of Appeals noted that, "as a practical matter, there are times when the expert's opinion has essentially no probative value unless the jury assumes the truth of some or all of this underlying information or data. For this reason . . . Evidence Rule 705(c) directs the trial judge to prohibit the expert from testifying about these underlying matters 'if the danger that [the expert's testimony concerning these matters] will be used for an improper purpose outweighs their value as support for the expert's opinion.'" *Vann v. State*, 229 P.3d 197, 209 (Alaska Ct. App. 2010) (quoting Alaska Rule of Evidence 705(c)).

In recent years, the Alaska Supreme Court has narrowed the application of the *Daubert* standard, noting a distinction between scientific and experience-based evidence. *See Marron,* 123 P.3d 992. In *Marron,* the plaintiff's expert witness was a general accident reconstructionist without a bachelor's degree—or an engineering degree of any kind. He did, however, have highly specialized training in accident reconstruction, had taken various accident reconstruction courses, and was a member of several professional societies. The court held that it was appropriate to admit his testimony because, as a result, the jury was able to evaluate the evidence in a more informed fashion than it would have without the expert testimony. *Id.* at 1004. Moreover, *a Daubert* analysis was not required because application of the *Daubert* standard is limited to "expert testimony based on scientific theory as opposed to testimony based upon the expert's personal experience." *Id.*; *see also Ratliff v. State,* 110 P.3d 982, 986 (Alaska Ct. App. 2005) (holding that shoeprint comparison and analysis did not need to be evaluated under the *Daubert/Coon* standard because the analysis rests on visual comparisons of samples, not the scientific method, and thus the expertise was gained by experience).

In 2012, the Alaska Supreme Court further clarified the difference between scientific and experience-based testimony. *See Thompson,* Nos. S-14142, S-14162 (Alaska Sept. 28, 2012). The *Thompson* case involved a negligence action based on damages suffered in a car accident. The plaintiff sought to introduce his treating physicians' testimony that they inferred, based on the plaintiff's statements that his symptoms began after the accident, that his injuries were caused by the accident. In order to resolve whether a *Daubert* analysis was required, the court addressed the distinction between scientific and experience-based testimony. Although there is no "clear divide," experience-based testimony "generally . . . 'depend[s] on a more subjective application of the expert's practical experience to the particular facts of the case,'" whereas scientific testimony "'may be subjected to objective testing.'" *Id.* (quoting *Marron,* 123 P.3d at 1006); *see also Starkey v. State,* 272 P.3d 347, 353 (Alaska Ct. App. 2012) (holding that testimony regarding statistical analysis of marijuana raids was experience-based rather than scientific because it "rested on fairly straightforward mathematics—and some implicit or unarticulated assumptions about the facts of the . . . underlying cases."). The *Thompson* court held that the plaintiff's treating physicians were experience-based experts because they had experience in treating similar injuries and were familiar with the plaintiff's injury in particular. *Thompson,* Nos. S-14142, S-14162 (Alaska Sept. 28, 2012). Thus, a *Daubert* analysis was not required. Experience-based expert testimony is admissible whenever an expert witness has "substantial experience in the relevant field and the testimony might help the jury." *Id.* (quoting *Marsingill,* 128 P.3d at 160).

Although a *Daubert* analysis is not required, the Alaska Supreme Court has emphasized the importance of ensuring the reliability of experience-based expert testimony. *See Barton v. North Slope Borough School District,* 268 P.3d 346, 351 (Alaska 2012). In *Barton,* the plaintiff broke her leg after colliding with a player who ran out of bounds during a high school football game. The plaintiff sued the school district, alleging that it negligently designed and operated the football field. To prove her claim, the plaintiff offered expert testimony from a landscape architect who would state her opinion that the football field was negligently designed, based on standards set forth in a sports manual. Before holding that the evidence was admissible, the court emphasized that this type of "non-technical, experience-based expert testimony . . . [must] meet the standards outlined in other evidentiary rules." *Id.* For example, the evidence must be presented by a properly qualified expert, the underlying facts or data must be of a type reasonably relied on by other experts in the field, and the evidence must be relevant." *Id.* (citing Alaska Rules of Evidence 702(a), 703).

b. Expert-Related Rules and Procedural Issues in Alaska State Courts

In Alaska, evidentiary rules limit each party to three expert witnesses per issue in any given case, a number that may be increased or decreased upon a showing of good cause. Alaska Rule of Evidence (ARE) 702(b). The recovery of costs for a witness called to testify as an expert is limited to $150 per hour. Alaska Rule of Administration 7(c). A witness may qualify as an expert by "knowledge, skill, experience, training, or education." ARE 702(a). However, Rule 702 does not include a licensing requirement. *See Martha S. v. Alaska Dept. of Health & Social Servs.*, 268 P.3d 1066, 1076–77 (Alaska 2012) ("[T]here is no requirement that a witness possess a particular license or academic degree in order to qualify as an expert.") (quoting *Handley v. State*, 615 P.2d 627, 630 (Alaska 1980)).

Alaska law requires detailed pretrial disclosure relating to experts and their expected testimony. Parties must disclose the identity of their experts and must, if the expert is retained for the purpose of providing expert testimony, also provide a written report containing a "complete statement" of all opinions to be expressed as well as the "basis and reasons therefor." Alaska Rule of Civil Procedure (RCP) 26(a)(2). Although sanctions are authorized for violations of this provision, the Alaska Supreme Court held that an expert's testimony should not be excluded if there is a lesser meaningful sanction available. *Maines v. Kenmorth Trucking Co.*, 155 P.3d 318, 326 (Alaska 2007); *cf. Harris v. State*, 195 P.3d 161, 180 (Alaska Ct. App. 2008) (distinguishing the propriety of a lesser sanction in *Maines* because "'more than two months remained until the scheduled trial date' and thus 'ample time [sic] remained to cure any problems [caused by the discovery violation.]'") (quoting *Maines*, 155 P.3d at 326).

An expert's report must also contain the data or other information on which the expert's opinion is based, any exhibits the expert may use as a summary of or support for her opinions, and the expert's qualifications—including a list of publications authored by the expert in the preceding ten years. RCP 26(a)(2)(B). In addition, a statement of the compensation paid to the witness and a listing of all cases in which the expert has testified at trial in the preceding four years are required. *Id.* In some cases, experts may be required to provide their tax returns if relevant to show potential bias. *See Noffke v. Perez*, 178 P.3d 1141, 1149–52 (Alaska 2008) (rejecting the plaintiff's argument that such a requirement would have a chilling effect on expert witnesses).

The discovery requirements under Rule 26(a)(2)(B) do not apply to experts who testify as a party's treating physician due to their unique role. *See Thompson*, Nos. S-14142, S-14162 (Alaska Sept. 28, 2012). "'Retained experts are presumed to be under the control of the party retaining them and are thus presumed to be cooperative,' but no such presumption is justified regarding a treating physician, whose testimony is based on experience attending to the patient rather than being hired to review a file and develop an opinion." *Id.* (quoting *Fletcher v. S. Peninsula Hosp.*, 71 P.3d 833, 845 n.59 (Alaska 2003).

The Alaska legislature has passed several laws that provide special expert admissibility rules for particular subject matters. For instance, in an action based on professional negligence, Alaska law bars expert testimony on an appropriate standard of care unless the expert meets a list of qualifications. *See* RCP, Chapter 20, Article 2. The expert must be a "professional" who is licensed in Alaska or in another state or country, trained and experienced in the same discipline or school of practice as the defendant or in an area directly related to the particular field or matter at issue, and certified by a board recognized in Alaska as having expertise and training directly related to the matter at issue. *Id; see also Ayuluk v. Red Oaks Assisted Living, Inc.*, 201 P.3d 1183, 1192 (Alaska 2009) (holding that the challenged expert met these criteria because she was a registered nurse for almost forty years and served on the Alaska Board of Nursing).

Similarly, a provision of the Alaska Rules of Criminal Procedure (ARCP) governs admissibility of expert testimony relating to criminal street gang activity, providing that expert testimony is admissible to show common characteristics of persons who are gang members, rivalries between gangs, and gang practices and customs, among other matters. *See* ARCP, Chapter 45, Article 2. Finally, Alaska law also provides for special "expert advisory panels" in health care malpractice actions. RCP 72.1. Either party in such an action may request that the court appoint a three-person expert advisory panel to conduct an investigation of the claim at issue and render an opinion. *Id.*

2. *Expert Evidence in Arizona State Courts*

a. *Daubert* Now Sets the Standard for Admissibility of Scientific Evidence

The Arizona Supreme Court recently reversed the Arizona courts' longstanding refusal to adopt the *Daubert* standard by amending the Arizona Rules of Evidence (ARE) to mirror the federal rule. The new ARE 702, which took effect on January 1, 2012, provides:

A witness who is qualified as an expert by knowledge, skill, experience, training, or education may testify in the form of an opinion or otherwise if:

(a) the expert's scientific, technical, or other specialized knowledge will help the trier of fact to understand the evidence or to determine a fact in issue;
(b) the testimony is based on sufficient facts or data;
(c) the testimony is the product of reliable principles and methods; and
(d) the expert has reliably applied the principles and methods to the facts of the case.

The comment to the 2012 amendment of Arizona's rule, which was derived in part from the Advisory Committee Notes to the federal Rule 702, echoes the *Daubert* standard by "recogniz[ing] that trial courts should serve as gatekeepers in assuring that proposed expert testimony is reliable and thus helpful to the jury's determination of facts at issue." ARE 2012, cmt. to 2012 Amend. Arizona's new Rule 702 is intended to be "broad enough to permit testimony that is the product of competing principles or methods in the same field of expertise." *Id.* "Where there is contradictory, but reliable, expert testimony, it is the province of the jury to determine the weight and credibility of the testimony." *Id.*

So far, an unreported decision by the Court of Appeals was the only Arizona decision to have applied the newly amended ARE 702. *State v. Burke*, 2012 WL 1470103 (Ariz. App. Div. 1, April 26, 2012.) In *Burke*, the defendant had been convicted in 2010 of several offenses involving sexual conduct with a minor. 2010 WL 1470103 at *1. In August of 2011, the Arizona Court of Appeals overturned those convictions. *Id.* The 2012 amendments to ARE 702 took effect prior to the defendant's retrial, and the state brought a motion in limine based on Daubert to exclude the testimony of defendant's expert, Dr. Phillip Esplin. *Id.* Dr. Esplin, a licensed psychologist who specialized in forensic psychology and interview techniques for and investigation of child sex crimes, proposed to testify about "false memory syndrome." *Id.*

The defendant "made no attempt to explain the admissibility of Dr. Esplin's testimony under the substantially revised Arizona Rule of Evidence 702 now in effect." *Id.* at *1. The trial court held a hearing and "ultimately ruled that Dr. Esplin would be able to testify as an expert and that his testimony could include testimony about 'false memory'," although the trial court did identify a series of questions and answers from Dr. Esplin's testimony in the defendant's first trial that "impinged on the jury's role in determining credibility." *Id.* The state brought a special action before the Court of Appeals, which agreed to review the trial court's decision because "this is an issue of first impression and statewide importance." *Id.* at *2.

The Court of Appeals began its opinion with a discussion of the 2012 amendments to ARE 702, which marked "a notable departure from Arizona's former test of admissibility of expert testimony that was detailed in *Logerquist v. McVey*, 196 Ariz. 470, 1 P.3d 113 (2000)." *Burke*, 2012 WL 1470103 at *2. The former Arizona test under *Logerquist* was "a very low threshold for the admissibility of scientific evidence" based on the *Frye* standard. *Id.* at *2 n.2. The Court of Appeals in Burke expressly looked to federal case law for guidance applying the new ARE 702. *Id.*; *see also* 17A A.R.S. Rules of Evid., Prefatory Comment (2012) ("Where the language of an Arizona rule parallels that of a federal rule, federal court decisions interpreting the federal rule are persuasive but not binding with respect to interpreting the Arizona rule.").

Relying on the United States Supreme Court's decision in *Kumho*, the Arizona Court of Appeals held that, "when considering the admissibility of expert testimony, the trial judge has the discretion both to avoid unnecessary reliability proceedings in ordinary cases where the reliability of an expert's methods is properly taken for granted, and to require appropriate proceedings in the less usual or more complex cases where cause for questioning the expert's reliability arises." *Burke*, 2012 WL 1470103 at *2 (internal quotations omitted). Failing to hold a hearing on reliability constitutes an abuse of that discretion "when the evidentiary record is insufficient to allow the court to make a proper reliability determination under Rule 702." *Id.*

The Court of Appeals concluded that the trial court should have held such a hearing before making a determination on the admissibility of Dr. Esplin's expert testimony regarding "false memory syndrome." *Id.* at *2. The trial court failed to do so, although it "did review the testimony from the first trial, and may have [had] some personal recollection of the general methodologies used by Dr. Esplin." *Id.* The Court of Appeals held that the record before the trial court "was insufficient to permit it to make a legally adequate determination that Dr. Esplin's testimony was admissible." *Id.* at *3. "The trial court therefore abused its discretion by failing to perform its gatekeeping role as required by [new] Rule 702." *Id.*

Prior to the 2012 amendment to ARE 702, a line of Arizona decisions had set forth limits to the *Frye* standard, confining it to only cases involving "novel" scientific theories. *See State v. Lucero*, 207 Ariz. 301, 85 P.3d 1059 (2004) (holding that a party challenging a scientific method must show that either the challenged evidence was "a novel scientific method or was a formerly accepted method newly fallen into disrepute in the scientific community"); *Logerquist*, 196 Ariz. at 486, 1 P.3d at 129; *see also State ex. rel Romley v. Fields*, 201 Ariz. 321, 35 P.3d 82 (Ct. App. 2001) (holding that actuarial models in hearings under the Sexually Violent Persons Act are not "novel scientific evidence or process[es]" under *Frye*). Although no Arizona decision has yet addressed these types of cases, their precedential value remains to be seen in light of the 2012 amendments to the ARE that encourage Arizona courts to look to *Daubert* and federal decisions applying it.

The 2012 amendments to the Arizona Rules of Evidence also included a change to conform ARE 704 to the federal Rule 704 regarding opinions on an ultimate issue. Prior to 2012, ARE 704 did not include Subsection (b) found in the federal Rule 704, which states, "In a criminal case, an expert witness must not state an opinion about whether the defendant did or did not have a mental state or condition that constitutes an element of the crime charged or of a defense. Those matters are for the trier of fact alone." Subsection (b) was added to the Arizona rule in 2012, although the comments to the 2012 amendments stated, "The new language in the Arizona rule is considered to be consistent with current Arizona law." ARE 704, cmt. to 2012 Amend.

The 2012 amendments to the ARE made additional changes regarding experts, but these changes were simply to conform to the federal restyling of the Rules of Evidence. The comments to each revised Arizona rule made clear that there was no intent to change any result in any ruling on admissibility.

b. Expert-Related Rules and Procedural Issues in Arizona State Courts

When a party in a civil case anticipates calling an expert witness, the Arizona Rules of Civil Procedure (ARCP) require the party to disclose the name and address of that witness, as well as "the subject matter on which the expert is expected to testify, the substance of the facts and opinions to which the expert is expected to testify, a summary of the grounds for each opinion, the qualifications of the witness and the name and address of the custodian of copies of any reports prepared by the expert" within forty days after a responsive pleading is filed. ARCP 26.1(a)(6), (b)(1). Arizona law does not require the expert to prepare and sign a report, as required by the Federal Rules, nor does it require the expert to disclose publications within the last ten years or a list of other cases in which the expert has testified. As the comments to the ARCP make clear, the Arizona rules committee originally considered requiring disclosure of all cases in which an expert had testified within the prior five years. ARCP 26.1(a), Cmte. Cmt. to 1991 Amend. While recognizing that this type of information might be important "in certain types of litigation," "[o]n balance, it was decided that it would be burdensome to require this information in all cases." *Id.*

In medical malpractice claims, Arizona law historically has not required the expert testifying as to the proper duty of care to be of the same specialty as the defendant. The expert may base his testimony on "education, experience, observation, or association with that specialty." *Taylor v. Di Rico*, 124 Ariz. 513, 518, 606 P.2d 3, 8. (1980). Similarly, the Arizona Court of Appeals has held that an expert need only have "some knowledge or experience" regarding the issue at hand, and that an expert does not need to be a medical doctor in order to testify about physical injuries. *See Lohmeier v. Hammer*, 148 P.3d 101, 108 (Ariz. Ct. App. 2006). Following the 2012 amendments to ARE 702, however, such rules may only apply to the extent the proponent of the expert testimony can establish that it satisfies *Daubert. See State v. Burke*, 2012 WL 1470103 (Ariz. App. Div. 1, April 26, 2012.)

3. *Expert Evidence in California State Courts*

a. Evidentiary Standards

The California Supreme Court recently held that California Evidence Code section 801(b) permits expert testimony only if the expert "provide[s] a reasonable basis for the particular opinion offered" and the opinion is not "based on speculation or conjecture." *Sargon Enters., Inc. v. Univ. of S. Cal.*, No. S191550, 2012 WL 5897314, at *14 (Sup. Ct. Cal. Nov. 26, 2012) ("*Sargon*") (pending publication); *see also Lockheed Litigation Cases*, 115 Cal. App. 4th 558, 561 (2004) (expert opinion must "be based on matter that provides a reasonable basis for the opinion"); *Miranda v. Bomel Const. Co., Inc.*, 187 Cal. App. 4th 1326, 1342 (2010) (citing Cal. Evid. Rule 801(b)) (applying a reasonable basis standard for medical expert testimony).

In *Sargon*, the plaintiff sued for breach of contract, alleging that the defendant mishandled clinical trials for new dental implants. *Sargon*, 2012 WL 5897314, at *1. An expert witness testified that the botched trials cost the plaintiff upwards of over a billion dollars in potential lost profit. *Id.* However, the expert's lost profit prediction depended on the plaintiff capturing a significant share of the dental implant industry. *Id.* at *2. The California Supreme Court determined that the expert's opinion was unfounded because it was "unduly speculative" to assume the plaintiff would obtain sufficient market space to justify the expert's prediction. *Id.* at *1. The court excluded the expert's testimony, noting that trial court judges have a strong "gatekeeper" role in determining the admission of expert evidence. *Id.*

The California Supreme Court in *Sargon* also noted that California Evidence Code section 802 allows courts to inquire into the reasons behind an expert's opinion. *Id.* at *15. Thus, under both rules, "trial courts act as a gatekeeper to exclude expert opinion testimony that is (1) based on matter of a type on which an expert may not reasonably rely, (2) based on reasons unsupported by the material on which the expert relies, or (3) speculative." *Id.*

California courts, as *Sargon* reaffirmed, apply a different test for expert opinions regarding "new" scientific techniques. *Id.* at n.6 ("Nothing we say in this case affects our holding in *Leahy* regarding new scientific techniques."). The court's citation to *Leahy* referred to the 1994 decision where the California Supreme Court rejected *Daubert* and reaffirmed the use of what was then known as the "*Kelly/Frye*" test. *See People v. Leahy*, 8 Cal. 4th 587, 882 P.2d 321 (1994).[6] In *Leahy*, the defendant was convicted of driving under the influence of alcohol. At trial, a police officer testified that he administered a horizontal gaze nystagmus (HGN) field sobriety test to the defendant and described the results. The California Supreme Court affirmed the Court of Appeal's reversal of the conviction and remanded for a determination as to whether the HGN test had achieved "general acceptance" in the scientific community, *i.e.*, whether it met the *Kelly/Frye* standard. *Id.* at 591–92, 882 P.2d at 665.

(1) Expert Evidence Must Be Both "New" and "Scientific" for Kelly/Frye to Apply.

In *Leahy*, the California Supreme Court held that *Kelly/Frye* applied to "new scientific techniques." *Leahy*, 8 Cal. 4th at 605, 882 P.2d at 332. Although the HGN technique for determining sobriety had been used by police for more than thirty years, the court held that it was nevertheless "new" for purposes of determining admissibility. *Id.,* 882 P.2d at 332. The court stated, "[i]n determining whether a scientific technique is 'new' for *Kelly* purposes, long-standing use by police officers seems less significant a factor than repeated use, study, testing and confirmation by scientists or trained technicians." *Id.* at 605, 882 P.2d at 332.

A technique is "scientific" if "the unproven technique or procedure appears in both name and description to provide some definitive truth which the expert need only accurately recognize and relay to the jury." *Id.*, 882 P. 2d at 333. This "common sense" approach serves the purpose of protecting the jury from new or experimental techniques which convey a misleading aura of certainty and obscure the technique's experimental nature. *People v. Stoll*, 49 Cal. 3d 1136, 1155–56 (1989). The HGN test's "pretentiously scientific name," the technical nomenclature surrounding it, and the "aura of certainty" created by an officer's description all indicated to the *Leahy* court that it was scientific in nature and therefore subject to *Kelly/Frye*. *Leahy*, 8 Cal. 4th at 606–07, 882 P.2d at 333; *see also People v. Mitchell*, 110 Cal. App. 4th 772, 793, 2 Cal. Rptr. 3d 49, 66 (2003) (finding that utilizing dogs trained in scent identification to identify the defendant's scent on other evidence was analogous to a machine that could calibrate and read physical evidence, and was therefore scientific); *cf. People v. Eubanks*, 53 Cal. 4th 110, 141 (2011) (finding that *Kelly* did not apply to testimony regarding the analysis of alcohol and drug levels in blood, since the practice was so well known in science and the law that no reasonable juror would give the testimony unquestioned deference).

---

[6] With the United States Supreme Court's repudiation of *Frye*, the test in California is now known commonly by the name of the state case, *People v. Kelly*, 17 Cal. 3d 24, 549 P.2d 1240 (1976), which stands for the identical doctrine. *See Leahy*, 8 Cal. 4th at 612, 882 P.2d at 337.

On the other hand, combining existing, accepted techniques does not trigger *Kelly/Frye* when neither technique is so foreign to everyday experience that they are difficult for a layperson to understand. *People v. Cowan*, 50 Cal. 4th 401, 113 Cal. Rptr. 3d 850, 236 P. 3d 1074 (2010). In *Cowan*, an expert combined two existing techniques—ballistics comparisons and identifying tool marks using elastic molds—to compare a pistol barrel with several bullets fired during the crime. *Id.* Because the combination of these two techniques was not beyond the common understanding of a lay juror, the combination was not new to science and *Kelly/Frye* did not apply. *Id.* at 470–71.

Further, California appellate courts have explained that *Kelly/Frye* applies not only to new scientific "techniques," but also "to new methodologies." *People v. Nolan*, 95 Cal. App. 4th 1210, 1215, 116 Cal. Rptr. 2d 331, 334 (Ct. App. 2002). The *Kelly/Frye* standard therefore only allows admission of expert evidence based on a new application of a scientific technique or methodology if the new application's reliability has been foundationally established, it is demonstrated that correct scientific procedures were used, and the new scientific technique is shown to have general acceptance in its field. *People v. McWhorter*, 47 Cal. 4th 318, 364, 97 Cal. Rptr. 3d 412, 451 (2009).

On the other hand, if the new method is merely a variation in an established technique, rather than a separate, distinct and new scientific technique, then the *Kelly/Frye* analysis is unnecessary. *People v. Cook*, 40 Cal. 4th 1334, 1345 (2007). Consequently, new devices or mechanisms created to implement established scientific methods—such as a new breathalyzer device or urinalysis testing device—are not considered distinct and new methodologies or techniques, and are therefore not subject to a *Kelly/Frye* hearing. *People v. Nolan*, 95 Cal. App. 4th 1210, 1215, 116 Cal. Rptr. 2d 331, 334 (Ct. App. 2002); *cf. People v. Henderson*, 107 Cal. App. 4th 769, 781, 132 Cal. Rptr. 2d 255 (Ct. App. 2003) (holding that a new method of DNA testing, capillary electrophoresis, was not simply a different test for performing the same procedure as the previous gel electrophoresis, but rather was a distinct and new scientific technique that required a determination of general acceptance under *Kelly/Frye*).

Improvements to existing methodologies are also not considered new scientific techniques for purposes of a *Kelly/Frye* hearing. *People v. Jackson*, 163 Cal. App. 4th 313, 325, 77 Cal. Rptr. 3d 474, 482 (2008). In *Jackson*, the defendant appealed the admission of DNA evidence procured by a new testing kit that had not been subjected to the *Kelly/Frye* analysis. *Id.* at 324, 77 Cal. Rptr. 3d at 481. Even though several changes were made in the new kit, the court affirmed the admission of the evidence because it was not shown that these changes affect the scientifically accepted methodology of the DNA testing, or that a materially distinct technique was used. *Id.* at 325, 77 Cal. Rptr. 3d at 482. Because the changes made to the kit seemingly improved the test's accuracy and efficiency, it was determined to be a "new and improved" version of a generally accepted methodology, and therefore a separate *Kelly/Frye* hearing was unnecessary. *Id.*

The *Kelly/Frye* standard requires the proponent of the expert evidence to establish a foundation of the reliability of the new application or method. *McWhorter*, 47 Cal. 4th at 364, 97 Cal. Rptr. 3d at 451. In *McWhorter*, the California Supreme Court determined that forensic image enhancements of photographs performed by an expert in the field of electronic processing of visual and audio recorded data were subject to the *Kelly* test. *Id.* at 364–367, 97 Cal. Rptr. 3d at 450–453. The forensic image enhancement expert could not demonstrate the reliability of the new technique of using a computer program to "emboss" a crime scene photo because the expert could neither identify the program that he had used to emboss the photo nor explain how the program's "emboss" function worked. *Id.* Without this foundation of reliability, the evidence was inadmissible. *Id.* at 367, 97 Cal. Rptr 3d at 453.

When the reliability of the scientific evidence is apparent to the lay juror, however, no *Kelly/Frye* analysis is necessary. If the procedure merely isolates physical evidence whose existence, appearance, nature, and meaning are obvious to a layperson, then the reliability of the process and its subsequent result is not subject to the *Kelly/Frye* standard for admissibility. *People v. Farnam*, 28 Cal. 4th 107, 160 (2002). In *Farnam*, the reliability of a computerized system comparing latent prints to fingerprints in the computer's database was apparent at trial. Because the jury could make its own comparisons between the latent prints found at the crime scene and the defendant's fingerprints, the scientific evidence and accompanying expert testimony did not implicate *Kelly/Frye. Id.* In these circumstances, jurors are permitted to use their own common sense and judgment in evaluating the weight of the evidence, without relying on expert testimony interpreting the evidence. *Id. See also People v. DePriest*, 42 Cal. 4th 1, 39–40 (2007) ("[S]hoe print evidence [does] not implicate the concerns underlying the *Kelly* rule" because "[j]urors could judge for themselves whether the sole patterns on these items looked the same."); *People v. Hoyos*, 41 Cal. 4th 872, 911, 63 Cal. Rptr. 3d 1, 36 (2007) ("[B]lood spatter testing does not require *Kelly* scrutiny.").

In *Leahy*, the California Supreme Court also clarified the meaning of "general acceptance" under *Kelly*, holding that it equates to a consensus drawn from a typical cross-section of the relevant, qualified scientific community. *Leahy*, 8 Cal. 4th at 587, 882 P.2d at 337. As a result, in evaluating whether a scientific technique meets the "general acceptance" standard, California courts consider the quality, as well as the quantity, of the scientific literature and opinion supporting or opposing the technique. A simple "numerical majority" of expert opinion regarding the technique is insufficient. *Id.* at 611, 882 P.2d at 336. This assures that those most qualified to assess the overall validity of a scientific method will have the determinative voice in its admissibility. *People v. Superior Court (Vidal)*, 40 Cal. 4th 999, 1014, 56 Cal. Rptr. 3d 851, 859 (2007) (citing *Kelly*, 17 Cal. 3d at 31).

Several California appellate decisions have addressed the question of evaluating "general acceptance." In *Ramona v. Superior Court*, 57 Cal. App. 4th 107, 66 Cal. Rptr. 2d 766 (Ct. App. 1997), an alleged victim of childhood sexual abuse brought suit against her father, relying on "repressed memories" retrieved through the aid of psychotherapy and use of the drug sodium amytal. Expressing its disbelief in the general acceptance of a "truth serum," the Court of Appeal directed the trial court to grant summary judgment, as well as costs, to the defendant. *Id.* at 121, 66 Cal. Rptr. 2d at 777.

In *People v. Allen*, 72 Cal. App. 4th 1093, Cal. Rptr. 2d 655 (Ct. App. 1999), the Court of Appeal reaffirmed that California courts may look to out-of-state cases in order to determine whether expert evidence has achieved general acceptance in the scientific community. The court noted that it has "sometimes looked beyond the trial record, examining California precedent, cases from other jurisdictions, and the scientific literature itself, to ascertain whether a particular technique is generally accepted." *Id.* at 1099, 85 Cal. Rptr. 2d at 659 (quoting *People v. Brown*, 40 Cal. 3d 512, 530, 726 P.2d 516, 523 (1985)). *See also Leahy*, 8 Cal. 4th at 606, 882 P.2d at 332 (using the number of legal challenges to the HGN test in other states as evidence that use of the test was not "settled in law").

Determining the existence of a "clear majority" is not always easy. In *People v. Reeves*, 91 Cal. App. 4th 14, 109 Cal. Rptr. 2d 728 (Ct. App. 2001), the Court of Appeal explained that that one expert's "lone dissent is not sufficient to generate a controversy where the remainder of the scientific community has reached consensus." *Id.* at 41, 109 Cal. Rptr. 2d at 748–49. Because it is impractical "to require that the views of a cross-section of the relevant scientific community be presented personally by each scientist testifying in open court," scientists have long been permitted to speak to the courts through their published writings in scholarly treatises and journals. *San Diego County Health & Human Servs. Agency v. Carlos R.*, 205 Cal. App. 4th 111, 123, 140 Cal. Rptr. 3d 222, 233 (Ct. App. 2012). In addition, the court may receive further testimony from disinterested and qualified experts on the issue of the technique's general acceptance in the pertinent scientific community. *Id.* An expert witness may not qualify as disinterested, however, if they are the technique's leading proponent or there is a vested career or promotional interest. *Id. See also People v. Brown* (1985) 40 Cal. 3d 512, 533 (1985) ("Testimony by a self-serving expert witness (e.g., the creator of the new test) may be insufficient to establish general acceptance within the scientific community.").

In *Carlos R.*, the Court of Appeal held that a court may rely on scientific literature alone in determining that there exists no generally accepted scientific consensus about the reliability of a technique (in *Carlos R.*, a polygraph examination). 205 Cal. App. 4th at 121, 140 Cal. Rptr. 3d at 232 (2012). While acknowledging that it may be preferable for a court to hear from disinterested experts before deciding the admissibility of scientific evidence, relying solely on scientific literature is acceptable where there is little doubt about continuing controversy in the relevant scientific community. *Id. See also Leahy*, 8 Cal. 4th at 611 ("If a fair overview of the literature discloses there is significant public opposition to the technique as unreliable, the court may rely on the literature alone to conclude there is no general consensus at the present time.") (quoting *People v. Shirley*, 31 Cal. 3d 18, 56 (1982)).

Also, in *People v. Nelson*, 43 Cal. 4th 1242, 1263 (2008), the California Supreme Court rejected the argument that the general acceptance analysis involves determining the "best" technique or methodology available. The question is whether a significant number of scientists publicly oppose a technique as unreliable not whether some scientists believe that an alternative or better technique may be available. *Id.*

Finally, California courts have clarified that *Kelly/Frye* tests only the *validity* of new scientific techniques or methodologies, not the way in which they are applied. In *O'Neill v. Novartis Consumer Health, Inc.*, 147 Cal. App. 4th 1388, 55 Cal. Rptr. 3d 551 (Ct. App. 2007), the plaintiffs argued that the pharmaceutical ingredient PAP caused several strokes. They cited the Yale Study, an epidemiological study about the effects of PAP, to support their position. The defendants presented two experts who testified that several of the cases in the Yale Study were misclassified, and that this impacted the results. The plaintiffs argued that this evidence did not meet the admissibility requirements of *Kelly/Frye*. The Court of Appeal, however, held that the defendant's experts' testimony was properly admitted, because the "evidence that some cases . . . were misclassified was not based on new scientific methodology; it was a challenge to the professionalism with which the methodology was applied." *Id.* at 1398, 55 Cal. Rptr. 3d at 560. *See also People v. Cua*, 191 Cal. App. 4th 582, 591, 119 Cal. Rptr. 3d 391, 399 (2011) ("In general, criticisms about the quality of [scientific] testing go to the weight of the evidence.").

A California appellate court's determination that a *Kelly/Frye* analysis is necessary for a certain technique or methodology is not static and "do[es] not stand for the proposition that certain techniques or procedures are subject to *Kelly's* foundational requirements whenever they arise, forevermore." *People v. Johnson*, 139 Cal. App. 4th 1135, 1149, 43 Cal. Rptr. 3d 587, 595 (Ct. App. 2006). Once a published appellate decision has *affirmed* admission of a scientific technique, however, then that technique's general acceptance is considered established. *People v. Doolin*, 45 Cal. 4th 390, 447 (2009). Unless new evidence is presented that demonstrates a change in the attitude or consensus of the scientific community, further *Kelly/Frye* hearings on the technique's general acceptance are unnecessary. *Id.*

(2) Admissibility of Medical Opinion Testimony

As noted above, California courts distinguish between medical opinion testimony and novel scientific techniques or methodologies. Medical opinion testimony, such as an opinion on a diagnosis or causation of an injury, is typically not subject to the *Kelly/Frye* test. *See Roberti v. Andy's Termite Pest Control, Inc.*, 113 Cal. App. 4th 893, 902–04, 6 Cal. Rptr. 3d 827, 832–34 (Ct. App. 2003) (stating that the court has "never applied the *Kelly-Frye* rule to expert medical testimony" because "a medical expert witness draws from accepted methods of scientific research" and does not use a new scientific technique).

Expert medical testimony, however, is still subject to an admissibility analysis. As a threshold matter, California courts may evaluate medical opinion testimony under tests familiar to all jurisdictions. In California, as elsewhere, questions of "the admissibility of evidence . . . [is] to be decided by the court." Cal. Evid. Code § 310(a). "The court in its discretion may exclude evidence if its probative value is substantially outweighed by the probability that its admission will . . . create substantial danger of undue prejudice, of confusing the issues, or of misleading the jury." *Id.* § 352.

The California Evidence Code also provides guidance for evaluating *expert* testimony in particular. An expert offering medical opinion testimony must be qualified as an expert. *See* Cal. Evid. Code § 720(a) ("A person is qualified to testify as an expert if he has special knowledge, skill, experience, training, or education sufficient to qualify him as an expert on the subject to which his testimony relates."). However, "even when [a] witness qualifies as an expert, he or she does not possess a carte blanche to express any opinion within the area of expertise." *Jennings v. Palomar Pomerado Health Systems, Inc.*, 114 Cal. App. 4th 1108, 1117, 8 Cal. Rptr. 3d 363, 368 (Ct. App. 2003). Specifically, under Section 801 of the California Evidence Code:

> If a witness is testifying as an expert, his testimony in the form of an opinion is limited to such an opinion as is . . . [b]ased on matter . . . that is of a type that reasonably may be relied upon by an expert in forming an opinion upon the subject to which his testimony relates.

Id. § 801(b).

As noted, California courts have interpreted Evidence Code section 801(b) to mean that "the matter relied on must provide a reasonable basis for the particular opinion offered, and that an expert opinion based on speculation or conjecture is inadmissible." *Sargon*, 2012 WL 5897314, at *14 (pending publication); *see also Lockheed Litigation Cases*, 115 Cal. App. 4th 558, 561, 10 Cal. Rptr. 3d 34, 35 (Ct. App. 2004) (affirming the exclusion of plaintiffs' experts evidence because the epidemiological evidence on which the expert purported to rely "provided no reasonable basis for the opinion that Plaintiffs' alleged exposure to chemicals . . . resulted in an increased risk of cancer"); *Dee v. PCS Prop. Mgmt., Inc.*, 174 Cal. App. 4th 390, 405, 94 Cal. Rptr. 3d 456, 466 (2009) (affirming the exclusion of expert testimony that plaintiff's illness was caused by exposure to mycotoxins when no evidence was offered that the plaintiff actually was exposed to mycotoxins, and the expert testimony based on speculation and conjecture "relied on an incorrect premise, and thus . . . lacked evidentiary value.").

California courts have also stressed the requirement that medical expert testimony be based on a "reasonable degree of medical certainty." In *Ochoa v. Pacific Gas and Electric Co.*, 61 Cal. App. 4th 1480, 72 Cal. Rptr. 2d 232 (Ct. App. 1998), the plaintiff alleged that the defendant's failure to discover a gas leak in the plaintiff's house caused or exacerbated several physical ailments. The Court of Appeal held that the trial court properly excluded the plaintiff's expert's testimony because his opinion was founded primarily on the fact that he did not know of any other possible cause for the plaintiff's symptoms. *See id.* at 1487, 72 Cal. Rptr. 2d at 236. The expert's opinion that "some unspecified gas is 'probably' the culprit for the increase in the severity of [the plaintiff's] respiratory problems" did not meet the requirement that an expert opinion be delivered with a "reasonable degree of medical certainty."[7] *Id.*

---

[7] Also instructive on this point is *Cottle v. Superiors Court*, 3 Cal. App. 4th 1367, 5 Cal. Rptr. 2d 882 (Ct. App. 1992). In this toxic tort action, plaintiffs challenged the trial court's exclusion of evidence of personal injuries. The California Court of Appeal held that the trial court had inherent power to exclude doctors' testimony that four plaintiffs suffered from various disabilities as a result of exposure to hazardous waste buried beneath their homes because the expert evidence failed to establish that plaintiffs' claims were founded on a reasonable medical probability. One doctor's "statements that similar problems 'have been associated with,' 'could be directly related to effects of,' 'may occur in children as a result of,' and 'may be related to' exposure do not establish causation to a degree of reasonable

Thus, to ensure that expert testimony is well founded, and not likely to mislead a jury, California courts "may, and upon objection *shall*, exclude testimony in the form of an opinion that is based in whole or in significant part on matter that is not a proper basis for such an opinion." Cal. Evid. Code § 803 (emphasis added). For example, an expert may not base an opinion on guess, surmise, conjecture, or assumptions of fact that do not have evidentiary support. In *Jennings*, for example, a doctor testified that bacteria growing around a retractor had caused the plaintiff's infection. The court found, however, that the doctor's conclusion was grounded in assumptions and speculation on exactly how this could have happened. See *Jennings*, 114 Cal. App. 4th at 1118, 85 Cal. Rptr. 3d at 369–70. The court explained that experts may not give conclusory opinions without explanation: "An expert's conclusory opinion that something did occur, when unaccompanied by a reasoned explanation . . . does not assist the jury to determine what occurred, but instead supplants the jury by declaring what occurred." *Id.* Thus, the *Jennings* court concluded that the plaintiff's expert's "opinion [was] too conclusory to support a jury verdict on causation." *Id.* at 1120, 85 Cal. Rptr. 3d at 371. *See also People v. Richardson*, 43 Cal. 4th 959, 1008 (2008) (affirming the exclusion of an expert's testimony regarding the time the crime occurred based on the detective's estimate of the water level in a bathtub the next day, as reliance on estimates with so many variables and uncertainties lacks evidentiary support).

A number of California courts have come to similar conclusions. *See, e.g., Cole v. Town of Los Gatos*, 205 Cal. App. 4th 749, 766, 140 Cal. Rptr. 3d 722, 737 (Ct. App. 2012), *review denied* (July 11, 2012), *reh'g denied* (May 24, 2012) ("Assertions of matter outside [the expert]'s personal knowledge, [that] took the form of absolute assertions of fact . . . were indeed [inadmissible], if only to ensure that they were not inadvertently allowed to become proof of the stated facts."); *Bozzi v. Nordstrom, Inc.*, 186 Cal. App. 4th 755, 762 (Ct. App. 2010) ("[The expert] relied on nothing more than syllogistic reasoning to conclude that if an escalator stops abruptly, it must have been defectively designed or maintained."); *Garibay v. Hemmat*, 161 Cal. App. 4th 735, 743, 74 Cal. Rptr. 3d 715, 721 (Ct. App. 2008) ("[The expert] had no personal knowledge of the underlying facts of the case, and attempted to testify to facts derived from medical and hospital records which were not properly before the court . . . [t]herefore his declaration of alleged facts had no evidentiary foundation."); *Andrews v. Foster Wheeler LLC*, 138 Cal. App. 4th 96,108, 41 Cal. Rptr. 3d 229, 239 (Ct. App. 2006) ("[A]n expert's opinion rendered without a reasoned explanation of why the underlying facts lead to the ultimate conclusion has no evidentiary value because an expert opinion is worth no more than the reasons and facts on which it is based.").

In addition to a relevant foundation for the expert's opinions, expert testimony must be "[r]elated to a subject that is sufficiently beyond common experience that the opinion of an expert would assist the trier of fact." Cal Evid. Code § 801(a). Because the purpose of expert testimony is to provide an opinion beyond the common experience, the expert witness must possess uncommon, specialized knowledge outside that of the lay juror. *People v. Chapple* 138 Cal. App. 4th 540, 547 (2006).

---

medical probability." *Id.* at 1387, 5 Cal. Rptr. 2d at 894. Rather than such inconclusive language, specific statements that "tie the [plaintiffs' physical] changes to the chemicals [under their homes) as separate from other chemicals in the environment" were required. *Id.* at 1386, 5 Cal. Rptr. 2d at 893. *See also Saelzler v. Advanced Group*, 400, 25 Cal. 4th 763, 23 P. 3d 1143 (2001) (reversing the California Court of Appeal and granting summary judgment because the expert's opinions were not based on reliable evidence and were "simply too tenuous" to raise a triable issue of fact); *Merrill v. Navegar, Inc.*, 26 Cal. 4th 465, 490, 28 P. 3d 116, 132 (2001) (reversing the California Court of Appeal and granting summary judgment where plaintiff's evidence of causation amounted to "little more than guesswork," reasoning that "it is insufficient" when plaintiff's evidence "leaves the question of causation in the realm of mere speculation and conjecture") (quotation marks and citation omitted).

This is not a difficult standard to achieve, however, as expert opinion testimony is excluded only when it would add "nothing at all" to the jury's common fund of information, and a reasonable juror could reach a conclusion just as intelligently as the witness. *People v. Jones*, 54 Cal. 4th 1, 43, 140 Cal. Rptr. 3d 383, 434 (2012) (internal citation omitted). Also, to the extent that the testimony is a mere legal conclusion, then it does not require the opinion of an expert to assist the trier of fact, and therefore is not admissible evidence. *People v. Baker*, 204 Cal. App. 4th 1234, 1245, 139 Cal. Rptr. 3d 594, 603–04 (2012) (expert testimony that the arson in question posed a substantial danger of physical harm to others was a legal conclusion and therefore not a question the expert was competent to answer).

b. Constitutional Issues

In *People v. Geier*, 41 Cal. 4th 555, 161 P. 3d 104 (2007), the California Supreme Court addressed, for the first time, the constitutionality of expert testimony based on scientific evidence produced by someone other than the testifying expert. In *Geier*, the defendant was accused of multiple murders and forcible rape. The prosecution's DNA expert testified that DNA recovered from a victim matched the defendant's DNA. The defendant argued that the expert's testimony violated his Sixth Amendment confrontation right because it was based on testing that the expert did not personally conduct. *Id.* at 593–94.

Generally, out-of-court statements offered against a criminal defendant are inadmissible under the confrontation clause unless the witness is unavailable and the defendant had a prior opportunity to cross-examine the witness. This applies only to "testimonial evidence," however. *Id.* at 598 (citing *Crawford v. Washington*, 541 U.S. 36 (2004)). Testimonial evidence has been defined as statements recounting past events, "the primary purpose of [which] is to establish or prove past events potentially relevant to later criminal prosecution." *Id.* at 603–04 (citing *Davis v. Washington*, 547 U.S. 813, 126 S. Ct. 2266, 2273–74 (2006)).

After discussing many other state and circuit court decisions that differed in their conclusions regarding whether scientific evidence constitutes testimonial evidence, the *Geier* court concluded that scientific evidence such as a DNA report does *not* constitute testimonial evidence. The court explained that, despite the fact that a DNA report could reasonably be anticipated to be used at a later criminal trial, the DNA analyst's observations "constitute a contemporaneous recordation of observable events rather than the documentation of past events." *Id.* at 605.[8] The court cited to decisions concluding that scientific evidence in routine forensic reports did not constitute testimonial evidence. *Id.* at 599–602. The court further noted that DNA analysts analyze samples not to generate incriminating evidence against defendants, but rather as part of their job; the analysis itself is neutral and has the power to either convict or exonerate a defendant. *Id.* at 607. Thus, *Geier* permits experts to testify at trial regarding scientific evidence prepared by another person so long as that evidence is prepared merely as a "contemporaneous recordation of observable events."

In light of subsequent Supreme Court developments on the scope of the confrontation clause (*see Melendez-Diaz v. Massachusetts*, 557 U.S. 305 (2009); *Bullcoming v. New Mexico*, 131 S.Ct. 2705 (2011); and *Williams v. Illinois*, 132 S.Ct. 2221 (2012)), the California Supreme Court revis-

---

[8] The court also noted that the expert, as director of the laboratory, oversaw all testing and supervised the analysts who actually perform the analyses. The court described the lab's protocols for DNA analysis as well as the analysts' handwritten notes documenting the testing procedures, and then concluded that the "record is sufficiently complete that Dr. Cotton or another analyst could reconstruct what the analyst who processed the samples did at every step." *Id.* at 594–95.

ited its confrontation clause jurisprudence in two companion cases, *People v. Dungo*, 55 Cal. 4th 608, 286 P.3d 442 (2012), and *People v. Lopez*, 55 Cal. 4th 569, 286 P.3d 469 (2012). In *Lopez*, the California Supreme Court held that the prosecution's use of testimonial out-of-court statements "ordinarily violates the defendant's right to confront the maker of the statements unless the declarant is unavailable to testify and the defendant had a prior opportunity for cross-examination." *Lopez*, 286 P.3d at 477. The court explained that an out-of-court statement is "testimonial" if made with some degree of formality or solemnity, and if its primary purpose pertains in some fashion to a criminal prosecution. *Id.*

In *Lopez*, the court held that a laboratory report calculating the defendant's blood alcohol level was not testimonial because it was insufficiently formal or solemn. 286 P.3d at 477. The court noted that, although the laboratory technician initialed the document, he did not sign, certify, or swear to the truth of the contents of the contested report. *Id.* at 479. The court observed that, unlike the laboratory certificates that were found to be testimonial in *Melendez-Diaz* and *Bullcoming*, the challenged laboratory report was neither sworn before a notary nor formalized in a signed document. *Id.*

In *Dungo*, a forensic pathologist testifying for the prosecution described to the jury objective facts about the condition of the victim's body as recorded in the autopsy report and accompanying photographs. 286 P.3d at 444. The court held that introduction of the expert's testimony did not give rise to a right by the defendant to question the preparer of the autopsy report. *Id.* As in *Lopez*, the court held that the confrontation clause was not violated because the underlying autopsy report was not sufficiently formal or solemn to be considered testimonial. The court held that the report, which described the condition of the victim's body and drew conclusions about the victim's cause of death, merely recorded objective facts, which is "less formal than statements setting forth a pathologist's expert conclusions." *Id.* at 459.

The court also found that the report was not testimonial for a second reason; its primary purpose was not criminal prosecution. 286 P.3d at 450. Rather, criminal investigation "was only one of several purposes." *Id.* Accordingly, the court found that no confrontation clause right of the defendant was violated by his inability to cross-examine the preparer of the autopsy report. *Id.*

c. Expert-Related Rules and Procedural Issues in California State Courts

California has detailed rules governing the exchange of expert witness information. The identities and opinions of experts retained solely as consultants, as well as the materials they create to explain or interpret their findings, are entitled to qualified work-product protection. *Williamson v. Sup. Ct. (Shell Oil)*, 21 Cal. 3d 829, 834, 582 P.2d 126, 129 (1978). However, "testifying" experts retained to offer opinions at trial are subject to discovery.

The California Code of Civil Procedure (CCP) creates a timeline for making demands for exchange of expert witness lists. Any party may obtain discovery by serving a written demand for exchange of expert witness lists. *See* CCP § 2034.210(a); 2034.230(a). Demand must be made ten days after the initial trial date is set or seventy days before that trial date, whichever is later. *See* CCP § 2034.220. The exchange must be made on or before the date specified in the demand, which must be twenty days after the service of the demand, or fifty days before the initial trial date, whichever is closer to the trial date. *See* CCP § 2034.230(b). Exchange of the witness lists among the parties must be simultaneous, occurring either at a meeting of the attorneys for the parties involved or by mailing the list on or before the date set for the exchange. *See* CCP §§ 2034.210(a), 2034.260(a). Although the parties can agree to set an earlier date for the exchange of information, and a trial court may order an earlier simultaneous exchange on a showing of good cause, the court may not order a unilateral exchange. *See Hernandez v. Superior Court*, 112 Cal. App. 4th 285, 287, 4 Cal. Rptr. 3d 883 (Ct. App. 2003) (holding that unilateral exchanges of information are not permitted under the statute and that general fairness requires adherence to the statutory procedures, as they were "designed to place the parties 'on roughly equal footing'").

Courts have shown to be intolerant of any efforts of gamesmanship in the expert exchange process. *Fairfax v. Lords*, 138 Cal. App. 4th 1019, 1022, 41 Cal. Rptr. 3d 850, 852 (Ct. App. 2006). In *Fairfax*, the defendant submitted a document entitled "First Designation of Expert Witnesses" that included no witness names. *Id*. Instead, the document stated that the client "hereby gives notice that he is not designating any retained experts for the first exchange of expert witness information" but that he "expressly reserves the right to designate experts in rebuttal to [the other side's] designations." *Id*. The Court of Appeal reversed the allowance of a "Second Designation of Expert Witnesses" by pointing out in the first sentence of the opinion that "simultaneous" means "occurring at the same time." *Id*. at 1019, 41 Cal. Rptr. 3d at 852. Further, when a party intentionally manipulates the discovery process to ensure that expert reports and writings are not created until after the agreed upon date for the exchange—and the late or incomplete disclosure was not exacerbated by the party seeking exclusion—the court may exclude the expert's opinions. *Boston v. Penny Lane Centers, Inc.*, 170 Cal. App. 4th 936, 952 (Ct. App. 2009).

An expert list must set forth the name and address of each expert whose opinion the party furnishing the list—the "designating party"—expects to offer into evidence at trial. *See* CCP § 2034.260(b)(1). In addition, an "expert witness declaration" must be prepared and attached to the expert list for each designated expert who is either a party to the action, an employee of a party, or who has been "retained by a party for the purpose of forming and expressing an opinion." *See* CCP §§ 2034.210(b); 2034.260(c). The purpose of the declaration "is to give fair notice of what an expert will say at trial." *Bonds v. Roy*, 20 Cal. 4th 140, 146, 973 P.2d 66, 70 (1999). Therefore, an expert "may be precluded from testifying at trial on a subject that was not described in the exchanged expert witness declaration." *DePalma v. Rodriguez*, 151 Cal. App. 4th 159, 164, 59 Cal. Rptr. 3d 479, 482 (2007).

Adequate notice allows the parties to assess which experts should be deposed, to "fully explore the relevant subject area at any such deposition," and to select an expert who can best respond with a competing opinion. *Bonds*, 20 Cal. 4th at 147, 973 P.2d at 70. The declaration, which must be signed by the designating party's attorney (not the expert), must include a brief statement of the expert's qualifications, a brief narrative statement of the general substance of the testimony that the expert is expected to give, and a representation that the expert has agreed to testify at trial and that he will be prepared to testify (simply quoting the language of the statute to that effect is sufficient). *See* Weil & Brown, *Cal. Practice Guide: Civil Procedure Before Trial* § 8:1668.5 (The Rutter Group 2012). The declaration must also include a statement of the expert's fee for providing deposition testimony and for consulting with the retaining attorney. *See* CCP § 2034.260(c)(5). Where a party submits an expert witness declaration that fails to disclose the general substance of the testimony the party wishes to elicit from the expert at trial, testimony that is beyond the scope of the declaration may be excluded. *Bonds*, 20 Cal. 4th at 146, 973 P.2d at 69.[9]

A party's expert may not offer testimony at trial that exceeds the scope of his deposition testimony if the opposing party has no notice or expectation that the expert will offer the new testimony, or if notice of the new testimony comes at a time when deposing the expert is unreasonably difficult. *Easterby v. Clark*, 171 Cal. App. 4th 772, 780, 90 Cal. Rptr. 3d 81, 89 (2009). If the opposing has such notice or expectation, the fact that an expert's testimony at trial differs from his deposition testimony goes to the expert's credibility like any other witness, and does not by itself without serve

---

[9] The demand for expert discovery under § 2034.210 may also include a demand for an exchange of discoverable reports and writings made by the designated expert. All discoverable reports are to be exchanged at the same time as the expert lists and declarations. *See* CCP § 2034.270.

as ground for exclusion. *Id*. In *Easterby*, the expert witness declared during deposition that he could not identify with a reasonable degree of medical probability the event that necessitated plaintiff's surgery. *Id*. at 775. Approximately three months before the start of trial, the plaintiff's informed defendants via correspondence that the same expert witness received additional information subsequent to the deposition and would be testifying on the event that led to the plaintiff's surgery, and subsequently did so at trial. *Id*. Thus, the elements of unfair surprise and prejudice were not present in the new testimony, and the court of appeal reversed the exclusion of the expert testimony and remanded for further proceedings. *Id. See also DePalma v. Rodriguez*, 151 Cal. App. 4th 159, 166, 59 Cal. Rptr. 3d 479, 483 (Ct. App. 2007) ("[T]he general substance of [the medical expert]'s opinion at the deposition was that one would not expect plaintiff to have suffered "any" injury. Therefore, his subsequent testimony at trial regarding the lack of any expectation of specific knee or shoulder injury resulted in no unfair surprise for plaintiff. [The medical expert] simply did not exceed the general scope of his deposition testimony.").

The California Supreme Court has addressed whether treating physicians—doctors who have seen a party on a professional basis for reasons other than to prepare for trial—are considered "retained experts" for purposes of the designation and disclosure requirements of CCP § 2034.260(b). *See Schreiber v. Estate of Kiser,* 22 Cal. 4th 31, 989 P.2d 720 (1999). The court concluded that treating physicians are not "retained experts," because they are not retained by a party for the purpose of litigation. Instead, treating physicians learn of plaintiffs' injuries and medical history because of the underlying doctor—patient relationship. Thus, they need not submit expert declarations, even if their testimony will include opinions with respect to subjects such as causation and standard of care. In reaching this decision, the *Schreiber* court noted that one of the reasons for requiring expert declarations is to give the opposing party notice of the identity and qualifications of the witness before trial. In contrast to retained expert witnesses, the identity of treating physicians is not privileged. In fact, it is likely that the treating physician will have been deposed before any expert disclosure is even required. The court further clarified that no expert declarations are required for treating physicians even though they can express opinions regarding causation and the standard of care. Accordingly, the court has advised opposing counsel "to ask a treating physician in deposition whether he holds any views on those subjects, and if so, in what manner he obtained the factual underpinning of those opinions." *Id*. at 39, 989 P.2d at 726.

Subsequent Court of Appeal opinions further discussed the implications of *Schreiber*. In *Fatica v. Superior Court,* 99 Cal. App. 4th 350, 120 Cal. Rptr. 2d 904 (Ct. App. 2002), the court granted a writ of mandate and ordered the trial court to permit expert opinion testimony from the plaintiff's treating physician. *Id*. at 352, 120 Cal. Rptr. 2d at 905–06. The *Fatica* defendant had argued that the plaintiff's treating physician should be precluded from testifying on matters unrelated to his direct treatment of the plaintiff because the physician was not prepared to, and did not, give any opinion testimony at his deposition. The trial court agreed. *See id.,* 120 Cal. Rptr. 2d at 905–06. Citing the *Schreiber* decision, however, the *Fatica* court confirmed that treating physicians are "percipient experts" whose testimony is not limited to personal observations. *Id*. at 353, 120 Cal. Rptr. 2d at 906. The court further noted that, while the defendant may have been "sandbagged" by the fact that the treating physician was unprepared to give opinion testimony at his deposition, the trial court did not need to "rush" to preclude his testimony at trial and could have ordered the expert to submit to a further deposition. *Id.,* 120 Cal. Rptr. 2d at 906.

In *Kalaba v. Gray,* 95 Cal. App. 4th 1416, 116 Cal. Rptr. 2d 570 (Ct. App. 2002), the California Court of Appeal also discussed the holding in *Schreiber* that treating physicians need not submit "expert witness declarations." *Id*. at 1422–23, 116 Cal. Rptr. 2d at 575–76. The plaintiff in *Kalaba* had failed to identify her treating physicians by name and address and had merely stated in her expert witness designations that she reserved the right to call "all past or present examining and/or treating physicians." *Id*. at 1423, 116 Cal. Rptr. 2d at 576. The trial court precluded the plaintiff's treating physicians from testifying, and the plaintiff appealed. On appeal, the *Kalaba* court found there had been "no compliance with the letter or the spirit of section 2034" and affirmed the exclusion of the plaintiff's treating physicians. *Id.* Thus, although a treating physician need not submit an expert declaration, parties must still identify the treating physician in their designation of experts in order for the physician's testimony to be admissible as expert testimony. It is not enough to simply designate "all treating physicians past or present." *Id.*

In *Dozier v. Shapiro*, 199 Cal. App. 4th 1509, 133 Cal. Rptr. 3d 142 (Ct. App. 2011), the California Court of Appeal affirmed the preclusion of treating physician testimony once the treating physician was transformed into a retained expert. While acknowledging that the information required by the expert declarations is unnecessary for treating physicians performing their traditional role, the court noted that the treating physician had received materials from counsel after his deposition to enable him to testify at trial about the defendant's adherence to the proper standard of care. *Id.* at 1521, 133 Cal. Rptr. 3d at 152. Since this was a subject on which the treating physician had formed no opinions in connection with his physician-patient relationship with the plaintiff, his role at trial was not that of a treating physician, but became that of a retained expert. *Id.* Accordingly, plaintiff was required to designate the physician as a retained expert, disclose the required information in the declaration, and disclose the substance of the physician's anticipated testimony at trial. *Id.* Because the record was clear that the treating physician had not formulated an opinion on adherence to the standard of care at the time of his deposition, "his later-formulated opinions on that subject were based on information he was provided by counsel after his deposition for the purpose of the lawsuit, rather than on the basis of his physician-patient relationship as Dozier's treating physician." *Id.* Therefore, his testimony at trial was properly precluded. *Id.*

4. Expert Evidence in Hawaii State Courts

a. A Modified *Daubert* Test Governs Admissibility

Hawaii courts utilize a modified version of *Daubert's* multifactor test that explores the dual issues of whether expert testimony is "relevant and reliable." *State v. Maelega*, 80 Haw. 172, 181, 907 P.2d 758, 767 (1995). In evaluating the admissibility of expert opinion testimony, Hawaii courts frequently consider the five factors that were laid out in *State v. Montalbo*, 73 Haw. 130, 138, 828 P.2d 1274, 1280–81 (1992), two of which go to relevance and three of which go to reliability: (1) whether the evidence will assist the trier of fact to understand or determine a fact in issue, (2) whether the evidence will add to the common understanding of the jury, (3) whether the underlying theory is generally accepted as valid, (4) whether the procedures used are generally accepted as reliable if performed properly, and (5) whether the procedures were applied and conducted properly in the present instance. *Maelega*, 80 Haw. at 181, 907 P.2d at 767 (citing *Montalbo*, 73 Haw. at 138, 828 P.2d at 1280–81); *see also State v. Werle*, 121 Haw. 274, 282 (2009) (same). Although the Hawaii Supreme Court has not adopted the *Daubert* test in construing Hawaii's evidence rules, "it has found the *Daubert* factors instructive." *State v. Escobido-Ortiz*, 109 Haw. 359, 410 (Haw. Ct. App. 2005).

In *State v. Vliet*, 95 Haw. 94, 19 P.3d 42 (2001), the Hawaii Supreme Court reaffirmed that relevance and reliability are the touchstones of admissibility for expert testimony. Although the court did not overrule the five factors from *Montalbo*, it did clarify that trial courts do not need to use any specific factor(s) in every case. Instead, trial judges have "broad latitude" in deciding in a particular case how to determine whether the particular expert testimony is reliable. *Id.* at 110, 19 P.3d at 58. Further, a trial court is not required to conduct a reliability inquiry in every case that involves expert testimony. If no objection is made to the testimony, the court may normally dispense with such an inquiry. *Id.* Further, because trial courts are given broad discretion, their decisions regarding reliability will be subject to review for abuse of discretion. In contrast, the trial court's relevancy determination is subject to Hawaii's stricter "right/wrong standard." *Id.* at 107, 19 P.3d at 55.

The Hawaii Supreme Court has elected to follow the United States Supreme Court's decision in *Kumho Tire Co., Ltd. v. Carmichael,* 526 U.S. 137, 119 S. Ct. 1167 (1999), in interpreting its test as applying to all types of "specialized knowledge." *Vliet,* 95 Haw. at 108–09, 19 P.3d at 56–57. Thus, Hawaii law does not require trial courts to differentiate between scientific, technical, or otherwise specialized knowledge before determining admissibility.

b. Expert-Related Rules and Procedural Issues in Hawaii State Courts

Although Hawaii's evidence rules generally parallel the federal rules, Hawaii has promulgated a rule of its own regarding the cross-examination of experts. *See* Haw. R. Evid. (HRE) 702.1. This rule allows experts to be "cross-examined to the same extent as any other witness and, in addition, may be cross-examined as to: (1) the witness' qualifications, (2) the subject to which the witness' expert testimony relates, and (3) the matter upon which the witness' opinion is based and the reasons for the witness' opinion." HRE 702.1(a). The commentary to the rule, which states that it "restates existing law," explains that the rule "provides the appropriate latitude" for cross-examination of an expert, because the "broad testimonial range" allowed to experts "suggests the need for an equally broad cross-examination." HRE 702.1(a) cmt.

When the expert is testifying as to an opinion, the Hawaii rule allows "the expert to be cross-examined in regard to the content or tenor of any scientific, technical, or professional text, treatise, journal, or similar publication" if the witness used the publication in forming his or her opinion, or if the publication qualifies for admission under HRE 803(b)(18). HRE 702.1(b). The commentary to the rule notes that this subsection also restates existing law and is meant to "clarif[y] the permissible use of texts and treatises on cross-examination." *Id.*

Previously, Hawaii law allowed expert testimony regarding the credibility of a witness in child abuse cases as an exception to its general rule that credibility testimony is inadmissible. However, in 1990, the Hawaii Supreme Court overruled this exception. *See State v. Batangan,* 71 Haw. 552, 558, 799 P.2d 48, 52 (1990) (overruling *State v. Kim,* 64 Haw. 598, 645 P.2d 1330 (1982)). Therefore, experts' opinions regarding a child's believability are no longer allowed. Nevertheless, experts may still explain "'seemingly bizarre' behavior" by child victims such as "delayed reporting, inconsistency, or recantation." *Id.*

5. *Expert Evidence in Idaho State Courts*

a. *Daubert* Guides Issues of Admissibility

Admissibility of expert testimony in Idaho is governed by Idaho Rule of Evidence (IRE) 702, which asks whether the proffered testimony would "assist the trier of fact to understand the evidence." *See State v. Gleason,* 123 Idaho 62, 66, 844 P.2d 691, 694 (1992). The Idaho Supreme Court has approved consideration of the *Daubert* factors as "guidance" in conducting the "inquiry envisioned by Rule 702." *State v. Parkinson,* 128 Idaho 29, 34, 909 P.2d 647, 652 (Ct. App. 1996).[10]

---

[10] The Idaho Supreme Court expressly rejected the *Frye* test in the early 1990s. *See State v. Gleason,* 123 Idaho 62, 66, 844 P.2d 691, 694 (1992) (holding that admission of testimony regarding the horizontal gaze nystagmus test was not reversible error); *State v. Rodgers,* 119 Idaho 1047, 1049, 812 P.2d 1208, 1210 (1991) (upholding the trial court's decision to admit blood spatter evidence); *State v. Crea,* 119 Idaho 352, 355–56, 806 P.2d 445, 448–49 (1991) ("We decline to adopt the *Frye* criterion as the basis for admission of scientifically derived evidence. . . .").

Idaho courts, however, are not tied to a strict analysis of the *Daubert* factors. Rather, a highly deferential and flexible standard of admissibility based on IRE 702 remains the rule. In general, "doubt about whether an expert's testimony will be useful should generally be resolved in favor of admissibility unless there are strong factors such as time or surprise favoring exclusion." *See State v. Rodgers,* 119 Idaho 1047, 1050, 812 P.2d 1208, 1211 (1991) (quoting IRE 702 cmt.).

The Idaho Supreme Court provided an example of the flexibility of the IRE 702 analysis in *Coombs v. Curnow,* 148 Idaho 129, 219 P.3d 453 (2009). In *Coombs,* the court held that relevant considerations in determining whether to admit the expert testimony at issue included whether the theory could be tested, whether it had been subjected to peer-review and publication, the potential rate of error, general acceptance of the theory, "the close oversight and observation of the test subjects, the prospectivity and goal of the studies, . . . the presence of safeguards in the technique, . . . analogy to other scientific techniques whose results are admissible, . . . the nature and breadth of inferences drawn, . . . the extent to which the basic data are verifiable by the court and jury, . . . [the] availability of other experts to test and evaluate the technique, [and] the probative significance of the evidence in the circumstances of the case." *Id.* at 141.

The Idaho Supreme Court has also confirmed that expert testimony may be admissible despite arguably failing to satisfy the *Daubert* factors. In *Weeks v. Eastern Idaho Health Services,* 143 Idaho 834, 153 P.3d 1180 (2007), a patient entered a hospital after suffering a hemorrhage and hematoma in her brain. At the hospital, a catheter was inserted to drain excess fluid. At some point, a mixture of drugs (including dopamine and amiodarone) was connected to the catheter instead of the intravenous line to which it should have been connected, and the patient died. *Id.* at 1182. The trial court excluded causation testimony from the plaintiff's expert on the grounds that the expert was unqualified and that his testimony was not "based upon sound scientific principles," and it granted summary judgment for the hospital. *Id.* at 1183. Reversing, the state Supreme Court noted the undoubted qualifications of the expert and stated that "[t]he focus of the . . . inquiry is on the principles and methodology used." *Id.* at 1184 (quotation marks and citations omitted). The question was whether the expert had a "scientific basis" for his opinion. *Id.*. The expert admitted that he was "unable to determine the exact effect of the medication on [the patient's] brain" but nevertheless testified that the infusion at issue '"would cause a deleterious effect, 'just from the fact of fluid going in when it should be going out.'" *Id.* at 1185. Despite the uncertainties involved, the court found that the expert's testimony amounted to more than mere "speculation." *Id.* It thus held that the trial court "erred in failing to admit [the expert's] testimony as to the . . . effects of the infusion because he based his testimony upon sound scientific principles." *Id.* at 1186.

As the drafting committee emphasized in the commentary to IRE 702, doubts should be resolved in favor of admissibility. In *Coombs,* for example, the court held that expert testimony linking the administration of a drug to a certain consequence does not need to be directly supported by medical evidence so long as the expert can determine conclusively the effect the medication had on the patient. *Coombs,* 148 Idaho at 141. The court found that, notwithstanding the absence of peer-reviewed articles supporting the expert's testimony, it was sufficiently reliable because it was based on the expert's familiarity with basic principles of medicine and studies suggesting a possible link between the administered drug and symptoms that could lead to the decedent's cause of death. *Id.* at 142–43.

In *State v. Merwin,* 131 Idaho 642, 962 P.2d 1026 (1998), the Idaho Supreme Court rejected a claim by the defendant that studies relating to head trauma relied on by prosecution were inadmissible. *See id.* at 646, 962 P.2d at 1030. Merwin claimed that the studies were unreliable because they were "case studies" instead of "controlled experiments" and because they were allegedly contradicted by other studies. *Id.,* 962 P.2d at 1030. The *Merwin* court reiterated that, under IRE 702, it would only look at whether the studies "possessed *sufficient indicia* of reliability" (emphasis added), and it stressed that a lower court's decision to admit evidence will not be disturbed except for a "clear abuse of discretion." *Id.,* 962 P.2d at 1030. *See also Walker v. American Cyanamid Co.,*

130 Idaho 824, 832, 948 P.2d 1123, 1131 (1997) (noting trial court's "broad discretion" to admit technical economic testimony).

A trial court's discretion is not, however, unlimited. In *Swallow v. Emergency Medicine of Idaho,* 138 Idaho 589, 67 P.3d 68 (2003), the Idaho Supreme Court held that an expert's opinion can be excluded when there is no scientific basis for that opinion, even if the witness has been determined to be an expert in that field. The reasoning and methodology underlying an expert's opinion must be "scientifically sound" in order for the opinion to be admissible. *Id.* at 592–93, 67 P.3d at 71–72. In *Swallow,* the court affirmed the exclusion of the testimony of an expert witness, a doctor, that high doses of a particular drug had caused the plaintiff's heart attack. The plaintiff produced no evidence—"tested, published, peer-reviewed, or otherwise shown to be reliable"—that the drug taken by the plaintiff could cause a heart attack. The doctor had relied only on ten FDA adverse-reaction reports—effectively anecdotal reports by physicians—over eight years in which a patient had suffered cardiac arrest after taking the drug. There was no indication that there was a greater incidence of heart attacks among those taking the drug than would be expected to occur by chance. The court found that the doctor's opinion was "nothing more than speculation based on a temporal concurrence of events." *Id.* at 594, 67 P.3d at 73.

b. Expert-Related Rules and Procedural Issues in Idaho State Courts

The Idaho Code has a special section regarding expert testimony on the issue of a criminal defendant's mental condition. The code permits expert evidence only if it is fully subject to the adversarial process. *See* Idaho Code § 18-207(4). At least ninety days before trial, parties must give notice of their intent to raise the issue of the defendant's mental condition and their intent to call experts. *Id.* § 18-207(4)(a). A party must also furnish a written synopsis of an expert's findings or a copy of the expert's report. *Id.* § 18-207(4)(b).

Further, in Idaho, the prevailing party in a civil action has a right to seek reimbursement of certain costs incurred in prosecuting or defending the action, including the cost of expert witnesses. *See* Idaho R. Civ. P. 54(d)(1). Expert costs can include "[r]easonable expert witness fees for an expert who testifies at a deposition or at a trial," but the amount is "not to exceed the sum of $2,000 for each expert witness for all appearances." Idaho R. Civ. P. 54(d)(1)(C)(8). To the extent that the expert's fees exceed $2,000, a party may seek an award of these "discretionary" costs "upon a showing that said costs were necessary and exceptional costs reasonably incurred, and should in the interest of justice be assessed against the adverse party." Idaho R. Civ. P. 54(d)(1)(D). "The grant or denial of discretionary costs is 'committed to the sound discretion of the district court,' and will only be reviewed by an appellate court for an abuse of that discretion." *Inama v. Brewer,* 132 Idaho 377, 383–84, 973 P.2d 148, 154–55 (1999) (quoting *Fish v. Smith,* 131 Idaho 492, 493, 960 P.2d 175, 176 (1998)) (citation omitted).

6. Expert Evidence in Montana State Courts

a. *Daubert* Applies to "Novel" Scientific Evidence

The Montana Supreme Court's approach to expert testimony is governed by *Barmeyer v. Montana Power Co.,* 202 Mont. 185, 657 P.2d 594 (1983). In *Barmeyer,* decided a decade before *Daubert,* the court rejected the *Frye* rule and established a flexible standard under Montana Rule of Evidence (MRE) 702 (which, at the time, was identical to its federal counterpart). *Id.* at 193–94, 657 P.2d at 598. The court observed that "it is better to admit relevant scientific evidence in the same manner as other expert testimony and allow its weight to be attacked by cross-examination and refutation." *Id.* Although *Barmeyer* was later overruled on other grounds, its test remains the touchstone of admissibility for

Montana state courts. *See State v. Cline,* 275 Mont. 46, 54, 909 P.2d 1171, 1177 (1996) (noting the "continuing vitality of *Barmeyer*" in finding that the trial court did not abuse its discretion by allowing expert testimony regarding the age of defendant's fingerprint). The Montana Supreme Court has held that the *Barmeyer* standard is more lenient than the federal approach, except in cases of "novel" scientific evidence, in which case the *Daubert* standard is applied. *Cline,* 275 Mont. at 55, 909 P.2d at 1177.

The Montana Supreme Court has noted that the *Barmeyer* standard reflects the "liberal trend" toward admissibility of "scientific evidence in general." *Hulse v. Department of Justice, Motor Vehicle Division,* 289 Mont. 1, 28, 961 P.2d 75, 91–92 (1998). That is, it reflects a preference for "liberal admissibility subject to stringent cross examination." *Id.* One observer has criticized the *Barmeyer* approach on these grounds:

> Thus, for example, a trial judge might conclude that the expert's opinion has not been tested, is neither subject to peer review nor publication, is subject to a high potential rate of error, and is not generally accepted in the scientific community. Thus, this judge may conclude that this opinion is patently inadmissible under *Daubert*. However, this same judge might nonetheless also conclude that, under *Barmeyer*, these infirmities go only to the weight of the opinion, and, may further assume that potential prejudice could be alleviated by vigorous cross examination.[11]

Although the *Barmeyer* analysis is more lenient than the *Daubert* analysis, but the *Daubert* standard still applies in cases with "novel" scientific evidence. After *Daubert* was decided, the Montana Supreme Court noted that the *Daubert* factors were "consistent with our previous holding in *Barmeyer* concerning the admission of expert testimony of *novel* scientific evidence." *State v. Moore,* 268 Mont. 20, 42, 885 P.2d 457, 471 (1994) (emphasis added) (applying *Daubert* factors in upholding admission of expert testimony regarding restriction fragment length polymorphism DNA analysis), *overruled on other grounds by State v. Gollehon,* 274 Mont. 116, 906 P.2d 697 (1995). The Montana Supreme Court clarified this statement in *State v. Cline,* in which it held: "Certainly all scientific expert testimony is not subject to the *Daubert* standard and the *Daubert* test should only be used to determine the admissibility of novel scientific evidence." *Cline,* 275 Mont. at 55, 909 P.2d at 1177.

Accordingly, in *Hulse v. Department of Justice, Motor Vehicle Division,* the court found that the horizontal gaze nystagmus (HGN) field sobriety test is not novel, and thus admissibility of evidence regarding the test is not subject to a *Daubert* inquiry. Instead, a "conventional" inquiry under *Barmeyer* and Rule 702 should be conducted to determine admissibility. *Hulse,* 289 Mont. at 30, 961 P.2d at 93–94 (disagreeing with the Ninth Circuit and "reassert[ing] our holding in *Cline* that the *Daubert* test should only be used to determine the admissibility of novel scientific evidence").[12]

The Montana Supreme Court continues to use the distinction between novel and non-novel scientific evidence. *See State v. Price,* 339 Mont. 399, 401–02, 406, 171 P.3d 293, 296, 299 (2007)

---

[11] Robert L. Sterup, Into the Twilight Zone: Admissibility of Scientific Expert Testimony in Montana After Daubert, 58 MONT. L. REV. 465, 488 (1997).

[12] Although *Hulse* sheds light on the respective roles of *Daubert* and *Barmeyer* in Montana, it did not answer the question of how trial courts are to separate "novel" science from other scientific applications. See R. L. Sterup, 58 MONT. L. REV. at 485–47, 489 ("The Daubert factors are designed to assist the trial judge in determining whether a particular scientific principle is generally accepted, verifiable, subject to a high rate of error and so forth. To ask the trial court to determine whether the science is novel before applying Daubert is to deprive him of the very framework of analysis Daubert was meant to provide."). The only guidance provided by the Montana Supreme Court is that novelty should be assessed "from a very narrow perspective." *State v. Clark,* 347 Mont. 354, 366, 198 P.3d 809, 819 (2008).

(affirming a trial court's admission of expert testimony on the "physiological and psychological injuries suffered as a result of [a] stun gun attack," explaining that "[m]edical diagnosis is not 'novel scientific evidence' and therefore the *Daubert* standard does not apply"); *Gilkey v. Schweitzer*, 295 Mont. 345, 983 P.2d 869 (1999) (finding *Daubert* inapplicable to testimony by a physician regarding the amount of information that should be provided to a patient before performing a medical procedure, because the testimony was not based on a novel scientific theory).

The Montana Supreme Court has identified yet another limit on the reach of *Daubert* in Montana state courts. In *State v. Clifford*, 328 Mont. 300, 121 P.3d 489 (2005), the court set forth three questions relevant to assessing the reliability of an expert's testimony: "(1) whether the expert field is reliable, (2) whether the expert is qualified, and (3) whether the qualified expert reliably applied the principles of that reliable field to the facts of the case." *Id.* at 306–07, 121 P.3d at 494–95. The court found, however, that under the Montana rules, only the first two of these inquiries are the subject of a *Daubert* analysis; the third goes to the weight of the evidence and may be attacked by cross-examination. *Id.*, 121 P.3d at 495. Specifically, the court explained that "[u]nder a *Daubert* analysis, the reliability of [an expert's] application of his expert field to the facts is immaterial in determining the reliability of that expert field." *Id.* at 307, 121 P.3d at 495. Thus, if a witness is a qualified expert in a field that has been found to be reliable, he or she may testify without a rigorous admissibility evaluation of how the methods of that field were applied to the facts. *Id.* (noting that this approach differs from the analysis under the Federal Rules of Evidence).

b. Expert-Related Rules and Procedural Issues in Montana State Courts

The Montana Rules of Evidence (MRE) are essentially analogous to the Federal Rules of Evidence (FRE), with a few discrete exceptions. For example, the MRE contain no provision like FRE 706, which provides for court-appointed experts. *See* MRE chapter 10, chapter compiler's comments.

Additionally, the Montana Code (MC) specifically limits expert witness fees to $10 per day plus mileage. *See* MC § 26-2-501; § 26-2-505 (stating that expert witnesses shall receive the same compensation as other witnesses); *see also In Matter of Ivan Mustard Trust*, 2000 WL 739683, at *4, 8 P.3d 124 (Mont. 2000). The Montana Supreme Court has explained that, "[o]f course, a party can pay an expert witness any fee he or she chooses, but a district court cannot award costs in excess of $10 per day per witness." *Witty v. Pluid*, 220 Mont. 272, 274, 714 P.2d 169, 171 (1986).

However, the Montana Supreme Court has also held that the $10 limit on an expert's fee is inapplicable in workers' compensation cases. *See Kloepfer v. Lumbermens Mutual Casualty Co.*, 272 Mont. 78, 899 P.2d 1081 (1995). The statute regulating workers' compensation cases allows "reasonable costs and attorney's fees" to be awarded. *See id.* at 82, 899 P.2d at 1083. Thus, "the costs payable in Workers' Compensation Court under the reasonable costs standard are not necessarily comparable to the standard applied in normal district court cases." *Id.*, 899 P.2d at 1084. The *Kloepfer* court reasoned that "[m]edical depositions have been consistently used in workers' compensation cases and the costs of such testimony have been routinely allowed by workers' compensation judges." *Id.* Therefore, the court "conclude[d] that the workers' compensation statutes do not require . . . a claimant's award [be diminished] by making the claimant pay the high costs of medical depositions which are a requirement in many cases for obtaining benefits." *Id.* at 82–83, 899 P.2d at 1084.

7. *Expert Evidence in Nevada State Courts*

a. State Law Determines Admissibility

To date, the Nevada Supreme Court has declined to adopt the *Daubert* test. *See Higgs v. State*, 222 P.3d 648, 650 (Nev. 2010); *Krause Inc. v. Little*, 117 Nev. 929, 934, 34 P.3d 566, 569 (2001);

Yamaha Motor Co. v. Arnoult, 114 Nev. 233, 242–43, 955 P.2d 661, 667 (1998).[13] Nor has the Nevada Supreme Court endorsed *Frye. See Santillanes v. State,* 104 Nev. 699, 703 n.3, 704, 765 P.2d 1147, 1150 n.3 (1988) (observing that "in the sixty-five years since *Frye* was decided we have neither cited to nor adopted the decision'"). Rather, Nevada state courts assessing the admissibility of scientific evidence and expert testimony rely solely on the touchstones of "trustworthiness and reliability." *Id.* at 703, 765 P.2d at 1150.

The open-ended nature of "trustworthiness and reliability" allows Nevada courts to conduct a broad inquiry in their role as gatekeeper. Indeed, the Nevada Supreme Court's reluctance to adopt *Daubert* stems from its perception that the *Daubert* standard is not permissive enough. In *Hallmark v. Eldridge,* 124 Nev. 492, 498, 189 P.3d 646, 650 (2008), the court used *Daubert* as "persuasive authority", stating that "NRS [Nev. Rev. Stat.] 50.275, ... as we have construed it, tracks Federal Rule of Evidence (FRE) 702." *Hallmark v. Eldridge,* 124 Nev. 492, 498, 189 P.3d 646, 650 (2008). However, two years later, the court criticized the language in *Hallmark,* stating that *Daubert* is only persuasive "to the extent that [it] espouses a flexible approach to the admissibility of expert witness testimony." *Higgs v. State,* 222 P.3d 648, 657 (Nev. 2010). Otherwise, "to the extent that courts have construed *Daubert* as a standard that requires mechanical application of its factors, we decline to adopt it." *Id.* at 657–58. In *Higgs,* the court emphasized that the law in Nevada continued to give judges "wide discretion" in the admissibility of expert testimony, and it stated that it would not adopt the *Daubert* standard "as a limitation on judges' considerations." *Id.* at 658. Thus, the Nevada courts' test may perhaps be best described as a modified *Daubert* inquiry, with an emphasis on flexibility.

Although general scientific acceptance is relevant to the admissibility analysis in Nevada courts only insofar as it goes to the trustworthiness or reliability of the testimony, *Santillanes,* 104 Nev. at 704, 765 P.2d at 1150, the Nevada Supreme Court has nevertheless accorded preeminent weight to the question of whether the evidence at issue is generally accepted within the relevant scientific community. For example, in *Bolin v. State,* 114 Nev. 503, 528, 960 P.2d 784, 800 (1998), the Nevada Supreme Court held that, because the "overwhelming weight of authority has established that DNA analysis utilizing the polymerase chain reaction (PCR) technique is reliable for use within the forensic context," the DNA evidence offered by the state was admissible. Similarly, in *State v. Holmes,* 112 Nev. 275, 914 P.2d 611 (1996), the court relied primarily on the fact that a number of scientific writings agreed that radioimmunoassay hair analysis—a method of drug testing—was accepted in the field of forensic toxicology in finding the test admissible. *Id.* at 280–81, 914 P.2d at 614–15 ("RIA testing ... is now an accepted and reliable scientific methodology for detecting illicit drug use."); *see also American Elevator Co. v. Briscoe,* 93 Nev. 665, 670–71, 572 P.2d 534, 538 (1977) (noting that the polygraph has not received the necessary "recognition" or "general scientific acceptance" to be considered trustworthy and reliable).

---

[13]   In *Arnoult,* the Nevada Supreme Court specifically declined to require a *Daubert*style inquiry in the context of nonscientific expert testimony or evidence, and suggested that the court's inquiry may be different in cases of scientific expert testimony versus nonscientific expert testimony. *See Arnoult,* 114 Nev. at 243, 955 P.2d at 667 (noting that *Daubert* applies only when the expertise at issue implicates the "natural 'laws of science'" and is "governed by the scientific method"). However, *Arnoult* was decided before the United States Supreme Court's decision in *Kumho Tire Co., Ltd. v. Carmichael,* 526 U.S. 137, 119 S. Ct. 1167 (1999), and in *Higgs v. State,* 222 P.3d 648 (Nev. 2010), the Nevada Supreme Court adopted a broad and open-ended test for all expert testimony, so it is unclear to what extent the Nevada Supreme Court would still accept a distinction between scientific and nonscientific evidence.

b. Expert-Related Rules and Procedural Issues in Nevada State Courts

Nev. Rev. Stat. Ann. (NRS) § 50.275 states: "If scientific, technical, or other specialized knowledge will assist the trier of fact to understand the evidence or to determine a fact in issue, a witness qualified as an expert by special knowledge, skill, experience, training, or education may testify to matters within the scope of such knowledge." In *Higgs v. State*, 222 P.3d 648, 657 (Nev. 2010), the Nevada Supreme Court identified three "overarching requirements for admissibility of expert witness testimony," based on the language of NRS § 50.275: the (1) qualification, (2) assistance, and (3) limited scope requirements. *Id.* at 658. According to NRS § 50.275, (1) the expert "must be qualified in an area of scientific, technical, or other specialized knowledge," (2) his or her specialized knowledge must "assist the trier of fact to understand the evidence or to determine a fact in issue," and (3) his or her testimony must be limited "to matters within the scope of [his or her specialized] knowledge." *Hallmark*, 124 Nev. at 498, 189 P.3d at 650 (internal quotations omitted). According to the *Higgs* court, "[these] requirements ensure reliability and relevance, while not imposing upon a judge a mandate to determine scientific falsifiability and error rate for each case." *Higgs*, 22 P.3d at 659.

Nevada's statutes regarding expert witnesses, NRS §§ 50.265–.365, roughly track FRE 701–705. However, Nevada has several additional statutes pertaining to expert witnesses. For example, NRS § 50.310 provides that the director of a medical laboratory who wishes to testify to the results of a medical test must provide an affidavit containing "the evidentiary foundation upon which the results of the test are based, including the description of the test, the personnel involved and the controls employed in conducting the test." NRS §§ 50.315–.310 provide detailed procedural rules regarding the admissibility of evidence regarding the existence or identity of, or a party's use of, alcohol or other drugs. Finally, NRS § 50.345 provides, "In any prosecution for sexual assault, expert testimony is not inadmissible to show that the victim's behavior or mental or physical condition is consistent with the behavior or condition of a victim of sexual assault."

Nevada also has detailed regulations regarding the time and manner in which parties exchange expert witness information in criminal cases. *See* Nev. Rev. Stat. Ann. (NRS) § 174.234 (2006). Each party is required to identify its expert witnesses and to file and serve on the opposite side, not less than twenty-one days before trial or at such other time as the court may direct, a written notice containing a brief statement of the subject matter on which the expert witness is expected to testify and the substance of her testimony, a copy of the curriculum vitae of the expert witness, and a copy of all reports made by or at the direction of the expert witness. *Id.; compare* Nev. R. Civ. P. 16.1(a)(2)(B) (listing rules for expert disclosures in civil cases).

Nevada, which allows the award of costs to the prevailing party as a matter of course, *see* NRS § 18.020, includes as such costs the "[r]easonable fees of not more than five expert witnesses in an amount of not more than $1,500 for each witness," § 18.005(5). The court may award a greater sum if it "determ[ines] that the circumstances surrounding the expert's testimony were of such necessity as to require the larger fee." *Id.*

8. *Expert Evidence in Oregon State Courts*

a. State Law Governs Admissibility

The Supreme Court of Oregon has declined to follow explicitly either *Daubert* or *Frye,* instead continuing to apply its own approach, developed in 1984 in *State v. Brown,* 297 Or. 404, 408–09, 687 P.2d 751, 754–55 (1984). In *Brown,* the Supreme Court of Oregon abandoned "special tests" like that of *Frye* for determining the admissibility of scientific evidence, in favor of applying "traditional evidence law" as codified in the Oregon Evidence Code (OEC):

In applying OEC 401, 702 and 403, this court must identify and evaluate the probative value of the evidence, consider how it might impair rather than help the fact finder, and decide whether truthfinding is better served by exclusion or admission.

Brown, 297 Or. at 409, 687 P.2d 755. In finding that polymerase chain reaction DNA evidence is admissible, the court held that code provisions dealing with relevance (OEC 401), the opinions of experts (OEC 702), and the exclusion of relevant evidence on the grounds of prejudice, confusion, or undue delay (OEC 403) should serve as the litmus tests for admissibility. *See Brown*, 297 Or. at 408–09, 687 P.2d at 754–55; *see also State v. Southard*, 347 Or. 127, 133, 318 P.3d 104, 107 (2009) (holding that test for admissibility of expert testimony is that testimony must be relevant, that it must possess "sufficient indicia of scientific validity and be helpful to the jury," and that the prejudicial effect cannot outweigh the probative value); *State v. Middleton*, 294 Or. 427, 437, 657 P.2d 1215, 1221 (1983) (holding that admissibility of expert testimony requires findings that the witness is qualified as an expert, that the subject is a proper subject for expert testimony, and that the offered testimony is relevant and will be helpful to the jury).

In determining the relevance of proffered scientific evidence under OEC 401 and OEC 702, the *Brown* court identified seven factors to be considered as guidelines: (1) the technique's general acceptance in the field, (2) the expert's qualifications and stature, (3) the use that has been made of the technique, (4) the potential rate of error, (5) the existence of specialized literature, (6) the novelty of the invention, and (7) the extent to which the technique relies on the subjective interpretation of the expert. *Id.* at 417, 687 P.2d at 759. These factors are then to be balanced against the exclusionary principles reflected in OEC 403. The court has also noted, however, that the factors are not exclusive, and are not intended to serve as a mechanical checklist. *See State v. Lyons*, 324 Or. 256, 271, 924 P.2d 802, 811 (1996).[14] Rather, "[w]hat is important is ... analysis of each factor by the court in reaching its decisions on the probative value of the evidence." *Brown*, 297 Or. at 417–18, 687 P.2d at 759–60.

Brown was decided before the United States Supreme Court decided *Daubert* but, since *Daubert* has been decided, the Oregon Supreme Court has cited to *Daubert* with approval. "Faced with a proffer of expert scientific testimony, an Oregon trial court, in performing its vital role as 'gatekeeper' pursuant to OEC 104(1), should ... find Daubert instructive." *State v. O'Key*, 321 Or. 285, 306, 899 P.2d 663, 680 (1995). Specifically, the Oregon Supreme Court stated:

> Both *Daubert* and *Brown* reject a "bright line test," and the "multifactor" observations they offer suggest a flexible approach to admission or exclusion of scientific evidence. Both Daubert and Brown allow Frye's "general acceptance" standard to be considered as one factor in the trial court's decision about admissibility. In addition, both suggest other (some

---

[14] Indeed, the *Brown* court approvingly noted a total of eleven factors that Oregon courts may consider: (1) the potential error rate in using the technique, (2) the existence and maintenance of standards governing its use, (3) the presence of safeguards in the characteristics of the technique, (4) analogies to other scientific techniques whose results are admissible, (5) the extent to which the technique has been accepted by scientists in the field involved, (6) the nature and breadth of the inference adduced, (7) the clarity and simplicity with which the technique can be described and its results explained, (8) the extent to which the basic data are verifiable by the court and jury, (9) the availability of other experts to test and evaluate the technique, (10) the probative significance of the evidence in the circumstances of the case, and (11) the care with which the technique was employed in the case. *Brown*, 297 Or. at 418 n.5, 687 P.2d at 760 n.5 (citing Mark McCormick, *Scientific Evidence: Defining a New Approach to Admissibility*, 67 IOWA L. REV. 879, 911–12 (1982)).

overlapping) indicia of legitimacy, none of which is dispositive. Both decisions view the validity of a particular scientific theory or technique to be the key to admissibility. Both require trial courts to provide a screening function to determine whether the proffered scientific evidence is sufficiently valid to assist the trier of fact.

Id. at 307, 899 P.2d at 680. Based on this "degree of congruence" between *Brown* and *Daubert*, the Court adopted the *Daubert* methodology insofar as it promoted the listed principles.

The Oregon Supreme Court continues emphasize the leniency of its test for the admissibility of expert testimony. In *Marcum v. Adventist Health System/West*, 345 Or. 237, 193 P.3d 1 (2008), the plaintiff, in preparation for an MRI, received an injection of gadolinium contrast. The plaintiff claimed that the injection had been improperly performed and that she suffered persistent pain at the injection site, ultimately diagnosed as Raynaud's syndrome. The trial court excluded the plaintiff's expert's medical causation testimony and directed a verdict for the defendants. The Court of Appeals affirmed, on the basis that "the expert had failed to show, either through studies ... or through a scientifically demonstrable mechanism of causation" that the gadolinium injection caused the plaintiff's injury. *Id.* at 242, 193 P.3d at 3. The Court of Appeals went through the proffered expert testimony in detail, noting that the plaintiff's expert "admitted that there is no medical literature reporting a causal link between gadolinium extravasation and Raynaud's syndrome." *Marcum v. Adventist Health System/West*, 215 Or. App. 166, 176 P.3d 1214, 1220 (Ct. App. 2007). Although the expert had performed experiments on the effects of gadolinium on mice, he conceded that "it is 'difficult to have a complete extrapolation of the mice results to human beings.'" *Id.* Moreover, the expert "acknowledged that the medical community does not fully understand the cause of Raynaud's syndrome." *Id.* at 177, 168 P.3d at 1221. Finding the expert's testimony unreliable, the Court of Appeals affirmed the exclusion of the testimony.

The Oregon Supreme Court reversed, stating that "the Court of Appeals asked for too much." *Marcum*, 345 Or. at 252, 193 P.3d at 8. In contrast to cases that looked at the scientific reliability of specific techniques or tests, the Oregon Supreme Court noted that the evidence in *Marcum* involved a complex question of medical causation. *Id.* at 245–46, 193 P.3d at 5. Given the rarity of the injury at issue and the difficult of performing any sort of controlled experiment on the subject, "the absence of a well-understood mechanism of causation" could not be grounds for excluding the expert's testimony. *Id.* at 250, 193 P.3d at 7. The "weaknesses in the expert's theory" went to the weight of the testimony, not its admissibility. *Id.* at 253, 193 P.3d at 9.

Nonetheless, there are still cases in which expert testimony is found to be inadmissible. In *State v. Southard*, 347 Or. 127, 318 P.3d 104 (2009), the trial court allowed a staff member at a medical facility for child abuse victims to testify that a child's verbal reports indicated that the child had indeed been abused. The Oregon Supreme Court reiterated the test for admissibility of expert testimony, noting that the testimony must be relevant, that it must possess "sufficient indicia of scientific validity and be helpful to the jury," and that the prejudicial effect cannot outweigh the probative value. *Id.* at 133, 218 P.3d at 107. The court found no problem with the relevance or reliability of the testimony, but, in an admittedly "narrow" ruling, held that the evidence should have been excluded on prejudice grounds. *Id.* at 132, 218 P.3d at 113. The expert testimony analyzed the credibility of the victim's report, and did so using "essentially the same criteria that we expect juries to use every day ... to decide whether witnesses are credible." *Id.* at 140, 218 P.3d at 112. The issue of credibility is one that the jury was capable of determining on its own, and thus the probative value of the expert's testimony was small. However, the diagnosis of a "credentialed expert" had the power to make the jury abnegate its duty to make credibility determinations and instead defer to the expert, and this was highly prejudicial to the defendant. *Id.* at 140–41, 218 P.3d at 112.

The Oregon Supreme Court has explained that the *Brown* factors are used only in determining the admissibility of "scientific evidence." In *State v. Marrington*, 335 Or. 555, 73 P.3d 911(2003), the court attempted to define what makes evidence scientific. The court stated that "the term 'scientific' ... refers to evidence that draws its convincing force from some principle of science, mathematics, and the like." *Id.* at 561, 73 P.3d at 914 (quoting *Brown,* 297 Or. at 407, 687 P.2d at 754). A key factor in determining whether evidence is scientific is whether the trier of fact would "perceive the evidence as such" because, when evidence is perceived as scientific, it possesses more persuasive power. In *Marrington,* a child victim claimed that the defendant had sexually assaulted her, but the victim waited more than a month before telling anyone about the assault. An expert witness, a psychologist, testified that delay in reporting incidents is common when children disclose sexual abuse.[15] The defendant attempted to argue that the testimony was scientific evidence and thus should be subject to the *Brown* factors to determine admissibility. *Id.* at 560–61, 73 P.3d at 914. The court noted that experts with experience in the behavioral sciences have the potential to influence triers of fact just as do experts in the "hard sciences." As a result of the witness's advanced degrees, certification as a counselor, and her research and testimony regarding the empirical confirmation of her testimony, the court determined that the witness's testimony had the ability to influence a jury as "scientific." Thus, she was considered an expert witness presenting scientific evidence subject to *Brown. Id.* at 562–64, 73 P.3d at 915–16; *see also State v. Perry,* 347 Or. 110, 120–21, 218 P.3d 95, 101 (2009) (holding that witness's testimony was subject to *Brown* analysis when she "was presenting herself as an expert in her field whose knowledge was based, at least in part, on studies, research, and scientific literature").

However, in another child sexual abuse case, *State v. Clemens,* 208 Or. App. 632, 145 P.3d 294 (Ct. App. 2006), the Oregon Court of Appeals found that testimony based only on personal experience and training is not scientific evidence when it is not based on "the application of a scientific method to collected data." *Id.* at 639, 145 P.3d at 297. In *Clemens,* the investigating officer testified that "the victim's statement was generally consistent with the nonchronological reporting patterns of child abuse victims." *Id.* at 635, 145 P.3d at 295. The defendant protested that this was scientific evidence improperly admitted without a determination of admissibility under the *Brown* factors. *Id.* The court found that, in contrast to *Marrington,* where the witness had a postgraduate degree in psychology and based her knowledge on research and literature in the field, the officer in *Clemens* did not have any specialized education or knowledge in the field of psychology or child behavior. This determination was made despite his relevant training and experience gained in conducting many child sexual abuse investigations. *Id.* at 639, 145 P.3d at 297. The court explained that because the officer's testimony did not use "the vocabulary of scientific research," was based on personal experience, and thus has "no increased potential to influence the trier of fact as a scientific assertion." *Id.* (internal quotations omitted). Thus, the court explained, the evidence was not subject to the *Brown* factors for admissibility.

Similarly, in *State v. Rambo*, 250 Or. App. 186, 279 F.3d 361 (Ct. App. 2012), the court found that a police officer's testimony that the defendant had been under the influence of drugs was not expert testimony that required analysis under *Brown*, despite the fact that the officer referred to blood alcohol tests and horizontal gaze nystagmus tests. The Supreme Court held that the testimony was based on the officer's training and experience and not "from the mantle of science." *Id.* at 195, 279 P.3d at 366. The officer's reliance on "scientific" evidence in forming his opinions did not automatically turn his opinions into scientific expert testimony. *Id.* Ultimately, as one court summarized, to be considered scientific evidence, testimony "must be opinion evidence that is proffered by an expert witness and possesses significantly increased potential to influence jurors as a scientific

---

[15] It should be noted that Oregon evidentiary rules contain a special provision allowing any party to introduce evidence establishing a pattern, practice, or history of abuse of a person, as well as expert testimony to assist the fact finder in understanding the significance of the evidence. OEC 404-1(1).

assertion." *State v. Owens*, 207 Or. App. 31, 39, 139 P.3d 984, 988 (Ct. App. 2006) (holding that blood test evidence of a defendant's blood alcohol content did not require expert testimony to be admissible). [16]

b. Expert-Related Rules and Procedural Issues in Oregon State Courts

The Oregon Rules of Civil Procedure lack an equivalent of Fed. R. Civ. P. 26(a)(2)'s requirement that a party disclose the identity of testifying experts and a written report of that expert's opinions. *See* Or. R. Civ. P. (ORCP) 36. The Oregon Supreme Court has thus held that "the legislature did not intend to authorize pretrial disclosure of either an expert's name or the substance of the expert's testimony," and that "the trial court lacked authority to require the parties to disclose that information in advance of trial." *Stevens v. Czerniak*, 336 Or. 392, 404–05, 84 P.3d 140, 147 (2004); *but see Gwin v. Lynn*, 344 Or. 65, 72, 176 P.3d 1249, 1253 (2008) ("[N]othing in the wording of the rule ... suggests that a witness who has been personally or directly involved in events relevant to a case may not be deposed as to facts of which the witness has personal knowledge, simply because that person will be, as to other matters, an expert witness at trial.") One exception to this rule is found in ORCP 44(C), which mandates that a plaintiff claiming personal injury "shall deliver to the requesting party a copy of all written reports and existing notations of any examinations relating to injuries for which recovery is sought."

In criminal cases, however, the Oregon Revised Statutes (ORS) required disclosure of "reports or statements of experts, made in connection with the particular case, including results of physical or mental examinations and of scientific tests, experiments, or comparisons." ORS §§ 135.815, 135.835. However, even when expert reports or statements are not disclosed as required by statute, defense witnesses' testimony should be excluded as a sanction only when "no lesser sanction would accomplish the aim of the statute, and then only if the state would be prejudiced if the witness or witnesses were permitted to testify even though the statute had not been complied with." *State v. Cunningham*, 197 Or. App. 264, 274, 105 P.3d 929, 935 (Ct. App. 2005) (quoting *State v. Mai*, 294 Or. 269, 277, 616 P.2d 315, 320 (1982)); *see also State v. Fain*, 132 Or. App. 488, 492, 888 P.2d 1052, 1053 (Ct. App. 1995).

Given the limits on pretrial expert discovery in civil cases, Oregon's summary judgment statute permits a party to oppose summary judgment with only an attorney affidavit based on facts or opinions obtained from the expert witness, without requiring expert testimony at that stage of the litigation. Specifically, ORCP 47(E) states:

> If a party, in opposing a motion for summary judgment, is required to provide the opinion of an expert to establish a genuine issue of material fact, an affidavit of the party's attorney stating that an unnamed qualified expert has been retained who is available and willing to

---

[16] Considerations of the *Brown* factors aside, Oregon courts maintain that at least one kind of expert testimony is generally inadmissible. In Oregon, a witness, expert or otherwise, may not give an opinion on whether he believes another witness is telling the truth. As Oregon's Supreme Court has explained, "[Oregon] reject[s] testimony from a witness about the credibility of another witness, although we recognize some jurisdictions accept it." *State v. Middleton*, 294 Or. 427, 438, 657 P.2d 1215, 1221 (1983) (footnote omitted). However, expert testimony generally describing how a person under the circumstances might typically react can be admissible. See *id.* at 434–36, 657 P.2d at 1219–20. The court has noted that "[m]uch expert testimony will tend to show that another witness either is or is not telling the truth. This, by itself, will not render evidence inadmissible." *Id.* at 435, 657 P.2d at 1219 (internal citation omitted).

testify to admissible facts or opinions creating a question of fact, will be deemed sufficient to controvert the allegations of the moving party and an adequate basis for the court to deny the motion.

ORCP 47(E); *see also Piskorski v. Ron Tonkin Toyota, Inc.,* 179 Or. App. 713, 718, 41 P.3d 1088, 1091 (Ct. App. 2002) (quoting ORCP 47(E)).

9. Expert Evidence in Washington State Courts

a. *Frye* and State Law Determine Admissibility

In Washington state, a party may introduce expert scientific evidence so long as the expert is qualified, relies on generally accepted theories and techniques, and assists the trier of fact. *Katare v. Katare,* 175 Wn.2d 23, 38, 283 P.3d 546, 554 (2012). Although the admissibility of scientific evidence is largely within a trial court's discretion, the Washington Rules of Evidence, together with the *Frye* standard, are the two key tools Washington courts use to determine the admission of expert scientific evidence. *Id.*

The Washington Supreme Court has explicitly rejected *Daubert. See State v. Copeland,* 130 Wash. 2d 244, 259–61, 922 P.2d 1304, 1314–15 (1996). In *Copeland,* the court considered the admissibility of evidence generated by the so-called product rule, a method used to calculate the probabilities of a genetic profile randomly occurring in the general population. In finding the evidence admissible, the court criticized *Daubert's* "drawbacks," noting the "difficult task" trial courts will face in conducting an inquiry into the "complexity and controversy" of scientific matters. *Id.* at 260, 922 P.2d at 1315. According to the *Copeland* court, under *Daubert* "judges will be required to understand not only the specific scientific evidence, but also the world of science." *Id.,* 922 P.2d at 1315. "The problem and potential problems" raised by *Daubert* thus prompted the court to reaffirm its adherence to the *Frye* standard when determining the admissibility of novel scientific evidence. *Id.,* 922 P.2d at 1315.[17]

Instead of *Daubert,* Washington courts use a two-part inquiry to determine whether expert scientific evidence is admissible. First, they ask whether the evidence satisfies the *Frye* general acceptance standard. *See Anderson v. Akzo Nobel Coatings, Inc.,* 172 Wn.2d 593, 603, 260 P.3d 857, 862 (2011). Under this prong, the primary goal of a court is to determine "whether the evidence offered is based on established scientific methodology." *Id.* More specifically, Washington courts examine expert testimony to determine "(1) whether the scientific theory on which the evidence is based is generally accepted in the relevant scientific community, and (2) whether the technique used to implement that theory is also generally accepted by that scientific community." *Id.*[18] Scientific

---

[17] In civil cases, the Washington Supreme Court has neither expressly adopted *Frye* nor expressly rejected *Daubert. Anderson,* 172 Wn. 2d at 602, 260 P.3d at 862; *see also Reese v. Stroh,* 128 Wash. 2d 300, 907 P.2d 282 (1995) (declining to adopt a suggestion by the state Court of Appeals that *Daubert* be adopted in civil cases only). However, "for the moment, it seems safe to presume that *Frye* continues to apply in civil cases until the Washington Supreme Court explicitly says otherwise." KARL B. TEGLAND, WASHINGTON PRACTICE: EVIDENCE LAW & PRACTICE § 702.19, at 88 (5th ed. 2007).

[18] The Washington Supreme Court has noted that courts in some states engage in a further admissibility inquiry—whether the technique or method was appropriately applied on the particular occasion at issue—but explained that in Washington, this inquiry "goes to weight, not to admissibility." *State v. Gentry,* 125 Wash 2d. 570, 586, 888 P.2d 1105, 1117.

opinion does not need be unanimous, but if there is "significant dispute among qualified scientists in the relevant scientific community" then the evidence may not be admitted. *Id.*

Second, Washington courts ask whether the evidence meets the requirements of Washington Rule of Evidence (WRE) 702. *Id.* Courts turn to the question of admissibility under WRE 702 "only after novel scientific evidence is found admissible under *Frye*." *Id.; see also State v. Gentry*, 125 Wash. 2d. 570, 587, 888 P.2d 1105, 1118 (1995) ("Once a *Frye* determination is made, a defendant's objection to the particular testing procedures utilized in a given case should be analyzed under the usual standards for admission of evidence. The admissibility of expert testimony is governed by [WRE] 702.") (footnote omitted). This second inquiry itself requires two subinquiries: (1) Is the proffered witness "qualified as an expert," and (2) would the proposed testimony "assist the trier of fact." WRE 702.

The Washington Supreme Court regularly reaffirms this two-part approach in its decisions, and does so across a broad spectrum of scientific evidence matters. *See State v. McCuistion*, 169 Wn.2d 633, 646, 238 P.3d 1147, 1153 n. 8 (2010) (finding that expert opinions pertaining to sexually violent persons remain subject to challenge for admissibility under the rules of evidence and *Frye*); *State v. Roberts*, 142 Wash. 2d 471, 520–521, 14 P.3d 713, 740–41 (2000) (upholding the admission of "blood splatter" evidence as generally accepted in the scientific community and helpful to the trier of fact); *State v. Cheatam*, 150 Wash. 2d 626, 646, 81 P.3d 830, 840 (2003) ("[E]xpert psychological testimony may be admitted to assist juries in understanding phenomena not within the competence of the ordinary lay juror."); *State v. Stenson*, 132 Wash. 2d 668, 714–15, 940 P.2d 1239, 1263 (1997) (upholding admission of phenol tests used to detect blood stains over the defendant's objection that the results were not helpful to the jury); *State v. Janes*, 121 Wash. 2d 220, 235, 850 P.2d 495, 503 (1993) (holding that "battered child syndrome" is generally accepted in the scientific community and is thus admissible to explain the relationship between surrogate father and son); *cf. State v. Riker*, 123 Wash. 2d 351, 358–59, 869 P.2d 43, 47 (1994) (finding no general acceptance warranting the admission of expert testimony concerning the "battered person syndrome" to explain the defendant's actions outside of a battering relationship).

In considering whether a given scientific theory has achieved general acceptance under *Frye*, Washington courts must undertake "a more searching review—one that is sometimes not confined to the record" and may embrace scientific literature, secondary legal authority, and cases in other jurisdictions. *State v. Cauthron*, 120 Wash. 2d 879, 888–89, 846 P.2d 502, 506 (1993) (quoting *People v. Reilly*, 196 Cal. App. 3d 1127, 1134 (1987)) (holding that evidence regarding restrictive fragment length polymorphism method of DNA typing is admissible if supported by valid probability statistics). If the theory is generally accepted, then any concerns about the possibility of error or mistake in the particular case at hand should be addressed under WRE 702 or by the trier of fact. *See id.* at 890, 846 P.2d at 507.

Washington courts need not, however, always engage in the two-part test outlined above. The Washington Supreme Court has instructed trial courts to evaluate evidence preliminarily under WRE 702 "whenever possible" to avoid "time-consuming, expensive *Frye* hearings." *State v. Gregory*, 158 Wash. 2d 759, 830, 147 P.3d 1201, 1238 (2006); *see also State v. Bander*, 150 Wn. App 690, 712 (Ct. App. 2009) ("The Supreme Court has repeatedly held that challenges to DNA evidence of this nature do not concern admissibility under *Frye* but, rather, concern admissibility under ER 702 and the weight that the trier of fact may accord to the evidence."). For example, in cases involving expert evidence related to an insanity defense, the Washington Supreme Court makes it clear that "ER 702 continues to control court analysis," and expert evidence that does not help the trier of fact will be inadmissible even with a *Frye* hearing. *State v. Klein*, 156 Wn.2d 102, 118, 125 P.3d 644, 651 (2005).

Further, Washington courts have warned that the two prongs of the admissibility inquiry should not be "inappropriately merged." *State v. Greene*, 92 Wash. App. 80, 95–96, 960 P.2d 980, 988–89

(Ct. App. 1998) (affirmed in part and reversed in part by *State v. Greene,* 139 Wash. 2d 64 (1999)). In *Greene,* the Washington Supreme Court considered the question of whether evidence of the defendant's dissociative identity disorder (DID) was admissible. The trial court held that it was not, because the available scientific studies did not address whether a person with DID is "insane." In reversing the trial court, the Court of Appeals observed that the question under *Frye* is whether DID is a generally accepted mental disorder. *Id.* at 97–98, 960 P.2d at 988–89.

The Washington Supreme Court agreed with the Court of Appeals in *Greene* that one appropriate question for consideration was whether DID is generally accepted in the scientific community. *Greene,* 139 Wash. 2d. at 71, 984 P.2d at 1028. However, although the court found that DID was generally accepted, it also explained that this did not necessarily lead to admission of the testimony. Even if evidence is generally accepted in the community, it still must be helpful to the trier of fact in order to be admissible under Evidence Rule 702. *Id.* at 73, 984 P.2d at 1028–29. To be helpful to a trier of fact, a diagnosis must be capable of forensic application to assess the defendant's mental state at the time of the crime. A diagnosis must relate a mental condition to a defendant's inability to appreciate the nature of his or her actions and the failure to form the specific intent required to commit the crime. *Id.* at 73–74, 982 P.2d at 1028–29. In *Greene,* the court held that the trial court properly excluded the DID diagnosis because although it was generally accepted, it was "not possible to reliably connect the symptoms of DID to the sanity or mental capacity of the defendant" in order to help the jury. *Id.* at 79, 984 P.2d at 1032. Therefore, at times Washington courts may properly exclude evidence under WRE 702 despite a finding of general acceptance under *Frye. See also State v. Martin,* 169 Wn. App. 620, 622, 281 P.3d 315, 316 (Ct. App. 2012) (affirming a lower court's decision that even if the "betrayal trauma theory" argued by the defendant was generally accepted within the scientific community under *Frye,* it was not established as a theory relevant to adult domestic violence and thus not helpful to the issue of intent in a domestic violence case); *Janes,* 121 Wash. 2d at 232–33, 850 P.2d at 501–02 (distinguishing the issue of whether the "battered child syndrome" satisfies *Frye* from the issue of whether evidence of the syndrome would aid the trier of fact under WRE 702).

Finally, in Washington, review of a decision to admit or exclude novel scientific evidence is *de novo,* unlike other states that review decisions regarding scientific evidence only for an abuse of discretion. *See* State *v. Dunn,* 125 Wash. App. 582, 590, 105 P.3d 1022, 1026 (Wash. Ct. App. 2005) (citing *State v. Cauthron,* 120 Wash. 2d 879, 889, 846 P.2d 502, 505 (1993)). Although it is clearly settled that *de novo* is the standard of review for cases that conduct a *Frye* hearing, "it is not clear what standard of review should be applied to a trial court's decision not to conduct a *Frye* hearing at all." *Gregory,* 158 Wn.2d at 830, 147 R.3d at 1239 (2006). The question appears to turn on whether the court resolves for itself the same questions ultimately addressed after a *Frye* hearing. *In re Berry,* 160 Wn. App. 374, 378, 248 P.3d 592, 595 (Ct. App. 2011) (reasoning that *de novo* review of expert evidence was appropriate even though a *Frye* hearing was not granted by the trial court).

b. Expert-Related Rules and Procedural Issues in Washington State Courts

Washington adopted its Rules of Evidence in 1979, and "generally patterned" its evidence rules after the Federal Rules of Evidence. *Brundridge v. Fluor Federal Servs., Inc.,* 164 Wn.2d 432, 450, 191 P.3d 879, 891 (2008). Under the Washington Rules, "[i]f scientific, technical, or other specialized knowledge will assist the trier of fact to understand the evidence or to determine a fact in issue, a witness qualified as an expert by knowledge, skill, experience, training, or education, may testify thereto in the form of an opinion or otherwise." WRE 702. As explained above, however, Washington courts have not interpreted and applied WRE 702 in the same way that the United States Supreme Court has interpreted and applied FRE 702.

As do many states, Washington also has rules governing expert disclosures. For example, Washington Criminal Rule 4.7 requires prosecutors to disclose to defendants, on written demand, reports or statements made in connection with the case; this includes the results of mental or physical exams and scientific tests, as well as "any reports or statements of experts made in connection with the particular case." Wash. Cr. R. 4.7(a)(1)(iv). The prosecution must also disclose "any expert witnesses whom the prosecuting attorney will call at the hearing or trial, the subject of their testimony, and any reports they have submitted to the prosecuting attorney." Wash. Cr. R. 4.7(a)(2)(ii). Violation of this discovery rule, however, "does not require exclusion of undisclosed evidence as a sanction." *State v. Perez*, 137 Wash. App. 97, 109, 151 P.3d 249, 255 (Ct. App. 2007). Rather, whether to impose such a sanction is within the trial court's discretion, and continuances may be granted to provide the party time to disclose the evidence. *Id.* Similarly, subject to constitutional limitations Rule 4.7 may require defendants to disclose "any reports or results, or testimony relative thereto, of physical or mental examinations or of scientific tests, experiments, or comparisons, or any other reports or statements of experts which the defendant intends to use at a hearing or trial." Wash Cr. R. 4.7(g).

CHAPTER X
EXPERT EVIDENCE IN THE TENTH CIRCUIT

by

Linnea Brown
Temkin Wielga Hardt LLP
1900 Wazee St., Suite 303
Denver, CO 80202
(303) 382-2901
brown@twhlaw.com

A. KEY DECISIONS APPLYING *DAUBERT*, *JOINER* AND *KUMHO TIRE*

1. U.S. Court of Appeals for the Tenth Circuit

The Tenth Circuit applies the *Daubert*, *Kumho*, and *Joiner* trilogy in a predictable matter. As required by the U.S. Supreme Court, the Tenth Circuit reviews *de novo* whether the district court applied the proper legal test in admitting or excluding expert testimony. *United States v. Avitia-Guillen*, 680 F.3d 1253, 1256 (10th Cir. 2012) (citing *Goebel v. Denver & Rio Grande W. R.R. Co.*, 215 F.3d 1083, 1087 (10th Cir. 2000)). The focus of the Tenth Circuit's *de novo* inquiry is on "whether the district court actually performed its gatekeeper role in the first instance." *Id.*; *United States v. Roach*, 582 F.3d 1192, 1206 (10th Cir. 2009) (quoting *Dodge v. Cotter*, 328 F.3d 1212, 1223 (10th Cir. 2003)). Once the Tenth Circuit is satisfied that the district court "did not abdicate its gatekeeping role," it reviews, under an abuse of discretion standard, the application of Rule 702 and *Daubert* by the district court admitting or excluding expert testimony. *Avitia-Guillen*, 680 F.3d at n. 2; *see United States v. Garcia*, 635 F.3d 472, 476 (10th Cir. 2011) ("If the district court applied the correct legal standard, we then review the manner in which the court performed its gatekeeping role, deciding whether to admit or exclude testimony, for abuse of discretion."). Further, as with other evidentiary matters, the proponent of the expert testimony bears the burden of showing that its proffered expert's testimony is admissible. *United States v. Nacchio*, 555 F.3d 1234 (10th Cir. 2009); *Student Marketing Group Inc. v. College Partnership, Inc.*, 247 Fed. Appx. 90 (10th Cir. 2007).

a. Reversals for Failure to Make Specific Findings or Too Greatly Limiting the *Daubert* Record

The Tenth Circuit has repeatedly recognized that trial courts have broad discretion as to how they conduct the *Daubert* gatekeeping function—including whether to hold evidentiary hearings or use other procedures. As do other circuits, the Tenth Circuit emphasizes that, regardless of the latitude district courts have regarding how to exercise their gatekeeping function, they cannot avoid performing that role in a manner that provides an adequate appellate record.

For instance, in *United States v. Roach*, the defendant filed a motion *in limine* seeking to prevent the government from presenting an expert witness based on his credentials under *Daubert*. 582 F.3d at 1196. The district court denied the motion without ruling on the expert's qualifications or reliability, and later instructed the jury that they should consider the witness an expert anyway. *Id.* at 1199. The Tenth Circuit held that the district court abused its discretion, holding that the statements made to the jury contained no factual findings. *Id.* (affirmed on other grounds).

Dodge v. Cotter, 328 F.3d 1212 (10th Cir. 2003), provides another useful example of the Tenth Circuit's analysis. The *Dodge* case arose out of toxic tort lawsuits involving a uranium milling facility in Colorado. In this appeal, defendants challenged the admission of plaintiffs' experts' testimony in two trials. In the pretrial proceedings, Cotter submitted a forty-seven-page motion with "an appendix of several thousand pages" containing expert reports, deposition testimony, and more than 200 articles and studies relied on by the experts. *Id.* at 1223. The trial court returned the motion and appendix and instructed Cotter to file a revised motion and appendix "neither of which could exceed twenty pages." *Id.* Cotter again sought leave to file additional materials but the trial court denied its motion and Cotter then filed the shorter brief and appendix.

The trial court then held a *Daubert* hearing but denied Cotter's request at the hearing to offer testimony from Cotter's experts about plaintiffs' experts work. The trial court based its decision on Cotter's failure to notify the court of its intention to offer live testimony sufficiently in advance. Thus, the *Daubert* hearing consisted solely of arguments by counsel based on a limited paper record. After the arguments, the trial court recognized "the need to hear from the experts themselves" and thus reserved ruling on each expert until trial. *Id.* at 1225. The court also again denied Cotter's request to proffer an appendix of all of the reports and studies relied upon by the contested experts. At trial, the court did conduct in camera *voir dire* of the disputed experts but did not make detailed findings as to the reliability of their testimony.

In reviewing the record, the Tenth Circuit reversed and remanded as to the experts. First, the Tenth Circuit concluded that the trial court findings "lack the degree of specificity that would allow us to determine whether the district court properly applied the relevant law." *Id.* at 1226. The Tenth Circuit continued: "in the absence of specific, detailed findings, it is impossible for us on appeal to determine 'whether the district court carefully and meticulously reviewed the proffered scientific evidence or simply made an off-the-cuff decision to admit the expert testimony.'" *Id.* (citations omitted).

Second, the Tenth Circuit indicated its inclination that "the [trial] court abused its discretion by unreasonably limiting the evidence upon which to base its [*Daubert*] decision." *Id.* at 1228. The Tenth Circuit noted that:

> Although each of the court's decisions taken by itself might be within its discretion, taken together, these decisions placed an unreasonable limitation on the information available to the court and in our view exceeded the bounds of permissible choice in the circumstances. In a case like this one, where the expert testimony is crucial to the ultimate outcome, is vigorously challenged, and has several obvious areas of concern, we think it unreasonable to limit so severely both the underlying documentation and the use of live witness testimony upon which the court might base a decision. This is not a case where the parties agreed that the *Daubert* issues could be decided on a stipulated record, nor was it an "ordinary case[] where the reliability of an expert's methods [could] properly [be] taken for granted." On the contrary, in this case, we fail to see how the *Daubert* issues could be reliably decided without a meaningful hearing, which of necessity depends upon the use of live witness testimony as opposed to attorneys' arguments.

Id. at 1228–29 (citations omitted). The Tenth Circuit did not base its reversal and remand on this ground, however, because it already based it on the absence of specific findings. *Dodge* provides useful authority for the requirement that the trial court permit development of an adequate *Daubert* record even if doing so presents a burden to the court and that the trial court's decision is likely to be reversed if not based on specific findings. *See also Burlington Northern & Santa Fe Railway Co. v. Grant*, 505 F.3d 1013 (10th Cir. 2007) (reversed trial court due to failure to make specific findings on which it based its *Daubert* exclusion); *Goebel,* 215 F.3d at 1088 (trial court denied motion without explanation; appellate court held that trial court must "adequately demonstrate by specific findings on the record that it has performed its duty as a gatekeeper").

b. Deference to Trial Court Under Abuse of Discretion Standard

When the trial court has provided "specific, on-the-record findings that testimony is reliable under *Daubert*," the Tenth Circuit usually defers to the trial court. *Roach,* 582 F.3d at 1207. The Tenth Circuit most often describes the abuse of discretion standard as:

> "[A]rbitrary, capricious, whimsical, or manifestly unreasonable" or when we are convinced that the district court "made a clear error of judgment or exceeded the bounds of permissible choice in the circumstances."

Dodge, 328 F.3d at 1223 (citing *Atlantic Richfield Co. v. Farm Credit Bank*, 226 F.3d 1138, 1163–64 (10th Cir. 2000)). As explained in *Roach,* conclusory statements made by the district court, without any factual findings indicating the basis for the court's determination, "make it impossible on appeal to determine whether the district court carefully and meticulously reviewed the proffered scientific evidence or simply made an off-the-cuff decision to admit the expert testimony." 582 F.3d at 1207. Accordingly, those courts abuse their discretion and warrant reversal. *Id.*

Recently, the Tenth Circuit elaborated on what was required by a district court to demonstrate when it has performed its duty as gatekeeper. *See Avitia-Guillen,* 680 F.3d at 1259. After examining a survey of cases, including *Goebel, Roach, Nacchio* and *United States v. Velarde,* 214 F.3d 1204 (10th Cir. 2000), the court concluded that the key inquiry is "whether the appellate court can determine whether the district court 'properly applied the relevant law.'" *Id.* (quoting *United States v. Nichols,* 169 F.3d 1255, 1262 (10th Cir. 1999)). In *Avitia-Guillen,* the relevant law in question was Rule 702. The Tenth Circuit went on to conclude that since the district court said the expert was qualified to testify as a fingerprint examiner based on her "training, education, background, and experience," the record was sufficient to demonstrate that it applied the relevant law and did not abuse its discretion. *Id.*

The *Avitia-Guillen* court also drew a distinction between a challenge involving an expert's credentials rather than her methodology. *Id.* at 1259. The court noted that while *Goebel* involved a challenge to an expert's "methodology in a complicated area of medical science," the case at hand dealt with an expert's qualifications to testify over a commonly used method of identification. *Id.* Furthermore, the district court in *Avitia-Guillen* specifically referenced Rule 702 as the standard it was applying, whereas no such announcement was made in *Goebel. Id.* The court went on to reason that this case was more similar to *Roach,* which also dealt with an expert's credentials. *Id.* Unlike *Roach,* where the evidence decision was overturned, the district court in this case did provide an explanation, albeit one that the Tenth Circuit admitted was "very brief." *Id.* at 1260. Nonetheless, the brief explanation was enough for the Tenth Circuit to conclude that the district court did not abuse their discretion. *Id.* The court was careful to note, however, that in other cases, "particularly when dealing with an expert's methodology, [it] may require more extensive factual findings." *Id.*

Older cases also help to illustrate what the Tenth Circuit looks for when determining whether there has been an abuse of discretion. In *Miller v. Pfizer,* 356 F.3d 1326 (10th Cir. 2004), *cert. denied,* 543 U.S. 917 (2004), the trial court's *Daubert* proceedings including full briefing, appointment of two independent experts, and a hearing at which plaintiff's expert was allowed "to engage in a dialogue with the independent experts" though he was restricted to relying only on the materials previously provided. *Id.* at 1330. Plaintiffs in *Miller* alleged product liability claims concerning their son's suicide and its alleged connection with Zoloft. On appeal, plaintiff challenged the trial court's refusal to allow additional supplementation of his expert's opinions as well as an abuse of discretion in excluding their expert. The Tenth Circuit however determined that plaintiff had had ample opportunities to and in fact did supplement. It stated that the "the orderly conduct of litigation demands that expert opinions reach closure" and "the day of the hearing was a bit late to try to buttress the theory of their case by producing a new analysis by their retained expert of long-available data." *Id.* at 1334. Finally, in considering plaintiffs' claim that the trial court's evaluation exceeded the scope of a proper *Daubert* review, the Tenth Circuit explained: "[w]hat the Millers call nitpicking, we would call being thorough" and upheld the exclusion of plaintiffs' expert. *Id.* at 1335.

In *Norris v. Baxter Healthcare Corp.*, 397 F.3d 878 (10th Cir. 2005), plaintiff brought a product liability claim involving silicone breast implants and the trial court granted defendant's motion for summary judgment after concluding that plaintiff's causation experts were unreliable and therefore inadmissible. The Tenth Circuit upheld the trial court's decision:

> This is not a case where there is no epidemiology. It is a case where the body of epidemiology largely finds no association between silicone breast implants and immune system disease.
>
> . . .
>
> Plaintiff and her experts' efforts to discredit the epidemiology are not peer-reviewed, are not developed independent of litigation, and are not generally accepted by the relevant scientific community. . . .Plaintiff and her experts have to base their positions on reliable studies and methodology. In failing to properly address the previous and contrary views, Plaintiff's experts made their opinions and testimony unreliable as to the issue of general causation.
>
> . . .
>
> Plaintiff's experts attempted to demonstrate specific causation without first demonstrating general causation. Both of plaintiff's experts agree that, at best, silicone-associated connective disuse disease is an untested hypothesis. At worst, the link has been tested and found to be untenable. Therefore, there is no scientific basis for any expert testimony as to its specific presence in plaintiff.

Id. at 882, 886, and 887. *See also Hollander v. Sandoz Pharmaceuticals Corp.*, 289 F.3d 1193 (10th Cir. 2002) (upholding trial court's exclusion of expert testimony attempting to link Parlodel (bromocriptine) with postpartum stroke, after detailed review of trial court's analysis of scientific literature and expert opinions).[1]

---

[1] "In summary, . . . the Hollanders have done the best they could with the available data and the scientific literature. The data on which they rely might well raise serious concerns in conscientious clinicians seeking to decide whether the benefits of the drug outweigh its risks. However, in deriving their opinions that Parlodel caused Ms. Hollander's stroke. . . . Drs. Kulig, Iffy, and Jose all made several speculative leaps. As a result, the district court did not abuse its discretion in excluding their testimony under *Daubert*." *Id.* at 1213 (citation omitted).

Consistent with *Daubert*, the Tenth Circuit has also held that "any step that renders the expert's analysis unreliable . . . renders the testimony inadmissible. This is true whether the step completely changes a reliable methodology or merely misapplies that methodology." *Mitchell v. Gencorp Inc.*, 165 F.3d 778, 782 (10th Cir. 1999).

c. *Daubert* in Other Civil Cases

In *Champagne Metals v. Ken Mac Metals*, 458 F.3d 1073 (10th Cir. 2006), the Tenth Circuit upheld the district court's exclusion of plaintiff's economist, finding that the expert based his opinion on data from a different market than the one on which he was offering opinions and that the idea that they could be interchangeable was solely the argument of counsel. In a footnote, the Tenth Circuit also addressed a common expert issue—an expert's attempting to prove facts instead of offering expert opinion. "Expert testimony that fails to make clear that certain facts the expert describes as true are merely assumed for the purpose of an economic analysis may not assist the trier of fact at all and, instead, may simply result in confusion. Thus, it was not 'manifestly unreasonable' for the district court to conclude that Dr. Murray's opinions lacked foundation because they were based on 'the self-serving statement[s] of an interested party.'" *Id.* at 1077 n.4.

The Tenth Circuit has reversed a trial court finding that the admission of expert testimony under Rule 701(c) (opinion testimony by lay witnesses) constituted an abuse of discretion. *James River Insurance Co. v. Rapid Funding, LLC*, 658 F.3d 1207, 1216 (10th Cir. 2011).

d. *Daubert* in Criminal Cases

Criminal cases use *Daubert* and the abuse of discretion standard, but will reverse an erroneous admission of evidence "only if the court's error was not harmless—that is, if 'it had a substantial influence on the outcome or leaves one in grave doubt as to whether it had such effect.'" *Roach*, 582 F.3d at 1207 (quoting *United States v. Bornfield*, 145 F.3d 1123, 1131 (10th Cir. 1998)). For example, in *Roach*, although the Tenth Circuit determined that the district court abused its discretion when it admitted expert testimony without providing any factual findings, it also concluded that the government met its burden of showing that the expert's testimony did not substantially affect the verdict. *Id.* at 1208. Therefore, since admitting the expert's testimony was harmless, it did not result in a reversal of the defendant's conviction. *Id.*

In *United States. v. Rodriguez-Felix*, 450 F.3d 1117 (10th Cir. 2006) *cert. denied*, 2006 U.S. LEXIS 7742 (U.S., Oct. 10, 2006), the Tenth Circuit again upheld the district court's decision—this time to exclude the testimony of an expert in the reliability (or unreliability) of eyewitness identification. The Tenth Circuit recognized that expert testimony on the reliability of eyewitness identification may be critical at trial and that identification can be subject to significant witness error or manipulation. *Id.* at 1123. Using the abuse of discretion standard, the Tenth Circuit upheld the district court conclusion that the expert's report provided insufficient information from which to conclude that the opinions were reliable—including no information about whether the research was his own or that of others, whether it was subjected to peer review, whether it was published, or whether it was accepted by others in the field. In addition, the Tenth Circuit affirmed the trial court's other basis for exclusion—relevancy—finding that the testimony would not assist the trier of fact. The Tenth Circuit found that the testimony did not fall outside the "juror's common knowledge and experience," such as lapses in time between the incident and the identification reducing the reliability of the identification. *Id.* at 1126.

The Tenth Circuit determined that such testimony is unlikely to assist the jury other than in specialized circumstances in which the factors affecting the identification fall outside a typical juror's experience and that cross-examination provides an equally or more effective tool for testing the reliability of eyewitness identification at trial. *Id.*

B. EXPERT RELATED RULES AND PROCEDURAL ISSUES

The Tenth Circuit generally does not permit gamesmanship in expert designations, disclosure or discovery. The Tenth Circuit is pragmatic and focused on parties meeting their obligations fairly and using the Federal Rules as adopted.

1. *Expert Designation and Expert Reports*

With regard to the designation of experts, the Tenth Circuit expects parties to understand that Rule 26 requires all witnesses whose testimony may include expert opinions to be designated as expert witnesses. The Tenth Circuit also recognizes the distinction between designating a witness who may provide expert testimony and providing an expert report. In *Nester Commercial Roofing, Inc. v. American Builders and Contractors Supply Co.*, No. 06-6290, 2007 U.S. App. LEXIS 23829 (10th Cir. Oct. 10, 2007), the court affirmed the trial court's exclusion of plaintiff's CPA's testimony on lost profits. The Tenth Circuit held that although the plaintiff did not need to provide an expert report from its CPA, its failure to designate its CPA as a witness who may offer expert testimony properly resulted in the exclusion of the expert portion of the CPA's testimony. *Id.* at *12. Plaintiff's CPA was not retained or specially employed to provide expert testimony and thus fell within the exceptions to the Rule 26(a)(2)(B) requirement of providing an expert report. *Id.* Rule 26(a)(2)(A), however, has no equivalent exception to the requirement of disclosing the identity of "any person who may be used at trial to present evidence under Rules 702, 703, or 705." In its opinion, the Tenth Circuit acknowledged its previous opinions in which it has held that "[w]itnesses need not testify as experts just because they are experts—the nature and object of their testimony determines whether the procedural protestations of Rule 702 apply." *Nester,* 2007 U.S. App. LEXIS 23829 at *12 (citing *United States v. Caballero*, 277 F.3d 1235, 1247 (10th Cir. 2002)).

In *Watson v. United States*, 485 F.3d 1100 (10th Cir. 2007), the court reiterated that:

> While the Rule focuses on those who must file an expert report, by exclusion it contemplates that some persons are not required to file reports and that these include individuals who are employed by a party and do not regularly give expert testimony.

Id. at 1107.[2]

The Tenth Circuit continued its discussion addressing plaintiff's claim that such an interpretation would be "grossly unfair." *Id.* The court noted that those who drafted Rule 26, as well as Congress in its adoption, sought to balance "fulsome and efficient disclosure of expert opinions" with other considerations such as "the resources that might be diverted from patient care if treating physicians were required to issue expert reports as a precondition to testifying" and that second guessing those policy judgments is not the court's role. *Id.* The court then pointed out that the Federal Rules of Civil Procedure "do supply other mechanisms, besides formal reports, for extracting the views of an expert witness like Dr. Goforth; sandbagging is not necessarily inevitable." *Id.* at 1108. The court identified depositions, individual document demands to the expert, and the party's own Rule 26(a)(1)(B) document disclosures as well as the catch-all "other discovery the court deems necessary and appropriate" as potential discovery mechanisms." *Id.*

---

[2] Caution should be used in evaluating the exclusions from the expert report requirement. *See, e.g., Washington v. Arapahoe County Department of Social Services*, 197 F.R.D. 439, 441 (D. Colo. 2000) (treating physician required to prepare report where expert testimony goes beyond his observations during treatment) and *Wreath v. United States*, 161 F.R.D. 448, 450 (D. Kan. 1995).

In *Jacobsen v. Deseret Book Co.*, 287 F.3d 936 (10th Cir. 2002), the court addressed a situation in which defendant's experts provided only preliminary and incomplete expert reports and the trial court denied plaintiff's motion for additional time to file rebuttal reports or to strike the incomplete reports. Defendants acknowledged that their expert reports were incomplete but argued that they could not be completed because plaintiff had not provided certain information. Defendants also argued that the incomplete reports did not preclude rebuttal reports "with 'the same level of generality 'as the incomplete reports.'" *Id.* at 952. The Tenth Circuit concluded that the district court abused its discretion in denying plaintiffs' motion to strike the incomplete reports. Preliminary reports do not satisfy Rule 26(a)(2) and can result in exclusion of the expert's testimony—regardless of the reasons for the incompleteness. *Id.*; *accord Kern River Gas Transmission Co. v. 6.17 Acres of Land*, 156 Fed. Appx. 96, 102–103 (10th Cir. 2005). In general, prejudice to the opposing party resulting from its not knowing the substance of the expert's testimony is considered so significant and incurable that the expert with the incomplete report will likely be excluded.

With regard to expert report disclosures, the Tenth Circuit expressed its pragmatism in *103 Investors I, L.P. v. Square D Co.*, 372 F.3d 1213 (10th Cir. 2004) in which the trial court twice extended defendant's expert report deadline but failed to extend the associated subsequent deadline for plaintiff's rebuttal expert reports and then excluded any of plaintiff's expert rebuttal testimony.

> The plaintiff's rationalization for the untimeliness of its filed report appears to us to be perfectly adequate; quite simply, Investors could not have been expected to file a rebuttal expert report prior to the report it sought to rebut.

Id. at 1217. The Tenth Circuit also considered whether the proffered rebuttal reports included new negligence theory, concluded the rebuttal report clearly rebutted plaintiff's expert assertions, and thus reversed for an abuse of discretion on both grounds. *Id.*

In the Tenth Circuit, a party may not submit an affidavit containing expert testimony in connection with a motion for summary judgment unless the affiant has been first designated as an expert witness under Rule 26(a)(2). *Bryant v. Farmers Ins. Exchange*, 432 F.3d 1114, 1124 (10th Cir. 2005). Even then, when submitting affidavits to justify opposition to summary judgment, courts will reject an expert's report if they do not comply with the requirements set out in Rule 56(f). *Cohlmia v. St. John Medical Ctr.*, 693 F.3d 1269, 1286 (10th Cir. 2012).

2. *Expert Qualifications*

District courts in the Tenth Circuit "[have] 'wide discretion' in determining whether a witness's experience is sufficient to qualify him as an expert." *Ronwin v. Bayer Corp.*, 332 Fed. Appx. 508, 513 (10th Cir. 2009) (quoting *United States v. Arney*, 248 F.3d 984, 991 (10th Cir. 2001)). Although an expert's qualifications may be deemed sufficient for a prior case, district courts still have "an obligation to assess the methodology that [the expert employs] in the case at hand." *Mooring Capital Fund, LLC v. Knight*, 388 Fed. Appx. 814, 820 (10th Cir. 2010) (quoting *United States v. Nacchio*, 555 F.3d 1234, 1258 (10th Cir.) (en banc), *cert. denied*, 130 S.Ct. 54, 175 L.Ed.2d 21 (2009)).

The Tenth Circuit has also addressed an unusual situation: What to do when an expert witness says he is not really so expert? At an expert witness's deposition, the same expert had offered testimony that plaintiff argued was an admission that the expert was not an expert. The Tenth Circuit declined to overturn the trial court's admission of the expert's testimony.

> And tempting though it might be to supplement our traditional case- and fact-specific inquiry with Ms. Watson's automatic rule that no witness who denies having the requisite expertise may testify, doing so would risk turning a substantive and serious examination by

a district court judge about a proffered witness's suitability into a game of gotcha, allowing lawyers to set cross-examination traps for unwary individuals who do not make their living testifying in court but who nonetheless may have a very great deal to offer fact finders. While overly modest expert witnesses may not be exactly an everyday sort of problem in our legal system, neither can we ignore the prospect of mistakenly excluding a witness who really is expert but simply too demure to trumpet his or her qualifications under cross-examination.

Watson, 485 F.3d at 1105–06.

3. Sanctions for Expert Disclosure Infractions

As a general rule, when a party fails to comply with Rule 26(a)'s disclosure requirements, that party "is not allowed to introduce the expert witness's testimony... at trial" unless it is justified or harmless under Rule 37(c)(1). *ClearOne Communications, Inc. v. Biamp Sys.*, 653 F.3d 1163, 1176 (10th Cir. 2011). Courts in the Tenth Circuit consider four factors when making that determination: (1) the prejudice or surprise to the impacted party, (2) the ability to cure the prejudice, (3) the potential for trial disruption, and (4) the erring party's bad faith or willfulness. *Id.*; *see also Jacobsen*, 287 F.3d at 953 (citing *Woodworker's Supply, Inc. v. Principal Mut. Life Ins. Co.*, 170 F.3d 985, 933 (10th Cir. 1999)). Whether a Rule 26(a) violation is justified or harmless "is entrusted to the broad discretion of the district court." *Neiberger v. Fed Ex Ground Package Sys., Inc.*, 566 F.3d 1184, 1192 (10th Cir. 2009) (quoting *Woodworker's Supply*, 170 F.3d at 993). Like other aspects of expert disclosure, the Tenth Circuit reviews sanctions imposed by a district court for an abuse of discretion. *Id.*

Over the last several years, federal courts within the Tenth Circuit have addressed a variety of discovery issues related to experts, including whether a witness's opinions required expert disclosures. *Arble v. State Farm Mut. Ins. Co.*, 272 F.R.D. 604 (2011) (expert to testify solely for *Daubert* purposes and not for trial); *Qwest Corp. v. Elephant Butte Irrigation Dist.*, 616 F.Supp. 2d 1110 (D. N.M. 2008) (basic calculations using addition, subtraction, and division understandable to a lay person not expert testimony so no report necessary).

Whether a "preliminary" expert report complies with Fed. R. Civ. Pro. 26 has also been an issue before the Tenth Circuit. *See Kern River Gas Transmission Co. v. 6.17 Acres of Land*, 156 Fed. Appx. 96, 102 (10th Cir. 2005) (did not comply); *Cohlmia v. Ardent Health Services, LLC*, 254 F.R.D. 426, 431, n. 6 (did not comply).

The Tenth Circuit has also ruled on whether an expert's report complies with the requirements of Fed. R. Civ. Pro. 26(a)(2). *See Gillum v. United States*, 309 Fed. Appx. 267 (10th Cir. 2009) (report did not comply; however, trial court abused its discretion in excluding expert's testimony which exclusion resulted in grant of summary judgment and was thus too extreme a sanction).Depending on the circumstance, a party may be able to provide a supplemental report of a previously designated expert or an original report of a new expert. *Rimert v. Eli Lilly and Co.*, 647 F.3d 1247, 1256 (10th Cir. 2011) (naming new expert after *Daubert* exclusion of previous expert); *Baumann v. American Family Mut. Ins. Co.*, 278 F.R.D. 614 (D. Colo. 2012) (death of expert); *Cohlmia v. Ardent Health Services, LLC*, 254 F.R.D. 426 (2008); and

Finally, courts in the Tenth Circuit have addressed whether the rate and hours spent in preparation for a deposition are reasonable and thus chargeable to the deposing party. *Fiber Optic Designs, Inc. v. New England Pottery, LLC*, 262 F.R.D. 586 (D. Colo. 2009) (citing cases supporting three different approaches to preparation time fees and addressing increased rate for deposition).

C. EXPERT WITNESS ISSUES UNDER STATE LAW

1. *Colorado*

Colorado rejected the *Frye* test in *People v. Shreck*, 22 P.3d 68 (Colo. 2001), recognizing the evolving nature of science and the importance of flexibility of analysis:

> We also find that this rigidity is ill-suited for determining the admissibility of scientific evidence, which, by its nature is ever-evolving. Under *Frye*, once a scientific principle or discovery becomes generally accepted, it forever remains accepted, despite improvements or other development in scientific technologies. Conversely, because it will take time for any scientific technique to become generally accepted, the *Frye* test restricts the admissibility of reliable evidence that may not yet qualify as "generally accepted" under *Frye*.

Id. at 76. In *Shreck*, the court held that Colo. R. Evid. 702 would govern the admissibility of scientific evidence. As must federal courts under *Daubert*, in Colorado courts must "focus on the reliability and relevance of the proffered evidence" and determine "(1) the reliability of the scientific principles, (2) the qualifications of the witness, and (3) the usefulness of the testimony to the jury."[3] In making these determinations, the court's "inquiry should be broad in nature and consider the totality of the circumstances in each specific case." *Shreck*, 22 P.3d at 70. The court stated that the specific *Daubert* factors may or may not be pertinent to a given case and that this position was consistent with the court's "previous declination to 'give any special significance to the Daubert factors.'" *Id.* at 78 (citing *Brooks v. People*, 975 P.2d 1105, 1114 (Colo. 1999)). Courts often refer specifically to *Shreck* when applying this standard. *See Jackson v. Unocal Corp.*, 262 P.3d 874, 886 (discussing the lack of a "*Shreck* hearing" at the class action certification stage); *Estate of Ford v. Eicher*, 250 P.3d 262, 265 (Colo. 2011) (discussing the trial court's refusal to conduct a "*Shreck* analysis").

Colorado courts must "issue specific findings as it applies the [Colo. R. Evid.] 702 and 403 analysis." *Shreck*, 22 P.3d at 70. However, trial courts are not required to conduct an evidentiary hearing under *Shreck* provided they have sufficient information to make findings under Colo. R. Evid. 403 and 702 and factors pertinent to a *Shreck* analysis. *People v. Rector*, 248 P.3d 1196, 1201 (Colo. 2011). Furthermore, trial courts have discretion to determine whether a party's request gives rise to a *Shreck* analysis at all. *Id.* Appellate courts will review a trial court's expert evidence decision for an abuse of discretion and will reverse "only when that decision is manifestly erroneous." *Id.* at 1200.

Expert testimony does not need to be offered to either a reasonable probability or reasonable certainty. Instead, expert testimony may be admissible when the opinion is stated at "I think," "I believe," "it may," "it is possible," or similar language. In *State v. Ramirez*, 155 P.3d 371 (Colo. 2007), the court held that the "reasonable probability" or "reasonable certainty" standard for expert opinions was "outdated and inappropriate." The court held that the standards for the admissibility of expert opinions are those in Rules 702 and 403 and not those from common law (from which the reasonable probability or reasonable certainty standard originated) that pre-dated Colorado's adoption of its Rules of Civil Procedure. In its analysis, the court importantly distinguished between cases in

---

[3] Like most other jurisdictions, in Colorado "[u]sefulness means that the proffered testimony would be useful to the fact finder to either understand other evidence or to determine a fact in issue." *See, e.g., Masters v. People*, 58 P.3d 979 (Colo. 2002); *State v. Martinez*, 74 P.3d 316 (Colo. 2003).

which the issue pertained to the sufficiency of the evidence to uphold a conviction or judgment and those in which the issue pertained to the admissibility of expert testimony.

In *Ramirez*, the court upheld the admission of testimony by a pediatric nurse practitioner who performed a sexual-assault examination of the victim. Her examination had four possible findings: normal, non-specific (which could be a normal finding but also could be associated with sexual abuse), suspicious (e.g., may have been caused by sexual abuse, but could have been caused by something else), and definitive (a rare finding of definite sexual abuse). In this case, the expert's examination resulted in a "suspicious" finding. After reiterating the analysis required under Rules 702 and 403, including emphasis on the issue of whether the expert testimony would be useful to the finder of fact, the court applied the analysis. The court explained that:

> Testimony is not speculative simply because an expert's testimony is in the form of an opinion or stated with less than certainty, i.e., 'I think' or 'it is possible.' If such were the case, most expert testimony would not be admissible, as rarely can anything be stated with absolute certainty, even within the realm of scientific evidence.
>
> . . .
>
> Thus, in determining that an expert's testimony is unreliable and should therefore not be admitted under CRE 702, it is not enough for a court to conclude that the testimony is 'speculative.' . . . the standard of admissibility under CRE 702 is reliability and relevance, not certainty.

Id. at 378. The court stated: "Speculative testimony under CRE 702 is opinion testimony that has no analytically sound basis." *Id.* In other words, the court focused not on words that previously would have triggered a "speculation" objection, but instead on the underlying reliability and usefulness of the expert opinion—and that an expert's testimony about what is possible or what the expert believes may be admissible if it is both reliable and useful to the fact finder.

In *Ramirez*, the court distinguished the case from *People v. Wilkerson*, 114 P.3d 874 (Colo. 2005), in which an expert's opinion was that an accidental shooting could happen 51 percent of the time. This expert opinion in *Wilkerson* was excluded because the expert did not have empirical or methodological justification in the record. In contrast, in *Ramirez*, the nurse practitioner did not offer any "statistical, numerical, nor quantifiable conclusions" related to her findings. *Id.* at 381 n. 10. Finally, the court cautioned that "even though the proffered testimony may be admissible upon the liberal standards of CRE 702, the court must also apply its discretionary authority under CRE 403" and that "evidence should be excluded when it has an undue tendency to suggest a decision on an improper basis." The Colorado Supreme Court has issued more recent opinions in which it applies its *Ramirez* holdings, such as *People v. Rector*, 248 P.3d 1196 (Colo. 2011) (also addresses Rule 704); *Estate of Ford v. Eicher*, 250 P.3d 262 (Colo. 2011).

In Colorado, expert testimony need not be admissible to be used by the court in deciding class certification. *Unocal Corp.*, 262 P.3d at 874. Instead, the courts need only to "rigorously analyze" the class certification evidence. *Id.* at 886. Class certification "is a case management tool and neither [Rule 23] nor [Colorado] case law imposes a specific burden of proof on the trial court's certification decision." *Id.* at 881. In *Jackson*, the court declined to adopt a preponderance of the evidence standard to class certification decisions. *Id.* at 884. The court acknowledged that the preponderance standard squares with "the additional discovery and definitive nature of certification under amended Fed. R. Civ. P. 23." However, the court declined to follow the trend in federal circuit courts of appeal both because of the difference between the federal and Colorado Rule 23, and because those cases are not persuasive in light of Colorado's "policy of liberally constructing [Rule 23] in favor of class certification." *Id.* at 883–884.

In re Application for Water Rights of Park County Sportsmen's Ranch, 105 P.3d 595 (Colo. 2005), provides an example of the application of Rule 702 in Colorado in a civil, scientific context. The Colorado Supreme Court upheld the water court's exclusion of expert testimony because of errors in technique, including failure to perform a sensitivity analysis, failure to properly calibrate the model, failure to explain anomalous results and residual errors, and failure to complete an independent peer review of the model.

2. Kansas

The admission of expert testimony in Kansas is pursuant to statute and *Frye v. United States*, 293 F. 1013 (D.C.Cir. 1923). The pertinent Kansas statute provides that:

> If the witness is testifying as an expert, testimony of the witness in the form of opinions or inferences is limited to such opinions as the judge finds are (1) based on facts or data perceived by or personally known or made known to the witness at the hearing, and (2) within the scope of the special knowledge, skill, experience, or training possessed by the witness.

K.S.A. 60-456(b)(2006). In criminal cases, admitting expert testimony generally lies within the discretion of the trial court, and if a court does abuse its discretion, the error remains subject to a harmlessness analysis. *State v. Gaona*, 270 P.3d 1165, 1173–74 (Kan. 2012).

In Kansas, an exception to the *Frye* test is when the expert's opinion is "pure opinion." That is an opinion which an expert "developed from inductive reasoning based on the expert's own experiences, observations, or research." *State v. Shadden*, 290 P.3d 436, 448 (2010) (reversed admission of scientific opinion based on failure to conduct *Frye* analysis on "psychomotor field test" and distinguished it from "common knowledge" of mannerisms of intoxicated person for which no *Frye* analysis is necessary). In *Kuhn v. Sandoz Pharmaceuticals Corp.*, 14 P.3d 1170, 1179 (Kan. 2000), the court reversed the trial court's exclusion of plaintiffs' causation expert testimony. The Kansas Supreme Court decided that the causation testimony at issue was not scientific opinion subject to *Frye* analysis, but was instead "pure opinion" and thus admissible. The court explained that pure opinion does "not hinge on the validity of a scientific principal, device, test, or procedure developed by another" and that "[w]eight will depend on the accuracy of observation, the extent of training, and the reliability of the experts' interpretations." *Id.* at 1182.[4] In *State v. Patton*, 120 P.3d 760 (Kan. 2005), the Kansas Supreme Court reiterated the *Kuhn* distinction and rationale:

> The *Frye* test does not apply to pure opinion testimony, which is an expert opinion developed from inductive reasoning based on the expert's own experiences, observations, or research. The validity of pure opinion is tested by cross-examination of the witness. The distinction between pure opinion testimony and testimony based on a scientific method or procedure is rooted in a concept that seeks to limit application of the *Frye* test to situations where there is the greatest potential for juror confusion.
>
> The distinction between pure opinion testimony and testimony relying on scientific technique promotes the right to a jury trial. Judges generally are not trained in scientific fields and, like jurors, are lay persons concerning science. A Kansas jury has a constitutional

---

[4] Further, *Kuhn* noted that Kansas does not require a finding of general causation in order to find specific causation and distinguished those cases requiring general causation as being those involving either mass exposures or "large existing epidemiological records." *Id.* at 1185.

mandate to decide between conflicting facts, including conflicting opinions of causation. The district judge under K.S.A. 60-456(b) controls expert opinion evidence that would unduly prejudice or mislead a jury or confuse the question for resolution. Cross-examination, the submission of contrary evidence, and the use of appropriate jury instructions form a preferred method of resolving a factual dispute.

120 P.3d. at 783.

In *Kuxhausen v. Tillman Partners*, L.P., 291 Kan. 314 (2010), the court returned to expert causation testimony in the context of chemical exposure. The court first reiterated Kansas law that "[i]t is necessary that the facts upon which an expert relies for his or her opinion should afford a reasonably accurate basis for his or her conclusions as distinguished from mere guess or conjecture. Expert witnesses should confine their opinions to relevant matters which are certain or probable, not those which are merely possible." *Id.* at 318 (internal citations omitted). The court found that "the factual basis for the [causation] opinion was lacking." *Id.* at 319. The court then upheld the exclusion of the causation opinion stating:

> In this case, Dr. Kanareck's opinion is ultimately based on nothing more than *post hoc ergo propter hoc* logic: the symptoms follow the exposure; therefore, they must be due to it. Such reasoning is nothing more than speculation."

Id. at 320. In contrast with *Kuhn*, *Kuxhausen* does not characterize the causation opinion as pure opinion testimony. On March 9, 2012, the Kansas Supreme Court granted review of *In the Matter of Girard*, 257 P.3d 1256 (Kan. App. 2012) in which the Court of Appeals stated "We are duty bound to follow Kansas Supreme Court precedent and will not apply the tests set forth in *Daubert* until instructed to do so." *Id.* at 1110.

3. New Mexico

In 2012, New Mexico amended Rule 11-702 NMRA, to make the style consistent with the 2011 federal amendments to F.R.E. 702. However, New Mexico did not made the substantive 2000 federal rule amendments "in light of the differences between federal law and New Mexico law regarding whether *Daubert* applies to nonscientific testimony." Advisory Committee Notes. The key difference between the federal and New Mexico rules is that New Mexico has not adopted *Kumho* and, therefore, New Mexico limits the application of a *Daubert* analysis to expert testimony that is "scientific."

In 1993, the New Mexico Supreme Court abandoned the *Frye* test. *State v. Alberico*, 861 P.2d 192 (N.M. 1993). Consistent with *Daubert*, *Alberico* cautioned that "[i]t is improper to look for scientific acceptance only from reported case law because that amounts to finding a consensus in the legal community based on scientific evidence that is sometimes many years old." *Id.* The court continued with a discussion of the scientific validity and scientific reliability:

> Reliability has been defined as a measure of bringing about consistent results, and validity is seen as proof of the technique's ability to show what it purports to show.
>
> We view validity and reliability as being scientifically interrelated, with the concept of validity encompassing the concept of reliability. In other words, if a particular scientific technique brings about consistent results, that is one element of validity, that is, proof of the technique's ability to show what it purports to show. While one concept embraces the other in a scientific sense, however, legally the two concepts are related to two separate eviden-

tiary issues. Validity is the measure of determining whether the testimony is grounded in or a function of established scientific methods or principles, that is, scientific knowledge. Reliability is akin to relevancy in considering whether the expert opinion will assist the trier of fact.

Id. at 167. The court then provided a few factors that courts could consider in determining validity—such as "the technique's relationship with established scientific analysis, the availability of specialized literature addressing the validity of the technique, and whether the technique is generally accepted." *Id.* at 203–04. The court emphasized that "we will not attempt to etch into stone a list of criteria as the *sine qua non* for the admissibility of scientific evidence, but these criteria will serve as guidelines for our lower courts and allow for further development in this area of our case law. *Id.* at 204. Although *Alberico* did not list the four *Daubert* factors, other New Mexico courts have relied upon them.[5] *See, e.g., State v. Fry*, 126 P.3d 516, 540–41 (N.M. 2005).

In *State v. Torres*, 976 P.2d 20 (1999), the New Mexico Supreme Court limited the requirements of *Alberico/Daubert* to scientific knowledge. Then, in *State v. Torrez*, 210 P.3d 228, 234 (N.M. 2009), the court again distinguished between "the standards applicable to determining the admissibility of expert *scientific* testimony with those for admitting expert testimony based on the *specialized knowledge* of the expert witness. *Torrez* held that "[t]he requirements that scientific expert testimony be "grounded in valid, objective science' and "reliable enough to prove what it purports to prove" are inapplicable to expert testimony that is based on the expert's specialized knowledge." *Id.* at 234 (internal citations omitted). The court further explained:

> In other words, even with nonscientific expert testimony, the trial court must exercise its gatekeeping function and ensure that the expert's opinion is reliable. However, when testing the reliability of nonscientific expert testimony, rather than testing an expert's scientific methodology as required under *Daubert* and *Alberico*, the court must evaluate a nonscientific expert's personal knowledge and experience to determine whether the expert's conclusions on a given subject may be trusted.

> While this inquiry is similar to a determination of whether an expert is qualified to opine on a given subject, the two inquiries are not identical. The first inquiry, testing an expert's qualifications, requires that the trial court determine whether an expert's skills, experience, training, or education qualify him or her in the relevant subject. Although the second inquiry uses these same factors, the court uses them to test the validity of the expert's conclusions. In this way, an expert may be qualified to offer opinions on a subject, but those opinions may nevertheless be unreliable in that they do not provide what they purport to prove.

Id. at 234–235. A number of recent New Mexico cases apply these principles. *See, e.g., Andrews v. United States Steel Corp.*, 250 P.3d 887 (N.M. 2011); *Parkhill v. Alderman-Cave Milling & Grain Co. of New Mexico*, 245 P.3d 585 (N.M. App. 2010) (causation testimony in chemical exposure case).

---

[5] Medical testimony in worker's compensation administrative cases are not subject to *Daubert*-type analysis in New Mexico due to special evidentiary rules in those proceedings. *Banks v. IMC Kalium Carlsbad Potash*, 77 P.3d 1014, 1021 (N.M. 2003).

4. Oklahoma

Oklahoma State Title 12, section 2705 provides that an expert may testify "by opinion or inference and give reasons therefor without previous disclosure of the underlying facts or data, unless required to disclose the underlying facts or data on cross-examination or by the court." *Covel v. Rodriguez*, 272 P.3d 705, 710 (Okla. 2012).

In the civil context, in *Christian v. Gray*, 65 P.3d 591 (Okla. 2003), the court adopted *Daubert* and *Kumho* as "appropriate standards for Oklahoma trial courts for deciding the admissibility of expert testimony in civil matters." *Id.* at 600. However, in doing so, it limited the application of those standards:

> We agree with the Court of Criminal Appeals that a *Daubert* inquiry will be limited to circumstances where the reliability of an expert's method cannot be taken for granted. Thus, a *Daubert* challenge includes an initial determination of whether the expert's method is one where reliability may be taken for granted.

Id. at 599–600. Moreover, while *Daubert* is still used in Oklahoma state civil matters, a *Daubert* challenge requires a trial court "to make a determination of the reliability of an expert's evidence *when it is sufficiently challenged.*" *Covel*, 272 P.3d at 708 (citing *Christian*, 65 P.3d at 599) (emphasis in original).

As with most other courts that apply *Daubert*, in *Christian* the Oklahoma Supreme Court held that "the *Daubert* factors are not a rigid standard applicable in every case." *Id.* "The *Daubert* factors "may" bear on a judge's gatekeeping determinations" but that will "all depend 'on the nature of the issue, the expert's particular expertise, and the subject of his testimony.'" *Id.* (quoting Fed. Judicial Center., Reference Manual on Scientific Evidence 19 (2d ed. 2000)); *see also Scruggs v. Edwards*, 154 P.3d 1257, 1262 (Okla. 2007) (noting that *Daubert* provides a "nonexhaustive list of factors" that are "flexible" and not intended to be rigidly applied to every case). Consistent with federal case law, the court stated that "[w]hen a trial court applies *Daubert* and determines that a particular method is required for the admissibility of a particular expert's conclusions the order should state those facts that the trial court relied upon in making that determination." *Christian*, 65 P.3d at 610.

In *Taylor v. State*, 889 P.2d 319 (Okla. Crim. Ct. App. 1995), the Oklahoma Court of Criminal Appeals[6] adopted *Daubert* for determining the admissibility of novel scientific evidence in criminal trials. The court concluded its opinion by stating:

> This court has now independently determined that DNA match evidence obtained through RFLP analysis and DNA statistics calculated through the standard population genetics formulas, pass the *Daubert* test. Therefore, from this point forward, trial courts faced with DNA profiling evidence produced through these means need not conduct a *Daubert* pretrial admissibility hearing. We emphasize that while this evidence is now generally admissible, its weight and credibility remain subject to attack through cross-examination and testimonial challenges.

Id. at 338–39.

After *Kumho*, in *Harris v. State*, 13 P.3d 489 (Okla. Crim. Ct. App. 2001), the court found *Kumho's* application of *Daubert* to nonscientific expert testimony persuasive. However, the court

---

[6] The Oklahoma Court of Criminal Appeals is the highest court for criminal cases. The Oklahoma Supreme Court does not handle criminal appeals. 20 Okla. Stat. § 40 (2007).

limited the application of *Daubert* to "novel" expert testimony and finding that because the expert testimony at issue was not novel and had "long been recognized" that no *Daubert* inquiry need be done. *Id.* at 493; *see also Anderson v. State*, 252 P.3d 211, 213 (Okla. Crim. Ct. App. 2010) (reinforcing that *Taylor* and *Daubert* are not applicable to nonscientific evidence).

5. Utah

In 2007, Utah amended its Rule of Evidence 702. Now Utah R. Evid. 702(a), (a) is substantively identical to F.R.E. 702, while sections (b) and (c) do not appear in the federal rule. As with F.R.E. 702, Utah. R. Evid. 702 applies to all expert testimony and does not distinguish between scientific and other expert opinion. Overall, "[a]lthough Utah law foreshadowed in many respects the developments in federal law that commenced with *Daubert*, the 2007 amendment preserves and clarifies differences between the Utah and federal approaches to expert testimony." Utah Advisory Committee Note. *See, e.g., Gunn Hill Dairy Properties, LLC v. Los Angeles Dept. of Water & Power*, 269 P.3d 980 (Utah App. 2012). Just as with federal law, trial judges in Utah have a gate-keeping function.

Before the 2007 amendment the key Utah case was *State v. Rimmasch*, 775 P.2d 388 (Utah 1989). Some of the expert opinion principles from *Rimmasch* remain Utah law, as reflected below, though some of them no longer reflect Utah law. In *Eskelson v. Davis Hosp. & Med. Center*, 242 P.3d 762 (2010), the Utah Supreme Court explained, in detail:

> In amending rule 702, the court did not intend to make it more difficult to admit expert testimony, but rather to clarify the requirements for admission. Aspects of the *Rimmasch* test continue to be applicable under amended Rule 702. For example, rule 702(b), like *Rimmasch*, requires a determination to determine whether a party has met its threshold burden to show the reliability of the principles that form the basis for the expert's testimony and the reliability of applying those principles to the facts of the case. And, similar to the *Rimmasch* standard, rule 702(c) allows the court to take judicial notice of principles that have been accepted by the relevant expert community.
>
> The advisory committee notes make clear that the new rule 702 'assigns to trial judges a "gatekeeper" responsibility to screen out unreliable expert testimony'—not just scientific expert testimony. When applying the new rule 702, judges should approach expert testimony with 'rational skepticism.' But the 'degree of scrutiny [that should be applied to expert testimony by trial judges] is not so rigorous as to be satisfied only by scientific or other specialized principles or methods that are free of controversy or that meet any fixed set of criteria fashioned to test reliability.' Importantly, both subsections (b) and (c) require the plaintiff to make only a 'threshold showing' of reliability.

Id. at 766; *see also State v. Clopten*, 223 P.3d 1103 (Utah 2009).

In *State v. Sheehan*, 273 P.3d 417 (Utah. App. 2012), the trial court admitted expert testimony offered by the State concerning fingerprint identification. The trial court excluded defendant's fingerprint expert testimony without making an independent evaluation of defendant's expert's testimony under Utah. R. Evid. 702. In addressing potential exclusion of the defendant's expert's opinion, the court emphasized that:

> Quite simply, there are two separate reliability determinations: admissibility, which is a legal determination the court makes, and the weight assigned to the evidence admitted at trial, which is a factual determination made by the fact finder.

In *Gunn Hill,* 269 P.3d 980 (Utah App. 2012), the court concluded:

> Under the rule, the line between assessing reliability and weighing evidence can be elusive. But the trial court may not cross that line when assessing threshold reliability for purposes of ruling on admissibility pursuant to rule 702. The court's role is only preliminary; the fact finder bears the ultimate responsibility for evaluating the accuracy, reliability, and weight of the testimony.

Id. at 995.

6. Wyoming

In *Bunting v. Jamieson,* 984 P.2d 467 (Wyo. 1999), the Wyoming Supreme Court expressly adopted *Daubert* and *Kumho* for admissibility of all expert testimony. *Accord Springfield v. State,* 860 P.2d 435, 443 (Wyo. 1993) (Wyoming evidence rule parallels federal and thus *Daubert* parallels Wyoming law). Then in *Seivewright v. State,* 7 P.3d 24 (Wyo. 2000), the court continued its adoption of *Daubert* gatekeeping:

> "First, the district court must determine whether the methodology or technique used by the expert to reach his conclusions is reliable. If so, the court must determine whether the proposed testimony "fits" the facts of the particular case."

Id. at 29. Furthermore, "a trial judge need not and should not determine the scientific validity of the conclusions offered by an expert witness. Rather, to decide admissibility, the trial judge should only consider the soundness of the general scientific principles or reasoning on which the expert relies and the propriety of the methodology applying those principles to the specific facts of the case." *Id. Seivewright* also holds that a court is not required to hold an evidentiary hearing on the admissibility of expert testimony. *Id.* at 30. In *Williams v. State,* 60 P.3d 151 (Wyo. 2002), the court reiterated its opinion in *Bunting* that "the important determination that must be squarely addressed by the trial court is whether or not the analysis of the expert in question is 'grounded on something other than 'subjective belief or unsupported speculation' and if such opinion employs the same level of intellectual rigor that characterizes the practice of an expert in the relevant field." *Id.* at 158 (quoting *Bunting,* 984 P.2d at 475–76).

In *Chapman v. State,* 18 P.3d 1164 (Wyo. 2001), the court addressed a complex criminal issue in which the defendant asserted that the trial court erred in permitting expert testimony that the victim had suffered post-traumatic stress disorder (PTSD) as part of the explanation of the victim's behavior. Although the court disagreed with the defendant's position that the theory of PTSD in the context of child sexual abuse was not reliable and held that the trial court did not err in its admission, it cautioned that testimony which could be interpreted as vouching for the credibility of the victim-witness must be admitted with care.

In *Reichert v. Phipps,* 84 P.3d 353 (Wyo. 2004), the court reversed the trial court's exclusion of expert testimony linking the physical trauma from a car accident with the development of fibromyalgia. Despite the trial court's conclusion that this causal opinion lacked support in the medical community and thus was unreliable, the Supreme Court concluded that where an expert's opinion is based on the patient's medical history, the physician's treatment of the patient, a differential diagnosis, and some support in the medical literature, then the opinion met the admissibility threshold. *Id.* at 362; *accord Easum v. Miller,* 92 P.3d 794, 804 (Wyo. 2004) (reversed trial court's exclusion of expert who used differential diagnosis to rule out causes other than the electrical shock for plaintiff's subsequent reflex sympathetic reflex).

In an interesting juxtaposition to *Reichert*, in *Hoy v. DRM, Inc.*, 114 P.3d 1268 (Wyo. 2005), the Wyoming Supreme Court upheld the trial court's exclusion of expert testimony concerning a causal link between construction activities and the temporally related collapse of a leach field. Perhaps a persuasive difference in the cases is that in *Hoy* the excluded expert made admissions that supported the exclusion while in *Reichert* most of the evidence on unreliability came from the opposing experts. The court stated, "[a]n expert cannot rely just upon their status as an expert to bootstrap the admission of their opinion testimony. There must be some indicia of reliability." *Id.* at 1283.

In *Cramer v. Powder River Coal, LLC*, 204 P.3d 974 (Wyo. 2009), the court upheld the trial court's decision to exclude expert opinion on the issue of whether defendant violated certain regulations. The trial court admitted expert testimony about the regulations, but excluded expert opinion on whether defendant had violated them. The Wyoming Supreme Court agreed that such testimony would not assist the trier of fact because the jury was capable of understanding the regulations and making the determination of whether defendant had violated the regulations—without expert opinion.

CHAPTER XI
EXPERT EVIDENCE IN THE ELEVENTH CIRCUIT

by

John L. North[1]
Daniel A. Cohen
D. Anne Jarrell
Misty Peterson
D. Alan White, Ph.D.
Paul G. Williams
Kasowitz Benson Torres & Friedman LLP
Two Midtown Plaza, Suite 1500
1349 West Peachtree St., N.W.
Atlanta, GA 30309
jnorth@kasowitz.com
dcohen@kasowitz.com
ajarrell@kasowitz.com
mpeterson@kasowitz.com
awhite@kasowitz.com
pwilliams@kasowitz.com

A. KEY DECISIONS APPLYING *DAUBERT*

1. *Decisions of the Eleventh Circuit*

The Eleventh Circuit, within the last few years, has broken no new ground in defining the district court's gatekeeping functions outlined in *Daubert v. Merrell Dow Pharmaceuticals, Inc.*, 509 U.S. 579, 589, 113 S.Ct. 2786, (1993) and the Federal Rules of Civil Procedure. It did continue its trend of giving strong deference to district court decisions on evidentiary matters. Similarly, it continued its trend of not publishing most of its opinions applying the *Daubert* standard.

In *Boca Raton Community Hospital, Inc.*, the Eleventh Circuit exhibited its preference to give "the district court 'considerable leeway'" in exercising its discretion as to whether to admit expert evidence." Boca *Raton Cmty. Hosp., Inc. v. Tenet Health Care Corp.*, 582 F.3d 1227, 1232 (11th

---

[1] We recognize and appreciate the efforts by the authors of Eleventh Circuit summaries for previous monographs. Their efforts, amongst other things, chronicle the development of *Daubert* caselaw from *Kumho Tire Co. v. Carmichael*, 526 U.S. 137, 152, 119 S.Ct. 1167, 1176, 143 L.Ed.2d 238 (1999), wherein the Eleventh Circuit applied *Daubert* beyond just the scientific evidentiary context, and *U.S. v. Frazier*, 387 F.3d 1244, 65 Fed. R. Evid. Serv. 675 (11th Cir. 2004), *cert. denied*, 544 U.S. 1063, 125 S. Ct. 2516, 161 L. Ed. 2d 1114 (2005), wherein the Eleventh Circuit firmly established its previous pattern of providing significant deference to district court rulings on the admissibility of expert evidence.

Cir. 2009) (citing *Kumho* for the proposition that "evaluating the reliability of expert testimony is uniquely entrusted to the district court under Daubert"). However, it is an unusual *Daubert* case in that the analysis turned on the "fit" of the expert's opinion, whereas, most cases turn on "reliability." Plaintiff, an acute care hospital ("Boca"), sought class action status against its health care provider network Tenet Health Care Corporation ("Tenet"), alleging Tenet conspired to defraud Boca by overcharging for Medicare reimbursements. As both organizations participate in the Medicare reimbursement program, Boca alleged that Tenet's illegal scheme not only defrauded Medicare, but also adversely affected payments to Boca.

Under the Medicare system at the time, Medicare paid health care providers like Boca and Tenet a fixed rate for procedures, based on the patient's diagnosis. For treatments that cost significantly more than the fixed rate, Medicare allowed for a supplemental payment under its outlier program. Under that program, the hospital would have something akin to a deductible; it would incur a cost for a set amount above the fixed rate (called the "threshold"), after which the outlier program would be triggered. Medicare set the threshold annually and did not disclose its methodology. Boca alleged that Tenet "gam[ed] the outlier program to get more reimbursements from Medicare than its extraordinary cost cases justified." Boca claimed that Tenet's overcharging resulted in Medicare increasing the loss threshold for all hospitals, meaning Boca received less than it should have as a direct result of Tenet's actions.

Boca proffered a financial expert to show that it was injured and had sustained resulting monetary damages. The district court excluded the opinion, finding the "expert's methodology did not fit Boca's liability theory" and, therefore, failed its *Daubert* analysis. The court found that Boca's theory was based on overcharging but its expert's calculations did not distinguish between lawful charges and unlawful charges. *Id.* at 1232. The method the expert used did not inform what amount contributed to the increase in the loss threshold. As a result, the method was "inadequate and speculative" because it did not establish that the amount of Tenet's charges were unlawful and, therefore, could not establish injury. *Id.*

On appeal, the Eleventh Circuit rejected Boca's claim that the "district court misunderstood the outlier program in general and its expert opinions' methodology in particular." *Id.* at 1233. The Eleventh Circuit upheld the district court's ruling on the same basis as the lower court: "if an expert opinion does not have a 'valid scientific connection to the pertinent inquiry' it should not be included because there is no 'fit.'" *Id.* (citing *Daubert*, 509 U.S. at 587, 113 S.Ct. at 2796). "[L]ike an oversized coat, the expert opinion covered too much . . . Having tailored a trim-fitting liability theory for the body of its case . . . , (plaintiff) cannot hang a baggy injury and damages theory on it." *Id.*

A simple slip-and-fall case provides the backdrop for the rare case of an Eleventh Circuit reversal and a strident dissent to the denial of an *en banc* rehearing request in *Rosenfeld v. Oceania Cruises, Inc.*, 654 F.3d 1190 (11th Cir. 2011), reh'g denied *en banc*, 682 F.3d 1320 (11th Cir. 2012).[2] Also, notably, this case turns on the "helpfulness" prong of the *Daubert* analysis. Plaintiff, a passenger on a cruise ship at the time of her alleged injuries, claimed she fell on ceramic tile near a buffet serving station. She alleged the defendant cruise line was negligent in failing to provide the proper floor surface for such an area.

During pretrial motions, in support of her contentions, plaintiff sought to introduce the expert testimony of a floor-safety specialist who would testify that "under wet conditions, the ceramic-tile surface surrounding [the buffet area] had an inadequately low coefficient of friction." *Id.* at 1192. According to the expert, a flooring with this low coefficient of friction was not safe for the buffet area "because it posed a high risk for those passing through" to slip and fall. In its pretrial order, the district court precluded the testimony, finding it would not be helpful to the court "in understanding a matter of scientific, technical, or specialized expertise." *Id.* at 1192.

---

[2] This case is all the more unusual in that it is a published decision.

At trial, plaintiff petitioned to introduce the expert's testimony; the district court denied her oral motion. During instructions to the jury, the district court stated that plaintiff was alleging defendant was negligent and that her injury was caused by defendant's choice of inadequate flooring. The jury returned a verdict for the defendant. Plaintiff appealed the district court's exclusion of the expert's testimony and its denial of plaintiff's request for a new trial. *Id.*

On appeal, the Eleventh Circuit framed the issue under *Frazier* and Rule 702 as to whether the district court abused its discretion in finding that the plaintiff's expert's proffered testimony as to the "safety of a defendant's choice of flooring, determined by the surface's coefficient of friction" was unhelpful. *Id.* at 1193. Helpfulness, in this case, referred to the third factor discussed in *Frazier*, based upon *Daubert*: whether the "testimony assists the trier of fact, through the application of scientific, technical, or specialized expertise, to understand the evidence or to determine a fact in issue." *Id.* (citing *Frazier*, 387 F.3d at 1260). Through this lens, the Eleventh Circuit found, with little discussion, that "matters of slip resistance and surface friction are 'beyond the understanding and experience of the average lay citizen.'" *Id.* at 1194 (quoting *United States v. Rouco*, 765 F.2d 983, 995 (11th Cir. 1985)). As such, it was error to prevent the expert testimony from going to the jury. The court then found the error was "not harmless" because without the expert's testimony, "the jury could not have found that the floor near the [ ] buffet was necessarily unsafe when wet." *Id.* The failure to allow this evidence was "particularly problematic" for the court because the jury instructions specifically instructed that the plaintiff's negligence claim was premised upon her allegations that her injury was caused by defendant's "failure to choose an adequate flooring surface." *Id.* at 1194. Based on these findings, the court reversed the district court's ruling and ordered a new trial allowing the expert's testimony on the "adequacy" of the flooring choice.

The plaintiff/appellant sought an *en banc* rehearing of the decision, which was denied without comment. *Rosenfeld*, 682 F.3d 1320 (11th Cir. 2012). However, the former chief judge of the Eleventh Circuit, Circuit Judge Tjoflat, who was not on the original panel, issued a lengthy and harsh dissent. He acknowledged that a slip-and-fall case does not "ordinarily present a question of exceptional importance" so as to demand an *en banc* review, but found that this case was an exception. In his dissent, he methodically laid out his view of how the panel's opinion failed to "maintain the integrity of the court's decision making process." *Id.* at 1341. He not only disagreed with the substance of the evidentiary ruling, but he also found error with the procedural posture of the appeal from the district court's ruling. Judge Tjoflat based his dissent on three points: the appellant did not preserve her right to appeal at the trial level; the panel misapplied Rule 702 to the proffered evidence; and finally, the panel erred in ruling without the evidence of the trial transcript. While Judge Tjoflat's position did not gain any support among his fellow justices, it is instructive procedurally and substantively.

As to the first issue, Judge Tjoflat revisited the facts and noted that there was no transcript taken of the trial proceedings. However, the record did reflect that the district court ruled twice on the admissibility of the plaintiff's expert: once at pretrial *in limine* motions, and once during trial. At the close of evidence, as reflected in the district court's order, plaintiff moved for a new trial based upon the district court's pretrial refusal to allow her expert to testify as to the safety of the flooring. The district court denied the motion. *Id.* at 1325. The plaintiff never moved for a new trial based on the district court's denial to admit the expert evidence during trial. "[A]n in limine ruling is, for all intents and purposes, superseded by the trial judge's final ruling on the evidence *at trial*." *Id.* at 1326 (emphasis in the original). Judge Tjoflat opined that appellant waived her right to seek a new trial because she did not preserve the claim—arguing that the Eleventh Circuit cannot "address a claim that has been abandoned on appeal or one that is being raised for the first time on appeal, without any special considerations." *Id.* at 1326 (quoting *Access Now, Inc. v. SW. Airlines Co.*, 385 F.3d 1324, 1335 (11th Cir. 2004)).

As to the second issue, Judge Tjoflat assumed for the sake of argument that the appellant had not waived her right to appeal the denial of the admissibility of the expert testimony. With that assumption, along with the assumption that the "sans-transcript record" was sufficient to allow for a review of the evidentiary ruling, the judge found the court erroneously applied Rule 702. The judge reframed the dispute from whether the plaintiff's injuries were caused by defendant's "failure to choose an adequate flooring surface" to whether her injuries were caused by "the wetness of the floor." *Id.* at 1330,1332. In its pretrial order, the district court stated that plaintiff sought to introduce the expert's testimony to 'show that the floor, when wet, [was] unreasonably dangerous." *Id.* at 1330. There was no dispute that the plaintiff fell. Therefore, according to the judge, "[w]hat the jury had to decide—in terms of the cause of the fall—was 'whether [she] fell because she slipped on a wet floor or for some other reason' like running, wearing high heels, not paying attention." *Id.* at 1331.

In this light, the judge explained that there is no need for an expert to opine because it is "common sense" that the existence of water on the surface would have contributed to slipping and falling. "The test for determining the appropriateness of expert testimony is 'the common-sense inquiry whether the layman would be qualified to determine intelligently and to the best possible degree the particular issue without enlightenment from those having a specialized understanding of the subject involved in the dispute.'" *Id.* (quoting *Pelster v. Ray*, 987 F.2d 514, 526 (8th Cir. 1993)) (quoting FED. R. EVID. 702, Advisory Committee's Note). And, assuming the basis for introduction of the evidence was the same at trial as it was at pretrial, the district court, according to Judge Tjoflat, was not in error. The expert's testimony "could not have assisted the jury [with] resolving the wetness issue" and therefore, the district court's ruling was not an abuse of discretion.[3]

Finally, assuming that an error had occurred, Judge Tjoflat took exception to the Eleventh Circuit's finding that the error was prejudicial and "so grave as to warrant a new trial." *Id.* at 1332. He argued strongly that it was the movant's affirmative responsibility to bring forth evidence of prejudice, and the lack of a trial transcript precluded such a showing in this case. *Id.* at 1333. "The panel essentially accepted one party's briefs as if they were a record of the trial. In doing so, the panel neglected the requirement that an appellant affirmatively show prejudice—which the appellant here deliberately avoided doing by replacing transcribed trial testimony with her appellate lawyer's say-so representations of what happened at trial. In this respect, the panel erred gravely." *Id.* at 1337. The dissent closed by urging that, without the proper evidence, the Eleventh Circuit had no basis for finding any such error affected the appellant's substantial rights.

In a criminal case involving terrorism claims, the Eleventh Circuit returned to the issue of the reliability of an expert's testimony under *Daubert* when it is based upon his experience alone. *United States v. Augustin*, 661 F.3d 1105 (11th Cir. 2011) *cert. denied*, 132 S. Ct. 2118, 182 L. Ed. 2d 881 (2012). In *Augustin*, five defendants were convicted on various counts involving terrorism and conspiracy to destroy buildings and levy war against the United States. Among the many bases for appeal was a claim by two of the defendants that the district court erred under Rule 702 in qualifying an expert witness based solely upon his experience. At issue was whether the witness who was claiming an expertise based "primarily or solely" upon experience sufficiently explained "how that experience le[d] to the conclusion reached, why that experience [wa]s a sufficient basis for the opinion, and how that experience [wa]s reliably applied to the facts." *Id.* at 1125 (quoting *Frazier*, 387 F.3d at 1260 (11th Cir. 2004) (en banc)). After untangling the defendants and the facts, the Eleventh Circuit found that the decision was within the district court's discretion and that the testimony was not "unduly prejudicial." *Id.* at 1126.

Defendant Batiste was the leader of the Miami branch of Chicago-based Moorish Science Temple. The group "mixed political and religious ideology with martial arts training." *Id.* at 1111. The other defendants were included among Batiste's followers. Part of the government's evidence

---

[3] Judge Tjoflat does not address the conflict with the jury instructions, which characterized the negligence issue as one of the selection of flooring instead of the condition of the flooring.

included recorded conversations with an FBI informant in which Batiste compared his situation to that of non-defendant Jeff Fort, "the leader of one of the biggest gangs based on Islamic philosophy [ ] who went to jail in the 1980s for terrorism because he was being helped by Libya." *Id.* at 1112 (internal quotations omitted). Fort was the leader of the Chicago group called Almighty Black P. Stone and/or El Rukns that was influenced by the Moorish Science Temple. During the trial, the government sought to qualify Agent Dan Young, Bureau of Alcohol, Tobacco, and Firearms (ATF) as an expert in gangs. Specifically, the government wanted Agent Young to testify about Fort, his organization and his terrorist activities. *Id.* Defendants Batiste and Abraham opposed the qualification. The district court found that Agent Young had "extensive experience" with Fort's organization "and other Chicago street gangs," and that his testimony was "relevant in educating the jury as to the background and significance of defendant Batiste's statements regarding Jeff Fort" and Fort's activities. *Id.* at 1125.

On appeal, Batiste and Abraham argued that Agent Young's experience was not sufficient: he had no firsthand knowledge of Fort and his experience was limited to "law enforcement reports generated by ATF, Chicago police, and an article by a Chicago professor." *Id.* The Eleventh Circuit rejected the defendants' argument finding that Rule 702 "does not define expert in a narrow sense." *Id.* (citing FED. R. EVID. 702, Advisory Committee's Note). Detailing Young's résumé more fully, it then found "Young's expertise for the purposes of this trial did not need to extend to every detail and intricacy particular to Fort's personal history and organization." *Id.*

The Eleventh Circuit then turned to Batiste's and Abraham's contention that the testimony was highly prejudicial and minimally probative because the government pulled out the single reference Batiste made to Fort that was contained within "hundreds of hours of recorded conversations." Batiste argued that the expert's testimony likened him to Fort and suggested a level of understanding and detail about Fort that Batiste did not convey in his statement. The Eleventh Circuit found that the admission of the recording with the informant made the "explanation of Fort's significance relevant." *Id.* The Eleventh Circuit further ruled, without comment, that the evidence was not "unduly prejudicial" and, while acknowledging the district court could have limited Agent Young's testimony, it was not an abuse of discretion not to do so. *Id.* at 1126.

In a very brief, unpublished decision, the Eleventh Circuit ruled on an issue of first impression in a criminal case as to the reliability of reverse projection photogrammetry. *United States v. Kyler*, 429 F. App'x 828 (11th Cir. 2011). At issue was the identification of the defendant as the bank robber captured on film during the robbery of a bank. The government's expert used the technology to determine that the bank's video footage showed that the robber in the video was the same height as the defendant. Defendant appealed from the jury's verdict convicting him of armed bank robbery, asserting, among other things, that the district court did not properly evaluate the expert's testimony under *Daubert*.

The Eleventh Circuit, without explaining the technology or the basis of the expert's claims that the technology was reliable, reviewed the district court's admittance of the evidence under the "plain error" standard instead of the "abuse of discretion" because the defendant did not preserve his objection contemporaneously with the district court's ruling. *Id.* at 829. Under the "plain error" standard, the appellant had to demonstrate "(1) error, (2) that is plain, and (3) that affects substantial rights." *Id.* at 830 (citations omitted). After outlining the requirements of *Daubert*, the Eleventh Circuit addressed only the reliability prong.

First, the court found that the appellant had not demonstrated plain error because he did not point to a ruling of the Eleventh Circuit Appeals Court or the Supreme Court "rejecting reverse projection photogrammetry as not sufficiently reliable under *Daubert*." *Id.* The court then pointed to a Ninth Circuit ruling which upheld expert testimony based upon the technology as reliable under *Daubert*.

In a continuing trend, the Eleventh Circuit again found expert testimony relying on differential diagnosis methodology unreliable.[4] In *Hendrix ex rel. G.P. v. Evenflo Co., Inc.*, the Eleventh Circuit invoked the oft-quoted maxim: "[t]he courtroom is not the place for scientific guesswork, even of the inspired sort. Law lags science; it does not lead it." 609 F.3d 1183, 1203 (11th Cir. 2010) (internal citations omitted). It did so in its extensive analysis of differential diagnosis methodology which excluded the plaintiff's experts' testimony.

Hendrix was a products liability case wherein the plaintiff alleged that defendant's infant car seat was defective and resulted in permanent injuries to a newborn child, which did not manifest until a few years later. Plaintiff sought to introduce the testimony of two medical experts to show that the injuries sustained in the accident led to the child's subsequent development of autism spectrum disorder (ASD) and syringomyelia, a spinal cord defect. Both experts used differential diagnosis methodology to determine the cause of the child's injuries. The district court granted partial summary judgment for defendant, ruling that the plaintiff's experts' methodology on the causation of ASD was unreliable under a *Daubert* analysis, and therefore excluded it. However, it held that the experts could testify as to causation of syringomyelia. The plaintiff chose to dismiss the remaining claims and appeal the district court's ruling excluding the ASD causation testimony.

The Eleventh Circuit reviewed the district court's ruling under an abuse of discretion standard.[5] First, it addressed plaintiff's claim that the district court erred in requiring the experts to show "that traumatic brain injury could ever cause ASD." Plaintiff posited that the proper inquiry was whether "traumatic brain injury could ever cause one or more of the individual neurologic deficits that led" to the child's ASD diagnosis. *Id.* at 1191–92. The Eleventh Circuit held that the district court was not required to undertake such an analysis, but even if it did, the plaintiff's own experts failed to provide the necessary testimony. In reviewing plaintiff's first causation expert, the court found error with the doctor's application of his "elaborate causation theory explicitly and unambiguously to [the child's] ASD diagnosis generally and not to [his] impairments individually." *Id.* at 1192. The court found similar error with the second expert's methodology. "Not only did [plaintiff's] two medical experts opine only about the cause of [the child's] ASD diagnosis taken as a whole, [plaintiff's] arguments to the district court also did not attempt to parse the causation issue with respect to any of [the child's] individual impairments." *Id.* at 1193.

The Eleventh Circuit then turned to its *Daubert* analysis, finding that the only issue was reliability.[6] "We have previously noted that, when applied under circumstances that ensure reliability, the differential etiology (diagnosis) method can provide a valid basis for medical causation opinions." *Id.* at 1195 (citing *McClain v. Metabolife Int'l, Inc.*, 401 F.3d 1233, 1252 (11th Cir. 2005)). The court then described the two-step process of a proper differential etiology analysis and examined, at length, the experts' opinions.

---

[4] The Eleventh Circuit in *McClain v. Metabolife International, Inc.*, 401 F.3d 1233 (11th Cir. 2005), applied *Daubert* to reverse the trial court's admission of differential diagnosis testimony because it was not based on reliable proof of general causation.

[5] In a footnote, the Eleventh Circuit explained that while cases and practitioners often use the phrase "differential diagnosis," the court would employ "the more precise term 'differential etiology.'" *Id.* at n 5.

[6] As noted by the court, the Eleventh Circuit requires district courts to conduct a three-part inquiry about whether: "(1) the expert is qualified to testify competently regarding the matters he intends to address; (2) the methodology by which the expert reaches his conclusions is sufficiently reliable as determined by the sort of inquiry mandated in *Daubert*; and (3) the testimony assists the trier of fact, through the applications of scientific, technical, or specialized expertise, to understand the evidence or to determine a fact in issue." *Hendrix ex rel. G.P. v. Evenflo Co.*, 609 F.3d 1183, 1194 (11th Cir. 2010) (citing *Frazier*, 387 F.3d at 1260).

The first step of a differential etiology analysis requires the expert to create a comprehensive list of all possible explanations for the injuries or condition at issue. *Id.* "[T]he district court must ensure that, for each possible cause the expert 'rules in' at the first stage of the analysis, the expert's opinion on general causation is devised from scientifically valid methodology." *Id.* (internal citations omitted). In keeping with its deference to district courts, the Eleventh Circuit reminded that it affords the "district court substantial discretion to decide how to test the reliability of the general causation evidence presented" by plaintiffs' experts.

In the second step of a differential etiology analysis, the "expert must eliminate all causes but one . . . appl[ying] the facts of the patient's case to the list created in the first step in order to form an opinion about the actual cause of the patient's symptoms, i.e., to determine specific causation." *Id.* at 1197. Citing to the Ninth Circuit, the Eleventh Circuit held that if an expert at this stage did not provide an explanation for ruling out the alternative causes listed in step one, a district court could exclude the expert's testimony. *Id.* (citing to *Clausen v. M/V NEW CARISSA*, 339 F.3d 1049, 1058 (9th Cir. 2003)). The court then reviewed extensively, step by step, the plaintiff's experts' testimony and found them both lacking thus upheld the lower court's finding that plaintiff "failed to present scientifically reliable evidence that traumatic brain injury can ever cause autism." It further agreed with the lower court's exclusion of "the experts' theories because of a lack of reliable proof of general causation between the alleged injury and the purported cause of that injury." *Id.* at 1203.

Similarly, in the unpublished decision *Weller v. United States*, the Eleventh Circuit upheld the district court's exclusion of plaintiff's experts' differential diagnosis for lack of reliability. 379 F. App'x 910, 911 (11th Cir. 2010) *cert. denied*, 131 S. Ct. 362, 178 L. Ed. 2d 150 (U.S. 2010).[7] In *Weller*, the decedent's estate brought suit against the United States government under the Federal Tort Claims Act. While not explained in the opinion, the underlying briefs detail that the decedent died while in the care of a VA Medical Center. *See Cathie Weller, individually and as the personal representative of the Estate of James Hetherington, Plaintiff/Appellant, v. United States of America, Defendant/Appellee*, 2010 WL 1705550, at *6 (11th Cir. 2010). The cause of death was listed as "toxic epidermal necrolysis due to multiple prescribed medications, therapeutic complication." *Id.* at *7. Both parties moved for summary judgment.

In granting defendant summary judgment, the district court held that the plaintiff's causation experts were "unreliable" under a *Daubert* analysis and excluded the evidence. Both experts had based their causation opinion upon the differential diagnosis methodology. In excluding the testimony, the district court found that neither expert had "compiled a comprehensive list of potential causes of the decedent's illness or explained why potential alternative causes were ruled out." 379 F. App'x at 911. The district court further found that the methodology was not applied reliably and that, as a result, the experts' testimony would not assist the trier of fact. *Id.* With little analysis, the Eleventh Circuit upheld the district court's ruling under the abuse of discretion standard. *Id.*

2. *District Court Cases*

The Eleventh Circuit comprises the Northern, middle, and Southern districts in each of the states of Alabama, Florida, and Georgia.

---

[7] But see a similarly unpublished case wherein the Eleventh Circuit upheld the district court's admission of plaintiff's causation expert who utilized differential diagnosis analysis. *S. States Co-op., Inc. v. Melick Aquafeeds, Inc.*, 476 F. App'x 185, 188 (11th Cir. 2012) (Defendant manufacturer claimed plaintiff's expert "failed to complete step two [of the differential diagnosis] because he did not scientifically rule out alternative causes for the slowing of fish growth, but instead 'assumed them away.'" The district court allowed the testimony to go to trial and the jury returned a verdict for the fish-farmer plaintiff.)

a. Alabama District Court Cases

Like Georgia and Florida, the district courts of Alabama follow the directives of the Eleventh Circuit in determining the admissibility of expert testimony. There are three districts within Alabama. The Alabama district courts recognize their role as gatekeepers, charged with "screening out experts whose methods are untrustworthy or whose expertise is irrelevant to the issue at hand," and guided by "the well-established principle that 'the proponent of the expert testimony carries a substantial burden under Rule 702' to lay the proper foundation to show admissibility of that testimony by a preponderance of the evidence." See *Foreman v. American Road Lines, Inc.*, 623 F. Supp. 2d 1327, 1332 (S.D. Ala. 2008) (discussed in further detail *infra*). Thus, Alabama's district courts have applied Rule 702 and the *Daubert* rubric to bar (or to admit) offered expert testimony in a variety of areas.

(1) The Northern District of Alabama

In *McCreless v. Global Upholstery Co.*, for example, the plaintiff attempted to sit in a one-year-old chair manufactured by the defendant, but the chair seat rapidly dropped and tilted forward, causing her to be thrown from the chair and to sustain painful back injuries. 500 F. Supp. 2d 1350 (N.D. Ala. 2007). Plaintiff's expert opined in his report that the pneumatic piston used to raise and lower the chair seat was not working properly and that a bracket attaching the pneumatic piston to the seat was fractured. *Id*. Defendants filed a motion to exclude the expert's testimony because it would not assist the trier of fact and because the expert failed to base his conclusions on proper scientific methods.

According to the Northern District, there was no dispute that the bracket attaching the piston to the seat of the chair in which plaintiff attempted to sit fractured, but the mere fact that the bracket was broken, without any evidence as to when it broke or what actually caused it to break, could not provide a basis for establishing liability on the part of the defendants. *Id*. at *4 (citing *Embody v. Medtronic, Inc.*, 238 F. Supp. 2d 1291, 1295 (N.D. Ala. 2003)). The Northern District further stated that, although plaintiff's expert had impressive credentials relating to materials engineering, plaintiff had failed to demonstrate how the expert's expertise in materials science qualified him to express an opinion regarding force dynamics, classical mechanics, or mechanical engineering. *Id*.

In regard to the expert's opinion that the cause of the seat bracket failure was the poor manufacture of the bracket, the Northern District determined that the opinion must be excluded because the expert's methods and procedures used to reach this conclusion were not sufficiently reliable. *Id*. at *5. The procedure the expert followed in reaching this opinion consisted of visual analyses and physical measurements of the broken seat components. *Id*. The expert's methods did not meet any of the four requirements for admissibility set out in *Daubert*. *Id*.[8]

Finally, the Northern District rejected the expert's opinion that alternative designs would have prevented the failure of the seat bracket and the ensuing accident. *Id*. at *6. The Northern District stated that the expert had employed no methods or procedures to reach this opinion; the expert did not conduct any experiments and did not testify that a chair incorporating either of his proposed alternative designs had been tested or even created. *Id*. Thus, the Northern District granted the defendants' motion to exclude all testimony from plaintiff's proposed expert.

In *Cook v. Sunbeam Products Inc.*, the plaintiff brought a products liability action against the defendant manufacturer of an electric blanket, alleging that its defective design led to a fire that

---

[8] In particular, the expert failed to test or attempt his theory on another chair manufactured by defendant. There also was no evidence that his technique had been subjected to peer review in publications or otherwise.

caused the death of his wife. 365 F. Supp. 2d 1189, 1190 (N.D. Ala. 2005). Plaintiff offered the testimony of an expert who opined that the defendant had manufactured other products that were defective, and, because the fire started in the decedent's bedroom while the accused electric blanket was present, the facts were consistent with the theory that the blanket caught fire because it too was defective. *Id.* at 1192.

Defendant filed a motion to exclude the proposed expert's testimony, and the Northern District granted the motion. The proposed expert admitted that he was unqualified to give an expert opinion on the cause and origin of fires, conceded that he had no formal training in the area, and could not say what caused the fire. *Id.*[9] Second, investigations into the cause of the fire by state and local authorities independently determined that the most probable cause of the fire was smoking in bed. *Id.* Third, plaintiff failed to show that the expert's opinion regarding the fire's origin was based upon any acceptable methodology applicable to fire investigation. *Id.* The expert merely stated his opinion that other products manufactured by defendant are defective and therefore the blanket the decedent was using also may have been defective and caused the fire. *Id.*[10] According to the Northern District, the critical inquiry was not whether one of defendant's electric blankets had ever caused injury due to a defective condition, but whether the electric blanket used in the decedent's bedroom was defective, and, if so, whether the defect caused the fire that resulted in the decedent's death. Because plaintiff's expert utilized no systematic or reliable methodology to reach his conclusion, his testimony would confuse and mislead the jury and was therefore inadmissible. *Id.* at 1193.

(2) The Middle District of Alabama

In *Benkwith v. Matrixx Initiatives, Inc.*, the plaintiff brought suit against the manufacturer of Zicam No-Drip Liquid Nasal Gel, alleging that it caused her to lose her senses of smell and taste. 467 F. Supp. 2d 1316, 1319 (M.D. Ala. 2006. Zicam is a homeopathic cold remedy intended to place zinc gluconate, which is supposed to reduce the length and severity of a cold, in direct contact with the nasal epithelial membrane. *Id.*[11] Plaintiff alleged that, after using Zicam for several colds, she realized that she had lost her senses of smell and taste. *Id.*[12] The defendants in the case filed a motion to exclude the testimony of plaintiff's expert, who opined that Zicam is capable of causing loss of the senses of taste and smell[13] and that use of Zicam caused plaintiff's condition.

The Middle District recognized that, since the scientific community did not accept that zinc gluconate was toxic to the human olfactory epithelium, the court had to analyze plaintiff's expert's

---

[9] The expert did not inspect the scene of the fire, did not perform a cause and origin analysis, and did not review the report or deposition testimony of the insurance inspector who investigated the fire.

[10] "That proposed testimony is based upon nothing more than speculation and conjecture; such an expert opinion is not reliable." (citing *Weisgram v. Marley Co.*, 169 F.3d 514, 519 (8th Cir. 1999)).

[11] A pump delivers the gel to the nasal membrane. The directions state that the applicator tip should be placed one-eighth of an inch past the nasal opening and angled outward. The user should pump the applicator once in each nostril and to avoid irritation, refrain from "sniffing up" the gel.

[12] According to plaintiff, she felt a burning sensation between her eyes each time she used Zicam.

[13] The latter condition is called anosmia.

methodology in regard to general causation. *Id.* at 1323.[14] The Middle District determined that the expert's methods did not meet the minimum level of scientific rigor required by *Daubert* to be reliable enough to be placed before the finder of fact in regard to general causation. The Middle District did not accept the expert's methodology for showing that Zicam, when used as directed, could reach the olfactory epithelium. *Id.* at 1324.[15] The expert relied on experiments with two cadavers to show that the Zicam could reach the olfactory epithelium, but the Middle District found that the experiments were not sufficiently reliable because of differences in membranes between a cadaver and those of a living human, with the cadaver having wider nasal passageways. *Id.* at 1325.[16]

The Middle District also rejected the expert's conclusion that zinc gluconate was toxic to the olfactory epithelium such that it could cause anosmia (loss of smell). The court found a number of problems with the expert's methodology including that the expert: relied on studies that did not employ proper methodology, tried to analogize results from studies on other substances that were too different from zinc gluconate, and improperly dealt with the dose-response relationship. *Id.* at 1326–30. Finally, the Middle District concluded that the expert failed to show any support for his contention that, if a dose of Zicam reached the olfactory epithelium, it would be sufficient to cause permanent anosmia. *Id.* at 1330.[17]

In addition to rejecting the expert's assertion of general causation, the Middle District found that the expert's conclusion of individual causation in relation to the plaintiff's condition was lacking. To find individual causation, the expert relied on temporal association as well as the burning sensation plaintiff experienced following her use of Zicam. *Id.* at 1331.[18] The Middle District noted that reliance on a temporal relationship in attempting to prove a causal relationship leads to a *post hoc ergo propter hoc* fallacy, which assumes causality from a temporal sequence. *Id.* The expert's reliance on the burning sensation felt by plaintiff after her use of the Zicam suffered from the same fallacy and also was rejected by the court. In sum, the Middle District excluded the expert's causation opinion because it simply did not meet the standards for the admissibility of expert scientific testimony. *Id.* at 1332.

In *Bloodsworth v. Smith & Nephew, Inc.*, the plaintiff underwent a total left hip replacement procedure during which the treating physician implanted a prosthetic hip system manufactured by the defendant. 476 F. Supp. 2d 1348, 1350 (M.D. Ala. 2006). After the surgery, plaintiff suffered complications, requiring several additional surgeries. *Id.* at 1351. Plaintiff brought a lawsuit against defendant alleging that the prosthetic hip liner was implanted in a defective condition and caused the system to fail. *Id.*

To support her theory of the case, the plaintiff intended to rely on the proposed expert testimony of her treating orthopedic surgeon. Defendant filed a motion to exclude the expert's

---

[14] The court noted that "[g]eneral causation is concerned with whether an agent increases the incidence of disease in a group and not whether the agent caused any given individual's disease."

[15] The court rejected the expert's reliance on a 1937 article as not supporting his theory.

[16] The court also criticized the timing of the experiments, which were conducted after the start of the litigation and after the expert had already concluded that Zicam could reach the olfactory epithelium. "This experiment appears to have been undertaken more to bolster a conclusion than to test a hypothesis. It [] does not meet the requirements of Rule 702."

[17] Plaintiff's expert relied on studies relating to application of zinc sulfate to animals' olfactory tissue by scientists or children's olfactory epithelia by trained rhinology experts, which the court noted to be very different from the directed application of Zicam.

[18] According to the expert, because there was no suggestion that plaintiff previously experienced anosmia, the only possible causes could be the Zicam use and a cold virus. He concluded that plaintiff never developed a cold, an assumption that the court rejected.

testimony as inadmissible under *Daubert* and Rule 702. Defendant also filed a motion for summary judgment, arguing that because expert testimony is critical in establishing that the hip liner is defective in design and that any design defect caused plaintiff's injuries, and because plaintiff produced no admissible expert testimony on these issues, plaintiff had presented no triable issue of fact. *Id.* at 1353.

The Middle District determined that plaintiff's proposed expert had testified only that he thought that the prosthetic hip liner's design was incorrect. He had not described or identified any specific defect in the design of the liner or "even given a hint" as to what he believed was "incorrect" about the design. *Id.* at 1355. The doctor's opinion was "totally unsubstantiated by any facts, explanation or critique," and he was reluctant to offer an opinion that the liner's design rendered the product defective. *Id.*[19] The Middle District therefore granted defendant's motion to exclude the expert's testimony. As this decision left plaintiff with no evidence supporting her contention that the prosthetic hip liner was defective and that it caused her injuries, the Middle District also granted defendant's motion for summary judgment. *Id.* at 1355–56 (citing *Cook ex rel. Estate of Tessier v. Sheriff of Monroe County, Fla.*, 402 F.3d 1092, 1113 (11th Cir. 2005)).

(3) The Southern District of Alabama

In *Foreman v. American Road Lines, Inc.*, three plaintiffs brought claims arising from a railroad collision in a consolidated action for psychological trauma and emotional injuries, as well as permanent loss of earnings capacity. *Foreman v. American Road Lines, Inc.*, 623 F. Supp. 2d 1327, 1329 (S.D. Ala. 2008). The plaintiff Harris sought to exclude the opinion testimony of the defendant's expert, Dr. Davis, a clinical psychologist, concerning the existence and severity of Harris's psychological and emotional injuries, and the extent to which such injuries restricted Harris's ability to work, in relevant part on the basis that Dr. Davis's opinions failed to comport with the reliability threshold defined in *Daubert*. 623 F. Supp. 2d at 1329–1330.

In evaluating Harris, Dr. Davis took a history from Harris, administered objective psychological tests for evaluation purposes, reviewed medical and psychological records, as well as vocational and employment-related documentation, and performed a clinical interview. *Id.* at 1332. While the objective testing scores revealed significant psychological issues, Dr. Davis's ultimate diagnostic impression was merely of mild post traumatic stress disorder; he thus opined that there were no psychological restrictions on Harris's ability to work. *Id.* at 1332, 1334. Harris argued that Dr. Davis improperly relied on a combination of clinical observations, test results, and professional judgment in forming his opinions, rather than just the objective testing, and thus Dr. Davis's statements should be excluded. *Id.* at 1332.

After discussing the general standard for determining the admissibility of expert testimony under Rule 702 and the *Daubert* factors, the Southern District recognized that "the rules relating to *Daubert* issues are not precisely calibrated and must be applied in case-specific evidentiary circumstances that often defy generalization:" *Id.* at 1333 (citing *United States v. Brown*, 415 F.3d 1257, 1266 (11th Cir. 2005)).

> For that reason, courts have stressed that the *Daubert* inquiry is "a flexible one," that the *Daubert* factors are mere guidelines for applying Rule 702, and that "expert testimony that does not meet all or most of the *Daubert* factors may sometimes be admissible" based on

---

[19] The Middle District rejected plaintiff's effort to save the expert's opinion on the basis of his education and experience as an orthopedic surgeon alone. The court concluded that mere reference to the expert's education and experience was not a substitute for failing to disclose the factual basis of the expert's opinion.

the particular case.[20] In performing a *Daubert* analysis, then, "the court's focus must be solely on principles and methodology, not on the conclusions they generate . . . it matters not whether the proposed expert testimony is scientifically correct, so long as it is shown to be reliable."

Id. at 1333 (citations omitted).

While Harris contended that Dr. Davis's opinions conflicted with the objective psychological test results, the Southern District found that there was "no evidence, and no reason to believe, that Dr. Davis's methodology in evaluating Harris was unreliable, or that it differed materially from methodology applied by clinicians in the psychological field every single day," and thus plaintiff's motion to exclude these statements was denied. *Id.* at 1335. To the extent that Dr. Davis's opinions diverged from the objective tests administered to Harris, the Southern District recognized that such differences could serve as fodder for robust cross-examination, but did not warrant outright exclusion of his testimony. *Id.*

b. Florida District Court Cases

Florida district courts tailor their *Daubert* analysis to the requirements established by the Eleventh Circuit. Accordingly, in determining the admissibility of expert testimony, the district court must consider whether:

(1) the expert is qualified to testify competently regarding the matters he intends to address; (2) the methodology by which the expert reaches his conclusions is sufficiently reliable as determined by the sort of inquiry mandated in *Daubert*; and (3) the testimony assists the trier of fact, through the application of scientific, technical, or specialized expertise, to understand the evidence or to determine a fact in issue.

City of Tuscaloosa v. Harcros Chems., Inc., 158 F. 3d 548, 562 (11th Cir. 1998) (footnote omitted). The following Florida district court decisions exemplify this analysis.

(1) The Northern District of Florida

In *Equal Employment Opportunity Commission v. West Customer Management Group*, No. 3:10cv378/MCR/CJK, 2012 WL 4458340 (N.D. Fla. Sept. 26, 2012), the Northern District of Florida considered a plaintiff's allegations that he was rejected for employment as a customer service representative due to his Jamaican heritage. *Id.* at *1. The defendant, a provider of customer service for corporate clients, required its representatives to have completed high school or earned a GED, to have acquired basic computer skills, and to have "the ability to communicate using a clear, distinct voice." *Id.* After interviewing for a customer service position, the plaintiff was told that he did not qualify for the job because of a lack of computer skills; the plaintiff also alleged that the interviewer told him he had a "thick accent" that "would make matters worse to a customer." *Id.* Following the interview, the interviewer completed a "candidate disposition form" on which he wrote that the plaintiff "was 'very difficult to understand' and had a 'heavy accent.'" *Id.* at *2.

While the defendant argued that it refused to hire the plaintiff for a combination of reasons that included the defendant's lack of computer skills, statements indicating poor customer relations in past position, and difficulty communicating clearly, *Id.* at *1–2, the plaintiff maintained that he was refused a position on the basis of his national origin and filed an EEOC discrimination charge

---

[20] *Id.* at 1333 (citing *Brown*, 415 F.3d at 1267–68).

against the defendant. *Id.* at *1. In response, the defendant moved for summary judgment, arguing that there was no evidence of discrimination and that it had "articulated a legitimate business reason for not hiring" the plaintiff. *Id.* at *3. In return, the plaintiff sought to introduce the expert testimony of Dr. Shurita Thomas-Tate, a speech pathologist specializing in "variations of English." *Id.*

After evaluating the plaintiff's speech patterns through a variety of methods, Dr. Tate was prepared to testify that the plaintiff communicated with a high level of intelligibility. *See id.* Furthermore, given the plaintiff's age of fifty-one, and the fact that he had lived in the United States for over two decades, Dr. Tate was of the opinion that it was unlikely his speech patterns would have changed since the time of his interview (which would rebut any argument by the defendant that the plaintiff's speech had improved in the intervening years). *See id.* Dr. Tate ultimately concluded that the plaintiff's accent did not hinder his ability to communicate effectively. *Id.* The defendant moved to strike the proffered expert testimony as not scientifically reliable. *Id.* at *3–5.

In addressing the motion to strike, the Northern District noted that, although the defendant attacked Dr. Tate's testimony as failing to meet all three prongs of the analysis set forth in *City of Tuscaloosa*,[21] it needed only to address the third factor, considering whether the expert testimony would be helpful in assisting the trier of fact. 2012 WL 4458340, at *5. Noting that "[t]he advisory committee notes to Rule 702 describe this as a 'common-sense inquiry,'" the Northern District found that Dr. Tate's testimony would not be helpful because the intelligibility of plaintiff's speech patterns was "the type of common-sense determination that an untrained layman is qualified to make intelligently without the aid of an expert." *Id* The Northern District noted that the plaintiff's claim did not involve a "speech disorder" or "technical peculiarities," and that accordingly a determination of whether the plaintiff's accent was so unintelligible as to legitimize the defendant's refusal to hire him was "squarely within the competency of the average juror." *Id.* Accordingly, the Northern District granted the defendant's motion to exclude Dr. Tate's testimony regarding the intelligibility of the plaintiff's speech. *Id.* at *6.

However, the Northern District did find that at least a portion of Dr. Tate's testimony, in which she opined that the plaintiff's speech patterns would not have changed during the years since his 2008 interview, would be helpful to a jury, and accordingly was "an appropriate subject for expert testimony in this case." *Id.* at *6. Having satisfied the "helpfulness" prong, the Northern District observed that it was now required to determine whether Dr. Tate was qualified to offer such an opinion, *See id.* at *6, and invited the parties to submit supplemental briefing on the matter. *Id.* at *6.

(2) The Middle District of Florida

In *Rembrandt Vision Technologies, L.P. v. Johnson and Johnson Vision Care, Inc.*, 282 F.R.D. 655 (M.D. Fla. 2012), the Middle District of Florida was confronted with the "abrupt and still unexplained implosion" of the plaintiff's expert during cross-examination. *Id.* at 668. In this case, plaintiff Rembrandt claimed that the defendant's contact lenses infringed its patent for "soft gas permeable" contact lenses. *Id.* at 657. The Middle District construed the patent claim term "soft gas permeable contact lens" to mean a contact lens with a "Shore-D" hardness measurement of less than five. *Id.* To establish the Shore-D hardness measurement of the allegedly infringing contact lenses, the plaintiff retained an expert to determine the hardness of the products at issue. *Id.*

The expert testified that he had measured the hardness of the defendant's contact lenses by stacking twenty-four individual lenses on a steel ball having a diameter that matched the curvature of the lenses, and utilizing a Shore-D durometer to perform measurements in sets of ten replicates each. *Id.* Upon cross-examination, however, the expert admitted that he was not an expert in Shore-D testing and had not referred to the patent itself when designing his testing procedures. *Id.* at 658.

---

[21] *See City of Tuscaloosa*, 158 F.3d at 562 and accompanying text.

Furthermore, the expert could not accurately recall the established testing standards he had relied upon in developing his procedures, and also could not explain how the procedures he developed satisfied such standards. *See id.*[22]

Upon further cross-examination, it also became apparent that the expert either had not followed the testing procedures that were outlined in his expert report, or had inaccurately reported the procedures that were followed. *Id.* at 658–61.[23] The plaintiff's expert then "suddenly changed course in the middle of cross-examination," *Id.* at 659, and testified that instead of stacking twenty-four contact lenses upon a steel ball, he had actually cut twenty-four contact lenses into separate quarters and then stacked those sections upon a flat surface to perform his measurements. *Id.* at 658–61. Exacerbating the confusion over his testing methods, the expert then admitted that he had not recorded any of these alternative procedures in a lab notebook during the Shore-D tests, and that accordingly "a scientist reviewing his work would not be able to reproduce his testing methodology." *Id.* at 660. Furthermore, the expert admitted that any scientist reviewing the procedures detailed in his expert report would recognize that they were "not consistent with the applicable scientific standards." *Id.* at 661.

The defendant moved to exclude the expert's testimony regarding his Shore-D testing under *Daubert*, and because this constituted the entirety of the plaintiff's evidence regarding the Shore-D hardness of the allegedly-infringing contact lenses, moved for summary judgment of non-infringement. *See id.* The Middle District deferred ruling on the motions until the conclusion of the infringement phase of the trial. *Id.* Following a jury verdict of non-infringement, the district court also granted both of the defendant's motions as an "alternative" basis of judgment. *Id.* at 669.

In analyzing the expert's testimony under *Daubert*, the Middle District rejected the plaintiff's argument that inconsistencies revealed during cross-examination should go to the weight and credibility of the evidence, rather than its admissibility. *See id.* at 666. The district court found that even if it accepted the trial testimony as truthful, the plaintiff had not met its burden of establishing the reliability of the expert's methodology for several reasons. *See id.* at 666–67.

As an initial matter, because the expert had cut the sample lenses into quarters, the district court concluded that it was impossible for him to have satisfied accepted Shore-D testing standards, as his measurements inevitably were conducted too close to the sample edges. *Id.* at 666. The Middle District also found that the expert's methodology was unreliable because he failed to maintain a record of his testing procedures that would permit confirmation of his results. *Id.*

Finally, the Middle District rejected the plaintiff's unusual argument that the expert's testing was reliable because the results of the tests were reliable. *See id.* In essence, the plaintiff argued that the expert's testimony "should be allowed so long as the court conclude[d] that his results [were] correct." *Id.* The Middle District disagreed, observing that a court's gatekeeping function is not dependent upon determining whether an opinion is *correct*; instead, the court must "determine whether the expert has used a reliable *methodology*." *Id.* (emphasis in the original). Looking to the Eleventh Circuit's holdings, the district court reminded the plaintiff that "district courts must conduct 'an exacting analysis of the *foundations* of the expert opinions.'" *Id.* (quoting *United States v. Frazier*, 387 F.3d 1244, 1260 (11th Cir. 2004) (emphasis in the original)). As such, the fact that a scientific test provides an expected result is "not relevant to the issue of whether [an expert has] employed a scientifically reliable methodology to reach his opinion." *Id.*

---

[22] In attempting to explain the nonconformity of his testing procedures, the expert stated that perhaps a missing comma in the governing scientific standards was to blame. *See id.*

[23] In attempting to explain discrepancies in his expert report, the expert repeatedly claimed that inconsistencies were the result of typos.

In sum, the Middle District concluded that the expert's explanations for the inconsistencies in his Shore-D testimony "bordered on the fanciful," and "led to derailment of the trial as to this issue," and that it was thus compelled to exclude the expert's testimony. *Id.* at 668.

(3) The Southern District of Florida

In *Berner v. Carnival Corporation*, 632 F. Supp. 2d 1208 (S.D. Fla. 2009), the plaintiff brought an action for injuries suffered in a physical altercation on the defendant's cruise ship. *Id.* at 1209. The plaintiff alleged that he was punched by another passenger in a hallway, and witnesses testified that the plaintiff was then stomped on by the assaulting passenger's girlfriend, who was wearing stiletto heels. *Id.* The plaintiff alleged that he suffered facial injuries and traumatic brain injury in the attack, and sued the defendant cruise line for failure to exercise reasonable care to ensure passenger safety. *Id.* The plaintiff sought to introduce the testimony of Jamie R. Williams, Ph.D., a biomechanical engineer who would testify that the plaintiff struck his head during the altercation with sufficient force to have caused traumatic brain injury. *Id.* at 1209–10.

The defendant moved to exclude Dr. Williams's testimony under *Daubert*, arguing that Dr. Williams's expertise as a biomechanical engineer did not qualify her to testify to the causation of a medical condition such as traumatic brain injury. *Id.* at 1210–11. The Southern District disagreed, noting that although Dr. Williams was not qualified to testify that the events in question actually *caused* a traumatic injury, or even that the plaintiff actually had *sustained* a traumatic brain injury, Dr. Williams was qualified to testify that the force with which the plaintiff's head struck the floor was *sufficient to have caused* traumatic brain injury. *See id.* at 1211–13. Having considered the treatment of medical causation testimony offered by biomechanical engineers in other courts, the district court stated that "[b]iomechanical engineers are qualified to testify about how forces may affect or injure an individual." *Id.* at 1213.

The defendant next attacked Dr. Williams's methodology as unreliable and speculative. *See id.* at 1213–15. While admitting that her calculations regarding the force with which the plaintiff's head actually struck the floor were sufficiently supported by the Newtonian laws of physics,[24] the defendant nevertheless claimed that Dr. Williams erred in determining that such force was sufficient to cause traumatic brain injury. *Id.* at 1213–14.

In reaching her conclusion, Dr. Williams compared her calculated impact energy to a medical study comparing impact force with incidence of concussion in Australian rules football *Id.* The defendant first objected that concussions were not synonymous with traumatic brain injury, but the district court rejected that argument, noting that Dr. Williams's report identified medical references from the Center for Disease Control and Prevention and the Mayo Clinic, indicating that a concussion was indeed a form of brain injury. *See id.* at 1215. The defendant then objected that the circumstances of injury in the Australian rules football study were so different from the conditions surrounding the plaintiff's injury as to belie comparison. *See id.* The Southern District found this argument similarly unpersuasive, observing that the results of the study appeared accurate and reliable, and were "published in a journal of repute, [which] may be subjected to peer review." *Id.* The Southern District further noted that the defendant would be able to explore through cross-examination any differences between the Australian rules football study and the circumstances of the plaintiff's injury. *Id.* Ultimately, the Southern District concluded that Dr. Williams had used "well-reasoned and established methodologies to conclude that the impact energy . . . was sufficient to cause a mild to moderate traumatic brain injury," and denied the defendant's motion to exclude. *Id.* at 1215–16.

---

[24] *See id.* at 1214 ("Carnival accepts the principles Dr. Williams used to determine the impact energy of [the plaintiff's] head striking the floor.").

c. Georgia District Court Cases

Georgia district courts follow the mandates of the Eleventh Circuit when addressing the admissibility of expert testimony. Georgia's district courts consistently emphasize the gatekeeping nature of the *Daubert* analysis, while reiterating that most challenges to proposed expert testimony are best kept for a thorough and sifting cross-examination, rather than resolved through outright exclusion of such testimony.

(1) The Northern District of Georgia

The Northern District of Georgia analyzed defendants' motion to exclude expert testimony in *Parker v. Brush Wellman, Inc.*, 2010 U.S. Dist. LEXIS 97702, 83 Fed. R. Evid. Serv. (Callaghan) 778 (N.D. Ga. Sept. 17, 2010). The Northern District's opinion addressed two separate cases that were consolidated for pretrial discovery purposes. 2010 U.S. Dist. LEXIS 97702, at *8. The plaintiffs all worked at Lockheed Martin's Marietta, Georgia, facility and alleged they were exposed to beryllium over a period of forty years while working on or around C-130, C-5 and F/A-22 aircraft built at the plant. *See id.* at *8, *12. The U.S. Air Force required beryllium parts in those aircraft for safety or maintainability reasons that could implicate national security issues. *See id.* at *9–10. Lockheed had implemented numerous safety precautions pertaining to beryllium exposure, including medical monitoring of those who worked around the beryllium and it also issued beryllium warnings to any employee who worked on beryllium-producing tasks. *See id.* at *10–11. Plaintiffs asserted a failure to warn claim against defendants, each of which allegedly manufactured component parts for Lockheed using copper-beryllium or aluminum-beryllium alloys. *See id.* at *12.

Defendants moved to exclude plaintiffs' expert's testimony on the grounds that his reports lacked evidentiary basis, sufficient facts or reliable scientific methodology, as required by Rule 702. *See id.* at *13. The expert had opined that it was "'virtually certain' that plaintiffs 'would' have been exposed to beryllium levels greater than the OSHA accepted rate," but defendants claimed that all of his supporting bases were conclusory and hypothetical. *Id.* at *17–18. The defendants also argued that, while the expert's report purportedly was based on his experience and anecdotal evidence, the expert merely opined that plaintiffs may have been exposed to beryllium generally without indicating the level, frequency, duration, or particle size of any such exposure. *See id.* at *18.

In beginning its examination of the *Daubert* issue, the Northern District noted that: "The trial court, as the gatekeeper, must determine that the testimony is 'sufficiently tied to the facts of the case that it will aid the jury in resolving a factual dispute.'" *Id.* at *14 (quoting *Daubert v. Merrell Dow Pharms.*, 509 U.S. 579, 591 (1993)). The Northern District stated that the Eleventh Circuit has distilled existing rules into a three-part inquiry, instructing courts to consider whether:

(1) the expert is qualified to testify competently regarding the matters he intends to address; (2) the methodology by which the expert reaches his conclusions is sufficiently reliable as determined by the sort of inquiry mandated in *Daubert*; and (3) the testimony assists the trier of fact, through the application of scientific, technical, or specialized expertise, to understand the evidence or to determine a fact in issue.

Id. at *14–15 (citing *City of Tuscaloosa v. Harcros Chemicals, Inc.*, 158 F.3d 548, 562 (11th Cir. 1998)).

The Northern District also stated that relevant factors for assessing the reliability of expert testimony include, but are not limited to, "(1) whether the expert's theory can be and has been tested, (2) whether the theory has been subjected to peer review and publication, (3) the known or potential rate of error of the particular scientific technique, and (4) whether the technique is generally accepted in the scientific community." *Id.* at *15 (quoting *U.S. v. Frazier*, 387 F.3d 1244, 1262 (11th Cir. 2004)).

Because beryllium was generally recognized by the medical community to cause the types of harm alleged by plaintiffs, the Northern District focused its *Daubert* analysis on individual causation to the plaintiffs. *See id.* at *15–16. The Northern District cited the Eleventh Circuit's opinion in *McClain v. Metabolife International, Inc.*, 401 F.3d 1233 (11th Cir. 2005), for the proposition that a plaintiff in a toxic tort case must demonstrate the levels of exposure that are hazardous to humans as well as the plaintiff's actual level of exposure to the defendant's toxic substances before he or she can recover from that defendant. *See* 2010 U.S. Dist. LEXIS 97702, at *16 (citing *McClain*, 401 F.3d at 1241). Further, when examining a toxic tort expert's reliability, "the link between an expert's opinion and the dose relationship is a key element although some ambiguity about individual responses is expected." *Id.* at *16–17 (quoting *McClain*, 401 F.3d at 1241, n.6) (internal citations omitted).

The Northern District agreed with defendants' contention that the expert's opinion lacked the evidentiary basis, sufficient facts or reliable methodology to meet the standards of Rule 702. *See id.* at *17. The expert produced no reliable scientific evidence that—even if plaintiffs had used defendants' products—such use actually caused plaintiff's injuries. *See id.* Further, the expert's opinion was purely hypothetical, was not tested, and was filled with equivocal phrases asserting it was likely plaintiffs would have been exposed to beryllium without supporting evidence of actual exposure. *See id.* at *17–18.

The Northern District noted that the "hallmark of the science of toxic torts is the dose-response relationship. Exposure is only the opportunity for contact. Dose is what enters the body." *Id.* at *18 (quoting *McClain*, 401 F.3d at 1240). Plaintiffs' expert generally opined that the plaintiffs may have been exposed to beryllium, but the expert did not indicate the level, frequency, duration, or particle size of any such exposure that would demonstrate the dose received from each defendant's products. *See id.* The expert actually noted currently available information regarding the relative risk of beryllium particulate exposure to cause chronic beryllium disease (CBD) may depend more on particle size and chemical composition than the total mass of beryllium exposure, but the expert did not test defendants' products to demonstrate whether those products produced a bioavailable beryllium particle or if such a particle was even procurable. *See id.* The Northern District held that plaintiffs' failure to demonstrate defendants' products produced bioavailable beryllium caused their claims to fail. *See id.* at *19, n. 2. The Northern District also found that plaintiffs' expert failed to produce any evidence that even a low-dose exposure resulted from defendants' products and that the expert had admitted he could not opine as to whether any given product was the source of exposure. *See id.* at *20.

The Northern District further held that plaintiffs' expert's methodology did not meet the Eleventh Circuit's reliability standards. *See id.* The expert's theory had not been appropriately tested, had not been subjected to peer review and did not have a known or potential error rate. *See id.* at *20–22. Moreover, the expert admitted there were no published studies documenting levels of beryllium released by workers using beryllium-aluminum in the aircraft industry. *See id.* at *22. Therefore, the Northern District determined plaintiffs' expert's technique did not meet the reliability requirement of *Daubert*, nor did it prove plaintiffs' actual exposure to defendants' products. *See id.* The Northern District also found that because plaintiff's expert produced no empirical evidence, his testimony would not meet the third *Daubert* prong to provide assistance to the trier of fact. *See id.* For all of these reasons, the Northern District granted defendants' motions to exclude plaintiffs' expert's testimony. *See id.* at *23.

In re Androgel Antitrust Litigation (No. II), 2012 U.S. Dist. LEXIS 140259, 12–13 (N.D. Ga. Sept. 28, 2012, was a multidistrict litigation proceeding involving antitrust actions, that included a patent dispute, which were consolidated for pretrial proceedings. *See id.* at *9. The issue before the

Northern District involved a patent for a testosterone replacement gel. *See id.* at *12. In addition to plaintiffs' antitrust claims, the plaintiffs had challenged the subject patent being listed in the Orange Book, a publication that includes information about each FDA-approved drug. *See id.* at *13–14, *21. Plaintiffs contended that the "gel" state of the patent at issue was a basic and novel property of the invention—an assertion with which defendants disagreed.

Plaintiffs moved to exclude portions of one defense expert's report that asserted the "[t]he formation of a gel and the viscosity of the gel are not 'basic and novel' properties of the invention." *Id.* at *48. Plaintiffs contended that the defendants' expert admitted during his deposition that the gel state was a basic and novel characteristic of the invention, thereby contradicting his report. *See id.* at *49.

The Northern District stated that before a court admits expert testimony under Rule 702, it must consider: "(1) whether the expert is qualified to competently testify regarding the matters he intends to address; (2) whether the methodology used to reach his conclusions is sufficiently reliable; and (3) whether the testimony is relevant, in that it assists the jury to understand the evidence or determine a fact in issue." *Id.* at *62 (quoting *Watt v. Butler*, 744 F. Supp. 2d 1315, 1319 (N.D. Ga. 2010) (citing *Daubert v. Merrell Dow Pharms., Inc.*, 509 U.S. 579, 589 (1993)).

Without further discussion of the *Daubert* factors, the Northern District held the alleged inconsistency was not grounds to exclude the defendants' expert's opinion under *Daubert* or Rule 702. *See id.* at *62–63. The Northern District explained that "contradictory expert testimony is grounds for cross-examination, not exclusion." *Id.* at *63 (citing *Janopoulos v. Harvey L. Walner & Assocs.*, Ltd., 866 F. Supp. 1086, 1096 (N.D. Ill. 1994) ("[D]iscrepancies in [expert's] testimony and declaration go to the weight rather than the admissibility of his opinions."). The Northern District further noted that the plaintiffs did not explain how the alleged inconsistency affected the expert's qualifications or methodology nor did they show the expert's opinion was irrelevant. *See id.* Therefore, the Northern District found the defendants' expert's report was admissible. *See id.* The Northern District did note that for purposes of the motion to exclude, it was not necessary to decide whether the expert's deposition testimony actually contradicted the expert report, although its earlier discussion of the issue indicated it found no such contradiction. *See id.* at *63, n. 17, *49–50.

(2) The Middle District of Georgia

In *Dishman v. Wise*, 2009 U.S. Dist. LEXIS 57888 (M.D. Ga. July 7, 2009), the Middle District of Georgia granted defendant's motion to exclude plaintiff's expert's opinion testimony in a medical malpractice case. *See id.* at *1. Plaintiff was injured while driving his motorcycle and the initial examining physician ordered X-rays of the plaintiff. *See id.* at *2. The X-rays were sent to the defendant doctor for review. He interpreted the X-rays as "radiographically normal." *See id.* The plaintiff continued to experience discomfort after the accident and sought a second opinion. *See id.* After the new physician determined plaintiff had a fractured finger, the physician referred plaintiff to an orthopedic hand surgeon who surgically repaired plaintiff's hand. *See id.* Although the range of motion in plaintiff's hand was partially restored, he continued to suffer arthritis, stiffness, and pain in the hand. *See id.* at *2–3.

Plaintiff sued the initial diagnosing doctor for multiple counts of negligence regarding defendant's initial failure to correctly diagnose plaintiff's injury. *See id.* at *3. Plaintiff relied solely upon the deposition testimony of the treating orthopedic hand surgeon to support his claim that defendant's delay in diagnosis caused plaintiff's injuries. *See id.* at *3–4. Defendant did not dispute that plaintiff's expert was qualified to testify as an expert based on her experience as an orthopedic surgeon, but rather argued that her opinion testimony was not reliable as required by *Daubert*. *See id.* at *7–9.

The Middle District reiterated *Daubert*'s admissibility guidelines and noted that plaintiff bears the burden of laying a proper foundation for his expert's testimony's admissibility by a preponderance of the evidence. *See id.* at *4–5. Plaintiff's expert was one of his treating physicians and, as such, "a treating physician 'may testify regarding his observations and decisions during treatment of a patient, [but] once the treating physician expresses an *opinion* unrelated to treatment which is 'based on scientific, technical, or other specialized knowledge,' that witness is offering expert testimony for which the court must perform its essential gatekeeping function as required by *Daubert*.'" *Id.* at *5 (quoting *Wilson v. Taser Intern., Inc.*, 303 Fed. App'x 708, 712 (11th Cir. Dec. 16, 2008)). The Middle District held that because plaintiff's expert had opined that an earlier diagnosis would have resulted in a better physical outcome for plaintiff, the expert was testifying regarding causation and the testimony must therefore satisfy the requirements of Rule 702 and *Daubert*. *See id.* at *6.

The Middle District held that plaintiff's expert's testimony failed to pass the four non-inclusive factors used to assess the reliability of expert testimony: "(1) whether the expert's methodology has been tested or is capable of being tested, (2) whether the technique has been subjected to peer review and publication, (3) the known and potential error rate of the methodology, and (4) whether the technique has been generally accepted in the proper scientific community." *Id.* (quoting *McDowell v. Brown*, 392 F.3d 1283, 1298 (11th Cir. 2004) (citing *Daubert*, 509 U.S. at 595)). Plaintiff's expert did not show that her opinion was testable, she did not offer any error rate for her opinion, she did not provide any evidence that her opinion had been peer reviewed or that she used a peer-reviewed source to reach her opinion, and she did not show the general acceptance of her opinion. *See id.* at *9. Neither plaintiff nor the expert submitted any medical literature, studies, or other information suggesting the methods she employed had been subjected to meaningful scrutiny, were generally accepted in the medical community or otherwise been established as reliable. *See id.* The gist of plaintiff's expert's opinion was that the quicker an injured joint was repaired, the less chance there was of developing complications. *See id.* at *10. Plaintiff's expert referenced research showing most people will have better outcomes if they are treated sooner rather than later, but the expert never identified or provided any such supporting research. *See id.* at *11. Accordingly, the Middle District was unable to review the research upon which the expert relied in forming her opinion and the Middle District held the expert's opinion failed the second prong of the Rule 702 test.

The Middle District also held that plaintiff's expert's testimony was not helpful to the trier of fact because it was nothing more than what the parties' lawyers could argue in closing arguments. *See id.* The Middle District noted that the Eleventh Circuit's decision in *McDowell v. Brown* was directly on point, as that case similarly dealt with a physician expert's unsupported opinion that the sooner an injury was treated, the better. *See id.* at *11–12 (citing *McDowell*, 392 F.3d at 1283). The Middle District quoted *McDowell*, stating:

> The district court was correct in finding that 'the earlier, the better' theory was 'too vague' to assist the trier of fact. Indeed, the notion of early treatment is well within common knowledge that would be obvious to the average juror, but has nothing to do with causation. As such, this 'the earlier, the better' theory adds nothing absent some testimony connecting the delay to the causation or aggravation of an injury.

Id. at *12 (quoting *McDowell*, 392 F.3d at 1299–1300).

Furthermore, plaintiff's expert did not definitively connect the delay in treatment to the cause or aggravation of the injury, but instead testified that the initial injury could have resulted in the same injuries for which plaintiff was seeking damages from defendants. *See id.* at *13. Plaintiff's expert further testified that she could not tell if plaintiff would have been better if he had been diagnosed and treated sooner. *See id.* The Middle District held that a mere guess that earlier treatment would have improved plaintiff's condition failed the test for expert opinion and her testimony was inadmissible under Rule 702. *See id.* at *13–14.

Finally, the Middle District addressed plaintiff's argument that his expert's opinion was admissible based on her education and experience as an orthopedic surgeon. *See id.* at *14. The Middle District stated that experience may provide a sufficient foundation for expert opinion, but that does not mean "experience, standing alone, is a sufficient foundation rendering reliable *any* conceivable opinion the expert may express. If the witness is relying solely or primarily on experience, then the witness must explain how that experience leads to the conclusion reached, why that experience is a sufficient basis for the opinion, and how that experience is reliably applied to the facts." *Id.* (quoting *United States v. Frazier*, 387 F.3d 1244, 1261 (11th Cir. 2004) (emphasis in original)). Plaintiff's expert, however, did not explain how her experience as an orthopedic surgeon led to her conclusion that earlier treatment would have been better nor was there any evidence or testimony showing a reliable application of her experience to the facts of the case. *See id.* at *14–15. "The trial court's gatekeeping function requires more than simply 'taking the expert's word for it.'" *Id.* at *15 (quoting *Frazier*, 387 F.3d at 1261). Accordingly, the Middle District held that plaintiff's expert's experience-based opinion was inadmissible and granted defendant's motion to exclude her testimony. *See id.* at *15–16.

(3) The Southern District of Georgia

In *Great Northern Insurance Company v. Ruiz*, 688 F. Supp. 2d 1362 (S.D. Ga. Feb. 5, 2010), the Southern District of Georgia denied defendant contractor's motion to strike the plaintiffs' expert's testimony, opining that a residential fire at a home under construction was caused by spontaneous combustion of rags left behind by the painters. Defendant argued that the expert's opinions neither were based upon facts or evidence in the record, nor were they based upon a reliable methodology. *See id.* at 1369.

Plaintiffs retained an electrical engineer and a fire scene investigator to determine the cause of the fire. *See id.* at 1366. The electrical engineer determined the fire was not caused by any electrical systems in the area. *See id.* The electrical engineer's opinion was not disputed. At issue was the plaintiffs' other expert, a fire scene investigator, who visited the site of the fire multiple times, conducted interviews, sifted through debris, analyzed burn patterns, and reviewed video evidence of the fire from a nearby security camera, among other things. *See id.* at 1366–67. The fire scene expert determined, based on his investigation, his personal experience in the field, and the process of elimination, where the fire originated and that the fire was caused by the spontaneous combustion of rags left behind by the painters. *See id.* He testified that the rags were stained with Zar, an oil-based wood stain that is prone to spontaneous combustion if not disposed of properly according to the product's material safety data sheet. *See id.* at 1367.

In examining the issue, the Southern District noted that the Eleventh Circuit has held that "Rule 702 mandates that district courts perform a critical 'gatekeeping' function in determining the admissibility of scientific and technical expert evidence." *Id.* at 1369 (citing *United States v. Frazier*, 387 F.3d 1244, 1260 (11th Cir. 2004). The Southern District went on to state that trial courts must engage in a three-part inquiry when determining the admissibility of expert testimony under Rule 702:

> (1) whether the expert is qualified to testify competently regarding the matters he intends to address; (2) whether the methodology by which the expert reaches his conclusions is sufficiently reliable as determined by the sort of inquiry mandated in *Daubert*; and (3) whether the testimony assists the trier of fact, through the application of scientific, technical, or specialized expertise, to understand the evidence or to determine a fact in issue.

See id. at 1369–1370 (citing *Frazier*, 387 F.3d at 1260. It also reiterated that the burden is on the party offering the expert to lay the proper foundation for the expert's opinion's admissibility and it must be shown by the preponderance of the evidence. *See id.* at 1370.

The defendant did not dispute the fire investigator expert's qualifications, but instead argued that the expert's opinions, neither were based upon sufficient facts or evidence in the record, nor were they based upon a reliable methodology. *See id.* Defendant also argued that because there was no direct evidence that the painters had left oil-stained rags, the expert's opinion should be stricken. *See id.* The Southern District addressed each argument in turn.

The Southern District held that, although an expert may lack direct evidence of the cause of the fire, he may rely upon circumstantial evidence to support his theory. *See id.* at 1371. In this case, the Southern District concluded that the record contained evidence that the painters were the last people to leave the scene before the fire, there were remnants of clean rags found in the home after the fire, several products, including wood stain, were left by the painters on the day of the fire, and another subcontractor had testified that the painters had a habit of leaving their oil-stained rags in the home overnight. *See id.* Furthermore, the expert "went through a process of eliminating alternative explanations, [and] concluded that no other explanation existed to explain the cause of the fire." *Id.* The Southern District stated:

> It is true that relevant testimony from a qualified expert is admissible only if the expert knows of facts which enable him to express a reasonably accurate conclusion as opposed to conjecture or speculation. However, *absolute certainty is not required*. Expert testimony is admissible which connects conditions existing later to those existing earlier provided the connection is concluded logically. Whether this logical basis has been established is within the discretion of the trial judge and the weaknesses in the underpinnings of the expert's opinion go to its weight rather than its admissibility.

Id. at 1371–1372 (emphasis in original) (quoting *Jones v. Otis Elevator Co.*, 861 F.2d 655, 662–63 (11th Cir. 1988). Accordingly, the Southern District held that the fire investigator expert's testimony was based upon sufficient facts so that it should not be excluded on that basis. *See id.* at 1370. The Southern District also determined that fire investigator expert's testimony was based upon a reliable methodology. *See id.* at 1372. The Southern District stated:

> To evaluate the reliability of scientific expert opinion, [courts should] consider, to the extent practicable: (1) whether the expert's theory can be and has been tested, (2) whether the theory has been subjected to peer review and publication, (3) the known or potential rate of error of the particular scientific technique, and (4) whether the technique is generally accepted in the scientific community. These factors are illustrative, not exhaustive; not all of them will apply in every case, and in some cases other factors will be equally important in evaluating the reliability of proffered expert opinion.

Id. (quoting *Frazier*, 387 F.3d at 1262). The Southern District then cited the Eleventh Circuit's ruling in *United States v. Santiago*, in which it upheld the trial court's acceptance of a fire expert's use of the scientific method to identify a fire's origin and rule out other potential causes of the fire (after examining the building, reviewing surveillance video and conducting interviews) before determining the fire was incendiary. *See id.* (citing *United States v. Santiago*, 202 Fed. App'x 399 (11th Cir. 2006)). Based on that precedent, the Southern District held that, because plaintiffs' expert used virtually the same methodology already upheld by the Eleventh Circuit, it would not strike the expert's testimony. *See id.* at 1372–73.

The Southern District further held that, even if the Eleventh Circuit's holding in *Santiago* was not considered, the fire investigator expert's testimony still survived a *Daubert* reliability inquiry because the expert's theory could easily be tested, spontaneous combustion is well-documented, and the facts and methods upon which plaintiffs' expert relied are of the kind reasonably relied upon by fire investigation experts. *See id.*

The Southern District also rejected defendant's argument that the fire investigator expert's testimony should be excluded on the grounds that he was not a spontaneous combustion expert because that was not the basis for the expert's opinion. *See id.* Instead, the Southern District held that the expert's opinion was admissible because it was "based upon his ability to determine the origin of the fire and his ability to rule out all causes of the fire except for the spontaneous combustion of oil-stained rags. This determination, through process of elimination, is not only accepted and utilized by the community of fire investigators, but also has been accepted by several courts." *Id.* at 1374. While the Southern District did note that the fire investigator's lack of knowledge regarding the conditions necessary for spontaneous combustion may impact his credibility as an expert, it stated that this deficit could be dealt with on cross-examination and did not support excluding his expert testimony in its entirety. *See id.* Accordingly, the Southern District denied defendant's motion to strike the plaintiffs' fire investigator's expert witness testimony.

B. EXPERT-RELATED RULES AND PROCEDURAL ISSUES

The district courts within the Eleventh Circuit have promulgated the following expert-related local rules that should be read in conjunction with the applicable provisions of the Federal Rules of Civil Procedure.

1. Alabama—Northern District

Local Rule 26.1(a)(2): Required Disclosures; Expert Testimony.
Unless otherwise ordered by the court in a particular case, the requirements of FED. R. CIV. P. 26(a)(2), relating to disclosure of expert testimony, do not apply in cases initially filed in, removed to, or transferred to this court before December 1, 1993, and by written stipulation the parties may agree to other times for providing information about expert testimony, to exempt one or more experts from the requirement of a written report, or to modify the information to be contained in the written reports. Unless otherwise ordered by the court in a particular case, the plaintiff shall make its disclosures under Rule 26(a)(2) at least ninety days before the date the case is set for trial or to be ready for trial and the defendant shall make its disclosures under Rule 26(a)(2) within thirty days after the plaintiff's disclosures.

2. Alabama—Middle District

The Middle District of Alabama does not have specialized rules regarding expert witnesses. Former M.D. Ala. Local Rules 26.1 and 26.2 were vacated effective December 1, 2000, by amendments to the Federal Rules of Civil Procedure and General Order 3069.

Local Rule 16.1(a)(1)(F): Inspection of Vehicles, Vessels, or Aircraft
If any vehicle, vessel, or aircraft was allegedly used in the commission of any offenses charged, the government shall permit the defendant's counsel and any expert selected by the defense to inspect it, if it is in the custody of any governmental authority.

3. Alabama—Southern District

Local Rule 5.5(a): Civil Discovery Material and Exhibits in all Civil Actions Other Than Inmate § 1983 Actions
(a) Service of Discovery Material. Initial disclosures, expert witness disclosures, pretrial disclosures, interrogatories, requests for production, requests for admissions and responses thereto, and notices of depositions shall be served in accordance with FED. R. CIV. P. 5(b), but shall not be filed with the clerk unless otherwise ordered by the court or for use at trial or in connection with motions. The party responsible for service of the discovery material shall retain the original and become custodian of the discovery material.

Local Rule 16.13(b)(1)(F): Inspection of Vehicles, Vessels, or Aircraft
If any vehicle, vessel, or aircraft was allegedly utilized in the commission of any offenses charged, the government shall permit the defendant's counsel and an expert selected by the defense to inspect it, if it is in the custody of any governmental authority.

Local Rule 26.1(a)(2): Implementation of FED. R. CIV. P. 26.
Expert Testimony and Pretrial Disclosures. Unless otherwise ordered by the court, the parties shall disclose the information described in FED. R. CIV. P. 26(a)(2-3) at the times and in a sequence established by the FED. R. CIV. P. 16(b) scheduling order(s) entered in each particular action.

Local Rule 83.8(d) Appointed Criminal Defense Attorneys.
(d) Authorization for Expert or Other Services. Prior court authorization is required before obtaining services or incurring any expense such as reporters' transcripts, interpreter, investigator, psychiatrist, or other expert services. The attention of counsel is called to the maximum fees therefore contained in 18 U.S.C. §3006A(e)(3). Appropriate forms may be obtained from the office of the clerk.

4. Florida—Northern District

Rule 26.3: Discovery—Criminal.
(B) Discovery Upon Defendant's Request. At the earliest opportunity and no later than five (5) working days after the date of arraignment, the defendant's attorney shall contact the government's attorney and make a good faith attempt to have all properly discoverable material and information promptly disclosed or provided for inspection or copying. In addition, upon request of the defendant, the government shall specifically provide the following within five (5) working days after the request:

. . .

(5) **Expert Witnesses Under FED. R. CRIM. P. 16(a)(1)(G).** A written summary of testimony the government intends to use under Rules 702, 703, or 705 of the Federal Rules of Evidence.

(C) **Defendant's Discovery Obligations.** If the defendant requests disclosure under subdivisions (a)(1)(C),(D), or (E) of FED. R. CRIM. P. 16, or if the defendant has given notice under FED. R. CRIM. P. 12.2 on an intent to present expert testimony on the defendant's mental condition, the government shall make its requests as allowed by FED. R. CRIM. P. 16 within three (3) working days after compliance with the defendant's request or after receipt of defendant's notice of intent to present expert testimony on the defendant's mental condition pursuant to FED. R. CRIM. P. 12.2, and the defendant shall provide the following within five (5) working days after the government's request:

Documents and Tangible Objects Under FED. R. CRIM. P. 16(b)(1)(A). Books, papers, documents, photographs, tangible objects, or copies or portions thereof, which the defendant intends to introduce as evidence-in-chief at trial.

Reports of Examinations and Tests Under FED. R. CRIM. P. 16(b)(1)(B). Results or reports of physical or mental examinations, and of scientific tests or experiments, or copies thereof, which the defendant intends to introduce as evidence-in-chief at trial, or which were prepared by a witness whom the defendant intends to call at trial and which relate to that witness's testimony.

Expert Witnesses Under FED. R. CRIM. P. 16(b)(1)(C). A written summary of testimony the defendant intends to use under Rules 702, 703, or 705 of the Federal Rules of Evidence.

(D) **Other Disclosure Obligations of the Government.** The government's attorney shall provide the following within five (5) days after the defendant's arraignment or promptly after acquiring knowledge thereof:

. . .

(5) **Inspection of Vehicles, Vessels, or Aircraft.** If any vehicle, vessel, or aircraft was allegedly utilized in the commission of any offenses charged, the government shall permit the defendant's counsel and any experts selected by the defense to inspect it, if it is in the custody of any governmental authority.

(F) Obligations of the Defendant.

(1) **Insanity**. If a defendant intends to rely upon the defense of insanity at the time of the alleged crime, or intends to introduce expert testimony relating to a mental disease, defect, or other mental condition bearing upon the issue of guilt, or, in a capital case, punishment, the defendant shall give written notice thereof to the government within ten (10) working days after arraignment.

5. *Florida—Middle District*

Local Rule 3.06(c)(6): Final Pretrial Procedures.
The pretrial statement shall be filed with the court no later than seven (7) days before the date of the final pretrial conference (or at such other time as the court may direct), and shall contain:

(6) a list of all expert witnesses including, as to each such witness, a statement of the subject matter and a summary of the substance of his or her testimony.

6. *Florida—Southern District*

Local Rule 16.1(b)(6): Compliance with Pretrial Orders
Regardless of whether the action is exempt pursuant to Federal Rule of Civil Procedure 26(a)(1)(B), the parties are required to comply with any pretrial orders by the court and the requirements of this

local rule including, but not limited to, orders setting pretrial conferences and establishing deadlines by which the parties' counsel must meet, prepare and submit pretrial stipulations, complete discovery, exchange reports of expert witnesses, and submit memoranda of law and proposed jury instructions.

Local Rule 16.1(e)(10): Pretrial Stipulations
It shall be the duty of counsel to see that the pretrial stipulation is drawn, executed by counsel for all parties, and filed with the court no later than seven (7) days prior to the pretrial conference, or if no pretrial conference is held, seven (7) days prior to the call of the calendar. The pretrial stipulation shall contain the following statements in separate numbered paragraphs as indicated:

(10) Each party's numbered list of trial witnesses, with their addresses, separately identifying those whom the party expects to present and those whom the party may call if the need arises. Witnesses whose testimony is expected to be presented by means of a deposition shall be so designated. Impeachment witnesses need not be listed. Expert witnesses shall be so designated.

Local Rule 26.1(b): Service and Filing of Discovery Material
Initial and expert disclosures and the following discovery requests, responses, and notices must not be filed with the court or the clerk of the court, nor proof of service thereof, until they are used in the proceeding or the court orders filing: (1) deposition transcripts, (2) interrogatories (including responses and objections), (3) requests for documents, electronically stored information or things or to permit entry upon land (including responses and objections), (4) requests for admission (including responses and objections), and (5) notices of taking depositions or notices of serving subpoenas.

Local Rule 88.10(b)(3): Criminal Insanity Defense
If a defendant intends to rely upon the defense of insanity at the time of the alleged crime, or intends to introduce expert testimony relating to a mental disease or defect or other mental condition bearing on guilt or, in a capital case, punishment, he or she shall give written notice thereof to the government.

Local Rule 88.10(l): Inspection of Automobile, Vessel or Aircraft
The government shall permit defendant, his counsel and any experts selected by the defense to inspect any automobile, vessel, or aircraft allegedly utilized in the commission of any offenses charged. Government counsel shall, if necessary, assist defense counsel in arranging such inspection at a reasonable time and place, by advising the government authority having custody of the thing to be inspected that such inspection has been ordered by the court.

Local Rule 88.10(n): Federal Rules of Evidence 702, 703, or 705
The government shall, upon request of the defendant, disclose to the defendant a written summary of testimony the government reasonably expects to offer at trial under Federal Rules of Evidence 702, 703, or 705. This summary must describe the witnesses' opinions, the bases and the reasons therefore, and the witnesses' qualifications. If the defendant seeks and obtains discovery under this paragraph, or if the defendant has given notice under Federal Rule of Criminal Procedure 12.2(b) of an intent to present expert testimony on the defendant's mental condition, the defendant shall, upon request by the government, disclose to the government a written summary of testimony the defendant reasonably expects to offer at trial under Federal Rules of Evidence 702, 703, 705 or Federal Rule of Criminal Procedure 12.2(b), describing the witnesses' opinions, the bases and reasons for these opinions, and the witnesses' qualifications.

Local Rule II.A.2: Persons Who May Attend Depositions
As a general proposition, pretrial discovery in civil matters must take place in public unless compelling reasons exist for denying the public access to the proceedings. Each lawyer may ordinarily

be accompanied at the deposition by one representative of each client and one or more experts. If witness sequestration is desired, a court order entered prior to the deposition is required. Lawyers may also be accompanied by records custodians, paralegals, secretaries, and the like, even though they may be called as technical witnesses on such questions as chain of custody or the foundation for the business record rule or other technical matters. While more than one lawyer for each party may attend, only one should question the witness or make objections, absent contrary agreement.

Appendix B: Standard Form Interrogatories
Interrogatory 3: Please provide the name of each person whom you may use as an expert witness at trial.
Interrogatory 4: Please state in detail the substance of the opinions to be provided by each person whom you may use as an expert witness at trial.

7. *Georgia—Northern District*

LPR 6.2. Exchange of Preliminary Constructions[25]
(a) Not later than twenty (20) days after the exchange of proposed terms, for construction, the parties shall simultaneously exchange a preliminary proposed construction of each claim term, phrase, or clause which any party has identified for claim construction purposes. Each such preliminary claim construction shall also, for each element which any party contends is governed by 35 U.S.C. § 112(6), identify the structure(s), act(s), or material(s) in the specification corresponding to that element.
(b) At the same time the parties exchange their respective preliminary claim constructions they shall each also provide a preliminary identification of extrinsic evidence, including without limitation, dictionary definitions, citations to learned treatises and prior art, and testimony of percipient and expert witnesses intended to support the respective claim constructions. The parties shall identify each such item of extrinsic evidence by production number or produce a copy of any such item not previously produced. With respect to any such witness, percipient or expert, the parties shall also provide a brief description of the substance of that witness' proposed testimony.
(c) The parties shall thereafter meet and confer for the purposes of narrowing the issues and finalizing preparation of a joint claim construction statement.

LPR 6.3. Joint Claim Construction Statement
(a) Not later than one hundred and thirty (130) days after the filing of the joint preliminary report and discovery plan, the parties shall complete and file a joint claim construction statement,
(b) The joint claim construction statement shall contain the following information:
  (1) The construction of those claim terms, phrases, or clauses on which the parties agree;
  (2) Each party's proposed construction of each disputed claim term, phrase, or clause, together with an identification of all references from the specification or prosecution history that support that construction, and an identification of any extrinsic evidence known to the party on which it intends to rely either to support its proposed construction of the claim or to oppose any other party's proposed construction of the claim;
  (3) The anticipated length of time necessary for the claim construction hearing;
  (4) Whether any party proposes to call one or more witnesses, including experts, at the claim construction hearing, the identity of each such witness, and for each expert, a summary

---

[25] The Northern District of Georgia is the only Eleventh Circuit district court to adopt local patent rules.

of each opinion to be offered in sufficient detail to permit a meaningful deposition of that expert. No other Rule 26 report or disclosure shall be required for testimony directed solely towards claim construction.

LPR 7: EXPERT WITNESSES
LPR 7.1. Disclosure of Experts and Expert Reports
(a) For issues other than claim construction to which expert testimony shall be directed, expert witness disclosures and depositions shall be governed by this rule.
(b) No later than thirty (30) days after (1) the normal close of discovery pursuant to the discovery track to which the case was assigned, or (2) the close of discovery after claim construction, which ever is later, each party shall make its initial expert witness disclosures required by Rule 26 on the issues on which each bears the burden of proof;
(c) No later than thirty (30) days after the first round of disclosures, each party shall make its initial expert witness disclosures required by Rule 26 on the issues on which the opposing party bears the burden of proof;
(d) No later than ten (10) days after the second round of disclosures, each party shall make any rebuttal expert witness disclosures permitted by Rule 26.

LPR 7.2. Depositions of Experts
Depositions of expert witnesses disclosed under this rule shall commence within seven (7) days of the deadline service of rebuttal reports and shall be completed within thirty (30) days after commencement of the deposition period. If the party taking the deposition agrees to pay the reasonable travel expenses of the expert, and absent good cause otherwise shown, the party designating the expert shall make its expert witness available for deposition in this district.

LPR 7.3. Presumption Against Supplementation or Amendment
Because of the complexity of the issues often present in patent cases, amendments or supplementation to expert reports after the deadlines provided here are presumptively prejudicial and shall not be allowed unless (a) the tendering party shows cause that the amendment or supplementation could not reasonably have been made earlier and (b) all reasonable steps are made to ameliorate the prejudice to the responding party.

Local Rule 16.4.B(18): Content of Consolidated Pretrial Order with Respect to Experts.
Each proposed consolidated pretrial order shall contain the information outlined below. No modifications or deletions shall be made without the prior permission of the court. A form pretrial order prepared by the court and which counsel shall be required to use is contained in appendix B. Copies of the form pretrial order containing adequate space for response are available at the public filing counter in each division.

The proposed order shall contain:

(18) (a) A separate listing, by each party, of all witnesses (and their addresses) whom that party will or may have present at trial, including expert (any witness who might express an opinion under Federal Rule of Evidence 702), impeachment and rebuttal witnesses whose use can or should have been reasonably anticipated. Each party shall also attach to the party's list a reasonably specific summary of the expected testimony of each expert witness.
(b) A representation that a witness will be called may be relied upon by other parties unless notice is given fourteen (14) days prior to trial to permit other parties to subpoena the witness or obtain the witness' testimony by other means.

(c) Witnesses not included on the witness list will not be permitted to testify, unless expressly authorized by court order based upon a showing that the failure to comply was justified. The attorneys may not reserve the right to add witnesses.

Local Rule 26.1: Initial and Expert Disclosures
A. Applicability. The parties to civil actions shall make the initial disclosures required by FED. R. CIV. P. 26(a)(1) at or within thirty (30) days after the initial appearance of a defendant by answer or motion. Expert disclosures shall be made as required by FED. R. CIV. P. 26(a)(2) and by LR 26.2(C). Pretrial disclosures (FED. R. CIV. P. 26(a)(3)) are addressed in LR 16.4, consolidated pretrial order.

C. Supplementation and Amendment of Disclosures. The duties of a party to supplement and amend prior to initial, expert or pretrial disclosure are set forth in FED. R. CIV. P. 26(e).

Local Rule 26.2.C: Discovery Period for Expert Witnesses.
Any party who desires to use the testimony of an expert witness shall designate the expert sufficiently early in the discovery period to permit the opposing party the opportunity to depose the expert and, if desired, to name its own expert witness sufficiently in advance of the close of discovery so that a similar discovery deposition of the second expert might also be conducted prior to the close of discovery.

Any party who does not comply with the provisions of the foregoing paragraph shall not be permitted to offer the testimony of the party's expert, unless expressly authorized by court order based upon a showing that the failure to comply was justified.

Any party objecting to an expert's testimony based upon *Daubert v. Merrell Dow Pharms., Inc.*, 509 U.S. 579, 113 S. Ct. 2786 (1993), shall file a motion no later than the date that the proposed pretrial order is submitted. Otherwise, such objections will be waived, unless expressly authorized by court order based upon a showing that the failure to comply was justified.

Local Rule 30.1: Expert Witnesses.
Limitations regarding the timing of expert depositions and listing of potential and expected expert witnesses at trial (*see* FED. R. CIV. P. 26(a)(2)), are set forth in local rules 26.2C and 16.4B(18), respectively.

8. Georgia—Middle District

The Middle District of Georgia does not have any specialized rules for expert witnesses in civil matters.

Local Rule VI A-C: Investigative, Expert and Other Services
A. Services Provided Upon Request. Counsel (whether or not appointed under the *Criminal Justice Act*) for any person who is financially unable to obtain investigative, expert or other services necessary for adequate representation may request the court to provide such services in an *ex parte* application directed to a judicial officer, as provided in 18 U.S.C. §3006A(e)(1). Upon a finding by the judicial officer, after appropriate inquiry, that such services are necessary and that the person for whom they are sought is financially unable to obtain them, the court shall authorize counsel to obtain such services.
B. Services Provided Without Prior Request. Pursuant to 18 U.S.C. §3006A(e)(2), counsel appointed under the *Criminal Justice Act* may obtain, subject to late review, investigative, expert or other services without prior authorization if necessary for the adequate representation of his client. The total cost of services obtained without prior authorization may not exceed $300.00 and expenses reasonably incurred. However, the court may, in the interest of justice and upon finding that timely procurement of necessary services could not await

prior authorization, approve payment for such services after they have been obtained, even if the cost of such services exceeds $300.00. Such expenditures without prior court authorization are not favored, and any application for court approval of such prior expenditures must clearly show why prior authorization could not have been obtained, in addition to demonstrating the necessity of such expenditures for adequate representation and financial inability on the part of the party for whom the services were obtained.

C. Submission of Requests. Requests for investigative, expert, or other services shall be submitted to the court by counsel (or by a *pro se* party) upon such forms designated and provided by the clerk of court, and the signing of said forms by counsel and by claimants shall affirm and certify as to the truth of the representations made therein. Said requests shall include the hourly or daily rate of the investigator, expert, etc. and an estimate of the total expenditure for services rendered. The judicial officer considering such requests may impose a limit on the amount which may be expended or promised for such services within the maximum prescribed by 18 U.S.C. §3006A(e)(3).

9. *Georgia—Southern District*

Local Rule 26.1(d)(ii) & (iii): Time Limitations

(d) Unless otherwise stated in the scheduling order issued pursuant to FED. R. CIV. P. 16(b):
    (ii) the plaintiff must furnish the expert witness reports required by FED. R. CIV. P. 26(a)(2)(B) and provide the disclosures required by FED. R. CIV. P. 26(a)(2)(C) within 60 days after the FED. R. CIV. P. 26(f) conference or, in cases exempt from the FED. R. CIV. P. 26(f) conference, within 60 days after the filing of the last answer of the defendants named in the original complaint;
    (iii) the defendant must furnish the expert witness reports required by FED. R. CIV. P. 26(a)(2)(B) and provide the disclosures required by FED. R. CIV. P. 26(a)(2)(C) within 90 days after the FED. R. CIV. P. 26(f) conference or 60 days after filing his answer, whichever is later, or in cases exempt from the FED. R. CIV. P. 26(f) conference, within 90 days after the answer.

C. STATE LAW EXPERT ISSUES

1. *Expert Evidence in Alabama State Courts*

Alabama's approach to the admissibility of expert evidence has changed dramatically in recent years. Courts had applied *Frye*, *Daubert*, and/or Rule 702 of the Alabama Rules of Evidence, depending on the type of expert evidence proffered (as discussed in further detail below), to admit or exclude it. However, for most types of civil state court cases filed on or after January 1, 2012, the Alabama legislature recently adopted a *Daubert*-like admissibility standard and amended the former *Frye*-based ALA. CODE § 12-21-160; the Alabama Supreme Court followed suit by amending ALA. R. EVID. 702 ("Rule 702") to make it "consistent" with the new version of ALA. CODE § 12-21-160. Thus, civil litigation practitioners will have to be well-versed in both sets of standards for the foreseeable future.

a. Alabama Previously Applied Three Standards for Admitting Expert Evidence

For cases filed prior to January 1, 2012, Alabama state courts apply three different standards for admitting expert evidence. For these cases, the admissibility of scientific expert testimony is governed by the *Frye* "general acceptance" test. *Kyser v. Harrison*, 908 So. 2d 914, 920 (Ala. 2005). For nonscientific expert testimony, Alabama courts apply Rule 702[26] of the Alabama Rules of Evidence:

---

[26] The entirety of former Rule 702 has been included in the new Rule 702 as section (a).

"[i]f scientific, technical, or other specialized knowledge will assist the trier of fact to understand the evidence or to determine a fact in issue, a witness qualified as an expert by knowledge, skill, experience, training, or education may testify thereto in the form of an opinion or otherwise." *Minor v. State*, 914 So. 2d 372, 401 (Ala. Crim. App. 2004). Further, ALA. CODE § 12-21-160 provided that "[t]he opinions of experts on any question of science, skill, trade, or like questions are always admissible, and such opinions may be given on the fact as proved by other witnesses."

ALA. CODE § 36-18-30, expressly using the *Daubert* factors, applied only to the admissibility of DNA and genetic marker evidence:

> Expert testimony or evidence relating to the use of genetic markers contained in or derived from DNA for identification purposes shall be admissible and accepted as evidence in all cases arising in all courts of this state, provided, however, the trial court shall be satisfied that the expert testimony or evidence meets the criteria for admissibility as set forth by the United States Supreme Court in *Daubert, et. Ux., et. Al., v. Merrell Dow Pharmaceuticals, Inc.*, decided on June 28, 1993.

ALA. CODE § 36-18-30; *Turner v. State*, 746 So. 2d 355, 361 n.7 (Ala. 1998); *Calhoun v. State*, 932 So. 2d 923, 947 (Ala. Crim. App. 2005).

In 1998, the Alabama Supreme Court adopted the *Daubert* factors in *Turner v. State*, setting forth the following two-prong test that must be satisfied before DNA evidence can be introduced: "'I. Are the theory and the technique (i.e., the principle and the methodology) on which the proffered DNA forensic evidence is based 'reliable'? II. Are the theory and the technique (i.e., the principle and the methodology) on which the proffered DNA evidence is based 'relevant' to understanding the evidence or to determining a fact in issue?'" *Calhoun v. State*, 932 So. 2d 923, 947 (Ala. Crim. App. 2005) (quoting *Turner*, 746 So. 2d at 358–361 (Ala. 1998)). *Turner* offered a *Daubert* approach to both the reliability and the relevance inquiry. Factors indicating reliability include testing, peer review, rate of error, and general acceptance; the relevance determination turns on the "fit" between the DNA evidence proffered and the facts of the case." *Turner*, 746 So. 2d at 358–61.

Noting the flexibility of the *Daubert* factors, Alabama courts have found that a failure to testify concerning one of the factors, such as the testing method used or the rate of error for the testing method, does not necessarily render the evidence insufficient to meet the reliability prong under *Daubert*. *Lewis v. State*, 889 So. 2d 623, 672 (Ala. Crim. App. 2003) (citations omitted) (determining that "the rate of error is but one factor to be considered in determining the admissibility of DNA evidence and . . . the absence of testimony regarding this factor will not, alone, render DNA evidence inadmissible"); *Calhoun*, 932 So. 2d at 947 (finding that the failure to state the name of the test used goes to the credibility of the DNA evidence rather than its admissibility). The Alabama Court of Criminal Appeals has addressed the admissibility of nuclear-DNA and mtDNA evidence (both matching evidence and population-frequency-statistical evidence), and found that so long as the expert "testified to testing, peer review, publication, controls, and general acceptance in the scientific community," such evidence was admissible. *Lewis*, 889 So. 2d at 673–74.[27]

While not adopting *Daubert* for non-DNA cases *per se*,[28] even prior to the amendment of Rule 702, the Alabama Supreme Court had in fact demonstrated a willingness to consider *Frye* and

---

[27] The court did not state whether it was taking judicial notice of this type of evidence.

[28] *See, e.g., Vesta Fire Ins. Corp. v. Milam & Co. Constr., Inc.*, 901 So. 2d 84, 106 (Ala. 2004) (stating that the court "has not yet explicitly adopted the *Daubert* test . . . and decline[s] to adopt *Daubert* under the circumstances of this case."); *Bagley v. Mazda Motor Corp.*, 864 So. 2d 301, 310 (Ala. 2003) (noting that it is an accurate statement that Alabama courts "have never recognized that *Daubert* is controlling in any case . . . other than those involving the admission of DNA evidence.").

Daubert in tandem in certain such cases. *See Gen. Motors Corp. v. Jernigan*, 883 So. 2d 646, 661 (Ala. 2003) (stating that although the court declined to adopt *Daubert*, the disputed expert testimony was admissible under either *Frye* or *Daubert*); *Ex parte Layton*, 911 So. 2d 1052, 1057 (Ala. 2005) (holding that the expert evidence at issue "fail[ed] to comply with either the standard enumerated in *Frye* or the standard enumerated in *Daubert*."). For instance, in *General Motors Corp. v. Jernigan*, General Motors (GM) challenged the expert testimony of an automotive design engineer who opined that an alternative design would have performed better and prevented the injuries suffered by a passenger. 883 So. 2d at 659. GM argued that this testimony should have been excluded because the expert "did not test, build, model, or draw his proffered alternative designs," and his "untested and subjective opinion" was therefore inadmissible." *Id.* at 662. The court disagreed, noting that the expert relied on GM's test results, evidence from the collision and considerable expertise in the area. *Id.* at 663. The court determined that the type of testimony proffered was comparable to the advisory committee notes to Rule 702 of the Federal Rules of Evidence, which had been amended to incorporate *Daubert*, and contained a statement demonstrating that an expert may be qualified on the basis of experience alone. *Id.* at 661. Applying this standard, the court concluded that the engineer's significant "experience and expertise were factors the jury could properly consider in this case, regardless of whether [the court] reviewed his testimony under the standard enunciated in *Daubert* or the standard enunciated in *Frye*." *Id.* at 662–663.

The Alabama Court of Criminal Appeals took a similar approach in *Barber v. State*, 952 So. 2d 393 (Ala. Crim. App. 2005). After determining that testimony concerning fingerprint identification was admissible under Rule 702 of the Alabama Rules of Evidence, the court also applied *Daubert* to the facts of the case. The appellant argued that print identification did not meet the standards outlined in *Daubert* because (1) the underlying premises upon which the print identification was based were not proven by testing, (2) there was not a known error rate for the technique, and (3) there was no objective threshold standard to guide examiners in making a positive identification. *Id.* at 417. The court noted that every circuit that had considered fingerprint identification in the post-*Daubert* era found such evidence admissible. *Id.* at 418 (citations omitted). Furthermore, the factors outlined in *Daubert* were flexible, there was a strong general acceptance of fingerprinting techniques, and under *Daubert*, a trial judge "need not expend scarce judicial resources reexamining a familiar form of expertise every time opinion evidence is offered." *Id.* at 419–420. Thus, based on the testimony presented and decisions from other jurisdictions, the court determined that the testimony was admissible "even applying the *Daubert* standard." *Id.* at 422.

b. Alabama Expert Evidence Admissibility In Most Civil Cases Filed On or After January 1, 2012

(1) New Rule 702

As mentioned earlier, the Alabama legislature rewrote the former ALA. CODE § 12-21-160 to provide the following:

(a) *Generally.* If scientific, technical, or other specialized knowledge will assist the trier of fact to understand the evidence or to determine a fact in issue, a witness qualified as an expert by knowledge, skill, experience, training, or education, may testify thereto in the form of an opinion or otherwise.

(b) *Scientific evidence.* In addition to requirements set forth in subsection (a), expert testimony based on a scientific theory, principle, methodology, or procedure is only admissible if:

(1) The testimony is based on sufficient facts or data,

(2) The testimony is the product of reliable principles and methods, and (3) The witness has applied the principles and methods reliably to the facts of the case.

(c) Nothing in this section shall modify, amend, or supersede any provisions of the Alabama Medical Liability Act of 1987 and the Alabama Medical Liability Act of 1996, commencing with Section 6-5-540, et seq., or any judicial interpretation thereof.

(d) This section shall apply to all civil state court actions commenced on or after January 1, 2012. In criminal actions, this section shall only apply to non-juvenile felony proceedings in which the defendant that is the subject of the proceeding was arrested on the charge that is the subject of the proceeding on or after January 1, 2012. This section shall not apply to domestic relations, child support, juvenile, or probate cases.

(e) The provisions of this section, where inconsistent with any Alabama Rule of Civil Procedure, Alabama Rule of Criminal Procedure or Alabama Rule of Evidence, including, but not limited to, ALA. R. EVID. 702, shall supersede such rule or parts of rules.

Accordingly, as of January 1, 2012, Rule 702 was amended by the Alabama Supreme Court to include a section (b), setting forth additional requirements for expert evidence in certain situations and making the rule "consistent" with the statute:

(a) If scientific, technical, or other specialized knowledge will assist the trier of fact to understand the evidence or to determine a fact in issue, a witness qualified as an expert by knowledge, skill, experience, training, or education may testify thereto in the form of an opinion or otherwise.

(b) In addition to the requirements in section (a), expert testimony based on a scientific theory, principle, methodology, or procedure is admissible only if:

(1) The testimony is based on sufficient facts or data;

(2) The testimony is the product of reliable principles and methods; and

(3) The witness has applied the principles and methods reliably to the facts of the case.

The provisions of this section (b) shall apply to all civil state-court actions commenced on or after January 1, 2012. In criminal actions, this section shall apply only to non-juvenile felony proceedings in which the defendant was arrested on the charge or charges that are the subject of the proceedings on or after January 1, 2012. The provisions of this section (b) shall not apply to domestic-relations cases, child-support cases, juvenile cases, or cases in the probate court. Even, however, in the cases and proceedings in which this section (b) does not apply, expert testimony relating to DNA analysis shall continue to be admissible under Ala. § 36-18-30.

(c) Nothing in this rule is intended to modify, supersede, or amend any provisions of the Alabama Medical Liability Act of 1987 or the Alabama Medical Liability Act of 1996 or any judicial interpretation of those acts.

(2) Rule 702(a)

Because the text of the former Rule 702 was not amended and is included in the new Rule as section (a), this indicates that the general admissibility requirements applicable to all experts are unchanged; the *Daubert*-based requirements added by section (b), then, only are applicable to scientific experts and evidence. For nonscientific experts, just as before the amendment of Rule 702, then, there are only two admissibility requirements: the witness must (1) be "qualified as an expert," and (2) give testimony which will "assist the trier of fact to understand the evidence or to determine a fact in issue." The advisory committee's notes explicitly state that preexisting judicial authority interpreting Rule 702 remains applicable to Rule 702(a).

(3) Rule 702(b) and the Daubert-Based Admissibility Criteria

For civil state court cases, filed on or after January 1, 2012, scientific experts must satisfy the requirements of both Rule 702(a) and Rule 702(b). As discussed above, scientific evidence in Alabama had long been the subject of *Frye's* general acceptance test; now a *Daubert*-based standard has been embraced fully for purposes of scientific evidence.

Henceforth, scientific evidence, to be admitted in Alabama courts, must satisfy the three requirements stated in Rule 702(b): it must be (1) based on sufficient facts or data, (2) the product of reliable principles and methods, and (3) applied reliably to the facts of the case. These criteria are the same as those added to the corresponding Federal Rule 702 after the United States Supreme Court's decisions in *Daubert* and its progeny; therefore, it appears clear that the Alabama legislature and Supreme Court intended to adopt a *Daubert*-based admissibility test to replace the *Frye* "general acceptance" test in cases where scientific evidence is sought to be introduced (or excluded). Alabama courts now must determine whether scientific evidence meets the three prongs of Rule 702(b), rather than relying on simply whether such evidence is "generally accepted" by other experts in the field.

The admissibility criteria imposed generally on all scientific evidence by Rule 702(b) is the same *Daubert* criteria imposed on DNA evidence by ALA. CODE § 36-18-30; the latter statute applies to DNA evidence even in domestic-relations cases, child-support cases, juvenile cases, and cases pending in the probate courts. The advisory committee's notes specifically recognize the identical nature of these criteria, and further state that the amendment to Rule 702 "is not intended to effect any change in the line of well developed judicial authority that has applied and interpreted the *Daubert* test pursuant to § 36-18-30 [pertaining to the admissibility of DNA evidence]." Because, and as noted above, Alabama courts have been analyzing the admissibility of DNA evidence under the *Daubert* standard for several years under § 36-18-30, those cases may serve as a template for applying Rule 702(b)'s requirements going forward.

(4) Exceptions to Rule 702(b) (Where the Daubert-Based Standard Will Not Apply)

As noted above, the provisions of section (a) apply in all cases where Rule 702 was previously applied. The provisions in section (b), however, do not apply in all cases.

Rule 702(b) applies in all civil state-court actions commenced on or after January 1, 2012, except domestic relations cases, child support cases, juvenile cases, or probate cases. In criminal actions, section (b) applies only in adult felony proceedings in which the defendant was arrested on or after January 1, 2012. The provisions of the Alabama Medical Liability Act of 1987 and the Alabama Medical Liability Act of 1996, § 6-5-540 et seq., Ala. Code 1975, and any judicial interpretation of those provisions remains unaffected by this amendment as well.

If Rule 702(b) does not apply, then it appears the *Frye* standard will continue to apply to determine the admissibility of scientific evidence (except for DNA evidence which is, of course, subject to § 36-18-30 in all cases).

(5) Alabama Allows Expert Testimony on Ultimate Facts

Unlike some jurisdictions, Alabama courts generally allow experts to testify on the "ultimate issue to be decided by the trier of fact." *See, e.g., Harrington v. State*, 858 So. 2d 278, 296 (Ala. Crim. App. 2003), *reh'g denied*, 2003; *Fitch v. State*, 851 So. 2d 103, 117 (Ala. Crim. App. 2001); *Henderson v. State*, 715 So. 2d 863, 864 (Ala. Crim. App. 1997). For instance, in *Harrington v. State*, the Alabama Court of Criminal Appeals held that testimony concerning whether a defendant accused of manslaughter suffered from battered spouse syndrome was admissible because this testimony "did not resolve the ultimate issue of [the defendant's] intent or the reasonableness of her belief in the need to defend herself." 858 So. 2d at 295. The court, however, noted that "this court has repeatedly acknowledged an erosion of the rule that once precluded expert testimony on the ultimate issue." *Id.* at 296. Thus, even if this testimony had been directed to the ultimate issue, it would have been admitted because "it would have aided the jury in its resolution of the case." *Id. Harrington* thus illustrates the inclusive approach taken by Alabama courts to the introduction of expert testimony.

c. Expert Related Rules and Procedures in Alabama State Court

Expert discovery under the Alabama Rules of Civil Procedure (ARCP) is initiated by the parties, not the court. Under Rule 26(b)(5), a party may submit interrogatories requiring the opposition to identify any expert witnesses expected to be called at trial, together with a description of the subject matter upon which the expert will testify and a summary of the grounds for each opinion. ALA. R. CIV. P. 26(b)(5)(A)(i). Failure to timely identify an expert in response to such interrogatories may result in the expert's testimony being disallowed. *Tuck v. Health Care Auth. of the City of Huntsville*, 851 So. 2d 498, 504 (Ala. 2002) (holding that, even if the expert is substituted for a previously identified expert who was disqualified, "it is not an abuse of discretion to disallow an expert's testimony when the expert was not timely identified in answers to interrogatories . . . . especially where . . . the credentials of the expert . . . were being vigorously challenged").

Discovery related to facts known or opinions held by an expert retained in anticipation of litigation but who is not expected to testify at trial may only be obtained in two circumstances. ALA. R. CIV. P. 26(b)(5)(B). First, the findings of an expert who has performed a physical or mental examination of a party or person in custody may be obtained by the person required to submit such examination under ARCP 35(b). Second, a party may seek discovery related to an expert not expected to be called at trial if "exceptional circumstances" are shown. *Id.* "Exceptional circumstances" are defined as situations in which "it is impracticable for the party seeking discovery to obtain facts or opinions on the same subject by other means." *Id.*[29]

Under ARCP 26(b)(5)(C), a party seeking discovery of an expert expected to be called at trial is required to bear the reasonable cost of the expert's time spent responding to interrogatories. If the expert is retained in anticipation of litigation, but is not expected to be called at trial, the party

---

[29] The Alabama Supreme Court held that a doctor being sued for medical malpractice related to the death of an infant was not required to disclose the name of an independent physician she consulted who could possibly be called as an expert witness. *Ex parte Cryer*, 814 So. 2d 239, 248–249 (Ala. 2001), *reh'g denied* (citing the former version of the statute, ALA. R. CIV. P. 26(b)(4)(B)).

seeking discovery is responsible for "a fair portion of the fees and expenses reasonably incurred by the latter party in obtaining facts and opinions from the expert." ALA. R. CIV. P. 26(b)(5)(C).

Alabama Rule of Evidence 706 provides for compensation to court-appointed experts. If a court appoints an expert *sua sponte* or on the motion of a party, the expert is entitled to "reasonable compensation" in an amount to be determined in the court's discretion. Likewise, the court has the discretion to determine the proportionate responsibility for the expert's costs between the parties. Liability for expert costs is not imposed on the judiciary. Nor does the judiciary bear any responsibility for the payment of court-appointed experts for indigent defendants. ALA. CODE § 15-12-21.

Alabama courts allow an expert to be appointed for indigent criminal defendants when the defendant can show "a reasonable probability that the expert would be of assistance in the defense and that the denial of expert assistance would result in a fundamentally unfair trial." *Ex parte Moody*, 684 So. 2d 114, 119 (Ala. 1996) (per curiam), *modified, reh'g overruled*, 682 So. 2d 448. The indigent defendant must be given an *ex parte* hearing for the judge to determine whether the expert is necessary to answer a "substantial issue or question" raised by the prosecution or to support "a critical element of the defense." *Id.* A defendant who makes such a showing is entitled only to a competent expert, not one of the defendant's choosing. *Id.* Court-appointed experts are available to defendants on any issue for which this showing can be made. *Id.*

2. *Expert Evidence in Florida State Courts*

a. Florida remains among the minority of state courts using the test set forth in *Frye v. United States*, 293 F. 1013, 1014 (D.C. Cir. 1923), to determine the admissibility of expert evidence

(1) Florida's Frye Test—An Overview

In determining the admissibility of expert evidence, Florida courts continue to adhere to the almost ninety-year-old standard set forth by the D.C. Court of Appeals in *Frye v. United States*.[30] The Supreme Court of Florida has persisted in relying upon *Frye* even though Florida is one of only a minority of states to do so,[31] and has maintained this reliance in the face of repeated calls to

---

[30] *See, e.g., Murray v. State*, 3 So. 3d 1108, 1117 n.5 (2009) ("Florida follows the *Frye* test to determine the admissibility of new or novel scientific evidence"); *Williamson v. State*, 994 So. 2d 1000, 1010 (2008) (trial court correct in recognizing "our adherence to *Frye*"); *Marsh v. Valyou*, 977 So. 2d 543, 547 (2007) ("Despite the Supreme Court's decision in *Daubert*, we have since repeatedly reaffirmed our adherence to the *Frye* standard for admissibility."). Federal courts and a majority of the states determine the admissibility of expert evidence according to the guidelines set forth by the Supreme Court in *Daubert v. Merrell Dow Pharmaceuticals, Inc.*, 509 U.S. 579 (1993).

[31] *See* Maggie Tamburro, *Daubert, Frye . . . or Both? Tracking Florida's Buy-In*, BULLS-EYE BLOG (Mar. 12, 2012), www.ims-expertservices.com/blog/2012/daubert-frye-or-both/ (asserting that only nine states (California, Florida, Illinois, Kansas, Maryland, Minnesota, New York, Pennsylvania, and Washington) and the District of Columbia continue to insist on *Frye* over *Daubert*); Kenneth W. Waterway & Robert C. Weill, *A Plea for Legislative Reform: The Adoption of Daubert to Ensure the Reliability of Expert Evidence in Florida Courts*, 36 NOVA L. REV. 1, 2 (2011) ("Florida is among a shrinking minority of states still clinging to the antiquated 'Frye test'").

abandon the standard from commentators,[32] the Florida legislature,[33] and its own justices.[34] At the same time, the Florida courts have carved out a number of exceptions to the applicability of *Frye*.

The Supreme Court of Florida has outlined a four-step process for the consideration of admissibility under *Frye*. *Ramirez v. State*, 651 So. 2d 1164, 1167 (1995). First, the court must determine whether the proffered expert testimony will assist the jury in understanding evidence or deciding upon a fact in issue. *Id.* Second, the court must determine whether the science underlying the expert testimony is "sufficiently established to have gained general acceptance" in its field. *Id.* (internal quotes and citations omitted).[35] "General acceptance" means "acceptance by a clear majority of the members of the relevant scientific community, with consideration by the trial court of both the quality and quantity of those opinions." *Hadden*, 690 So. 2d at 576 n.2. Third, the court must determine whether a particular witness is qualified to render expert testimony. *Ramirez*, 651 So. 2d at 1167. Finally, if the court allows the witness to testify as to his or her expert opinion, it is up to the jury to determine the weight the opinion should be given. *Id.* Admissibility of expert evidence is at the trial judge's sole discretion. *Ramirez v. State*, 810 So. 2d 836, 844 (2001).

The proponent of expert evidence bears the burden of establishing its admissibility by a preponderance of the evidence. *See Williamson v. State*, 994 So. 2d 1000, 1009–10 (2008). To preserve the issue of admissibility for appeal, an opposing party must object on the basis that the "novel scientific evidence offered is unreliable." *See Hadden* 690 So. 2d at 580.[36] Absent a proper

---

[32] *See* Waterway & Weill, *supra* note 31 at 2–3 (condemning the *Frye* test as an insufficient "check on the integrity of expert evidence," and calling upon the Florida legislature to statutorily adopt the *Daubert* standard "to place Florida on equal footing with most other jurisdictions and federal courts.").

[33] On February 24, 2012, the Florida house, for the second consecutive year, passed HB243, a bill that would change the courtroom standards for admission of expert evidence from *Frye* to a *Daubert*-based test. Despite the support of such proponents as the Florida chamber of commerce, the bill failed to pass the Florida senate, and the house and senate were unable to reach an agreement on a compromise bill. *See* Tamburro, *supra* note 31; *see also* Gary Blankenship, *JNC, Expert Witness, Foreclosure Bills All Die*, THE FLORIDA BAR NEWS (Apr. 1, 2012), http://www.floridabar.org/DIVCOM/JN/jnnews01.nsf/8c9f13012b96736985 256aa900624829/4e88f8e8f348cf87852579cd00421c19!OpenDocument; Chris Wilkerson, *Legislature Fails Again to Change Expert Witness Testimony Standard*, TAMPA BAY BUSINESS JOURNAL (March 30, 2012, 6:00 AM), http://www.bizjournals.com/tampabay/print-edition/2012/03/30/legislature-fails-again-to-change.html?page=all (noting the Florida chamber of commerce's position that the current *Frye* standard "puts Florida businesses in constant danger of being pulled into lawsuits because plaintiff attorneys gravitate to Florida courts where they are able to present 'junk science'").

[34] "Because, like the United States Supreme Court, I find no basis for concluding that *Frye* has survived Florida's adoption of an evidence code similar to the federal code, I would recede from our cases continuing to apply *Frye* . . . ." *Marsh v. Valyou*, 977 So. 2d 543, 551 (2007) (Anstead & Pariente, JJ., specially concurring).

[35] *See also Frye v. United States*, 293 F. 1013, 1014 (D.C. Cir. 1923). In determining "general acceptance," courts are instructed to look to "disparate sources-e.g., expert testimony, scientific and legal publications, and judicial opinions." *See Ramirez v. State*, 810 So. 2d 836, 844 (2001) (citing *Hadden v. State*, 690 So. 2d 573, 579 (1997)).

[36] While such an objection may be raised either at trial or in a motion *in limine*, Florida courts recognize the latter as the more proper approach. *See Janssen Pharm. Prods., L.P. v. Hodgemire ex rel. Hodgemire*, 49 So. 3d 767, 771 (Fla. Dist. Ct. App. 2010) (citing *Ramirez*, 651 So. 2d at 1168 n.4).

objection from the challenging party, it is not error for a court to admit expert evidence without conducting a *Frye* hearing. *E.g.*, *Taylor v. State*, 62 So. 3d 1101, 1118 (2011). Admissibility decisions under *Frye* are reviewed de novo, *see King v. State*, 89 So. 3d 209, 228 (2012) (quoting *Marsh v. Valyou*, 977 So. 2d 543, 547 (2007); *Hadden v. State*, 690 So. 2d 573, 579 (1997), with "general acceptance" considered at the time of appeal. *Id.*

(2) Florida's Frye Test in Practice—Limited Use

As discussed above, the Supreme Court of Florida's adherence to the *Frye* standard over that of *Daubert* has not been without controversy.[37] However, as several commentators have observed, the impact of choosing between *Frye* and *Daubert* may, in practice, have little effect upon the ultimate admissibility of expert evidence.[38] It is perhaps of greater importance that Florida courts have developed a number of exceptions that significantly limit *Frye's* application.[39] In such cases, the testimony at issue is admitted without having to satisfy the requirements of *Frye*,[40] and as the Supreme Court of Florida repeatedly has stated, because of these exceptions "*Frye* is inapplicable in the vast majority of cases."[41] Florida courts need not determine admissibility according to *Frye* where proffered expert evidence is not based upon new or novel scientific techniques;[42] where proffered evidence represents the "pure opinion" of an expert witness;[43] or where an expert reaches conclusions based upon underlying scientific methodology that itself meets the *Frye* test.[44] The following section describes these exceptions and analyzes recent Florida cases applying them.

---

[37] *See supra* notes 30–34 and accompanying text. There is even disagreement over which is actually the stricter standard. *Compare Marsh*, 977 So. 2d at 546–47 (2007) ("Courts and commentators have since debated whether the *Daubert* standard is more lenient or more strict.") *with Brim v. State*, 695 So. 2d 268, 271–72 (1997) ("Despite the federal adoption of a more lenient standard in *Daubert* . . . we have maintained the higher standard of reliability as dictated by *Frye*.") *with* Waterway & Weill, *supra* note 31 at 2 ("[*Frye*] does not provide trial judges with the legal tools for ensuring that 'expert' witnesses are qualified and that their testimony is relevant, reliable, and appropriate for a jury.").

[38] *See, e.g.*, Edward K. Cheng & Albert H. Yoon, *Does Frye or Daubert Matter? A Study of Scientific Admissibility Standards*, 91 VA. L. REV. 471, 511 (2005) (finding "no evidence that *Frye* or *Daubert* makes a difference" in scientific admissibility determinations); David W. Barnes, *General Acceptance Versus Scientific Soundness: Mad Scientists in the Courtroom*, 31 FL. ST. U. L. REV. 303 (2004) (arguing that the decisions of the Supreme Court of Florida mandate the use of a "Frye-plus" test that is similar to *Daubert*).

[39] *See* Waterway & Weill, *supra* note 31 at 9 (2011) (complaining of "an essentially unbroken line of [Supreme Court of Florida] cases proclaiming that Florida follows the general acceptance test but restricting the test's reach to the point of near non-usability").

[40] *See infra* notes 41, 47, 48, and 55; *see also Murray v. State*, 3 So. 3d 1108, 1117 (2009) and accompanying text.

[41] *See King*, 89 So. 3d at 228 (quoting *Marsh*, 977 So. 2d at 547); *Spann v. State*, 857 So. 2d 845, 852–53 (2003); *U.S. Sugar Corp. v. Henson*, 823 So. 2d 104, 109 (2002); *Hood v. Matrixx Initiatives, Inc.*, 50 So. 3d 1166, 1173 (Fla. Dist. Ct. App. 2010).

[42] *See infra* note 41 and accompanying text.

[43] *See infra* note 48 and accompanying text.

[44] *See infra* note 55 and accompanying text.

i. Frye does not apply where the science is not new or novel

The Supreme Court of Florida repeatedly has affirmed that a court need not conduct a *Frye* analysis if the proffered expert evidence does not involve new or novel science.[45] While what constitutes "new or novel" remains undefined,[46] Florida courts considering the question look to both the novelty of the science at issue[47] and whether such evidence previously has been admitted by other Florida courts. *See Murray v. State*, 3 So. 3d 1108, 1117 (2009) (evidence involving microscopic hair comparisons exempted from *Frye* analysis because of previous Florida Supreme Court decision that such science was not new or novel); *Ibar v. State*, 938 So. 2d 451, 467–68 (2006) (footwear impression expert evidence not new or novel, having been in existence for more than 100 years and discussed in an 1893 decision of the Supreme Court of Florida); *Still v. State*, 917 So. 2d 250, 251 (Fla. Dist. Ct. App. 2005) (finding a *Frye* hearing not required for admission of scientific evidence involving GPS technology, noting that Florida courts previously had admitted such evidence).

In 2012, the Supreme Court of Florida followed the previously admitted evidence route in *King v. State*, 89 So. 3d 209 (2012). At issue was expert "tool-mark identification" testimony linking pistol shell casings known to have been fired from the defendant's gun with a shell casing found near the victim. *Id.* at 227–28. The defendant argued that the admissibility of such expert testimony, in the absence of a known weapon, should have been subjected to a *Frye* inquiry. *Id.* at 229. The Supreme Court rejected this argument, finding that "research reveals that both Florida courts and other state and federal courts have admitted this evidence since at least 1969." *Id.* Accordingly, the trial court did not err in declining to conduct a *Frye* hearing with respect to such evidence. *Id.* at 228–29 (2012).

---

[45] *See, e.g., King,* 89 So. 3d at 228 (emphasis in original) (quoting *Marsh,* 977 So. 2d at 547) ("By definition, the *Frye* standard *only applies* when an expert attempts to render an opinion that is based upon *new or novel scientific techniques.*"); *Ibar v. State,* 938 So. 2d 451, 467 (2006) ("*Frye* sets forth the test to be utilized when a party seeks the admission of expert testimony concerning new or novel scientific evidence. In this case, however, there was no new or novel scientific theory being presented by the shoe print expert. Thus . . . *Frye* is [in]applicable."); *Spann,* 857 So. 2d at 852 ("In the vast majority of cases, no *Frye* inquiry will be required because no innovative scientific theories will be at issue.").

[46] *See* Waterway & Weill, *supra* note 31 at 12 ("No Florida court has or can reasonably define 'new or novel' in the context of science.").

[47] *See McDonald v. State,* 952 So. 2d 484, 498 (2006) ("Visual and microscopic hair comparison is not based on new or novel scientific principles and, therefore, does not require a *Frye* analysis."); *Spann,* 857 So. 2d at 852 (forensic handwriting identification not new or novel science requiring a *Frye* analysis); *Medina v. State,* 920 So. 2d 136, 138 (Fla. Dist. Ct. App. 2006) (agreeing with the trial court that scientific evidence involving GPS technology is not new or novel and thus not subject to a *Frye* hearing); *Davis v. Caterpillar, Inc.,* 787 So. 2d 894, 898 (Fla. Dist. Ct. App. 2001) (reversing trial court's order striking expert testimony regarding blind spot monitoring technology in part because such testimony "did not involve any novel scientific principle").

ii. Frye does not apply where an expert offers a "pure opinion."

Florida courts long have recognized that testimony providing an expert's "pure opinion" does not warrant a *Frye* analysis.[48] The Supreme Court of Florida, in oft-repeated language, explained the reason for this distinction in *Flanagan v. State*:

> While cloaked with the credibility of the expert, [pure opinion] testimony is analyzed by the jury as it analyzes any other personal opinion or factual testimony by a witness. [Non-opinion expert testimony], on the other hand, by its nature necessarily relies on some scientific principle or test, which implies an infallibility not found in pure opinion testimony. The jury will naturally assume that the scientific principles underlying the expert's conclusion are valid. Accordingly, this type of testimony must meet the *Frye* test . . . .[49]

In determining whether expert testimony is "pure opinion," Florida courts look to whether the testimony is based upon the expert's personal experience or training, as opposed to relying upon a "study, test, procedure, or methodology that constitute[s] new or novel scientific diagnosis." *See Marsh*, 977 So. 2d at 548–49 (quoting *Gelsthorpe*, 897 So. 2d at 510–11).[50] "Pure opinion" testimony often is seen in the medical context, particularly where a doctor renders an expert opinion based upon "personal experience or training" after reviewing a party's medical history and performing differential diagnosis. *See, e.g., Marsh*, 977 So. 2d at 548–49 (medical expert testimony linking trauma to fibromyalgia exempt from *Frye* as pure opinion where testimony was based upon a review of plaintiff's medical history, clinical examination, published research, differential diagnosis, and the experts' own experience); *Gelsthorpe*, 897 So. 2d at 510 (medical expert's testimony that child suffered brain damage resulting from defendant physicians' failure to promptly perform caesarian delivery exempt from *Frye* as pure opinion because it was based upon differential diagnosis and analysis of medical records). However, examples outside of the medical context also are seen.[51]

---

[48] *See Marsh v. Valyou*, 977 So. 2d 543, 548 (2007) ("It is well-established that *Frye* is inapplicable to 'pure opinion' testimony."); *Hadden v. State*, 690 So. 2d 573, 578–79 (1997) ("[T]he *Frye* standard for admissibility of scientific evidence is not applicable to an expert's pure opinion testimony which is based solely on the expert's training and experience."); *Flanagan v. State*, 625 So. 2d 827, 828 (1993) ("pure opinion testimony . . . does not have to meet *Frye*, because this type of testimony is based on the expert's personal experience and training."); *Gelsthorpe v. Weinstein*, 897 So. 2d 504, 509 (Fla. Dist. Ct. App. 2005) ("[T]he *Frye* standard is not applicable to 'pure opinion testimony.'").

[49] *Flanagan*, 625 So. 2d 827, 828 (1993). *But see* Neil D. Kodsi, *Confronting Experts Whose Opinions are Neither Supported nor Directly Contradicted by Scientific Literature*, FLA. B.J., June 2006, at 80 (observing that the exception may discourage rigorous scientific analysis by exempting from *Frye* opinion testimony based upon an expert's experience and training, while subjecting identical testimony to a *Frye* analysis if actual confirmatory tests or studies have been performed).

[50] *See also* Kodsi, *supra* note 49 (discussing the dangers inherent in this distinction).

[51] *See, e.g., Torres v. State*, 999 So. 2d 1077 (Fla. Dist. Ct. App. 2009) (expert testimony of former FBI agent based upon his professional experience with victims of child molestation admissible as "pure opinion"); *State v. Sercey*, 825 So. 2d 959, 981–82 (Fla. Dist. Ct. App. 2002) (drug testing experts' testimony regarding the timing of defendant's use of marijuana prior to a blood draw exempt from *Frye* as "pure opinion" because it was based on the experts' knowledge and experience); *Davis v. Caterpillar, Inc.*, 787 So. 2d 894, 898 (Fla. Dist. Ct. App. 2001) (reversing the trial court's decision to exclude expert testimony; witness allowed to testify that "based on his experience" a piece of construction equipment was unreasonably dangerous because it lacked means for monitoring a rear blind spot).

In 2008, the Supreme Court of Florida addressed the "pure opinion" exception in *Williamson v. State*, 994 So. 2d 1000, 1008–11 (2008). In that case, the state introduced the testimony of an expert in "individual decision-making" and "extreme and extraordinary techniques of influence and control" to explain the actions of the key witness in a murder trial. *Id.* The expert testified that the witness's actions displayed "a pattern of someone who has . . . been terrorized, [and acted] in response to a credible threat, not only to himself, but . . . to members of his family." *Id.* at 1009. The defendant, who was convicted based in part upon the witness's testimony, challenged the trial court's summary denial of his postconviction claim that his trial counsel was ineffective for failing to request a *Frye* hearing to examine the "novel science" upon which the expert had relied. *Id.* at 1008.

In denying the defendant's claim, the trial court determined that the expert testimony was "pure opinion," and accordingly not subject to a *Frye* analysis. *See id.* at 1010. The Supreme Court of Florida disagreed, finding that the expert in fact had provided "syndrome testimony," which necessitated a *Frye* analysis to determine "whether it was sufficiently established to have general acceptance in the particular field in which it belongs." *Id.*[52] The claim was remanded to the trial court, in part for a determination of whether the expert's evidence was "generally accepted." *Id.*

The Florida Court of Appeals for the Fourth District found *Frye* inapplicable based on the pure opinion exception in *Hood v. Matrixx Initiatives, Incorporated*, 50 So. 3d 1166 (Fla. Dist. Ct. App. 2010), *petition for review denied*, 66 So. 3d 303 (2011). There, the plaintiffs brought an action to recover for injuries arising from the use of Zicam nasal gel, an over-the-counter cold remedy. *Id.* at 1168. At trial, the plaintiffs sought to introduce the expert medical testimony of Dr. Bruce Jafek to demonstrate that Zicam toxicity caused one of the plaintiffs to lose his sense of smell. *Id.* The trial court granted the defendants' motion to exclude this testimony after conducting a *Frye* analysis and concluding that the methods and techniques utilized by the expert in forming his opinion had not gained the general acceptance of the scientific community. *Id.* at 1170–72. Because Dr. Jafek was to provide the plaintiffs' only expert evidence regarding causation, the trial court also granted the defendants' motion for summary judgment. *Id.* at 1172.

The Court of Appeals reversed. Observing the oft-repeated maxim that *Frye* is "inapplicable to the 'vast majority' of cases," the Court of Appeals proceeded to analyze the proffered evidence in light of the Supreme Court of Florida's holding in *Marsh*. *Id.* at 1173–75; *see also Marsh v. Valyou*, 977 So. 2d 543, 549 (2007) (medical expert testimony linking trauma to fibromyalgia exempt from *Frye* as pure opinion where testimony was based upon a review of plaintiff's medical history, clinical examination, published research, differential diagnosis, and the experts' own experience). While recognizing that at least six federal courts had found Dr. Jafek's conclusions regarding olfactory damage caused by Zicam inadmissible under the *Daubert* standard, the Court of Appeals nevertheless stated that "[o]ur understanding of *Marsh* is that where the scientific literature recognizes an association or possible etiology between a medical condition and a predicate event, a medical expert may render a medical causation opinion based upon a differential diagnosis." *Matrixx,*

---

[52] The Supreme Court of Florida noted that on two earlier occasions it had considered and rejected "expert syndrome testimony" for failing to satisfy the requirements of *Frye*. *See Hadden v. State*, 690 So. 2d 573, 580–81 (1997) (syndrome testimony in child abuse cases is not pure opinion testimony); *Flanagan v. State*, 625 So. 2d 827, 828 (1993) ("[S]exual offender profile evidence is not generally accepted in the scientific community and does not meet the *Frye* test for admissibility.").

50 So. 3d 1166 at 1173–75.[53] Accordingly, the majority of Dr. Jafek's testimony was exempt from *Frye* as "pure opinion,"[54] and the case was remanded for further proceedings. *Matrixx*, 50 So. 3d at 1176.

    iii. Frye does not apply to expert conclusions based upon underlying methodology that itself satisfies Frye

Finally, Florida courts have held that a *Frye* inquiry is appropriately directed only to the scientific principles and methodologies relied upon by an expert in forming an opinion, and not to the opinion itself.[55] Put simply, Florida courts have held that while the scientific principles and methodology supporting expert evidence must be generally accepted in the relevant field, the same standard does not apply to any conclusions an expert derives from such principles and methodology. *U.S. Sugar Corp.*, 823 So. 2d at 109–10. In allowing this exception, Florida courts have recognized that "[o]therwise, the utility of expert testimony would be entirely erased, and 'opinion' testimony . . . would simply be the recitation of recognized scientific principles to the fact finder." *See id.* at 110.

In 2010, the Florida Court of Appeals for the Fifth District applied this rationale in *Janssen Pharmaceutical Products, L.P. v. Hodgemire ex rel. Hodgemire*, 49 So. 3d 767 (Fla. Dist. Ct. App. 2010), *petition for review denied*, 64 So. 3d 1260 (2011). In that case, a husband serving as the Personal Representative of the Estate of his deceased wife ("plaintiff") brought suit against defendant drug manufacturers, alleging that the wife died of a fatal overdose of fentanyl delivered by a defective transdermal patch manufactured by one of the defendants. *Id.* at 769. The plaintiff sought to introduce expert testimony regarding "postmortem redistribution," a process wherein drugs stored in the tissues of the body are released back into the bloodstream after death. *Id.* at 770. Based upon an understanding of postmortem redistribution, the manufacturer-specified dosage provided by a properly functioning transdermal fentanyl patch and the dosage required for fentanyl toxicity, the

---

[53] The court went on to note that "[t]he fact that the precise causation is still under investigation does not make the expert opinions in this case 'new or novel' or inadmissible under the more demanding requirements of *Frye*." *Id.* at 1174. This is a direct quote from a 2009 decision of the Florida District Court of Appeals for the Fourth Circuit, *Andries v. Royal Caribbean Cruises, Limited*, in which the court also had found "pure opinion" medical causation testimony admissible under the *Marsh* rationale. 12 So. 3d 260 (Fla. Dist. Ct. App. 2009) (reversing the trial court's award of summary judgment to defendants after improperly barring such testimony).

[54] Interestingly, the court specifically noted that "[t]o the extent that Dr. Jafek relied upon 'new and novel' experiments that he personally conducted regarding Zicam . . . evidence regarding such experiments is not admissible as 'pure opinion.'" *Id.* at 1175. This situation reflects the concerns of some commentators that the "pure opinion" exception favors the admission of scientific evidence that is not supported by experimental data. *See* Kodsi, *supra* note 49.

[55] *See Castillo v. E.I. Du Pont De Nemours & Co., Inc.*, 854 So. 2d 1264, 1269 (2003) ("We must consider whether the scientific principles upon which the [plaintiffs'] experts based their opinions are generally accepted in the scientific community."); *U.S. Sugar Corp. v. Henson*, 823 So. 2d 104, 110 (2002) ("We wish to highlight the principle that under *Frye*, the inquiry must focus only on the general acceptance of the scientific principles and methodologies upon which an expert relies in rendering his or her opinion."); *Berry v. CSX Transp., Inc.*, 709 So. 2d 552, 567 (Fla. Dist. Ct. App. 1998) ("[W]e hold that, under *Frye* and its Florida progeny, when the expert's opinion is well-founded and based upon generally accepted scientific principles and methodology, it is not necessary that the expert's opinion be generally accepted as well.").

experts concluded that the plaintiff's wife in fact had died from a lethal dose of fentanyl that was delivered by a defective patch. *Id.* at 769–70. After hearing this and other testimony, the jury found for the plaintiff. *Id.* at 770.

The defendants appealed, challenging the trial court's conclusion that the proffered testimony was not subject to *Frye*. *Id.* at 771. The defendants focused upon the final conclusions drawn by the plaintiff's experts, arguing that the scientific literature reflected "wide individual variability" that precluded the use of postmortem redistribution analysis for predicting results for a single individual. *Id.* at 772. The Court of Appeals rejected this argument, observing that because both parties conceded that the science and methodology underlying postmortem redistribution analysis with fentanyl was generally accepted, *Frye* did not require the experts' opinion based upon such studies to be generally accepted. *See id.* (citing *United States Sugar Corp. v. Henson*, 823 So. 2d 104, 109 (2002)). Accordingly, the Court of Appeals affirmed the trial court's decision to allow expert testimony regarding postmortem redistribution analysis and fentanyl toxicity. *Id.* at 773.

b. Beyond the Exceptions—Recent Florida Cases Applying the Frye test for admissibility of Expert Evidence

While the preceding sections have dealt with the variety of exclusions precluding the application of *Frye*, in certain circumstances, Florida courts nevertheless can and do analyze expert evidence under the "general acceptance" standard mandated by the *Frye* analysis. This section discusses two recent cases.

In *Overton v. State*, 976 So. 2d 536 (2007), a convicted murderer sought review of the trial court's denial of his motion for postconviction relief in which he alleged, among other things, ineffective assistance of counsel due to his attorney's failure to participate adequately in a *Frye* hearing regarding the admissibility of short tandem repeat (STR) DNA testing. *Id.* at 549–50. The Supreme Court of Florida held that even assuming deficiency of counsel, the defendant was not prejudiced, in part because the DNA testing at issue satisfied the requirements of *Frye*. *Id.* at 552–53.

The Supreme Court analyzed the DNA testing evidence using the two-pronged analysis it previously had developed in *Hayes v. State*, 660 So. 2d 257, 264–65 (1995), for considering the admissibility of DNA test results under *Frye*. *Overton*, 976 So. at 550, 553. Under the two-pronged *Hayes* analysis, both the DNA test at issue as well as the testing procedures utilized to perform the DNA test must meet the *Frye* "general acceptance" standard. *Hayes*, 660 So. at 264–65. With respect to the first prong, the Supreme Court found "strong evidence that the underlying scientific principle with STR DNA testing was generally accepted at the time of [the defendant's] trial." *Overton*, 976 So. at 553. With respect to the second prong, there also was evidence demonstrating that the protocols and procedures utilized by the testing lab that performed the STR DNA testing were generally accepted by the scientific community as being sufficient to protect against contamination and error. *See id.* Accordingly, because the STR DNA testing at any event would have been admissible under *Frye*, the defendant could have suffered no prejudice from his counsel's alleged failure to participate more fully in the trial court's original *Frye* hearing, and the Supreme Court affirmed the trial court's denial of postconviction relief for ineffective assistance of counsel. *Id.* at 553, 575.

In *Brewington v. State*, No. 2D10-458, 2012 WL 3822109 (Fla. Dist. Ct. App., Sept. 5, 2012), the Florida Court of Appeals for the Second District considered the admissibility of expert testimony purporting to offer a novel theory involving battered woman syndrome. *Id.* at *1. The case involved the tragic death of the defendant's three-year-old son, which resulted from beatings the child received from the defendant's boyfriend. *Id.* In connection with this crime, the defendant was charged with aggravated manslaughter of a child. *Id.* At trial, the state presented evidence that the defendant was aware her boyfriend was beating her son and yet failed to seek medical care. *Id.* In response, the defendant, who testified that she also had been abused by her boyfriend and that she was afraid of him, sought to present evidence that she suffered from "battered woman syndrome," which prevented her from realizing what was taking place or acting to save her child. *Id.* The trial court ruled such evidence inadmissible under *Frye. Id.* at *2.

While noting that courts in other state jurisdictions had allowed "battered woman syndrome" evidence in similar cases, the Court of Appeals nevertheless agreed that "the trial court was constrained by *Frye*." *Id.* at *3–4. In its decision, the trial court had found that the defense's expert witness

> (1) had not shown that the effect of battered woman syndrome in the context of failing to aid a child was capable of objective testing, (2) had not shown that battered woman syndrome in this context had been subject to peer review and publication, and (3) had not shown that the scientific or psychological community generally accepted battered woman syndrome to negate the mens rea element for a woman charged with failing to protect a child from abuse.

Id. at *2.[56] Agreeing with the trial court that the defendant had "failed to establish, by a preponderance of the evidence, that the theory that battered woman syndrome can negate mens rea for failing to protect a child has been sufficiently tested and generally accepted by the relevant scientific or psychological community," the Court of Appeals affirmed the decision to exclude the evidence for failure to meet the "exacting" standard of *Frye. Id.* at *3–4.

c. Expert Related Rules and Procedural Issues

(1) Florida Evidence Code

Florida's evidence statutes relating to expert witnesses essentially mirror their federal counterparts. Specifically, Fla. Stat. Ann. §§ 90.702, 90.703, 90.704 and 90.705 address the same topics as Rules 702, 704, 703 and 705, respectively, of the Federal Rules of Evidence. Opponents to the continued application of the *Frye* standard for the admission of expert evidence have pointed to this similarity in arguing that the *Frye* standard should be abandoned in favor of *Daubert*.[57]

---

[56] Interestingly, in determining the admissibility of the proffered evidence, the trial court essentially undertook a *Daubert* analysis by not only questioning the general acceptance of the defendant's theory (a prong common to both *Frye* and *Daubert*) but also considering whether the theory was capable of objective testing or had been subject to peer review and publication (which are a part of the *Daubert* analysis). *Compare Daubert v. Merrell Dow Pharmaceuticals, Inc.*, 509 U.S. 579 (1993) *with Frye v. United States*, 293 F. 1013, 1014 (D.C. Cir. 1923).

[57] "While this court has continued to apply *Frye* in determining the admissibility of scientific expert opinion testimony after the adoption of the Florida Rules of Evidence, it has done so without confronting the fact that those rules do *not* mention *Frye* or the test set out in *Frye*."). *Marsh v. Valyou*, 977 So. 2d 543, 551 (2007) (Anstead & Pariente, JJ., specially concurring) (emphasis in original). Judge Anstead continues by stating that "[b]ecause, like the United States Supreme Court, I find no basis for concluding that *Frye* has survived Florida's *adoption of an evidence code similar to the federal code*, I would recede from our cases continuing to apply *Frye*." *Id.* (emphasis added) *But see Hadden v. State*, 690 So. 2d 573, 578 (Fla. 1997) ("Our specific adoption of that test after the enactment of the evidence code manifests our intent to use the *Frye* test as the proper standard for admitting novel scientific evidence in Florida, even though the *Frye* test is not set forth in the evidence code.").

On cross-examination of an expert, counsel may use "[s]tatements of facts or opinions on a subject of science, art, or specialized knowledge contained in a published treatise, periodical, book, dissertation, pamphlet, or other writing . . . if the expert witness recognizes the author or the treatise, periodical, book, dissertation, pamphlet, or other writing to be authoritative." FLA. STAT. § 90.706 (2012). Moreover, if the trial court finds the literature to be authoritative and relevant, it may be used for purposes of cross-examination even if the expert does not recognize it. *Id.* Attempts to bolster the expert's testimony by references to consultations with other experts or such authoritative literature is not permitted on direct examination. *Linn v. Fossum*, 946 So.2d 1032, 1039 (Fla. 2006). *But see J.V. v. Dept. of Children and Family Services*, 967 So.2d 354 (Fla. Dist. Ct. App. 2007) (rule does not preclude expert from relying upon facts and data "reasonably relied upon by experts in the subject," such as medical reports authored by other physicians).

Florida does not have a statutory provision equivalent to Rule 706 of the Federal Rules of Evidence, but Fla. Stat. Ann. § 916.115 does address the appointment of expert witnesses in criminal matters. Specifically, the statute provides that the department of corrections shall maintain and annually provide to the courts a list of persons qualified to serve as experts. FLA. STAT. § 916.115(1)(b) (2012). A court may appoint no more than three experts to determine a defendant's mental condition, including issues of competency to proceed, insanity, and involuntary hospitalization or placement. FLA. STAT. § 916.115(1) (2012). The court shall pay for any expert appointed by court order, FLA. STAT. § 916.115(2) (2012), with the exception that any fees associated with the development of testimony in support of an asserted affirmative defense of insanity by an expert appointed by the court upon motion of defense counsel is charged to the defense. *Id.* Both the public defender's office and the state attorney's office are permitted to retain experts, and the fees associated with such experts are payable by the retaining office. FLA. STAT. § 916.115(2)(a),(b) (2012). The fees of an expert retained by a defendant who has been appointed private counsel, or who has been deemed indigent and is represented by unappointed private counsel or is proceeding pro se will be paid by the Justice Administrative Commission. FLA. STAT. § 916.115(2)(c),(d) (2012). Witness fees paid to experts shall be taxed as costs in the case. FLA. STAT. § 916.115(2)(f) (2012).

In both civil and criminal cases, expert witnesses are entitled to a fee, including the costs of exhibits used, "in an amount agreed to by the parties, and the same shall be taxed as costs." FLA. STAT. § 92.231(2) (2012). In criminal cases and in matters where services are provided for the state, expert witnesses "shall be compensated in accordance with standards adopted by the Legislature." FLA. STAT. § 92.231(2),(3) (2012). This statute does not mandate an award of costs, including expert witness fees, to a prevailing party, but does provide a mechanism through which a party may seek such costs.[58] In 2005 the Supreme Court of Florida adopted the Statewide Uniform Guidelines for Taxation of Costs in Civil Actions, to guide courts in determining what costs (if any) should be awarded to a prevailing party. *In re Amendments to Uniform Guidelines for Taxation of Costs*, 915 So. 2d 612 (2005). While advisory, and recognizing that "[t]he taxation of costs in any particular proceeding is within the broad discretion of the trial court," the Guidelines place the burden on the party seeking costs to show such costs were "reasonably necessary either to defend or prosecute the

---

[58] *See Massey v. David*, 979 So. 2d 931, 941 (2008) ("The substantive right to taxation of expert witness fees as costs was created in section 92.231(2) . . . ."); *see also Winter Park Imports, Inc. v. JM Family Enters., Inc.*, 77 So. 3d 227, 231–232 (Fla. Dist. Ct. App. 2011) (taxation of costs within the court's "broad discretion"; courts are "not precluded from considering the time an expert expended in preparing for deposition, including the time reasonably and necessarily spent when conferring with counsel and in formulating his or her expert opinion through examination, investigation, testing, and/or research"; however such fees must be "reasonably necessary").

case." *Id.* at 614. The guidelines also provide specific examples of the types of costs that both should and should not be awarded. *Id.* at 614–17.

(2) Civil Discovery Regarding Expert Witnesses

The Florida Rules of Civil Procedure are devoid of specific provisions regarding the timing of the disclosure of expert witnesses and the production of expert reports. Rule 1.200 provides that the court and parties may address "disclosure of expert witnesses and the discovery of facts known and opinions held by such experts" during a case management conference. FLA. R. CIV. P. 1.200(a)(8). This rule also provides that "the limitation of the number of expert witnesses" may be considered during a pretrial conference. FLA. R. CIV. P. 1.200(b)(4). A pretrial order is to be prepared "reciting the action taken at [the pretrial] conference" and "shall control the subsequent course of the action unless modified to prevent injustice." FLA. R. CIV. P. 1.200(d).

Florida Rule 1.280 governs discovery generally, including certain aspects of expert witness discovery. Rule 1.280(b)(5) permits a party to use interrogatories and depositions to discover the facts and opinions of a testifying expert, the scope of his or her employment in the case and corresponding compensation, the expert's general litigation experience, other cases in which the expert has testified, and the portion of the expert's time spent serving as an expert witness. FLA. R. CIV. P. 1.280(b)(5). Experts are required to produce business or financial records only in the most "unusual or compelling circumstances," and may not be forced to "compile or produce nonexistent documents." FLA. R. CIV. P. 1.280(b)(5)(A). Discovery of non-testifying experts typically requires a showing of "exceptional circumstances." FLA. R. CIV. P. 1.280(b)(5)(B). A party seeking discovery from an expert witness must "pay the expert a reasonable fee for time spent in responding" to discovery as provided in Rule 1.280, unless "manifest injustice would result." FLA. R. CIV. P. 1.280(b)(5)(C).[59]

Rule 1.390 governs the depositions of expert witnesses in Florida state courts. First, the rule defines an "expert witness" for purposes of this rule as "a person duly and regularly engaged in the practice of a profession who holds a professional degree from a university or college and has had special professional training and experience, or one possessed of special knowledge or skill about the subject upon which called to testify." FLA. R. CIV. P. 1.390(a). The rule provides that expert witnesses shall be subject to deposition at any time prior to trial in accordance with the rules for taking depositions of lay witnesses. FLA. R. CIV. P. 1.390(b). The expert shall be paid a reasonable witness fee for his or her deposition appearance. FLA. R. CIV. P. 1.390(c). The amount of the fee is determined by the court, and such fees may be taxed as costs. *Id.*

A unique aspect of this rule is that an expert deposition may be used at trial in lieu of live testimony without regard to the expert witness's residence. FLA. R. CIV. P. 1.390(b). That is, a party may elect to depose an expert witness rather than offer his or her testimony live at trial without needing to prove that the witness is "unavailable." *Id.* The purpose of this rule appears to be to reduce the costs associated with using expert witnesses. *See Owca v. Zeminski*, 137 So. 2d 876, 877 (Fla. Dist. Ct. App. 1962) (discussing prior iteration of nearly identical rule).

(3) Expert Discovery in Criminal Matters

A criminal defendant may choose to participate in limited discovery as provided by Rule 3.220 of the Florida Rules of Criminal Procedure by serving a "notice of discovery" on the prosecuting

---

[59] Under certain circumstances and/or at the discretion of the court this rule also requires the party seeking discovery to pay "a fair part of the fees and expenses reasonably incurred by the [responding] party in obtaining facts and opinions from the expert." *See id.*

attorney. FLA. R. CRIM. P. 3.220(a). Filing the "notice of discovery" has the effect of "bind[ing] both the prosecution and defendant to all discovery procedures contained in [Rule 3.220]." *Id.* Within fifteen days after service of the notice, the prosecutor is required to serve a written "discovery exhibit" that discloses, among other things, the identity of testifying expert witnesses and makes available to the defendant for inspection or copying any expert reports or statements made in connection with the case. FLA. R. CRIM. P. 3.220(b). Fifteen days after receiving the prosecutor's "discovery exhibit," the defendant in turn is required to furnish similar information to the prosecutor. FLA. R. CRIM. P. 3.220(d). The rule further outlines procedures for depositions, FLA. R. CRIM. P. 3.220(h), a continuing duty to disclose, FLA. R. CRIM. P. 3.220(j), protective orders, FLA. R. CRIM. P. 3.220(l), *in camera* and *ex parte* proceedings, FLA. R. CRIM. P. 3.220(m), and sanctions for discovery abuses, FLA. R. CRIM. P. 3.220(n).

(4) Medical Experts—Licensure of Out-Of-State Medical Experts and Disciplinary Provisions for Deceptive or Fraudulent Testimony

Effective October 1, 2011, Florida law requires any out-of-state physician, doctor of osteopathy, or dentist wishing to provide expert testimony to obtain an expert witness certificate from the Florida Department of Health. FLA. STAT. §§ 458.3175, 459.0066, 466.005 (2012). This certificate "shall be treated as a license in any disciplinary action, and the holder of an expert witness certificate shall be subject to discipline by the board." FLA. STAT. §§ 458.3175(3), 459.0066(3), 466.005(3) (2012). Both in-state and out-of-state testifying medical experts may be disciplined for providing a "corroborating written medical expert report" without proper investigation, or for giving "deceptive or fraudulent expert witness testimony." FLA. STAT. §§ 458.331(1)(jj) & (oo) (2012). Such discipline may include denial of license; suspension, revocation, or restriction of license; imposition of administrative fines; restriction of practice; and other remedial measures. FLA. STAT. § 456.072(2) (2012).

3. Expert Evidence in Georgia State Courts

On January 1, 2013, Georgia implemented a new Georgia Evidence Code. *See* Georgia Senate Bill 3, enacted February 16, 2005; *see also Daubert v. Merrell Dow Pharm., Inc.*, 509 U.S. 579 (1993). The new rules continue the old rules application of *Daubert* principles in civil cases. Under the new code, the old Title 24 of the Georgia code was completely replaced and restructured by the new rules, and contains virtually all pertinent evidence rules. *See* Paul S. Milich, *Georgia's New Evidence Code—An Overview*, 28 GA. STATE U. L.REV. 6 (2011). The numbering of the new Title 24 is based upon the federal rules, with the new citation first identifying Georgia Title 24, then the Federal Rule of Evidence Article (*e.g.*, 7 for Opinions and Expert Testimony), and then the federal rule number. *See id.* Thus, the new cite to Georgia's rule for the qualification of expert testimony is O.C.G.A. § 24-7-702 and the rule for the bases of an expert's opinion testimony is O.C.G.A. § 24-7-703.

While this new Georgia Evidence Code largely parallels the Federal Rules of Evidence, the language and its application, it does not track exactly, creating important differences. For example, the *Daubert* standard in the new Rule 702 is expressly limited to civil cases only. It remains to be seen whether or how the *Daubert* standard may be applied in the criminal context.[60] The pre-2013 admissibility standard for expert scientific opinions in criminal cases was, and may continue to be, the standard articulated by the Georgia Supreme Court in *Harper v. State* in 1982—the "shall always be admissible" standard. 292 S.E.2d 389 (Ga. 1982); O.C.G.A. § 24-9-67; *see also Vaughn v. State*,

---

[60] The former O.C.G.A. § 24-9-67, addressing expert opinion in criminal cases, has been newly codified as O.C.G.A. § 24-7-707 (which does not have a F.R.E. analog).

646 S.E.2d 212 (Ga. 2007) (holding Harper continues to apply in criminal cases). Moreover, the new Rule 702 explicitly does not apply in civil actions brought under O.C.G.A. § 22-1-14 (eminent domain—valuation of condemned property), *see* O.C.G.A. § 24-7-702(a), and shall not be strictly applied in cases brought under Georgia Code Title 34, Chapter 9 (workers' compensation) or Title 50, Chapter 13 (pertaining to administration of Georgia's government bureaucracy). *See* O.C.G.A. § 24-7-702(g). Just as with the federal rule, the new code sections allow experts to rely on hearsay evidence in some circumstances.[61]

a. Civil Cases

With the enactment of O.C.G.A. § 24-9-67.1 as part of the Tort Reform Act, the Georgia legislature adopted much of Federal Rules of Evidence 702 and 703. As expressly stated in the that code section, the legislature intended that the Georgia state courts follow *Daubert*, as delineated in FRE 702 (except in criminal matters), and other federal cases applying the standards announced therein, in civil actions. O.C.G.A. § 24-9-67.1(b) (f). Cases decided under the former O.C.G.A. § 24-9-67.1 will continue to have precedential value because the new code merely restructures the statute to more closely follow the federal rules' structure. However, commentators have noted that the structure is not exactly aligned with the federal statutes and caution that only future rulings applying the new code will inform how closely the Georgia courts follow federal precedent.[62]

In *Condra v. Atlanta Orthopaedic Group, P.C.*, 285 Ga. 667, 669–672, 681 S.E.2d 152, 153–156 (2009), the Georgia Supreme Court applied O.C.G.A. § 24-9-67.1 to overrule its prior decision in *Johnson v. Riverdale Anesthesia Associates, P.C.*, 275 Ga. 240, 563 S.E.2d 431 (2002). *Condra* was a medical malpractice case in which plaintiffs' experts opined that medication the defendant physician had prescribed for plaintiff's condition (1) was inappropriate, (2) that it caused her to develop a rare and serious bone marrow disease, (3) that the disease could have been avoided had the physician conducted blood count monitoring during plaintiff's treatment, and (4) that the failure to conduct blood count monitoring was a breach of the standard of care. 285 Ga. at 667, 681 S.E.2d at 153. Defendants' experts testified that failing to conduct blood count monitoring was not a breach of the standard of care, but one defense expert testified in his deposition that it was his usual practice to conduct blood count monitoring when he prescribed the medication at issue. 285 Ga. at 668, 681 S.E.2d at 153. The trial court granted defendants' motion *in limine* preventing plaintiffs from cross-examining the experts as to their personal practices. *See id.*

The Georgia Court of Appeals upheld the trial court's ruling, relying upon the precedent set in *Johnson v. Riverdale Anesthesia Associates, P.C.*, 285 Ga. at 669, 681 S.E.2d at 153. In *Johnson*, the court held that testimony regarding a medical expert's personal practices was inadmissible as both impeachment evidence and substantive evidence regarding the applicable standard of care. 275 Ga. at 241, 563 S.E.2d at 433. The *Johnson* court reasoned that because the applicable standard of care in medical malpractice actions were those practices generally employed by the medical profession rather than those of an individual provider, evidence of an expert's personal practices was irrelevant in establishing the standard of care. *See id.*

The Georgia Supreme Court overruled its prior decision in *Johnson* because the newly enacted O.C.G.A. § 24-9-67.1 (now O.C.G.A. §§ 24-7-702 – 703) "places particular emphasis on a proffered medical experts' professional experience and practice in assessing his or her qualification to serve

---

[61] Experts may rely on facts or data that are otherwise inadmissible in evidence, "if of a type reasonably relied upon by experts in the particular field in forming opinions or inferences upon the subject." O.C.G.A. § 24-7-703.

[62] *See, e.g., Paul S. Milich, Georgia's New Evidence Code—An Overview,* 28 GA. STATE U. L.REV. 6 (2011)

as an expert witness." 285 Ga. at 669, 681 S.E.2d at 154. The Georgia Supreme Court reasoned that because O.C.G.A. § 24-9-67.1(c)(2)(A)'s threshold inquiry focused on the expert's practice and experience in the pertinent field for at least three of the last five years, "it would defy logic to find such experience categorically irrelevant in assessing the credibility of the expert's testimony." 285 Ga. at 670, 681 S.E.2d at 154. The Georgia Supreme Court held that "[t]he relevance and importance of a medical expert's personal choice of a course of treatment is highly probative of the credibility of the expert's opinion concerning the standard of care." *Id.* The Georgia Supreme Court also noted that:

> Under the *Daubert* line of cases, the trial judge is charged with the responsibility of evaluating the credibility of the expert's testimony. Such evaluation is made possible through, among other things, vigorous cross-examination.
>
> The right of . . . cross examination . . . is a substantial right, the preservation of which is essential to the proper administration of justice, and extends to all matters within the knowledge of the witness, the disclosure of which is material to the controversy.

285 Ga. at 671, 681 S.E.2d at 155 (citing *Daubert v. Merrill Dow Pharmaceuticals, Inc.*, 509, U.S. 579, 589, 595–596 (1993) and *News Publishing Co. v. Butler*, 95 Ga. 559, 559, 22 S.E. 282 (1895). Accordingly, the *Condra* court held that "evidence regarding an expert witness' personal practices, unless subject to exclusion on other evidentiary grounds, is admissible both as substantive evidence and to impeach the expert's opinion regarding the applicable standard of care." 285 Ga. at 669, 681 S.E.2d at 154.

In *An v. Active Pest Control South, Inc.*, 313 Ga. App. 110, 720 S.E.2d 222 (2011), the Georgia Court of Appeals addressed the issue of whether courts must decide issues of an expert opinion's admissibility before ruling on summary judgment motions. In *An*, the plaintiff homeowner had sued an exterminator for professional negligence and breach of contract after her home was infested by termites. The plaintiff identified potential experts, including an entomologist and a general contractor with expertise in estimating the costs of residential construction and repair. 313 Ga. App. at 112–113, 720 S.E.2d at 224. Defendant exterminator asserted that the expert opinions were unreliable, and therefore inadmissible, and moved to exclude the opinions pursuant to O.C.G.A. § 24-9-67.1. 313 Ga. App. at 113, 720 S.E.2d at 224–225. Defendant contemporaneously filed a motion for summary judgment arguing, among other things, that plaintiff would be unable to prove at trial that termites caused any damage to the home after defendant had treated it, nor able to prove the extent of any such damage. *See id.* The trial court heard argument on all of the motions and granted defendant's motion for summary judgment without addressing the pending motions to exclude the expert opinions. *See id.*

The Georgia Court of Appeals held that because the trial court had not ruled on the motion to exclude plaintiff's experts' opinions, those opinions were still in the record and would, if admitted, provide sufficient grounds for a jury to find the plaintiff had been injured and to value her injuries. 313 Ga. App. at 116, 720 S.E.2d at 226–227. The Georgia Court of Appeals stated "questions of admissibility generally are committed to the sound discretion of the trial courts." 313 Ga. App. at 115, 720 S.E.2d at 226. The Georgia Court of Appeals further opined:

> Whether an expert opinion ought to be admitted under O.C.G.A. § 24-9-67.1 is a question that is especially fit for resolution by a trial court because it requires a consideration of the facts and data upon which the opinion is based, whether the opinion is a product of "reliable principles and methods," and whether the opinion was reached by a reliable application of those principles and methods to the facts of the case. See O.C.G.A. § 24-9-67.1 (b).

All these things may require fact finding, and trial judges are better suited to find facts than appellate judges. Perhaps for these reasons, the appellate courts consistently have said that it is the trial judge that is to act as a gatekeeper and assess the reliability of proposed expert testimony.

Id. (citing, e.g., *Daubert v. Merrell Dow Pharmaceuticals, Inc.*, 509 U. S. 579, 589 ("[T]he trial judge must ensure that any and all scientific testimony or evidence admitted is not only relevant, but reliable."); *Condra v. Atlanta Orthopaedic Group*, 285 Ga. 667, 671, 681 S.E.2d 152 (2009) ("Under the Daubert line of cases, the trial judge acts as the gatekeeper in determining the admissibility of expert opinion . . . .")).

The Georgia Court of Appeals held that the trial court should have addressed questions of admissibility before ruling on summary judgment because the questions of admissibility were, at least to some extent, dispositive of questions of summary judgment. 313 Ga. App. at 115, 720 S.E.2d at 227. However, the Georgia Court of Appeals limited its holding by stating it may not always be necessary to rule on motions to exclude expert testimony prior to ruling on summary judgment if the issue would not be dispositive, noting that O.C.G.A. § 24-9-67.1 does not specify a time by which a court must decide motions to exclude expert testimony, except that it must be before the final pretrial conference. *See* 313 Ga. App. at 117, n.9, 720 S.E.2d at 227, n.9 (citing OCGA § 24-9-67.1 (d)). Similarly, "when the admissibility of an expert opinion has been challenged, and the admissibility of that opinion may be dispositive of a motion for summary judgment, . . ., it does not serve judicial economy to decide the motion for summary judgment without passing upon the admissibility of the expert opinion." *Id.*

In *Butler v. Union Carbide Corporation*, 310 Ga. App. 21, 25–31, 712 S.E.2d 537, 541–545 (2011), the Georgia Court of Appeals upheld a trial court's exclusion of plaintiff's medical expert's testimony on the grounds that it was unreliable. In *Butler,* plaintiff-appellant was the administratrix of her deceased husband's estate. She sued defendant manufacturer, asserting claims of product liability, negligence, and loss of consortium arising from her husband's malignant mesothelioma allegedly resulting from his occupational exposure to products containing asbestos. 310 Ga. App. at 21, 712 S.E.2d at 538.

Plaintiff's expert pathologist testified at deposition that defendant's product contributed to the causation of the decedent's mesothelioma because "each exposure to asbestos above 'background' levels, or those present in ambient air, contributed to causing the disease." 310 Ga. App. at 21, 712 S.E.2d at 538–539.[63] The trial court determined that plaintiff's expert failed to properly use the scientific method to make scientifically valid decisions in reaching his specific causation opinion as mandated by *Daubert*. 310 Ga. App. at 24, 712 S.E.2d at 540. To reach this conclusion, the trial court analyzed plaintiff's expert's deposition and *Daubert* hearing testimony by applying four nonexclusive *Daubert* factors used to determine reliability: "(1) whether the theory or technique can be tested, (2) whether it has been subjected to peer review, (3) whether the technique has a high known or potential rate of error, and (4) whether the theory has attained general acceptance within the scientific community." *Id.* The trial court held the expert's opinion failed the first element because he relied on the theory that any exposure to the asbestos in defendant's product would contribute to the development of mesothelioma, but he also testified that the theory was essentially untestable and in fact, had not been tested. *See id.* Additionally, the trial court found that plaintiff's expert's testimony failed the third element because "a nontestable hypothesis . . . cannot have an error rate." *Id.* The trial court considered the second element, peer review, to be relevant but not dispositive, and far less

---

[63] A certified industrial hygienist had testified that "exposure to asbestos from [defendant's product] was more than two fibers per cubic centimeter 'on an eight hour time weighted average basis.'" *Id.* at 22–23, 712 S.E.2d at 539.

crucial than the "testable," "tested" and "error rate" elements. *See id.* Regarding the fourth factor, general acceptance within the scientific community, the trial court noted that plaintiff's expert's opinion relied heavily on this factor, but that any general acceptance shown for his opinion was far outweighed by its lack of scientific validity. *See id.* Finally, the trial court found that plaintiff's expert was the "quintessential expert for hire" and therefore exercised its discretion "to apply the *Daubert* factors with greater rigor." *Id.* The trial court excluded plaintiff's expert's specific causation testimony because it failed the *Daubert* test for scientific knowledge and therefore was "not 'the product of reliable principles and methods' under O.C.G.A. § 24-9-67.1 (b) (2)." *Id.*

In her appeal, plaintiff argued that the trial court abused its discretion in striking her expert's specific causation opinion for three reasons: (1) the expert used generally accepted, reliable methodology, (2) his opinion was based on reliable science, and (3) his opinions were widely accepted. 310 Ga. App. at 26, 712 S.E.2d at 541. The Georgia Court of Appeals noted that the trial court "properly utilized federal authority, including *Daubert*, as permitted by O.C.G.A. § 24-9-67.1 (f) when determining whether the expert's testimony met the requirements of O.C.G.A. § 24-9-67.1 (b) . . . that such authority imbues trial courts with 'substantial discretion in deciding how to test an expert's reliability' . . . [and that the statute places] the burden of establishing the reliability of the expert's opinion on the proponent. *Id.* at 25–26; 712 S.E.2d at 541.

The Georgia Court of Appeals first addressed plaintiff's argument that her expert used generally accepted, reliable methodology, noting that the literature did not support the expert's specific causation opinion based on the evidence in the record. 310 Ga. App. at 26, 712 S.E.2d at 541–542. The evidence showed that plaintiff's exposure to defendant's product was limited, as it comprised one percent or less of the total amount of such products to which the decedent was exposed. 310 Ga. App. at 26, 712 S.E.2d at 542. Furthermore, during the expert's deposition, he did not opine that any specific company's product caused the decedent's disease, but rather that his cumulative occupation exposure to all such products contributed to the disease. *See id.* At the *Daubert* hearing, plaintiff's expert testified that the decedent's exposure to defendant's product over "just a few weeks" could have reached a cumulative exposure level that studies showed to be statistically significant, despite being a low dosage. *Id.* However, the evidence showed the decedent had only been exposed to defendant's product for eight days. 310 Ga. App. at 26–27, 712 S.E.2d at 542. Moreover, the expert admitted that when forming his opinion he had relied upon a study that "did not address whether a component of a cumulative exposure of asbestos is causative." 310 Ga. App. at 27, 712 S.E.2d at 542. Similarly, the Georgia Court of Appeals found that the other studies upon which the expert relied did not support his opinion. *See id.* The Georgia Court of Appeals also noted that the Texas Court of Appeals had previously found the scientific literature upon which the expert relied to be inconclusive, which supported the trial court's conclusion that plaintiff's expert's "'no threshold' theory was scientifically unreliable." *Id.* (citing *Smith v. Kelly-Moore Paint Co.*, 307 S.W.3d 829, 837–839 (Tex. App. 2010)).

The Georgia Court of Appeals also referred to the Texas appellate court's opinion to rebut plaintiff's argument that her expert's opinions were widely accepted, noting that the Texas court had rejected plaintiff's expert's "any exposure" theory. 310 Ga. App. at 28, 712 S.E.2d at 543. The Georgia Court of Appeals stated that "nothing in the record or case law precluded the trial court from exercising its discretion to weigh this factor less heavily than the other three *Daubert* factors," noting the U.S. Supreme Court's statement that "the question of 'whether *Daubert*'s specific factors are, or are not, reasonable measures of reliability in a particular case is a matter that the law grants the trial judge broad latitude to determine.'" *Id.* (quoting *Kumho Tire Co. v. Carmichael*, 526 U.S. 137, 153 (1999)).

The Georgia Court of Appeals further noted the trial court's determination that plaintiff's expert was a "quintessential expert for hire" was supported by the record and it was therefore within the trial court's discretion "to apply the *Daubert* factors with greater rigor." 310 Ga. App. at 28, 712 S.E.2d at 543.

Plaintiff-appellant also argued that the trial court abused its gatekeeper function under *Daubert* by assessing her expert's credibility. *See id.* The Georgia Court of Appeals noted that the gatekeeper function is not intended to supplant the adversary system or the role of the jury; but rather, "vigorous cross-examination, presentation of contrary evidence, and careful instruction on the burden of proof are the traditional and appropriate means of attacking shaky but admissible evidence." 310 Ga. App. at 28–29, 712 S.E.2d at 543 (quoting *Quiet Technology DC-8 v. Hurel-Dubois UK Ltd.*, 326 F.3d 1333, 1341 (11th Cir. 2003). However, that discussion was intended "to warn trial courts not to 'evaluate the credibility of opposing experts and the persuasiveness of competing scientific studies.'" 310 Ga. App. at 29, 712 S.E.2d at 543 (quoting *Quiet Technology, DC-8*, 326 F3d at 1341). The Georgia Court of Appeals noted the trial court was not weighing conflicting experts' testimony, but rather determined that, although plaintiff's expert was a qualified doctor, "he ha[d] not properly utilized the scientific method to make scientifically valid decisions in reaching his specific causation opinion as required by *Daubert.*" *Id.* The Georgia Court of Appeals upheld the trial court's exclusion of plaintiff's expert's specific causation opinion and affirmed the trial court's grant of summary judgment to defendant due to the lack of any other evidence of specific causation. 310 Ga. App. at 30–31, 712 S.E.2d at 544–545.

In *Horton v. Hendrix*, a daughter challenged the mental competence of her deceased mother at the time she executed a will devising all of her estate to a newly created trust. 291 Ga. App. 416, 416–418, 662 S.E.2d 227, 230–231 (2008). The daughter appealed the trial court's exclusion of a portion of her medical expert's testimony because it was based solely on unadmitted medical records of the mother. 291 Ga. App. at 422, 662 S.E.2d at 234. The Georgia Court of Appeals affirmed the trial court's decision finding no abuse of discretion. *See id.* Without extensive analysis, the Georgia Court of Appeals determined that an expert's opinion based solely upon on review of medical records is hearsay and held: "Not even an expert can give an opinion based entirely upon reports which have been prepared by others and which are not in evidence. A testifying expert is not to serve as a conduit for the opinions of others." *Id.* (quoting *Webb v. Thomas Trucking, Inc.*, 255 Ga. App. 637, 642, 566 S.E.2d 390, 396–397 (2002)). Thus, after the implementation of O.C.G.A. § 24-9-67.1, Georgia courts continue to hold that, while an expert's opinion may consider data gathered by others, it still must be based upon that expert's own findings and not be a mere conduit.

b. Criminal Cases

Prior to the enactment of the new Georgia evidence code, the Georgia legislature left the criminal standard untouched when it adopted the *Daubert* standard for civil cases. The new Georgia evidence code largely parallels the Federal Rules of Evidence and in general applies to both civil and criminal cases. However, as discussed above, an important exception applies in the expert rules application. Rule 702 does not apply to criminal cases.

c. Expert Related Rules and Procedures in Georgia State Court

Generally, Georgia's Rules of Civil Procedure reflect the Federal Rules of Civil Procedure. Georgia Rule of Civil Procedure 26 differs from Federal Rule of Civil Procedure 26, however, in that a party must use interrogatories to gather information on the opponent's expert, the opinions to which the expert expects to testify, and a summary of the grounds for each opinion. O.C.G.A. § 9-11-26(b)(4). *Compare* Fed. R. Civ. P. 26(a)(2). Georgia also requires the party requesting discovery under O.C.G.A. § 9-11-30, -31, and -34 from an expert to "pay a reasonable fee for the time spent in responding to discovery by that expert." O.C.G.A. § 9-11-26(b)(4)(A)(ii).[64] Those code sections describe oral depositions, depositions by written questions, and requests for production of documents and things. O.C.G.A. § 9-11-30, -31, and -34.

Georgia Rule 26 also provides that facts known and opinions held by experts that are retained in anticipation of litigation but who will not be called as witnesses at trial are only discoverable in two limited circumstances. O.C.G.A. § 9-11-26(b)(4)(B). First, when a mental or physical condition is in issue, the opposing party may request a mental or physical examination of a party. O.C.G.A. § 9-11-35(b). The physician's or psychologist's report from the examination must be disclosed to the party who underwent the exam if the party requests a copy of the report. O.C.G.A. § 9-11-35(b). Second, the nontestifying expert's work may be discoverable upon a showing of exceptional circumstances under which it would be "impracticable for the party seeking discovery to obtain facts or opinions on the same subject by other means." O.C.G.A. § 9-11-26(b)(4)(B).[65]

---

[64] Federal Rule of Civil Procedure 26(b)(4)(C) allows the court to require the party seeking discovery from an expert to pay a reasonable fee for time spent responding to the discovery; however, in practice this procedure is not always used.

[65] *See, e.g., Dep't of Transp. v. Bacon Farms, L.P.*, 608 S.E.2d 305, 309 (Ga. Ct. App. 2004) (finding no abuse by the trial court in refusing to compel discovery of valuation expert that had withdrawn as expert in case, the proponent stipulated it would not use the information, and the adversary did not show any exceptional circumstances to warrant compelling the discovery).

CHAPTER XII
EXPERT EVIDENCE IN THE DISTRICT OF COLUMBIA*

by

Christine G. Rolph
Scott C. Jones
Latham & Watkins LLP
555 Eleventh Street, N.W., Suite 1000
Washington, D.C. 20004
(202) 637-3367
christine.rolph@lw.com
scott.jones@lw.com

A. EXPERT EVIDENCE IN THE DISTRICT OF COLUMBIA CIRCUIT

1. Key Decisions Applying *Daubert v. Merrell Dow Pharm., Inc.*, 509 U.S. 579 (1993)

The Supreme Court's treatment of expert testimony issues in *Daubert* was consistent with precedent in the D.C. Circuit. As such, *Daubert* did not unsettle expert evidence practice in the jurisdiction. The lead case applying *Daubert* in the D.C. Circuit is *Ambrosini v. Labarraque*, 101 F.3d 129 (D.C. Cir. 1996) [hereinafter *Ambrosini*]. This section begins by discussing the *Ambrosini* decision. Next, it provides detail on a number of related expert testimony cases in the D.C. Circuit. Finally, the section turns to a discussion of the procedural rules regarding expert testimony which are relatively unique to the D.C. Circuit.

a. *Ambrosini v. Labarraque*, 101 F.3d 129 (D.C. Cir. 1996)

The D.C. Circuit extensively incorporated *Daubert* into its expert evidence jurisprudence in *Ambrosini*, a case where the circuit court addressed the admissibility of expert evidence regarding whether Depo-Provera, a brand name, progestogen-only contraceptive, caused a minor-plaintiff's birth defects. The court employed *Daubert* to determine the admissibility of two types of expert evidence: evidence linking Depo-Provera to birth defects generally (general causation) and evidence linking Depo-Provera to the minor plaintiff's injuries specifically (specific causation). The decision

---

* The authors acknowledge the work of Gregory S. Kaufman in drafting a prior version of the chapter which appeared in Scientific Evidence Review Monograph No. 6, as well as the work of Jess Lennon, who provided research and drafting assistance in the preparation of this chapter.

focused on whether weaknesses in the quality of the experts' methodologies and conclusions should act as a bar to that testimony's admissibility, or, rather, as considerations for the fact finder to weigh.[1]

Initially, the district court granted summary judgment to the defense after refusing to admit the testimony of plaintiffs' two expert witnesses on causation—an epidemiologist and a teratologist. The epidemiologist sought to offer testimony that Depo-Provera could cause birth defects like those sustained by the minor plaintiff. The teratologist sought to offer testimony that Depo-Provera specifically caused the minor plaintiff's birth defects.[2]

The district court applied the *Daubert* two-prong test to determine whether the testimony was admissible. The first of *Daubert*'s two prongs concerns the reliability of the methodology employed by the expert, while the second asks whether the expert's testimony is likely to assist the trier of fact. The district court began by considering the epidemiologist's testimony on general causation. The district court ruled that, while the epidemiologist's methodology for determining that Depo-Provera could cause birth defects was reliable, the testimony was nevertheless inadmissible because it was unlikely to assist the trier of fact. The district court stated that the testimony was unhelpful for two reasons: (1) the epidemiologist did not address "the relative risk between exposed and unexposed populations . . . of the birth defects from which [plaintiff] suffers," and (2) the epidemiologist's opinion that the drug "can cause" the type of birth defects plaintiff did not meet the plaintiff's ultimate burden of proof for causation. *Ambrosini*, 101 F.3d at 135.

The district court also excluded the testimony of the teratologist. First, as to general causation, the court rejected the methodology employed by the teratologist to find that Depo-Provera can cause birth defects. The court held that the teratologist unfairly minimized the epidemiological studies showing no causal relationship between the drug and birth defects, but then failed to offer a rationale for ignoring those studies. *Id.* at 137. Second, as to specific causation, the district court found fault with the teratologist's methodology, which was limited to a review of the medical file and failed to take sufficient steps to rule out alternative causes of the birth defects. *Id.*

On appeal, the circuit court reversed. The court ruled that the lower court erred by blurring the distinction between *Daubert*'s threshold admissibility requirements and the "persuasive weight" to be assigned to expert testimony:

> The *Daubert* analysis does not establish a heightened threshold for the admission of expert evidence, but rather focuses on the court's "gatekeeper" role as a check on "subjective belief" and "unsupported speculation." . . . Even if the burden placed on the "gatekeeper" may seem heavy at times, there is nothing in *Daubert* to suggest that judges become scientific experts, much less evaluators of the persuasiveness of an expert's conclusion. Rather, once an expert has explained his or her methodology, and has withstood cross-examination

---

[1] As a procedural matter, the defense previously moved for summary judgment, arguing that the plaintiffs had shown no reliable scientific evidence demonstrating causation. Plaintiffs responded with affidavits from an epidemiologist testifying as to general causation and a teratologist testifying as to both general and specific causation. *Ambrosini v. Labarraque*, 966 F.2d 1464 (D.C. Cir. 1992). The district court's initial grant of summary judgment to the defendants was reversed by the circuit court, which found that the district court had not conducted a sufficient inquiry into the bases of the plaintiffs' experts' opinions. On remand, the district court again granted summary judgment to the defendants. See *Ambrosini v. Upjohn Co.*, No. 84-3483, 1995 WL 637650 (D.D.C. Oct. 18, 1995), *rev'd*, *Ambrosini*, 101 F.3d 129.

[2] Teratology is described as "that science which is concerned with the development of malformations or abnormal development in animals and human beings." *Upjohn*, 1995 WL 637650, at *6.

or evidence suggesting that the methodology is not derived from the scientific method, the expert's testimony, so long as it "fits" an issue in the case, is admissible . . .

Id. at 134 (internal citations omitted); *see also id.* at 131. The circuit court concluded that *Daubert* only envisions a limited "gatekeeper" role for the court, rather than encouraging an independent assessment of the evidence for accuracy and persuasiveness.

Applying this standard, the circuit court first revisited the admissibility of the epidemiologist's testimony under the *Daubert* test. First, the court confirmed as reliable under *Daubert* the epidemiologist's methodology which it noted was a conventional "totality of the data" technique examining the entire medical literature on the subject. *Id.* at 136. Although the court expressed concern that some of the expert's calculations were unpublished, the epidemiologist had stated that there was no need for publishing the work because the material was not novel, the drug was off the market, and there was not sufficient interest in the field. The court found that this response was sufficient to sustain the *Daubert* analysis. *Id.* at 136–37.

However, the key concern for the epidemiologist's testimony had been whether it would survive the second *Daubert* prong. Here, the D.C. Circuit corrected the lower court's analysis, stating that the second *Daubert* prong tests *mere relevance*. Testimony need not satisfy the plaintiff's burden on the ultimate issue to comply with the *Daubert* standard; the testimony must simply relate to a contested issue and aid the fact finder in resolving the claim. *Id.* at 135–36. Thus, although the epidemiologist's inability to be clear about the probability of specific causation might prove fatal to the plaintiff's claim at trial, it would not act as a bar to admissibility. *Id.* The court ruled that because the epidemiologist's findings would still be helpful to the trier of fact, the testimony was admissible.

The circuit court then turned to the teratologist's testimony, addressing his conclusions on general causation and specific causation independently. With regard to general causation, the circuit court credited the expert's methodology, which relied on specific animal, pharmacological, and human studies. *Id.* at 137. Although none of the studies specifically concluded that the drug caused the type of birth defects suffered by the plaintiff, the court noted that the expert purported to follow the "traditional methodology of experts in his field, after considering all the data and evidence," to arrive at his conclusion of causation. *Id.* Indeed, the expert's identification of the research he reviewed and the explanation of his techniques were satisfactory under the logic of *Ferebee v. Chevron Chemical Co.*, 736 F.2d 1529 (D.C. Cir. 1984), decided thirteen years earlier.

In *Ferebee*, the circuit court stressed that "a cause-effect relationship need not be clearly established by animal or epidemiological studies before a doctor can testify that, in his [or her] opinion, such a relationship exists." *Id.* at 1535. In other words, if an expert is well-qualified in her field, her conclusions will not be barred because they are the first of their kind. There need not be a critical mass of prior supporting data to satisfy *Daubert*'s first prong. Thus, here, where the expert's method involved the synthesis of multiple studies, the fact that no single study had been conclusive did not affect admissibility. *Ambrosini*, 101 F.3d at 137.

The *Ambrosini* court found further support for the teratologist's general causation testimony from the reasoning of *Mendes-Silva. Mendes-Silva v. United States*, 980 F.2d 1482 (D.C. Cir. 1993). There, the circuit court noted that "[w]hen the underlying basis or methods of an expert's opinion are of a type reasonably relied upon by the experts in the field, the court must allow the opinion to be assessed by the fact finder—even if the opinion reaches a novel conclusion." *Id.* at 1485. Thus, neither the fact that the teratologist could not point to a specific epidemiological study proving his conclusions, nor that his conclusions were novel, would render his testimony inadmissible. The methodology was of a type reasonably relied upon by experts in the field.

The circuit court's review of the teratologist's testimony on specific causation focused on reliability. The court found that the teratologist's use of differential diagnosis was a reliable method used within the relevant field. *Ambrosini*, 101 F.3d at 140. Further, while the expert's review of alternative causes may not have been exhaustive, the fact that the doctor's differential analysis did not eliminate all possible alternatives would not bar admission of the evidence. The expert's conclusions would still be helpful to the jury, just less so. The court explained that the fact finders were responsible for determining the persuasive weight of the testimony. *Id.*

Thus, the court concluded: "*Daubert* instructs that the admissibility inquiry focuses not on conclusions, but on approaches, and the record shows that both [experts] employed scientifically valid methodologies. . . . Their conclusions were neither the 'subjective belief' or 'unsupported speculation' that *Daubert* and the Federal Rules would preclude a fact finder from hearing . . . ." *Id.* In reversing the trial court's grant of summary judgment to defendant, the *Ambrosini* court summarized by stating:

> The district court's error . . . did not lie in its mischaracterization of the experts' methodologies but instead in its misconception of the limited "gatekeeper" role envisioned in *Daubert*. By attempting to evaluate the credibility of opposing experts and the persuasiveness of competing scientific studies, the district court conflated the questions of the admissibility of expert testimony and the weight appropriately to be accorded such testimony by a fact finder.

Id. at 141 (internal citations omitted). Together, the *Ambrosini* court's treatment of the two experts' opinions confirmed the liberalizing effect of *Daubert* on the admissibility of expert testimony. Under *Ambrosini*, the gatekeeper role stretches only to questions of the reliability and relevance of expert testimony.

Importantly, the facts of *Ambrosini* can be distinguished from the facts forming a proper bar to admissibility in *Richardson v. Richardson-Merrell, Inc.*, 857 F.2d 823 (D.C. Cir. 1988). In *Richardson*, parties wrestled over the admissibility of expert testimony regarding the putative teratogenic effects of Bendectin. In that case, three distinct reasons compelled a ruling of inadmissibility. First, the expert admitted that his methodology was not generally accepted. *Ambrosini*, 101 F.3d at 139. Second, there was an overwhelming body of contradictory epidemiological evidence. *Richardson*, 857 F.2d at 830. And third, the doctor provided unreviewed recalculations of data gathered by others, while in *Ambrosini*, the teratologist's testimony involved a more trustworthy assessment of the limitations of peer-reviewed studies. *Id.* at 831.

b. Other Cases

The following cases are relevant when determining the contours of expert evidence admissibility in the federal courts of the D.C. Circuit.

(1) Is the expert's opinion reliable?

(a) *Lakie v. SmithKline Beecham*, 965 F. Supp. 49 (D.D.C. 1997)—Plaintiff claimed that benzene found in denture adhesives caused him personal injuries. The court admitted expert testimony as to specific causation based on a differential analysis that ruled out alternative causes of the plaintiff's injuries. Despite the lack of direct, foundational epidemiological evidence for general causation, the court admitted the testimony, in part, because there was indirect evidence upholding general causation. Other studies had linked benzene exposure to similar bone marrow disorders. Further, the court admitted the specific causation testimony even though the expert's analysis failed to eliminate some possible alternative causes of the plaintiff's injuries. The court explained that the existence of alternative causes should affect the weight that fact finders assign to the expert's testimony, not its admissibility.

(b) *Raynor v. Merrell Pharm., Inc.*, 104 F.3d 1371 (D.C. Cir. 1997)—Plaintiff brought a personal injury claim against Merrell Pharmaceuticals for birth defects allegedly caused by the drug Bendectin. Plaintiff offered expert testimony based on two sets of research—*in vivo* animal studies and *in vitro* studies—to determine general causation, and followed with testimony based on differential diagnosis to show specific causation. The court held the testimony inadmissible. First, the court explained that the *in vivo* animal studies and *in vitro* studies could only be verified through epidemiological research. A wealth of epidemiological research had already been collected and was contrary to these studies. Second, the court explained that testimony on specific causation has "legitimacy only as follow-up to admissible evidence" that the substance in question *could* cause the injury. *Id.* at 1376. The methodologies of the experts, thus, could not form the foundation of scientific knowledge necessary to make the expert testimony admissible.

(c) *Bell v. Gonzales*, No. 03-163, 2005 WL 3555490 (D.D.C. Dec. 23, 2005)—Plaintiff alleged that he was reassigned from his job after his employers learned that he had consulted a counselor regarding his having Tourette's syndrome (TS). The plaintiff presented an expert who testified that the timing of plaintiff's injuries (increased obsessive compulsive behavior and exacerbated TS characteristics) supported his opinion that the distress brought on by the plaintiff's discriminatory reassignment caused his injuries. The defense countered that *Daubert* required the expert to conduct a differential analysis, ruling out alternative causes, to establish specific causation. The court resolved the dispute in favor of the plaintiff, explaining that alternative causation is one of a number of permissible methods for showing specific causation. While possible alternative causes are relevant, expert testimony will not be excluded merely because there may be other causes involved.

(d) *Jenkins v. United States*, 307 F.2d 637 (D.C. Cir. 1962)—Appellant was convicted of assault with a deadly weapon and related crimes. The trial court excluded the opinions of two psychiatrists because they were formed without personal knowledge of all the facts on which their opinions were based. The psychiatrists' conclusions relied, in part, on retesting of the appellant conducted by another doctor on their staff. The court of appeals reversed, explaining that "the better reasoned authorities admit opinion testimony based, in part, upon reports of others which are not in evidence but which the expert customarily relies upon in the practice of his profession." *Id.* at 641. Because it is the "well known practice of psychiatrists" to rely on a psychologist's report when conducting a diagnosis, the methodology was sound and the expert testimony should have been admitted. *Id.* at 642.

(e) *United States v. Stagliano*, 729 F. Supp. 2d 222 (D.D.C. 2010)—Defendants were accused of distributing obscene videos in interstate commerce. They sought to introduce a psychologist's opinion that, based on his experience treating patients, the videos did not lack serious scientific value. The court excluded the testimony, explaining that where an expert witness seeks to offer *scientific* testimony, the reliability of that testimony must be demonstrated by the traditional *Daubert* factors,[3] rather than nontraditional factors, such

---

[3] The traditional *Daubert* factors include: (1) "whether the theory or technique can be and has been tested," (2) "whether the theory or technique has been subjected to peer review and publication," (3) "the method's known or potential rate of error," and (4) "whether the theory or technique finds general acceptance in the relevant scientific community." *Ambrosini*, 101 F.3d at 134 (citing *Daubert*, 509 U.S. at 593–94).

as personal knowledge and experience. However, where an expert offers nonscientific testimony, its reliability may be demonstrated via nontraditional factors.

(2) Will the testimony assist the trier of fact?

  (a) United States v. Naegele, 471 F. Supp. 2d 152 (D.D.C. 2007)—Defendant offered multiple experts to aid in his defense of indictments arising out of bankruptcy proceedings. One expert on voice recording and enhancement technology was presented to testify whether the defendant's voice in a particular recording was intelligible. The court excluded the testimony, explaining that because the jury was competent to determine whether the plaintiff's voice was intelligible, the expert's testimony would not assist the trier of fact. The court also excluded expert testimony regarding the complexity of certain bankruptcy forms. The court held that the jury was competent to determine whether the forms were confusing, since filling out forms is within the common experience of jurors.
  (b) United States v. Libby, 461 F. Supp. 2d 3 (D.D.C. 2006)—Defendant faced charges of obstruction of justice, false statements, and perjury. The defendant attempted to offer expert testimony to show the plausibility of his faulty memory defense. In excluding the testimony, the court held, in part, that an expert's testimony regarding the rate of error in human recollection would be inadmissible because the subject matter—human forgetfulness—was within the common knowledge of the jury. Thus, expert testimony would not assist the trier of fact.

(3) Qualifications of the expert

  (a) Groobert v. President & Dirs. of Georgetown Coll., 219 F. Supp. 2d 1 (D.D.C. 2002)— In this wrongful death action, plaintiff sought compensation for lost future earnings. The plaintiff introduced a stock photographer to testify about the future earnings of the decedent, who had also been a stock photographer. The defendant complained that the expert had no training in evaluating the career paths of photographers. Nevertheless, the district court held that the photographer's experience in the art field was a sufficient basis for giving an expert opinion on future earnings in that field. One may become qualified as an expert through skill, training, education, or experience.
  (b) Rogers v. Ingersoll-Rand, 971 F. Supp. 4 (D.D.C. 1997)—Plaintiff brought a products liability personal injury action against the defendant. The defendant notified the plaintiff less than two weeks before trial of its intent to call a witness to testify regarding new tests conducted on the product at issue. The defendant claimed that the witness was a lay witness, as opposed to an expert, but the trial court disagreed and excluded the testimony. In denying defendant's motion for a new trial, the district court explained that a witness who draws inferences that a jury would be unable to draw from ordinary experience is an expert witness, regardless of designation by the offering party.
  (c) Coleman v. Parkline Corp., 844 F.2d 863 (D.C. Cir. 1988)—Plaintiff sued an elevator cab manufacturer for securing elevator domes in a manner that contributed to an injury she sustained while unloading the domes. The plaintiff offered, and the trial court admitted, a witness who had an engineering degree, had formerly worked for the Occupational Safety and Health Administration and the Institute of Safety Analysis, and had considerable experience with investigating accidents, determining their causes, and making suggestions about their prevention. However, the expert did not have personal

experience in the subject of his testimony—securing and unloading elevator cab domes. Nevertheless, the circuit court upheld the admission of the testimony, explaining that experts need not have personal familiarity with the subject of the testimony. Rather, the rule simply requires an expert witness to wield expertise that permits the witness to draw conclusions that aid the trier of fact.

2. *Expert-Related Rules and Procedural Issues*

The D.C. Circuit has published a limited set of additions to the Federal Rules of Civil Procedure (Fed. R. Civ. P.) and the Federal Rules of Evidence (Fed. R. Evid.) which apply to expert witnesses.

Under Rule 16.3, litigants must confer within twenty-one days prior to when a scheduling conference is held or a scheduling order is due. This rule parallels Fed. R. Civ. P. 26(f), and serves as the anchor for subsequent sections that enumerate the topics which must be considered at the pretrial conference. Rule 16.3(c)(9) outlines the treatment of expert witnesses at the pretrial conference, explaining that counsel must confer over whether the requirement of the exchange of expert witness reports and information pursuant to Rule 26(a)(2) of the Fed. R. Civ. P. will be modified, and whether and when depositions of the expert witnesses will occur.

Beyond conferring over discretionary expert witness procedures, under Rule 16.5(a)(2), counsel are required to file and serve a pretrial statement not less than fourteen days prior to the final pretrial conference. Rule 16.5(b)(5) explains that in this statement, litigants should include a schedule of witnesses to be brought and a brief description of the testimony they intend to offer, including an estimate of the time it will take to elicit that testimony. Witnesses who are deemed experts must be designated by an asterisk.

An additional expert rule specific to the D.C. federal courts addresses the assessment of expert witness fees. Rule 54.1(d)(12) instructs the clerk to tax fees of court-appointed expert witnesses when they are requested to do so in the bill of costs. A crucial distinction is made between court-appointed experts and those experts who are not court-appointed. As the court made clear in *Machesney v. Larry Bruni, P.C.*, 905 F. Supp. 1122, 1138 (D.D.C. 1995), if an expert is not court-appointed, this provision is inapplicable and the fees will not be taxed as costs by the prevailing party.

B. EXPERT EVIDENCE IN LOCAL DISTRICT OF COLUMBIA COURTS

1. *Key Decisions*

The D.C. Superior Court and D.C. Court of Appeals do not apply the Federal Rules of Evidence. Further, D.C. courts do not rely on legislatively created evidentiary rules. Thus, the common law on evidence controls expert evidence issues within the District. One should be careful to note that pre-1975 local federal cases may continue to inform contemporary common law practices.

Despite having different sources, federal and D.C. rules on expert evidence overlap substantially. As the key decision of *Dyas v. United States*, 376 A.2d 827 (D.C. 1977), reveals, some of the philosophy of the *Daubert* test is represented in *Dyas*'s three-step treatment of expert testimony. However, relevant distinctions between the common law of D.C. and federal expert evidence law exist, especially regarding court determinations of the reliability of expert testimony, and such variations are noted throughout this section.

a. *Dyas v. United States*, 376 A.2d 827 (1977)

The leading expert case pertaining to the local courts of D.C. is *Dyas v. United States*.[4] The *Dyas* court addressed whether a trial judge had improperly excluded a defendant's expert testimony on the issue of the reliability of eyewitness identifications. While using language slightly different than that of *Daubert*, the court's treatment closely followed the second, "fit" prong of the *Daubert* two-part standard. Specifically, the court questioned whether the testimony was within the ken of the average layman and likely to duplicate the work of thorough cross-examination of the eyewitness, thereby rendering the testimony unlikely to aid the triers of fact. *Id.* at 832.

The court of appeals began by outlining its three-part test for admissibility of expert testimony:

(1) the subject matter "must be so distinctively related to some science, profession, business, or occupation *as to be beyond the ken of the average layman*"; (2) "the witness must have sufficient skill, knowledge, or experience in that field or calling as to make it appear that his opinion or inference *will probably aid the trier in his search for truth*"; and (3) expert testimony is inadmissible if "the state of the pertinent art or scientific knowledge does not permit a reasonable opinion to be asserted even by an expert."

Id. (quoting MCCORMICK ON EVIDENCE § 13, at 29–31 (E. Cleary ed., 2d ed. 1972)).

The court took a close look at the first two prongs of the test. It initially questioned whether the subject of the testimony—the reliability of eyewitnesses—fell outside the ken of the average layman. Drawing the same conclusion as a Ninth Circuit case on the issue, the court excluded the expert testimony because the subject matter was well within the experience of the average layman. *See United States v. Amaral*, 488 F.2d 1148, 1153 (9th Cir. 1973). More plainly, the court stated that the jury was perfectly capable of determining for itself the reliability of a witness's testimony.

Operating in tandem, the second prong of *Dyas* worked to bar admissibility because well-developed cross-examination would be sufficiently probative of the reliability of the identification by the eyewitness. *Dyas*, 376 A.2d at 832. In other words, because determining the credibility of witness testimony is within the common experience of the jury, cross-examination of an eyewitness would suffice to assist the jury in determining the witnesses' reliability. Expert testimony would be unnecessarily duplicative and therefore unhelpful to the trier of fact.

The first two prongs of the *Dyas* test proved dispositive here. As applied, these two prongs—involving the likelihood of the testimony assisting the trier of fact—closely resemble the second prong of the *Daubert* test. However, because the first two prongs of the *Dyas* test controlled, *Dyas* did not elaborate on the issue of *reliability*—the province of the first *Daubert* prong and *Dyas*'s third prong.

Dyas's third prong answers the reliability question differently from *Daubert*. Rather than adopt the federal standard on reliability, the D.C. Court of Appeals reaffirmed that "[i]n our jurisdiction, the seminal case of *Frye v. United States* . . . is the starting point in addressing questions of admissibility of scientific evidence." *United States v. Jenkins*, 887 A.2d 1013, 1021 (D.C. 2005). Thus, when

---

[4] In *Dyas*, a jury convicted the defendant of armed robbery. On appeal, *Dyas* complained that the trial judge had improperly denied him the chance to present expert testimony questioning the general reliability of eyewitnesses. *Dyas*, 376 A.2d at 828–29. Because the admission of expert testimony is committed to the broad discretion of the trial court, the D.C. Court of Appeals applied a "manifestly erroneous" standard. *Dyas*, 376 A.2d at 831 (quoting *Salem v. U.S. Lines Co.*, 370 U.S. 31, 35 (1962)).

testing the reliability of expert testimony, *Dyas*'s third prong instructs counsel to turn to *Frye*, not *Daubert*. *Frye* applies a "general acceptance" test for reliability. *Frye v. United States*, 293 F. 1013, 1014 (D.C. Cir. 1923). To be admissible, expert testimony must rely on methods that already have gained sufficient recognition within the relevant community of experts. *Id.* at 1013–14.

Despite the *Dyas* holding, there is not a *per se* rule that expert testimony regarding eyewitness credibility does not satisfy the *Dyas* test. *Benn v. United States*, 978 A.2d 1257, 1277 (D.C. 2009). Rather, "the decision to admit or exclude expert testimony must be made on a case-by-case basis, grounded on the proffer made and on its potential to assist the jury in the *particular case before the court.*" *Id.* at 1273 (emphasis added).[5]

While the *Dyas-Frye* standard diverges from federal court jurisprudence regarding Fed. R. Evid. 702, D.C. courts have in large part adopted Fed. R. Evid. 703[6] and 705.[7] The District of Columbia's banner Fed. R. Evid. 703 case is *In re Melton*, 565 A.2d 635 (D.C. 1989), *rev'd on other grounds*, 597 A.2d 892 (D.C. 1991). There, the court of appeals debated whether statements by a patient's family qualified as information of the type customarily and reasonably relied upon by experts in psychiatry.

While prior cases had upheld similar bases for expert testimony, the court specifically referenced the language of, and commentary to, Fed. R. Evid. 703 in reaching the same conclusion. In particular, the court approved of an example case offered in the advisory committee notes to Fed. R. Evid. 703, which specifically validated the use of similar evidence as the basis of a physician's testimony.[8]

---

[5] For instance, "[w]hen other evidence points to the verity of a victim's identification of the accused, such as the victim's depiction of the gun in a sketch immediately after the crime and the police's recovery of a gun in the motel matching that description, that evidence is a legitimate consideration for the trial judge in exercising judgment on whether to exclude such expert testimony" as not being beyond the ken of the jury. *Patterson v. United States*, 37 A.3d 230, 238 (D.C. 2012).

[6] At the time of adoption, Fed. R. Evid. 703 read as follows: "The facts or data in the particular case upon which an expert bases an opinion or inference may be those perceived by or made known to [the expert] at or before the hearing. If of a type reasonably relied upon by experts in the particular field in forming opinions or inferences upon the subject, the facts or data need not be admissible in evidence." Fed. R. Evid. 703 (1975) (amended Oct. 1, 1987; Dec. 1, 2000).

[7] At the time, the 1975 iteration of Fed. R. Evid. 705 controlled: "The expert may testify in terms of opinion or inference and give his reasons therefor without prior disclosure of the underlying facts or data, unless the court requires otherwise. The expert may in any event be required to disclose the underlying facts or data on cross-examination." Fed. R. Evid. 705 (1975) (amended Oct. 1, 1987; Dec. 1, 1993).

[8] The advisory committee notes states: "[A] physician in his [or her] own practice bases his [or her] diagnosis on information from numerous sources and of considerable variety, including statements by patients and relatives, reports and opinions from nurses, technicians and other doctors, hospital records, and X-rays. Most of them are admissible in evidence, but only with the expenditure of substantial time in producing and examining various authenticating witnesses. The physician makes life-and-death decisions in reliance upon them. *His [or her] validation, expertly performed and subject to cross-examination, ought to suffice for judicial purposes.*" Fed. R. Evid. 703 advisory committee's note (1975) (emphasis added).

For the purpose of determining what constitutes reasonable and customary reliance within a field, the *Melton* court adopted a two-part test.[9] Under this test, a trial judge will admit expert opinion based on hearsay testimony under Fed. R. Evid. 703 when "(1) the judge is persuaded that experts in the field commonly rely on the particular type of hearsay information in addressing the specific type of problem raised in the case before the court, and (2) the judge concludes that the information (if not admissible for its truth under an exception to the hearsay rule) is of a type for which the underlying reliability of the data can be sufficiently explored through cross-examination of the testifying expert." *In re Melton*, 597 A.2d at 904 (emphasis omitted).

D.C. courts adopted the reasoning of Fed. R. Evid. 705 in *Clifford v. United States*, 532 A.2d 628 (D.C. 1987). There, the court of appeals debated whether the trial court improperly excluded the appellant's expert testimony because the appellant had refused to disclose test results on which the expert based his opinions. *Id.* at 630. The appellant, John Clifford, had been convicted for assault with intent to commit a sexual act. Clifford sought to introduce the testimony of a clinical psychologist who would explain that, on the basis of an interview and test protocols, Clifford was unlikely to engage in the alleged activity absent drug inducement. *Id.* at 631. The trial court refused to admit the testimony.

In reviewing the trial court's decision to exclude the expert's opinion, the court of appeals observed that precedent in the jurisdiction already was consistent with the language of Fed. R. Evid. 705. *Id.* at 633. The court then proceeded to credit the rationale behind each aspect of the rule, making a particular effort to validate the use of cross-examination, as opposed to hypotheticals, to investigate the factual basis upon which expert testimony was based. *Id.* ("Although hypothetical questions are still permitted under the federal rules, the aim of Rule 705 is to replace the need for hypotheticals with reliance on cross-examination to bring out the basis of an expert's testimony. Use of the adversary process should allow the opposing attorneys to explore an expert's reasoning more selectively and, hence, more efficiently while reducing the opportunities for deceptive manipulation of the testimony"). While noting approval of the entirety of the rule, the court specifically adopted "the provision of Fed. R. Evid. 705 under which the trial court may order that a party proffering expert testimony turn over for inspection by the opponent any report or document on which the expert relied in forming the opinion to which he or she will testify." *Id.* at 635. Finding the judge's order acceptable under Fed. R. Evid. 705, the appellate court refused to overturn the trial court's decision to exclude the evidence because Clifford refused to comply with the order to turn over documents on which his expert relied.

b. Other Cases

(1) "Beyond the ken of the average layman"

Middleton v. United States, 401 A.2d 109 (D.C. 1979)—Appellants challenged the exclusion of expert testimony as to the frequency of chipped front teeth in the adult male population. Siding with the trial court, the decision explained "that the frequency of gapped or chipped teeth (with its attendant implications concerning the reliability of the eyewitness testimony) was not beyond the ken of the lay trier." *Id.* at 130.

---

[9] At the *en banc* hearing following *In re Melton*, the court counseled that Fed. R. Evid. 703 issue determinations should be handled prior to seating the jury. If counsel anticipates that such an issue will arise, she should file a motion *in limine* or seek a ruling from the court to avoid disruption of testimony. *In re Melton*, 597 A.2d 892, 907 (D.C. 1991).

(2) *"Sufficient skill, knowledge, expertise"*

   (a) *District of Columbia v. Anderson*, 597 A.2d 1295 (D.C. 1991)—The court considered whether a podiatrist could offer testimony regarding the standard of care in a medical malpractice action. The court held that a nonmedical witness is not necessarily prohibited from presenting testimony on medical issues, so long as the proffered witness has sufficient knowledge and experience to offer an opinion that could aid the trier of fact.

   (b) *Johnson v. District of Columbia*, 728 A.2d 70 (D.C. 1999)—Appellant offered a plumber as its expert witness testifying about the standard of care regarding commercial water heater regulations. The plumber had no background in water heater design and showed a lack of knowledge of the regulations allegedly violated. Thus, the trial court and appellate court found that the plumber lacked sufficient knowledge and expertise to offer expert testimony on the subject. *But see Jenkins v. United States*, 307 F.2d at 644 ("[I]f experience or training enables a proffered expert witness to form an opinion which would aid the jury, in the absence of some countervailing consideration, his testimony will be received").

(3) *"Aiding the trier of fact"*

   St. Lewis v. Firestone, 130 A.2d 317 (D.C. 1957)—The trial court had admitted testimony from a fire investigator stating his opinion that the decedent had been smoking carelessly in bed. The court of appeals found error because the expert had not discovered any evidence shedding light on the cause of the fire or the supposed negligence of the decedent. Because "[n]o skilled training or special knowledge obtained from experience was applied in arriving at his conclusion, . . . anyone of ordinary training and intelligence would be equally capable of an opinion." *Id.* at 319. Such guesswork would be unhelpful to the triers of fact, who could just as easily and accurately draw their own conclusions.

(4) *"State of the art or scientific knowledge does not permit a reasonable opinion to be asserted"*

   (a) *United States v. Jenkins*, 887 A.2d 1013 (D.C. 2005)—A trial court granted the defense's *Frye* motion seeking to exclude results from a DNA test. The defense argued that there was controversy within the scientific community as to the validity of the three prevailing DNA match methodologies, demonstrating that the methodology used had not gained general acceptance within the field. The court of appeals disagreed, however, explaining that experts in the field were not debating the *validity* of the methodologies, but rather were concerned with which methodology of DNA matching was most *probative*. The court reversed and remanded, stating that the controversy within the scientific community went to relevancy—a matter the jury is best equipped to handle.

   (b) *Douglas v. United States*, 386 A.2d 289 (D.C. 1978)—Defendant offered testimony of a psychologist which asserted that because the defendant had no history of sexual deviancy, he was unlikely to have committed the particular offense. The court of appeals upheld the trial court's finding of inadmissibility on the grounds that the psychology was too inexact. Scientific knowledge could not "determine with sufficient reliability that an individual did *not* commit a certain act, based solely on the presence of some characteristics and the absence of certain observable symptoms." *Id.* at 296.

(5) *Rule 703 or Rule 705 Issues*

   (a) *Jenkins v. United States*, 307 F.2d 637 (D.C. Cir. 1962)—Appellant challenged the trial court's decision to exclude the opinions of two psychiatrists because they were formed, in part, without personal knowledge. The court of appeals reversed, explaining that "the better reasoned authorities admit opinion testimony based, in part, upon reports of others which are not in evidence but which the expert customarily relies upon in the practice of his profession." *Id.* at 641. *See also L.C.D. v. District of Columbia*, 488 A.2d 918 (D.C. 1985).

(b) *Wash. Metro. Area Transit Auth. v. Davis*, 606 A.2d 165 (D.C. 1992)—Expert testimony offered by plaintiff regarding potential lost earnings of a deceased nine-year-old was found inadmissible due to an insufficient basis. The expert's calculations assumed that the nine-year-old would become a professional (doctor, lawyer, or government employee with G16 status), despite the fact that she was a C-average student, no one in her immediate family completed college, and she had expressed interest in a lesser paying field. Absent an authoritative source for determining that the child would have graduated from graduate school, the basis for the testimony was merely personal opinion, "rather than scientific or expert in nature." *Id.* at 178.

(c) *Lyons v. Barrazotto*, 667 A.2d 314 (D.C. 1995)—The D.C. Court of Appeals considered whether it was an abuse of discretion for a trial court to grant a new trial on the basis that it had previously admitted into evidence medical reports and results prepared by nontestifying experts, which helped form the basis of the testimony offered by two experts. Finding an abuse of discretion, the court explained that the hearsay evidence was correctly admitted for the limited purpose of explaining the basis of the experts' testimony, and that its prejudicial effect did not substantially outweigh its probative value.[10]

2. *Expert-Related Rules and Procedural Issues*

The Superior Court Rules of Civil Procedure (SCR—Civil Rules) touch on a number of subjects related to expert evidence. The SCR—Civil Rules cover the following areas: discovery, court-appointed experts, expert fees, and taped expert depositions.

Discussion of the procedures governing the use of expert testimony in the D.C. courts properly begins with SCR-Civil Rule 16(b). Rule 16(b) requires parties to hold a scheduling and settlement conference as soon as practicable following the filing of the complaint. The conference provides the judge the opportunity to set a scheduling conference order that will include the dates for the exchange of SCR-Civil Rule 26(b)(4) expert testimony statements.

The discovery process generally follows Rule 26; subsection (b)(4) speaks specifically to the treatment of expert testimony. Rule 26(b)(4) requires a party to identify each individual expected to be called as an expert, state the subject matter of the expert's testimony, reveal the substantive facts and opinions to which the expert will testify, and explain the grounds for the expert's conclusions.

Practitioners should be wary of the implications of Rule 26(b)(4) statements. First, designating a witness as an expert entitles all litigants to the expert's opinions. In *Street v. Hedgepath*, the D.C. Court of Appeals explained how broadly this principle reaches when it held "that *ex parte* interviews with a treating physician are a permissible means of informal discovery when the plaintiff has put

---

[10] It should be noted that "whereas the common law of evidence in the District of Columbia favors the admission of an expert's testimony about the hearsay bases of his opinions and permits its presentation on direct examination unless its legitimate probative value is substantially outweighed by the risk of unfair prejudice . . ., Rule 703 now disfavors the admission of such testimony and requires its exclusion unless the risk of unfair prejudice is substantially outweighed by its legitimate probative value." *In re Amey*, 40 A.3d 902, 913 (D.C. 2012) (emphasis omitted).

the medical condition of that physician's patient at issue by filing a lawsuit." 607 A.2d 1238, 1247 (D.C. 1992).

On the other hand, failure to include an expert witness or the subject on which she is expected to testify has ramifications as well. First, witnesses whose names are not found in the pretrial statement generally will only be allowed to testify for impeachment or rebuttal purposes. SCR-Civil Rule 16(e) ("Except for plaintiff's rebuttal case or for impeachment purposes, no party may offer at trial the testimony of any witness not listed in the pretrial statement of the parties . . . ."). Thus, one court has held that expert testimony could not be offered because it did not properly constitute rebuttal evidence. *See Cooper v. Safeway Stores, Inc.*, 629 A.2d 31 (D.C. 1993). Typically, counsel may offer a supplement to its pretrial statement to add an expert witness. SCR-Civil Rule 26(f)(1)(B). *See Daniels v. Beeks*, 532 A.2d 125 (D.C. 1987) (finding an abuse of discretion where the trial court denied a party's request to supplement a pretrial statement with an expert witness). When addressing incomplete pretrial statements on expert testimony, D.C. courts consider two competing factors in their determination of admissibility—first, whether the opposing party will be prejudiced by the delay and, second, whether the party in error acted willfully. *See Regional Redevelopment Corp. v. Hoke*, 547 A.2d 1006 (D.C. 1988). Other factors also may be considered, including the effects of inclusion on trial orderliness and the value of the testimony to the jury's deliberation.

The leading pronouncement on the multifactor decision process for admitting expert evidence omitted from pretrial statements can be found in *Weiner v. Kneller*, 557 A.2d 1306 (D.C. 1989). In *Weiner*, the plaintiff offered an expert witness to refute the contention that the decedent's condition had been incurable, rendering moot the argument that medical malpractice led to her death. *Id.* at 1308. The defense was advised of this witness through oral disclosure, but without the filing of a supplementary statement, as required by SCR-Civil Rules 26(b)(4) and 26(f)(1)(B). *Id.* In considering whether the trial court properly excluded this testimony, the *Weiner* court laid out the following five-factor test for determining whether to include the expert testimony:

> (1) whether allowing the evidence would incurably surprise or prejudice the opposing party, (2) whether excluding the evidence would incurably prejudice the party seeking to introduce it, (3) whether the party seeking to introduce the testimony failed to comply with the evidentiary rules inadvertently or willfully, (4) the impact of allowing the proposed testimony on the orderliness and efficiency of the trial, and (5) the impact of excluding the proposed testimony on the completeness of information before the court or jury.

Id. at 1311–12. While noting that the appellants had the burden of proving a preponderance of these factors, the court still found the testimony improperly excluded. Because there was no surprise or prejudice attendant to the new testimony, and the evidence was important to the appellant's case, the court ruled that the testimony should have been admitted. *Id.* at 1312.

While facts known and opinions held by testifying experts are broadly available by discovery, *non*testifying experts will not be subject to discovery as a general rule. Rule 26(b)(4)(B) provides in pertinent part that such facts and opinions are available only "as provided in Rule 35(b) [addressing physical and mental examinations of a person] or upon a showing of exceptional circumstances under which it is impracticable for the party seeking discovery to obtain facts or opinions on the same subject by other means." SCR-Civil Rule 26(b)(4)(B).

As a matter of convenience, expert testimony need not be presented on the stand. D.C. has promulgated SCR-Civil Rule 32(a)(4), which permits a videotaped deposition of any expert witness (including a treating or consulting physician) to be used for any purpose, even though the expert is able to testify. SCR-Civil Rule 32(a)(4). Rule 32(a)(4) requires "notice" to be given that the deposition videotape will be used at trial. The rule also carves out an exception, permitting the court to limit the videotaped deposition's use "for good cause shown."

D.C. has promulgated Rule 28 of the Superior Court Rules of Criminal Procedure ("SCR-Criminal Procedure") to authorize courts to appoint expert witnesses. There is not a corresponding civil rule for the appointment of experts, but it is widely recognized that trial courts are vested with the power to appoint experts in appropriate situations. *See In re Eric L. Cummings*, 471 A.2d 254, 257 (1984).

When addressing the issue of expert witness fees, practitioners should refer to SCR-Civil Rule 26(b)(4)(C) which explains that, apart from exceptional cases of manifest injustice:

> (i) the court shall require that the party seeking discovery pay the expert a reasonable fee for time spent in responding to discovery under subdivisions (b)(4)(A)(ii) and (b)(4)(B) of this rule; and (ii) with respect to discovery obtained under subdivision (b)(4)(A)(ii) of this rule the court may require, and with respect to discovery obtained under subdivision (b)(4)(B) of this rule the court shall require, the party seeking discovery to pay the other party a fair portion of the fees and expenses reasonably incurred by the latter party in obtaining facts and opinions from the expert.

SCR-Civil Rule 26(b)(4)(C).

If a witness must be subpoenaed, practitioners should refer to SCR-Civil Rule 45, which explains that the party demanding the subpoena should take reasonable steps to prevent any undue burden falling on the witness, SCR-Civil Rule 45(c)(1), and that, for unretained experts, the court may modify, quash, or limit the subpoena. SCR-Civil Rule 45(c)(3)(B). Costs attendant to obtaining expert witnesses may be awarded to the prevailing party. Rule 54(d)(1) explains: "Except when express provision therefor is made either in an applicable statute or in these Rules, costs other than attorneys' fees shall be allowed as of course to the prevailing party unless the court otherwise directs."

And finally, D.C. Code § 11-2605 makes a specific ascription to indigent defendants, entitling them to expert assistance whenever an adequate defense so necessitates. *See Jackson v. United States*, 768 A.2d 580, 587 (D.C. 2001) (explaining that a reasonableness standard is used to assess indigents' requests for expert assistance).

CHAPTER XIII

THE NAS AND THE COURTS: A THREE-YEAR PERSPECTIVE

by

Jules Epstein
Associate Professor of Law
Widener University School of Law
4601 Concord Pike
P.O. Box 7474
Wilmington, DE 19803
(302) 477-2031

In a 2009 report, the National Research Council (NRC) of the National Academy of Sciences (NAS) raised serious concerns about the scientific foundation underlying typical forensic examiner testimony on pattern and impression evidence. STRENGTHENING FORENSIC SCIENCE IN THE UNITED STATES: A PATH FORWARD, *available at* https://www.ncjrs.gov/pdffiles1/nij/grants/228091.pdf. In particular, the report concluded that:

> no forensic method other than nuclear DNA analysis has been rigorously shown to have the capacity to consistently and with a high degree of certainty support conclusions about "individualization" (more commonly known as "matching" of an unknown item of evidence to a specific known source). Chapter 3, p. 87.

Said more simply, claims such as that a bullet was fired from one firearm *to the exclusion of all others in the universe of firearms*, or that a fingerprint came from one individual *to the exclusion of all others*, lacked a sufficient research foundation to be valid and reliable.

The report also took to task the legal community, providing the following assessment of how courts and lawyers addressed the admissibility and/or limits of forensic evidence:

a) "Review of reported judicial opinions reveals that, at least in criminal cases, forensic science evidence is not routinely scrutinized pursuant to the standard of reliability enunciated in *Daubert*." Report, Chapter 3, p. 87.
b) "[J]udges and lawyers . . . often lack the scientific expertise necessary to comprehend and evaluate forensic evidence." *Id.*, at 85.
c) "[E]very effort must be made to limit the risk of having the reliability of certain forensic science methodologies judicially certified before the techniques have been properly studied and their accuracy verified." *Id.*, at 86.

Overall, the report concluded that "the courts continue to rely on forensic evidence without fully understanding and addressing the limitations of different forensic science disciplines." *Id.*, at 85

More than three years have passed since the release of the report. To some extent it has refocused courts and lawyers on how to treat forensic "matching" evidence. But relatively few reported court decisions have referenced the report[1], and still fewer in the context of admissibility issues. *See, e.g., Melendez-Diaz v. Massachusetts*, 129 S. Ct. 2527, 2536 (U.S. 2009) (referencing report in context of determining whether forensic lab reports constitute "testimonial" hearsay).

This article considers whether those decisions reflect a new judicial "understanding and addressing [of] the limitations" of these disciplines. The conclusion is mixed, and varies discipline to discipline. The limited and varied response to the report may also be a by-product of how the challenges were framed, *i.e.*, as requests for total exclusion rather than restrictions on the nature of the conclusions drawn, and on *Daubert*'s relatively low threshold for admissibility. *Daubert v. Merrell Dow Pharms.*, 509 U.S. 579, 590 (U.S. 1993). *Daubert* expressly acknowledged that expert opinion testimony could be "shaky" but still admissible: "Vigorous cross-examination, presentation of contrary evidence, and careful instruction on the burden of proof are the traditional and appropriate means of attacking shaky but admissible evidence." *Id.* at 596. And in the succeeding case *Kumho Tire Co. v. Carmichael*, 526 U.S. 137, 152 (U.S. 1999), the court emphasized that "the trial judge must have considerable leeway in deciding in a particular case how to go about determining whether particular expert testimony is reliable." As one court explained the limits of these holdings:

> issues of credibility and persuasiveness...are relevant only in valuing the testimony, not in determining its admissibility . . . [I]t is not the trial court's role to decide whether an expert's opinion is correct. The trial court is limited to determining whether expert testimony is pertinent to an issue in the case and whether the methodology underlying that testimony is sound.

Deputy v. Lehman Bros., Inc., 345 F.3d 494, 506 (7th Cir. Wis. 2003) (internal citation and quotation omitted).

Whatever the reason, the limited impact of the report may be unsurprising. This article concludes with a discussion of two instances where courts have imposed a structure on the presentation of scientific evidence. Establishing practices and procedures as a "systems approach" may do more to ensure that forensic testimony is reliable.

A. LATENT PRINT EVIDENCE

The NAS report first concluded that fingerprint examination is not supported by "peer-reviewed, published studies establishing [its] scientific bases and validity" and lacks "rigorous protocols to guide . . . [experts'] subjective assessments of matching characteristics." Report at 8. The report elaborated that, "[a]lthough there is limited information about the accuracy and reliability of friction ridge analyses, claims that these analyses have zero error rates are not scientifically plausible . . ." *Id.* at 146. Regarding the Analysis, Comparison, Evaluation, and Verification (ACE-V) methodology for print comparison used by the FBI and many other agencies and examiners, the report stated that "ACE-V does not guard against bias; is too broad to ensure repeatability and transparency; and does not guarantee that two analysts following it will obtain the same results." *Id.* "For these reasons," the report cautioned, "merely following the steps of ACE-V does not imply that one is proceeding in a scientific manner or producing reliable results." *Id.*

---

[1] Report as of June 5, 2012, only 53 federal or state decisions had referenced the Report. LEXIS search "strength! w/2 forensic w/2 science and date aft 3/1/2009," in the federal and state court database, conducted June 5, 2012.

Notwithstanding these concerns, reported decisions show courts faced with challenges to latent print testimony continue to admit this testimony in an unqualified fashion. In *United States v. Watkins*, 450 Fed. Appx. 511 (6th Cir. Ohio 2011), the challenge to fingerprint evidence was inhibited by the fact that trial occurred before the issuance of the report. Nonetheless, the appellate court concluded that the admissibility decision was proper even in light of the report's conclusions and the fact that the expert testified that the error rate for this discipline is "zero." The court explained that, "assuming arguendo that the ACE-V method is not error-free, the fact that the fingerprint examiner testified that it was 100 percent accurate does not by itself mean that the district court erred in determining that the ACE-V method was scientifically valid." 450 Fed. Appx. at 515. This unqualified acceptance of latent prints was also affirmed by federal district courts in Michigan, California, and Virginia. *United States v. Stone*, 2012 U.S. Dist. LEXIS 8973 (E.D. Mich. Jan. 25, 2012) (rejecting call for outright exclusion); *United States v. Love*, 2011 U.S. Dist. LEXIS 58390 (S.D. Cal. June 1, 2011); *United States v. Council*, 777 F. Supp. 2d 1006 (E.D. Va. 2011).

The Virginia decision deserves examination, in part for the proof offered in support of the challenge. The defense presented testimony from professor Jennifer Mnookin, a law professor and scholar in science and the law. As described by the district court,

> [h]er research focuses on scientific evidence, particularly forensic science evidence and the validation of the scientific processes underlying forensic science evidence. She is currently a member of a working group of the National Institute of Justice and the National Institute of Standards and Technology that studies the effect of human factors on friction ridge analysis.

777 F. Supp. 2d at 1009. Professor Mnookin testified that "ACE-V does not describe a scientific process . . . , lacks objective criteria to determine whether a print is fit for analysis and comparison and, therefore, relies almost entirely on the experience and intuition of the examiner." *Id.* at 1010. The district court acknowledged that "Dr. Mnookin's criticisms of ACE-V's scientific validity track the conclusions offered by the NRC report." *Id.* Nevertheless, the testimony was ruled admissible:

> [E]ven widening the circle to include commentators such as Dr. Mnookin and the members of the committee that drafted the NRC report barely changes the balance of opinion. Adding those commentators to the equation does not outweigh the acceptance friction ridge analysis has gained . . .

Id. at 1011.

The resistance to admissibility challenges has been extended to the exclusion at trial of expert testimony explaining the limits of the current state of knowledge in the field of latent print analysis. In *People v. Gonzalez*, 2012 Cal. App. Unpub. LEXIS 1294 (Cal. App. 4th Dist. Feb. 22, 2012), the defense sought leave to present professor Simon Cole, whose doctorate is in science and technology studies, to testify that:

> that fingerprint evidence is not reliable is based upon several factors. The first is that he has searched for but found no studies validating the accuracy of fingerprint identification. In addition, he noted that there are no accepted standards for determining a match. The second is the conclusions of the prepublication version of a report from the National Academy of Sciences entitled "Strengthening Forensic Science in the United States."

Id. at **6–7. Cole's proffered testimony was excluded at trial on the ground that it "would not assist the jurors." *Id.* at *7. This decision was upheld on appeal.

It deserves note that the challengers in the cited federal cases sought outright exclusion of the latent print testimony. It is unclear whether more limited challenges, such as to examiners reporting an individualization to the exclusion of all others or barring testimony claiming a zero error rate, will have a different outcome. Overall, however, the report has had seemingly no impact on trial court acceptance of latent print evidence.

B. BALLISTICS EVIDENCE

The NAS report explained that in ballistics examinations, the comparison between crime scene evidence [a fired cartridge casing or an actual bullet or bullet fragment], and a sample from a suspect firearm, "the decision of the toolmark examiner remains a subjective decision based on unarticulated standards and no statistical foundation for estimation of error rates." Report at 153–154. The report elaborated:

> Toolmark and firearms analysis suffers from the same limitations discussed above for impression evidence. Because not enough is known about the variabilities among individual tools and guns, we are not able to specify how many points of similarity are necessary for a given level of confidence in the result. Sufficient studies have not been done to understand the reliability and repeatability of the methods. The committee agrees that class characteristics are helpful in narrowing the pool of tools that may have left a distinctive mark. Individual patterns from manufacture or from wear might, in some cases, be distinctive enough to suggest one particular source, but additional studies should be performed to make the process of individualization more precise and repeatable.

Id., at 154.

Unlike with latent prints, some courts have been prone to scrutinize ballistics evidence more and (at least slightly) restrict the conclusiveness of the examiner's findings, albeit not uniformly. *See, e.g., People v. Melcher*, 2011 Cal. App. Unpub. LEXIS 7222 at *29 (Cal. App. 1st Dist. Sept. 23, 2011)(affirming the trial court ruling that the NAS report conclusions did not warrant a "Kelly/Frye" hearing and admitting the ballistics testimony). In *Melcher*, the trial court did preclude the expert from saying that no other gun in the world could have left the same markings, but permitted testimony that "the chance of another weapon creating the same pattern was so remote as to be 'practically impossible.'" *Id.* at *30.

A series of federal district court *in limine* rulings have cabined ballistics testimony to some extent. One court permitted the conclusion that the cartridge and bullet fragment found at the crime scene were fired by the suspect's weapon, but ruled that the expert should not be permitted to express his opinions with any degree of certainty. *United States v. Willock*, 682 F. Supp. 2d 512 (D. Md. 2010). In *Willock*, the limitation regarding degree of certainty was not imposed by the court but agreed to by the parties. A more elaborate set of restrictions was imposed in *United States v. Taylor*, 663 F. Supp. 2d 1170 (D.N.M. Oct. 9, 2009), where ballistics "match" testimony was permitted, but not to a degree of scientific certainty and not to the absolute or practical exclusion of all other firearms. The permissible qualifier was that the opinion was "within a reasonable degree of certainty in the firearms examination field." *Id.* at 1180.

Other courts have responded similarly. *See, e.g., United States v. Mouzone*, 2009 U.S. Dist. LEXIS 100718, 98–99 (D. Md. Oct. 29, 2009). While the most recent holding strongly approved of ballistics match evidence, despite acknowledging the NAS report, it did so in a case where the government did not "seek to present an opinion that the recovered bullet and shells originated from the respective firearms seized from defendants 'to the exclusion of all other firearms in the world'." *United States v. Otero*, 2012 U.S. Dist. LEXIS 53198 at **9–10 (D.N.J. Mar. 15, 2012). Instead, the government took the more limited position that "that its expert, Deady, should be permitted to give testimony on his firearms identification 'to a reasonable degree of certainty'." *Id.*

In sum, the foregoing cases demonstrate that, whether by judicial fiat or prosecution concession, the NAS report has led to some limits on the absoluteness and certainty components of ballistic "match" evidence.

C. QUESTIONED DOCUMENTS (HANDWRITING) ANALYSIS

The NAS report did not endorse the current state of questioned document analysis as strongly based in science or supported by appropriate studies.

> The scientific basis for handwriting comparisons needs to be strengthened. Recent studies have increased our understanding of the individuality and consistency of handwriting and computer studies and suggest that there may be a scientific basis for handwriting comparison, at least in the absence of intentional obfuscation or forgery. Although there has been only limited research to quantify the reliability and replicability of the practices used by trained document examiners, the committee agrees that there may be some value in handwriting analysis.

Report, at 166–167.

Prior to the issuance of the report, some federal judges had imposed substantial limitations on the nature of the conclusions a handwriting expert could draw. As one court concluded:

> I find Harrison's testimony meets Fed. R. Evid. 702's requirements to the extent that she restricts her testimony to similarities or dissimilarities between the known exemplars and the robbery note. However, she may not render an ultimate conclusion on who penned the unknown writing.

United States v. Hines, 55 F. Supp. 2d 62, 70–71 (D. Mass. 1999) (limiting expert conclusion and collecting cases with similar rulings). Other, however, courts held to the contrary. *See, e.g., United States v. Mooney*, 315 F.3d 54, 63 (1st Cir. 2002) (affirming the district court's acceptance of handwriting expert "match" testimony and the that court's decision to not follow *Hines*). Nonetheless, in 2012, and after consideration of the report, one court approved of the "match" testimony in handwriting (albeit under a *Frye* "general acceptance" standard), and explicitly "reject[ed] appellant's argument that the NRC report represents a scientific consensus as to handwriting identification materially different from that established at the evidentiary hearing." *Pettus v. United States*, 37 A.3d 213, 226 (D.C. 2012).

To date, there has been no reported decision that has relied on the NAS report to restrict the nature of a handwriting analyst's conclusion.

D. TOWARDS A "SYSTEMS" APPROACH

The report acknowledged that the adversary process, and the crucible of a particular fact-driven case, may not be the ideal forum for addressing the state of scientific knowledge:

> [T]he adversarial process relating to the admission and exclusion of scientific evidence is not suited to the task of finding "scientific truth." The judicial system is encumbered by, among other things, judges and lawyers who generally lack the scientific expertise necessary to comprehend and evaluate forensic evidence in an informed manner, trial judges

(sitting alone) who must decide evidentiary issues without the benefit of judicial colleagues and often with little time for extensive research and reflection, and the highly deferential nature of the appellate review afforded trial courts' *Daubert* rulings. Furthermore, the judicial system embodies a case-by-case adjudicatory approach that is not well suited to address the systematic problems in many of the various forensic science disciplines.

Report, at 110.

Where the NAS report may have impact in the litigation context is where courts establish practices and protocols for the presentation of forensic evidence. To date, two instance of this have occurred.

Judge Nancy Gerter of the district of Massachusetts issued a "procedural order" directing how "trace evidence" is to be handled in criminal cases before her, directing that a party:

a) identify whether or not they seek to introduce trace evidence,
b) state whether or not either party seeks a Daubert/Kumho hearing prior to trial, and
c) state the witnesses required for the Daubert/Kumho hearing and the exhibits that the parties seek to admit.

No later than two months before the pretrial conference, counsel must also indicate:

i) if counsel is appointed, whether expert funds are sought to deal with the trace evidence;
ii) whether all discovery obligations under the local rules have been met or whether additional discovery required.

Procedural Order: Trace Evidence, Case 1:08-cr-10104-NG at 1 (D. Mass. 2010); *available at* http://www.mad.uscourts.gov/boston/pdf/ProcOrderTraceEvidenceUPDATE.pdf.

The Massachusetts Supreme Court went further in the context of a challenge to ballistics evidence. In doing so, it has provided a systems model for forensic evidence cases. In 2011, the Massachusetts Supreme Court set forth its protocol for future cases, in part in light of the report:

i) First, before trial, the examiner must adequately document the findings or observations that support the examiner's ultimate opinion, and this documentary evidence, whether in the form of measurements, notes, sketches, or photographs, shall be provided in discovery, so that defense counsel will have an adequate and informed basis to cross-examine the forensic ballistics expert at trial.
ii) Second, before an opinion is offered at trial, a forensic ballistics expert should explain to the jury the theories and methodologies underlying the field of forensic ballistics.
iii) Third, in the absence of special circumstances casting doubt on the reliability of an opinion, and once these two things have been done, a forensic ballistics expert may present an expert's opinion... Where a qualified expert has identified sufficient individual characteristic toolmarks reasonably to offer an opinion that a particular firearm fired a projectile or cartridge casing recovered as evidence, the expert may offer that opinion to a "reasonable degree of ballistic certainty."

Commonwealth v. Pytou Heang, 942 N.E.2d 927, 944–945 (Mass. 2011). The Massachusetts Supreme Court also emphasized that "[t]he lack of a firm scientific basis proving the uniqueness of individual characteristic toolmarks is a proper subject for both direct examination and cross-examination." *Id.* at 944 n. 28.

E. CONCLUSION

If the report is correct as to the limitations of the forensic disciplines discussed above, and especially as to whether the discipline is error free and can truly make an individualized source attribution, then courts either have not kept up with the science or the *Daubert* and *Frye* standards for assessing reliability have questionable utility in this arena (except for the limited strictures imposed in some firearms identification cases).

Repeated case by case challenges may slowly ensure testimony consistent with the current state of each discipline's proven capacity. Otherwise change will have to come elsewhere, such as from within the forensic disciplines themselves or when expert working groups strive to identify the current state of a discipline and the proper means of expressing findings.[2] For now, however, one conclusion of the report seems to remain true: "The present situation, however, is seriously wanting, both because of the limitations of the judicial system and because of the many problems faced by the forensic science community." Report, at 110.

---

[2] *See, e.g.*, Latent Print Examination and Human Factors: Improving the Practice through a Systems Approach, NIST (February 2012) http://www.nist.gov/customcf/get_pdf.cfm?pub_id=910745

CHAPTER XIV
EXPERT WITNESS QUALIFICATIONS AND TESTIMONY*

by

Carol Henderson
Kurt Lenz

A. INTRODUCTION

The field of scientific interpretation of evidence and its portrayal in popular media has progressed to the point that expert testimony at trial is not only commonly accepted by judge and jury, but also expected. This article addresses the factors that influence the selection of an expert, including the importance of investigating the expert's credentials and making an informed assessment of the credibility that the expert's qualifications will project to a judge and jurors.

While this article is written from a United States perspective, many of the issues discussed here are applicable to expert witness testimony worldwide. This article does not, however, address the legal standards for the admissibility of expert testimony, or attorneys' ethics in dealing with experts.

B. SELECTING AN EXPERT

Many variables should be considered in selecting an expert witness, including the expert's availability, cost, experience, and reputation. When an expert serves as a consultant or in the pretrial phases of litigation, the criteria for selecting that expert may be limited to the expert's competency in the field. As a trial witness, however, the expert's integrity, charisma, and overall effectiveness as a witness must also be considered.

Thus, consideration should be given not only to the expert's formal training but also to the expert's personality, demeanor, and capacity to organize, express, and interpret complex concepts for the jury. The weight accorded to the expert's opinion by the judge or jury will be determined in large part by the expert's perceived character, objectivity, and impartiality.

Of course, the quality of the expert's credentials remains an important factor to consider as well. A thorough evaluation of an expert should take into account such matters as (1) the membership requirements of the associations to which the expert belongs, (2) how the expert's credentials compare to those of the opposing expert, (3) whether the journals in which the expert's articles appear are held in high regard in the field, and (4) whether the conclusions in those articles were subject to peer review. Studies of jurors' perceptions of experts can be particularly helpful in guiding this evaluation.

Care should always be taken to verify the credentials of one's own expert, as well as those of an adversary's expert, for, although it is unlikely that an expert has faked credentials, it has occurred. Indeed, experts have come under increased scrutiny in recent years for fabricating or inflating their qualifications.

---

*   The materials in this chapter have been adapted, with permission, from the authors' prior work in *Expert Witnesses: Qualifications and Testimony*, in *Encyclopedia of Forensic Sciences* 2d Ed. (Jay A. Siegel et al eds.) (Elsevier Academic Press forthcoming 2013).

1. Qualifications

The court must determine whether a proffered witness is qualified to testify as an expert, and that determination will not be overturned except for an abuse of discretion. *Kumho Tire Co. Ltd. v. Carmichael*, 526 U.S. 137, 143 (1999); *But see, e.g., Radlein v. Holiday Inns, Inc.*, 971 So.2d 1200 (La. App. 4 Cir. 2007) (holding that the trial court's decision will not be reversed unless there is a clear showing of error). Federal Rule of Evidence 702 states that a witness may qualify as an expert on the basis of knowledge, skill, training, experience, or education. An expert witness must possess only one of these traits for the judge to find the expert qualified to give an opinion. In making this evaluation, the judge may consider the expert's educational background, work experience, publications, awards, teaching, speaking, or other professional engagements, prior expert-witness testimony, and membership in professional associations.

Often, the expert may have to educate the attorney proffering the expert regarding the significance of particular experience, achievements, and certifications to ensure that they are appropriately presented to the judge. An expert must be prepared to explain board certification and licensure requirements to the judge in detail.

2. Experience as an Expert Witness

Experience and training are often more significant than academic background and are accorded more weight by jurors, according to at least one study evaluating juror perceptions of fingerprint experts. Charles Illsley, *Juries, Fingerprints, and the Expert Fingerprint Witness*, presentation at the International Symposium on Latent Prints at the FBI Academy (July 1987). However, experience as an expert witness, standing alone, does not qualify someone as an expert in later cases. One court rejected the opinion of a witness who had testified as an expert 126 times. *Bogosian v. Mercedes-Benz of North America Inc.*, 104 F.3d 472, 477 (1st Cir. 1997). Another court noted that, "it would be absurd to conclude that one can become an expert by accumulating experience in testifying." *Thomas J. Kline, Inc. v. Lonillard, Inc.*, 878 F.2d 791, 800 (4th Cir. 1989), *cert. denied*, 493 U.S. 1073 (1990). Conversely, a lack of previous experience as an expert witness does not disqualify one from testifying as an expert, because "even the most qualified expert must have his first day in court." *U.S. v. Locascio*, 6 F.3d 924, 937 (2d Cir. 1993), *cert. denied*, 511 U.S. 1070 (1994).

3. Education and Training

An expert may be qualified on the basis of academic credentials, including the expert's undergraduate, graduate, and postgraduate work. An expert's academic credentials should only be issued by accredited educational institutions and programs, because the proliferation of the Internet, while laudable for so many reasons, has also rekindled the old-fashioned diploma mill. *See* The Technical Working Group on Education and Training in Forensic Science, *Education and Training in Forensic Science: A Guide for Forensic Science Laboratories, Educational Institutions and Students*, National Institutes of Justice Special Report (June 2004). One such business, Diplomas 4U, once provided bachelors, masters, MBA, or PhD degrees in its customers' field of choice; advertisements assured that no one would be turned down and that there would be no bothersome tests, classes, books, or interviews. After studying this issue, the National Academy of Sciences has concluded that it is crucially important to improve undergraduate and graduate forensic science programs with, among other things, attractive scholarship and fellowship offerings, and funding for research programs to attract research universities and students in fields relevant to forensic science. Committee on Identifying the Needs of the Forensic Sciences Community, National Research Council, *Strengthening*

Forensic Science in the United States: A Path Forward (NAS report), National Academy of Sciences, pp. 238–239 (August 2009).

An expert should continuously perform research and publish in the expert's field, preferably in peer-reviewed publications. Teaching experience is another of the qualifications that judges will evaluate: all forms of teaching—regular, specialty, guest lecturing, visiting professorships, continuing education, and short courses—weigh in as credentials. An expert should also keep up to date with developments in his or her field of expertise by reading the current literature, enrolling in continuing education seminars, joining professional societies, and attending professional meetings.

4. Membership in Professional Associations

A study published by the U.S. Department of Justice in 1987 found that jurors perceived those fingerprint experts who belonged to professional associations to be more credible than other experts, and presumed experts would belong to such groups. Illsley, *supra*. It is therefore important for an expert to remain active and participate in professional societies; the expert's credibility is diminished if the expert has not recently attended a professional meeting. Professional associations that only require annual dues payment to become a member are not as prestigious as associations that are joined by special invitation only, by approval of special referees, or by passing an examination.

Thus, an expert should be selective about which professional associations to join. The NAS report calls for standardized accreditation and/or certification, as well as a uniform code of ethics:

> Although some areas of the forensic science disciplines have made notable efforts to achieve standardization and best practices, most disciplines still lack any consistent structure for the enforcement of 'better practices,' operating standards, and certification and accreditation programs. . . . Accreditation is required in only three states . . . [and] [i]n other states, accreditation is voluntary, as is individual certification. . . .". NAS report at 213

Thus, the NAS report calls for the creation of a federal agency to develop tools to advance reliability in forensic science, to ensure standards that reflect best practices, and serve as accreditation tools for laboratories and as guides for the education, training, and certification of professionals. NAS report at 214.

C. INCREASED SCRUTINY OF EXPERTS

Experts have come under increased scrutiny for either fabricating or inflating their qualifications. In Florida, in 1998, a person who had been testifying as an expert in toxicology for three years for both the prosecution and defense in criminal cases was prosecuted for perjury for testifying with fraudulent credentials. *See* Henry Fitzgerald, Jr., *Phony "Expert" Jailed for 3 Years*, Ft. Lauderdale Sun-Sentinel 3D (Dec. 1, 1998). The expert claimed to possess masters and doctorate degrees from Florida Atlantic University, but when a prosecutor sought to confirm the claims, he discovered that the registrar's office had no record of the expert attending or receiving a degree from the university.

In another case, a Harvard medical professor was sued for trademark infringement for falsely claiming to be board-certified by the American Board of Psychiatry and Neurology (ABPN) in five trials. *ABPN v. Johnson-Powell*, 129 F.3d 1 (1st Cir. 1997). The board sought to seize the expert's witness fees and treble damages, but the court denied that relief because it believed the expert was unlikely to infringe in the future.

In 2007, a court granted the plaintiff a new trial in her product liability action when it was discovered that the pharmaceutical company's cardiology expert had misrepresented his credentials by testifying that he was board certified in internal medicine and cardiovascular disease when in fact those certifications had expired. *In re Vioxx Products*, 489 F. Supp. 2d 587 (E.D. La. 2007).

In addition to perjury prosecutions for false qualifications, some jurisdictions also prosecute for academic fraud. For example, in Florida, a person who misrepresents association with, or academic standing at, a postsecondary educational institution is guilty of a first-degree misdemeanor. Fla. Stat. § 817.566 (2004).

Courts have also overturned convictions where the experts testified outside their field of expertise. Instances include a medical examiner testifying to shoe-pattern analysis and an evidence technician with no ballistics expertise giving testimony about bullet trajectory. *See Gilliam v. State*, 514 So. 2d 1098 (Fla. 1987); *Kelvin v. State*, 610 So. 2d 1359 (Fla. App. 1 Dist. 1992).

There is evidence to suggest that, since the Supreme Court's decisions in *Daubert v. Merrell Dow Pharmaceuticals, Inc.*, 509 U.S. 579 (1993), and Kuhmo Tire Co., courts have been more willing to exclude expert testimony. The Federal Judicial Center compared a 1998 survey of 303 federal judges with a 1991 survey. Mark Hansen, *Admission Tests: Fewer Post-Daubert Judges Allow Experts to Testify Without Limitations in Civil Trials, Study Finds*, A.B.A. J. 28 (Feb. 2001). In 1998, 41 percent of the judges claimed to have excluded expert testimony, whereas only 25 percent of the judges did so in 1991. A 2001 RAND study similarly concluded that judges were becoming more vigilant gatekeepers; for example, in the U.S. Third Circuit Court of Appeals, the exclusion rate in products liability cases rose from 53 to 70 percent. Lloyd Dixon and Brian Gill, *Changes in the Standards in Admitting Expert Evidence In Federal Civil Cases Since Daubert Decision*, RAND Monograph (2001). This contradicts most of the reported case law following Daubert, which seems to indicate that the exclusion of expert testimony remains the exception, not the rule. *See* Fed. R. Evid. 702, Adv. Cmte. Note to the 2000 Amendment. (2000).

D. WEIGHT OF THE EVIDENCE

Once a judge decides that an expert may testify, the jury must then decide the weight to accord the expert's opinion. Jurors have become familiar with the role of the expert witness at trial through the coverage of high-profile cases in the popular media and fictional television depictions such as *CSI*. Studies have shown that jurors have increased expectations for scientific evidence, and that in cases based on circumstantial evidence, jurors are more likely to acquit a defendant if the government did not provide some form of scientific evidence. *See, e.g.,* Hon. Donald E. Shelton, Young S. Kim, and Gregg Barak, *An Indirect-Effects Model of Mediated Adjudication: The CSI Myth, the Tech Effect, and Metropolitan Jurors' Expectations for Scientific Evidence*, 12 Vanderbilt J. Ent. & Tech. L. 1 (2009); Young S. Kim, Gregg Barak, and Donald E. Shelton, *Examining the "'CSI-effect' in the Cases of Circumstantial Evidence and Eyewitness Testimony: Multivariate and Path Analyses*, 37 J. Crim. Justice 452 (2009); *see also* National Clearinghouse for Science, Technology and the Law at Stetson University College of Law, *Bibliography of Resources Related to the CSI Effect*, http://www.ncstl.org/education/CSI%20Effect%20Bibliography (accessed on December 3, 2012). Expert witnesses and attorneys should be aware of studies regarding jurors' perceptions of expert witnesses, and how those perceptions have evolved over time.

For example, a 1994 study revealed that the characteristics of experts that were most important to jurors in determining the experts' credibility were (1) the expert's willingness to draw firm conclusions, and (2) the expert's ability to convey technical information in plain language that a layperson could understand. Daniel W. Shuman, et al., *An Empirical Examination of the Use of Expert Witnesses in the Courts—Part II: A Three City Study*, 35 Jurimetrics 193 (1994). Another study concluded that an expert's believability is linked to the expert's qualifications, familiarity with the facts of the case, good reasoning, and perceived impartiality. Daniel W. Shuman, et al., *Assessing the Believability of Expert Witnesses: Science in the Jurybox*, 37 Jurimetrics 23 (1996). Jurors were also influenced by independent research that corresponded with the expert's opinion.

A 1998 study exposed jurors as a more skeptical, cynical group. *Jurors: A Biased, Independent Lot*, Nat'l L.J. A1 (Nov. 2, 1998). Among the findings, the study concluded that 50 percent of those surveyed thought that expert witnesses say only what they are paid to say; 33 percent did not believe police testimony; and 75 percent said they would set aside what a judge says the law requires and reach a verdict the jurors felt was right. Yet another study concluded that using expert testimony to counter the prosecution's expert in criminal cases caused jurors to be skeptical of all expert testimony, rather than simply sensitizing them to flaws in the prosecution expert's testimony. Lora M. Levett & Margaret B. Kovera, *The Effectiveness of Opposing Expert Witnesses for Educating Jurors About Unreliable Expert Evidence*, J. L. & Human Behavior (Pub. online Oct. 17, 2007). In fact, jurors rendered more guilty verdicts when they heard defense expert testimony than when they did not. This study throws into question the Supreme Court's assumption in *Daubert* that opposing expert testimony effectively safeguards against "junk" science in the courtroom.

Increasing awareness of errant experts and exonerations of the wrongly accused has influenced how jurors perceive scientific evidence. For example, background beliefs about the possibility of laboratory errors and intentional tampering affect the weight jurors afford a DNA report, and jurors with such beliefs gave probability estimates less weight. Jason Schklar and Shari Seidman, *Juror Reactions to DNA Evidence: Errors and Expectancies*, 23 J. L. & Human Behavior 159 (1999). A separate poll regarding forensic fraud and its impact on potential jurors found that 32 percent think wrongful convictions happen frequently; 23 percent said that wrongful convictions are rarely an accident. Ed Godfrey, *Poll Shows Oklahomans Distrust System*, The Daily Oklahoman A1 (May 27, 2001).

Experts must understand that effective communication with jurors requires organized content, and the effective use of visual presentation techniques including, whenever possible, demonstrative exhibits that incorporate large, user-friendly data presentation monitors and systems for use both by the court and individual jurors, as well as interactive electronic timelines and e-documents that allow jurors to feel they are in control of and have access to all information regarding the facts of the trial. Data also suggests that when testifying to jurors, experts should attempt to associate themselves with a more collaborative, personalized role such as a teacher, rather than a more hierarchal and impersonal profession such as a scientist. Sonya Hamlin, *Who Are Today's Jurors and How Do You Reach Them?*, Litigation 9 (Spring 2000). Surveys confirm these conclusions distinguishing jurors from Generations X and Y from past generations. Bob Van Voris, *Jurors to Lawyers: Dare to be Dull*, Nat'l L.J. A1 (Oct 23, 2000). For example, while 64 percent of jurors overall believe the police tell the truth when they testify, only 51 percent of jurors between eighteen and twenty-four years old share that belief. Sixty percent overall and 72 percent of those aged eighteen to twenty-five viewed presentations using videos, simulations, and computers positively.

E. CONCLUSION

Expert testimony will continue to play an important role in the future. Expert witnesses have been facing increased scrutiny in the U.S. and worldwide. For more effective expert testimony, lawyers and experts must be aware of the factors that the courts will evaluate in order to determine whether an expert is qualified or not, as well as jurors' changing perceptions of experts.

INDEX

103 Investors I, L.P. v. Square D Co., 381
$141,770.00 in United States Currency, United States v., 254–255
985 Assocs., Ltd. v. Daewoo Elecs. Am., Inc., 64

Abdi, United States v., 199
Abernathy v. State (Mississippi), 154
Abuse of discretion standard
  First Circuit, 1–3, 4, 8
  Second Circuit, 28
    Connecticut state courts, 61
    Vermont state courts, 65
  Fourth Circuit, 110–111
  Fifth Circuit, Mississippi state courts, 154
  Sixth Circuit, 159
  Ninth Circuit, 340–341
  Tenth Circuit, 377–379
  Eleventh Circuit, 393–395
  Eighth Circuit, 229–230
Acca v. Clemons Props., Inc., 54
Acceptance Insurance Companies Securities Litigation, In re, 253, 291
Access Now, Inc. v. SW. Airlines Co., 395
Accident reconstruction
  First Circuit, 17–18
  Fourth Circuit, Virginia state courts, 129
  Fifth Circuit
    Mississippi state courts, 154–155
    Texas state courts, 148
  Sixth Circuit, 159–160, 169–170
  Eighth Circuit, 251–252, 265, 285, 288, 295–296
    Iowa state courts, 303
    Nebraska state courts, 314, 316
Accounting testimony
  Sixth Circuit, 185
  Seventh Circuit, 221
  Eighth Circuit, 247–251, 270–271
    Nebraska state courts, 291, 314
ACE-V methodology, 460–461
Acid-phosphate tests, 256
Acosta-Mestre v. Hilton Int'l of Puerto Rico, Inc., 9
Adams v. Cooper Industries, Inc., 172, 185
Adams v. NVR Homes, Inc., 115–116, 120
Adcock v. Miss. Transp. Comm'n, 154
Adesina v. Aladan Corp., 26
Affidavits and declarations
  Second Circuit, 36

  Sixth Circuit, 205
  Seventh Circuit, 213, 224
  Eighth Circuit
    Iowa state courts, 269
    Minnesota state courts, 309
    Nebraska state courts, 291
  Ninth Circuit
    Nevada state courts, 365
    Oregon state courts, 369
  Tenth Circuit, 381
Agha v. Feiner, 92, 98
Aguilar, United States v., 333
Aguilera v. Mount Sinai Hosp. Med. Ctr., 224
Ahlberg v. Chrysler Corp., 239–240
Akerson v. Falcon Transport Co., 5
Akkerman v. Mecta Corp., 330
Alabama district courts, 400–404, 414–415
Alabama state courts, 421–427
Alaska state courts, 341–345
Alatorre, United States v., 336, 337
Alberico, State (New Mexico) *v.*, 386–387
Alessio v. Crook, 201
Alfa Corp. v. OAO Alfa Bank, 31
Alienation of affections actions, 297
Allen, People v., 350
Allen v. Brown Clinic, P.L.L.P., 233
Alsbach v. Bader, 309
Alt, State (Minnesota) *v.*, 305
Alvarado v. Diamond Offshore Mgmt. Co., 140
Alzanki, United States v., 6
Amador-Galvan, United States v., 331
Amaral, United States v., 452
Ambrosini v. Labarraque, 445–448
Amendments to Uniform Guidelines for Taxation of Costs, In re, 436–437
American Elevator Co. v. Briscoe, 364
American Fam. Ins. Group v. JVC Americas Corp., 282
American & Foreign Ins. Co. v. General Electric Co., 166
American Honda Motor Co. v. Allen, 208
Americans with Disabilities Act (ADA) cases, 275–276
Amorgianos v. Nat'l R.R. Passenger Corp., 25, 26, 27, 28, 64

Analytical gap test
  First Circuit, 14, 148
  Second Circuit, 28, 33–34
  Fifth Circuit, 135, 147, 148, 156
  Sixth Circuit, 173
  Eighth Circuit, 245, 299
    Nebraska state courts, 313
  Ninth Circuit, 325
Anderson, United States v., 332
Anderson v. Akzo Nobel Coatings, Inc., 370–371
Anderson v. Hess Corp., 293–294
Anderson v. Raymond Corporation, 242
Anderson v. State (Oklahoma), 389
Andrews v. Foster Wheeler LLC, 353
Andrews v. United States Steel Corp., 387
Androgel Antitrust Litigation (No. II), In re, 409–410
Animal studies, 326–327, 449
Antitrust cases
  Sixth Circuit, 173–175
  Seventh Circuit, 208–209
  Eighth Circuit, 249, 251, 274–275, 284, 286
  Eleventh Circuit, 409–410
An v. Active Pest Control South, Inc., 440
Aon Consulting, Inc. v. Midlands Financial Benefits, Inc., 314
Aozminski, United States v., 188
Apollo, Commonwealth (Pennsylvania) *v.*, 103
Appeals, preserving challenges
  First Circuit, 9
  Eighth Circuit, 253, 262
Application for Water Rights of Park County Sportsmen's Ranch, In re, 385
Appraisers and appraisals
  Fourth Circuit, 116
  Fifth Circuit, 136
    Mississippi state courts, 157
  Sixth Circuit, 185–186
  Eighth Circuit
    Missouri state courts, 309
    South Dakota state courts, 320
Arble v. State Farm Mut. Ins. Co., 382
Aredia and Zometa Products Liability Litigation, In re, 180
Arizona state courts, 345–347
Arkansas district courts, 263–267
Arkansas state courts, 299–302
Armstead v. State (Maryland), 125
Arney, United States v., 381
Arnold v. Amada North America, Inc., 287
Arousal tests, 120
Arroyo, Commonwealth (Pennsylvania) *v.*, 104
Asbestos litigation, 57, 305, 329, 441

Association of Mexican-American Educators (AMAE) v. California, 337–338
ATA Airlines, Inc. v. Federal Express Corp., 209, 210
Atlantic Richfield Co. v. Farm Credit Bank, 377
Audio recording evidence, First Circuit, 13
Augustin, United States v., 396–397
Avance v. Kerr-McGee Chem., LLC, 154
Avent v. Commonwealth (Virginia), 128
Avila v. Willits Environmental Remediation Trust, 323, 326, 328
Avitia-Guillen, United States v., 375, 377
Ayala-Pizarro, United States v., 6
Ayers v. Robinson, 221
Ayuluk v. Red Oaks Assisted Living, Inc., 345

Bado-Santana v. Ford Motor Co., 5
Bahena, United States v., 257
Bailey, State (Minnesota) *v.*, 306
Baker, People v., 354
Baker Valley Lumber, Inc. v. Ingersoll-Rand, 22–23
Baker v. Dalkon Shield Claimants Trust, 4
Baker v. John Morrell & Co., 273
Ballance v. Wal-Mart Stores, Inc., 108
Ballinger v. Atkins, 108
Ballistics evidence
  California state courts, 349
  Massachusetts state courts, 20
  NAS report, 462–463
  Nebraska state courts, 314
  New Jersey state courts, 96
  North Dakota state courts, 294
Balodis, Commonwealth (Pennsylvania) *v.*, 100
Bander, State (Washington) *v.*, 371
Bank Brussels Lambert v. Credit Lyonnais (Suisse), 35, 42
Bankruptcy cases, 273, 450
Barabin v. AstenJohnson, Inc., 329
Barber v. Mercer, 147
Barber v. State (Alabama), 423
Barerra-Medina, United States v., 335
Barmeyer v. Montana Power Co., 361–362
Barna v. Commissioner of Public Safety, 305
Barnette, United States v., 110, 120
Barrett v. Rhodia, Inc., 231–232
Barton v. North Slope Borough School District, 343–344
Bastys v. Rothschild, 36
Batangan, State (Hawaii) *v.*, 359
Battered child syndrome, 307–308, 371, 372
Battered woman syndrome, 96, 103, 434–435
Bauldwin, State (Nebraska) *v.*, 316

Baumann v. American Family Mut. Ins. Co., 382
Baycol Prods. Litig., In re, 232–233, 253–254, 277–278
Bealor, State (New Jersey) *v.*, 98
Beard, State (West Virginia) *v.*, 130
Beard v. Meridia Huron Hospital, 202
Beasley, United States v., 110, 124, 255–256
Bednar v. Bassett Furniture Mfg. Co., Inc., 232
Behavioral-science experts, 94
Belk v. Meyer, 121
Bell v. Gonzales, 449
Benavidez-Benevidez, United States v., 331
Benedi v. McNeil-P.P.C., Inc., 118
Benjamin v. Kerik, 32
Benkwith v. Matrixx Initiatives, Inc., 401–402
Bennett v. Richmond, 227
Benn v. United States, 453
Benzene exposure cases
   First Circuit, 3–4, 11
   Second Circuit, 50–51
   Fifth Circuit, 134
      Mississippi state courts, 156
      Texas state courts, 149–150
   Sixth Circuit, 183
Berg Litig., In re, 328
Berner v. Carnival Corporation, 407
Berry, In re, 372
Berry, State (New Jersey) *v.*, 93
Berry v. City of Detroit, 162, 188
Best v. Lowe's Home Centers, Inc., 159, 181–182, 183, 184
Betz v. Pneumo Abex, 101
Beverly, United States v., 196–197
"Beyond the ken," 93, 454
Bielskis v. Louisville Ladder, Inc., 207, 208, 210–211
Binakonsky v. Ford Motor Co., 108, 118
Biomedical and biomechanics experts
   First Circuit, 10
   Third Circuit
      Delaware state courts, 90
      New Jersey state courts, 95
      Pennsylvania state courts, 104
   Fifth Circuit, Mississippi state courts, 154
   Sixth Circuit, 176–178
Birkhead v. State (Mississippi), 155
Bite-mark analysis, 96, 305
Black Cloud, United States v., 256
Black v. Rhone-Poulenc, 120
Blackwell, State (Maryland) *v.*, 125
Black Wolf, United States v., 299
Blades v. Monsanto Co., 237, 254
Bland v. Verizon Wireless, 233

Blasioli, Commonwealth (Pennsylvania) *v.*, 101
Blood alcohol testing
   Fourth Circuit, 119
   Eighth Circuit, 262
   Alaska state courts, 342–343
   California state courts, 355
   Connecticut state courts, 60
   Delaware state courts, 89
   Iowa state courts, 303
   Minnesota state courts, 305, 307
   New Jersey state courts, 96
   Oregon state courts, 368–369
   South Dakota state courts, 318, 319
Bloodstains
   Ninth Circuit, 332
   Arkansas state courts, 300
   Missouri state courts, 312
   North Carolina state courts, 126
   Washington state courts, 371
Bloodsworth v. Smith & Nephew, Inc., 402–403
Blue Dane Simmental Corp. v. American Simmental Assoc., 251
Boca Raton Cmty. Hosp., Inc. v. Tenet Health Care Corp., 393–394
Boehm v. Willis, 65
Bogosian v. Mercedes-Benz of North Am., Inc., 9
Bolin v. State (Nevada), 364
Bonds, United States v., 196
Bonds v. Roy, 356
Bonner v. ISP Technologies, Inc., 234–236
Borawick v. Shay, 42
Bornfield, United States v., 379
Bossier v. State Farm Fire & Cas. Co., 172
Boss v. Nissan North America, Inc., 114
Boston v. Penny Lane Centers, Inc., 356
Bowen v. E. I. DuPont de Nemours & Co., Inc., 86, 87, 91
Bowersfield v. Suzuki Motor Corp., 84
Bradway, Commonwealth (Massachusetts) *v.*, 21
Brady v. Ballay, Thornton, Maloney Med. Assocs., Inc., 105
Braun v. Lorillard Inc., 208
Breast Implant Cases, In re, 45
Breast implant litigation
   Second Circuit, 45
      New York state courts, 57
   Ninth Circuit, 326, 337
   Tenth Circuit, 378
Breathalyzer tests. *See* Blood alcohol testing
Brenman v. Demello, 92, 93
Brewington v. State (Florida), 434–435
Brien, United States v., 6
Brock v. Caterpillar, Inc., 166–167

Brooklyn Floor Maint. Co. v. Providence Wash. Ins. Co., 56
Brooks, State (Vermont) *v.*, 64
Brooks v. Outboard Marine Corp., 30–31
Brooks v. People, 383
Brooks v. SSM Health Care, 310
Brown, People v., 350
Brown, State (Oregon) *v.*, 365–368
Brown, United States v., 403
Brown v. Crown Equipment Corp., 200
Brown v. Raymond Corp., 167
Browne v. Smith, 54
Brundridge v. Fluor Federal Servs., Inc., 372
Bryant v. City of Chicago, 215
Bryant v. Farmers Ins. Exchange, 381
Buckman v. Bombardier Corp., 114–115
Buck v. Ford Motor Co., 184–185
Bullard, State (North Carolina) *v.*, 125–126
Bullcoming v. New Mexico, xxx–xxxi
Bunting v. Jamieson, 390
Burke, State (Arizona) *v.*, 345–346, 347
Burke, State (North Dakota) *v.*, 317
Burley v. Kytec Innovative Sports Equipment, 320
Burlington Northern & Santa Fe Railway Co. v. Grant, 377
Burns Philp Food, Inc., v. Cavalea Cont'l Freight, Inc., 214
Burton v. Danek Med. Inc., 75
Burton v. Wyeth-Ayerst Labs., 139
Bush v. Michelin Tire Corp., 162
Butler v. State (Missouri), 312
Butler v. Union Carbide Corporation, 441
Buzzerd v. Flagship Carwash of Port St. Lucie, Inc., 80
Bynum, United States v., 107, 118–119

Caballero, United States v., 380
Calderin-Rodriguez, United States v., 262
Calderon-Segura, United States v., 332–333
Caldwell v. Warren, 155
Calhoun v. State (Alabama), 422
California state courts, 347–358
Callahan v. Cardinal Glennon Hosp., 312
Calleia, State (New Jersey) *v.*, 100
Campbell v. Keystone Aerial Surveys, Inc., 137
Candlewood Timber Group, LLC v. Pan Am. Energy, LLC, C.A., 92
Capano, State (Delaware) *v.*, 90
Caraker v. Sandoz Pharmaceuticals Corp., 219
Carbotrade S.p.A. v. Bureau Veritas, 45
CardioVention, Inc. v. Medtronic, Inc., 279
Carlen v. Minn. Comprehensive Epilepsy Program, P.A., 281

Carmona, United States v., 26
Carnegie Mellon University v. Hoffmann-LaRoche, Inc., 325–326
Carovski v. Jordan, 41
Carroll v. Litton Systems, Inc., 115
Carr v. Deeds, 112–113
Carter, State (Nebraska) *v.*, 316
Carter v. City of Philadelphia, 82, 83
Cartier, Inc. v. Four Star Jewelry Creations, Inc., 37
Casey v. Geek Squad, 109–110
Casillas, State (Nebraska) *v.*, 314
Causation, general
   First Circuit, 3–4, 14
   Third Circuit, 74
   Fifth Circuit, 134, 141
   Sixth Circuit, 159, 168, 179, 183, 185
   Seventh Circuit, 219
   Eighth Circuit, 236, 263, 276, 280, 290
   Ninth Circuit, 328
   Eleventh Circuit, 399, 402
   District of Columbia, 448–449
   New York state courts, 51
Causation, specific
   Third Circuit, 75
   Fifth Circuit, 141
   Sixth Circuit, 159, 183, 185
   Eighth Circuit, 231, 232, 233, 253
   Ninth Circuit, 330
   Eleventh Circuit, 399
   District of Columbia, 445, 446, 447, 448, 449
   Georgia state courts, 441–442, 443
   Minnesota state courts, 276–277, 307
   Nebraska state courts, 291, 293
   New York state courts, 51
Cauthron, State (Washington) *v.*, 371
Cavallo v. Star Enterprise, 108, 109, 117–118
Cawthorn, United States v., 261
Cebenka v. Upjohn Co., 89
Cela v. Goodyear Tire & Rubber Co., 55
CERCLA actions, 244
Cerruti 1881 S.A. v. Cerruti, Inc., 45
Champagne Metals v. Ken Mac Metals, 379
Champion v. Outlook Nashville, Inc., 162, 187–188
Chapman v. LaBone, 269
Chapman v. State (Wyoming), 389
Chapple, People v., 353
Cheairs v. State (Louisiana), 152
Cheatam, State (Washington) *v.*, 371
Chemical exposure cases. *See* Toxicology/toxic tort cases
Chemistry experts, 118–119. *See also* Toxicology/toxic tort cases

Children's Broadcasting Corp. v. Walt Disney Co., 251
Child sexual-abuse accommodation syndrome, 96
Childs v. Gen. Motors Corp., 73
Chin v. Port Authority of N.Y. & N. J., 28
Chiropractors, 104, 235
Chmiel, Commonwealth (Pennsylvania) *v.*, 101, 102
Christiansen v. Silfies, 105
Christian v. Gray, 388
Citizens Financial Group, Inc. v. Citizens National Bank of Evans City, 77
Civil rights actions, 189–190, 250, 273
Claar v. Burlington Northern Railroad Co., 324, 333
Clark Equip. Co. v. Habecker, 80
Class actions
    Sixth Circuit, 199
    Eighth Circuit, 250, 254, 274–275, 286
        South Dakota state courts, 319
    Ninth Circuit, 336
    future issues, xxxii
Clausen v. M/V New Carissa, 328, 399
Clayton v. County of Cook, 225
Clay v. Ford Motor Co., 169–170
ClearOne Communications, Inc. v. Biamp Sys., 382
Clemens, State (Oregon) *v.*, 368
Clemente v. Blumenberg, 49–50
Clifford, State (Montana) *v.*, 363
Clifford v. United States, 454
Cline, State (Montana) *v.*, 362
Clopten, State (Utah) *v.*, 389
Cloud v. Pfizer, Inc., 327
Coca-Cola Bottling Co. of Memphis, Tenn. v. Gill, 300–301
Coffee v. Dowley Manufacturing Company, Inc., 166
Coffey v. County of Hennepin, 282
Coffin v. Orkin Exterminating Co., Inc., 9–10
Cohen, United States v., 332
Cohlmia v. Ardent Health Services, LLC, 382
Cohlmia v. St. John Medical Ctr., 381
Coleman v. Parkline Corp., 450–451
Cole v. Homier Distributing Co., Inc., 247
Cole v. Town of Los Gatos, 353
Coley, State (Tennessee) *v.*, 201
Collins, United States v., 260
Collins v. Greater N.Y. Sav. Bank, 52
Colon ex rel. Molina v. BIC USA, Inc., 41–42
Colorado state courts, 383–385
Comber v. Prologue, Inc., 118
Comcast Corp. v. Behrend, xxxii
Commonwealth v. _____. *See Name of party*
Concord Boat Corp. v. Brunswick Corp., 251
Condra v. Atlanta Orthopaedic Group, P.C., 439, 441

Confidentiality agreements, 139
Congiusti v. Ingersoll-Rand Co., 99
Connecticut state courts, 59–63
Conroy, United States v., 263
Conspiracy theories, 198
Constellation Power Source, Inc. v. Select Energy, Inc., 40
Constitutional issues, California state courts, 354–355
Construction by Singletree Inc. v. Lowe, 54
Consumer surveys. *See* Surveys
Contract disputes
    Sixth Circuit, 185, 186, 187
    Eighth Circuit, 248, 250
        South Dakota state courts, 318
    Ninth Circuit, California state courts, 347–348
Cook, People v., 349
Cook ex rel. Estate of Tessier v. Sheriff of Monroe County, Fla., 403
Cook v. American Steamship Co., 193
Cook v. Sunbeam Products Inc., 400–401
Cooley v. Lincoln Electric Co., 181
Coombs v. Curnow, 360
Coon, State (Alaska) *v.*, 341–342
Cooper v. Brown, 332
Cooper v. Laboratory Corp. of America Holdings, Inc., 119
Cooper v. Safeway Stores, Inc., 457
Cooper v. Smith & Nephew, Inc., 109, 117
Cooper v. Wal-Mart Transp., 137
Copeland, State (Tennessee) *v.*, 195, 200
Copeland, State (Washington) *v.*, 370
Coratti v. Wella Corp., 51
Cordoba, United States v., 121, 330–331
Corey, State (South Dakota) *v.*, 319
Cortes-Irizarry v. Corporacion Insular de Seguros, 7, 8, 83
Council, State (South Carolina) *v.*, 127
Council, United States v., 461
Court-appointed experts
    Second Circuit, 45
        New York state courts, 57
    Seventh Circuit, Wisconsin state courts, 228
    Ninth Circuit, 337–339
    Eleventh Circuit
        Alabama state courts, 427
        Florida state courts, 436
    District of Columbia, 457–458
Covel v. Rodriguez, 388
Cowan, People v., 349
CQ, Inc. v. TXU Mining Co., 135
Craftsmen Limousine, Inc. v. Ford Motor Co., 249
Cramer v. Powder River Coal, LLC, 391
Crawford v. Washington, xxx–xxxi, 354

Crews, Commonwealth (Pennsylvania) *v.*, 102–103
Crisp, United States v., 121–123
Cross-examination of experts
    First Circuit, xxxi, 4, 17, 24
    Second Circuit, 42
        Vermont state courts, 64
    Third Circuit, Delaware, 92
    Fourth Circuit, 116, 122
        South Carolina state courts, 127
    Seventh Circuit, Illinois, 223
    Eighth Circuit, 234, 248, 295
    Ninth Circuit, Hawaii state courts, 359
    Tenth Circuit, 379
        Oklahoma state courts, 388
    Eleventh Circuit, 405–406, 410
        Florida state courts, 436
    District of Columbia, 454
Crowhorn v. Boyle, 88
Crowley v. Chait, 83
Cua, People v., 351
Cunningham, State (Oregon) *v.*, 369
Cunningham, United States v., 199
Cunningham v. McDonald, 89
Czyszczon v. Universal Lighting Technologies, Inc., 212–213

Daly, State (Nebraska) *v.*, 316
Damages experts
    Fifth Circuit, 135, 137, 138–139, 140
        Mississippi state courts, 152–153
    Sixth Circuit, 163, 185–187
    Seventh Circuit, 220–221
    Eighth Circuit, 247–251, 279, 283–284, 290
        Arkansas state courts, 301
        Missouri state courts, 310
        Nebraska state courts, 315–316
    Eleventh Circuit, 394
Dancy v. Hyster Company, 242, 243
Daniels, State (Missouri) *v.*, 312
Daniels v. Beeks, 457
Daras, United States v., 119
Darling v. J.B. Expedited Services, Inc., 170
Darren M., In re, 223
Daubert factors
    First Circuit
        federal courts, 1–18
        state courts, 19–23
    Second Circuit
        federal courts, 25–34
        state courts, 58–65
    Third Circuit
        Delaware state courts, 85–86
        federal courts, 69–70, 78–79

Fourth Circuit
    federal courts, 107–124
    North Carolina state courts, 126
    South Carolina state courts, 127
    Virginia state courts, 128
    West Virginia state courts, 130
Fifth Circuit
    federal courts, 133–136
    state courts, 146, 152
Sixth Circuit, 204–206
    federal courts, 159
    Kentucky state courts, 201–202
    Michigan state courts, 203
    Ohio state courts, 202
    Tennessee state courts, 200
Seventh Circuit, 207–221
    Indiana state courts, 226
    Wisconsin state courts, 227
Eighth Circuit
    Arkansas state courts, 299–302
    federal courts, 229–299
    Iowa state courts, 302–303
    Minnesota state courts, 304
    Nebraska state courts, 313–316
    North Dakota state courts, 317
    South Dakota state courts, 318–320
Ninth Circuit, 323–335
    Alaska state courts, 341–344
    Arizona state courts, 345–347
    Hawaii state courts, 358–359
    Idaho state courts, 359–361
    Montana state courts, 361–363
    Nevada state courts, 363–365
    Oregon state courts, 365, 366–367
    Washington state courts, 370
Tenth Circuit, 375–379
    Colorado state courts, 383
    New Mexico state courts, 386–387
    Oklahoma state courts, 388
    Utah state courts, 389
    Wyoming state courts, 390
Eleventh Circuit, 393–414
    Alabama state courts, 421, 422–424, 425
    Georgia state courts, 438–443
District of Columbia Circuit, 445–451
Daubert hearings
    Second Circuit, 33, 41–42
    Third Circuit, 83
    Sixth Circuit, 165–166
    Eighth Circuit, 262–263
    Ninth Circuit, 336–337
    Louisiana state courts, 152
    South Dakota state courts, 319

Daubert v. Merrill Dow Pharmaceuticals, Inc.,
    xxvii, xxviii, 460. *See also specific court
    applications*
David E. Watson, P.C. v. United States, 238, 247
Davidson v. Besser Co., 288–289
Davis, State (Missouri) *v.*, 312
Davis, United States v., 109, 123, 256–257
Davison v. Cole Sewell Corp., 165
Davis v. Combustion Eng'g, Inc., 194
Davis v. Kraff, 223
Davis v. Washington, 354
Davi v. Class, 319
Day v. McIlrath, 304
Deal v. Hamilton County Board of Education, 194
Deceptive trade practices, 290
Dedeaux Utility Co. v. City of Gulfport, 157
Dee v. PCS Prop. Mgmt., Inc., 352
*Degelman Indus. Ltd. v. Pro-Tech Welding &
    Fabrication, Inc.*, 36
Deitch v. May, 53
De Jager Const., Inc. v. Schleininger, 163
Delaware state courts, 85–92
Demaree v. Toyota Motor Corp., 169
DeMeyer v. Advantage Auto, 47–48
Demjanjuk, United States v., 194
Dengler, Commonwealth (Pennsylvania) *v.*, 101
De novo review
    Seventh Circuit, 207, 220, 222, 223
    Tenth Circuit, 375
    Florida state courts, 429
    Washington state courts, 372
DePalma v. Rodriguez, 356, 357
Depositions of experts
    First Circuit, 24
    Second Circuit
        Connecticut state courts, 62–63
        New York state courts, 56, 57–58
    Third Circuit, 83–84
        Pennsylvania state courts, 105
    Fourth Circuit, North Carolina state courts,
        126–127
    Fifth Circuit
        Louisiana state courts, 151
        Mississippi state courts, 153
    Sixth Circuit, 205
    Seventh Circuit, Illinois state courts, 225
    Eighth Circuit, South Dakota state courts, 320–321
    Ninth Circuit, California state courts, 356–357
    Tenth Circuit, 381–382
    Eleventh Circuit, 417–418, 419
        Florida state courts, 437, 438
    District of Columbia, 457
DePriest, People v., 350

Deputy v. Lehman Bros., Inc., 460
Derico v. Int'l Bus. Mach. Corp., 45
DES Cases, In re, 45
Design Strategy, Inc. v. Davis, 36
*DG&G, Inc. v. FlexSol Packaging Corp. of
    Pompano Beach*, 238
Dhillon v. Crown Controls Corp., 211
Diaz, United States v., 9, 199
*Dickenson v. Cardiac and Thoracic Surgery of
    Eastern Tennessee*, 160, 178
Dickie v. Shockman, 296–297
Dico, Inc., United States v., 244
Differential diagnosis
    Third Circuit, 75–76
    Fourth Circuit, 116–117
    Sixth Circuit, 159, 181–185
    Seventh Circuit, 219
    Eighth Circuit, 236, 237, 282–283
    Ninth Circuit, 328
    Tenth Circuit, 390
    Eleventh Circuit, 398–399
        Florida state courts, 431
    District of Columbia, 449
Dinkins, State (South Carolina) *v.*, 127
Dion v. Graduate Hosp., Univ. of Penn., 105
DiPetrillo v. Dow Chemical Co., 23
Disclosure requirements
    Second Circuit, 34, 35–38, 42–45
        Connecticut state courts, 62–63
        New York state courts, 52–57
        Vermont state courts, 65–66
    Fourth Circuit, 112–113
    Fifth Circuit, 141, 144
        Mississippi state courts, 153
    Seventh Circuit, Illinois state courts, 225
    Eighth Circuit, 263
        Minnesota state courts, 309
    Ninth Circuit, 339–340
        Alaska state courts, 344
        Arizona state courts, 346
        California state courts, 355–356
        Nevada state courts, 365
        Oregon state courts, 369
        Washington state courts, 373
    Tenth Circuit, 381, 382
    Eleventh Circuit, 414, 415, 419, 420
        Florida state courts, 437
        Georgia state courts, 444
Discovery
    First Circuit, 19
    Second Circuit
        Connecticut state courts, 63
        Vermont state courts, 65–66

Discovery *(continued)*
   Third Circuit, Pennsylvania state courts, 105
   Fifth Circuit
      Louisiana state courts, 150–151
      Mississippi state courts, 153
      Texas state courts, 145–146
   Seventh Circuit
      Illinois state courts, 225
      Indiana state courts, 227
      Wisconsin state courts, 228
   Eighth Circuit
      Arkansas state courts, 302
      Iowa state courts, 304
      Minnesota state courts, 308–309
      Missouri state courts, 312–313
      Nebraska state courts, 316–317
      North Dakota state courts, 318
      South Dakota state courts, 320–321
   Ninth Circuit
      Alaska state courts, 344
      California state courts, 355–356
      Oregon state courts, 369–370
   Eleventh Circuit, 415–416, 417, 420
      Alabama state courts, 426–427
      Florida state courts, 437–438
   District of Columbia, 456–457
Discovery Operating, Inc. v. BP America Prod. Co., 150
Discrimination actions, 250. *See also* Racial discrimination suits
Dishman v. Wise, 410–411
Dissociative identity disorder, 372
District of Columbia, 445–458
   key decisions, 445–456
   rules and procedural issues, 456–458
District of Columbia v. Anderson, 455
DNA evidence
   First Circuit, 12
      Massachusetts state courts, 19
   Second Circuit, New York state courts, 46–47
   Third Circuit, Pennsylvania state courts, 102–103
   Fourth Circuit, Maryland state courts, 125
   Sixth Circuit, 196–197
   Eighth Circuit, 255–256
      Arkansas state courts, 300
      Minnesota state courts, 305, 306
      Missouri state courts, 312
      Nebraska state courts, 316
      North Dakota state courts, 317
      South Dakota state courts, 319
   Ninth Circuit
      California state courts, 349, 354
      Nevada state courts, 364
      Oregon state courts, 366
      Washington state courts, 371
   Eleventh Circuit
      Alabama state courts, 422, 425
      Florida state courts, 434
Dodge v. Cotter, 375, 376–377
Doe v. McFarlane, 310
Dokken, Estate of, 320
Domingo v. T.K., 326
Donaldson v. Cent. Ill. Pub. Serv. Co., 222, 223
Dongguk Univ. v. Yale Univ., 44
Doolin, People v., 351
Doriguzzi, State (New Jersey) *v.*, 93, 94
Dorsey, United States v., 107–108, 109, 124
Doss v. NPC Int'l, Inc., 141–142
Dot-intensity analysis, 96
Douglas v. United States, 455
Downing, United States v., 69, 79
Downs v. Perstorp Components, Inc., 172, 182
Dozier v. Shapiro, 358
Drug-dog testimony, 199, 254–255, 306–307
Drug investigations
   Third Circuit, 79
      Delaware state courts, 88
      New Jersey state courts, 94, 98
   Fourth Circuit, 124
   Eighth Circuit, 254–255, 258–259, 261
      Iowa state courts, 269–270
      Nebraska state courts, 292
   Ninth Circuit, 329, 333–334
      Nevada state courts, 364
Duke v. Lowe's Home Ctrs., Inc., 141
Dunbar v. Shaklee Corp., 237
Duncan v. City of Cedar Rapids, 304
Dungo, People v., 355
Dunkle, Commonwealth (Pennsylvania) *v.*, 100
Dunn, State (Washington) *v.*, 371
Dunn v. Medina Mem'l Hosp., 53
Dunn v. Nexgrill Industries, Inc., 252
Duphily v. Del. Elec. Coop., 92
Dura Automotive Systems of Indiana, Inc. v. CTS Corp., 213–216
Duran v. Cullinan, 223–224
Dyas v. United States, 451–454

Easterby v. Clark, 356–357
East Tennessee Natural Gas v. 7.74 Acres in Wythe County, Virginia, 116
Easum v. Miller, 390
Econometrics, 135
Economic testimony
   Fourth Circuit, 120–121
   Sixth Circuit, 163, 186, 187

Eighth Circuit, 247–251
   Missouri state courts, 310
Edelman, State (South Dakota) *v.*, 318, 319
Ed Peters Jewelry Co. v. C & J Jewelry Co., 8
Edwards, State (Nebraska) *v.*, 316
E.E.O.C. v. Freeman, 186
EEOC v. Green, 8
EEOC v. West Customer Management Group, 404–405
E. I. DuPont de Nemours & Co. v. Robinson, 147, 148, 149
Eighth Circuit, 229–321
   key cases, 229–299
      civil cases, 229–254
      criminal cases, 254–263
      district courts, 263–299
   state law issues, 299–321
Einheber v. Bodenheimer, 55
Elcock v. Kmart Corp., 71–72, 73, 83
Eldredge v. City of St. Paul, 275–276
Eleventh Circuit, 393–444
   key decisions, 393–414
   rules and procedural issues, 414–421
   state law issues, 421–444
Elliot v. Amadas Ind., Inc., 142–143
Ellipsis, Inc. v. The Color Works, Inc., 187
Ellis v. Costco Wholesale Corp., 323, 336
Embody v. Medtronic, Inc., 400
Emotional harm, Eighth Circuit, 246–247, 273
Engineered Products Co. v. Donaldson Company, Inc., 271
Engineering/product design testimony
   First Circuit, 8–9
   Second Circuit, 29–30, 33
      New York state courts, 48–50
      Vermont state courts, 67
   Third Circuit, 70, 71
      Pennsylvania state courts, 101
   Fourth Circuit, 111, 113–115
      West Virginia state courts, 130
   Fifth Circuit, 136–137, 142
   Sixth Circuit, 162–163, 164–169, 177–178, 190
   Seventh Circuit, 210–213
   Eighth Circuit, 237–243, 265–266, 270, 286–287, 293, 296
   Eleventh Circuit, 423
Environmental engineering/hydrology
   Third Circuit, 76–77
   Fourth Circuit, 115–116
   Seventh Circuit, 213–214
   Eighth Circuit, 244
Epidemiological studies
   First Circuit, 4, 11
   Second Circuit, New York state courts, 51
   Third Circuit, New Jersey state courts, 98
   Fourth Circuit, 117–118, 120
   Ninth Circuit, 324–325
   District of Columbia, 447, 449
   Nebraska state courts, 315
Eric L. Cummings, In re, 458
ERISA actions, 161
Ervin v. Johnson & Johnson, Inc., 217
Escobido-Ortiz, State (Hawaii) *v.*, 358
Eskelson v. Davis Hosp. & Med. Center, 389
Estate of Ford v. Eicher, 383, 384
Estate of James Hetherington, Plaintiff/Appellant, v. United States of America, Defendant/Appellee, 399
Eubanks, People v., 348
Evans, United States v., 262
Excessive force, 187–188, 281
Experience-based testimony
   Eighth Circuit, 259
   Alaska state courts, 341, 343–344
   Texas state courts, 147
Expert qualifications
   Third Circuit, 70–72
      Delaware state courts, 87–88
      New Jersey state courts, 98–99
      Pennsylvania state courts, 103–104
   Fifth Circuit, 133, 136–137, 139–140, 142
      Louisiana state courts, 152
      Texas state courts, 146–147
   Sixth Circuit, 159–164
   Seventh Circuit
      Illinois state courts, 224–225
   Eighth Circuit
      Arkansas state courts, 300–301
      Iowa state courts, 303
   Ninth Circuit
      Alaska state courts, 344–345
      Arizona state courts, 345
   Tenth Circuit, 381–382
   District of Columbia, 450–451
Expert reports
   First Circuit, 24
   Second Circuit, 35
   Third Circuit, 84
   Fifth Circuit, 141–142
      Louisiana state courts, 151
      Texas state courts, 150
   Sixth Circuit, 205
   Ninth Circuit, Alaska state courts, 344
   Tenth Circuit, 381, 382
   Eleventh Circuit, 419
   work-product protection, 42
Experts in field, 89

Extrapolation of data, 223–224
Eyewitness identification
    Third Circuit
        New Jersey state courts, 93–94
        Pennsylvania state courts, 103
    Fourth Circuit, 123
    Sixth Circuit, 195–196
        Tennessee state courts, 200–201
    Eighth Circuit, 258, 263
    Ninth Circuit, 331
    Tenth Circuit, 379

False advertising, 15, 125
False confessions, 97
False memory testimony, 345–346
Family Health of Del., Inc. v. Brar, 89, 91
Fargo, City of v. McLaughlin, 317
Farm Bureau Mut. Ins. Co. of Arkansas, Inc. v. Foote, 299–300
Farnam, People v., 349–350
Fast v. Applebee's International, Inc., 286
Fatica v. Superior Court, 357
Faulkner, State (Missouri) *v.*, 312
Faulty memory defense, 450
Fedelich v. Am. Airlines, 16–17
Federal Rule of Criminal Procedure, 141
Federal Rule of Evidence, xxvii–xxviii. *See also under* Rule
Federal Rules of Civil Procedure. *See* Rules and procedural issues
Federal Trade Commission v. Enforma Natural Products, Inc., 338–339
Fees and costs
    Second Circuit, 38–41
        Connecticut state courts, 62–63
    Seventh Circuit
        Illinois state courts, 225–226
        Wisconsin state courts, 228
    Eighth Circuit, 254
    Ninth Circuit
        Idaho state courts, 361
        Montana state courts, 363
        Nevada state courts, 365
    Eleventh Circuit
        Florida state courts, 436–437
        Georgia state courts, 443–444
    District of Columbia Circuit, 451, 458
FELA (Federal Employer's Liability Act) cases, 163–164, 184, 216, 266, 313
Feldman v. N.Y. State Bridge Auth., 56
Feliciano, United States v., 331
Feliciano-Hill v. Principi, 5
FEMA Trailer Formaldehyde Prods. Liab. Litig., In re, 140

Fener v. Operating Engineers Construction Ind. v. Misc. Pension Fund (Local 66), 136
Fenner Investments Ltd. v. Hewlett-Packard, 138
Fensterer v. State (Delaware), 89
Ferebee v. Chevron Chemical Co., 447
Ferrante v. Sciaretta, 99
Ferriso v. Conway Org., 38
Fertig, State (New Jersey) *v.*, 94
Fiber Optic Designs, Inc. v. New England Pottery, 382
Fickle v. State (Nebraska), 314
Fifth Circuit, 133–157
    key decisions, 133–143
    rules and procedures, 143–144
    state law issues, 144–157
Figueroa v. Orleans, 155
Fingerprint evidence
    First Circuit, Massachusetts state courts, 20–21
    Second Circuit, Connecticut state courts, 60
    Third Circuit, 78
        Delaware state courts, 87
    Fourth Circuit, 121–122
        Virginia state courts, 128
    Eighth Circuit, 260
    Ninth Circuit, 332–333
        California state courts, 349–350
    Eleventh Circuit, 423
    NAS report, 460–462
Finley, United States v., 331–332
Firearms identification evidence. *See* Ballistics evidence
Fire cause and origin experts
    Sixth Circuit, 170–172, 191–192
    Eighth Circuit, 244–246, 251–252, 272, 275, 282, 299
        Nebraska state courts, 314–315
        South Dakota state courts, 319
    Eleventh Circuit, 412–414
    District of Columbia, 455
Fireman's Fund Ins. Co. v. Canon U.S.A., Inc., 244, 251–252
First Circuit
    key decisions, 1–18
    local practice tips, 23–24
    rules and procedural issues, 7–8, 18–19
    state law issues, 19–23
First Premier Bank v. Kolcraft Enterprises, 319
First Union National Bank v. Benham, 252–253
First Western Bank Wall v. Olsen, 320
Fish v. Smith, 361
Fit requirement
    First Circuit, 15
    Third Circuit, 69, 79–81
    Fourth Circuit, 109–110

Sixth Circuit, 163, 175, 187
Seventh Circuit, 215, 221
Eighth Circuit, 258
  Nebraska state courts, 313
Eleventh Circuit, 394
  Alabama state courts, 422
District of Columbia Circuit, 452
Fitzgerald, United States v., 120
Fitzpatrick v. Louisville Ladder Corp., 292–293
Flaherty v. Connecticut, 40
Flanagan v. Altria Group, Inc., 163
Flanagan v. State (Florida), 431
Fleet Mgmt., United States v., 75
Flesner v. Bayer, 232
Fletcher v. S. Peninsula Hosp., 344
Florence v. Commonwealth (Kentucky), 202
Florida district courts, 404–407, 415–418
Florida state courts, 427–438
Footprint evidence, 261–262
Ford, State (South Carolina) *v.*, 127
Ford, United States v., 79
Ford Motor Co. v. Ammerman, 227
Foreman v. American Road Lines, Inc., 400, 403–404
Forensic evidence, NAS report, 459–464. *See also specific types of evidence*
Forensic pathologists, 104, 140
Foret, State (Louisiana) *v.*, 152
Forklifts of St. Louis, Inc. v. Komatsu Forklift USA, Inc., 253
Fortune Dynamic Inc. v. Victoria's Secret Stores Brand Mgmt. Inc., 335
Forty, State (Vermont) *v.*, 65
Fosamax Prods. Liab. Litig., In re, 32
Foster v. Richardson, 147
Fourth Circuit, 107–131
  key decisions, 107–124
  state law issues, 124–131
F. P. Woll & Co. v. Fifth & Mitchell St. Corp., 84
Frabizio, United States v., 13–14
Franklin Corp. v. Tedford, 156
Frankson v. Brown & Williamson Tobacco Corp., 48
Franz v. New England Disposal Techs, 43–44
Frazier, United States v., 395, 412–413
Freeman, United States v., 334
Freeman v. Case Corp., 108, 113
Freitas v. Michelin Tire Corp., 33
Frisby, State (New Jersey) *v.*, 93
Fritter v. Dafina, Inc., 38
Frost, State (New Jersey) *v.*, 98
Fry, State (New Mexico) *v.*, 387
Frye v. United States, xxvii–xxviii. *See also* General acceptance test
Fuesting v. Zimmer, Inc., 211–212
Fugate v. Commonwealth (Kentucky), 201

Fullerton v. Gen. Motors Corp., 10
Furlan v. Schindler Elevator Corp., 73–74

Galloway v. Big G Express, Inc., 168
Gammill v. Jack Williams Chevrolet, 147
Gaona, State (Kansas) *v.*, 385
Garcia, United States v., 375
Garibay v. Hemmat, 353
Garland v. Rossknecht, 319
Garnier v. Ill. Tool Works, 40
Garriott v. NCsoft Corp., 135
Gary, United States v., 122
Gary's Implement, Inc. v. Bridgeport Tractor Parts, Inc., 315–316
Gas chromatography/mass spectrometry (GC/MS) testing, 119, 254–255
Gass v. Marriott Hotel Services, Inc., 178
Gatekeeper role of judge
  First Circuit, 3–4, 7–8, 12, 13, 14, 16
  Second Circuit, 25–26, 30–31
    Connecticut state courts, 59
    Vermont state courts, 64, 66
  Fourth Circuit, 108
  Fifth Circuit, 141
  Seventh Circuit, 208
  Ninth Circuit, 323, 333
    California state courts, 348
    Oregon state courts, 366
  Tenth Circuit, 375, 377
    Oklahoma state courts, 388
    Utah state courts, 389
    Wyoming state courts, 390
  Eleventh Circuit, 393, 400
  District of Columbia Circuit, 447
  introduction, xxviii–xxix
Gatewood, United States v., 270
Gaydar v. Sociedad Instituto Gineco-Qururgico Y Planificacion Familiar, 5
Gayz v. Kirby, 54
Geier, People v., 354
Gelsthorpe v. Weinstein, 431
General acceptance test
  introduction, xxvii–xxviii
  First Circuit
    Maine state courts, 22
    Massachusetts state courts, 19–20
  Second Circuit, New York state courts, 46–52, 58
  Third Circuit, 69
    New Jersey state courts, 94–97
    Pennsylvania state courts, 100–103
  Fourth Circuit
    Maryland state courts, 125
    West Virginia state courts, 131

General acceptance test *(continued)*
 Sixth Circuit
  Ohio state courts, 202
  Tennessee state courts, 200
 Seventh Circuit, Illinois state courts, 221–223, 227
 Eighth Circuit
  Minnesota state courts, 304–308
  Missouri state courts, 309–312
  North Dakota state courts, 317
 Ninth Circuit
  Alaska state courts, 341–342
  Arizona state courts, 346
  California state courts, 348–351
  Montana state courts, 361
  Nevada state courts, 364
  Oregon state courts, 365
  Washington state courts, 370–372
 Tenth Circuit
  Colorado state courts, 383
  Kansas state courts, 385–386
  New Mexico state courts, 386
 Eleventh Circuit
  Alabama state courts, 421–423, 425
  Florida state courts, 427–435
 District of Columbia, 453
General Electric Co. v. Joiner, xxvii, xxix. *See also specific court applications*
General Motors Corp. v. Jernigan, 423
Genetically Modified Rice Litigation, In re, 283–284
GenOn Mid-Atlantic, LLC v. Stone & Webster, Inc., 44
Gentry, State (Washington) *v.*, 371
Gentry v. Mangum, 130, 131
George v. Ford Motor Co., 25–26
Georgia district courts, 408–414, 418–421
Georgia state courts, 438–444
Gerardi v. Verizon N.Y., 54
Gianakos, United States v., 257
Giangrasso v. Ass'n for the Help of Retarded Children, 49
Gibson Guitar Corp. v. Paul Reed Smith Guitars, 163
Gier By and Through Gier v. Educational Service Unit No. 16, 246–247
Gilbert v. Daimler Chrysler Corp., 203
Giles v. Miners, Inc., 243
Gilkey v. Schweitzer, 363
Gillum v. United States, 382
Ginsberg v. St. Michael's Hosp., 99
Giordano v. Market Am., Inc., 47
Gipson, United States v., 255
Glaser v. Thompson Medical Co., 179
Glastetter v. Novartis Pharms. Corp., 236, 254
Gleason, State (Idaho) *v.*, 359
Glyman, Commonwealth (Massachusetts) *v.*, 21
Goddard v. State (Missouri), 311–312
Goebel v. Denver & Rio Grande W. R.R. Co., 375, 377
Goeb v. Tharaldson, 304–305
Golden v. Union Pac. R.R. Co., 313
Gold v. Dalkon Shield Claimants Trust, 38, 45
Goldwater v. Postmaster Gen., 41
Gollehon, State (Montana) *v.*, 362
Gonzalez, People v., 461
Gonzalez v. Exec. Airlines, Inc., 15–16
Goode, State (North Carolina) *v.*, 126
Goodman v. Staples, 340
Goodridge v. Hyster Co., 90
Goodwin v. MTD Prods., Inc., 220
Goodyear v. Hyster Co., 88
Government experts, 81
Grace, United States v., 341
Grady v. Frito-Lay, Inc., 100–101, 102
Graham v. Playtex Prods., Inc., 41
Grant v. Bristol-Myers Squibb, 337
Grant v. Ford Motor Co., 154, 155, 156
Grant v. Pharmavite, 290–291
Graves v. Toyota Motor Corp, 142
Grdinich v. Bradlees, 37–38
Great Northern Insurance Company v. Ruiz, 412–413
Greatwalker, United States v., 257
Greene, State (Washington) *v.*, 371–372
Green v. Alpharma, Inc., 301–302
Green v. Cessna Aircraft Co., 22
Gregg v. Indian Motorcycle Corporation, 270
Gregory, State (Washington) *v.*, 371
Gricco, United States v., 78–79
Griffin, State (Connecticut) *v.*, 61
Griffith, United States v., 334
Grimes v. Hoffmann-LaRoche, Inc., 15
Grimmond, United States v., 110
Grinnell Mut. Reins. Co. v. Heritage Ins. Agency, 282
Grisso test, 61
Groobert v. President & Dirs. of Georgetown Coll., 450
Group Health Plan, Inc. v. Philip Morris USA, Inc., 250
Guardia v. Lakeview Regional Medical Center, 152
Guerre-Chaley v. State (Alaska), 342–343
Guidichessi v. ADM Milling Co., 303
Guild v. Gen. Motors Corp., 29
Gulf South Pipeline Co. v. Pitre, 157
Gunn Hill Dairy Properties, LLC v. Los Angeles Dept. of Water & Power, 389, 390
Gunshot residue (GSR) tests, 306

Gurry v. McDaniel, 331
Guthrie, State (South Dakota) *v.*, 318–319
Gutierrez, State (Nebraska) *v.*, 314

Habecker v. Clark Equipment Co., 80, 84
Hadden v. State (Florida), 428
Hair analysis
   Second Circuit, Connecticut state courts, 60
   Eighth Circuit, Missouri state courts, 312
   Ninth Circuit, Nevada state courts, 364
   Eleventh Circuit, Florida state courts, 430
   Sixth Circuit, 197
Hall, United States v., 215
Hallam, Village of v. L.G. Barcus & Sons, Inc., 314
Hallmark v. Eldridge, 364, 365
Hall v. Baxter Healthcare Corp., 326
Hall v. Kurz Enters., 22
Hammond v. Int'l Harvester Co., 70
Handley v. State (Alaska), 344
Handwriting analysis
   First Circuit, Massachusetts state courts, 21
   Third Circuit, 78–79
   Fourth Circuit, 122–123
   Sixth Circuit, 197
   Eighth Circuit, 293
      North Dakota state courts, 317
   NAS report, 463
Hanford Nuclear Reservation Litigation, In re, 327–328, 330, 336
Hangarter v. Provident Life and Accident Ins. Co., 336
Hankey, United States v., 333, 335
Hankins v. Ford Motor Co., 143
Hansen v. United States, 181
Hans v. Mem. Hosp. at Gulfport, 155
Harbor Software, Inc. v. Applied Sys., Inc., 45
Hardyman v. Norfolk & W. Ry. Co., 182, 184
Harper v. State (Georgia), 438
Harrigan v. Del. Transit Corp., 90
Harrington v. State, 426
Harris, United States v., 123
Harris v. Long Island R.R. Co., 50
Harris v. State (Alaska), 344
Harris v. State (Oklahoma), 388–389
Hartford Ins. Co. v. Gen. Elec. Co., 17
Hartley v. St. Paul Fire & Marine Insurance Co., 170–171
Harvey, State (New Jersey) *v.*, 94, 95
Harvey v. Allstate Insurance Co., 191–192
Hasan, State (Connecticut) *v.*, 60
Havasy v. Resnick, 105
Hawaii state courts, 358–359
Hawthorne Partners v. AT&T Technologies, Inc., 186

Hayden v. Gordon, 54
Hayes v. Carroll, 146–147
Hayes v. State (Florida), 434
Health-care fraud, 198–199
Hearsay
   Second Circuit, 32, 49
   Sixth Circuit, 171
   Eleventh Circuit, Georgia state courts, 439, 443
   District of Columbia, 454, 456
   U.S. Supreme Court, xxx
Hedonic damages
   Fourth Circuit, West Virginia state courts, 130
   Sixth Circuit, 187
   Seventh Circuit, 221
Hein v. Merck & Co., Inc., 187
Heller v. Shaw Indus., Inc., 69, 73, 74–75, 76, 80, 85
Henderson, People v., 349
Henderson, State (New Jersey) *v.*, 93, 94
Hendrix ex rel. G.P. v. Evenflo Co., Inc., 398
Heparin Products Liability Litigation, In re, 181
Herd v. Town of Pawling, 55
Hermanek, United States v., 333–334, 337
Hernandez, State (North Dakota) *v.*, 317
Hernandez v. Superior Court, 355–356
HGN test. *See* Horizontal gaze nystagmus (HGN) test
Hickerson v. District Pride Mobility Products Corp., 245
Higgins v. Diversey Corp., 108
Higgs v. State (Nevada), 363, 365
High Fructose Corn Syrup Antitrust Litigation, In re, 208–209
Hill v. Koppers, Inc., 143
Hill v. Mills, 156
Hines, United States v., 463
Hinkson, United States v., 341
Hisenaj v. Kuehner, 95
Hobbs v. Harken, 310
Hodgson, State (Minnesota) *v.*, 305
Hofer, State (South Dakota) *v.*, 318
Hoffman v. Caterpillar, Inc., 215
Hoffman v. Constr. Protective Servs., 340
Hofmann v. Toys "R" Us-N.Y. Ltd. P'ship., 49
Hoganson v. Mernard, Inc., 167
Holbrook v. Lykes Bros. Steamship Co., 70–71, 72, 82
Hollander v. Sandoz Pharmaceuticals Corp., 378
Holmes, State (Nevada) *v.*, 364
Hood v. Matrixx Initiatives, Incorporated, 432–433
Hopper v. M/V UBC Singapore, 136–137, 139
Horizontal gaze nystagmus (HGN) test
   Third Circuit
      New Jersey state courts, 94, 96
      Pennsylvania state courts, 103

Horizontal gaze nystagmus (HGN) test *(continued)*
   Fourth Circuit, 124
   Eighth Circuit
      Nebraska state courts, 314
      North Dakota state courts, 317
   Ninth Circuit
      California state courts, 348
      Montana state courts, 362
      Oregon state courts, 368–369
Hormone replacement therapy (HRT), 263–264, 282–283, 307
Horn, United States v., 123–124
Horton v. Hendrix, 443
Hose v. Chicago & Northwestern Transp. Co., 237
Hottinger v. Trugreen Corp., 226
Hough v. State Farm Insurance Company, 180
Houlihan v. Invacare Corp., 37
Hoult v. Hoult, 7–8
Houser, State (Nebraska) *v.*, 316
Housley v. Orteck International, Inc., 268
Houston v. State (Arkansas), 300
Houwman v. Gaiser, 297
Howard v. Clark, 331
Howell v. State (Tennessee), 201
Hoyos, People v., 350
Huchting, State (Missouri) *v.*, 312
Hulse v. Department of Justice, Motor Vehicle Division, 362
Human factors
   Fifth Circuit, 140
   Sixth Circuit, 169–170
   Seventh Circuit, 211
   Eighth Circuit, 237–243
      South Dakota state courts, 320
Hunt v. City of Minneapolis, 253
Huss v. Gayden, 133
Hutchinson v. American Family Mut. Ins., 302, 303
Hutchins v. Fletcher Allen Health Care, Inc., 65
Hybrid fact-opinion testimony, 118–119
Hyundai Motor America v. Applewhite, 154, 156

Ibar v. State (Florida), 430
Idaho state courts, 359–361
Iles v. Ogden, 152–153
Illinois state courts, 221–226
Impastato, United States v., 141
Imperial Trading Co. v. Travelers Property Cas. Co., 140
Inama v. Brewer, 361
In camera review, 44–45
Independent Fire Ins. Co. v. Sunbeam Corp., 152
Indiana state courts, 226–227
Indigent defendants, 427, 436, 458

Inductively coupled plasma-atomic emission spectrography (ICP) tests, 256–257
Industrial hygienists, 50
Industrial Silicon Antitrust Litig., In re, 76
Industry standards, 77
Innis Arden Golf Club v. Pitney Bowes, Inc., 35
In re. *See Name of party*
Insanity defense
   Eighth Circuit, 260
   Ninth Circuit, Washington state courts, 371
   Eleventh Circuit, 416, 417
      Florida state courts, 436
Insurance. *See also* Fire cause and origin experts
   Fifth Circuit, 137
      Mississippi state courts, 155
   Eighth Circuit, 261, 268, 280, 282, 284, 291
   Ninth Circuit, 340
Intellectual property cases
   First Circuit, 16
   Third Circuit, 77
   Fifth Circuit, 135, 136, 138–139
   Sixth Circuit, 163, 190, 191, 194
   Eighth Circuit, 247–248, 251, 271, 272, 279, 284
   Ninth Circuit, 335
Interplan Architects, Inc. v. C. L. Thomas, Inc., 138
Interrogatories
   First Circuit, 19
   Third Circuit
      Delaware state courts, 92
      Pennsylvania state courts, 105
   Fourth Circuit, North Carolina state courts, 126–127
   Fifth Circuit
      Louisiana state courts, 151
      Mississippi state courts, 153
   Sixth Circuit, 205
   Seventh Circuit
      Illinois state courts, 225
      Indiana state courts, 227
      Wisconsin state courts, 228
   Eighth Circuit, 258
      Arkansas state courts, 302
      Minnesota state courts, 308–309
      Nebraska state courts, 316–317
      South Dakota state courts, 320
   Eleventh Circuit, 418
In The Interest of T.A., Child, 318
Investor Resource Svcs., Inc. v. Cato, 155
Iowa district courts, 267–274
Iowa state courts, 302–304
IP Innovation LLC v. Red Hat, Inc., 138
Iron Cloud, United States v., 262
Isely v. Capuchin Province, 192
Ivan Mustard Trust, In Matter of, 363

Jackson, City of v. Spann, 157
Jackson, People v., 349
Jackson v. Nutmeg Techs., Inc., 51
Jackson v. State (Arkansas), 301
Jackson v. United States, 458
Jackson v. Unocal Corp., 383, 384
Jacobsen v. Deseret Book Co., 381, 382
Jacobson v. $55,900 in U.S. Currency, 306–307
Jahn v. Equine Services, PSC, 178–179
James River Insurance Co. v. Rapid Funding, 379
Janes, State (Washington) *v.*, 371, 372
Janis, United States v., 260
Janopoulos v. Harvey L. Walner & Assocs., Ltd., 410
Janssen Pharmaceutical Products, L.P. v. Hodgemire ex rel. Hodgemire, 433–434
Jarvis v. Ford Motor Co., 29
Jaurequi v. Carter Mfg. Co., Inc., 243
Jawara, United States v., 335
J.B.D.L. Corp. v. Wyeth-Ayerst Laboratories, Inc., 174–175
J.B. Hunt Transport, Inc. v. General Motors Corp., 252
Jeanes v. Allied Life Ins. Co., 271
Jenkins, United States v., 455
Jenkins v. United States, 449, 455–456
Jenner v. Dooley, 319
Jennings v. Palomar Pomerado Health Systems, Inc., 352, 353
Jensionowski v. Beck, 13
Jenson v. Eveleth Taconite Co., 246
Jimenez v. GNOC Corp., 97
Jimico Enters. v. Lehigh Gas Corp., 40
Jinro America, Inc. v. Secure Investments Inc., 335
John Doe 76C v. Archdiocese of Saint Paul and Minneapolis, 308
John's Heating Svc. v. Lamb, 342
Johnson, People v., 351
Johnson, United States v., 256
Johnson v. Commonwealth (Kentucky), 202
Johnson v. District of Columbia, 455
Johnson v. Greenberg, 54
Johnson v. Knoxville Community School District, 303
Johnson v. Manitowoc Boom Trucks, Inc., 159, 164–165
Johnson v. Riverdale Anesthesia Associates, P.C., 439–440
Johnson v. Vane Line Bunkering, Inc., 75
John v. Im, 128
Joint E. & S. Dist. Asbestos Litig., In re, 45
Jolly v. State, 90
Jones, People v., 354
Jones, State (Minnesota) *v.*, 306

Jones, State (South Carolina) *v.*, 127
Jones, United States v., 193, 197
Jones v. Constantino, 105
Jones v. Otis Elevator Co., 413
Jones v. United States, 326
Jordan, United States v., 257
Jouve v. State Farm Fire & Cas. Co., 142
J.Q., State (New Jersey) *v.*, 93
Junk v. Terminix Int'l Co., 231, 267–268
J.V. v. Dept. of Children and Family Services, 436

Kalaba v. Gray, 357–358
Kansas state courts, 385–386
Kass v. W. Bend Co., 29
Katare v. Katare, 370
Katt v. City of New York, 32–33
Kayne, United States v., 6
Kearney v. Philip Morris, Inc., 12–13
Keightley, State (Missouri) *v.*, 312
Kelly, People v., 348–351
Kempner Mobile Elecs., Inc. v. Southwest Bell Mobile Sys., 207
Kemp v. State (New Jersey), 97
Kennedy v. Collagen Corp., 326
Kenosha v. Heublein, 215
Kentucky Speedway, LLC v. National Association of Stock Car Auto Racing, Inc., et al., 174
Kentucky state courts, 201–202
Kern River Gas Transmission Co. v. 6.17 Acres of Land, 381, 382
Key pathway analysis, 191–192
Khan v. Singh, 97
Khoury v. Philips Medical Systems, 238
Kilgore v. Carson Pirie Holdings, Inc., 191
Kilhullen v. Kansas City S. Ry., 154–155
Kilpatrick v. Breg, Inc., 180
Kim, State (Hawaii) *v.*, 359
Kime, United States v., 258
Kinder, State (Missouri) *v.*, 312
King v. Burlington Northern Santa Fe Ry. Co., 315
King v. Enterprise Rent-A-Car Company, 189
King v. State (Florida), 429, 430
Kinney, State (Vermont) *v.*, 64
Kirchner v. Wilson, 316
Kirsch, State (Connecticut) *v.*, 60
Kivland v. Columbia Orthopaedic Group, LLP, 311
Klatsky v. Lewis, 55
Klawitter, State (Minnesota) *v.*, 305
Klein, State (Washington) *v.*, 371
Kloepfer v. Lumbermens Mutual Casualty Co., 363
Klutman v. Sioux Falls Storm, 320
Knotts v. Black & Decker, Inc., 171
Knous v. ConAgra Foods, Inc., 173
Koch Ref. Co. v. Jennifer L. Boudreaux MV, 139

Kolesar v. United Agri Products, Inc., 184
Koplewitz v. Hamilton, 66
Koutnik v. Brown, 216
Kozak v. Medtronic, Inc., 139
Krause Inc. v. Little, 363
Kromah, State (Minnesota) *v.*, 306
Krueger v. Johnson & Johnson, 273–274
Krygier v. Airweld, Inc., 53
Kudabeck v. Kroger Company, 235
Kuhn v. Sandoz Pharmaceuticals Corp., 385–386
Kuhn v. Wyeth, Inc., 230–231
Kumho Tire Co. v. Carmichael, xxvii, xxix–xxx. *See also specific court applications*
Kuper v. Lincoln-Union Elec. Co., 319
Kurncz v. Honda North America, Inc., 187
Kuxhausen v. Tillman Partners, 386
Kyler, United States v., 397
Kyser v. Harrison, 421

Lagola v. Thomas, 92
Lake Cherokee Hard Drive Technologies, LLC. v. Bass Computers, Inc., 139
Lakie v. SmithKline Beecham, 448–449
Lamere v. N.Y. State Office for the Aging, 39, 40
Landrigan v. Celotex Corp., 98
Langan, United States v., 195
Lanigan, Commonwealth (Massachusetts) *v.*, 19–20
Lapsley v. Xtek, Inc., 207, 210
Larry Reed & Sons, United States v., 261
Larson v. Kempker, 235
Lasky v. Union Electric Co., 309
Latent print evidence. *See* Fingerprint evidence
Lauria v. Nat'l R.R. Passenger Corp., 70
Lauzon v. Senco Products, Inc., 239, 242–243, 292–293
Lawrence v. Raymond Corp., 164
Layton, Ex parte, 423
L.C.D. v. District of Columbia, 456
L.C.H. v. T.S., 342
Leaf v. Goodyear, 302
Leahy, People v., 348, 350, 351
Leblanc, United States v., 197–198
LeBlanc v. Chevron USA, Inc., 134
Ledin v. State (Minnesota), 305
Leep, State (West Virginia) *v.*, 131
Lee v. Metropolitan Govt. of Nashville and Davidson County, et al., 162
Lee v. Nat'l RR Passenger Corp. (Amtrak), 142
Legal experts, 268–269, 270–271
Lemler, State (South Dakota) *v.*, 319
Lemmermann v. Blue Cross Blue Shield of Wisconsin, 218–219
Lemmon v. Wyeth, LLC, 282–283

Lennon v. Norfolk and Western Ry. Co., 220
Levy v. United States, 136
Lewis v. CITGO Petroleum Corp., 207
Lewis v. State (Alabama), 422
Libby, United States v., 450
Libel suits, 326–327
Licciardi v. TIG Ins. Grp., 19
Lidle v. Cirrus Design Corp., 35
Lightman, United States v., 77
Lincoln, City of v. Realty Trust Group, 313
Linkage analysis, 97
Linn v. Fossum, 436
Lissak v. Cerabona, 55
Lobsters, Inc. v. Evans, 14
Lockheed Litigation Cases, 347, 352
Loeffel Steel Products, Inc. v. Delta Brands, Inc., 208
Loftus, State (South Dakota) *v.*, 319
Logerquist v. McVey, 346
Lohmeier v. Hammer, 347
Long v. Missouri Delta Med. Ctr., 310
Lopez, People v., 355
Lopez-Martinez, United States v., 336
Lopez v. Scribner, 337
Lost-profits analysis, 137, 146, 187, 247
Loudermill v. Dow Chemical Co., 235
Louisiana federal courts, 139–141, 144
Louisiana state courts, 150–153
Love, State (Missouri) *v.*, 312
Love, United States v., 461
Loving, State (Minnesota) *v.*, 306
Lowe, United States v., 12
Lucero, State (Arizona) *v.*, 346
Luminol. *See* Bloodstains
Lupton, United States v., 220
Lust v. Merrell Dow Pharmaceuticals, 325
Lynch v. Trek Bicycle Corp., 25
Lyons v. Barrazotto, 456
Lytle v. Ford Motor Co., 226

MacDonald, State (Maine) *v.*, 22
Machesney v. Larry Bruni, 451
Machmuller, State (South Dakota) *v.*, 318
Mack, State (Minnesota) *v.*, 305
Mack Trucks, Inc. v. Tamez, 147
MacLennan, State (Minnesota) *v.*, 307–308
Maelega, State (Hawaii) *v.*, 358
Magee v. Paul Revere Life Ins. Co., 41
Maggi v. RAS Development, Inc., 223
Magistrini v. One Hour Martinizing Dry Cleaning, 80
Maher v. Quest Diagnostics, Inc., 59, 60, 61–62
Maine District Court, 9–11, 18

Maine state courts, 22
Maines v. Kenmorth Trucking Co. (Alaska), 344
Major League Baseball Props., Inc. v. Salvino, Inc., 25
Malpractice claims, professional, 252–253. *See also* Medical malpractice
Mamah, United States v., 215
Mancuso v. Consolidated Edison Co., 45
Mannarino v. United States, 40
Maras v. Avis Rent A Car System, Inc., 279–280
Marcum v. Adventist Health System/West, 367
Marcus, State (New Jersey) *v.*, 97
Margolies v. McCleary, Inc., 248
Maritime Overseas Corp. v. Ellis, 149
Marks, In re Commitment of, 150
Marmo v. IBP Inc., 292
Marmo v. Tyson Fresh Meats, Inc., 234–235, 254
Marriage of Alexander, In re, 222
Marriage of Jawad, In re, 222
Marrington, State (Oregon) *v.*, 367–368
Marron v. Stromstad, 341, 343
Marsh v. Valyou, 429, 431
Marsingill v. O'Malley, 341, 343
Martha S. v. Alaska Dept. of Health & Social Servs., 344
Martin, State (Washington) *v.*, 372
Martin, United States v., 263
Martinez, United States v., 198, 256
Marvin Lumber and Cedar Co. v. PPG Industries Inc., 249
Maryland Casualty Co. v. Therm-O-Disc, Inc., 111–112
Maryland state courts, 125
Mascarenas v. Miles, 289
Mason, State (Nebraska) *v.*, 314
Mason v. Rizzi, 90
Massachusetts District Court, 11–14, 18–19, 464
Massachusetts state courts, 19–21
Mathis, United States v., 80, 81
Mattis v. Carlon Elec. Prods., 299
Mauro v. Owens-Corning Fiberglas Corp., 99
Mayhorn v. Logan Medical Foundation, 130
Maze v. Regions Bank, Inc., 283
McCabe et al. v. Macauley et al., 268–269
McCalla v. Harnischfeger Corp., 99
McClain v. Metabolife International, Inc., 398, 409
McClendon, State (Connecticut) *v.*, 61
McCreless v. Global Upholstery Co., 400
McCuistion, State (Washington) *v.*, 371
McCulloch v. Hartford Life & Accident Ins. Co., 40
McDaniel v. CSX Transportation, Inc., 200
McDermott v. Alvey, Inc., 55
McDonald v. Mem. Hosp. at Gulfport, 155

McDowell v. Brown, 411
McGovern ex rel. McGovern v. Brigham & Women's Hosp., 14
McGrew v. State, 226, 227
McGuire et al. v. Davidson Manufacturing Corporation, 273
McGuire v. Seltsam, 310
McIntosh v. Monsanto Company, 284
McKee v. Bowers Window & Door Co., 155
McKeown v. Pitcock, 155
McKnight By and Through Ludwig v. Johnson Controls, Inc., 253
McKown, People v., 222
McLean, State (New Jersey) *v.*, 93
McNeel v. Union Pac., 313
McNeil-PCC, Inc. v. Merisant Co., 16
McPike v. Corghi S.P.A., 265–266
McSwain v. Sunrise Medical, Inc., 142
M.C. v. Yeargin, 311
McWhorter, People v., 349
Medalen v. Tiger Drylac U.S.A., Inc., 280–281
Medical causation
    First Circuit, 14
    Third Circuit, 74–75
    Fourth Circuit, 116–118
    Fifth Circuit, Mississippi state courts, 155
    Sixth Circuit, 159, 178–185, 193
    Seventh Circuit, 216–220
        Indiana state courts, 227
    Eighth Circuit, 230–237, 263–264, 266–267, 268, 279–280, 281, 282–283, 288, 289, 290–291, 293–294
        Arkansas state courts, 301–302
        Minnesota state courts, 307
        Missouri state courts, 311
        South Dakota state courts, 320
    Ninth Circuit, 324–330
        Alaska state courts, 342
        California state courts, 351–354
        Idaho state courts, 360
    Tenth Circuit, 390
    Eleventh Circuit, 407
        Florida state courts, 431, 432
Medical examiners, 118
Medical malpractice
    First Circuit, 14, 15
    Second Circuit, Connecticut state courts, 61–62
    Third Circuit, New Jersey state courts, 97
    Fifth Circuit
        Mississippi state courts, 155, 156
        Texas state courts, 146–147
    Sixth Circuit, 160
    Seventh Circuit, Illinois state courts, 224–225

Medical malpractice *(continued)*
   Eighth Circuit, 281
      Minnesota state courts, 309
   Ninth Circuit, 326
      Arizona state courts, 347
   Eleventh Circuit, 410–412
   District of Columbia, 455
Meemic Ins. Co. v. Hewlett-Packard Co., 168
Melberg v. Plains Marketing, L.P., 295–296
Melcher, People v., 462
Melendez-Diaz v. Massachusetts, xxx–xxxi, 460
Melendez v. Roman Catholic Archdiocese of N.Y., 56
Melton, In re, 453–454
Mendler v. Aztec Motel Corp., 77
Mendoza-Paz, United States v., 333, 337
Mensink v. American Grain, et al., 302
Mental state or condition
   Eighth Circuit, 258
   Ninth Circuit, 331–332
   Eleventh Circuit, 415–416, 417
   Arizona state courts, 346–347
   Florida state courts, 436
   Idaho state courts, 361
   New Jersey state courts, 100
   Washington state courts, 372
Menz v. New Holland North America, Inc., 285
Mercer v. Pittway Corp., 302
Mercer v. Rockwell Intern. Corp., 172–173
Merrell Dow Pharms., Inc. v. Havner, 149
Merwin, State (Idaho) *v.*, 360
Messner v. Northshore University HealthSystem, 208
Metabolife Int'l v. Wornick, 326–327
Metavante Corp. v. Emigrant Savings Bank, 208, 220
Meterlogic, Inc. v. KLT, Inc., 250
Metropolitan Life Insurance Company v. Bancorp Services, 284
Metropolitan Prop. & Cas. Ins. Co. v. Clayco Constr. Group, LLC, 141
Metropolitan St. Louis Equal Housing Opportunity Council v. Gundaker Real Estate Co., 287–288
Meyer, United States v., 269–270
Meyers v. Nat'l R.R. Passengers Corp., 216–217
M. G. Bancorporation, Inc. v. Le Beau, 85–86
MGE UPS Systems, Inc. v. GE Consumer and Indus., Inc., 135
MGM Well Services, Inc. v. Mega Lift Systems, LLC, 137
Michael v. Mr. Heater, Inc., 220
Michigan state courts, 203–204

Middleton, People v., 47
Middleton, State (Oregon) *v.*, 366
Middleton v. United States, 454
Mid-South Retina, LLC v. Conner, 155
Mike's Train House, Inc. v. Lionel, LLC, 190
Milanowicz v. Raymond Corp., 73
Millenium Expressions, Inc. v. Chaus Mktg., Ltd., 37
Millenkamp v. Davisco Foods, Int'l, 336
Miller Brewing Co. v. Ed Roleson, Jr., Inc., 301
Miller v. Baker Implement Co., 254
Miller v. Bike Athletic Company, 202
Miller v. Brass Rail Tavern, 103–104, 105
Miller v. Eldridge, 202
Miller v. Genie Ind., Inc., 143
Miller v. Pfizer, 377–378
Miller v. United States, 76
Mills-Stevens v. Travelers Ins. Co., 22
Milward v. Acuity Specialty Prods. Grp., Inc., 3–4
Mims v. Electronic Data Systems Corp., 190
Minix v. Canarecci, 207
Minnesota District Court, 274–282
Minnesota state courts, 304–309
Minor v. State (Alabama), 422
Miranda v. Bomel Const. Co., Inc., 347
Mirror Worlds, LLC v. Apple, Inc., 138
Mississippi federal courts, 141–143, 144
Mississippi state courts, 153–157
Mississippi Transp. Comm'n v. Buchanan, 157
Mississippi Transp. Comm'n v. McLemore, 153–154, 155
Missouri district courts, 282–289
Missouri state courts, 309–313
Mitchell, People v., 348
Mitchell, United States v., 70, 72
Mitchell v. Barnes, 154
Mitchell v. Commonwealth (Kentucky), 201
Mitchell v. Gencorp Inc., 379
Mitchell v. United States, 4
Modelski v. Navistar Int'l Transp. Corp., 224
Moeller, State (South Dakota) *v.*, 319
Moeller v. Weber, 319
Mohney v. USA Hockey, Inc., 177
Moltner v. Starbucks Coffee Co., 25
Montalbo, State (Hawaii) *v.*, 358
Montana state courts, 361–363
Montes v. Union Pacific R.R. Co., 289
Montgomery, United States v., 260
Montgomery Cnty. v. Microvote Corp., 73
Moody, Ex parte, 427
Mooney, United States v., 463
Moore, State (Montana) *v.*, 362
Moore, State (New Jersey) *v.*, 98
Moore v. Gatica, 147

Moore v. P&G - Clairol, Inc., 218
Moore v. State (Arkansas), 300
Mooring Capital Fund, LLC v. Knight, 381
Morales v. American Honda Motor Co., 159, 192, 193–194
Morgan, State (South Carolina) *v.*, 127
Morgan v. United Parcel Service, 250
Morin v. United States, 329–330, 336
Mouzone, United States v., 462
Mukhtar v. California State University, 328, 334–335
Multiple chemical sensitivity, 9–10, 34, 118, 282
Multiple regression analysis, 76
Murillo, United States v., 333
Murray v. Payne, 154
Murray v. State (Florida), 430
Myers v. Illinois Central R.R. Co., 207, 216

Nacchio, United States v., 375, 381
Naeem v. McKesson Drug Co., 208, 220
Naegele, United States v., 450
Nagib v. Meridian Medical Technologies, Inc., 169
National Academy of Sciences (NAS) report, 459–465
National Bank of Commerce of El Dorado v. Associated Milk Producers, Inc., 237
National Bank of Commerce of El Dorado v. Dow Chem., 266–267
National Research Council, 459–464
Native Americans, 161–162, 257, 258, 298
Nebraska District Court, 289–293
Nebraska Nutrients v. Shepherd, 315
Nebraska Plastics, Inc. v. Holland Colors Americas, Inc., 248–249
Nebraska state courts, 313–317
Negligence claims
 First Circuit, 1–3, 9–10
 Fourth Circuit, 129
 Fifth Circuit, 147
  Mississippi state courts, 156
 Sixth Circuit, 160, 165, 166, 170–171, 178–179, 181
 Seventh Circuit, 211–212, 216
 Eighth Circuit, 242, 262, 266, 268, 273–274
  Arkansas state courts, 300, 344–345
 Ninth Circuit, Alaska state courts, 343–344
 Tenth Circuit, 381
 Eleventh Circuit, 410
  Georgia state courts, 440
Neiberger v. Fed Ex Ground Package Sys., Inc., 382
Nelson, People v., 351
Nelson v. American Home Products Corp., 288
Nelson v. Tenn. Gas Pipeline Co., 193

Nelson v. Wal-Mart Stores, Inc., 264–265
Nemeth, State (Ohio) *v.*, 202
Nemir v. Mitsubishi Motors Corp., 177–178
Nesbitt, State (New Jersey) *v.*, 100
Nester Commercial Roofing, Inc. v. American Builders and Contractors Supply Co., 380
Neurontin Product Liability Litigation, In re, 51–52
Nevada state courts, 363–365
Newcomer v. Workmen's Comp. Appeal Bd., 100
Newell Rubbermaid, Inc. v. Raymond Corp., 164
New Hampshire District Court, 14–15, 18
New Hampshire state courts, 22–23
Newhart v. State, 227
New Haverford P'ship v. Stroot, 86
New Jersey state courts, 92–100
Newkirk v. Conagra Foods, 328
New Mexico state courts, 386–387
News Publishing Co. v. Butler, 440
New York State Courts, 46–58
New York State Silicone Breast Implant Litig., In re, 57
New York v. Solvent Chem. Co., 40
Nichols, United States v., 261
Nichols v. American Nat. Ins. Co., 246
Nilavar v. Mercy Health System-Western Ohio, 174
Nimely v. City of New York, 25, 28, 29
Ninth Circuit, 323–373
 key decisions, 323–335
 rules and procedural issues, 336–341
 state law issues, 341–373
Nisus Corporation v. Perma-Chink Systems, Inc., 194
Noffke v. Perez, 344
Nolan, People v., 349
Non-retained experts, Missouri state courts, 312–313
Norman v. State (Delaware), 88
Norris v. Baxter Healthcare Corp., 378
North Carolina state courts, 125–127
North Dakota District Court, 293–297
North Dakota state courts, 317–318
Northern States Power Co. v. Burlington Northern & Santa Fe Rwy. Co., 309
Northern Trust Co. v. Burandt and Armbrust, LLP, 222
North Star Mutual Ins. Co. v. Zurich Ins. Co., 280
Novel scientific evidence. *See* General acceptance test
Nunez v. Allstate Ins. Co., 133
Nutra Sweet Co. v. X-L Eng'g Co., 208, 214

Obeta, State (Minnesota) *v.*, 308
Obrey v. Johnson, 335

Occupational medicine experts, 163–164
Ochoa v. Pacific Gas and Electric Co., 352
Oddi v. Ford Motor Co., 69, 72, 73, 82
Odom, State (New Jersey) *v.*, 93
Oglesby v. General Motors Corp., 109, 113
O'Hara v. Travelers, 142
Ohio, State of ex rel. Montgomery v. Trauth Dairy, Inc., 175
Ohio state courts, 202–203
Ohio v. Roberts, xxx–xxxi
Oklahoma state courts, 388–389
Olin Corp. v. Certain Underwriters at Lloyd's London, 26
Olson v. Ford Motor Co., 234, 253
Omeprazole Patent Litig., In re, 28
O'Neill v. Novartis Consumer Health, Inc., 351
Opinion testimony
    First Circuit, 6
        Massachusetts state courts, 20, 21
    Second Circuit, 31
    Third Circuit, New Jersey state courts, 100
    Fifth Circuit, Mississippi state courts, 141, 142
    Sixth Circuit, 161, 176
    Seventh Circuit, 215, 216
    Eighth Circuit, 237, 244, 253, 271
        Arkansas state courts, 300
        Iowa state courts, 302
        Minnesota state courts, 278
        Nebraska state courts, 314
    Ninth Circuit
        California state courts, 348, 351–354, 357
        Hawaii state courts, 358
    Tenth Circuit, 379
        Colorado state courts, 384
        Kansas state courts, 385, 386
    Eleventh Circuit, 403, 410
        Florida state courts, 431, 433
        Georgia state courts, 438
    District of Columbia Circuit, 449
Oregon state courts, 365–370
Orians, United States v., 331
Overton v. State (Florida), 434
Owca v. Zeminski, 437

Pacamor Bearings, Inc. v. Minebea Co., Ltd., 14–15
Packers and Stockyards Act violations, 297–298
Packer v. SN Servicing Corp., 39
Padillas v. Stork-Gamco, Inc., 83
Paige v. Miss. Baptist Med. Ctr., 155
Paoli R.R. Yard PCB Litig., In re, 69, 70, 72, 73, 75, 76, 82, 83, 84, 85, 182
Parah v. Lakeside Pharmacy, Inc., 66
Parker v. Brush Wellman, Inc., 408

Parker v. Mobil Oil Corp., 46, 50–51
Parkhill v. Alderman-Cave Milling & Grain Co. of New Mexico, 387
Parkinson, State (Idaho) *v.*, 359
Parmenter v. J & B Enterprises, Inc., 155
Parmentier v. Novartis Pharmaceuticals Corporation, 282–283
Pasteur, Commonwealth (Massachusetts) *v.*, 21
Patent infringement, 139, 194, 271, 284
Patrick, United States v., 13
Patterson, Commonwealth (Massachusetts) *v.*, 20–21
Patterson v. Balsamic, 36–37
Patterson v. Tibbs, 156
Patton, State (Kansas) *v.*, 385
Paul v. Missouri Pacific R.R. Co., 266
Paz v. Brush Engineered Materials, Inc., 134
PBM Products, LLC v. Mead Johnson & Co., 120–121
Peitzmeier v. Henessey Industries, Inc., 243, 265–266
Pelling, United States v., 332
Pelster v. Ray, 396
Pennsylvania state courts, 100–106
People v. _____. *See Name of party*
Perry, State (Oregon) *v.*, 368
Perry Lumber Co. v. Durable Services, 314–315
Perry v. New Hampshire, 263
Personal injury cases
    Second Circuit, Vermont state courts, 65
    Fifth District
        Louisiana state courts, 139
        Mississippi state courts, 157
    Eighth Circuit, 285, 289, 295–296
    District of Columbia, 448–449, 450
    Vermont state courts, 65
Person v. Shipley, 226, 227
Pestel v. Vermeer Mfg. Co., 242
Peters, State (Wisconsin) *v.*, 227
Petruzzi's IGA Supermarkets Inc. v. Darling-Del. Co., 76, 82
Pettus v. United States, 463
Pfizer, Inc. v. Advanced Monobloc Corp., 89
Phenolphthalein tests, 97
Phillips v. Gelpke, 100
Phillips v. Industrial Machine, 316
Photographic evidence, 13–14, 124, 349
Physician's assistants, 333
Physician testimony. *See also* Medical causation
    Second Circuit, Vermont state courts, 65, 66
    Third Circuit, 70–71, 75, 80
        Delaware state courts, 88
        New Jersey state courts, 99
    Fifth Circuit, 137–138

Eighth Circuit, 273, 276–277, 293
   Missouri state courts, 310–312
Ninth Circuit, California state courts, 357–358
Eleventh Circuit, 402–403
   Florida state courts, 438
   Georgia state courts, 439–440
District of Columbia, 453
Piccinonna, United States v., 121
Pineda-Torres, United States v., 334
Pineda v. Ford Motor Co., 72
Pioneer Hi-Bred International, Inc. v. Ottawa Plant Food, Inc., 272
Pipitone v. Biomatrix, Inc., 140
Piskorski v. Ron Tonkin Toyota, Inc., 370
Plaza, United States v., 78
Pluck v. BP Oil Pipeline Co., 183
Police experts
   Third Circuit, 79
      Delaware state courts, 88
      New Jersey state courts, 98–99
   Fourth Circuit, West Virginia state courts, 130
   Sixth Circuit, 162, 187–188
   Eighth Circuit, 259
      Minnesota state courts, 305–306
   Ninth Circuit, Oregon state courts, 368–369
Polidore v. McBride, 17–18
Polski v. Quigley Corp., 229
Polygraph tests
   First Circuit, 13
   Third Circuit, Pennsylvania state courts, 103
   Fourth Circuit, 121
   Sixth Circuit, 197
   Eighth Circuit, 257–258, 268, 298
      Minnesota state courts, 305
      North Dakota state courts, 317
   Ninth Circuit, 330–331
      Nevada state courts, 364
Pomella v. Regency Coach Lines, Ltd., 170
Pomerantz Paper Corp. v. New Cmty. Corp., 97
Pope v. City of New York, 44
Porter, State (Connecticut) *v.*, 59–60, 61
Posado, United States v., 121
Positron emission tomography (PET), 260
Post-traumatic stress disorder (PTSD)
   First Circuit, 15–16
   Third Circuit, New Jersey state courts, 94
   Sixth Circuit, 192
   Eighth Circuit, Missouri state courts, 311
   Tenth Circuit, 390
Post-trial motions, Sixth Circuit, 206
Poulin v. Yasner, 59
Poulsen, United States v., 198–199
Powers, United States v., 109, 120

Practice tips
   First Circuit, 23–24
   Second Circuit, 45–46
   Sixth Circuit, 204–206
   New York state courts, 57–58
   Vermont state courts, 66–67
Prater v. CSX Transportation, Inc., 163–164
Prater v. State (Arkansas), 300
Premises liability actions, 191
Prempro Prods. Liab. Litig., In re, 233, 263–264
Prentice v. Dalco Elec., Inc., 59, 60
Preponderance of evidence standard, 111–112
Presley v. Lakewood Engineering and Manufacturing, 244–245
Pretrial conferences. *See also Daubert* hearings
   First Circuit, 6, 18
      New Hampshire state courts, 23
   Eighth Circuit, Minnesota state courts, 309
   Eleventh Circuit, 416–417, 437
   District of Columbia, 451
Pretrial orders
   Third Circuit, 84
   Eleventh Circuit, 394, 416–417, 419–420
      Florida state courts, 437
Previto v. Ryobi North America, Inc., 141
Price, State (Montana) *v.*, 362–363
Pride v. BIC Corp., 165–166
Primiano v. Cook, 323, 329
Prince-Oyibo, United States v., 121
Prince v. Michelin North America Inc., 286–287
Product design. *See* Engineering/product design testimony
Product liability cases
   First Circuit, 15, 17
   Second Circuit, 29–30
   Fifth Circuit, 142–143
      Mississippi state courts, 156
      Texas state courts, 147–148
   Sixth Circuit, 159, 162, 166–169, 171, 177, 179, 184–185, 193–194
   Seventh Circuit, 218, 219
   Eighth Circuit, 234, 237–238, 241–243, 271–272, 273, 275, 276–278, 280–281, 286–287, 288–289, 290–291, 292–293, 294–295, 299
   Tenth Circuit, 378
   Eleventh Circuit, 398, 400–401
   District of Columbia, 450
Pro Service Automotive, LLC v. Lenan Corp., 240
Psychology/psychiatry testimony
   First Circuit, 6, 15–16
      Maine state courts, 22
      Massachusetts state courts, 21

Psychology/psychiatry testimony *(continued)*
   Second Circuit, Connecticut state courts, 61
   Third Circuit, 71–72
   Fourth Circuit, 119–120
   Sixth Circuit, 197–198
   Seventh Circuit, 214–216
   Eighth Circuit, 246–247, 258, 297, 298
      Iowa state courts, 303
      Minnesota state courts, 307–308
      Missouri state courts, 310
      South Dakota state courts, 318–319, 320
   Ninth Circuit, 331–332
      Alaska state courts, 342
   Eleventh Circuit, 403–404
   District of Columbia, 449, 455–456
Puerto Rico District Court, 15–17, 18
Pugh v. Louisville Ladder, Inc., 115
Pulice v. Smith and Nephew Richards, Inc., 267
Punitive damages, 139
Pure opinion exception to *Frye*, 431–434
Pytou Heang, Commonwealth (Massachusetts) *v.*, 20, 464

Quad City Bank & Trust v. Jim Kercher & Associates, P.C., 303
Quattrocchi, State (Rhode Island) *v.*, 23
Quenneville v. Buttolph, 65
Questioned documents, 463
Quiet Technology DC-8 v. Hurel-Dubois UK Ltd., 443
Qwest Corp. v. Elephant Butte Irrigation Dist., 382

Racial discrimination suits
   Sixth Circuit, 189, 190
   Eighth Circuit, 250, 264–265, 285–286, 287–288
   Ninth Circuit, 334–335
Radman v. Harold, 125
Rambo, State (Oregon) *v.*, 368–369
Ramirez, State (Colorado) *v.*, 383–384
Ramirez, United States v., 292
Ramirez-Robles, United States v., 331
Ramirez v. State (Florida), 428
Ramona v. Superior Court, 350
Ramsey v. Consol Rail Corp., 214
Ranes v. Adams Laboratories, Inc., 303
Ratliff v. State (Alaska), 343
Ratner v. Gen. Motors Corp., 99
Ratner v. McNeil-PPC, Inc., 51
Raymond, United States v., 11
Raymond v. USA Healthcare Center-Fort Dodge, 268
Raynor v. Merrell Pharm., Inc., 449
Raytheon Co. v. Indigo Sys. Corp., 136

Reali v. Mazda Motor of Am., Inc., 10
Rebelwood Apartments RP, LP v. English, 154, 157
Rector, People v., 383, 384
Redlightning, United States v., 333, 341
Reed, State (Connecticut) *v.*, 60
Reed, United States v., 334
ReedHycalog UK, Ltd. v. Diamond Innovations Inc., 138–139
Reed v. Binder, 84
Reed v. State (Maryland), 125
Reeves, People v., 350
Regional Redevelopment Corp. v. Hoke, 457
Register, State (South Carolina) *v.*, 127
Regression analysis, 76, 135–136, 250, 298
Reichert, in *Hoy v. DRM, Inc.*, 391
Reichert v. Phipps, 390
Reinfeld v. Hutcheson, 319–320
Relevance standard. *See also* Fit requirement
   Second Circuit, Connecticut state courts, 59–60
      Wisconsin state courts, 227
   Third Circuit, Delaware state courts, 88–89
   Fourth Circuit, 108, 109
   Seventh Circuit, Wisconsin state courts, 227
   Eighth Circuit, Arkansas state courts, 300
   Ninth Circuit, 329
      Hawaii state courts, 358–359
Reliability standard
   First Circuit, 12, 14
   Second Circuit, 27–34
      Connecticut state courts, 59
      New York state courts, 58
   Third Circuit, 74–79
      Delaware state courts, 88–89
      New Jersey state courts, 94–98
   Fifth Circuit
      Mississippi state courts, 155–156
      Texas state courts, 147–149
   Sixth Circuit, Ohio state courts, 202
   Seventh Circuit, Indiana state courts, 226
   Eighth Circuit
      Arkansas state courts, 301
      Minnesota state courts, 304–308
   Ninth Circuit, 323–324, 329
      Hawaii state courts, 358–359
      Montana state courts, 363
   Daubert's multi-factor test, xxviii
   District of Columbia, 448–450, 452–453
Religious experts, 261
Rembrandt Vision Technologies, L.P. v. Johnson and Johnson Vision Care, Inc., 405–406
Renucci v. Mercy Hosp., 54
Reports. *See* Expert reports
Repressed memory evidence, 12, 192, 308

Res ipsa loquitur, 97, 293
Reynolds, United States v., 258
Rhode Island District Court, 17–18
Rhode Island state courts, 23
Rhodes v. Rhodes, 157
Ricco v. Riva, 227
Rice v. Cincinnati, New Orleans and Pacific Ry. Co., 162–163
Richardson, People v., 353
Richardson, United States v., 256
Richardson v. Richardson-Merrell, Inc., 448
RICO actions, 163
Riker, State (Washington) *v.*, 371
Rimert v. Eli Lilly and Co., 382
Rimkus Consulting Group, Inc. v. Cammarata, 137
Rimmasch, State (Utah) *v.*, 389
Rincon, United States v., 331
Ritt, State (Minnesota) *v.*, 305–306
Roach, United States v., 375, 377, 379
Roberson v. City of Philadelphia, 74
Roberti v. Andy's Termite Pest Control, Inc., 351
Roberts, State (Washington) *v.*, 371
Roberts, United States v., 200
Robertson, United States v., 259
Robertson v. Norton Co., 243
Robidoux v. Oliphant, 224
Robinson, State (Nebraska) *v.*, 314
Robinson v. Suffolk Cnty. Police Dep't, 35
Rodriguez, United States v., 256
Rodriguez Cirilo v. Garcia, 16
Rodriguez-Felix, United States v., 379
Rodriguez v. State (Delaware), 87
Rogers, State (Idaho) *v.*, 360
Rogers v. Ingersoll-Rand, 450
Rolen v. Hansen Beverage Co., 179
Rolls-Royce Corp. v. Heros, Inc., 138
Roman Nose, State (Minnesota) *v.*, 306
Romley, State ex. rel. v. Field, 346
Ronwin v. Bayer Corp., 381
Rook v. 60 Key Centre, Inc., 55
Rosamond v. Great American Ins. Co., 141
Rosenfeld v. Oceania Cruises, 394–396
Rosen v. Ciba-Geigy Corp., 208
Rose v. Truck Centers, Inc., 168
Ross, United States v., 261–262
Rouco, United States v., 395
Rouse, United States v., 257, 258, 298
R & R Sails, Inc. v. Insurance Co. of Pennsylvania, 340
R.S., In re, 94, 95
Rubanick v. Witco Chem. Corp., 95, 97, 98
Ruiz-Troche v. Pepsi Cola of Puerto Rico Bottling Co., 1–3

Rule 104(a)
    Third Circuit, 82
Rule 403
    First Circuit, 12
    Third Circuit, 82
Rule 702
    First Circuit, 3, 5, 6–7, 11, 12, 15
    Second Circuit, 28
    Third Circuit, 82
    revisions based on *Daubert*, xxx
Rule 706
    Second Circuit, 45
    Ninth Circuit, 337–339
Rule 901
    First Circuit, 12
Rules and procedural issues
    First Circuit, 7–8, 18–19
    Second Circuit, 34–45
        Connecticut state courts, 62
        New York state courts, 52–57
        Vermont state courts, 65–66
    Third Circuit, 82–85
    Fourth Circuit, 112–113
    Fifth Circuit, 137–138, 141–142, 143–144
        Louisiana state courts, 150–153
        Mississippi state courts, 153, 154
        Texas state courts, 144–146, 149–150
    Sixth Circuit, 192–194, 199–200
        Kentucky state courts, 202
        Michigan state courts, 203–204
        Ohio state courts, 203
        Tennessee state courts, 201
    Seventh Circuit, Illinois state courts, 224
    Eighth Circuit, 253–254, 262–263
        Arkansas state courts, 302
        Iowa state courts, 304
        Minnesota state courts, 308–309
        Missouri state courts, 312–313
        Nebraska state courts, 316–317
        North Dakota state courts, 318
    Ninth Circuit, 336–341
        Alaska state courts, 344–345
        Arizona state courts, 347
        California state courts, 355–358
        Hawaii state courts, 359
        Idaho state courts, 361
        Montana state courts, 363
        Nevada state courts, 365
        Oregon state courts, 369–370
        South Dakota state courts, 320–321
        Washington state courts, 372–373
    Tenth Circuit, 380–382

Rules and procedural issues *(continued)*
    Eleventh Circuit, 414–421
        Alabama state courts, 426–427
        Florida state courts, 435–438
        Georgia state courts, 443–444
    District of Columbia Circuit, 451, 456–458
Rushing, United States v., 261
Russell v. K-Mart Corp., 92
Russell v. State (Alaska), 342
Rutherford, United States v., 293
Rutigliano v. Valley Bus. Forms, 75
Rutland, United States v., 82

Safety experts
    Third Circuit, 70, 80, 90
    Fifth Circuit, 140
    Sixth Circuit, 161, 170
    Eighth Circuit, Iowa state courts, 302
Saginaw Chippewa Indian Tribe v. Granholm, 161–162
Salander v. Cent. Gen. Hosp., 53
Saldana, State (Minnesota) *v.*, 308
Saldana v. Kmart Corp, 80–81
Salmon, State (Missouri) *v.*, 312
Samaan v. St. Joseph Hosp., 5–6
Samaniego v. City of Kodiak, 342
Sample v. Monsanto Company, 286
San Antonio, City of v. Pollock, 149
Sandata Tech., Inc. v. Infocrossing, Inc., 35
Sanders v. Ahmed, 312
San Diego County Health & Human Servs. Agency v. Carlos R., 350–351
Sandoval-Mendoza, United States v., 329
Santana, United States v., 6–7
Santiago, United States v., 413–414
Santillanes v. State, 364
Sappington v. Skyjack, Inc., 238–239
Sargon Enters., Inc. v. Univ. of S. Cal., 347–348, 352
Satellite images, 261
Savage v. Union Pacific Railroad Co., 266
Schaaf v. Caterpillar, Inc., 296
Schafersman v. Agland Coop, 313–314
Schiff, United States v., 81
Schipp v. Gen. Motors Corp., 265
Schmidt v. City of Bella Villa, 229
Schneider v. Fried, 71, 80, 85
Schneider v. State (Minnesota), 306
Schott, et al. v. I-Flow Corp., et al., 179–180
Schreiber v. Estate of Kiser, 357
Schreiner, State (Missouri) *v.*, 314
Schubert v. Nissan Motor Corp., 8
Schudel v. Gen. Elec. Co., 326
Schultz v. Capital Int'l Sec., Inc., 111

Schultz v. Glidden Co., 217
Schultz v. State (Maryland), 125
Schumacher v. Tyson Fresh Meats, Inc., 297–298
Scientific knowledge
    First Circuit, 10, 12, 17
        Rhode Island state courts, 23
    Second Circuit, 25, 59
    Fourth Circuit, 107–108
        West Virginia state courts, 130
    Fifth Circuit, Mississippi state courts, 155–156
    Sixth Circuit, 166, 170, 175, 176, 197
        Kentucky state courts, 201
    Eighth Circuit, Iowa state courts, 303
    Ninth Circuit, 331
    Tenth Circuit, New Mexico state courts, 387
    Eleventh Circuit, Georgia state courts, 442
    Daubert's multi-factor reliability test, xxviii
    District of Columbia Circuit, 452, 455
    future issues, 463–464
Scientific Working Group for Forensic Document Examination, 79
Scott, State (Tennessee) *v.*, 200
Scott v. City of Chicago, 215
Scrap Metal Antitrust Litigation, In re, 173–174
Scroggin v. Wyeth, 233
Scruggs v. Edwards, 388
Scwartz, State (Minnesota) *v.*, 305
Sdoulam, United States v., 259
Seaman v. Seacor Marine L.L.C., 134
Searles v. Fleetwood Homes of Pa., 22
Second Circuit, 25–67
    key decisions, 25–34
    local practice tips, 45–46
    rules and procedural issues, 34–45
    state law issues, 45–67
Section 1983 claims, 16
Securities fraud, 81, 136, 291
S.E.C. v. Nadel, 44–45
Seivewright v. State (Wyoming), 390
Senior, Commonwealth (Massachusetts) *v.*, 20
Sentinel Management Co. v. Aetna Cas. & Surety Co., 305
Sepulveda, United States v., 6
Sepulveda-Barraza, United States v., 334
Seventh Circuit, 207–228
    key decisions, 207–221
    state law issues, 221–228
Shadden, State (Kansas) *v.*, 385
Shaffer v. Amada America Inc., 242, 287
Shahzade v. Gregory, 12
Shaken baby syndrome, 96
Shalom Hospitality, Inc. v. Alliant Energy Company, et al., 273

Sharpe v. Director, Office of Workers' Compensation Programs, 111
Shay, United States v., 6
Sheehan, State (Utah) *v.*, 389–390
Sheet Metal Workers' National Pension Fund v. Palladium Equity Partners, LLC, 161
Sheridan v. Catering Management, Inc., 313
Sherwin, United States v., 197
Sherwin-Williams Co. v. Gaines ex rel. Pollard, 156
Shirley, People v., 351
Shoeprint analysis, 79
Shreck, People v., 383
Shuck v. CNH American, LLC, 245
Siegel v. Fisher & Paykel Appliances Holdings, Ltd., 167
Sigler v. American Honda Motor Co., 159
Sigur v. Emerson Process Management, 140
Silverberg v. Community General Hospital, 54
Simon Prop. Group L.P. v. mySimon, Inc., 216
Simons, In re Commitment of, 221–222, 223
Simo v. Mitsubishi Motors North America, Inc., 114
Sinskey, United States v., 256
Sixth Circuit, 159–206
    criminal cases, 195–200
    key decisions, 159–192
        expert qualifications, 159–164
        methodology, 164–192
    practice tips, 204–206
    procedural issues, 192–194
    state law issues, 200–204
Slip-and-fall cases, 77, 80–81, 87, 394–396
Smelser v. Norfolk Southern Railway, 159, 176–177
Smith, United States v., 195, 333
Smithers, United States v., 195–196
Smith v. Cangieter, 240
Smith v. Gen. Elec. Co., 14
Smith v. Kelly-Moore Paint Co., 442
Smith v. Pfizer Inc., 180–181
Smith v. Rasmussen, 246
Smith v. State Farm Fire & Casualty Co., 113
Snyder v. Case, 316
Sodium amytal tests, 96
Softel, Inc. v. Dragon Med. & Scientific Commc'n, Inc., 36
Solorio-Tafolla, United States v., 259, 263
Sorabella, State (Connecticut) *v.*, 59
Sorenson v. St. Paul Ramsey Med. Ctr., 309
Source Code Evidentiary Hearings in Implied Consent Matters, In re, 307
Southard, State (Oregon) *v.*, 366, 367
South Carolina state courts, 127
South Dakota District Court, 297–299

South Dakota Microsoft Antitrust Litigation, In re, 319
South Dakota state courts, 318–321
Speculation, 109, 129
Speech pathologists, 405
Spencer v. Commonwealth (Virginia), 127–128
Spencer v. Wal-Mart Stores East, LP, 87
Spin Doctor Golf, Inc. v. Paymentech, L.P., 146
Spotted Elk, United States v., 259
Spreadsheet Automation Corp. v. Microsoft Corp., 138
Springfield v. State (Wyoming), 390
Stagliano, United States v., 449–450
Standards of review. *See specific standards*
Starkey v. State (Alaska), 343
State Bd. of Registration for the Healing Arts v. McDonagh, 310
State v. _____. *See Name of party*
Statistical methodology, 135–136, 247–251, 285–286
Stenson, State (Washington) *v.*, 371
Stepp, United States v., 199
Sterling v. Interlake Indus., Inc., 35–36
Stevens v. City of Virginia, 281
Stevens v. Czerniak, 369
Stibbs v. Mapco, Inc., 274
Stigliano v. Connaught Labs., 99
Still v. State (Florida), 430
Stilwell v. Smith & Nephew, Inc., 329
St. John, State (Connecticut) *v.*, 61
St. Jude Medical, Inc. Silzone Heart Valves Prods. Liab. Litig., In re, 278–279
St. Laurent v. Metso Minerals Indus., Inc., 15
St. Lewis v. Firestone, 455
Stohr, State v., 303
Stoll, People v., 348
Stone, United States v., 198, 461
Stout, State (Missouri) *v.*, 309
Strach v. Doin, 53
Street-gang investigations, 98–99, 124, 301, 333
Street v. Hedgepath, 456–457
Streich, State (Vermont) *v.*, 64
Stroud v. Hennepin County Med. Ctr., 309
Student Marketing Group Inc. v. College Partnership, Inc., 375
Sturgis v. Bayside Health Ass'n. Chartered, 92
Suanez v. Egeland, 95
Sullivan v. U.S. Dep't of the Navy, 328
Superior Court (Vidal), People v., 350
Supreme Pork, Inc. v. Master Blaster, Inc., 319
Surace v. Caterpillar, Inc., 71, 72
Surles ex rel. Johnson v. Greyhound Lines, Inc., 160–161

Surveys
   First Circuit, 16
   Third Circuit, 77, 78
   Fourth Circuit, 120–121
   Sixth Circuit, 186, 191
   Seventh Circuit, 209, 216
   Eighth Circuit, 276, 285–286
   Ninth Circuit, 335
Sutera v. Perrier Grp. of Am., Inc., 11
Suzlon Wind Energy Corp. v. Shippers Stevedoring Co., 137
Swain, State (Missouri) *v.*, 312
Swallow v. Emergency Medicine of Idaho, 361
Swanson, State (North Dakota) *v.*, 317
Sylla-Sawdon v. Uniroyal Goodrich Tire Co., 253
Symington v. Daisy Manufacturing Co., Inc., 294–295
Synergetics, Inc. v. Hurst, 247–248

Talkington v. Atria Reclamelucifers Fabrieken BV, 108
Tamraz v. Lincoln Electric Co., 182–183
Target Market Publishing, Inc., v. ADVO, Inc., 221
Tarmac Mid-Atlantic, Inc. v. Smiley Block Co., 129
Tasers, 140, 162
Taylor, United States v., 462
Taylor v. Di Rico, 347
Taylor v. State (Florida), 429
Taylor v. State (Oklahoma), 388
Taylor v. Teco Barge Line, Inc., 161
TCE Systems, Inc. v. Thomas & Betts Corp., 186
Teligent, Inc., In re, 37
Tenet Hospitals Ltd. v. Boada, 147
Tennessee state courts, 200–201
Tenth Circuit, 375–391
   key decisions, 375–379
   rules and procedural issues, 380–382
   state law issues, 383–391
Teratology, 267, 446–448
Terrorism, 199, 396–397
Terry v. Caputo, 202
Tesco Corp. v. Weatherford Int'l, Inc., 137
Texans CUSO Ins. Group, LLC, In re, 137
Texas federal courts, 136–139, 143–144
Texas state courts, 144–150
Tharo Systems, Inc. v. Cab Produkttechnik GmbH & Co Kg, 185
Therrien v. Town of Jay, 5
Third Circuit, 69–106
   key decisions, 69–81
      expert qualifications, 70–72
      fit requirement, 79–81
      introduction, 69–70
      reliability, 72–79

   rules and procedural issues, 82–85
   state law issues, 85–106
Thomas, United States v., 124
Thomas v. City of Chattanooga, 189
Thomas v. City of Winnfield, 140
Thomas v. FAG Bearings Corp., et al., 289
Thompson v. Cooper, 341, 343
Thompson v. Gordon, 225
Thompson v. Merrell Dow Pharms., Inc., 98
Thompson v. State Farm Fire and Casualty Co., 171
Thomson v. Gummiwerk Kraiburg Elastik Beteiligungs GmbH & Co. et al., 271–272
Thorpe, State (Nebraska) *v.*, 314
Thurman v. Missouri Gas Energy, 288
Title VII actions, 186
Tittsworth v. Robinson, 129
TMI Litig. Cases Consol. II., In re, 72
Tobacco litigation, 163, 235, 250
Tool-mark identification, 430
Torres, State (New Jersey) *v.*, 92, 93, 98–99
Torres, State (New Mexico) *v.*, 387
Townsend, State (New Jersey) *v.*, 92
Toxicology/toxic tort cases
   First Circuit, 1–2, 3
   Third Circuit, New Jersey state courts, 97
   Fourth Circuit, 117–118, 120
   Fifth Circuit, 133, 134–135, 141, 143
      Mississippi state courts, 156
   Sixth Circuit, 172–173, 178, 184, 185, 192–193, 198
   Seventh Circuit, 217–219
   Eighth Circuit, 230–237, 266, 280–281, 290–291, 292, 293–294
      Nebraska state courts, 313
   Ninth Circuit, 324, 326, 327–328
   Tenth Circuit, 376
      Kansas state courts, 386
   Eleventh Circuit, 408–409
      Florida state courts, 433–434
Toyota Motor Corp. v. Gregory, 202
Trademark disputes. *See* Intellectual property cases
Transamerica Life Ins. Co. v. Lincoln Nat. Life Ins. Co., 271
Transcontinental Ins. Co. v. Crump, 149
Trapani v. Treutel, 155
Travelers Indemnity Co. v. Industrial Paper & Packaging Corp., 171–172
Traylor, State (Minnesota) *v.*, 306
Trevor Anthony Brown, State (Minnesota) *v.*, 309
Trickett v. Ochs, 66–67
Trier of fact, assisting
   First Circuit, 15
      Maine state courts, 22
      Rhode Island state courts, 23

Second Circuit, 25
    Vermont state courts, 64
Third Circuit, 80
    Delaware state courts, 86, 90
    New Jersey state courts, 92, 100
    Pennsylvania state courts, 100
Fourth Circuit, 107, 109, 120–121
    South Carolina state courts, 127
Fifth Circuit
    Louisiana state courts, 152
Sixth Circuit, 159
    Tennessee state courts, 201
Ninth Circuit
    California state courts, 353–354
    Idaho state courts, 359
    Nevada state courts, 365
District of Columbia, 450, 455
Rule 702, xxviii, xxx
Triplett, United States v., 262
Troupe v. McAuley, 155
Trustees of the Chicago Painters and Decorators Pension, Health and Welfare and Deferred Saving Plan Trust Funds v. Royal Int'l Drywall and Decorating, Inc., 207–208
Tucker v. Rees-Memphis, Inc., 155
Tuck v. Health Care Auth. of the City of Huntsville, 426
Tuf Racing Prods., Inc. v. Am. Suzuki Motor Corp., 221
T-Up, Inc. v. Consumer Protection Division, 125
Turner v. Iowa Fire Equip. Co., 236–237
Turner v. State (Alabama), 422
Tuscaloosa v. Harcros Chems., Inc., 404, 405
Tyus v. Urban Search Management, 214–215

Unfair competition, 15
Union Carbide v. Ever-Ready, Inc., 191
Unique Concepts, Inc. v. Brown, 45
United States v. _____. *See Name of party*
Unrein v. Timesavers, Inc., 241–242
Uribe v. Sofamor, S.N.C., 293
USGen New England, Inc. v. Town of Rockingham, 63–65
U.S. Sugar Corp. v. Henson, 433, 434
Utah state courts, 389–390
Utz v. Running & Rolling Trucking, Inc., 154

Vadala v. Teledyne Indus., Inc., 8–9
Valencia, United States v., 135
Valentine v. Conrad, 202
Valentine v. Pioneer Chlor Alkali Co., 326
Vandeweagh, State (New Jersey) *v.*, 94
Vann v. State, 343
Vaughn v. State (Georgia), 438–439

Velarde, United States v., 377
Velasquez, United States v., 78–79
Vermont state courts, 63–67
Versata Software Inc. v. SAP America, Inc., 138
Vesey, United States v., 258–259
Viagra Prods. Liab. Litig., In re, 276–277
Victor O., State (Connecticut) *v.*, 61
Virginia state courts, 127–129
Virgin Islands v. Sanes, 81
Vliet, State (Hawaii) *v.*, 358–359
Vocational rehabilitation, 71–72, 316, 319
Voiceprint analysis, 96
Voice recordings, 450
Voir dire, 4, 92
Volatile organic compounds (VOCs), 76–77, 80
Volkswagen of America, Inc. v. Ramirez, 148

Wackenhut Corp. v. Fortune, 157
Wackman v. Rubsamen, 134–135
Wagner v. County of Maricopa, 324
Wagner v. Hesston Corp., 240–241
Wagoner v. Exxon Mobile Corp., 141
Wahl v. American Honda Motor Co., 48–49
Walker, Commonwealth (Pennsylvania) *v.*, 103
Walker, United States v., 79
Walker v. American Cyanamid Co., 360–361
Walker v. American Home Shield Long Term Disability Plan, 337
Walker v. Consol. Rail Corp., 220
Wal-Mart Stores, Inc. v. Dukes, 274–275, 336
Wal-Mart Stores, Inc. v. Merrell, 150
Walstad, State (Wisconsin) *v.*, 227
Wanderer v. Johnston, 339
Warnings, 267–268
    First Circuit, 15
    Second Circuit, 33
    Third Circuit, 71
    Fifth Circuit, 140, 143, 155
    Sixth Circuit, 167
    Eighth Circuit, 237–243, 267–268, 289, 296, 297, 320
Washington Metro. Area Transit Auth. v. Davis, 456
Washington state courts, 370–373
Wash Solutions, Inc. v. PDQ Mfg., Inc., 248
Waters, United States v., 257, 262
Watkins, United States v., 461
Watson v. State, 227
Watson v. Theo Alloys Int'l, Inc., 130
Watson v. United States, 380, 381–382
Watts v. Radiator Specialty Co., 156
Watt v. Butler, 410
Webb v. Thomas Trucking, Inc., 443
Weeks v. Eastern Idaho Health Services, 360
Weiner v. Kneller, 457

Weisgram v. Marley Co., xxxii, 245–246
Weller v. United States, 399
Wells v. Howe Heating & Plumbing, 320
Wells v. SmithKline Beecham Corp., 134
Wendt v. Host Int'l, Inc., 335, 339
Werle, State (Hawaii) *v.*, 358
Werth v. Hill-Rom, Inc., 275
Wesely v. Flor, 309
Wesley, People v., 46–47, 51
West, State (Connecticut) *v.*, 60
Westberry v. Gislaved Gummi AB, 109, 111, 116–117
Westby v. Schmidt, 318
Westfield Insurance Co. v. Harris, 110–111
West Philadelphia Therapy Ctr. v. Erie Ins. Grp., 104
West Tennessee Chapter of Associated Builders and Contractors, Inc. v. City of Memphis, 189
West Virginia state courts, 129–131
Wheat v. State (Delaware), 90
Wheeling Pittsburgh Steel Corp. v. Beelman River Terminals, Inc., 244
Whirlpool Corp. v. Camacho, 147–148
Whirlpool Properties, Inc. v. LG Electronics United States, Inc., 191
White, United States v., 123
White Horse, United States v., 258, 298
Whitehouse Hotel L.P. v. Comm'r, 136
Whiting v. Boston Edison Co., 13
Whitson v. State, 300
Wholesale Grocery Prods. Antitrust Litig., In re, 274–275
Wick v. Wabash Holding Corp., 26
Wikipedia, 31
Wilke, People v., 222
Wilkerson, People v., 384
Willert v. Ortho Pharm. Corp., 282
Williams, United States v., 257
Williams et al. v. Security National Bank of Sioux City, Iowa, 270–271
Williamson v. State (Florida), 428, 432
Williamson v. Sup. Ct. (Shell Oil), 355
Williams v. Hedican, 303
Williams v. Illinois, xxx–xxxii
Williams v. State (Wyoming), 389
Willis v. Kia Motors Corp., 143
Willock, United States v., 462
Wilson, United States v., 110, 112
Wilson v. Clark, 224
Wilson v. Taser Intern., Inc., 411
Wilt v. Buracker, 130, 131
Winters v. Fru-Con Inc., 207, 211
Wisconsin state courts, 227–228
Wiseman, State ex rel. (West Virginia) *v. Henning*, 131

Wong v. Regents of the University of California, 340
Woodard v. Custer, 204
Woodhull v. County of Kent, 189–190
Wood v. Minn. Mining & Mfg. Co., 239, 243
Woodworker's Supply, Inc. v. Principal Mut. Life Ins. Co., 382
Workers' compensation cases, 313, 319–320
Work-product doctrine, 42–44
Worthy v. McNair, 155
W.R. Grace & Co.-Conn. v. Zotos International, Inc., 42
Wright Asphalt Prods. Co. v. Pelican Refining Co., 137
Wright v. State (Delaware), 88
Wright v. Willamette Indus., Inc., 232, 266
Wrongful death actions
 First Circuit, 14
 Second Circuit, Vermont state courts, 66
 Fifth Circuit, 134–135, 140
  Louisiana state courts, 152–153
 Sixth Circuit, 165–166
 Eighth Circuit, 245–246, 283
 Vermont state courts, 66
Wsol v. Great No. Asset Mgmt., Inc., 221
WWW, Inc. v. Wounded Warriors, Inc., 290
Wynacht v. Beckman Instruments, Inc., 181
Wyoming state courts, 390–391

Yamaha Motor Co. v. Arnoult, 364
Yapp v. Union Pacific Railroad Company, 285–286
Yarchak v. Trek Bicycle Corp., 74
Yax v. Dev. Team Inc., 54
Yelverton v. Yelverton, 157
Yeti by Molly Ltd. v. Deckers Outdoor Corp., 339–340
Younglove Construction, LLC v. PSD Development, LLC, et al., 185–186
Young v. All Erection & Crane Rental, Corp., 295
Yousef, United States v., 41

Zach v. Centocor and Johnson & Johnson, 268
Zandi v. Wyeth, 307
Zaremba v. General Motors Corp., 28, 29–30
Zeigler v. Fisher-Price, Inc., 272
Zenith Electronics Corp. v. WH-TV Broadcasting Corp., 212
Zerega Ave. Realty Corp. v. Hornbeck Offshore Transp., 28
Ziegenfus v. John Veriha Trucking, 43
Zito v. Zabarsky, 46
Zurn Pex Plumbing Products Liability Litigation, In re, 237–238, 247, 254
Zuzula v. ABB Power T & D Co., 168–169
Zwillinger v. Garfield Slope Hous. Corp., 33–34